THEOLOGICAL DICTIONARY

OF THE

NEW TESTAMENT

EDITED BY

GERHARD FRIEDRICH

Translator and Editor

GEOFFREY W. BROMILEY, D. LITT., D. D.

Volume VIII

T—Y

WM. B. EERDMANS PUBLISHING COMPANY

GRAND RAPIDS, MICHIGAN

THEOLOGICAL DICTIONARY OF THE NEW TESTAMENT

Translated from
THEOLOGISCHES WÖRTERBUCH ZUM NEUEN TESTAMENT
Achter Band: T-Y, herausgegeben von Gerhard Friedrich

Published by
W. KOHLHAMMER VERLAG
Stuttgart, Germany

First printing, May 1972

Second printing, June 1974

ISBN 0-8028-2252-9

PHOTOLITHOPRINTED BY CUSHING - MALLOY, INC.
ANN ARBOR, MICHIGAN, UNITED STATES OF AMERICA
1974

Preface

The publishers and editor have decided to conclude Volume VIII at the letter Y, since the addition of the other articles would have made the concluding volume too bulky.

The preparation of the work has not gone ahead as quickly as projected and desired. There are various reasons for this. For one thing, the editor in recent years has been so much claimed by academic responsibilities that he has not been able to devote sufficient time to writing. Publishing and printing changes have also caused delays. Furthermore, it was not easy to get in outstanding articles to time, since the present situation has not been particularly favourable for the investigation of scientific questions in peace and detachment.

In the main the Theological Dictionary has been composed from an etymological standpoint. When deadlines could not be kept in earlier volumes, the editor could always choose not to treat delinquent articles by stems but to fit them in later with a corresponding material group or according to the first letter in the term. In the later stages, however, this option has run out, and delays have been caused on this account too.

It is all the more gratifying, then, that translations of the whole work into English and Italian have been pressing ahead rapidly. It is to be expected that soon after the conclusion of the project the Dictionary will be completely available in three languages.

The editor always takes pleasure in thanking the various contributors and helpers for their unselfish labours. By their special knowledge and their diligence in correcting proofs and checking references and quotations they have made an essential contribution to the reliability of the Theological Dictionary. I mention with gratitude the following who have given editorial assistance: H. R. Balz, G. Bertram, P. Boendermaker, E. Dammann, A. Dihle, G. Egg, G. Fohrer, E. P. D. Gooding, A. Hiller, G. Kelber, H. Krämer, C. F. D. Moule, E. Nestle, K. Reinhardt, K. H. Rengstorf, E. Risch, K. H. Schelkle, G. Schlichting, W. Schneemelcher, K. Staab, and H. Traub.

In recent years W. Michaelis and G. Schrenk have been called home. I mention their names with gratitude and respect.

G. Friedrich

Kiel, January 5 1969.

Editor's Preface

The post-war volumes of the Theological Dictionary of the New Testament are distinguished from the first four by many special features. Gerhard Friedrich succeeds Gerhard Kittel as editor. The fall of Hitler has made possible wider international contacts, especially with scholars of the English-speaking world. The series begins to benefit not only from newer developments in biblical and theological studies but also from exciting discoveries like the Dead Sea Scrolls.

These changes have certain important implications for the Dictionary. Some of the judgments in earlier articles have had to be reconsidered. A place has had to be found for additional material. Points not originally thought to be significant have had to be discussed. In a work extending over so many decades some of this would have been inevitable in any case. The break between the Kittel and the Friedrich volumes, however, has made an even more imperious demand, even at the risk of adding to the final size of the work.

Naturally the purpose, design and structure of the Dictionary remain the same. Nor is there any change in either its proper use or its enduring value. Added interest is imparted, however, by the fact that the post-war volumes bring us increasingly into the sphere of modern research and debate. Readers of the present version will also profit by the fact that few of even the most important articles in these later volumes have ever been offered previously in English translation.

A great debt is again owed to Professor F. F. Bruce of Manchester University for his invaluable and indefatigable labours in proof reading. If some errors still slip through the net — and we are grateful to readers who call attention to these — there is the consolation that Dr. Bruce in particular has been able to correct not a few errors in the original German.

Attention may be drawn at this point to five corrections that should be made in page references: On p. 188, note [5] the reference should now be → 195, 20 ff.; on p. 191, 1 → 200, 20 ff.; on p. 191, note [36] → 201, 30 ff.; and on p. 191, 34 → 194, 6 ff. and 199, 16 ff.

Pasadena, California, 1972.   *G. W. Bromiley*

Contents

Contributors

Editor:

Gerhard Friedrich, Kiel.

Contributors:

Horst Balz, Kiel.
Otto Bauernfeind, Tübingen.
Georg Bertram, Giessen.
Carsten Colpe, Göttingen.
Gerhard Delling, Halle.
Gottfried Fitzer, Vienna.
Georg Fohrer, Erlangen.
Leonhard Goppelt, Munich.
Walter Grundmann, Jena and Eisenach.
Helmut Köster, Harvard University, USA.
Eduard Lohse, Göttingen.
Ulrich Luck, Bethel.
Christian Maurer, Berne.
Otto Michel, Tübingen.
Karl Heinrich Rengstorf, Münster.
Harald Riesenfeld, Uppsala.
Wilhelm Schneemelcher, Bonn.
Johannes Schneider, Berlin.
Wolfgang Schrage, Bonn.
Eduard Schweizer, Zürich.
Gustav Stählin, Mainz.
Konrad Weiss, Rostock.
Ulrich Wilckens, Hamburg.
Peter Wülfing von Martitz, Cologne.

τάγμα → τάσσω

---

† ταπεινός, † ταπεινόω, † ταπείνωσις,
† ταπεινόφρων, † ταπεινοφροσύνη

Contents: A. The Use of the Word Group in the Greek and Hellenistic World: 1. Etymological Derivation and Original Meaning; 2. ταπεινός; 3. ταπεινόω; 4. ταπείνωσις; 5. ταπεινόφρων, ταπεινοφροσύνη; 6. The Meaning of the Derivates. B. The Use of the Word Group in the Septuagint: 1. The Hebrew Originals of the Greek Terms; 2. ταπεινόω; 3. ταπεινός; 4. ταπείνωσις; 5. The Greek and the Biblical Understanding. C. Humility in Judaism: 1. The Qumran Sect and Apocalyptic Judaism; 2. Rabbinic Literature; 3. Hellenistic Judaism. D. The Statements about Humility and Lowliness in the New Testament: 1. Occurrence of the ταπεινός Group in the New Testament; 2. ταπεινόω; 3. ταπεινός; 4. ταπείνωσις; 5. ταπεινοφροσύνη; 6. ταπεινόφρων. E. Humility in the Post-Apostolic Fathers: 1. ταπεινός; 2. ταπεινόω; 3. ταπείνωσις; 4. ταπεινοφρονέω; 5. ταπεινοφροσύνη; 6. ταπεινοφρόνησις; 7. ταπεινόφρων; 8. The Shift in the Sense of the Terms in the Post-Apostolic Fathers.

A. The Use of the Word Group in the Greek and Hellenistic World.

1. Etymological Derivation and Original Meaning.

Etym. research has yielded no plain result.[1] The first instance in Pind. Nem., 3, 82 shows the basic meaning to be "low," "flat"; cf. also Hdt., IV, 191, 3; Xenoph. Eq., 1, 4; 10, 6; cf. Lat. humilis.

2. ταπεινός.

a. "Lowly," "mean," "insignificant," "weak," "poor," e.g., of the trivial power or significance of a city or country, state or statesman, Demosth. Or., 4, 23; 9, 21; Isoc. Or., 4, 68 and 141; 8, 116; Plut. De Demosthene, 1 (I, 846c), of the position a man occupies, Demosth. Or., 57, 45; Isoc. Or., 3, 42; Epict. Diss., III, 24, 36, of bodily form: τὸ σχῆμα σεμνὸς κοὐ ταπεινὸς οὐδ' ἄγαν εὔογκος ὡς ἂν δοῦλος, Eur. Fr., 688, 2 f. (TGF, 576) opp. σεμνός, of a man's power and influence, Hdt., VII, 14; Demosth. Or., 1, 9, of prison (opp. ὑψηλός of the judge's seat), Epict. Diss., II, 6, 25, of stars near the horizon, Artemid. Onirocr., II, 8 (p. 91, 16), of the couched lance as distinct from the raised lance ταπεινὰ καὶ μὴ ὑπερφανῆ, Xenoph. Eq. Mag., 5, 7, of an insignificant river (opp. μέγας), Polyb., 9, 43, 3, of poverty in worldly goods, Isoc. Or., 8, 125; Anonymus Fr., 547, 6-8 (TGF, 947): ἡ δὲ μεσότης ἐν πᾶσιν ἀσφαλεστέρα. τὸ μήτε λίαν ἐν ταπεινῷ τῆς τύχης (or ψυχῆς) μέρει φέρεσθαι μήτ' ἐν ὑψηλῷ. A man, people, or state may be

---

ταπεινός κτλ. Bibl.: Cr.-Kö., Liddell-Scott, Pape, Pass., Pr.-Bauer, s.v.; A. Dihle, Art. "Demut" in RAC, III, 735-778; L. Gilen, "Die Demut des Christen nach d. NT," Zschr. f. Aszese u. Mystik, 13 (1938), 266-284; A. v. Harnack, "Sanftmut, Huld u. Demut in d. alten Kirche," Festschr. J. Kaftan (1920), 113-129; S. Rehrl, Das Problem d. Demut in d. profangriech. Lit. im Vergleich zu LXX u. NT (1961); A. Schlatter, "Jesu Demut," BFTh, 8 (1904); E. Schweizer, "Erniedrigung u. Erhöhung bei Jesus u. seinen Nachfolgern," AbhThANT, 28[2] (1962); L. Stachowiak, "Refleksse nad biblijnym posecrem pokory," Ruch Biblijny i Liturgicrny, 13 (1960), 199-216; K. Thieme, Die chr. Demut (1906); also "Die ταπεινοφροσύνη Phil. 2 u. R. 12," ZNW, 8 (1907), 9-31; Trench, 84-89.
[1] Schwyzer, I, 489.

small and insignificant intrinsically, but it may also be made lowly, e.g., by the military force and superior power of others, Xenoph. Hist. Graec., II, 4, 23; An., II, 5, 13; Isoc. Or., 15, 195 says of philosophy: ταπεινὴν ποιῶν τὴν φιλοσοφίαν, and the word is used in Plat. Leg., V, 728e with respect to the human soul and human courage. But the last example leads on already to a further sense.

b. With respect to the spiritual and moral state of man ταπεινός means "lowly," "servile," often with other terms which show that ταπεινός is used disparagingly. For the aristocratic culture of ancient Greece the worth of a man was determined by his parentage. A noble mind and virtue were inherited and could not be acquired → VI, 38, 12 f. ταπεινός expresses both the low estate of the man who lives in poor and petty relations, esp. the slave, and also the base disposition resulting therefrom. The ref. is not to the ethically negative characteristic of craftiness and falsehood nor to subjection to impulses but rather to the obsequiousness of the servant due to social status. Acc. to Hom. Od., 17, 322 f. all-seeing Zeus robs a man of half his worth ἀρετή when he brings close to him the day of servitude. This basic thought persists in spite of Sophist-Socratic criticism of aristocratic culture. Plat. Leg., VI, 774c calls δουλεία ταπεινὴ καὶ ἀνελεύθερος, cf. also Leg., V, 728e; VII, 791d. It is required of princess Andromache when she has become a slave: δεῖ σ' ἀντὶ τῶν πρὶν ὀλβίων φρονημάτων πτῆξαι ταπεινὴν προσπεσεῖν τ' ἐμὸν γόνυ, Eur. Andr., 164 f.; she is to display the lowly and submissive disposition which befits a slave. Xenoph. Cyrop., V, 1, 5 speaks of the noble figure of a prisoner καίπερ ἐν ταπεινῷ σχήματι ἑστηκυῖα, cf. also Eur. Fr., 688, 2 f. → 1, 24 f. Acc. to Aristot. Pol., IV, 11, p. 1295b, 18-21 those who have grown up in poverty are wholly of an ignoble disposition ταπεινοὶ λίαν and can exercise only menial dominion. Aristot. Eth. Nic., IV, 8, p. 1125a, 2 says the ταπεινοί are thorough flatterers and he closely associates ταπεινός and ἀγεννής, ibid., IV, 8, p. 1124b, 22.

Under the critical influence of the Sophists Eur. coined the statement that the name alone distinguishes a valiant slave from a free man, Ion, 854, cf. also Andr., 638; Hel., 729-733. A man's worth is recognised apart from his social position; for Socrates (→ VI, 38, 14 ff.) virtue can be taught and hence anyone can attain to a high and free disposition. Yet nothing is changed as regards the use of ταπεινός. Aristot. Pol., VIII, 2, p. 1337b, 8-15 attacks anything "that makes the body or spirit of free men unable to nurture or develop virtue... also financial matters. They hamper the spirit and make it ταπεινήν, unserviceable." Xenoph. Mem., III, 10, 5 contrasts τὸ μεγαλοπρεπές τε καὶ ἐλευθέριον καὶ τὸ ταπεινόν τε καὶ ἀνελεύθερον. To the question whether this is to be imitated the answer is given that men δι' ὧν τὰ καλά τε καὶ ἀγαθὰ καὶ ἀγαπητὰ ἤθη φαίνεται are to be viewed more favourably ἢ δι' ὧν τὰ αἰσχρά τε καὶ πονηρὰ καὶ μισητά. τὸ ταπεινόν belongs to the αἰσχρά τε καὶ πονηρὰ καὶ μισητά. The link with αἰσχρός is found also in Demosth. Or., 18, 178; Plut. Cato Minor, 32 (I, 774e), that with φαῦλος in Isoc. Or., 10, 12 and that with κάκιστος in Plut. De Nicia, 26 (I, 540 f.). These associations strengthen the negative character of ταπεινός. Thuc., II, 61, 2 speaks of διάνοια ταπεινή in the sense of lack of spirit. Demosth. Or., 18, 108 states in opposition to criticism of his policy: κακόηθες οὐδέν ἐστι πολίτευμα ἐμόν, οὐδὲ ταπεινόν, οὐδὲ τῆς πόλεως ἀνάξιον.

Epict. (→ VI, 38, 28 ff.) goes on to argue that all men, whatever their social status, are sons of one deity and citizens of one world and must meet in friendship. The man who is conscious of the divine relationship which underlies his human dignity does not speak basely or frivolously μηδὲ ταπεινοὺς μηδ' ἀγεννεῖς τινας διαλογισμούς, Diss., I, 9. 10. The scoundrel and calumniator are a baser ταπεινότερον animal than the fox, for they have forgotten the human dignity based on their relation with Zeus, Diss., I, 3, 8. Attachment to earthly things, which are not man's true possession since they can be taken from him, makes man a servant who becomes ungodly and unavoidably base in disposition ἀνάγκη δὲ καὶ ταπεινὸν εἶναι καὶ μικροπρεπές, Diss., IV, 7, 11; cf. III, 24, 56 (→ 5, 35 ff.) as opposed to μεγαλόψυχος - μεγαλόφρων etc. IV, 7, 8 f., cf. IV, 1, 2 and 54; 12, 20. All that alienates man from himself and makes him dependent, even though it be the urge for undisturbed studies, makes him small, IV, 4, 1; of a petty nature, cf. also II, 14, 22; 16, 18; III, 2, 14; 24, 58. The usage in Epict., confirmed by contemporaries, [2] is the more significant inasmuch as he belongs to a time close to the NT and the thoughts he utters are similar to many NT sayings.

c. ταπεινός can express the "difficult situation" of a man or society, also the "lowly status" to which they may reduce themselves for some reason, e.g., as petitioners. In Plut. one finds the phrase ταπεινὸν or ταπεινὰ πράττειν or ταπεινῶς ζῆν, "to live in relations which are lowly and bad," De Aristide, 27 (I, 335e); De Sulla, 1 (I, 451c); 7 (I, 456b) etc., [3] cf. already Eur. Herc. Fur., 1413; Demosth. Or., 61, 45; cf. 13, 25: it is not possible μικρὰ καὶ φαῦλα πράττοντας μέγα καὶ νεανικὸν φρόνημα λαβεῖν ὥσπερ οὐδὲ λαμπρὰ καὶ καλὰ πράττοντας μικρὸν καὶ ταπεινὸν φρονεῖν. Gk. thought, with its orientation to the mean, is opposed both to those who injure or illegally harm and wound (ὑβρίζω) others and also to those who remain patient and apathetic and suffer humiliation, the ταπεινοί. Orestes, become ταπεινός, stands over against Neoptolemos, who meets him as ὑβριστής, Eur. Andr., 977-980. Demosth. Or., 21, 186 reckons with the πολλοὶ λόγοι καὶ ταπεινοί of Midias and demands: ἔστι δ', ὅσῳ περ ἂν αὐτὸν νῦν ταπεινότερον ποιῇ, τοσούτῳ μᾶλλον ἄξιον μισεῖν αὐτόν. The main fault for Demosth. is that Midias is not really ταπεινός but makes himself so to win favour. Aristot. Rhet., II, 3, p. 1380a, 23-33 knows of human pity for the ταπεινοί (→ 5, 17 ff.), who are contrasted with the ὑβρισταί. This pity is exploited by those who like the two Quinctii come before the people as ταπεινοὶ καὶ δεδακρυμένοι to arouse sympathy, Plut. De Quinctio Flaminino, 19 (I, 379e), cf. also Tib. Gracch., 16 (I, 832c). Menelaos in Eur. Iph. Aul., 339 accuses Agamemnon of making himself ταπεινός to all in order to obtain his high rank by obsequiousness. This shows clearly why the ταπεινός becomes a flatterer. Eur. Fr., 81 (TGF, 384) demands: ταπεινὰ γὰρ χρὴ τοὺς κακῶς πεπραγότας λέγειν, cf. Eur. Tro., 1025-8. Plut. Apophth., 11 (II, 193a) tells how Epaminondas after the victory over the Lacedaemonians shows himself αὐχμηρὸς καὶ ταπεινός to the public; when asked why, he replies: "Yesterday I felt proud, as was right; to-day I scourge the immoderateness of my joy." Here becoming ταπεινός is compensation for the exaggerated joy of victory; it is meant to preserve the proper mean. Plut. Ser. Num. Vind., 3 (II, 549d) speaks of the κακία which as an evil human mind can be brought by divine chastisement to understanding (σύννους), humility (ταπεινή) and fear of God (κατάφοβος πρὸς τὸν θεόν). Here abasement, as the abasing of man's wickedness, can have positive significance even though it is not a positive good. [4] Isoc. Or., 4, 152 ref. to Persian satraps who are τὰ μὲν ταπεινῶς τὰ δ' ὑπερηφάνως ζῶντες; both are abhorred, cf. also Epict. Diss., II, 1, 11. Acc. to Plut. Aud. Poet., 9 (II, 28a) the right attitude is to withstand fate and hold one's head high καὶ ποιεῖν ὑψηλὸν ἑαυτὸν καὶ ἀταπείνωτον, i.e., not to surrender one's honour. It is not surprising, then, that the Gks. detested the eastern practice, widely followed among the Persians, of prostration before rulers, cf. Hdt., III, 86; Alexander, when he tries to introduce it, meets with resistance, Arrian Anabasis, [5] 4, 10, 5-12, 5. In pedagogy the humiliating of children, called ταπεινά like domestic animals in P. Gen., I, 14, 6, is rejected, Sen. De ira, 2, 19-21, cf. also Plut. Praec. Coniug., 8 (II, 139b).

---

[2] Rehrl, 30 f.

[3] Ibid., 31.

[4] Ibid., 44 f. Rehrl misunderstands this ref. in acc. with his dogmatic presuppositions, cf. Dihle, 742. Rehrl, 134-6 builds up from Plut. a picture of the humble man which the term ταπεινός itself does not support. Ibid., 140 he speaks of respect, esteem, awe, humility, wonder, subjection, and he concludes that "humility is thus sustained by these religious virtues." The impossibility of deducing all this from ταπεινός itself raises the basic question whether Rehrl does not put humility in this total picture in order to find there what he is looking for, esp. as he has a presupposed view of it on scholastic premisses. If Dihle begins with Augustine, Rehrl begins with Thomas Aquinas, cf. 13-23. But there is a gt. difference between them, for while Rehrl finds in Thomas the dogmatic basis which is to be confirmed, Dihle sees in Augustine the pt. where antiquity ends, and he sketches the development which leads up to this pt.

[5] Ed. A. G. Roos (1907).

d. ταπεινός can also mean sometimes "modest" and "obedient." Xenoph. Ag., 11, 11 describes the virtues of Agesilaos and calls him *inter al.*: καὶ τῷ μεγαλόφρονι οὐ σὺν ὕβρει ἀλλὰ σὺν γνώμῃ ἐχρῆτο· τῶν γοῦν ὑπεραύχων καταφρονῶν τῶν μετρίων ταπεινότερος ἦν. If the meaning here is "modest," the term takes on the sense of "obedient" in Isoc. Or., 3, 56: The obedience of subjects to government — ταπεινοὺς μὲν εἶναι χρὴ πρὸς τὴν ἀρχὴν τὴν ἐμήν — is the presupposition of its success and its ordering of the affairs of the citizens. Xenoph. Resp. Lac., 8, 2 says of the Lacedaemonians: τῷ ταπεινοὶ εἶναι μεγαλύνονται. They regard obedience in state, army and family as the highest good; this obedience must not be a mere sham (Plut. De Dione, 33 [I, 973a]) or compliant self-surrender (Plut. Adulat., 19 [II, 60 f.]).

e. Oceanus demands of Prometheus that he be ταπεινός *vis-à-vis* the gods, Aesch. Prom., 320, but Prometheus counts on Zeus humbling himself, 908. The context shows that in the saying of Oceanus ταπεινός means "to become obedient," "to adjust to." It has this sense in the well-known ref. Plat. Leg., IV, 716a, where it occurs with κεκοσμημένος: ταπεινὸς καὶ κεκοσμημένος, i.e., in relation to the laws originating in δίκη. It is contrasted with an attitude characterised as ἐξαρθεὶς ὑπὸ μεγαλαυχίας and is finally called ὕβρις, and it expresses prudence. The man who adjusts compliantly to δίκη is one who follows the deity τῶν συνακολουθησόντων... τῷ θεῷ, IV, 716b. It is best not to speak of humility here; the term is controlled by κεκοσμημένος and means "to adjust to" rather than "to humble or to abase oneself." [6] As the context shows plainly, the ref. is to the mean which is provided for man in the deity [7] and which he achieves in common following thereof. [8]

3. ταπεινόω. [9]

ταπεινόω is found in the act., mid. and pass. from Hippocr. Κῳακαὶ προγνώσιες, 7, 208 (Littré, V) etc.

a. It means "to make small or little," "to humiliate," "to weaken," e.g., the spleen, Plat. Tim., 72d, the power of a state, Xenoph. Hist. Graec., V, 3, 27; Plut. Lucull., 21 (I, 505c), the renown of the Athenians, Xenoph. Mem., III, 5, 4.

b. Men "exploit," "oppress," Epict. Diss., III, 24, 75; Plut. C. Gracch., 9 (I, 838d), they "humble," "put down," Polyb., 3, 116, 8 they "humiliate others by breaking their spirit," Plut. Cim., 12 (I, 485e); Mar., 41 (I, 430a). Aristot. Rhet., II, 12, p. 1389a, 32 is aware that the course of life can rob man of his courage and high spirit and leave him dispirited (τεταπείνωνται) ὑπὸ τοῦ βίου πω, cf. II, 13, p. 1389b, 25: διὰ τὸ τεταπεινῶσθαι ὑπὸ τοῦ βίου. Philodem. Philos. Περὶ κακιῶν [10] Col. 15, 5-7 calls it ἄδικον διὰ τοῦ ταπεινοῦν ἑτέρους ἑαυτὸν μετεωρίζειν and right to console and uplift τοὺς ταπεινουμένους (11, 30), statements governed by the equal dignity of every man for this Epicurean philosopher. Plat. Lys., 210e says one must deal with the young so as to bring them to obedience and modesty ταπεινοῦντα καὶ συστέλλοντα and not to leave them indisciplined and arrogant χαυνοῦντα καὶ διαθρύπτοντα. It is necessary to control human

---

[6] What is said → n. 4 applies also to this passage and its interpretation by Rehrl, 40-43. Dihle, 754 ref. to Orig. Cels., III, 61 and VI, 15; Celsus stresses κεκοσμημένος and sees here the opp. of Christianity, which injures and insults man's dignity.

[7] In contrast to Protagoras, for whom man is the measure of all things.

[8] Dihle, 742 f. thinks the background of the reception of the biblical and Chr. view of humility in the Hell. world is the fixed Roman social order with the sharp social distinctions based on position in the *civitas*. For this "*humilior* is an official term for the little man," 743.

[9] The noun ταπεινότης (from ταπεινός) does not occur in the NT or post-apost. fathers, and in the LXX we find it only at Sir. 13:20 B: βδέλυγμα ὑπερηφάνῳ ταπεινότης (A reads: ταπείνωσις, so ταπεινότης is not solidly attested). On its use in Gr. lit. cf. Thuc., VII, 75; Demosth. Or., 10, 74; Isoc. Or., 4, 118; 7, 4; Xenoph. Hist. Graec., III, 5, 21; Plat. Polit., 309a; Aristot. De Virtutibus et vitiis, 7, p. 1251b, 15 and 25; Rhet., II, 6, p. 1384a, 4 etc.

[10] Ed. C. Jensen (1911).

desire so that like a restive steed it obeys the discretion of the charioteer ταπεινωθείς ἕπεται, Plat. Phaedr., 254e. Men should subject themselves to reason ταπεινωθέντες, Plat. Theaet., 191a. Like ταπεινός (→ 4, 14 ff.), ταπεινόω has also in Plat. the sense "obediently to fit into a given order." Xenoph. An., VI, 3, 16 says: καὶ ὁ θεὸς ἴσως ἄγει οὕτως, ὃς τοὺς μεγαληγορήσαντας ὡς πλέον φρονοῦντας ταπεινῶσαι βούλεται, ἡμᾶς δὲ τοὺς ἀπὸ τῶν θεῶν ἀρχομένους ἐντιμοτέρους ἐκείνων καταστῆσαι. Epict. Diss., I, 6, 40 sees man endowed with powers which enable him to bear all things without being oppressed or downcast (→ lines 32 ff.) μὴ ταπεινούμενοι μηδὲ συγκλώμενοι ὑπ' αὐτοῦ. A rightly brought up young man does not let himself be dispirited by poor clothes ταπεινώσῃ nor does he swagger ἐπάρῃ in fine raiment, because he knows the God in whose company he is, Diss., II, 8, 15 f.; cf. also II, 16, 16; III, 23, 10; 26, 35. Acc. to Plut. Aud. Poet., 13 (II, 35d) knowledge of the poets helps to μεγαλοφροσύνη and keeps from ταπεινοῦσθαι, cf. also Cons. ad Apoll., 29 (II, 116e).

That man should humble or belittle himself is rejected. Plut. De exilio, 1 (II, 599b) seeks in misfortune men who teach us that τὸ λυπεῖσθαι καὶ τὸ ταπεινοῦν ἑαυτόν is quite unnecessary, vain and irrational. ἑαυτὸν ταπεινοῦν is practised to gain the favour of the people (→ 3, 14 ff.), Plut. Quaest. Rom., 49 (II, 276d). Aristot. Rhet., II, 3, p. 1380a, 23-33 says that one should not contradict those who disparage themselves — mid. ταπεινουμένους — since they show themselves to be weaker and meaner. Plut. Quaest. Rom., 10 (II, 266 d) reckons with the possibility that concealing the head in sacrifice and prayer achieves the end of humbling oneself before the gods. Here ταπεινοῦν ἑαυτόν has a positive sense, but for Plut. this is only one way of explaining the practice, and he seems to prefer others. [11]

4. ταπείνωσις.

ταπείνωσις means "reducing," "diminution," of a bodily swelling, Aristot. Part. An., IV, 10, p. 689a, 25, of a man by fate, Philodem. Philos. Περὶ κακιῶν (→ n. 10), Col. 10, 34; Polyb., 9, 33, 10. ὑψώματα καὶ ταπεινώματα of the stars cause ἀμαύρωσις "weakening," "obscuring" ἢ ταπείνωσις "humiliation," "depression" in man, Plut. Sept. Sap. Conv., 9 (II, 149a). Epict. Diss., III, 22, 104 uses it similarly of the mind.

5. ταπεινόφρων, ταπεινοφροσύνη. [12]

a. ταπεινόφρων is attested in Plut.; he rejects the view that fate makes gt. men fearful and poor-spirited ταπεινόφρονας while good fortune produces ἀνδρείαν καὶ φρόνησιν, Alex. Fort. Virt., 4 (II, 336e). Fortune may afflict a man with sickness, take away his goods, kindle the hatred of a people or tyrant, but it cannot make him bad, fearful, abject ταπεινόφρονα, ignoble or envious, Tranq. An., 17 (II, 475e).

b. Outside the NT ταπεινοφροσύνη occurs in Epict. Diss., III, 24, 56: He who is not tied by things man cannot control but despises them, and judges aright, and keeps his impulses and desires in rein, is incapable of flatteries and a mean and petty disposition ταπεινοφροσύνη; in context this denotes weakness and pusillanimity. [13]

6. The Meaning of the Derivates.

The derivates of ταπεινός confirm its meaning and use. They, too, are always employed negatively except that in Plat. (→ 4, 14 ff.) they also acquire the nuance of obedient integration into a given order which man sees to be rational and in Plut., though the sense is negative, it can move in the direction of man's subjection to deity → 5, 19 ff.

---

[11] Hence Rehrl's depiction (62-65) needs to be considerably qualified → n. 4, 6.
[12] Trench, 84-87.
[13] Epict. Diss., I, 9, 10 has the verb ταπεινοφρονέω; in Chr. writings it occurs for the first time only in the post-apost. period.

B. The Use of the Word Group in the Septuagint.

1. The Hebrew Originals of the Greek Terms.

In the LXX ταπεινός and derivates are much more common than in Gk. and Hell. literature. ταπεινός is prominent and esp. the verb ταπεινόω; the former occurs 67 times for 12 Hbr. stems, while ταπεινόω occurs some 165 times for 20 Hbr. groups with their different verbal forms. [14] The most prolific use is in Is. and Ps. ταπείνωσις occurs 39 times for four Hbr. equivalents, [15] while ταπεινοφρονέω and ταπεινόφρων are found only once each.

The prominence of the verb in the use of the group shows that the main ref. is to an action rather than a state, and that this includes its results. This is confirmed by the Hbr. equivalents. Among them special significance attaches to the group עָנָה, עָנִי, עָנָו, עָנִי and עֲנָוָה. [16] To get at their meaning it is as well to begin with the verb, since the adj. and noun correspond to this. [17] The basic sense of the verb is "to stoop," "to stoop low." The lion at his prey is not afraid and does not stoop at the noise of the approaching shepherd, Is. 31:4. Sheep without a shepherd flee and bow down, Zech. 10:2. The basic sense then gives us "to humble oneself," Ps. 119:67; ni Is. 53:7; hitp Gn. 16:9, also "to show oneself to be humbled," hitp 1 K. 2:26; Ps. 107:17. The verb is used intr. "to be humbled" q Ps. 116:10; ni Is. 58:10 and Ps. 119:107. The causative pi "to humble someone" ref. to an individual, Gn. 16:6; 31:50; Ex. 22:21, 22 etc., or a whole people, Gn. 15:13; Ex. 1:11 f. etc. With the verb one finds 2 adj.: עָנִי derives from עָנָה "to be humbled" and means "humbled" by necessity or sickness ("afflicted") or by poverty and want ("poor"); עָנָו derives from עָנָה "to humble oneself" and means basically "bent" under what is overhanging or what happens. This is confirmed by the Gk. rendering of the two words. עָנִי is usually transl. πένης (→ VI, 38, 40 ff.), πτωχός (→ VI, 888, 3 ff.), [18] also ἀσθενής and ταπεινός but עָנָו is only rarely transl. πένης (Ps. 10:17; 22:26) or πτωχός (Is. 29:19; 61:1; Ps. 69:33) and is mostly rendered by πραΰς (→ VI, 647, 9 ff.) and ταπεινός. ταπεινός is thus used for both adj. and means both the lowly estate of the afflicted and also the disposition of the one who humbles himself, whether negatively as "subservient" or positively as "modest," "humble," "compliant."

The situation is the same with the nouns. עֳנִי means the "affliction" which bows man down, Gn. 16:11; 29:32; 1 S. 1:11, while עֲנָוָה (always post-exilic apart from Zeph. 2:3) ref. to the disposition of the one who humbles himself and means "compliance" or "humility," Prv. 15:33; 18:12; 22:4; cf. also Sir. 3:17; 4:8; 10:28; 13:20; 45:4. In the LXX עֳנִי is rendered by ταπείνωσις and also by πενία, πτωχεία, θλῖψις etc., while עֲנָוָה is transl. πραΰτης.

2. ταπεινόω.

a. ταπεινόω means act. "to bow down," "to make low," "to humble": πενία ἄνδρα ταπεινοῖ Prv. 10:4; mountains and hills are to be laid low for the triumphant way in

---

[14] The chief Hbr. equivalents of ταπεινός are אֶבְיוֹן, דַּךְ, דַּכָּא, דַּל, עֹמֶק מוּךְ, עָנִי and עָנָו, also רוּשׁ, שָׁפֵל and derivates; ταπεινόω transl. עָנָה and derivates, דָּכָה, דָּכָא, בָּלָה, כָּנַע, זָלַל, דָּלַל which is preferred in Ch., also מוּךְ and מָכַךְ, עָנָה, which is esp. common in the historical books and Hos., then שׁוּה and שָׁפֵל.

[15] The Hbr. equivalents of ταπείνωσις are דַּכָּא, עֳנִי and תַּעֲנִית, עֹצֶר, שֶׁפֶל.

[16] Cf. E. Kutsch, עֲנָוָה (Demut). Ein Beitrag zum Thema „Gott u. Mensch im AT," Mainz (1960).

[17] Kutsch, op. cit., 49 takes issue here with A. Rahlfs, עָנִי u. עָנָו in d. Ps. (1892) and H. Birkeland, Ani u. anaw in d. Ps. (1933). Rahlfs starts with the lowliness of the servant compared to his master, while Birkeland sees in the adj. a state of diminished power, ability, or worth. Both thus define the meaning in terms of a state rather than thinking of an act or event.

[18] The statements here need to be modified in the light of Kutsch's researches (→ n. 16).

the desert, Is. 40:4; Bar. 5:7; the one who sits on the high throne is contrasted with the one who is humbled to earth and ashes, Sir. 40:3. In the mid. it means "to become poor," Lv. 25:39, "to sink down," "to humble oneself," Qoh. 10:18.

b. When humiliation is by force ταπεινόω takes on the sense "to bend," "to harass," "to oppress," Gn. 15:13 (associated with δουλόω and κακόω); 31:50; Ex. 1:12; Dt. 26:6; Ju. 12:2 A; 1 Βασ. 12:8; 2 Βασ. 7:10; 1 Ch. 17:9; Jdt. 5:11; Is. 51:23; 60:14; ψ 9:31; 93:5, cf. 105:42 f.: καὶ ἐταπεινώθησαν ἐν ταῖς ἀνομίαις αὐτῶν. ταπεινόω can also mean "to overthrow," "to weaken," Ju. 16:5, 6, 19; 1 Ch. 20:4; 2 Ch. 13:18. It may then have the sense "to destroy," "to blot out," 1 Βασ. 26:9; Mal. 2:12. Any power brought to bear on man can be expressed by ταπεινόω, "to force": ἐταπείνωσαν ἐν πέδαις τοὺς πόδας αὐτοῦ, ψ 104:18. Along the same lines the LXX uses ταπεινόω for "to force" a woman, so Gn. 34:2; Dt. 22:24, 29; Ju. 19:24; 20:5; 2 Βασ. 13:12, 14; Lam. 5:11. Since it can also be employed for "to use sexually," Dt. 21:14; Ez. 22:10 f., the basic sense is plainly "to humble a woman" with an emphasis on the unlawfulness of the act, 2 Βασ. 13:12.

c. ταπεινόω ἐμαυτόν or mid. pass. ταπεινόομαι "to abase oneself," "cast oneself down," as in the direction of the angel to Hagar: ταπεινώθητι ὑπὸ τὰς χεῖρας αὐτῆς (sc. Sarah), Gn. 16:9; Est. 6:13; ψ 38:3. LXX has the repeated phrase ταπεινώσατε τὰς ψυχὰς ὑμῶν, "to humble one's soul," "to fast," Lv. 16:29; cf. 16:31; 23:27, 29, 32; Jdt. 4:9; Is. 58:3, 5 and ψ 34:13 f., in which it is esp. clear that the decisive issue in such fasting (→ III, 837, 28 ff.; IV, 927, 25 ff.) is not just the observance in which self-humbling finds visible expression but more particularly the subjection of the mind to God's will and judgment, which alone gives to the outward exercise any value before God. This fasting expresses abasement before God. [19] Manasseh, the king of Israel led away into captivity by the Assyrians, seeks God's face καὶ ἐταπεινώθη σφόδρα ἀπὸ προσώπου θεοῦ τῶν πατέρων αὐτοῦ, and he is heard, 2 Ch. 33:12 f., cf. also the saying of God to Josiah in 2 Ch. 34:27. Of Amon, Manasseh's son, however, it is said that he did not humble himself like his father, 2 Ch. 33:23; [20] cf. also 2 Εσδρ. 8:21 and Sir. 2:17: οἱ φοβούμενοι κύριον ἑτοιμάσουσιν καρδίας αὐτῶν καὶ ἐνώπιον αὐτοῦ ταπεινώσουσιν τὰς ψυχὰς αὐτῶν, also Jer. 13:18; Da. 10:12; Sir. 3:18; 7:17.

In fasting a man humbles himself before God but not before other men. Only in a few passages, always in the later Wisdom lit., do we read of abasement before men; in Prv. 13:7 the hitp means "to make oneself poor." Many make themselves poor but have gt. riches (Mas.); LXX gives the moral and religious sense: There are men who humble themselves at gt. wealth. Here, too, there is contrast between ταπεινοῦντες ἑαυτοὺς and πλουτίζοντες ἑαυτούς, cf. also Prv. 25:7 and Sir. 4:8; 12:11; 29:5; Lk. 14:7-11; these passages are critical of this self-abasement. In the OT, then, we find no glorifying of self-abasement. There is prophetic criticism of fasting customs and stress is laid on the proper attitude of the heart to God and His will, Jl. 2:12 f.; Is. 58:5 ff.

---

[19] Two Gk. inscr. of Jewish origin from the 2nd/1st cent. B.C. which show the influence of the LXX on the religious life of Hell. Judaism contain prayers for vengeance; they ref. to the fasting of the gt. Day of Atonement. In them we read: πᾶσα ψυχὴ ἐν τῇ σήμερον ἡμέρᾳ ταπεινοῦται μεθ' ἱκετείας, Deissmann LO, 352-8. ταπεινόω has the sense of Lv. 23:29: "to mortify oneself," "to fast," cf. Lv. 16:29, 31 and ψ 34:13.

[20] The "humility" ענוה of the king who bows before deity and worships it, esp. by building a temple and establishing its cultus in thanksgiving for granted victories, is widespread in the Near East, cf. S. Mowinckel, "Die vorderasiat. Königs- u. Fürsteninschr.," Eucharistion f. H. Gunkel, I, FRL, 36, 1 (1923), 278-322; Kutsch, op. cit., 105-120. In LXX the main OT passages ψ 44:5; 131:1-5; Zech. 9:9 are transl. by πραΰτης or πραΰς → VI, 647, 32 ff. "In the introductions in ψ 15:1; 55:1; 56:1; 59:1 'ΑΣ read מכתם "expiation" (?) from the roots מוך and תמם and transl. ταπεινοφροσύνη (or ταπεινός, cf. ταπεινὸς τῇ καρδίᾳ Is. 35:4 'A in the same sense), τέλειος etc. (on מוך cf. Lv. 25:25 Σ; 25:39; 27:8 LXX). There was thus developed the picture of the Messianic king (David) as the prince of peace, Is. 9:5, 6" [Bertram].

d. Of special significance are the many statements in which God is the subject of action. That God lays low the high and mighty is part of His work in history as experienced by Israel, as is also His choosing and exalting of the lowly, 1 Βασ. 2:7; Ez. 21:31; Sir. 7:11; cf. 2 Βασ. 22:28; Hos. 14:9. [21]

Israel knows this in its own history, 3 Βασ. 8:35; 2 Ch. 6:26; 28:19; 32:26; Is. 64:11; ψ 89:15; God humbles it for its sin, ψ 146:6, and ὕβρις, Hos. 5:5; 7:10; cf. Job 22:12; 40:11. The same applies to Israel's foes when it receives help from God, Ju. 4:23; 5:13 A; 1 Βασ. 7:13; 1 Ch. 17:10; Ez. 17:24; Da. 7:24; ψ 54:20; 71:4; 80:15; 88:11. Individuals also experience it in their own lives, Rt. 1:21; 1 Ch. 4:10; Tob. 4:19. [22] This divine work of God in history may be educational, as attested esp. in the Wisdom lit.: πρὸ συντριβῆς ὑψοῦται καρδία ἀνδρός, καὶ πρὸ δόξης ταπεινοῦται, Prv. 18:12, cf. also 29:23: ὕβρις ἄνδρα ταπεινοῖ, also Sir. 13:8; 18:21. The most ample expression of God's abasing and exalting work in history is to be found in the earlier prophecy of Is. Is. proclaims in the name of God: πάντας ὑπερηφάνους ταπεινώσω, Is. 1:25, cf. 10.33. On the day of Yahweh it takes place that "the proudly uplifted eyes of men will become humble and the pride of men will be brought low. But the Lord alone is exalted on that day," 2:11. In the LXX this threat becomes the principle of God's sole exaltation in face of which man is base: οἱ γὰρ ὀφθαλμοὶ κυρίου ὑψηλοί, ὁ δὲ ἄνθρωπος ταπεινός· καὶ ταπεινωθήσεται τὸ ὕψος τῶν ἀνθρώπων, καὶ ὑψωθήσεται κύριος μόνος ἐν τῇ ἡμέρᾳ ἐκείνῃ.

The prophet directs this message against Jerusalem and Zion, not against their foes, Is. 3:8, 17, 26; 29:4. The humiliation of all the arrogant takes place in face of Hades, so that their abasement is approaching death and destruction, Is. 5:14 f. [23] What is stated in prophecy and penetrates Israel's awareness finds a strong echo in the laments of Lam. 1:5, 8, 12; 2:5; 3:32-34 and esp. the Ps. The Ps. are governed by the realisation: ὁ θεὸς κριτής ἐστιν· τοῦτον ταπεινοῖ καὶ τοῦτον ὑψοῖ, ψ 74:8. The Psalmist sees and confesses that he is punished with sickness for his sin: ἐκακώθην καὶ ἐταπεινώθην, ψ 37:9; πτωχός εἰμι ἐγὼ καὶ ἐν κόποις ἐκ νεότητός μου, ὑψωθεὶς δὲ ἐταπεινώθην καὶ ἐξηπορήθην, ψ 87:16; cf. also ψ 106:12, 17. With the sickness which oppresses and humbles him he is overshadowed by death ψ 43:20, which humbles him to the dust ψ 43:26, cf. 142:3. But he is also aware that God does not repel the man who accepts abasement and humbles himself beneath God's hand: καρδίαν συντετριμμένην καὶ τεταπεινω-μένην ὁ θεὸς οὐκ ἐξουθενώσει, ψ 50:19, so that he will rejoice again, 50:10. He sees that God is humbling him in order to set him in a right relationship to Himself; when he is abased man finds that, thrown back on God, he is like a child before Him. This is clear in a confession which comes close to the message of Jesus: φυλάσσω τὰ νήπια ὁ κύριος· ἐταπεινώθην, καὶ ἔσωσέν με, ψ 114:6. Deliverance leads to the testimony: ἐπίστευσα, διὸ ἐλάλησα· ἐγὼ δὲ ἐταπεινώθην σφόδρα, ψ 115:1, which acc. to the HT means "I spoke the truth when I said, I was greatly bowed down," Ps. 116:9; cf. also ψ 141:7. Hence abasement and affliction can finally be regarded as salvation: ἀγαθόν μοι ὅτι ἐταπείνωσάς με, ὅπως ἂν μάθω τὰ δικαιώματά σου, ψ 118:71, cf. also v. 67, 75, 107. When God brings a man down He is not acting out of the caprice which overthrows justice, Lam. 3:35; Job 37:23, as men do, Ex. 23:2; Dt. 16:19 (always ענה). He is working out His saving purposes for that man. Man has to learn God's commandment and find the relation of obedience to it. God's faithfulness abases man, as the Psalmist recognises in

---

[21] The Gks. see a similar divine action, cf. Hes. Op., 5-8: He (Zeus) readily grants strength, but readily encumbers the strong as well; he readily makes the fortunate small and lifts up the hidden. He readily makes the crooked straight and causes the proud to wilt. He, Zeus, the Thunderer from the heights, who dwells in the highest chambers; cf. also Eur. Tro., 612 f.: ὁρῶ τὰ τῶν θεῶν, ὡς τὰ μὲν πυργοῦσ' ἄνω τὸ μηδὲν ὄντα, τὰ δὲ δοκοῦντ' ἀπώλεσαν.

[22] Is. 58:10: ψυχὴ τεταπεινωμένη, which needs the help of fellow-men, cf. also Is. 51:21 and Da. 3:39 LXX: πνεῦμα τεταπεινωμένον.

[23] Cf. also the oracle on the nations Is. 25:11 f. and 26:5 f.

Ps. 119: "I know, O Lord, that thy judgments are righteousness, and that thou in faithfulness hast afflicted me," Ps. 119:75 (LXX καὶ ἀληθείᾳ ἐταπείνωσάς με, ψ 118:75). Hence Yahweh does not bring down for ever, Lam. 3:31 f.; when man repents, the affliction ceases, 3 Βασ. 8:35 f. This is rooted in the experience of Israel to which Dt. 8:2 f., 16 refers. Israel, when afflicted by Yahweh, has to learn that it does not live by bread alone but by the Lord who creates with His Word. LXX here transl. עָנָה by κακόω "to cause to go badly." The pt. of God's abasement is thus to set the one abased in a right relation to Himself.

3. ταπεινός.

a. In the LXX, as in Gk. lit., ταπεινός means "low," "flat," "under": Joshua conquers τὸ ὄρος Ισραηλ καὶ τὰ ταπεινά, Jos. 11:16, cf. also Ju. 1:15; 1 Macc. 6:40; ψ 112:6 f.; 137:6. Connected with this basic sense is the use of ταπεινός for leprosy deep below the skin: καὶ ἡ ὄψις τῆς ἁφῆς ταπεινὴ ἀπὸ τοῦ δέρματος τοῦ χρωτός, Lv. 13:3, cf. v. 4, 20, 21, 25, 26, also 14:37. ταπεινός is used fig. for "low" as opp. to high in Qoh. 10:6.

b. ταπεινός "bowed," "mean," "small," "base," is mostly negative as in Gk. usage (→ 2, 6 ff.), Sir. 25:23; 29:8; a man's little worth as compared to others, Lv. 27:8; also ἀρχὴ ταπεινὴ παρὰ πάσας τὰς ἀρχάς, Ez. 29:14 f.; cf. Da. 3:37, where the small significance of the Israelites on the whole earth is attributed to their sins. Gideon calls his house ταπεινοτέρα ἐν Μανασση, Ju. 6:15A.

The special OT situation comes to light in Ju. 6:15: God chooses precisely the small and insignificant for His plans. The same applies to David: κἀγὼ ἀνὴρ ταπεινὸς καὶ οὐχὶ ἔνδοξος (1 Βασ. 18:23). Jdt. 9:11 has the confession: ταπεινῶν εἶ θεός. In Zeph. 2:3 πάντες ταπεινοὶ γῆς are summoned to seek the Lord. ταπεινοί are those who keep God's statutes, i.e., who do what is right in relation to God, cf. Ps. 119:67. In Zeph. 2:3 the summons to the ταπεινοί or עֲנָוִים is set in the midst of threats (1:2-18 and 2:4-15) and in the context of a call to repentance (v. 1) in view of the limited time available before God's wrath breaks forth, v. 2. Those addressed separate themselves from the "people which is not ashamed" (v. 1) and which is called to repentance, by doing what is right before God. They are summoned to seek the Lord, i.e., to seek צֶדֶק and עֲנָוָה; they are thus to hold fast to what they are that they might be kept in the judgment. עֲנָוָה is a right attitude to God which obediently asks concerning His law and will. In keeping is the promise of Zeph. 3:12 that God will leave in Israel λαὸν πραῢν καὶ ταπεινόν, i.e., עַם עָנִי וָדָל, which seeks refuge in the name of the Lord. Probably connected with the election of the ταπεινοί is the insight: οὗ ἐὰν εἰσέλθῃ ὕβρις, ἐκεῖ καὶ ἀτιμία· στόμα δὲ ταπεινῶν μελετᾷ σοφίαν, Prv. 11:2, cf. also Sir. 11:1.

c. ταπεινός means "bowed down," "oppressed," "held down," e.g., by foreign political and military powers, Jdt. 16:11; 1 Macc. 14:14; by the oppression of the rich and mighty, Am. 2:7; Is. 58:4. God is the One who hears the desire of the poor and is ready to establish right ὀρφανῷ καὶ ταπεινῷ, ψ 9:38 f. Correspondingly it is God's demand κρίνατε ὀρφανὸν καὶ πτωχόν, ταπεινὸν καὶ πένητα, ψ 81:3; note the close connection of ταπεινός and ὀρφανός with πτωχός (→ VI, 888, 3 ff.) and πένης (→ VI, 38, 40 ff.), cf. also ψ 73:21: τεταπεινωμένος (דַּךְ), κατῃσχυμμένος (נִכְלָם), πτωχός (עָנִי), πένης (אֶבְיוֹן). Poverty and lowliness are directly related; for poverty is one of the things that bow man down, cf. also Am. 8:6 or Sir. 13:21 f.: ταπεινός with opp. πλούσιος, but in v. 23 πτωχός and πλούσιος, also Is. 61:1 S * ταπεινοῖς for πτωχοῖς. Prv. 30:14 ref. to the wicked generation which seeks κατεσθίειν τοὺς ταπεινοὺς ἀπὸ τῆς γῆς καὶ τοὺς πένητας αὐτῶν ἐξ ἀνθρώπων, cf. also Is. 32:7; Jer. 22:16.

d. Against this background stands the message: God saves and exalts the lowly and oppressed and overthrows and destroys high and arrogant oppressors: σὺ λαὸν ταπεινὸν σώσεις καὶ ὀφθαλμοὺς ὑπερηφάνων ταπεινώσεις, ψ 17:28. This is true not only when the oppressed are in a situation of external oppression but also when the oppression is from within: ἐγγὺς κύριος τοῖς συντετριμμένοις τὴν καρδίαν καὶ τοὺς ταπεινοὺς τῷ πνεύματι σώσει, ψ 33:19. For oppression through external relations causes an oppressed spirit and heart. It is the eternal nature of God, who is exalted above all nations and all heavens, that He, "our God, who dwells on high, looks down to what is low," accepting the poor, ψ 112:4-7, cf. also ψ 137:6. Hence He sees ἐπὶ τὴν προσευχὴν τῶν ταπεινῶν and does not despise their prayer, ψ 101:18, cf. Sir. 35:17-19. μεγάλη ἡ δυναστεία τοῦ κυρίου καὶ ὑπὸ τῶν ταπεινῶν δοξάζεται, Sir. 3:20. In Wisdom lit. this experience yields the insight: κύριος ὑπερηφάνοις ἀντιτάσσεται, ταπεινοῖς δὲ δίδωσιν χάριν, Prv. 3:34 (→ 19, 14 ff.; 24, 2 f.); [24] cf. Sir. 10:15; Job 5:11; 12:21; also Ez. 17:24 and 21:31: ἐταπείνωσας τὸ ὑψηλὸν καὶ τὸ ταπεινὸν ὕψωσας. It is again Is. (→ 8, 12 ff.) who especially develops this message, 2:11. The work of the coming One is seen in the light of it. The Messiah establishes right for the weak דל (LXX ταπεινός) and pronounces sentence for the oppressed of the land לְעַנְוֵי־אָרֶץ LXX τοὺς ταπεινοὺς τῆς γῆς, 11:4. The LXX shows that for it the ταπεινός is the righteous man who does what is right before Yahweh; his opposite is the ἀσεβής, cf. also Sir. 12:5. In sayings in Is. the effect of this message is clear. The promise is given: δι᾽ αὐτοῦ σωθήσονται οἱ ταπεινοὶ τοῦ λαοῦ, in the HT: "There the poor of his people have a refuge," 14:32. God is invoked as πάσῃ πόλει ταπεινῇ βοηθός, in the HT: "A stronghold to the lowly, a stronghold to the poor in his distress," 25:4. 26:4-6, on the other hand, speaks of the humbling of the lofty and the triumph of the lowly over them. In Dt. Is. this message is developed in such a way that witness is borne especially to comfort for the humble and oppressed who in the despondency of their hearts put their trust solely in God's help: ἠλέησεν ὁ θεὸς τὸν λαὸν αὐτοῦ καὶ τοὺς ταπεινοὺς τοῦ λαοῦ αὐτοῦ παρεκάλεσεν, 49:13. The permanence of the covenant of peace is promised to the ταπεινή, 54:10 f. At the end of Is. is a divine saying testifying to the election of the distressed in their oppression: God's eyes are on τὸν ταπεινὸν καὶ ἡσύχιον καὶ τρέμοντα τοὺς λόγους μου, 66:2. The ὅσιοι καὶ ταπεινοὶ καρδίᾳ are summoned to praise God, Da. 3:87. πραΰς and ταπεινός, expressing forbearance and submission to God, occur together in Is. 26:6; Zeph. 3:12; cf. also Prv. 16:19.

4. ταπείνωσις.

ταπείνωσις means "humble, difficult situation," "lowliness," then the resulting disposition of the soul, "sorrow," "grief"; this finds its expression in "fasting."

There is ref. to the oppressed situation of the people in Egypt in Dt. 26:7; 2 Εσδρ. 19:9; ψ 135:23; to oppression by foreign nations in Canaan in 1 Βασ. 9:16, then in the exilic and post-exilic periods in Est. 4:8; Jdt. 6:19; 7:32; 13:20; Lam. 1:3, 7, 9. Dt. Is. can proclaim to the people: ἐπλήσθη ἡ ταπείνωσις αὐτῆς, λέλυται αὐτῆς ἡ ἁμαρτία, 40:2. The prayer of the high-priest Simon recalls God's continual help: ἐπεὶ δὲ πλεονάκις θλιβέντων τῶν πατέρων ἡμῶν ἐβοήθησας αὐτοῖς ἐν τῇ ταπεινώσει, 3 Μacc. 2:12. Concerning the sorrow produced by the lowly situation one reads that on account of the

---

[24] The text of Prv. 15:33 (16:1) is uncertain: "The fear of the Lord is instruction and wisdom; and before honour is humility," cf. προσπορεύεται δὲ ταπεινοῖς δόξα in Cod A א.

desecration of the temple καὶ οἱ ἱερεῖς σου ἐν πένθει καὶ ταπεινώσει (fasting), 1 Macc. 3:51; in the prayer of the three in the fiery furnace: ἐν ψυχῇ συντετριμμένῃ καὶ πνεύματι ταπεινώσεως προσδεχθείημεν, Da. 3:39 Θ (LXX πνεύματι τεταπεινωμένῳ).

There is often ref. to the situation of individuals, e.g., Hagar when expelled by Sarah in Gn. 16:11; unloved Leah in Gn. 29:32; Jacob serving Laban in Gn. 31:42; Joseph in Egypt in Gn. 41:52; the childlessness of Hannah, the mother of Samuel, 1 Βασ. 1:11; David under the curse of Shimei in his flight before Absalom in 2 Βασ. 16:12; [25] Ezra in 2 Εσδρ. 9:5. Some statements in the Ps. may be mentioned in this connection. Threatened by death, the Psalmist asks the Lord to look on the ταπείνωσις brought on him by his enemies and to deliver him, ψ 9:14. ταπείνωσις can thus denote the destiny of death by which man is brought to dust, ψ 89:3. In Sir. 11:12 עָפָר צַחֲנָה "dust of corruption" is transl. by ταπείνωσις. This ταπείνωσις has its cause in sin: ἰδὲ τὴν ταπείνωσίν μου καὶ τὸν κόπον μου καὶ ἄφες πάσας τὰς ἁμαρτίας μου, ψ 24:18. In ταπείνωσις God's Word and instruction helps to life, ψ 118:50, 92. Hence he who trusts and keeps it can pray: ἰδὲ τὴν ταπείνωσίν μου καὶ ἐξελοῦ με, ὅτι τὸν νόμον σου οὐκ ἐπελαθόμην, ψ 118:153. Joy is the response to the experience of such deliverance: ἀγαλλιάσομαι καὶ εὐφρανθήσομαι ἐπὶ τῷ ἐλέει σου, ὅτι ἐπεῖδες τὴν ταπείνωσίν μου, ἔσωσας ἐκ τῶν ἀναγκῶν τὴν ψυχήν μου, ψ 30:8.

What is prayer and experience in the Ps., threat and promise in the prophets, and event in the history books, is said to be the insight of wisdom in the Wisdom lit. Acc. to Prv. 16:19 it is better to handle those who are in oppression with patience and gentleness πραΰθυμος μετὰ ταπεινώσεως than to share the prey with the arrogant. Sir. discerns in God's action His purpose to guide and instruct: ἐν ἀλλάγμασιν ταπεινώσεώς σου μακροθύμησον· ὅτι ἐν πυρὶ δοκιμάζεται χρυσὸς καὶ ἄνθρωποι δεκτοὶ ἐν καμίνῳ ταπεινώσεως, Sir. 2:4 f., cf. also 11:12; 13:20; 20:11, statements which are deductions from the basic insight of 2:4 f.

In Is. 53:8 the LXX says concerning the Servant of the Lord: ἐν τῇ ταπεινώσει ἡ κρίσις αὐτοῦ ἤρθη, HT: He was led from prison and judgment. The LXX views the entire fate of the Servant as ταπείνωσις and bears testimony: The ταπείνωσις which he has taken on him removes judgment from him and is the reason for his exaltation full of salvation. This idea has its basis in the original Hebrew. What is summed up as ταπείνωσις in the LXX is to be found in v. 7. The Servant of the Lord is mistreated and he submits. This is illustrated by the sheep which is led to the slaughter and the lamb before its shearers. His obedience is displayed hereby, and this is the ground of his exaltation, as the LXX, anticipating Is. 53:10-12 HT, says.

5. The Greek and the Biblical Understanding.

The different estimation of the word group ταπεινός in Greek literature and the Bible is governed by the different understanding of man. The Greek concept of free man leads to contempt for lack of freedom and subjection. This qualifies ταπεινός and derivates negatively. In Israel and post-exilic Judaism, however, man is controlled by God's action. Man must listen to God and obey Him, so that he can

---

[25] 2 Βασ. 16:12 LXX obviously presupposes בְּעָנְיִי; Mas. has ketib בַּעֲוֺנִי and qere בְּעֵינִי. A similar reading occurs at Is. 3:8, where the LXX introduces a new sense, the violating of God's honour being replaced by the humbling of the glory of Jerusalem and Judah or the people, cf. also 3:17; Job 22:12; ψ 21(22):22. In Is. 40:2 LXX again introduces ταπείνωσις arbitrarily for צבא with ἁμαρτία (עָוֺן). Cf. also Jer. 2:24; Ju. 5:13 A; Job 12:21; ψ 38:3; 87:16 [Bertram].

call himself God's servant. This gives to the group ταπεινόω-ταπεινός-ταπείνωσις a positive sense to the degree that it expresses the doing of acts by which man is set in a right relation to God.

C. Humility in Judaism.

1. The Qumran Sect and Apocalyptic Judaism.

a. The men of the Qumran group calls themselves "the poor" אביונים and "the lowly" or "afflicted" ענוים, a term constantly found in their writings → VI, 896, 34 ff. [26] In this way they express on the one side their dependence on God's mercy and grace in His choice of the poor and lowly while on the other side they express hereby their resolve to be wholly faithful to the covenant by observing the Law; for they want to be the faithful in Israel. [27] "Thou savest the life of the afflicted עני in the place of lions whose tongues are sharp as swords. And Thou, my God, didst hold their teeth closed that they should not tear the life of the mean and afflicted נפש עני ורש," 1 QH 5:13 f., [28] cf. also 5:16 (Sir. 2:4 f.), 18, 20-22: the "poor of grace" אביוני חסד with ענוים; 14:3: the "humble of spirit" ענוי רוח. The pettiness of man in face of death, which is plain in Is. 5:14 f.; ψ 89:3, is echoed in Qumran in 1 QH 6:34; 11:12.

In the Rule ענוה is demanded. Its meaning corresponds to ταπεινοφροσύνη in the later NT writings (→ 21, 32 ff.) and some post-apost. fathers (→ 25, 7 ff.). For this humility is a disposition which members of the union should observe toward one another and which is essential to unity. "All should act in true unity, gracious humility ענוה טוב, loving concern, and right thinking toward their neighbours in the community of holiness and as sons of the eternal fellowship," 1 QS 2:24. Acc. to 1 QS 4:3 f. this רוח ענוה, like longsuffering, pity, kindness, understanding and perception, is a gift of "the spirit of light and truth." The men of Qumran are under obligation to "nurture faithfulness, union and humility ענוה, righteousness, equity, and devotion," 1 QS 5:3 f. They are to correct one another "in truth and humility ענוה and loving concern," 5:25. But one also finds in Qumran a ענוה which is practised vis-à-vis the mighty and which conceals a mind of hatred towards them, 9:21-23; 11:1.

b. Some passages from the Gk. version of Test. XII may be grouped with the Qumran statements. Among them in Test. B. 5:5 is the saying about the righteous man who humbles himself in prayer — εἰ καὶ πρὸς ὀλίγον ταπεινωθῇ — and who is thus exalted to greater glory than that of Joseph. The adj. ταπεινός occurs in G. 5:3; acc. to the context it means "patient," "longsuffering": ὁ γὰρ δίκαιος καὶ ταπεινὸς αἰδεῖται ποιῆσαι ἄδικον. ταπείνωσις occurs 5 times and seems to be the equivalent of ענוה. In G. 5:3 we read: ἡ δικαιοσύνη ἐκβάλλει τὸ μῖσος, ἡ ταπείνωσις ἀναιρεῖ τὸ ζῆλος, ταπείνωσις is "patient waiting on God's help" and renunciation of one's own passion in acts. The meaning in Jud. 19:2 is the "abasement which goes with conversion" and which involves recognition of sin. Judah confesses that he has lost his children for the sake of money and would die childless without ἡ μετάνοιά μου καὶ ἡ ταπείνωσίς μου καὶ αἱ εὐχαὶ τοῦ πατρός μου. In Jos. 10:2 ταπείνωσις is "the conversion of the heart accompanied by fasting." Joseph's descendants must seek after prudence and purity ἐν ὑπομονῇ καὶ προσευχῇ μετὰ νηστείας ἐν ταπεινώσει καρδίας in order that the

---

[26] Cf. J. Maier, Die Texte vom Toten Meer, II (1960), 203, s.v. "Demut," "Demütige," "Elende," "Niedrige," "Arme"; also the excursus on the piety of poverty, 83-87. The transl. in what follows is based on Maier.

[27] Cf. W. Grundmann, "Der Lehrer d. Gerechtigkeit v. Qumran und d. Frage nach der Glaubensgerechtigkeit in der Theol. d. Ap. Pls.," Revue de Qumran, 2 (1960), 238-247.

[28] This illustration of Daniel in the lions' den (Da. 6:23) is used in early Christianity, e.g., in catacomb art, as a symbol of preservation and deliverance from death.

Lord may dwell among them. Joseph himself in 18:3 bears witness to the good fortune
to which he was led διὰ τὴν ταπείνωσιν καὶ τὴν μακροθυμίαν μου. The priestly
orientation of Test. XII may be seen in the admonition in R. 6:10: πρὸς τὸν Λευὶ
ἐγγίσατε ἐν ταπεινώσει καρδίας ὑμῶν, ἵνα δέξησθε εὐλογίαν ἐκ τοῦ στόματος
αὐτοῦ. ταπείνωσις is the subjection of the heart to God and it is extended to the
priests as those whom God has commissioned; it may also be practised in relation to others,
as Test. Jos. 18:3 shows.

c. Jewish apocalyptic is not far from the spirit of Qumran. It does not contribute
any new insights. Worth noting is a passage in 4 Esr. in which we have a divine oracle
that reads: "Thou hast often compared thyself with sinners; no more. Rather wilt thou
receive renown before the Most High because, as is due, thou hast humbled thyself and
not reckoned thyself among the righteous; therefore thou wilt have the greater honour.
For in the last time the dwellers on earth must be humbled by many severe humiliations
because they have walked in wicked pride," 8:47-50. [29] This text ref. to apocalyptic
humbling which comes on the earth through many plagues (cf. Is. 2 and 3). It also speaks
of the reward which the humble receive, cf. 4 Esr. 8:50-54. Humility has its own proper
value in the sense of a virtue which receives a special reward. The admonitions of En.
are against the rich whose heart convicts them as sinners and who tread down the lowly,
Eth. En. 96:4 f., 8; they also hold out to the poor and humble the promise of God's re-
compensing aid.

2. Rabbinic Literature.

For the Rabb. humility is of special importance. R. Jehoshua bLevi in debate with
R. Pinchas bJair, who called "piety" חכירות the greatest of all virtues, described "humility"
ענוה as the greatest, with an appeal to Is. 61:1, bAZ, 20b, cf. bAr., 16b. [30] There is
developed here what was suggested in 4 Esr. 8:47-50 (→ lines 9 ff.) regarding the value
of humility. R. Pinchas says of keeping the Torah that it leads to bodily cleanness, this to
Levitical cleanness, this to temperance, this to holiness, this to humility ענוה, this to
abhorrence of sin, this to piety (as mystical contemplation), this to endowing with the
Holy Spirit (as prophetic inspiration), this to the resurrection of the dead, Sota, 9, 15.
In this ordo salutis on the basis of keeping the Torah humility has a high place. The
humble man is a "son of the world to come," bSanh., 88b; "to him whose mind is humble
שדעתו שפלה Scripture reckons it as though he were to bring all offerings at once," says
bSota, 5b quoting Ps. 51:17. Yet it is not just that keeping the Torah leads to humility;
humility is necessary for the attaining and retaining of knowledge of the Torah. Among
48 things essential for this Ab., 6, 5 mentions humility ענוה. This finds expression in a
life of denial in which a man "makes himself a desert on which all tread," bErub., 54a;
bNed., 55a; [31] hereby he receives the Torah by which God becomes his portion: "and
when God is his portion he rises to greatness." But if he becomes proud of this, God
humbles him. Nevertheless, if he repents, God exalts him, bErub., 54a; bNed., 55a. For
"the words of the Torah remain only in the man who looks on himself as if he were
nothing," bSota, 21b, f. Tanch. כי תבא, 24b: [32] "The Torah does not remain with the
proud but with him whose mind is humble נמוכה." Part of humility is modesty in relation
to other men. This rests on the principle that man should learn from the mind of his
Creator: "Come and see that God's way is not that of flesh and blood. The way of flesh

[29] Cf. Str.-B., IV, 21 f. and Grundmann, op. cit. (→ n. 27), 246 f.
[30] Cf. Str.-B., I, 194 and 789, n. 2.
[31] Cf. AbRNat, 11: "When a man humbles himself for the sake of the Torah, i.e., makes
himself contemptible, and eats dates and carob-beans, and clothes himself in dirty garments,
and sits and watches at the door of scholars, those who pass by say: There is a fool. But at
the last thou dost find the whole Torah in him." Humility thus finds outward expression.
[32] Cf. Str.-B., I, 191-4.

and blood is that the lofty has regard to the lofty but the lofty does not have regard to the lowly. God's way is not thus: He is lofty and has regard to the lowly השפל," bSota, 5a, quoting Ps. 138:6. R. Meir advises: "Be humble שפל רוח (Prv. 16:19; → 10, 33 ff.) toward all men," Ab., 4, 10. The Rabb. thus continue along the lines of the later Wisdom lit. and extend what was limited to members of the order in Qumran, practising humility before men as well as God, → 12, 17 ff. This is demanded in face of death: "Be very humble שפל רוח; for what man has to expect is worms," Ab., 4, 4. Saul's humility was lauded. It is said of him that "he was patient, i.e., forbearing and humble in spirit עניו ושפל רוח, and that for this reason he became king," Pesikt., 5, 44a. The combination of long-suffering and humble subjection of heart is based on the OT (→ 10, 32 ff.) and occurs also in the NT (→ 20, 10 ff.). ענוה as a right position before God includes gentleness and patience. These express humility of heart. The opp. is a boisterous and arrogant nature. The ענוה of many Rabbis is extolled similarly. [33]

The Rabb. know that God exalts him who humbles himself and humbles him who exalts himself, cf. what is said about attaining and retaining the Torah → 13, 24 ff. In this connection one finds ταπεινόω and ταπείνωσις in the LXX (→ 8, 1 ff.; 10, 39 ff.) and the NT (→ 16, 11 ff.; 21, 19 ff.). From R. Hillel we have the saying: "My humbling השפלתי is my exalting הגבהתי, my exalting my humbling," Lv. r., 1, 5 (105c). One often finds the statement: "He who humbles himself עצמו המשפיל, him God will exalt, and he who exalts himself, him God will humble משפילו," bErub., 13b. This includes confession of the sin of which one is guilty before God. [34] AbRNat, 11 has the saying: "He who exalts himself on account of the words of the Torah, will finally be abased שפל and he who abases himself שפל on account of the words of the Torah will finally be exalted." Prv. 3:34 is often quoted in the Rabb., cf. also the NT (→ 19, 14 ff.) and post-apost. fathers (→ 24, 5 f.). [35]

The debate between Rabb. and Christians deserves special notice. Proper to the disciple of Abraham is "a benevolent eye, a modest disposition, a humble spirit רוח נמוכה; proper to the disciple of Balaam, which includes the Christian, is a malevolent eye, a greedy mind, a proud spirit," Ab., 5, 19. In Christianity, however, the Rabb. are accused of contradiction between their theories, which contain praise of humility, and their practice, which is arrogant, Mt. 23:1-12 → 16, 7 ff.

3. Hellenistic Judaism.

a. From Hell. Judaism prior to Philo two ref. from Ep. Ar. are worth noting. Here the advice to the traveller to appear more lowly rather than more lofty to those to whom one journeys is based on the following argument: "God accepts all that abases itself τὸ ταπεινότερον προσδέχεται κατὰ φύσιν and the human race is usually gracious to those who subject themselves," Ep. Ar. 257. To the king who asks his guests at a feast how one can avoid arrogance the reply is given: "When a man pays heed to equality and remembers on every occasion that as a man he rules over those like him καὶ ὁ θεὸς τοὺς ὑπερηφάνους καθαιρεῖ, τοὺς δὲ ἐπιεικεῖς καὶ ταπεινοὺς ὑψοῖ," 262 f. Here the experiences of Israel in Prv. and Sir. and the insights of the Gks. are put in proverbial form.

b. Philo uses ταπεινός, also ταπεινόω, ταπείνωσις and ταπεινότης, in the Gk. sense and he also adopts the biblical insights. Thus he knows a ταπείνωσις which is ἀμφίβολος. The one ταπείνωσις, mentioned along with δουλεία and κάκωσις in Rer.

[33] Ibid., 197-9.
[34] Cf. the examples in Schl. Mt. on 18:4; examples of exalting and abasing, Str.-B., I, 774 and 921.
[35] Str.-B., III, 768.

Div. Her., 268, occurs acc. to Poster. C., 46 when, as the powers of the soul decline, κατὰ τὰ ἐξ ἀλόγων παθῶν ἐγγενόμενα νοσήματά τε καὶ ἀρρωστήματα ταπεινούμεθα. Philo then adds: ἢ κατ' ἀρετῆς ζῆλον στέλλοντες ἑαυτοὺς ἀπὸ οἰδούσης οἰήσεως (sc. ταπεινούμεθα). The first ταπείνωσις is due to weakness of soul, the other arises out of the tested power which is followed for man by atonement ἱλασμός, Poster. C., 46-48. In this connection the biblical τὰς ψυχὰς ταπεινοῦν "to fast" [36] is expounded as μεγαλαυχίαν ἀποτίθεσθαι, ἧς ἡ ἀπόθεσις ἀδικημάτων ἑκουσίων καὶ ἀκουσίων ἐργάζεται παραίτησιν, 48. Along the lines of Gk. usage Philo knows the ταπεινὴ καὶ χαμαίζηλος ψυχή which is ruled and humiliated by the impulses and must be moved to the height and greatness of virtue, Leg. All., III, 19; Det. Pot. Ins., 16; cf. also Poster. C., 73 f.; Deus Imm., 167. In such a soul there dwells, e.g. pusillanimity, of which he says: ταπεινὸν δὲ ἡ δειλία, ἡ δὲ ἀνδρεία ταπεινώσει καὶ δειλία πολέμιον, Leg. All., I, 68, while ὁ μὲν τέλειος ὢν βραχὺ καὶ ταπεινὸν οὐδὲν φρονεῖ, III, 134, In the holy words of God and the laws of men who are friends of God there is οὐδὲν ταπεινὸν οὐδ' ἀνάξιον, Det. Pot. Ins., 13; for τὸ μὴ ταπεινῶς καὶ χαμαιζήλως ὑπερμεγέθως δὲ καὶ ὑπεραύλως καὶ ὑψηλῶς νοεῖν περὶ θεοῦ ἔμφασιν τοῦ ὑψίστου κινεῖ, Leg. All., III, 82. But since God, endowed with a series of predicates expressing His majesty, οὐδὲ τὸν ταπεινότατον ὑπεριδεῖν ὑπέμεινεν (Decal., 41), there is the other, καλὴ ταπείνωσις, which includes the exclusion of every non-rational thought, Fug., 207. Biblical usage and content may be seen in the following passages. Measuring his own vanity, which is grounded in mortality, in his constitution of dust and ashes, and in the contemplation of the all-surpassing height of the divine blessings, man, ταπεινὸς γεγονώς, καταβεβλημένος εἰς χοῦν, gains confidence and courage to draw near to God, Rer. Div. Her., 29. This abasement is the essential transition to proximity to God. For one who gauges his own littleness τὴν ἰδίαν ταπεινότητα will be all the greater before the "judges of truth," Poster. C., 136. Persuasion of the pettiness and vanity (τὴν ταπεινότητα καὶ οὐδενείαν) of the cleverness of human understanding goes hand in hand with conviction as to the all-surpassing loftiness and majesty of the unbegotten spirit, Congr., 107. These statements are governed by the awareness of the gt. distance and distinction between the Creator and His creature which gives rise to the biblical statements and also by confidence that the goal of our lives is to be found in this God.

c. Joseph. uses the word group ταπεινός, ταπεινόω, ταπείνωσις, ταπεινοφροσύνη negatively like the Gks. He has ταπεινός, "base," "little," "poor-spirited" in Bell., 4, 319 and 365; 6, 395; Ant., 5, 115; 7, 95; 10, 11; 13, 415, ταπεινόω "to abase" in Ant., 5, 186; 9, 174; pass. "to be abased" in Ant., 18, 147, ταπείνωσις "abasement," "humiliation" in Bell., 2, 604; Ant., 2, 234, and ταπεινοφροσύνη "lowly mind" in Bell., 4, 494.

D. The Statements about Lowliness and Humility in the New Testament.

1. Occurrence of the ταπεινός Group in the New Testament.

Of the group the adj. ταπεινός occurs 8 times in the NT, ταπεινόω 14 times, ταπείνωσις 4, ταπεινοφροσύνη 7 and ταπεινόφρων once. The distribution of the words is as follows: 4 in Mt., 7 in Lk. with 2 in Ac., 13 in Pauline works: 1 in R., 4 in 2 C., 4 in Phil., 3 in Col., 1 in Eph., also 4 each in Jm. and 1 Pt. In all there are 34 instances in the NT. The group does not occur at all in the Johannine writings, Mk., 1 C., Gl., Hb., the smaller Cath. Ep. (Jd., 2 Pt.), nor the Past. In view of the OT background of the NT it is as well here again to begin with the verb ταπεινόω, esp. as this is also used the most.

---

[36] LXX usage also has an influence in the use of ταπεινόω for "to force," though this is allegorically interpreted in Mut. Nom., 194; there are ref. to the LXX in nearly all the passages we mention.

2. ταπεινόω.

a. Luke extends the quotation from Is. 40:3 ff. with which he introduces the work of John the Baptist and adopts the statement: καὶ πᾶν ὄρος καὶ βουνὸς ταπεινωθήσεται (3:5). This is characteristic of Lk. The introductory infancy story (1:48, 52) shows that Lk. takes figuratively what Is. says about God's eschatological acts towards men.

b. In three passages one finds in the account of the message of Jesus in the Synoptists the saying: "Whosoever shall exalt himself shall be abased; and he that shall humble himself shall be exalted," Mt. 23:12; Lk. 14:11; 18:14. The saying has an OT basis (→ 8, 1 ff.) and there are Rabb. par. → 14, 13 ff. It is a two-membered mashal whose very form betrays its Jewish origin. [37] In using it Jesus adopts a basic experience of the Israelite and non-biblical world but makes it into a saying expressing God's eschatological work, as may be seen from the future forms ταπεινωθήσεται and ὑψωθήσεται; [38] the name of God lies concealed in the pass. Mt. 23:12 (→ IV, 654, 22 ff.) is at the end of a passage which starts with the contradiction between the teaching and practice of the Rabbis and which warns the disciples against the danger of presumption to which these have fallen victim (but → 14, 25 ff.). God will exalt the one who makes himself the servant of others, cf. Lk. 22:25-27; Mk. 9:35; 10:42-44 par. Mt. 20:25-27. But He will abase the one who exalts himself above others. In Lk. 14:11 the saying comes at the end of an illustration which is modelled on Prv. 25:6 f. (→ 7, 34 f.) and for which there is a Rabbinic parallel. [39] The starting-point in Lk. is the ambition of the invited guests, 14:7. The conclusion demands submission to God's decision rather than arrogant anticipation of it. Lk. 18:14 is at the end of the parable of the Pharisee and the publican (18:9-14). The publican humbles himself before God by his position μακρόθεν, by his gestures, and by his prayer. [40] If this is based on Ps. 51:1, the promise of this psalm (51:17) is also his. This is declared by the verdict of Jesus, to which is added the saying about God's eschatological work. The humility of the publican, which contrasts with the arrogance of the Pharisee, has its basis in self-knowledge and consists in entire self-committal to God's grace. But this puts the publican in a right relation to God. A special turn is given to this thrice attested saying in Mt. 18:4: ὅστις οὖν ταπεινώσει ἑαυτὸν ὡς τὸ παιδίον τοῦτο, οὗτός

[37] Bultmann Trad., 84: "The basic forms of the OT and Jewish mashal ... may be seen clearly," and 108: "obviously a current saying which was appended now here and now there to the tradition."
[38] Bultmann Trad., 109 says that "the spirit of this piety is that of the popular belief in God which along with recognition of God's sovereign rule affirms compensatory justice in world events"; yet one should not ignore the eschatological character of the saying expressed in the future tense. On this Dihle, 748 rightly says: "The quotation from the OT, which is common in the NT, to the effect that God will abase the haughty and accept the humble, was at first the simple expression of historical religious experience, then among the 'anawim it came to express the sense of the special election of the poor and humble, but the eschatological character of NT proclamation gives it an entirely new sense." Cf. also the helpful study by R. Bultmann, "Allg. Wahrheiten u chr. Verkündigung," ZThK, 54 (1957), 244-254.
[39] Str.-B., II, 204; In the Rabb. version the saying has as its conclusion the statement of Hillel: "My humbling is my exalting, my exalting my humbling" → 14, 16 ff.; cf. Jeremias Gl.6, 191: "I.e., v. 11 is an ancient saying which Jesus had before Him and which is also connected with table precedence in Rabb. literature." On the passage as a whole cf. Grundmann Lk. on 14:7-11.
[40] Cf. Grundm. Lk. on 18:9-14; Jeremias Gl.6, 139-143.

ἐστιν ὁ μείζων ἐν τῇ βασιλείᾳ τῶν οὐρανῶν. The saying is put in context by the ὡς τὸ παιδίον τοῦτο → V, 648, 4 ff.[41] Jesus is speaking to adults. He is conscious of their lost childlikeness before God. He thus gives humility a special nuance. It is to become a child again before God, i.e., to trust Him utterly, to expect everything from Him and nothing from self.[42] This is the only way to become great in the kingdom of God → IV, 531, 37 ff. The distinctive version as compared with Mt. 23:12; Lk. 74:11; 18:14 (→ IV, 652, 38 ff.; 1003, 9 ff.) makes it likely that we have here the meaning Jesus attached to the common saying.[43] In this connection it is worth noting that Jesus neither practises nor demands the visible self-abasement in life-style, gesture, or clothing which was familiar and customary in the world around. Indeed, He is critical of such practices, cf. Mt. 6:16-18; 11:18 f.; Mk. 2:18 f. The newness of this is stressed by the Evangelists, who put Mk. 2:21 f. and par. immediately after 2:18 f.

c. Paul in Corinth is accused of a petty disposition and servile appearance → 2, 6 ff. (2 C. 10:1). This is based on his refusal to take advantage of the apostle's privilege of being supported by the congregation. Paul calls this refusal a self-abasement whose aim is "that you may be exalted" — ἐμαυτὸν ταπεινῶν ἵνα ὑμεῖς ὑψωθῆτε, 11:7. By offering the Gospel free he demonstrates his freedom for service, 1 C. 9:4-18.[44] He makes himself small in order to exalt them, cf. also 1 C. 4:10; 2 C. 4:12.[45] On his approaching visit to the church he fears a fresh humiliation by it which in the last resort will come from God — μὴ πάλιν ἐλθόντος μου ταπεινώσῃ με ὁ θεός — unless there is within it the conversion of those who persist in their sins, 2 C. 12:19-21.[46] This humiliation consists not only in the contempt which he suffers in the community but also in the threat to his crown and repute (→ VII, 628, 32 ff.) through a congregation which has fallen into sin. In a passage which formally consists of two three-line units (Phil. 4:12 f.)[47] Paul says: οἶδα καὶ

[41] It is to be noted that after the parable of the Pharisee and the publican, which closes with the saying about exalting and abasing, Lk. puts the blessing of the children, which contains a more developed version of the saying in Mt. 18:3 about becoming childlike as a presupposition of receiving the kingdom of God, Lk. 18:15-17. In contrast Mt. 19:13-15 has the blessing of the children without this saying. He has what is probably the original form of this in 18:1-4 and he combines it with an independent form of the saying about exalting and abasing.

[42] This amounts to what Jeremias Gl.⁶, 190 puts in the words: "If you do not learn to say Abba, you cannot find entry into God's royal dominion." He says of the authority of Jesus: "He speaks to His heavenly Father with the childlikeness, confidence and intimacy of a little child to its father," → I, 5, 3 ff.; V, 984, 18 ff. This new relation to God expressed in the Abba implies a wholly new attitude to the child → V, 639, 31 ff., cf. J. Leipoldt, "Vom Kinde in d. alten Welt," Reich Gottes u. Wirklichkeit, Festschr. f. E. Sommerlath (1961), 343-351. Schl. Mt. on 18:4 shows that the Rabb. understand ταπεινώσει ἑαυτόν as confession of guilt, cf. also Jeremias Gl.⁶, 190, n. 2. But in Mt. ταπεινώσει ἑαυτόν requires a broader interpretation.

[43] As against Jeremias Gl.⁶, 190: "Perhaps a reconstruction of Mt. 23:12b" → n. 42.

[44] Cf. E. Käsemann, "Eine paul. Variation des 'amor fati,'" ZThK, 56 (1959), 138-154; W. Grundmann, "Pls. aus dem Volke Israel, Ap. d. Völker," Nov. Test., 4 (1961), 287.

[45] Cf. Schl. K. on 2 C. 11:7: "The ὑψωθῆναι of the community takes place as he declares to it God's saving message. This is man's supreme exaltation. But since he does this after the manner of a gift δωρεάν, he makes himself poor and small thereby."

[46] On the question of the relation of 2 C. 10-13 to 1-9 cf. P. Schmiedel, Die Briefe an die Korinther, Handkomm. z. NT, II² (1892), 74-82; A. Jülicher-E. Fascher, Einl. in d. NT⁷ (1931), 98-101; G. Bornkamm, "Die Vorgesch. d. sog. 2 K.," SAH, 2 (1961).

[47] Cf. Loh. Phil. on 4:12 and also 1:29; G. Friedrich, Der Brief an d. Philipper, NT Deutsch, 8⁹ (1962) on 4:12.

ταπεινοῦσθαι (→ IV, 655, 8 ff.), οἶδα καὶ περισσεύειν. By the substitution of ὑστερεῖσθαι for ταπεινοῦσθαι at the end of the fifth line it acquires the sense: "to live in poor circumstances," "to live in want," "to be straitened."[48] This ability arises out of his initiation into Christ which confers on him the needed strength → II, 313, 6 ff.; cf. IV, 828, 1 ff.

This attitude of Paul is part of his discipleship of the Kurios. Of the latter it is said in the hymn in Phil. 2:6-11:[49] ἐταπείνωσεν ἑαυτὸν γενόμενος ὑπήκοος μέχρι θανάτου (2:8). This hymn provides a basis for the preceding exhortation (2:1-5). The hymn and the exhortation are linked together by ταπεινοφροσύνη (2:3; → 21, 32 ff.) and ἐταπείνωσεν ἑαυτόν (2:8), → II, 278, 30 ff. The hymn is governed by the underlying theme of humiliation and exaltation (→ 8, 1 ff.) and it focuses on Jesus Christ, of whom we read on the one side: ἐταπείνωσεν, but on whom there is effected on the other side: διὸ καὶ ὁ θεὸς αὐτὸν ὑπερύψωσεν (2:9 → III, 354, 1 ff.). If this theme is given an emphatically eschatological accent in the NT, this hymn refers not merely to the historical event but also to the eschatological turning-point in the absolute. First a mythical expression describes the Christ event as a free self-emptying of divine likeness and then in a statement expressing the historical facts the same event is portrayed as free obedience even to death. The ἑαυτὸν ἐκένωσεν of the incarnation becomes a concrete historical event in the ἐταπείνωσεν ἑαυτόν.[50] When Paul adds θανάτου δὲ σταυροῦ, the ἐταπείνωσεν ἑαυτόν reaches its sharpest climax in the scandal of the cross. Humiliation and death, a free act here, are combined thereby → 8, 22 f.; 11, 11 ff. God for His part replies to this with exaltation, but it is itself the governing factor in the Christian life.[51]

d. In Jm. 4:10 we have the imperative ταπεινώθητε ἐνώπιον κυρίου, καὶ ὑψώσει ὑμᾶς (cf. 4:7) on the basis of the quotation of Prv. 3:34 LXX (→ 10, 12 ff.) in 4:6 → 19, 14 ff. The imperative means: Submit to God. The demand is crowned by a promise: καὶ ὑψώσει ὑμᾶς. The exaltation is the grace which God gives to the

---

[48] So Friedrich, loc. cit. Loh. Phil. on 4:12 thinks "the delight of the martyr" is expressed in v. 12 f. The ταπεινοῦσθαι relates to the affliction of suffering and imprisonment, which is greater than that of economic distress, so that we have here the tension between inner being and possession on the one side and outer existence and non-possession on the other — a tension indissolubly bound up with Paul's apostolic work. But the context both before and after speaks of the help of the Philippians and forces us to think of this first (the flourishing of v. 10) even though there might be a further ref. to imprisonment and trial. When Loh. says that Phil. has the ταπειν-group more than any Pauline letter one should remember that the meaning varies, that 2 C. 10-12 does in fact use it more often, and that the two letters were written close together, though Phil. belongs to Ephesus. One is tempted to suppose that the striking use in Phil., 2 C. and Col. as compared with the other epistles, in which the only instances are Eph. 4:2 and R. 12:16, is due to the judgment of 2 C. 10:1, which hit Paul hard and caused him gt. concern.

[49] Cf. the comm. on Phil. 2:1-11, also E. Lohmeyer, "Kyrios Jesus. Eine Untersuchung zu Phil. 2:5-11," SAH, 1927/28, 4 (1928); E. Käsemann, "Krit. Analyse v. Phil. 2:5-11," Exeget. Versuche u. Besinnungen, I (1960), 51-95; G. Bornkamm, "Zum Verständnis d. Christus-Hymnus Phil. 2:6-11," Stud. z. Antike u. Urchr.² (1963), 179-187; F. Hahn, "Christologische Hoheitstitel," FRL, 83 (1963), 120 f.; E. Larsson, Christus als Vorbild (1962) 235-263.

[50] Cf. Käsemann, op. cit. (→ n. 49), 77: The ref. is not to the mind of Jesus nor is a virtue attributed to him; what we have here is rather "the exhibiting of an objective fact, that of abasement."

[51] Friedrich, op. cit. on 2:5: "The Christ story is not an isolated individual event; it is a final happening which governs the life and acts of men." Cf. also Larsson, op. cit. (→ n. 49), 232-235, 263-275.

man who subjects himself to Him. The context shows that this submission is to be construed as a purifying act of penitence. [52] Similarly, or at least under the influence of Prv. 3:34 LXX (→ 10, 12 ff.; 19, 14 ff.), 1 Pt. 5:5 f. speaks of subjection to God: ταπεινώθητε οὖν ὑπὸ τὴν κραταιὰν χεῖρα τοῦ θεοῦ, ἵνα ὑμᾶς ὑψώσῃ ἐν καιρῷ, 5:6. As the context shows, this consists in man's putting his whole confidence in the grace of God, who cares for those who subject themselves to Him. In both passages we have traces of a common Christian exhortation, though this may be applied in different ways.

3. ταπεινός.

a. Very close to the figuratively understood declaration in Lk. 3:5 is the saying in the Magnificat: καθεῖλεν δυνάστας ἀπὸ θρόνων καὶ ὕψωσεν ταπεινούς, 1:52. This has an OT basis and it refers to the eschatological work of God → III, 412, 15 ff. It has fundamental significance in Luke's work as a whole → 16, 2 ff.

b. 1 Pt. 5:5 and Jm. 4:6 quote Prv. 3:34 (→ 10, 12 ff.) in the LXX version: ὁ θεὸς ὑπερηφάνοις ἀντιτάσσεται, ταπεινοῖς δὲ δίδωσιν χάριν. [53] Instead of κύριος both passages have ὁ θεός, most probably because κύριος is a term for Christ and their concern is with God's eschatological acts. They do not follow the basic text with its variation in the first line: "As concerns mockers, he mocks; to the lowly he gives grace," Targum: "He overthrows mockers, but gives grace to the humble." [54] They use the saying as the starting-point for different hortatory sayings (→ 18, 25 ff.) so that Prv. 3:34 LXX is seen to have fundamental significance for primitive Christian exhortation → 19, 6 f. Jm. 1:9 says: καυχάσθω δὲ ὁ ἀδελφὸς ὁ ταπεινὸς ἐν τῷ ὕψει αὐτοῦ. ὁ δὲ πλούσιος in the continuation defines ὁ ἀδελφὸς ὁ ταπεινός as the brother who is bowed down by poverty, the עָנִי, which might just as well be rendered by πτωχός as ταπεινός, → VI, 38, 42 f.; 888, 10 ff.; 892, 24 ff. This poor man is rich through his exaltation, cf. Mt. 5:3; 11:5; Lk. 4:18; Jm. 2:5.

c. Paul hears from Corinth the criticism that he was κατὰ πρόσωπον μὲν ταπεινὸς ἐν ὑμῖν, ἀπὼν δὲ θαρρῶ εἰς ὑμᾶς (2 C. 10:1), i.e., "servile," "abject," "ineffectual," "inferior" [55] in presence, though bold at a distance. Here ταπεινός has the derogatory negative sense found in the Greeks, e.g., always in Epictet. Paul gives his views on this → 17, 14 ff. He bears witness to something confessed by those of the old covenant, namely that God is ὁ παρακαλῶν τοὺς ταπεινούς (2 C. 7:6; cf. Is. 49:13), i.e., He consoles the humble. In content ταπεινός is defined by ἔξωθεν μάχαι, ἔσωθεν φόβοι (2 C. 7:5). Paul gives the admonition: μὴ τὰ ὑψηλὰ φρονοῦντες, ἀλλὰ τοῖς ταπεινοῖς συναπαγόμενοι, R. 12:16. Whether τὰ ὑψηλά are revelations and secret thoughts such as are sought after in Gnostic

---

[52] The imp. ταλαιπωρήσατε καὶ πενθήσατε καὶ κλαύσατε in v. 8 may ref. to this. Cf. Wnd. Jk., ad loc.; but cf. Schl. Jk. on 4:9: "Effort and submission . . . not a rule to remind us of Pharisaic statutes (fasting, sack-cloth and ashes, torn garments)."

[53] ταπεινός is here the opp. of ὑπερήφανος "the arrogant man."

[54] Cf. Str.-B., III, 768, also I, 203.

[55] "ταπεινός is never the term for a purely spiritual process. It ref. always to what a man has and can do. He has, they said, no power; he can only talk, beseech and admonish; he cannot act; no one has any reason to fear him," Schl. K., ad loc. Yet beseeching and admonishing are regarded by them as the expression of a mean and servile mind. Outer appearance and inner attitude combine in the judgment that Paul is ταπεινός.

circles, [56] or whether the reference is to the pride of Gentile Christians in relation to Israel (cf. 11:20), is an open question. Either way the point is that the members of the Roman church are not to lift up their eyes to what is high and lofty, nor are they to be carried away by this, but they are to turn to τοῖς ταπεινοῖς. If the dative is to be taken as a neuter, as the opp. τὰ ὑψηλά suggests, Paul has in mind the small and insignificant services by which the one can help the other. If the reference is to οἱ ταπεινοί to whom the services are to be rendered, the meaning is that thought is to be given to the brethren. [57] What is said here finds expression in the concept ταπεινοφροσύνη → 21, 32 ff.

d. In the Saviour's invitation we read: μάθητε ἀπ' ἐμοῦ, ὅτι πραΰς εἰμι καὶ ταπεινὸς τῇ καρδίᾳ, Mt. 11:20. The OT had prepared the way for the association of πραΰς καὶ ταπεινός, and this also occurs in Judaism → 10, 33 f.; 14, 6 ff. [58] Jesus is ταπεινός towards God, "yielded" to Him; the τῇ καρδίᾳ which is added to ταπεινός (→ 10, 32 f.) makes it plain that He is this, not in virtue of a necessity which is imposed on Him and to which He is subject, but in freedom and assent to this way of God with Him. He is also ταπεινός towards men, whose servant and helper He becomes, Lk. 22:27; Mt. 20:28; Mk. 10:45. This aspect of His being ταπεινός is expressed by πραΰς. [59] He gives Himself to fellowship with sinners and the despised. He thus becomes a model for His people. This saying is constitutive for Mt.'s picture of Christ → VI, 649, 17 ff. [60]

4. ταπείνωσις.

a. On the occasion of Philip's encounter with the treasurer of the queen of Ethiopia (Ac. 8:32-35) Is. 53:7 f. is quoted according to the LXX → 11, 28 ff. In v. 8 witness is herewith borne to the Servant of the Lord as the one who was humiliated and exalted. Luke understands God's eschatological acts on His Son and Christ as exaltation through humiliation, cf. Lk. 9:20-22; 12:49 f.; 24:7, 26, 46; Ac. 2:36. This is repeated in His people, Lk. 9:23-27; Ac. 14:22. [61] The divine work includes the replacement of judgment, which is humiliation, by exaltation. This is displayed especially in Jesus Christ, and according to Ac. 8:26-40 it is for Luke the heart of Scripture.

---

[56] This is shown by συναπαγόμενοι, which suggests thought as ecstatic rapture; through the ref. to τοῖς ταπεινοῖς it acquires a significantly critical accent. The small and minor service counts for more before God than ecstasy, cf. Mi. R., ad loc.

[57] Schl. R. on 12:16 thus thinks of the small and weak in the community.

[58] Cf. on πραΰς Str.-B., I, 197-199.

[59] Schl. Mt. on 11:29 draws attention to the difference between this image of Jesus as teacher and that of the Jewish teacher.

[60] Cf. G. Barth, "Das Gesetzesverständnis des Evangelisten Mt.," Überlieferung u. Auslegung im Mt.-Ev., ed. G. Bornkamm, G. Barth and H. J. Held[3] (1963), 97, 122, 139, n. 1; G. Strecker, "Der Weg der Gerechtigkeit," FRL, 82 (1962), 173 f. The influence of sayings about Christ's lowliness and self-abasement may be seen in some Chr. additions to Test. XII, so B. 10:7: "worshipping the king of heaven, who has appeared on earth in the form of a lowly man ἐν μορφῇ ἀνθρώπου ἐν ταπεινώσει." Through Him, acc. to D. 5:13, the Holy One of Israel rules over Jerusalem and Israel in lowliness and poverty ὁ Ἅγιος Ἰσραὴλ βασιλεύων ἐπ' αὐτῆς ἐν ταπεινώσει καὶ πτωχείᾳ, cf. B. 9:5: ἔγνων δὲ οἷος ἔσται ταπεινὸς ἐπὶ γῆς καὶ οἷος ἔνδοξος ἐν οὐρανῷ. In D. 6:9 one may see clearly the influence of Mt. 11:29: ὁ Σωτὴρ τῶν ἐθνῶν. ἐστὶ γὰρ ἀληθὴς καὶ μακρόθυμος, πρᾷος καὶ ταπεινός, καὶ ἐκδιδάσκων διὰ τῶν ἔργων τὸν νόμον Κυρίου.

[61] Cf. Grundm. Lk. on 9:18-27 and Exc. 454-7.

b. Confession is made in the Magnificat: ἐπέβλεψεν ἐπὶ τὴν ταπείνωσιν τῆς δούλης αὐτοῦ, Lk. 1:48, cf. 1 Βασ. 1:11. Understanding of this depends on who the speaker is. If the reference is to Elisabeth, [62] ταπείνωσις denotes "childless-ness," which was a disgrace in Israel. Elisabeth has experienced grace through the child she has conceived, cf. 1:25; ἐπεῖδεν there too. If as in most MSS the reference is to Mary ταπείνωσις means "lowliness," this being strengthened by the genitive τῆς δούλης αὐτοῦ, cf. v. 38. The fact that God chooses the humble hand-maiden, the virgin, who is of no account in the eyes of the world, to be the mother of His Son, is the reason for the thankful joy in God which the speaker confesses (1:46 f.) and the cause of the honour which she will be paid (1:48). The fact that God has regard to the low estate of His handmaiden gives rise to the hope that His eschatological action, which casts down the mighty from their thrones and lifts up the humble (1:52; → 8, 1 ff.; 10:1 ff.; 16:1 ff.), is now beginning — an expectation which commences in the infancy stories and is confirmed by the appearance of the Baptist, 3:5. [63] In this way Luke makes the election of the lowly and the abasement of the rich and mighty a basic feature of God's historical action from the eschato-logical perspective.

c. Paul calls the mortal body τὸ σῶμα τῆς ταπεινώσεως in Phil. 3:21. Often in the OT (→ 8, 22 f.; 11:11 ff.), the Dead Sea Scrolls (→ 12, 15 ff.) and the Rabbis (→ 14, 5 ff.) ταπείνωσις is the proximity of death or subjection to it. σῶμα τῆς ταπεινώσεως is the body which falls victim to humiliation in death, cf. 1 C. 15:42-44. The statement that this body will be fashioned after the likeness (→ VII, 958, 2 ff.) of the body of His glory is governed by the resurrection of Jesus from the dead, 1 C. 15:43; R. 6:4.

d. The demand that the ἀδελφὸς ὁ ταπεινός should glory in his exaltation (→ 19, 22 ff.) is followed by: ὁ δὲ πλούσιος ἐν τῇ ταπεινώσει αὐτοῦ, ὅτι ὡς ἄνθος χόρτου παρελεύσεται (Jm. 1:10; → VI, 330, 6 ff.). The reason (1:11) makes it clear that the ταπείνωσις of the rich is his subjection to death, which brings to nothing all the loftiness and affluence of the wealthy, → VI, 911, 5 ff. [64] Jm. is speaking of the eschatological inversion of all things which is already at work, Jm. 2:5.

5. ταπεινοφροσύνη.

a. In Phil. 2:3 Paul requires ταπεινοφροσύνη from the community. Not "self-seeking" ἐριθεία nor "vainglorious boasting" κενοδοξία as self-glory should control their mutual relations but ταπεινοφροσύνη. The opposite gives this the sense of unselfishness. The two sentences which follow show that it is the resolution to subject oneself to others and to be more concerned about their welfare than one's

---

[62] So a b l * hr and Iren. A. v. Harnack, "Das Magnificat der Elisabeth (Lk. 1:46-55) nebst einigen Bemerkungen z. Lk. 1 u. 2," Stud. zur Gesch. d. NT u. d. Alten Kirche, I (1931), 62-85 considers an original καὶ εἶπεν which was then amplified in different ways, Mary gradually establishing itself with advancing Mariology, though Elisabeth would have been more correct. But other factors, too, favour Mary.

[63] For development of this insight cf. Grundm. Lk., ad loc.

[64] Dib. Jk. on 1:9-11; Schl. Jk. on 1:9-11, cf. 120: "As he gives thanks for temptation, so also for the decay and death of man. This would not be possible, of course, if everything perished. For then all glory would end. But Jm. had Is. 40:6 in view, and his readers too knew the Scriptures."

own, v. 4. [65] The term ταπεινοφροσύνη thus catches up what Jesus said about greatness through service, → II, 84, 1 ff. It is given its distinctive shape by Jesus' own conduct, which in Phil. 2:5-11 is viewed from a standpoint which serves as the basis of Paul's admonition, 2:1-4 → 18, 6 ff. By the Christ event the submission of man to God is made also the content of relations between men, since God Himself acts thus in Christ. Man now subordinates himself to others in service. This has nothing whatever to do with self-disparagement or servility. In such ταπεινοφροσύνη others are taken seriously because God Himself takes men seriously and refers them to one another by His acts. Only by ταπεινοφροσύνη, refraining from self-assertion, can the unity of the congregation be established and sustained. Without ταπεινοφροσύνη it would crumble. ταπεινοφροσύνη thus acquires its positive significance through the unity of Christ's community, which is above individuals. It has, then, much the same sense as ענוה in 1 QS → 12, 17 ff. In this way a possibility was fulfilled which the Greeks had not perceived and which even transcends the statements of the OT and Judaism. [66] An example of such ταπεινοφροσύνη is Paul himself in Ac. 20:19 when before God he displays it to the church at Ephesus and to believers in Asia. [67]

b. In Col. ταπεινοφροσύνη is used three times in different ways. In 2:18, 23 it is a concept of the Colossian heresy [68] and it either means "fasting" (→ 7, 17 ff.; → IV, 933, 16 ff.) or "mortification," which is supported by 2:21 and the association with ἐθελοθρησκία and ἀφειδία σώματος (v. 23), or it expresses a sense of inferiority which underlies the cult of angels in the sense that the lofty and remote deity is inaccessible and unreachable for man on earth and man thus sees himself as delivered up to angelic powers. [69] Either way ταπεινοφροσύνη denotes cultic practice rather than a disposition → I, 86, 1 ff. [70] Paul calls this carnal (v. 18), since it is a self-selected cultus which involves scorn for those who do not take part in it. In contrast to it he demands a different kind of ταπεινοφροσύνη. The admonition to put on sincere pity, kindness, humility, gentleness and forbearance — a group of five [71] (3:12) — describes the reality of the new man as He has appeared in Jesus Christ as the image of God, Col. 1:15; 3:10. Since the four terms which surround ταπεινο-

---

[65] Cf. Loh. Phil. on 2:3 f. Friedrich, op. cit., ad loc. considers the possibility that "the first signs of the boastful Gnostic pride of perfection were already appearing in Philippi." If so Paul had a concrete situation in view. Cf. also Larsson, op. cit., 213-5 and Thieme ταπεινοφροσύνη, 18, who takes ταπεινοφροσύνη to be essentially "the readiness for a lower position, lesser regard, the absence of any desire to be great or distinguished, to have external honour or public esteem or a name, to mean something, to play a role." He distinguishes it from a sense of inferiority, with which it has nothing whatever to do.

[66] Dihle, 751 says: "In Gk. ethics man, as he protects his own worth, has also to acknowledge the worth and claim of the other man. The NT idea that man should be basically the subject and servant of his neighbour is without precedent." Schlier Eph.³ on 4:2 draws attention to the ecclesiological significance of ταπεινοφροσύνη: "It is worth noting that the term ταπεινοφροσύνη plays a great part where the unity of the church is acutely threatened."

[67] Cf. H. Schürmann, "Das Testament des Pls. f. die Kirche," Unio Christianorum, Festschr. f. L. Jaeger (1962), 108-146.

[68] On the heresy in Colossae cf. Loh. Kol. Einl., 3-8; Dib. Gefbr., Exc. 38-40; H. Conzelmann, Der Br. an die Kol., NT Deutsch, 8⁹ (1962), Exc. 146-8; G. Bornkamm, "Die Häresie des Kolosserbr.," Das Ende des Gesetzes⁴ (1963), 139-156.

[69] Cf. Dib. Gefbr. on Col. 2:18.

[70] Loc. cit.

[71] Bornkamm, op. cit. (→ n. 68), 151.

φροσύνη in the middle relate to conduct toward others (3:13 f.) [72] they, too, have the same reference. Hence Col.3:12 is very close to Phil. 2:3 (→ 21, 32 ff.) and it confirms the insight gained there. In the exhortation of Eph. 4:2 we find it at the head of modes of behaviour [73] which agree with Col. 3:12 but are not in a group of five and are not orientated to love as σύνδεσμος τῆς τελειότητος, [74] but rather to ἑνότης τοῦ πνεύματος ἐν τῷ συνδέσμῳ τῆς εἰρήνης. In controversy with the Colossian error ταπεινοφροσύνη in 3:12, and even more so in Eph. 4:2, takes on the character of a Christian virtue.

c. In 1 Pt. 5:5, after the epistle has addressed the elders of the community and the young in it, we have the following admonition to all: πάντες δὲ ἀλλήλοις τὴν ταπεινοφροσύνην ἐγκομβώσασθε, and Prv. 3:34 is advanced as a basis → 19, 14 ff. Humility as readiness for service is to be mutual, and it is to be put on like a loin cloth, ἐγκομβώσασθε. [75] Each in the community knows that he may seek the service of the other, and each is pledged like a waiting slave to this service; the members of the community live for one another. In the context (→ 19, 2 ff., 14 ff.) ταπεινοφροσύνη is here the heart of Christian existence in which life is ordered to willing service for others and the believer lets himself be assigned to his proper place by the hand of God (1 Pt. 5:6) → III, 912, 23 ff.

6. ταπεινόφρων.

1 Pt. concludes its admonitions to slaves, wives and husbands (2:18-3:7) with the general demand (3:8): τὸ δὲ τέλος πάντες ὁμόφρονες, συμπαθεῖς, φιλάδελφοι, εὔσπλαγχνοι, ταπεινόφρονες (P 𝔓 φιλόφρονες). In this series of five (cf. Col. 3:12) ταπεινόφρονες comes at the end, the only NT instance of this position. If a fellowship is to arise which is orientated to the model of Christ, which is of one accord and governed by mercy and brotherly love, and which fulfils its calling (v. 9), then there is need of a disposition which is ready for service to others and which does not lift up itself above others, cf. also 1 Pt. 5:5; lines 9 ff.

E. Humility in the Post-Apostolic Fathers.

1. ταπεινός.

In the prayer in 1 Cl., 59, 4, which comes from the Jewish synagogue, we read: τοὺς ταπεινοὺς ἐλέησον. The meaning of ταπεινός here is "oppressed," "poor," "afflicted";

---

[72] ταπεινοφροσύνη and πραΰτης, which are sharply separated among the Gks., who took a positive view of πραΰτης as distinct from ταπεινοφροσύνη (→ VI, 646, 5 ff. and Rehrl, 31), are in direct proximity to one another.

[73] Here, too, ταπεινοφροσύνη and πραΰτης stand directly alongside one another → VI, 650, 13 f.

[74] Love is the comprehensive unity of the attitudes mentioned; it is also the completion, cf. 1 C. 13:8, 13. In Eph. 4:2, however, it is itself an attitude etc. But cf. Larsson, op. cit. (→ n. 49), 221, n. 1, who appeals to G. Rudberg, "Syndesmos," Coni. Neot., 3 (1939), 19-21; in his view the meaning is: "that love may hold Christians together."

[75] "ἐγκομβοῦσθαι, to tie the ἐγκόμβωμα or girdle, as servants do in making ready for their work," Wnd. Pt., ad loc. The figure reminds us of Jn. 13:4 f., so that here as elsewhere in 1 Pt. one may discern the image of the Lord behind the admonitions. It is worth noting that one may see Jn. 21:15-17 (cf. 1 Pt. 1:8) behind 1 Pt. 5:2 f. The Johannine Peter tradition is thus to be seen. The elders as shepherds under the chief shepherd also remind us of the link between Jn. 10 and 21:15-17. The command to be examples to the flock reminds us of Jn. 13:12-17. In gen., with ref. to Col. 3:12, → II, 339, 11 ff.

it thus corresponds to עָנִי. Just before v. 3, echoing Job 5:11, says of God: τὸν ποιοῦντα ταπεινοὺς εἰς ὕψος. 1 Cl., 30, 2 quotes Prv. 3:34 LXX (→ 10, 12 ff.; 19, 10 ff.); the quotation is followed by a command to cleave to the ταπεινοί because God gives them grace. Esther's τὸ ταπεινὸν τῆς ψυχῆς saved the whole people, 1 Cl., 55, 6; so highly does God rate the humility which expects all help from Him. Barn., 3, 3 quotes Is. 58:6 f. freely and says: καὶ ἐὰν ἴδῃς ταπεινόν, οὐχ ὑπερόψῃ αὐτόν.

2. ταπεινόω.

In the Jewish prayer in 1 Cl., 59, 3 ff. v. 3 (→ 23, 30 ff.) says of God with Is. 3:11: τὸν ταπεινοῦντα ὕβριν ὑπερηφάνων and (cf. Is. 10:33): καὶ τοὺς ὑψηλοὺς ταπεινοῦντα. Awareness of God's abasing and exalting is thus determinative here too and forms the background for the request for mercy on the afflicted (v. 4). ψ 50:10 is quoted in 1 Cl., 18, 8 and ψ 50:19 in 18, 17. Barn., 3, 1-5 quotes Is. 58:4-10; 3, 1 echoes Is. 58:5: ἄνθρωπον ταπεινοῦντα τὴν ψυχὴν αὐτοῦ, and 3, 5 Is. 58:10: καὶ ψυχὴν τεταπεινωμένην ἐλεήσῃς. Barn., 4, 4 quotes Da. 7:24 and 4, 5, quoting Da. 7:7 f., says: ὡς ἐταπείνωσεν ὑφ' ἓν τρία τῶν μεγάλων κεράτων. Herm. m., 4, 2, 2 demands that good be done and calls for a fast to expiate sin and for penitential self-chastisement: καὶ ταπεινοῖ τὴν ἑαυτοῦ ψυχὴν καὶ βασανίζει, ὅτι ἥμαρτεν.

3. ταπείνωσις.

This is used of Moses in 1 Cl., 53, 2 when he stayed 40 days and nights on the mount ἐν νηστείᾳ καὶ ταπεινώσει; ταπείνωσις is the abasement before God which accompanies and finds expression in fasting, i.e., עֱנוּת. It is also used of Esther in 1 Cl., 55, 6 and elucidated by τὸ ταπεινὸν τῆς ψυχῆς. 1 Cl., 16, 7 quotes Is. 53:8.

The three terms which are most prominent in the biblical writings have a consistently biblical sense in the post-apost. fathers. They occur mostly in OT quotations and they are focused on fasting and penitential acts. They are thus orientated to a developing order of life and discipline in the Church. This is why some terms which are seldom used in the Bible come to the forefront to emphasise the character of the emerging order.

4. ταπεινοφρονέω.

At the beginning of 1 Cl. the Corinthians are praised: πάντες τε ἐταπεινοφρονεῖτε μηδὲν ἀλαζονευόμενοι, ὑποτασσόμενοι μᾶλλον ἢ ὑποτάσσοντες, 2, 1. Admonitions to humility precede the gt. exposition of the history of the fathers in 1. Cl., 13, 1: ταπεινοφρονήσωμεν οὖν, consisting in the penitential renunciation of sins. Acc. to 1 Cl., 13, 3 this ταπεινοφρονεῖν is subjection to the Word of Scripture and the Lord. Those who fulfil it belong to Christ: ταπεινοφρονούντων γάρ ἐστιν ὁ Χριστός, 1 Cl., 16, 1 who Himself is ταπεινοφρονῶν, v. 2. In proof Is. 53:1-12 is quoted and there is ref. to the exemplariness of Christ ὑπογραμμὸς ὁ δεδομένος ἡμῖν: εἰ γὰρ ὁ κύριος οὕτως ἐταπεινοφρόνησεν, τί ποιήσωμεν ἡμεῖς οἱ ὑπὸ τὸν ζυγὸν τῆς χάριτος αὐτοῦ δι' αὐτοῦ ἐλθόντες; 16, 17, cf. also 48, 6. It is said of the fathers: εὐηρέστησαν ταπεινοφρονοῦντες τὰ πρὸς τὸν πατέρα καὶ θεὸν καὶ κτίστην καὶ πάντας ἀνθρώπους, 62, 2. The quotation of Prv. 3:34 LXX in 30, 2 is followed by an admonition which reminds us of Col. 3:12 (→ 22, 27 ff.): ἐνδυσώμεθα τὴν ὁμόνοιαν ταπεινοφρονοῦντες, ἐγκρατευόμενοι, 30, 3. The significant warning ὁ ταπεινοφρονῶν [76] μὴ ἑαυτῷ μαρτυρείτω in 38, 2 shows how stress on a humble disposition as a virtue can lead to boasting. Herm. s., 5, 3, 7 demands fasting and almsgiving, gives concrete directions for these, and concludes: καὶ οὕτω ταπεινοφρονήσεις. A reward is promised for this. Remission of sins

---

[76] It is possible here to read ταπεινόφρων as noun for the part. ταπεινοφρονῶν, so Pr.-Bauer, s.v.

does not immediately follow repentance ἀλλὰ δεῖ τὸν μετανοοῦντα βασανίσαι τὴν ἑαυτοῦ ψυχὴν καὶ ταπεινοφρονῆσαι ἐν πάσῃ πράξει αὐτοῦ ἰσχυρῶς καὶ θλιβῆναι ἐν πάσαις θλίψεσι ποικίλαις, 7, 4; the reward is given only to him who endures in afflictions — μόνον παράμεινον ταπεινοφρονῶν καὶ λειτουργῶν τῷ κυρίῳ ἐν πάσῃ καθαρᾷ καρδίᾳ, 7, 6. Here, then, ταπεινοφρονέω means humble and persevering submission to fasting, almsgiving and affliction.

5. ταπεινοφροσύνη.

ταπεινοφροσύνη is the mind expressed in ταπεινοφρονεῖν. 1 Cl., 30, 8 reads: ἐπιείκεια καὶ ταπεινοφροσύνη καὶ πραΰτης παρὰ τοῖς ηὐλογημένοις ὑπὸ τοῦ θεοῦ. [77] They are the opp. of θράσος καὶ αὐθάδεια καὶ τόλμα. Jacob is an example of ταπεινοφροσύνη acc. to 1 Cl., 31, 4. It is required of the bishop (44, 3) and of anyone who holds a leading position in the congregation, 48, 6. ταπεινοφροσύνη with ἐπιείκεια consists in subjection to God's will and thus expresses what ענוה is for the Jews, 56, 1; 58, 2. It is thus the express aim of the upbringing of children: μαθέτωσαν, τί ταπεινοφροσύνη παρὰ θεῷ ἰσχύει, 21, 8. For Herm. v., 3, 10, 6: πᾶσα ἐρώτησις ταπεινοφροσύνης χρῄζει, ταπεινοφροσύνη is a presupposition for the answering of prayer; this is confirmed in s., 5, 3, 7 → 24, 44 ff. In Jewish thinking, too, fasting leads to the answering of prayer.

6. ταπεινοφρόνησις.

Since ταπεινοφροσύνη means fasting in Herm. (→ lines 14 ff.), a humble mind as subjection to the commandments of the Lord is expressed by the new term ταπεινοφρόνησις. If life is given to those who keep the Lord's commandments these do not act περὶ πρωτείων ἢ περὶ δόξης, but περὶ μακροθυμίας καὶ περὶ ταπεινοφρονήσεως (vl.) ἀνδρός, s., 8, 7, 6.

7. ταπεινόφρων.

1 Cl., 19, 1 uses τὸ ταπεινόφρον as noun. The ref. is to the humble and modest ὑποδεές manner of the fathers which has provided an example to improve men; the meaning is the same as that of ταπεινοφροσύνη (→ lines 7 ff.). [78] Barn., 19, 3 warns against self-exaltation and demands: ἔσῃ δὲ ταπεινόφρων κατὰ πάντα. Acc. to Herm. m., 11, 8 it may be said of him who has the Spirit from above: πραΰς ἐστιν καὶ ἡσύχιος καὶ ταπεινόφρων καὶ ἀπεχόμενος ἀπὸ πάσης πονηρίας. The man who has ταπεινοφρόνησις is ταπεινόφρων and this is the work of God's Spirit. Ign. Eph., 10, 2 demands: πρὸς τὰς μεγαλορημοσύνας αὐτῶν (sc. of men) ὑμεῖς ταπεινόφρονες, par. πρὸς τὰς ὀργὰς αὐτῶν ὑμεῖς πραεῖς.

8. The Shift in the Sense of the Terms in the Post-Apostolic Fathers.

Humility was at first an eschatological expectation and a manner of life controlled by Christ. But with the relaxing of eschatological tension and awareness it become a disposition which produces specific conduct, i.e., penitence and fasting, and the word may be used for this conduct. This shift in sense took place under Jewish Christian influence in the Roman church, as may be seen from 1 Cl. and Herm. Apart from Barn. with his OT

---

[77] On the linking of the stems ταπειν- and πραΰ- (→ 10, 33 f.; 14, 6 ff.) cf. Mt. 11:29; Col. 3:12; Eph. 4:2 and 1 Cl., 30, 8, also Herm. m., 11, 8; Ign. Eph., 10, 2. 2 C. 10:1 should also be noted in this connection.

[78] Possibly one should also ref. to 1 Cl., 38, 2 here → n. 76.

quotations the other post-apost. writings, with trifling exceptions, do not use words of the group ταπειν-. In 1 Cl. and Herm. humility as penitence and fasting has an established place in Christianity understood as a *nova lex*. The new development is partly influenced by the fear of moral decay in Roman society, which had its effect on the Christian community too. This fear was evoked by the impact of the Chr. message. But the new development had a profound influence on early Christianity. [79]

Grundmann

---

[79] Cf. Dihle, 752-778, also O. Schaffner, *Christliche Demut* (1959), 35-78.

τάσσω, τάγμα, ἀνατάσσω,
ἀποτάσσω, διατάσσω, διαταγή,
ἐτιταγή, προστάσσω, ὑποτάσσω,
ὑποταγή, ἀνυπότακτος,
ἄτακτος (ἀτάκτως), ἀτακτέω [1]

---

† τάσσω.

1. τάσσω in Gk. means "to appoint," [2] "order," hence a. "to arrange," e.g., religious festivals and their celebration, Plat. Leg., VII, 799a, "to determine," e.g., the law-giver "lays down" what is bad or good, [3] Leg., V, 728a, or ὁ νόμος οὕτω τάττει, La., 199a, the ἄρχοντες command, Leg., VI, 762c, similarly of the Jewish Law, Jos. Ap., 2, 203 f., 206; b. "to appoint," officers draw up soldiers for battle, Plat. Ap., 28e, ἀρχὰς τὰς ἐφ' ἑκάστοις τεταγμένας are authorities appointed for various tasks, Aristot. Pol., IV, 14, p. 1298a, 23, officials are τεταγμένοι ἐπί τινι, appointed to something, Plat. Leg.,

---

τ ά σ σ ω κτλ. Bibl.: On R. 13 → VI, 516, Bibl.; esp. → V, 440, n. 401; L. Cerfaux-J. Tondriau, "Le culte des souverains dans la civilisation gréco-romaine," *Bibliothèque de Théologie*, III, 5 (1957); O. Cullmann, *Der Staat im NT*[2] (1961; E.T.); G. Delling, *R. 13:1-7 innerhalb d. Briefe d. NT* (1962); M. Dibelius, "Rom u. d. Christen im ersten Jhdt.," *Botschaft u. Gesch.*, II (1956), 177-228; F. J. Dölger, "Zur antiken u. frühchr. Auffassung d. Herrschergewalt von Gottes Gnaden," *Ant. Christ.*, III (1932), 117-127; also "Herrschergewalt hat Gottes Macht," *ibid.*, 128-131; O. Eck, "Urgemeinde u. Imperium," BFTh, 42, 3 (1940); A. A. T. Ehrhardt, *Politische Metaphysik v. Solon bis Aug.* (1959); W. Elert, "Pls. u. Nero," *Zwischen Gnade u. Ungnade* (1948), 38-71; H. Fuchs, *Der geistige Widerstand gg. Rom in d. antiken Welt* (1938); E. R. Goodenough, "The Political Philosophy of Hellenistic Kingship," *Yale Class. Stud.*, I (1928), 52-102; L. Goppelt, "Der Staat in d. Sicht d. NT," *Macht u. Recht*, ed. H. Dombois and E. Wilckens (1956), 9-21; also "Die Freiheit zur Kaisersteuer," *Festschr. f. K. D. Schmidt* (1961), 40-50; M. Hengel, "Die Zeloten," *Arbeiten bes. z. Gesch. d. Spätjudt. u. Urchr.*, 1 (1961), 93-114; E. Käsemann, "R. 13:1-7 in unserer Generation," ZThK, 56 (1959), 316-376 (with bibl.); G. Kittel, *Christus u. Imperator* (1939); W. L. Knox, "Church and State in the NT," JRS, 39 (1949), 23-30; J. Koch-Mehrin, "Die Stellung d. Christen zum Staat nach R. 13 u. Apk. 13," *Ev. Theol.*, 7 (1947/48), 378-401; O. Kuss, "Pls. uber d. staatliche Gewalt," *Theol. u. Glaube*, 45 (1955), 321-334; C. D. Morrison, *The Powers That Be* (1960); F. Neugebauer, "Zur Auslegung v. R. 13:1-7," *Kerygma u. Dogma*, 8 (1962), 151-172; E. Peterson, *Der Monotheismus als politisches Problem* (1935); K. H. Schelkle, "Staat u. Kirche in d. patristischen Auslegung v. R. 13:1-7," ZNW, 44 (1952/53), 223-236; A. Strobel, "Zum Verständnis v. R. 13," ZNW, 47 (1956), 67-93; F. Taeger, *Charisma*, I (1957), II (1959); N. Wasser, *Die Stellung d. Juden gegenüber den Römern nach d. rabb. Literatur*, Diss. Zürich (1933); A. Young, "The Stoic Creed on the Origin of Kingship and of Laws," *The Class. Weekly*, 28 (1934/35), 115-8.
[1] Worth noting is the absence of τάξις, διάταξις etc., though these were common in the philosophical, popular and literary speech of Hellenism gen. [Dihle].
[2] "Order or arrange with ref. to a specific place, position, or relation *vis-à-vis* others," acc. to H. Schmidt, *Synonymik d. gr. Sprache*, I (1876), 210 f. The compound διατάσσω is first attested in Hes. Op., 276 → 34, 16 f.; the noun ταγός "(military) leader," Hom. Il., 23, 160 vl., also a term of office in Thessaly, Xenoph. Hist. Graec., VI, 4, 28 etc. Etym. uncertain, cf. Boisacq, Hofmann, *s.v.* [Risch].
[3] And this is also in fact moral good or evil.

XII, 952e, cf. ὁ τεταγμένος σατράπης, Jos. Ap., 1, 135. Priests are appointed as supervisors and judges, 2, 187, God will appoint an angelic guard for the righteous, Gr. En. 100:5, the senses are appointed to serve, Epict. Diss., II, 23, 7 and 11, a man is "set" in his place (post) before God, Ench., 22, cf. already Socrates: οὗ ἄν τις ἑαυτὸν τάξῃ ἡγησάμενος βέλτιστον εἶναι ἢ ὑπ' ἄρχοντος ταχθῇ, ἐνταῦθα δεῖ... μένοντα κινδυνεύειν, Plat. Ap., 28d; there is ref. to the Great Bear ἣν ὁ κύριος θεὸς ἔταξε to circle around the sacred pole, Preis. Zaub., I, 4, 1306 f., cf. 1278 f.; the ταχθέντες (sic) δυνάμεις appointed for the day of judgment on the spirits of Beliar are in the third heaven, Test. L. 3:3. c. ὥρᾳ τεταγμένῃ, "at the appointed time," Epict. Diss., III, 15, 3 (cf. 24, 86); ἐν τεταγμένῃ πολιτείᾳ, "in an ordered state," Plat. Resp., X, 619c, par. κοσμέω, Gorg., 504a; "to establish an order" in the cosmos, e.g., Aristobul. in Eus. Praep. Ev., 13, 12, 11 f.; Corp. Herm., 5, 4 (cf. 11, 9); cf. στοιχεῖα πάντα τεταγμένα σοῖσι νόμοισι, Preis. Zaub., I, 4, 440 (cf. 1961); through the appointed courses of the stars, days, months and years came into being, Philo Op. Mund., 60, rain and wind come κατὰ τεταγμένας καιρῶν περιόδους, Poster. C., 144. d. The mid. sense is "to fix for oneself," Plat. Leg., V, 733e.

2. In the LXX the verb is most commonly used for שׂים or שׂום. It means a. "to ordain," "issue a prohibition," Da. 6:13 f. Θ; b. "to appoint" someone as something, 2 Macc. 8:22; 1 Βασ. 22:7, e.g., judges over the people, 2 Βασ. 7:11, Levites in their ministry, 1 Ch. 16:4; τεταγμένος ἐπὶ τῶν πραγμάτων, Εσθ. 3:13 f.; cf. 3 Macc. 7:1; 2 Macc. 6:21; 3 Macc. 5:14 and τῶν ἐπ' ἐξουσίαις τεταγμένων of those "put" in positions of power, obviously by God, 4 Εσθ. 8:12e; c. "to set," e.g., God sets limits for the sea, Jer. 5:22, or with ref. to the statutes of David, 1 Εσδρ. 1:15; d. "to draw up," "set up," e.g., troops, 2 Macc. 15:20, men, 4 Βασ. 10:24, idols, Jer. 7:30, cf. Ez. 14:4, 7, altars, Jer. 11:13; cf. τεταγμένη as the division of an army (→ 31, 14 f.), Cant. 6:4, 10; τεταγμένος "well-ordered," of government (→ line 9 f.) Sir. 10:1. In the mid. a. "to command" (God as subj.) Ex. 29:43, "to make dispositions," the last will Is. 38:1, τὸ ταχθέν, "charge," Ep. Jer. 61; b. "to appoint (for oneself)," 2 Macc. 10:28; "to fix," e.g., of time, 2 Βασ. 20:5; Job 12:5; 14:13; a day, 2 Macc. 3:14; 14:21, a plan, 1 Macc. 5:27; 12:26. The peculiarities due to transl. from the HT need not all be adduced here; example "to turn" one's gaze on something, 4 Βασ. 12:18 (cf. ἐστήρισεν Lk. 9:51); Da. 11:17 Θ; "to set" the heart on something, Hag. 1:5; Ez. 44:5, "to make" Zech. 7:14; Hos. 2:5; Zech. 10:3 etc.

3. In the NT as in non-biblical Greek τάσσω means "to determine," Ac. 15:2, "to appoint," Ac. 28:23; [5] 12:21; → line 9 f., "to order," Mt. 28:16 mid.; on 1 C. 16:15 → 27, 11 ff.; lines 3 ff. [6] The officer who commands others is himself under orders (Lk. 7:8) and thus knows from two-sided experience what it means concretely to be subject to authority with no possibility of resistance, → 41, 9 ff.

Elsewhere God is the One who orders or appoints, though only in the passive in the NT and with no mention of God in Ac. God has arranged the commission which results for Paul from his experience on the Damascus Road → VI, 863, 5 ff. (Ac. 22:10, cf. 14 f.). According to Ac. 13:48 the man who is a Christian [7] is ordained to eternal life. [8] The idea that God's will to save is accomplished in Christians with

---

[4] Cf. V. Ryssel in Kautzsch Apkr. u. Pseudepigr., ad loc. Linguistically cf. ἐπὶ σκηπτουχίᾳ ταχθείς, Aesch. Pers., 297 f. Εσθ. 8:12a-x was probably written from the very first in Gk., O. Eissfeldt, Einl. in d. AT³ (1964), 801 f.

[5] Cf. τάξας... ἡμέραν, Jos. Ant., 9, 136.

[6] On 1 C. 16:15 cf. formally ὅσοι... εἰς ὑπηρετικὴν ἑκόντες αὐτοὺς τάττουσι, Plat. Polit., 289e; cf. Ap., 28d; other examples in Pr.-Bauer, s.v.

[7] ὅσοι hardly means that a specific no. was appointed but distinguishes converts from other hearers.

[8] Formally cf. Test. L. 3:3; on ἐκλέγομαι κτλ. in Ac. → IV, 174, 23 ff.; 179, 1 ff.; ἐκλεκτός does not occur in Ac.

their conversion is obviously not connected with the thought of predestination (→ IV, 192, 1 ff.) but rather with that of conferring status (→ 31, 20 ff.); cf. οὐκ ἀξίους, Ac. 13:46.

According to R. 13:1 existing [9] secular powers are "instituted" by God and derive their authority from Him. This is why Christianity subjects itself to their rule (43, 25 ff.), conscious of the divine appointment (→ 36, 15 ff.) [10] and the implied commission of the authorities (→ 43, 24 ff.). This is given unrestricted emphasis, obviously in opposition to a contrary tendency (→ 36, 15 ff.) Immediately after there is express mention of the obligation (→ III, 618, 21 ff.) to pay taxes, R. 13:7. [11]

The meaning of τεταγμέναι in R. 13:1 cannot be expounded apart from a proper understanding of ἐξουσίαι. [12] The widespread expression οἱ ἐν (ταῖς) ἐξουσίαις means "those in office," Aristot. Eth. Nic., VIII, 7, p. 1158a, 28; 9, p. 1159a, 19; "in positions of government," Diod. S., 1, 58, 3. ὑπατικὴ ἐξουσία is "consular power," Diod. S., 14, 113, 6 (here in the hands of those who are not consuls), τὴν ὕπατον ἐξουσίαν παραλαβόντων means "to hold as the consulate," Dion. Hal. Ant. Rom., 7, 1, 1; δημαρχικῆς ἐξουσίας is said of the holder of the tribunicia potestas (here Augustus), Ditt. Syll.[3], II, 780, 4 (6 B.C.), [13] cf. also → II, 563, n. 15. The officebearer of the Essenes is not to ἐξυβρίζειν εἰς τὴν ἐξουσίαν, against the position conferred on him, Jos. Bell., 2, 140, cf. Εσθ. 8:12e (→ 28, 22). [14] Cf. the phrase λαμβάνω ἐξουσίαν, "to receive authority," Jos. Bell., 2, 117. Ditt. Or., II, 665, 16 f. speaks of men who greedily and shamelessly abuse their office; the sense "powers" is obviously close here and in other places. As regards non-biblical use of ἐξουσία in the political sphere one can hardly carry through a simple lexical integration and thus suggest a single word by which to render R. 13:1. Note must be taken of the great breadth of meaning the term can have outside the NT and in principle in R. 13 too, at least so far as we are concerned with our non-Greek sense of language. The context implies some limitation. On the one hand ἐξουσία in R. 13:1 is not abstract [15] even though the statements claim a more general validity → 43, 25 ff. Yet ἐξουσία here does not ref. merely to a single authority [16] or official, [17] even though R. 13 is speaking of the actual authorities with which Christians had to do at the time. Again, these are not just the authorities of the Roman state which exercised power through

---

[9] There is no reason to add a "still" here (Dibelius, 184).

[10] The piling up of words of the ταγ-group calls for notice; apart from ὑποτάσσω (→ 43, 25 ff.) we have διαταγή (→ 36, 15 ff.) and also ἀντιτάσσομαι → 36, 20 ff.

[11] Cullmann, 42 sees an allusion to Mk. 12:17 and par. R. 13:1-7 is not opposed to 1 C. 6:1-6, since the organised secular order is not called in question there, E. Dinkler, "Zum Problem d. Ethik bei Pls.," ZThK, 49 (1952), 174; the statements have a different orientation, cf. Schl. K., 190.

[12] Meanings irrelevant to R. 13 are naturally omitted, → II, 562, 3 ff.

[13] Cf. also Jos. Ant., 16, 162; 19, 287. Also D. Magie, De Romanorum iuris publici sacrique vocabulis solemnibus in Graecum sermonem conversis (1905), Index, s.v. ἐξουσία, also s.v. ἀρχή. Further examples Strobel, 79: ἐξουσία corresponds to potestas (acc. to Strobel "office").

[14] In the LXX there is no use of ἐξουσία akin to R. 13 (→ II, 561, 24 ff.), not even where we have the HT. In additions to Da. the word often means "power," "dominion" possessed by someone, 4:31 (twice), 37a-b.

[15] Neither "authority" in the abs. nor the state, Käsemann, 324.

[16] ἐξουσία can sometimes be understood thus: θεραπεύειν γάρ, οὐκ ἐρεθίζειν χρὴ τὰς ἐξουσίας → II, 564, 15 f. But the choice here shows precisely why respect must be shown to the Roman governors. οἱ μὲν ῥαβδοῦχοι κελευσθέντες ὑπὸ τῆς ἐξουσίας "the lictors had received orders from the authorities," Dion. Hal. Ant. Rom., 11, 32, 1. The meaning "official position" is obvious if authority is to be valid ἐπὶ πάσης ἐξουσίας καὶ παντὸς κριτηρίου, P. Oxy., II, 261, 15 (55 A.D.), cf. I, 97, 5 (115-6 A.D.).

[17] In R. 13:3 ἄρχων (→ I, 489, 8 ff.) is certainly not chosen without awareness of the connection with dominion ἀρχή, cf. οἱ ἄρχοντες, "the (Roman) rulers," Jos. Ant., 16, 174.

its governors; they include those of the Hell. *polis,* and it is in this light that we are to understand R. 13, including the plur. of v. 1. In R. 13 the power of the state is decisively [18] seen as the watcher over good and evil on God's commission, [19] and it is presupposed that in principle at least it is able to use a just standard in its judgments and decisions, → 44, 24 ff. [20]

R. 13 does not object that the ruling powers promote the pagan cultus with all their might (on this cf. R. 1:21-25), nor that in practice their official acts are in part inseparably bound up with this. [21] Again, it does not charge that power is abused [22]

---

[18] There is no ref., e.g., to the state doing good.

[19] R. 13 has nothing whatever to do with the widespread idea of the king as "living law" (→ IV, 1032, 35 ff.).

[20] That man gen. knows the good, that the non-chr. norm is primarily the Chr. one too, is a common thought in Pl., R. 2:14 f.; 1:32, cf. Phil. 4:8, where what is gen. accepted ethically is required of Christians too; Pl. obviously assumes a certain consensus in ethical judgment.

[21] This does not apply only to the emperor cult and its preparatory stages → VII, 1009, 15 ff., cf. on this G. Herzog-Hauser, Art. "Kaiserkult," Pauly-W. Suppl., 4 (1924), 806-853. The paying of divine honours to emperors, which does not affect their human quality (Taeger, I, 257; cf. Menand. Fr., 600 [Koerte, II, 193]: νόμος γονεῦσιν ἰσοθέους τιμὰς νέμειν) took on specific cultic forms esp. in the East. In Rome the principle could be championed that divine honour should be paid to the ruler only after death, Tac. Ann., 15, 74, 3; Taeger, II, 306. Divine honours could be paid to heroes; it is said of Philopoimen (slain 183 B.C.): μετὰ τὴν τελευτὴν... τὰς ἰσοθέους τιμὰς ἠλλάξατο, Diod. S., 29, 18, 1st cent. practice went against the Roman principle, esp. in the case of Caligula and Domitian, also Nero, to whom in the yr. of his accession (i.e., before R. was written) the senate resolved to dedicate a statue of the same size as that of the god in the temple of Mars, Tac. Ann., 13, 8, 1; on Nero cf. also G. Schumann, *Hell. u. griech. Elemente in d. Regierung Neros,* Diss. Leipzig (1930), 27-32. Neither these events in Rome nor the more far-reaching developments in the East caused the author of the NT epistles to limit his recognition of the divine ordination of the state. With few exceptions the Roman state did not require of Jews a proof of loyalty by emperor worship, obviously because it was seen that their exclusive monotheism predated their attachment to the Roman empire. In this respect Christians had no claim to exemption once they parted company with the Synagogue as well as the state and thus declared themselves to be a newly arisen group within the Rom. empire [Dihle].

[22] Cf. Cullmann, 42. That the attitude of R. 13 is governed by the prevailing political situation (cf. the many ref. to the *pax romana* or Nero's restraint in the early part of his reign, cf. Taeger, II, 305) is against the tenor of the statements → 43, 25 ff. Obviously Paul was acquainted with the unfavourable attitude of many provincial governors, esp. in Palestine. For the abuse of power and law by Tiberius, Caligula, Nero, Pilate, Felix etc. cf. in detail Elert, 45-48, for Nero's path to power, 44 f. Paul alludes to unpleasant personal experiences in, e.g., 2 C. 11:25 (→ VI, 971, 5 ff.). But neither negative (Dibelius, 185) nor positive (Kittel, 21) factors affect the judgment of R. 13, which is thoroughly theological. The word optimism (cf. "enthusiasm" Knox, 29) is the wrong one for it, Kittel, 37 and 40. Obviously there was misunderstanding in the early Church. Roman rule was supposedly set by God in the service of His saving work, since by means of it He put an end to continuous wars and bound cities and nations together by trade. This is why the apostle enjoined submission to the powers that be acc. to Diodore of Tarsus on R. 13:1 (Staab, 107), Peterson, 83 and n. 139. 141; Orosius goes even further, Peterson, 88-93. But cf. 1 Cl., who is often thought to be alluding to the Domitian persecution in 1, 1, but did not let this affect adversely what he says about intercession for rulers, 61, 1 f.; at most v. 2b might contain a hint of tensions; Eck, 80; Kittel, 30; Knox, 25, n. 15. How the *pax romana* might be estimated in loyal statements can be seen from the comparison in an address to Rome between the τάξις which Zeus' rule brought after ἀταξία among the Titans and the blessings of Roman government (concretely the empire) after the confusion which preceded it, Ael. Arist. Or., 26, 103 (Keil). Platonically it is the demiurge who brought the disorganised visible world out of ἀταξία to the τάξις of the cosmos, Plat. Tim., 30a; in Philo much the same is said of God the Creator: εἰς τάξιν ἐξ ἀταξίας... ἄγων, Plant., 3, cf. Som., I, 241, but in him too Augustus is ὁ τὴν ἀταξίαν εἰς τάξιν ἀγαγών, Leg. Gaj., 147 (cf. Peterson, 29-31, 112 f.). There is not even a hint of all this in R. 13.

by one or other of those that bear office. [23] There is a clear connection between 13:7 and 13:8, [24] which leads on from obligations to those in authority to obligations characterising the relations between man and man. [25] On Rev. 13 → III, 134, 23 ff.

4. In the post-apost. fathers the verb occurs 4 times but only in the part. of the pass. perf.: the course of the stars "ordained" by God, 1 Cl., 20, 2; the "set" times of cultic practice, 40, 1 f.; the author of 1 Cl. stresses order in other places too, cf. στάσις, → VII, 571, 18 ff. On the ways of light angels are posted to direct him, Barn., 18, 1 cf. 1 QS 3:20 f., 24 f. In Mart. Pol., 10, 2 the saying of the martyr to the governor carries a plain ref. to R. 13:1, 7: δεδιδάγμεθα ... ἀρχαῖς καὶ ἐξουσίαις (→ 44, n. 27) ὑπὸ τοῦ θεοῦ τεταγμέναις τιμὴν κατὰ τὸ προσῆκον τὴν μὴ βλάπτουσαν ἡμᾶς ἀπονέμειν.

† τάγμα.

1. τάγμα usually means the result of τάσσειν, [1] what is "ordered," "fixed": a. what is appointed in the sense of established, e.g., νόμου τάγμα, Ps.-Plat. Def., 414e, cf. Aristot. Pol., IV, 9, p. 1294b, 6; "set sum," Oec., II, p. 1349a, 24; b. often a specific group, a military division or troop, Ep. Ar., 26, different from ἡγεμόνες, Jos. Bell., 6, 255, cf. ἐκ τοῦ τάγματος τοῦ παρ' ἡμεῖν γυμνασίου "belongs" to the ephebes, P. Oxy., IX, 1202, 18 (217 A.D.); hence gen. "group," "host," host of things that may be perceived by the senses, Philo Migr. Abr., 209, cf. 100: ἐκ τοῦ τάγματος τῶν ἀθέων ὑπάρχειν, Sext. Emp. Math., IX, 54; Jos. calls both the Essenes in Bell., 2, 122 and 125 and the Sadducees in 2, 164 τάγμα; c. the "position" someone assumes, in the sense of "rank," τάγματος βουλευτικοῦ "of the rank of councillor," CIG III, 1, 4412b, 4 f., cf. 4411b, 4 f.; ἀνὴρ ... τοῦ πρώτου τάγματος "of the highest rank," Ditt. Syll.[3], II, 796, 7 f. (35/36 A.D.); φύσεως καθ' ἑαυτὰ τάγμα ἔχοντα, "who ... have the rank of self-subsistent entity," Epic. Ep., 1, 71 (Usener). [2]

2. In the LXX the noun occurs only in the sense of "unit" for דֶּגֶל [3] "ensign" and then "unit" in Nu. 2:2 ff.; 10:14 ff., for רַגְלִי "pedestrian" in 1 S. 4:10; 15:4; חַוָּה "camp" is obviously presupposed in 2 S. 23:13 (Mas. חַיָּה). There is no other instance in the LXX.

3. In the NT the word occurs only in 1 C. 15:23. If the meaning here had necessarily to be "unit," then only one group of the resurrected would perhaps be mentioned in v. 23. [4] But it is highly possible that the sense is: each in his "position,"

---

[23] Cf. also Pol., 12, 3: Orate etiam pro regibus et potestatibus et principibus atque pro persequentibus et odientibus vos.
[24] Ltzm. R., ad loc. speaks of a "skilful transition," but the significance is material rather than formal (→ V, 564, 29 ff.; 564, 1 ff.). We have a play on words with a paradoxical point, cf. Mi. R. on 13:8.
[25] On the other hand the connection between R. 13:1-7 and vv. 11-14 is no closer than is usual in Pauline theology. The eschatological motivation of ethics in vv. 11-14 does not restrict vv. 1-7, as against Dibelius, 184; cf. Cullmann, 42 f. Obviously the political order, like every other, will end with the final winding up of this aeon. But Pl. has no particular reason to say this in R. 13. In the context he is obviously not concerned with the "eschatological qualification of his loyalty" (Dibelius, 185); indeed, what is at issue gen. is something far different from loyalty.

τάγμα. [1] Debr. Griech. Wortb. § 311. Cf. P. Chantraine, Formation des noms en grec ancien (1933), 179-190 [Risch].
[2] Quoted in Diog. L., X, 71, cf. O. Apelt, Leben u. Meinungen berühmter Philosophen, Philos. Studientexte, 6, 2 (1955), 255.
[3] The word is common in 1 QM, cf. Y. Yadin, The Scroll of the War of the Sons of Light against the Sons of Darkness (1962), Index, s.v., also s.v. τάγμα.
[4] Schl. K., 412: "an individual is no τάγμα."

"rank." [5] Christ has the rank of ἀπαρχή, cf. v. 20. The resurrection of His people takes place simultaneously with the *parousia* of Christ as participation in His rule. Nothing is said about the rest of mankind in the context, v. 22b. [6] The primary issue in 1 C. 15 is the resurrection of Christians, who receive a new corporeality → VI, 420, 4 ff.; cf. 1 Th. 4:14-17. For further details *v.* τέλος → 56, 26 ff.

Formally ἕκαστος ἐν τῷ ἰδίῳ τάγματι corresponds exactly to איש בתכונו 1 QS 6:8. The division of members of the community into ranks or orders plays a big role in 1 QS, cf. 6:9, 10, 22; 7:21; 8:19; 9:2, 7. תכון also has in 1 QS the sense of "statute," "decision," 5:3; 9:21 etc. תכון is gen. "what is ordered," in other nuances too → 31, 12 ff.

4. In the post-apost. fathers we find the expression ἕκαστος ἐν τῷ ἰδίῳ τάγματι in 1 Cl. in the sense of "rank": each of the military ranks carries out what has been ordered by the one above it, τὰ ἐπιτασσόμενα, 37, 3, and similarly in the community each should perform his ministry in his own rank, 41, 1. The "group" is τάγμα in Herm. s., 8, 5, 1-6, cf. τάγματα τάγματα "in units," 8, 2, 8; 4, 2 and κατὰ τάγματα, 8, 4, 2. στρατιωτικὸν τάγμα is a detachment of soldiers, Ign. R., 5, 1. The word does not occur in the Apologists.

† ἀνατάσσω.

The verb is rare; it means "to order fully," "to arrange," Ep. Ar., 144; ἑαυτόν "to order oneself," "to take up a strong position," M. Ant., III, 5, 2; "to revoke," "to repeal," Dio C., 78, 18, 5; in the mid. "to go through," "to repeat" what has been learned, Plut. De sollertia animalium, 12 (II, 968c); "to note in orderly fashion," not necessarily systematically but in such a way that others can profit, Hippiatrica Berolinensa, [1] 1, 1; "to record again," Ezra with ref. to destroyed works of the OT, Iren. in Eus. Hist. Eccl., V, 8, 15. The word does not occur in the LXX, [2] the post-apost. fathers, or the Apologists.

The author of Lk. in the prologue describes the work of his predecessors [3] as an ἀνατάξασθαι διήγησιν "concerning the events enacted among us (by God → VI, 310, 4 ff.)," → VI, 639, 12 ff. [4] In his judgment this work of theirs took place in agreement with the oral tradition of eye-witnesses (→ V, 373, 13 ff.) to the community. ἀνατάξασθαι διήγησιν can hardly mean that the πολλοί set the oral tradition in writing. In literary contexts at least διήγησις means the ordered account

---

[5] Ltzm. K., *ad loc.* "class"; H. Schwantes, *Schöpfung d. Endzeit* (1963), 29: "rank."
[6] Test. B. 10:6-8 makes a distinction: Enoch, Seth, Abraham etc. will rise again, τότε καὶ ἡμεῖς ἀναστησόμεθα..., καὶ οἱ πάντες ἀναστήσονται, οἱ μὲν εἰς δόξαν, οἱ δὲ εἰς ἀτιμίαν.

ἀνατάσσω. Bibl.: H. Cadbury, *Comm. on the Preface of Luke*, Jackson-Lake, I, 2 (1922), 494 f.; J. Mansion, "Sur le sens d'un mot grec: ἀνατάσσω," *Serta Leodiensia*, 44 (1930), 261-7; H. Schürmann, "Evangelienschr. u. kirchliche Unterweisung," *Miscellanea Erfordiana, Erfurter Theol. Stud.,* 12 (1962), 48-73; Zn. Lk., 43-5.
[1] Ed. E. Oder-C. Hoppe, Corpus Hippiatricorum, I (1924), 1.
[2] Cf. ἀναγράφω in LXX at 1 Εσδρ. 1:22, 31 (par. ἱστορέω), 40: τὰ ἱστορηθέντα... ἀναγέγραπται [Bertram].
[3] The author of Lk. would not have written a new διήγησις had he not thought he could do better. But there is no censure in 1:1. In contemporary history it was customary to ref. to predecessors, e.g., Diod. S., 1, 1, 1-3 (critically), cf. 1, 3, 1: "on this account I also...," and 2: ἐπεχείρησαν ἀναγράφειν. Cf. the bibl. in Pr.-Bauer, *s.v.*
[4] Diod. S., 1, 3, 2 etc. use πράξεις for this in similar basic statements, cf. also Polyb., 5, 31, 4 f. etc.

or presentation of an event. [5] In any case the idea of what is set forth in order is contained in the total expression ἀνατάξασθαι διήγησιν, → II, 909, 9 ff. The activity of ἀνατάσσεσθαι is emphatically differentiated from that of oral transmission; to put in writing necessarily confers order on the material. [6]

† ἀποτάσσω.

1. In Gk. this means a. "to delegate, appoint for," Aristot. Pol., VI, 8, p. 1322a, 26; "assign to," Polyb., 6, 35, 6 etc.; Philo Vit. Mos., I, 38; "set aside," Jos. Ant., 19, 337; "separate," in calculations Jos. Bell., 3, 69; "lop off" a sum from certain revenues, Inscr. Magn., 101, 47; b. mid. "to separate," Philostr. Vit. Ap., VI, 11 (217, 25); "to part," e.g., Elisha with Elijah's permission says farewell to his parents before becoming Elijah's μαθητής, Jos. Ant., 8, 354; with dat. "to leave someone," Jos. Ant., 11, 344; "to dismiss someone," P. Oxy., II, 298, 31 (1st cent. A.D.); "to renounce" ἀποτάσσομαί σου τῆς φιλίας, "I break off friendship with thee," Corpus Fabularum Aesopicarum, [1] 35, 1; then often "waive" in Philo, [2] "to separate oneself from sense perceptions," Leg. All., II, 25, cf. III, 41; Moses ὅλη τῇ γαστρὶ ἀποτάττεται (Ex. 34:28), cf. III, 142, he also bids farewell to the other πάθη, 145; the soul detaches itself from the corporeal, 238; for the sake of God, the logos etc. to give up all else worth striving for, Quaest. In Ex., II, 68; to give up nourishment for 3 days in order to pray, Jos. Ant., 11, 232; δείπνοις, Stob. Ecl., III, 279, 11; certain priestesses renounce ταῖς μίξεσιν, Soranus Gynaeciorum, I, 32, 1 (CMG, IV, 21, 28 f.).

2. In the LXX the verb occurs in the following passages: a. act. "to appoint" as officers, 1 Εσδρ. 6:26, "to detach" troops as a garrison, 1 Macc. 4:61; 6:50; 11:3, for patrolling, 15:41; "to separate," Jer. 20:2; b. the mid. "to turn from," Qoh. 2:20.

3. In the NT we find only the mid.: "to part from," least emphatically in Ac. 18:18, 21; perhaps stronger in 2 C. 2:13 (cf. 12b), also "to depart," Mk. 6:46 → line 11 f. The man who makes formal parting from his folks a presupposition of ἀκολουθεῖν (→ I, 213, 34 ff.) is said by Jesus not to be fit for the kingdom of God, Lk. 9:61 f.; cf. 1 K. 19:20 f. In Lk. 14:33 Jesus demands the radical renunciation of all possessions [3] from the man who wants to join Him. On the verb here → lines 14 ff. On the whole topic → VI, 327, 18 ff.; 905, 5 ff.

---

[5] τὸ συνεχὲς τῆς διηγήσεως, Ep. Ar., 8, cf. also 1, 322. The διήγησις is to be distinguished from a preface 2 Macc. 2:32 (par. ἱστορία) or digression, 6, 17 (ἐλευστέον ἐπὶ τὴν διήγησιν). In a letter we read ἐν τῇ διηγήσει τῶν πεπραγμένων, "in the account of the events," Dio C., 78, 37, 6; cf. the "presentation" of the case (along with witnesses) in a judicial speech, Plat. Phaedr., 266e. In historians διήγησις is the current term for historical depiction, e.g., Polyb., 5, 31, 4. It also bears the sense of presentation in Sir. (→ II, 909, n. 3) though usually in the sense of instruction rather than narrative.
[6] On the other hand the verb hardly implies repetition in Lk. 1:1, as against Zn. Lk., 43-45.

ἀποτάσσω. [1] Ed. A. Hausrath, I, 1 (1940), 50, 11.
[2] Ref. in R. Reitzenstein, Historia Monachorum u. Historia Lausiaca (1916), 104.
[3] No other understanding of τὰ ὑπάρχοντα seems to be possible. The expression always (14 times) denotes earthly goods in the NT. In the many LXX instances (15 in Gn.) it bears the same sense for a whole series of Hbr. equivalents (and often without); it is thus presupposed to be a fixed term. Many instances are in pap. from the 3rd cent. B.C. to the Byzantine period, τὰ ὑπάρχοντα, "property," Preisigke Wört., II, 643. Cf. also Philo Leg. All., III, 197; Sacr. AC, 43 (Gn. 25:5); v. further Pr.-Bauer, s.v. → VI, 318, Bibl.

4. In the post-apost. fathers the mid. denotes "full separation": it is good to follow the angel of righteousness and to break free from the angel of wickedness, Herm. m., 6, 2, 9. The future aeon, i.e., concretely the one who lives thereby, bids farewell to vices, 2 Cl., 6, 4; the Christian must part from this aeon and consort with the future aeon, he cannot have both for his friends, v. 5; he must say farewell to lusts, 16, 2. Life is renounced, Ign. Phld., 11, 1. The Apologists use the verb only 3 times: Christians have taken leave of pagan wisdom, Tat. Or. Graec., 1, 3, of idols, Just. Apol., 49, 5, of everything worldly, Dial., 119, 6.

† διατάσσω.

1. διατάσσω is attested from Hes. (→ line 17 f.) and means a. act. "to order," e.g., ἔστι τις ὁ διατάσσων τὴν τοιαύτην τάξιν, an ordered host looking on the cosmos, Aristot. Fr., Vol. V, p. 1476a, 19,[1] also an army in Jos. Ant., 5, 27 etc.; Augustus has brought the πρόνοια which "orders" our lives, Ditt. Or., II, 458, 33-35; providence which "orders" all things has set someone on the throne, Ael. Arist. Or., 35, 14[2] (Keil); then "ordain," "decide," "dispose," "regulate," e.g., τὰ πράγματα, Jos. Ant., 9, 6; κατὰ τὰ διατεταγμένα, P. Oxy., IV, 718, 25 (2nd cent. A.D.); "establish," Aristot. Eth. Nic., I, 1, p. 1094b, 2; τόνδε γὰρ ἀνθρώποισι νόμον διέταξε Κρονίων, Hes. Op., 276; of the OT law-giver, Ep. Ar., 162 and 170, cf. 147; God as He who "determines" things, Epict. Diss., I, 12, 15, e.g. summer and winter, virtue and vice, 16, also personal happenings, 25; "to give directions," ὡς ὁ Ζεὺς διέταξεν, τοῦτο ποίησον, III, 7, 36; ὡς διέταξεν ὁ δυνάμενος (sc. God), IV, 12, 25. Ordering by people who have to decide, Ditt. Syll.³, II, 818, 6 etc.; Ditt. Or., I, 326, 27 etc. In Jos. God ordains διὰ Μωυσέος, Ant., 5, 98, or Moses does, 4, 308; 5, 91, or kings, 7, 367.[3] b. Mid. "to dispose," "to ordain," Aristot. Probl., 29, 4, p. 950b, 19, in Jos. (→ line 22 f.) corresponding to the act., e.g., Ant., 11, 77 and 100. In Philo Moses "ordains," Spec. Leg., IV, 102, or the Law, Virt., 18, or Scripture.[4] ·

2. In the LXX the verb is comparatively rare and is used for several terms,[5] → 40, 34 ff. It means a. act. "to order," God has ordered everything in nature by measure, number and weight, Wis. 11:20, "to arrange," e.g., priests, 2 Ch. 5:11, or "to draw up" troops, Jdt. 2:16; 2 Macc. 5:3; 12:20; 14:22; 3 Macc. 5:44, "to allot," e.g., a ration, 3 Βασ. 11:18; Da. 1:5 Θ, "to determine," Ez. 21:24; 44:8, "to measure," 42:20; b. mid. "to determine," 1 Βασ. 13:11, "to command," 4 Macc. 8:3.

3. In the NT the word[6] is used without emphasis in Luke's writings in the sense "to order, command," Jesus in Lk. 8:55 and Paul in Ac. 20:13. With reference to the acts of earthly rulers it means "to issue an edict," the emperor in Ac. 18:2, "to

---

διατάσσω. [1] Cf. also W. D. Ross (1955), 80.
[2] Cf. M. P. Charlesworth, "Providentia et Aeternitas," HThR, 29 (1936), 107-132, esp. 119, n. 37.
[3] Further examples in Thackeray Lex. Jos., s.v.
[4] Philo does not usually specify in this case. More examples Leisegang, VII, 1, s.v.
[5] [Rengstorf].
[6] Compounds of τάσσω meaning "order" are not used quite interchangeably in the LXX. συντάσσω is restricted to Mt., where it occurs only in the expression "as he had directed" of Jesus in 21:6; 26:19 in two stories which in part are par. formally and of God in 27:10 in an OT quotation. On the other hand ἐπιτάσσω does not occur in Mt. Nor are other compounds common. κελεύω (7 times) is more often used, elsewhere only Lk. 18:40 and frequently in Ac. (of all verbs of command apparently the most common, 17 times in Ac.; the closest is the "Pauline" παραγγέλλω). Mt. sometimes uses ἐντέλλομαι too (→ II, 545, 8 ff.); Paul does not have this. The idea of ordering is also contained in λέγω. On παραγγέλλω → V, 763, 16 ff.

give official instructions," an officer in Ac. 23:31, a procurator in 24:23; cf. παρὰ τὸ διατεταγμένον in Lk. 3:13 → 34, 16, "to charge with," e.g., a master vis-à-vis his slave in Lk. 17:9, then (v. 10) applied to God's concrete directions which fill life with works of obedience, → IV, 718, 1 ff. In Ac. 7:44 the reference is to God's specific instructions for the making of the tent of revelation (Ex. 25:40) [7] by Moses → τύπος. The σκηνή (→ VII, 375, 5 ff.) has its origin in God's directions. [8] In Mt. 11:1 (the only instance in Mt.) the imparting of detailed instructions for the disciples' missionary work is called διατάσσειν [9] → 34, 22. Paul with his ὁ κύριος διέταξεν in 1 C. 9:14 is referring to one of the special orders of Jesus in His address on sending out the disciples, Mt. 10:10; Lk. 10:7 → I, 757, 15 ff. We have detailed instructions of the apostle with reference to the collection in 1 C. 16:1, the regulation of questions of worship in 11:34, the attitude to secular status in 7:17. διατάσσεσθαι is obviously part of the apostolic office, 1 C. 7:17; 16:1; for 1 C. → 37, 8 ff. The more precise content of διεταξάμην in Tt. 1:5 is brought out in v. 6 (ff.). The verb also means "to ordain" in Gl. 3:19. The Torah was not just mediated by angels. It was "ordained" or "decreed," and this through [10] Moses as the mediator to the Israelites → IV, 618, 16 ff. The presence of angels at the giving of the Law is generally maintained in Judaism, but we seldom hear of their co-operation. [11] At any rate the divine origin of the Law is not affected by Jewish statements. Where these suggest the co-operation of angels, this is only for the sake of God's transcendence. There is hesitation to let God have direct dealings with man. Instead angels play a mediating role. Paul concludes from the giving of the Torah by angels that God allowed angels to formulate its statutes; the Law is only decreed by angels. [12] But the fact that it is not ordained directly by God in its details does not mean for Paul that it was not instituted by God in intention, cf. → V, 740, 8 ff. [13] Note should also be taken of the compound ἐπιδιατάσσομαι (→ II, 129, 26 ff.), "to decree additionally," i.e., "to make further decrees supplementary to those already given," Gl. 3:15. [14]

4. In the post-apost. fathers Ign. (always mid.) emphasises that he is not ordained like someone who represents (Eph. 3, 1), like an apostle (Tr., 3, 3), like Peter and Paul (R., 4, 3); on 1 C. 7:17; 16:1 → lines 12 f. Moses recorded in the Holy Scriptures what was ordained for him, 1 Cl., 43, 1. The sea, whose limits God has set, does what He has "appointed" (act.) for it, 20, 6. Soldiers execute εὐτάκτως and ὑποτεταγμένως "what is commanded" τὰ διατασσόμενα, 37, 2; on the group ταγ- in 1 Cl., cf. also → 31, 4 ff.; 47, 3 ff. Heaven, earth, sea and all things in them "ordained" by God, Dg., 7, 2. The verb also occurs in the mid. in Herm. v., 3, 1, 4.

---

[7] Cf. Philo Vit. Mos., II, 74 f.; Leg. All., III, 102. For the Rabb. interpretation cf. Str.-B., III, 702-4.

[8] As distinct from the temple acc. to M. Simon, St. Stephen and the Hellenists (1958), 50-53, 56.

[9] As distinct from διδάσκω, which is not a specific Matthean term, in v. 1 → II, 139, 1 ff.

[10] Formally cf. διὰ φωνῆς κυρίου ἐν χειρὶ Μωυσῆ in Nu. 10:13; cf. "to speak by the hand" of someone in 3 Βασ. 12:15; Zech. 7:7.

[11] For Jos. → 36, n. 4 In Jub. 6:22; 30:12(21) there is ref. to a writing of the (first) Law, the Torah, for Moses by the angel of the presence, whereas Jub. is meant in 1:27 (and 2:1: dictation to Moses). The ref. are in Str.-B., III, 556, Rabb. material ibid., 554-6.

[12] Cf. Hb. 2:2: δι' ἀγγέλων λαληθείς, but v. 3: λαλεῖσθαι διὰ τοῦ κυρίου.

[13] Paul does not think dualistically; the Gnostics, to whose statements Schlier Gl. on 3:19 refers, took a very different line.

[14] Cf. προσδιατάσσομαι Inscr. Graecae ad res Romanas pertinentes, IV, 661, 17, ed. G. Lafaye, R. Cagnat etc. (1927).

† διαταγή.

1. διαταγή is the "instruction": ποιούμενος κατὰ τὴν τοῦ κελεύοντος δια-
ταγὴν μὴ ἀντιτασσόμενος of slaves, Vett. Val., IX, 11 (p. 355, 17 f.); medical
prescription, e.g., Rufus in Oribasius Collectiones medicae, VI, 38, 13 (CMG, VI,
1, 1, p. 190, 13); decree; order, e.g., concerning the use of graves, Inscr. Graecae
ad res Romanas pertinentes, [1] IV, 661, 17 (85 A.D.); 734, 12; 840, 3; the customary
term for an official decree, pap., e.g., by the emperor or governor, is διάταγμα,
cf. Hb. 11:23. [2]

2. The only LXX instance is at 2 Εσδρ. 4:11: ἡ διαταγή (in the original text
"copy") τῆς ἐπιστολῆς to Artaxerxes.

3. In the NT the noun occurs at Ac. 7:53; Stephen's address ends with the
statement that the Jews certainly accepted the Torah as [3] the directions of angels
but they did not keep it, i.e., its statutes were given them not just as human decrees
but through God's messengers (→ I, 83, 38 ff.) and hence as God's instructions. [4]
On the different emphasis in Gl. 3:19; Hb. 2:2 → IV, 866, n. 210. The man who
withstands the official authority ordained by God (→ 29, 4 ff.) is in conflict with
God's "ordinance" acc. to R. 13:2. Obviously this does not mean that every govern-
mental decree is God's ordinance. διαταγή refers rather to God's "ordaining"
according to v. 1b.

> Opposition to the powers that be is thus understood here as a radical opposition in
> principle, or at least as permanent opposition in practice. This is supported, if not by the
> pres. ἀντιτασσόμενος, at any rate by the perf. ἀνθέστηκεν. Judicial power acts as such
> at God's commission, v. 3 f. [5]

4. In the post-apost. fathers the word occurs only in 1 Cl., 20, 3: By divine "direction"
(→ VII, 571, 31 ff.) sun, moon and stars describe their foreordained courses with no
deviation τοὺς ἐπιτεταγμένους ... ὁρισμούς, → 31, 4 f.; 46, 8 f. In the Apologists the
word simply denotes the "decreeing" of the Torah by Moses in Just. Dial., 67, 7.

† ἐπιταγή.

1. This word, attested from the 2nd cent. B.C., means "ordinance," "disposition,"
Ditt. Or., I, 333, 9 (2nd cent. B.C.); Polyb., 13, 4, 3, "order" of a superior, Ep. Ar., 103,
"statute," e.g., νόμων ἐπιταγαί, Diod. S., 1, 70, 1; ἐξ ἐπιταγῆς, Ditt. Or., II, 674, 1;
[κατὰ τὴ]ν ἱερωτάτην αὐτοῦ (sc. the emperor) ἐπιταγὴν ἔγραψα, Ditt. Syll.[3], II,
821 D, 2 (90 A.D.). In the course of the year everything takes place as ordained κατὰ
ἐπιταγήν, Eth. En. 5:2; κατ᾿ ἐπιταγήν on votive offerings means "at the behest" of the
deity, Ditt. Syll.[3], III, 1153, 4; 1171, 3; κατ᾿ ἐπιταγὴν τοῦ θεοῦ ἀνέθηκα εἰκετεύων, [1]

δ ι α τ α γ ή. [1] Ed. G. Lafaye, R. Cagnat etc. (1927); cf. also Deissmann LO, 70 f.
[2] Cf. S. Lösch, *Diatagma Kaisaros* (1936), 9 f.; J. Irmscher, "Zum Διάταγμα Καίσαρος
v. Nazareth," ZNW, 42 (1949), 172-184, esp. 176.
[3] The constr. with εἰς may be explained both from the *koine* and also from the Semitic ל
it probably does not stand for a modal ἐν with dat., though even if it did no other sense is
possible.
[4] Cf. Jos. Ant., 15, 136: We have learned the most beautiful and sacred (→ II, 231, 8 ff.)
of the δόγματα contained in the laws δι᾿ ἀγγέλων παρὰ τοῦ θεοῦ.
[5] The authority is God's διάκονος (v. 4), perhaps His instrument; διάκονος certainly
has this sense in Jos. Bell., 3, 354; 4, 388 and 626; Philo Poster. C., 165; Vit. Mos., II, 199.

ἐ π ι τ α γ ή. [1] F. W. Hasluck, "Poemanenum," JHS, 26 (1906), 23-31, Text 28, Inscr. 6.

cf. κατ᾽ ἐπιταγὴν τοῦ κυρίου, Herm. v., 3, 8, 2. The word occurs only here in the post-apost. fathers and not in the Apologists; on the verb → 36, 25 f.; 32, 12; 46, 14 f.

2. In the LXX the noun means God's "ordinances" in Wis. 18:15; 19;6, those of the ruler in 14:17; 1 Εσδρ. 1:16; Da. 3:16; 3 Macc. 7:20; these are the only instances.

3. In the NT the word occurs only in the Pauline corpus, and always (except at 1 C. 7:25; Tt. 2:15) in the expression κατ᾽ ἐπιταγήν. The usage adduced — 36, 29 ff. shows that it denotes especially the direction of those in high office who have something to say. [2] In the use in 1 C. one may see how even detailed norms of Christian conduct developed in primitive Christianity. For such norms the dominical tradition is an absolutely authoritative source; the presence of an ἐπιταγὴ κυρίου (→ III, 1092, 7 ff.) decides, 1 C. 7:25; [3] → 35, 8 ff. If in contrast Paul calls his own directions a mere counsel, he goes on to give it its own weight in what follows. The οὐ κατ᾽ ἐπιταγήν of 7:6 rules out the misunderstanding that he was making marital intercourse a general ethical requirement in v. 5; this is why he adds v. 7, → II, 342, 10 ff. In 2 C. 8:8 the "not by command" stands in contrast to the idea of voluntariness. How naturally Paul assumes that it is his apostolic right to give instructions may be seen from διατάσσω → 35, 13 f.; cf. ἐπιτάσσω Phlm. 8. On the basis of God's "command" the declaration of the secret which has now been revealed takes place. R. 16:26, the word of proclamation has been entrusted to the apostle, Tt. 1:3, and he is the apostle of Jesus Christ, 1 Tm. 1:1; cf. διὰ θελήματος θεοῦ, Col. 1:1; Eph. 1:1; similarly Gl. 1:1, 15. In Tt. 2:15 ἐπιταγή means the impress of the pastoral word. On κατ᾽ ἐπιταγήν → 36, 32 ff.

† προστάσσω.

1. The word is often used for "to order (validly)" of those who have the right to command, [1] so rulers, Plat. Resp., I, 339d, legislators, V, 746a, the law, 745a, similarly pap., [2] also God: ἐμοὶ ... προστέτακται ὑπὸ τοῦ θεοῦ, Plat. Ap., 33c, nature, Phaed., 80a, kings, Jos. Ap., 2, 141, the Athenians, through laws, 172, the Jewish laws, 149, the Law, 202, Plato as law-giver, 257, Moses, 12, God, Ant., 1, 51 and 59 (in an individual direction), also God in Philo Vit. Mos., II, 63, νόμος, Spec. Leg., III, 73, the λόγος θεῖος; [3] men should command women, Test. R. 5:5. In Stoicism the word has the special sense "to impart an ethical direction or norm." The law can only forbid and not command the wicked because they are unable to do what is truly right, Plut. Stoic. Rep., 11 (II, 1037c-d). But cf. Philo: It is unnecessary to command or forbid the perfect man who is κατ᾽ εἰκόνα of God (→ II, 392, 11 ff.), Leg. All., I, 94. One also reads that it is the

[2] The verb is used similarly in the Synpt., where it often denotes the powerful command of Jesus to demons, Mk. 1:27 par.; 9:25; Lk. 8:31.
[3] Cf. v. 10, where Paul ref. to himself the dominical tradition preserved in Mk. 10:11 par.

προστάσσω. Bibl.: A. Pelletier, "Flavius Josèphe adaptateur de la Lettre d'Aristée," Études et Commentaires, 40 (1962), 61, 277-282. On Ac. 17:26: H. Conzelmann, "Die Rede d. Pls. auf dem Areopag," Gymnasium Helveticum, 12 (1958), 18-32; M. Dibelius, Aufsätze z. Ag.[4] (1961), 30-35; W. Eltester, "Gott u. d. Natur in d. Areopagrede," Nt.liche Studien f. R. Bultmann, ZNW Beih., 21[2] (1957), 202-227, esp. 204-209; B. Gärtner, "The Areopagus Speech and Natural Revelation," Acta Semin. Neotest. Upsaliensis, 21 (1955), 146-152; M. Pohlenz, "Pls. u. d. Stoa," ZNW, 42 (1949), 69-104, esp. 84-88; W. Schmid, "Die Rede d. Ap. Pls. vor d. Philosophen u. Areopagiten in Athen," Philol., 95 (1943), 79-120, esp. 99-104; for further more recent lit. Eltester, 205 f., n. 6; Haench. Ag on 17:16 ff.

[1] "προστάσσω est bien le verbe de l'autorité suprême," Pelletier, 277, cf. 61.
[2] Cf. Preisigke Wört., s.v.
[3] Further examples in Leisegang, VII, 2, 690.

task of the king "to command what is necessary and to forbid what is unlawful," Vit. Mos., II, 4, through laws, 5; κατορθοῖ κατὰ τὴν τοῦ ὀρθοῦ λόγου πρόσταξιν, applies to the perfect, Leg. All., I, 93.

2. In the LXX the word means "to command," of God in Lv. 10:1; Jon. 2:1; 4:6-8; of Moses in Ex. 36:6; Dt. 27:1; kings in 2 Ch. 31:13; 1 Εσδρ. 5:68 etc.

3. The fixity of usage outside the NT may be noted in the NT too. The apostle orders the baptism of those on whom the Holy Ghost has descended, Ac. 10:48. Moses in the Torah gave statutes which are to be kept, Mk. 1:44 and par. The angel of God gives an individual instruction, Mt. 1:24. In Ac. 10:33 the content of Peter's preaching is called that which is laid upon him by God, here in a statement which is neutral in respect of content [4] and asserts both the authority and also the dependence of the apostle. God is the One who orders in Ac. 17:26 (→ V, 453, 22 ff.).

In this compressed statement [5] only catch-words are used. [6] One interpretation takes the ordained times to be seasons [7] and this is lexically possible; [8] its main material support is found in the Creator sayings in v. 24 f. with an appeal partly to pagan philosophical thought [9] and partly to OT Jewish thought. [10] More likely is a ref. to ordained divisions of the years rather than seasons. The idea that God's creative sway [11] and even His special providential care for men may be seen in the ordered temporal progression of day, month and year is to be found in the OT and Judaism, Gn. 1:14; Ps. 104:19; Jub. 2:8 f.; cf. En. 82:7-10. [12] The third interpretation, [13] which may be traced back to similar non-chr. and

---

[4] That the ref. is to God's commission is clear in a man for whom the God of Judaism had been presented as the One who gives instructions.

[5] For v. 26 cf. Bibl.

[6] Cf. Schmid, 99. Par. materials for all expositions.

[7] Wdt. Ag., ad loc.; Dibelius, 32, 35; Eltester, 206-9; Haench. Ag., ad loc.; → n. 12.

[8] Gärtner, 147, n. 2 doubts the force of the passage adduced in → III, 458, 1 ff.; 459, 25 (IG, 14, 1018, 3 is late and obscure). But Philo Mut. Nom., 266 is plainly against those who take καιροί to be seasons. Eltester, 208 quotes Op. Mund., 59 (interpretation of Gn. 1:14); in Op. Mund., 55 καιροί means lexically the divisions of years, while ἐτήσιοι goes with it in Spec. Leg., III, 188. Thus the sense "seasons" can be deduced in Philo only from the context. Elsewhere Philo clearly distinguishes between τῶν καιρῶν αἱ περίοδοι and ἐτήσιοι ὧραι, II, 57 (the former is common in Philo, Op. Mund., 43; Rer. Div. Her., 282; Poster. C., 144). In the 2nd cent. A.D. Moeris says towards the end (ed. J. Becker, Harpocration et Moeris [1833], 214, 19): ὥρα ἔτους is Attic, καιρὸς ἔτους Hellenistic.

[9] Dibelius, 35.

[10] Eltester, 207-9. The inclination now is rather to see Ac. 17:26 in the light of (Hell.) Judaism.

[11] Those who ref. καιρούς to cyclical order in nature think v. 26 bases God's knowability on His rule as Creator.

[12] Dibelius, 32 f. thinks the establishment of boundaries ref. to the ancient doctrine of zones (only 2 of 5 are habitable). Eltester, 213-224 sees a ref. to the borders of land and sea, cf. OT and Judaism. In this as in the understanding of καιροί he is followed by W. Nauck, "Die Tradition u. Komposition d. Areopagrede," ZThK, 53 (1956), 15-18 with additional OT materials. Cf. also W. Eltester, "Schöpfungsoffenbarung u. natürliche Theol. im frühen Christentum," NTSt, 3 (1956/57), 100 f. F. Mussner, "Einige Par. aus d. Qumrantexten z. Areopagrede," BZ, NF, 1 (1957), 128 f. ref. to 1 QM 10:12-15: God creates the earth and its division into deserts etc., He creates the seas and rivers, the separation of the peoples, the inheritance of countries. Conzelmann, 25 deduces from the materials in Mussner with ref. to Ac. 17:26 that "the new Dead Sea texts show that in current Judaism historical and natural times and boundaries could be naïvely associated."

[13] Esp. the older philologists (but v. H. Hommel, "Neue Forschungen zur Areopagrede Acta 17," ZNW, 46 [1955], 161-3), e.g., K. Reinhardt, Art. "Poseidonios," Pauly-W., 22 (1953), 819: "to be understood in the light of Chr. eschatology," but also theologians, cf. Gärtner, 147-151.

in the first instance Jewish thoughts, takes the ordained times to be the epochs of the history of the peoples on the basis of v. 26. Only here do we read that God caused (→ VI, 463, 13 f.) [14] mankind to dwell on the whole surface (→ VI, 777, 5 ff.) of the earth — a direct reminiscence of Dt. 32:8: [15] ὡς διέσπειρεν (sc. God) υἱοὺς Αδαμ, [16] ἔστησεν ὅρια ἐθνῶν κατὰ ἀριθμὸν ἀγγέλων θεοῦ (national angels, cf. Da. 10:13, 20 f.) and cf. also the rendering of Gn. 10:32; 11:8 f. by Jos. Ant., 1, 120: [17] men dispersed into the lands into which God led them. With this dispersion of mankind over the whole earth (Gn. 11:4, 8 f.) — which in the light of the OT is seen as God's work in history — God did not leave the race to itself but worked in its history by establishing ordered times and spatial limits [18] with the goals described in v. 27. [19] Ac. speaks elsewhere of historical epochs, [20], [21] mostly within salvation history, yet still from the standpoint of God's ordination, 1:7; 3:20 f.

4. In the post-apost. fathers the verb ref. to the work of those who legitimately command: ὡς τὸ θέλημα προστάσσει, i.e., the will of God (→ III, 61, 28 ff.), Ign. Pol., 8, 1; an angel gives direction, Herm. s., VII, 1 and 5, the instruction to live single after divorce, m., 4, 1, 10. God "ordered" that all should live together in concord (→ VII, 571, 27 ff.), so already in nature, 1 Cl., 20, 11. As specific times are set for cultic acts, so priests are assigned their place in the cultus, 40, 4 and 5. The community also has the right to give instructions to the individual, 54, 2. The noun πρόσταγμα is commonest in the post-apost. fathers in 1 Cl., always with ref. to God's directions, 2, 8; 3, 4; 20, 5; 37, 1; 40, 5; 50, 5; 58, 2.

† ὑποτάσσω.

A. In the Greek World.

There are no pre-Hell. examples. 1. The act. means a. "to place under" (opp. προτάττω), Plut. Quaest. Conv., IX, 2, 2 (II, 737e), in pap. "to affix under" in a writing, [1] also inscr., e.g., Ditt. Or., I, 168, 29; "to arrange under a rubric," Polyb., 18, 15, 4; b. "to subordinate," φύλαρχος ὑποτεταγμένος τῷ ἱππάρχῳ, Aristot. Fr., 392,

---

[14] Specifically on ἐποίησεν Eltester, 211, n. 13, esp. exegesis in the early Church. For the distribution of the earth to the peoples cf. Jub. 8:11 - 9:15, also 10:28-36.

[15] There are many ref. to this.

[16] Cf. ἐξ ἑνός Ac. 17:26; Pohlenz, 101: "genuinely Pauline."

[17] For ref. Gärtner, 151.

[18] For the historical boundaries of the people as set by God cf. Sir. 39:23: God's wrath drives the peoples out of their possessions and changes watered land into salt wastes, cf. also 1 QM 10:14 f.; → n. 12.

[19] ζητεῖν... is dependent on v. 26; → n. 14.

[20] Cf. esp. the vl. προτεταγμένους at Ac. 17:26, which Pohlenz, 87, n. 37 and Schmid, 103, n. 81 prefer, though they can hardly be right textually. Cf. χρόνον προτάξας "fixing a time (term) in advance," Soph. Trach., 164.

[21] Ac. 14:17 does not force us to take καιροί in 17:26 as seasons. The word is fixed in 14:17 (though it does not really mean seasons here) and the material context is different.

ὑ π ο τ ά σ σ ω. Bibl.: C. E. B. Cranfield, "Some Observations on R. 13:1-7," NTSt., 6 (1959/60), 241-9; E. Kähler, Die Frau in den paul. Briefen unter bes. Berücksichtigung des Begriffes d. Unterordnung (1960); K. H. Rengstorf, "Die nt.lichen Mahnungen an die Frau, sich dem Manne unterzuordnen," Verbum Dei manet in aeternum, Festschr. f. O. Schmitz (1953), 131-145; also "Mann u. Frau im Urchr.," Arbeitsgemeinschaft f. Forschung d. Landes Nordrhein-Westfalen, Geisteswissenschaften, 12 (1954), 22-49; E. G. Selwyn, The First Ep. of St. Peter[2] (1946), esp. 419-439.

[1] Cf. Preisigke Wört., s.v.

V, p. 1543a, 12-14, God set the monarchy under the priesthood, Test. Jud. 21:2, God set all creatures in the three elements under man, Philo Op. Mund., 84 (Gn. 1:26), the wise man renounces things of second rank, Leg. All., III, 26, politically and militarily τὴν Θηβαΐδα... ὑποτάξας, Ditt. Or., II, 654, 7 (1st cent. B.C.), cf. Jos. Ap., 1, 119; pass. "to be subject" par. νικάομαι, Sext. Emp. Math., XI, 102, wives who submit to their husbands ὑποτάττουσαι ... ἑαυτάς are extolled, Plut. Praec. Coniug., 33 (II, 142e); οἱ ὑποτεταγμένοι "the subordinate," Plut. Apophth. Lac., 66 (II, 213c), in the Essenes, Jos. Bell., 2, 140, often "subjects," Ep. Ar., 205, 207 etc. (6 times in all); Epict. Diss., IV, 2, 10; Artemid. Onirocr., IV, 44 (p. 227, 20), more sharply "one without rights" par. or synon. δοῦλος, Vett. Val., II, 31 (p. 103, 10 f., 16 f.); in magic: "Subject all demons to me, that each... may be obedient," Preis. Zaub., I, 5, 164-166, cf. 4, 3080; to God as Ruler of the universe πάντα ὑποτέτακται, II, 13, 579 f.; Apollo, ᾧ ὑπετάγη πᾶσα φύσις, I, 2, 101, cf. τὰ γὰρ κοσμικὰ στοιχεῖα λόγῳ πάντα αὐτῷ ὑπετάσσετο, Ps.-Callisth., I, 1, 3. Epict. (Diss., I, 4, 19), who knew from experience what dependence on men means, views ὑποτάσσειν ἄλλοις ἑαυτόν negatively; the one whom nothing more (desires etc.) affects of which he is still a slave τίνι ὑποτέτακται, cf. III, 24, 71; IV, 4, 33; the craving for wealth, power, leisure, erudition ταπεινοὺς ποιεῖ καὶ ἄλλοις ὑποτεταγμένους, IV, 4, 1. But it is necessary to submit to spiritual laws (IV, 3, 12) or God (IV, 12, 11). God "has subordinated my will to me alone by giving a norm" of action, IV, 12, 12; in practice this means, e.g., that it is seemly for the servant of Zeus to submit to the god in concern for men, III, 24, 65. That being subject to men is not to be disparaged may be seen from thanks for subjection to a ruler or father in M. Ant., I, 17, 5.

2. The mid. means a. "to subject oneself" out of fear, Herodian. Hist., II, 2, 8, "to be subservient," of a servile disposition, Jos. Bell., 4, 175,[2] "to acknowledge as lord," 2, 433; b. "to submit voluntarily," πρέπον γάρ ἐστι τὴν γυναῖκα τῷ ἀνδρὶ ὑποτάσσεσθαι, says Alexander to his mother, who in spite of a wrong done her by Philip should seek reconciliation, Ps.-Callisth., I, 22, 4; gen. a commendable attitude by which one gains the sympathy of others, par. ταπεινόομαι, Ep. Ar., 257. In the first instance, then, ὑποτάσσομαι does not mean so much "to obey" — though this may result from self-subordination — or to do the will of someone but rather "to lose or surrender one's own rights or will."

B. In the Septuagint.

In the LXX, in respect of which all examples are given, the verb is not very common, but it stands for 10 Hbr. equivalents. In 13 instances there is correspondence of content, while in 5 others the relation is looser. The verb means 1. act. "to place under," subordinate," Da. 11:39 Θ, e.g., fighting groups, 2 Macc. 8:9, 22, ὑποτεταγμένοι "subordinate" officials, Εσθ. 3:13a, "subjects" 3:13b; 8:12c; 3 Macc. 1:7; cf. 3 Βασ. 10:15 (= 2 Ch. 9:14); "to subject," e.g., God makes creatures subject to man, Ps. 8:6 (→ 41, 22 ff.), the people subject to David ψ 143:2, nations, 17:48, the nations to the Israelites, 46:4; cf. 59:10 = 107:10, "to overcome," Moses overcame Pharaoh, Wis. 18:22, cf. 2 Macc. 4:12; pass. "to be subject," 3 Macc. 2:13, "to become subject," Wis. 8:14, πᾶσαι ἐξουσίαι αὐτῷ (the one like unto a man) ὑποταγήσονται, Da. 7:27; cf. 11:37; 2. mid. (with pass. aor.): "to subject oneself," "to acquiesce in" δόγματι Da. 6:14 Θ, "to acknowledge someone's dominion or power," Yahweh's and His people's, 1 Ch. 22:18, on a change of government, 29:24, "to submit," 2 Macc. 13:23, "to surrender to God," ψ 36:7; 61:2, 6 (all 3 instances "to be still" in the HT), "to humble oneself before him," 2 Macc. 9:12.

---

[2] Ref. in Rengstorf Mahnungen, 132 f.

C. In the New Testament.

In the NT the word is restricted to Luke, the Pauline corpus, Hb., Jm. 4:7 and 1 Pt. Statistically, then, it is a Hell. term. This agrees with what was said about the LXX → 40, 34 ff. The main use of the act in the NT is certainly influenced by the LXX → lines 19 ff. But lexically ὑποτάσσω does not correspond here to the HT ("to lay at the feet").

For a material understanding of the verb in the NT its considerable range of meaning should be noted, especially in the middle. Originally it is a hierarchical term which stresses the relation to superiors. But one should note that the subordination expressed may be either compulsory or voluntary. In the former case the main idea may be that of either power or conquest on the one side or lack of freedom on the other. In the NT the verb does not immediately carry with it the thought of obedience, → I, 223, 34 ff.; VI, 9, 24 ff. → 40, 29 ff. To obey or to have to obey, with no emphasis, is a sign of subjection or subordination. The latter is decisive as regards the content of the word.

1. In the active the verb occurs in R. 8:20: κτίσις [3] on account of Adam (→ III, 1031, 32 ff.) "became [4] subject," "was given up," to vanity, to the lostness of its existence before God. [5] The statement corresponds to that in R. 5:12. [6]

All the other active statements are christological. They stand in express relation to Ps. 8:6 [7] in 1 C. 15; Hb. 2; Eph. 1. The christological interpretation of this v. is based on Ps. 110:1, [8] as may be seen from 1 C. 15:25, 27. But it could well be pre-Pauline. [9] In the argument of 1 C. 15:26 f. Ps. 8:6 is important because of the πάντα, which justifies the addition of πάντας to Ps. 110:1 in v. 25: He subjects all things, including death as the last enemy → II, 813, 38 ff. [10] The reference is to its forcible

---

[3] In Judaism בר(א)נש is a gen. term for man, acc. to W. Lütgert, Die Liebe im NT (1905), 2 as distinct from the Israelite.

[4] ὑπετάγη, which might mean "subjected himself," cf. R. 10:3; 1 Pt. 2:13 etc., is controlled by οὐχ ἑκοῦσα. To be sure, all have sinned and death is the result, R. 15:12c and d; but this nexus goes back to Adam, 5:12a, b. In some sense, of course, God does the subjecting, but this is not necessarily expressed in the form ὑπετάγη (pass. as substitute for God's name) even though ἐφ' ἐλπίδι naturally ref. to the hope given by God. In any case, however, the διὰ τὸν ὑποτάξαντα aimed at Adam presupposes that the whole nexus is appointed by God.

[5] ματαιότης (→ IV, 523, 11 ff.) is never just corruption in the NT; it is a spiritual state, not a physical. It is not identical with → φθορά in v. 21; death is the correlate of the meaninglessness of existence without God.

[6] O. Cullmann, "Unsterblichkeit d. Seele u. Auferstehung d. Toten," ThZ, 12 (1956), 126-156 conjectures (142 f.) a relation to Gn. 3:17; but the ref. is only to the field which no longer produces fruit as a matter of course, not to death etc. For the connection between the death of the race and that of Adam cf. the material in Str. -B., III, 227 f.

[7] Ps. 8:6 obviously bears no special significance in Judaism; it is certainly not important messianically.

[8] On Ps. 110 in older Rabb. lit. cf. Str.-B., IV, 452-465.

[9] But 1 C. 15 shows that the messianic interpretation of Ps. 8:6 does not have to presuppose the understanding of Jesus as Son of Man in the sense of the primal Man. At first only Ps. 8:6 is used, supplementing Ps. 110:1. Hb. 2 is the first and only passage to adduce Ps. 8:4-6. The estimation of Ps. 8:2 in Mt. 21:16 possibly presupposes a non-messianic Rabb. interpretation, Str.-B., I, 854 f. Even if all Ps. 8 were taken messianically, the Messiah would not have to be the primal Man. Ps. 8:5a is clearly viewed as a humiliation statement in Hb. 2:9a.

[10] Cf. on 1 C. 15:27 (though with no discernible influence) Da. 7:27 → 40, 43 f. and linguistically Jos. Bell., 2, 361: you alone regard it as shameful δουλεύειν οἷς ὑποτέτακται τὰ πάντα (sc. the Romans) and 5, 396: Ῥωμαίοις ὑπέταξεν ὁ θεὸς τοὺς οὐκ ἀξίους ἐλευθερίας (cf. Schl. Jk., 253, n. 2).

disarming by God. How this is done we are not told. [11] In v. 24c - v. 27a, where the idea of God's sole causality is the obvious presupposition, the idea of Christ's supreme rule (ὑποτάσσω is here complementary to βασιλεύω) is emphasised. At the end Christ's power is not restricted in any way. Materially Paul has to add that the idea of God's subjection to Christ is quite impossible. God is the One who does the subjecting, v. 27 → 41, 23 f. On v. 28b → lines 35 ff. 1 C. 15, including Ps. 8:6, is obviously presupposed materially in Phil. 3:21. Here, too, it is especially by the overcoming of death that Christs's unlimited final power is demonstrated. But in this case it is He who does the subjecting. In Hb. 2:7 f., in controversy with angel-christology, God does the subjecting as in 1 C. 15. In both passages there is stress on πάντα, and in both full subjection is plainly still ahead. Ps. 8:5 f. [12] is emphatic-ally viewed as a prophecy of the Son (cf. 1 C. 15:28), but it is split temporally: v. 6a relates to earthly life (Hb. 2:9), while v. 6b and 7b relate to life beyond this earth (Hb. 2:8b). What is meant is that Christ's rule begins with His exaltation (v. 5) but is not yet consummated nor, of course, universally manifested, v. 8c. With no specific reference to the subjection of hostile powers the idea of the position of power which God has granted Christ is also linked with Ps. 8:6 in Eph. 1:22a; [13] here Ps. 8:6 is related to the enthronement which has already been accomplished, not to the eschatological event which is still to take place. In 1 Pt. 3:22 both Ps. 110:1 and Ps. 8:6b influence even formally the brief confessional-type statement, while in 1 C. 15 and Hb. 2 we have theological developments of what is confessed. [14] 1 Pt. 3:22 is directly related to the events connected with the exaltation, and in this respect it is close to Eph. 1:22. The spread [15] of the statement in relation to the verb of Ps. 8:6 suggests that very early on it became a constituent part of the primitive Christian confession.

2. The middle, which is used with the passive aorist (→ n. 4), occurs once in the sense of compulsion and means "to have to submit," Lk. 10:17, 20 [16] → 41, 9 ff. Elsewhere it denotes voluntary subordination in a rich development of non-biblical beginnings.

a. Paul uses the verb in formulation of important theological statements: By nature [17] the strivings of the σάρξ resist submission to God's demand, R. 8:7. On the other hand pious Judaism, by clinging to observance of the Torah as a way of salvation, resists the saving work of God in Christ, 10:3 → II, 206, 23 ff. In both cases submission is refused because renunciation of one's own (sinful or pious) will is demanded. The most significant statement in the middle occurs in the play

---

[11] Acc. to v. 27b the meaning in context is at least that Christ does not win the victory in His own power. Possibly the idea is that God subjects to Christ's dominion those who have been conquered by Christ in God's power. But one should respect the restraint of the sayings. In Rev. too the victories of Christ are affirmed but not described. God obviously does the subjecting in Rev. For Paul in Phil. 3:21 → lines 7 ff.

[12] Not linked here with Ps. 110, though this plays a big role elsewhere in Hb.; → lines 9 ff.

[13] Par. καθίσας ... ὑπεράνω, v. 20 f.

[14] If one may speak of a formula, this is expanded in Eph. 1:22.

[15] This is the greater the more the four letters are separated as regards composition.

[16] On the other hand Mk. 1:27 and 4:41 par. have ὑπακούω, which is not lexically identical with ὑποτάσσομαι, cf. → I, 223, 34 ff. with → 41, 12 ff.; Cranfield, 242 f. Schl. Lk. on 10:17-20 has a string of Palestinian par. but none for ὑποτάσσομαι.

[17] οὐ δύναται, i.e., it is not in a position to achieve the voluntary subjection in which alone there can be ἀρέσκειν.

on the active in 1 C. 15:28. [18] The supreme power of the Son is not an end in itself; it is merely granted [19] to Him in order that He may render it back to God after completing His task, v. 24. For with His own visible subjection to God He also subjects to God all the things that have been subjected to Him by God. This statement is demanded by Paul's view of God (v. 28c) and especially by his concept of God's absolute power. [20] It is hardly by chance that Paul here uses for the one and only time the absolute "the Son." The Son in the absolute is the One who to the very limit gives God the precedence which is His due.

b. In keeping, though in marked gradation, is the extensive use of the middle in NT exhortation, especially in respect of relation between men. [21] In Jm. 4:7 absolute submission to God is impressively contrasted with resistance to the devil. [22] In Hb. 12:9 natural submission to the rod of the earthly father is a metaphor for the same salutary attitude in relation to God, → V, 621, 26 ff.; 1014, 5 ff.

c. Lk. 2:51 stresses that the growing Jesus subordinated Himself to His parents, cf. v. 40 and 8:21. Within His special mission the earthly Jesus adapts Himself to the earthly orders. As in the right relation of sons or daughters to parents, for which ὑποτάσσομαι is not used elsewhere (→ I, 223, 34 ff.), so also in the commonly required subjection of wife to husband according to the biblical understanding (Col. 3:18; Eph. 5:22-24; 1 Pt. 3:1; Tt. 2:5) the issue is keeping a divinely willed order, [23] cf. 1 Cor. 11:3; 14:34 (Gn. 3:16); also 1 Pt. 3:6, with a reference in v. 5 to the ὑποτάσσεσθαι of the women of the OT. According to Paul this position of the wife should also be maintained in church assemblies in the prevention of self-willed speaking (as distinct from 1 C. 11:5), 14:34 → I, 787, 34 ff. ὑποτάσσεσθαι has here no direct personal opposite; it simply denotes the status of women as such.

d. The same acquiescence in a divinely willed order is at issue in R. 13:1-7, this time in submission to the authorities → 29, 4 ff. ὑποτάσσομαι is here a counterpart to ὑπερέχω, [24] which is the formal basis of the demand for subjection, R. 13:1; 1 Pt. 2:13. [25] In ὑποτάσσεσθαι the supremacy of the ὑπερέχων is acknowledged to be legitimate. Materially self-subjection is based (R. 13:5; cf. 1 Pt. 2:14) on the task of the authority which it discharges in fact even though it be a pagan govern-

---

[18] The statement bears no relation to the point of the passage but simply arises out of the emphasis of the verb in the preceding sentences. O. Cullmann, *Die Christologie d. NT*[3] (1963), 300, *ad loc.*: "Here is the key to all NT Christology."

[19] And thus loaned, cf. Mt. 28:18 → V, 895, 18 ff.

[20] It may be asked whether the ἐν here does not also express relation, → II, 543, 3 ff.

[21] For at least preparatory hints of this outside the Bible → 40, 28 f. The signification of the Gk. term makes necessary the use of the concept "order" from this point on to the end of the art.

[22] On ἀνθίσταμαι - ὑποτάσσομαι cf. R. 13:1 f. → 36, 20 ff. Only externally, then, is Jm. 4:7 related to ψ 36:7 etc. → 40, 46 f.

[23] The primary reason is that woman is created after man and for his sake, cf. esp. 1 C. 11:7-9 with ref. to Gn. 2:18, 22 f. The context makes it unlikely that 1 C. 11:3 has Gn. 3:16 in mind. There may be an allusion to this in 1 C. 14:34, and there is an undoubted ref. to Gn. 3:6, 13 in 1 Tm. 2:14.

[24] οἱ ὑπερέχοντες is a fixed term for rulers, Diog. L., VI, 78, cf. Pr.-Bauer, *s.v.* for other examples, also 1 Tm. 2:2.

[25] In 1 Pt. 2:13 the βασιλεύς is the real bearer of rule, cf. v. 14; there is no such distinction in R. 13. For further details on 1 Pt. 2:13 → 45, 4 ff. On ὑπερέχων cf. the paradoxical statement Phil. 2:3.

ment, namely, that of recognising good [26] (→ II, 587, 36 ff.) and punishing evil, R. 13:3 f. Since in its judicial activity the government is God's instrument (→ 36, n. 5), an instrument of His wrath (v. 4 f. → V, 440, 21 ff.), it is materially essential to subject oneself to it on the basis of the binding of the conscience to God's will, v. 5 → VII, 915, 35 ff.

Tt. 3:1 [27] seems perhaps to be taking up R. 13:1. In detail 1 Pt. 2:13 f. reminds us of R. 13:1-7 in at any rate v. 14b. [28] R. 13 itself would also appear to be an interpretation [29] of Jesus' answer to the question as to His attitude to Roman rule, Mk. 12:17 and par. [30] The question of the attitude to the Roman state — not the state as such — was inherited by Christianity from Judaism. Since Christianity did not take the promise to Israel to be earthly and political, the problem changed into that of the attitude to government generally. The answer is not that the present state maintains certain presuppositions for the external existence of Christianity and on this ground we are not against it, → 30, n. 22. The answer is rather that the authorities are ordained as such by God, and hence ὑποτάσσεσθαι is demanded not merely from Christians but from all men, R. 13:1. There is in this respect a uniform parenetical tradition in the NT epistles.

e. The submission of slaves to their masters is demanded (1 Pt. 2:18; Tt. 2:9), but not because slavery is ordained by God (materially cf. 1 Tm. 6:1). Slavery is accepted as a social reality which primitive Christianity was not in a position to abolish externally. Among Christians it could be overcome by brotherhood in ἀγάπη, but it could not be set aside legally (1 Tm. 6:2), so that there had to be acknowledgment of dependence, → II, 272, 17 ff.; 899, 6 ff. In ὑποτάσσεσθαι to state, husband, and master the primary point is recognition of the existing relation of superordination. [31]

f. The direction in 1 Pt. 5:5a is based on a given order, that of the precedence of elders over the young, even though the point is proper conduct within the community (→ VI, 665, 25 ff.), cf. the demand for subjection to brethren who have deserved especially well of the community in 1 C. 16:16. The admonition in 1 Pt. 5:5a

---

[26] The imparting of ἔπαινος is a function of the government in antiquity, cf. A. Strobel, "Zum Verständnis v. R. 13," ZNW, 47 (1956), 67-93, esp. 80-83. Further examples Ditt. Syll.³ and Inscr. Magn., Index, s.v. ἐπαινέω. Naturally we have inscr. extolling esp. worthy citizens, e.g., a physician: ἐπαίνων... ἠξιώθη, Ditt. Syll.³, II, 620, 37 (c. 190 B.C). Note μὴ κομίζων κατηγορίαν ἀνθυπάτων ἀλλ' ἔπαινον, 783, 29 f. (c. 25 B.C.). Materially cf. Philo: The Law fulfils its task in two ways by honouring good and punishing evil, Leg. Gaj., 7.

[27] On the combination of ἀρχαί and ἐξουσίαι for official powers cf. Lk. 12:11 and on this esp. Strobel, op. cit., 72-79 (rich materials 75-79).

[28] G. Kittel, Christus u. Imperator (1939), 52 suggests dependence on R. 13; Selwyn, 426-9 indicates the broad material agreement between statements about "civic obedience" in R., 1 Pt. and Tt., but would trace them back, with other admonitions under the rubric subiecti (→ n. 35), to a common source ("code of subordination"). 1 Pt. 2:14 is certainly closely related to v. 15, as may be seen from the catch-word ἀγαθοποιέω, which plays an important role in 1 Pt.

[29] Kittel, op. cit., 7 f., 19.

[30] Not just the εἰκών (→ II, 387, 32 ff.) but also the ἐπιγραφή "Tiberius Caesar Divi Augusti Filius Augustus" cf. E. Stauffer, Christus u. d. Cäsaren² [1948], 133) must have caused great offence to the strict Jew. Jesus simply says that the emperor's claim to payment of taxes, which is an acknowledgment of his sovereignty, is valid.

[31] As regards marriage this may be seen in the distinction between ὑποτάσσεσθαι or φοβεῖσθαι, which is demanded of the wife, and ἀγαπᾶν which is demanded of the husband, Eph. 5:24 f., 33.

is supplemented by the demand for mutual ὑποτάσσεσθαι (→ II, 339, 13 ff.) or general ταπεινοφροσύνη (→ 23, 9 ff.). To the former there corresponds the imperative in Eph. 5:21: "Submit to one another" in the fear of Christ, and then the broader command in 1 Pt. 2:13: "Submit to every ordinance of man," which stands expressly (→ III, 1034, 33 ff.) [32] at the head of admonitions ordering the relations between men generally. [33] In view of 1 Pt. 2:12, which refers to the conduct of Christians to those without, non-Christians are especially in view in v. 13a: every human creature, → n. 3; I, 366, 22 ff. This is a possibility of ordering human life in society generally such as one finds outside Christianity only in Ep. Ar., 257, → 40, 29 ff. 1 Pt. 2:13 thus goes beyond Eph. 5:21, where the admonition has primarily the life of the community in view. Mutual submission distinguishes the conduct of the pneumatics towards one another in divine worship, 1 C. 14:32. [34]

g. The remaining use of ὑποτάσσομαι in NT exhortation suggests that the general rule demands readiness to renounce one's own will for the sake of others, i.e., ἀγάπη, and to give precedence to others. This word which belonged originally to the sphere of worldly order is now filled with new content as a term of order. Clearly this means that, e.g., the relation of the owner to the slave takes on a new aspect even though the legal position remains unchanged. Even the ὑποτάσσεσθαι of those who are properly subordinate does not stay the same when done under the control of dependence on the Lord, though externally it is rendered in exactly the same way as by others (cf. Tt. 2:9); for the demand now has a specific Christian basis, Col. 3:18; 1 Pt. 2:13; Eph. 5:21 f., cf. Eph. 5:24: as the community is subject to Christ. In exhortation the middle embraces a whole series of meanings from subjection to authority on the one side to considerate submission to others on the other. As regards the detailed meaning this can finally be decided only from the material context. The demand for mutual submission among Christians shows especially that ὑποτάσσομαι bears a material relation to Christian ταπεινοφροσύνη, → 21, 33 ff.; 40, 29 f. The findings as a whole suggest that the term ὑποτάσσομαι played a general catechetical-type role in primitive Christian exhortation. [35] Yet the distinctions in meaning in the various material contexts should not be overlooked, nor should the differences from the closely related words ταπεινός κτλ. (→ 16, 1 ff.) and ὑπακούω (→ I, 223, 34 ff.).

D. In the Early Church.

In the post-apost. fathers the verb plays a greater role in Ign. and 1 Cl. → 47, 1 ff. In Ign. Pol., 2, 1; Eph., 5, 3 not to resist (ἀντιτάσσεσθαι) the bishop is "to subject oneself" to God. Elsewhere the ref. is to subjection to the bishop and presbyters, Eph., 2, 2; Mg., 2; Tr., 2, 1 f.; 13, 2; Pol., 6, 1. "Subordinate yourselves to the bishop and to one

---

[32] Selwyn takes ἀνθρωπίνη κτίσις to be a comprehensive term for state, home, and family as institutions established by man.

[33] The relation of πάσῃ ... κτίσει and βασιλεῖ κτλ. in 1 Pt. 2:13 f. corresponds to that between πάντας and τὸν βασιλέα in v. 17.

[34] Cf. H. Greeven, "Propheten, Lehrer, Vorsteher bei Pls.," ZNW, 44 (1952/53), 1-43, esp. 13.

[35] Cf. P. Carrington, The Primitive Christian Catechism (1940), 42 f. etc. and Selwyn, 419-439, who groups the parenetical statements linked to the three verbs under the rubric subiecti, → n. 28.

another as Jesus Christ to the Father according to the flesh and the apostles to Christ and the Father and the Spirit," Mg., 13, 2, "to the bishop as to the grace of God and the presbytery as to the law of Jesus Christ," Mg., 2, "to the bishop as to Jesus Christ," Tr., 2, 1 etc. Subjection to the presbyters is demanded in 1 Cl., 57, 1 (→ VII, 571, 27 f.), cf. μάθετε ὑποτάσσεσθαι in 57, 2, to the leaders of the community, 1, 3. God gave dominion to those who govern the state, so Christians acknowledge the honour given to them, and submit to them, and are not in opposition to God's will, 61, 1, cf. R. 13:2 f., 7; on 1 Cl., 37, 2 → 35, 32 f. The demand to submit to God's will in 34, 5 obviously means act. subjection. The heavens which move by God's direction peaceably submit to Him, 20, 1. Finally there is a gen. demand that each submit to his neighbour in 38, 1, cf. the examples in v. 2, cf. 1 Pt. 2:13; Eph. 5:21, also the admonition ὑποτασσόμενοι μᾶλλον ἢ ὑποτάσσοντες in 1 Cl., 2, 1. Dg., 7, 2 says that all things are subject to God, heaven, earth, and sea, and all that therein is. God for His part, out of His love for man, has subjected all things (on earth) to him, 10, 2, His whole creation, Herm. m., 12, 4, 2. Slaves are required — there is an accompanying admonition to masters not to give orders in bitterness (ἐπιτάσσω) — to submit to their masters ὡς τύπῳ θεοῦ in reverence and fear, Did., 4, 10 f., in part literally the same, Barn., 19, 7.

In the Apologists apart from Athenag. Suppl., 18, 2 (all things are subject to God and the Son) only Just. uses the verb: God has put the earth under man, Epit., 5, 2; act. "to attach" a writing, Apol., 68, 4; mid. in a quotation from Da. 7:27 in Dial., 31, 7. "To subject oneself" to demons or not, Dial., 85, 3, to Christians, 76, 6; elsewhere the subjection of all rule, Dial., 39, 7, all enemies, Apol., 40, 7, and demons, Dial., 30, 3; 85, 2; 121, 3, to Christ.

† ὑποταγή.

1. As nomen actionis ὑποταγή means "submission," Dion. Hal. Ant. Rom., 3, 66, 3; then "subordination," "dependent position," par. δουλεία, Artemid. Onirocr., I, 73 (p. 66, 14), also "slavery," Vett. Val., II, 34 (e.g., p. 106, 17: τῆς ὑποταγῆς ἀπολυθέντες).

2. In the LXX the word occurs only in Wis. 18:15A, a slip for ἐπιταγή "command."

3. In the NT the only use of ὑποταγή is in the Pauline corpus. Along the lines of 1 C. 14:34 (→ 43, 19 f.) it means "submission" in the sense of renunciation of initiative (1 Tm. 2:11 par. ἡσυχία);[1] ἐν ὑποταγῇ ἔχειν "to have in subjection" (1 Tm. 3:4) refers to all sons and daughters living in the house → V, 130, 17 ff. Paul regards as an act of submission the confession of the Christian message which Gentile Christians make with the collection for the Jerusalem church (2 C. 9:13; → V, 215, 23 ff.). The reference is to "acquiescence" (→ 40, 29 f.; 45, 11 f.), to the overcoming of a certain inner resistance to the demand of the Jerusalem leaders (Gl. 2:10) or of Paul, and to integration into the entire Christian fellowship, → III, 808, 24 ff.; IV, 282, 18 ff. In Gl. 2:5 τῇ ὑποταγῇ would denote tactical yielding[2] without οἷς οὐδέ,[3] otherwise[4] it is the (required) act of submission, cf. καταδουλόω in v. 4. In general → VI, 83, 16 ff.

ὑ π ο τ α γ ή. [1] v. 11 f. perhaps in the sense of silence, or at any rate quietness, cf. 2 Th. 3:12 → 48, 1 ff.
[2] Not under compulsion (v. 3), but to take the wind out of the sails of the false brethren, v. 4. The terms used in v. 4 f. support this, esp. καταδουλόω and ἀλήθεια.
[3] Zn. Gl., 90-93; 288-298 specifically on the reading.
[4] With οἷς οὐδέ Schlier, Ltzm. Gl., ad loc.

4. In the post-apost. fathers the noun refers to unanimous submission ἐν μιᾷ ὑποταγῇ to those who lead the community, Ign. Eph., 2, 2; its necessity is deduced from the ὑποταγὴ μία of members within the body, 1 Cl., 37, 5. κανὼν τῆς ὑποταγῆς applies to women, 1, 3. The noun does not occur in the Apologists.

† ἀνυπότακτος.

1. This is not found before 200 B.C. It does not occur in the LXX. It means "not subject," qui sui iuris est, [1] i.e., the king alone, Artemid. Onirocr., II, 30 (p. 125, 13), opp. the slave, II, 53 (p. 152, 13); "free," the will of (the just) man is ἀδούλευτος and ἀνυπότακτος while the other is "subject" to him ὑποτεταγμένα, Epict. Diss., II, 10, 1; "not capable of being subjected," fidelity and chastity, IV, 1, 161; "not subject to specific (here geographical) ideas," Polyb., 3, 36, 4; 5, 21, 4; "not subject to the rules," of songs, Zenobius, II, 15 (CPG, I); "not subjecting oneself," "rebellious," cf. Haman's accusation of the ἔθνος of the Jews to the Persian king: τοῖς νόμοις ἀλλόκοτον καὶ τοῖς βασιλεῦσιν ἀνυπότακτον, Jos. Ant., 11, 217.

2. In the NT the word occurs in the sense of "not subject" in Hb. 2:8 → 42, 9 ff. In the Past. it means "refractory," "insubordinate," [2] "rebellious" against one's father, Tt. 1:6; "not subjecting" oneself to sound teaching (cf. ἀντιλέγοντες v. 9) or its proponents (1:10). [3] At the head of a list of vices it occurs with ἄνομος, 1 Tm. 1:9, "not submissive" either in practice or principle. Here too, as in current usage, it has the sense of "rebellious" or "refractory" against God's will, → III, 654, 12 f.; IV, 1087, ἄνομος, n. 1.

† ἄτακτος (ἀτάκτως), † ἀτακτέω.

1. ἄτακτος means "disordered," matter before creation in Philo Op. Mund., 22; cf. Corp. Herm., 5, 4; in Jos. often in a military sense, e.g., disorderly retreat, Bell., 3, 113; the Idumaeans are a θορυβῶδες καὶ ἄτακτον ἔθνος ("undisciplined") with ref. to violent changes, 4, 231; "unbridled" of ἡδοναί, Plat. Leg., II, 660b; ἄτακτος Ἀφροδίτη, VIII, 840e; what is ἄτακτον is ὄχλος, Philo Praem. Poen., 20; the φιλήδονος is among other things ἄπολις, στασιώδης, ἄτακτος, ἀσεβής, ἀνίερος, Sacr. AC, 32; the one part of man's soul is irrational, subject to passions and errors, and ἄτακτος, Plut. De Virtute Morali, 3 (II, 442a); μηδὲν ἄτακτον ποιήσητε (opp. let your works be ἐν τάξει), Test. N. 2:9. In the LXX the adj. occurs only in 3 Macc. 1:19 in the sense "unseemly," in Σ "waste," of the land, Dt. 32:10; Ez. 12:20. The adv. means "without order or plan," synon. παρὰ φύσιν, Aristot. Cael., III, 2, p. 301a, 4; the crowd would rather live ἀτάκτως than σωφρόνως, Pol., VI, 4, p. 1319b, 32; ἀνόμως καὶ ἀτάκτως "without law or order," Jos. Ap., 2, 151; ἀτάκτως φέρομαι means "to roam about in disorderly fashion," Philo Sacr. AC, 45. The adv. ref. to the wild course of a driver in 4 Βασ. 9:20 Σ.

ἀτακτέω means "to set oneself outside the order," "to evade one's obligations," Demosth. Or., 3, 11; "not to fulfil one's divinely appointed duties," Xenoph. Oec., 5, 15; 7, 31; the ruler can τάττειν and punish τὸν ἀτακτοῦντα, Cyrop., VIII, 1, 22; often military: "to act without discipline," VII, 2, 6; Jos. Ant., 17, 296; "to act irresponsibly," i.e., against the provisions of a will, P. Eleph., 2, 13 (3rd cent. B.C.); in context "to evade work which is ordered," P. Oxy., II, 275, 25 (66 A.D.); with ἀργέω ("to do nothing") and ἀσθενέω, IV, 725, 40 (183 A.D.). The verb does not occur in the LXX.

ἀνυπότακτος. [1] Cf. Thes. Steph., s.v.
[2] So everywhere Pr.-Bauer, s.v., cf. Schl., ad loc.
[3] Dib. Past. has "undisciplined" as in v. 6.

2. In the NT the adjective occurs in 1 Th. 5:14, the adverb in 2 Th. 3:6, 11 and the verb in 2 Th. 3:7. Non-Christian examples show that the word group is well-known and important and that it relates to several spheres but especially to that of human conduct, both ethical on the one side and political in the broader sense on the other. In both it characterises a man as one who sets himself outside the necessary and given order. In view of the attested breadth of meaning one must be on guard against taking it too narrowly in the Thessalonian Epistles. In 2 Th. 3 one might easily conclude from v. 7 that the primary reference of the group is to laziness. But outside Christianity the verb, [1] when applied to work, does not in the first instance lay emphasis on sloth but rather on an irresponsible attitude to the obligation to work. Certainly the τινές in v. 11 are not guilty of mere inaction but of a busy unrest [2] which obviously finds expression outside the community. [3] The admonition to ἡσυχάζειν in 1 Th. 4:11 f. goes hand in hand with that to daily work and with the reference to the ἔξω. How serious are the dangers which arise for the community out of the conduct of the τοιοῦτοι may be seen from the directions in 2 Th. 3:6 (→ VII, 589, 35 ff.), 14. ἀτάκτως περιπατεῖν in 3:6, 11 shows that the τινές with their aloofness from working for their keep are outside the civil order, which applies to Christians too. They are also outside the requirements of the ethical catechism they accepted as neophytes, v. 6, cf. v. 10 and already 1 Th. 4:11. In the Thessalonian Epistles, then, the group is to be taken primarily in a secular sense: an undisciplined life in the secular sphere contradicts the direction under which the Christian stands, 2 Th. 3:6a, 12a. In view of the connections between 2 and 1 Th. the group is to be taken in 1 Th. 5:14 as in 2 Th. 3, cf. also 1 Th. 2:9.

3. In the post-apost. fathers the adj. occurs only in a passage which takes up the train of thought in R. 1:24-28 and 3:26: Up to the event of salvation in Christ God permitted men to be driven about in disorderly movement, ἀτάκτοις φοραῖς φέρεσθαι, Dg., 9, 1. The adv. occurs only in a saying about cultic acts, which according to the will of God are not to be performed in a disorderly way, 1 Cl., 40, 2. The verb does not occur. In the Apologists we find only the adj., Athenag. Suppl., 25, 3.

Delling

τεκνίον, τέκνον → V, 636, 24 ff.

ἄτακτος κτλ. [1] "To fight shy of work" is a sense expressly attested for the verb.
[2] The groups περιεργ- and ἡσυχ- also occur in the Pauline corpus only in Th. (apart from the Past.). Those concerned about uprightness seek ἡσυχάζοντα ... καὶ εἰρηνικὸν βίον, Philo Abr., 27 (cf. 1 Tm. 2:2).
[3] Dob. Th. on 1 Th. 4:11 ref. to Dio C., 60, 27, 4: τὴν ... ἡσυχίαν ἄγων καὶ τὰ ἑαυτοῦ πράττων, "who keeps quiet and concerns himself only with personal matters."

τέλος, τελέω, ἐπιτελέω, συντελέω,
συντέλεια, παντελής,
τέλειος, τελειότης, τελειόω,
τελείωσις, τελειωτής

† τέλος.

A. The Understanding of the Term in the Greek World. [1]

1. First [2] τέλος as nomen actionis means a. "achievement," e.g., Ζεὺς δ᾽ ἐπέκρανεν
τέλος, Aesch. Suppl., 624, "execution of a resolve," Ditt. Syll.[3], II, 793, 7 (21 A.D.),
"fulfilment" of a law, Aristot. Pol., VI, 8, p. 1322b, 13, a ruling, 1322a, 6, "carrying out"
of an OT prophecy, Jos. Bell., 4, 387, τέλος ἐπιθεῖναι "to add execution" to the words,
Isoc. Or., 6, 77, τέλος ἔχειν "were carried out" (opp. neglect), ibid., 7, 25, of a motion,
Demosth. Or., 58, 46 etc.; cf. also the request for good "success" in all acts, τέλος ἐσθλὸν
ἐπ᾽ ἔργοις, Orph. Hymn. (Quandt), 57, 12 (41) etc.; so often the one petition at the
end of a prayer after many invocations; through Dikaiosyne the wisdom of virtue comes
to happy fruition, 63, 11 (45); b. then τέλος means "power": deity has the power to
determine τέλος ἔχει δαίμων βροτοῖς, τέλος ὅπᾳ θέλει, Eur. Or., 1545; τέλος
ἔχοντες, "with full powers," Thuc., IV, 118, 10; οἱ ἐν τέλει, "the influential," Jos.
Bell., 1, 243; Ant., 14, 302, or "those in office," 4, 171. On the basis of discharging an
official task the word comes to mean the "office" itself, Aesch. Ag., 1202, e.g., τὸ
ὀροφυλακικὸν τέλος the office of frontier-guard, Ditt. Syll.[3], II, 633 93 f. (c. 180 B.C.),
of the general, Xenoph. Cyrop., I, 5, 7; "official power" (authority), An., II, 6, 4 (plur.);
also "decision," Aesch. Eum., 243, hence "what is valid," par. κύριον, Aristot. Pol., VI,
2, p. 1317b, 6. Cf. also → 51, 1 ff., 6 ff.

2. On the other side τέλος means "completion" as a state, "perfection," e.g., τέλος
ἔχειν, Plat. Leg., VI, 772c; Jos. Ant., 10, 58, God has the upper limit, the final step, of
θεία μοῖρα, Ps.-Plat. Epin., 985a, "the final step" of νοητόν is the good abs., Plat.
Resp., VII, 532b, "the supreme stage" of happiness is God ἄκρα καὶ τέλος, Philo Cher.,
86, also "crowning," e.g., τέλος προσέθηκαν ἀσέβειαν (Ex. 32:2-6), Spec. Leg., III,
125, ἐμπεσεῖν εἰς τέλος κακῶν, "caught in extreme evil," Test. D. 6:5. Common senses

τ έ λ ο ς. Bibl.: N. Messel, "Die Einheitlichkeit d. jüd. Eschatologie," Beih. z. ZAW,
30 (1915), esp. 60-69; P. J. du Plessis, Τέλειος. The Idea of Perfection in the NT, Diss.
Kampen (1959); Str.-B., IV, 799-1015; Volz Esch., esp. 135-147.
[1] Cf. du Plessis, 36-56; D. Holwerda, "ΤΕΛΟΣ," Mnemosyne, IV, 16 (1963), 337-363
thinks the basic sense is "beam of a balance," "scales," Hes. Theog., 638, "pan of the scales,"
Soph. Oed. Col., 422 (337-340).
[2] It is hard to pin down the original sense. Already in the Iliad it ranges from "fulfilment"
(mostly τέλος θανάτοιο of the death which overtakes a man, e.g., Hom. Il., 3, 309) to
"military post," "detachment," 10, 56. 470; 11, 730 = 18, 298; the idea of ritual correctness is
also important esp. in the deriv. → τέλειος and τελήεις. Hence most etym. dict. thinks
several terms have come together in τέλος, esp. * qᵘelos "turning-point" (πέλομαι, though
this is not certain) and * telos, "promotion," "achievement" (τελα-, ταλα-), cf. Boisacq,
Hofmann, s.v., Schwyzer, I, 512 (only πέλομαι). The post-Homeric and almost exclusively
poetic τέλλω "to fulfil" is itself not wholly clear [Risch].

are a. the "mark" in a race, Philo Som., I, 171, the "goal" of the way of Abraham to Moriah is a pious act, Abr., 172; what someone has in view, e.g., the aim of the husbandman is his reward, Agric., 5. In Gk. philosophy τέλος can be used for the "goal" of man's being (for the Stoa → φύσις); [3] in this sense it is used esp. after Aristot.; Plato still prefers σκοπός, → VII, 413, 26 ff. It also occurs in the theological consideration of nature which is concerned to demonstrate that everything which is brought forth by nature and which takes place in it has a purpose. [4] In this connection cf. the sense of bodily "maturity," e.g., horses τέλος ἔχειν, "to be full-grown," Plat. Leg., VIII, 834c. b. An ambivalent sense is "result," Isoc. Or., 6, 50, "issue," Polyb., 1, 61, 2; Jos. Vit., 154; τῆς πράξεως (τοῦ πράγματος), Test. A. 1:9; 2:1, 4; τὸ γὰρ τέλος εἶναι τοῦ θεοῦ, Jos. Bell., 5, 459; "Now I hope, the issue, of course, is with God," Menand. Fr., 114 (Körte); ἦν θεὸς ἀγαθὸν τέλος διδῷ, Xenoph. Cyrop., III, 2, 29, the "final result," e.g., of polytheistic ideas: ὧν ἀθεότης τὸ τέλος, Philo Exsecr., 162, "the end product of considering spiritual things is ἀλήθεια, that of considering visible things is δόξα," Praem. Poen., 28, "the final state," e.g., τοιαῦτα τῶν εὐσεβῶν τὰ τέλη, the "ultimate destiny" of the righteous (things turn out well for them), Philo Jos., 122, cf. τὰ τέλη τῶν ἀνθρώπων δεικνύουσι τὴν δικαιοσύνην αὐτῶν, Test. A. 6:4, God has given man two ways and δύο τέλεα, 1:3, ἴδετε ... τοῦ ἀγαθοῦ ἀνδρὸς τὸ τέλος, B. 4:1. c. "Conclusion": adv. prep. expressions with τέλος denote totality, whether in time or not, so εἰς τέλος "fully," "entirely" (opp. partially), Ditt. Or., I, 90, 12, "finally" (?), P. Tebt., I, 38, 11 (113 B.C.), διὰ τέλους "for ever," P. Petr., II, 13, 19, 8 (258-3 B.C.), "continually," "unceasingly," Menand. Fr., 276, 16; 287, 4 (Körte); Ditt. Syll.³, II, 747, 51; μέχρι τέλους, "fully," "totally," P. Tebt., II, 379, 17 (265 A.D.), ἀπὸ ἀρχῆς μέχρι τέλους, "from beginning to end," 420, 18 f. (3rd cent. A.D.). In the adv. acc. (no art.) [5] the word means "finally," Corpus Fabularum Aesopicarum, [6] 290, 3; 292, 8; Jos. Vit., 196; Test. Jos., 8, 2. d. It then means "end" gen. in the sense of "cessation," "end of life," τέλος ἔχειν, "to be dead," Jos. Ant., 17, 185; Bell., 7, 155; οἱ τέλος ἔχοντες, "the dead," Plat. Leg., IV, 717e; τέλος ἔχει, of a ship which has sunk; "it has gone," P. Petr., II, 40a, 23 (3rd cent. B.C.); abs. "it is over," Menand. Sam., 203 (Körte), "conclusion" of the Pentateuch, Philo Vit. Mos., II, 290. On ἀρχὴ καὶ τέλος in relation to eternity → I, 479, 27 ff. [7] In Jos. Ant., 8, 280 the formula is seen in the light of the confession of God as Creator: God is not created by men but is His own work and the beginning and end of all, i.e., He fixes the beginning and end τῶν ἁπάντων, all things being dependent on Him; cf. God is sufficient ἀρχὴ καὶ μέσα καὶ τέλος for Himself and all things τῶν πάντων, Ap., 2, 190. Already outside the NT, then, it should be noted that the senses can merge into one another, so that sometimes several translations are possible. [8]

---

[3] A. Bonhöffer, *Die Ethik d. Stoikers Epict.* (1894), 7-15, 163-188; G. Delling, "Telos-Aussagen in d. gr. Philosophie," ZNW, 55 (1964), 26-42, esp. 29-36; A. Döring, "Doxographisches zur Lehre vom τέλος," *Zschr. f. Philosophie u. philosophische Kritik*, 101 (1893), 165-203; E. Grumach, "Physis u. Agathon in d. alten Stoa," *Problemata*, 5 (1932), esp. 35-43; W. Jaeger, "Das Ziel d. Lebens in d. gr. Ethik von der Sophistik bis Aristot.," NJbchKlAlt, 16 (1913), 687-705; M. Pohlenz, *Die Stoa*, I (1948), 111-118; II (1949), 64-68; H. Preisker, *Das Ethos d. Urchr.* (1949), 13-16; K. Reinhardt, *Poseidonios* (1921), 248-262; W. Wiersma, Περὶ τέλους. *Studie over de leer van het volmaakte leven in de ethiek van de oude Stoa*, Diss. Groningen (1937); also "Τέλος u. καθῆκον in d. alten Stoa," *Mnemosyne*, III, 5 (1937), 219-228.

[4] R. Eucken, *Die Methode d. aristot. Forschung* (1872), 67-121; Pohlenz, *op. cit.* I, 98-100, 430 f.; II, 55-58; Reinhardt, *op. cit.*, 327-335; W. Theiler, *Zur Gesch. d. teleologischen Naturbetrachtung bis auf Aristot.* (1925); P. Wendland, *Philos Schrift über d. Vorsehung* (1892), esp. 68-82; Delling, *op. cit.*, 36-41.

[5] Already in Hdt. and Thuc., examples in Liddell-Scott, *s.v.* [Risch].

[6] Ed. A. Hausrath, I, 2 (1956).

[7] Further examples in O. Weinreich, "Aion in Eleusis," ARW, 19 (1916/19), 174-190, esp. 181 f.

[8] Cf. also Liddell-Scott, *s.v.*, where there is a lot of material in different groups.

3. τέλος is also "obligation" → 49, 18 ff., e.g. ἔξω τοῦ τέλους τούτου, outside this obligation, the obligation to do certain things for the state, Demosth. Or., 20, 19, hence "tax," [9] e.g., Jos. Bell., 2, 4, of the farmer, τελῶν μεγάλων, Artemid Onirocr., V, 31; in a play on words τελειωθείς-τέλος-τελεσφόρος, Philo Migr. Abr., 139; cf. Rer. Div. Her., 120 f., both on Nu. 31:28 → 52, 35 f.

4. Then τέλος (→ 58, 1 ff.) means "offering" for the gods, [10] e.g., τέλη ἔγκαρπα, Soph. Trach., 238, πάγχαλκα τέλη, Ant., 143; θεοῖσι μικρὰ θύοντες τέλη, Eur. Fr., 327, 6 (TGF, 458); [11] ὄψιν καὶ τέλη μυστηρίων means "the celebration" of the mysteries at Eleusis, Eur. Hipp., 25; transf. μεγάλα τέλη of initiations which purify the soul, Plat. Resp., VIII, 560e. Obviously the occasional description of the γάμος as τέλος has nothing to do with the mystery initiations. [12] In τέλος... γάμοιο, Hom. Od., 20, 74 τέλος is the "fulfilment," of sacrifices πρὸ παίδων καὶ γαμηλίου τέλους, Aesch. Eum., 835; similarly the ref. in νυμφικὰ τέλη, Soph. Ant., 1240 f., is to "acts" in the marriage festival. [13] Thus the description of marriage as τέλος is to be understood in terms of the sense → 50, 1 ff. To dream of death is an intimation of marriage to the unmarried, for death and marriage are both τέλος for men, Artemid. Onirocr., II, 49; death as τέλος, III, 58; Aristot. Metaph., IV, 16, p. 1021b, 28 f. says expressly that τέλος is used in this sense because death is a termination.

5. Finally τέλος is a "detachment," "group" (→ n. 2), e.g., Solon divided the whole πλῆθος of the Athenians into 4 τέλη, Aristot. Fr., 350, Vol. V, p. 1537a, 16 and 23; then squadrons of ships, Thuc., I, 48, 3; κατὰ τέλη, VI, 42, 1; Polyb., 11, 11, 6.

B. τέλος in the Septuagint. [14]

Semitic equivalents [15] are סוֹף only Qoh. 3:11; 7:2; 12:13, cf. ἕως τέλους Da. 7:26 (6:27 Θ), קֵץ Ju. 11:39; 4 Βασ.19:23; 2 Ch. 18:2; 2 Εσδρ. 23:6; cf. Da. 9:26 Θ; 11:13 Θ; קָצֶה 2 Βασ. 24:8; 4 Βασ. 8:3; 18:10; cf. קְצָת Da. 1:15, 18 Θ; 4:34 Θ; apart from 4 Βασ. 19:23 [16] קַץ etc. are used for τέλος only in precise or gen. indications of time, e.g., μετὰ τὸ τέλος τῶν ἑπτὰ ἐτῶν, 4 Βασ. 8:3, also with other prep. In adv. expressions διὰ τέλους "constantly" == תָּמִיד [17] Is. 62:6, ἕως τέλους "fully" for עַד מְאֹד ψ 37:7, εἰς τέλος "totally" for the combination of abs. inf. and fin. verb, Am. 9:8; on Gn. 46:4 → n. 21. The noun is primarily temporal when εἰς τέλος transl. לָעַד, 1 Ch. 28:9; Ps. 9:18b Cod A (BS: εἰς τὸν αἰῶνα) and (commonly) לָנֶצַח "for ever," "eternally," "constantly," Job 14:20; 20:7; 23:7; ψ 9:7, 19a, 32; 43:24; 48:10; 51:7; 67:17; 73:1, 10, 19; 76:9; 78:5;

---

[9] For details cf. W. Schwahn, Art. "Τέλη," Pauly-W., 5a (1934), 226-310.
[10] τελετή first means "execution," then religious "actions," e.g., sacrifices etc. on into the Chr. era, cf. C. Zijderveld, Τελετή. Bijdrage tot de kennis d. religieuze terminologie in het Grieksch, Diss. Utrecht (1934), 97 f. → IV, 804, n. 10.
[11] Cf. Liddell-Scott, s.v., I, 6. But in Aesch. Pers., 204 τέλη probably ref. to the work of the gods concerned.
[12] Cf. H. Bolkestein, "Τέλος ὁ γάμος," Mededeelingen d. Koninklijke Akademie van Wetenschappen Afd. Letterkunde, Deel 76B (1933), 21-47. Also W. Erdmann, Die Ehe im alten Griechenland (1934), 136.
[13] γάμος and τέλος are not equated in any of these passages.
[14] Cf. du Plessis, 56-67.
[15] Oddly enough τέλος is not used for אַחֲרִית, though this can mean the "end" that overtakes someone (Köhler-Baumg., s.v.), Dt. 32:20; Ps. 73:17; Lam. 1:9 etc. (for the LXX transl. → II, 698, 1 ff.), also the "issue" of a matter (Köhler-Baumg., s.v.), Is. 41:22; 46:10; 47:7; Qoh. 7:8; it is mostly rendered ἔσχατα, Prv. 14:12 τελευταῖα.
[16] Here HT means spatial limit; LXX makes little of it; the par. Is. 37:24 has μέρος → IV, 594, 26 ff. For details cf. Hatch-Redp., s.v. μέρος.
[17] διὰ παντός is often used for this, Johannessohn Präp., 236 f. This par., too, shows that in some temporal statements τέλος indicates totality.

88:47; 102:9; Hab. 1:4 or just נִצַּח ψ 12:2; 15:11, cf. ψ 73:3, where LXX alters the request. But the situation is different when ἕως εἰς τέλος is used for עַד־תֻּמָּם "wholly," "entirely," Dt. 31:24, 30; Jos. 8:24 A; 10:20, also תמם Nu. 17:28; Jos. 3:16. Non-adv. εἰς τέλος = תְּמִים in Jos. 10:13. Thus τέλος is used for derivates of תמם only in the Hexateuch. Cf. in Ez. 20:40; 36:10 εἰς τέλος for כָּלָה „totally," in ψ 73:11 for כָּלֶה "altogether," in 2 Ch. 12:12; 13:1; Sir. 10:13 for similar terms, also ἐπὶ τέλος ἀγαγεῖν (→ n. 18) for עֲשׂוֹת הַכֹּל 1 Ch. 29:19.

1. Act. τέλος is "execution," 3 Macc. 1:26; cf. 3:14; 5:19; 1 Ch. 29:19. [18]

2. τέλος means a. "goal" perhaps Job 23:3; b. "result," "reward," [19] 2 Macc. 5:7; "final result," "conclusion" — human knowledge can go no further — Qoh. 12:13; "issue," 4 Macc. 12:3; in the plur. the "end" of each one, Wis. 3:19; c. "conclusion," "close," Qoh. 7:2, so not only in statements of time for קֵץ etc. (→ 51, 23 ff.) and elsewhere (→ 51, 30 ff.) but also in totality sayings (→ 52, 2 ff.). In this sense τέλος is contrasted with ἀρχή (cf. also Is. 19:15): God's work is totally hidden from man ἀπ' ἀρχῆς καὶ μέχρι τέλους, Qoh. 3:11; God grants understanding of cosmic events εἰδέναι... ἀρχὴν καὶ τέλος καὶ μεσότητα χρόνων, Wis. 7:18. With no obvious equivalent the word occurs in Da. 9:27 for the end of a period of time, also with no HT Wis. 11:14: ἐπὶ τέλει τῶν ἐκβάσεων, cf. 3 Macc. 4:15; 5:49, in the sense "to lead to an end" 3 Macc. 3:14; 5:19; P. Tebt., I, 14, 8 (114 B.C.), and quantitatively πρὸς τέλος ἀφικνέομαι "to come to the extreme limit," 2 Macc. 6:15 קֵץ in the eschatological sense is not transl. by τέλος in the LXX. Where τέλος is used for קֵץ in Da. 9:26b Θ; 11:13 Θ we do not have the eschatological tt., cf. συντέλεια → 65, 34 ff. Surprisingly often (some 60 times) τέλος occurs in adv. combinations, → 51, 26 ff. In one series τέλος is put with prep. with nothing corresponding in the extant HT, esp. εἰς τέλος, [20] "finally," "for ever," "completely," Gn. 46:4; [21] ψ 17:36; [22] Job 20:28; Ez. 15:4, 5; 22:30; Sir. 12:11. In works with no HT τέλος again occurs in adv. combinations: εἰς τέλος "perfectly," "wholly and utterly," Jdt. 7:30; 14:13, "to the limit," Ps. Sol. 1:1; cf. 2:5, "fully" or "finally," 2 Macc. 8:29, διὰ τέλους, "continually," "perpetually," Εσθ. 3:13g; μέχρι τέλους "constantly" of God's anger or wrath, Wis. 16:5 or "in full measure," 19:1. [23] The adv. expressions sometimes have a gt. breadth of meaning so that it is hard to say whether the ref. is to time or extent and should be transl. "finally," "constantly" etc. or "totally," "entirely" etc.; τέλος becomes a term of completeness. [24] Adv. τὸ τέλος means "finally," "ultimately" in 2 Macc. 13:16; 3 Macc. 4:14; without art. 2 Macc. 5:5. d. "cessation," Bar. 3:17, Wis. 14:14.

3. τέλος means "tax," "tribute," "toll," for מֶכֶס Nu. 31:28, 37-41 (κυρίῳ destined for Yahweh), for מִכְסָה Lv. 27:23, for מַס Est. 10:1, also 1 Macc. 10:31; 11:35.

4. In the headings of more than 50 Ps. we read εἰς τὸ τέλος for לַמְנַצֵּחַ, [25] perhaps "for the cultus." [26] τέλος is then an "act" in divine worship.

---

[18] Cf. du Plessis, 57: ἐπὶ τέλος ἀγαγεῖν corresponds to τελέω.
[19] So A. Kamphausen in Kautzsch Apkr. u. Pseudepigr., ad loc.
[20] On εἰς τέλος in the LXX gen. cf. Dob. Th., 115, n. 3.
[21] Johannessohn Präp., 303 finds here a combination of finite verb and inf. abs., cf. Am. 9:8.
[22] BHK suggests לָצֶנַח in the HT of the LXX; this is possible but in view of the other passages (esp. Ez.) by no means certain.
[23] du Plessis, 57. Cf. the opp. πεῖρα τῆς ὀργῆς, 18:25.
[24] Cf. du Plessis, esp. 57-60.
[25] Cf. O. Eissfeldt, Einl. in d. AT³ (1964), 612; Köhler-Baumg., s.v. Cf. S. Mowinckel, Psalmenst., 4 (1923), 22; Tg. לְשַׁבָּחָא "to praise," v. Levy Chald. Wört., s.v.
[26] So also the Hbr. equivalent Ges.-Buhl, s.v. נצח; possible acc. to du Plessis, 61 f. K. Bornhäuser, "Das Wirken d. Christus," BFTh, II, 2 (1924), 212-4 takes the term eschatologically: the final victory of the Messiah, 214.

C. The End in Jewish Apocalyptic.

The lack of unanimity in Jewish expectation of the future finds reflection in the varied use of the term "end." In Rabb. lit. two OT expressions form the basis: קֵץ and אַחֲרִית הַיָּמִים. The latter denotes primarily "the time which follows," Gn. 49:1; Nu. 24:14; Dt. 31:29 (with a ref. here to the exile), "the latter days," Jer. 48:47; 49:39. But already in Nu. 24:14 it is natural to think of the "last time," and there are many instances of this, Jer. 23:20; 30:24; Ez. 38:16 (cf. at the "end" of the years, 38:8); Dt. 4:20 (time of the return of Israel to Yahweh and of final salvation as in Hos. 3:5; Is. 2:2 [Mi. 4:1]), and Da. 10:14. Many later writers took קֵץ eschatologically in many passages outside Da., cf. esp. Ez. 21:30, 34; 35:5; Hab. 2:3, and plainly in Sir. 36:7 (הֶחִישׁ קֵץ) [27] and Da. Here קֵץ is almost a tt. in the combination קֵץ הַיָּמִין Da. 12:13, עֵת קֵץ 8:17; 11:35, 40; 12:4, 9 and abs. 8:19; 11:27; 12:6, 13. In context the ref. is always to the last tribulation or to a last epoch distinct from history in gen.; in Da. 12:13 the ref. is to the resurrection. Acc. to 11:27 the final events, which at any rate in Da. include the last tribulation and the coming of the age of salvation, arrive at a time which God has ordained and which may be calculated, 12:7. On the other hand Sir. 36:7 (→ n. 27) has the prayer: Hasten the end and establish the time. Here the bringing in of salvation is understood as the fulfilment of OT promises, 36:14 f.

In the Qumran writings there is no sure evidence of the use of just קֵץ as a tt. [28] On the other hand אַחֲרִית הַיָּמִים occurs for the "end-time," e.g., in the setting of a specific order for this, 1 QSa 1:1. 1 QpHab says of contemporary or imminent events that they belong to the "end of the days," 2:5 f.; 9:6. Is. 8:11 is referred to the end of the days in 4 Q Florilegium 1:15, [29] Ps. 2:1 to "the elect of Israel at the end of the days" in 4 Q Florilegium 1:19. 1:2 speaks of a house built at the "end of the days": the expression also occurs in 1:12 and perhaps 1 Q 14:6, 2 (DJD, I, 77). It probably lies behind ἐν ταῖς ἐσχάταις ἡμέραις in Test. Jud. 18:1; D. 5:4; cf. S. 8:2; Jos. 19:10.

In post-Chr. apocalyptic an abs. use of "end" may be seen clearly in 4 Esr. along with the use of combinations. The "end of the times" is an unlimited period in 3:14, cf. S. Bar. 21:8; 30:3; 59:4; Ezra is instructed concerning its events, 4 Esr. 14:15; cf. "end of the days" in 4 Esr. 12:9 [30] and "end" in 6:15. A single generation experiences the "end," 5:41; God fixes the time, 6:1. It includes gt. distress, 13:20, the coming of the Messiah, 12:32 (here

---

[27] Acc. to R. Smend, *Die Weisheit Jesus Sirach, hbr. u. deutsch* (1906), 30, c. 33:10.

[28] If the end-time is to be denoted by קֵץ, אחרון is added in 1 QpHab 7:7, 12; 1 QS 4:1b, cf. 4 QpNa 4:3 (ed. E. Lohse, *Die Texte aus Qumran* [1964], 261-7); apart from אֵין קֵץ in QpNa 2:6 קֵץ is "end" only spatially, 1 QH 6:31. In 1 QS קֵץ means gen. "time," cf. P. Wernberg-Møller, *The Manual of Discipline* (1957), 48, n. 34; 71, n. 68 (time, period), cf. K. Elliger, *Stud. z. Hab.-Komm. vom Toten Meer* (1953), 183, n. 1, who also transl. קֵץ by "time" in 1 QpHab. In Damasc. קֵץ ref. mostly to the sect's present, cf. H. Braun, *Spätjüd.-häret. u. frühchr. Radikalismus,* I (1957), 111, n. 1; additions denote a ref. to the future. The same applies to the other texts, e.g., 4 QpNa 3:3. "The term קֵץ in the meaning of period belongs to the phraseology which is characteristic of the language of the Dead Sea Scrolls as well as of the Damascus Fragments," N. Wieder, "The Term קֵץ in the Dead Sea Scrolls and in Hebrew Liturgical Poetry," *Journal of Jewish Studies,* 5 (1954), 22-31, esp. 22, with instances of the same usage from Jewish piyyutim, 23-31. Cf. F. Nötscher, "Zur Terminologie d. Qumran-Texte," *Bonner Bibl. Beiträge,* 10 (1956), 167-9. But cf. A. Strobel, "Untersuchungen zum eschatologischen Verzögerungsproblem," *Nov. Test. Suppl.,* 2 (1961), 8 and 10. For the transition from "end" to "time" cf. Jer. 34:14; Dt. 15:1 (after the passage of), cf. M. Wallenstein, "Some Lexical Material in the Judean Scrolls," VT, 4 (1954), 211-4, esp. 213. For more on קֵץ in the Scrolls → χρόνος.

[29] Ed. and transl. J. M. Allegro, "Fr. of a Qumran Scroll of Eschatological Midrašim," JBL, 77 (1958), 351-4; ed. A. M. Habermann, *Megilloth Midbar Yehuda* (1959), 173 f.; ed. and transl. Lohse, *op. cit.,* 255-9.

[30] The expression also occurs in S. Bar. 10:3; 25:1.

again the "end of the days"), the judgment 12:21; 7:84, 87; cf. 7:113, the transforming of the foundations of the earth, 6:16, and salvation, 13:18 ("end-time"). The word "end" is obviously understood in antithesis: the end of the first (this) world and the beginning of the coming world, 6:7; 7:113.

In Rabb. lit. אַחֲרִית הַיָּמִים is elucidated by קֵץ, so Gn. 49:1 in bPes., 56a etc., [31] קֵץ being taken eschatologically. קֵץ can thus denote the final time, קִצִּין plur. the calculated times, bSanh., 97b; [32] the meaning is restricted. Calculations of the end relate esp. to the coming of the Messiah. [33]

D. τέλος in the New Testament.

Not all the statements can be arranged with lexical certainty. Sometimes where one meaning is more or less sure another may be involved too. In the non-prepositional use of τέλος at any rate the context usually offers the basic sense.

1. To understand τέλος and especially τελέω (→ 57, 17 ff.) it is important to keep in view the originally dynamic character of the noun. The sense attested → 49, 7 ff. underlies Lk. 22:37. What concerns me [34] must actually be "carried out, ful-filled"; [35] on τέλος ἔχειν → 49, 11 f.

2. a. As the "goal" (→ 50, 1 ff.) of the instruction imparted to the community (→ V, 764, 12 ff.) active love is mentioned in 1 Tm. 1:5, obviously in opposition to certain speculations, v. 4, 6 f. In this the community finds its fulfilment, which is thus radically outside itself. According to 1 Pt. 1:9 the *telos* of faith in Christ (v. 8) is eschatological salvation, v. 5. In 1 C. 10:11 the context (→ III, 623, 34 ff.; 625, 14 ff.) suggests that τὰ τέλη τῶν αἰώνων refers more precisely to "the aims [36] of the times." Of these times an especially prominent one was was the wilderness age of Israel (vv. 1-10). They find fulfilment in the present events determined by Christ.

There are in the NT no statements about the *telos* of men which stand in formal analogy to Greek sayings (→ 50, 3 ff.). [37] The NT puts the matter differently and sayings which are teleological in content do not set man in the centre, → II, 428, 12 ff.; → II, 327, 16 ff. [38]

---

[31] Cf. Str.-B., IV, 1014.

[32] *Ibid.*, 993.

[33] *Ibid.*, 1003, 1006 etc.

[34] Lk. elsewhere has τὰ περὶ Ἰησοῦ etc., cf. 24:19, 27; 22:37 ℜ, also Ac. 18:25; 23:11; 28:31 with verbs of knowing and speaking.

[35] γεγραμμένον agrees with this in v. 37a, cf. also τελεσθῆναι in v. 37a. On τέλος ἔχειν *perfici*, cf. Ditt. Syll.[3], I, 157, 4 and n. 3 etc.

[36] Cf. formally ἐκβάσεις καιρῶν καὶ χρόνων, Wis. 8:8; on the meaning of the expression → n. 39. But cf. 1 QpHab 7:13: "All the times of God will come to their (appointed) measure." The rendering "to which the mysteries of eternity have come" is an impossible transl.; it is championed by M. M. Bogle, "1 C. 10:11. A Suggestion," Exp. T., 67 (1955/56), 246 f.

[37] R. 6:21 f. can hardly have been understood thus by the author (→ 55, 5 ff.) or the readers or hearers, esp. as the sayings are always negative apart from R. 6:22, and could only be taken as definitions of *telos* in an ironically paradoxical sense.

[38] Cf. E. Stauffer, "»Ἵνα u. d. Problem des teleologischen Denkens bei Pls.," ThStKr, 102 (1930), 232-257; G. Delling, "Zur paul. Teleologie," ThLZ, 75 (1950), 705-710, esp. 708-710.

b. In Mt. 26:58 (no par.) τέλος can mean issue" [39] in an ambivalent sense, and similarly in Jm. 5:11, where it refers to the final end which God set for Job's sufferings. [40] The "end result" of the curse on the land which produces thorns and thistles is according to Hb. 6:8 its burning, cf. Am. 7:4; Dt. 32:22, or, construed differently, this is the "final fate" of this land, → III, 643, 28 ff. [41] τέλος is also used in R. 6:21 f. for the eschatological "result" of man's acts, [42] for man's "final destiny," especially in final perdition, Phil. 3:19 (→ I, 397, 1 ff.); 2 C. 11:15, where the end is characterised accordingly as the ungodly work of those mentioned. In this connection one should also adduce 1 Pt. 4:17, where final destiny is hinted at in the question. The way had been prepared both linguistically (→ 50, 15 ff.) and materially for the sense of "final destiny" as the issue determined by God's judgment. As regards the OT this is true already in the Ps., e.g., ψ 72:17, [43] and then in Judaism especially one finds the spread of the idea of a double fate in the hereafter.

c. The sense "end" (→ 50, 33 ff.) as conclusion in antithesis to commencement is not very likely in Lk. 22:37 (→ 54, 14 f.). The self-designation of God in Rev. 21:6 (cf. 1:8) or Christ in Rev. 22:13: ἐγὼ ... ἡ ἀρχὴ καὶ τὸ τέλος primarily denotes His eternity but then His absolute majesty; [44] formally it interprets the preceding A and Ω or πρῶτος and ἔσχατος; materially it cannot be understood apart from these (→ I, 1, 27 ff.; 484, 12 ff.). [45] The sense of "conclusion" connects τέλος with the eschatological events which have yet to take place, at any rate in the Synoptics and 1 C. 15. Here the context suggests the parousia especially (Mk. 13:7 and par. and also Mt. 24:14, cf. Mk. 13:21-27). Calculating this is impossible, but is is also unnecessary, Mk. 13:32 f., 24-27. 1 C. 15:24 (→ 56, 26 f.) has in view the transferring of the βασιλεία to God by Christ after the vanquishing of the "powers" [46] with which the conclusion of Christ's work is in fact reached, v. 28. 1 Pt. 4:7 might well have in view the conclusion of all earthly occurrence.

In prepositional phrases — which never have the article — the reference is not linguistically to the apocalyptic tt., though materially the still awaited end is or might be in view. One should think rather in terms of the non-biblical adverbial use also attested in the LXX → 50, 19 ff.; 52, 22 ff. τέλος with εἰς (the most common), ἕως (only in Paul), ἄχρι, μέχρι (only in Hb.) means first ("up") "to

---

[39] In the NT ἔκβασις occurs only at Hb. 13:7; 1 C. 10:13, in LXX Wis. 2:17; 8:8: the way periods and times pass, their "end results"; 11:14.

[40] Strobel, op. cit., 259 thinks τέλος has at least two senses here as "end" and (eschatological) "goal."

[41] The one interpretation holds good if ἧς goes with γῆ, the other if it goes with κατάρα.

[42] This is meant by καρπός in v. 21a, which is taken up in the plur. in v. 21b c (ἐφ' οἷς or ἐκείνων). Cf. also the formal par. τὸ δὲ τέλος ... εὐσέβεια, Philo Vit. Cont., 88. The sense of "final destiny" is intrinsically possible in R. 6:22.

[43] Other examples → 50, 9 ff. Obviously in the OT the ref. is to man's earthly destiny, but the idea of the final or definitive is quite plain.

[44] Cf. also on Jos. Ant., 8, 280 → 50, 31 ff.

[45] Polar expressions like beginning and end to denote totality or extension are common in many languages in archaic, popular, or poetic diction. Only thinking influenced in some way by philosophy feels within such expressions a contradiction of the idea of God's eternity [Dihle].

[46] Cf. Stauffer Theol., 198, who, of course, takes τέλος to be a final goal, n. 720. It is unlikely that τὸ τέλος is used as an adv. (→ 56, 8 ff.) in 1 C. 15:24. Acc. to W. D. Davies, Paul and Rabbinic Judaism (1955), 299 τὸ τέλος means "the final consummation"; cf. H. Molitor, "Die Auferstehung d. Christen u. Nichtchristen nach d. Ap. Pls.," NTAbh, 16, 1 (1933), 44-53.

the end" or "to the full." The context must decide whether the expressions are to be taken temporally or quantitatively. Thus εἰς τέλος means "to the end," "for ever" ([→ 52, 4 f.] Mk. 13:13 and par.; Mt. 10:22), [47] "fully," "in full, supreme measure" [48] (Jn. 13:1; 1 Th. 2:16 [in the present]), [49] "finally" (Lk. 18:5). [50] ἕως τέλους means "fully" (→ 51, 28 f.), "wholly and utterly" (2 C. 1:13 [with the opp. ἀπὸ μέρους, v. 14]; also 1 C. 1:8). ἄχρι τέλους means "continually," "to the last" (Rev. 2:26; Hb. 6:11; μέχρι τέλους bears the same sense (Hb. 3:14 and vl. in v. 6). Adv. τὸ τέλος occurs in the sense "finally" (→ 50, 24 f.; 52, 32 f.) with an element of crescendo in 1 Pt. 3:8.

d. τέλος means "cessation" (→ 50, 26 ff. perhaps also 1 Pt. 4:7), of ζωή (Hb. 7:3 → I, 482, 27 ff.), of δόξα on the face of Moses (2 C. 3:13 → VI, 776, 6 ff. and n. 42), of the dominion of the Messiah (Lk. 1:33), cf. also τέλος ἔχει "it is up" with him, with Satan or his power (Mk. 3:26 → 50, 28 f.). For the believer the Law is set aside as a way of salvation by the Christ event — Χριστός means especially the crucifixion and resurrection, R. 7:4; 10:4 → IV, 1075, 37 ff. [51]

The narrower context esp. supports this interpretation of R. 10:4. Here νόμος corresponds to man's own righteousness, which the pious Jew seeks, v. 3; God's righteousness stands in contrast with the νόμος; this is the righteousness which God creates, His justifying work. In R. 10:4 νόμος is esp. the Law by keeping which one is just before God. This possibility of justification before God is abolished by Christ's cross. νόμος and δικαιοσύνη in R. 10:4 denote the Jewish way of salvation which is set aside in Christ. The two are mutually exclusive for Paul. Cf. on this antithesis Gl. 3:21; 2:21.

3. "Tribute," "tax" (→ 51, 1 ff.) is the meaning of τέλος in Mt. 17:25; R. 13:7 → 29, 8 ff.

4. The sense of "act of initiation" (→ 51, 8 ff.) does not occur in the NT, nor is "detachment" (→ 51, 19 ff.) attested here. In 1 C. 15:23 Paul says: ἕκαστος ἐν τῷ ἰδίῳ τέλει (→ 51, 19 ff.), but τέλος in v. 24 means "end" rather than "remaining group," [52] → 55, 23 ff.

E. The Usage of the Post-Apostolic Fathers.

In gen. the usage is not very specific. Faith and love are the beginning and "end" of ζωή, Ign. Eph., 14, 1; hope of life is the beginning and end of our life, the righteousness of judgment is the beginning and end, Barn., 1, 6, cf. ἐν ἀρχῇ καὶ ἐν τέλει, "from

---

[47] The interpretation "to the end" is attempted by Strobel, op. cit., 279 f.

[48] Cf. Bl.-Debr. § 207, 3.

[49] Formally par.: ἔφθασε δὲ αὐτοὺς ἡ ὀργὴ τοῦ θεοῦ εἰς τέλος, Test. L. 6:11; the passage is not among the Qumran findings thus far. The reading τοῦ θεοῦ in DEFG it vg etc. was added at 1 Th. 2:16 under the influence of the brief saying. The above interpretation agrees with R. 9-11 as a whole → V, 434, 18 ff.

[50] Jeremias Gl.[6] (1962), 153 advocates "totally" (relating to ὑπωπιάζω, which he interprets as "to achieve"); I do not take ὑπωπιάζω in a transf. sense → II, 426, n. 25.

[51] H. Hellbardt, "Christus das Telos d. Gesetzes," Ev. Theol., 3 (1936), 331-346 takes τέλος in R. 10:4 as at once "end," "purpose," and "goal," 345 f. "Final goal" is suggested by R. Bring, "Die Erfüllung d. Gesetzes durch Christus," Kerygma u. Dogma, 5 (1959), 1-22, esp. 10 f., cf. already F. Flückiger, "Christus des Gesetzes τέλος," ThZ, 11 (1955), 153-7. For bibl. on Paul's understanding of the Law cf. Schlier Gl.[12], 176 f., n. 2, cf. the exc. 176-188.

[52] This sense has not yet been attested, not even by the passages in Pr.-Bauer, s.v. Cf. W. G. Kümmel in Ltzm. K.[4], 193 (on p. 80, 24).

beginning to end," "all the time," Ign. Mg., 13, 1. Man's acts have a specific final result, each going to his own place, to death or life (R. 6:21 f.), Ign. Mg., 5, 1. For Ign. martyrdom means that he is made worthy εἰς τέλος εἶναι, i.e., to be "at the goal," R. 1:1. τέλος is eschatological in Herm. v., 3, 8, 9, also in the abs. ἔχει τέλος "the end is there," which is par. to συντέλεια, perhaps also Ign. Mg., 6, 1: Christ was before the aeons with the Father and appeared ἐν τέλει, "in the last time" or "finally"; εἰς τέλος may mean "to the last" in Ign. Eph., 14, 2; R., 10, 3 but "always" is also possible. τέλος ἔχειν means "to come to an end" in Herm. v., 2, 2, 5, "to be at an end" in 3, 3, 2. The remaining instances have prepositional expressions, μέχρι τέλους "continually," "without end," of the punishment of eternal fire, Dg., 10, 7. εἰς τέλος is the commonest in the sense of being "finally" saved, 2 Cl., 19, 3, of the διαθήκη being "fully" [53] set aside, Barn., 4, 7, "wholly," "totally" godless, 10, 5, hating evil "completely," 19, 11. The sense in Herm. is always "fully," "wholly and entirely," e.g., to fall away from God "completely" in v. 3, 7, 2; s., 6, 2, 3; 8, 8, 2, to fall "totally" victim to death, m., 12, 2, 3; s., 8, 6, 4.

† τελέω.

A. The Use Outside the Bible.

The verb [1] means:

1. a. gen. "to carry out" one's own will or that of others; acc. to Plato the order of the universe may be traced back to the resolves of one will ἀγαθῶν πέρι τελουμένων, which relate to ἀγαθά and are "put into effect" acc. to a plan and purpose (→ 50, 3 ff.), Leg., XII, 967a; Isis says: δ ἂν ἐμοὶ δόξῃ, τοῦτο καὶ τελεῖται, Isidis aretalogia Cymaea, [2] 46; one may thus read: τοῦτο μὲν ὡς ἐβουλόμην τετέλεσται, P. Oxy., III, 413, 174 f.; not to give up a plan but "to execute" it, Gr. Hen. 6:4; gen. "to do," e.g., things for the polis, Inscr. Magn., 163, 15-17, or the transl. of the OT, Ep. Ar., 308, help for members, 242. τετελεσμένος means "complete," "perfect," Xenophanes Fr., 34, 3 (Diels, I, 137, 4). b. "To carry out" what is said (opp. "to promise"), τελέσαι ἔργῳ Aesop., [3] 34, 3, 8 f.; "to fulfil" a promise, Jos. Ant., 11, 315; "to put a curse into effect," God, 8, 362. c. "To carry out the instructions of others," e.g., orders by soldiers, Jos. Bell., 2, 495, the statutes of the law-giver, Plat. Leg., XI, 926a, or God's will: ἅγιος ὁ θεός, οὗ ἡ βουλὴ τελεῖται ἀπὸ τῶν ἰδίων δυνάμεων, Corp. Herm., 1, 31, cf. 13, 19; σοῦ ... βουλομένου πάντα τελεῖται, 13, 21; prayers, Aesch. Ag., 973; → 68, 32 ff.

2. "To bring to an end," e.g., of years, Aristot. Hist. An., VII, 1, p. 581a, 14; ὁ αἰὼν ὁ μέγας τελεσθήσεται, Gr. En. 16:1.

3. "To fulfil obligations," τὰ καθήκοντα τελεῖσθαι, "what one is under obligation to pay," P. Tebt., I, 5, 31 (118 B.C.), cf. 6, 32 (140/139 B.C.); esp. taxes: τέλη τελέω, Ditt. Syll.[3], III, 912, 25 (3rd cent. B.C.); 941, 8 (3rd cent. B.C.), tribute of subjection, Jos Ant, 10, 2, or the subject, 10, 155; slaves daily "render" to their owner φόρον ... ἀναγκαῖον, Philo Agric., 58; then also — both very common in the pap. — gen. "to pay," e.g., χρήματα ("fee"), Plat. Ap., 20a etc.; τὰ τελεύμενα are "expenses," Democr. Fr., 279 (Diels, II, 203, 13).

---

[53] So K. Thieme, Review of R. Mayer's Zum Gespräch mit Israel in ThLZ,, 88 (1963), 838. Cf. Barn., 4, 8: Israel annulled God's covenant of salvation by turning to idols.

τελέω. [1] The older form is τελείω, found, e.g., in Hom.; it arose out of * τελεσjω, cf. Schwyzer, I, 724 [Risch]. τελέω is a very ancient, important, and widespread term which in the prose and common speech of the post-class. period was increasingly supplanted by practically equivalent compounds like ἐκ-, συν- (→ 62, 23 ff.) and διατελέω, so that the simple form could have a lofty sound [Dihle].
[2] Ed. W. Peek, Der Isishymnus v. Andros u. verwandte Texte (1930), 124.
[3] Corpus Fabularum Aesopicarum, I, 1, ed. A. Hausrath (1962), 49.

4. "To carry out" religious acts, e.g., feasts, sacrifices, games, Inscr. Magn., 56, 11-15, sacrifices etc. for the dead, ὅσα προσήκει τελεῖσθαι, Plat. Leg., XII, 958d, θυσίαν, Plut. Thes., 16, 3 (I, 7a), daily prayers and offerings, of the Jewish high-priest, Philo Spec. Leg., III, 131; "to sacrifice," e.g., a hecatomb, Aesop. (→ n. 3), 28, 1, 2; hence abs. "to serve" as a priest, Ditt. Syll.³, III, 1012, 29 and 31 (2nd/1st cent. B.C.); but also "to instal" as a priest (not "to consecrate"): "In order that the priestess may be regularly installed, τελεσθῇ," lines 21-23, cf. 20: "The *polis* appoints." Another sense is "to practise" magic, of a witch, Aesop., I, 1 (→ n. 3), 56, 1, 2, ποιοῦσα in 3, 2, "to carry out a practice," Preis. Zaub., I, 3, 440, "to consecrate an object to magic," I, 4, 787 etc., "to endow a man (II, 13, 610) or object with power," so in a request to the deity, I, 4, 1690, "to fulfil" the requirements of the magician τέλεσον, δαῖμον, I, 4, 2094 etc. With special ref. to the mysteries τελέω means originally "to carry out" the secret acts, cf. ἐπιτελέω (→ 61, 18 ff.), abs., e.g., Demosth. Or. 18, 259, then "to consecrate" men, pass. οἱ τελούμενοι τὰ μυστήρια, "those who receive consecration" (Andania), Ditt. Syll.³, II, 736, 15 (92 B.C.), ὅσαι ἐπὶ Δήμητρα τετέληνται (Eleusis), III, 1024, 22 (c. 200 B.C.); of the consecration of the Corybants, Plat. Euthyd., 277d. After death, certain mysteries promise, the κεκαθαρμένος τε καὶ τετελεσμένος will dwell with the gods, Plat. Phaed., 69c. Plat., of course, finds the true consecration in the constant elevation to ὄν ὄντως "true being," which follows ἀνάμνησις of pre-earthly existence; during this recollection there takes place the most blessed consecration in the vision of God; he who practises it aright is the τελέους ἀεὶ τελετὰς τελούμενος and he alone will be essentially τέλεος, Phaedr., 249c; 250b.

Acc. to Philo Spec. Leg., I, 319 (on Dt. 23:18 → 59, 4 ff.) no Jew can take part in mystery rites μήτε τελείτω μήτε τελείσθω, cf. the argument in 319-323. Philo uses τελέομαι formally like the LXX (→ 58, 1 ff.) for the adoption of the worship of false gods by the Israelites (Nu. 25:3), Mut. Nom., 107; Spec. Leg., I, 56. But he can also use the verb quite freely with ref. to the Jewish religion: acc. to Ex. 29 οἱ τελούμενοι ἱερεῖς are priests to be consecrated, Vit. Mos., II, 150; Moses is introduced by God into sacred rites by the revelation of the divine will, Gig., 54; the Therapeutae are consecrated to the mysteries of the religious life by study of the Law, the Prophets, the Ps. etc., Vit. Cont., 25; often τελέομαι means penetration to the higher stages [4] of religious knowledge, e.g., by deeper insight into the special meaning of OT sayings, Cher., 48, participation in the gt. rites, Abr., 122; Decal., 41. Non-religiously τελέω in a transf. sense means "to introduce into the mysteries" of the art of government, Leg. Gaj., 56; φιλοσοφία τετελεσμένοι of non-Jewish wisdom, Mut. Nom., 36.

B. The Septuagint.

In the LXX,[5] from which all examples are given, τελέω means 1. a. "to carry through," Tob. 7:9B; 2 Macc. 4:23; 3 Macc. 5:27 (Sir. 7:25; 38:27, eventually in the sense "to complete"); b. "to actualise," e.g., a word (on Rt. 3:18 → line 42 f.), "to fulfil" a saying of God, 2 Εσδρ. 1:1 for כלה q and Δα. 4:33 for סוף, cf. συντελέω → 63, 29 ff.; 2. "to complete," "to bring to an end," "to conclude," a building, 2 Εσδρ. 5:16 שלם peal, 16:15 שלם q, 6:15 שיצא, the harvest, Rt. 2:21, a ῥῆμα (a matter unless the transl. ref. it to v. 13 → line 38), 3:18, ταῦτα, 2 Εσδρ. 9:1; τελέω ἐν... means "to deal with," 10:17 (in all 4 instances כלה pi); cf. also 7:12 for גמר peal, no HT equivalent 1 Εσδρ. 8:65, cf. 2 Εσδρ. 9:1; also Jdt. 8:34, works 1 Macc. 4:51, walls 13:10; νεότης τελεσθεῖσα ταχέως, Wis. 4:16; on Sir. → line 37 f. In the passages → lines 40 ff. apart from Wis. 4:16 the idea is again that of real actualisation but with a stronger emphasis on completion. The sense "to render," "to pay" (→ 57, 34 ff.) does not occur. 3. The religious sense is

---

[4] There is perhaps an allusion to this in Vit. Mos., I, 62; the ref. is at any rate to ethical progress.

[5] Cf. du Plessis, Τέλειος. *The Idea of Perfection in the NT,* Diss. Kampen (1959), 71 f.

presupposed, but only with ref. to heathen cults and negatively, in the mid. pass. "to dedicate oneself to the service of a god" ἐτελέσθη Ισραηλ τῷ Βεελφεγωρ Nu. 25:3, cf. ψ 105:28, of individuals τετελεσμένον τῷ... Nu. 25:5 (all 3 passages for צמד ni), τετελεσμένη the "qedesha" Hos. 4:14; for the LXX קדש is connected with τελ-, τελεσφόρος and τελισκόμενος "consecrated," Dt. 23:18; also τελετή 3 Βασ. 15:12 (for מקדש in Am. 7:9).

C. The New Testament.

The word has various nuances in the NT. [6]

1. a. Obviously the answer of the Kurios in 2 C. 12:9a is formulated in general terms: [7] The power which is real power "comes to perfection" [8] in weakness, "is truly efficacious" in it, i.e., precisely [9] in weakness when nothing aids it, when it has even to overcome obstacles. What is meant is the power (→ I, 491, 30 ff.) of Christ (v. 9c); on ἀσθένεια concretely → VII, 411, 19 ff. Gl. 5:16 forbids "carrying out" a will which is opposed to the πνεῦμα and hence alien to it, v. 17 → VII, 133, 10 ff. Jesus is oppressed by contemplation of the approaching baptism of judgment (→ I, 538, 28ff; VI, 944, 11 ff.; VII, 884, 4 ff.) until it is "accomplished," Lk. 12:50. The word from the cross in Jn. 19:30 is explained by v. 28: Everything that God commissioned Jesus to do has been "completed," [10] the saving work whose earthly completion according to Jn. is at the cross. 2 Tm. 4:7 says that the apostle, now close to death, has "carried through his course" (→ τρέχω) to success (στέφανος, v. 8, par. ἀγών, v. 7). [11] τελέομαι is used three times in Rev. in statements about the seven plagues, which are a most intense form of the penalties visited on mankind in the end-time; [12] the wrath of God is "executed" [13] in them (15:1) and His secret plan (→ IV, 824, 6 f.) "fulfilled" (10:7). While this takes place the temple of God is inaccessible until they are "accomplished" (15:8 → IV, 888, 23 ff.). This is also the meaning in Rev. 11:7 → IV, 502, 13 ff.

b. [14] Divine sayings which ordain the future are "put into effect" (→ 57, 26 ff.), e.g., those about the awaited events of the last time in Rev. (17:17) or those about

---

[6] On πληρόω, which is par. in use but not synon. by origin or specific content, → VI, 297, 11 ff.

[7] Without μου (as against 𝔎 etc.). Cf. esp. Wnd. 2 K., ad loc.

[8] Possibly also "to its goal." In the basic statement a definite transl. is hardly possible nor can one decide for certain between the mid. and pass.

[9] Not "only," as often affirmed, cf. Ltzm. K., ad loc. "a pre-condition"; Wnd. 2 K., ad loc.: "necessary"; W. Grundmann, Der Begriff d. Kraft in d. nt.lichen Gedankenwelt (1932), 104: "a necessary presupposition."

[10] Bultmann J. on 19:28 ref. to statements about Jesus' ἔργα in Jn. Cf. esp. the sing. at 4:34; 17:4 (→ 81, 18 ff.). Acc. to O. Cullmann, "Der joh. Gebrauch doppeldeutiger Ausdrücke als Schlüssel zum Verständnis d. vierten Ev.," ThZ, 4 (1948), 370 Jn. 19:30 contains both the chronological sense of "ended" and also the theological sense of "achieved." On the relation to τελειωθῇ in 19:28 → 82, 12 ff.

[11] Unlike πληρόω in Ac. 13:25 → VI, 297, 9 ff.

[12] The judgment on Babylon and the parousia follow.

[13] Cf. συνετέλεσεν κύριος θυμὸν αὐτοῦ Lam. 4:11, cf. Ez. 5:13.

[14] On the par. use of πληρόω in the sense of → n. 6 → VI, 295, 7 ff. In the specific use of τελέω, πληρόω etc. discussed there and above, there is a significant distinction in the introductory formulas to Scripture quotations in the NT and Rabb. Judaism, cf. B. M. Metzger, "The Formulas introducing Quotations of Scripture in the NT and the Mishnah," JBL, 70 (1951), 297-307, esp. 306 f.

the death of Jesus in the OT (Lk. 22:37; [15] 18:31; [16] Ac.13:29); in both sets the plan of God is executed → VI, 296, 5 ff.

c. [17] Lk. 2:39 stresses the fact that the parents of Jesus "carried out" conscientiously (πάντα) the purification rites of Lv. 12 → III, 429, n. 5. [18] The uncircumcised also "carry out" the prescriptive will of God as it is known to the Jew from the Torah, R. 2:27 → IV, 1069, 31 ff. The royal law according to Jm. 2:8 ff. (→ I, 591, 22 ff.; IV, 1080, 33 ff.) is "fulfilled" especially in the law of love, expressly described as that of the OT, Lv. 19:18.

2. The persecuted disciples in their flight [19] will not have "finished" the list of Israel's cities [20] before Jesus comes in His redeeming parousia (→ VI, 845, 1 ff.); this is promised in Mt. 10:23. In a stylistic arrangement[21] Mt. has five sermon-complexes which he marks off clearly by a stereotyped conclusion: καὶ ἐγένετο ὅτε ἐτέλεσεν ὁ Ἰησοῦς . . . , 7:28; 11:1; 13:53; 19:1; 26:1: here, in the last speech, πάντας τοὺς λόγους. [22] In chronological notes the pass. is used to mark the conclusion of a divinely appointed time, Rev. 20:3, 5, 7; cf. the ἄχρι in v. 3, 5.

3. Finally the verb means "to pay what one owes" (→ 57, 34 ff.), "to make obligatory offerings" to the temple chest (Mt. 17:24) or the state (R. 13:6, → 29, 8 f.).

D. The Post-Apostolic Fathers.

Apart from Barn., 7, 3 (an OT event, the offering of Isaac, understood as a type which was "fulfilled" in Christ), the word occurs here only in Herm., where it is common

---

[15] There is ref. here to Is. 53:12. On τελεσθῆναι and τέλος → 54, n. 35. On δεῖ → II, 23, 12 ff., also E. Fascher, "Theol. Bemerkungen zu δεῖ," Nt.liche Stud. f. R. Bultmann, Beih. z. ZNW, 21 (1954), 228-254.

[16] 22:37 is obviously from Luke's special material, and probably the version of 18:31 too, unless Lk. himself put in τελεσθήσεται here, → VI, 296, n. 61.

[17] On the par. use of πληρόω in the sense of → n. 6 → VI, 292, 23.

[18] Formally this should properly go under → lines 9 ff.

[19] Persecution is the special theme of the narrower context. H. Schürmann, "Zur Traditions- u. Redaktionsgesch. v. Mt. 10:23," BZ, NF, 3 (1959), 82-88 views the passage with Lk. 12:11 f. as "a unity forged in the history of the tradition," 85; "both sayings were originally apocalyptic persecution sayings," 86. Cf. ad loc. W. G. Kümmel, Verheissung u. Erfüllung[3] (1956), 55-60, who surveys the position of A. Schweitzer, Leben Jesu[5] (1951), 405-410 and the gen. "solution of consistent eschatology," Cf. both works for further bibl.

[20] This is what οὐ μὴ τελέσητε means here whether related to the flight or to the missionary work; as against E. Grässer, "Das Problem d. Parusieverzögerung in d. synpt. Ev. u. in d. Ag.," Beih. z. ZNW, 22 (1957), 137, cf. Kümmel, op. cit., 55. The pt. of 10:23 is not the time of the parousia (cf. Schl. Mt., ad loc.) but the promise to the afflicted. Acc. to E. Bammel, "Mt. 10:23," Stud. Theologica, 15 (1961) 92 the saying itself in any form in which it can be reconstructed has nothing whatever to do with missionary work.

[21] The expression does not always fit the context too well, esp. 13:53, cf. 19:1 (the only NT instances of μεταίρω); it is significant in context at 7:28. The sermons are introduced differently, 5:1 f.; 10:(1,) 5; 13:1-3; 18:1 (-3); 24:3. K. Stendahl draws conclusions as to the structure and thrust of Mt. in "The School of St. Matthew," Acta Semin. Neotestam. Upsaliensis, 20 (1954), 24-27.

[22] καὶ ἐγένετο ὅτε does not occur elsewhere in Mt., with gen. abs. only in 9:10. M. Johannessohn, "Das bibl. καὶ ἐγένετο u. seine Gesch.," ZvglSpr., 53 (1925), 161-212 believes (195) Mt. follows the LXX in the expression discussed → lines 11 ff., cf. 1 Βασ. 18:1; 24:17; 2 Βασ. 13:36, but he is also aware of differences, 195 f. In particular the significance and fixed form in Mt. argue against dependence.

for "to carry out," "to perform," a fast in s., 5, 1, 5; 5, 3, 8, a sudden idea, τὸ καλόν, 5, 2, 7, an order, 5, 2, 4, a service, m., 2, 6; 12, 3, 3; s., 2, 7; then "to complete" a work, s., 2, 7; 9, 10, 2, a building, v., 3, 4, 1 f. etc., an explanation, v., 3, 7, 4; also with part. "to cease doing something," 1, 4, 1.

† ἐπιτελέω.

1. Outside the Bible ἐπιτελέω is a strengthened form of τελέω (→ 57, 17 ff.) with no special distinction in use. It means a. "to carry out," e.g., ἐπιτελεῖτε ὡς καθήκει (→ III, 437, 23 ff.), P. Oxy., III, 483, 34 (108 A.D.), καθῆκον ἔργον, Philo Cher., 14, "to achieve," Som., I, 90. Moses asks as to the causes by which things "come into being" in creation, Fug., 161; processes in the universe "take place" acc. to God's laws, Op. Mund., 61; "to do" something unwillingly, Corp. Fabul. Aesopicarum, [1] 247, 10. Saying and "doing" things are set in juxtaposition in Epict. Diss., III, 24, 111. There is a similar pairing — to promise and "to accomplish" — in Aristot. Eth. Nic., IX, 1, p. 1164a, 5 f. and 30. Sarapis is μόνος . . . ἕτοιμος τῷ τινος δεομένῳ τοῦτ᾽ ἐπιτελεῖν, Ael. Arist. Or., 45, 22 (Keil); ἵνα μοι τὰς ἐντολὰς ἐπιτελέσῃς, we read in Preis. Zaub., I, 4, 1539 f.; "to fulfil," a vow, Hdt., I, 86, 2, "to fulfil oneself," an oracle (pass.), I, 13, 2, "to carry out" what is commanded, Epict. Diss., III, 22, 57. b. "To pay," cf. τελέω (→ 57, 34 ff.), e.g., tribute φόρον, Hdt., V, 49, 6. c. "To perform" religious actions, abs., e.g., ἐπετέλουν αὐτῷ annually to the divinely honoured north wind, Ael. Var. Hist., 12, 61; ἱερουργίας, P. Tebt., II, 294, 24 f. (146 A.D.); Jewish priests carry out religious acts in the tabernacle, Philo Ebr., 129, the high-priest "executes" prayers and offerings, Som., I, 215; θυσίαν Jos. Ant., 1, 58; Ptolemy III Euergetes in Jerusalem, Ap., 2, 48; a funeral, 2, 205; the Jews "celebrate" glorious feasts of light, i.e., the Dedication and Tabernacles, [2] 118. The idea that in the mysteries the act is performed "for" a deity may be seen too in the statement: ὀμνύω τοὺς θεούς, οἷς τὰ μυστήρια ἐπιτελεῖται, Ditt. Syll.[4], II, 736, 2 f. (92 B.C.). ἐπιτελέω is also used with ref. to contests, Dion. Hal. Ant. Rom., 7, 73, 1.

2. In the LXX (all ref. given) the verb means a. gen. "to accomplish," of God, Nu. 23:23 (פעל), "to carry out," Da. 11:16 (כלה q), "to do something to someone," Ju. 21:10 A (עשׂה), "to carry through," 1 Εσδρ. 6:4 (twice); 8:16, 21, 91, so τρόπον, 2 Macc. 12:8, royal service, 15:5, a commission, 14:29, a resolve, 3:23, a purpose, 3:8, a βούλημα, 15:5, commands ῥήματα of the ruler, Jdt. 2:13, λεγόμενα, Est. 8:14, vows, Ju. 11:39 A (עשׂה); cf. of a promise οὕτως ἐπιτέλεσον, κύριε (cf. Lv. 26:44), 3 Macc. 6:15, "to fulfil" a request, Ps. Sol. 6:6, "to execute" a threat of judgment, ἄρξομαι καὶ ἐπιτελέσω, 1 Βασ. 3:12 (כלה pi); b. to begin and also "to end," Zech. 4:9 (HT בצע pi), "to conclude," of building, esp. the temple, 1 Εσδρ. 4:55; 5:70 (ἀποτελεσθῆναι B); 6:13, 27; the sense is always that of carrying through to a finish; c. "to celebrate" a feast, a wedding, Tob. 12:1 א, μνημόσυνον, a feast of remembrance, Est. 9:27; "to offer," a whole offering, Lv. 6:15 (קטר ho).

3. In the NT ἐπιτελέω has the following senses.

a. "To perform," "to establish" (Hb. 8:5 → VII, 375, 15 ff.). παθήματα such as are experienced by the recipients of 1 Pt. (1 Pt. 5:9) come upon, or more strictly are accomplished on, Christians, [3] → V, 934, 34 f. The holiness given to the ἅγιοι

ἐπιτελέω. [1] Ed. A. Hausrath, I, 2 (1956), 66.
[2] On light in these festivals cf. Str.-B., II, 539-541, 806 f.
[3] Dat. incommodi, cf. E. G. Selwyn, *The First Epistle of St. Peter* (1958), ad loc. Cf. the dat. incommodi in Ael. Arist. (→ line 14 f.) etc. Ref. is often made to Plat. Leg., X, 910e: δίκην (punishment) τούτοις ἐπιτελούντων, but there is no great affinity of sense to 1 Pt. 5:9.

(→ II, 583, 5 ff.) is something they "actualise" by cleansing themselves from all that defiles both body and spirit, 2 C. 7:1. In other instances in Paul the idea is that of carrying out what is planned (R. 15:28) or begun, cf. the collection for Jerusalem in 2 C. 8:11, where "accomplishment" is contrasted with the resolve and the first steps (ποιῆσαι), or "execution" [4] with the design which has its source in a ready mind, → VI, 699, 19 ff. God's grace is also "actualised" toward the Corinthians in the collection, v. 6. The exclusive work of God "among you" is made no less plain in Phil. 1:6 than the fact that the "carrying out" of this work right up to the *parousia*, i.e., the judgment (→ II, 952, 7 ff.), is decisive. [5]

b. The temporal sense "to finish" is to be found in Gl. 3:3. Here the recipients, after the "commencement" of the churches took place in the work of the Holy Spirit (→ VI, 428, 14 ff.), are now in danger of "ending" (mid.) with trust in human action (σαρκί).

c. The reference in Hb. 9:6 is to priestly functions in the tabernacle.

4. In the post.-apost. fathers the verb is used for "to accomplish" of sacrifices, Dg., 3, 5, celebration of the anniversary of a martyrdom, Mart. Pol., 18, 3. The only other use (12 times) is in 1 Cl. for "to carry out" what is commanded in 37, 2 f., one's ministry in 20, 10, an act in the fear of God, 2, 8, cultic functions, 40, 2 f.; once of an OT saying (Dt. 32:15) ἐπετελέσθη τὸ γεγραμμένον, "it was fulfilled," 1 Cl., 3, 1.

† συντελέω.

1. Non-Biblical Usage.

The word [1] means "to fulfil" obligations, "to make common contributions," "to contribute," Demosth. Or., 20, 28, hence "to belong to a group," 23, 213, "to contribute" chariots in equipping someone, Xenoph. Cyrop., VI, 1, 50; each of the gods contributes something to life on earth, e.g., Helios, Selene, etc., Luc. Bis Accusatus, 1, cf. Deorum concilium, 15, then "to pay," e.g., ἀργύριον, Aristot. Oec., II, p. 1353a, 2 etc.; b. "to accomplish together," e.g., τῷ χρησμῷ, "to co-operate" with the oracle, Luc. Alex., 36 (→ line 23 f.), gen. "to carry out," συντέλεσόν μοι τὸ δεῖνα πρᾶγμα, Preis. Zaub., I, 3, 85, 90 f. and 92 f., cf. 121, "to accomplish," e.g., acts, Ep. Ar., 234, ἀδικίαν, 152 "to execute," e.g., building a temple, συνετέλεσεν... εὐαρέστως, Ditt. Syll.[3], II, 587, 9 f. (c. 196 B.C.), a race-track δρόμον, 463, 14 (c. 246 B.C.), works of art, Ep. Ar., 51. 57. 81, a literary work, the OT, 312 (but cf. Ez. 16:14 → 63, 27); abs. the word means "to work," 258; συντελέομαι means "to take place," movement "takes place" in space, Sext. Emp. Math., X, 154. συντελεσθέντα means "events," Dion. Hal. Ant. Rom., 7, 73, 5. Then we have the special sense "to carry out" a task οἱ ἄγγελοι συντελοῦντες τὸ συνταχθὲν αὐτοῖς, Gr. En. [2] 102:3, resolves, Ditt. Syll.[3], I, 485, 37 (3rd

---

[4] Decision whether the intention is truly carried out depends on giving acc. to ability, ἐκ τοῦ ἔχειν, cf. Schl. K., 598.
[5] There is transition from the congregation to the individual in v. 7. We find no trace of a cultic sense (which ἐνάρχομαι and ἐπιτελέω might have) in either Phil. 1:6, Gl. 3:3 or 2 C. 8:6, 11 (cf. προενάρχομαι in v. 10), as against J. B. Lightfoot, *St. Paul's Ep. to the Galatians* (1892), *ad loc.*

συντελέω. [1] Obviously developed in class. Gk. [Dihle].
[2] Ed. C. Bonner, "The Last Chapters of Enoch in Greek," *Stud. and Documents,* 8 (1937).

cent. B.C.), legal ordinances, II, 578, 63 (2nd cent. B.C.). The word is also used in a stronger sense: the Stoics say that "deeds find their fulfilment" τὰς καλὰς πράξεις συντελεῖσθαι in the 4 types of the καλόν (the just, the brave, the moderate, the understanding) as the τέλειον ἀγαθόν, Diog. L., VII, 100; "to end," [3] "to finish," something executed, Luc. Verae historiae, II, 23; f. "to perform" feasts, sacrifices, etc., θυσίαν... τῷ θεῷ, Ditt. Syll.[3], II, 604, 8 (192 B.C.) etc., offerings and sacrifices, 736, 39 (92 B.C.), the Eleusinian rites, 540, 23 f. (215/214 B.C.), giving of oracles, III, 1157, 18 and 42 (c. 100 B.C.), ἀγιστείας, Ps.-Plat. Ax., 371d, πανήγυριν, Jos. Ant., 15, 269, τοὺς γάμους (→ 51, 11 f.), Luc. Alex., 35.

2. The Septuagint.

Only a few examples of common usage will be given here, with more instances of the special employment of the term. The word is most often used for forms of כלה. It is not attested in the sense "to contribute," "to pay" → 62, 22 ff. It means a. [4] "to achieve," "to carry out" (→ 62, 26 ff.), e.g., God is ὁ συντελῶν πάντα, Is. 44:24; διαθήκην "to reach an agreement" between king and people. Ιερ. 41(34):8, 15; παρὰ... κυρίου ταῦτά μοι συνετελέσθη, Job 19:26; in prayer for a young couple: "Fulfil their life in health," Tob. 8:17, cf. Job 21:13; συντελεσθέντα are "events," Tob. 12:20 AB; συντελέω τὰ ἔργα τὰ καθήκοντα means "to render the forced labour prescribed," Ex. 5:13, cf. 14; "to carry out," "to do," e.g., πονηρά, Gn. 44:5, ἄνομα, Job 35:14; Prv. 1:19; Is. 32:6; with εἰς "to have to do with a woman," Test. Jud. 13:3. A special sense is "to perform fully," "to complete," of a wedding in Gn. 29:27, the world, i.e., creation in Prv. 8:31, heaven and earth (pass.) in Gn. 2:1; God "executes" His wrath to the very end, Lam. 4:11; Ez. 5:13; 6:12; 7:5; 13:15; 20:8; Da. 11:36 (also Θ). Worth noting is συντετέλεσται "something is decided," 1 Βασ. 20:7, 9, 33 (on Is. 28:22 → 64, 8 f.; n. 6), cf. act. 2 Βασ. 21:5. In the sense "to do perfectly," "to complete," it is used with the inf. ἀποδεκατῶσαι, Dt. 26:12, διαβῆναι, Jos. 4:11, or part. διαβαίνων, Jos. 3:17; 4:1, διαμερίσας, 21:42a, προσφέρων, Ju. 3:18. συντετελεσμένον means "complete," "perfect," Ez. 16:14. b. "To carry out" what is spoken, God speaks and it takes place ἅμα συνετελέσθη (HT different), Is. 46:10; of the words of God, Lam. 2:17; Tob. 14:4 א; Δα. 4:33 Θ, the νόμος, Sir. 34:8, prophecies of the end, Da. 12:7, cf. ὅραμα, 9:24, commissions, Ep. Jer. 61; 3 Macc. 5:4. c. "To end," "to finish," God finishes His works, Gn. 2:2, buildings esp. 3 Βασ. 3:1 etc.; begun and not completed, 1 Ch. 27:24; abs. "to be complete(d)," 2 Ch. 29:17; 24:14. "To end a stretch of time," Da. 10:3; pass. "to come to an and," aor. "to be at an end," e.g., συνετελέσθησαν αἱ ἡμέραι πένθους, Dt. 34:8, days of a marriage, Tob. 8:20 AB; 10:7 AB, feast-days, Job 1:5. In the sense "to stop doing something" it is construed with the part., e.g., προσευχόμενος, 3 Βασ. 8:54, προφητεύων, 1 Βασ. 10:13; "to be complete," e.g., ἐξιλασκόμενος, Lv. 16:20; or inf., e.g., καταφαγεῖν, Gn. 43:2 etc. The word also means "to cause to cease," pass. "to cease," "to disappear," Is. 18:5, cf. συντελεσθήσεται ἡ βασιλεία τοῦ ἐχθροῦ, Test. D. 6:4 (v. Mk. 3:26). Another special use is "to put an end to," "to destroy," act. 1 Βασ. 15:18; 2 Βασ. 22:38; ψ 118:87; Zech. 5:4; Jer. 5:3; 14:12; 15:16; Ez. 7:15; cf. Ps. Sol. 7:15; Test. L. 5:4 (not 1 Εσδρ. 1:53, on this cf. 2 Ch. 36:19); in the pass. 2 Ch. 18:10; Sir. 45:19; Na. 2:1; Is. 1:28; Jer. 14:15; 16:4; Ez. 5:12; 6:12; 11:15; 13:14; cf. Test. Jud. 22:2. d. "To carry out" cultic acts, e.g., to sacrifice animals συντελεῖν αὐτούς, Tob. 8:19 א; θυσίας, 3 Macc. 5:43, cf. 1 Εσδρ. 1:16; "to celebrate" a festival, 2 Ch. 30:22, though this is not to be regarded as technical usage, and certainly not in Ez. 43:23 etc.

---

[3] In the one example in Leisegang, s.v. Philo, influenced by the interchange in Gn. 29:27 f., distinguishes between συντελέω and ἀναπληρόω (or συμπλήρωσις) "to fulfil" and "to complete," Ebr., 53.

[4] The ref. show συντελέω is one of the words which replace τελέω, → 57, n. 1 [Dihle].

3. The New Testament.

Here the word means a. "to execute," "accomplish." Satan "practises" every (form of) temptation on Jesus, though naturally without success, Lk. 4:13. God "fulfils" the new order promised in Ιερ. 38(31):31, Hb. 8:8; → II, 132, 3 ff. [5] R. 9:28 offers an abbreviated quotation from LXX Is. 10:22 f. How it was understood may be seen from R. 9 (→ IV, 210, 27 ff.): God "fulfils" a saying, He "puts into effect" His word concerning the remnant.

כלה ונחרצה is variously transl. in Is. 28:22; 10:22 f.; Da. 9:27. [6] In Da. 9:27 the two Hbr. words are both rendered by συντέλεια, obviously in the sense of destruction (cf. συντέτμηται καὶ συντετέλεσται "totally destroyed" in Da. 5:27 f.) On the other hand συντετελεσμένα... πράγματα in Is. 28:22 suggests "firmly resolved deeds" which God will do on the whole earth (on ΣΘ → n. 6). Hence in Is. 10:22 f. λόγον might ref. to the matter, and hence συντελῶν in v. 22 would mean "carrying out" and συντέμνων in v. 22 or συντετμημένον in v. 23 would denote the short time or swiftness with which God will act, cf. συντόμως ἀπόλλυμαι in Prv. 13:23; 23:28, σύντομον... τέλος Wis. 14:14. Is. 10:22 f. was perhaps taken as a promise in LXX, but not in R. 9:28, [7] though the meaning of both verbs is the same as that postulated for Is. 10:22 f. [8]

In the disciples' question in Mk. 13:4 and par. Mark's συντελεῖσθαι is interpreted in Lk. 21:7 by a simple γίνεσθαι. But the συντελεῖσθαι of Mk. 13:4 plainly carries the thought of the events of the last time, cf. also the πάντα, which is not in Lk.

b. "To end," pass. "to come to an end," Lk. 4:2; → 63, 33 f.; "when the seven days came to an end," Ac. 21:27.

4. The Post-Apostolic Fathers.

Only Herm. and Barn. use the verb. In Herm. it means "to carry out," e.g., a process relating to divorce in m., 4, 1, 11, written instructions in s., 5, 3, 7, then more often "to finish," e.g., expositions in m., 12, 3, 2; s., 8, 11, 1; 9, 29, 4, a building in s., 9, 5, 2. Barn. has the word only in quotations, 12, 1; 16, 6; 15, 3 f. or with ref. to a quotation, 15, 4 (twice; cf. Gn. 2:2).

† συντέλεια.

1. Outside the Bible this means [1] a. "a common accomplishment" for public purposes, Demosth. Or., 20, 23, or a voluntary one, Dio C., 54, 30, 5; then gen. state "taxes," 48, 31, 1; "payment," Ps.-Aristot. Rhet. Al., 3, p. 1423b, 1; b. "common performance," "co-

---

[5] συντελέσω is also used in Ιερ. 38(31):31 Σ. In Hb. 8:8-10 three different verbs, συντελέω, ποιέω, διατίθεμαι, are used for LXX (διαθήκην) διατίθεσθαι, Ιερ. 38(31):31-33. In the rendering of כרת ברית in Ιερ. a distinction is made with respect to those concerned between διατίθεμαι (Yahweh makes a covenant with the people, Ιερ. 38[31]:31-33; 39[32]: 40; 41 [34]:13) and συντελέω (the king makes a covenant with the people, 41[34]:8, 15).

[6] Cf. further J. Ziegler, "Untersuchungen zur Septuaginta d. Buches Isaias," At.liche Abh., 12, 3 (1934), 140; E. Bammel, "Mt. 10:23," Stud. Theol., 15 (1961), 87, who suggests a shortening of the time.

[7] 'Α at v. 23 has τελευτὴν καὶ συντομήν for LXX λόγον συντετμημένον, and ΣΘ have συντέλειαν... καὶ συντομήν (also in Is. 28:22); they each take both words to denote "destruction".

[8] On the various possibilities v. Mi. R., ad loc.

συντέλεια. [1] Found from the 5th cent. B.C., properly an abstr. of συντελής [Risch].

operation," Plat. Leg., X, 905b (only here in Plat.); then gen. "execution," as distinct from preparations for building the temple, Jos. Ant., 15, 389; "execution" of the literary plan of the Antiquitates, Jos. Ant., 20, 262, "completion," e.g., συντέλειαν εἴληφεν ὁ Παρθενών of the ἀποκατάστασις of a temple, Ditt. Syll.³, II, 695, 13 f. (2nd cent. B.C.); then the "tense of the completed act" (the aor. as opp. to the iterative impf.), Philo Rer. Div. Her., 17; Moses called the no. 7 συντέλειαν "completion" καὶ παντέλειαν "perfection" (par. τελείωσις → 84, 32 f.); Gn. 2:1 (→ 63, 21 f.) is exegeted thus, Spec. Leg., II, 58, cf. also Dio C., 44, 48, 2 → VI, 307, 4 ff. c. "Conclusion," "ending" of the war, Ditt. Or., I, 327, 6 (2nd cent. B.C.); Polyb., 4, 28, 5. d. "Performance" of sacrifices and offerings, Ditt. Syll.³, II, 736, 60 and 182-5 (92 B.C.).

2. In the LXX (all instances given) the word means a. "execution" of the crossing of the Jordan, Jos. 4:8 (HT different), also 1 Βασ. 8:3 ² (בְּצַע cf. בצע "to accomplish") and Hab. 3:19 (no HT equivalent), also of a work of art, 3 Βασ. 6:25 (קֶצֶב); Sir. 38:28 (twice, no HT), "in gathering," Ex. 23:16 (אָסִיף, cf. συντελέω Lv. 23:39); "totality," 3 Βασ. 6:22 (HT תֹּם), e.g., of the fear of God, Sir. 21:11 (no HT), κακίας, Ez. 22:12 (as opp. to HT), τῆς πόλεως the "entire" city, Ju. 20:40 (כָּלִיל), also "perfection," ψ 118:96 (תִּכְלָה), "completion" of attire, Sir. 45:8; 50:11 (in both instances HT ³ כָּלִיל), "satiety" in drinking, 1 Βασ. 20:41 (גדל), "fulfilling" of a word of God, 1 Εσδρ. 2:1. b. "Conclusion," e.g., συντέλειαν λειτουργῶν, Sir. 50:14 (כלה pi), of a building, 1 Εσδρ. 6:19, a work, Sir. 37:11 (מוֹצָא); "end," Job 26:10 (תִּכְלִית), as distinct from beginning, Dt. 11:12 (אַחֲרִית); "expiration" of a year, 2 Ch. 24:23, "end" of the phase of the moon, Sir. 43:7 (in both cases HT תְּקוּפָה "turning"); μέχρι συντελείας "to the last" (?), Sir. 47:10 (Hbr. perhaps "year by year"); "cessation," Sir. 22:10; "end" of the days of one's life, Sir. 33:24 (no HT), of words, Sir. 43:27 (קֵץ), cf. Ἀα. 4:28, 31, also of years, Ἀα. 4:34, war, Da. 9:27, of a man, Sir. 11:27 (אַחֲרִית), of the ungodly, 21:9; adv. in εἰς συντέλειαν, "completely," "for ever," Sir. 40:14 (לָנֶצַח); for other Da. passages → lines 34 ff. c. "Destruction," cf. συντελέω (→ 64, 8 ff.), 2 Εσδρ. 19:31; Na. 1:8 f.; Zeph. 1:18; Jer. 4:27; 5:10, 18; Ιερ. 26(46):28 (συντέλεια par. ἐκλιπεῖν both for כָּלָה); Da. 9:27 (also Θ); Ez. 11:13; 13:13; 20:17 (in these 12 instances for כָּלָה), ⁴ 4 Βασ. 13:17, 19; 2 Εσδρ. 9:14; ψ 58:13 f.; Da. 12:7 (all 6 for כלה pi), cf. Job 30:2 (HT כֶּלַח); Ez. 21:33 (כול hi); Am. 8:8; 9:5; Hab. 1:9 and also 1:15 ⁵ (in these 4 instances for כֹּל); Am. 1:14; Na. 1:3 (in both cases for סוּפָה "stormy wind"); Da. 9:27 (cf. συντελέω → 64, 8 ff.) and also 11:36 (in both cases חרץ ni); finally 1 Macc. 3:42 (par. ἀπώλεια); Εσθ. 4:17s.

3. As an apocalyptic tt. συντέλεια is common in Da. LXX for קֵץ to denote the "end," so καιρὸς συντελείας for קֵץ עֵת at 11:35; 12:4 (also Θ), and with no corresponding HT 12:7; ὥρα συντελείας 11:40 (but ὥρα καιροῦ 8:17), while Θ prefers καιροῦ πέρας 8:17; 11:35, 40; 12:9. Da. LXX also uses συντέλεια for קֵץ the eschatological "end" at 8:19, cf. too 11:27; 12:6 (in all these Θ πέρας) and 12:13a (Θ the same); συντέλεια ἡμερῶν is the transl. of קֵץ הַיָּמִין at 12:13b (also Θ). συντέλεια for "end" in a more gen. sense occurs for קֵץ at 9:26 (twice); 11:6, 13, 45; ⁶ συντέλεια καιρῶν with no HT 9:27. The noun is always an apocal. tt. in Test. XII; Zeb. 9:9 ref. to rejection ἕως καιροῦ συντελείας (→ line 35 f.); B. 11:3: ἕως συντελείας τοῦ αἰῶνος. Levi is not guilty of the transgression of the temple cultus by his sons ἐπὶ τῇ συντελείᾳ τῶν αἰώνων, i.e.,

---

² In context the doing of evil, cf. συντελειῶν in Gr. En. 106:18, ed. C. Bonner, "The Last Chapters of Enoch in Gk.," *Stud. and Documents,* 8 (1937).

³ On Sir. cf. R. Smend, *Die Weisheit d. Jesus Sirach* (1906).

⁴ On the other hand συντέλεια καιροῦ reinterprets כָּלָה in Da. 9:27 Θ.

⁵ In context "gathering" is also possible, cf. Ex. 23:16.

⁶ We cannot deal here with the many problems of translation in these LXX passages. There is much variation in Θ, cf. also → 51, 24 f.; 52, 21 f.

at the time of the author, L. 10:2, cf. R. 6:8. συντέλεια corresponds to קץ, but sometimes in the transl. the idea of completion in the sense of eschatological fulfilment may be stronger; in Judaism the "end" is the conclusion and related events.

4. In Rabb. lit. סוֹף הָעוֹלָם occurs in Sanh., 4, 5. גמר הקץ in 1 QpHab 7:2 is formally different: Hab. is not instructed about the "consummation of the time," but what is in view is its end; [7] cf. συντέλεια καιροῦ in Da. 9:27 Θ.

5. In the NT the word occurs only in eschatological sayings. συντέλεια τοῦ αἰῶνος (or in Hb. τῶν αἰώνων) is traditional and stereotyped → 65, 41 ff. [8] Hb. 9:27 stresses that the saving work accomplished in Christ is itself the event of the end-time. By juxtaposition of the extended times from creation and the final event the ἅπαξ (→ I, 381, 16 ff.), the definitiveness, and the perfection of the sacrifice of Jesus are underlined, → V, 918, 7 ff.

The version συντέλεια τοῦ αἰῶνος [9] is peculiar to Mt. (→ VII, 232, 2 ff.). It occurs in interpretations of parables, 13:39 (without τοῦ), 40, 49 (both in the fixed form οὕτως ἔσται ἐν τῇ συντελείᾳ τοῦ αἰῶνος). It is used by the disciples [10] in 24:3 and is again in the material peculiar to Mt. in 28:20. Materially it refers to eschatological events which have still to take place (24:3; 28:20); of these judgment is especially mentioned, 13:39 f., 49.

6. In the post-apost. fathers συντέλεια occurs only in Herm. as a traditional term, e.g., in the question εἰ ἤδη συντέλειά ἐστιν, whether the "end" has already come, v., 3, 8, 9, and in the over-full expression ἐπ' ἐσχάτων τῶν ἡμερῶν τῆς συντελείας, at the "end" God's Son has been manifested, s., 9, 12, 3. In the Apologists only Tat. has the word; the resurrection of bodies follows μετὰ τὴν τῶν ὅλων συντέλειαν, Or. Graec., 6, 1, that of soul and body ἐπὶ συντελείᾳ τοῦ κόσμου, 13, 1, judgment follows ἐν ἡμέρᾳ συντελείας, 17, 1.

† παντελής.

1. Outside the Bible the word means a. "completing all," e.g., of the no. 10 (with παντοεργός "effecting all"), Philolaos Fr., 11 (Diels, I, 411, 9 f.), of Zeus (cf. τέλειος → 68, 33 ff.), Aesch. Sept. c. Theb., 116, of χρόνος, Choeph., 965; "fully effective," of popular decisions, Suppl., 601; "all-powerful" of a μοναρχία, Soph. Ant., 1163; b. "complete," "full," of freedom, Plat. Leg., III, 698a, of ἀρετή, Aristot. Eth. Nic., IV, 7 f., p. 1124a, 8 and 29, of φιλία, [1] Eth. M., II, 11, p. 1209a, 16; "complete," of equipment, Aesch. Choeph., 560, common in Philo, often par. ὁλόκληρος (→ III, 766, 41 ff.), also "intact," "unblemished," of the priest, Spec. Leg., I, 80, the κόσμος, Abr., 44. The ref. may also be ethical; only a ὁλόκληρος καὶ παντελής can look into the holy of holies, Ebr., 135. Only man's unselfish intention to worship God with his sacrifice is ὁλόκληρος καὶ παντελής, Spec. Leg., I, 196; fasting is a sign παντελοῦς εὐσεβείας, II, 197; of God (→ 52, 2 ff.; 52, 11 ff.), Jos. Ap., 2, 190. The adv. is common; it means "absolutely," e.g., with οὐδέν, Jos. Ap., 1, 199 (→ 67, 11 ff.). Later one finds εἰς τὸ παντελές instead

---

[7] Thus far this is the only instance in the Dead Sea Scrolls. On 1 QpHab 7:2 cf. K. Elliger, *Stud. zum Hab.-Komm. vom Toten Meer* (1953), 190 f. K. G. Kuhn, "Die in Palästina gefundenen hbr. Texte u. d. NT," ZThK, 47 (1950), 209, suggests "completion of the end-time"; but → 53, n. 28.

[8] On πλήρωμα τοῦ χρόνου Gl. 4:4 → VI, 305, 17 ff.

[9] Cf. A. Feuillet, "Le sens du mot Parousie dans l'évangile de Matthieu," *The Background of the NT and Its Eschatology, Festschr. f. C. H. Dodd* (1956), 261-280, esp. 269-272.

[10] The linguistic link suggests that the term in Mt. was evoked by the συντελεῖσθαι of Mk. (→ 64, 18 ff.). But the words are used in lexically different senses.

παντελής. [1] "Uniting all values," F. Dirlmeier, Aristot. Magna Moralia (1958), 77 with n. 8.

of παντελῶς, [2] e.g. "completely" obliterated of a kingdom, Philo Deus Imm., 173, disappeared, Leg. Gaj., 144 (often in the same sense κατά...); it occurs with ἀνενέργητος in Sext. Emp. Math., VII, 30; Moses forbids divorce "altogether," Jos. Ant., 3, 274, drives lepers "completely" out of the city, 264 etc., [3] cf. πρὸς τὸ παντελές "fully," 1, 97, εἰς τὸ παντελές, "completely" extirpated, Ael. Nat. An., 17, 27; "for ever," "permanently," Var. Hist., 7, 2; Ditt. Or., II, 642, 2 (3rd cent. A.D.), "always" corresponding to לעלמא in a burial inscr. in two languages from Palmyra (193 A.D.). [4]

2. In the LXX παντελής occurs only in Macc. and as an adj. ref. to the "complete" enjoyment of deliverance, 3 Macc. 7:16. As an adv. it means "totally" forbidden in 2 Macc. 3:12, to be "completely" at one's last gasp, v. 31, to trust "wholly" in the Lord, 7:40, after a "very" short time, 11:1, "fully" bled, 14:46. Αλλ has it in a negative saying in Ju. 3:2 (the transl. takes לֹא....רַק to means "not at all"): παντελῶς... ἀνεπιστήμονες. 'Α has ἀπώλετο παντελές in Job 30:2 (HT יֻבַּל!).

3. In the NT the word is used only in the adverbial phrase εἰς τὸ παντελές. The bowed down woman cannot stand up "fully" (if one takes it with ἀνακῦψαι) or "at all" (if with μή, cf. vg omnino; εἰς τὸ παντελές comes emphatically at the end), Lk. 13:11. In the former case συγκύπτουσα would be weakened, while in the latter it is stressed → II, 427, n. 30. Again, the emphasis on her being bound (v. 12, 16), which does not suggest partial liberation, favours the second interpretation. In the context of Hb. 7:25 that which endures in the person and work of the High-priest Jesus is emphasised, vv. 11-25, esp. 24 f. σῴζειν εἰς τὸ παντελές is elucidated by πάντοτε... ἐντυγχάνειν, v. 25. The One who saves "for ever" (→ I, 381, 16 ff.; 383, 30 ff.) is also, however, the One who saves "altogether," so that the saying about the "totality" of the saving work can hardly be expounded in only a single direction.

4. The Apologists have παντελής only in εἰς τὸ παντελές, "absolutely," Tat. Or. Graec., 6, 1; παντελῶς "generally," Just. Epit., 10, 8.

† τέλειος.

A. Review of Usage outside the Bible. [1]

1. The adj. means a. "whole," of sacrifices, "without blemish," Hom. Il., 1, 66, then "complete" in compass, with no part outside, nothing which belongs left out, Aristot.

---

[2] Other adv. phrases with εἰς and adj. in Mayser, II, 2 (1933/34) § 119, IV.

[3] For details Pr.-Bauer, s.v.

[4] Cf. J. Cantineau, "Textes funéraires Palmyréniens," Rev. Bibl., 39 (1930), 546 f., Text B.

τ έ λ ε ι ο ς. Bibl.: W. Bauer, Mündige u. Unmündige bei d. Ap. Pls., Diss. Marburg (1902); A. Fridrichsen, "Fullkomlighetskravet i Jesu fürkunnelse," Svensk Teol. Kvartalskrift, 9 (1933), 124-133; also "Helgelse och fullkomlighet hos Paulus," Den nya kirkosynen (ed. Y. Brilioth [1945]), 62-91; C. Guignebert, "Quelques remarques sur la perfection (τελείωσις) et ses voies dans le Mystère paulinien," RevHPhR, 8 (1928), 412-430; J. Kögel, "Der Begriff τελειοῦν im Hb.," Festschr. f. M. Kähler (1905), 35-68; O. Moe, "Fullkommenhetstanken i den NT," Tidsskr. f. Teol. og Kirke, 26 (1955), 25-35; T. Osnes, Fullkommenhetstanken i d. NT (1954); P. J. du Plessis, Τέλειος. The Idea of Perfection in the NT, Diss. Kampen (1959), on this K. Prümm, "Das nt.liche Sprach- u. Begriffsproblem d. Vollkommenheit," Biblica, 44 (1963), 76-92; B. Rigaux, "Révélation des mystères et la perfection à Qumran et dans le NT," NTSt, 4 (1957/58), 237-262; R. Schnackenburg, "Die Vollkommenheit d. Christen nach d. Ev.," Theol. Jbch. (1961), 67-81; C. Spicq, L'Epître aux Hébreux, II³ (1953), 214-9; cf. also the Bibl. → 79, n.

[1] du Plessis, 74-77. Derived from τέλος (cf. P. Chantraine, La formation des noms en Grec ancien [1933], 49 f.), the word could later be associated with τελέω. In Attic and elsewhere one often finds τέλεος for τέλειος [Risch].

Metaph., IV, 16, p. 1021b, 12 f. τέλειος can then be par. to ὅλος, Phys., III, 6, p. 207a, 9 and 13, cf. ὅλον οὗ μηδέν ἐστιν ἔξω, 11 f. It is used of a materially exhaustive investigation, Plat. Resp., VIII, 545a, of the cosmos which contains all kinds of living creatures, Tim., 41c; to complete the "full" year in its measure, 39d; ἐν βίῳ τελείῳ, in the course of a "full, unshortened" human life, Aristot. Eth. Nic., I, 6, p. 1098a, 18; a "more complete" eclipse, Philo Vit. Mos., I, 123; of the soul and its "full" faculties: πάντοτε τῇ ψυχῇ χρῆται οὔσῃ τελείᾳ ὁ σπουδαῖος, Diog. L., VII, 128. Herod wants to demonstrate "full" εὐσέβεια by building the temple, Jos. Ant., 15, 387. The designation of some numbers as τέλειαι ref. to those which represent the sum of their divisors, [2] e.g., 6 (3+2+1), Philo Op. Mund., 13 f., 89; Leg. All., I, 3 and 15, or 28 (14+7+4+2+1), Op. Mund., 101; Spec. Leg., II, 40. Cf. also 4 in Op. Mund., 47; Virt., 158, 10 in Spec. Leg., I, 177 f.; II, 41 and 201; Decal., 20, and 12 in Praem., 65 etc.

b. "Perfect," e.g., in the stages of learning — beginning, advance, and maturity, Philo Agric., 165, cf. → VI, 710, 8 ff. Aristot. attempts a def.: "Perfect" is that beyond which there is no further advance in excellence or quality in its genus, which lacks nothing of its own excellence. In this sense the word is not primarily ethical; it is purely formal and may ref. to a physician, a flautist, an informer, or a thief, Metaph., IV, 16, p. 1021b, 15-19. Hence τέλειον εἶναι τῆς τοῦ πράγματος ἀρετῆς means "to reach the limit of professional ability," Plat. Leg., I, 643d. A citizen "in the full sense of the word" is one who knows how to rule and to be ruled with justice, 643e; cf. V, 730d. Plat. can also use τέλειος negatively, τελέους πρὸς ἀρετὴν ἢ πρὸς κακίαν γεγονέναι, Leg., III, 678b, cf. the antithesis of "perfectly good" and "perfectly bad," τέλειον ἀγαθὸν ἢ τέλειον κακόν Philo Mut. Nom., 227. Acc. to Sophist opinion "perfect" ἀδικία is more useful than "perfect" righteousness, Plat. Resp., I, 348b. The man who can spin fine discourses is a "perfect" Sophist, Crat., 403e. The use of τέλειος in respect of values (→ 69, 18 ff.) has its roots just as much in sense a. (→ 67, 30 ff.) as b. (→ lines 13 ff.).

c. We then find the sense "brought to or arrived at the τέλος," "actualised," in the contrast between γνώμη "intention" and τέλειον "finished act" (of Cain, cf. Gn. 4:11), Philo Det. Pot. Ins., 96; of curses: τέλεα καὶ ἐπήκοα γενέσθαι, Plat. Leg., XI, 931b, prayers: ἐφ᾽ αἷς οἱ θεοὶ τέλιον (→ n. 5) ἐπακούσαντες παρέσχον, BGU, IV, 1080, 5 f. (3rd cent. A.D.).

2. The adj. can then mean "actualising," Aesch. Eum., 382; in this sense it is commonly a divine attribute [3] meaning "mighty," [4] "efficacious" (cf. τέλος → 49, 7 ff.), esp. Zeus; Zeus the mightiest power of the mighty (the gods), Aesch. Suppl., 525 f.; Ζεῦ τέλειε, τὰς ἐμὰς εὐχὰς τέλει, Ag., 973 etc. On Ael. Arist. Or., 43, 31 (Keil) → 86, n. 7. It is used of gods and goddesses in this sense of "mighty," Aesch. Sept. c. Theb., 167; of Apollo who works lavishly, Theocr. Idyll., 25, 22. God is in no respect ἀργός (→ I, 452, 3 ff.); He is τέλειος (a play on "active"/"perfect"), i.e., He does all things, Corp. Herm., 11, 13.

3. Biologically "full-grown," "mature," e.g., sheep in Hdt., I, 183, 2, transf. animals often in the pap., cf., κάμηλος τελεία, BGU, I, 153, 15 and 33 (152 B.C.); of man, "adult," "mature," e.g., θυγατέρα... τέλιον [5] οὖσαν, BGU, IV, 1100, 9 f. (1st cent. B.C.) as

---

[2] Cf. Liddell-Scott, s.v., with examples from other sources.

[3] Cf. O. Höfer, Art. "Teleia, Teleios," Roscher, V, 254-9; S. Eitrem, Art. "Teleioi Theoi," Roscher, V, 259; H. Bolkestein, "Τέλος ὁ γάμος," Mededeelingen d. Koninklijke Akad. van Wetenschappen Afd. Letterkunde, Deel 76B (1933), 7-15.

[4] Transl. "authoritative" by M. A. Bayfield, "On Some Derivatives of τέλος," Class. Rev., 15 (1901), 446 f.; cf. ἀνὴρ τέλειος "master of the house," Aesch. Ag., 972; on this sense cf. E. Fraenkel, Aesch. Ag., II (1950), ad loc.

[5] I.e., τέλειον. The use of τέλειος or τέλεος for the fem. too is widespread. cf. Liddell-Scott, s.v. [Risch].

opp. to νήπιος, Philo Sobr., 9; Artemid. Onirocr., III, 27, in antithesis to childish play, III, 1; cf. the series τὸ βρέφος ... ὁ νεανίας, ὁ τέλειος ἀνήρ, Philo Cher., 114; as opp. to παιδίον, Plut. Quaest. Conv., V, 7, 1 (II, 680e); τέλειον γίνεσθαι, "to become full-grown," Cons. ad Apoll., 34 (II, 119e); the young Moses is τελειότερος than usual at his age, Philo Vit. Mos., I, 19.

4. Examples are sometimes quoted for the sense "belonging to dedication," "dedicated," 6, 7 but they do not really prove it. Thus τέλεοι τελεταί "perfect" rites (of philosophy) in Plat. Phaedr., 249c (→ IV, 808, n. 55) is used in a transf. sense like τέλεα (sc. μυστήρια), "supreme" mysteries (of love, in distinction to the first stages) in Symp., 210a. In context the command τέλει τελείαν τελετήν means "make the stone all-effective," Preis. Zaub., II, 12, 306 f.; the τέλειος λόγος is the "supreme," final 8 instruction or revelation, Corp. Herm., 9, 1. τέλειοι ἄνθρωποι have become "full men" 9 by understanding the κήρυγμα, being immersed in the νοῦς and receiving a share of knowledge, 4, 4 → IV, 811, 34 ff. 10 The equation of τέλειοι with οἱ γεγαμηκότες in Hesych., s.v.; Poll., III, 38 is also no help, for here τέλειος means "complete." Of the whole group only τέλος and esp. τελέω stand in any relation to the mysteries. Nor apart from allusions was the usage extensive in the pre-Chr. and NT age.

B. The Concept of the Perfect Man in Philosophy.

The formal understanding of τέλειος as in → 68, 13 ff. is limited ethically to the positive use in a value-system and links up with what is said in → 67, 30 ff. It is here that τέλειος takes on special significance for the Gk. understanding of man; the point is the total humanity and the full ἀρετή which are to be achieved. That is τέλεια whose τέλος σπουδαῖον is "worthwhile" and morally good; κατὰ γὰρ τὸ ἔχειν τὸ τέλος τέλεια, says Aristot. Metaph., IV, 16, p. 1021b, 23-25; things "which have a meaningful purpose" are thus τέλεια.

In content τέλειος is filled out variously.

1. For Plato 11 the τέλεος ... ἄνθρωπος is he who has attained φρόνησις, "firm and true views," insight and philosophical knowledge, and the goods which these things carry with them, Leg., II, 653a. How this perfection is reached we are told in Phaedr.: The man who by recollection of what he once saw in God's proximity presses on to the world of ideas and thus reaches up to true being, he alone is τέλεος, 249c; for the soul was truly τελέα before it acquired an earthly body, 246b-c. When Plat. describes the cosmos, the εἰκὼν τοῦ νοητοῦ θεὸς αἰσθητός, as τελεώτατος in Tim., 92c, or as the self-sufficient and most perfect God in 68e, this includes the idea of completeness, as elsewhere; the cosmos should be as perfect as possible seeing it consists of complete parts, 32d. Rather

---

6 It is not listed in the detailed art. in Liddell-Scott, s.v. Cf. Bauer, 5-7 as against Heinr. 1 K., 92-4 and others; Spicq, 218, n. 2. Cf. also Osnes, 36-38. du Plessis, 16-20 has an account of the debate.

7 Ref. is often made to Reitzenstein Hell. Myst., 338 f., but he is more cautious than many who quote him regarding the instances he adduces. Cf. U. Wilckens, Weisheit u. Torheit (1959), 54, who also ref. to → IV, 803, 19 ff., though τέλειος occurs there only → 808, n. 55; 811, 34 ff. On τέλειος in Gnosticism cf. Wilckens, 53-59; H. M. Schenke, Der Gott "Mensch" in d. Gnosis (1962), 57 f.

8 It relates to the νοῦς → IV, 957, 5 ff. Cf. Reitzenstein Hell. Myst., 339.

9 Ibid., 338, cf. 339.

10 Of other instances quoted in favour of τέλειος as a tt. in the mysteries τέλειαι καθάρσεις in Philo Vit. Mos., II, 196 means perfect rather than dedicatory purifications, while in Deus Imm., 132 the Jewish priest is cleansed and unblemished (not dedicated). du Plessis, 81-85 deals with some passages from Hipp. Ref. but concludes that "the basic notion is rather more the perfection of being," 85.

11 Osnes, 41-46.

different, however, are statements about the τέλειον in the ethical sphere. The ref. here is to the absolutely good as the τέλεον, Phileb., 61a. This is intrinsically the good, the ἱκανὸν καὶ τέλεον; it needs nothing else; it is "perfect," 66b; 67a. Phileb. is written to show that this cannot at any rate be desire.

2. In Aristot. [12] the ref. is to the τελεία ἀρετή which is present when an ethical choice is made μετὰ φρονήσεως, Eth. M., II, 3, p. 1200a, 3 f. φρόνησις for its part is one of the virtues which is τελεία only in conjunction with others, line 9; τὸ γὰρ τέλειον ζητοῦμεν ἀγαθόν, ἡ δὲ φρόνησις μόνη οὖσα οὐ τέλειον, I, 2, p. 1184a, 36 f. Thus righteousness can be called τελεία only in a specific sense and not an absolute οὐχ ἁπλῶς, since on the one side it is not just practised by man in relation to himself but also in relation to others, and on the other it is the employment of perfect ἀρετή, Eth. Nic., V, 3, p. 1129b, 25-33. Since ἀρετή is not a norm outside man but what is at issue is the actualising of the ἀρετή essential to man, the question of the τέλειον stands above that of τελεία ἀρετή. τέλειον in the abs. is what is chosen for its own sake, and this is εὐδαιμονία, I, 5, p. 1097b, 33 f.; it is τέλειον δή τι ... καὶ αὔταρκες and hence τῶν πρακτῶν ... τέλος, p. 1097b, 20 f. τέλειον (opp. ἀτελές) is that in possession of which we need nothing more. It is the τέλος τέλειον, the good absolutely, Eth. M., I, 2, p. 1184a, 8-14, which is the same as εὖ πράττειν καὶ εὖ ζῆν, I, 3, p. 1184b, 8 f., which consists ἐν τῷ κατὰ τὰς ἀρετὰς ζῆν, I, 4, p. 1184b, 29 f. The fact that the content of the term varies may be seen in the def. of the state in another passage: "The polis is the fellowship of families and localities in a full and self-sufficient life ... and that is to live happily," Polit., III, 9, p. 1280b, 40 - p. 1281a, 2; cf. p. 1280b, 33-35. On τέλειος in the Peripatetics, Stob. Ecl., II, 131 f.

3. Stoicism [13] develops an Aristotelian principle when it stresses the fact that only he who has all the moral talents ἀρετάς is τέλειος, and only the deed which accords with all the ἀρεταί, in which they all co-operate, is τελεία, Plut. Stoic. Rep., 27 (II, 1046e, f). The σπουδαῖος (→ VII, 560, 39 ff.), i.e., the Stoic who uses the ἀρεταί, lacks nothing for the τέλειος βίος, he has all ἀγαθά, Stob. Ecl., II, 99, 6; 100, 7 f., 11 f. On τέλειον καθῆκον → III, 439, 6 ff. [14]

4. In Philo [15] one sees different influences even in the use of the adj. in the teaching on values. With the Stoa Philo can distinguish the perfect virtues which only the τέλειος has from the μέσα τῶν καθηκόντων, Sacr. AC, 43. He can describe φρόνησις, ἀνδρεία, δικαιοσύνη as τέλεια ἀγαθά, 37, or the καλόν as τέλειον ἀγαθόν, Poster. C., 95. But then with Aristot. Eth. Nic., X, 7, p. 1177a, 17 f. he can call academic vision, or philosophy, the most perfect good, Op. Mund., 54. Again, with Plat. (→ 79, 29 ff.) he can call the vision of true being the most perfect thing, Ebr., 83 ("Israel" means the vision of God, 82). But the most perfect good can also be ἐγκράτεια in Spec. Leg., I, 149 or καρτερία, which grants the perfect good of ἀφθαρσία while desire brings death, in Agric., 100; the τέλειον ἀγαθόν is the ἀγαθότης in whose train are the individual virtues, Migr. Abr., 36 f. The σοφία which comes from God and is revealed by Him (Migr. Abr., 38-42) is the τελεία ὁδός which leads to God, Deus Imm., 142 f. (→ V, 64, 9 ff.). ἐλπίς is a perfect good as the expectation of ἀγαθά, for it binds thought to God, Poster. C., 26; but so, too, is πίστις as the gift of true hope, Migr. Abr., 44. If already one sees here how Philo's system of values is controlled by his religious thought, this is esp. clear when he speaks of the perfect good in the strict sense. Here God is τὸ τέλειον... καὶ πρὸς ἀλήθειαν ἀγαθόν, Gig., 45 (though this saying does not suffice for an

---

[12] Or in his school; Aristot.'s authorship of Eth. M. is open to question.
[13] Osnes, 47-54 deals mainly with Epict. and Sen. in his section on Stoicism. In gen. cf. M. Pohlenz, Die Stoa, I (1948), 123-131.
[14] Cf. on this A. Bonhöffer, Die Ethik d. Stoikers Epict. (1894), 212-216.
[15] W. Völker, Fortschritt u. Vollendung bei Philo v. Alex. (1938), 318-348; Osnes, 54-60.

understanding of the OT κύριος predicate, as Philo here emphasises on Lv. 18:6); God is τὸ πρῶτον ἀγαθὸν καὶ τελεώτατον (cf. Spec. Leg., I, 277), by whom τὰ ἐπὶ μέρους ἀγαθά are sent, Decal., 81. Himself the good, He is full of ἀγαθὰ τέλεια (Spec. Leg., II, 53) and the Giver of "perfect" goods, Leg. All., III, 135. From the standpt. of human conduct the "perfect" good is θεοσέβεια (opp. φιλαυτία), Congr., 130, ὁσιότης, Sacr. AC, 10, μνήμη θεοῦ, Spec. Leg., II, 171. To live as pleases God is τελεώτατον as compared with being just and perfect; it is the crown of supreme εὐδαι-μονία, Deus Imm., 118. The Mosaic Law means that εὐδαιμονεῖν comes through the deployment (→ 70, 11 ff.) of "perfect" virtue, Agric., 157. The use of virtue is happiness rather than mere possession, and it is impossible unless God makes it fruitful, Det. Pot. Ins., 60. God plants virtues in the soul along with the corresponding deeds, and He thus leads the soul to perfect felicity, Plant., 37. On the other hand, with the perception of eternal wisdom God with no effort on man's part suddenly and unexpectedly grants him a treasure of perfect happiness, Deus Imm., 92. The pinnacle of the "most perfect" felicity for man is ultimately God, Plant., 66. He is at any rate the Father of τελεία φύσις, "perfect" being, who sows εὐδαιμονεῖν in the souls of men, Leg. All., III, 219. To become a τελειοτάτη φύσις is the goal of men, Cher., 9, cf. Som., I, 59; God's φύσις is τελειοτάτη in the abs., Cher., 86. He who possesses "wholly perfect" φύσις is free of every πάθος, every passionate emotion, Ebr., 135. The τέλειος has removed θυμός and the ἡδοναί from his soul — in distinction from the προκόπτων, [16] Leg. All., III, 140, cf. 144 and 147. ὁ τέλειος τελείαν ἀπάθειαν ἀεὶ μελετᾷ, 131, ὅλα τὰ πάθη δι' ὅλων ἀπέκοψεν, 134: "The perfect man must be pure in word and deed and his whole conduct," Vit. Mos., II, 150. The one who lives in full purity already receives in the body a share in eternal life, Spec. Leg., II, 262 (on Ex. 20:12). With the negative statements we find sonorous positive ones as well. The τέλειος regards the ethically beautiful alone as a good, Sobr., 15; all the notes of the good sound together in him, thought, word and deed being in harmony, Poster. C., 88. He will be moved of himself to virtuous action without needing instruction, Leg. All., III, 144; cf. I, 94. Finally Philo, interpreting Lv. 16:17, ventures to say that "the perfect man is neither God nor man, he stands between unbegotten and corruptible modes (the progressing man stands between the living and the dead)," Som., II, 234; the perfect mode which is constant in virtues stands closest to the divine δύναμις, Abr., 26. But such statements are greatly qualified by others. First, the perfect man, having come into being (unlike God), does not escape error, Spec. Leg., I, 252; "we" do not belong to the τελειότεροι whose nourishment is the whole word of God (Dt. 8:3), Leg. All., III, 176. Philo includes himself among the ἀτελεῖς, 207. None but God is τέλειος in any matter, Rer. Div. Her., 121. The perfect is not to be found in anything created except by the working of God's grace, Plant., 93. Hence he may be regarded as τέλειος ἀνήρ who takes living and effective note of the ordinances of the Torah, Spec. Leg., IV, 140 (on Dt. 6:7; 11:19), who is taught in the truth as it is declared in God's revelation, I, 63, cf. 65. When outstanding OT figures were described by the adj. τέλειος Philo was probably influenced to some degree by the Jewish understanding. Gn. 6:9 suggested this for Noah; this was taken to mean that he possessed all virtues and constantly exercised them, Abr., 34. To the "perfect" Abraham — he was this after the change of name (Gn. 17:5), Leg. All., III, 244 — God gives the comprehensive promise of Gn. 22:16 f. (Leg. All., III, 203). The attribute also occurs in connection with the "leading" of Isaac to God (Gn. 22), Deus Imm., 4; a fuller statement is that Abraham's φύσις was τελειοτέρα ἢ κατὰ ἄνθρωπον, Virt., 217. With ref. to Isaac in interpretation of Gn. 21:16 the conjunction of "perfect in virtues" and "mature" plays a role, Sobr., 8 f. Moses is τέλειος in Leg. All., II, 91; he is the "wholly perfect" Moses in Ebr., 94 as compared with the "perfect" Aaron, Det. Pot. Ins., 132. He is ἀνὴρ τὰ πάντα... τελειότατος, Vit. Mos., I, 1, "the perfect" sage,

---

[16] Cf. G. Stählin, "Fortschritt u. Wachstum," *Festgabe f. J. Lortz*, II (1958), 13-25; on the group προκοπ- and τέλειος in Philo esp. 18-20 (→ VI, 709, 26 ff.).

Leg. All., III, 140, the "most perfect" of the prophets, Decal., 175, the νοῦς τέλειος, Agric., 80; he is τελεία ψυχή which went to God directly apart from any visible event, Sacr. AC, 10. In the formally traditional [17] ref. to the τελειότατος κόσμος in Op. Mund., 14, cf. 9; Plant., 6 and 131; Rer. Div. Her., 199; Conf. Ling., 87 (qualified here: the most perfect of sensorily perceptible things), Philo was perhaps influenced by Gn. 1. [18]

C. τέλειος and Equivalents in the Septuagint and the Dead Sea Scrolls.

1. In the LXX [19] (all instances given) the word means "unblemished," "undivided," "complete," "whole"; it is thus used esp. for שָׁלֵם, תָּמִים and cognates. [20] For this τέλειος [21] occurs esp. with καρδία (elsewhere πλήρης → VI, 284, 37 f.), so of the heart which is "undivided" πρὸς κύριον or μετὰ κυρίου in exclusive worship, without idolatry, wholly obedient to God's will, 3 Βασ. 8:61; 11:4, (10B); 15:3, 14; 1 Ch. 28:9 (only here with ἐν καρδίᾳ, elsewhere in predicate clauses); of "total" carrying away, Jer. 13:19 (→ n. 20); the whole offering, Ju. 20:26; 21:4B (sc. θυσίας, A in both vv. σωτηρίου). For תָּמִים it is used of the people which should serve Yahweh wholly and undividedly τέλειος ἔσῃ ἐναντίον κυρίου, Dt. 18:13; of Noah who was "blameless" in his generation (par. δίκαιος) and pleased God, Gn. 6:9; [22] cf.: Νωε εὑρέθη τέλειος δίκαιος צדיק נמצא תמים Sir. 44:17; gen. of individuals, 2 Βασ. 22:26. We also find the sense "without bodily defect," the Passover lamb for תָּמִים, Ex. 12:5, the beloved for תָּם, Cant. 5:2; 6:9, "infallible" oracles (?) for plur. of תֹּם (→ II, 61, 31 f.) 2 Εσδρ. 2:63. For תַּכְלִית "fulness" it is used of "total" hate in ψ 138:22, while it means "practised" for the מֵבִין "master" (opp. μανθανόντων) in 1 Ch. 25:8. With no HT it occurs only in Wis. 9:6 in debate with the Gk. attitude: "If anyone were perfect in man's judgment it would be of no account if he lacked the wisdom of God," cf. Philo (→ 70, 40 ff.; 71, 12 ff.). The sense "dedicated" does not occur. The adv. means "wholly," "fully" in 2 Macc. 12:42; 3 Macc. 3:26; 7:22; Jdt. 11:6.

---

[17] Cf. Plat. (→ 69, 32 ff.) and εἷς καὶ μόνος καὶ τέλειος οὗτος οὐρανός ἐστιν, Aristot. Cael., I, 9, p. 279a, 10 f.

[18] For the concept of perfection in Gnosticism cf. du Plessis, 85-93 and esp. Osnes, 64-82; → n. 7.

[19] du Plessis, 94-103; Osnes, 24-27, 107-111, on שָׁלֵם and תָּמִים 33-36, 87-94 and C. Edlund, "Das Auge d. Einfalt," Acta Seminarii Neotest. Upsaliensis, 19 (1952), 28-79; W. Trilling, "Das wahre Israel," Stud. z. Alten u. Neuen Testament³ (1964), 194.

[20] תָּמִים and cognates are the original of τέλειος only 7 times. This group is almost always the original of ἄμωμος (50 times). τέλειος is practically never found in Ps. or Prv. (only ψ 138:22 → line 22), nor does it occur in the prophets except at Jer. 13:19, for שָׁלֵם. שָׁלֵם occurs 27 times in the HT but only 4 times in 1 K. and once at 1 Ch. 28:9 is it transl. τέλειος; on the other hand it is 7 times transl. πλήρης → VI, 283, 35 f. The other instances are divided among various Gk. words [Bertram].

[21] Cf. τελειόω (→ 80, 31 f.) for the verb שׁלם. Other equivalents of שׁלם have no ethical or religious significance.

[22] Cf. εὐαρέστει ἐναντίον ἐμοῦ καὶ γίνου ἄμεμπτος, Gn. 17:1; δίκαιος... ἀνὴρ καὶ ἄμεμπτος, Job 12:4 (in both cases ἄμεμπτος for תָּמִים); cf. 1:8; 9:20 (in both cases ἄμεμπτος for תָּם). ἄμωμος is common for תָּמִים (→ IV, 830, 27 ff.) but mostly it has a different sense (though cf. ψ 17:24). δίκαιος (adv.) occurs for תָּמִים only at Prv. 28:18; ἐν εὐθύτητι Jos. 24:14; Sir. 7:6; on ὅσιος → V, 491, 21 f. Other LXX transl. of תָּמִים are of no particular relevance here. Edlund, op. cit., 51-61 discusses the rendering by ἁπλοῦς, esp. in 'A and Σ (some 15 times), 61; ἁπλότης, common in Test. XII (also in the phrase ἁπλότης τῆς καρδίας), he sees as a transl. of תֹּם "totality," 78 f., details, 62-78. On the OT cf. Schnackenburg, 68 f.

2. In the Dead Sea Scrolls [23] תמים in 1 QM 7:5 ref. to him who is "without defect" in spirit and body, cf. Cant. → 72, 20 f.; אנשי התמים in 1 QS 8:20 [24] or the mere adj. in 3:3 denotes members of the group; this [25] is a house of "totality" and truth, 8:9; cf. 9:6. For the rest תמים occurs in combinations denoting the walk, these being mostly found word for word in the OT, esp. Ps. and Prv.: תמימי דרך 1 QM 14:7; 1 QH 1:36; 1 QS 4:22 (or תמימי הדרך 1 QSa 1:28), cf. Ps. 119:1; Prv. 11:20, התהלך תמים 1 QS 1:8; 1 QSb 5:22; Damasc. 2:15 (3:2), הלך תמים 1 QS 2:2; 3:9; 9:19; 1 QSb 1:2, cf. Ps. 15:2 (LXX ἄμωμος); Prv. 28:18 (LXX δικαίως), הלך בתמים 1 QS 9:6, 8, cf. Ps. 84:11 (LXX ἐν ἀκακίᾳ), [26] הלך בתמים דרך 1 QS 8:18, 21; 9:9, cf. Ps. 101:6, (ב)תמים דרך, 1 QS 8:10; 9:5, cf. Ps. 101:2; [27] with suffix 1 QS 9:2. A blameless walk is possible only acc. to the statutes of the community which were revealed to it as exposition of the Torah, 1 QS 2:2; 3:9 f.; 9:9, 19, cf. also 8:1 f.: "Without blemish in all that has been revealed on the basis of the whole Torah." He who belongs to the group but does not walk in the "entirety" of the way, intentionally omitting a word from the "whole" commandment, [28] may not participate in the fellowship of the pure, 8:17 f.; cf. 8:20-22; 9:1 f. Walking "perfectly" means "full observance" of the right norm; [29] walking "without blemish" is not deviating to the right hand or the left, not transgressing one of the words of God, 3:10 f. The word obviously stands in some relation to the Qumran concept of purity; the community of the "faultless" is also that of the pure, → n. 24, 26. The contexts in which תמים appears in the Qumran writings show clearly that the ref. is to total fulfilment of God's will, keeping all the rules of the community. שֶׁלֵם for LXX τέλειος occurs in the Scrolls (as in 1 Ch. 28:9) in the expression לב שלם ...ב [30] "with... undivided heart," 1 QH 16:7, 17, cf. ἐν τελείᾳ καρδίᾳ μεταμελουμένους καὶ πορευομένους ἐν πάσαις ταῖς ἐντολαῖς αὐτοῦ, Test. Jud. 23:5 (the only instance of τέλειος in Test. XII).

D. τέλειος in the New Testament.

1. In Greek thought and usage τέλειος often means "totality" — 67, 30 ff. This justifies the rendering of corresponding Hebrew terms by τέλειος, primarily in Mt. The one who does the "whole" will of God (→ lines 19 ff.) is תָּמִים; the heart which is "undivided" in obedience to God (→ 72, 11 ff.; line 21 ff.) is שָׁלֵם. [31] The attitude

---

[23] du Plessis, 104-115; F. Nötscher, Gotteswege u. Menschenwege in d. Bibel u. in Qumran (1958), 51, 77, 80, 82; 84-88; Rigaux, 237-240; on Damasc. cf. Osnes, 105-7; on Rabb. lit., 94-104.

[24] Cf. אנשי תמים (ה)קדש Damasc. 20:2, 5, 7 (9:30, 32, 33); Rigaux, 238.

[25] Not a leading group in it, as du Plessis, 107 thinks.

[26] To walk בתמים קדש, in "full" holiness, Damasc. 7:5 (8:21).

[27] No man has a pure walk תום דרך (cf. Prv. 13:6) if God does not help him thereto by the Spirit, 1 QH 4:30-32. Only material on תמים is adduced → lines 1 ff.; cognates are used similarly, cf. the bibl. → n. 23.

[28] Cf. H. Bardtke, Die Handschriftenfunde am Toten Meer, I (1952); II (1958); but he usually has "perfect" and only occasionally "pious," "faultless," etc. for תמים.

[29] Not works of supererogation. G. Barth, "Das Gesetzesverständnis des Evangelisten Mt.," Überlieferung u. Auslegung im Mt.-Ev. (ed. G. Bornkamm, G. Barth, and H. J. Held[3] [1963]), 91 f. speaks of a "super" contained in the Qumran תמים, but while this is correct historically it does not characterise the understanding of the group itself.

[30] In several Qumran works the word שלם also means "to complete," "to supplement," "to replace," "to repent," "to repay."

[31] H. Ljungman, "Das Gesetz erfüllen," Lunds Univ. Årskrift, I, 50, 6 (1954), 89-91 on Mt. 5:48 pts. out that תָּמִים at Dt. 18:13 is rendered שלים in Tg.O.

behind the question: "What lack I yet?" (Mt. 19:20),[32] which is based formally on what precedes (ταῦτα πάντα ἐφύλαξα), is overcome by the τέλειον εἶναι (v. 21), which materially includes both. The rich young ruler is not undivided in relation to God. "Being whole" manifests itself in concrete behaviour; to be undivided in relation to God includes detaching oneself from that which separates from God, → 72, 11 ff.[33] The context in each case supplies the reference. In Mt. 5:48[34] the "whole" applies to conduct in relation to men. God is fully "undivided" in this → V, 991, 19 ff. He pours out His blessings on the πονηροί (→ VI, 558, 11 ff.), the ἄδικοι (→ I, 151, 25 ff.), v. 45. As[35] God is unrestricted in His goodness, so according to v. 48 the disciples of Jesus should be[36] "total" in their love, bringing even their enemies (→ II, 813, 29 ff.; VI, 316, 26 ff.) within its compass, v. 44 f.[37]

2. In the Catholic Epistles, too, τέλειος means "whole," "complete," thus plainly in Jm. 1:4 par. to ὁλόκληρος (→ III, 767, 21 ff.) and ἐν μηδενὶ λειπόμενος. The man is "whole"[38] who does the "whole" work, and the ὑπομονή in which faith works itself out (v. 3; → IV, 588, 17 ff.) in trials (→ II, 258, 17 ff.) is not to be (ἐχέτω)[39] without its "total" work. The man who is proved by faith in sufferings is not thereby dispensed from the "whole" work, i.e., from "total" obedience;[40] he himself is whole only with the whole work. That man does the whole work who continually (→ IV, 578, 19 ff.) takes such note of the full, "entire" law of liberty (Jm. 1:25; → II, 502, 7 ff.; V, 815, 22 ff.) that he does it (→ VI, 478, 37 ff.); doing

---

[32] Cf. "one thing thou lackest" in Mk. 10:21; Lk. 18:22; it is not by chance that the phrase is put on the lips of the rich young ruler in Mt.

[33] Here the detachment is primarily from possessions; this is the "critical point" for the ruler, Osnes, 127. v. 24 f. shows that it has paradigmatical significance.

[34] In Lk. 6:36 (→ V, 161, 30 ff.) the application is made directly. On the 2 passages cf. J. Dupont, "'Soyez parfaits' (Mt. 5:48), 'soyez miséricordieux' (Lk. 6:36)," Sacra Pagina, 2 (ed. J. Coppens, A. Descamps, E. Massaux, Biblioth. Ephemeridum Theolog. Lovaniensium, 12/13 [1959]), 150-162. On τέλειος in Mt. cf. Barth, op. cit., 89-93, 95 f.; Osnes, 115-162; Trilling, op. cit., 192 f., 194-196; G. Kretschmar, "Ein Beitrag zur Frage nach dem Ursprung frühchristlicher Askese," ZThK, 61 (1964), 27-67, esp. 53-59; Schnackenburg, 70-81; H. Braun, Spätjüd.-häretischer u. frühchr. Radikalismus, II (1957), 54 and 56 (on Mt. 19:21), also 43, n. 1, where he discusses the distinction from Qumran; E. Fuchs, "Die vollkommene Gewissheit," Nt.liche Stud. f. R. Bultmann, Beih. z. ZNW, 21 (1954), 130-136 on Mt. 5:48. Further bibl. in H. Braun, "Qumran u. d. NT," ThR, NF, 28 (1962), 97-234, esp. 114 and 139. Acc. to M. Black, An Aramaic Approach to the Gospels and Acts[2] (1954), a paranomasia between ἀσπάζομαι/ שְׁלַם and τέλειος/ שְׁלִים lies behind Mt. 5:47 f.

[35] vv. 43-48 are a self-contained passage; v. 48 belongs only to this and not to vv. 21-47 gen., though this is concerned with wholeness too, cf. Osnes, 122-125; Trilling, 195 f.

[36] This is the pt. of the fut. ind.; we have here the legal language of the OT, Bl.-Debr. § 362, Lv. 19:2 is an OT par. only formally (on this cf. 1 Pt. 1:16); on τέλειος ἔση ἐναντίον κυρίου in Dt. 18:13 cf. Gn. 17:1 (→ n. 22; 73, 8 f.). In Midr. Ps. on 119:1 Dt. 18:13 is taken to mean "as he (sc. Yahweh) is without stain," Osnes, 103 f.

[37] περισσόν in v. 46 f. does not involve anything above the norm; love for ἀγαπῶντες and ἀδελφοί is not an achievement in the context. περισσόν means "the unusual," → VI, 61, 22 ff.

[38] Schl. Jk. on 1:4 recalls the Rabb. צַדִּיק גָּמוּר but differentiates Jm. 1:4 from it; on the concept → II, 186, 12 ff.; in the Rabb. it is primarily negative and means "free from defects," Str.-B., II, 210, cf. bSanh., 99a. Cf. also Str.-B., IV, 1231.

[39] Jm. is not saying that perseverance effects the full work. The similarity of terms should not mislead us into interpreting Jm. 1:3 f. in the light of R. 5:3-5. F. Mussner, Der Jk., Herders Theol. Komm., 13 (1964), ad loc. speaks of an "eschatological perfectionism" in τέλειος, ὁλόκληρος and ὑπομονή.

[40] There is naturally a material connection with 2:14-17.

is the point of the passage. When Jm. speaks of the whole law which grants freedom when it is done, [41] he undoubtedly has especially in view the νόμος as it is summarised in the law of love (→ 60, 6 ff.; → IV, 1081, 25 ff.; 1082, 2 ff.; VI, 293, 1 ff.; 305, 3 ff.). Yet he is not thinking only of this. For him the whole man is also (3:2) the one who has himself fully (→ III, 338, 4 ff.) in rein, v. 3. The essence of this self-control is control of the tongue (→ I, 721, 2 ff.) or the word, which for its part has such decisive effects, vv. 6-12. Again, the τέλειος ἀνήρ does not vacillate ἐν λόγῳ, 3:2, though Jm. recognises that no one does the whole will of God (πολλὰ γὰρ πταίομεν ἅπαντες). The series of statements shows how important the word τέλειος is for Jm. in his own sense. What is "whole" and "without fault" comes from God, Jm. 1:17; [42] hence temptation cannot have its origin in Him, → VII, 760, 26 ff.

"Full," "unlimited" love, "which lacks nothing of its totality," leaves no room for fear, 1 Jn. 4:18. This is said generally of the love (cf. v. 19a) in which the Christian has fellowship with God (v. 16b). But it is plain that this love comes from God (v. 16a, 19b) and that abiding in this love is abiding in the love of God (v. 16b); the love of the Christian is a putting of this love into effect (vv. 19-21). Hence v. 18, too, is probably referring in the first instance to the love which has come from God [43] in the sending of the Son (cf. v. 10), which drives out the fear of judgment (v. 17) that is only too well-founded in the light of ἁμαρτίαι (v. 10), and which will not, of course, remain without an answer → 81, 29 ff.

The command to be "completely" (cf. ἐν πᾶσιν, 2 Tm. 4:5) sober in 1 Pt. 1:13 is ethically related and eschatologically grounded (as an adv. only here).

It should not be overlooked that the use of τέλειος in the sense expounded was made possible by a formally similar use of the word in non-biblical Greek, → 67, 30 ff.

3. In the Pauline corpus the meaning "whole" is suggested at 1 C. 13:10 by the antithesis to ἐκ μέρους. Spiritual gifts — γνῶσις [44] and prophecy are mentioned — do not give full knowledge [45] of God → IV, 596, 22 ff. This will be granted to the Christian only with the immediacy of face-to-face, v. 12. Col. 4:12 is referring to the solid position occupied by Christians as those who are "whole," "complete" (par. πεπληροφορημένοι → VI, 285, 10 ff.) in the total will of God (cf. 1:9, a

---

[41] Cf. Schl. Jk. on 1:25. For explanation in terms of 1 QS 10:6, 8, 11 cf. E. Stauffer, "Das 'Gesetz der Freiheit' in d. Ordensregel v. Jericho," ThLZ, 77 (1952), 527-532, cf. → V, 815, n. 13. For more details W. Nauck, "Lex insculpta (חרות חוק) in der Sektenschr.," ZNW, 46 (1955), 138-140; cf. M. Weise, Kultzeiten u. kultischer Bundesschluss in d. "Ordensregel" vom Toten Meer (1961), 49 f. חֵרוּת (Ex. 32:16 of the Decalogue) is read here by P. Wernberg-Møller, The Manual of Discipline (1957), 144, n. 19; Bardtke, I, ad loc.; M. Burrows, The Dead Sea Scrolls (1957), ad loc. and others; cf. 1 QH 12:3: "Thou hast engraved חרתה on them the covenant of thy salvation with the stylus of life" (Bardtke, II, 226). Jos. Ap., 2, 178 speaks of the νόμοι engraved in souls.

[42] Hardly a regular hexameter, nor intended as such; on the possibilities cf. W. Hatch, "Note on the Hexameter in Jm. 1:17," JBL, 28 (1909), 149-151. On the saying cf. Philo Leg. All., III, 134 f.: The τέλεια ἀγαθά which God gives the τέλειος enable him without effort to detach himself entirely from the passions.

[43] Osnes, 254 f.

[44] The ref. in 1 C. 13:8 is to the λόγος γνώσεως which is grouped with other charismata in 12:8, cf. the list in 13:2.

[45] γινώσκω in the broader, fuller sense; prophecy, too, mediates only γινώσκειν ἐκ μέρους; the γνῶσις received by the pneumatic now is not τελεία.

statement about the content of intercession for the community, → VI, 291, 12 ff.). Yet in the main the feeling of antiquity (→ V, 642, 28 ff.) was that only an "adult" can be a "full" man; hence these senses can overlap in Paul. Thus in Col. 1:28 he describes it as the goal of his preaching and teaching to present every man before God or Christ (→ V, 840, 19 ff.) as "complete," "full-grown," under the direction of Christ and His cross and resurrection; [46] the "whole" man is the one who lives in the power of the cross and resurrection of Jesus. In accordance with the previous sentence τέλειος seems sometimes to be used explicitly in antithesis to νήπιος etc. (→ 68, 41 ff.); formally this is especially clear in 1 C. 14:20: παιδία... ταῖς φρεσίν [47] — ταῖς... φρεσὶν τέλειοι. [48] Concerning tongues the judgment of those addressed is compared to the immature thinking and imagining of a child [49] and the judgment of mature Christians is set in contrast to it. On Eph. 4:13 → VI, 302, 22 ff. [50] Since the reference here is to the judgment of the τέλειοι, a similar understanding seems natural in Phil. 3:15: [51] mature Christians judge in the way set forth in 3:3-14. [52] Nor is this understanding to be ruled out at 1 C. 2:6 [53] even though Paul is here adopting a term of his adversaries. [54, 55] The mature are those who understand the message of the cross, namely, as [56] the wisdom of God, and who embrace it in faith, → IV, 819, 12 ff. [57] There seems no reason to suppose that in R. 12:2 Paul is adopting the concept of the τέλειον, along with the ἀγαθόν (→ I, 11, 15ff.), as we find it in the Greek value-system, → 79, 19 ff. [58] In any case the word is governed here by the preceding τὸ θέλημα τοῦ θεοῦ. [59] Knowledge of the "perfect," "entire" will

---

[46] Cf. F. Neugebauer, In Christus (1961), 103, 177.

[47] Cf. τῇ κακίᾳ νηπιάζετε. The idea of moral immaturity is implied.

[48] Philip V of Macedonia showed himself to be, not a παιδίον νήπιον, but a τέλειος ἀνήρ, Polyb., 5, 29, 2. There is a chiasmus in both cases.

[49] Cf. 1 C. 13:11; → IV, 919, 8 ff. Those who regard good fortune as constant are νήπιοι, children with no understanding or discernment, Philo Leg. Gaj., 1.

[50] "Full-grown," "total," acc. to S. Hanson, "The Unity of the Church in the NT," Acta Seminarii Neotest. Upsaliensis, 14 (1949), 159, cf. 158-160. Further bibl. Rigaux, 251, n. 2. On the Gnostic view in H. Schlier, Christus u. d. Kirche im Eph. (1930), 27-35 cf. → II, 943, 7 ff.; on the history of the interpretation of τέλειος in Paul in the light of Gnosticism, du Plessis, 20-32.

[51] "Arrivés à l'âge d'homme," Spicq, 216.

[52] There is no trace of a dialectical tension between τετελείωμαι in v. 12 and τέλειος in v. 15; cf. W. Lütgert, "Die Vollkommenen im Phil. u. d. Enthusiasten in Thessalonich," BFTh, 13, 6 (1909), 17-23; here the apostle's "perfection" is seen in his steadily pressing on to the goal, 23. It is not to be ruled out that Paul was perhaps using a term current in Philippi.

[53] Independently of 3:1 f., though children are contrasted with the pneumatics here, → n. 55.

[54] These might thus style themselves full Christians or full men. Paul could also be using the term in the latter sense, though with a different view of what constitutes a "full" man.

[55] Materially, of course, τέλειος means here the same as πνευματικός, Spicq, 217; Osnes, 173-5; Wilckens, op. cit., 53. The message of the cross is indeed accessible only to pneumatics, 1 C. 2:10-13.

[56] W. Grundmann attempts to establish a distinction between Paul's preaching of the cross and his preaching of wisdom, "Die ΝΗΠΙΟΙ in d. urchr. Paränese," NTSt, 5 (1958/59), 188-205, esp. 191.

[57] Wilckens, 53 and 60 transl. "perfect" but interprets τέλειος in 1 C. 2:6 by Gnostic mystery terminology, 54, cf. 53-60. Bauer, 11 has "ripened."

[58] Grammatically τὸ ἀγαθὸν κτλ. can be taken as an attribute of τὸ θέλημα... cf. Ltzm., Mi. R., ad loc., though they do not transl. attributively, Dihle thinks only an attributive understanding is possible.

[59] Cf. materially Philo Deus Imm., 118, which is shaped by bibl. thought, → 71, 6 ff.

of God [60] in the concrete situation is developed by renewal (→ III, 453, 21 ff.) of the power of judgment through the Holy Spirit.

4. In Hb. a distinction is made in 5:14 between initial doctrines (→ VII, 687, 8 ff.) for νήπιοι and the full fare for τέλειοι (cf. 5:12 - 6:1), for the "full-grown," who have received the λόγος δικαιοσύνης, instruction regarding the will of God (→ II, 198, 15 f.) and who through the ensuing exercising of the power of moral discernment have the ability to judge between good and evil. [61] In 9:11 τέλειος refers to the heavenly sanctuary (→ VII, 375, 22 ff.). It is more perfect than the earthly and provisional temple, in which no full purging from sins can be effected → 83, 1 ff. τέλειος is mainly a value term in this use.

5. As shown, the sense of "dedicated" along the lines of a supposed mystery-usage (→ 69, 6 ff. with n. 6-10) [62] is neither directly attested nor even presupposed in the NT. But neither does τέλειος denote here "the perfect (man)" in the sense of an ethics which grounds the concept in humanity, → 79, 19 ff. Plainly the meaning "complete," "whole," controlled the usage in Mt. (→ 73, 27 ff.) and the Catholic Epistles (→ 74, 12 ff.), τέλειος being parallel to certain Hebrew adjectives (→ 72, 9 ff.; 73, 19 ff.). [63] It should not be forgotten that this use does find very formal parallels in the Greek sphere (→ 67, 30 ff.), even, in part, to the point of some philosophical statements. In the other NT Epistles, esp. in the Pauline corpus, we find alongside this use of τέλειος especially the meaning "mature" (→ 76, 3 ff.), which initially is not far from that of "whole," "complete." One does not find in the NT any understanding of the adjective in terms of a gradual advance of the Christian to moral perfection [64] nor in terms of a two-graded ideal of ethical perfection. Totality is demanded of the Christian in acts too.

---

[60] εὐάρεστον then denotes what is well-pleasing to God, cf. Eph. 5:10 and does not, like προσφιλῆ in Phil. 4:8, relate to general judgment; it is certainly defined in a Chr. way in Col. 3:20. Cf. Wis. 9:10: The wisdom sent by God teaches what is well-pleasing to God. That (or he) is εὐάρεστος with which (whom) God is pleased, which (who) is right to Him, e.g., Enoch in Wis. 4:10; εὐαρεστέω is used in LXX for a term which denotes action (→ I, 455, 20 ff.; 457, 19 ff.). It occurs sometimes outside the Bible in a long list of terms describing the ἀγαθόν acc. to the Stoic view, Cl. Al. Prot., VI, 72, 2; Strom., V, 110, 3; Eus. Praep. Ev., 13, 13, 37 (the author supposedly Cleanthes); here man is the measure of what is pleasing. But in context one need not think of the judgment of others (cf. Phil. 4:8) but only one's own, what is pleasing to "me."

[61] Cf. H. P. Owen, "The 'Stages of Ascent' in Hb. 5:11 - 6:3," NTSt, 3 (1956/57), 243-253: the mature are to be this in order to be able to receive solid nourishment, 244; three stages are distinguished, of which that of the τέλειοι is the ethical-practical, the third the religious-theoretical. In reality ethical consolidation leads to ripeness for the λόγος δυσερμήνευτος, v. 11. The distinction in Hb. 5:11 - 6:3 is in fact hortatory. The author presents lofty teaching of the νήπιοι, 5:10 f. He thus intends 5:11-14 to be taken as a summons to maturity, → 79, 8 f.

[62] H. Preisker, Das Ethos d. Urchr. (1949), 129-134, though he sees connections with תמים, advocates in the main an eschatological NT understanding of τέλειος in the sense of control by the telos, the end or goal. This is probably a modern etymologoumenon.

[63] Cf. more recently G. Wagner, "Das religionsgesch. Problem v. R.6:1-11," AbhThANT, 39 (1962), 287 f., with bibl. → IV, 824, 16 ff.

[64] The image of growth is not meant in this sense (→ αὐξάνω under ὑπεραυξάνω), nor that of bringing forth fruit, → III, 615, 10 ff.

E. τέλειος in the Post-Apostolic Fathers.

Here, too, the adj. means a. "that from which nothing is missing," "total," e.g., "full" knowledge in 1 Cl., 1, 2; Barn., 1, 5, "complete," exact foreknowledge, 1 Cl., 44, 2, also the "full," "supreme," σκάνδαλον, Barn., 4, 3, "completed" sins, Herm. v., 1, 2, 1; Barn., 8, 1. τὸ τέλειον is the "supreme measure," e.g., τῶν ἁμαρτιῶν, Barn., 5, 11, or τῆς γνώσεως "complete" knowledge, 13, 7. Christ is the "full," "entire" hope of Christians, Ign. Sm., 10, 2, cf. "full" grace, 11, 1. Then b. "perfect," sometimes professionally, so τέλειος ἀθλητής, Ign. Pol., 1, 3. Fasting is "perfect" through keeping the commandments, Herm. s., 5, 3, 6. Ign. Sm., 11, 2 ref. to the work which is "perfect" on earth and in heaven, and continues: τέλειοι ὄντες τέλεια καὶ φρονεῖτε, 11, 3; a "perfect" temple for God is the community which has become spiritual, Barn., 4, 11. 1 Cl., 55, 6 ref. to Esther being "perfect" in faith. Ign. is made strong by Jesus Christ, who became the τέλειος ἄνθρωπος (obviously in acts), Sm., 4, 2; Ign. Eph., 15, 2 describes the "perfect" Christian. The saying in Did., 1, 4: If someone smites thee on the right cheek, turn to him the other also καὶ ἔσῃ τέλειος, is obviously influenced by Mt. 5:39, 48. How being perfect is understood in Did., namely, in the sense of special achievement, may be seen from 6, 2: If you can bear the whole yoke of the Lord, τέλειος ἔσῃ. c. τέλειος is used as a par. of ἔγκαρπος in 1 Cl., 44, 5; 56, 1; one may ask whether the sense here is not "effective."

† τελειότης.

1. This word, which is not common outside the Bible, [1] denotes a state of being τέλειος in the sense of a. "completeness," e.g., τελειότης (opp. ἀτέλεια) μεγέθους, Aristot. Phys., VIII, 7, p. 261a, 36. Acts are not judged by speed but by τελειότης, Corpus Fabularum Aesopicarum [2], 251, 6; b. "completion" in contrast to commencement and progress, by the powers of the soul one achieves ἀρχάς τε... καὶ προκοπὰς καὶ τελειό-τητας in laudable acts, Philo Agric., 157, cf. the contrasting of προκοπαί and τελειότητες in 168; Conf. Ling., 72 etc. μετάνοια in the sense of βελτίωσις is under τελειότης, Abr., 26. The προκόπτων reaches τελειότης through divine blessings, Mut. Nom., 24, which God alone can give, Fug., 172. [3] In Philo, who uses the word a good deal, τελειότης is not a purely ethical concept. [4] Applied to man, it denotes the highest stage of humanity which is reached with the vision of God, Ebr., 82 → 70, 35 f. The product of the highest stage of τελειότης is the praise of God, Plant., 135. In the strict sense no man is τέλειος; true τελειότητες belong only to the One, Rer. Div. Her. 121. [5] The words of God's revelation do not correspond to the measure of His τελειότης but are suited to man's capacity to hear (on Ex. 20:19), Poster. C., 143. Philo Rer. Div. Her., 156 ref. to the "perfection" of creation. A final sense c. is biological "ripeness" or "maturity," of men etc., Aetius Placita, V, 23. [6]

2. In the LXX (all passages given) the word means a. "wholeness," δυνάμεως τελειό-της (God's) "almightiness," Wis. 12:17, "integrity" of conduct between men, Ju. 9:16, 19 (in both instances for תָּמִים), moral blamelessness, Prv. 11:3 A (HT תֻּמָּה); b. "com-pleteness," concern for wisdom brings complete understanding, φρονήσεως τελειότης, Wis. 6:15; c. on Jer. 2:2 → 85, 13 f.

τελειότης. [1] Attested from Democr. Fr., 187 (Diels, II, 183, 9): ψυχῆς... τελειότης, cf. Ps.-Plat. Def., 412b and Aristot. Phys., III, 6, p. 207a, 21 [Risch].
[2] Ed. A. Hausrath, I, 2 (1956).
[3] That it is God, not man, who does the supreme work in man is stressed by Philo in Leg. All., I, 49; II, 46 f.; even confession of God is God's work, I, 82.
[4] Cf. the broad understanding of the Stoic principle: ἡ δ' ἀρετὴ τελειότης ἐστὶ τῆς ἑκάστου φύσεως, which is found in ethics but is accorded very gen. validity, Chrysipp.. Fr., 257 (v. Arnim, III, 61, 38 f.).
[5] The plur. use in Philo shows that completion or the highest stage may be found in the various relations of action or being, cf. also τέλειος (→ 69, 27 ff.) in Aristot. and Plat.
[6] Ed. H. Diels, Doxographi Graeci (1879), 434 f.

3. a. In the NT at Col. 3:14 the preceding hortatory description of proper conduct between Christians (v. 12 f.) is rounded off with a demand to add love, [7] the bond of completeness, to all that has been said. From a NT standpoint it might well be said that by love the Christian virtues are bound together in a whole. [8] In the context, which emphasises the unity of the community (vv. 11-15), it is more likely that the reference is to the community: enacted love unites it within itself [9] "into [10] a whole." [11]

b. In distinction from ἀρχή (Hb. 5:12; 6:1) τελειότης is in Hb. the "highest stage" [12] of Christian teaching [13] (6:1).

4. In the post-apost. fathers the noun occurs only in 1 Cl. We read in 50, 1 that love has the quality of perfection; it is perfect and supreme. In 53, 5 the perfection of the love of Moses for his people is extolled. The word is not found in the Apologists.

† τελειόω.

1. Non-Biblical Usage.

Like other verbs in -όω, τελειόω is factitive [1] and means "to make τέλειος"; it is esp. common in the pass. "to become τέλειος," and the participial forms largely correspond

---

[7] Grammatically τὴν ἀγάπην is naturally dependent on ἐνδύσασθε, v. 12, but it is open to question whether the metaphor of putting on clothes is continued in v. 14. In the OT and Philo the garment in a metaphorical sense denotes something which governs the existence or conduct of the one clothed. On the formula ὅ ἐστιν, "that is," cf. Bl.-Debr. § 132, 2.

[8] The true view of what is morally beautiful, righteous and good is the more divine σύνδεσμος ἀρετῆς μερῶν, Plat. Polit., 309c, 310a. The Pythagoreans call φιλία the σύνδεσμος of all virtues acc. to Simpl. in Epict., 30 (Dübner, 89, 16 f.). Cf. the statements of philosophy about the unity of virtue → 70, 24 ff.

[9] σύνδεσμος (→ VII, 854, 14 ff.) is not just a tie or band around something, and certainly not as an article of clothing (→ V, 302, 21 ff.); it is in the first instance that which binds, e.g., wood in a building, Thuc., II, 75, 5, children in marriage, Aristot. Eth. Nic., VIII, 14, p. 1162a, 27. Medically it can denote the ligaments, Col. 2:19; Da. 5:6 Θ. On Col. 3:14 cf. H. Chadwick, "All Things to All Men," NTSt, 1 (1954/55), 261-273, esp. 273.

[10] Obj. gen., cf. Bl.-Debr. § 163.

[11] Cf. T. Osnes, Fullkommenhetstanken i d. NT (1954), 209, ad loc. 207-211, also G. Rudberg, "Parallela," Coni. Neot., 3 (1938), 19-21; A. Fridrichsen, "Charité et perfection. Observation sur Col. 3:14," Symb. Osl., 19 (1939), 41-45. It is natural in Col. to think of the body of Christ, cf. Osnes, 209-211; v. also Col. 2:19; but this figure of speech is hardly the basis of 3:14.

[12] For the distinction cf. formally Philo, though he relates the stages differently → 78, 23 ff. Lexically τελειότης in Hb. 6:1 is not used in the same way as τέλειος in 5:14 → 77, 3 ff.

[13] E. Käsemann, Das wandernde Gottesvolk³ (1959), 117-124 coins the phrase λόγος τέλειος.

τ ε λ ε ι ό ω . Bibl.: M. Dibelius, "Der himmlische Kultus nach d. Hb.," Botschaft u. Gesch., II (1956), 160-176; T. Häring, "Über einige Grundgedanken d. Hb.," Monatsschr. f. Pastoraltheol., 17 (1920/21), 260-276; also "Noch ein Wort zum Begriff τελειοῦν im Hb.," NkZ, 34 (1923), 386-9; E. Käsemann, Das wandernde Gottesvolk³ (1959), 82-90; J. Kögel, "Der Begriff τελειοῦν im Hb.," Festschr. f. M. Kähler (1905), 35-68; O. Michel, "D. Lehre von d. chr. Vollkommenheit nach d. Anschauung d. Hb.," ThStKr, 106 (1934/35), 333-355; O. Moe, "Der Gedanke d. allg. Priestertums im Hb.," ThZ, 5 (1949), 161-9; T. Osnes, Fullkommenhetstanken i det NT (1954), 206-233; P. J. du Plessis, Τέλειος. The Idea of Perfection in the NT, Diss. Kampen (1959); E. Riggenbach, "Der Begriff d. τελείωσις im Hb.," NkZ, 34 (1923), 184-195; C. Spicq, L'Epître aux Hébreux, II³ (1953), 214-225; F. Torm, "Om τελειοῦν i Hb.," Svensk Exeget. Årsbok, 5 (1940), 116-125; A. Wikgren, "Patterns of Perfection in the Ep. to the Hebrews," NTSt, 6 (1959/60), 159-167; Wnd. Hb., Exc. on 5:9.

[1] Debr. Griech. Wortb. § 198; Schwyzer, I, 727. The verb is Ionic, but common in class. Attic [Dihle].

to τέλειος. The word[2] means a. "to bring to completeness, wholeness." Aristot. Eth. Nic., X, 3, p. 1174a, 15 f., "to complete," e.g., τελειώσαντος θεοῦ, Philo Det. Pot. Ins., 39. Pray for the one for whom things are going better than for you ἵνα τελειωθῇ, that he may "receive full" happiness, Test. G. 7:1.[3] b. Also act. "to do fully," ἐτελέωσε ποιήσας he has carried out fully, Hdt., I, 120, 2; "to complete," e.g., of building the tower, Philo Conf. Ling., 155; pass. "to be completed," a work of art. Epict. Diss., II, 8, 25, the cosmos, Philo Op. Mund., 89; cf. also the series "to begin," "to advance," "to be finished," ἀρχομένοις, προκόπτουσι, τετελειωμένοις, Agric., 159, cf. 160, 165. Philo often uses the word for moral "perfection"; God grants it (opp. ἀτελεῖς), Agric., 169; "to reach the highest stage" of humanity by renouncing the world of sense perceptions in order to have a part in that of the νοῦς, Migr. Abr., 214. Corresponding to the use of τέλειος (→ 70, 27 f.) is the σπουδαῖος or τελειωθείς in Stoicism, opp. φαῦλος, who is ἀτελής; these are the only possibilities of existence acc. to Cleanthes, Stob. Ecl., II, 65, 10 f. cf. καθῆκον τελειωθέν, 86, 11 f. It can be said of time: πάντων τούτων χρόνος ἐτελεώθη, it was fulfilled and thus terminated, Plat. Polit., 272d; cf. of Aaron, ὅταν τελευτᾷ, τουτέστιν ὅταν τελειωθῇ, Philo Leg. All., III, 45. Then act. c. "to put into effect," a prophecy, Jos. Ant., 15, 4, "to carry out" a divine direction, Philo Abr., 62; pass. "to be put into effect," e.g., a word of God, a prophecy, Vit. Mos., I, 283; II, 275, a design, Ditt. Syll.[3], II, 685, 35 f. (139 B.C.), a desire (opp. ἀτελής "unfulfilled"), Epict. Diss., IV, 4, 35. Good and its opp. are done through the λόγος of God, Philo Cher., 35; miraculous events, Vit. Mos., II, 261. d. Act. "to bring to maturity," the bird in itself does not bring any being to maturity, Aristot. Gen. An., III, 2, p. 752b, 21; of animals and plants, God τρέφει καὶ αὔξει καὶ τελειοῖ, Philo in Eus. Praep. Ev., 8, 14, 43; pass. "to ripen," common in Aristot., also Plat.; τελειωθέντες means "full-grown" (opp. νήπιοι), of wolves, Corpus Fabul. Aesop.,[4] 225, 2 and 7, "adult," e.g., παιδείᾳ τε καὶ ἡλικίᾳ, Plat. Resp., VI, 487a; with opp. παῖς, Aristot. Pol., VIII, 5, p. 1339a, 31-33, "procreative," Philo Leg. All., III, 245,[5] cf. I, 10. The fruit of the fig-tree does not "ripen" in an hour, Epict. Diss., I, 15, 8.[6]

2. The Septuagint.

In the LXX (all instances given) the verb means a. "to make perfect," the beauty of Tyre, Ez. 27:11 (for כלל); that God's blessing "may be perfect," Sir. 7:32 (for שלם); τελειοῦμαι "to be untouched," to prove blameless," when tempted by wealth, Sir. 31:10 (שלם), God, 2 Βασ. 22:26 (תמם hitp), act. "to make free from stain," Δα. 3:40.[7] The phrase τελειόω τὰς χεῖράς τινος (→ n. 11) in Ex. 29:9, 29, 33, 35; Lv. 8:33; 16:32;[8] Nu. 3:3 is to be understood[9] along the same lines; in Ex. 29:33 LXX it is elucidated by ἁγιάζω, cf. τελείωσις (→ 85, 26 f.), Lv. 8:33. It is always used for the Hbr. "to fill

---

[2] First found in Hdt., e.g., I, 120, 2 [Risch].
[3] Formally cf. Hdt., III, 86, 2: The miraculous signs ἐτελέωσέ μιν made Darius, who was seeking the monarchy, king.
[4] Ed. A. Hausrath, I, 2 (1956).
[5] In a play on the sense of "humanly perfect"; there is a similar play in e.g., Leg. All., III, 45 and 74.
[6] Osnes, 29 ref. to the sense "to dedicate" in Orph. Fr. (Kern), 301-3 (p. 315-7), but the verb does not occur there.
[7] τελειῶσαι ὄπισθέν σου in v. 40d is originally a marginal gloss on v. 40b, hence a material par. to ἐξιλάσαι ὄπισθέν σου here (v. 40d may also be related to 40c); cf. τελειόω and ἐξιλάσκομαι in Lv. 8:33 f.
[8] Naturally there is no connection between this and πίμπλημι τὰς χεῖρας, Lv.9:17; 16:12, as against Osnes, 121. Comparison shows the transl. of Lv. was aware of the distinction in rendering מלא.
[9] At Ex. 29:29 Ἀ has πληρῶσαι, Σ τελειωθῆναι. At Lv. 16:32 Αλλ has οὗ ἐπληρώθη ὁ τόπος for LXX ὃν ἂν τελειώσουσιν τὰς χεῖρας αὐτοῦ.

the hands" [10] except at Lv. 4:5: ὁ ἱερεὺς ὁ χριστὸς ὁ τετελειωμένος τὰς χεῖρας, where it is an addition to the HT, and Lv. 21:10, where "to fill the hands" is transl. by τελειόω alone: τετελειωμένου ἐνδύσασθαι τὰ ἱμάτια, the acc. "the hands" being regarded as superfluous. That someone's hands are made free from stain, or that he is made free from stain, [11] means finally that the one concerned is "able to practise the cultus," cf. Lv. 21:10. b. "To complete," the Lord's house (opp. laying the foundation), 2 Ch. 8:16 (for inf. pi of כלה); παρὰ τοῦ θεοῦ ἡμῶν ἐγενήθη τελειωθῆναι τὸ ἔργον τοῦτο, 2 Εσδρ. 16:16 (עשה); cf. 3 Βασ. 7:10 A (HT at 7:22 תמם) of the λειτουργία, "to carry through to the end," Sir. 50:19b, ἕως τελειωθῆναι (αὐτόν) "to the last remnant," 3 Βασ. 14:10 (LXX col. of the Hexapla); "to conclude," the seal of martyrdom "completed" a life of fidelity to the Law, 4 Macc. 7:15. In this connection cf. what is said about the righteous who die young: τελειωθεὶς ἐν ὀλίγῳ ἐπλήρωσεν χρόνους μακρούς, Wis. 4:13, cf. ἐν ἀναπαύσει ἔσται, v. 7, also v. 10. [12] c. "To carry through," ἔργον, 2 Εσδρ. 16:3 (vl. for τετελεκώς Sir. 7:25), God carry out thy design, Jdt. 10:8.

3. The New Testament.

In the NT τελειόω means a. "to fulfil," "to carry out," e.g., a required course (→ τρέχω) in the sense of a received commission, Ac. 20:24. [13] It also occurs in this sense in Jn. Dt. 8:3 (cf. Mt. 4:4) is reconstructed in Johannine fashion in Jn. 4:34 and referred to Jesus. The life of Jesus consists in doing the will of God (→ III, 55, 17 ff.), i.e., in carrying out the work of salvation (→ II, 642, 37 ff.), in doing this in the works, the preaching and the deeds which are given Him by the Father and the performing of which is witness that He is sent by the Father, 5:36. In the execution of "the" historical work by Jesus there thus takes place the glorifying of the Father on earth, 17:4. Jn. stresses that Jesus fulfils only that which is assigned to Him by God, cf. δείκνυμι (→ II, 28, 9 ff.), βλέπω (5:19) and διδάσκω (8:28 cf. 5:30; 8:38).

b. In Jn. τελειόω (→ lines 17 ff.) occurs in active aorist forms, but elsewhere we find passive perfect forms, e.g., in 1 Jn., where τελειόω denotes the completeness or perfection of the love of God or of the Christian in love, 4:18. The ἀγάπη τοῦ θεοῦ has "come to entirety" in the man who keeps God's Word, i.e., His command-

---

[10] Elsewhere transl. πληρόω κτλ. (→ VI, 287, 35 ff.) but not in the Pent. In Ez. 43:26, where it ref. to the altar in the HT, help was sought by relating it to the priest: πλήσουσιν χεῖρας αὐτῶν.

[11] Riggenbach's view (186) that τὰς χεῖρας is an acc. of relation is continually repeated (Osnes, 30, du Plessis, 121). If this were so we should not have a ref. to those who are cultically qualified in respect of their hands in the formulations of Ex. 29:9, 33, 35; Lv. 8:33 and Ex. 29:29 (for here the αὐτούς which goes with χρισθῆναι can hardly be referred also to τελειῶσαι). Only in Lv. 16:32 (→ n. 9) and Nu. 3:3: οὓς ἐτελείωσαν τὰς χεῖρας αὐτῶν does τελειόω clearly have with χεῖρας a personal obj. The transl. here is mechanical since both אשר and the suffixes are rendered, cf. the same in Lv.16 f., also ἐν οἷς ἡγιάσθησαν ἐν αὐτοῖς in Ex. 29:33. There is an acc. of relation at Lv. 4:5 in an addition of the translator, but in the pass. This is impossible, however, at Ex. 29:9, 33, 35; Lv. 8:33. In any case the primary ref. of τελειοῦν with τὰς χεῖρας is to the act of the priest. This may be seen from the fact that the verb is not taken from the usage of the mysteries (cf. τελέω → 58, 11 ff.). Lv. 21:10 shows that the ref. is naturally to the cultic cleanness of the whole person.

[12] Cf. Philo Leg. All., III, 45, where with ref. to Nu. 20:25 it is said that Aaron when he died, i.e., "was perfected," mounted up to Hor, i.e., light.

[13] The apostle gives his life to this. Cf. δρόμον τελέω (→ 69, 19 ff.), 2 Tm. 4:7 and πληρόω, Ac. 13:25 → VI, 297, 9 f.

ments (v. 4), 1 Jn. 2:5, in those who love one another, 4:12. What is meant by ἀγάπη τοῦ θεοῦ is God's love for us, which manifests its completeness in the fact that it allows us to look forward without fear to the Last Judgment, 4:17; → 75, 13 ff. If a man lives in this fear, his being is not fully controlled by love (→ 81, 27 f.), 4:18. The choice of the verbal form instead of the adjective underlines the fact that only in παρρησία (→ V, 879, 33 ff.) in the judgment, only in brotherly love, in obedience, does the love of God achieve totality in the lives of Christians.

The word has a similar meaning in the passive perfect in Jn. In 17:23 Jesus prays that His disciples may be "perfect" in one, i.e., "wholly and utterly" one, → II, 434, 19. [14] This takes place through the "I in them and thou in me," cf. v. 21. The fact that Jesus is sent by the Father, and that the Father loves the community of Jesus, may be perceived in the "full" unity of the community. Scripture as witness to Christ (5:39) in respect of the passion of Jesus "comes to completeness" (→ VI, 295, 9 f.) in the final event of the crucifixion to which there is direct reference in the OT (Ps. 22:15; 69:21) according to Jn. 19:28 [15, 16] (→ V, 289, 8 ff.; VI, 295, 41 f.). On the basis of works Abraham's faith "came to fulness," "became complete," Jm. 2:22. This may be seen in the sacrifice of Isaac, Gn. 22. In this the Scripture (Gn. 15:6) was fulfilled. This expressed in advance the divine verdict, which was then confirmed by the offering up of Isaac, Jm. 2:23. For James this proves the thesis of 2:22b.

c. The use of τελειόω in Hb. for the most part follows a special use of the verb in the LXX → 80, 34 ff. Here, too, τελειόω τινά [17] means "to put someone in the position in which he can come, or stand, before God" (Hb. 7:19; 10:1), [18] whether in the narrower sense as a priest who may perform his cultic functions before God or in the broader [19] sense as a non-priest, 10:14. [20] Here again the τετελειωμένος (7:28) is χριστός (as in Lv. 4:5 LXX; 21:10), the high-priest (though → III, 279, 26 ff.). Naturally in Hb., both here and elsewhere, cultic [21] terminology is used to clarify the very different mode of operation in the new order of salvation: οὐδὲν ... ἐτελείωσεν (→ IV, 1079, 4 ff.) ὁ νόμος (7:19) or in acknowledgment

---

[14] Cf. Bl.-Debr. § 145 with bibl. ἕν is the controlling word in vv. 21-23.

[15] τελειωθῇ ref. materially to v. 29.

[16] This presupposes that the ἵνα clause goes with what follows, cf. Bl.-Debr. § 478, also Kühner-Blass-Gerth, II, 2, 607, 5: The thought of the ἵνα clause is underlined by putting it first. It would be odd if the allusion to two psalms so firmly connected with the passion tradition were not intentional, → II, 226, 7 ff. and n. 1.

[17] It is obvious why Hb. no longer has τὰς χεῖρας; the way had been prepared for dropping this, cf. Lv. 21:10.

[18] Cf. the relation of ἐτελείωσεν ... ἐγγίζομεν ... in Hb. 7:19; the latter is also part of the vocabulary of the LXX (→ II, 330, 27 ff.), cf. Hb. 7:25 (→ II, 683, 26 f.). προσέρχεσθαι is only allowed for priests, Nu. 17:5, cf. 8:19, and only for those free from defects (Lv. 21:17 f., 21) lest by their προσέρχεσθαι they desecrate God's sanctuary, Lv. 21:23; this is why those who draw near unlawfully are subject to death, Nu. 18:3. Priests drawing near to God must "sanctify" themselves, ἁγιασθήτωσαν, Ex. 19:22. προσέρχεσθαι ref. to all the τετελειωμένοι in Hb., esp. 7:25; 10:1. The elect of the race may always stand before God, 1 QS 11:16 f.

[19] This sense also occurs in the LXX if Δα. 3:40 (→ 80, 32) is correctly understood. If not, this meaning derives from "to make free from stain."

[20] Here, too, τελειόω goes directly with ἁγιάζω, cf. Ex. 29:33.

[21] Häring Grundgedanken, esp. 267-273, stresses the cultic character of the τελειόω group in Hb., though he tries to explain the LXX use by analogy with τελέω in the sense "to dedicate." Dibelius, esp. 165-8, and Moe, 165-8 agree that the use is cultic. The difficulties of an "ethical" interpretation find fresh illustration in Wikgren, 160-5.

of the cultic law of the OT which foreshadows the definitive order: It could not permanently "qualify" the priest [22] "for cultic ministry" (10:1); the offerings prescribed by it were unable κατὰ συνείδησιν (→ VII, 918, 28 ff.) τελειῶσαι (9:9). For Hb. the need of τελειοῦν is no longer based on what is at least also a cultic defect of the priest; it is based solely on his sinfulness, cf. καθαίρω, [23] → III, 426, 1 ff. If the τελειοῦσθαι which Jesus experienced does not mean liberation from guilt, the categories used even with reference to Him are ethical. God has qualified Jesus, the → υἱός (5:8 f.; 7:28), "to come before him" in priestly action. He has done so by the suffering (2:10) in which Jesus confirmed His obedience, 5:8 f. [24] As the One qualified (τελειωθείς) [25] for priestly ministry before God, as the One eternally qualified (εἰς τὸν αἰῶνα τετελειωμένος, 7:28), He is the absolute High-priest, 5:9 f. → V, 917, 18 ff. By His high-priestly work (→ προσφέρω) before God Christ has once and for all "qualified" those for whom He acts [26] "to come directly before God" (10:14; cf. 7:19) in the heavenly sanctuary as men whose sin is expiated. [27] This goes far beyond what took place in the OT cultus, which allowed a direct approach to God in the inner temple only for the priest and not the whole people. [28]

d. τελειόω is used differently in Hb. 11 f. If the πρεσβύτεροι who rested wholly on faith (11:2) did not attain to that which was promised (→ II, 584, 23 ff.), if they did not come to the true πατρίς (v. 14), to the heavenly πόλις (v. 10, 16), i.e., the proximity of God (12:22), this may also be expressed by saying that "they did not reach the perfection" which is given only in the saving work of Christ (μὴ χωρὶς ἡμῶν, 11:40). But they have now received a share in the consummation, 12:23; → II, 190, 27 ff.; VI, 445, 28 f. [29] If Paul has not yet received the prize of victory,

---

[22] τὸν λατρεύοντα, 9:9, cf. Moe, 165; τοὺς λατρεύοντας, 10:2.

[23] κεκαθαρμένος καὶ τέλειος, which are par. terms for the priest, are also to be taken cultically, Philo Deus Imm., 132, cf. τέλειος → 69, n. 10.

[24] E. Benz, "Der gekreuzigte Gerechte bei Plato, im NT u. in d. alten Kirche," AAMainz, 1950, 12 (1950), 1029-74, esp. 1061, claims that there is "linguistic convergence" between Hb. 2:10 and Plat. Resp., II, 362a, which says of the righteous: τελευτῶν πάντα κακὰ παθὼν ἀνασχινδυλευθήσεται. But as regards τελευτῶν and τελειῶσαι this is merely an affinity of sound even if here in Plato τελευτῶν does actually mean "to complete," "to reach his goal," as Benz thinks, 1062. On J. Jeremias, "Hb. 5:7-10," ZNW, 44 (1952/53), 107-111, cf. M. Rissi, "Die Menschlichkeit Jesu nach Hb. 5:7 u. 8," ThZ, 11 (1955), 28-45; A. Strobel, "Die Psalmengrundlage der Gethsemane-Parallele Hb. 5:7 ff.," ZNW, 45 (1954), 252-266. G. Friedrich, "Das Lied vom Hohenpriester im Zshg. v. Hb. 4:14 - 5:10," ThZ, 18 (1962), 95-115 takes τελειωθείς in Hb. 5:9 to mean "one who has reached the goal"; "τελειόω has this sense only here," 107.

[25] As the One who has shown Himself completely innocent by doing God's will (10:7), He is qualified for actual discharge of the high-priestly office. The unblemished High-Priest (cf. ἀμίαντος 7:26; → IV, 647, 19 f.) offers Himself as unblemished ἄμωμον (תָּמִים) victim, 9:14. The whole vocabulary is cultic in origin.

[26] οἱ ἁγιαζόμενοι is a characteristic expression in Hb. (cf. 2:11) for the people for whom the High-priest Jesus intercedes.

[27] In materially the same sense τελειόω can be used for ἁγιάζω as the work of the High-priest in Hb. 2:11; 10:14. This, like τελειοῦν, takes place by offering before God, 10:10 cf. v. 29 and 13:12.

[28] δικαιόω in Pl. and τελειόω in Hb. are in some sense par. and come from the same Jewish background. The difference between them is connected with the difference between legal and cultic thinking.

[29] Naturally "complete" here may be used in the sense of Wis. 4:13 (δίκαιος, which is also used for an OT saint in Hb. 11:4; elsewhere in Hb. only at 10:38 in an OT quotation), i.e., at the goal of heavenly rest → 81, 11 ff.

if he is still pressing on, this means that "I have not yet reached the full and final thing" [30] (Phil. 3:12, but cf. → V, 622, 15 ff.); this will take place only in the resurrection, v. 11. [31] The threat of Herod Antipas does not prevent Jesus from carrying through His work in the time set for Him (ἀποτελῶ σήμερον καὶ αὔριον); then He will be "perfected," i.e., His work will be "brought to a conclusion" by God (Lk. 13:32). [32, 33] The parents of Jesus "fulfilled" the days of the Passover, of their participation in it, Lk. 2:43. For similar statements → VI, 130, 25 ff.; 294, 20 ff.; 297, 6 ff.

e. The verbs τελέω and τελειόω coincide in the NT especially in the sense "to carry through," "to complete" (→ 59, 13 ff.; 81, 16 ff.). Whereas this is the chief meaning of τελέω, the thought of totality is stronger in the case of τελειόω, → 81, 27 ff. The findings suggest for τελέω the meanings of τέλος, "goal," "issue," "end" (→ 54, 17 ff.) and for τελειόω those of τέλειος, "whole," "complete," "perfect" (→ 73, 26 ff.).

4. The Post-Apostolic Fathers.

Here, too, the verb means a. "to carry out," e.g., one's ministry in the community of the Lord, Herm. s., 9, 26, 2, the creation of man and woman, 1 Cl., 33, 6, "to fulfil" revelations and visions, Herm. v., 4, 1, 3. Faith, as opp. to doubt, promises all things and "effects" all things, Herm. m., 9, 10. The eschatological resolve of God will be speedily carried out, 1 Cl., 23, 5. Resurrection is "effected" in the Gospel, [34] Ign. Sm., 7, 2. Every word of the martyr Polycarp "was fulfilled" and will be fulfilled, Mart. Pol., 16, 2. b. "To complete," perhaps in the sense of bringing together, since the passage goes on to speak of the Church, Did., 10, 5, or in the pass. "to come to completion," in sins, Barn., 14, 5, also "to ripen," 6, 19 (cf. the context). c. "To bring (or pass. to come) to perfection," in one's love, Did., 10, 5; pass. "to become perfect," Did., 16, 2, cf. τέλειος → 78, 15 f.

† τελείωσις.

1. Outside the Bible. The word [1] is a nomen actionis and denotes the act or accomplishment of τελειοῦν. It means a. "actualisation," "execution," e.g., τῆς φύσεως, of man's nature, Aristot. Eth. Nic., VII, 13, p. 1153a, 12 (→ lines 32 ff.), of a resolve, an oath, Philo Spec. Leg., II, 9, of the words of the prophets (on Dt. 33), Philo Vit. Mos., II, 288. b. "Completion," "making into a whole" (opp. beginning) of the parts of the cosmos, Spec. Leg., II, 58, cf. Decal., 99; in the 8th seventh comes the fulfilment of spiritual

---

[30] Cf. formally the similar association in Philo Leg. All., III, 74: ὅταν τελειωθῇς καὶ βραβείων... ἀξιωθῇς. The one who has reached the goal receives the reward of victory.
[31] As a Pharisee Paul thought he had the whole, v. 5 and esp. v. 6; in the context v. 12 has a polemical ring.
[32] Pass., cf. J. Blinzler, "Die literarische Eigenart d. sog. Reiseberichtes im Lk.," Synpt. Stud. Festschr. f. A. Wikenhauser (1953), 46, n. 67, ad loc. 42-47.
[33] Personal pass. constr. There is no ref. to the end of the life of Jesus; only v. 33 begins to speak of the journey to Jerusalem. Blinzler, op. cit. (→ n. 32), 45 would cut out σήμερον καὶ αὔριον καί in v. 33 as a doublet of v. 32.
[34] Obviously in distinction from a mere prediction of the resurrection by the prophets; Bau. Ign., ad loc. ref. to Phld., 9, 2.

τελείωσις. [1] An Ionic word which did not come in by way of Attic but passed directly into the koine [Dihle].

powers (νοῦς and λόγος), Op. Mund., 103, "perfection" in virtues, Noah, Deus Imm., 122, "perfection" with σπουδή and βελτίωσις, Agric., 166. c. "Conclusion," e.g., τοῦ ἔργου, Ditt. Syll.³, II, 799, 1, 29 (38 A.D.); in Gr. En. sometimes "end" in gen., 10:14; ἀπ' ἀρχῆς μέχρι τελειώσεως, 2:2. d. Biologically "ripening," Aristot. Gen. An., IV, 8, p. 776b, 1 etc.; the processes of generation, growth and maturing take place through earth and water, Phil. Spec. Leg., III, 58; of καρποί, II, 204; cf. Virt., 145; the rise of man's procreative power with the end of the 2nd seventh, Leg. All., I, 10 etc.

2. In the LXX. Here (all instances given → lines 25 ff.) the word means a. "execution" of a plan, τῶν λόγων, Jdt. 10:9; also in the phrase τελείωσις τοῦ σωτηρίου for םֶלֶשׁ plur.), 2 Ch. 29:35; ² b. "completion," Sir. 34:8, probably for כָּלִיל: ³ wisdom becomes perfect through a reliable mouth; c. "conclusion," "completion" of the building of the temple, 2 Macc. 2:9, cf. ἕως τελειώσεως αὐτῶν in 'Α (instead of ἕως εἰς τέλος LXX), Dt. 31:24; d. "time of becoming sexually mature," obviously understood thus by the transl. (with νεότης) for כְּלוּלֹת, ⁴ Jer. 2:2 AB (א τελειότης).

3. In the NT τελείωσις occurs twice. a. Mary is called blessed because she trusts that through God there will be execution of the words of the angel which come from God, Lk. 1:45. b. Though the Levitical priesthood the state is not reached in which "one can come before God," Hb. 7:11. In context the reference is to the priest who is not qualified by the Aaronic order to intercede for the people ⁵ before God, → 82, 22 ff.; 83, 4 ff.

Hb. 7:11 adopts a common LXX tt. Its meaning may be seen from the special use of τελειόω in the sense of "to qualify for the cultus," → 81, 4 ff. The use of τελείωσις for the corresponding act derives from the equation מִלֵּא–מִלְֻּאִים. The latter is ready a tt. in the OT, though its meaning is not intrinsically clear and has to be deduced from the context. ⁶ Ex. 29:26, 27, 31 speaks of κριὸς (τῆς) τελειώσεως v. 26 ΣΘ: τῶν τελειώσεων, 'Α: τῆς πληρώσεως), cf. also Lv. 8:22, 29. ⁷ In Lv. 8:28 we have ὁλοκαύτωμα τῆς τελειώσεως (so also HT, in 8:26, ⁸ 31 the basket τῆς τελειώσεως, in v. 33 the day of τελείωσις (τελειώσεως Αλλ), in 7:37 the νόμος... τῆς τελειώσεως (the 2 latter corresponding to the HT). מִלְֻּאִים alone is transl. by θυσία τῆς τελειώσεως in Ex. 29:34. The whole way of using τελείωσις in these verses shows that LXX understands by it an action connected with the instituting of the priests in their ministry. More precise interpretation is yielded by τελειόω → 80, 34 ff. The expression is common in

---

² The LXX usually has σωτήριον for this, also θυσία (τοῦ) σωτηρίου, Ex. 32:6; Lv. 9:4; Dt. 27:7; Jos. 9:2b (HT 8:31); 2 Ch. 31:2. Since this is often based on the HT the addition of θυσία in the vv. mentioned was natural. In 2 Ch. 29:35 τελείωσις corresponds to θυσία but under Αλλ we find τελειώσεων at Lv. 4:35; 6:5, and τελειώσεων at Lv. 7:29 for םֶלֶשׁ plur.

³ So already V. Ryssel in Kautzsch Apokr. u. Pseudepigr., ad loc.; cf. συντέλεια → 65, 16 ff. and συντελέω → 63, 12.

⁴ Perhaps in analogy to the use of words in the group τελ- for words of the group כלה etc. (→ n. 3; 52, 4 ff.; 58, 39, 43 f.; 61, 28 f., 35; 72, 22; 80, 30 f. etc.

⁵ The people had received the Law on the basis of this priesthood, cf. the transl. in Wnd. Hb., ad loc.

⁶ The noun is used elsewhere for "border" and is transl. πλήρωσις in Ex. 35:27; 1 Ch. 29:2, γλυφή in Ex. 25:7; 35:9 (hence always with care).

⁷ Always in agreement with HT; only in Ex. 29:22 did LXX (perhaps) put in τελείωσις independently.

⁸ So also Orig. in the LXX column of the Hexapla; the others (οἱ λοιποί) offer in the Hexapla τῶν ἀζύμων (corresponding to the HT).

dispersion Judaism. Philo has it with express appeal to the context ἐν τῷ Λευιτικῷ, Rer. Div. Her., 251, declaring thereby his historical understanding of the term τελείωσις in Lv. 8. κριὸς τῆς τελειώσεως is quoted as fully familiar in Leg. All., III, 130 and Migr. Abr., 67 in an allegorical exposition which alludes to the sense of "fulfilment," while in Vit. Mos., II, 149 κάθαρσις ἀγνευτική is named as the content of the dedication. [9]

4. The word does not occur in the post-apost. fathers or the Apologists.

† τελειωτής.

1. τελειωτής is the one who accomplishes τελειοῦν. Thus far the only instances are Chr. (from Hb. 12:2 on) [1] and the word is rare, though used with various material connections. On the one side God is called τελειωτής as the One who works in natural events (cf. τέλειος → 68, 33 ff. as a divine attribute, also → n. 7), Orig. Princ., III, 1, 19, (232, 1), or ὁ τῶν τελουμένων τελειωτής καὶ δεσπότης as the One who calls to ministry and witness by the Holy Ghost, Ps.-Method. De Simeone et Anna, 5 (MPG, 18 [1857], 360B). On the other side man is also called τελειωτής as the one who accomplishes baptism, making the candidate τέλειος or helping him to τελειότης, Greg. Naz. Or., 40, 44 (MPG, 36 [1858], 421C). In view of the very different meaning it may be said that the use in the post-NT writings certainly does not go back to Hb. One may suspect formation of the nomen agentis from the verb, and Hb. 12:2 did not have to be the pioneer in this.

2. As regards interpretation of the word in Hb. 12:2 it is best to consult the context first. [2] Hb. 11 has given several illustrations of πίστις from the host of believers before Christ. In 12:2 Jesus is set forth as the One in whom this host may be seen in prototype (ἀρχηγός) [3] and also as the One who has "brought" believing [4] "to completion" (→ 80, 1 ff.), i.e., given it a perfect basis [5] by His high-priestly work. Through this, πίστις, which is firm confidence in the fulfilment of God's promise (11:13, 33), [6] has become full assurance. Yet one cannot rule out the possibility, again in the light of the context, that ἀρχηγός and τελειωτής, [7] being

---

[9] In the narrower context the terminology is in part that of the mysteries. Philo uses this elsewhere for the Jewish religion (cf. Moses as a hierophant) though without seriously making the latter a mystery religion. Thus in II, 150 Philo explains priestly dedication in ethical rather than mystery terms.

τελειωτής. [1] [Risch].

[2] If this is an adopted expression — a "liturgical redeemer designation," Mi. Hb., ad loc. — there are naturally broader possibilities of interpretation.

[3] One cannot adduce 2:10 as an argument against this understanding. In Hb. πίστις is not to be equated with σωτηρία, since it does not specifically denote the content of Chr. faith. The thought of the prototype is not ruled out by the relative clause in 12:2; cf. Moses in 11:24-26 (→ V, 241, 26 ff.) and also 12:3.

[4] Cf. A. Schlatter, Der Glaube im NT[5] (1963), 531 f. The very different explanations of τελειωτής in Hb. 12:2 even to the extreme of "mystagogue" (M. Dibelius, "Der himmlische Kultus nach d. Hb.," Botschaft u. Gesch., II [1956], 171) often disregard the fact that the meaning of πίστις must be kept in view, esp. as it is used elsewhere in Hb. → n. 3.

[5] Schlatter, op. cit., 532.

[6] In a share in the city above, 11:10, 16, cf. 11:14.

[7] Cf. the formally par. ἀρχή and τέλος (e.g., Hb. 7:3 → 56, 10 f.), v. also Ael. Arist. Or., 43, 31 (Keil): Zeus, who has power over all things, is the only author and finisher of all things ἀρχηγέτην καὶ τέλειον μόνον ... τῶν πάντων.

linked by the common article and the common genitive attribute, are more strongly parallel in Hb. 12:2, so that τελειωτής denotes the One who "exercises complete" faith as demonstrated by suffering, a point which is given such heavy stress in Hb. (e.g., 5:7 f.; cf. 12:3). On this reading the two terms refer primarily to the passion of Jesus on its personal side.

Delling

† τελώνης

Contents: A. State Tax-Farming and Tax-Farmers in Antiquity: I. The Main Types of Tax-Farming in Antiquity: 1. Athens; 2. Ptolemaic Egypt; 3. Rome. II. Tax-Farming in Palestine. III. The Social Position and Moral Evaluation of the Tax-Farmer: 1. In Antiquity Generally; 2. In Judaism. B. Jesus and Toll-Collectors.

τ ε λ ώ ν η ς. Bibl.: Gen.: Liddell-Scott, Pape, Pass., Thes. Steph., *s.v.*; also H. v. Herwerden, Lex. Graec. suppletorium et dialecticum² (1910); Sophocles Lex., *s.v.*; D. Dimitrakos, Μέγα λεξικὸν τῆς Ἑλληνικῆς γλώσσης, VIII (1952), *s.v.* On A. I, 1: A. Boeckh, *Die Staatshaushaltung d. Athener*³ (1886); K. Riezler, *Finanzen u. Monopole im alten Griechenland* (1907); H. Francotte, *Les finances des cités grecques* (1909); G. Busolt and H. Swoboda, *Gr. Staatskunde,* II³ *Hndbch. kl. AW,* IV, 1, 1 (1926), 1131-1149, 1210-1239; A. Andreades, *Gesch. d. gr. Staatswirtschaft,* I (1931); W. Schwahn, Art. τελῶναι, Pauly-W., 5a (1934), 418-425; also art. τέλη, *ibid.,* 226-310; H. Michell, *The Economics of Ancient Greece*² (1957). On A. I, 2: Ostraka, 130-663; C. Préaux, *L'économie royale des Lagides* (1939). On A. I, 3: G. Humbert, *Les douanes et les octrois chez les Romains* (1867); H. Naquet, *Des impôts indirects chez les Romains sous la République et sous l'Empire* (1875); A. G. Dietrich, *Beiträge zur Kenntnis des röm. Steuerpächtersystems* (1877); M. R. Cagnat, *Étude historique sur les impôts indirects chez les Romains* (1882); J. Marquardt, *Röm. Staatsverwaltung,* II² (1884) (1957)³, 148-316; F. Thibault, *Les douanes chez les Romains* (1888); A. G. Dietrich, *Die rechtliche Natur der societas publicanorum* (1889); F. Kniep, *Societas publicanorum* (1896); M. Rostovtzeff, "Gesch. d. Staatspacht in d. röm. Kaiserzeit," *Philol. Suppl.,* 9, 3 (1904) 312-512; V. Ivanov, "De societatibus vectigalium publicorum populi Romani," *Zapiski de la section classique de la Société impériale archéol. de Russie* (1910); W. Schwahn, Art. "tributum," Pauly-W., 7a (1939), 1-78; S. de Laet, Portorium. *Étude sur l'organisation douanière chez les Romains à l'époque du Haut-Empire* (1949); H. Vittinghoff, Art. "portorium," Pauly-W., 43 (1953), 346-399; also Art. "portitor," *ibid.,* 346. On A. II: L. Herzfeld, *Handelsgesch. d. Juden des Altertums* (1865), 159-162; L. Goldschmid, "Les impôts et droits de douane en Judée sous les Romains," *Revue des Études Juives,* 34 (1897), 192-217; S. Krauss, *Talmudische Archäol.,* II (1911), 372-6; W. Otto, Art. "Herodes," Pauly-W. Suppl., 2 (1913), 1-158; F. C. Grant, *The Economic Background of the Gospels* (1926), 87-91; E. Bikermann, *Institutions des Séleucides* (1938), 107-132; F. M. Heichelheim, *Roman Syria. An Economic Survey of Ancient Rome,* IV (ed. T. Frank [1938]), 123-258; M. Rostovtzeff, *Die hell. Welt,* I (1955), 257-278, 361-368; II (1955), 640-645, 758-783; 789-793; A. Schalit, *König Herodes* (1969), Index, *s.v.* "Zöllner." On A. III and B.: A. Wünsche, *Neue Beiträge zur Erläuterung d. Ev.* (1878) on Mt. 5:46; 9:10; 18:17; 21:31; Lk. 3:12; 18:13; L. Abrahams, *Studies in Pharisaism and the Gospels,* I (1917), 54-61; C. C. Burkhardt, "Zöllner u. Sünder," *Schriften u. Vorträge* (1917), 307-335; C. G. Montefiore, *The Synoptic Gospels,* I (1927), 53-57; J. Jeremias, "Zöllner u. Sünder," ZNW, 30 (1931), 293-300; H. C. Youtie, "Publicans and Sinners," *Michigan Alumnus Quarterly Review,* 43 (1937), 650 f.; E. Sjöberg, *Gott u. d. Sünder im palästinischen Judt.* (1938), 125-169; A. Edersheim, *Sketches of Jewish Social Life* (1950), 51-8; H. G. G. Herklots, *Publicans and Sinners* (1956); Str.-B., I, 377-380; Jeremias Gl.⁶ (1962), 124-145; *Jerusalem z. Zt. Jesu*³ (1962), 337-347; M. Avi-Yonah, "Gesch. d. Juden im Zeitalter d. Talmud." *Studia Judaica,* 2 (1962), 69, 98-102; J. Jeremias, Art. "Zöllner u. Sünder," RGG³, VI, 1927 f.; R. Hummel, "Die Auseinandersetzung zwischen Kirche u. Judt. im Mt." *Beiträge z. evangelischen Theol.,* 33 (1963), 22-26.

The noun τελώνης [1] is made up of τέλος "toll," "indirect tax" and the verb ὠνέομαι, "I buy." [2] It denotes a person who purchases from the state the rights to official taxes and dues (cf. τέλη ὠνοῦνται παρὰ τῆς πόλεως, Xenoph. Vect., 4, 19) and who collects these from the people who owe them. [3]

A. State Tax-Farming and Tax-Farmers in Antiquity.

I. The Main Types of Tax-Farming in Antiquity.

1. Athens.

The system of farming out sources of state income such as taxes, tolls, houses, parcels of ground, mines etc. goes back to the Gk. city states and their *polis* constitution. Originally the farming was a private agreement between the state and the tax-farmers. But already in class. Athens the city regulated tax-farming by laws fixing its requirements and the duties and privileges of the tax-farmers. [4] It was not concerned, however, how the farmer collected the taxes or whether he kept books. From the standpt. of practical finance tax-farming guaranteed the city an adequate income without its having to collect the taxes owed or to bother about administration. It could have its money at the beginning of the fiscal year and thus avoided the difficulties which might otherwise arise, for in the days of classical Athens — as distinct from Ptolemaic Egypt — there was no way of estimating accurately in advance what would be the income from tolls and other taxes and then using this to cover current expenditures with the help of notes or loans. [5] Furthermore if the state had tried to collect and administer its own taxes it would have had to use trained officials who could acquire the necessary knowledge and experience only after a long period in office. But a long period in office did not fit in with the basic principles of the *polis* constitution, which provided for officials who would quickly succeed one another. Only with the help of the tax-farming system could the city avoid these constitutional problems. [6] The system had the disadvantage that the farmers had to impose more taxation than would be paid to the city in order to make an adequate profit and were thus driven over-readily to unlawful practices. The state treasury could also be hurt if all those interested in the business banded together and agreed in advance to make a lower bid in order to split the resultant profit, Andoc., I, 133d.; Plut. De Alcibiade, 5 (I, 194a). [7] In Athens, for which we have the best sources of information, [8] the main farming, apart from mines and landed properties, was in the area of customs

---

[1] τελώνης is found the first time in Aristoph. Eq., 248.

[2] On the formation of this determinative compound cf. P. Chantraine, "La formation des noms en grec ancien," *Collection linguistique,* 38 (1933), 29; Schwyzer, I, 451, 4. Much as with ἀρτοπώλης "baker" (Poll. Onom., VII, 21) we have the noun ἀρτοπώλιον "baker's shop" (Aristoph. Ra., 112), so with τελώνης we have τελώνιον (cf. Chantraine, 57), first found in Posidippus (3rd cent. B.C.), Fr., 13 (CAF, III, 339) meaning "custom-house." Cf. Liddell-Scott, Moult.-Mill.. *s.v.*

[3] Dimitrakos, 7149: ὁ ἀγοράζων τὰ εἰς τὸ δημόσιον τέλη καὶ εἰσπράττων αὐτὰ ἀπὸ τῶν ὀφειλετῶν. In Gk. purchase and farming are often not distinguished, cf. Ostraka, I, 525, n. 3.

[4] οἱ νόμοι οἱ τελωνικοί, Demosth. Or., 24, 96 and 101. These laws contained provisions relating to the rate of taxes and the list of taxable goods, cf. the νόμος τελωνικός of Palmyra (Ditt. Or., II, 629) which dates from Roman times. For details cf. Laet, 356-360. On tax-farming laws gen. cf. W. Schwahn, Art. νόμος τελωνικός, Pauly-W., 17 (1936), 843-5.

[5] Michell, 355-7.

[6] Rostovtzeff Staatspacht, 337.

[7] Boeckh, I, 405 f.

[8] *Ibid.,* 366-414; Busolt and Swoboda, 1210-1239; Schwahn τελῶναι, 418-425.

and business taxes. [9] Farming [10] was controlled by a special board, the πωληταί, [11] on the basis of an agreement within the appropriate laws. [12] An individual might come forward as a tax-farmer τελώνης or else a company of interested parties; a company could more easily raise the necessary capital at the rate of half the sale-price. The contract went to those who offered most, Andoc., I, 134; Plut. De Alcibiade, 5 (I, 194a). When a company took over a tax, only its head, ἀρχώνης, was responsible to the state. He and his backers were enrolled in the tax-farming lists, Aristot. De republica Atheniensium (→ n. 11), 47, 2; Andoc., I, 134. [13] The arrangement was usually for a year, Andoc., I, 133; Aeschin. Tim., 119. [14] A quick turnover in tax-farmers promoted competition. But since collection of taxes presupposed long experience, the same people constantly figure as lessees. [15] Because the sums formed an important part of the national revenue and were destined to cover urgent expenditure, the lessee had to provide backers who would guarantee the prompt payment of the agreed amount with their person and property and make up any deficiency, Andoc., I, 73 and 134; Demosth. Or., 24, 102. There were two dates for payment; during the first prytaneia a first instalment, the προκαταβολή, was due, Aristot. De rep. Athen., 47, 2; Suid., IV, 2461 (Adler); [16] only after this was the farmer allowed to gather the taxes. The rest, the προσκατάβλημα, was apparently paid in the sixth prytaneia, Demosth. Or., 24, 97 f. [17] Atimia [18] and imprisonment were penalties for tardy payment. If the debt was not paid by the ninth prytaneia the sum due was doubled, the goods of the debtor were seized, and the backers were held liable, Andoc., I, 73; Demosth. Or., 24, 60. 144. In spite of these harsh conditions tax-farming seems to have been a lucrative business in Athens and brought in more than the 12 % the banks paid at that time. [19] If as a result of over-riding circumstances like war or pestilence the yield fell short, the people of Athens after investigation could remit the debt. [20] Tax-farmers were granted immunity from military service in Athens so that they could devote themselves without interruption to their business. [21] To collect the taxes they used employees and slaves ἐκλέγοντες, Demosth. Or., 24, 144. [22] If there were reasons for suspicion ships and crates could be searched and goods on which

---

[9] "All regular taxes were farmed out," Boeckh, I, 188. The lessees used to be described acc. to the nature or rate of the dues, e.g. πεντηκοστολόγοι, Demosth. Or., 21, 133; Poll. Onom., IX, 29, εἰκοστολόγοι, Aristoph. Ra., 363, πορνοτελῶναι, Philonides Fr., 5 (CAF, I, 255); cf. Aeschin. Tim., 119 f.

[10] πρᾶσις, P. Rev., 55, 16; this expression was probably a common one already in Athens. Cf. the expression ὠνὰς πρίασθαι ἐκ τοῦ δημοσίου, Andoc., I, 73.

[11] On the poletai cf. Aristot. De republica Atheniensium (ed. F. G. Kenyon [1892]), 47, 2 f.; Busolt and Swoboda, 1141; T. Lenschau, Art. "Poletai," Pauly-W., 42 (1952), 1350-1361.

[12] On συγγραφαί cf. W. Schwahn, Art. συγγραφαί, Pauly-W., 4a (1932), 1369-1376.

[13] Cf. on this Rostovtzeff Staatspacht, 334.

[14] Mines were farmed out for at least 3 yrs., Aristot. De rep. Athen., 47, 2.

[15] Rostovtzeff Staatspacht, 335.

[16] Boeckh, I, 412. The prytaneia was the period in office of one of the 10 (or after the 3rd cent. 12) divisions of the council of 500 (βουλή) corresponding to the 10 or 12 Attic phylai. The prytanes formed the leaders and business section of the council and held office in a sequence determined by lot. According to the division of the yr. a prytaneia lasted 36-39 days, or later (with 12 instead of 10) 29-30 (32) days. Cf. on this Busolt and Swoboda, 1028 f.

[17] Cf. CIA, II, 1059; on this Schwahn τελῶναι, 419.

[18] This meant the loss of civil dignities and the right to come before the courts as witness or accuser. Residence was still permitted. Cf. Busolt and Swoboda, 950.

[19] Schwahn τελῶναι, 420. In the difficult period after the Peloponnesian War Andocides could outbid his rivals, who offered 30 talents, by another 6 talents and still make a profit, Andoc., I, 134.

[20] Schwahn τελῶναι, 420.

[21] Boeckh, I, 408; Schwahn τελῶναι, 420 f.

[22] Boeckh, I, 407; Schwahn τελῶναι, 421.

tax had not been paid impounded, *ibid.*, 21, 133; Zenobius Centuria, I, 74 (CPG, I). [23]
The tax-farmers could lodge a complaint, φάσις, against smugglers with the *thesmothetai,*
Poll. Onom., VIII, 47. [24] If this succeeded the goods concerned were confiscated and the
evaders punished, Poll. Onom., VIII, 47 f. [25] Complaints against tax-farmers were handled
by the apodects, Aristot. De republ. Athen., 52, 3. [26] The tax-farming procedure in the
other Gk. city states seems to have been the same as in Athens, cf. the Protogenes inscr.
from Olbia, Ditt. Syll.[3], I, 495 (c. 230 B.C.).

2. Ptolemaic Egypt.

The Hell. kingdoms of the Diadochi adopted tax-farming. The basic structure remained
the same, as may be seen esp. from Egypt. sources. [27] In Ptolemaic Egypt tax-farming
was regulated by royal legislation. The state signed a contract of sale πρᾶσις (or ὠνή)
with an individual or company. The "chief lessee" and representative of such a company was
called ἀρχώνης, the tax-farmer gen. τελώνης, tax-farming was ἀγοράζω, * πρίαμαι,
λαμβάνω or ἐγλαμβάνω τὴν ὠνήν, while farming out was πωλέω or πιπράσκω. [28]
Almost all regular taxes were farmed out. [29] The changes made in the Egypt. system as
compared with the Athenian were caused by the fact that Egypt did not have a *polis*
constitution but was an absolute monarchy. Whereas Athens had as little as possible to
do with tax-farming and the collection of taxes, the Egypt. state supervised this even
down to details. For this purpose it established a considerable bureaucracy which on the
basis of long experience could estimate the probable yield of every tax. [30] One of the
royal officials, usually the οἰκονόμος, farmed out the taxes. [31] The taxes of a whole
province νομός, a district μερίς, or a locality κώμη, might be farmed out. [32] Officials
could not be farmers themselves, nor in all probability could slaves, P. Rev., 15, 1-10. [33]
But anyone else who offered the appropriate security was accepted; nationality was of

---

[23] Schwahn τελῶναι, 421.
[24] Cf. E. Berneker, Art. φάσις, Pauly-W., 38 (1938), 1897 f. The θεσμοθέται in Athens
were the last 6 archons who formed a kind of judicial court with varied jurisdictional responsibilities, cf. Aristot. De rep. Athen., 59, 1-6. They kept watch over constitutional and legal
decisions and formed a final court in actions against the state and its agencies. Accusations
φάσεις connected in some way with the interest of the state also came within their competence,
so probably disputes about tolls and taxes. Cf. on this G. Glotz, Art. "Thesmothetai,"
Darembg.-Saglio, V (1917), 242-5; K. Latte, "Thesmotheten," Pauly-W., 6a (1937), 33-37;
Busolt and Swoboda, 1096-1100.
[25] Schwahn τελῶναι, 421.
[26] The apodects, a financial board working under the council of 500, received payments
for the πόλις, esp. from farmers of tolls and mines and buyers of state lands. They could
prosecute tax-farmers. Cf. Busolt and Swoboda, 1139-1141; Schwahn τελῶναι, 421.
[27] The many pap. which have been discovered, esp. in Wilcken Ptol., I, 112 (203/202
B.C.) and P. Hibeh, I, 29 (265 B.C.), offer a detailed picture of the situation in Egypt.
Cf. Préaux, 450, n. 1.
[28] ὠνή P. Rev., 17, 14; (δια)πρᾶσις, P. Oxy., I, 44, 4 (1st cent. A.D.); P. Rev., 55, 16;
P. Zois, 1, 24 (138 B.C.), ed. C. Wessely, *Die griech. Pap. d. kaiserlichen Sammlungen Wiens*
(1885), 15; cf. Ostraka, 531; ἀρχώνης P. Rev., 34, 11-15; λαμβάνω τὰ τέλη, P. Par., 62, 1,
12 (before 170 B.C.); cf. Ostraka, 548; * πρίαμαι, P. Rev., 34, 2; 56, 14; ἐγλαμβάνω
(ἐκλαμβάνω) τὴν ὠνήν, P. Par., 62, 4, 9 f.; cf. Ostraka, 521, 539, n. 1; πωλέω, P. Rev.,
57, 3; πιπράσκω, Jos. Ant., 12, 169.
[29] Ostraka, 515 f.; on exceptions cf. Mitteis-Wilcken, I, 1, 180.
[30] Rostovtzeff Staatspacht, 339; Ostraka, 493-496.
[31] Ostraka, 517 f.; Schwahn τελῶναι, 421.
[32] νομός P. Rev., 60, 3; μερίς P. Petr., II App. (1894), p. 3; κώμη P. Rev., 54, 12;
P. Petr., II, 46 (200 B.C.); cf. Ostraka, 520.
[33] Ostraka, 522.

no account. [34] Those interested could study the publicly displayed conditions, the contracts of the previous year, and the tax rolls, P. Rev., 26, 11-17; 33, 9-18. [35] The best bids won, Jos. Ant., 12, 177; the government probably fixed a minimal rate. [36] A contract was made between the state and the lessee in which the latter undertook to pay the amount to the state in the course of a year. [37] He did not have to make a large first instalment, as in Athens. But within thirty days of the acceptance of his bid he had to produce guarantors ἐγγύους καθιστάναι, otherwise the contract was invalid, P. Rev., 34, 2-4; 56, 14; P. Par., 62, 1, 13-16; 2, 1 f. (before 170 B.C.). [38] The guarantors were investigated by the royal officials, P. Par., 62, 2, 9-13. [39] Probably each individual guarantor sponsored only one part of the sum.[40] It seems that third parties, βεβαιωταί, guaranteed the mortgages of the guarantors, P. Par., 62, 2, 7-11 (before 170 B.C.). [41] It may be assumed that the guarantors had some share in the profits. [42] Every lessee had to have an office λογευτή- ριον, P. Rev., 11, 13; [43] all revenues were brought and entered up here. Control of receipts was exercised both by the lessee and also by a state official, the ἀντιγραφεύς, P. Rev., 10, 10-13. [44] The lessee himself collected the taxes (P. Rev., 15, 10-16), [45] using his own employees for this. [46] These were the tax-collectors λογευταί, [47] servants ὑπηρέται [48] and those who kept receipts συμβολοφύλακες, P. Rev., 13, 1 f. There was also an office-manager ἔφοδος, P. Rev., 12, 17 f.; cf. P. Tebt., I, 30, 27 (115 B.C.). [49] The wages of these subordinates were fixed by law, P. Rev., 12, 14-18. The sums collected in the λογευτήριον were transferred to the royal bank and credited to the lessee's account (P. Rev., 34, 7-21), [50] though he himself did not control this. If at the end of the year, when the royal official had balanced his books, there was a surplus, ἐπιγένημα, this belonged to the tax-farmer; a deficit ἔγδεια was charged either to himself or his sponsors, P. Rev., 17, 1-19, 16; 34, 8-21. But since the tax-farmer could be glad if receipts covered the sum ἀναπληροῦν τὰς ὠνάς (P. Par., 62, 5, 3, before 170 B.C.), the state granted him in this case a share at the rate of 5-10% of the contracted sum, ὀψώνιον, P. Par., 62, 5, 3 (before 170 B.C.). [51] The tax-farmer does not seem to have had a right to distrain the goods of those who were tardy in paying their taxes; he could only give their names to the royal officials μηνύω, P. Hibeh, 29, 5 f. (265 B.C.); BGU, VIII, 1730, 9 (50/49 B.C.); Ditt. Or., II, 665, 29; also συκοφαντέω, P. Rev., 5, 1-3; cf. P.

---

[34] In the 2nd cent. B.C. we read of many Jewish as well as Greek and Egypt. tax-farmers. Cf. Ostraka, 523 f.; J. Juster, Les Juifs dans l'Empire Romain, II (1914), 257; L. Fuchs, Die Juden Ägyptens in ptolemäischer u. röm. Zeit (1924), 63 f.; V. Tcherikover, Hellenistic Civilisation (1959), 340 f.

[35] Ostraka, 527 f.

[36] Ostraka, 528.

[37] Ostraka, 531. The arrangement was for one year, P. Par., 62, 1, 1-3 (before 170 B.C.); it began on New Year's Day; cf. Ostraka, 518.

[38] Ostraka, 547-9.

[39] Royal officials could not put up pledges, P. Rev., 15, 2-5; cf. Ostraka, 549.

[40] Ostraka, 550 f.

[41] Ibid., 553 f.

[42] Ibid., 551-3.

[43] Rostovtzeff Staatspacht, 342; Ostraka, 557.

[44] Ostraka, 558-560, 639 f.; Rostovtzeff Staatspacht, 341.

[45] Ostraka, 560 f.; Schwahn τελῶναι, 424 f.; but cf. Préaux, 564; Rostovtzeff Hell. Welt, I, 257.

[46] For the personnel cf. P. Rev., 11, 16 f.; 13, 1-4; also Préaux, 456, n. 3.

[47] P. Rev., 12, 14; 13, 2; P. Petr., II App. (1894), p. 3; cf. Ostraka, 557.

[48] These sometimes collect taxes and sometimes are entrusted with other duties, P. Rev., 55, 18; cf. Ostraka, 557.

[49] Cf. Ostraka, 558.

[50] Ibid., 60-80, 560 f.

[51] Cf. ibid., 532-534.

Oxy., I, 36, 3, 4 f.; these could then seize the amounts by force. [52] The aim of tax-farming in Egypt, then, was not to relieve the state of the burden of collection or to make the income available at the beginning of the fiscal year; its sole purpose was to guarantee a fixed sum to the state. State tax officials and the tax-farmers exercised mutual control, so that revenue could be collected with no serious loss to the state treasury. [53]

3. Rome.

In Rome, too, tax-farming developed. It did so for the same reasons and in the same forms as in Athens → 89, 7 ff. Since the Roman magistrates were also in office only for short terms no civil service could arise which might have managed state property and collected dues and customs. [54] The senate supervised state finances and it commissioned the censors to farm out sources of income. Laws, the *leges censoriae*, regulated tax-farming. The tax-farmers [55] had to produce guarantors who could share the profits. Thus tax-farming companies arose. At first the state made a contract only with an individual, the head of the company. [56] It is hard to say for certain how far tax-farming in Rome was shaped by Gk. influences. [57] Tax-farming took a different course in Rome when from the end of the 3rd cent. B.C. the possessions of the Roman state increased to such a great extent. [58] Vast capital was needed to pay the required sum if the taxes of a whole region or the Spanish mines were taken up. There thus arose a tax-farming class [59] which dealt only with the farming and managing of state revenue and undertook extensive financial operations with its profits. Livy mentions that already in 212 the senate had to take the tax-farmers into account [60] and that in 168, when Macedonia was reconstructed, no one could withstand their influence. [61] Things went so far that the tax-farming companies did not just unite temporarily but constituted themselves as corporations, i.e., as legal persons with their own capital, inventory and slaves. [62] Their highest point of power was reached when Gaius Gracchus in 123 B.C. committed to them the collection

---

[52] *Ibid.*, 561-569; Mitteis-Wilcken, I, 1, 310 f.; Rostovtzeff Staatspacht, 343 f. In any case measures could be taken against delinquents by tax-farmers only with the help or knowledge of the authorities; imprisonment for debt was a possibility. Cf. R. Taubenschlag, *The Law of Greco-Roman Egypt in the Light of the Papyri²* (1955), 689.

[53] Préaux, 450 f.; Rostovtzeff Hell. Welt, I, 211 and 258.

[54] Rostovtzeff Staatspacht, 367 f.; but Schwahn tributum, 64 f. thinks tax-farming developed in Rome because wealthy citizens wanted to ensure a share in plundering the provinces.

[55] Lat. *publicanus* from *publicum* "public property," Gk. δημοσιώνης, Strabo, 12, 3, 40. Cf. on this Kniep, 1-11; Rostovtzeff Staatspacht, 375-7; Laet, 18 f.

[56] Lat. *manceps* corresponds to Attic ἀρχώνης, cf. Rostovtzeff Staatspacht, 368 f.; Laet, 97-103; A. Steinwenter, Art. "manceps," Pauly-W., 27 (1928), 987-994.

[57] Rostovtzeff Staatspacht, 368; Laet, 111 f.

[58] Rostovtzeff Staatspacht, 369 f.

[59] *Ordo publicanorum.* The gt. tax-farmers belonged to the equestrian class. Senators were not allowed to engage in business since they supervised national finances; cf. A. Stein, *Der röm. Ritterstand* (1927), 7-13.

[60] *Patres ordinem publicanorum in tali tempore offensum nolebant,* Liv., 25, 3, 12.

[61] *Ubi publicanus esset, ibi aut ius publicum vanum aut libertatem sociis nullam esse,* Liv., 45, 18, 4. On the situation in Macedonia cf. Schwahn tributum, 42.

[62] The *societas publicanorum* consisted of shareholders (*affines* or *participes*) who put up the capital, shared the profits and accepted liability for obligations to the state. These selected people to conduct the company's business, a *magister* who lived in Rome, made contracts with the state and supervised the accounts, also *promagistri* who were located in the various provinces whose taxes were farmed out to the company and who saw to the collection of taxes, receiving instructions from the *magister.* There were also several employees (*portitores*), mostly slaves, who collected sums due and performed other appropriate duties, cf. on this Laet, 102-108.

of direct taxes in the Asian province formed from the kingdom of Pergamon. [63] In 48 or 47 Julius Caesar took back this right from them in Asia, Judea and possibly Syria. [64] The power of the tax-farmers began a slow decline from this year onwards. At the end of the republic expenditures rose sharply due to a standing army, paid officials, and support of the capital. The publicans by their lack of moderation had damaged state finances and ruined the provinces. [65] Augustus and his successors took up the task of financial reorganisation. This included restriction of the power of the tax-farming corporations. Possibly under Tiberius the farming of direct taxation was taken away from them completely. [66] Nero passed further important laws. [67] The finance-procurators appointed by the emperors and serving only at their pleasure were in a position to check the ability of the provinces to pay and also to supervise the profits of the publicans; in this way they could effectively control the latter. [68] Finally the end of the companies came in the 2nd cent. A.D.; from now on most taxes were collected by imperial officials and the *portorium* was put in the hands of general tax-farmers, *conductores*. [69] From the end of the 2nd cent. the *portorium*, too, was collected directly. [70]

II. Tax-Farming in Palestine.

a. The first ref. to tax-farming in Palestine is from the time of Ptolemy II Philadelphos, 308-246 B.C. For the native population the village was an economic and taxation unit whose taxes were probably farmed out to a general tax-farmer μεμισθωμένος τὴν κώμην, cf. Preisigke Sammelbuch, V, 8008, 17. Jos. Ant., 12, 155 tells [71] how

---

[63] Laet, 72 f.; Rostovtzeff Hell. Welt, II, 640-645; Schwahn tributum, 44. The power of the tax-farmers was enhanced by the fact that from Gaius Gracchus to Sulla the assizes were largely controlled by knights, who had thus to judge members of their own class. Cf. W. Kübler, Art. "Equites Romani," Pauly-W., 6 (1909), 289-292; T. Mommsen, *Röm. Staatsrecht*, III, 1[3] (1952), 529-532; Stein, *op. cit.*, 13-21. Even provincial governors, who all belonged to the senatorial class, had reason to fear the power of the tax-farmers and members of their class, as is shown by the condemnation of Publius Rutilius Rufus in 92 B.C. Cf. H. Last, "The Enfranchisement of Italy," *The Cambridge Ancient History*, 9 (ed. S. A. Cook, F. E. Adcock and M. P. Charlesworth [1932]), 176; Rostovtzeff Hell. Welt, II, 766.

[64] Laet, 72, n. 3; Rostovtzeff Hell. Welt, II, 789-793.

[65] At first it was the task of the censors to decide disputes between the state and tax-farmers or tax-farmers and tax-payers. After Sulla the censors were to all practical purposes abolished and this task passed to the consuls and praetors in Rome and the governors in the provinces. But often the economic power of the publicans made effective control impossible. Cf. Laet., 108 f; Rostovtzeff Hell. Welt, II, 758-783.

[66] Rostovtzeff Staatspacht, 379; 415-417; Laet, 371 f. To collect direct taxes the tax-farming companies in the east of the empire signed contracts with the individual communities and cities in which the latter pledged to pay a specific sum and themselves collected the tolls. When the companies were restricted to indirect taxes the self-governing bodies retained this responsibility and the state dealt with them without intermediaries, cf. Laet, 372; Schwahn tributum, 66 f. The guarantee was given by the community councils or individuals who probably belonged to the councils, so that state revenues were in any case assured. Cf. M. Rostovtzeff, *Gesellschaft u. Wirtschaft im röm. Kaiserreich* (1929), II, 100-103.

[67] Tac. Ann., 13, 50 f. Nero ordered *inter al.*: 1. public notice to be given of the terms of each tax; 2. publicans to have only a year to lodge complaint against delinquents; 3. the praetor in Rome and legates in the provinces to have the right and duty of deciding complaints against publicans *extra ordinem;* cf. Mommsen, II, 2, 1020 f.; on the whole matter Laet, 120 f.

[68] Laet, 373; Vittinghoff portorium, 389-391.

[69] Laet, 384-403; Vittinghoff portorium, 385-8. *Portorium* is the term for any due to be collected at a place of passage. It includes customs, taxes on specific goods entering, leaving, or passing through towns, and tolls for the use of roads, bridges, and other public structures, cf. Vittinghoff portorium, 348; Laet., 16 f.

[70] Laet, 403-415.

[71] On κεφάλαιον cf. Ostraka, 241, n. 3; in criticism of Jos. Ant., 12, 154 f. and on the chronological problems, cf. Tcherikover, *op. cit.*, 128-130.

Antiochus III (241-187 B.C.) made peace with the Egypt. king after his victory at Paneas, gave him his daughter Cleopatra to wife, and threw in Coele-Syria, Samaria, Judea and Phoenicia as a dowry. Since the "tributes" φόροι of these territories were to be shared between the kings, in each town leading citizens ἐπίσημοι (cf. Ant., 12, 169) bought the collection of taxes, raised the amount laid down τὸ προστεταγμένον κεφάλαιον, and paid it to the kings. These leadings citizens were not so much entrepreneurs as representatives of their native cities who paid the kings a total sum of taxes fixed in advance, not on the basis of bids. In return they received the right to collect the taxes in their native cities. The aim was not to run a business for profit but to satisfy the claims of the two kings. Things seem to have been much the same in the story of the clever Joseph son of Tobias in Ant., 12, 158-222.[72] Acc. to this account the Egypt. king annually farmed out the indirect taxes, τέλη, of Syria and Phoenicia to leaders of the towns in these areas, Ant., 12, 169.[73] If one ignores the part played by Joseph, which differs from the usual forms,[74] these people too are not entrepreneurs but more or less official representatives of their towns[75] who because of their unusual private resources[76] were able to farm the taxes on their cities in order to meet the demands of the king. Whether they used a private organisation to collect the taxes due or whether municipal officials took care of this, it is hard to say. The wording of Ant., 12, 155: τὰς ἰδίας ... ὠνοῦντο πατρίδας φορολογεῖν, seems to support the former possibility. The tax-farming price was fixed between them and the officers of the crown[77] with some royal pressure. There was only one representative for each town, for if the tax-farmers were really commissioned by the towns these would certainly not empower several represent-atives who by their competition would only run up the price. Only with the extraordinary intervention of Joseph, who offers not merely for his own city but for all the cities together, is there an auction. But he, too, has to provide guarantors, Ant., 12, 177. His resources are not enough to enable him to pay the sum at once nor to offer security for the total amount due, as with the representatives of the cities.[78] As regards the taxation

---

[72] In criticism of this story cf. A. Büchler, *Die Tobiaden u. d. Oniaden im 2 Macc. u. in der verwandten jüd.-hell. Lit.* (1899), 43-106; Schürer, I, 183, 195 f.; II, 99 f.; Rostovtzeff Staatspacht, 359 f.; Ostraka, 520-522; Rostovtzeff Hell. Welt, I, 266 f., 273, 276; Tcherikover, *op. cit.,* 127-142; further ref. in R. Marcus, *Josephus,* 7 (1957), 767 f. The story of Joseph shows how the Hell. type of the extraordinary man who energetically and ruthlessly exploits the factors in a historical situation could occur already in Judaism at the end of the 2nd cent. The presupposition of his activity is the economic and fiscal system in the outlying areas of Ptolemy's empire. Τωβίας or Τουβίας, who is also mentioned as Joseph's father in the Zenon-Pap. (CPJud, I, Index, s.v. Τουβίας), belonged to the Jewish nobility on the one side but on the other was closely related politically and economically to Ptolemy II Phila-delphos. On the history of the Tobias family cf. J. Regner, Art. "Tobias," Pauly-W., 6a (1937), 1629-1632; O. Plöger, "Hyrkan im Ostjordanland," ZDPV, 71 (1955), 70-81; CPJud, I, 116-118, 121-129.

[73] This took place in Alexandria. Cf. on this P. Zenon, I, 59037, 6 (257/58 B.C.), ed. C. C. Edgar (1925); Rostovtzeff Hell. Welt., I, 266; Préaux, 420, n. 9.

[74] Rostovtzeff Staatspacht, 360 and Hell. Welt, I, 276 thinks Joseph went to Alexandria as a representative of the high-priest Onias to farm all the taxes of Judea. But the text merely says that he went there because of the tribute Onias had not paid, cf. Büchler, *op. cit.,* 98. This tribute was probably not farmed out but paid as a fixed sum by the high-priest, Jos. Ant., 12, 158 f., cf. 169 and 175. It so happened Joseph arrived when the τέλη were being farmed out, cf. the fact that the farmers had made a bid for the τέλη of Judea before Joseph made his comprehensive offer. Ant., 12, 175 f.

[75] Rostovtzeff Staatspacht, 360 f.

[76] οἱ δυνατοὶ οἱ ἐν ἑκάστῃ πόλει, Jos. Ant., 12, 169, cf. also 175 and Bell., 292.

[77] The king's presence at the farming out is perhaps to be regarded as part of the popular narrative style, Jos. Ant., 12, 177.

[78] Rostovtzeff Staatspacht, 361, in analogy to the practice of the publicans in Asia, thinks Joseph did not collect the taxes but made a contract with the cities for payment of a specific sum which they had then to collect.

which the Jews had to pay to the Seleucid kingdom in the 2nd cent. we receive information from Aristot. Oec., II, p. 1345b, 7 - 1346a, 24, the ref. in 1 Macc. 10:29 f. and the accounts in Jos. Ant., 12, 138-153; 13, 49-57. [79] Here, too, several taxes are farmed out; there is perhaps a ref. to this in 1 Macc. 13:39. [80] We do not know whether the Hasmoneans used the tax-farming system.

b. In 63 B.C. Pompey conquered Jerusalem, robbed the people of political liberty, and laid on the much reduced Jewish state a tribute for whose collection and payment the high-priests were probably responsible, Jos. Bell., 1, 154-158; Ant., 14, 73-76. As a result of the disorders of 57 B.C. the Syrian governor Gabinius intervened again in Jewish affairs and restricted Hyrcanus to his high-priestly office. He divided the Jewish people into five districts σύνοδοι or συνέδρια, each grouped around a city, Jos. Bell., 1, 167-170; Ant., 14, 89-91 and all for the purpose inter al. of collecting taxes. [81] At this period the Jews made acquaintance with the Roman societates publicanorum → 93, 12 ff. From Cic. De provinciis consularibus, 5, 10 one may perhaps deduce that in 56 Judea and Syria formed a single tax area whose total taxes were entrusted to a tax-farming society. The society did not raise the taxes itself but made contracts with the individual towns and communities in which these undertook to pay lump sums which they had then to collect. How this was done we do not know. [82] When Caesar came to Syria in 47 B.C. at the close of the Alexandrian War he changed the position in Judea in favour of Hyrcanus II and Antipater, who had rendered him important services in Egypt. He appointed Hyrcanus ethnarch of the Jews and Antipater procurator of Judea, Jos. Ant., 14, 143; Bell., 1, 199. In an edict of 47 B.C. he reduced Jewish taxes. Probably he exchanged the harvest dues, formerly payable in cash, for a fourth part of the produce of each second year, Jos. Ant., 14, 202-210. [83] He remitted taxes in the sabbatical year and he gave back the city of Joppa to Hyrcanus, though the latter had to give the Romans each year 20,675 bushels of grain for this district and the harbour tolls of the city. [84] The payment, including that for Joppa, had to be made in Sidon, perhaps because this was the headquarters of the company of publicans which farmed the Syrian and Judean taxes. [85] In a second edict at the beginning of 44 B.C. (cf. Jos. Ant., 14, 200 f.) Caesar abolished with the current term the system of farming out the taxes to a society in Judea. [86] We have no exact information on the further changes made by Caesar. Probably the ethnarch Hyrcanus or the procurator Antipater was made responsible for the payment of the taxes. [87]

---

[79] The most important taxes were a. a fixed sum paid directly to the royal treasury by the governments of the associated provinces, the φόρος, b. a poll tax, c. the crown tax, d. the salt tax, e. harvest dues, f. customs. Cf. Bikermann, 106-132; Rostovtzeff Hell. Welt, I, 361-8.

[80] Bikermann, 128.

[81] This seems to follow from Jos. Bell., I, 170. Jos. alternates expressions when describing the relations of individual districts to the cities. In respect of Amathus he says: οἱ δὲ ἵνα συντελῶσιν εἰς 'Αμαθοῦντα, loc. cit. Cf. on this Rostovtzeff Staatspacht, 476, n. 310; Schürer, II, 243 and the ref. in Marcus, op. cit., 780 f.

[82] On this cf. Cicero De provinciis consularibus, 5, 10. Probably Gabinius tried to squeeze out the publicans altogether. Cf. Laet, 86 f.; Rostovtzeff Hell. Welt, II, 776-8.

[83] Cf. on this Heichelheim, 231.

[84] Cf. A. Büchler, "Die priesterlichen Zehnten u. d. röm. Steuern in den Erlassen Cäsars," Festschr. f. M. Steinschneider (1896), 101; Laet, 87 f.

[85] Rostovtzeff Staatspacht, 477; cf. also Hell. Welt, II, 792.

[86] μήτε ἐργολαβῶσί τινες, Jos. Ant., 14, 201. In Asia, too, Caesar took farming of the tribute from the publicans. Cf. Juster, op. cit., I, 140; Schwahn tributum, 44; Rostovtzeff Hell. Welt, II, 792 f.

[87] When Cassius came to Syria in 44 B.C. and assembled troops he laid on Judea a tribute of 700 talents which Antipater had to collect, Jos. Bell., 1, 220-222; Ant., 14, 271-276.

c. Herod at the beginning of his reign had to pay a tribute for Idumea and Samaria. [88] But this was remitted in 30 B.C. by Augustus, so that his kingdom was free of Roman taxes from that time on. [89] He could now control his own finances. [90] There are no details on how he collected his taxes. The slaves mentioned by Jos. as collectors [91] were royal slaves. It would seem, then, that Herod did not farm out his taxes but collected them directly. [92] The ethnarch Archelaus and the tetrarch Herod Antipas had their own financial arrangements. The latter used the farming system. The dues collected in Capernaum at the time of Jesus flowed into his coffers. [93] In 6 A.D. Archelaus was deposed by Augustus and his ethnarchate was made into the Roman province of Judea. A prefect or procurator of equestrian rank took over the administration. Along with command of Roman troops and jurisdiction he had esp. the control of finances. [94] As an imperial province Judea did not pay its taxes into the *aerarium populi Romani,* which was under the supervision of the senate, but into the imperial treasury, the *fiscus,* Mk. 12:14-17 and par. [95] In the Roman provinces two kinds of direct taxes were collected, [96] the one on produce, the *tributum agri,* [97] which was paid partly in cash and partly in kind, the other a poll tax, the *tributum capitis.* [98] In NT times direct taxes were not farmed out in Judea. [99] It seems as though the Sanhedrin, under the supervision of the procurator, had to see to the collection of taxes and was responsible for their payment. Acc. to Jos. Bell., 2, 405 the leaders and councillors, exhorted thereto by Agrippa, set out to collect delinquent taxes. When the people grumbled against Agrippa and he left Jerusalem for this reason, he sent the leaders and most influential people to Gessius Florus at Caesarea in order that the latter might select from among them those who should collect the taxes, Jos. Bell., 2, 407. The fact that direct taxes were a gt. burden on the land in the time of Augustus may be seen from the request which Syria and Judea made for remission of taxes in 17 A.D., Tac. Ann., 2, 42. In addition there were the indirect taxes, e.g., the *portorium* and a tax on all purchases and leases in Jerusalem, Jos. Ant., 17, 205; 18,

---

[88] Otto, 26.

[89] *Ibid.,* 55.

[90] He could start new taxes (Jos. Ant., 17, 205), grant remission (Jos. Bell., 1, 426-8; Ant., 15, 365; 17, 299-316) and control the land of his kingdom (Otto, 58 f.), though one may assume that at least sometimes he was subject to Roman supervision as regards taxation. Cf. E. Stauffer, "Die Dauer des Census Augusti," *Stud. z. NT u. zur Patristik, Festschr. f. E. Klostermann* (1961), 11, n. 4.

[91] Jos. Ant., 17, 307 f.: τῶν δούλων, οἳ ἐπ' ἐκπράξει τῶν φόρων ἐξίοιεν.

[92] We read here of φόροι, i.e., produce or poll taxes. Herod perhaps farmed out other sources of revenue. Otto, 94 thinks the φίλοι of the king and their δοῦλοι whom Jos. mentions in Ant., 17, 308 might have been either royal officials and their servants or tax-farmers and their private slaves.

[93] τελώνιον in Mk. 2:14 and par. is a customs house. Cf. on this P. Par., 62, 8, 3 (before 170 B.C.); Ditt. Or., II, 496, 9, also Moult.-Mill., Liddell-Scott, Pr.-Bauer, *s.v.* The τελώνιον at which Levi (Mt.) sat was probably a simple exchange-table on which receipts were written and payments received; cf. καθῆσθαι ἐπὶ τὸ τελώνιον. The tax-collector could get up and go away without ado. On the other hand בֵּית חֲמֶכֶס in bSukka, 30a was perhaps a proper building.

[94] Schürer, I, 454-479; H. G. Pflaum, Art. "procurator," Pauly-W., 45 (1957), 1240-1246, 1267-1269.

[95] Laet, 364.

[96] Schürer, I, 511-513.

[97] Justinianus Digesta, 50, 15, 4, 2 (ed. T. Mommsen and P. Krüger, Corpus iuris civilis, I11 [1908]). The basic tax was raised either as a quota on the harvest or as a fixed sum independent of it. Cf. Schwahn tributum, 10 f., 62.

[98] The Roman poll tax was raised either a. as a variable capital tax (1% per annum in Syria, Appian. Rom. Hist. Syriaca, 50; cf. Tac. Ann., 13, 51; Cic. Att., 5, 16) or b. as a general poll tax. It was collected independently of the census from those who paid no other taxes. In Syria acc. to Ulpian in Just. Digesta, 50, 15, 3 men of 14 to 65 paid and women of 12 to 65, cf. Ostraka, 242 f.; Schwahn tributum, 68 f.

[99] Schürer, I, 474; II, 235 f.; Rostovtzeff Staatspacht, 378-381, 415-417.

90. [100] These indirect taxes, esp. the *portorium*, were mostly farmed out in Judea under the empire. [101] While the whole land was divided into various tax-districts, which usually followed geographical rather than administrative boundaries, and which were sometimes let out as a whole to tax-farming corporations (→ 93, 12 ff.), [102] there was separate development in Egypt, Judea and Syria in respect of the *portorium*. [103] In their administrative regulations the Romans took into account as far as possible the institutions which already existed in lands annexed by them. Thus in the eastern part of the empire they used the system of small tax-farming which had long flourished there. [104] Sometimes only a single customs post might be farmed out. On the other hand a lessee might also take over a larger area. Finally there were also corporations with a president at the head. [105] Natives usually came forward as tax-farmers, cf. Egypt. [106] Roman citizenship was not necessary.

d. Dues were collected in the following places. At the coast: 1. Gaza, Plin. Hist. Nat., 12, 32, 63-65. [107] Many caravans from the East and South-East reached a Roman customs station for the first time at Gaza and had to pay here the 25 % toll obviously imposed on all trade with the Orient. [108] 2. Ascalon. Here dwelt the publican (Bar) Ma'yan acc. to the Talmud → n. 106. [109] 3. Joppa. The Romans probably took over in 6 A.D. the customs station here, which is attested for the time of Hyrcanus II, Jos. Ant., 14, 206. [110] 4. Caesarea. Jos. Bell., 2, 287 and 292 mentions the tax-farmer John in 66 A.D.; he was one of the most influential Jews of the day and leased the highly remunerative harbour tolls. [111] Inland: 1. Jerusalem. Herod's impost on sales and leases continued in Roman times. It was ended by Vitellius in 36 A.D., Jos. Ant., 18, 90. 2. Jericho. The ἀρχιτελώνης Zacchaeus (→ n. 105 f.) collected tolls on goods coming to Judea from Perea, Lk. 19:1 f. If Jericho was not directly at the border [112] it could hardly be avoided by those travelling from Perea to Jerusalem, to Bethel, or to the North. 3. Capernaum. Here customs were probably collected on goods brought into the tetrarchy of Herod Antipas from the Decapolis. [113] How tax-farming was carried out in Judea we do not know. Probably the procurator laid it in the hands of subordinates. It has been deduced from Lk. 19:8 [114] that the Jewish tax-farmers did not have the right of executive collection in the case of those who refused to pay. As under the Egypt. system (→ 92, 27 ff.) Roman officials had to collect arrears by force. The tax-farmers could only report smugglers and

---

[100] Cf. Laet, 420-422.

[101] *Ibid.*, 421.

[102] *Ibid.*, 363 f.; Vittinghoff portorium, 351-373.

[103] Laet, 331-344.

[104] Rostovtzeff Staatspacht, 480; Vittinghoff portorium, 388 f. Individual leases explain the gt. no. of publicans, cf. Mk. 2:15 f. par. These collected other indirect taxes as well as customs, but not those paid in money (ἀργυρικά), e.g., poll taxes and harvest dues, in the time of Gessius Florus, Jos. Bell., 2, 405-407. Cf. also Schwahn tributum, 69 f. But one has always also to consider the possibility of sub-leasing in Palestine, as in Egypt, Ostraka, 547.

[105] Cf. ἀρχιτελώνης in Lk. 19:2. This word is not attested elsewhere. It perhaps denotes a head publican who joined with partners to take up a larger lease, cf. Rostovtzeff Staatspacht, 480.

[106] Zacchaeus of Jericho in Lk. 19:2, John of Caesarea in Jos. Bell., 2, 287 and Bar Ma'yan of Ascalon in jSanh., 6, 9 (23c, 32), jChag., 2, 2 (77d, 47f.) were Jews.

[107] Laet, 333 f.

[108] Laet, 335 f. deduces this esp. from the fact that this high rate is attested for Leukekome on the Red Sea, Seleucia on the Tigris, and Palmyra.

[109] The story of Bar Ma'yan was perhaps a familiar one in NT days, cf. Jeremias Gl.⁶, 178.

[110] Laet, 341.

[111] Cf. H. Dessau, *Gesch. d. röm. Kaiserzeit*, II, 2 (1930), 801 f.

[112] Rostovtzeff Staatspacht, 481.

[113] Krauss, 699, n. 438 suggests frontier tolls. Schl. Mt. on 9:9, with a ref. to Ditt. Or., II, 496, 8-11, conjectures dues for fishing rights. Cf. also Rostovtzeff Hell. Welt, I, 232.

[114] Rostovtzeff Staatspacht, 343 f., 480.

delinquents to them, cf. συκοφαντέω, Lk. 19:8 → VII, 758, 1 ff. Rabb. sources do not tells us much about tax-farming in Judea. [115]

III. The Social Position and Moral Standing of the Tax-Farmer.

1. In Antiquity Generally.

Throughout antiquity tax-farmers were feared (Herond. Mim., 6, 64) and disliked. [116] At root no one pays taxes and dues willingly to the state, especially to an alien government. Apart from this there were two reasons especially why the τελῶναι of antiquity were viewed with contempt.

a. Tolls and customs, with few exceptions, were collected for purely fiscal purposes, i.e., to fill the state coffers. [117] Thus traders encountered great difficulties even though the rates were not themselves excessive. [118] Every Gk. πόλις was naturally a separate taxing district. Furthermore the Roman empire not only raised tolls at the frontiers but was also sub-divided into a series of individual customs areas, and even within these areas there might be customs houses at some points where traders had to pay yet again, though less than at the borders. [119] The Romans simply took over the toll stations of towns and states which they had conquered during the yrs. and exploited them to their own profit. [120] In Rome there were also more or less dependent states which still managed their own finances and collected their own tolls. [121] It thus happened that on long journeys goods were often taxed many times over. In gen. provincials did not understand very well that the *pax Romana* whose advantages they enjoyed had to be paid for by financing through various dues the gigantic apparatus of Roman government.

b. Since the tax-farmer had paid or pledged to pay to the state a specific sum he had to collect more than this if he was not to suffer financial loss or even incur severe penalties. It is obvious that this system forced the tax-farmer to gather in more than was legally imposed. Furthermore he had to protect himself at all costs against fraud, Plut. De curiositate, 7 (II, 518e). These conditions gave rise to continual disputes, Artemid. Onirocr., III, 58. The rates of taxation and sometimes the manner of collection were regulated by law, but the statutes were not always known to provincials. It was possible to inspect the contracts which the state made with publicans, cf. Cic. Ep. ad Quintum

---

[115] τελώνης is transl. מוֹכֵס (from מֶכֶס "toll," "due," Aram. מִיכְסָא), cf. Accad. *miksu* and Syr. *maksa,* also מֶכֶס, Nu. 31:28, 37, the tax collected from war-booty for God. In the Palmyrenian tariff τελώνης is transl. מכסא, Corpus Inscr. Semiticarum, II, (ed. J. B. Chabot *et al.* [1926]), 3913, 2, col. 1, 38. 46. 47 etc.; cf. Levy Wört., III, Jastrow, II, *s.v.* מוֹכֵס does not specifically mean "tax-farmer" but more gen. "tax-collector," whether publican, publican's agent, or state official. The מוֹכֵס often mentioned with the גַּבָּאי has nothing to do with tolls but collects direct taxes, Gn. r., 42 on 14:1; Est. r., 2 on 1:1.

[116] Poll. Onom., VI, 128 lists 19 unworthy occupations, among which are 6 varieties of publicans and tax-collectors; in IX, 32 as many as 35 words are mentioned for reviling a tax-farmer, but only 10 can be found with which to praise him.

[117] There are, of course, individual instances of taxes for economic reasons, esp. in the Ptolemaic empire, Préaux, 371-379. The high taxes at the eastern frontier of the Roman empire hit oriental trade and were designed to check the outflow of gold to the Orient, cf. Plin. Hist. Nat., 12, 41, 84; Laet, 306-311, 333-8; also Vittinghoff portorium, 381-384.

[118] In gen. tolls were at a fixed percentage of all goods (*ad valorem*). The rate often attested for Gk. cities in the class. age was 2%. The Seleucids collected 10%, the Romans except on the eastern frontier 2% or up to 5%. Cf. Laet, 47, n. 1; 450 f.; Vittinghoff portorium, 378-381.

[119] Laet, 366-369.

[120] Laet, 55-8, 97-9; Vittinghoff portorium, 375-8.

[121] So, e.g., the tetrarchies of Herod Antipas and Philip, also the city of Palmyra.

fratrem, I, 1, 35. [122] But in practice the tax-collectors were often the only ones with precise knowledge of the relevant statutes. It was thus a significant improvement when Nero ordered that the pertinent regulations should be posted up for general inspection at every customs house, Tac. Ann., 13, 51. The bilingual inscr. found in Palmyra was obviously for this purpose. [123] Since there were often disputes between tax-payers and tax-farmers (Ditt. Or., II, 629, 6-10), the council decreed that goods not hitherto listed in the customs law should be inscribed on a stone pillar (II, 629, 11-13). Authorised municipal officials were to supervise the way tax-farmers conducted their business (II, 629, 14 f.). In gen. any traveller passing a Roman customs point had to declare all articles he had with him. Means of transport, articles for personal use, things belonging to the *fiscus* and supplies for the army were duty-free. [124] On the basis of the traveller's declaration, the *professio*, the collectors estimated the value of dutiable goods and thus fixed the rate of tax. Where there were special rates for goods this was simple enough. But when the tax was *ad valorem* there was plenty of scope for arbitrariness. [125] The collectors had the right to search goods and people if they suspected an attempt at fraud. [126] Even letters and private papers were not protected, Plaut. Trinummus, 794; Terentius Phormio, 150. [127] We also learn, however, that the tax-farmers had to bear any loss caused by search if no fraud could be detected, P. Oxy., I, 36, 2, 6-15. Goods not declared could be confiscated, *ibid.*, I, 36, 2, 11 f.; Quint. Declamationes, 341 and 359. These probably accrued to the tax-farmers. [128] Special bitterness was caused when goods on which duty had not been paid were reported by third parties who often received a bonus for this. [129] Ignorance of the regulations did not protect a traveller against confiscation. [130] A collector who confiscated anything wrongfully had to restore double the value of the goods. But if the matter was not taken up within a year simple replacement was enough. If force was used in illegal confiscation, threefold restitution had to be made, Justinianus Digesta, 39, 4, 1; 39, 4, 9, 5. But if it was merely a case of misunderstanding the collector could simply restore the excess demanded, 39, 4, 16, 14. The tax-farmers were also accountable for anything their subordinates did, 39, 4, 1, 5. [131] With all these regulations one may suspect that a simple traveller who had been defrauded often failed to lodge a complaint with the praetor in Rome or the governor in the province concerned because he did not know the proper rules or channels. This system of tax-farming was thus the main reason why for centuries we find testimony to the poor reputations of tax-farmers.

Aristot. Rhet., II, 23, p. 1397a, 23-27 quotes the saying of a tax-farmer Diomedon: "If tax-farming is no disgrace to you (the authorities), it is no disgrace to us." But this view could not carry the day, since the abuses of collection were too flagrant. It is noteworthy that the inhabitants of the province of Asia in gratitude put up statues to Titus Flavius Sabinus with the inscr. καλῶς τελωνήσαντι, Suet. Caes., VIII, 1. Tax-farmers were gen. accused of inordinate greed. Aristoph. Eq., 248 called the hated

---

[122] Laet, 100 f., 382 f.

[123] In the yr. 1881; cf. Laet, 90, 356-360. In Egypt, too, the law had sometimes to be publicly displayed in the τελώνιον, PRev, 9, 2-5. Cf. Mitteis-Wilcken, I, 184 and 211.

[124] Laet, 427-431.

[125] Laet, 439, n. 2 thinks there were probably lists for individual goods, but none is attested, and cf. Quint. Declamationes (ed. C. Ritter [1884]), 340, where there is plenty of room for personal judgment in estimating the value of a slave.

[126] Plut. De curiositate, 7 (II, 518e) speaks of objections to the inspection of baggage by tax-collectors. But they were allowed to do this by law and suffered the loss if they did not do so.

[127] Ed. S. Prete (1954).

[128] Laet, 440 f.

[129] Laet, 441; cf. Taubenschlag, *op. cit.*, 553.

[130] Justinianus Digesta, 39, 4, 16, 5: *Licet quis se ignorasse dicat, nihilo minus eum in poenam vectigalis incidere divus Hadrianus constituit.* The tax-farmer had not intentionally to give false information so that he could confiscate goods, but he also did not have to furnish any particulars. Cf. for this 39, 4, 16, 6.

[131] Laet, 445.

Paphlagonian a tax-collector, a dog, a very Charybdis, sucking up everything and never satisfied. Plut. Aquane an ignis utilior, 12 (II, 958d) calls sleep a tax-gatherer which robs us of half life. In an edict of the Roman governor in Egypt there is ref. to the greed of tax-farmers in their dealings with travellers. [132] Dio Chrys. Or., 14, 14 (Budé) thinks it incompatible with true freedom to follow certain trades like that of the tax-farmer. [133]

2. In Judaism.

In Judaism, too, tax-farmers were regarded as people who tried to get money dishonestly. Rabbinic pronouncements of the post-Christian period give us a picture of the position of the publican which does not contradict what we are told in the Synoptic Gospels.

a. They treat tax-collectors, tax-farmers and thieves as in a special way unclean.

It is noted first that they have many contacts with Gentiles. They are then counted among the 'Am ha'ares, bBek., 30b; bAZ, 39a. [134] They are the opp. of the chaberim who joined forces to make it possible to carry out the rules of tithing and Levitical purity, Demaj, 2, 2 f.; TDemaj, 2, 2; bAZ, 39a; bBek., 31a. Publicans and tax-collectors were always under suspicion of uncleanness, Kelim, 15, 4: The handle of the tax-supervisor's staff is unclean. The question is often debated whether or how far a house becomes unclean when tax-collectors and thieves enter it, Toh., 7, 6; TToh., 7, 6; 8, 5 f.; Chag., 3, 6. [135] Acc. to TDemaj, 3, 4 the tax-collector is open to suspicion that he has not tithed properly. The business of the tax-collector was incompatible with the status of a chaber or it robbed him of the status of the trustworthy (נֶאֱמָ), TDemaj, 3, 4; jDemaj, 2, 3 (23a, 11-13); bBek., 31a. [136]

b. Publicans and tax-collectors were regarded as thieves or even robbers.

In TBM, 8, 25 it is laid down to whom a thing belongs which the member of a caravan has saved from an attack by robbers. Then along the same lines it is stated to whom the toll belongs if it is not exacted from a caravan. BQ, 10, 2 lays down that an ass that publicans have given someone as a substitute for the one they have taken, or a garment that robbers have given someone in place of the one they have seized, belongs to the person concerned since it may be assumed that the former owner has accepted the loss. The rules about the uncleanness of tax-gatherers are dealt with alongside those

---

[132] Pap. in the Princeton Univ. Collections, II (ed. E. H. Kase, *Princeton Univ. Studies in Papyrology,* I [1936]), 20, 1; cf. U. Wilcken, "Urkundenreferat," APF, 12 (1937), 232.

[133] Tax-farmers were regarded as ἅρπαγες in their life and acts, Xeno Comicus Fr., 1 (CAF, III, 390), also πονηροί, Diogenes Cynicus Ep., 36, 2 (Epistolographi, 249), ἀναιδεῖς, Artemid. Onirocr., I, 23, or ἀσχήμονες, Plut. Apophth. Lac., 63 (II, 236b), αἰσχροκερδεῖς, Aspasius In ethica Nicomachea Comm., IV, 3, Comm. in Aristot. Graeca, 19, 1 (ed. G. Heyblut [1889] 102, 21); Dio Chrys. Or., 14, 14 (Budé). They were mentioned along with shopkeepers, Artemid. Onirocr., I, 23; IV, 57, usurers, Aspasius (loc. cit.), deceivers, Artemid. Onirocr., IV, 57, beggars and thieves, Luc. Pseudolog., 30, brothel-keepers, Aspasius and Dio Chrys. (loc. cit.); Luc. Menippus, 11, and robbers, Artemid. Onirocr., IV, 57, cf. also Vett. Val., I, 1 (p. 2, 11); Iambl. Babylonica Fr., 93 (ed. E. Habrich [1960]). The feelings of antiquity regarding tax-farmers may best be seen in the fact that in the preaching of the early Church the powers which threaten the soul of man on its ascent after death are depicted as tax-farmers, Ps.-Cyrillus Homiliae diversae, 14 (MPG, 77 [1864], 1073A-1076A). Cf. Mandaean ideas, Lidz. Joh., 174, 17; 175, 19 etc.

[134] Str.-B., II, 494-519; A. Büchler, *Der galiläische Am-haarez d. zweiten Jhdt.* (1906); R. Meyer, "Der Am-haarez," *Judaica,* 3 (1947), 169-210.

[135] Cf. also bChag., 26a. If only גבאין are mentioned here and not מוכסין this is perhaps because publicans collected their tolls at specific places and did not often enter houses, whereas tax-gatherers had to collect their dues from individual tax-payers, cf. BQ, 10, 1.

[136] There is no instance of a chaber being a publican. One would sometimes collect direct taxes, since in this way he could protect the Jewish population from exploitation, bSanh., 25b.

concerning the uncleanness of thieves, Toh., 7, 6; TToh., 8, 5 f. As regards restitution publicans and tax-gatherers are in the same category as robbers and usurers, bBQ, 94b; cf. TBM, 8, 26. This legal classification of tax-collectors and tax-farmers with thieves and robbers was because of their exactions and extortions. They collected more than was due, Lk. 3:13. Others had no rates that could be checked, bNed., 28a; bBQ, 113a. [137] Others again exacted tolls by false accusations, Lk. 19:8; cf. Shab., 8, 2; bShab., 78b. Finally there were some who posed as publicans with no state authorisation or lease, bNed., 28a; bBQ, 113a.

c. Whereas direct taxes (→ 97, 14 ff.) were regarded as a sign of subjection (Jos. Ant., 18, 4), [138] indirect taxes, especially tolls (→ 97, 25 ff.) seem to have been viewed more as injustice and chicanery. [139]

Protection against publicans took the form of false declarations which were not at all binding, bBB, 127b; jQid., 4, 7 (66a, 40-42). [140] False protestations and oaths were regarded as legitimate as a means of avoiding their clutches. [140] From their funds no money was to be exchanged nor gifts for social purpose disbursed, BQ, 10, 1. By denying them the right to appear as witnesses the Rabb. put them on a level with gamblers, usurers, those who flew pigeons for wagers, traders in the fruits of the fallow year, robbers, the violent, shepherds and slaves, bSanh., 25b; RH, 1, 8. They were regarded as people who in following their profession not only disregarded the Rabb. exposition of the Law but gen. transgressed the commandment of God. [142] As in the case of the robber the whole family was classified with him legally, so the family of the publican was treated in the same way as

[137] If קִצְבָּה is understood concretely as table or poster the ref. is to publicans who had not posted up the regulations in their stations.

[138] Cf. also Tert. Apol., 13, 6: *Hae sunt notae captivitatis;* cf. M. Hengel, *Die Zeloten* (1961), 132-145.

[139] We are pointed in this direction by the saying of Shim'on b Jochai that the Romans built such wonderful bridges only to be able to collect tolls at them, bShab., 33b. Cf. Avi Yonah, 63 f. In the days of Gamaliel II the toll was called one of the four burdens with which the Romans oppressed Israel, AbRNat, 2, 4; cf. Avi Yonah, 94; but cf. J. Goldin, *The Fathers acc. to Rabbi Nathan* (1956), 116. Perhaps the ref. on the fast roll to the fact that publicans (דִּימוֹסָנָאֵי = δημοσιῶναι = *publicani*) were to be expelled from Judea and Jerusalem on the 25th Siwan relates to the beginning of the rebellion of 66. The ref. is to the farmers of indirect taxes. Cf. also H. Lichtenstein, "Die Fastenrolle," HUCA, 8-9 (1931-32), 302 f. On דִּימוֹסָנָאֵי cf. Krauss Lehnw., 206.

[140] He who at a toll post has declared a man to be his son and then says he is his slave is trustworthy since he has done it to escape the slave tax. He is not trustworthy if he does not do this. Cf. also Suet. De rhetoribus, 1.

[141] Ned., 3, 4: One swears to murderers, confiscators or publicans that something is a priestly due or an imperial possession even though it is not. The Gemara, 28a explains what form of oath should be used. Many Rabb. thought cheating the customs justifiable only when the publicans were notorious rogues, bNed., 28a; bBQ, 113a; bSanh., 25b. bAZ, 13a discusses the question whether a Jew should wear a wreath to avoid paying customs which are remitted on the occasion of a festival in a pagan city. When efforts were being made to restore tolerable relations with Rome after the collapse of the Bar Cochba revolt, R. Jehuda I passed on to his son the rule of prudence that one should not evade tolls, bPes., 112b; cf. Avi Yonah, 79. There is a ruling forbidding customs evasion in a Bar. in bBQ, 113a: אסור להבריח את המכס; cf. Kil. 9, 2. But this ref. only to wearing clothes of various raw materials over one another so as to claim exemption on the ground of personal use. The laws of the Sassanids were expressly regarded by R. Shemu'el as binding on Bab. Jews: "The law of the dominion is law" דִּינָא דְמַלְכוּתָא דִּינָא. This ruled out customs evasion, bNed., 28a; bBQ, 113a. Cf. N. N. Glatzer, *Gesch. d. talmudischen Zeit* (1937), 89 f. The discussion in bBQ, 113-114a shows how Judaism wrestled with the problems that arose for men committed to God's commandment when under alien rule. Perhaps Paul's statements in R. 13:1-7 presuppose a similar discussion in his day among Jews and Jewish Christians in Rome.

[142] Jeremias Jerusalem, 345 f.

the publican himself, S. Lv. on 30:5 (91c); bShebu., 39a; jKet., 2, 10 (26d, 32 f.); jSanh., 1, 4 (19b, 19). The Rabb. demanded in principle that a thief or robber who wanted to "convert" should restore goods illegally taken or make good any loss; otherwise his conversion could not be recognised as complete, bBQ, 94b. The basis of the relevant legislation on this pt. is Lv. 6:1 ff., which orders restitution of the full value plus an extra fifth of any goods taken by fraud. Since tax-gatherers and tax-farmers were regarded as thieves and robbers they had to make appropriate restitution too if they wished to repent. This was not easy, since they had caused loss not just to one person but to several, and they might not even know all of them, TBQ, 10, 14. For this reason the conversion of tax-gatherers, publicans and shepherds was regarded as difficult, TBM, 8, 26; bBQ, 94b. To make it easier it was laid down that they should make restitution to known persons and the rest of their ill-gotten gains could be used for the common good, TBM, 8, 26. [143]

d. No doubt there were also in Palestine tax-farmers who conducted their business properly and could earn the respect of their fellow-men. Among them was the publican John who tried to settle the dispute with Gessius Florus, Jos. Bell., 2, 287. [144] So many men took part in the burial of the publican Bar Ma'yan that work stopped in the city, though there was no one at the funeral of a pious scholar who died at the same time, jChag., 2, 2 (77d, 42-57); jSanh., 6, 9 (23c, 30-43). [145]

B. Jesus and Toll-Collectors.

τελώνης occurs only in the Synoptic Gospels: 1. in the logia tradition at Mt. 11:18 f. and par., also Mt. 5:46 f.; 2. in the Mk. tradition at 2:14-17 and par. (→ n. 104); 3. in the special Mt. tradition at 10:3; 18:17; 21:31 f.; 4. in the special Lk. tradition at 3:12 f.; 7:29; 15:1; 18:9-14; 19:2. The noun τελώνιον occurs only at Mt. 2:14 par. (→ 97, 7 ff. and n. 93). It is worth noting that the Johannine tradition omits Jesus' dealings with tax-collectors. For what the NT teaches us about administrative techniques → 97, 6 ff.; 13; 98, 7 ff.; 21 ff.; 102, 4 ff.

Primitive Christianity obviously agreed wholeheartedly with the Rabbis and the Jewish people in thinking that publicans alienated themselves in a special way from God and His will by the circumstances of their profession. In Mt. 5:46 f. publicans and sinners are mentioned in the corresponding concluding clauses of a double saying. The rules which they follow in dealings with their ilk serve as a measure whereby to show of what little worth is conduct which recognises only one's peer as a neighbour and orientates itself exclusively by what the other does. Publicans and sinners are the opposite of children of the kingdom of God. [146] The

---

[143] A Bar. quoted in bBQ, 94b says one should not take anything from robbers and usurers when they want to make restitution. The wise are not satisfied with those who take anything. R. Jochanan (d. 279 A.D.) explained this ruling by adducing an illustration from the time of Rabbi.

[144] Schl. Theol. d. Judt., 186 thinks the high regard for John was possible only because the Jews in Caesarea were not yet under Pharisaic influence. Cf. also Jeremias Jerusalem, 345 f.

[145] The Rabb. narrator thinks the honourable burial was unmerited. It was revealed in a dream that Bar Ma'yan would be rewarded in this way for the only good deed he did in his life, so that he could then be led off to his punishment in the hereafter. The story is told wholly from the Rabb. standpt., but it is a popular one and found wide acceptance.

[146] The Lucan form of the logia Lk. 6:32-34 evidences a more Hell. development as regards individual terms, since it has χάρις, ἁμαρτωλός and ἀγαθοποιέω for μισθός, τελώνης and ἀσπάζομαι. It is a bit tame compared with the tautness and vividness of Mt. Its own pt. is to be found esp. in the emphasising of the contrast to the ἁμαρτωλοί mentioned (catechetical tradition). The third member of the Lucan group is adopted in Just. Apol., 15, 10, but with τελῶναι for ἁμαρτωλοί. It was natural enough to mention publicans along with money-transactions. Cf. also Plut. Lucull., 7 (I, 496b); 20 (504c); Pomp., 25 (I, 632a); De vitando aere alieno, 5 (II, 829c).

proverbial association of publicans and sinners is also found in the community order of Mt. 18:15-20. Publicans and sinners are the two groups of men who do not belong to the community: notoriously sinful Israelites who have separated themselves from the true Israel, and Gentiles; excommunicated members of the community are on their level. [147] It is notable that there are traces of a particularly negative estimation of toll-collectors in Mt. On the other hand it may be pointed out that Matthew is the only one to be called ὁ τελώνης in the list of the twelve apostles. Furthermore the judgment of publicans in Mt. 5:46 f.; 18:17 is not an independent one. The current evaluation is taken up without explanation into the line of argument, → II, 372, 15 ff. Lk's approach is not in the last analysis much different. For the toll-collectors mentioned in Lk. 18:9-14 and 19:1-10 are examples of how Israelites who are very far from God miraculously find the way to conversion. Not the publican himself, but his conversion is a model for Lk. [148] Jesus' own judgment is to the point here, for publicans are also in view when He speaks of the lost sheep of the house of Israel, Mt. 9:36; 10:6; 15:24 and cf. Lk. 19:10. The Synoptic Gospels tells how many people who belonged to those circles in the Jewish people whose conversion was said by the Rabbis to be especially difficult were gripped by the preaching of Jesus, Mk. 2:14 f. and par.; Lk. 15:1; 19:1-10. The decisive point is that neither Jesus Himself nor John the Baptist (Lk. 3:12 f.) denied them access into the saved eschatological community. The possibility of conversion is extended to the tax-gatherer too, and Jesus stresses the fact that there is special joy (→ VI, 492, 1 ff.) in heaven (Mt. 18:13 f.; Lk. 15:7, 10) precisely over the conversion of sinners of this kind. Jesus does not adopt the remnant teaching and He rejects for the present time any exclusion of specific groups, Mt. 13:24-30, 47-50. [149] He starts rather with full recognition of all Israel and with membership of the children of Abraham, Lk. 19:9. There is at this point a plain distinction from Essenism and Pharisaism. In execution of this particular commission the express summons of the Gospel is to publicans and sinners and to table-fellowship with them. This is why Jesus is called "gluttonous, and a winebibber, a friend of publicans and sinners," Mt. 11:19; Lk. 7:34. The term ἁμαρτωλός, which is used along with τελώνης, is a comprehensive word for the man whose way of life is fundamentally and perpetually in contradiction to God's demands. But it is also employed from the standpoint of the community with reference to groups standing under a specific verdict. Publicans were reviled as ἁμαρτωλοί first by the Pharisees, then by the mass of the people which had to suffer under them in everyday life, cf. Lk. 18:11; 19:7. [150]

Particular offence must have been caused by the accepting of a publican into the band of disciples. The call of Levi (→ 97, 7 f.; 98, 24 f.; IV, 234, 17 ff.) is

---

[147] The association of these groups gives evidence of a Jewish Christian outlook and is certainly Palestinian in origin. Like the Qumran sect the Christian community seems to have regarded itself as the true Israel, cf. on this W. Trilling, "Das wahre Israel," Stud. zum Alten u. Neuen Test., 10³ (1964), 116 f.; cf. also Hummel, 25 f.

[148] The words ἅρπαξ, ἄδικος, μοιχός, τελώνης on the lips of the Pharisees suggest fixed usage but they undoubtedly have a material basis, Lk. 18:11. In Lk. 19:2 Zacchaeus is esp. characterised by the fact that he is not just ἀρχιτελώνης but also πλούσιος. For Lk. wealth is plainly something which separates man from God.

[149] Cf. on this J. Jeremias, "Der Gedanke d. 'Heiligen Restes' im Spätjudt. u. in d. Verkündigung Jesu," ZNW, 42 (1949), 191-193; cf. also E. Gulin, "Zum Ursprung d. Sünderliebe Jesu," Acta Academiae Aboensis Humaniora, 7, 10 (1931), 1-18; N. A. Dahl, Das Volk Gottes (1941), 161.

[150] Jeremias ZNW, 30, 294 f.; Jeremias Gl.⁶, 132.

described in the same way as that of other disciples, cf. Mk. 2:14 with Mk. 1:16-20 and par. After it Jesus takes part in the feast in a house to which many publicans and sinners are invited. [151] In this story it is presupposed that participation in a feast is regarded as a form of particularly close fellowship, Mk. 2:15-17 and par. [152] Lk. 19:1-10 describes with special emphasis how Jesus put up at the house of the head tax-farmer (→ 98, 10 ff.) Zacchaeus in Jericho. Zacchaeus himself, in accordance with Rabbinic statutes, voluntarily swore that he would make restitution to any whom he had wronged and also give a certain amount of money to the poor. [153] In some cases the rate of restitution would be higher than that required. [154] It is worth noting that full salvation is promised to this house by Jesus even before the penitent restitution is actually made. Elsewhere, too, Jesus pronounces a word of salvation to confirm that this kind of conversion, and the publican's prayer of repentance (→ I, 331, 30 ff.), is accepted by God, Lk. 18:14. [155] In this connection it may be noted that quite obviously neither John nor Jesus demanded in principle that toll-collectors should give up their profession. [156]

The conversion of publicans and sinners is not only defended by Jesus, Lk. 15:1-32; Mt. 20:13-16. [157] It is also used as a model and a warning, Mt. 21:28-31. [158] In the parable of the Pharisee and the publican Jesus makes a particularly sharp attack (→ I, 331, 30 ff.) on the Rabbis, Lk. 18:9-14. The Berakah of the Pharisee has become praise of self rather than praise of God, whereas the publican can utter only a brief prayer of penitence. Jesus' verdict on the two cannot be detached from the situation of eschatological conflict. The Gospels set the public acceptance of publicans and sinners by Jesus in the Galilean period of His ministry, Mk. 2:13-17 and par. In the later Jerusalem period only isolated though astonishing instances of this kind are reported, Mk. 14:3-9; Lk. 7:36-50; 19:1-10.

Michel

---

[151] The text in Mk. 2:15-17 must be taken to imply that the feast was held in Levi's house (as plainly in Lk. 5:29). The difficult syntax of Mk. 2:15; Mt. 9:10 suggests that the call of Levi and the feast with the publicans were originally separate. Perhaps it was presupposed in the independent story of the feast that Jesus was the Host, cf. Loh. Mk., *ad loc.*; Jeremias Gl.⁶, 225.

[152] There were special rules to protect table-fellowship in Essenism, Jos. Bell., 2, 129, the Rabbinate, Demaj, 2, 3; TDemaj, 2, 2 f.; bSanh., 23a; bBer., 43b and primitive Christianity (the Lord's Supper).

[153] Cf. TBM, 8, 26.

[154] Acc. to Lv. 6:1 ff. in property offences, including seizure, 120% of the value of the object had to be returned. In cases of cattle rustling there had to be restitution four- or fivefold acc. to Ex. 21:37, cf. Str.-B., II, 250. Fourfold restitution for seizure through false accusation reminds us of Egypt. penalties. Cf. Taubenschlag, *op. cit.*, 553.

[155] Rabb. lit., too, mentions a form of conversion consisting only of a prayer, bSanh., 103a; jSanh., 10, 2 (28c, 48-72). From those in the professions listed in bSanh., 25b the Rabb. demanded, of course, a renunciation of their profession. One may assume that this also applied to publicans even though bSanh., 25b does not expressly say so, since these were mentioned along with notorious sinners.

[156] Cf. Schl. Lk., 212 f.

[157] From the introduction in Lk. 15:1 f. it seems that Lk. took the three parables that follow to mean that Jesus was justifying His dealings with publicans and sinners and inviting His opponents to rejoice with Him. This might well be materially correct. Cf. Jeremias Gl.⁶, 124-139.

[158] προάγω corresponds to Aram. אֳקָדֵם and can be taken in a temporal as well as an exclusive sense, Tg. Job, 41, 3. Cf. Jeremias Gl.⁶, 126, n. 2.

τέμνω, ἀποτομία, ἀπότομος,   διχοτομέω → II, 225, 17 ff.
ἀποτόμως, κατατομή,   περιτέμνω, περιτομή, ἀπερίτμητος
ὀρθοτομέω   → VI, 72, 17 ff.

† τέμνω.

The simple τέμνω [1] "to cut" is common in Gk. from Homer, but does not occur in the NT or the post-apost. fathers. This is undoubtedly accidental, for the LXX uses the word sometimes, [2] it is common in the pap., [3] and it turns up again in Chr. works, for the first time in Just. [4]

† ἀποτομία,   † ἀπότομος   † ἀποτόμως.

A. Non-Biblical Use.

1. ἀπότομος, from ἀποτέμνω, means "sharply cut," [1] but the adj. and derived adv. in -ως are hardly ever used in this basic sense. More common is the derived sense "steep," "unapproachable," of places on inaccessible crags (opp. ἐπιβατός), καὶ τὰ μὲν τρία τῶν κώλων ἐστὶ ἀπότομα, κατὰ δὲ τὸ ἒν ἐπιβατόν, Hdt., IV, 62, 1; cf. Plat. Critias, 118a; Hdt., I, 84, 3; also Philostr. Vit. Ap., III, 4 (I, 86, 23). [2] Fig. of the height from which there is no escape and which one reaches before plunging to one's doom, Soph. Oed. Tyr., 876 f. Important in the development of the transf. sense is the use for "sharp" weapons, Inscr. Graec. ad res Romanas pertinentes, III, 360, 9, [3] hence "keen" contests, CIG, II, 2880, 11-13; [4] cf. Inscr. Magn., 163, 10-11. [5]

In a transf. sense ἀπότομος almost always means "exact," so Plut. De tuenda sanitate praecepta, 15 (II, 131c.). As distinct from par. ἀκριβής "exact" in the sense of "careful," "conscientious" (cf. Ac. 26:5) it means "exact" in the sense of "strict," "sharp," un-alterable," cf. παρορᾶν τὸ τῶν νόμων ἀπότομον καὶ τὴν τῆς ἀληθείας ἀκρίβειαν, Diod. S., 1, 76, 1. Like ἀκριβής, ἀπότομος can be used neutrally with no judgment on the matter thus described: ἀπότομόν τινα συγκεφαλαίωσιν ἐποιήσατο τῶν ὑπαρ-χόντων πρὸς ὑμᾶς δικαίων, Polyb., 9, 32, 6; τοῖς δὲ περὶ τοὺς λόγους (i.e., prose authors) οὐδὲν ἔξεστι τῶν τοιούτων (namely all that is allowed to poetic licence), [6] ἀλλ' ἀποτόμως καὶ τῶν ὀνομάτων τοῖς πολιτικοῖς μόνον καὶ τῶν ἐνθυμημάτων καὶ περὶ αὐτὰς τὰς πράξεις ἀναγκαῖόν ἐστι χρῆσθαι, Isoc. Or., 9, 10; ὅτι τῶν πραγμάτων οὔτε καλῶν οὔτε αἰσχρῶν ἀποτόμως ὄντων, ἀλλὰ παρὰ τοὺς χρω-

---

τ έ μ ν ω .   [1] Outside Attic mostly τάμνω, on the etym. Boisacq and Hofmann, s.v.
[2] Lv. 25:3, 4 and Is. 5:6 (for ומר); 4 Βασ. 6:4 and Da. 2:34, 45 (for גזר); also Ex. 36:10; Wis. 5:12; 4 Macc. 9:17; 10:19. Ἀ, Σ and Θ also use it a few times.
[3] Cf. Preisigke Wört., s.v.
[4] Apol., 9, 2; 44, 7; 55, 3; Dial., 44, 4; 93, 3; 120, 5; 128, 4; 131, 3; in quotation from Da. 2:34 (→ n. 2) in Dial., 70, 1; 76, 1; 114, 4.

ἀ π ο τ ο μ ί α κ τ λ .   [1] Also with a pass. sense; for the construction cf. Schwyzer, I, 430.
[2] Liddell-Scott, s.v. takes τὰ ἀπότομα to mean "precipices." On the corresponding use of the adv. cf. Philostr. Vit. Ap., II, 5 (I, 45, 19).
[3] Ed. R. Cagnat and G. Lafaye (1906); cf. also Moult.-Mill., s.v. ἀποτόμως, who writes ad loc.: It "is believed to describe regular sharp weapons dealt out to gladiators for combat, in place of the blunt ones which the blasé populace found insufficiently exciting."
[4] The observation of the ed., ad loc.: μονομαχίαι ἀπότομοι sunt severae.
[5] Further examples in Liddell-Scott, s.v.
[6] Cf. 9, 9: τοῖς μὲν γὰρ ποιηταῖς πολλοὶ δέδονται κόσμοι.

μένους τὸ πλεῖστον διαλλαττόντων, Demosth. Or., 61, 4. But ἀπότομος is also used
to denote a strictness which is beyond all measure or reason, so that it takes on the sense
of "pitiless," "unmerciful," e.g., of Ἀνάγκη, whose merciless will is without moderation:
οὐδέ τις ἀποτόμου λήματός ἐστιν αἰδώς, Eur. Alc., 981 f., or of the pitiless severity
of a law: τὸν δὲ πηρωθέντα ἢ καθόλου τι ἐλάττωμα ἔχοντα ἐν τῷ σώματι μεθισ-
τάνειν ἑαυτὸν ἐκ τοῦ ζῆν ἀναγκάζουσι κατά τινα νόμον ἀπότομον, Diod. S., 2,
57, 5: cf. also 1, 76, 1 → 106, 23 f.; similarly to denote a personal attitude εἰσελθόντες
εἰς τὴν σύγκλητον πάντες κατηγόρουν ἀποτόμως τοῦ Φιλίππου, Polyb., 18, 11, 2;
of Crassus: καὶ τοῖς φίλοις ἐδάνειζεν ἄνευ τόκων, ἀπῆτει δ' ἀποτόμως τοῦ χρόνου
παρελθόντος εἰς ὃν ἐδάνεισε (vl.), Plut. Crass., 3 (I, 544b).

2. The noun ἀποτομία obviously does not occur until the Hell. period. Only occasionally does it mean (like the verb) "cutting off." [7] Once (cf. the adj. ἀπότομος → 106,
12 f.) it ref. to the "difficulty" of a journey. [8] But in an overwhelming majority of instances
ἀποτομία means "strictness." It thus corresponds to the last sense of ἀπότομος → 106,
21 ff. In respect of the law the "pitiless severity" called ἀποτομία may be viewed
positively: διὰ δὲ τῆς ἀποτομίας τῶν νόμων διέσωσε τοὺς νόμους ὁ νομοθέτης,
Diod. S., 12, 16, 3. Of the Egyptians, among whom parents could lay total claim to the
goods of daughters, it is said: παρ' οἷς ἄκρατός ἐστιν ἡ τῶν ν[ό]μων ἀποτομ[ί]α,
P. Oxy., II, 237, 7, 40 (186 A.D.). Here again ἀποτομία does not mean immoderate
severity [9] but the claim to inexorable validity which belongs to the law by right. [10] Such
ruthless severity is less appropriate, of course, in one's own attitude and conduct: δεῖ
τοὺς πατέρας τὴν τῶν ἐπιτιμημάτων ἀποτομίαν τῇ πραότητι μιγνύναι, Plut. Lib.
Educ., 18 (II, 13d); cf. πάντων μάλιστα ἡ περὶ τὰ δίκαια καὶ τὴν φυλακὴν τῶν
νόμων ἄκρατός τε καὶ ἀπαράπειστος καὶ οὐθὲν τῷ ἐπιεικεῖ διδοῦσα ἀποτομία,
Dion. Hal. Ant. Rom., 8, 61, 2. Legal strictness without πραότης and ἐπιείκεια is a mark
of the tyrant: πρὸς Διονύσιον τὸν τύραννον κατὰ Φαλάριδος τοῦ τυράννου ἐροῦμεν
καὶ τῆς Φαλάριδος ἀποτομίας, Ps.-Demetr., 292. Finally, then, ἀποτομία means "un-
compromising hardness" in carrying out a resolve once made, in contrast to moderate
and reasonable agreement, e.g., in the Hell. novel the mother of Dareios beseeches her
son to subject himself to Alexander: ἔασον οὖν ἐλπίδα ἐπὶ τὸ κρεῖττον καὶ μὴ
ἀποτομίᾳ χρησάμενος ἀναμφιβόλως τοῦ ζῆν στερηθῇς... ὅθεν ἐλπίζω εἰς συν-
θήκας ὑμᾶς ἀγαθὰς ἐλεύσεσθαι, Ps.-Callisth., 2, 12, 4.

B. The Septuagint and Judaism.

1. Only ἀπότομος and ἀποτόμως occur in the LXX, and even these only in Wis.
They are used for the unbending "severity" of God in His judgment of the wicked and
the mighty: ὅτι κρίσις ἀπότομος ἐν τοῖς ὑπερέχουσιν γίνεται, Wis. 6:5. The means
of divine judgment are also called ἀπότομος, e.g., His wrath in 5:20, His word which
mercilessly executes judgment in 12:9, cf. 18:15, [11] the water of the sea in 5:22. The
context of these expressions makes it plain that God is represented here as a sovereign
monarch who judges justly but does not have to give account to any for His acts, cf.
12:12-14. If on the one side He is a father admonishing the righteous, on the other side
his penal judgment is like that of a Greek tyrant (→ lines 25 ff.): τούτους μὲν γὰρ ὡς
πατὴρ νουθετῶν ἐδοκίμασας, ἐκείνους δὲ ὡς ἀπότομος βασιλεὺς καταδικάζων
ἐξήτασας, 11:10. It is thus evident that in this one LXX book which uses ἀπότομος

---

[7] Demosthenes Ophthalmicus Medicus (1st cent. A.D.) in Aetius Amidenus, VII, 81.
[8] ... τ]ὴν ἀποτομίαν τῆς ἀναβάσεως (sc. the journey towards the Nile), BGU, 1208,
16 f. (27/26 B.C.).
[9] Cf. Moult.-Mill., s.v.
[10] Perhaps one should also adduce here BGU, IV, 1024, 5, 13 (4th/5th cent. A.D.),
where the reading is ἀποτομία acc. to Moult.-Mill.: ἐνόμισας λανθάνειν τ[ὴ]ν νόμων
ἀπο[τ]ομίαν, but cf. the BGU ed.: ἐνόμισας λανθάνειν... [τὴ]ν [...]ν ἀπο[δη]μίαν.
[11] Though this occurs in a passage which uses the image of divine armour there is no
reason to find echoes of the basic sense "sharp" of swords etc. → 106, 17 ff.

the word describes the "unrelenting severity" of the divine judgment in the same way as it is used in Gk. lit. for the inexorability of the law, the pitilessness of *ananke,* or the unyielding hardness of the tyrant (→ 107, 15 ff.), a quality which in neither area is befitting in man.

2. The noun ἀποτομία does not occur in the LXX but it is found twice in Σ with ref. to Nineveh and Babylon and in both cases with the basic sense of "cruelty": ὦ πόλις αἱμάτων ὅλη ψευδὴς ἀποτομίας πλήρης (LXX ἀδικίας πλήρης for כֻּלָּהּ כַּחַשׁ), Na. 3:1; καὶ ἡ ἀποτομία μου κατὰ Βαβυλῶνος, Ιερ. 38(51):35 (LXX αἱ ταλαιπωρίαι for וּשְׁאֵרִי אֶל בָּבֶל).[12]

3. ἀποτέμνω is common in Jos. and one also finds the adj. ἀπότομος twice in the sense of "steep," "inaccessible," of the city of Jotapatah πάντοθεν φάραγξιν ἀπείροις ἀπότομος, Bell., 3, 158, of Sinai which men cannot climb because of the steepness of its slopes τῶν κρημνῶν τὸ ἀπότομον, Ant., 3, 76. The adj. is also used once in a transf. sense for the "tyrannical harshness" of Herod ἐκείνῳ γὰρ πονηρὸν ἦν ἦθος ἐπὶ τιμωρίαν ἀπότομον, Ant., 19, 329. Philo uses the noun in the same sense for "merciless and crushing ferocity," Flacc., 95; Spec. Leg., II, 94.

C. The New Testament.

1. The adverb ἀποτόμως occurs in 2 C. 13:10. Paul is giving an unusually sharp warning here. His concern in the letter is to settle the matter so as to avoid the only other alternative: ἵνα παρὼν μὴ ἀποτόμως χρήσωμαι κατὰ τὴν ἐξουσίαν. To translate ἀποτόμως by "strictly" is not satisfactory here, for the meaning can hardly be that Paul has not acted strictly enough in this letter or in the recent visit,[13] but will do so in the future. What ἀποτόμως denotes is surely a completely different dimension of Paul's authority, namely, the power of crushing judgment, which is not the intention of the gift of this authority, but which is materially implicit in it: ἣν ὁ κύριος ἔδωκέν μοι εἰς οἰκοδομὴν καὶ οὐκ εἰς καθαίρεσιν. If this is so, ἀποτόμως has the same sense here as in Wis. → 107, 34 ff. It denotes the inflexibly sharp judgment which might in this case result in the destruction of the community.[14] In contrast Tt. 1:3 has in view the very sharp correction which will make heretics sound in faith again.

2. The noun ἀποτομία occurs in the NT only at R. 11:22.[15] Here we find it twice as the opposite of χρηστότης. As the admonition μὴ ὑψηλὰ φρόνει, ἀλλὰ φοβοῦ (R. 11:20) follows wisdom style[16] (cf. Wis. 6:5 — 107, 35 ff.), so the warning juxtaposition of God's goodness and severity is one of the main themes of Jewish wisdom. There can thus be no doubt but that ἀποτομία here is to be understood in the same way as ἀπότομος in Wis. (→ 107, 41 ff.): Those who do not cleave to God's goodness are threatened by "the inflexible hardness and severity" of the Judge as the only alternative. The severity of the divine judgment is thus described here by an expression which was used already in Greek for the pitiless severity of the law (→ 107, 15 ff.) and which was applied by Paul to God's judicial work under the influence of the usage of Wis.

---

[12] The HT is hard to expound. Perhaps ἀποτομία has here again the sense of judgment without grace.

[13] On the relation of 2 C. 10-13 to the intermediate visit *v.* G. Bornkamm, "Die Vorgeschichte d. sog. 2 K.," SAH, 1961, 2 (1961), 16-23.

[14] Cf. the condemnation of the incestuous person in 1 C. 5:1-5. There, too, Paul's absence plays some part.

[15] Nor does the word occur in other primitive Chr. writings outside the NT.

[16] Cf. Mi. R., *ad loc.*

D. The Post-Apostolic Fathers.

ἀπότομος occurs once in the post-apost. fathers. It is a merit of righteous presbyters not to use their judicial authority without clemency: μὴ ἀπότομοι ἐν κρίσει, εἰδότες, ὅτι πάντες ὀφειλέται ἐσμὲν ἁμαρτίας, Pol., 6, 1. Thus a righteous presbyter should not act like a tyrant in his judgment, or, to adopt the usage of Wis. (→ 107, 35 ff.), he is not to anticipate God's judicial severity in his own office.

† κατατομή.

A. Non-Biblical Greek.

The noun κατατομή derives from κατατέμνω[1] and means "incision," "sectional plane," but is is much less common than the verb[2] and in its use it is obviously restricted for the most part to the scientific and technical world,[3] e.g., in describing plants λωτὸς ("water-lily") ... διέζωσται ταῖς κατατομαῖς τὸν αὐτὸν τρόπον τῇ μήκωνι, Theophr. Hist. Plant., IV, 8, 10; the smoothly polished surface of a tree: λεῖα ἐκπεποιημένα ἄνευ κατατομῆς, IG, I², 372, 134 f.; cf. 373, 231. A related sense is the "surface" or "sectional plane" of a stone: ἐπέγραψεν ἐπὶ τὴν κατατομὴν τῆς πέτρας, Philochorus Fr,. 138 (FHG, I, 407): μέταλλον καὶ κατατομήν, IG, II/III², 1582, 70.[4] There is no evidence of any transf. use of κατατομή. One thus finds no basis for the sense at Phil. 3:2 in the use of the noun. Important here, however, is a special use of the verb κατατέμνω, which in its basic sense "to cut in pieces" is also employed for the cutting up of meat, esp. sacrificial meat: πρόβατα καὶ ἔπειτα ταῦτα θύσαντες καὶ κατατα-μόντες τὰ κρέα, Hdt., IV, 26, 1; ἵν' εἰσάγοιτο σπλάγχνα κατατετμημένα, Aristoph. Av., 1524. This explains the common use of the verb in ironic or malicious observations. It is said of sailors who all think they can steer: φάσκοντας μηδὲ διδακτὸν εἶναι, ἀλλὰ καὶ τὸν λέγοντα ὡς διδακτὸν ἑτοίμους κατατέμνειν ("to cut into strips"), Plat. Resp., VI, 488b; ὡς μεμίσηκά σε Κλέωνος ἔτι μᾶλλον, ὃν κατατεμῶ τοῖσιν ἱππεῦσι καττύματα, Aristoph. Ach., 300 f.; of Socrates, who taught that one should renounce family ties etc.: ταῦτ' οὖν ἔλεγεν οὐ τὸν μὲν πατέρα ζῶντα κατορύττειν διδάσκων, ἑαυτὸν δὲ κατατέμνειν, Xenoph. Mem., I, 2, 55. In this usage "to cut into strips" is used ironically or spitefully for "to crush," "to kill." There is a similar ironic-metaphorical usage in the following instances: from a speech against Demosthenes ὥστε τὴν μιαρὰν κεφαλὴν ταύτην ... μυριάκις κατατέτμηκε, "he has hacked off his own filthy head a thousand times,"[5] Aeschin. In Ctesiphontem, 212, or the charge against Socrates: ἕκαστον τῶν ὄντων ἐν τοῖς λόγοις κατατέμνοντες "while they (Socrates and his friends) chop up all things with words," Plat. Hi., I, 301b. This ironic use may not be without significance for an understanding of κατατομή in Phil. 3:2.

κ α τ α τ ο μ ή. Bibl.: J. B. Lightfoot, *St. Paul's Ep. to the Philippians*[6] (1891) on 3:2; R. Bultmann, *Der Stil d. paul. Predigt u. die kynisch-stoische Diatribe* (1910), 105; Loh. Phil. on 3:2; Pr.-Bauer, *s.v.*; F. W. Beare, *The Ep. to the Phil.* (1959) on 3:2; H. Koester, "The Purpose of the Polemic of a Pauline Fragment," NTSt, 8 (1962/63), 319-322; H. v. Campenhausen, "Ein Witz des Ap. Pls. u. d. Anfänge des chr. Humors," *Aus d. Frühzeit des Christentums* (1963), 104 f.

[1] On the formation of κατατομή cf. Schwyzer, I, 460.

[2] κατατέμνω in the sense "to cut in pieces," e.g., καὶ ὁ ἡγεμὼν αὐτός τε κατέτεμνε τὰ γέρρα, Xenoph. An., IV, 7, 26, "to divide by cutting up" ἡ γὰρ Βαβυλωνίη χώρη πᾶσα ... κατατέτμηται [ἐς] διώρυχας, Hdt., I, 193, 2; cf. Xenoph. An., II, 4, 13; IG, II/III², 1668, 7; but also the partition of a city: Ἱππόδαμος (a famous city-builder of the 5th cent. B.C.), ὃς καὶ τὴν τῶν πόλεων διαίρεσιν εὗρε καὶ τὸν Πειραιᾶ κατέτεμεν, Aristot. Pol., II, 8, p. 1267b, 22 f.

[3] On the use of the word for a part of the theatre cf. Liddell-Scott, *s.v.*

[4] Liddell-Scott, *s.v.*: "perhaps a mine and a quarry face."

[5] The meaning is that he intentionally attracted injuries to make capital out of his wounds when accusing others of wilful damage.

B. The Septuagint.

The noun κατατομή does not occur at all in the LXX but we sometimes find the verb κατατέμνω, always for the forbidden rite of slitting the skin. κατετέμνοντο κατὰ τὸν ἐθισμὸν αὐτῶν ἐν μαχαίραις ... ἕως ἐκχύσεως αἵματος, 3 Βασ. 18:28; ἐπὶ σίτῳ καὶ οἴνῳ κατετέμνοντο, Hos. 7:14; as a mourning practice πάντες βραχίονες κατατετμημένοι, Is. 15:2; [6] cf. Lv. 19:28. The Hbr. original of κατατέμνω in the first two passages is דדּ hitp, 1 K. 18:28; Hos. 7:14. [7] The transl. of this by κατατέμνω is even more consistent in the later translations, cf. ᾿Α and Σ at Ιερ. 48(41):5 (LXX κόπτομαι), Σ at Jer. 16:6 (LXX ἐντομίδας ποιέω), ᾿Α, Σ Θ at Dt. 14:1 (LXX φοιβάω). Apart from these verses דדּ hitp occurs in the OT only at Mi. 4:14; Jer. 5:7; 47:5; here other terms are used for it in LXX. [8] Thus κατατέμνω is a precise and common rendering of דדּ hitp in the Gk. Bible. In sum 4 (or 5) of 7 (or 8) instances have it in LXX or ᾿Α, Σ and Θ. Finally, Ιερ. 31(48):37 is important. HT here has in parallelism גרע for cutting off the beard and גְּדָה for cultic incisions. The LXX transl. by ξυρέω and κόπτω, ᾿Α by κατατέμνω [9] and καταπλήττω, but Σ by ξυρέω and κατατομή. This is the only instance of the use of the substantive κατατομή in a cultic connection, and it is undoubtedly significant that the word could be used in a recension of the Gk. OT for the forbidden practice of cultic incisions. This use of the noun and the corresponding use of the verb in the Gk. OT is at least an indication of a fairly well established technical usage. [10]

C. The New Testament.

κατατομή occurs in the NT only at Phil. 3:2. The verb is absent altogether. Neither noun nor verb is found elsewhere in primitive Christian literature. We have in Phil. 3:2 a polemic against Jewish Christian Gnosticism. [11] These adversaries undoubtedly advocated and propagated circumcision. [12] Paul describes them as κύνες, κακοὶ ἐργάται, and κατατομή. In so doing he apostrophises und presses to absurdity a claim of his adversaries, namely, that they are missionaries accredited by the Spirit and that they possess circumcision, cf. Phil. 3:3. κατατομή indubitably refers to the latter ground of the opponents' boasting, namely, περιτομή. One should not take this to mean that Paul has in mind the fact that propaganda for circumcision causes "division" κατατομή in the community. [13] Nor is he alluding to the fact that circumcision works to the destruction of his adversaries. [14] The word κατατομή is never used in such a sense in Greek elsewhere. The only other possibility is that we have a paronomasia in Phil. 3:2. In an ironic play on words

[6] The idea is that of slitting the arm, whereas the HT ref. to cutting off the beard.

[7] The גרד of the HT at Hos. 7:14 should be emended to גדד, cf. BHK, ad loc.; H. W. Wolff, Dodekapropheton, Bibl. Komm., 14:1 (1961), 136, on incisions in the rite of adjuration, 163.

[8] LXX transl. Mi. 4:14 by ἐμφράσσω, Jer. 5:7 by καταλύω, and Ιερ. 29(47):5 by κόπτω.

[9] So acc. to MS 86, but ξύρησις acc. to Syrohexapla, cf. J. Ziegler, Jeremias, Vetus Testamentum Graecum auctoritate Societatis Litterarum Gottingensis editum, 15 (1957), ad loc.

[10] Neither verb nor noun is found in Philo or Joseph.

[11] W. Schmithals, "Die Irrlehrer d. Phil.," ZThK, 54 (1957), 313. Older exegesis mostly favours a ref. to Jews, so also Dib. Ph. and Loh. Phil., ad loc. For a discussion of the whole question cf. Schmithals, also Köster, 318 f.

[12] Paul describes his opponents herewith as men who value circumcision, who are themselves circumcised, and who — possibly — include the practice of circumcision among their wicked works, Schmithals, 313.

[13] K. Barth, Erklärung d. Phil. (1928), ad loc. thinks this interpretation is over-clever.

[14] So Dib. Ph., ad loc.: "The adversaries are people for whom περιτομή becomes κατατομή and hence destruction."

Paul brings against his adversaries the objection that their vaunted circumcision (περιτομή) is in reality dissection (κατατομή). [15] Paul himself, by using the nuances of κατατομή and κατατέμνω, fin⌐s here an ironic play on words for his polemic. [16]

This development may be readily understood against the background of the use of ironic playing on words in the diatribe, [17] the use of the verb κατατέμνω in ironic statements in Greek generally (→ 109, 22 ff.), and finally the fact that in the Gk. OT κατατέμνω denotes ritual maimings which were abhorrent to a Jew, → 110, 2 ff. [18] All three factors are present in the idea of "dissection," and the word is intentionally ambiguous as an ironic term of abuse. The nature of the play on words reminds us of the ironic demand in Gl. 5:12 περιτέμνω - ἀποκόπτω, → III, 853, 27 ff. [19] In both cases we have bitter and aggressive irony rather than genuine humour. [20] This is produced by the sharpness of the theological controversy, nor does it shrink from wounding statements. Paul was never timid in debate.

† ὀρθοτομέω.

This occurs only in the Gk. Bible [1] and even here only a few times: Prv. 3:6; 11:5; 2 Tm. 2:15.

1. At root is a usage current in profane Gk. in which τέμνω ὁδόν means "to lay down a way," "to build a road," e.g., Ἀρχέλαος... ὁδοὺς εὐθείας ἔτεμε, Thuc., II, 100, 2; also "to open a way," e.g., μίαν ὁδὸν τέμνειν ἄχρις ἂν ὅτου ἔλθωσιν εἰς τόπους οἰκουμένους, Jos. Ap., 1, 309; ἡ τετμημένη ὁδός is "the finished road," Plut. Galb., 24 (I, 1064c); Hdt., IV, 136, 2. Esp. important is the fact that ἡ τετμημένη ὁδός can also mean fig. the passable way, e.g., of legislation: καὶ θαρροῦντα τὴν νῦν ἐκ τῶν παρόντων λόγων τετμημένην ὁδὸν τῆς νομοθεσίας πορεύεσθαι, Plat. Leg., VII, 810e.

2. In the LXX we do not find τέμνω ὁδόν, but twice ὀρθοτομέω ὁδόν denoting "to open a way": ἐν πάσαις ὁδοῖς σου γνώριζε αὐτήν (sc. τὴν δικαιοσύνην), ἵνα ὀρθοτομῇ τὰς ὁδούς σου, Prv. 3:6, and δικαιοσύνη ἀμώμους ὀρθοτομεῖ ὁδούς, Prv. 11:5. In content this corresponds to the fig. use of τέμνω ὁδόν elsewhere in Gk. lit. The use of ὀρθοτομέω [2] for the simple τέμνω is based on the underlying Hbr. יׁשׁר pi (אֹרַח or דֶּרֶך). The Hebr. expression אֹרַח or דֶּרֶך יְשָׁרָה "the straight way" on which Yahweh leads His people or the righteous is transl. in the LXX by ὁδὸς εὐθεῖα 1 Βασ. 12:23; ψ 106:7; Prv. 20:11, or by ὁδὸς ὀρθή, Ιερ. 38(31):9; Prv. 16:25. [3] Similarly in the LXX κατευθύνοντες at Prv. 9:15 or κατορθοῦντες at Prv. 2:7 corresponds to Hbr. מְיׁשָׁרִים or יְשָׁרׅים as a term for those who tread this way. Thus ὀρθοτομέω ὁδόν instead

---

[15] For ancient and modern examples of such play on words cf. Lightfoot, ad loc. Loh. Phil., ad loc. also ref. to S. Glass, Philologia Sacra (1705), 1989-2075, and he gives OT examples. The most familiar example adduced here is: καὶ τὴν μὲν Εὐκλείδου σχολὴν ἔλεγε χολήν, τὴν δὲ Πλάτωνος διατριβὴν κατατριβήν, Diog. L., VI, 24.

[16] "Paul denies this title to the Jews and replaces it with the jeering title of his own coinage," Beare, 104.

[17] Cf. on this Bultmann, 105.

[18] Lightfoot and Loh. Phil., ad loc. rightly ref. to his factor.

[19] Cf. on this Campenhausen, 104 f.

[20] Ibid., 105; Bultmann, 105.

ὀρθοτομέω. Bibl.: Pr.-Bauer, Moult.-Mill., s.v.; Dib. Past. and W. Lock, The Pastoral Ep., ICC (1924) on 2 Tm. 2:15.

[1] For the use in ecclesiastical Gk. dependent on the Bible cf. Sophocles Lex., s.v. ὀρθοτομέω and ὀρθοτομία.

[2] To be derived from a virtual ὀρθοτόμος "cutting straight."

[3] On ὀρθός etc. in the LXX → V, 449, 24 ff.

of the usual τέμνω ὁδόν has its roots in the Hbr. usage of Wisdom lit. and is to be regarded as a typical LXX expression. The whole stress is on the ὀρθο-, [4] so that one should transl. "to make (the way) straight."

3. ὀρθοτομέω does not occur in later Jewish lit. But we find closely related terms like κατευθύνω and κατορθόω, also the rarer εὐθύνω and ὀρθόω, which are already used in the LXX for ישׁר and which are still in the first instance linked closely with the idea of the way → V, 50, 7'ff., cf. Test. Jud. 26:1; S. 5:2. This usage continues in Hbr. witnesses too, cf. 1 QS 4:2; 1 QH 12:34. [5] But the fig. idea that this ὁδός is the way of life on which the righteous walks becomes less pronounced, and the way or ways are simply God's commandments. The metaphorical content of the relevant terms is thus forfeited. τοῖς κατευθύνουσι τὰς ὁδοὺς αὐτοῦ in Test. Jud. 26:1 [6] thus means "those who follow his commandments aright." [7]

4. In the one NT instance of ὀρθοτομέω (2 Tm. 2:15) the figurative idea of the way is so pale that a theological concept can be the direct object: ὀρθοτομοῦντα τὸν λόγον τῆς ἀληθείας, cf. Herm. v., 3, 5, 3 → n. 7; → lines 23 ff. Whereas the false teachers engage in irreligious theological chatter which can only destroy their hearers and which leads to an ungodly walk (2:14, 16), Timothy is to be a workman of God who need not be ashamed since he "does what is right with reference to the word of truth." This cannot mean in the context that Timothy should "trim" [8] or "handle" [9] the word of truth rightly. The view that he is to deliver the word of truth correctly in proclamation [10] is also impossible in view of the parallels adduced. [11] One can no longer take into account the metaphorical aspect, nor can the word of truth be the object of Timothy's ὀρθοτομέω in the simple sense. Rather one is to construe the expression along the lines of κατορθόομαι τὰς ἐντολὰς (Herm. v., 3, 5, 3) and ὀρθοποδέω πρὸς τὴν ἀλήθειαν τοῦ εὐαγγελίου (Gl. 2:14 → V, 451, 16 ff.). In his conduct Timothy must "speak the word of truth aright," i.e., follow it. When he puts his acts under the word of truth he is worthy before God and he need not be ashamed, 2 Tm. 2:15. He is superior to the false teachers, not because he can present the word better, nor because he offers it in a theologically legitimate form, but because he follows this word of truth aright in his own life, and thus confirms it.

Köster

---

[4] Cf. the par. καινοτομέω "to establish something new"; examples in Dib. Past. on 2 Tm. 2:15.

[5] In primitive Chr. lit. plainest in Herm., cf. v., 2, 2, 6.

[6] So acc. to Cod β, S¹ for מישרים, which can claim priority as compared with κατέχουσιν in Cod α (as against Charles, ad loc.); cf. also the passages from 1 QS and 1 QH → 112, 8.

[7] ἐντολαί can easily replace ὁδοί, cf. Herm. v., 3, 5, 3: καθωρθώσαντο τὰς ἐντολὰς αὐτοῦ.

[8] "To cut the word of truth according to the right norm which is given in the Gospel," B. Weiss, *Die Briefe Pauli an Tm. u. Tt.* (1902), ad loc. This is impossible, since the word of truth and the Gospel are one and the same thing.

[9] To be rejected are attempts to expound ὀρθοτομέω here in terms of the hewing of stones for the building of the Church. This is linguistically impossible and furthermore the idea is absurd.

[10] So Pr.-Bauer, *s.v.* and most comm., ad loc. Pr.-Bauer paraphrases: "cause the road to cut the district in a straight line."

[11] One may thus doubt also whether the equation of ὀρθοτομία and ὀρθοδοξία by the fathers on the basis of 1 Tm. 2:15 really corresponds to the original sense, cf. Eus. Hist. Eccl., IV, 3, 1 and Sophocles Lex., *s.v.* The liturgical use in teaching about episcopal responsibilities as an admonition to vigilance as to correct doctrine rests on a later misunderstanding of the v., cf. Lock on 2:15.

† τέρας   → σημεῖον, VII, 200, 24 ff.

Contents: A. Non-Biblical Greek Usage: 1. The Usage as Such; 2. The Theological
·Reference; 3. On the Trend and Development of the Usage; 4. σημεῖα καὶ τέρατα. B. The
Old Testament and Greek Judaism: 1. τέρας as a Translation of מוֹפֵת in the Septuagint;
2. τέρας in Non-Biblical Greek Judaism: a. Philo; b. Josephus; c. The Pseudepigrapha;
d. σημεῖα καὶ τέρατα. C. Post-Biblical Judaism: 1. The Dead Sea Scrolls; 2. Rabbinic
Judaism. D. The New Testament: 1. Reasons for the Absence of τέρας Alone; 2. σημεῖα
καὶ τέρατα - τέρατα καὶ σημεῖα. E. The Early Church.

A. Non-Biblical Greek Usage.

1. The Usage as Such.

The word occurs in literature from Hom. and is obviously part of the older Gk.
vocabulary, since it is already widespread and fairly common in early times. Yet the
origin and original meaning are obscure. An attempt to link τέρας with Assyr. *tertu*
(omen), [1] which, if one ignores linguistic factors, finds support in some peculiarities of
usage, is questionable. [2] Acc. to a common view [3] τέρας is etym. akin to πέλωρ, "terrible
miraculous sign," then "monster." [4] But it is more accurate [5] to limit oneself to the claim
that the two words belong to the same linguistic field and overlap in meaning, but are
not co-extensive. Thus in connection with one of the first instances of τέρας, in the
description of the αἰγίς, the terror-kindling shield of Zeus, the Γοργείη κεφαλὴ δεινοῖο
πελώρου is mentioned as one of the emblems, and this is then characterised as the Διὸς
τέρας αἰγιόχοιο, Hom. Il., 5, 741 f. Here, then, τέρας denotes the fear-arousing force
of a monster. The same applies in Il., 2, 278-332, where Odysseus recalls a dreadful
μέγα σῆμα observed by all at the beginning of the campaign against Troy, calls it δεινὰ
πέλωρα, and adopts the verdict of the seer Calchas, who saw in the unusual event a

---

τ έ ρ α ς . Bibl.: On A.: Liddell-Scott, Pass., *s.v.*; A. E. Housman, "On the Paeans of
Pindar," Class. Rev., 22 (1908), 8-12; C. F. v. Nägelsbach, *Homerische Theologie*[2] (1861),
168-194; P. Stein, ΤΕΡΑΣ, Diss. Marburg (1909); H. Stockinger, *Die Vorzeichen im homer.
Epos. Ihre Typik u. ihre Bedeutung* (1959). On B.: Köhler-Baumg., *s.v.* מוֹפֵת; C. A. Keller,
Das Wort OTH als "Offenbarungszeichen Gottes," Diss. Basel (1946); L. Köhler, *Theol.
d. AT*[2] (1947), 85 f.; Schl. Theol. d. Judt., 69. On D.: Pr.-Bauer, *s.v.*; G. Delling, *Jesu
Wunder in d. Predigt* (1940), 14-16; A. Fridrichsen, "Observationen z. NT aus Aelians Varia
Historia," *Symb. Osl.,* 5 (1927), 60-66; Trench, 218-221. On E.: H. Schlingensiepen, "Die
Wunder d. NT. Wege u. Abwege ihrer Deutung bis zur Mitte des fünften Jhdt.," BFTh, II,
28 (1933).
   [1] H. Lewy, "Etymologien," ZvglSpr, 58 (1931), 30 f.
   [2] So P. Kretschmer, "Literaturbericht f. d. Jahr 1930," *Glotta,* 21 (1933), 181.
   [3] The explanation advanced by H. Osthoff, "Etym. Beiträge z. Mythologie u. Religionsgeschichte 2: πέλωρ u. τέρας," ARW, 8 (1905), 51-68 has been adopted by Boisacq and
Hofmann, *s.v.*
   [4] On the forms and meaning of πέλωρ (adj. πελώριος) in early epic cf. H. Troxler,
Sprache u. Wortschatz Hesiods, Diss. Zürich (1964) [Risch].
   [5] Osthoff's explanation *(op. cit.,* 56) rests cn the assumpticn that the λ in πέλωρ is from
ρ and the τ of τέρας from qᵘ; but the Aeolic form τερέων (plur. gen.) in Alcaeus Fr., line
101 (ed. E. Lobel - D. Page [1955], 286) is against this [Risch].

τέρας μέγα and related it to the approaching ten-year war of the Gks. to take the city. Here πέλωρον or πέλωρ denotes a *stupendum* as such, but the stress in the case of τέρας is on the terror awakened by the sight of the *stupendum*. [6] On the other hand, in distinction from σῆμα, which as a formal concept pts. to the need for attention and consideration (→ VII, 203, 1 ff.), the tendency with τέρας is to submit what is perceived to the question of its divine purpose and to explain or interpret it. In this regard, as the second example shows, the *tremendum* in τέρας may be an omen which for all its dreadfulness pts. to something good.

The use in non-biblical Gk. everywhere corresponds to the character of τέρας in the oldest stratum of its occurrence. It plays no decisive role, whether the ref. be to unusual natural phenomena which awaken terror like a clap of thunder in a clear sky (Hom. Od., 20, 101-104) or whether it be to dreadful monsters like the hell-hound Cerberus (Soph. Trach., 1098), the sphinx (Eur. Phoen., 806), the Minotaur (Isoc. Or., 27), [7] or a monster born contrary to the natural order (Plat. Crat., 393b, 394d). Even when this word which is so strongly controlled by feeling is used more weakly as part of an expression [8] this fits in with the use corresponding to the structure of the term.

For the understanding and use of τέρας in Aristot. the aspect of παρὰ φύσιν is determinative. [9] Aristot. perhaps followed Plato (→ line 13 f.), unless he adopted an earlier established use of the term in the technical vocabulary of science and medicine, as in Hdt., I, 59 and also the tragedians (→ line 12 f.) and Aristoph. (e.g., Pax, 755-759): τέρας is what is παρὰ φύσιν. [10]

2. The Theological Reference.

a. In connection with its earliest use τέρας seems to have a clear theological reference. This is because for Hom. τέραα [11] are always seen in causal connection with the gods. [12]

---

[6] Conclusive in this regard is Pind. Pyth., 1, 25 ff.: The Typhon moving in Etna, a mythological monster with a hundred dragon-heads spewing out fire, sends out terrible rivers (of fire) through the crater of Hephaestus, with the result: τέρας μὲν θαυμάσιον προσιδέσθαι, θαῦμα δὲ καὶ παρεόντων ἀκοῦσαι. Only direct impression establishes a τέρας (Housman, 9 for Pind. Paeanes, 4, 39 τέρας δ' ἐόν: "his own miraculous experience"), while for those who know it through witnesses we have no more than θαῦμα. The differentiated use of πέλωρ and τέρας together in Hom. influences the Homeric-style epic of Apoll. Rhod., e.g., Argonautica, IV, 1364 f. (Seaton): ἔνθα τὸ μήκιστον τεράων Μινύησιν ἐτύχθη. ἐξ ἁλὸς ἤπειρόνδε πελώριος ἔκθορεν ἵππος... In content τέρας is here a sign denoting deliverance, though it needs interpretation to be understood.

[7] Cf. already on the Gorgon → 113, 18 ff., Typhon → n. 6. On the monsters mentioned cf. also Stein, 17-19 and on others 22-25.

[8] E.g., Plat. Theaet., 163d: τέρας γὰρ ἂν εἴη ὃ λέγεις. There are related expressions in Plat. Men., 91d; Hi., I, 283c; Theaet., 164b; Phaed., 101b etc. Here the word ref. to something that deviates from gen. perception or opinion and is thus shocking, cf. also Stein, 25 f. Eur. Hel., 260 offers an instructive pre-platonic example in Helen's own conclusion as to her unusual origin: τέρας γὰρ ὁ βίος καὶ τὰ πράγματ' ἐστί μου... Cf. also K. Kerényi, "Die Geburt d. Helena," *Albae Vigiliae*, NF, 3 (1945), 9-28.

[9] Cf. the materials in Stein, 7-16.

[10] The def. of τέρας as παρὰ φύσιν naturally presupposes the concept of nature developed from the late 5th cent. B.C. in philosophy, science, and gen. culture. On this basis παρὰ φύσιν has a good sense with ref. to τέρας when the attempt is made to fix the relation of the unusual to the ordered whole. But the character of the term as a blanket concept (Osthoff, *op. cit.*, 52 f.) implies its inadequacy for the fixing of a specific sense. Thus the def. in Ps.-Ammon. Adfin. Vocab. Diff., 135: Τέρας Σημείου διαφέρει. τὸ μὲν γὰρ Τέρας, παρὰ φύσιν γίνεται· τὸ δὲ Σημεῖον παρὰ συνήθειαν, which is adopted by Suid. and Etym. M., *s.v.*, raises doubts. Cf. already the protest of Trench, 219, though he fails to note that the ancient lexicographers were influenced by Aristot. and hence construed the original concrete use in early epic in terms of the later more abstract use.

[11] Hom. has τέραα for τέρατα.

[12] v. Nägelsbach first made express ref. to this.

Events or things which smite men as τέραα [13] are always thought to be of divine origin, Il., 4, 398; cf. 4, 408; 6, 183; Od., 12, 394. Hom. mentions only Zeus as the divine author of τέραα. When we have a τέρας Zeus has a hand in it even though another god, Athene in Il., 5, 733-752, Eris in 11, 3-14, or Poseidon, Od., 3, 173-178, cf. 16, 402 f., is given prominence. When an eagle lets go a snake it has lifted into the air, the Trojans see in this a Διὸς τέρας αἰγιόχοιο, Il., 12, 209. Further passages in which this phrase occurs (Il., 5, 742; Od., 16, 320), cf. Διὸς τέρας (Od., 20, 101; Eur. Phoen., 1189, also Aristoph. Pax, 42; Callim. Hymn., 1, 69), make it clear that a given formula is used which binds the τέρας to Zeus. Among the τέραα that the epic tradition ascribes to him is esp. thunder, Od., 20, 103 etc. Then there is the rainbow, Il., 11, 27 f.; 17, 547 f., the shooting star, 4, 75 f., the eagle as Zeus' bird, 12, 200; cf. 8, 245-252; 24, 283-298, but also with special emphasis the αἰγίς with a Gorgon head (→ 113, 18 ff.), which is specifically a πολέμοιο τέρας, Il., 11, 4; 5, 737-742. [14]

b. Yet the linking of the τέρας with Zeus in early Gk. epic seems to be secondary, an attempted harmonising of certain phenomena originally felt merely as *tremendum* with belief in the Olympian gods. [15] In connection with a τέρας Zeus is often described as son of Kronos, Il., 4, 75 f.; 11, 27 f.; cf. Od., 20, 101 f. This [16] and the fact that τέρας can even serve in the classics as a tt. for fabled beings (→ 114, 12 f. with n. 7) suggest that the origin of τέρας is to be sought in a world and a religion which are pre-homeric and are stamped by popular belief. If this is correct, it is elements of popular religion that Homeric epic tries to interpret by means of τέρας, yet in such a way that their origin is still plain to see.

c. In Hom. the τέρας is only for men and not animals, → n. 13. In it men experience in a world in which all effort is directed to the search for the essence of nature both their dependence on higher powers and also their closeness to them on the basis of humanity. For this reason it is in their interest to attain clarity as to the relevance of the τέρας which is set before them. At this point τέρας comes to be connected with the concept of the sign or omen. The μάντις now becomes indispensable. But with the τέρας which raises questions Hom. also knows that to which prayer is directed. One sees here the attempt to find the terrifyingly unusual as meaningful and hence to divest it of its sinister character. Thus Calchas calls the τέρας θεοπροπέων (Il., 2, 308-332 → 113, 22 ff.) in the sense that its significance lies solely in the number, 2, 322. [17] More important, because related to the cultus, are scenes like those in which Priam in Il., 24, 283-321 and Odysseus in Od., 20, 98-104, when they pray to Father Zeus, receive a τέρας which gives them certainty as to what is about to happen. Yet a mysterious element still clings even to these τέραα.

3. On the Trend and Development of the Usage.

a. What has been said yields a picture which is most instructive for the history of the use of τέρας outside the biblical sphere to the degree that the intellectual history of the Gk. world is in some sense mirrored in it. In the course of this history a complex

---

[13] Cf. Il., 11, 28: τέρας μερόπων ἀνθρώπων.

[14] Zeus also controls lightning, but this does not seem to be in the category of τέρας for Hom.; he calls it σῆμα in Il., 2, 353 etc. In spite of τὸ τέρας ... Διὸς Σκαταιβάτου in Aristoph. Pax, 42 this seems to be a decisive point (so also Stein, 61 f.) against the thesis of H. Usener, "KERAUNOS" *Rhein. Mus.*, NF, 60 (1905), 13, who appealing to Aristoph. argued that τέρας is "intrinsically lightning."

[15] If Hes. Theog., 743 f. says of Tartaros: δεινὸν δὲ καὶ ἀθανάτοισι θεοῖσι τοῦτο τέρας, this is perhaps influenced by the recollection that no one is not exposed to what is evoked by the sense of insecurity, not even the gods.

[16] On Kronos cf. Nilsson, I², 511: "He is mythological, not cultic," unlike the Olympians.

[17] Cf. on this v. Nägelsbach, 174 f.

deriving from popular religion (→ 115, 17 ff.), that before which one shrinks and trembles because it is so sinister, is so far mastered by rational interpretation in the Homeric world that the one concerned has the chance to attain clarity concerning his situation; at the same time, with the help of belief in the Olympian gods, esp. Zeus (→ 115, 2 ff.), this complex is cultically integrated. The result is that τέρας becomes a concept which by its original range makes possible the recognising of the extraordinary as such and a rational reaction to it. But some basic elements remain and may be noted, e.g., in Cicero when he uses the Gk. term to show what a dangerous threat Caesar was at the height of his conflict with Pompey: hoc τέρας horribili vigilantia, celeritate, diligentia est; plane quid futurum sit, nescio, Cic. Att., 8, 9, 4. [18] All the same, by the beginning of the A.D.-period the term seems to have played out its once important role in the gen. consciousness, as may be seen fairly clearly from the development of the usage up to this time.

b. Xenophon often speaks of the various manifestations from which the divine will may be read off, Mem., I, 1, 3; Symp., 4, 48; Eq. Mag., 99, and he mentions dreams, voice- and way-oracles, the flight of birds etc. But he avoids τέρας in this connection. [19] Since this happens regularly, it can hardly be accidental. It may be due to an aversion connected with the def. of τέρας as a term for something which is παρὰ φύσιν, → 114, 17 ff. When the mythical Triton is a τέρας in Apollonius Rhodius Argonautica, IV, 1620 f. (Seaton), or a shooting star in III, 1377 f., or when a τέρας has to be interpreted if it is to yield up its secret and serve as an omen, the word is obviously a traditional epic element here after the model of Hom. (→ 113, 11 ff.) but without the survival of the pre-homeric elements still to be found in Hom. himself. In Polybius the word does not occur at all, though he uses related terms. One suspects that it does not fit into the world-view of this sober historian and politician. [20] Epictet. has it only in Diss., III, 1, 27 and here with the long-established (→ 114, 17 ff.) idea of παρὰ φύσιν. Plut. [21] is dependent on convention and tradition and also makes concessions to the liking of his age for the supernatural. [22] Yet in him τέρας [23] is comparatively rare like τερατώδης, τεράστιος, τερατεύομαι and τερατοσκόπος and there are many layers of use in accordance with the strands of tradition combining in him. Philosophical terminology has some influence when De Gaio Julio Caesare, 63 (I, 737e) says of a sacrifice which has no heart that it is a τέρας; οὐ γὰρ ἂν φύσει γε συστῆναι ζῷον ἀκάρδιον. But when the μάντις at once comes into action [24] regard is paid to contemporary superstition (cf. also Apophth. Lac., 2 [II, 224e]) which expects τεράτων ἀποτροπή of the expert, Fab. Max., 18 (I, 184c). Sometimes a φάσμα μέγα καὶ τερατῶδες, an uncanny phenomenon, is also called τέρας, De Dione, 55 (I, 982b-c). But in Fac. Lun., 25 (II, 940d) τέρας is almost synon. with μῦθος. Sometimes there is criticism of superstition as when a protest is lodged against assuming a τέρας on the ground that there is nothing here παρὰ φύσιν, Alex., 75 (I, 706b). Aelius Aristides never tires of praising the θεοὶ σωτῆρες for their miraculous

---

[18] One is tempted to regard τέρας here as no more than colloquial usage within the rational urbaneness of class. and Hell. breeding. But it is no accident that the word appears in another linguistic setting, and with an ironical accent, in the correspondence of two classically educated Romans.

[19] In this he agrees with Aesch. Prom., 484 ff.; cf. Stein, 54 f.

[20] Passages with τερατεία, 2, 17, 6; 58, 12 etc. or τερατεύομαι, 2, 56, 10 display a clear use of these words in sensum malum.

[21] Cf. H. Almquist, "Plut. u. d. NT," Acta Seminarii Neotestamentici Upsaliensis, 15 (1946), 1-24. H. Braun, "Plutarchs Kritik am Aberglauben im Lichte d. NT," Gesammelte Stud. zum NT u. seiner Umwelt (1962), 120-135.

[22] Ibid., 15 f.

[23] In Plut. τέρας is as good as synon. with τέρασμα in Col., 28 (II, 1123b) as a term for monsters or mythological figures.

[24] Cf. also De Sulla, 7 (I, 456a-c): καθαρὰ καὶ φανερὰ σημεῖα as τέρατα (= omina) need interpretation by the τερατοσκόπος.

help. But in so doing he avoids τέρας. The reason seems to be that the word had taken on negative content in aretalogy and was no longer the right term to present the reality of a divine wonder. [25]

4. σημεῖα καὶ τέρατα.

Cf. → VII, 206, 37 ff. For further examples showing the material closeness of τέρας and σημεῖον (σῆμα) → 113, 22 ff., also, e.g., Plut. De Dione, 24 (I, 968b): πολλὰ τερατώδη ... σημεῖα, and → n. 24.

B. The Old Testament and Greek Judaism.

1. τέρας as a Translation of מוֹפֵת in the Septuagint.

a. τέρας occurs in the LXX 46 times, also a few extra times in the other Gk. versions. In 34 of the 38 instances where there is a Hbr. original the Hbr. word is מוֹפֵת; in two others we have a form of פֶּלֶא, Ex. 15:11; Is. 28:29 (→ 118, 20 ff.), while שַׁמָּה is the equivalent in ψ 45:9 ("that which causes astonishment or terror") and the corresponding Aram. תְּמַהּ in Δα. 3:99 Θ, [26] though there seem to be special reasons for the choice here (→ VII, 217, 31 ff. on Da. 3:32 f.). This fairly uniform picture [27] is confirmed by the fact that in the LXX מוֹפֵת is not transl. by τέρας only 4 times, Ex. 7:9; 11:9 f.; 2 Ch. 32:24; σημεῖον is used in these verses → VII, 209, 3 ff. Finally θαυμάσιος is used for מוֹפֵת at Σιρ. 36:5; elsewhere in 43:25; 48:14, cf. 16:11 this word is used for תְּמַהּ. [28]

In the other versions 'A at Zech. 3:8 has ἄνδρες τέρατος in place of LXX ἄνδρες τερατοσκόποι for אַנְשֵׁי מוֹפֵת, members of the priestly college. [29] This is the only ref. of any interest. For the rest, apart from Δα. 6:28 Θ, where אָתִין וְתִמְהִין, ignored by LXX, is rendered by σημεῖα καὶ τέρατα, there is agreement with the LXX.

b. Nothing certain can be said about the original meaning of מוֹפֵת. [30] Of parallel terms אוֹת deserves some attention, since מוֹפֵת is co-ordinated with it in 18 of the 36 passages in which it occurs in the OT, → VII, 210, 20 ff. The nature of the combination suggests that the words have a common reference which they reflect differently. Analysis of the material shows that in fact they both relate to an event or factor which falls outside the realm of the ordinary and which thus demands

---

[25] The profane miracle story replaces τερατῶδες by ψεῦδος, cf. A. Kiefer, Aretalogische Studien (1929), 24.

[26] Ed. J. Ziegler, Septuaginta Gottingensis, 16 (1954).

[27] We are leaving out of account the use of τέρατα for אוֹת in Sir. 45:19 and for נִפְלָאוֹת in Sir. 48:14. There seems to be here a use of the Gk. word which departs from the normal use (in which it is attached to מוֹפֵת → lines 10 ff.) inasmuch as it seems to be governed by the idea of the unusual in analogy to the Gk. παρὰ φύσιν, → 114, 17 ff.

[28] Sir. 48:12 in the second half of the v. puts מוֹפְתִים after אוֹתוֹת in the first half. There is nothing corresponding to this in the Gk. transl.

[29] Cf. BHK and the comm., ad loc., also O. Procksch, Theol. d. AT (1950), 458: "Men of the sign for the initiation of the Messianic time." For the older Jewish understanding of the v. → 123, 21 ff.

[30] Unlike the older dict. and Ges.-Buhl, s.v., where ref. is made to a hypothetical root אפה and comparative Arab. material, Köhler-Baumg., s.v. has nothing about the etym. of מוֹפֵת. For a long time nothing par. was known in other Semitic languages, but we now seem to have this in a Phoenician inscr. from Cyprus (1st half of the 9th cent. B.C.?) in the form mpt, cf. W. Albright "New Light on the Early History of Phoenician Colonization," The Bulletin of the American Schools of Orient. Research, 83 (1941), 14-22; Keller, 155, n. 40. One should probably read מִפַת אִישׁ[ן (Albright, 16, n. 5), cf. אַנְשֵׁי מוֹפֵת in Zech. 3:8 (→ lines 19 ff. and → 123, 5 ff.) and מוֹפֵת הַדוֹר in bChul., 103b (→ 123, 23 ff.).

attention and consideration. אוֹת lays emphasis upon the impression (→ VII, 211, 5 ff.; 213, 12 ff.) but in contrast מוֹפֵת puts the whole stress on the knowledge which what is thus designated either mediates or is designed to mediate. Furthermore מוֹפֵת as distinct from אוֹת, being a formal concept (→ VII, 212, 37 ff.), is furnished with a theological reference; for its ultimate author is always God and it denotes things which are not just of significance for the future but which also display God's historical power. מוֹפֵת thus has a revelatory character to the degree that it helps to set forth the fact that God makes concrete decisions in the present that are determinative for the future. [31]

In 2 K. 20:1-11; Is. 38:1 f. Hezekiah on the basis of his prayer to God receives the message that 15 yrs. are added to his life and in confirmation a sign is given to him (אוֹת → VII, 213, 12 ff.). In the par. account in 2 Ch. 32:24, 31 [32] we find מוֹפֵת for אוֹת v. 24, cf. v. 31. Acc. to the context the substitution is caused by the fact that here the event is seen as whole and hence the accent is on the miracle, which in the first instance consists in Hezekiah's cure on the basis of a new decision of God's will. As compared to this the sign which gives the king personal assurance can and should retreat into the background. Analysis of the text shows that there can be no question of treating מוֹפֵת and אוֹת as synonyms. To be sure, a מוֹפֵת can serve as אוֹת as in the case of the sun going backwards, → lines 10 ff. But unlike the latter מוֹפֵת always has to do with something out of the ordinary. Hence it can be brought into close connection with נִפְלָאָה, which denotes what seems to be impossible, but is possible to God, Ps. 105:5; 1 Ch. 16:12; [33] hence it may be used when one is speaking of God's wonderful acts. [34]

The fact that God always stands ultimately behind a מוֹפֵת is shown by passages in which אוֹת is not added, e.g., Ex. 4:21 (→ n. 32); 7:9; 11:9 f. Esp. instructive is the prophetic story in 1 K. 13:1-5, since here מוֹפֵת is co-ordinated with אִישׁ אֱלֹהִים "according to God's direction" דְּבַר יהוה. Fundamentally we still have the same framework when in Ez. 12:1-16; 24:15-27; cf. Is. 20:3 a prophet, on the basis of what he does at God's command, himself becomes a מוֹפֵת, [35] or when a righteous man, whom God has directed, thanks God by calling himself a מוֹפֵת "for many" לְרַבִּים, Ps. 71:7; cf. Ps. 4:3; 17:7 (פלא). In Jl. 2:30 f. מוֹפְתִים in heaven and earth stand at the disposal of Him who has made them; they usher in the last time because the orders of nature reverse themselves in them.

Finally testimony is given to the special ref. of מוֹפֵת to the revelation of God's will by passages like Ps. 105:5; 1 Ch. 16:12; cf. Ex. 7:4. Here מוֹפְתִים is always linked with מִשְׁפָּטִים. One may gather from this that it is of the essence of a מוֹפֵת that in it God comes into His own, reaching His goal in the establishment of His universal rule, → III, 926, 4 ff. If מוֹפְתִים represent divine judgments, it is only at a first glance that the divine sovereignty disclosed in them is negative. In fact it is positive, for they aim at the manifestation of His righteousness, → III, 932, 24 ff. This explains why it is that in the OT מוֹפֵת always carries with it the idea of God's activity pressing on to the final

---

31 The thesis of Keller, 60 that the use of מוֹפֵת is "in essentials the same as that of *oth*" cannot be sustained. מוֹפֵת and אוֹת are characteristically different in meaning. Cf. what follows.

32 Cf. also Ex. 4:21 (הַמּוֹפְתִים) with a ref. back to 4:17 (הָאֹתֹת). The question of the source of the verses is of no importance here.

33 Cf. on this Procksch, *op. cit.*, 457.

34 On פלא in this sense, Procksch, 456-8.

35 Keller, 60 f. sees no distinction between the parabolic action of the prophet called אוֹת in Ez. 4:3 and those which come under the category מוֹפֵת in Ez. 12:1-16 and 24:15-27. He fails to note that what the prophet does in 4 f., in distinction from the later actions, could not be described as unusual or contrary to every norm.

goal, so that it has nothing whatever to do with an omen, [36] nor can it be regarded as a prediction of aid. [37]

c. The use of τέρας in the LXX is unequivocally governed by the content of מוֹפֵת in the OT. What this word means is an indispensable and effective element in God's self-attestation when the word of His messengers does not break through in a decisive situation. To this degree τέρας belongs here to the theology of revelation, → 118, 3 ff. The element of the unusual which belongs to it by derivation (→ 114, 2 ff.) is maintained. But it is now based on the biblical concept of God as the Creator and Lord of all events and thus transferred from the sphere of the marvellous and unnatural (→ 114, 10 ff.), demarcated from the world of myth, and protected against conceptual abstraction (→ 114, 17 ff.). In its whole range, then, the use and meaning of τέρας in the LXX differs characteristically from the employment of the term in secular Greek.

In rendering מוֹפֵת (→ 117, 11 ff.) the translators obviously paid careful attention to the fact that they must not obliterate the boundary between the specific senses of τέρας and σημεῖον. This may be seen, e.g., from the fact that in Ex. 4:17, 21 אוֹת and מוֹפֵת are rendered acc. to their varying senses by σημεῖον and τέρας even though in fact the ref. is to the same thing. The situation is similar when in Ex. 7:9 a translation which is plainly interpreting acc. to the context uses σημεῖον ἢ τέρας for a simple מוֹפֵת, a procedure also followed in Ex. 11:9 f. (→ VII, 220, 15 ff.). [38] But it also makes good sense when at Dt. 11:3 God's אֹתֹת וּמַעֲשִׂים become σημεῖα καὶ τέρατα, for מַעֲשִׂים in the Mas. has to do with the kind of divine self-declaration which elsewhere in Dt. is denoted by מוֹפֵת. Things are similar in Is. 24:16 when זִמְרֹת [39] is transl. by τέρατα and ψ 45:9 when שַׁמָּה = τέρας (→ 117, 12 f.), for in both instances the stress is on the fact that God Himself will act, or acts, miraculously. The changing of forms of פלא into τέρας at Ex. 15:11; Is. 28:29 (→ 117, 12 f.) fits in here from the material standpt. The same also applies, of course, to passages which present a divinely authorised messenger as מוֹפֵת/τέρας, e.g., Ez. 12:6 etc. (→ 118, 26 ff.). In all these cases τέρας serves in its own way to make known the sovereign divine being of God in its uniqueness. Naturally this is true in the full sense only when we have the fixed expression σημεῖα καὶ τέρατα with its recollection of the exodus of the chosen people from Egypt, → VII, 221, 7 ff., also → 122, 24 ff.

In this framework it is to be noted that τέρας plays no essential role in those LXX writings which are Greek by origin.

Only Bar. and Wis. offer instances. [40] Two of the four in Wis. have the term in the expression σημεῖα καὶ τέρατα (122, 24 ff.) at 8:8; 10:16, cf. also Bar. 2:11 → VII,

---

[36] Köhler, 85 f. defines מוֹפֵת as "omen" when in fact it indicates the present, God's readiness and ability to act here and now.

[37] Keller, 61 champions this view, again assimilating (→ n. 35) מוֹפֵת and אוֹת, and thus robbing each of its distinctiveness.

[38] There is a model for the Gk. expression in Dt. 13:2 f. S. Nu., 23 on 6:3 notes on this: אוֹת הוּא מוֹפֵת ומופת הוא אות, but adds: אלא שדברה תורה שתי לשונות. The pt. is that the two words mean the same here, as also in Nu. 6:3. But in spite of K. G. Kuhn, Der tannaitische Midr. S. Nu. (1959), 76 f., ad loc. there is no suggestion that they are synonyms.

[39] Cf. the comm., ad loc.

[40] We also find τὰ σημεῖα καὶ τὰ τέρατα τὰ μεγάλα in the addition to Est. 10:3 in v. 3 f. But like much else in the addition, e.g., kinship of thought to the Qumran findings, this Deuteronomism (cf. Dt. 7:19; 29:2; also 6:22) compels us still to keep open the question of a Hbr. original, with O. Eissfeldt, Einl. in d. AT³ (1964), 801 f. and against M. Weise, Art. "Zusätze zum Estherbuch" in RGG³, II, 708.

221, 16 ff. But in Wis. 17:14; 19:8, too, the ref is to the wonderful acts of God which reveal Him; in the first case it is said of the Egyptians τέρασιν ἠλαύνοντο φαντασμάτων, [41] while the second says of the Israelites that they saw θαυμαστὰ τέρατα at the Red Sea. [42] The absence of τέρας from Macc. is the more remarkable in view of the fact that God is called τερατοποιός in 2 Macc. 15:21; 3 Macc. 6:32. When one considers that a description of God as ποιῶν τέρατα in the Red Sea Song of Ex. 15:11 is adopted here, the avoidance of τέρας in pertinent passages like 1 Macc. 4:9 is especially striking. Possibly it rests on an aversion of Gk. Judaism to the word as such — in distinction from the traditional formula σημεῖα καὶ τέρατα. This might be explained fairly easily in the light of the history of the use of τέρας in Gk. gen. → 115, 36 ff. Possibly παράδοξος (→ II, 255, 5 ff.) sometimes served in later Gk. Judaism to express what was still meant by τέρας for the LXX translators, so Wis. 16:17; Jdt. 13:13; 3 Macc.6:33. [43]

2. τέρας in Non-Biblical Greek Judaism.

a. Philo. [44]

Like σημεῖον (→ VII, 221, 34 ff.) τέρας is comparatively rare. More common is τεράστιος, sometimes also τερατώδης. Of derivates we also find τερατεύομαι, τερατολογία, τερατοσκόπος, τερατουργία, τερατουργός. In a few instances Philo has the formula σημεῖα καὶ τέρατα, → VII, 222, 35 ff.

The original connection of τέρας with the uncanny and terrifying (→ 114, 2 ff.) may still be seen in Philo. Thus he ref. occasionally to τέρατα παλίμφημα as the abhorrent product of abnormal relations between men and animals, like the centaurs and other hybrid creatures. In this respect he follows the usage of class. Gk. lit. (→ 114, 12 ff.), Spec. Leg., III, 45. He says of the serpent that tempted Eve and the serpent that was lifted up in the desert and protected the people from death when they looked upon it that they are like φάσμασιν καὶ τέρασι if one takes the stories literally; but the mythical element disappears, and the truth comes to light, when the deeper sense is disclosed, Agric., 96 f. [45] When angels take human form in the story of Abraham, Philo calls this τερατωδέστατον, Abr., 118. The τερατοσκόπος whose job it is to unfold the meaning of τέρατα, Philo in complete consistency with his belief in God and in rejection of manticism sets alongside the οἰωνόμαντις as a ματαιάζων, Conf. Ling., 159; cf. Spec. Leg., IV, 48. But in addition to this negative characterisation he can even range him with the ἐγγαστρίμυθος [46] who for him is quite other than an advocate of the truth, Som., I, 220. τερατεύομαι has for Philo the sense "to tell fables," "to recount marvels," Rer. Div., 97; Decal., 76; Aet. Mund., 48; the object can be more precisely defined as μύθου πλάσμα. [47]

For the noun τέρας we may find the adj. τεράστιος, which can have the implication that what is denoted is παρὰ φύσιν (→ 114, 17 ff.), Plant., 4; Abr., 118; Vit. Mos., II,

---

[41] The terrors of the Egypt. darkness are depicted with the help of the idea that night is the time of ghostly apparitions. Yet we have here not just the influence of certain bibl. ideas, cf. Ps. 91:5 f. (with a ref. to Ex. 11:4 f.?) but also special traditions also found in Philo: God τοὺς ἐπιτιθεμένους κατέπληξε σημείοις καὶ τέρασι καὶ φάσμασι καὶ τοῖς ἄλλοις ὅσα κατ' ἐκεῖνον τὸν χρόνον ἐθαυματουργεῖτο, Spec. Leg., II, 218. On the relation of τέρας and φάσμα in Philo → lines 23 ff.

[42] On this cf. Σιρ. 36:5 with θαυμάσιος for מוֹרָא.

[43] Σιρ. 43:25 has παράδοξος for פֶּלֶא with θαυμάσιος for חָכְמָה (on the latter → 117, 12 ff.).

[44] On miracles in Philo cf. G. Delling, "Wunder - Allegorie - Mythus bei Philon v. Alexandreia," Wissenschaftliche Zschr. d. Martin-Luther-Univ. Halle-Wittenberg, Gesellschafts- u. sprachwissenschaftliche Reihe, VI, 5 (1957), 713-739.

[45] For the understanding and treatment of myth in Philo, ibid., 727-729.

[46] On this remarkable figure, the in some sense pneumatically begotten prophet or seer, cf. H. Leisegang, Pneuma hagion (1922), 35-40.

[47] For this reason Philo can characterise as μυθοπλάσται those who pursue τερατεύεσθαι, Aet. Mund., 68.

266; Spec. Leg., IV, 129. Where this word or another of the group is used, rather strangely it does not have a negative accent, since in adoption of the vocabulary of the Gk. Bible for God's miraculous acts the terms are part of the theological dictionary. [48] Thus for Philo, too, God is the Author of the τέρατα done by Moses. This finds clear expression when Vit. Mos., I, 90 says that in the situation of Ex. 5:2 Moses began δεικνύειν... ἃ προὐδιδάχθη τέρατα, or when in Vit. Mos., I, 80 his hand and staff are called τὰ τῶν τεράτων ὄργανα. [49] We are still within this framework when the effect of Moses' hands uplifted in prayer in the battle against the Amalekites (Ex. 17:8 ff.) is brought into material connection with a τερατωδέστατόν τι... πάθος, Vit Mos., I, 217, or when the law-giving at Sinai, promulgated with a trumpet-blast from heaven, is for this reason characterised as a τεράστιον καὶ μεγαλουργηθὲν [50] ἔργον, Spec. Leg., II, 188.

The relation of τέρας and σημεῖον in Philo corresponds to what we said about that of מוֹפֵת and אוֹת in the OT. In Philo, too, a τέρας can also be a σημεῖον, esp. when God Himself is patently behind it, Vit. Mos., I, 77. 80. 178, [51] though σημεῖον in Philo does not itself stand in direct proximity to a miracle, → VII, 222, 35 f.

As concerns the occurrence of τέρας as a whole, Philo, when using the term in a good sense, always shows that he is governed by recollection of the liberation from Egypt and Israel's wilderness period. In his usage in sensum bonum he is thus to be described as a biblicist. τέρας is for him a word which notwithstanding its occasional use after the manner of early epic (→ 114, 23 ff.) is adapted in a singular way to emphasise, within God's total self-revelation, the means of revelation as such. It helps him to demonstrate, according to his chief concern, the fact that Judaism on the basis of the Mosaic revelation possesses the highest form of the knowledge of God and in connection with this also has the highest morality.

b. Josephus. [52]

Joseph. is more precise than Philo in his use of τέρας. It would seem that he intentionally uses the term in imitation of its employment in Gk. epic, → 113, 11 ff.; 114, 23 ff. The use of τέρας is even perhaps one of the stylistic elements in Jos. in which he is controlled by ancient models. [53] It is true that the term can sometimes mean "monster," Ant., 4, 291. But even in such cases there is no mythological ref. [54] The sole determinative factor is the idea of παρὰ φύσιν (→ 114, 17 ff.), i.e., of a creature which is outside God's created order and opposed to it. To this degree τέρας is co-ordinated with and governed by the biblical belief in God in Jos. too.

In Jos. as in Philo τέρατα help esp. to the knowledge of God. But in Jos. the knowledge they make possible or deepen is not connected so much with God's absoluteness as with His sovereignty over all events. In particular they almost always have a ref. to the

---

[48] Philo cannot imagine a nature which is divorced from God or in tension with Him since God is for him the Author of every order in nature or society. To this degree what is or seems to be παρὰ φύσιν — the expression occurs only in Abr., 46 acc. to Leisegang, s.v. — is for him in tension only with man's expectation or judgment, not in contradiction with a divinely ordained causality. Cf. on this whole problem Delling, op. cit., 718-721.
[49] It amounts to the same thing when Vit. Mos., I, 91 speaks of τῶν τεράτων ἐπίδειξις through Moses: Moses is the one through whom God shows himself to be the One who acts.
[50] On the word group μεγαλουργ- in Philo cf. Delling, op. cit., 733, n. 26.
[51] The cloud in which God is with His people is a σημεῖον τερατωδέστατον.
[52] On what follows cf. G. Delling, "Josephus u. das Wunderbare," Nov. Test., 2 (1958), 291-309. Unfortunately this does not go closely into the terms used.
[53] Cf. on this R. J. H. Shutt, Studies in Josephus (1961), 79-109 with special ref. to Ant.
[54] This must be stressed because strange and terrifying natural events are called τέρατα by Jos. (→ 122, 2 ff.), i.e., things which already come under the term τέρας in Homer → 115, 9 ff.

divinely chosen people of Israel and Israel's relation to God in connection with its insight into God's plan and purpose for it. To this degree τέρατα in Jos. are close to the category of predictive signs except that it is God who in them indicates the future which He Himself exclusively controls. In this respect the use in Bell. is esp. typical. [55] Within a believing consideration of history and the world one sees here that, in certain situations which compel us to look to God, overnight storms (Bell., 4, 287), unusual phenomena in the heavens (6, 288 ff.) or a strange happening in the temple (6, 292) can be divine τέρατα in the same way as the bush which burned but was not consumed (Ex. 3) was for Moses a τέρας θαυμάσιον, Ant., 2, 265. To this extent God's πρόνοια and δύναμις are expressed in His τέρατα, Ant., 2, 286; 20, 167 f., no matter whether these be the Egypt. τέρατα or those preceding the destruction of the city and the temple. [56] In view of this it is naturally decisive that there be the insight to make possible a correct evaluation of the situation lit up by the τέρας, for a τέρας may be interpreted in various ways. The λόγιος is thus needed in explanation, Bell., 6, 295, or best of all the ἱερογραμματεύς, 6, 291, since familiarity with Scripture is the best presupposition for the understanding of a τέρας, in which God becomes as it were directly actual in relation to the future. To this extent God's τέρατα in Jos. always serve the interests of His direction, and this in a way which is governed by the nature of the OT' exodus narratives in the account of God's מוֹפְתִים. On the relation between τέρας and σημεῖον in Jos. → VII, 224, 17 ff. [57]

c. The Pseudepigrapha.

In the pseudepigr. τέρας plays either no part at all or only an insignificant one. [58] The Sibyllines avoid it even when its use might seem to be suggested by the theme, terrible events in heaven and on earth which are a reason for serious apprehension, 3, 672 ff.; cf. 3, 796 and 804. Lat. Esr. in such instances does not have a term corresponding to τέρας but *signum* ══ σημεῖον, → VII, 232, 24 ff. [59] τέρας does not occur in Test. XII.

d. σημεῖα καὶ τέρατα.

Concerning what is said in → VII, 221, 7 ff. it may now be stated on the basis of an investigation of מפת and τέρας that the theological importance of the phrase σημεῖα καὶ τέρατα in the LXX rests essentially on the second member, which expresses the conviction that God's way and goal governs all that happens. It is important that Jos., if he never uses the expression for the Egypt. signs and wonders but only for the signs of

---

[55] τέρας occurs only in Bell. and Ant., not Ap. and Vit. As regards our total assessment this is a not unimportant factor since it raises the question whether a τέρας can be for Jos., only something which has significance for the larger history.

[56] Even the τέρας of a miraculous preservation of Herod on the collapse of a dining-room in Bell., 1, 331 (→ VII, 224, 17 ff.) is traced to God's πρόνοια by Jos. in the par. Ant., 14, 462. Cf. also Ant., 20, 168 and on the whole matter Delling, *op. cit.*, 297, 303-305.

[57] It is worth noting that the Jewish historian Artapanos, who wrote a Gk. work περὶ ᾿Ιουδαίων (extant only in fragments) in the 1st cent. B.C. — a work which Jos. had before him — is very close to Jos. in his use of τέρας including its differentiation from σημεῖον. This may be seen with sufficient certainty from the part of his account of Moses preserved by way of Alexander Polyhistor. in Eus. Praep. Ev., 9, 27. 29. 31 f. On Artapanos cf. K. Merentites, ῾Ο ᾿Ιουδαῖος Λόγιος ΑΡΤΑΠΑΝΟΣ (1961).

[58] Due to the lack of indexes only rough figures are possible.

[59] A. Hilgenfeld, *Messias Judaeorum* (1869), 74, 102 tries to work back from *initia (sc. temporum) manifesta in prodigiis et virtutibus,* 9:6 to a Gk. ... ἐν τέρασι καὶ δυνάμεσι and from *tunc ostendet eis plurima portenta,* 13:50 to a Gk. τότε δείξει αὐτοῖς [πολλῷ], πλείονα τέρατα, but he has to wrestle with many uncertain factors of some difficulty.

the destruction of the city and temple, seems in retrospect to lay against those responsible for the fate of both the same charge as against Pharaoh in Egypt, namely, that of refusing faith in God by disregarding these signs, → VII, 224, 17 ff.

C. Post-Biblical Judaism.

1. The Dead Sea Scrolls.

In distinction from אוֹת (→ VII, 225, 18 ff.) מוֹפֵת is very seldom used here. In the text to hand it occurs only three times. The heavily damaged 1 QH 15:20 has אות ומופת (→ VII, 226, 20 ff.). The other two passages 1 QH 7:21 אנשי מופת (cf. Zech. 3:8 and → 117, 19 ff.) [60] and 1 QH 13:16 with the statement that man born of woman when he offends will be eternally [...] ומופת דורות, [61] are fairly obscure. But 1 QH 13:16 and 1 QH 7:21 are certainly independent of the developed plur. formula אותות ומופתים → VII, 216, 8 ff. Here, too, מופת is connected with God's work of revelation. On מופת דורות and אנשי מופת → lines 23 ff.

2. Rabbinic Judaism.

Here מופת has almost disappeared. The Palestinian Pentateuch Targum replaces it by נס, נסא, e.g., Ex. 11:9 f. or פרישא, פרישתא, e.g., Ex. 7:3; Dt. 26:8 or 7:19; 29:2, or סימן, e.g., Ex. 7:9; Dt. 13:2; 28:46, or a combination of the first two words mentioned, 34:11. [62] In this replacement there is no uniform rendering of the Deuteronomic אותות ומופתים, so that in the Tg. Pal. the pregnancy of this expression is lost.

The essentially later Targum Onkelos keeps מופת or מופתא in a no. of passages, e.g., Dt. 13:2 f.; את או מופת or אתא ומופתא; Is. 20:3: את ומופת; Dt. 6:22: אתין ומופתין. Elsewhere it is replaced by אתא, Ex. 7:9, cf. also Tg.J. I on 1 K.13:3, 5; Tg.Pro. on Jl. 2:30. The reason for the replacement is that the specific sense of מופת was no longer present. The word does not occur in the Mishnah. Tosefta has preserved a fr. of an obviously ancient exposition of אנשי מופת, Zech. 3:8 (→ 117, 19 ff.) with a ref. to Dt. 13:2: אין מופת אלא נביאה. T. Hor., 2, 9. [63] The Babyl. Talmud, for which, as for the Tannaites (Mishnah, Tos., Tannait. Midr.), [64] the current word for "wonder" is נס or Aram. נסא, [65] bears testimony to the unusual nature of מופת when in bChul., 103b R. El'azar bPedat in a disputation in the last third of the 3rd cent. calls his colleague R. Assi [66]

---

[60] Others on the basis of Is. 8:18 ref. to the members of the community of the Teacher of Righteousness who speaks in 1 Q, so S. Holm-Nielsen, *Hodayot, Psalms from Qumran* (1960), 135, n. 35. Cf. also G. Jeremias, *Der Lehrer d. Gerechtigkeit* (1963), 186 and 189 f.

[61] Cf. J. Carmignac, "Citations de l'AT dans les Hymnes de Qumran," *Revue de Qumran,* 2 (1959/60), 360 with ref. to Dt. 28:46; A. Dupont-Sommer, "Le Livre des Hymnes découvert près de la mer Morte (1 QH)," *Semitica,* 7 (1957), 87, n. 2 with ref. to Ps. 71:7; → VII, 216, 27 ff. with ref. to Is. 8:18.

[62] Ref. acc. to Codex Neofiti 1 of the Vatican Library.

[63] Par.: jHor., 48b, 50 f.; bHor., 13a (with נביא for :ביאה). Rabb. Judaism seems to have devoted much attention to Zech. 3:8 → 117, 19 ff. and lines 5 ff.

[64] A good example: "Ten wonders (נסים) were done for our fathers in Egypt...," Ab., 5, 4; also M. Ex. ויהי בשלח 4 on Ex. 14:16.

[65] This applies also to the Egypt. wonders. Thus bShab., 97a says concerning the two miracles with Aaron's rod in Ex. 7:8 ff., נס בתוך נס "wonder on wonder." The saving of the Jews by Esther is סוף כל הניסים in bYoma, 29a. jTalmud, like bTalmud, has נס, נסא cf. Levy Wört., *s.v.*

[66] On him cf. Bacher Pal. Am., II, 151-156, 165-173.

מופת הדור. Since the Hbr. formula is kept in an Aram. passage, one may see in it a traditional expression [67] in praise of a man on whom the eyes of his contemporaries rest, [68] but one which was felt to be archaic. [69]

D. The New Testament.

1. Reasons for the Absence of τέρας Alone.

τέρας does not occur alone in the NT. This is not accidental. Proof may be found in the quotation from Jl. 2:30 in Ac. 2:19. Adding to both HT and LXX, the author in the second part has introduced an interpretative σημεῖα, so that we now find the formula τέρατα καὶ σημεῖα, which is used a few times in Ac. (→ VII, 239, 15 ff.) in place of the customary σημεῖα καὶ τέρατα, 2:22, 43; 6:8; 7:36. [70] This requires closer investigation not merely because the combination which includes τέρας very obviously fulfils an indispensable function in the NT but also because the second element, σημεῖον, became even more important in Jn. (→ VII, 243, 14 ff.) in relation to the world outside.

One might think it was due to σημεῖον and some power of absorption it exerted that τέρας is so much in the background in the NT. [71] Yet an argument against this is that even more colourless words than τέρας have been retained to denote miraculous events, e.g., θαυμάσιον (→ III, 37, 45 ff.), ἔνδοξον (Lk. 13:17), and παράδοξον (→ II, 255, 7 f.), but also δύναμις (→ II, 301, 27 ff.). Furthermore, another factor is of greater significance. It is true that in the transition from the B.C. to the A.D. period the word was hardly used at all in non-Jewish Gk. But in Gk. Judaism (→ 119, 3 ff.; 121, 34 ff.) it had at this time been given a special accent referring it to God's self-revelation as the Creator and the Governor of all events, and especially of the destiny of the people chosen by Him. On the other hand, it should not be overlooked in this connection that מופת, for which τέρας was used in the LXX, had practically ceased to play any role at all in contemporary Judaism.

Probably it is not due to τέρας alone, but to that which primitive Christianity had to denote and to the way in which the first Christians understood and expounded this, if to them τέρας did not seem to be very well adapted to be received into their vocabulary of proclamation for the ends they had in view. This applies to some degree not only to the miracles of Jesus and their evangelical-kerygmatic significance but also to miracles in the very earliest Christianity.

In the stories of the wonderful acts of Jesus stress is obviously laid from the very first on the fact that it is He Himself who performs them. This may be the reason why the Synoptic Gospels call them δυνάμεις, i.e., something which discloses what He can

---

[67] Cf. 1 QH 13:16 → 123, 4 f.

[68] In modern Hbr. מופת הדור is an outstanding, exemplary man.

[69] Rashi on bChul., 103b simply ref. to Zech. 3:8: מופת הדור: גדול הדור כמו אנשי מופת המה. In post-Talmudic Hbr. and esp. in Chassidism מופת came back into vogue, cf. E. Ben Jehuda, *Thesaurus totius Hebraitatis,* 6 (1948), *s.v.*

[70] Possibly an ancient Rabb. theologoumenon influenced this form of the quotation (→ VII, 228, 1 ff.; cf. Abraham Ibn Ezra [1092-1167] in his comm. on Jl. 2:30, ed. M. Friedländer [1873-7]).

[71] Cf., e.g., Delling, 16: "The special NT expression for the physically healing and life-giving act of Jesus is however 'the sign'." In such statements a specific theological aspect is also presupposed.

do. [72] It seems that δύναμις (→ II, 299, 15 ff.) is selected in order to give to ἔργον an unambiguous, i.e., christological, interpretation as applied to the miraculous deeds of Jesus, Mt. 11:2; cf. Lk. 24:19. In this respect δύναμις in the Synoptists stands in much the same interpretative role to ἔργον as does σημεῖον in Jn. → VII, 248, 6 ff. [73] But in the use of τέρας in the Gk. Bible and works influenced by it the great emphasis is always on God as the author of the acts in question, → 124, 21 ff. One has thus to reckon with the possibility that τέρας is not used for the miracles of Jesus in order not to restrict Jesus' autonomy. [74]

This picture receives some correspondence and confirmation when it finds repetition in the way that primitive Christianity speaks of the miracles of the apostolic age. Here, too, δύναμις replaces τέρας for miraculous acts. But the δυνάμεις (→ II, 311, 14 ff.) are the result of the operation of the Holy Spirit (→ VI, 423, 12 ff.) in whom God has continued the work of Jesus, 1 C. 12: 1 ff.; Gl. 3:5. For this reason they are ascribed to the apostles (→ I, 440, 30 ff.) who represent Jesus, 2 C. 12:12. Yet on occasion δύναμις can even seem to be used to clarify the expression σημεῖα καὶ τέρατα, 2 C. 12:12.

2. σημεῖα καὶ τέρατα — τέρατα καὶ σημεῖα.

In respect of τέρας it is worth noting that Acts uses not only σημεῖα καὶ τέρατα (4:30; 5:12; 14:3; 15:12) but also τέρατα καὶ σημεῖα (2:19, 22, 43; 6:8; 7:36) → VII, 240, 34 ff. Even when one considers that there are ancient models for both and that both occur in the LXX, their juxtaposition in the same NT book is remarkable. The question arises whether we do not have in them different traditions or different assessments of the primitive Christian situation, especially as the expression in the second form is to be found especially in the Pentecost narrative, → VII, 242, 20 ff. Another factor in relation to the two versions is perhaps that in connection with the σημεῖα καὶ τέρατα passages the accent is more on God as the One who by His operations gives a new and specific stamp to the present (the catchword is → χείρ), while in the τέρατα καὶ σημεῖα passages there seems to be stronger emphasis on what God can do, on the degree to which the present stands under the sign of His advance and pressure, and to that extent invites to conversion and turning to Him (the catchword is δύναμις, → II, 306, 1 ff.).

If there is something in this, it is no accident that Paul, when he refers to σημεῖα καὶ τέρατα (R. 15:19; 2 C. 12:12; 2 Th. 2:9), has δύναμις in the vicinity even when speaking of the manifestation of antichrist (2 Th. 2:9), the point being at least to make it clear that what matters is the power deployed by him, → II, 653, 23 ff.

E. The Early Church.

The post-apost. fathers only have σημεῖα καὶ τέρατα (→ VII, 261, 1 ff.), never τέρας alone. *Portentum*, which corresponds to this, is also absent from the Lat. versions.

---

[72] Cf. with Mk. 6:5 esp. Mt. 11:20.

[73] That σημεῖον replaces the Synoptic δυνάμεις in Jn. is supported not least by the fact that Jn. does not use δύναμις of Jesus, though he has the verb δύναμαι, e.g., δύνασθαι σημεῖα ποιεῖν, Jn. 3:2.

[74] The setting may well be the controversy with Judaism, which contested the Messiahship of Jesus. Such a ref. is a more convincing reason for the avoidance of τέρας than the idea that the term was not used to denote Jesus' miracles lest the suspicion might arise they were essentially παρὰ φύσιν, as τέρας might easily suggest to educated Greeks → 114, 17 ff. and n. 10.

The apocr. Acts present a similar picture. Here there is no independent use of τέρας, [75] as distinct from σημεῖον → VII, 261, 1 f. In Act. Joh., 39 there is ref. to τεράστια that John has seen, and he at once explains the term by the apposition ἰάσεις νόσων, thus using it in a good sense. In the Apologists τέρας is used only by Athenag. Suppl., 20, 2. In the context of a recapitulation of Gk. traditions concerning the origin of the gods it serves here to denote a mythological monster and thus shows the author to be an educated man in the sense of his day, since he is employing an expression of ancient epic poetry in exactly the same way as Cic. Att. does, → 116, 7 ff. [76]

Rengstorf

---

[75] In a longer list in Act. Joh. 106 one finds ... πόσα τέρατα, ἰάσεις πόσας, πόσα σημεῖα ... But one should perhaps read τεράστια for τέρατα as in 39.

[76] The remarkable late Midr. אגדתא שמעון כיפא, which contains a Jewish Peter story and is preserved in various recensions (A. Jellinek, *Bet ha-Midrasch*, V [1872], 60-69; VI [1877], 9-14) not only has Peter do several signs (אות) but also tells how an אות או מופת was asked of him in Antioch, V, 60, 27 ff.; VI, 11, 25 ff. In another passage a מופת is asked of him in validation and he accedes in an אות, VI, 13, 14 ff. The distinction between א׳ת and מופת is plain, but as things are one can hardly assume that it is borrowed from popular Chr. Peter stories, since Chr. usage offers no point of connection.

τέσσαρες, τέταρτος, τεταρταῖος,
τεσσεράκοντα, τεσσερακονταετής

τέσσαρες, τέταρτος, † τεταρταῖος.

A. Four in Antiquity.

1. Linguistic Problems.

τέσσαρες, Attic τέτταρες, Ionic τέσσερες, Doric τέτορες, Aeolic (Hom.) πίσυρες, Boeotic πέτταρες, [1] is connected with the Indo-Eur. stem * qᵘetᵘor. The geminates - σσ - or - ττ - rest on - τϝ -, [2] - ϝ - being squeezed out in τετρα- or τεταρ-. [3] Under the influence of non-Attic dialects the *koine* gen. has - σσ -, more rarely - ττ -, e.g., P. Petr., III, 45, 4, 1 (p. 136). [4] The neut. τέσσερα for τέσσαρα is rare in pap. and inscr. prior to 200 A.D. [5] In the NT one finds τέσσερα at Jn. 19:23 ℵ A; Rev. 4:6 A; 4:8 ℵ A; 5:8 ℵ A; 5:14 A; 19:4 ℵ, cf. also τεσσεράκοντα (→ 138, 16 ff.), which almost always occurs too in the oldest witnesses, [6] but elsewhere only forms of τεσσαρ- except for Rev. 4:4 A. One is not to assume Ionic influence, cf. Hdt., I, 51, 3; II, 31 etc. [7] but a gen. intermingling of forms by popular dissimilation of the unemphatic - α - between the emphatic - ε - and - α - and after the disruptive - ρ -. [8] Hence there is no shift in sound [9]

τ έ σ σ α ρ ε ς κτλ. Bibl.: Liddell-Scott, Pape, Pass., Pr.-Bauer, Hofmann, *s.v.;* Mayser, I, 57, 224, 315; II, 74; Moult.-Mill., I, 45 f., 243 f.; II, 66 f., 170; W. Burkert, "Weisheit u. Wissenschaft. Stud. zu Pythagoras, Philolaos u. Platon," *Erlanger Berichte zur Sprach-u. Kunstwissenschaft,* 10 (1962), 61-64, 90-95, 170-3, 442-452; F. Dornseiff, "Das Rotas-Opera-Quadrat," ZNW, 36 (1937), 228-230, 234-238; L. Dürr, *Ezechiels Vision im Lichte der vorderasiat. Altertumskunde* (1917), 54-60; F. Heiler, "Erscheinungsformen u. Wesen d. Religion," *Die Religionen d. Menschheit,* 1 (1961), 166; C. G. Jung, "Zur Psychologie westlicher u. östlicher Religion," *Gesammelte Werke,* 11 (1963), 179-209; E. Kautzsch, Art. "Zahlen bei d. Hebräern," RE, 21³ (1908), 603, older bibl., 598; G. Sauer, "Die Sprüche Agurs. Untersuchungen u. Bdtg. einer bibl. Stilform unter bes. Berücksichtigung v. Proverbia c. 30," BWANT, 84 (1963), 71-111.

[1] Hofmann, *s.v.;* Schwyzer, I, 82.

[2] Schwyzer, I, 227, 301, 319.

[3] *Ibid.,* 301, cf. 590. [Line 7 f. by Krämer].

[4] Mayser, I, 222 and 224; II, 74; A. Thumb, *Die griech. Sprache im Zeitalter des Hell.* (1901). 78.

[5] Radermacher, 43; Thackeray, 62; Pr.-Bauer, *s.v.* Progressive assimilation and popular slovenliness are assumed by Mayser, I, 51; II, 74; Schwyzer, I, 255 f., as in LXX and NT esp. Cod A and ℵ, cf. Helbing, 5; Thackeray, 62 f.

[6] Moult.-Mill., II, 170 f.; Bl.-Debr. § 29, 1.

[7] Cf. O. Hoffmann, *Die griech. Dialekte,* III (1898), 248 f.; P. Kretschmer, "Beiträge zur griech. Lautlehre aus Vaseninschr." ΑΝΤΙΔΩΡΟΝ, *Festschr. J. Wackernagel* (1923), 194 f.; otherwise τεσσερ- would have prevailed in all forms in the NT, Moult.-Mill., II, 170 f. as against Bl.-Debr. § 29, 1.

[8] Thackeray, 73 f.; K. Foy, "Griech. Vokalstud.," *Beiträge zur Kunde d. idg. Sprachen,* 12 (1887), 52 and 56.

[9] Cf. Kretschmer, *op. cit.,* 194.

but τέσσερ- is to be regarded as a choice from among different dialects on euphonic or rhythmic grounds. [10] But this is uncertain in the NT period (→ 127, 11 f.), for the MSS often have figures which were then written out acc. to later usage. [11] In the acc. τέσσαρες for τέσσαρας, cf. Rev. 4:4 A and LXX, is to be regarded as a penetration of the nominative. [12]

2. In the Greek Sphere.

The gen. meaning of four in religious history has its origin in the orientation to four sides which, as before, behind and to right and left, are suggested by man's physical constitution. [13] The four corners of heaven or the world embrace the whole of man's horizon. There thus arises the transf. meaning of quaternity as the basis of a concept of totality, [14] for in distinction from trinity it offers a natural schema as an artistic form. [15] But only occasionally is four a sacred number. [16]

a. Four is often a small round no.: the four virtues are first mentioned in Aesch. Sept. c. Theb., 610, cf. Pind. Nem., 3, 74: τέσσαρας ἀρετάς. Stoic psychology ref. to four basic emotions, Diog. L., VII, 110 (→ 133, 24 f.); there are four types of sovereignty, Aristot. Pol., III, 14, p. 1285b, 20, of constitution, Plat. Resp., VIII, 544a-545c, cf. the division of work, II, 369d-370a, also Hom. Od., 9, 335; Il., 2, 618; Diod. S., 13, 7, 1; Pind. Olymp., 8, 68; Nem., 2, 19; Aristot. De animalium incessu, 1, p. 704a, 11; 7, p. 707a, 18 and 22; τετράδραχμον is a small current coin, Diog. L., II, 34, cf. IG, 9, 1, 333, 4, τετράτρυφος a "piece of bread" which can be divided into four, Hes. Op., 441 f. One often finds the series three - four (→ 132, 12 ff.), e.g., τρὶς μάκαρ... καὶ τετράκις, Hes. Fr., 81, 7, v. also Hom. Il., 1, 128; of the torments of Tantalus μετὰ τριῶν τέταρτον πόνον, Pind. Olymp., 1, 60.

---

[10] E. Risch, Review of the Engl. transl. of Bl.-Debr. [9, 10] (1961), Kratylos, 9 (1964), 86.
[11] This is esp. true of A and א (→ n. 5), cf. Moult.-Mill., II, 17; Bl.-Debr. § 46, 2 with the ref. of P. Katz in the Engl. transl. (1961); Thackeray, 63.
[12] Helbing, 53 f.; Mayser, I, 59 and 315; II, 74; Thackeray, 73 f., 148 f.; Bl.-Debr. § 46, 2; Moult.-Mill., I, 33 and 36; II, 130 and 170 think the influence of a North-West Gk. dialect possible, but Moult.-Mill., I, 243 f. also stresses that τέσσαρες must be regarded as distinct from about 200 A.D. "as the only cardinal which ever had a separate acc. form."
[13] O. Rühle, Art. "Zahlen," RGG², V, 2064; W. Wundt, Völkerpsychologie, VI, 3² (1915), 355.
[14] Acc. to Jung, 182 quaternity is an archetype which in religious history precedes the idea of trinity, cf. 192 f., 204; also Psychologie u. Religion (1947), 94-116; Symbolik des Geistes (1953), 417-427; L. Parneth, Zahlensymbolik im Unbewusstsein (1952), 150-168.
[15] Jung, 182. Babyl. cosmology has the 4 phases of the moon, 4 forms of the sun's appearance, 4 turning-pts. in the year, cf. Heiler, 166; F. C. Endres, Mystik u. Magie d. Zahlen³ (1951), 123 f.; Dürr, 58 f. There are many par. for 4 as a no. of natural order in ancient Chinese, Indian, Persian, Egypt. and Islamic religion, cf. Rühle, 2064 f.; Heiler, 166; Endres, 126 f.; A. Schimmel, Art. "Zahlensymbolik," RGG³, VI, 1862 with bibl.; H. Bonnet, Reallex. d. ägypt. Religionsgeschichte (1952), 874. On 4 in Red Indian cults and the myths and sagas of primitive peoples cf. L. Lévy-Bruhl, Les fonctions mentales dans les sociétés intérieures⁹ (1951), 240; Endres, 133; Roscher, VI, 393 with bibl. Acc. to Wundt, op. cit., II, 3 (1909), 4 is the sacred no. of the new world. On divine fours in ancient religions cf. K. Sethe, "Von Zahlen u. Zahlworten," Schr. d. Wissenschaftlichen Gesellschaft in Strassburg (1916), 31; Bonnet, 315, 366, 870, 874; 129, 46 ff. An Accad. title is šar kibratim arbaim "King of the Four Areas of the World," cf. F. Thureau-Dangin, "Die sumer. u. akkad. Königsinschr.," Vorderasiatische Bibliothek, I, 1 (1907), 165-169; J. Hehn, "Siebenzahl u. Sabbat bei d. Babyloniern u. im AT," Leipziger Semitistische Stud., II, 5 (1907), 76 f., cf. 13 f. The quadrilateral plays a role in architecture, cf. Roma quadrata (→ 134, 23 f.), Ennius Annales, 158 (ed. J. Vahlen [1903]) and the expression "quarter of a city."
[16] Paneth, 156 f.; Jung, 183; → n. 15.

b. Common of times and terms: Something decisive happened on the fourth assault, Hom. Il., 5, 438, cf. 16, 705, dangers on the fourth day, Polyb., 3, 52, 2. Counting back in quarter-years, P. Lond., II (p. 119, 22) (145 A.D.) or after four yrs., P. Flor., 86, 9 (1st cent. A.D.), a contest every four yrs., CIG, II, 1, 2741, 15 f., reckoning the Olympiads, Timaeus Fr., 60 (FGrHist, IIIb, 619), four seasons, Diod. S., 1, 26, 5; ἔσχατον ἐν μησὶν τεσσεράσιν, Ditt. Syll.³, II, 633, 98 (2nd cent. B.C.) is a limited span. Common in sicknesses, e.g., fatal issue ἐν τρισὶν ἢ τέτταρσιν ἡμέραις, Isoc. Or., 12, 267, four days fever τεταρταῖος πυρετός, which often leads to a dangerous crisis, Hippocr. Περὶ κρισίων, 36 (Littré, IX, 286), hence in magic formulae and threats of punishment, Ditt. Syll.³, III, 1239, 20; P. Tebt., II, 275, 21, in a Chr. prayer for liberation from fever and other pains τριτεον τεταρτεον for all days, P. Oxy., VIII, 1151, 37. The dangerous nature of the τεταρταῖος πυρετός is connected with the no. four as a symbol of the heaviness of the earth, Plat. Tim., 86a → 130, 8 ff. The child moves in its mother's womb after conception τῷ μὲν ἀρσένι τρεῖς μῆνες, τῇ δὲ θηλείῃ τέσσαρες, Hippocr. Περὶ φύσιος παιδίου, 21 (Littré, VII, 510). After the fourth yr. of sexual maturity a woman should marry, Hes. Op., 698, cf. four as the no. of wedding and marriage, Plut. Is. et Os., 30 (II, 363a).[17] Leading Egypt. women are embalmed after death only τριταῖαι ἢ τεταρταῖαι, Hdt., II, 89, 1. The fourth day of the month[18] is supposedly the birthday of Heracles[19] and is thus linked to a hard life: τετραδισταί· οἱ ἐπίπονον βίον ζῶντες, Etym. M., 754, 15; Anecd. Graec., s.v.; Suid., s.v. Hence τετράδι μὲν τ' οἴχου, Hesych., s.v. τετράδι γέγονας is a fixed expression ἐπὶ τῶν ἄλλοις πονούντων, Zenobius, VI, 7 (CPG, I) Suid., s.v.; Phot. Lex., s.v.; Plato Comicus Fr., 100 (CAF, I, 628); Philochorus Fr., 85 (FGrHist, IIIb, 123). In the passages just mentioned Hermes from Philochorus on is also connected with the fourth day, cf. Cl. Al. Strom., VII, 75, 2; Theophr. Char., 16, 10; Athen., 14, 78 (p. 459, 11 ff.).[20] As an apotropaic countermeasure one should be very merry on this day, Athen., 6, 42 (p. 43, 10), open a cask, Hes. Op., 819, hold carouses, Theophr. Char., 16, 10; Alexis Fr., 258 (CAF, II, 391); Menand. Fr., 320 (CAF, III, 92), cf. Hesych., s.v.;[21] one should also build light ships, Hes. Op., 809 and conduct one's wife into the house, 800.[22]

c. In myths the common idea of the four ages of the world, which is found in the Babyl. creation epic and as far as Peruvian and Mexican legends,[23] is presupposed in Hes. Op., 109-201, for here the mounting series of four metals is used only secondarily for the four ages,[24] cf. Plat. Resp., VIII, 546e; Ovid Metam., 1, 89 ff. Hermes is often called τετράγωνος to express his perfection and omnipresence, e.g., Cornut. Theol. Graec., 16 (23, 11 ff.) with ref. to his ἐδραῖόν τι καὶ ἀσφαλὲς ἔχειν, Apollodorus Fr., 129 (FGrHist, IIb, 1078) in virtue of his four discoveries, cf. Lydus De mensibus IV, 76;[25] Thuc., VI, 27, 1; Paus., IV, 33, 3; VIII, 39, 6, also the Hermes hymns, P. Lond., I, 46, 400 ff. (4th cent. A.D.); I, 121, 668 ff. (3rd cent. A.D.). The four-cornered Hermes pillars expressed his significance and universality[26] and even presented him as four-headed without producing a monster,[27] cf. Hesych. s.v. Ἑρμῆς, Phot. Lex., s.v.; Eustath. Thessal. Comm., in Il., 1353 on Il., 24, 336: ἡ τετρὰς δέ, φησιν, ἱερὰ τοῦ θεοῦ → 131, 9 ff.. the

---

[17] Four is often found in connection with women, cf. G. Germain, *Homère et la mystique des nombres* (1954), 50 f.; P. Geigenmüller, "Plutarchs Stellung zur Religion u. Philosophie seiner Zeit," NJbchKlAlt, 47 (1921), 269; Burkert, 450.

[18] Cf. F. Poland, Art. "τετραδισταί," Pauly-W., 5a (1934), 1070 f.

[19] Cf. J. B. Keune, Art. "Herakles," Pauly-W. Suppl., 3 (1918), 1016 f.

[20] Cf. S. Eitrem, Art. "Hermes," Pauly-W., 8 (1913), 763 f.

[21] Poland, op. cit., 1071.

[22] Cf. S. Eitrem, op. cit., 774, where a connection with the relation between Hermes and Aphrodite is assumed → lines 33 ff.

[23] Roscher, VI, 393; Heiler, 159 f.; Wundt, op. cit., 299 f., 354-6.

[24] Cf. Roscher, VI, 382 f., 389-391, 394.

[25] Ed. R. Wünsch (1898).

[26] Eitrem, 773, 777 f.

[27] H. Usener, *Kleine Schriften*, IV (1913), 354.

τετρακόρης τε θεᾶς four-eyed [28] Proserpine, Epigr. Graec., 406, 11, Apollo τετράχειρ καὶ τετράωτος, III, 1, 4000, 15; IG, 5, 1, 683 (2nd/3rd cent. A.D.); 5, 1, 259; Sosibius Fr., 11 (FHG, II, 627), Hecate τετρακέφαλος, Lydus De mensibus (→ n. 25), III, 8, Aphrodite Paus., IX, 40, 3, a Kronos altar τετραπρόσωπον, Plut. Parallela minora, 9 B (II, 308a), cf. the heaping up of predicates τετραπροσωπε τλιη τετραωνυμε τετραοδιτι in a magic pap.; [29] the all-sidedness of Argus τέτρασιν ὀφθαλμοῖσιν ὁρώμενον ἔνθα καὶ ἔνθα, Hes. Fr., 188. [30]

d. In the Platonic and Pythagorean tradition number is in the first instance a symbol, but in Aristot. its numerical value is to the fore. [31] Four is the symbol of a three-dimensional pyramid for what is solid στερεόν, Xenocrates Fr., 39; [32] Theon., 101, 11 f.; [33] Speusippus, Fr., 4 (Diels, I, 401); Sext. Emp. Math., X, 278, cf. the criticism of Aristot. Metaph., 13, 3, p. 1090b, 20 ff. Acc. to Aristot. An., I, 2, p. 404b, 23-27 Plato [34] equates the first four numbers with the qualities of the soul νοῦς, ἐπιστήμη, δόξα and αἴσθησις which are fashioned after the elements, [35] cf. the four virtues (→ 128, 13 ff.; 133, 26 f.) ἀνδρεία, σωφροσύνη, φρόνησις (or σοφία), δικαιοσύνη, Plat. Resp., IV, 427e; 428a; 429a-434c; Aristot. Pol., VII, 1, p.1323a, 23 f.[36] As ἰσάκις ἴσον four also means righteousness, Aristot. Magna Moralia, I, 1, p. 1182a, 14; Metaph., 1, 5, p. 985b, 29; Alex. Aphr. In Aristot. Comm., 28. [37] The doctrine of the four elements [38] (→ VII, 672, 9 ff.) is traced back to Empedocles, cf. Fr., 6 (Diels, I, 311) τέσσαρα γὰρ πάντων ῥιζώματα, which he equates with four gods, cf. Aristot. Metaph., 1, 4, p. 985a, 32; Plot. Enn., VI, 2, 2. Only the demiurge himself could unlock their mutual embrace, Plat. Tim., 32b-c. The four elements play a special role in Mithraism, Dio Chrys. Or., 36, 39-46. [39] The Pythagoreans honoured the τετρακτύς [40] which as the sum of the first four numbers yields 10 and is thus the basis of the decimal system, [41] Theon. (→ n. 33), 87, 4; Luc. Vit. Auct., 4; Hierocl. Carm. Aur., 20 (p. 128, 4 f.); in Sext. Emp. Math., IV, 3 it is τελειότατος ἀριθμός, cf. VII, 94. [42] There was also a second tetractus formed from the sum of the first four even and odd numbers = 36, Theon., 94, 10 ff.; Plut. De animae procreatione, 11 (II, 1017d); 14 (II, 1019b); 30 (II, 1027 f.); Is. et Os., 75 (II, 381f. - 382a). This contains all the harmonies of basic musical relations, [43] Theon., 93, 17; Sext. Emp. Math., VII, 95,

[28] Usener, op. cit., 353, perhaps also as dea quadrifrons, cf. U. Wilamowitz in Epigr. Graec., 406, 11.
[29] Gk. magic pap. of Paris and London, ed. C. Wessely, Denkschr. d. kaiserlichen Akad. d. Wissenschaften, Philologisch-Hist. Kl., 36, 2 (1888), p. 108, 2560 f.; cf. G. Kruse, Art. "Tetracheir, Tetragonos, Tetrakore," Pauly-W., 5a (1934), 1070, 1075, 1076 f.
[30] Cf. transf. of the lion, Aristot. Physiognomica, 5, p. 809b, 16, the "blameless" τετράγωνος man, Simonides Fr., 37, 3 (ed. D. L. Page, Poetae Melici Graeci [1962], No. 542), cf. Plat. Prot., 344a; Suid., s.v.; Aristot. Eth. Nic., 11, p. 1100b, 21.
[31] J. Stenzel, Zahl u. Gestalt bei Plat. u. Aristot.³ (1959), 25 and 42, 104-124; W. Jaeger, Aristot. (1923), 181-199; Burkert, 441-456.
[32] Ed. R. Heinze (1892), 173, 16 ff.
[33] Ed. E. Hiller (1878).
[34] Cf. Burkert, 23-25.
[35] On fourness as the principle of the perceptible Stenzel, op. cit., 96 f. Since the soul knows all being, it must also consist of the principle of being.
[36] Jaeger, op. cit., 291.
[37] Ed. M. Hayduck, Comm. in Aristot., 1 (1891), 38, 8 ff. on Metaph, 1, 5, p. 85b, 26.
[38] Cf. Burkert, 62 f., 275 with n. 119.
[39] Cf. further F. Cumont, Die Mysterien des Mithra. Ein Beitrag z. Religionsgesch. d. röm. Kaiserzeit⁴ (1963), 104-107.
[40] K. Staehle, Die Zahlenmystik bei Philo v. Alex. (1931), 14; K. v. Fritz, Art. "Pythagoreer," Pauly-W., 24 (1963), 200-203; Burkert, 450.
[41] Represented as an isosceles triangle, Burkert, 452 f.; F. Hultsch, Art. "Arithmetica," Pauly-W., 2 (1896), 1087-1090.
[42] Not to be confused with the perfect numbers of the ancient arithmeticians. Cf. F. Hultsch, "Erläuterungen z. d. Bericht des Jamblichos über die vollkommenen Zahlen," NGG, Philologisch-Hist. Kl., 1894 (1895), 246; Fritz, op. cit., 202.
[43] Burkert, 63 f., 452.

τὴν τῶν ὅλων φύσιν, Theon., 94, 4. It is the content of the Pythagorean oath as παγὰ ἀενάου φύσεως ῥιζώματ' ἔχουσα, Sext. Emp. Math., IV, 2; VII, 94; Luc. Vit. Auct., 4; Hierocl. Carm. Aur., p. 2, 47 f.; cf. Sext. Emp. Math., IV, 3 and 9; VII, 95 and 100; [44] Hierocl. Carm. Aur., 20 (p. 130, 9 f.). All symbolical number-values are ascribed to it, e.g., of the τεσσάρων στοιχείων, Hesych., s.v.; Hierocl. Carm. Aur., 20 (p. 128, 16 f.); Theon., 97, 4 ff., as the number of perfection, Plut. Is. et. Os., 48 (II, 370e), the four phases of the moon, Suid., s.v., the seasons, Theon., 98, 11 f.; Hierocl. Carm. Aur., 20 (p. 128, 16 f.). It is the *logos* τῆς συστάσεως, Sext. Emp. Math., IV, 4-6 and contains φύσιν παντὸς μεγέθους, Theon., 97, 7 ff., ὃ δὲ τετράς, γῆ, 97, 7, indeed it is the Demiurge himself and identical with the visible God, Hierocl. Carm. Aur., 20 (p. 130, 16 f., cf. 127, 1 f.): ἔστι γάρ ... ἡ τετράς, θεὸς νοητός, αἴτιος τοῦ οὐρανίου καὶ αἰσθητοῦ θεοῦ. [45]

B. Four in the Old Testament and Judaism.

1. In the Old Testament.

In the OT four has no speculative features but mostly expresses totality and universality. [46]

a. In the universality of Yahweh's creation the basis of four as a perfect number (→ 128, 7 ff.) is the statement about the four quarters of heaven (→ n. 15) as a totality statement, cf. the four rivers of Paradise which denote the totality of the world, Gn. 2:10-14, [47] the division of the kingdom by God εἰς τοὺς τέσσαρας ἀνέμους τοῦ οὐρανοῦ, Da. 11:4, cf. on this Ιερ. 25:16 (49:36); Ps. 107:3; Gn. 13:14, of the end upon the τέσσαρας πτέρυγας "pillars" or "borders" of the land of Israel, where an original concept of the whole earth is related to Israel, [48] Ez. 7:2, cf. Is. 11:12; Ez. 37:9; 42:15-20; 47:1 ff., of the four Jerusalem gatekeepers, 1 Ch. 9:24, 26, cf. 26:12 ff. In the night visions of Zech. 1:8-11 the four colours of the apocalyptic horses correspond to the four districts of the earth, [49] cf. 2:10 and esp. 6:1-8, where the τέσσαρα ἅρματα correspond to the τέσσαρες ἄνεμοι.

Four is important in Ez.'s theophany, where the figures τεσσάρων ζῴων appear in the whirlwind (1:5), each with the four faces of a man, lion, ox and eagle (→ 134, 13 ff.; 135, 1 ff.) and four wings (1:6-11) along with four wheels within one another, 1:15-18, cf. 10:9-14, 21. [50] With no express mention of the four quarters of heaven the ref. here is to the universality of the power of Yahweh, [51] cf. also the four phenomena at Elijah's theophany in 1 K. 19:11 f. Four then comes to play a significant role in apocal. speculations (→ 133, 10 ff.; 134, 12 ff.). The τέσσαρες ἄνεμοι introduce the ascent of the τέσσαρα θηρία from the sea, Da. 7:2 f. Historical relations lie behind the four-headed leopard of Da. 7:6. But elsewhere four is the no. of totality, cf. 7:17; 8:8, 22 [52] and the allegory of the four empires in 2:31 ff. → 133, 9 f. [53] In Zech. 2:1, 3 the ref. of the

---

[44] Cf. W. Theiler, Review of H. Mutschmann, Sexti Empirici Opera, III (1954), *Gnomon*, 28 (1956), 284 f.

[45] Perhaps experiencing a mystery originally lies behind the tetractus, Burkert, 171 f.

[46] Sauer, 72.

[47] Cf. G. v. Rad, *Das erste Buch Mose, AT Deutsch*, 2⁶ (1961) on 2:10; H. Gunkel, *Die Urgeschichte u. die Patriarchen* (1911), 58.

[48] W. Zimmerli, *Ez., Bibl. Komm. AT*, 13 (1956), 169.

[49] H. Gunkel, "Zum religionsgeschichtlichen Verständnis d. NT," FRLANT, 1 (1903), 46.

[50] Dürr, 54-60; Zimmerli, *op. cit.*, 52-55, 60-62 pt. to Egypt. par. But in Ez. these ideas do not ref. to Yahweh Himself but to the throne-carrying creatures, cf. Gunkel, *op. cit.*, 44-47; K. Tallqvist, "Himmelsgegenden u. Winde," *Stud. Or.*, 2 (1928), 108-185; A. Jeremias, *Das AT im Lichte d. Alten Orients*³ (1916), 617-620, Index 663. In Ez. 1, unlike Is. 6:2, the cherubim have four wings, which gives even greater emphasis to four, cf. G. Fohrer, *Ez., Hndbch. AT*, 13² (1955), 8; Zimmerli, *op. cit.*, 53: "thrust of the number four."

[51] Cf. Zimmerli, 53.

[52] Cf. F. Nötscher, *Da., Echter-Bibel* (1953), ad loc., but cf. on 8:22.

[53] Cf. on this M. Noth, "Das Geschichtsverständnis der at.lichen Apokalyptik," *Gesammelte Stud. z. AT*² (1960), 254-273.

τέσσαρα κέρατα and τέσσαρας τέκτονας is to the totality of the world-powers, [54] cf. τέσσαρα εἴδη in Jer. 15:3.

b. As a round no.: the fourth yr. of a reign is often marked by special events, Zech. 7:1; Jer. 25:1; 28:1; 36:1; 46:2; 51:59; 1 K. 6:1 (→ 136, 35 ff.); 2 K. 18:9; 2 Ch. 3:2; cf. 2 S. 15:7. [55] One finds τετράμηνον as a round no. in Ju. 19:2 A; 20:47 A. Waiting ends with the ἡμέρᾳ τετάρτῃ in Ju. 14:15, cf. Neh. 6:4. A festal practice seems to stand behind Ju. 11:40. [56] We find a little group of four men in 2 K. 7:3; Da. 1:17; 3:25 etc., cf. Ex. 21:37; 2 S. 12:6; Dt. 22:12; Ju. 9:34; 1 K. 18:34; Ez. 14:21; Job 1:13 ff., always a small round no. Four is also common in connection with the specifications of the ark and the tabernacle, Ex. 25:12, 26, 34; 26:2, 8, 32 etc., but only in Ex. 17:1 f. is τετράγωνον τὸ θυσιαστήριον significant, cf. Ez. 40:41 f.; 43:16 f., 20.

c. The series three-four (→ 128, 20 ff.) denotes a greater no. but without specifying, [57] cf. Jer. 36:23; God punishes to the third and fourth generation, Ex. 20:5; 34:7; Nu. 14:18; Dt. 5:9, i.e., a few generations, [58] cf. Gn. 15:16; 2 K. 10:30; 15:12. The series is schematic in proverbs, Am. 1:3, 6, 9, 11, 13; 2:1, 4, 6, where the indefiniteness of the numbers is plain, since they do not correspond to the misdeeds of the peoples. The fourth member is distinct in Ezr. 8:32 f.; 2 Ch. 20:25 f.; Lv. 19:23-25, where the fruits are to be dedicated to the Lord in the fourth yr. and eaten only in the fifth; this is to be explained by cultic or primitive religious ideas. [59] Other three-four series close to Ugaritic literature [60] occur in Prv. 30:15, 18 (→ n. 57), 21, 24, 29; in an augmented list the stress here is on the four, [61] cf. Sir. 26:5; Jdt. 12:7, 10. The beginnings of the intellectual ordering of reality are to be seen in these sayings. [62]

2. In Judaism.

a. In Rabb. works four is a common round no. in enumerations: four things allowed in the camp, bErub, 17a, the four views of scriptural enquiry, bRH, 18b and the four cups at the Passover, bPes., 110a. Esp. important is AbRNat: [63] four categories of penitence, 29 (p. 88), of men and scholars, 40 (p. 126), cf. 40 (p. 127), four things for which men will be rewarded or punished in the hereafter, 40 (p. 119), cf. 36 (p. 108). Ab., 5, 9 ff. has a similar series of seven number sayings regarding stretches of time, dispositions etc. Acc. to jBer., 1 (4a, 7 f.) four men were given their names before birth and acc. to bChag., 14b four men have entered transitorily into Paradise. In jMeg., 1, 11 (71b, 53-55); jSota, 7, 2 (21c, 10-12); Est. r., 3 on 1:22 there is ref. to the idea of four languages which the world uses. [64] The fourth day of the week רביעיות is the day of demons, bPes., 112b, rain,

---

[54] Kautzsch, 603; R. Rignell, *Die Nachtgesichte d. Sach.* (1950), 52, cf. → 131, 17 ff.; 133, 9 f.; n. 15.
[55] Here we are to read τέσσαρα with Cod L Sy al, cf. H. W. Hertzberg, *Die Samuel-bücher, AT Deutsch,* 10² (1960), *ad loc.*
[56] K. Budde, *Das Buch d. Ri., Kurzer Hand-Comm. AT,* 7 (1897), *ad loc.*
[57] Sauer, 82. W. M. W. Roth, "The Numerical Sequence x/x+1 in the OT," *VT,* 12 (1962), 303 f. interprets these sequences in two half-verses in the light of the structure of Hbr. parallelism and assumes in some cases "a definite numerical value," 304, cf. Prv. 30:18 f.
[58] M. Noth, *Das zweite Buch Mose, AT Deutsch,* 5² (1961) on 20:5; W. Zimmerli, *Das Gesetz u. d. Propheten* (1963), 90 thinks that at most there would be four generations in the family at one time.
[59] A. Bertholet, *Lv.. Kurzer Hand-Comm. AT,* 3 (1901), 68 f. sees the rudiments of primitive ideas of field-gods using the fruits the first three years, but not M. Noth, *Das dritte Buch Mose, AT Deutsch,* 6 (1962), *ad loc.* Philo Abr., 13 finds here a confirmation of the sanctity of four by Moses, cf. Virt., 158 f.
[60] Sauer, 92-124, esp. 113 f.
[61] Cf. P. Volz, *Weisheit, Schr. AT,* III, 2 (1911), 48.
[62] G. v. Rad, *Theol. d. AT,* I⁴ (1962), 437 f.
[63] Ed. S. Schechter (1887); transl. J. Goldin, "The Fathers acc. to R. Nathan," *Yale Judaica Ser.,* X (1956).
[64] Cf. Krauss Lehnw., XIX with n. 1.

Lv. r., 35 on 26:3, and marriage, bKet., 1, 1 → 129, 29. The soul of a dead person comes back three days to the tomb and finally leaves it only on the fourth day. [65] Midr. Ps. 92:10 has four kingdoms (→ 134, 9 f.; 131, 33 ff.) present in Paradise. PREl, 4 interprets the creation of the firmament after the model of the throne on the four living creatures in Ez. 1; one is not to pry into the four mysteries acc. to Chag., 2, 1. Qumran has four waters of purification, 1 QS 3:4 f.; the community is divided fourfold into 1000, 100, 50 and 10, 2; 21 f.; 1 QSa 1:14 f., 29 f., though the hierarchical structure is different, 1 QS 2:19 ff.; 4:8 f. Apocal. uses the OT ref. to the four winds (→ 131, 17 ff.), Eth. En. 18:2 f.; 34:1; 36:1; 60:12; 4 Esr. 13:5, cf. S. Bar. 6:4, but esp. the ref. to the four kingdoms of Daniel (→ 131, 35 f.), 4 Esr. 11:39 f.; 12:11 f.; S. Bar. 39:5; Apc. Elias Hbr. 6:3. There is an echo of Ez.'s four creatures (→ 131, 27 ff.) in Eth. En. 40:2 ff., 9 f.; Gr. Bar. 6:2 ff.; cf. 8:4. The underworld is divided into four acc. to Eth. En. 22.

b. Philo in his lost work Περὶ ἀριθμῶν deals fully with Pythagorean number speculations (→ 130, 22 ff.), cf. Vit. Mos., II, 115. He speaks of the τέτταρα στοιχεῖα as the basic constituents of the world, Aet. Mund., 107; Abr., 162; Congr., 117; Decal., 53; Rer. Div. Her., 140, 152 f., 281; Op. Mund., 52; Quaest. in Ex., II, 86, and of man, Aet. Mund., 29; Rer. Div. Her., 282. [66] Naturally there is no idea of divinising four (→ 131, 9 ff.); God uses it as a number of *ratio divina ac sacra,* Quaest. in Ex., II, 87, and on the fourth day He made heaven with the stars, Op. Mund., 53, cf. 62; Plant., 117. Not the Gk. philosophers but Moses the all-wise saw the holiness of the no. four, Abr., 12 f., cf. Virt., 158 f.; Plant., 125 (on Lv. 19:24; → 132, 9 ff.). But Pythagorean influences predominate, cf. Op. Mund., 52; Plant., 123 and 125; ἀριθμῷ τελείῳ, Op. Mund., 47, cf. 51. Four is the no. of the στερεόν (→ 130, 1 ff.), Op. Mund., 49 and 98; Decal., 26, and of righteousness (→ 130, 16 ff.), Op. Mund., 51. There are four main emotions ἡδονή, ἐπιθυμία, λύπη, φόβος, Rer. Div. Her., 268; Abr., 236 and 244; Agric., 83; Praem. Poen., 71, also four virtues (→ 128, 13 ff.; 130, 14 ff.), Som., II, 243. Four contains ἄλλας ἀμυθήτους ἀρετάς, but its most important secret is the τετραγράμματον ὄνομα, for it is πάντα ἐν τετράδι, Vit. Mos., II, 115.

C. Four in the New Testament.

There are no number speculations of a Pythagorean type (→ 130, 22 ff.) in the NT at all. [67]

1. General Use.

In Mk. 2:3 and Ac. 10:11; 11:5 the use is technical. The four anchors of Ac. 27:29, thrown out in unusual fashion from the stern, are for esp. firm anchorage. [68] τετράμηνον in Jn. 4:35 is a short period, the minimum time of waiting between sowing and harvest. [69] ἀπὸ τετάρτης ἡμέρας in Ac. 10:30 is also a short space of time, lit. only three days acc. to the context, cf. 10:9, 23 f. [70] The ref. to the fourth watch of the night in Mk. 6:48 par. Mt. 14:25 is not to be regarded as typical for it denotes here the first dawn. The series of four in 2 Pt. 3:10 and Rev. 5:13 [71] suggest completeness.

---

[65] Str.-B., II, 544 f. with many examples.

[66] He can also speak of two or three elements, Vit. Mos., II, 121.

[67] One cannot accept the view of E. Laubscher, *Phänomene d. Zahl in d. Bibel mit bes. Berücksichtigung d. NT, vorab d. Offenbarung d. Joh.* (1955), 77, that the text of the Bible is of numerical composition.

[68] On this cf. F. F. Bruce, *The Acts of the Apostles*[2] (1952), ad loc.

[69] Bultmann J., ad loc., n. 1.

[70] Perhaps the three-day fast before baptism plays some part here, cf. H. Conzelmann, *Die Ag., Hndbch. NT,* 7 (1963), ad loc.

[71] R. Morgenthaler, "Die lk. Geschichtsschreibung als Zeugnis, I," AbhThANT, 14 (1949), 38-41, 135-141 finds many groups of four, esp. in Lk.

In the parable of the four parts of the field in Mk. 4:1 ff. and par. we have the familiar combination of three similar members with a fourth that is different; the fruitful earth is contrasted with the three non-fruitful types of ground. The τέσσαρας ἡμέρας which Lazarus had already spent in the grave (Jn. 11:17, cf. 39) express the definitiveness and irreversibility of death → 133, 1 ff.; III, 845, 8 ff.; → τρεῖς. Since the four sections of the Roman night watch consisted of four soldiers each τετραδίοις [72] (Ac. 12:4), this explains why when Jesus' clothes were distributed to the soldiers of the night watch at the foot of the cross they were divided into four parts, Jn. 19:23. [73] Fourfold restitution τετραπλοῦν (Lk. 19:8) means generous restitution → 132, 7 f.

2. In Apocalyptic Passages.

In Rev. the Ez. tradition (Ez. 1 → 131, 27 ff.) of τέσσερα ζῷα around God's throne-chariot is often used, Rev. 4:6, 8; 5:6, 8, 14; 6:1, 6; 7:11; 14:3; 15:7; 19:4. The four faces of each creature (→ 131, 28 f.) become four different figures, the lion, ox, eagle and man, in Rev. 4:7; → 135, 1 ff.; IV, 761, 14 ff. The motif of the four wheels (→ 131, 29 f.) is also changed so that the animals themselves now γέμουσιν ὀφθαλμῶν, Rev. 4:8, cf. 6. The four creatures are no longer viewed as carrying the divine throne; they surround it to the glorifying of the universal power of God. [74] The motif of the four horses (→ 131, 24 ff.; III, 338, 10 ff.; VI, 952, 27 ff.) is taken up in Rev. 6:1-8, where there is a distinctive combination with the first four seals, cf. the four destroying angels, 9:14 f. At the four γωνίαι of the earth (Rev. 20:8; → 131, 21 ff.) stand four angels as watchers over the τέσσαρας ἀνέμους, Rev. 7:1; → 131, 20 f., 26, 33 f.; 133, 8 ff. [75] The heavenly Jerusalem (→ 131, 23 f.) is a πόλις τετράγωνος, Rev. 21:16; → n. 15; III, 344, 1 ff. In the Synoptic apocalypse, too, one finds the motif of the four winds (→ 131, 20 f.) from which the elect are gathered, Mk. 13:27 par. Mt. 24:31; → n. 75).

D. In the Early Church.

In Did., 10, 5 we find the theme of the gathering of the saints from the four quarters of heaven (→ lines 24 ff.), while Barn., 4, 5 echoes the thought of Da. 7:7 f. → 131, 33 ff. Herm. v., 3, 13, 3 mentions the τέσσαρα στοιχεῖα → 130, 18 ff.; cf. also the four periods of salvation history up to the time of the apostles, s., 9, 4, 3; 5, 4; 15, 4; 16, 5 and τετράγωνος πέτρα ... ὥστε δύνασθαι ὅλον τὸν κόσμον χωρῆσαι in s., 9, 2, 1. Iren. Haer., I, 8, 6, cf. I, 14, 1; 15, 3; 16, 1; 18, 1 [76] expressly contests Gnostic numbers speculations with their two basic fours of revelation. In Haer., III, 11, 8, however, Iren. himself bases the fourness of the Gospels on the fact that the Church has spread to the four districts of the earth and the four quarters of heaven and thus needs four pillars for its support, the Gospels being mentioned and characterised after the four beasts (→ 134,

---

[72] As a military tt. cf. Philo Flacc., II, 111; Pr.-Bauer, s.v.
[73] Cf. Bultmann J., ad loc.
[74] E. Lohse, Die Offenbarung d. J., NT Deutsch, 11⁸ (1960) on 4:6 f. ref. to Babylonian astrology. But the motifs here are biblical and they are not to be pressed, cf. Loh. Apk., ad loc., who speaks of a "complete retreat of astral relations."
[75] For this reason the earth is not to be regarded as a square, so Loh. Apk., ad loc.; Lohse, op. cit., ad loc., for here and in 20:8 OT traditions are adopted, the OT πτέρυγες (→ 131, 21 ff.) being rendered by γωνίαι in Rev. 7:1; 20:8, → I, 791, 28 ff. These ref. make it plain that the number four is to be taken symbolically rather than geometrically, for in the OT passages it ref. both to the ends of the earth and also to those of the land, whose rough boundaries are certainly known. Hence the ref. in Rev. is to the allsidedness of the earth.
[76] C. Schneider, Geistesgeschichte d. antiken Christentums, I (1954), 285.

14 ff.) and compared to the four covenants of God. [77] The now common association of the names of the beasts with the Evangelists derives from Aug. De Consensu Evangelistarum, I, 6 (CSEL, 43), cf. Ambr. Expositio Evangelii secundum Lucam Prologus, 7 f. (CCh, 11). There are further speculations with the number four in Aug. Quaest. in Heptateuchum, IV, 2 (CSEL, 28); Enarratio in Ps. 86:4 (MPL, 37 [1841], 1104); Serm., 252, 10 f.; Hier. Comm. in Aggaeum, II, 753 (MPL, 25 [1884], 1401C); Hipp. Ref., V, 9 and 26; VI, 14, cf. 23 f.

† τεσσεράκοντα,   † τεσσερακονταετής.

A. Forty in Antiquity.

On the linguistic problems of the stems τεσσαρ- and τεσσερ- → 127, 6 ff. Forty plays an important role in many civilized and uncivilized peoples as a number for specific periods of days and years, for numbers of men and things. [1] It is gen. used as a round number. [2] in Bab. kissatum can be added, "totality," "fulness." [3] It is esp. important among the Mandaeans, [4] the Arabs and other Islamic peoples, [5] and African [6] and Red Indian tribes. [7]

In Gk. it is found a. as a round no., for 40 yrs. as a long time, e.g., of a war, Appian. Rom. Hist., 12, 118, 583, cf. Xenoph. Hist. Graec., V, 4, 13; P. Oxy., IV, 718, 11 f. (180 A.D.); Preisigke Sammelbuch, V, 8246, 9 f., 20 f. (240 A.D.); for a very long punishment, P. Flor., 61, 62 (85 A.D.); 40 days as a shorter time, Diod. S., 17, 111, 6; Hdt., II, 29, 5; Philostr. Vit. Ap., VIII, 19 (p. 335, 3 f.). It also occurs for groups of men, Hom. Il., 2, 524; Hdt., I, 166, 2; 202, 3, esp. important in military connections, CIG, I, 5187a, 6-8, cf. Diod. S., 1, 92, 2; IG, II/III², I, 334, 23 (c. 335 B.C.); Diog. L., VIII, 39; Porphyr. Vit. Pyth., 56.

b. It is the time of maturity. M. Ant., XI, I, 3 speaks of τρόπον τινὰ ὁ τεσσαρακοντού-της having seen... πάντα τὰ γεγονότα καὶ τὰ ἐσόμενα, i.e., on the ground of analogy,

---

[77] Cf. H. v. Campenhausen, "Iren. u. d. NT," ThLZ, 90 (1965), 6: "By means of the ref. to the deeper context the Gospels lose even the appearance of contingence and on the basis of the ancient 'Scripture' . . . are integrated theologically into God's eternal plan of salvation." Conjectures that four is the number of the material (→ 130, 9 ff.) and hence of the incarnation are wide of the mark, as against C. Bischoff, Die Mystik u. Magie d. Zahlen (1920), 203; Endres, op. cit. (→ n. 15), 131 f.

τεσσεράκοντα κτλ. Bibl.: J. Bergmann, "Die runden u. hyperbolischen Zahlen in d. Agada," MGWJ, 82 (1938), 370-372; F. Heiler, "Erscheinungsformen u. Wesen d. Religion," Die Religionen d. Menschheit, 1 (1961), 173 f.; E. Kautzsch, Art. "Zahlen bei d. Hebräern," RE, 21³ (1908), 603 f.; E. König, Art. "Number," Hastings DB, III (1900), 563 f.; also "Die Zahl Vierzig u. Verwandtes," ZDMG, 61 (1907), 913-917; P. H. Menoud, "'Pendant quarante jours' Act. 1:3," Neotestamentica et Patristica, Festschr. O. Cullmann (1962), 148-156; W. H. Roscher, "Die Zahl 40 im Glauben, Brauch u. Schrifttum d. Semiten," ASG, 27 (1909), 91-138; also "Die Tessarakontaden u. Tessarakontadenlehren d. Griechen u. anderer Völker," Berichte über die Abhandlungen der Königl. Sächsischen Gesellschaft der Wissenschaften zu Leipzig, Philologisch-Histor. Kl., 61 (1909, 17-206.

[1] Cf. esp. Roscher Tessarakontaden; also Zahl, passim. R. Hirzel, "Über Rundzahlen," ASG, 5 (1885), 1-74 begins with the 40 yr. period of the γενεαί of man, while Roscher Zahl, 97, 100-103 and Tessarakontaden, 21, n. 2 and 22-28 thinks the time of the uncleanness of woman after childbirth is basic. A. Jeremias, Das AT im Lichte d. Alten Orients³ (1916), 139 f. suggests the time of the absence of the Pleiades, i.e., an astrological origin cf. also Index, 662, his work Hndbch. d. altorient. Geisteskultur (1913), 152 f.; Heiler, 173 f. Acc. to Roscher Tessarakontaden, 50-54, however, the forty day period as a round no. lies behind this too.

[2] Cf. König Number, 564; Zahl, 913; Bergmann, 370.

[3] J. Hehn, "Siebenzahl u. Sabbat bei d. Babyloniern u. im AT," Leipziger Semitist. Stud., II, 5 (1907), 9 with n. 1, cf. 3, n. 1; Roscher Zahl, 95 f. → II, 628, 6 ff.

[4] Roscher Zahl, 98 f.

[5] Ibid., 116-138; Heiler, 174.

[6] Heiler, 173; F. C. Endres, Mystik u. Magie d. Zahlen³ (1951), 225.

[7] Roscher Tessarakontaden, 170-172; Endres, 226.

cf. VII, 49, where the 40 yrs. of human life tell us as much as ἔτη μυρία. Often men must be at least 40 yrs. old to take on important jobs, e.g., law-givers, IG, 5, 2, 357, 16 (3rd cent. B.C.); Ditt. Syll.³, I, 344, 45; Aristot. Respublica Atheniensium, 29 (p. 102),⁸ choregi, who only at 40 stand ἐν τῇ σωφρονεστάτῃ αὐτοῦ ἡλικίᾳ, Aeschin. Tim., 11, cf. 12, positions of leadership, Aristot. Respublica Athen., 29 (p. 103); 42 (p. 133), cf. BGU, I, 86, 4 (155 A.D.); Porphyr. Vit. Pyth., 9; P. Petr., I, 19, 6; P. Gen., I, 24, 11 (96 A.D.).

c. It occurs, too, for specific periods, acc. to Aristot. Hist. An., VII, 3, p. 583b, 4 the first movement of a child in its mother's womb takes place περὶ τὰς τεττεράκοντα ἡμέρας, and the σῶμα of the embryo may be discerned at the same time, Oribasius Fr. (Diels, I, 301), cf. Diog. L., VIII, 29, also the καθάρσεις after conception, Aristot. Hist. An., VII, 3, p. 583a, 28. A 40 day period occurs some 74 times in Hippocrates' works⁹ and it plays a special role in gynaecology and embryology, cf. Περὶ ἑπταμήνου, 9 (Littré, VII, 446); Περὶ φύσιος παιδίου, 18 (Littré, VII, 500 f., 504). Pregnancy normally lasts 7 × 40 days, Hippocr. Περὶ ὀκταμήνου, 10 (VII, 452). In many illnesses there is a crisis after 40 days, Περὶ κρισίων (IX, 289). There is ref. to Pythagoras' fast of 40 days in Diog. L., VIII, 40; Porphyr. Vit. Pyth., 57, to 40 days of rain in Ps.-Callisth., III, 26, 7 (p. 127, 3), 40 days when the Pleiades are not visible, Hes. Op., 385, cf. also Paus., I, 144; Dion. Hal. Ant. Rom., 9, 36, 3; Hdt., IV, 73, 1.

B. Forty in the Old Testament and Judaism.

1. In the Old Testament.

The use of forty in the OT cannot be adequately explained in terms of derivation from the Pleiades period.¹⁰ In most instances it is a typical round number, → 135, 10 ff.; n. 2.

a. The forty year period is in the OT connected with a generation schema, not in the sense of the interval between generations, but rather in that of the period within which a whole group of living adults is at work.¹¹ This is esp. true of the wilderness generation, where the 40 yrs. are often viewed as the time of testing and keeping by God, Ex. 16:35; Dt. 1:3; 2:7; 8:2, 4; 29:4; Am. 2:10; Neh. 9:21, so that a new generation could grow up, Nu. 14:33 f.; 32:14 ff., whereas the old as a punishment would not survive the wilderness period, Nu. 14:32; 32:11, 13; 33:38; Jos. 5:6; Ps. 95:10, cf. the 40 yrs. of punishment in Ez. 29:11-13. The same schema of the replacement of a present generation by a new one after 40 yrs. shapes the framework of Ju., cf. 3:11, 30; 5:31; 8:28; 13:1, and it also plays a certain part in the chronology of the so-called Deuteronomic history.¹² David reigns 40 yrs., 2 S. 5:4 f.; 1 K. 2:11; 1 Ch. 29:27,¹³ similarly Solomon, 1 K. 11:42; 2 Ch. 9:30, Joash, 2 K. 12:2; 2 Ch. 24:1; on 2 S. 15:7 → 132, n. 55. The 480 yrs. from the exodus to the building of the temple (1 K. 6:1) are not composed schematically of 12 generations of 40 yrs. each¹⁴ but are to be understood in the light of detailed chronological references.¹⁵

---

⁸ Ed. F. G. Kenyon³ (1892).

⁹ Roscher Tessarakontaden, 83 f., 85-131.

¹⁰ Kautzsch, 604; → n. 1.

¹¹ König Zahl, 913: "the graphic approximate term for the length of a generation," cf. König Number, 563; M. Noth, *Überlieferungsgeschichtliche Stud.*² (1957), 63: "After 40 yrs." almost none of those who have taken part in a specific historical event are still in public life."

¹² Cf. Noth, *op. cit.,* 62-69, esp. 68; W. Nowack, *Buch d. Ri., Rt. u. S., Handkomm. AT,* I, 4 (1902), XVIII-XX. For this reason the Mas. figure of 40 yrs. for the judgeship of Samuel in 1 S. 4:18 is probably older than LXX 20 yrs., cf. Noth, 65.

¹³ The date in 2 S. 5:5 might well be based on more specific records, cf. K. Budde, *Die Bücher d. S., Kurzer Hand-Comm. AT,* 8 (1902), ad loc.

¹⁴ On this cf. König Zahl, 914-917; Roscher Zahl, 115 f.

¹⁵ Noth, *op. cit.* (→ n. 11), 62-68; W. Vollborn, "Die Chronologie des Richterbuches," *Festschr. F. Baumgärtel* (1959), 192-196.

b. The number 40 also denotes maturity. The 40th yr. is important in a man's life
(→ 135, 23 ff.) as the yr. of marriage, Gn. 25:20; 26:34, cf. also accession to the crown
by Ishbosheth in 2 S. 2:10, the scout's office (Jos. 14:7) which lasted 40 days, Nu. 13:25.
In this connection one might mention that 120 yrs. (Gn. 6:3; Dt. 34:7, cf. 80 yrs. in Ex.
7:7) can be the span of human life. [16]

c. Forty can also be a typical round no. The flood narrative (J) has periods of
40 days, [17] Gn. 7:4, 12, 17; 8:6, cf. the time spent by Moses on the mountain Ex. 24:18;
34:28; Dt. 9:9, 18, 25; 10:10. Goliath taunts the host 40 days in 1 S. 17:16, cf. the time
of repentance for Nineveh, Jon. 3:4. Ez. has to lie on his right side 40 days to announce
the exile of Judah, [18] Ez. 4:6. This can only be a round figure after the analogy of the
wilderness period, [19] cf. Elijah's journey of 40 days through the desert in 1 K. 19:8. The
40 days of a mother's uncleanness after the birth of a boy are important, Lv. 12:4 → 136,
11 ff. [20] In lists 40 is used for larger numbers, cf. Ju. 12:14; 2 K. 8:9; Neh. 5:15. Acc. to
Dt. 25:3 forty stripes are the maximum punishment which can be suffered without dis-
honour, → 138, 18 ff. [21]

2. In later Judaism.

In later Jewish lit. only 7 is a more common number than 40. [22]

a. Often OT round numbers are elevated to typical periods, cf. the 40 days of Lv.
12:1 ff. (→ lines 11 ff.) in Jos. Ant., 3, 269; Nidda, 3, 7; Ohaloth, 18, 7 in connection
with the flood Gn. r., 32 on 4:7, the rules of purification bMen., 103b; Nu. r., 18 on 16:35,
in popular medicine bShab., 109b; jTaan., 4, 8 (68d, 4 r.) and agriculture jShebi, 4, 20
(35d, 48); bPes., 56a; Ed., 6, 1, 40 day fasting bBM, 33a; 85a; bMQ, 26a and praying
Beth Hamidrash, III, 78; [23] jTaan., 4, 8 (68b, 60 f.), cf. Vit. Ad., 6, 17; Gr. Bar. 4:14;
Apc. Abr. 12:1. Copying the 40 day stay of Moses on Sinai Ezra withdraws for 40 days
to copy the Law in 4 Esr.14:23, 36, 42, 44, and is then raptured in 14:49, similarly Baruch,
who is to be raptured after 40 days and who in the interim receives eschatological
admonitions, S. Bar. 76:2-4 (→ 139, 7 ff.). Forty day fasting is mentioned in bGit., 56a,
cf. also bSanh., 43a, Bar. 40 yrs are important as periods in office, cf. the high-priest
Simeon in bJoma, 39a, cf. jJoma, 6, 3 (43c, 64), Saul in Jos. Ant., 6, 378 and Jeroboam
in Ant., 9, 205 and 215. 40 yrs. before the destruction of the temple signs appeared,
bJoma, 39b; jJoma, 6, 3 Bar. (43c, 60 ff.), the Sanhedrin left, bAZ, 8b Bar.; bSanh., 41a
Bar. the ius gladii was taken from the Jews, jSanh., 1, 1 (18a, 36 f.); 14, 2 (24b, 42 f.),
perhaps a ref. to the subjugation of the Jews to Roman rule in 6 A.D. [24] A Rabb.
disciple had to be 40 yrs. old to make independent decisions, bSota, 22a; bAZ, 19b. [25]
The 120 yrs. of Moses' life are divided into 3 groups of 40 each in S. Dt., 357 (150a) on

---

[16] The idea of 3 generations of 40 yrs. each plays a part here → 135, 23 ff., 137,
35 ff.; n. 26.

[17] Cf. the 150 days of P, Gn. 7:24; 8:3.

[18] Cf. G. Fohrer, Die symbolischen Handlungen d. Propheten (1953), 36.

[19] Cf. W. Zimmerli, Ez., Bibl. Komm. AT, 13 (1956), 120.

[20] Roscher Zahl, 100-103 thinks this basic (→ n. 1), but it is an isolated ref. in the OT,
cf. B. Jacob, Das 1. Buch d. Tora (1934), 234 f.

[21] Only 39 of the maximum 40 lashes were given, Jos. Ant., 4, 238 and 248; Mak., 1, 1;
bMak., 2a, the no. 39 being explained by the "not more" יֹסִיף לֹא or the בְּמִסְפָּר of the Torah,
bMak., 22a b with a full discussion in which Jehuda advocates 40 lashes, cf. Mak. 3:10;
gematric explanation in Nu. r., 18 on 16:35, cf. the 40 less 1 chief tasks in Shab., 7, 2 f.;
bShab., 70b and 40 plus 1 as a minimum no. in bShab., 66b; Nidda, 3, 7. On this cf. Roscher
Zahl, 103; J. Blinzler, Der Prozess Jesu³ (1960), 159; Wnd. 2 K. on 11:24.

[22] Roscher Zahl, 100; RW, II, 715.

[23] Ed. A. Jellinek² (1938).

[24] Str.-B., I, 1026 f.; → VII, 865, 1 ff.

[25] On ordination and 40 yrs. cf. J. Jeremias, "War Paulus Witwer?" ZNW, 25 (1926),
311; E. Lohse, Die Ordination im Spätjudt. u. im NT (1951), 43.

34:7 (→ 138, 31 ff.), and cf. the similar way of describing the lives of Hillel, Jochanan b Zakkai and Akiba, Gn. r., 100 on 50:14, [26] cf. Test. S. 8:1; A. 1:1.

b. Gen. as a round number, e.g. learning and teaching 40 times, bKet., 22b; bBer., 28a; bMeg., 7b; bPes., 72a; jGit., 6, 1 (47d, 34); scourging, → n. 21. We find 40 as a round no. in jTaan., 4, 8 (69a, 7-9); bSota, 34a; Jos. Bell., 5, 189 and 205; Ep. Ar., 105; Jub. 3:9; 5:25; S. Bar. 29:5; Gr. Bar. 6:2; 1 QM 6:14; 7:1; ζωογονικωτάτη, Philo Vit. Mos., II, 84.

c. In Messianic contexts: Acc. to R. Akiba the interim Messianic kingdom as a time of conflict lasts 40 yrs. like the wilderness period, Pesikt. r., 1 (4a), cf. bSanh., 99a, [27] so, too, the time between the death of the Teacher of Righteousness and the coming of the divine kingdom in Damasc. 20:15 (9:40), cf. 1 QM 2:6, 9, where the eschatological war lasts 40 yrs. with 6 of preparation, the yr. of release and the period of conflict, cf. 4 Q Ps. 37:2, 8. [28] 40 days of judgment are affixed to the 40 yr. Messianic kingdom (Apc. Elias Hbr. 6:5) in 8:1, cf. the 200 yr. kingdom in 4 Esr. 7:28 f. Here the wilderness yrs. have become a Messianic type.

C. Forty in the New Testament.

40 is a round figure for the duration of an illness in Ac. 4:22 and for a group of people in Ac. 23:13, 21. The fact that Paul was five times given 40 less 1 stripes by the Jews (2 C. 11:24) is the first written instance of the omission of the 40th stroke → 137, 13 f. [29] The Jewish punishment is clearly distinguished from the Roman one here → VI, 971, 4 ff.

The number 40 is important in connection with salvation history, cf. the recollection of the wilderness period under the sign of God's wrath (Hb. 3:10, 17; → 136, 29 ff.) or His guidance (Ac. 13:18; → 136, 26 ff.); here ὡς τεσσερακονταέτη χρόνον denotes a typological rather than a chronological period. In the same synagogue sermon a 40 year rule is ascribed to Saul (Ac. 13:21) even though the OT tradition seems to give him only 2 years; [30] no data are given concerning David (→ 136, 33 f.). The 40 years of the wilderness period are thus regarded as a typical time for God's dealings with His people in election. In Stephen's address (Ac. 7:42) the quotation from Am. 5:25, which originally understood the 40 years of the desert wandering positively as a period without sacrifices, is now given a negative turn in accordance with the general tenor of the speech, → VII, 934, n. 40. [31] The liking of Lk. for 40 year periods is also shown by the adoption of the tradition of three 40 year periods in the life of Moses, Ac. 7:23, 30, 36; → 137, 4 f.; 137, 35 ff.

In the temptation story (Mk. 1:13 and par.) the forty days of the temptation (→ VI, 33, 2 ff.) are linked directly to the baptism by John and they are thus given programmatic significance as an anticipation of Jesus' true obedience to His Messianic commission → VI, 34, 15 ff. [32] In Mk. 1:13 the stay in the wilderness is a type of God's special nearness and also of testing → 136, 26 ff.; → II, 658, 3 ff. [33] When it is said that Jesus was μετὰ τῶν θηρίων and that the angels ministered to Him,

---

[26] Bergmann, 371; Roscher Zahl, 110, n. 32; Lohse, 43, n. 5.

[27] Cf. Str.-B., IV, 2, 817 and 825; III, 824-7 with many similar examples.

[28] Ed. E. Lohse, Die Texte aus Qumran (1964), 271.

[29] Wnd. 2 K., ad loc.

[30] 1 S. 13:1 is hotly contested and corresponds to later depreciation of Saul's period in office, cf. Noth, op. cit. (→ n. 11), 66. Jos. Ant., 6, 378 (→ 137, 29 ff.) has 40 yrs. but 10, 143 20 yrs.

[31] Cf. H. Conzelmann, Die Ag., Hndbch. NT, 7 (1963), ad loc.

[32] R. Schnackenburg, "Der Sinn d. Versuchung Jesu bei d. Synpt.," Theol. Quart., 132 (1952), 306 f., 310 f., 319.

[33] In this regard it makes no difference whether the ref. is to yrs. or days, cf. A. Feuillet, "L'épisode de la tentation d'après l'Év. selon S. Marc (1:12-13)," Estudios Biblicos, 19 (1960), 58.

this defines the desert as the place of eschatological paradisial peace, → VII, 796, 31 ff. [34] In Mt. 4:2 the reference to Jesus' fasting ἡμέρας τεσσεράκοντα καὶ τεσσεράκοντα νύκτας is additionally a link to Moses' fast on Mt. Sinai, → 137, 7 f.; IV, 931, 25 ff. [35] This also finds an echo in Lk. 4:2 f. Here, then, we have a Moses typology, → IV, 871, 4 ff. The linking of the πειράζων with the hunger resulting from the fast puts the true theme of temptation at the end of the 40 days.

The 40 days of the appearances of Jesus (→ II, 66, n. 3) to the apostles (Ac. 1:3) are to be taken as a round figure with striking parallels in apocalyptic, → 137, 24 ff. Ac. 1:3 is hard to reconcile with the account of the ascension in Lk. 24:51 to the degree that the latter mentions no interim period. [36] In Ac. 1:3 Luke is concerned, as at the beginning of the Gospel, to prove the reliability of what is recounted. [37] The message of the apostles is validated by the disclosures of the post-Easter Jesus λέγων τὰ περὶ τῆς βασιλείας τοῦ θεοῦ (v. 3); these take place in the 40 days of His earthly presence between death and ascension. Luke can use ἡμέρας πλείους for the same period. [38] It is hard to find any specific OT type for it. [39] But perhaps there is a connection with Jewish statements about reliable instruction → 138, 3 f.

D. In the Early Church.

The post-apost. fathers ref. only to Moses' stay on Sinai, 1 Cl., 53, 2; Barn., 4, 7; 14, 2. Tert. Apol., 21, 23 says Ac. 1:3 is the period of the reliable instruction of the disciples (→ lines 10 ff.); Aug. Serm., 263, 4 [40] suggests a ref. to Jesus' fasting, cf. also Orig. Fr. in Mt., 61 (GCS, 41, 39) with an emphasis on the likeness of 40 to the perfect 4. For further speculation on 40 as *integritas saeculorum* cf. Aug. Enarratio in Ps. 94:14 (MPL, 37 [1841], 1225 f.), as the fulness of the Law, in Joh. Ev. Tract., 17, 6 on Jn. 5:5. The τεσσερακοστή as a 40 day fast is already mentioned as a normal practice at Nicaea [41] and no doubt developed out of the ancient Easter fast in the light of the 40 day fasting of Jesus. [42]

Balz

---

[34] Schnackenburg, *op. cit.*, 308 f.; U. Holzmeister, "'Jesus lebte mit den wilden Tieren' Mk. 1:13," *Festschr. M. Meinertz* (1951), 85-92.
[35] 1 K. 19:8 is no par. since it does not have the point of the fast.
[36] On the problem H. Grass, *Ostergeschehen u. Osterberichte*[3] (1964), 43-51; U. Wilckens, *Die Missionsreden d. Ag.*[2] (1962), 57, n. 1; P. A. van Stempvoort, "The Interpretation of the Ascension in Luke and Acts," NTSt, 5 (1958/59), 30-42. Ac. 1:3 is Lucan, and hence the ascension ref. in Lk. 24:51 was later cut out in Cod ℵ* D it sy^s.
[37] Cf. Menoud, 151 f., 154, 156; W. Schmithals, *Das kirchliche Apostelamt* (1961), 234. On the Gospel of the forty days cf. A. Schneider, "Das Ev. d. vierzig Tage," *Gesammelte Aufsätze* (1963), 17-34.
[38] This time as a special time of salvation is distinguished from that which follows by the fact that the later appearances are from heaven, cf. H. Conzelmann, *Die Mitte d. Zeit*[5] (1964), 176-8; 189 f.; Grass, *op. cit.*, 48 f. In Ac. 10:41 Cod D etc. ἡμέρας τεσσεράκοντα is a secondary interpolation from 1:3, cf. Wilckens, *op. cit.*, 150, n. 2.
[39] M. Goguel, *La foi à la résurrection de Jésus dans le christianisme primitif* (1933), 354 thinks the 40 days of appearances are par. to those of temptation and sees in them entry on earthly or heavenly office, cf. Menoud, 150, n. 2.
[40] Cf. K. P. Köppen, "Die Auslegung d. Versuchungsgeschichte unter bes. Berücksichtigung d. Alten Kirche," *Beiträge z. Gesch. d. bibl. Exegese*, 4 (1961), 19, n. 3 with more examples.
[41] Cf. F. G. Cremer, "Die Fastenansage Jesu," *Bonner Bibl. Stud.*, 23 (1965), 41; B. Lohse, "Das Passahfest d. Quartadecimaner," BFTh, II, 54 (1953), 70, n. 1.
[42] Cremer, *op. cit.*, 40 f.

---

† τηρέω, † τήρησις, † παρατηρέω,
† παρατήρησις, † διατηρέω,
† συντηρέω

---

† τηρέω.

A. τηρέω Outside the New Testament.

1. The basic meaning [1] "to keep in view," "to take note," "to watch over." [2] Though the word is later synon. with → φυλάσσω, the meaning is originally more neuter, while φυλάσσω has rather more clearly the sense of "to watch over in order to protect." The meaning "to watch for" would be quite impossible in the case of φυλάσσω: παραστεί-χοντα, τηρήσας μέσον κάρα, διπλοῖς κέντροισί μου καθίκετο, Soph. Oed. Tyr., 808 f., cf. "to wait for," Thuc., III, 22, 1; IV, 26, 7; VI, 2, 4. Concretely the word means "to watch over," e.g., τὸ ἔξωθεν [τεῖχος] ἐτηρεῖτο, Thuc., II, 13, 7; τὸ χῶμα, P. Petr., II, 37, 1, 19; "to rule," e.g., πόλιν, Pind. Pyth., 2, 88; also abs. P. Greci e Latini, III, 168, 9 (118 B.C.), cf. 165, 4 (6th cent. A.D.). Of direct perception it means "to observe," e.g., τηρῶ... αὐτοὺς... κλέπτοντας, Aristoph. Eq., 1145 ff.; in scientists οἱ πάλαι τετηρηκότες, Aristot. Cael., II, 12, p. 292a, 7 f.; cf. μετακόσμησιν Soranus Gynaecia, I, 41, 4 (CMG, IV), cf. Vita Hippocratis, 13 (CMG, IV). Other senses are "to test," e.g., τετηρημένης ἐπ' αὐτοῖς τῆς θεραπείας, Gal. De sanitate tuenda, V, 10, 51 (CMG, V, 4, 2), cf. Hippocratis de acutorum morborum victu liber et Galeni comment., IV, 17 (Kühn, 15, 766); "to ward off," "to watch over" in a protective sense, e.g., αἵτινες τηροῦμεν ὑμᾶς, Aristoph. Nu., 579; cf. Pax, 201; of the keeping back of dogs, Ps.-Xenoph. Cyn., 6, 1; "to guard protectively," e.g., μᾶλλον τήρει τὰς τῶν λόγων ἢ τὰς τῶν χρημάτων παρακαταθήκας, Isoc. Or., 1, 22; cf. Plat. Resp., VI, 484c; "to protect," e.g., τὴν νῆσον, Ps.-Plat. Ax., 371a; τηρέω ἀπὸ τοῦ πυρός; [3] "to keep," Aristot. Eth. Nic., VIII, 1, p. 1155a, 9 (par. σῴζω); τηρέω ἔχων "to hold in custody," Aristoph. Nu., 752; "to keep," e.g., τήρησόν μοι αὐτὰ ἕως ἀναβῶ, P. Oxy., XIV, 1757, 23 f. (2nd cent. A.D.); "to keep oneself," ἐγὼ μόνος πάνυ ἐμαυτὸν τηρῶν in the sense of "living in retirement," P. Oxy., X, 1298, 7 (4th cent. A.D.); τηρῆσαι ἑαυτὸν ἁπλοῦν, M. Ant., VI, 30, 2; ἄμεμπτ[ον] ἐμα τὸν ἐτήρησα, BGU, IV, 1141, 25 (13 B.C.).

In a transf. sense one finds the meaning "to see to something," [4] e.g., τὸ τηρεῖν ὅπως κρεῖττον ἔσται τὸ βουλόμενον τὴν πολιτείαν πλῆθος τοῦ μὴ βουλομένου, Aristot. Pol., V, 7, p. 1309b, 16-18; τὴν θήραν τηρέω, "to apply oneself to the chase," Aristot. Hist. An., IX, 39, p. 623a, 13; "to watch for," e.g., καιρόν, Aristot. Rhet., II, 5, p. 1382b, 10; cf. Lys., 12, 71. Yet the main stress is on warding off, cf. δεῖ τηρεῖν ὅπως μηδὲν παρανομῶσι καὶ μάλιστα τὸ μικρὸν φυλάττειν, Aristot. Pol., V, 8, p. 1307b, 31 f. One also finds "to defend oneself," e.g., φυλάττειν ἐμὲ καὶ τηρεῖν ἐκέλευεν, ὅπως μὴ παρακρούσομαι μηδ' ἐξαπατήσω, Demosth. Or., 18, 276; "to observe," "to keep," e.g., ὅρκους, Democr. Fr., 239 (Diels, II, 193); εἰρήνην, Demosth. Or., 18, 89; πίστιν, Polyb., 6, 56, 13; 10, 37, 9; τὸ καθῆκον, 6, 56, 14; φιλίαν, Diod. S., 15, 30, 4; νόμους,

---

τ η ρ έ ω.   [1] First used in the Demeter hymn, Hom. Hymn. Cer., 142. In Alcman. Fr., 1, 77, τείρει (D. L. Page, Poetae Melici Graeci [1962], 4) is now read for τηρεῖ (Diehl, II², 13) [Risch]. The verb is obviously from τηρός, "he who watches over something," though this occurs only in Aesch. Suppl., 248 and the tradition is not quite certain, cf. Boisacq, Hofmann, s.v.; Walde-Pok., I, 508. Schwyzer, I, 726 thinks τηρέω is etym. "less or not clear."
[2] Cf. Cr.-Kö., Liddell-Scott, Moult.-Mill., s.v.
[3] F. Bilabel, "Ὀψαρτυτικά u. Verwandtes," SAH, 1919, 23 (1920), 10a, 16.
[4] Abs. "to pay attention," Mayser, II, 1, 82, 24.

11, 11, 4; of laws πάλαι τετήρηται, πάλαι πεφύλακται, Poll. Onom., V, 166; τὰ προγο-
νικὰ νόμιμα, Athen., 7, 50 (297d); τὰ ... δίκαια "marriage settlement," BGU, IV, 1098,
33 f. (1st cent. B.C.); τὴν δεξιάν, "promise," P. Oxy., III, 533, 18 (2nd/3rd cent. A.D.);
τὸν νόμον, Achill. Tat., VIII, 13, 4.

2. In the LXX τηρέω occurs 39 times, mostly in the Wisdom lit. The Hbr. equivalents
are esp. שׁמר and (only Prv.) נצר, but both are rendered in different senses by → φυλάσσω,
and indeed this is usual in the case of שׁמר. τηρέω means concretely "to aim at something,"
e.g., κεφαλήν and πτέρναν in Gn. 3:15 (both times for שׁוף); "to keep watch," "to pay
attention," 1 Εσδρ. 4:11; 2 Εσδρ. 8:29; "to watch over," e.g., σταθμούς, Prv. 8:34;
1 Macc. 4:61; 6:50; οἱ τηροῦντες, Cant. 3:3; 8:11 f.; "to observe," e.g., ἐπίνοιαν, Jer.
20:10; "to watch for," e.g., καιρόν, Jdt. 12:16; εὔκαιρον, 2 Macc. 14:29. In the sense
of protective watching it means "to guard" in Prv. 2:11 (for נצר); "to keep," e.g., ἀπὸ
γυναικός, 7:5 (for שׁמר); ψυχήν, 13:3; 16:17; 19:16; αὐτὸν ἄμεμπτον, Wis. 10:5. In a
transf. sense τηρέω occurs mostly in the Wisdom lit. "to observe," "to keep," e.g., τοὺς
λόγους μου, 1 Βασ. 15:11 (for קום; vl. ἔστησεν); νόμον, Tob. 14:9; ῥήματα, Prv. 3:1
and βουλήν, 3:21 (both times נצר); ἐντολάς, Sir. 29:1 (ποιεῖ Cod A); διαθήκην,
Da. 9:4 (φυλάσσω in Θ); "to notice," Prv. 15:32 (for שׁמע); "to observe," e.g., the
wind, Qoh. 11:4 [5] (שׁמר רוח).

3. In Philo τηρέω is rare; it means "to pay heed," e.g., τήρει δ' ὅτι οὐκ εἶπεν,
Leg. All., III, 184; on the basis of Gn. 3:15 "to aim at something," protectively (par.
διαφυλάσσω and διασῴζω), III, 188 f. or in a hostile sense (par. ἐπιτηρέω πρὸς
ἀναίρεσιν), loc. cit. Cf. also μηδὲ εἰς τὸν αἰῶνα μηνίσας τηρήσῃς τὰ κακά μοι,
Prayer Man. 13. It can mean "to watch over" in Test. Zeb. 4:3; Jos. Ant., 14, 366; "to
preserve," e.g., εἰς κόλασιν αἰώνιον, Test. R. 5:5; G. 7:5; ἑτέρῳ κατακλυσμῷ, Jos.
Ant., 1, 97; "to hold," e.g., φυλάξατε ... τὴν ἐντολὴν τοῦ κυρίου καὶ τὸν νόμον
αὐτοῦ τηρήσατε, Test. D. 5:1; τὴν πίστιν, Jos. Ant., 15, 134; of marital fidelity, Bell.,
2, 121; τὰς ἐντολάς, Ant., 8, 120; τὴν τῆς ἀληθείας παράδοσιν, Vit., 361.

4. In Rabb. lit. שׁמר and עשׂה can be par., and in such a way as to lead one to expect
that they are complementary. שׁמר stresses obedience to the traditional law (cf. קבל)
as distinct from carrying out individual commands: ללמוד וללמד לשׁמור ולעשׂות, T. Sota, 8, 10;
cf. S. Dt., 48 (84b) ond Dt. 11:22. Perhaps this relation is present already in Sir. 29:1:
ὁ ποιῶν ἔλεος δανιεῖ τῷ πλησίον, καὶ ὁ ἐπισχύων τῇ χειρὶ αὐτοῦ τηρεῖ ἐντολάς.

B. In the New Testament.

τηρέω occurs 60 times in the NT. In distinction from the LXX it is more common here
than → φυλάσσω, which is found only 32 times. The preference for τηρέω is esp. striking
in the Johannine writings. It occurs 18 times in Jn., φυλάσσω 3, and 7 in 1 Jn., φυλάσσω
only once.

1. Literal Meaning.

The verb is used in the NT in the following senses: a. lit. "to guard," e.g., a prison
in Ac. 12:6, prisoners or felons, Mt. 27:36, 54; Ac. 12:5; 16:23; 24:23; 25:4, 21b; cf. οἱ
τηροῦντες, Mt. 28:4; b. "to keep" until a given point in time, e.g., wine at the wedding-
feast, Jn. 2:10; [6] the eschatological inheritance awaited in hope, 1 Pt. 1:4; a pass. use is
also possible of people, e.g., Paul in prison, Ac. 25:21a; the fallen angels and unrighteous

---

[5] Cf. G. Bertram, "Hbr. u. gr. Qohelet," ZAW, 64 (1952), 47.
[6] Cf. P. Oxy., XIV, 1757, 23 (2nd cent. A.D.) → 140, 26 f.; also Moult.-Mill., s.v.; W. S.
Wood, "The Miracle of Cana," JThSt, 6 (1905), 438: "maintain," "keep going" (no new
examples).

men whom God keeps so that they will not escape judgment, 2 P. 2:4, 9; Jd. 6b, [7] also the world, 2 Pt. 3:7, → lines 10 ff.; on the other hand final punishment is reserved for the sinful world, 2 Pt. 2:17; Jd. 13; c. "to maintain," not found expressly in the NT but echoed in some expressions (→ 143, 10 ff., 18 ff.), and also with a negative "to forfeit," "to lose," [8] so Jd. 6a: the angels have not retained the sphere of dominion allotted to them τοὺς μὴ τηρήσαντας τὴν ἑαυτῶν ἀρχήν but lost it by their own fault; [9] d. "to protect," with ref. to the preserving or keeping of someone intact: [10] τηρεῖν τὴν ἑαυτοῦ παρθένον "to keep his virgin" (→ V, 836, 19 ff.) as such. [11]

2. Transferred Meaning.

a. The object of τηρέω in the sense "to preserve," "to protect," "to guard" is the disciple, or in the Church situation the Christian, who as he passes through the world is exposed to temptation and the danger of falling: τήρησον αὐτοὺς ἐν τῷ ὀνόματί σου (Jn. 17:11; → V, 272, 20 ff.); [12] ἐγὼ ἐτήρουν αὐτοὺς ἐν τῷ ὀνόματί σου... καὶ ἐφύλαξα (Jn. 17:12); [13] οὐκ ἐρωτῶ ἵνα... ἀλλ᾿ ἵνα τηρήσῃς αὐτοὺς ἐκ τοῦ (→ VII, 162, 31 f.) πονηροῦ (Jn. 17:15). [14] It is evident that there is parallelism between ἐν τῷ ὀνόματι (v. 12) and ἐκ τοῦ πονηροῦ (v. 15). Hence ἐν here does not have an instrumental sense [15] but a transferred spatial sense and can be rendered by "in the sphere of power of faith in thy name" as the opposite of the power of evil, which is to be kept at a distance → VI, 225, 10 ff. The same applies in Rev. 3:10, where the transfigured Christ protects His community against (ἐκ) eschatological temptation. [16] The Pauline wish that the spirits, souls and bodies of Christians may be kept blameless also has an eschatological thrust, this time with reference to fellowship with Christ at the parousia, 1 Th. 5:23. [17] The salutation in Jd. is addressed to the called, who will be kept for Christ, [18] i.e., for His eschatological reign. In the saying ὁ γεννηθεὶς ἐκ τοῦ θεοῦ τηρεῖ αὐτόν (1 Jn. 5:18) the

---

[7] Cf. also Test. R. 5:5, Gr. En. 7:1 and Wnd. Kath. Br., ad loc. The perf. τετήρηκεν indicates that the imprisonment still goes on.

[8] Cf. the dominical saying quoted in 2 Cl., 8, 5: εἰ τὸ μικρὸν οὐκ ἐτηρήσατε, τὸ μέγα τίς ὑμῖν δώσει; on this H. Köster, Synpt. Überlieferung bei d. apost. Väter (1957), 99-102.

[9] There is a play on words in Jd. 6, τηρέω being used twice in the same sentence with two different meanings and subjects, once negatively, the second time positively: The angels have not kept their job, hence God now keeps them fast. Cf. Rev. 3:10.

[10] The ref. can also be to things, e.g., τὴν σφραγῖδα, 2 Cl., 7, 6, τὴν σάρκα, 14, 3, cf. τὴν ἐκκλησίαν, 14, 3.

[11] Cf. Pr.-Bauer, s.v. γαμίζω and τηρέω, also Heracl. Hom. All., 19 (p. 30, 3): διὸ δὴ καὶ παρθένον αὐτὴν ἐτήρησαν and Achill. Tat., VIII, 18, 2: παρθένον γὰρ τὴν κόρην μέχρι τοῦτο τετήρηκα. S. Belkin, "The Problem of Paul's Background," JBL, 54 (1935), 52 suggests "to pay keep" for τηρέω. On this cf. esp. W. G. Kümmel, "Verlobung u. Heirat bei Pls.," Nt.liche Stud. f. R. Bultmann, Beih. ZNW, 21² (1957), 275-295.

[12] In D τηρέω occurs again, anticipated by dittography from v. 12.

[13] In Jn. 17:12 φυλάσσω is a synon. variation, but it should be noted that the prepositional ἐν τῷ ὀνόματι occurs with τηρέω. Cf. E. A. Abbott, Johannine Grammar (1906), 434 on the relation of τηρέω and φυλάσσω; he transl. ἐτήρουν by "I was always watching or keeping my eye on."

[14] ἐκ with τηρέω is non-class. It occurs again in Rev. 3:10 and with διατηρέω in Ac. 15:29, cf. ἵνα σε τηρήσῃ ἀπὸ γυναικὸς ἀλλοτρίας, Prv. 7:5. Cf. on this Bl.-Debr. § 149 and Abbott, op. cit., 251 f.

[15] So Bultmann J., ad loc.

[16] Cf. in this regard μὴ εἰσενέγκῃς ἡμᾶς εἰς πειρασμόν, Mt. 6:13.

[17] The logical subj. is God. Cf. on this use of τηρέω Wis. 10:5 of wisdom: ἐτήρησεν αὐτὸν ἄμεμπτον θεῷ, also Prv. 16:17; 19:16; BGU, IV, 1141, 25 (13 B.C.), also Deissmann LO, 275 f.

[18] The vl. ἐν (Χριστῷ) in some versions can be taken locally or instrumentally.

reference is to the protection against the devil and sin which is granted by Christ as the Son of God and by the life in the Spirit which He makes possible. [19] The reflexive use brings individual activity to the fore, as on the part of the apostle: ἐν παντὶ ἀβαρῆ ἐμαυτὸν ὑμῖν ἐτήρησα καὶ τηρήσω (2 C. 11:9); with reference to the Christian walk, which presupposes keeping at a distance from the world: σεαυτὸν ἁγνὸν τήρει, 1 Tm. 5:22; [20] θρησκεία καθαρά ... ἄσπιλον ἑαυτὸν τηρεῖν ἀπὸ τοῦ κόσμου, Jm. 1:27. [21] In the expression ἑαυτοὺς ἐν ἀγάπῃ θεοῦ τηρήσατε in Jd. 21 θεοῦ is a subjective genitive [22] (cf. Jn. 15:9; 1 Jn. 2:5; 3:17; 4:12); God's initiative is expressed in the genitive and man's response in the verb. [23]

b. With an impersonal object τηρέω denotes the actual maintaining of the essential functions or realities of Christian life, e.g., τὴν πίστιν "to keep faith" (2 Tm. 4:7), [24] a type of expression which also occurs in profane speech but which has here a special Christian content. [25] τηρεῖν τὴν ἑνότητα τοῦ πνεύματος in Eph. 4:3 presupposes that the unity created by the Spirit is given from the commencement and not something yet to be effected. [26] In the combination μακάριος ὁ γρηγορῶν καὶ τηρῶν τὰ ἱμάτια αὐτοῦ in Rev. 16:15 the verb is governed by the metaphor: the garment is equivalent to the state of salvation, which is to be maintained.

c. A meaning which is shown by its frequency to be characteristic of the NT is that of "to take note of," "to observe," "to fulfil," "to keep," especially with reference to doctrine or commandments and precepts. Thus in the saying of Jesus

---

[19] The reading αὐτόν in BA* et al. is undoubtedly original rather than ἑαυτόν. Schnckbg. J., ad loc. ref. ὁ γεννηθεὶς ἐκ τοῦ θεοῦ to the Christian and αὐτόν to God: "He who was (once) born of God (also) holds fast to Him." This singular use of τηρέω for the maintaining and preserving of fellowship with God is supposedly based on θεὸν ἔχω in 2 Jn. 9; cf. 1 Jn. 2:23; 5:12. But in J.² (1963), ad loc. Schnckbg. follows the view of K. Beyer, Semitische Syntax im NT, I, 1 (1962), 216 f. that the statement is a Semitism and is to be construed: "He who was born of God, him God keeps." Cf. also A. E. Brooke, Johannine Epistles, ICC (1912), 148 f.

[20] This can also be said without predicate acc.: τηρεῖ ἑαυτόν, 1 Jn. 5:18 vl.

[21] Cf. M. Ant., VI, 30, 2 and BGU, IV, 1141, 25 (13 B.C. → 140, 29 f.) and Deissmann LO, 275 f.

[22] Cf. Wnd. Kath. Br., ad loc.: "An attempt to combine divine and human activity in the religious life," also K. H. Schelkle, Die Petrusbr. Der Judasbr., Herders Theol. Komm. z. NT, 13, 2 (1961), ad loc.; but J. Chaine, Les Épîtres cath.² (1939), ad loc. advocates an obj. gen. C. Spicq, Agapè, II (1959), 352 locates the synthesis in the gen. θεοῦ: "Il s'agit très vraisemblablement d'un génitif 'compréhensif' unissant à la fois la charité de Dieu pour ses élus et la redamatio de ceux-ci comme dans II Cor. V 14 ... Assurément, l'amour de Dieu pour nous est premier, mais il est versé dans le coeur des croyants par le Saint-Esprit (Rom. V 5) et il demeure en eux (I Jo. III 17)."

[23] Close to the reflexive is τὴν σάρκα ἁγνὴν τηρήσαντες in 2 Cl., 8, 4 and 6; τὴν σάρκα ὑμῶν ὡς ναὸν θεοῦ τηρεῖτε, Ign. Phld., 7, 2. On the aor. imp. used effectively cf. Bl.-Debr. § 337, 2 and 2 Cl., 8, 6.

[24] Cf. BMI, III, 587b, 5 (2nd cent. A.D.): ὅτι τὴν πίστιν ἐτήρησα, cf. Deissmann LO, 262; also Jos. Ant., 15, 134, v. also Bell., 2, 121: μηδεμίαν (sc. γυναῖκα) τηρεῖν πεπεισμένοι τὴν πρὸς ἕνα πίστιν, and 6, 345; cf. Polyb., 6, 56, 13: οὐ δύνανται τηρεῖν τὴν πίστιν — δι' αὐτῆς τῆς κατὰ τὸν ὅρκον πίστεως τηροῦσι τὸ καθῆκον, also 10, 37, 9. Cf. also Dib. Past. on 2 Tm. 4:7.

[25] On this cf. Dib. Past. on 2 Tm. 4:7; C. Spicq, Les Épîtres past. (1947), ad loc.; also J. M. T. Barton, "Bonum certamen certavi ... fidem servavi," Biblica, 40 (1959), 878-884.

[26] This use of τηρέω is also a favourite one in the early Church, cf. of the seal of baptism: εἰληφότες τὴν σφραγῖδα ... καὶ μὴ τηρήσαντες ὑγιῆ, Herm. s., 8, 6, 3; with the same image as a basis also ἐὰν μὴ τηρήσωμεν τὸ βάπτισμα ἁγνὸν καὶ ἀμίαντον, 2 Cl., 6, 9, cf. 14, 3 and Kn. Cl., ad loc.; also τήρει οὖν τὴν ἁγνείαν καὶ τὴν σεμνότητα, Herm. m., 4, 4, 3. Cf. F. J. Dölger, Ichthys, II (1922), 476; Sphragis (1911), 86.

to the rich young ruler it is said of the main commandments of the Mosaic Law: τήρει τὰς ἐντολάς, Mt. 19:17. [27] τὸν νόμον Μωϋσέως in Ac. 15:5 is comparable. In a similar passage in Ac. 21:25 vl. τηρέω is synon. with φυλάσσω. [28] The keeping of feasts should also be mentioned in this connection τηρεῖν τὸ σάββατον, Jn. 9:16. [29] So, too, does following the teaching of the scribes and Pharisees (Mt. 23:3) [30] and their tradition (Mk. 7:9). [31]

In the Church period the "royal law" is to be kept, Jm. 2:10. [32] That traditional catechetical material in the primitive Palestinian community was regarded as stemming from Jesus' teaching of the disciples and taken to be normative for the walk of Christians in the form of ἐντολαί may be seen also from διδάσκοντες αὐτοὺς τηρεῖν πάντα ὅσα ἐνετειλάμην ὑμῖν, Mt. 28:20; → II, 545, 20 ff. [33] In the Past. Timothy is admonished to keep and use the commandment (→ II, 555, 41 ff.), [34] i.e., the normative traditional material, [35] without perversion in the interval up to the parousia: παραγγέλλω ... τηρῆσαί σε τὴν ἐντολὴν ἄσπιλον ἀνεπίλημπτον, 1 Tm. 6:13 f. [36]

This use of τηρέω is especially common in the Johannine writings. [37] In Jn. Christian action is controlled by the divine love. Responsive love for Christ cannot be limited to emotion. It finds expression rather in the obedient walk of Christians: ἐὰν ἀγαπᾶτέ με, τὰς ἐντολὰς τὰς ἐμὰς τηρήσετε, Jn. 14:15, [38] cf. 14:21. The ἐντολαί (→ II, 553, 40 ff.; VI, 227, 32 ff.) are for their part to be related to the "new commandment" of love, Jn. 13:34. [39] Here, too, the mode of expression presupposes acquaintance with a catechetical tradition. [40] The expressions ἔχω τὰς ἐντολάς and τηρέω τὰς ἐντολάς (Jn. 14:21) are parallel and correspond in the same way as ἀκούω and φυλάσσω (12:47) or ἀκούω and πιστεύω [41] (5:24). The ἐντολαί may be traced back to the revelation which Jesus brought. His obedience and love to the Father are the starting-point and model, Jn. 8:55; 15:10. This is expressed on the other side in the fact that to the ὁ τηρῶν τὰς ἐντολάς μου there

---

[27] Cf. τηρέω ἐντολάς Sir. 29:1; Jos. Ant., 8, 120.

[28] Cf. φυλάξατε τὴν ἐντολὴν τοῦ κυρίου καὶ τὸν νόμον αὐτοῦ τηρήσατε, Test. D. 5:1, also Jos. Ap., 2, 273; τηρεῖν τὰ νόμιμα, Jos. Ant., 8, 395; 9, 222.

[29] Cf. τηρέω with τὴν νηστείαν as obj., Herm. s., 5, 3, 5 vl.

[30] Cf. Loh. Mt., ad loc., who adduces LXX ref. with φυλάσσω and ποιέω.

[31] Cf. Jos. Vit., 361; also E. A. Abbott, Johannine Vocabulary (1905), 208.

[32] Cf. Herm. s., 8, 3, 3-5 and τὰ νόμιμα τοῦ θεοῦ, v., 1, 3, 4; τὰ δικαιώματα κυρίου, Barn., 10, 11. Cf. also μνήσθητε τῶν λόγων Ἰησοῦ τοῦ κυρίου ἡμῶν, 1 Cl., 46, 7.

[33] Loh. Mt., ad loc., n. 1 finds here an echo of the name Ναζωραῖος.

[34] So Dib. Past., ad loc., cf. Spicq, op. cit., ad loc.; cf. also 2 Pt. 2:20 f.; 3:2.

[35] Cf. in this respect B. Gerhardsson, Memory and Manuscript, Diss. Uppsala (1961), 290.

[36] On the aor. cf. Bl.-Debr. § 337, 2. φυλάσσω occurs in the same sense at 1 Tm. 5:21 and R. 2:26; Gl. 6:13. Cf. E. Käsemann, "Das Formular einer nt.lichen Ordinationsparänese," Exeget. Versuche u. Besinnungen, I3 (1964), 101-108.

[37] In Jn., 1 Jn. and Rev. τηρέω occurs in this sense 27 times. Loh. Apk. on 1:3 tries to explain the alternation of φυλάσσω and τηρέω in terms of the different meanings of the basic Hbr. terms שׁמר and נצר, but this does not help much, cf. → n. 51 and Abbott, op. cit. (→ n. 13), 369-388; Schnckbg J. on 1 Jn. 2:3.

[38] The fut. in BL al is the correct reading as shown by the verbal forms in the context, cf. esp. Bultmann J. and C. K. Barrett, The Gospel acc. to St. John (1955), ad loc.

[39] Cf. on Jn. 13:33-38 L. Cerfaux, "La charité fraternelle et le retour du Christ," Recueil L. Cerfaux, II (1954), 27-40.

[40] Cf. ὁ ἔχων ἀγάπην ἐν Χριστῷ ποιησάτω τὰ τοῦ Χριστοῦ παραγγέλματα, 1 Cl., 49, 1.

[41] So Bultmann J. on 14:21, n. 5.

corresponds a τὸν λόγον μου τηρήσει (Jn. 14:23 f.),[42] and this in a train of thought analogous to 14:15, 21. This τηρέω τὸν λόγον shows us what significance was accorded to the transmitted message of Jesus. Election predestines to faith and therewith to obedience, 17:6.[43] The word of revelation imparted by Jesus to the disciples is passed on by these with a summons to faith and obedience: εἰ τὸν λόγον μου ἐτήρησαν, καὶ τὸν ὑμέτερον τηρήσουσιν, Jn. 15:20. Keeping the word of Jesus in faith carries with it eternal life and therewith freedom from judgment and death, 8:51 f.[44] The saying of Jesus to Mary on the occasion of the anointing in Bethany ἄφες αὐτήν, ἵνα εἰς τὴν ἡμέραν τοῦ ἐνταφιασμοῦ μου τηρήσῃ αὐτό (Jn. 12:7) probably (→ VII, 925, n. 41) means "Let her alone, she has observed (i.e., done) this with a view to my death."[45]

The Johannine Epistles and Rev. use the same kind of expression and thinking as John's Gospel with reference to keeping the essential commandments as a sign of vital Christianity, e.g., τηρέω τὰς ἐντολάς of the commandments of Jesus in 1 Jn. 2:3, 4; 3:22, 24; 5:3,[46] or keeping the commandments of God in combination with witness for Jesus in Rev. 12:17, or keeping the commandments of God and demonstrating faith in Jesus in Rev. 14:12;[47] τηρέω τὸν λόγον in 1 Jn. 2:5; Rev. 3:8, τηρέω τὰ γεγραμμένα or τοὺς λόγους in Rev. 1:3; 22:7, 9[48] of the prophecies of Rev. as words of the exalted Christ which we are to preserve faithfully and to protect against falsification. The reference in Rev. 3:3 is to the safeguarding of the Christian tradition: μνημόνευε οὖν πῶς εἴληφας καὶ ἤκουσας, καὶ τήρει καὶ μετανόησον. The object of τήρει is to be supplied from the preceding sentence,[49] which in λαμβάνω, ἀκούω[50] uses the typical vocabulary of tradition.[51] The Christian life as concrete fulfilment of God's will is both a prerequisite of answered prayer and also a result of the Spirit's working, 1 Jn. 3:22, 24. Love for God is manifested in love for one's fellow-men and obedience to the commands which regulate human life together (→ VI, 227, 32 ff.), 1 Jn. 5:2 f. ὁ τηρῶν... τὰ ἔργα

---

[42] ὁ λόγος μου in v. 23 denotes the totality of revelation, οἱ λόγοι μου in v. 24 the details, cf. ἐντολαί. On this cf. Barrett, 390 and 421 and Abbott, op. cit. (→ n. 13), 621 f., also τοὺς λόγους μου οὐκ ἐτήρησεν, 1 Βασ. 15:11.

[43] On the form τετήρηκαν cf. Bl.-Debr. § 83, 1; in interpretation of the v. Barrett, ad loc.

[44] On the aor. ἐὰν τηρήσῃ Abbott, op. cit. (→ n. 31), 374.

[45] The reading τετήρηκεν "has saved up" is undoubtedly secondary, though preferred by H. Strathmann, Das Ev. nach J., NT Deutsch, 4[10] (1963) and R. V. G. Tasker, The Gospel acc. to St. John (1960), ad loc. Decision concerning the meaning of ἵνα τηρήσῃ is difficult; Bultmann J. and R. Schnackenburg, "Der joh. Bericht von d. Salbung in Bethanien," Münchener Theol. Zschr., 1 (1950), 48-52 propose: "to save up the ointment," but this is not satisfying, nor is "to think of," "to remember it" (sc. the act of anointing), a sense not found elsewhere in Jn. The explanation suggested above is explicitly developed in D. Daube, The NT and Rabbinic Judaism (1956), 317-320, cf. the discussion in Barrett, ad loc., who finds difficulty in connecting αὐτό with the act of anointing. Cf. also Bau. J., ad loc.

[46] Schnckbg. J., ad loc.

[47] On ἐντολαὶ θεοῦ cf. Deissmann LO, 322. τηρέω τὰς ἐντολὰς τοῦ θεοῦ (alternating with synon. φυλάσσω) occurs repeatedly in Herm. m., 7, 5; 12, 3, 4; 12, 6, 3; s., 5, 1, 5; 5, 3, 3 and 5; 6, 1, 4. This obviously echoes a form of expression common in the Johannine writings.

[48] Cf. μακάριοι οἱ ἀκούοντες τὸν λόγον τοῦ θεοῦ καὶ φυλάσσοντες, Lk. 11:28 and also H. B. Swete, The Apocalypse of St. John (1907), ad loc.

[49] Cf. Philo Leg. All., III, 184.

[50] On the tenses v. Had. Apk., ad loc.

[51] On this cf. Gerhardsson, op. cit., 280-288. Less convincing is the conjecture of Loh. Apk., ad loc., that τήρει abs. is used in the special sense "Be a נֵצֶר (Ναζωραῖος)," an observant.

μου in Rev. 2:26 is to be regarded as a stylistic development in which τηρέω τὰς ἐντολάς and ποιέω τὰ ἔργα (cf. Jn. 8:39 ff.; 6:28) are fused. [52]

† τήρησις.

1. In Gk. τήρησις means "attention," "vigilance," "watch," e.g., Thuc., VII, 13, 1; ἀφύλακτος ἡ τήρησις, Eur. Fr., 162 (TGF, 406); Mitteis-Wilcken, I, 2, 11B, 5 f. (2nd. cent. B.C.), "observation" in a scientific sense, e.g., ἐκ τηρήσεως ἐμπειρικῶς, Gal. Hippocratis de acutorum morborum victu liber et Galeni comment., IV, 55 (Kühn, 15, 830), cf. In Hippocratis praedictionum librum I, comment., I, 15 (Kühn, 16, 550); In Hippocratis Prognosticum comment. tria, III, 44, 307 f. (CMG, V, 9, 2); Soranus Gynaecia, I, 4, 2 (CMG, IV); Sext. Emp. Pyrrh. Hyp., I, 11, 23; II, 22, 246 and 254; in rhetorical instruction Apollon Dyscol. Synt., I, 60 (p. 52, 3 f.), "preservation," Polyb., 6, 11a, 10; τήρησις καὶ φυλακὴ χρημάτων, Diod. S., 3, 4, 4; cf. 1, 91, 6; Soranus Gynaecia, I, 32, 2 (CMG, IV); τοῦ ὕδατος, Ditt. Syll.³, II, 683, 60 (2nd cent. B.C.); τοῦ σπέρματος, Soranus Gynaecia, I, 46, 1 (CMG, IV). Transf. the word is used for preserving bodily well-being or health, Gal. De methodo medendi, 9, 14 (Kühn, 10, 646); Soranus Gynaecia, I, 28, 2 (CMG, IV), in the sense of "caring for" τῆς ὅλης οἰκίας, P. Oxy., VII, 1070, 51 (3rd cent. A.D.), "custody," Thuc., VII, 86, 2; Jos. Ant., 16, 321; 18, 235, [1] "prison," BGU, II, 388, 3, 7 (2nd/3rd cent. A.D.), "observing, keeping" laws, e.g. τήρησις τῶν θείων νόμων, Hierocl. Carm. Aur., 2, 2.

2. In the LXX the word occurs only in the apocr. It is used for military "protection," 1 Macc. 5:18; 3 Macc. 5:44, for "guarding" against robbery, 2 Macc. 3:40, and for the "keeping" of commands, e.g., νόμων, Wis. 6:18; ἐντολῶν Sir. 32:23.

3. In the NT the general sense of "custody" and the more concrete "prison" are possible in two descriptions of the imprisonment of apostles: [2] ἔθεντο εἰς τήρησιν εἰς τὴν αὔριον in Ac. 4:3, and ἔθεντο αὐτοὺς ἐν τηρήσει δημοσίᾳ [3] in Ac. 5:18. The "keeping" or "fulfilling" of God's commandments τήρησις ἐντολῶν θεοῦ (→ II, 552, 18 ff.) is for Paul a requirement of Christian life in contrast to circumcision as a sign of the relationship with God in Judaism, 1 C. 7:19, cf. Gl. 5:6; 6:15; R. 14:17.

† παρατηρέω.

1. In Gk. the word [1] is used for direct perception and means "to observe," so of the white-tailed eagle which chases a bird παρατηρῶν ἀναδυόμενον ἐκ τῆς θαλάσσης, Aristot. Hist. An., IX, 34, p. 620a, 8; with indirect question, Xenoph. Mem., III, 14, 4; cf. Epic. Ep., 2, 115, in the sense of "inquisitive attention," Philem. Fr., 100, 1 (CAF, II, 510), τόπους with armed forces "to keep under observation," Polyb., 1, 29, 4, "to watch for" criminals, Wilcken Ptol., I, 64, 9 (156 B.C.), transf. "to lurk," "to lie in wait," e.g., παρατηροῦσιν τοὺς εἰληφότας τι παρὰ τῆς τύχης, Ceb. Tab., 9, 2; ἐνεδρεύω καὶ παρατηρέω, Polyb., 18, 3, 2; cf. Aristot. Rhet., II, 6, p. 1384b, 7; pass. Dicaearchus

---

[52] Acc. to Loh. Apk., ad loc. we have here a bold, Johannine tinged combination, cf. also Swete, op. cit., ad loc. But Had. Apk., ad loc. thinks the community should hold fast and maintain τὰ ἔργα μου as Jesus did them as a model and decreed them as His works.

τήρησις. Bibl.: Mayser, I, 3², 71, 11; II, 2, 496, 10; Moult.-Mill., s.v.
[1] In Thuc., VII, 86, 2 and Jos. Ant., 18, 235 the concrete sense "prison" is also possible.
[2] Pr.-Bauer, s.v., leaves the question open, Jackson-Lake, I, 4, on 4:3 and 5:18 transl. "custody," Haench. Ag.,¹³ ad loc. opts for "prison."
[3] Jackson-Lake, I, 4, ad loc. takes δημοσίᾳ as an adv. But the Hbr. loan-word formed from it suggests an adjectival sense, cf. Str.-B., II, ad loc. and Pr.-Bauer, s.v.

παρατηρέω. Bibl.: Mayser, I, 3², 138, 9; 228, 22; Cr.-Kö., Liddell-Scott, Moult.-Mill., s.v.
[1] The prep. denotes the presence of the observer on the one side and the energy of participation on the other, → V, 727, n. 1.

Fr., 59, 16 (FHG, II, 258), "to pay heed to someone," e.g., τοὺς ἀναγινώσκοντας χρὴ παρατηρεῖν, Dion. Hal., Περὶ τῶν ἀρχαίων ῥητόρων, II, 53 (Usener-Radermacher, I, 245); παρετήρουν σφᾶς αὐτούς, Polyb., 11, 9, 9, pass. "to be kept under supervision," Menand. Fr., 543, 6 (Koerte, 179)," to watch," e.g. ὅπως τοῦτο μὴ γένοιτο παρατηρῶν, Demosth. Or., 18, 161, "to pay regard," "to note," e.g., παρατήρει μοι τοὺς χρόνους εἰς σύγκρισιν τῆς Μωϋσέως ἡλικίας, Cl. Al. Strom., I, 73, 6; ὅπερ καὶ ἐπὶ τῶν προφητεύειν νῦν δὴ λεγομένων παρατηρητέον, VI, 66, 5. In the sense of systematic watching the word then means "to be on the look-out" for omens, e.g., τὰ ἐκ τοῦ οὐρανοῦ γιγνόμενα παρατηρεῖν, Dio C., 38, 13, 6; scientifically of astronomers, Vett. Val., IV, 29 (205, 13); of the Indian gymnosophists δοκοῦσι δὲ παρατηρεῖν τὰ οὐράνια καὶ διὰ τῆς τούτων σημειώσεως τῶν μελλόντων προμαντεύεσθαί τινα, Cl. Al. Strom., III, 60, 4; of doctors, Gal. De sanitate tuenda, III, 8, 43 (CMG, V, 4, 2); De diaeta Hippocratis in morbis acutis, 5, 201; 9, 217 (CMG, V, 9, 1); Philodem. Philos. De ira, 9, 18 f. Finally one may ref. to the sense "to preserve," "to keep watch over," e.g., παρατηρεῖσθαι [2] αὐτήν (sc. τὴν φιάλην), P. Oxy., VI, 937, 16 (3rd cent. A.D.) and "to observe," "to keep," e.g., οὐδὲ τοὺς καιροὺς παρατηρήσει, Philodem. Philos. Περὶ οἰκονομίας, 17, 10 f.; cf. De ira, 19, 3; [3] παρατηρεῖν ἐν ἀμφοῖν τὰ μέτρια, Aristot. Rhet., III, 2, p. 1405b, 33; ἀκριβῶς παρατηρεῖσθε, namely, the commandments and prohibitions of laws, Dio C., 53, 10, 2. [4]

2. In the LXX the verb occurs only twice and this in the sense "to lurk," "to lie in wait for," ψ 36:12 (mid. for Hbr. מם) and then in the more special sense "to keep" in memory ἐὰν ἀνομίας παρατηρήσῃ, ψ 129:3. [5] In Θ it means "to watch lurkingly" at Sus. 12:15, 16; Da. 6:12. [6] In Σ one finds νὺξ παρατετηρημένη "to observe the night" at Ex. 12:42 (for לֵיל שִׁמֻּרִים) and "to pay heed," 1 S. 1:12; ψ 55:7. [7]

3. In other Jewish Gk. writings one finds the sense "to find by observation" in Jos. Bell., 2, 468, "to wait for observantly" in Test. Sol. 6:4 (94 *, 30); Ep. Ar., 246 [8] (mid.), "to observe," "to keep" of cultic observance αἱ νηστεῖαι καὶ λύχνων ἀνακαύσεις καὶ πολλὰ τῶν εἰς βρῶσιν ἡμῖν οὐ νενομισμένων παρατετήρηται (of non-Jews), Jos. Ap. 2, 282; τὰς ἑβδομάδας, Jos. Ant., 3, 91; τὴν τῶν σαββάτων ἡμέραν, 14, 264; ἡμέρας, sc. the days of Purim, 11, 294. In the last sense, for which there is no LXX precedent with the compound, παρατηρέω is plainly distinguished from the more usual simple form by the fact that the participation of the active subj. is more strongly expressed. The context of the Jos. ref. is always of such a kind as to stress the resolve to keep the commandments or celebrate the days.

4. In the NT the term occurs in the sense "to watch lurkingly," e.g., παρετήρουν αὐτὸν εἰ τοῖς σάββασιν θεραπεύσει αὐτόν, Mk. 3:2, where the par. Lk. 6:7 has the mid. παρετηροῦντο, cf. also ἦσαν παρατηρούμενοι αὐτόν in Lk. 14:1 [9] and without object παρατηρήσαντες ἀπέστειλαν in Lk. 20:20, [10] or with object: "to

---

[2] Bl.-Debr. § 316, 1 pts. out that the mid. παρατηρέομαι has the same sense as the act. Cf. on this A. T. Robertson, A Grammar of the Greek NT⁴ (1923), 804-806.

[3] P. Tebt., II, Ostracon, 10 (p. 337 [2nd cent. A.D.]) lists a number of days which an unknown person keeps παρατηρεῖ.

[4] In the secular literary koine this is the only instance of mid. παρατηρέομαι → n. 2.

[5] For Hbr. שמר, cf. also Lv. 19:18 Αλλ and Field, ad loc.

[6] In the latter v. LXX has τηρέω.

[7] On this cf. Field, ad loc.

[8] On this cf. H. G. Meecham, The Letter of Aristeas (1935), 290.

[9] On the periphrastic conjugation in the situational notes of the Lucan framework cf. G. Björck, ᾮΗν διδάσκων (1940), 44 f.

[10] But note the vl. ἀποχωρήσαντες in D Θ pc it and ὑποχωρήσαντες in W. On this cf. Kl. Lk., ad loc. For παρατηρέομαι, which means here "to wait the chance," cf. F. Field, Notes on the Translation of the NT (1899), 74 and also W. K. Hobart The Medical Language of St. Luke (1882), 153 f.

watch" and thereby to bar the gates of a city by guards παρετηροῦντο δὲ καὶ τὰς πύλας, Ac. 9:24. [11] The term also means "to keep" with reference to cultic observance: ἡμέρας παρατηρεῖσθε καὶ μῆνας καὶ καιροὺς καὶ ἐνιαυτούς, Gl. 4:10. [12] Paul says that relapse into Jewish observance is like a relapse into polytheism and means a loss of freedom.

The theme of the inappropriate keeping of days and times recurs in Pauline polemic at Col. 2:16, cf. R. 14:5. Paul is either arguing against keeping the Sabbath and the feasts prescribed in the Mosaic Law, which he regards as a loss of freedom [13] (→ IV, 641, 22 ff.) or he has in view apocryphal Jewish speculations about lucky or unlucky days and seasons whose superstitious observance expresses inner bondage. [14] The latter view is supported by Ps.-Clem. Hom., 19, 22, 2-9, a passage which, probably in direct controversy with Paul, deals thoroughly with the significance of observing specific times in the begetting of children. [15] Furthermore the compound, esp. in the mid., seems to have the sense of "anxious, scrupulous, well-informed observance in one's own interest," [16] which does not fit the traditional celebration of the Sabbath or other Jewish feasts but does fit regard for points or spans of time which are evaluated positively or negatively from the standpoint of the calendar or astrology. [17] Naturally it is conceivable that Jewish feasts, esp. in the Hell. sphere, were regarded and celebrated superstitiously. [18]

5. The fr. in the collections of sayings in P. Oxy., IV, 654, 35 f. might be completed as follows with the help of Logion 6 in the Copt. Gospel of Thomas (81, 17 f.), cf. 14 (83, 14-27): κ]αὶ τί παρατηρήσ[ομεν ὅταν δειπ/νῶμε]ν; [19] the sense here is that of cultic observance.

† παρατήρησις.

1. In the Gk. world the noun means "watching," "lying in wait," "inquisitive spying," e.g., Plut. Capitulorum descriptio, 9 (II, 266b); Polyb., 16, 22, 8. It means "observing" by scientists or physicians, e.g., Sext. Emp. Math., I, 153, in Egypt. or Babyl. astronomy, αἱ τῶν ἄστρων ἀρχαιόταται παρατηρήσεις, Diod. S., 1, 9, 6; 1, 28, 1; cf. 5, 31, 3; τὰ πλεῖστα ἐκ παρατηρήσεως καὶ ἐξ εἰκότων προειρηκότες, Cl. Al. Strom., I, 135, 2; Δημόκριτος δὲ ἐκ τῆς τῶν μεταρσίων παρατηρήσεως πολλὰ προλέγων, VI,

---

[11] παρετήρουν acc. to the textus receptus, cf. ἐφρούρει τὴν πόλιν in 2 C. 11:32 and Haench. Ag.[13] on 9:24, n. 3.

[12] The verb is in the mid. (→ n. 2) but p [46] has the vl. παρατηροῦντες. Tisch. NT, J. B. Lightfoot, St. Paul's Ep. to the Galatians[10] (1890) and Schlier Gl.[12], ad loc. take this as a question. Oe. Gl., ad loc. leaves a choice between a simple pres. and a pres. de conatu.

[13] Cf. also the authors in Schlier Gl.[12], 206, n. 1.

[14] So Schlier Gl.[12] on 4:10 with appeal to Eth. En. 75:3f.; 79, 2 etc. and a fr. of the Book of Elchasai in Hipp. Ref., IX, 16, 2 f. On Jewish sectarian calendar speculations cf. also M. Testuz, Les idées religieuses du livre des Jubilés (1960), 121-164. M. J. Lagrange, Saint Paul. Ép. aux Galates[2] (1925) on 4:10 pts. out that the very neutral terms days, months, times and years (as distinct from the formulation in Col. 2:16) are chosen so as to cover Hell. superstition in gen.

[15] In context one finds the following terms: ἀπαρατηρήτως, ἀκαίρως, καιρὸς ἐπιτήδειος, ἐπιτηρήσιμοι ἡμέραι, ἀμελήσαντες τὴν παρατήρησιν. Cf. on this Dg., 4, 5.

[16] Cf. Schlier Gl.[12], 203, n. 3 and Cr.-Kö., s.v.

[17] A. Strobel, "Die Passaerwartung als urchr. Problem in Lk. 17:20 f.," ZNW, 49 (1958), 163 f. thinks παρατηρέομαι in Gl. 4:10 means "the fixing of the calendar (by watching the heavens)." But on closer examination none of the supporting texts has the verb in this sense.

[18] Cf. Horat Sat., 1, 9, 69 ff. [Risch]. v. also Oe. Gl. on 4:10.

[19] Cf. J. A. Fitzmyer, "The Oxyrhynchus Logoi of Jesus and the Coptic Gospel acc to Thomas," Theol. Stud., 20 (1959), 528 f.; also Hennecke, I[3], 65.

π α ρ α τ ή ρ η σ ι ς. Bibl.: Cr.-Kö., Liddell-Scott, Moult.-Mill., Thes. Steph., s.v.; also H. J. Mette, Parateresis. Untersuchungen zur Sprachtheorie d. Krates v. Pergamon (1952), with R. Schröter's review, Gnomon, 27 (1955), 326-331.

32, 1, medical observation, [1] e.g., ἐκ παρατηρήσεως διδαχθῆναι, Gal. In Hippocratis Prognosticum comment. III, 15, 257 (CMG, V, 9, 2); cf. IG, [2] IV, 1, 687, 14 (c. 165 A.D.), empirical "observation" as distinct from logical deduction, e.g., τότε οὔτε παρατηρήσει οὔτε λογισμῷ χρώμεθα, Gal. De optima secta ad Thrasybulum liber, 10 (Kühn, 1, 127); παλαιᾷ τινι καὶ πολυχρονίῳ παρατηρήσει περὶ τούτων (sc. human sacrifices) πεπιστευκότες, Diod. S., 5, 31, 3; [2] in orators "attention" along with "information" (ἱστορία) and "practice" (ἄσκησις), Philodem. Philos. Volumina rhetorica, I, 20, 22, [3] cf. Procl. in Platonis Cratylum comment. 85. The word is then used for critical "scrutiny," e.g., ἐπὶ παρατηρήσει τῇ ἐμῇ εὑρίσκω, Orig. Orat., 3, 1; ὑπὸ... παρατηρήσεων καὶ ἐξετάσεων, Orig. Comm. in Joh., 13, 63 on 4:54. In science research lies behind an "observation," e.g., ἐκεῖνα μᾶλλον παρατηρήσεως ἄξια, Ps.-Long., Sublim., 23, 2, esp. "observations" in scientific works, e.g., Schol. in Aristoph. Ra., 1227; [4] Apollon. Dyscol. De pronomine, 51b (p. 41, 8); Ps.-Ammon. Adfin. Vocab. Diff., 127. It also means "self-scrutiny," "attention to self," "self-discipline," e.g., ἐπιστροφὴ ἐφ' αὐτὸν καὶ παρατήρησις, Epict. Diss., III, 16, 15; M. Ant., III, 4, 1, "watching," e.g., unreliable hostages, Aen. Tact., 10, 25; "watching over" a husband by his wife, Pythagoras Ep., 5, 1 (Epistolographi, 604), "observance," "keeping" of rules or commandments, e.g., οὐκ ἔκ τινος παρατηρήσεως, "not to keep to a given order (in a list)," Schol. in Hom. Il., 2, 494, [5] following the rules of rhetoric in reading poetical works, Dion. Thr. Art. Gramm., 2 (6, 21 f.), "observing" usage in the linguistic theory of Crates of Pergamon, [6] care in following the rules for choosing sacrifices οὕτως ἀκριβῆ ποιούμενοι τὴν παρατήρησιν, Plut. Is. et Os., 21 (II, 363b). There is an instance of the use of the prepositional μετὰ παρατηρήσεως which in context means "maintaining obedience," i.e., to one's father, Schol. in Soph. Ant., 637. [7]

2. In the LXX there are no instances of παρατήρησις, but it occurs in 'A at Ex. 12:42 in νὺξ παρατηρήσεως for לֵיל שִׁמֻּרִים (LXX νυκτὸς προφυλακή or ἐκείνη ἡ νὺξ αὕτη προφυλακὴ κυρίῳ), → 147, 23 f. [8] The meaning of παρατήρησις here is based on the possible sense of "observation," "watch," "night watch," "keeping" for שִׁמֻּרִים. [9]

3. In the NT παρατήρησις occurs only once at Lk. 17:20. The interpretation of the v. is important here in fixing the sense of παρατήρησις. [10] To the question of

---

[1] Cf. on this W. K. Hobart, The Medical Language of St. Luke (1882), 153.

[2] Cf. παρατήρημα, on this Liddell-Scott, s.v.

[3] Cf. also C. J. van Vooijs, Lexicon Philodemeum, II (1940), 47.

[4] Ed. F. Dübner, Scholia Graeca in Aristoph. (1855), 307.

[5] Ed. G. Dindorf, III (1877), 136, 32.

[6] Cf. on this Mette, 31 f. As against the dogmatic regulation of rhetoric Crates emphasises respect for actual usage συνήθεια: what matters is constant observation παρατήρησις.

[7] Ed. P. N. Papageorgios (1888), 249.

[8] Cf. on this Field, ad loc. and the express discussion and exposition of the passage in A. Strobel, "Die Passaerwartung als urchr. Problem in Lk. 17:20 f.," ZNW, 49 (1958), 164-174.

[9] On Jewish interpretations cf. Str.-B., I, 85; IV, 55, also Strobel, op. cit., 164-171. "The Passover night itself is often glorified by the Haggadah as a 'night of observations' לֵיל שִׁמֻּרִים i.e., as a night to which one pays attention because it is worth noting," Str.-B., IV, 54.

[10] For the history of exposition cf. esp. B. Noack, "Das Gottesreich bei Lk.," Symb. Bibl. Upsalienses, 10 (1948), 3-38. Apart from the comm., ad loc. cf. Str.-B., II, 236; A. Feuillet, "La venue du Règne de Dieu et du Fils de l'Homme," Recherches des Sciences Relig., 35 (1948), 544-565; E. Percy, Die Botschaft Jesu (1953), 216-223; R. Otto, Reich Gottes u. Menschensohn[3] (1954), 104-9; W. G. Kümmel, Verheissung u. Erfüllung[3] (1956), 26-9; Strobel, op. cit.; also "A. Merx über Lk. 17:20 f.," ZNW, 51 (1960), 133 f.; A. Rüstow, "'Εντὸς ὑμῶν ἐστιν, zur Deutung v. Lc. 17:20-21," ZNW, 51 (1960), 197-224; A. Strobel, "In dieser Nacht," ZThK, 58 (1961), 16-29; G. F. Hawthorne, "The Essential Nature of the Kingdom of God," Westminster Theol. Journal, 25 (1962/63), 35-47; F. Mussner, "Wann kommt das Reich Gottes?" BZ, NF, 6 (1962), 107-111; R. Sneed, The Kingdom's Coming: Luke 17:20 f., Diss. Washington (1962); A. Strobel, "Zu Lk. 17:20," BZ, NF, 7 (1963), 111-3; R. Schnackenburg, Gottes Herrschaft u. Reich[3] (1963), 92-4.

the Pharisees as to the when of the coming of God's kingdom Jesus replies: οὐκ ἔρχεται ἡ βασιλεία τοῦ θεοῦ μετὰ παρατηρήσεως οὐδὲ ἐροῦσιν· ἰδοὺ ὧδε ἤ· ἐκεῖ· ἰδοὺ γὰρ ἡ βασιλεία τοῦ θεοῦ ἐντὸς ὑμῶν ἐστιν.

One must ask whether παρατήρησις is related directly to the temporal πότε of the preceding question of the Pharisees whereas ἰδοὺ ὧδε ἤ· ἐκεῖ in distinction herefrom has a local sense, whether the reference is thus to the calculating of times on the one hand and the local establishment of visible signs on the other. It may be said in this regard that the temporal and local aspects are very close in all apocalyptic. For this reason it is as well to regard the two negative statements of the logion as virtually synon. [11] Another problem is whether to take the saying as fut., so that calculation or observation of the signs of apocalyptic events stands in contrast to the sudden (fut.) incursion of the kingdom of God. [12] Or is the ref. to the kingdom of God already come? [13] The latter view is to be preferred, and so is the interpretation "among you," "in your midst," or even "in your sphere," for ἐντὸς ὑμῶν. [14] Does this mean that in the two parts of the logion the calculable futurity of eschatological events acc. to Jewish expectations is contrasted with the presence already of God's rule in the coming of Jesus? Behind this kind of exposition is the improbable assumption that παρατήρησις means the calculation of future events with the help of signs. But the examples from profane literature (→ 148, 26 ff.) show that the sense which fits best is that of the rational-empirical observation and fixing of signs and symptoms. [15]

Lk. 17:20 f. thus means that whether the kingdom of God has already come cannot be decided on the basis of events which intimate and anticipate the final consummation as though the desire for rationally and empirically accessible signs and proofs could be satisfied therewith. [16] In the measure that the divine dominion is already at work it can be known and grasped only by faith. [17] The saying is one of the Synoptic statements concerning the mystery of the kingdom of God, which is not accessible to the Pharisaic demand for signs. [18] The expression οὐκ ἔρχεται ἡ βασιλεία (→ I, 585, 43 ff.) τοῦ θεοῦ μετὰ παρατηρήσεως shows that the attitude of the Pharisees expressed in their Messianic and eschatological expectations is quite

[11] It should be noted that the meaning "observation" is naturally suggested for παρατήρησις by the texts adduced above and also by the astronomical contents. In these texts παρατήρησις never means the calculation of future phenomena but the concrete observations which underlie such calculations.
[12] On the champions of this view cf. Kümmel, op. cit., 28 and the polemic in Otto, op. cit., 104-109.
[13] So Otto, 108 f.; Kümmel, 28 f.; Schnackenburg, op. cit., 94.
[14] On ἐντός cf. Pr.-Bauer, s.v., also Kümmel, 28 f. with bibl., and A. W. Argyle, "'Outward' and 'Inward' in Biblical Thought," ExpT, 68 (1956/57), 196-199; Rüstow, op. cit., 207-218, esp. 213 f.; Hawthorne, op. cit., 35-47.
[15] The introductory question πότε ἔρχεται ἡ βασιλεία τοῦ θεοῦ; means "When does one know the kingdom of God is there?" rather than "At what time will the kingdom of God come?"
[16] The negative half of the v. seems to have been shaped by Lk. or earlier tradition as a contrast to the Lord's saying in v. 21, cf. 17:23; Mk. 13:21; Mt. 24:23, 26. The difficulty of finding a Hbr. equivalent for μετὰ παρατηρήσεως suggests this prep. expression does not go back directly to a saying of Jesus but is to be ascribed to the Gk. stage of the Gospel tradition. On retransl. of μετὰ παρατηρήσεως into Hbr. cf. Str.-B., II, ad loc. and Dalman WJ, I, 116-119, also Strobel, op. cit., 163-174.
[17] Cf. esp. the fine discussion in Otto, 108 f.
[18] Cf. Lk., e.g., 8:9 f.; 10:23 f.; 11:16, 20, 29; 12:56. The typical Pharisaic striving for certainty, here in face of what is to come, serves as a foil, K. H. Rengstorf, Das Ev. nach Lk., NT Deutsch, 3⁹ (1962) on 17:20.

inadequate in face of what is effected by the coming of Jesus in the midst of His people. [19]

4. In the polemic of Ep. to Diognetus against Jewish ritualism παρατήρησις occurs in the traditional sense of "observing," "keeping" with ref. to cultic observance: τὴν παρατήρησιν τῶν μηνῶν καὶ τῶν ἡμερῶν ποιεῖσθαι, 4, 5, cf. Gl. 4:10 (→ 148, 2 ff.) and παρατηρέω (→ 147, 14 ff., 27 ff.).

† διατηρέω.

διατηρέω [1] occurs in the NT only in the sense "to keep": ἡ μήτηρ αὐτοῦ διετήρει πάντα τὰ ῥήματα ἐν τῇ καρδίᾳ αὐτῆς (Lk. 2:51), where the preposition expresses careful and permanent storing in the memory; [2] cf. Dg., 8, 10; διετήρει τὴν σοφὴν αὐτοῦ βουλήν, of God, who kept [3] His plan of salvation to Himself unchanged up to the coming of Christ. In the reflexive the word means "to keep oneself," "to abstain," ἐξ ὧν διατηροῦντες ἑαυτοὺς εὖ πράξετε, Ac. 15:29. [4]

† συντηρέω.

συντηρέω [1] means "to keep" in the memory ἡ δὲ Μαρία πάντα συνετήρει τὰ ῥήματα ταῦτα συμβάλλουσα ἐν τῇ καρδίᾳ αὐτῆς, Lk. 2:19; [2] the prep. gives the verb an intensive sense. One also finds the meaning "to think of someone" [3] and care for him, Herm. m., 8, 10, "to guard, protect someone," [4] Mk. 6:20; Herm. m., 5, 1, 7; s., 5, 6, 2 and pass. "to be preserved" [5] (wine-skins), Mt. 9:17; Lk. 5:38 textus receptus.

Riesenfeld

[19] For the syntactical position of μετὰ παρατηρήσεως cf. Cr.-Kö., *s.v.* The construction is a special one, since the prep. expression does not have the subj. of the sentence as subj.; with the verb it is the obj. of the prep. expression. Cf. καὶ μὴν ἔοικέν γε ἡδονὴ πολλάκις οὐ μετὰ δόξης ὀρθῆς ἀλλὰ μετὰ ψεύδους ἡμῖν γίγνεσθαι in Plat. Phileb., 37e, where desire is the obj. of true or false ideas. The inventive combinations of Strobel, *op. cit.* (→ n. 8), 163-183 and ZThK, 58 (1961), 16-29, who (following Jewish interpretations of Ex. 12:42) relates μετὰ παρατηρήσεως to cultic observance and eschatological expectations at the Easter feast, lay more weight on the expression than it can bear in Lk. Similarly Rüstow's suggestions, *op. cit.*, 197-224 are for the most part too speculative and presuppose special hypotheses concerning Lk. On μετὰ cf. also Pr.-Bauer, *s.v.*

δ ι α τ η ρ έ ω. Bibl.: Bl.-Debr. § 149; Mayser, I, 3², 137, 13 and 39; 213, 46; 234, 19; 240, 7; II, 1, 250; Moult.-Mill., *s.v.* A. T. Robertson, *A Grammar of the Greek NT*⁴ (1923), 627, 828.
[1] The word occurs 24 times in the LXX, mostly for נצר; διατηρήσις also occurs.
[2] Cf. διετήρουν τὴν πόλιν καὶ τὴν ἑαυτῶν πίστιν, Polyb., 1, 7, 7, cf. 7, 8, 7; Philo Aet. Mund., 35; ὁ δὲ πατὴρ αὐτοῦ διετήρησεν τὸ ῥῆμα, Gn. 37:11; cf. Da. 7:28 Θ vl.; τὸ ὄντως καλόν... διατηρεῖτε, Test. A. 6:3.
[3] Cf. Ep. Ar., 206; Jos. Ap., 1, 210.
[4] Cf. διατηρεῖ ἐκ θλίψεως τὴν ψυχὴν αὐτοῦ, Prv. 21:23, also ψ 11:8, and διατηρήσατε οὖν ἑαυτοὺς... ἀπὸ παντὸς ἔργου πονηροῦ, Test. D. 6:8, cf. Jn. 17:15.

σ υ ν τ η ρ έ ω. [1] The word occurs 35 times in the LXX, almost always in the apocr.
[2] Cf. συνετήρει παρ' ἑαυτῇ, Polyb., 30, 30, 5 of the reaction of an assembly to complaints; Sir. 39:2, also τὸ ῥῆμα ἐν τῇ καρδίᾳ μου συνετήρησα, Da. 7:28 Θ; similarly Test. L. 6:2. συντηρήσειν ὁμοίως τά τε τῆς αἱρέσεως αὐτῶν βιβλία καὶ τὰ τῶν ἀγγέλων ὀνόματα in Jos. Bell., 2, 142, as the second obj. shows, ref. to the keeping of the contents of the sectarian books in the memory. The late examples in M. Andreopuli, Liber Syntipae (ed. V. Jernstedt, *Mémoires de l'Académie Impériale des Sciences de St. Petersbourg*, 8, 11 [1912], 102, 1; 104, 9) are undoubtedly influenced by Lk. 2:19.
[3] Cf. BGU, IV, 1101, 14 (1st cent. B.C.); Preisigke Wört., *s.v.*
[4] Cf. Preisigke Wört.; Moult.-Mill., *s.v.*
[5] Cf. IG, 12, 5, 860, 44 (1st cent. B.C.); Jos. Bell., 1, 184.

τίθημι, ἀθετέω, ἀθέτησις,
ἐπιτίθημι, ἐπίθεσις, μετατίθημι,
μετάθεσις, παρατίθημι, παραθήκη,
[παρακαταθήκη], προτίθημι,
πρόθεσις, προστίθημι

τίθημι.

A. In Profane Greek.

τίθημι [1] is very common from Hom. (→ lines 17; 153, 7 ff.) in all popular and cultured strata and in many constructions and meanings. The mid. is mostly trans. but expresses a special relation of the event to the subj. The differentiated use of the verb is made possible by the fact that a second transf. sense is linked with the primary' local sense "to bring to a place," "to place, put, lay," so that placing is an effective disposing which determines the quality of what is placed and can thus mean "to establish," "to bring to a specific state," "to bring about," "to institute," "to make."

1. The Local Sense of τίθημι.

a. Here the construction is variable, e.g., the verb is connected with the acc., θεμείλια "to lay foundations," Hom. Il., 12, 28 f., ἱμάτιον "to lay down a cloak, garment," Plut. De Alcibiade, 8, 2 (I, 195b), or an adv. τὰ ἄνω κάτω and τὰ κάτω ἄνω τιθέναι, Hdt., III, 3, 3, or various prep. like ἀνά τινι [τι], ἐπί τινος or τινι or τι, ὑπό τινι or τι, παρά τι, but mostly εἰς and acc. or ἐν and dat., e.g. εἰς φυλακήν, "to throw someone in prison," P. Petr., II, 5a, 3 (3rd cent. B.C.); εἰς χεῖρά τινος δεξιάν, "to put one's right hand in someone's hand," Soph. Ai., 751; ἐν ὄμμασι τίθεμαι, "to hold before one's eyes," Pind. Nem., 8, 43; εἰς τεῦχος τὴν ψῆφον, "to put one's voting pebble in the urn," Aesch. Ag., 816, hence γνώμην τίθεμαι, "to give one's voice that something be done," Hdt., VII, 82; τίθημι εἰς ταφάς etc., "to inter," Soph. Ai., 1109 f. Of special expressions one may note b. from economic life τόκον τίθημι, "to pay the tax," Demosth. Or., 41, 9; οὐσίαν τίθεμαι παρά τινα, "to deposit money," Hdt., VI, 86a, 5; τά τε ληφθέντα καὶ τὰ τεθέντα, "debits and credits," Demosth. Or., 49, 5; c. The military expression τὰ ὅπλα τίθεμαι means different things acc. to context, e.g., Πελοποννησίοισι ... ἀντία ἔθεντο τὰ ὅπλα, "they camped over against the Peloponnesians ready for battle," Hdt., V, 74, 2; ὁπόσοιπερ ἂν ὅπλα ἱππικὰ ἢ πεζικὰ τιθῶνται, "which bear arms, i.e., serve with the cavalry or infantry," Plat. Leg., VI, 753b; μετὰ Ἀθηναίων θησόμενον τὰ ὅπλα, "to side with the Athenians," Thuc., IV, 68, 3; "to lay down" shields as a sign of readiness to negotiate, Xenoph. Hist. Graec., II, 4, 12, or of capitulation, Diod. S., 20, 31, 5; 45, 7. d. In contests ἄεθλα τίθημι is "to display, present the prizes publicly," Hom. Il., 23, 263; τὰ τιθέμενα are the prizes, Demosth. Or., 61, 25. e. Sacrally the verb is used

---

τ ί θ η μ ι κτλ. Bibl.: Liddell-Scott, Moult.-Mill., Pass., Pr.-Bauer, s.v.
[1] On the Indo-Eur. root dhē-, cf. Lat. facio (fecit: Gk. ἔθηκε), Germ. tun, Eng. do., cf. Boisacq, Hofmann, s.v., Pokorny, 235-9. κεῖμαι counts as a perf. pass. → III, 654, 17 ff. On the partial transition into the ω-conjugation cf. Bl.-Debr. § 94, 1.

of gifts donated to the gods in the temple, e.g., τίθημι ἀγάλματα, "to make votive offerings," Hom. Od., 12. 347. f. On the verge of the transf. sense, but still mainly local, is τίθημί τινί τι ἐν στήθεσσι, ἐν φρεσί etc. "to put, suggest, plant something in someone's heart," Hom. Il., 17, 470, but ἐνὶ φρεσὶ τίθεμαι, "to have in mind," "to think of doing," Od., 4, 729.

2. The Transferred Sense of τίθημι.

a. Spatial placing can already imply creative fashioning, e.g., δῶμα τίθεμαι "to raise, build a house," Hom. Od., 15, 241, or in personal relations ἣ φιλότητα μετ' ἀμφοτέροισι τίθησι Ζεύς; "or will Zeus establish friendship between the two parties?" Hom. Il., 4, 83 f., then plainly in the expression τίθεμαι παῖδα (υἱὸν) ὑπὸ ζώνῃ, "to put a child under one's girdle," "to conceive," Hom. Hymn. Ven., 255 and 282; placing which brings order into confused relations is found in the phrase τὰ παρ' ὑμῖν εὖ τίθει, Aristoph. Lys., 243; ἕως ἂν τὸν πόλεμον εὖ θῶνται, "until they had brought the war to a happy end," Thuc., VIII, 84, 5. In this connection one might mention periphrastic expressions like τίθεμαι θυσίαν, "to sacrifice," Pind. Olymp., 7, 42; τίθεμαι γάμον, "to hold a wedding," 13, 53. b. As the terms ὁ θεσμός (divine or human) "statute," "law" and νόμων θέσις "legislation" make clear, τίθημι plays an important role in the sphere of the law, e.g., τίθημι νόμον, "to establish a law," Soph. El., 580; Plat. Resp., I, 339c; pass. περὶ ὧν κεῖται θάνατος, "whereon the death penalty stands," Eur. Ion, 756; νόμος... τοῖς σύμπασιν κείμενος, Plat. Leg., X, 909d. c. Gods establish gen. or special ordinances and decrees, e.g. οὕτω νῦν Ζεὺς θείη, Hom. Od., 8, 465; τέλος δ' ἔθηκε Ζεὺς καλῶς, Soph. Trach., 26; οἱ ὑπὸ τῶν θεῶν κείμενοι νόμοι, Xenoph. Mem., IV, 4, 21; the Pelasgians trace back the term θεοί to the fact ὅτι κόσμῳ θέντες τὰ πάντα πρήγματα καὶ πάσας νομὰς εἶχον, "that they have set all things in order and undertaken the distribution of all goods," Hdt., II, 52, 1. d. There is also a positing in man's intellectual activity, e.g., the acknowledgment of a premise or possibility in philosophical discussion, θῶμεν οὖν, βούλει, δύο εἴδη τῶν ὄντων; "will you agree to presuppose two kinds of being?" Plat. Phaed., 79a; τίθημι ὡς ἀληθῆ ὄντα, "I will accept that it is true," 100a, also κείσθω, τούτων τεθέντων, "let it be presupposed," Aristot. An. Pri., I, 15, p. 34b, 23 and 26 etc., cf. ἡ θέσις the thesis accepted or to be defended, Plat. Resp., I, 335a. e. Worthy of special note is the construction with double acc. (ποιέω, ποιέομαι), "to make someone something," "to appoint," "to institute," e.g., τίθημί τινα ἄλοχόν τινος, "to make a woman someone's wife," Hom. Il., 19, 298, mid. ἄκοιτιν τίθεμαί τινα, "to make someone one's own wife," Bacchyl., 5, 169; υἱὸν τίθεμαί τινα, "to adopt," Plat. Leg., XI, 929c; also abs. τίθεμαί τινα, Plut. Aem., 5, 4 (I, 257); adj. εὐδαίμονα τίθημί τινα, "to make happy," Xenoph. Cyrop., IV, 6, 3; γέλωτα τίθημί τινα, "to make a mock of someone," "take him for a fool," Hdt., III, 29, 2; with evaluation δαιμόνιον αὐτὸ τίθημι ἐγώ, "I regard it as a divine dispensation," Soph. El., 1270; οὐ τίθημι ἐγὼ ζῆν τοῦτον, "I do not believe that this person lives," Soph. Ant., 1166; οὐδαμοῦ τίθημί τι, "to value, regard as nought," Eur. Andr., 210.

B. The Septuagint.

1. Occurrence.

The material Hbr. equivalent of τίθημι is שִׂים, which combines local and transf. elements and is thus predominantly transl. by τίθημι and compounds. This stands behind some 260 of 560 τίθημι ref., and the related שִׂית behind another 36. For נתן in its local sense "to put something somewhere" and, with double acc., "to make someone something," τίθημι is used 90 times, and for the second hi form הִגִּיַע "to set down in a place" 21 times. Fairly often τίθημι is used for a hi, e.g., הֵבִיא at Ex. 34:26, הוֹשִׁיב at 1 K. 2:24. As regards the construction of the verb the various Gk. translations offer the same diversity as profane Gk.

2. Meaning.

Both materially and linguistically the OT contains a few shifts of accent.

a. The most diverse local meanings like "to set down," "to erect," "to hang up," "to place," can be compared very well in the account of the erection of the tabernacle, where τίθημι alternates with ἵστημι, εἰσφέρω, ἐμβάλλω and also with various compounds of its own stem, Ex. 40. In detail attention may be drawn to τίθημι "to inter" in 1 K. 13:31, "to invest" funds in Sir. 29:11, "to gird on" a sword in Ex. 32:27, but θήσω τὴν ῥομφαίαν μου εἰς τὴν χεῖρα αὐτοῦ in Ez. 30:24 vl.; the fruits of the land are "brought" to the temple as a gift, Ex. 34:26, the confiscated booty of Achan is also set before the Lord, Jos. 7:23; τίθημι σκάνδαλα "to set snares, obstacles," Jdt. 5:1, also personally "to cause to fall," "to tempt to destruction," ψ 139:16, similarly τίθημι πρόσκομμα, Is. 29:21; παγίδα, ψ 118:110. Special OT expressions are τίθεμαι (τίθημι) τὴν ψυχήν μου ἐν χειρί μου, "to hazard one's life" for בְּכַפִּי נַפְשִׁי שִׂים, Ju. 12:3; 1 S. 19:5; 28:21; Job 13:14; τίθεμαι τὴν καρδίαν etc. "to direct one's attention to," "to note," ψ 47:14; negative imp. "do not worry about," 1 S. 9:20 etc.; τίθεμαι εἰς καρδίαν [ψυχήν], ἐν τῇ καρδίᾳ etc. "to take to heart," 2 S. 19:20; Jer. 12:11; Hag. 2:15; in a rather different sense τίθεσθαι ἐπὶ τὴν καρδίαν αὐτοῦ (sc. idols) "to set in the heart," Ez. 14:3, 4, 7; τίθημι τὸ πρόσωπον with inf. "to purpose," Ιερ. 49(42):17. b. In a transf. sense one finds "to appoint" overseers, 2 K. 11:18; "to bring shame on," 1 S. 11:2; τίθεμαι ἐμαυτῷ βουλὴν περί τινος, ἐπί τι, "to advise to come to a decision about something," Ju. 19:30; cf. 20:7; τίθημι γνώμην, "to issue an order," 2 Εσδρ. 4:19, 21. For publishing laws (→ 153, 16 ff.) one finds τίθημι πρόσταγμα, δικαιώματα, νόμον, μαρτύριον etc. Gn. 47:26; Ex. 15:25; ψ 77:5; 80:6; ἕως ἂν θῇ ἐπὶ τῆς γῆς κρίσιν, "until he has established justice on the earth," Is. 42:4; τίθημι διαθήκην τινί (→ II, 105, 17 ff.), "to conclude a covenant," "to reach an agreement," Ex. 34:10, 12, 15 etc. c. τίθημι with double acc. has a causative sense, "to make someone something," e.g., military leader, 1 Macc. 10:65, enemy, 1 S. 22:13; to make God one's refuge, ψ 51:9. The sense "to regard someone as something" does not occur, but cf. ἔθεντο αὐτὸν εἶναι ἀσεβῆ, "they represented him as an ungodly man," Job 32:3.

3. Both the content of OT literature and the special orientation of the verb explain why in more than a quarter of the instances God is the subject of τιθέναι. His creative, saving and judging action is denoted thereby. Especially in the Ps., then the Prophets and Gn., is this so. God sets the stars in the firmament, Gn. 1:17. He puts the primal floods in chambers, ψ 32:7. He sets a boundary for the ocean which it cannot pass, Job 38:10; ψ 103:9. He changes the rivers into deserts and the deserts into seas, ψ 106:33, 35. He transforms the mantle of heaven into sackcloth, Is. 50:3. His way of doing new things among men is seen in his making Abraham the father of many nations, Gn. 17:5 f. He also makes the seed of Jacob as the sand of the sea, Gn. 32:13. He causes His own name to dwell in specific places, 1 K. 9:3 etc. He makes the anonymous Servant of the Lord a chosen arrow and his mouth a sharp sword, Is. 49:2. He chooses Jeremiah as a prophet to the nations, Jer. 1:5. He makes David the firstborn among kings and establishes his throne for ever, ψ 88:28, 30. He sets the enemies of the priest-king like a footstool under his feet, ψ 109:1. To the individual He grants life and mercy, Job 10:12. He directs his soul to life ψ 65:9. He makes the poor man a bow of brass, ψ 17:35. He sets aside his tears (ψ 55:9) and his sins (ψ 89:8). As Judge He makes His enemies as a fiery oven ψ 20:10. He deals with them as with Oreb and Zeeb ψ 82:12. He makes the manufacturers of idols as nothing, Mi. 1:7. He causes sorrow as for an only child, Amos 8:10. But He also brings salvation ψ 11:6. He establishes a wall and a bulwark to defend Jerusalem, Is. 26:1. He will make those who are driven out the stem of the future and those who are rejected a strong people, Mi. 4:7. He who once set

Israel in its place (1 Ch. 17:9) and established it among the peoples (Ez. 5:5) will put it in its own land again (Ez. 37:14).

C. The New Testament.

The 101 [2] instances are spread over all the NT writings. No less than 39 are in Lk. and some stereotyped expressions occur among these. The word has a strong theological thrust in the Pauline corpus.

1. General. a. The basic local sense is found in many connections, e.g., a light is "put" on a lamp-stand, Mk. 4:21 and par.; the sick are "laid out" for healing, Mk. 6:56 etc.; wine is "served," Jn. 2:10; Moses "puts" the concealing mask on his face, 2 C. 3:13; the expression τίθημι τὰς χεῖρας is found for the laying on of hands, Mk. 8:25; 10:16 (Mk. elsewhere has the compound ἐπιτίθημι for this → 161, 2 ff.). b. Similarly men can be "buried," Mk. 6:29; 15:46 and par. etc., but cf. ἔθηκαν, "they laid her out" (sc. Tabitha), Ac. 9:37. c. Economically the word means "to invest money," Lk. 19:21 f.; each of you "set money aside" in self-denial, 1 C. 16:2. d. The term has a metaphorical sense in ἐν τίνι αὐτὴν παραβολῇ θῶμεν; "with what likeness shall we set it forth (i.e., God's rule)?" Mk. 4:30; there is Semitic influence in this and the following example: τὸ μέρος αὐτοῦ μετὰ τῶν ὑποκριτῶν (Lk. ἀπίστων) θήσει, Mt. 24:51 and par.; Paul offers the Gospel without charge, 1 C. 9:18; members of the community may give mutual offence (→ VII, 355, 12 ff.), R. 14:13. [3]

2. Some peculiarities in Luke: a. τίθημι τὰ γόνατα, "to bend the knees" (sc. in prayer, cf. genua ponere), apart from Mk. 15:19, where it is said of the soldiers in their mockery, occurs only at Lk. 22:41; Ac. 7:60; 9:40; 20:36; 21:5 (→ I, 738, 12 ff.). b. The OT τίθεμαι ἐν καρδίᾳ etc. (→ 154, 15 ff.) "to take note of," "to take to heart," "to intend," "to purpose," occurs only in Lk. 1:66; 21:14; Ac. 5:4, so too τίθεμαι εἰς τὰ ὦτά μου, Lk. 9:44; τίθεμαι ἐν τῷ πνεύματι, "to resolve" to do something, Ac. 19:21 and τίθεμαι βουλήν, "to make a resolve," Ac. 27:12. c. τίθημί τι παρὰ (πρὸς) τοὺς πόδας τινός, "to lay something at someone's feet," i.e., to give him control over it, Ac. 4:35, 37; 5:2.

3. Peculiar to John is the expression τίθημι τὴν ψυχήν μου ὑπέρ τινος, Jn. 10:11, 15, 17, 18a b; 13:37, 38; 15:13; 1 Jn. 3:16a b. In linguistic parallels one may discern two strands. The Greek-Hellenistic parallels which use τίθημι all denote taking a risk rather than full sacrifice of life: παρατίθεμαι τὴν ψυχήν, "to risk one's life" (→ 162, 9 f.). The OT τιθέναι τὴν ψυχὴν ἐν χειρὶ αὐτοῦ (→ 154, 12 f.) moves along similar lines. Greek terms for the actual sacrifice of life are ἐκπνέω, ἀφίημι, προβάλλω, προτείνω [4] etc. and — important in the present context — δίδωμι τὴν ψυχήν, Eur. Phoen., 998; Jos. Bell., 2, 201. A counterpart in Rabbinic Hebrew is נתן נַפְשׁוֹ (or מסר or יהב), which is mostly translated "to offer up one's life" (→ VI, 496, n. 104). [5] Against this twofold linguistic background one might suppose that John deliberately chose τίθημι τὴν ψυχήν to catch an echo of the sense of "hazarding one's life" at least at Jn. 10:11 (→ IV, 342, 18 ff.) [6] and also 13:37 f.;

---

[2] The tradition vacillates between τίθημι and compound. The simple is probably original at Mk. 8:25; Lk. 8:16b; Rev. 1:17, the compound at Mt. 14:3; Gl. 3:19.

[3] Cf. Lv. 19:14: ἀπέναντι τυφλοῦ οὐ προσθήσεις [Α προθήσεις] σκάνδαλον.

[4] Express examples in E. Fascher, "Zur Auslegung v. Joh. 10:17-18," DTh, 8 (1941), 43.

[5] Examples in Str.-B., II, 537; P. Fiebig, "Die MEx u. d. Joh.-Ev.," Angelos, I (1925), 58 f.; Schl. Mt. on 20:28; Schl. J. on 10:11. There are no non-Johannine par. for Schlatter's rendering of יְהַב by ἔθηκεν at the last of these passages.

[6] The readings δίδωσιν in p [45] אˣ D lat sy[s] bo at v. 11 and δίδωμι in p [45, 66] אˣ DW at v. 15 show assimilation to Mk. 10:45.

15:13⁷ (and cf. 1 Jn. 3:16b). Yet the emphasis in all these vv. is on the actual sacrifice of life, just as the only possible rendering in the other references is "to depart, give or offer up one's life." John thus adopts the form of the Greek expression τίθημι τὴν ψυχήν but gives it a new sense in order thereby to reproduce in his own way the Synoptic δίδωμι τὴν ψυχὴν λύτρον, Mk. 10:45 and par. → IV, 342, 12 ff. But in so doing he also goes back directly to the Hebrew of Is. 53:10 (→ VI, 544, 22 ff.) אִם־תָּשִׂים אָשָׁם נַפְשׁוֹ. τίθημι now corresponds exactly to the Hebrew שִׂים, while the ὑπέρ formula is a rendering of the Hebrew אָשָׁם → V, 710, 11 ff.

4. τίθημι belongs to a specific theological context in which it denotes God's action in past, present and future.

a. Important here is the OT verse from the royal psalm ψ 109:1, which is often quoted in the NT. It runs: Κάθου ἐκ δεξιῶν μου, ἕως ἂν θῶ τοὺς ἐχθρούς σου ὑποπόδιον τῶν ποδῶν σου. Both the context of 1 C. 15:23-28 and the embedding of the quotation in v. 25 show that the enthronement of Christ and the consequent subjection of hostile powers take place in time. The latter is the goal but it is also the crown and consummation of the βασιλεύειν of the Christ enthroned at Easter. ⁸ The way in which Paul introduces the saying into the text presupposes that it is a familiar one in the church, so the change in subject⁹ is not specially noted either with θῇ in v. 25 or ὑπέταξεν in v. 27. The differentiation of two events in the past and the future is also to be found in Hb. The present position of the Son as compared with the angels (1:13) is based on His exaltation (1:3; 8:1) and includes within it an almost peaceful waiting for the as yet unfulfilled subjection of His foes (10:13). In accordance with the Lucan design Acts and the inauthentic Marcan ending connect the quotation with the ascension, though the conclusion of the events of the end-time has yet to come (Ac. 2:33 f.; Mk. 16:19). Col. 3:1 is to be understood similarly. One need not decide whether the enigmatic debate as to the relation between Christ and the Son of David in Mk. 12:35 ff. and par. goes back to the earthly Jesus. ¹⁰ In any case the Rabbinic suppression of a Christological exposition of ψ 109:1 ¹¹ is connected with the fact that Christians saw here the exaltation of their Lord in the Easter event. Hence the emphasis of the pericope as we now have it in the Synoptic Gospels does not lie in the issue of Jesus' descent from David but in the question of the function of the Exalted Lord as indicated by the title Son of David and Kurios. The community of Jesus is not content with the restricted Jewish interpretation of ψ 109:1a which relates the mission of the coming Messiah only to political redemption. For Christians the Risen Lord is not just the Redeemer of Israel; He is the unique and all-embracing Kurios whom God has set over the whole world.

---

7 Cf. Bultmann J. on 10:11-13, n. 2. Bau. J. on 10:18 and Bultmann J. on 10:17, n. 3 think there is an analogy to putting off clothes and putting them on again, but though this cannot be ruled out in view of the allusive style of the Fourth Gospel it is very unlikely.
    8 On the tension between Christ's rule and the coming kingdom of God in connection with ψ 109:1 cf. O. Cullmann, *Die Christologie d. NT³* (1963), 229-239.
    9 God is the subject, not Christ, as against Ltzm. 1 K., *ad loc.*
    10 It is accepted as an authentic saying of Jesus by Loh. Mt., *ad loc.*; Schl. Mt. on 22:44; V. Taylor, *The Gospel acc. to St. Mark* (1955), 493; J. Jeremias, *Jesu Verheissung f. d. Völker²* (1959), 45; Cullmann, *op. cit.*, 87, 132-134; → II, 39, 11 ff. Bultmann thinks it is a community saying, Trad., 145 f.; Theol., 28 f.
    11 Cf. on this Str.-B., IV, 452-465, Exc. on Ps. 110.

b. The apostle Paul uses τίθημι and compounds very rarely. When he does it is particularly to describe God's work. This is true of the simple form in 8 of 13 instances. On the use of ψ 109 → 156, 11 ff. R. 4:17 quotes God's saying to Abraham which explains the patriarch's change of name, πατέρα πολλῶν ἐθνῶν τέθεικά σε, Gn. 17:5. The father of the people of God made up of both Jews and Gentiles also represents what faith is. The reference is now to faith in God who calls to life the promised posterity beyond the bounds of natural procreation and in the midst of a Gentile world already fallen victim to death. The election of Abraham is against the background of the new creation. A similar interrelation of election and new creation in the divine ordination may be seen in 1 Th. 5:9: God has not ordained us for wrath (→ V, 443, 1 ff.) but for the attainment of salvation. Also in the background is the perfect κεῖμαι, Phil. 1:16; 1 Th. 3:3. The verb has in view here the point at which God's transcendent decision and man's real existence converge. One sees this too when the existence of different members (→ IV, 561, 15 ff.) in Christ's body is traced back to divine ordination, 1 C. 12:18, 28. The mixed quotation in R. 9:33 calls Christ the divinely appointed stone of stumbling at which the paths of Israel and the Church cross. According to Is. 28:16 God Himself will "lay" the precious stone in Zion, and according to Is. 8:14 the Kurios will Himself be the stone of stumbling (on the OT passages → IV, 272, 22 ff.; VI, 97, 39 ff.; for the interpretation of R. 9:32 f. → IV, 276, 23 ff.). It is worth noting that Paul here has τίθημι for the LXX ἐμβάλλω, and 1 Pt. 2:6 (→ VII, 353, 5 ff.) follows suit. One may see from this how well adapted Paul thought the term was to express God's action in all its multiplicity. In 2 C. 5:19 as well the word takes on its special dimension from the fact that God is the subject: καὶ θέμενος ἐν ἡμῖν τὸν λόγον [12] τῆς καταλλαγῆς. The new creation on which the standards of the passing world are broken (v. 17) is built on God's reconciling act. This for its part contains two things, first God's act in Christ, and then the resultant commissioning of the apostles (v. 18 f.) with the ministry of reconciliation (→ I, 255, 12 ff.). And v. 19 underlines the fact that all this does not consist in just thinking and speaking about God but has its origin in God's own authoritative and effective ordination. [13] A similar polar duality of the divine ordination of the Gospel may be seen in 1 C. 3:10 f. → V, 140, 14 ff. On the one side it is Paul and on the other, as the passive κείμενον in v. 11 shows, it is God Himself who has laid the fondation of the community. The combination of these two statements presupposes not only that Paul follows the divinely laid foundation but also that God for His part binds Himself to the called apostle and thereby makes possible and ordains the paradox of the συνεργοὶ θεοῦ of v. 9.

c. The idea of divine ordination in concert with the goal of election may be seen also in later writings. Christ put Paul in service, or elected him to it, 1 Tm. 1:12. Paul is appointed a herald and apostle, 1 Tm. 2:7; 2 Tm. 1:11. Those who are disobedient to the Word take offence as ordained, 1 Pt. 2:8. Sodom and Gomorrah are set as a warning example to the wicked who come after, 2 Pt. 2:6. The eternal Son Himself is appointed the heir of all things, Hb. 1:2. Paul backs up his dedication to the Gentile mission by pointing out that the Servant of the Lord is appointed a light for the nations, Ac. 13:47. The setting up of church leaders is traced back to the Holy Spirit, Ac. 20:28. The fixing of the eschatological hour by the Father, which has already been done, is still concealed from the disciples, Ac. 1:7.

---

[12] Cf. the reading τὸ εὐαγγέλιον in p [46]. D * G offer mixed readings.
[13] ὡς ὅτι θεὸς ἦν ... καταλλάσσων ... καὶ θέμενος corresponds to a ὡς with gen. abs., Bl.-Debr. § 396, cf. also 2 C. 5:20.

D. The Post-Apostolic Fathers.

Unqualified use is common, esp. in Herm. in connection with the fitting, taking out and simple laying of stones in the building of the tower, v., 3, 2, 7; s., 9, 4, 5. 8; 8, 1. In detail one finds "to bow the knees" (→ 155, 20 ff.) in Herm. v., 1, 1, 3; 2, 1, 2; 3, 1, 5; "to set the Lord in one's heart," "to pay heed" to Him, m., 12, 4, 5; ἐν ἰσχύι τέθεικεν τὴν σάρκα αὐτοῦ, "the Lord has made his flesh mighty," Barn., 6, 3; βλέπετε ἐπὶ τίνων τέθεικεν, "see by whom (sc. examples, persons) he has shown . . . ," 13, 6.

Divine ordaining is found in OT quotations, 1 Cl., 15, 6; 36, 5; Barn., 5, 14; 13, 7 etc., also in free usage: God has established wisdom and knowledge of His secrets, Barn., 6, 10; He has put in us the gift of His doctrine, 9, 9; He has enjoined repentance, Herm. m., 4, 3, 4 and 5; He has ordained for Christians an order of suffering which they are not to evade, Dg., 6, 10; those who act as apostates He ordains to punishment and chastisement, 1 Cl., 11, 1.

† ἀθετέω,   † ἀθέτησις.

1. In profane Gk. ἀθετέω [1] means "to regard as nought," "to declare invalid," "to set aside," e.g., an agreement between cities, Ditt. Or., II, 444, 18, cf. the legal tt. ἀθέτησις, "declaration of invalidity," BGU, I, 44, 16 (102 B.C.); τινί "to deny one's assent" to something, Polyb., 12, 14, 6; pass. "to be stricken" from a list, P. Tebt., I, 74, 29 (2nd cent. B.C.); "to act treacherously towards someone," "to break with him," Polyb., 11, 36, 10.

2. In the LXX ἀθετέω has strongly the character of wilful repudiation of an institution and even more so of a person.

This may be seen already in the fact that of some 60 instances 22 render בגד "to act unfaithfully," "to be apostate," and 10 פשע "to fall away," "to be unfaithful." The others are divided among different verbs. The meanings are a. trans. "to disregard," "to pass over something," e.g., God's sacrifice, 1 Βασ. 2:17, "to break an oath," 2 Ch. 36:13; 1 Macc. 6:62, "not to pay heed to God's word and demands," Jer. 15:16; οἱ ἱερεῖς ἠθέτησαν νόμον μου, "they have rebelled against my law," Ez. 22:26; Is. 24:16; we enter the legal sphere when a command of the king is "transgressed" by individuals, Δα. 3:95 (28), a royal resolve is "annulled" by disobedience, 1 Macc. 11:36; 14:44 f., or "reversed" by the one who makes an agreement, 1 Macc. 15:27; 2 Macc. 13:25; 14:28; the Word of Yahweh οὐ μὴ ἀθετηθῇ, "will not be revoked," Is. 31:2; cf. ψ 88:35. God "brings to nought": ἀθετεῖ δὲ λογισμοὺς λαῶν καὶ ἀθετεῖ βουλὰς ἀρχόντων, ψ 32:10; He destroys man, Jdt. 16:5. b. Intrans. of relation to a person the verb means "to act unfaithfully towards someone," ἔν τινι, εἴς τινα, e.g., a woman, Ex. 21:8; "to fall away from someone," Ju. 9:23; Is. 33:1; 53:12 Σ; Jer. 3:20 etc.; ἀθετῶν ἠθέτησεν εἰς ἐμέ, "he has forsaken me," Jer. 5:11; Is. 1:2. Abs. the verb means "to act wickedly," Is. 21:2 etc.

3. In the NT ἀθετέω means a. "to invalidate a matter," "to declare it invalid," e.g. "in the same way no one annuls the legally effected will of a man nor adds thereto," Gl. 3:15. Only the testator during his lifetime has the right to annul or alter his

---

ἀ θ ε τ έ ω . [1] From ἄθετος (found from Aristot., e.g., Metaph., 4, 6, p. 1016b, 25, also inscr., e.g., P. Amh., II, 64, 12 [2nd cent. A. D.]), "not established," "not in the right place," "invalid."

will, → II, 129, 19 ff. [2] οὐκ ἀθετῶ τὴν χάριν τοῦ θεοῦ, says Paul in Gl. 2:21, thus acknowledging, by his desire to live in full unity with Christ as one who is dead to the Law, the fact that the grace of God is in force, whereas the Judaisers, according to whom righteousness is achieved by the Law, make void or invalidate, not God's grace as such, but its practical force. b. The following passages are under strong OT influence (→ 158, 21 ff.): If anyone violated a precept of Moses' Law he had to die without mercy, Hb. 10:28. The Pharisees and scribes rejected God's will, Lk. 7:30. The invalidation of God's ἐντολή does not take place by legal enactment but by the practical attitude of disobedience: "Full well you disregard the commandment of God (→ II, 549, 5 ff.) to keep your own tradition," Mk. 7:9. To the ἀθετέω there corresponds ἀφίημι (v. 8), the opposite being τηρέω (→ 144, 5 f.), "to keep by fulfilling," v. 9b. Mt. correctly has παραβαίνω for ἀθετέω in 15:3. By marrying again young widows "have broken their first loyalty" (sc. to Christ → I, 788, 33 ff.) τὴν πρώτην πίστιν ἠθέτησαν, 1 Tm. 5:12. God brings to nought the wisdom of the wise, 1 C. 1:19, cf. ψ 32:10 → 158, 32 f. c. The verb also means "to refuse, reject" a person. Thus Lk. 10:16 is marked by the contrast between hearing and accepting Christ in His messengers and resisting and rejecting Him, cf. also 1 Th. 4:8; Jn. 12:48. The rejection of the κυριότης in Jd. 8 probably signifies the rejection of the Kurios Himself, → III, 632, 19 ff.; 1097, 1 ff. Herod will not "reject," "turn down," the daughter of Herodias, Mk. 6:26.

ἀθέτησις is "abrogation," "annulment," e.g., of the Law, Hb. 7:18, or sin, 9:26.

4. All three passages in the post-apost. fathers refer to "rejection," "depising," God or Christ and His witnesses, Ign. Eph., 10, 3; Herm. m., 3, 2; ἀθετέω εἰς τὸν θεόν in Herm. v., 2, 2, 2 is an expression derived from the LXX, → 158, 34 ff.

ἀνατίθημι, προσανατίθημι, ἀνάθεμα, ἀνάθημα, κατάθεμα, ἀναθεματίζω, καταθεματίζω → I, 353, 13 ff.

διατίθημι → II, 104, 24 ff.; διαθήκη → II, 106, 13 ff.

ἐπιτίθημι, ἐπίθεσις.

1. In secular Gk. a. the verb means "to lay down," "to put to," "to set on," τί or τινί τι or ἐπί τινος etc., e.g., a sacrifice on the altar, Hom. Od., 21, 267, a wreath, Jos. Ant., 9, 149, "to lay on" blows, BGU, III, 759, 13 (2nd cent. B.C.), "to apply" means of healing, Ditt. Syll.³, 1173, 9; Jos. Ant., 9, 268, "to give additionally" a half talent of gold, Hom. Il., 23, 796, "to put" the crown on wisdom, Plat. Euthyd., 301e, "to impose" a punishment, Leg., VIII, 838c, "to give" a name, Hdt., V, 68, 1. The mid. can mean "to put on" a helmet, Hom. Il., 10, 30 f., "to take up" a matter, Plat. Gorg., 527d, "to make an attack on," Hdt., V, 31, 3, "to waylay," Jos. Ant., 1, 328; Philo Leg. Gaj., 371; τυραννίδι "to try to attain dominion," Lyc., 125, "to bring fear on someone," Xenoph. Cyrop., IV, 5, 41, "to give" someone something, BGU, IV, 1208, 1, 4 (27 B.C.). b. The noun ἡ ἐπίθεσις means "the putting up" of a statue, CIG, II, 1, 3124, 2, the "putting on" of a cover, Aristot. De iuventute et senectute, 5, p. 470a. 11; also "assault," Plat. Leg., III, 698b.

2. In the LXX one finds a. the verb some 270 times in various senses. As with τίθημι (→ 153, 43 ff.) שׂים and נתן are the chief of no less than 34 Hbr. equivalents. In detail one finds the sense "to lay" something on someone, Gn. 22:6, 9, "to put" plaster on a

[2] One cannot be sure whether Paul has in view Jewish, Hell. or some other law. Cf. the survey in E. Bammel, "Gottes διαθήκη u. das jüd. Recht," NTSt, 6 (1959/60), 313-319. Bammel himself suggests the Jewish legal institution of the מַתָּנָה.

wound, 2 K. 20:7, "to set" the Spirit on someone, Nu. 11:17, 25; Is. 44:3, "to lay" sicknesses, Dt. 7:15, "to impose" hard service, Dt. 26:6, "to impose" a tribute, 2 K. 18:14,
"to give" a name, Ju. 8:31 etc. In connection with the temple ministry it means "to bring"
fire on the altar, Lv. 1:7, "to smear" blood on the horns of the altar, Lv. 4:7, "to put on"
the high-priest the individual parts of his official attire, Lv. 8:7-9, "to lay out" the show-
bread, Lv. 24:6, "to wave" the wave offering before the altar, Lv. 14:24. In the mid. esp.
it means "to waylay" someone, Ex. 21:14, "to weave" a conspiracy, 2 Ch. 24:21, 25 f.,
"to act arrogantly" towards someone, Ex. 18:11, "to fall on" and plunder, 1 Βασ. 23:27;
27:8, 10, "to intend" to do something, Gn. 11:6, hence "to seek to win someone" (sc. to a
love-affair), Ez. 23:5, 7.

Especially common and many-faceted is ἐπιτίθημι τὰς χεῖρας (or τὴν χεῖρα)
ἐπὶ τὴν κεφαλήν, "to lay on hands," particularly for סמך "to lean upon the head."
This is done with the sacrifice to dedicate it to God, Ex. 29:10, 15; Lv. 1:4; 3:2, 8,
13 etc.) and with Levites to institute them in their ministry, Nu. 8:10. Blessing and
the appropriate gifts of the Spirit are imparted with this offical institution, Nu. 27:18,
23; Dt. 34:9; Gn. 48:17 f. In exceptional cases the laying of hands is in cursing, as
at the stoning of the blasphemer, Lv. 24:14. Only once is it connected with healing
the sick. The Gentile Naaman expects, though vainly, that Elisha will put his hand
on the leprous spot, 2 K. 5:11. The LXX ἐπιτίθημι omits here the magical element
in the Hbr. נוף "to wave over." There is also a tendency in this direction in 2 K. 13:16
where Elisha lays his hand on the king's hands to declare blessing to him in this way.

b. The noun ἐπίθεσις occurs 5 times: ἐπέθεντο αὐτῷ ἐπίθεσιν, "they concocted
a conspiracy against him," 2 Ch. 25:27, of a military attack, 2 Macc. 4:41; 5:5; 14:15.
Like the verb it can once indicate wooing, Ez. 23:11.

3. In the NT ἐπιτίθημι in half the 40 passages is a tt. for the laying on of hands,
while in the other instances it has various senses.

a. In detail one finds: "to lay" a sheep on one's shoulders, Lk. 15, 5, "to place on"
the crown of thorns, Mt. 27:29; Jn. 19:2, "to put" the title on the cross, Mt. 27:37, "to lay
on" blows, Lk. 10:30; Ac. 16:23, "to give" a name (→ 159, 34; 160, 3), Mk. 3:16 f., "to
impose" a yoke (i.e., of legalism), Ac. 15:28, cf. v. 10; Mt. 23:4, as a play on words: He
who "makes addition" to the words of Rev., on him God will "lay" as a punishment the
plagues described therein, Rev. 22:18. In the mid. it means that none shall "undertake"
to harm Paul, Ac. 18:10; another meaning is "to furnish" someone with what is needed,
28:10.

b. The rite of laying on hands is denoted 20 times by the verb, ἐπιτίθημι χεῖρά
(or χεῖρας) τινι (or ἐπί τινα, ἐπί τι), and 4 times by the noun ἐπίθεσις τῶν
χειρῶν. One must distinguish between laying on hands in healing, for which there
are parallels in the world of Hellenistic religion, [1] and laying on hands in blessing,
especially to impart the Spirit at baptism and ordination, which is inherited especially
from the OT and Judaism, [2] → line 11 ff. On the other hand the two rites are united
again in the fact that the divine and human hand is the most important instrument
to convey the powers of healing and blessing. Hence laying on hands is only one

ἐπιτίθημι, ἐπίθεσις. [1] Material in Weinreich AH; bibl. on laying on hands
in the NT in E. Lohse, Die Ordination im Spätjudt. u. im NT (1951), 69, n. 1.
[2] Lohse, op. cit., 19-27 and 102-108 for bibl. on OT, Jewish and Chr. laying on of hands.

form of the varied transfer of power by moving the hand, by touching, seizing and anointing (→ χείρ). In particular Mk., and to a lesser degree Lk., tells of the healings of Jesus by the laying on of hands, Mk. 5:23; 6:5; 7:32; 8:23, 25; 16:18; Lk. 4:40; 13:13. Yet in Mt. the mere touching of children (in Mk.) becomes a laying on of hands in blessing, Mt. 19:13, 15 and par. Ac. tells of healing by the laying on of hands only in one case by Paul, 28:8. On the other hand it understands the rite in connection with or amplification of baptism as an imparting of the Spirit, (8:17-19 [→ VI, 414, 16 ff.]; 9:12, 17; 19:6) or as authorisation for a particular task, the diaconate in 6:6 or missionary work in 13:3. The Past. connect the laying on of hands with the imparting of gifts of the Spirit (→ VI, 451, 20 ff.) by ordination, [3] 1 Tm. 4:14; 5:22; 2 Tm. 1:6. Hb. 6:2 probably has the transmission of office particularly in view as well.

4. In the post-apost. fathers one finds nothing new in the use of ἐπιτίθημι, cf. λίθοι ἐπιτιθέμενοι εἰς τὴν οἰκοδομήν, Herm. v., 3, 5, 2; ἐπιθεὶς αὐτῷ τοῦτο τὸ ὄνομα, Barn., 12, 8; ἐπίθεσις does not occur at all.

† μετατίθημι, † μετάθεσις.

1. In secular Gk. a. the verb means "to bring to another place," "to set in another place," either locally, e.g., τι... εἰς τόπον, Plat. Leg., X, 903d or metaphorically; we then find the sense "to change," "to alter," e.g., an agreement, Thuc., V, 18, 11; τὸ ῥηθέν, Plat. Polit., 297e; of the changing of the high-priestly office, Jos. Ant., 12, 387, the name, Jos. Ap., 1, 286. The mid. has the special sense "to change over," e.g., to another opinion, Hdt., VII, 18, 3; Plat. Resp., I, 345b, to go over to the Roman party, Polyb., 24, 9, 6; ὁ μεταθέμενος is the one who runs from one philosophical school to another, Diog. L., VII, 1, 37; 4, 166. b. μετάθεσις means "change of place," e.g., Epic. Fr., 61 (Usener, 118, 17 f.); Diod. S., 1, 23, 3. It then means "transformation," "alteration," e.g., θεὸς οὐδεμίαν ἐνδεχόμενος μετάθεσιν, Ps.-Aristot. Mund., 6, p. 400b, 29; "change of mind," Polyb., 1, 35, 7.

2. In the LXX a. the verb occurs 18 times for different Hbr. words and has a local sense, e.g., "to remove" a boundary, Dt. 27:17 etc., "to ward off" an attack, 3 Macc. 1:16, "to transplant" a people (or "to transform"? Mas. has אלפ "to do wonderful things") Is. 29:14, "to be translated" from the earth (לקח), as in the case of Enoch, Gn. 5:24; Wis. 4:10; Sir. 44:16; 49:14 vl. It also has a transf. sense and can mean "to convince," "to talk round," Sir. 6:9, "to fall away," e.g., μεταθέμενον ἀπὸ τῶν πατρίων ("customs of the fathers"), 2 Macc. 7:24. b. The noun is μετάθεσις, e.g., ἡ ἐπὶ τὰ Ἑλληνικὰ μετάθεσις, "the transition to the Greek custom," 2 Macc. 11:24.

3. In the NT a. the verb has a local sense and means "to conduct across," of the dead in Ac. 7:16, the rapture of Enoch, Hb. 11:5. It can also have a transf. sense and in this case means "to transform," e.g., God's grace into licence in Jd. 4, or passively "to be done away, altered," of the priesthood in Hb. 7:12 → III, 281, 40 ff.; the mid. means "to turn from," "to fall away," "to become apostate," e.g., ἀπὸ τοῦ καλέσαντος ὑμᾶς... εἰς ἕτερον (→ II, 703, 42 ff.) εὐαγγέλιον, Gl. 1:6. b. The noun is used for the "translation" of Enoch in Hb. 11:5, the "revocation" or "alteration" of the Law in 7:12, the "metamorphosis" of shaken (→ VII, 70, 13 ff.) creation in 12:27.

---

[3] On ἐπίθεσις τῶν χειρῶν τοῦ πρεσβυτερίου in 1 Tm. 4:14 as a technical word for ordination cf. J. Jeremias, "Zur Datierung der Pastoralbriefe," ZNW, 52 (1961), 101-104.

4. The post-apost. fathers use only the verb, in a local sense at Barn., 13, 5; Mart. Pol., 8, 2; Herm. v., 3, 7, 6, Enoch's translation, 1 Cl., 9, 3. The mid. means "to become of another mind," ἀπὸ τῶν χαλεπῶν ἐπὶ τὰ δίκαια, Mart. Pol., 11, 1.

παρατίθημι, † παραθήκη, [παρακαταθήκη].

1. Profane Greek.

a. The verb has a local sense "to set alongside," "before," also transf. e.g., "to place something before someone in elucidation," "to present," διῆλθές μοι παρατιθεὶς ἕκαστον τί εἴη ὄφελος, Xenoph. Cyrop., I, 6, 14, also mid., e.g., μῦθον, Plat. Polit., 275b, παράδειγμα, 279a; also "to hazard," e.g., κεφαλάς, Hom. Od., 2, 237; ψυχάς, 3, 74; 9, 255. b. Very important is the tt. παρατίθεμαί τινί τι, "to give someone something in trust," "to entrust," e.g., τοῦ παραθεμένου τὰ χρήματα, Hdt., VI, 86 β 1. From Hdt. on we also find the nouns παραθήκη (Hdt., VI, 86 β 1) and παρακαταθήκη (V, 92 η 2). The second is the Attic form, the first became more common in Hellenism. [1] Both mean "deposit," [2] i.e., "goods placed in trust" or "agreement in respect of entrusted goods," "a trust agreement," e.g., κατατίθεμαι παρα[κατα]θήκην παρά τινι, "to leave a deposit with someone," Lys., 32, 16; δέχομαι, "to receive," Plat. Resp., IV, 442e; ἀποστερέω, "to embezzle," Isoc. Or., 17, 50; ἀποδίδωμι, "to restore," 21, 16. In the ancient Gk. and Jewish sphere, as well as the ancient Roman, one finds the legal device whereby an object can be entrusted to another's keeping for a specific period. [3] This object was to be kept free, unused and undamaged until restoration. The trustworthiness of the trustee was thus most important. But there was, too, a stringent penalty for embezzlement, and the special wrath of the gods was also invoked. The legal formulae soon came to be used in a transf. sense, e.g., παρατίθεμαί τινά τινι, "to entrust someone to the care or protection of someone," Diod. S., 17, 23, 5; to submit words as entrusted goods, Hdt., IX, 45, 1; μᾶλλον τήρει τὰς τῶν λόγων ἢ τὰς τῶν χρημάτων παρακαταθήκας, Isoc. Or., 1, 22.

2. The Septuagint.

a. παρατίθημι occurs 42 times, mostly for שׂים, and is used chiefly in a local sense, esp. for the serving of foods, Gn. 18:8 etc.; then we find "to set forth," e.g., a law, Ex. 19:7, cf. Dt. 4:44 mid. On the threshold of the transf. use is "to lay down," e.g., arms for keeping 1 Macc. 1:35, with τινί for "with someone," 9:35. παρέθεντο εἰς ἐπισιτισμὸν εἰς παρασκευὴν πολέμου, "they furnished" (sc. the villages) with military stores, Jdt. 4:5; Gn. 41:36 'Α. b. As a term in commercial law "to give money to someone for safe-keeping," we find the mid. at Lv. 5:23; Tob. 1:14; 4:1, 20. The responsibility of the trustee for the money handed to him is regulated in Ex. 22:7-13. The introductory formula reads: ἐὰν δέ τις δῷ τῷ πλησίον ἀργύριον ἢ σκεύη φυλάξαι, "if a man shall deliver unto his neighbour money or stuff to keep," v. 7, cf. v. 10. An expiatory offering for irregularities committed is prescribed in Lv. 6:2 ff. In Ex. 22 παρακαταθήκη is used for מְלָאכָה, but in Lv. 5:21, 23 one finds παραθήκη for פִּקָּדוֹן, which fits the matter better and was adopted as the established term in later Judaism. In Jerusalem as in the surrounding Gentile world money belonging to widows and orphans was laid up in the temple treasury, 2 Macc.

παρατίθημι, παραθήκη, [παρακαταθήκη].
[1] Phryn. Ecl., 287 (Rutherford); Nägeli, 27; Pr.-Bauer, s.v.
[2] W. Hellebrand, Art. "παρακαταθήκη," Pauly-W., 18, 2 (1949), 1186-1202; R. Leonhard, Art. "Depositum," Pauly-W., 5 (1905), 233-6; Mitteis-Wilcken, II, 1, 257-9; J. Ranft, Der Ursprung d. katholischen Traditionsprinzips (1931), 192-206, 299-303; also Art. "Depositum," RAC, III, 778-784; C. Spicq, "S. Paul et la loi des dépôts," Rev. Bibl., 40 (1931), 481-502; also S. Paul, Les épîtres pastorales² (1947), 327-335, Exc. "Le bon dépôt."
[3] There is an instructive example of such an agreement in P. Oxy., VII, 1039 (210 A.D.).

3:10, 15. There is a distinctive metaphor in Tob. 10:13: παρατίθεμαί σοι τὴν θυγατέρα μου ἐν παρακαταθήκη, "I give my daughter to thee as an entrusted possession." When the psalmist in ψ 30:6 prays εἰς χεῖράς σου παραθήσομαι τὸ πνεῦμά μου (for פקד hi), as one who is persecuted, though innocent, he sets himself under the protection of the faithful God.

3. Later Judaism.

Rabb. rulings concerning the "deposit" (פקדון) are gathered together in BM 3:1-12, cf. also BQ, IX, 7b, 8. [4] Joseph. lays special emphasis on the honesty which, grounded on ·fear of God and the conscience, must hold sway in trusts, Ant., 4, 285 ff. Philo has even stronger accents in this respect in his express commentary on the pertinent OT statutes, Spec. Leg., IV, 30-38. [5] He sometimes uses παρακαταθήκη in a transf. sense as well: ἡ δὲ φυλακὴ παντελές, μνήμη τὰ ἀσκητὰ παραδοῦναι θεωρήματα τῶν ἁγίων, ἐπιστήμης καλὴν παρακαταθήκην φύλακι πιστῇ, "but watching is something complete, namely, giving over to the memory the views of sacred things won by practice, handing to the faithful guardian the entrusted possession of knowledge...," Det. Pot. Ins., 65. As the continuation in 67 shows, Philo moves on from the thought of keeping a παρακαταθήκη to that of keeping God's διαθήκη; he is led to do this by the common term → φυλάσσω. All that man is and has he should regard as something entrusted to him by God, Rer. Div. Her., 103-106.

4. The New Testament.

a. The verb occurs 19 times, mostly in the lit. sense, "to lay" food before someone, Mk. 6:41 and par., also παρέθηκεν παραβολήν, Mt. 13:24, 31, and cf. "to expound," "to allege," of teaching, Ac. 17:3. [6] Jesus in a saying from ψ 30:6 (→ lines 2 ff.), which was an evening prayer of pious Jews, commends His spirit into the hands of the Father, Lk. 23:46, cf. Ac. 7:59. The persecuted in their sufferings should entrust their lives to the faithful Creator, 1 Pt. 4:19. Paul at his departure entrusts the churches or elders to the abiding faithfulness of God, Ac. 14:23; 20:32.

b. The mid. παρατίθεμαι, "to commit," "to deposit," is a commercial term, Lk. 12:48. There is special teaching on the deposit of the faith in the Past. Here the verb expresses the concept of tradition when the παραγγελία, i.e., proclamation, teaching, is handed over to Timothy (1 Tm. 1:18), who for his part is to entrust it to faithful men who can teach others also, 2 Tm. 2:2. The threefold παραθήκη (vl. παρακαταθήκη) [7] is to be understood against this background, and the φυλάσσω everywhere associated with it reminds us of OT and Jewish traditions. [8] 1 Tm. culminates in the admonition of 6:20 ὦ Τιμόθεε, τὴν παραθήκην φύλαξον. In the context, which echoes an ancient ordination formula (vv. 12-16), there is reference to the parousia as the time up to which the ἐντολή (→ II, 555, 41 f.), i.e.,

---

[4] For details cf. Levy Wört., IV and Jastrow, II, s.v. פקד and פקדון.

[5] The discussion in the transl. of J. Heinemann, Die Werke Philos v. Alex., II (1910), 255-8.

[6] Ac. 28:23 A offers ἐξετίθετο παρατιθέμενος τὴν βασιλείαν τοῦ θεοῦ. ἐκτίθεμαι also occurs in Ac. 18:26 for "to expound," and cf. ὑποτίθεμαι in 1 Tm. 4:6.

[7] Some minuscules puristically replace NT παραθήκη by παρακαταθήκη.

[8] Acc. to Spicq la loi (→ n. 2), 490 f. and épîtres, 328 f. the Past. are based more on Rom. than Attic trust law. But Ranft, op. cit., RAC, III, 781 is right to ref. above all to the Jewish tradition.

the totality of Christian faith, [9] is to be kept undefiled and intact, v. 14. This and the impressive warning against heretics (v. 20) show that the content of the παραθήκη consists in the Gospel enshrined in the traditional confession and disputed by the false teachers. [10] 2 Tm. 1:12 and 1:14 form a whole. The reference is again to the traditional confession which Timothy has received at his ordination (v. 6) from the ordained apostles (v. 11) and which he himself is to pass on further (2:1 f.). The parallelism of 1:13 and 1:14 indicates that the commanded keeping of the παραθήκη is to take place with the assistance of the Holy Spirit and hence as an act of faith and love. Emphasis is thus placed on the element of responsibility for the authenticity and intactness of the entrusted deposit. The one to whom the good tradition is entrusted bears special responsibility, v. 14. v. 12 expresses a different thought: πέπεισμαι ὅτι δυνατός ἐστιν τὴν παραθήκην μου φυλάξαι εἰς ἐκείνην τὴν ἡμέραν. A first point to decide is whether παραθήκην μου means "the good thing that I have entrusted" [11] or "the good thing entrusted to me," → IV, 491, 23 ff. [12] Mention of the eschatological day (v. 12) and regard for the generations which follow (2:2) definitely suggest the second, passive interpretation. Christ is able to protect and keep the Gospel committed to the community not only up to the time of the first apostle who will soon depart, but through the storms of coming generations right up to the last day. The genuineness of continuity is established not by the transmitted teaching as such but by the One who is Himself its content. In terms of this insight the Past. can repulse the false doctrinal traditions of the Gnostics without absolutising their own tradition.

5. The Post-Apostolic Fathers.

Here παρακαταθήκη is used once for an entrusted deposit: Liars do not return the entrusted good which they have received, i.e., the true Spirit, Herm. m., 3, 2. There is nothing distinctive about the 4 passages in which the verb is used, Ign. Tr., 5, 1; Mart. Pol., 7, 2; Herm. s., 9, 10, 6; Dg., 5, 7.

† προτίθημι,   † πρόθεσις.

1. Profane Greek.

a. The verb προτίθημι "to set before," "to place before," is first used in a purely local sense, e.g., food in Hes. Theog., 537, also the sacral placing of foods in a temple, e.g., Ἀλεξανδρεῖς τῷ Κρόνῳ ἀφιεροῦντες προτιθέασιν ἐσθίειν τῷ βουλομένῳ ἐν τῷ τοῦ Κρόνου ἱερῷ, Athen., 3, 74 (110b). [1] The noun means "offering" and denotes the προθέσεις set before the gods at popular festivals, Ditt. Or., I, 90, 48 (2nd cent. B.C.).

---

9 Acc. to R. Seeberg, Der Katechismus d. Urchristenheit (1903), 110 παραθήκη, ὁμο-λογία, ἐντολή and πίστις denote one and the same thing from different standpoints.

10 Spicq épîtres (→ n. 2) on 6:20 suggests various translations, e.g., sound doctrine, the mystery of piety, the orally transmitted Gospel whether as a basis of life or an obj. of faith, the Chr. credo etc.

11 Schl. Past., Bengel, ad loc. It is a mistake with Wbg. Past., ad loc. and Ranft Traditions-prinzip (→ n. 2), 300, on the basis of Ign. Pol., 6, 2, to think of the reward which is ready for Paul as a heavenly possession.

12 Spicq épîtres, 327 f.; Dib. Past., J. Jeremias, Die Briefe an Tm. u. Tt., NT Deutsch, 9⁸ (1963), ad loc.

π ρ ο τ ί θ η μ ι, π ρ ό θ ε σ ι ς. 1 Cf. Deissmann B., 155 f. But the instance sometimes adduced from Ditt. Syll.³, II, 708, 15 cannot have a sacral sense: τισὶν δὲ τῶν πολειτῶν ε[ἰς] λύτρα προτιθείς.

b. The verb can then have the special sense "to lay before the public," e.g., τὰ μὲν ὀστᾶ προτίθενται τῶν ἀπογενομένων, "the bones of the dead men were displayed publicly," Thuc., II, 34, 2; cf. Eur. Alc.,, 664, "to make known publicly," e.g., τοὺς [προέδρους] προτιθέναι περὶ ὧν δεῖ βουλεύεσθαι, IG, IV, 1 ², 68, 80 (4th cent. B.C.). Similarly the noun means "public lying in state of the dead," Plat. Leg., XII, 947b, "public declaration" of written laws, Aristot. Pol., VI, 8, p. 1322a, 9. c. The meaning "to impose," "to make a task," occurs, e.g., in Soph. Ant., 216; mid. it means "to undertake as a task," e.g., ὅπερ νῦν προυθέμεθα σκέψασθαι, Plat. Phaedr., 259e etc.; cf. Jos. Ant., 18, 286; κατὰ τὴν ἐξ ἀρχῆς ἐπιβολὴν καὶ πρόθεσιν, "according to the original plan and purpose," Polyb., 5, 35, 2; cf. Jos. Ant., 19, 190; Philo Vit. Mos., 36; Epict. Diss., IV, 6, 26. d. One also finds the sense "to place before," e.g., a preface before a speech, Plat. Leg., IV, 723c; "to prefer" one thing to another, Hdt., III, 53, 4.

2. The Septuagint.

The verb occurs 15 times, ² the noun 19 times. The proper meaning is "to collect," e.g., temple treasures in 2 Macc. 1:15, "to lay before, out," e.g., the showbread (sc. before God), Ex. 29:23; 40:4, 23; Lv. 24:8; 2 Macc. 1:8. The noun πρόθεσις is used almost exclusively in this sense. Every Sabbath 12 pieces of showbread ἄρτοι προκείμενοι, ³ which were reserved for the priests on duty, were arranged as a constant and esp. holy offering on the gold-covered table, Ex. 25:23-30; Lv. 24:5-9. ⁴ The mid. of the verb carries with it deliberate attention to the matter or person before one, e.g., "to set, hold God before one's eyes," ψ 53:5; 85:14, "to undertake something," ψ 100:3; 3 Macc. 2:27. But it is only in the apocr. writings that the noun πρόθεσις takes on the corresponding sense of "attempt," "purpose," 2 Macc. 3:8; 3 Macc. 1:22; 2:26; 5:12, 29; cf. Ps. 10:17 Σ; Ep. Ar., 199; the ref. is always to human designs.

3. The New Testament.

The verb occurs 3 times in the middle, the noun 12 times.

a. The showbread is called οἱ ἄρτοι τῆς προθέσεως ⁵ (Mk. 2:26 and par.). When Hb. 9:2 lists not only the table but more specifically ἡ πρόθεσις τῶν ἄρτων as an object in the temple sanctuary, the reference is not so much to the act of placing as to something concrete, perhaps the bread laid on the table rather than the table itself. ⁶, ⁷

b. There are two possible interpretations of ὃν προέθετο ὁ θεὸς ἱλαστήριον in R. 3:25. On the ground that προτίθεμαι and πρόθεσις are used elsewhere in Paul only in the sense of a resolve that has been made, it is proposed on the one hand that here, too, we are to think of the counsel of God: "which God has foreordained

---

² In 4 other passages, 2 Ch. 28:13; Est. 9:27; Qoh. 1:16, 18, in which there is vacillation between προτίθημι and προστίθημι, the latter is to be preferred.

³ Cf. Εξ. 39:17; the terms for the showbread vary in both Gk.: ἄρτοι ἐνώπιοι in Ex. 25:30, ἄρτοι τοῦ προσώπου in 1 S. 21:7 etc., and Hbr.: לֶחֶם פָּנִים in Ex. 25:30, לֶחֶם הַמַּעֲרֶכֶת in 1 Ch. 9:32, לֶחֶם הַתָּמִיד in Nu. 4:7 etc.

⁴ Details in P. Volz, Die bibl. Altertümer² (1925), 118 f.; Str.-B., III, 718-733.

⁵ Cf. the D reading οἱ ἄρτοι τῆς προσθέσεως.

⁶ Cf. Pr.-Bauer, s.v.

⁷ Rgg. Hb., 238, n. 57; Bengel, Mi. Hb., ad loc.

or chosen as a means of expiation."[8] But the construction with a double accusative emphatically demands a verb of action and not just resolve. The context, too, depicts the execution rather than the planning of God's new righteousness, cf. v. 21, 27. For this reason, in spite of the many interpretations of ἱλαστήριον (→ III, 320, 25 ff.; V, 706, n. 399), there is widespread consensus for the rendering: "whom God has set forth publicly[9] as a means of expiation (mercy seat),"[10] — 165, 1 ff.

c. Human "resolving," "undertaking," "purposing," is expressed by προτίθεμαι in R. 1:13 and πρόθεσις in Ac. 11:23; 27:13. Timothy follows the doctrine and mode of life (→ I, 128, 16 ff.) of Paul but also among other things his πρόθεσις, i.e., his aspiration, mind, 2 Tm. 3:10.

d. Paul adopts πρόθεσις in a wholly new sense when he uses it for the primal decision of God whereby the saving event in Christ and the resultant way of the community to eschatological glorifying are established and set in motion. The matter itself is already present in the OT when we are told that God executes what He has resolved of old.[11] The final words of R. 8:28: οἴδαμεν δὲ ὅτι τοῖς ἀγαπῶσιν τὸν θεὸν πάντα συνεργεῖ (→ VII, 875, 12 ff.)[12] εἰς ἀγαθόν, τοῖς κατὰ πρόθεσιν κλητοῖς οὖσιν, are not a lame appendix but point to the sustaining ground of the hope of the community. The existence of the community rests on God's primal decision[13] in which His will to bring to eschatological glory is coincident with His will to affirm the community that stands over against Him in love. πρόθεσις is not a formal thing but has as its content the enduring faithfulness of the One who has decided here.[14] In v. 29 f. there is recapitulation of the event which in virtue of the innermost decision in the heart of God has been and will be executed in the "realities" of the created and fallen world. The decisions of προγινώσκειν and προορίζειν (→ V, 456, 17 ff.) made before and above all time already have as their goal the concrete community (→ II, 396, 24 ff.; VII, 787, 34 ff.) of the firstborn (→ VI, 880, 3 ff.) Son, v. 29. But God remains the subject of the calling and justification enacted in time, v. 30. Paul does not dwell on the dubious contingent aspects of the community but points to the real basis of the event as this is revealed

---

[8] So Peshitta, Orig., Chrys., Ambrosiaster, cf. M. J. Lagrange, S. Paul, Épitre aux Romains (1950), ad loc.

[9] Büchsel (→ III, 321, 17 ff.) wrongly locates the public character of the event in its proclamation.

[10] Zn. R., Ltzm. R., Mi. R.[12], Schl. R., ad loc.; T. W. Manson, "Ἱλαστήριον," JThSt, 46 (1945), 1-9; W. D. Davies, Paul and Rabbinic Judaism (1948), 240 f.; W. G. Kümmel, "πάρεσις u. ἔνδειξις," Heilsgeschehen u. Gesch. (1965), 264; L. Morris, "The Meaning of ἱλαστήριον in R. 3:25," NTSt, 2 (1955/56), 42; E. Käsemann, "Zum Verständnis v. R. 3:24-26," Exeget. Versuche u. Besinnungen, I[3] (1964), 96.

[11] E.g., Is. 25:1; 44:28; 46:10. The Gk. terms here are θέλημα and esp. for עֲצַת בּוּלָה, in Sirach also κρίσις, 16:26.

[12] p[46] B A sa Or[part] put ὁ θεός after συνεργεῖ. But with א C 𝕮 D G bo pl Cl Or[part] we should read the shorter text: "All things work together for good."

[13] κατὰ πρόθεσιν does not ref. to the assent of the called as some fathers proposed, Orig. Comm. in R., 7, 7 (MPG, 14 [1862], 1121 f.); Cyr. Procatechesis, I (33 [1893], 333 f.); Chrys. Hom. in R., 15, 1 (60 [1892], 541); Theod. Mops. In R., ad loc. (66 [1864], 832); Thdrt. Interpretatio epist. ad Romanos, ad loc. (82 [1864], 141). Nor is there, as Aug. Contra duas ep. Pelagianorum, II, 10, 22, MPL, 44 (1865), 536; Contra Julianum, V, 4, 14, MPL, 44 (1865), 792 believes, a distinction between the called and the chosen as in Mt. 22:14.

[14] The decisive difference from the predestination teaching of Jewish apoc. and esp. the Essenes, cf. 1 QS 3:14, 23; 11, 18 f. etc. lies in the content and the personal relation to God.

in Christ. [15] The aorist ἐδόξασεν thus anticipates prophetically the eschatological glorification which is not yet manifested but is at least begun in Christ. [16]

Through treating lightly all the privileges of birth or morality Esau (→ II, 953, 30 ff.) must serve his younger brother that thereby the project of God by election (→ IV, 179, 10 ff.) might stand, R. 9:11. God's πρόθεσις includes a Yes to Israel, yet even in this area it is not rigid, but in each instance decides freely in what way and by what human agents the promise will be fulfilled. There is a special development in Eph. 1:9 ff.: God has revealed the secret of His will to gather up all things in Christ κατὰ τὴν εὐδοκίαν (→ II, 747, 1 ff.) αὐτοῦ, ἣν προέθετο ἐν αὐτῷ "according to the decision of his good-pleasure established from the very first in him (sc. Christ)." προέθετο and κατὰ πρόθεσιν (v. 11) do not denote common resolving or undertaking (→ I, 635, 29 ff.; III, 57, 1 ff.). They are stamped by the προ- which characterises the whole hymn and which indicates the election of Christ's community before all creation, cf. πρὸ καταβολῆς κόσμου προορίσας (v. 5); προορισθέντες (v. 11). In this free decision of God which is primal both temporally and materially there lies the basis of the community's superiority over Gnostic redeemer figures and communities, [17] as echoed yet again in 3:11. The material concreteness of the primal decision of God's will is expressed in the hendiadys in 2 Tm. 1:9: κατὰ ἰδίαν πρόθεσιν καὶ χάριν. Yet there also threatens in this text the danger of severing the fixed decision from the person of God along the lines of a *decretum absolutum* when it is said of this gracious foreordination that it was granted before all ages in Christ and manifested in the present, v. 9.

4. The Post-Apostolic Fathers.

The post-apost. fathers have πρόθεσις only once: serving in a holy and blameless disposition, 1 Cl., 45, 7. The verb means "to undertake" in Herm. m., 12, 3, 5, while elsewhere it ref. to the divine ordination: ἦλθε δὲ ὁ καιρός, ὃν θεὸς προέθετο, Dg., 9, 2.

προστίθημι.

1. In secular Gk. one finds the meaning "to put to," "to add to," of things, e.g., "to put to," i.e., "shut" the doors, Hdt., III, 78, 3, "to add something," e.g., ἐάν τι ἀφέλωμεν ἢ προσθῶμεν ἢ μεταθῶμεν, Plat. Crat., 432a, "to make additions" to agreements or documents, Polyb., 21, 42, 27; mid. "to attach oneself to," e.g., τῇ γνώμῃ, Hdt., I, 109, 2, "to win for oneself," τί ἂν προσθείην; "what would I get by it?" Soph. Ant., 40. Of persons: Ἀθηναίοις προσθεῖναι σφᾶς αὐτούς, "to join the Athenians," "to take up the Athenian party," Thuc., III, 92, 2; mid. "to win over someone," "to bring him to one's side," Soph. Oed. Col., 404, τινὰ πολέμιον, "to make oneself an enemy," Xenoph. Cyrop., II, 4, 12, "to attach oneself to someone," Soph. Oed. Col., 1332; Jos. Vit., 87 and 123.

2. In the LXX a. some three quarters of the 290 odd ref. are a Hebraising rendering of יָסַף etc., e.g., προσέθηκεν τεκεῖν, Gn. 4:2; προσθεῖσα ἔτι ἔτεκεν, 38:5, also mid., e.g., προσθέμενος ἔλαβεν, Gn. 25:1 etc., in the oath τάδε ποιήσαι ὁ θεός τινι καὶ

---

[15] Mi. R.[12], 211, n. 2 rightly stresses that πρόθεσις is not a theological speculation but that the *extra nos* is safeguarded here.

[16] Acc. to Zn. R., Schl. R., *ad loc.* Paul has in view what has already taken place, while acc. to Ltzm. R., *ad loc.* we have anticipatory future certainty. But one must not make the tension into an either-or, cf. R. 5:10.

[17] Cf. C. Maurer, "Der Hymnus v. Eph. 1 als Schlüssel zum ganzen Brief," EvTh, 11 (1951/52), 154-157.

τάδε προσθείη, 1 S. 25:22. b. In the other instances the usage follows that of secular Gk. One need only note a few OT peculiarities. For the alternation with προτίθημι → 165, n. 2. Cf. also μὴ προστίθεσθε καρδίαν, "set not your heart on" in ψ 61:11. Worth noting is the idea of heaping up quantitatively understood praise or wrong, e.g., προσθήσω ἐπὶ πᾶσαν τὴν αἴνεσίν σου, I will increase thy praise," ψ 70:14; ἐπὶ ταῖς ἁμαρτίαις ἡμῶν, "to add even more to our sins," 2 Ch. 28:13; ἁμαρτίας ἐφ᾿ ἁμαρτίαις, Is. 30:1; Sir. 3:27, but πρόσθες ἀνομίαν ἐπὶ τὴν ἀνομίαν αὐτῶν, "reckon to their account fault on fault" (נתן\), ψ 68:28. For incorporation in a society one has προσθείη κύριος ὁ θεός σου πρὸς τὸν λαόν, 2 S. 24:3; cf. Dt. 23:16; προστεθήσονται... πρὸς τοὺς ὑπεναντίους, "they will make common cause with the foe" (יסף ni), Ex. 1:10; τοῖς ἔθνεσιν, "to join the peoples" (דבק) Jos. 23:12; aliens let themselves be accepted into the community of Israel (לוה; ספח ni), Is. 14:1; cf. Ez. 37:16; Jdt. 14:10; 1 Macc. 8:1 etc. αὐτῷ προστεθήσεσθε (דבק), "you should cling to him (sc. God)," Dt. 13:5. Some 20 times the pass. corresponds to אסף ni; "to be gathered to his fathers, to die," Gn. 25:8 etc., cf. Ac. 13:36.

3. In the NT a. some Hebraisms (→ 167, 37 ff.) are to be translated by a simple "again," "further," so Mk. 14:25 vl.; Lk. 19:11 etc. b. Then the verb is used for "to add" things, e.g., the additional measure in reciprocal measuring (Mk. 4:24), further words to a speech (Hb. 12:19), an act to speech (Lk. 3:20), a cubit to the span of life (→ II, 942, 22 ff.; Mt. 6:27 and par.); these things (sc. food and clothing) will be added, Mt. 6:33 and par., though it may be asked whether the meaning here is not just "to give," "to hand over." The same applies to Lk. 17:5: πρόσθες ἡμῖν πίστιν, "Lord, confer faith on us." Gl. 3:19 is to be understood in the context of Paul's doctrine of the Law. As compared with the line of promise from Abraham to Christ the Law is only a temporally restricted interlude which began after the promise (→ II, 582, 22 ff.; Gl. 3:17, cf. R. 5:20) and which was ended by the coming of the promised seed (Gl. 3:25, cf. R. 7:6; 8:1 f.). c. The incorporation of men into a society, as it is found already in the OT (→ lines 8 ff.), occurs 4 times in Ac. Neither 2:41 nor 2:47 has the obj. to which one is added: ὁ δὲ κύριος προσετίθει τοὺς σῳζομένους καθ᾿ ἡμέραν ἐπὶ τὸ αὐτό [1] (Ac. 2:47, cf. v. 41). προσετίθεντο πιστεύοντες τῷ κυρίῳ in 5:14 is to be translated after the analogy of καὶ προσετέθη ὄχλος ἱκανὸς τῷ κυρίῳ in 11:24: "Believers were continually added to the Lord." [2]

4. In the post-apost. fathers προστίθεμαι occurs in the sense of יסף "to continue," "to do further," Barn., 2, 5; 1 Cl., 12, 7, etc. Other meanings are "to add" nothing to a matter and to take away nothing, Barn., 19, 11; Did., 4, 13, "to add" debauchery to the sins, Herm. v., 2, 2, 2; προστίθημι ταῖς ἁμαρτίαις, "to apply oneself to sins," "to stay in them," "to increase them," 6, 1, 4 etc.; εἰς δὲ τὸ προσθεῖναι δικαιοσύνην καὶ γνῶσιν κυρίου, "to the augmenting of righteousness and the knowledge of the Lord," Did., 11, 2.

Maurer

προστίθημι. [1] The addition of the dat. obj. [ἐν] τῇ ἐκκλησίᾳ by D 𝔐 E pl is secondary. ἐπὶ τὸ αὐτό is an OT expression, not a substitute for an absent dat., cf. Haench. Ag.13, ad loc. One should transl. "altogether."
[2] So with Haench. Ag.13 against Bauernf. Ag., ad loc. In any case the pass. is to be preferred to the mid. "they joined." The pass. pts. to God as the logical subj.

---

† τιμή, † τιμάω

A. The Word Group in Greek and Hellenistic Literature.

I. Meanings.

Gen. τιμή [1] means 1. the "worth" one ascribes to a person, i.e., "satisfaction," "compensation," "evaluation," "honour"; 2. (only after Hom.) the value of a thing, "price," "purchase price."

In detail [2] τιμή denotes 1. legal "appraisal," "compensation," "penalty," "satisfaction," Hom. Il., 1, 159; 3, 286, 288, 459; 5, 552; Od., 22, 57 etc., but not often in prose; similarly τιμάω can mean "to assess an offence," "to fix the penalty due," with the penalty in the gen. θανάτου τιμάω, "to sentence to death," Plat. Gorg., 516a; cf. Leg., VIII, 843b; IX, 879b, 880c; Aristoph. Vesp., 106. 2. "Value," "honour," usually ascribed to an exalted personage, "regard" or "respect" paid to another, Xenoph. Mem., II, 1, 33. Similarly τιμάω means a. act. "to value," "to show honour," Hom. Od., 14, 203; 15, 365; Aesch. Suppl., 115; Isoc. Or., 9, 42; Xenoph. An., I, 9, 14; V, 8, 25; Cyrop., III, 3, 6; Hdt., VII, 213, 3; b. pass. "to be deemed worthy of an honour." Hom. Il., personages, e.g., Eur. Iph. Aul., 19; cf. οἱ τετιμημένοι, "men who are in high positions," Xenoph. Cyrop., VIII, 3, 9. 3. "Honorary office," then "office" gen., Hdt., I, 59, 6 etc.; τιμαὶ καὶ ἀρχαί, "honorary and state officials," Plat. Resp., VIII, 549c; Xenoph. Cyrop., I, 2, 15. τιμή is also used to denote a king's prerogatives, Hom. Od., 1, 117; Hes. Theog., 347. 4. "Dignity" and the related authority, e.g., divine, Hom. Od., 5, 335; Il., 9, 498; 15, 189, or royal, Il., 1, 278; 2, 197; 6, 193. 5. "Honorarium," Diog. L., V, 72; Preis. Zaub., I, 4, 2454. 6. "Honours," "distinctions," "awards," Hom. Il., 1, 510; 4, 410; 9, 608; Soph. Phil., 1062; Plat. Leg., I, 632b; τιμαὶ καὶ δωρεαί, Plat. Resp., II, 361c; similarly τιμάω means "to make a present," "to reward," Xenoph. An., VII, 3, 29; τιμάω καὶ δωρέομαι, "to distinguish and confer an award," Xenoph. Cyrop., III, 2, 28; VIII, 2, 10, with ἐπαινέω "to commend" and "to reward," I, 2, 12. 7. Very significant is the religious use: a. θεῶν τιμή, "worship of God," Plat. Leg., IV, 723e. The task of men is θεῷ τιμὴν διδόναι, Eur. Ba., 342, cf. Aesch. Choeph., 200; Eur. Heracl., 903; Soph. Oed. Col., 277, 1070 f.; Aristoph. Pl., 93, cf. also σέβομαι καὶ τιμάω, Xenoph. Mem., II, 3, 13; cf. Diod. S., 6, 4, 8; Dio Chrys. Or., 33, 45; 75, 8; Ael. Arist. Or., 13 (Dindorf, I, 297); cf. also τι[μ]ῶν σὴν ἀρετήν, ὦναξ, ὥσπερ τὸ δίκαιον, IG, 4, 950, 79; b. Of the gods taking an interest in men, Hom. Il., 15, 612; 17, 99; 23, 788; Pind. Olymp., 1, 55; Soph. Ant., 288. c. The belief that certain men are honoured and esp. blessed by the gods is an ancient one in Greece and it appears in Asia Minor

---

τ ι μ ή κ τ λ . [1] Behind the noun τιμή is τίω "to value," "to esteem highly," "to honour," which was known to Hom. (in prose replaced by τιμάω) and is usually combined with τίνω, "to make amends for" etc. (root qʷei and qʷi), cf. Boisacq, Hofmann, s.v. [Risch]. Cf. also M. Greindl, Κλεος, κυδος, ευχος, τιμη, φατις, δοξα, Diss. Munich (1938), 59, who thinks the original sense of τιμή is "compensation," also E. Pfister, "Die Hekata-Episode in Hesiods Theogonie," Philol., 84 (1929), 5.

[2] On the rich and many-faceted meaning of the word group cf. Liddell-Scott, Pape, s.v., For Hom. cf. H. Ebeling, Lex. Homericum, II (1963), s.v.

particularly in connection with Hecate and other deities. [3] Most instructive is the hymn to Hecate, Hes. Theog., 411-428, [4] whose theme is the τιμή of the goddess and her δύναμις. Because of this δύναμις she is invoked by men in sacrifice, [5] for the gods grant happiness, wealth and power in virtue of their own τιμή and δύναμις. This comes out strongly in Hom. Hymn., 3, 469 f. etc.; in 24, 4 f. τιμή is synon. with δύναμις, and the τιμή of the gods is lauded in 4, 37; 29, 3; τιμή and δύναμις are also closely connected in Plut. Def. Orac., 21 (II, 421e). d. In religious usage τιμαί are then the marks of esteem which characterise divine worship, [6] Ditt. Or., I, 56, 9: τιμαὶ τῶν θεῶν, i.e., institutions for worship of the deity, cultic feasts, sacrifices, e.g., Aesch. Pers., 622; Eur. Herc. Fur., 853; Soph. Oed. Tyr., 909; Oed. Col., 1007; then gen. for donations to the gods, Hes. Op., 142. 8. "Evaluation of a matter," "value," price," Plat. Leg., XI, 914c; P. Tebt., III, 703, 176 (3rd cent. B.C.) etc. In keeping is the verb τιμάω in the sense "to appraise," "to tax," "to rate," "to fix the value or price," Thuc., III, 40, 7; IV, 26, 7, also inscr., e.g., P. Greci e Latini, 4, 382, 15 (248/7 B.C.) and pap., e.g., P. Flor., II, 266 etc. [7] 9. The abs. use of the gen. τιμῆς "against payment, cash payment." Hdt., VII, 119, 2; P. Tebt., I, 5, 185, 194 (118 B.C.); BGU, III, 1002, 13 (55 B.C.) etc. [8]

II. The Concept of Honour.

τιμή has in the first instance a strong material orientation. Odysseus' honour is inseparably bound up with the restoration of control of his possessions, Hom. Od., 1, 117. Achilles' honour is functionally dependent on the number of gifts brought to him to persuade him to take part in the battle, Il. 9, 605. [9] Here bodily soundness, the undisputed exercise of social influence and uninfringed enjoyment of one's property are the basis of esteem. [10] Later the noun is used in a more strongly ethical context. A certain type of

---

[3] On this A. D. Nock, "Stud. in the Graeco-Roman Beliefs of the Empire," JHS, 45 (1925), 100 f.; also "Σύνναος Θεός," Harvard Stud. in Class. Philology, 41 (1930), 50; Reitzenstein Hell. Myst., 252-4. With Paus., X, 32, 13 (honoured by the goddess Isis) one may ref. esp. to the three Phrygian inscr. discussed in Nock, 100 (Waddington, III, 805; J. Keil and A. v. Premerstein, Zweiter Bericht über eine zweite Reise in Lydien 241, DA Wien, 54 [1911], 130; W. M. Ramsay, "The Cities and Bishoprics of Phrygia," JHS, 4 [1883], 419 f.); in these men in much the same terms are called τιμηθέντες ὑπὸ Σωτείρης Ἑκάτης. Cf. also Sappho Fr., 112 (ed. E. Lobel and D. Page [1955], 89); Schol. in Pind. Pyth., 3, 153a (ed. A. B. Drachmann, II [1910], 84, 22); Plut. Quaest. Graec., 28 (II, 297e); Cleanthes Fr., 537 (v. Arnim, I, 123, 2).
[4] Pfister, op. cit., 1-9.
[5] Pfister, 6: "Because she (the goddess) has δύναμις, she has τιμή, and her τιμή consists in her δύναμις."
[6] Cf. F. Stippel, "Ehre u. Ehrerziehung in d. Antike," Kulturphilosophische, philosophie-gesch. u. erziehungswissenschaftliche Stud., 7 (1959), 10: "The true nature of Gk. worship and Gk. piety is expressed in the honour paid to the deity: to be pious is to 'honour the gods.'"
[7] On the mid. cf. Mitteis-Wilcken, 224a.
[8] Cf. Bl.-Debr. § 179, 1.
[9] Cf. H. Schrade, Götter u. Menschen Homers (1952), 221-4; Stippel, op. cit., 6-15, W. Schadewaldt, Von Homers Welt u. Werk[3] (1959), 175, 182, 220.
[10] [Lines 18-23 based on Dihle.] Cf. also M. P. Nilsson, "Götter u. Psychologie bei Hom.," ARW, 22 (1923/24), 365: "Homer's concept of honour is shot through by naive delight in property and costly gifts. The greater the gift, the more the honour." Similarly Schrade, op. cit., 214, who stresses that Hom. has no sense of abstract honour, since for him it is always linked to material possessions or gifts. Stippel, op. cit., 15 maintains that the whole structure of Homeric man is most deeply and persistently influenced and interpenetrated by honour. In this connection ref. is made to the link with τιμωρία, τιμωρέω. The latter means "to have regard to one's honour," i.e., to reverse or avenge its violation. The sense "to punish" is possible only when justice which has executive power replaces individual action [Dihle].

moral conduct is prerequisite for the esteem a man enjoys. Gradually τιμή detaches itself from real possessions and becomes an abstract concept of honour. That the original elements in the meaning of the word were never wholly lost can be seen in the fact that in the *koine* τιμή can mean both "honour" and "price." If in the early Greek period [11] honour as esteem by society on account of concrete circumstances was one of the highest values among the nobility of the 8th cent. B.C. (Hom.), in the city states, esp. Sparta and Athens, the honour of the individual was also that of the *polis*. When under the influence of Sophism the individual came to be increasingly detached from the *polis* the concept of honour became much more individualistic, esp. in Isocrates. But Plato was the first to establish the personal ethical element in honour, or "inward honour," though without absolutely rejecting "outward honour" (the distinctions accorded a man by the world around). In relation to this wise moderation is to be commended. [12] Plato, then, finally anchored honour in the moral person. The most significant attempt to provide a scientifically grounded ethics of honour was that made by Aristot. The discussion in Eth. Nic., IV, 7, p. 1123b, in which he speaks of μεγαλοψυχία, is basic here. The high-minded man must be virtuous, for there is no honour without virtue. He thus possesses honour on the basis of inner worth. By reason of his ἀρετή honour is then shown him from without, by his fellow-citizens. If at bottom the high-minded man can only give himself the honour worthy of his virtue, he is in the last analysis above "outward honour." But there is no honour worthy of perfect virtue. In the Aristot. concept of honour, there is thus a strong individualistic tendency, though the solidarity of the *polis* is not destroyed, for man is by nature a creature destined for political society. Finally Stoicism brought the individualistic concept of honour to its full development. In it "inward honour," the sense of one's own worth, is decisive. Stoic philosophy was not against every kind of outward honour, but the wise man is relaxed in relation to it; he does not chase it and can do without it. This attitude corresponds to the inner freedom which rules his thought. From the various standpoints the teaching of honour was of great importance among the Greeks and Romans.

B. The Word Group in Hellenistic Judaism.

I. The Septuagint.

The OT requirement to honour parents (Ex. 20:12), and more broadly to act morally in accordance with Yahweh's commandments (Gn. 38:23; 1 S. 15:30; 2 S. 6:20), is not unlike the Gk. concept of τιμή (→ 169, 11 ff., 25 ff.), but this is an exception, and it is no surprise that in Hbr. there is no exact equivalent to τιμάω κτλ. Through the influence of the Alexandrian school the Gk. terms penetrated increasingly into the world of ideas developed by Judaism. In the LXX they are most common in the later writings which do not belong to the Hbr. canon. [13]

---

[11] On the history of the τιμή concept cf. esp. Stippel, *op. cit.*, 15-57 with examples and specialised bibl.

[12] Cf. on this W. Venske, *Plato u. der Ruhm. Ein Beitrag z. Gesch. d. griech. Ruhmesidee*, Diss. Kiel (1937), 30-34.

[13] In Palest. Aram. one finds the loan word טִים in the sense 1. "worth," "price," "value," 2. "equivalent," cf. Dalman Wört., Levy Wört., II, Krauss Lehnw., II, *s.v.*; cf. I, 216. On the Rabb. concept of honour cf. Str.-B., I, 917; II, 553-6, and esp. Ab., 2, 10; 4, 12, 21; bBer., 19b. For valuable insights into its ethical basis cf. J. Lewkowitz, Art. "Ehre," *Jüd. Lex.*, II (1928), 275 f.: "The commandment to pay heed to a man's honour applies not only to servants in relation to their masters, children in relation to their parents and citizens in relation to the king, but also between equals. The man of high degree must not violate the honour of those beneath him. Judaism seeks to ennoble human life by demanding self-esteem and regard for others."

1. τιμή is used for 12 Hbr. words, mostly יָקָר ,יְקָר ,עֵרֶך ,כָּבוֹד. [14] The most important meanings are a. "honour." In the first instance this is the honour which is due to God and which is to be and is shown Him; men are commanded to bring Him δόξα and τιμή ψ 28:1; 95:7; cf. Job 34:19. Then it is the honour which comes to man from God. God has crowned δόξῃ καὶ τιμῇ "with glory and honour" the man whom He created in His image, ψ 8:6. Earthly goods are almost always connected with honour. Sacred garments help to honour and adorn the high-priest, Ex. 28:2. In the description of the resplendent appearance of Aaron in Sir. 45:12 the head-piece which adorns him is called καύχημα τιμῆς. In Job 40:10 Job is challenged to come forward in divine majesty and deck himself with glory and pomp (δόξα καὶ τιμή). In the Wisdom lit. there is a stronger ethical emphasis. Thus to do good is to gain the esteem of others. Association with wisdom esp. confers praise among men and regard among the elders, Wis. 8:10. Sir. 3:11 declares that the fame a man has depends on the honour his father possesses. But in Sir. 10:28 the son is admonished humbly to render to himself only the honour he deserves. The fool has no honour, Prv. 26:1. Finally τιμή means showing honour to others. Wives owe respect to their husbands, Est. 1:20. The word also means b. "payment," Job 31:39, esp. honorarium for services (the doctor), Sir. 38:1, "price," Gn. 44:2; Nu. 20:19; Ep. Jer. 24 (the senseless acquisition of idols at a price), "compensation," "damages," Gn. 20:16, "ransom," τιμὴ τῆς λυτρώσεως, ψ 48:9, "payment" for the redemption of the firstborn, Ex. 34:20. Lv. 5:15, 18 gives instructions on assessing faults with a view to fixing the price of expiation. In Lv. 27:2-27 there are precise rulings on the estimation of vows and dues. Here τιμή is used for עֵרֶך. We then find c. "valuables," "treasure," e.g., Ez. 22:25 the unlawful taking of valuables; on Sir. 45:12 → line 7 f. d. The sense "tax" occurs once in 1 Macc. 10:29: the letter of king Demetrius assures the Jews that the tribute, the salt tax (τιμὴ τοῦ ἁλός) and the crown tax are remitted. e. In Da. we find the following combinations with similar terms: τιμὴ καὶ χάρις, 1:9; βασιλεία, ἰσχύς, τιμή and δόξα are given to the king by God, 2:37; similarly 5:18 Θ: God has given Nebuchadnezzar τὴν βασιλείαν καὶ τὴν μεγαλωσύνην καὶ τὴν τιμὴν καὶ τὴν δόξαν, cf. δόματα, δωρεαί and τιμή, 2:6 Θ. To the Son of Man was given ἡ ἀρχὴ καὶ ἡ τιμὴ καὶ ἡ βασιλεία, 7:14 Θ, cf. also δόξα καὶ τιμή, 1 Macc. 14:21; votive offerings πρὸς αὔξησιν καὶ δόξαν τοῦ τόπου καὶ τιμήν, 2 Macc. 5:16; Nebuchadnezzar declares Babylon is built εἰς τιμὴν τῆς δόξης μου, Δα. 4:30 (27); cf. also τιμὴ καὶ εὔνοια, 2 Macc. 9:21. f. Another sense is "royal dignity," Da. 5:20 Θ. g. Finally one finds "honourable conduct," i.e., martyrdom in 4 Macc. 1:10. 2 Macc. 4:15 tells how the high-priest Jason caused the priests to attend games contrary to the Law, "regarding native honours (τὰς μὲν πατρῴους τιμάς) [15] as nought but viewing Greek glories (τὰς δὲ Ἑλληνικὰς δόξας) as very splendid."

2. τιμάω [16] occurs for 6 Hbr. words, [17] chiefly כבד pi and pu, ערך hi and עֵרֶך, in the sense a. "to honour," e.g., God, Is. 29:13; Prv. 3:9 etc., the king, Wis. 14:17, parents, Ex. 20:12; Dt. 5:16, the old man, Lv. 19:32, the poor, Prv. 14:31, the loyal slave, Prv. 27:18, the doctor, Sir. 38:1, the temple, 2 Macc. 3:2, 12; 13:23; 3 Macc. 3:16. The commandment to honour parents is esp. pressed in Sir. 3:3, 5, 8 with a ref. to the blessing resting on observance of this commandment, cf. also Tob 4:3. Prv. 3:9 stresses the Law's demand

---

[14] Cf. in detail Schleusner, V, 511.

[15] The expression is difficult. It ref. to honourable conduct which is right by strict Jewish tradition or to honours corresponding to the statutes of the Law.

[16] Cf. Schleusner, V, 510.

[17] Apart from the 6 roots in Hatch-Redp., s.v. one might also mention חקר "to investigate," "prove" (cf. τιμάω "to appraise") in Prv. 25:2, 27; cf. also מְחִיר in Prv. 27:26; LXX often has δοξάζω and δόξα for כבד and כָּבוֹד where Σ has τιμάω and τιμή, e.g., 2 Βασ. 10:3; ψ 65:2; 72:24 [Bertram].

that one should honour the Lord with gifts from one's substance and with first-fruits of the whole harvest. Wis. 6:21 admonishes the rulers of the world to honour wisdom, cf. Prv. 4:8; "Exalt wisdom, and she shall bring thee to honour." Wis. 14:15, 17 warns against honouring the picture of a man, esp. the earthly king, as a god. 4 Mac. 17:20 says of martyrs that they are honoured not merely with heavenly honour but also by the fact that for their sakes the enemy has no further power over God's chosen people. Special note should be taken of ψ 138:17 where the pass. τιμῶμαι means "to be valuable." The HT is אֵל רֵעֶיךָ יָּקְרוּ־מַה־לִּי, "how precious (weighty, hard to grasp) are thy thoughts for me, O God"; LXX runs: ἐμοὶ δὲ λίαν ἐτιμήθησαν οἱ φίλοι σου, ὁ θεός. [18] τιμάω then means b. "to appraise," "determine the worth," Lv. 27:8-14 → 172, 21. It can also mean c. "to honour with money," "reward," Nu. 22:17, 37, and d. "to grant support," Est. 9:3.

II. Philo.

The following senses occur. 1. In Philo the τιμὴ θεοῦ and the τιμὴ γονέων are to the fore. Honour and veneration are due to God because He is the one true God, Leg. Gaj., 347, the Creator of all things, 293, the αὐτοκράτωρ, 301 and 305, the great King, Decal., 61. [19] Parents have a claim to honour, respect, esteem on the basis of the 4th (5th) commandment, Rer. Div. Her., 171; Vit. Mos., II, 207; Decal., 51, 106, 121, 165; Spec. Leg., II, 261; III, 21 etc. The aged, too, are worthy of highest honour, Sacr. AC, 77. Honour also belongs to the temple, Leg. Gaj., 16, and the Sabbath, Spec. Leg., II, 149. 2. "Dignity" (divine) is the sense in Vit. Mos., II, 67. 3. The word often means "value," "price," "tax (rate)," "assessment," in Spec. Leg., II, e.g., II, 32, 33, 36, 113, 233. 4. Worth noting and very typical of Philo are the combinations which interrelate inward and outward values, e.g., πλοῦτος, δόξα, ἀρχαί, τιμαὶ καὶ ὅσα τούτων ἀδελφά, Det. Pot. Ins., 122, δόξα, πλοῦτος, τιμαί, ἀρχαί, Cher., 117, χρυσός, ἄργυρος, δόξα, τιμαί, ἀρχαί, Leg. All., II, 107, ἀξίωμα, τιμή, εὔκλεια, Sacr. AC, 16; ἀρχαί, τιμαί, εὐδοξία, Praem. Poen., 107, δόξαι καὶ τιμαί, Abr., 264.

III. Josephus.

1. The noun, often plur., means predominantly in Jos. a. "honour," "honouring," esp. of prominent people and not infrequently with gifts, titles, or possessions, e.g. honouring with the title of Caesar in Bell., 2, 208 or king in 1, 461, cf. 194, 200, 207. The king can claim marks of honour by reason of his position, Ant., 6, 67. Then the ref. is b. to the "cultic honour" to be shown to God, Ant., 1, 156; acc. to 1, 172 νενομισμέναι τιμαί are due to God. The goal of εὐσέβεια is the "veneration" of God, 8, 208; 9, 53; 11, 120; the opp. is dishonouring disdain. [20] c. The word is used specially in Jos. for the "dignity" of the high-priest, Ant., 3, 188; 12, 42, 157 etc. d. "Distinction" and "reward," e.g., with raiment or other valuables, Bell., 2, 165, 488; 3, 408, "recognition" for something specific, Bell., 2, 96, cf. gen. δῶρα καὶ τιμή in Ant., 1, 297. e. "Price," e.g., for land, Bell., 2, 285, cf. 592; Ant., 2, 118, 120, 124; 4, 284; Vit., 153. f. Special expressions are ἐν τιμῇ ἔχω, "to hold in honour," Ant., 2, 39; εἰς τιμὴν παρελθεῖν, "to come to honour," 2, 57; ἀξιοῦμαι τιμῆς, "to be highly honoured," 2, 258. The favourite combination of τιμή with δόξα is also common in Jos., e.g., Ant., 12, 118.

---

[18] The LXX text probably rests on the fact it understood רֵע as "fellow," "friend," cf. Field, II, 294. On the HT cf. F. Baethgen, Die Ps., Handkomm. AT, II, 2² (1897), ad loc.
[19] Of the many examples ref. may be made to Vit. Mos., II, 173, 177, 273; Spec. Leg., I, 20, 57, 65, 70, 195, 317; II, 146; III, 29, 125; Virt., 179, 181; Leg. Gaj., 290.
[20] Cf. on this Schl. Theol. d. Judt., 99.

2. The verb τιμάω usually means a. "to honour," "to show honour." The obj. are men in Ant., 2, 123, first parents, 3, 92, then esp. the king, 6, 80; 9, 153; but the chief obj. is God, 6, 21. Like God, sanctuaries also have a claim to "cultic veneration," Ant., 1, 316. Another sense is b. "to reward," "to make presentations," Bell., 1, 511 and 646; Ant., 1, 314. c. Pass. "to stand in honour," Bell., 1, 16 and 576; Ant., 3, 49; οἱ ὑφ' Ἡρώδου τετιμημένοι are Herod's favourites, Bell., 2, 7; Moses is called ὁ ὑπὸ τοῦ θεοῦ τετιμημένος, "the honoured of God," Ant., 3, 38.

C. The Word Group in the New Testament.

I. τιμή.

1. Honour.

a. "Honour": In R. 12:10 Paul directs Christians to give one another the preference in honour. [21] In 1 Tm. 6:1 slaves are admonished (→ II, 899, 6 ff.) to show all honour to their masters in order that the opposite course should not prejudice the name of God and Christian teaching. [22] 1 Pt. 3:7 summons men to give their wives the honour due to them, since their weaker nature lays on the husband the obligation of loving regard, → I, 785, 31 ff.; III, 857, 18 ff. In 1 Th. 4:4 τιμή is the respect which is to be shown to the wife, to which she has a claim as a creature of God. [23] In R. 13:7 the apostle asks of Christians that they should concede to all men what they owe them. In particular they are to pay to the state not only the taxes it may claim but also due fear and respect, i.e., the ready recognition which finds expression in obedience. [24]

b. "Esteem," "dignity," "recognition": In Jn. 4:44 the Evangelist refers to a saying which Jesus once pronounced: A prophet finds no recognition in his own country. [25]

The combining of τιμή and δόξα, which is a familiar one in Hellenistic thought

---

[21] Mi. R.[12], ad loc. conjectures that Paul is hitting at the ambition of the charismatics and their false claim to leadership. The charismatic should esteem the honour of others more highly than his own. προηγοῦμαι can be transl. in different ways: 1. "to forestall others in matter of honour," 2. "to precede others in showing honour," "to surpass them" (in the sense of προτιμάω). We have here a par. to Phil. 2:3. Michel transl.: "Let each give preference to the other in showing honour." Acc. to O. H. Nebe, Die Ehre als theol. Problem (1936), 26 and 74 honour is a basic concept in public life and a basic order of life in society.
[22] Cf. J. Jeremias, Die Br. an Tm. u. Tt., NT Deutsch, 9⁸ (1963), ad loc.: "Slave service must be a witness to the Gospel by deed."
[23] So also Dob. Th. on 4:4 f. For explicit discussion cf. C. Masson, Les deux ép. de S. Paul aux Thess., Comment. du NT, 11a (1957) on 4:4, who equates ἐν τιμῇ with "dans l'honneur" and comments: "Un chrétien aura de ce qui est honorable et déshonorable une idée plus précise que le païen, car pour lui est déshonorable tout ce qui manque au respect dû à la personne et aux droits du prochain, tout ce qui est incompatible avec l'ἀγάπη."
[24] Jewish traditions already mention fear and honour when describing the relation of the righteous to the state, cf. Str.-B., III, 305, also 1 Pt. 2:17. Mi. R.[12], ad loc.: "The relation to the state authority is in the deepest sense one of obligation. It is not just a matter of financial dues in taxes and tolls but of inner attitude in respect and honour. There is allusion to R. 13:7 in Mart. Pol., 10, 2 which enjoins that due τιμή be shown the divinely instituted ἀρχαί and ἐξουσίαι.
[25] Jn. 4:44 is a variant of the dominical saying in Mk. 6:4 par.; the saying has a better basis in the Synoptic tradition than in Jn. On the history of exposition v. Bultmann J., 150, n. 6.

and usage (→ 172, 35 f.; 173, 21 ff., 40), occurs in christological statements in 2 Pt. and Hb. 2 Pt. 1:17 speaks of the transfiguration of Jesus. While the two terms do not occur in Mk. 9:2-8 and Mt. 17:1-8 — Lk. alone has ἐν δόξῃ in 9:31 — a decisive statement in 2 Pt. is that at the transfiguration on the mount Jesus received honour and glory from the Father. τιμή and δόξα are associated in Hb. 2:7, 9 and 3:3. Hb. 2:6-8a is a quotation from Ps. 8:5-7 LXX, where man's position in creation is denoted by the words δόξα and τιμή. But that which according to the wording of the Ps. must be applied to man generally or to the individual (υἱὸς ἀνθρώπου) is related by the author of Hb. to Christ, 2:9 (→ III, 1089, 26 ff.). Christ's passion is the presupposition of His crowning with glory and honour. [26] This crowning is obviously His institution into the high-priestly office. [27] The terms δόξα and τιμή thus refer not so much to the glorifying and exalting of Christ [28] as to His high-priestly dignity. [29] The reference might well be to the position of honour which He assumes as the heavenly High-priest. In Hb. 3:3 Christ and Moses are compared in respect of their δόξα and τιμή. As the Son of God Christ is far superior to the representative of the old covenant. Certainly the position of Moses was most honourable. To him was entrusted the guiding of the "house" of Israel, and of his faithfulness as a servant of God there is no doubt. But since he himself was only part of the house, he is far behind its founder in glory (dignity), → V, 125, 16 ff. [30] The superiority of Christ over Moses may be deduced from the very wording of Nu. 12:7. [31] When δόξα and τιμή are associated, δόξα is the higher term. τιμή in the sense of a position of honour constitutes only one part of δόξα. [32] In Hb. 5:4 τιμή has very plainly the sense of "dignity of office." Aaron did not take his high-priestly "dignity" to himself but received it by divine calling, Ex. 28:1 f. In the same way Christ was instituted in the high-priestly office by God (→ III, 275, 19 ff.; 277, 17 ff.). But this is an eternal priesthood after the order of Melchisedec. [33]

In 1 Pt. 2:7 Christians are said to possess "honour." [34] They get a share in the honour of Christ because they are fitted as living stones into the holy house whose foundation is Christ, the elect whom God holds in honour. The saying is not eschatological. [35] It refers rather to the present close connection between the λίθοι

---

[26] Cf. on this J. Héring, L'Ép. aux Hb., Comment. du NT, 12 (1954) on 2:7 The crowning is a sign of royal power and supernatural dignity. On δόξα and τιμή loc. cit.: "Le premier terme (δόξα) insiste un peu plus sur la dignité supernaturale, tandis que l'autre (τιμή) rappelle plutôt l'autorité sur tous les êtres."

[27] Cf. also Mi. Hb. on 2:9, n. 3.

[28] So Rgg. Hb. on 2:9; Héring, op. cit., 32.

[29] Cf. H. Strathmann, Der Br. an d. Hb., NT Deutsch, 9⁸ (1963) on 2:9.

[30] Cf. Héring on 3:3: "Nous supposons une ellipse: quoique Moïse fût fidèle, le Christ lui est supérieur, car il reçut une dignité supérieure (πλείονος... δόξης... ἠξίωται). Pourquoi? La réponse nous est donnée en v. 3b: Jésus a construit lui-même une maison, à savoir la nouvelle alliance, tandis que Moïse ne fût même pas l'architecte de l'ancienne."

[31] Cf. on this Mi. Hb., ad loc.

[32] Mi. Hb. on 5:4, n. 4 ref. to the fact that Jewish exegesis in Nu.r. on 16:35 (441) expresses the thought that Aaron received his high-priestly dignity from God. Thus the statement in Hb. is fashioned by the thought and wording of a distinct tradition.

[33] On this cf. Strathmann, op. cit. (→ n. 29) on 5:4-6 and C. Spicq, L'Ép. aux Hb., II² (1953), ad loc., who defines the τιμή (of Christ) as "dignité divine"; G. Friedrich, "Messianische Hohepriestererwartung in d. Synpt.," ZThK, 53 (1956), 310 f., cf. 303.

[34] The difficult passage (cf. F. W. Beare, The First Ep. of Peter² [1958], ad loc.) is to be construed in such a way that τιμή refers back to λίθον... ἔντιμον in v. 6.

[35] But cf. Kn. Pt., ad loc., who takes the view that ἡ τιμή is meant eschatologically.

ζῶντες and Christ the λίθος ζῶν. [36] To translate ἡ τιμή by "costly possession" does not quite do justice to the context. 1 Pt. 1:7 has in view the suffering of Christians. If they hold fast in suffering, there will be imparted to them at Christ's *parousia* ἔπαινος "praise," δόξα "glory," and τιμή "honour." [37] According to 1 C. 12:23, 24 special honour in the whole organism of the community is to be granted to those Christians to whom is given no striking χάρισμα. By the τιμή shown them they are set on an equal footing with other members of the community. [38] In the metaphor of the different vessels found in a big household 2 Tm. 2:20 f. makes it clear that the rise of false teachers (→ VII, 364, 29 ff.) is not surprising. [39] There are vessels which serve honourable uses (εἰς τιμήν) and others which serve dishonourable uses (εἰς ἀτιμίαν). The job of individual members of the community is to purge themselves of the refuse of error so that they may be vessels with an honourable calling, serviceable to God in every good work. The metaphor presupposes that τιμή can mean "(high) price" of things as well as "honour" of persons. Similarly R. 9:21 says: As the potter makes vessels εἰς τιμήν and others εἰς ἀτιμίαν from the same clay, so God in the sovereignty of His creative power has the freedom in execution of His purposes in human history to make some into vessels of wrath and others into vessels of mercy; [40] σκεῦος εἰς τιμήν is the vessel to which the use for which it is destined brings honour. According to R. 2:7, 10 δόξα, τιμή and ἀφθαρσία are the reward which men will receive in the Last Judgment if they have done good in fulfilment of God's will. [41] That this is not Paul's last word in the matter may be seen from R. 3:9-20.

2. Honorarium.

The interpretation of 1 Tm. 5:17 (→ VI, 666, 27 ff.; 702, 20 ff.) [42] is disputed. The saying may mean that presbyters should be more honoured than simple members of

---

[36] Cf. Beare, *op. cit., ad loc.*; K. H. Schelkle, *Die Petrusbr., Herders Theol. Komm. z. NT*, 13, 2 (1961), *ad loc.* thinks the passage has a present and eschatological sense. Cf. also E. G. Selwyn, *The First Ep. of St. Peter* (1961), *ad loc.*: "The meaning is that the honour which Christ has by virtue of God's choice is imparted to, and shared by, the faithful." Selwyn sees in v. 7 a midrash-type observation on the preceding promise to believers, "which it links up with the description of the Stone as 'held in honour.'" Wbg. Pt., *ad loc.*, relying more on v. 5, goes further: "The union with Christ is to serve the establishing of a holy priesthood whose members have the privilege of offering spiritual sacrifices which are well-pleasing to God through Christ."

[37] Cf. Wnd. Kath. Br., *ad loc.* Because δόξα is bracketed by ἔπαινος and τιμή Kn. Pt., *ad loc.* thinks it means only "fame" and not "radiance."

[38] Cf. on this J. Héring, *La Première Ép. de S. Paul aux Corinth., Comment. du NT*, 7² (1959), 113; "Ils jouissent de plus d'égards et deviennent par là respectables, au même titre que les autres, parce qu'on ne les expose pas."

[39] Acc. to Dib. Past., *ad loc.* 2 Tm. 2:20 is influenced by Wis. 15:7 as well as R. 9:21. In interpretation the author has in view the deceiver and the deceived.

[40] Mi. R.¹², 243, n. 2 thinks the words εἰς τιμήν replace a gen. On εἰς τιμήν τινος "to someone's honour," "that he may have honour," cf. εἰς τιμὴν Δήμητρος, Cornut. Theol. Graec., 28 (55, 7), εἰς τιμὴν Πτολεμαίου, Ditt. Or., I, 111, 26, also Ign. Eph., 2, 1; 21, 1 and 2; Mg., 3, 2; Tr., 12, 2; Pol., 5, 2 and εἰς λόγον τιμῆς "with regard, reference to," Ign. Phld., 11, 2.

[41] Cf. Schl. R., 85: "For the Jew and for the Greek there is only one way of salvation, only that of doing good."

[42] The expression διπλῆ τιμῆ is found in Ael. Arist. Or., 32, 3 (Keil).

the congregation in virtue of their outstanding service. [43] More likely, however, is the explanation that they are to receive double payment. [44]

3. τιμή in Col. 2:23.

Explanation of this passage is difficult, [45] for Paul is obviously adopting the slogans of Gnostic heresy without defining their content more precisely. τιμή is probably a current term in the vocabulary of the mysteries to denote election and deification. The false teachers plainly espouse the view that from the cult of the στοιχεῖα and observance of the precepts imposed on them there develops for participants in the cult an honour which consists in the vision of God. [46] Paul rejects this idea. He perhaps uses τιμή in an ironic sense by changing what was originally a positive term for the heretics into its opposite. But one cannot rule out altogether the possibility that τιμή retains the sense of "honour." [47] Another possibility is that of taking it in the sense of "worth." [48]

4. The Cultic Liturgical Use of the Word.

In doxological formulae τιμή is often combined with related terms. 1 Tm. 1:17, where we have it with δόξα, contains a liturgical prayer formula deriving from the treasury of the pre-Christian Hellenistic synagogue. Similarly the doxology in confession of God in 1 Tm. 6:16 follows the traditions of the Hellenistic synagogue. [49]

The most developed doxologies containing τιμή are in Rev. Thus the four creatures in 4:9 offer to God δόξα, τιμή and εὐχαριστία. This praise of God is

---

[43] So W. Michaelis, Das Ältestenamt (1953), 112-119, who pts. out that acc. to 1 Tm. 3:4, 12 the presbyters still kept their secular jobs; hence διπλῆ τιμή ref. only to "honour," cf. also his Past. u. Gefbr. (1930), 61-63.

[44] Jeremias, op. cit. (→ n. 22), ad loc. takes as his starting-pt. the view that in the Past. πρεσβύτεροι denotes age rather than office; v. 17 says quite clearly that those to whom an office is entrusted and who discharge it faithfully are to receive double payment, namely, in comparison with the aged and widows supported by the church. Double honour thus includes both honour and payment. Similarly Dib. Past., ad loc. thinks that an honorarium is undoubtedly meant.

[45] Theod. Mops. In epist. Pauli ad Coloss., ad loc. noted already: ἀσαφὲς μέν ἐστι — obscurus quidem versus, MPG, 66 (1864), 931 A.

[46] So G. Bornkamm, "Die Häresie d. Kol.," Das Ende d. Gesetzes⁴ (1963), 151. Loh. Kol. on 2:23, n. 2 says: "what this 'honour' means is uncertain," but he thinks the ref. is to the cultic goal of the "arbitrary service" and "humility," namely, "filling" with the fulness of deity. τιμή, as Reitzenstein Hell. Myst., 252-4 has shown, is a fixed term for the vision of deity, e.g., in Paus., X, 32, 13. Cf. also B. Reicke, "Zum sprachlichen Verständnis v. Kol. 2:23," Stud. Theol., 6 (1952), 39-52, and Pr.-Bauer, s.v., who with Bornkamm rejects the sense of "honour."

[47] T. K. Abbott, The Ep. to the Eph. and to the Col., ICC (1956), ad loc.; C. Masson, L'Épitre aux Col., Comment. du NT, 10 (1950), 138, n. 4; Dib. Gefbr., ad loc. and H. Conzelmann, Die kleinen Briefe d. Ap. Pls., NT Deutsch, 8⁹ (1962), ad loc. stand by the sense of "honour." Within this view the most convincing transl. is that of Dibelius, who thinks τιμή is the honour done to foods by asceticism: "(Things) which are all destined to be destroyed by use ... and not that honour be done to them in satisfaction of earthly sense."

[48] So, e.g., P. L. Hedley, "Ad Col. 2:20 - 3:4," ZNW, 27 (1928), 215; Ew. Gefbr., 405-7, who gives a brief instructive survey of earlier exeg. treatment of the passage. If τιμή is taken as "worth" the transl. runs: Human commands and doctrines are reputed to be special wisdom ... but are without value, since they serve only to satisfy the flesh, cf. also Haupt. Gefbr., 113-8, who thinks τιμή denotes subj. "evaluation" rather than obj. "worth." Cf. also → VII, 1066, n. 412.

[49] Cf. Jeremias, op. cit. on 6:15. Dib. Past., ad loc. also thinks this is a Jewish cultic formula. Undoubtedly the cultic speech of Gk. speaking Judaism influenced the Past.

in each instance concluded by the adoration of the elders (4:11) who confirm that God alone is worthy to receive δόξα, τιμή and δύναμις. This is the counterpart of the worship of Caesar in the ruler-cult. [50] Confession is made here that God and not the emperor is the Creator and Lord of all. In 5:12 f. the angelic choirs extol the omnipotence of the Lamb in a seven-membered [51] doxology. The Lamb is worthy to receive (→ IV, 6, 32 ff.) δύναμις, πλοῦτος, σοφία, ἰσχύς, τιμή, δόξα and εὐλογία. All creation joins in: εὐλογία, τιμή, δόξα and κράτος are due to God and the Lamb to all eternity. With slight variations 7:12 corresponds to 5:12, but it is addressed only to God. In prayerful reverence the voices of the angelic choirs magnify God's εὐλογία, δόξα, σοφία, εὐχαριστία, τιμή, δύναμις and ἰσχύς. All these songs of praise naturally had their place in the cultus of the earthly community too. [52]

5. Value, Price.

τιμή can be used with δόξα of earthly goods, Rev. 21:26 (echoing Is. 60:5). The members of the original community in Jerusalem hand over to the apostles' control the "money received" τὰς τιμὰς τῶν πιπρασκομένων [53] through the sale of lands and houses, Ac. 4:34. [54] Ananias and Sapphira are accused in Ac. 5:2, 3 of keeping back part of the "proceeds" from a field they sold. According to Ac. 19:19 the "value" of the magical books burnt in Ephesus was 50,000 silver drachmas. [55] In Ac. 7:16, which speaks of the grave that Abraham purchased for a "sum" of silver, the word is in the gen. pretii.

1 C. 6:20; 7:23 is theologically significant. The gen. is again a gen. pretii; ἠγοράσθητε τιμῆς means literally: "You have been bought (back) 'for a price,' [56] 'against' payment' [57] of the price asked" → I, 125, 22 ff. [58] Christ has acquired Christians as His possession, since He paid the price with His blood for their liberation from the dominion and power of sin. [59]

II. τιμάω.

1. "To honour": The commandment to honour parents (Ex. 20:12; Dt. 5:16) is more than once pressed by Jesus as a commandment which demands unconditional obedience, Mk. 7:10; 10:19; Mt. 15:4; 19:19; Lk. 18:20. According to Mk. 7:11, 12 and Mt. 15:5, 6 the fifth commandment includes financial support of parents in need,

---

[50] So also E. Lohse, Die Offenbarung d. Joh., NT Deutsch, 11⁸ (1960), ad loc. Acc. to Loh. Apk. on 4:11 "the hymn ... expresses the victorious awareness of the divine that the one true and mighty God is worshipped in all the confusing wealth of religions and cults."
[51] Cf. 1 Ch. 29:11.
[52] On this G. Delling, Der Gottesdienst im NT (1952), 67-71. Acc. to Jn.'s view the earthly ἐκκλησία worships with the host of angels, cf. A. T. Nikolainen, "Der Kirchenbegriff in d. Offenbarung d. Joh.," NTSt, 9 (1962/63), 361.
[53] There is a similar formulation in 1 Cl., 55, 2: τὰς τιμὰς αὐτῶν "the sum which they had received for themselves."
[54] Bibl. in Haench. Ag.¹³ on 4:32-37.
[55] For equivalents cf. Haench. Ag.¹³, ad loc.
[56] So Deissmann LO, 275.
[57] Pr.-Bauer, s.v. ἀγοράζω.
[58] Acc. to Deissmann LO, 274-278 Paul's metaphorical use is based on the purchase of a slave by the deity in ancient sacral law, but W. Elert, "Redemptio ab hostibus," ThLZ, 72 (1947), 267 argues that the formula used by Paul can relate to any kind of slave sale, including the ransoming of men thrust into slavery as prisoners of war.
[59] Paul does not say, of course, from what Christians are freed, but he is probably thinking (→ I, 125, 22 ff.) of the power of sin, cf. H. D. Wendland, Die Br. an d. Korinther, NT Deutsch, 7¹⁰ (1964), ad loc.

nor can a son evade this by appealing to the corban legislation, → III, 864, 13 ff. 1 Tm. 5:3 might also be mentioned in this connection. Here Timothy is told to honour widows. χήρας τίμα can be an injunction to treat widows with respect. [60] But since the reference is not to all widows in the community but only to "real widows" (v. 3, 5, 16), i.e., to those who have no relatives and none to care for them, and who also cannot count on remarriage, "honouring" includes material provision as well. [61] In Eph. 6:2, where there is again reference to the commandment, children are exhorted to honour their parents by obedience; the ὑπακούειν is to take place "in the Lord," cf. Col. 3:20. In 1 Pt. 2:17 we have an inclusive demand that one should pay all men the honour due, love the brethren, fear God and honour the king. In Ac. 28:10 Paul is honoured with many honours, or concretely gifts, after curing the father of Publius and other residents on the island of Malta. [62]

If τιμάω is used only in the negative for honouring God in the Synoptics (Mk. 7:6 and par in the quotation from Is. 29:13 LXX), the use of the term in John's Gospel is theologically significant. In Jn. 5:23 Jesus makes the claim that He should be honoured as God is. This is based on the fact that the Father has given Him the authority to discharge the office of eschatological judge. Hence men are under obligation to subject themselves to Him and His judgment. [63] In Jn. 8:49 Jesus in answer to Jewish charges declares that as the One sent by God He fulfils God's commission; by His obedience, which includes active acknowledgment and fulfilment of the divine will, He honours the Father. The Jews who do not believe in Jesus and hence do not keep His Word (8:51) refuse to pay Him the honour due. [64] But he who serves Jesus and is ready even to sacrifice his life in this service [65] will be honoured by the Father (12:26), [66] i.e., he is promised a share in the δόξα of Jesus. [67]

[60] Cf. Dib. Past., ad loc.
[61] So also Jeremias, op. cit., ad loc., who thinks, no doubt correctly, that the wording of the text carries intentional allusion to the fifth commandment.
[62] Gifts are a visible token of thanks for the rich blessing which the healed had received through the apostolic power of healing. Cf. G. Stählin, Die Apg., NT Deutsch, 5¹⁰ (1962), ad loc.; Haench. Ag.¹³, ad loc.; also F. F. Bruce, The Acts of the Apostles² (1952), ad loc. Sir. 38:1 offers a certain par. On the linguistic formulation cf. Ditt. Or., I, 51, 3: τοὺς τοιούτους τιμᾶν ταῖς πρεπούσαις τιμαῖς.
[63] Cf. on this Bultmann J., ad loc.: "One cannot honour the Father apart from the Son; the honour of the Father and the Son is identical; the Father is encountered in the Son, and the Father is only in the Son." Cf. also C. K. Barrett, The Gospel acc. to St. John (1958), ad loc.: "So complete is the identity in function and authority between the Father and the Son that it is impossible to honour God while disregarding Jesus," also W. Thüsing, "Die Erhöhung u. Verherrlichung Jesu im J.," NTAbh., 21 (1960), 42 and 44, ad loc. Thüsing, 44 says concerning the relation between τιμᾶν and δοξάζειν: "In comparison with τιμᾶν it may be said that δοξάζειν is par. to this but — in some passages at least — goes beyond it." In distinction from τιμᾶν the obj. of δοξάζειν is only the Father and the Son, Thüsing, 242, n. 8.
[64] Cf. Barrett, op. cit., ad loc.: "ἀτιμάζετε, not so much 'you insult' as the antithesis of τιμᾶν, 'you fail to give me due honour as the Father's Son.'"
[65] Ibid. on 12:26: "What kind of service may be implied by this διακονία may be seen from the fact that it follows and explains the saying about hating one's life. To serve Jesus is to follow him . . . , and he is going to death."
[66] Bultmann J., 325, n. 5 sees in v. 26 John's variant of Mk. 8:34 par.: "The Evangelist has shortened the version of the saying he had before him by leaving out the cross-bearing and expanded it by καὶ ὅπου κτλ." Cf. Barrett, 353 and Thüsing, 129, n. 26; 130; 131, n. 37.
[67] Cf. 4 Macc. 17:20, which says of martyrs standing before God's throne: καὶ οὗτοι ἁγιασθέντες διὰ θεὸν τετίμηνται, cf. Bultmann J., 326, n. 4. Barrett, ad loc. expounds: "John nowhere else uses τιμᾶν with God as subject, but cf. 5:23. Probably there is allusion to Mark 10:30, the reward of following; and 10:35-45, where (10:43) the reward of being great among the disciples is given to the διάκονος."

2. "To value": In Mt. 27:8 f. [68] the Evangelist tells us how the chief priests and elders used the thirty pieces of silver which Judas brought back to them. He sees in the purchase of the potter's field a fulfilment (→ III, 220, 11 ff.) of Zech. 11:12 f. [69] The quotation (v. 9 and 10) contains both the verb τιμάω "to assess the value" and the noun τιμή in the sense of the "sum realised." [70]

D. The Word Group in the Post-Apostolic Fathers.

In the post-apost. period Christians are summoned to honour the office-bearer in the church, the teacher of the divine word, Did., 4, 1, the presbyter, 1 Cl., 21, 6, the bishop, Ign. Sm., 9, 1. In Did., 15, 2 congregational officers are called οἱ τετιμημένοι ὑμῶν, "those distinguished among you." In 1 Cl., 44, 6 the congregational office is called the office which is held in honour ἡ τετιμημένη λειτουργία. In 1 Cl., 61, 1 and 2 τιμή is used of the divinely ordained position of the ruler; in 64 and 65, 2 it is used with δόξα etc.

J. Schneider

---

[68] Cf. E. F. Sutcliffe, "Mt. 27:9," JThSt, NS, 3 (1952), 227 f.

[69] Mt. ascribes the OT saying to Jer. J. Schniewind, *Das Ev. nach Mt., NT Deutsch,* 1[9] (1960), *ad loc.:* "The name Jeremiah comes from the fact that Jer. hears God's words in the potter's field (18:2, 3) and also sells his cousin's field at God's behest (32:6-15)."

[70] On τιμή as price and honour → 169, 4 ff.; 170, 11; 172, 16; 173, 20 and 41.

┌─────────────────────────────────┐
│ † τολμάω,   † ἀποτολμάω,   │
│ † τολμητής, † τολμηρός   │
└─────────────────────────────────┘

A. In the Greek World.

1. The verb τολμάω, found from Hom., is derived from τόλμᾱ "courage" (so Pind. Olymp., 9, 82; Attic τόλμᾳ). [1] Etym. the noun belongs to the root τελα/ταλα/τλᾱ "to lift up, carry, bear," cf. ἐτάλασσα, ἔτλην, τλητός etc., Lat. *tuli,* "I have borne," also *tollo, tolero,* "I lift, endure," Gothic þ*ulan,* Old High German *dolēn, dulden,* "thole" etc. [2] With the verb one usually finds the inf., more rarely an augmenting part. [3]

It means a. "to endure," "to suffer," "to put up with," [4] Hom. Od., 24, 162 f.: "But he (Odysseus) endured (ἐτόλμα) with patient (τετληότι) spirit being pelted and berated in his own house." [5] Later this sense, which derives from the stem, is rare, e.g., χρὴ τολμᾶν χαλεποῖσιν ἐν ἄλγεσι κείμενον ἄνδρα, Theogn., 555, or "to hold out in suffering," 355, 1029, cf. 591. Eur. Hec., 326 has Odysseus say: "There is among us no one more wretched than thou . . . ; endure this (τόλμα τάδ' . . .)," and the chorus bewails the lot of the slave: "Oh what a misfortune to be a slave, to have to suffer indignity (τολμᾷ θ' ἃ μὴ χρή)," 333, cf. Herc. Fur., 756; cf. the archaic expression in Plat. Leg., IX, 872e, δίκη ἐπίσκοπος sees to it the the one who has killed his father "must suffer" this similarly from his children (τολμῆσαι). [6]

b. It then means "to dare." The verb is common with θυμός, e.g., Hom. Il., 17, 68: "None of them has in his breast the courage to dare to oppose Menelaus," cf. 10, 232, τολμήεις θυμός in 10, 205; Od., 17, 284. The transition to "to dare" is plain here. The ref. is to perception of a danger and the courage to accept it. What is at issue is whether one will expose oneself to the danger or not, cf. Il., 8, 424; 13, 395; 12, 51 (horses); also Od., 24, 261 f. Later this is the main sense, e.g., Plat., where it is connected with an inf. denoting saying, cf. Phaedr., 241a; 247c; Leg., X, 895a; Resp., VI, 503b etc., naming, La., 197a; Gorg., 494e, and agreeing, Soph., 247b. There is a venture in the discussion because what is maintained is surprising, has not yet been proved, or has yet to be proved. Even if the one who proves it is sure of his proof, he is not sure of its effect on the listener or the sceptic. Hence τολμητέον δέ, Leg., X, 888a; cf. Theaet., 196d. But one also finds "to venture to do something" more gen., Polit., 300b; Symp., 182e; Resp., IX, 571c; Thuc., VII, 59, 3; Xenoph. An., III, 2, 29; Ditt. Syll.[3], III, 1106, 129 (300 B.C.); Eur. Hipp., 476 (with part.); the negation is common, cf. Plat. Gorg., 483a; Theaet., 190b.

τ ο λ μ ά ω κ τ λ . [1] Liddell-Scott, *s.v.* [Risch].

[2] Boisacq, Hofmann, *s.v.* ταλάσσαι, G. Curtius, *Grundzüge d. gr. Etymologie*[5] (1879), *s.v.;* Schwyzer, I, 360, 362.

[3] Schwyzer, II, 362, 365, 392 f.; Bl.-Debr.[11] § 392, 1a.

[4] Hofmann, *s.v.* τόλμη.

[5] Cf. also πολύτλας δῖος 'Οδυσσεύς in Hom., e.g., Il., 10, 248; Od., 5, 354, also the admonition to be patient τέτλαθι, Il., 1, 586; 5, 382 etc. or τλήσομαι ἄλγεα πάσχων, Od., 5, 362.

[6] Elsewhere Plat. has ὑπομένω, πάσχω for "to endure," e.g., Leg., IX, 869c.

c. We then find "to have the courage," "to be courageous." There is still so strong an emphasis on the element of daring or boldness that this is a better rendering than simply "to dare." Odysseus chooses four companions by lot who must summon up courage τολμήσειεν to plunge the stake with him into the eye of Polyphemus, Hom. Od., 9, 332. Prometheus laments that none opposes Zeus when he wills to destroy men, ἐγὼ δ' ἐτόλμησα, and Oceanos had the courage with him, Aesch. Prom., 235 and 331. τολμῶντες... ἄνδρες are courageous men, Thuc., II, 43, 1, and in Plat. Leg., IV, 706c we read: "They do not have the courage to venture their lives in opposition to the enemy assault (μὴ τολμῶντας... ἀποθνήσκειν)." The risk which courage takes may be due to danger, e.g., from the standpoint of the right, Plat. Leg., IX, 880b, or the gods, X, 888d. In any case courage gets the power to act only from necessity and fear, constraint and resolve, certainty of the rightness of motive and uncertainty of the outcome. The conviction of conscience that one's motives are right impels to the venture of action or rightly restrains from it. Socrates defends himself by the "inner voice" against the charge that he advises individuals but does not dare to give public counsel to the city, Plat. Ap., 31c.

d. The word can then mean "to dare" in the sense "to make bold," "to presume." τολμάω can have not only the intensive sense "to have the courage" in the good sense but also "to dare," "to presume" in the bad sense, cf. Poll. Onom., III, 134 f.; V, 125; VI, 130. In Soph. El., 471 it stands in a negative context: When her mother learns her plan, Chrysothemis will repent of her rashness, cf. Phil., 82, where Odysseus tries to encourage the frightened Neoptolemos to get the bow of Philotectes by stealth. Trach., 582 f. is similar: "To venture wickedness (sc. magic) (κακὰς δὲ τόλμας) I would neither understand nor would I seek to know it better, and I abhor women who venture it (τάς τε τολμώσας)"; Plat. Resp., VIII, 569b says: "The tyrant will presume to do violence to his father," cf. Leg., IX, 869a; 873a of the murder of parents and children, also Aristoph. Pl., 419 ff., with its threat of "poverty" on those who want to give "wealth" sight: "You venture an intolerable venture (τόλμημα γὰρ τολμᾶτον οὐκ ἀνασχετόν) which no no god and no man has ever ventured."

e. Positively or negatively one often finds the rhetorical "to venture to say," cf. Hom. Od., 24, 261 f., Plat. (→ 181, 24 f.) and Epict. Diss., II, 16, 42: "Stretch forth thy neck since bondage is done away, venture to say it with a glance at God," cf. also I, 23, 7; II, 20, 32 and Philodem. Philos. Rhetor., I, 341.

2. The compound ἀποτολμάω strengthens the sense, cf. Thuc., VII, 67, 1: "Though we have no experience, we have dared it courageously."

B. In the Septuagint.

The word is seldom found in the Gk. OT, only 7 times in all and never in the Historical Books or the Prophets. In the only 2 instances with Hbr. originals (Job 15:12; Est. 7:5) τολμάω is more a paraphrase than a transl.: for לקח "to carry away to something" in Job 15:12 and מלא לב "to fill the heart" in Est. 7:5; cf. Qoh. 8:11 'A. The verb means 1. "to dare" of a legal alteration in 3 Macc. 3:21, of fatal disobedience in 4 Macc. 8:18; 2. "to presume," the challenging conduct of an inferior towards a superior, e.g., the traitor's tricks against the noble high-priest in 2 Macc. 4:2, the queen's refractoriness in relation to her husband in Est. 1:18, Job's protest against God in Job 15:12, [7] Haman's anti-semitism in Est. 7:5 and the attack of a weak army on a strong one in Jdt. 14:13. The word has the sense of shameful insolence in Prv. 7:13 Σ.

---

[7] G. Fohrer, Das Buch Hi., Komm. AT, 16 (1963), 263, n. 12a: "passionate and uncontrolled protest against the righteous God."

C. In Philo and Josephus.

1. Philo seldom uses the term. [8] In him it means "to venture" with ref. to hypotheses and judgments in the field of knowledge. In a discussion of time one reads: "If one were to venture the assumption that it is older (sc. than the world), this would be unphilosophical," Op. Mund., 26. "Who would dare advance assured statements about what is not known for certain?" Som., I, 54.

2. In Jos. τολμάω and related words occur over 200 times. [9] The verb means a. "to have the courage," "to be confident," e.g., to pluck up courage to ask in Bell., 1, 561, not to have the confidence to send an embassage in 2, 280, cf. 1, 545. Esp. in many descriptions of battles the word is used for the courage to accept the dangers of a fight and the risk of an uncertain outcome or death, Bell., 1, 149, cf. 3, 147, 220; 6, 32. All the situations possible only in battle involve a venture, 3, 525; 4, 66, cf. Ant., 5, 67; 6, 177 etc.; pass. forms are also used, Bell., 4, 648, cf. 5, 5. An Eleazar is depicted as an esp. daring man νεανίας τολμῆσαι θρασύς, 7, 196. Apart from battle τολμάω is used in connection with daring deeds like the demolishing of the golden eagle in Bell., 1, 653 or the seeking of the crown ἀντιποιηθῆναι βασιλείας ἐτόλμησεν, 2, 59. b. Negatively the word means in Jos. "to dare," "to presume," "to be insolent," the reviling of the princesses ἐτόλμησεν ... ὑβρίσαι in Bell., 1, 568, the insolent carelessness of a murderer in 1, 627, cf. 4, 264. This kind of daring is directed against right and law, Bell., 2, 308. Acts of violence are also associated with the word: "Noaros had 70 men executed (τολμήσας τοὐργον) without the knowledge of Agrippa," Bell., 2, 483, cf. Ant., 7, 150 and the expressions αἴσχιστα τολμάω in Bell., 4, 351, or "actually perpetrated atrocities" τῶν ἑκάστοτε τολμωμένων in 1, 465, cf. also Ant., 8, 245 and Bell., 6, 212. Offences against God are also part of this τολμάω which passes the boundaries of all shame. "The sin (against God) which we have dared in our fury against our own brethren," Bell., 7, 332. "ὁ τὸν θεὸν ἀσεβεῖν τετολμηκώς, he is capable of all wickedness," 7, 263.

The motives behind ventures are courage (→ line 9 ff.), warlike passion, μεγίστη ἀνάγκη (Bell., 6, 120), or the aim of clothing a new perception of God in words, Ant., 1, 155; negatively they are conceit and presumption Bell., 1, 7, wantonness and wickedness Ant., 1, 73 and 188. Obstacles are terror Bell., 4, 331, fear and anxiety 3, 298, reason Ant., 1, 16, the fear of venturing anything dangerous or wicked before God, Ant., 1, 14; 9, 212.

D. In the New Testament.

τολμάω with ἀποτολμάω once occurs 15 times, or with Synoptic par. 17 times. In 10 or 12 instances there is an amplifying inf., while 7 or 9 instances are negative.

1. τολμάω in the Gospels, Acts and Jude.

In the Synoptists τολμάω occurs 3 or 4 times, in Ac. twice, in Jn. and Jd. once each.

a. It occurs only once without negation in the sense "to dare": Joseph of Arimathea dared and went (τολμήσας εἰσῆλθεν) to Pilate and asked him for the body of Jesus, Mk. 15:43. We must not think there was any risk here or that something unusual and hence venturesome was done. [10] The context yields the sense that this respected member of the Sanhedrin, unlike the many women (cf. v. 40 f. and v. 47), ventured to approach the Roman procurator directly.

---

[8] Leisegang does not list τολμάω.
[9] [Rengstorf].
[10] Loh. Mk., ad loc. ref. to the Roman custom of giving the corpse of an executed person to friends or relatives. But the two motives suggested by Loh. for the venture are not convincing.

b. In the other passages τολμάω is always used with a negative and it serves to denote fear or anxiety. Thus in the context of the debates of Jesus we read that "no one dared to ask him any more," Mk. 12:34 and par. Jesus has beaten back the attacks of His opponents and they are discouraged and do not venture to put any more questions. The note emphasises the supremacy and majesty of Jesus. In Jn. 21:12 the fear aroused by the miraculous encounter with the Risen Lord and the singular events connected therewith is the reason why "none of the disciples durst ask him, Who art thou?" [11] Similarly it is because of reverence for the sacred and for God's presence that in connection with God's revelation in the burning bush Ac. 7:32 says of Moses: "Trembling, he dare not look closely." [12] In Jd. 9 as well (→ IV, 866, n. 211) it is respect for God and the creatures belonging to Him which rules out blasphemy. In the dispute about Moses' body Michael dare not pronounce a railing judgment even against the devil. [13] On the other hand Ac. 5:13 reflects the situation of the imminent danger of clashing with the authorities in Jerusalem: "While the apostles were together with one accord in Solomon's porch, none of the others dare show that he was attached to them; [14] but the people magnified them (the apostles), and many became believers." "The rest" are the other Christians [15] mentioned previously. The reasons for this failure to venture are not far to seek. The author of Ac. simply makes the observation to prepare the way for the fact that the apostles will be arrested but not any of the other Christians.

2. τολμάω in Paul.

Paul makes more lavish use of the term in various senses. In him it means a. "to dare" in a weak sense: For the good man someone might dare to die (R. 5:7), i.e., there is no risk, one can count on it, someone might perhaps die. We then have b. "to dare" with the courage of confession, as when the brethren fearlessly venture to proclaim God's Word in spite of the apostle's imprisonment, Phil. 1:14, [16] or when the conviction that his action is right gives Paul courage against opponents who accuse him of a worldly manner of life, 2 C. 10:2. Paul is speaking here with the courage of a sense of apostleship. [17] Another sense is c. "to dare," "to presume." Paul says to his adversaries in Corinth: If in anything one of them, e.g., a full Jew or a servant of Christ, can make bold assertions, he, Paul, can make similar bold assertions, 2 C. 11:21. [18] τολμάω is used here in a form of speech which in the first

---

11 Bultmann J., ad loc.: "The point of the question, since they have already recognised Him, is obviously: Are you really He? What is denoted is the peculiar feeling of the disciples in the presence of the Risen Lord: He is the Lord and yet He is not; He is not the One they have known thus far and yet He is. A singular wall has been erected between Him and them."
12 Haench. Ag.[13], ad loc.
13 Wnd. Kath. Br.; Kn. Pt.; K. H. Schelkle, Der Judasbr., Herders Theol. Komm. NT, 13, 2 (1961), ad loc.
14 κολλάομαι "to seek closer intercourse with someone" (→ III, 822, 13 f.) does not correspond to the author's intention acc. to the situation.
15 Haench. Ag.[13], ad loc. rightly rejects the ref. of οἱ λοιποί to enemies (so G. Stählin, Die Ag., NTD, 5 [1962], ad loc.). He also sees clearly that κολλάομαι is to be taken spatially. His view that οἱ λοιποί are non-christians leads him to seek the reason for not venturing in the holy awe which keeps them at a distance from the group of Christians (but the ref. is only to the apostles). Cf. similarly Bauernf. Ag., ad loc.
16 Loh. Phil., ad loc.: "That it is a venture means that it remains unattainable by man."
17 θαρρέω and τολμάω are synon.; cf. also Wnd. 2 K., ad loc.
18 Ltzm. K., ad loc.

instance implies courtesy to the one addressed. But the polite way of praising the opposite speaker shows ironically or sarcastically that his speech is presumptuous → lines 5 ff. Completely ironical is Paul's saying that he himself does not dare to reckon himself among or equate himself with those who commend themselves (sc. as full apostles), 10:12. [19] Finally we have d. "to be bold, insolent." Paul thinks it quite inappropriate and an offence against the new position of the saints, who shall judge the world, [20] that one of them who has a dispute against another should presume to seek judgment from unbelievers instead of the saints, 1 C. 6:1. Conversely, Paul says from the midst of the new awareness of a man to whom grace has been given by God: "I will not dare to speak of those things which Christ hath not wrought by me... by word and deed," R. 15:18. [21]

In the NT the word group τολμάω has the same range of meaning as in profane Greek and Josephus, both in the good sense "to have the courage" and also in the bad sense "to presume." What makes a word or work a venture is danger or propriety; what prevents the venture is recognition of the supremacy of the other, reverence for God, or fear of the holy; the ὕβρις of self-reliance is ruled out by the encounter with Jesus as in Paul's formula: "Christ works through me." In the NT the word τολμάω does not denote the venture of existence, the ventures of life, or the venture of faith. [22]

3. ἀποτολμάω.

This is used only in R. 10:20 to strengthen the quotation formula [23] → IV,, 111, 25 ff.

4. τολμητής.

The only instance of the noun τολμητής is in a description of false teachers and apostates, and the word has a thoroughly negative sense: τολμηταὶ αὐθάδεις, "self-willed and presumptuous men," who have no respect for God or awe of what is holy, who do not shrink from railing against government, 2 Pt. 2:10. [24] Materially the meaning is the same as in Jd. 9 (→ 184, 10 ff.), [25] for 2 Pt. 2 evidently makes use of Jd.

---

[19] Wnd. 2 K., ad loc.

[20] Joh. W. 1 K., ad loc. τολμᾷ is called a strong term, and Bengel, ad loc. is quoted: grandi verbo notatur laesa maiestas Christianorum.

[21] Mi. R.[12], ad loc.

[22] I. Lepp, Wagnisse d. Daseins (1963), 71 f., 226, 238; K. Heim in H. Faber, "Grusswort, Theol. als Glaubenswagnis," Festschr. K. Heim (1954), 6; P. Wust, Ungewissheit u. Wagnis[2] (1946), 55, 285-8; R. Bultmann, "NT u. Mythologie," Kerygma u. Mythos, I (1948), 51 speaks of the "venture of the Easter faith."

[23] D * G E F, also d g e f, leave out ἀποτολμᾷ καί, probably on the basis of a 2nd cent. original. Such characterising of an author quoted from the OT is not common in Paul, cf. R. 9:25; 14:11 etc. For the apostle the prophet's word is God's word and not a special venture. Materially, stylistically and textually ἀποτολμᾷ καί is to be regarded as a later addition, cf. O. Michel, Pls. u seine Bibel (1929), 72 (a list of Paul's quotation formulae); Mi. R.[12], ad loc. leaves the vl. an open question.

[24] Wnd. Pt.; Kn. Pt.; Schelkle, op. cit. (→ n. 13), ad loc.

[25] In early Chr. writings outside the NT only the noun ἡ τόλμα, which is not used in the NT, occurs. 1 Cl., 30, 8 says at the end of an admonition: θράσος καὶ αὐθάδεια καὶ τόλμα τοῖς κατηραμένοις ὑπὸ τοῦ θεοῦ, "insolence, arrogance and presumption" as characteristics of those who are accursed by God [Schneemelcher].

5. τολμηρότερος.

In the case of this word, which occurs only in R. 15:15, [26] one is not to seek reasons why the apostle thinks he has written "a little boldly" to the Romans. [27] He is simply using an apologetic formula such as one finds also in Plato → 181, 24 ff. Behind it there naturally lies the conviction that he had something special to say.

Fitzer

---

[26] p[46] א C D E F G L P have the neuter, A B adverbial τολμηροτέρως. Mi. R.[12], *ad loc.* opts for the adverbial form.

[27] Mi. R.[12], *ad loc.* considers various answers to the question: "In what did the apostle's boldness consist? In the fact that he wrote the Roman church as a stranger, or in certain theses and formulations which were hard for the Roman church to accept?" But this is not a formal admission; it is just a manner of speaking and there is no special need to explain it.

τόπος

Contents: A. Usage in Greek Literature: 1. Simple Use in Common Speech: a. Territory,
Land; b. District, Town, Dwelling-Place; c. A General Term for Place; 2. Special Meanings:
a. Sanctuary; b. In Place of, Opportunity; c. Rhetorical Usage; d. Place in a Writing;
3. τόπος in Philosophical, Scientific and Cosmological Usage. B. Old Testament Usage:
1. General; 2. Linguistic Peculiarities: a. Basis; b. Place Where; c. This Place; d. מָקוֹם
with Possessive Pronoun; 3. Meanings of מָקוֹם in Comparison with the Greek τόπος:
a. Land, Locality; b. Town, Dwelling-Place; c. Other Places; 4. מָקוֹם as the Promised
Land; 5. מָקוֹם as a Term for Holy Places: a. Original Canaanite Shrines; b. Zion and the
Temple in Jerusalem; c. This Place in the Prophets; d. Post-Exilic Usage; 6. Places in
Creation. C. Later Jewish Usage: 1. Rabbinic Writings; 2. Philo. D. New Testament
Usage: 1. τόπος as a General Term for Place; 2. Special Senses: a. Temple; b. The Right
Place For, Opportunity; c. Place of Scripture. E. The Post-Apostolic Fathers.

A. Usage in Greek Literature.

1. Simple Use in Common Speech.

a. Territory, land: τόπος [1] first occurs in lit. in Aesch. and is then very common in
all authors. In the oldest clear use in the singular [2] it means "a defined place," then a
specific "territory," "area," or "land," e.g., Armenia, Xenoph. An., IV, 4, 4, Greece,
Aesch. Pers., 790; cf. Isoc. Or., 5, 107; cf. also Aristot. Meteor., I, 14, p. 352a, 34; I, 14,
p. 351a, 36; "every single place on earth," Aesch. Eum., 249. Jos. Ap., 1, 9 f. contrasts
"the lands" (οἱ τόποι is an authentic plur.) of the Egyptians, Phoenicians etc. and "the
territory of Greece" ὁ περὶ τὴν Ἑλλάδα τόπος. The plur. is used for a locality or land to
the degree that it is not a single unit; it is a gen. and indefinite term for a geographical
area, e.g., "in that locality," Xenoph. Cyrop., II, 4, 20, "from wintry pastures," Eur. Alc.,
67, "in the Greek world," Aesch. Pers., 796; cf. Ag., 191; Eum., 292, 703, "towards the
west," Prom., 350, cf. Pers., 447; Aristot. Meteor., I, 14, p. 351a, 19 and 35; αὐτόπτης
γάρ εἰμι τῶν τόπων, "I know the district," P. Oxy., VIII, 1154, 8 f. (1st cent. A.D.).
When a locality (area or place) is mentioned by name and thus defined we find the
sing., Xenoph. An., IV, 4, 4, the place where the tower of Babel was built, Philo Som., II,
286; cf. P. Tebt., II, 319, 8 and 26 (248 A.D.); 324, 11 f. (208 A.D.). But mostly indication of the place or land concerned follows in a prepos. phrase, and here we normally
have the plur., consistently so in the expression οἱ κατά... τόποι, "the district of..."

τ ό π ο ς . Bibl.: Liddell-Scott, Moult-Mill., Pr.-Bauer, Preisigke Wört., s.v.; C. Roberts,
T. Skeat, A. D. Nock, "The Gild of Zeus Hypsistos," HThR, 29 (1936), 40, 45 f.; P. Chantraine, "Remarques sur le parallélisme sémantique latin locus et grec τόπος," Mélanges
A. Ernout (1940), 51-60; E. R. Smothers, "Give Place to the Wrath," Catholic Biblical
Quart., 6 (1944), 205-215.
[1] Etym. uncertain, cf. Boisacq, Hofmann, s.v.; C. D. Buck, A Dict. of Selected Synonyms
in the Principal Indo-Eur. Languages (1949), 830. H. Osthoff, "Gr. u. lat. Wortdeutungen,"
Idg. Forsch., 8 (1898), 23 proposes derivation from * toqʷos and this seems to be supported
now by Mycenaean Gk., since in the (incomplete) tablet Gv 863 (M. Ventris and J. Chadwick, Documents in Mycenaean Gk. [1956], 273) from Cnossos toqo probably means "place"
(e.g., for vines, Ϝοινάσι) [Risch].
[2] Cf. the attestation in Mycenaean Gk. → n. 1.

e.g., "the land of Eryx," Diod. S., 4, 23, 2, "the land of Haran," "the neighbourhood of Haran," Philo Migr. Abr., 216; cf. P. Tebt., I, 8, 8 f. (c. 201 B.C.), "our neighbourhood," I, 27, 5 (113 B.C.). In other pap. the sing. and plur. alternate: ὁ περὶ Θράκην τόπος, "the area in the neighbourhood of Thrace," Demosth., 20, 59; οἱ περὶ τὴν γῆν τόποι, "the sphere around the earth," Aristot. Meteor., I, 3, p. 340a, 22; ὁ ἐπὶ Θράκης τόπος, "the locality toward Thrace," Aeschin. In Ctesiphontem, 73, cf. Fals. Leg., 9.

b. "District," "town," "dwelling-place." τόπος often seems to denote the specific smaller part of a greater whole, with χώρα as the broader term: "What took place in this sphere (ἐπὶ τούτου τοῦ τόπου), which is small, can also take place in bigger localities (περὶ μεγάλους τόπους) and whole lands (χώρας ὅλας)," Aristot. Meteor., I, 14, p. 352a, 14-17. Plato calls the 12 districts (μόρια) into which the land (χώρα) is to be divided οἱ τῆς χώρας τόποι, Plat. Leg., VI, 760c, cf. 760d e, 761d; ὁ τόπος ἡμῖν τῆς χώρας is the part of the land assigned to us, 705c, and in Ptolemaic Egypt τόπος was the term for the smallest unit of government under the νομός: "districts of the nomos,"[3] P. Tebt., I, 28 5 (c. 114 B.C.).[4] But in popular use τόπος does not have the function of denoting a specific area of a definite size. It can be used as an alternative to all kinds of terms for places. Thus it is a synon. of "town," "ward of a town," "house," "dwelling," and it can finally mean "place of abode" in a gen. sense. In detail it means "town," Diod. S., 2, 13, 6; cf. 1, 15, 6; 13, 64, 7; Jos. Ap., 1, 238; cf. 1, 86,[5] "district of a city," Jos. Ap., 2, 34 (Jewish quarters in Alexandria); cf. Diod. S., 20, 100, 4, "parcel of ground," Aeschin. Tim., 98 (in the same context another parcel is called χωρίον, 99), "houses," 123. In the pap. τόπος is often used for a "piece of land," also a "dwelling"; in tax receipts a lot which has not been built on is ψιλὸς τόπος, P. Oxy., III, 501, 14 (187 A.D.); 510, 12. 15 (101 A.D.); P. Tebt., II, 280, 6 (126 B.C.); 281, 16 f. (125 B.C.) etc.; a tax has to be paid for acquiring lots, P. Tebt., II, 281, 12 (125 B.C.); τόπος can also be used for the rented part of a building, the upper room, P. Oxy., VIII, 1127, 5 f., cf. 15, 22, 39 (183 A.D.), dining room, VIII, 1129, 10, cf. 17 (449 A.D.); cf. VIII, 1128, 23 (173 A.D.), or in the plur. the various parts of a rented property,[6] P. Oxy., III, 502, 34, cf. 16-21 (164 A.D.).[7] On τόπος as a gen. term for "dwelling" cf. Aeschin. Tim., 120: τόποι πρὸς διανομήν (for every living creature) are in the same context χωρίον and χώρα, Philo Det. Pot. Ins., 151 f.; cf. the alternation of τόπος, χώρα and γῆ, Migr. Abr., 176 f.; οἱ περὶ τὸν τόπον ἐκεῖνον are "the inhabitants of that district," Aristot. Meteor., II, 6, p. 364a, 3 f. A man bad at home was never any good in Macedonia: οὐ γὰρ τὸν τρόπον, ἀλλὰ τὸν τόπον μόνον μετήλλαξεν,[8] Aeschin. In Ctesiphontem, 78; cf. Philo Leg. All., II, 85.

c. A General Term for Place. In later usage all kinds of places are called τόπος. The sense is provided by the context and it is impossible even approximately to present all the possibilities of usage, Diod. S., 2, 7, 5; Philo Op. Mund., 161.[9] This multiplicity

---

3 But cf. Preisigke Sammelb., IV, 7337, 6 f.; Roberts-Skeat-Nock, 46, who suggest τόπος is a town which is not a πόλις. Further examples in Preisigke Wört., s.v. ἐπίσημος.

4 Further instances in Liddell-Scott, Preisigke Wört., s.v. Various special technical designations derive from this, e.g., τοπάρχης, τοπογραμματεύς, τοπαρχία, τοπογραμματεία, τοποτηρησία, Preisigke Wört., s.v.

5 ὁ τόπος Συχέμ in Philo Migr. Abr., 221, 224 derives from OT usage, Gn. 12:6 → 195, 22 ff.

6 Here the plur. τόποι corresponds exactly to the English "premises" used in similar contracts.

7 The derivative τοποθεσία often means in the pap. the area of a lot or field, v. Preisigke Wört., s.v.

8 Cf. C. D. Adams, The Speeches of Aeschines, Loeb Class. Library (1919), ad loc.: "he changed his position, not his disposition."

9 Cf. H. G. Güterbock, Kumarbi (1946), 36, who with ref. to the phrase "coming forth from the good place" in Hittite myth asks whether this means birth, but does not think "the good place" can be a Hittite paraphrase for the womb.

explains the stereotyped adverbial expressions in τόπος: πᾶς τόπος means "everywhere,"
Diod. S., 13, 22, 3, transf. "wholly and utterly," Philo Praem. Poen., 35, κατὰ τόπους [10]
"locally," Catal. Cod. Astr. Graec., VIII, 3, 186, 1 f. etc.; cf. Aristot. Meteor., II, 1,
p. 354a, 5; II, 8, p. 368b, 24 f. κατὰ τόπον "in the place in question," P. Oxy., VIII, 1101,
9 (367-370 A.D.); 1162, 1-2 (4th cent. A.D.), κατ᾿ ἄλλον τόπον, "elsewhere," Aristot.
Meteor., I, 13, p. 351a, 17 f., κατ᾿ οὐδένα τόπον, "nowhere," II, 1, p. 354a, 1. Very
common in the pap. is ἐπὶ τῶν τόπων, "on the spot," P. Oxy., III, 511, 9 f. (103 A.D.);
cf. ἡ ἐπὶ τόπων δημοσία τράπεζα, "the public bank on the spot," P. Tebt., II, 294,
16 f. (146 A.D.), cf. also P. Oxy., III, 485, 31 (178 A.D.); VIII, 1101, 20 (367-370 A.D.);
P. Tebt., II, 289, 6 (23 A.D.); 296, 13 (123 A.D.); 297, 16 (123 A.D.); [11] παρὰ τόπον,
"in the wrong place," "out of place," Strabo, 10, 2, 21. [12]

2. Special Meanings.

a. Sanctuary. The word is often used in cultic contexts with ref. to certain legal and
cultic actions at specific times and places. Thus the charge is brought against Ctesiphon
that by proposing to crown Demosthenes in the theatre he has not only transgressed the
laws ἀλλὰ καὶ τὸν τόπον μετενεγκών, Aeschin. In Ctesiph., 34, cf. 43 and 48. Epictet.
criticises the planting of mysteries in other places: σὺ δ᾿ ἐξαγγέλλεις αὐτὰ καὶ ἐξορχῇ
παρὰ καιρόν, παρὰ τόπον, Diss., III, 21, 16, cf. 21, 14. [13] Philo attacks those who pray
to God without asking μὴ τόπους εἰ βέβηλοι ἢ ἱεροί, μὴ καιροὺς εἰ ἐπιτήδειοι, μὴ
αὐτοὺς εἰ καθαροὶ σῶμα καὶ ψυχήν, Spec. Leg., II, 6, cf. the use in the explanation
of the expiatory offering, I, 240. In Gk. lit. τόπος is only seldom used for holy places.
The relevant passages are dependent on Jewish-Chr. usage or are disputed. The former
is the case when the synagogue is called ἱερὸς τόπος in Philo Omn. Prob. Lib., 81, cf.
Flacc., 49, also the Jerusalem temple in Leg. Gaj., 318. ἐπισημότατος τόπος for the
imperial temple in an edict of Augustus in Jos. Ant., 16, 165 simply reflects general usage
and is no proof of a technical use of τόπος for holy places. [14] The meaning in the
fragmentary letter of the prophet Cronius is uncertain: [ὅ]τι ἔξεσ[τι] πᾶσι ἐν ἀγνοῖς
τόποις γενέσθαι, P. Tebt., II, 616 (2nd. cent. A.D.). [15] Also disputed is ἀνέβην δὲ εἰς
Ῥώμην... καὶ παρεδέξατο ἡμᾶς ὁ τόπος ὡς ὁ θεὸς ἤθελεν, BGU, I, 27, 8 ff.
(2nd/3rd cent. A.D.). [16] But in one of the earliest Chr. pap. from Egypt τόπος probably
denotes a holy place: εἰ οὖν ἔκρεινας... δοῦναι τὴν ἄρ[ο]υραν τῷ τόπῳ, P. Oxy.,
XII, 1492, 8-11 (3rd/4th cent. A.D.). [17] Only in the following cent., however, does ἅγιος
τόπος become a common term for "grave," [18] "grave of a martyr," or the associated

---

[10] Plat. Leg., VI, 762b-c contains the fuller sense "in all districts."

[11] Cf. Moult.-Mill., s.v.; also the indexes of editions of the pap.

[12] ἄτοπος "irregularly," "rarely" corresponds to this sense of παρὰ τόπον; on παρὰ
καιρόν, παρὰ τόπον in Epict. Diss., III, 21, 16 → lines 16 ff.

[13] The reading and transl. of the second ref. are disputed; Liddell-Scott, s.v.: "by virtue
of the place."

[14] ἐπισημότατος "known" is also common with τόπος elsewhere and may have led to
its choice here, cf. ἐν τοῖς ἐπισημοτάτοις τόποις, P. Oxy., XVII, 2108, 7 (259 A.D.),
→ n. 82.

[15] Even for the most commonly adduced ref. Pap., 2710, 6 (HThR, 29 [1936], 40)
A. D. Nock thinks "temple" or "place of assembly" in the temple is most improbable, Roberts-
Skeat-Nock, 46.

[16] Probably τόπος here is not the city of Rome itself but the land of the mariners' society
(collegium naviculariorum); the θεός is the god of the society, and thus the pap. is not of
of Chr. origin, cf. U. Wilcken, Grundzüge u. Chrestomathie d. Papyruskunde, I, 2 (1912)
524 f.

[17] Cf. G. Ghedini, "῾Ο ΤΟΠΟΣ nel P. Oxy., 1492," Aegyptus, 2 (1921), 337 f.

[18] Eur. Heracl., 1041 cannot be regarded as an early example of this usage since one
should read τάφος for τόπος.

monastery. [19] On the other hand ἄσυλος τόπος was already common in Egypt at an earlier time, cf. P. Tebt., I, 5, 83 (118 B.C.); edict of Euergetes II. [20]

b. In Place of, Opportunity. This post-class. use develops out of the gen. sense of "place for something or someone"; there is a series of par. to this Gk. development in the Lat. locus. [21] The starting-pt. is the idea associated with τόπος that all things and people have their own special places, cf. seat at a meal, Jos. Ant., 12, 210, at school, Diog. L., VII, 22, the senator's seat in the theatre, Epict. Diss., I, 25, 27, cf. Res Gestae Divi Augusti, 7, 2 f., [22] fig. the place in the theatre of the world which one should leave willingly, Epict. Diss., IV, 1, 106. The par. to the Latin is evident in the Gk. expressions εἰς τόπον τινός (in alicuius locum) [23] "in place of," "instead of someone," and τόπον τινὸς ἔχω (in alicuius loco esse) [24] "to take someone's place or position." As regards the former cf. the rule that the town whose judge is chosen as president should send another judge εἰς τὸν τούτου τόπον, Diod. S., 1, 75, 4, Augustus: Nicolaus Damascenus Vita Caesaris, 4, [25] the member entering a society in place of a deceased person, Inscr. Perg., 374B, 21 ff. [26] In all these cases we have an expression which is to be taken adverbially "in his place," "in place of." The abs. "position" is not attested for τόπος in Gk. [27] On τόπον τινὸς ἔχω cf. φίλου οὐ δύνασαι τόπον ἔχειν, Epict. Diss., II, 4, 5, also Dion. Hal. De Demosthene, 23. Transf. τόπος as "room for something" means "opportunity," "occasion" and corresponds in this to a widespread Lat. use. [28] Sometimes local elements are still perceptible in τόπος, e.g., "room, opportunity for flight," Heliodor. Aeth., VI, 13, but mostly the use is quite abstract, e.g., par. ἀφορμή: "Where is there still reason (τόπος) for tears? What occasion (ἀφορμή) is there still for flattery?" Epict. Diss., I, 9, 20; cf. II, 13, 10; III, 24, 56; cf. the oldest instance of this usage, Polyb., 1, 88, 2. Common expressions are τόπον λαμβάνω, "to get the opportunity," Jos. Ant., 16, 190, τόπον δίδωμι, "to give opportunity, occasion," Plut. Adulat., 21 (II, 62d), cf. De cohibenda ira, 14 (II, 462b); Philo Mut. Nom., 270, [29] τόπον ἔχω, "to have an opportunity, possibility, ground," Epict. Diss., I, 24, 15; cf. 18, 12; IV, 10, 7; Jos. Ant., 16, 258. [30] Of this usage, which arose in Hell. Gk. under Lat. influence (→ n. 30), there are further instances in biblical Gk. → 200, 2 ff.

---

[19] Examples in Liddell-Scott, Preisigke Wört., s.v. This sense corresponds exactly to a special sense of Latin locus and is perhaps influenced by the Lat., cf. Chantraine, 53; CIL, 14, 1885, 1907, 1914, 3898, 1 and 3. In a phrase like δοῦναι τόπον (sc. εἰς τὴν ταφήν), IG, 12, 401, 14 τόπος is quite untechnical and just means "place for" a burial.

[20] Cf. Preisigke Wört., s.v. τόπος, ἄσυλος, ἀσυλία → n. 81.

[21] Cf. on what follows Chantraine, 51-60.

[22] Ed. H. Volkmann (1957). This can hardly be influenced by the Lat. (princeps senatus fui) as against Chantraine, 55.

[23] Cf. meque iis in patris locum successisse existimes, Cic. Ep. ad Brutum, I, 13, 1.

[24] But cf. alicuius loco aliquem habere, "to regard, hold someone as something": quid enim tam alienum ab humanis sensibus est quam eum patris habere loco, Cic. Ep. ad Brut., I, 17, 5; cf. Or. post reditum in senatu habita, 35; Caesar Comm. Belli Civilis, III, 21 (ed. A. Klotz [1964]).

[25] Cf. FGrHist, II, 392, 25 f.

[26] Quoted from Deissmann NB, 95.

[27] As against Pr.-Bauer, s.v.; there can be no question of a technical use to denote a place within a closed circle (Deissmann NB, 95).

[28] There are many Lat. examples, cf. locus peccandi, Terentius Andria, 233 (ed. R. Kauer and W. Lindsay [1926]), locus resecandae, Cic. Att., I, 18, 2, suspicioni locum dare, Cic. Or. pro Marco Caelio, 9; often negative Cic. Or. pro Lucio Murena, 12; Liv., 24, 26, 15, also Terentius Andria, 601, cf. Chantraine, 55 f.

[29] Further examples Smothers, 210-212.

[30] These verbal Gk. expressions can correspond to the Lat. nouns res and causa but also to verbal par., cf. locum dare, habere, cf. Chantraine, 57, also the examples → n. 28.

c. Rhetorical Usage. This is based on the idea that everything has its right place. Here, then, a τόπος is what will always recur in the same situation (cf. topic). Technically Aristot. first [31] uses the term for a στοιχεῖον "basic element" → VII, 679, 2 ff., i.e., that under which many rhetorical syllogisms are embraced, cf. Aristot. Rhet., II, 22, 13, p. 1396b, 22; II, 26, 1, p. 1403a, 18; also II, 22, 16, p. 1396b, 30 ff.; II, 23, 1, p. 1397a, 7. In Epict. ὁ πρῶτος, ὁ δεύτερος τόπος etc. denote the various fields of Stoic dialectic, Diss., II, 17, 15. 31-33; III, 2, 1. [32] But τόπος is not used non-technically in Gk. in this sense. [33] There is a unique combination of Gk. technical usage and the OT (→ 193, 1 ff.) in Philo Vit. Mos., II, 192, where the four instances in which the Law is given in question and answer are called τόποι. Very strained is the interpretation of "the place whereon thou standest is holy ground" (Ex. 3:5) as a ref. to the τόπος αἰτιολογικός, "searching the basis," Philo Fug., 163; cf. Som., I, 184. But even here the technical use is retained. [34]

d. Place in a Writing. This occurs in ref. to the military author Ephorus in Polyb., 12, 25 f., 1 and Strabo in Jos. Ant., 14, 114. Philo ref. to his own works, Virt., 16, cf. 22. He does not have τόπος for quotations from the OT.

3. τόπος in Philosophical, Scientific and Cosmological Usage.

Aristot. gave the basic though disputed philosophical def. of τόπος in Phys., IV, 1-4, p. 208a, 27 - 212a, 30. In the question περὶ τόπου ... εἰ ἔστιν ἢ μή, καὶ πῶς ἐστί, καὶ τί ἐστιν, IV, 1, p. 208a, 27-29 [35] his starting-pt. is that the commonest form of movement is κατὰ τόπον, "from one place to another," IV, 1, p. 208a, 31 f. But he rejects the popular view that, e.g., τόπος is something whose content one may change at will, IV, 1, p. 208b, 1-3, or which has existence apart from a given content, 6-8. The πρῶτος or ἴδιος τόπος (in contrast to εἶδος, μορφή and ὕλη) is what directly embraces and limits a thing: τὸ πέρας τοῦ περιέχοντος σώματος, IV, 4, p. 212a, 5 f.; IV, 2, p. 209b, 1 f. Its characteristics are as follows: a. place in the original sense includes that whose place it is but it is not itself part of a thing; b. the direct place of a thing is neither greater nor smaller than the thing; c. a thing can leave the place where it is and be separated from it; d. every place has an above and below and each body will by nature seek out its own place and stay there, IV, 3, p. 210b, 33 - 211a, 6. The idea of empty space is expressly called an impossibility by Aristot., IV, 6-9, p. 213a, 12 - 217b, 28. τόπος is never infinite space as such. It never remains empty if a thing changes its place. It belongs to the idea of place to be always proper to certain things. This idea is not without significance as regards scientific terminology (→ 192, 16 ff.) and it finds a par. in the OT (→ 194, 4 ff.; 199, 2 ff.). Even place in the broader sense, which is common to many things, is not unlimited; it is a precisely defined space adopted by several things in common. [36]

---

[31] The way is prepared for this usage in Isoc. Or., 10, 38; Aeschin. In Ctesiph., 216; on this whole section cf. Chantraine, 53-55.

[32] Further examples in Liddell-Scott,, s.v.

[33] As it is in Lat. along with the technical use adopted from the Gk., cf. secundo loco, "moreover," Cic. Fam., I, 6, 2, priore loco dicere, Cic. Or. pro Quinctio, 95, cf. 33. In this connection Lat. had no perceptible influence on Gk. cf. Chantraine, 55. ἔσχατος τόπος in Lk. 14:10 cannot be explained along these lines → 204, 23 f.

[34] τόπος also means "topic," "theme" in the following passages in Philo: Fug., 2, cf. 87; Leg. All., II, 65; Spec. Leg., I, 327; II, 29; Jos., 151; Som., I, 53.

[35] The same question is put for ἄπειρον, "infinite space," and it is discussed along with τόπος, Phys., IV, 6-9, p. 213a, 12 - 217b, 28 → lines 28 ff.

[36] In his doctrine of categories Aristot. does not use either τόπος or χρόνος as the term for a category. He speaks rather of the ποῦ and ποτέ of a thing, Cat., 4, p. 1b, 26; 9, p. 11b, 10 f.; An. Post., I, 22, p. 83a, 22; p. 83b, 17. In later lit., however, τόπος and χρόνος are gen. used in enumeration of the categories, cf. Philo Decal., 30 etc. (→ 201, 17 ff.); Stob. Ecl., I, 73, 15.

Geographically τόπος means a. (geographical) "position," Demosth., 4, 31; Philo Op. Mund., 17; Aristot. Meteor., II, 2, p. 356a, 27. In these examples τόπος in the geographical sense is abstracted from the things found there, a land, town, or river. b. "Territory," "district": τόπος here is used mostly plur. for localities about which gen. statements are made, e.g., τόποι ξηροὶ καὶ θερμοί as the parts where the south wind has its origin, Aristot. Meteor., II, 3, p. 358a, 30. c. "Zone," usually sing. for zones of the earth: ὁ τροπικὸς τόπος, Aristot. Meteor., I, 6, p. 343a, 14; ὁ πρὸς ἄρκτον τόπος, I, 6, p. 343a, 36; ὁ μεταξὺ τόπος τῶν τροπικῶν, I, 6, p. 343a, 8; cf. II, 5, p. 363a, 13. Aristot. used the same terms in scientific description of the cosmos. He distinguishes three cosmic zones, a central zone for the heavy element (earth), an outer zone for the encircling element (aether), and a third intermediate zone containing the two elements of water and air, Cael., I, 8, p. 277b, 14-17. Cf. also ὁ ἄνω τόπος, Aristot. Meteor., I, 3, p. 339b, 37; 340a, 25 f. etc., ὁ ἀνωτέρω τόπος, I, 3, p. 340b, 33, ὁ μεταξὺ γῆς καὶ οὐρανοῦ τόπος, I, 3, p. 340a, 6 f.; cf. a, 18; ὁ μεταξὺ τόπος τῶν ἄστρων καὶ τῆς γῆς, I, 3, p. 341a, 11. In this connection τόπος often means cosmic place, e.g., of a planet, I, 6, p. 343a, 2. But the main thought is not that of apparently free and unlimited space, for beyond heaven there is οὐδὲ τόπος οὐδὲ κενὸν οὐδὲ χρόνος, Cael., I, 9, p. 279a, 11 f. [37] Cosmically τόπος is still the limited sphere or place proper to a specific thing. In this connection arises the astrological use for "position" in the zodiac, Vett. Val., III, 3 (p. 139, 13) or for the zodiac itself, Hephaestio Astrologus, 1, 12; [38] cf. Corp. Herm., 5, 4.

In the usage of Hellenism various cosmological speculations came to be associated with the term τόπος. [39] Corp. Herm., 2, 3 f. discusses the size and constitution of the "place" in which the universe moves, ἀσώματος ... ὁ τόπος is not a place in the true sense, but, like God, it is νοῦς as the power which includes all things within it. [40] For the division of the cosmos into 4 places cf. Stob. Ecl., I, 407, 20 f. τόποι τέσσαρές εἰσιν ἐν τῷ παντί, namely, heaven for the gods, aether for the stars, air for ψυχαὶ δαιμόνιαι, [41] earth for men etc. [42] There is a similar use of τόπος in physiology. Aristot. expressly relates cosmological and physiological statements. As there are three spheres in the cosmos, the upper, middle and lower, Cael., I, 8, p. 277b, 14-18, so men have their centre above, four-footed beasts in the middle, plants below, De animalium incessu, 5, p. 706b, 3. Hippocr. and Gal. use τόπος "zone" of the body in their titles: περὶ τόπων τῶν κατὰ ἄνθρωπον. [43] In discussion of the three parts of the soul λογιστικόν — θυμικόν — ἐπιθυμητικόν it can be said that distinction may be made not only in respect of their functions (δυνάμει) but also in respect of their places (τόποις), Philo Leg. All., III, 115, cf. 116. In scientific usage, too, one may see how basic for the Gk. understanding of τόπος is the thought of limited space: the place cannot be separated from the thing which is now in it and completely fills it.

---

[37] Against Plat. Phaedr., 247c, which in speaking of the ὑπερουράνιος τόπος uses τόπος mythically in connection with the description of the intelligible world.

[38] Ed. A. Engelbrecht (1887).

[39] Sometimes we read of the heavenly place of the soul, Philo Som., I, 181, or the place of the ungodly, Iambl. Vit. Pyth., 30, 178, though there is no trace of a systematic use of τόπος for the place beyond, cf. the freeing of chained Kronos in magic, Preis. Zaub., I, 4, 3123.

[40] These statements about νοῦς are almost the same as those of Philo about God as τόπος → 200, 29 ff. But in Corp. Herm., 2, 12 God as cause is distinguished from the νοῦς as that which encloses all things in itself.

[41] Cf. Nock-Fest, IV, 59, n. 3.

[42] This division goes back to the ancient distinction of gods in heaven and men on earth; the aether as the seat of the stars is Aristotelian, Nock-Fest, IV, 59. Different is the Stoic division into fire, water, air and earth, which has nothing to do with the present theme, but cf. Stob. Ecl., I, 413, 21 - 414, 13; 460, 11 - 461, 16; τόπος is not used for this Stoic division.

[43] Further examples in Liddell-Scott, s.v.

B. Old Testament Usage.

1. General.

The Hbr. original of τόπος is מָקוֹם. This occurs some 400 times and in the vast majority of instances in transl. by LXX τόπος. [44] This rendering is even more consistent in the later transl. than the LXX. [45] מָקוֹם and τόπος largely correspond, though not completely, for LXX has τόπος in about another 180 instances [46] and more than 100 times in parts of the LXX for which there is no Hbr. original [47] or none can be pre-supposed.

2. Linguistic Peculiarities.

a. Basis. Whereas the Gk. concept starts with the thought of space (→ 187, 16 ff.) the idea of a marked place is basic to מָקוֹם. It means "site," "settlement," "place," and only in a derived sense "locality" or "district." Gk. τόπος is a geographical place containing something, OT מָקוֹם is a site where something is.

b. Place Where. This explains the most striking outward mark of OT usage, the linking of מָקוֹם with the relative אֲשֶׁר, and adv. indication of place peculiar to Hbr. Thus הַמָּקוֹם אֲשֶׁר . . . שָׁם simply means "where," esp. in prepos. expressions: עַד־הַמָּקוֹם אֲשֶׁר־הָיָה שָׁם אָהֳלֹה, "where his tent was," Gn. 13:3, וּרְאֵה מִן־הַמָּקוֹם אֲשֶׁר אַתָּה שָׁם "look from where thou standest," Gn. 13:14, cf. also Gn. 19:27; 22:3, 9; 39:20; 40:3; Nu. 10:29; 14:40; Ju. 20:22; 1 K. 5:23; Ezr. 1:4; Neh. 4:14; Qoh. 1:7; 11:3; Hos. 2:1; Jl. 3:7; Is. 7:23; Jer. 22:12 etc. Lit. transl. of these Hbr. expressions yields the LXX formulations ἕως τοῦ τόπου, οὗ, Gn. 13:3 etc., ἀπὸ τοῦ τόπου, οὗ, Gn. 13:14 etc., ἐπὶ τὸν τόπον, ὄν, Gn. 22:3 etc., εἰς τὸν τόπον, ἐν ᾧ, Gn. 39:20 etc. Often a very ungreek ἐκεῖ is added to render the שָׁם which mostly follows in Hbr., Gn. 40:3; Rt. 1:7 etc.; cf. the addition of כָּל־: πᾶς τόπος οὗ... ἐκεῖ "everywhere where," Gn. 20:13; also Dt. 11:24; Est. 4:3; Jer. 8:3 etc.; Ez. 34:12. This distinctive Hbr. usage occurs in the LXX even where no Hbr. original has been preserved, e.g., εἰς πάντα τόπον, οὗ ἂν ἐπορεύετο, 1 Macc. 13:20, [48] and sometimes in books which were written in Gk., cf. πᾶς δὲ τόπος, οὗ, 3 Macc. 3:29, though we also find here the better Gk. ἐν ᾧ τόπῳ ἔδοξαν τὸν ὄλεθρον ἀναλαμβάνειν, ἐν τούτῳ, 3 Macc. 6:30.

---

[44] The other renderings are mostly good ones in context: χώρα in Jos. 4:18; Job 2:11 vl., πόλις Gn. 18:26 vl.; Dt. 21:19 vl.; Job 2:11 vl., οἶκος Ex. 16:29 vl., γῆ Ex. 23:20; the MSS often vary here. A special case is Gn. 1:9; LXX συναχθήτω τὸ ὕδωρ ... εἰς συναγωγὴν μίαν presupposes as HT אֶל־מִקְוֶה אֶחָד for the present אֶל־מָקוֹם אֶחָד. The former is attested in Fr. 4 Q Gnh [F. M. Cross Jr.].

[45] In a couple of dozen cases in which LXX does not use τόπος 'Α Σ and Θ have it, e.g., Gn. 1:9; Rt. 4:10 'ΑΣ; Job 38:12 'ΑΘ; Is. 5:8; 26:21; 28:8; Jer. 17:12 'ΑΣ; Ez. 6:13 'Α; 41:11 Σ. The later transl. follow the same practice in Hbr. sayings for which there is no LXX, cf. Jer. 27(34):22; 29(36):14; 44(51):29.

[46] The no. cannot be given for certain since the MSS vary a good deal.

[47] In Sir. מָקוֹם can often be shown to be the original of τόπος, 4:5; 13:22; 38:12; 41:19.

[48] Often LXX transl. by τόπος adv. phrases in which there is no Hbr. מָקוֹם, e.g., for אֶל־אֲשֶׁר Ex. 32:34, אֶל־כָּל־אֲשֶׁר Jos. 1:16; cf. also Ju. 17:8, 9; 18:13 (B) and the transl. of Aram. וּבְכָל־דִּי דָאֲרִין in Da. 2:38 Θ, where LXX has ἐν πάσῃ τῇ οἰκουμένῃ.

c. This Place. In Hbr. the demonstrative is often added to denote the place referred to. It is open to question whether this is to be taken adverbially too in many instances. [49] This is possible in verses like Dt. 1:31: "Until you come to this place (here)," cf. 9:7; 11:5; 29:6, also in Jer. and Baruch's stories about Jer., cf. Jer. 22:11 f.; 24:5; 29:10; 42:18. Elsewhere הַמָּקוֹם הַזֶּה has a more technical sense → 195, 20 ff.

d. מָקוֹם with Possessive Pronoun. This use is found with things as well as men or peoples. A very close relation is expressed by it. מָקוֹם with suffix is the place to which something belongs, e.g., a stone in Gn. 29:3, cf. 1 S. 5:3; 2 Ch. 24:11; 1 K. 5:8 (3 Βασ. 5:1). Of men it denotes the place allotted to an individual or people; thus Jacob asks Laban for return אֶל־מְקוֹמִי וּלְאַרְצִי Gn. 30:25. The names of the tribal leaders of Esau are listed לִמְקֹמֹתָם Gn. 36:40. In this connection we may ref. to the many expressions in which someone comes from his מָקוֹם like the friends of Job (Job 2:11) or returns there like Abraham, Gn. 18:33, cf. Gn. 32:1; 1 S. 26:25; 29:4, and esp. the stereotyped אִישׁ לִמְקֹמוֹ, "let each go to his home," Ju. 7:7; 9:55, also 1 Βασ. 10:25, cf. Ex. 18:23; 1 Macc. 6:54; 11:38. In this distinctive use one may discern a material peculiarity of the OT idea of place. Every place is defined in relation to a thing which is found there, an event which took place there, or a man or people living there. The concrete reference and the idea of possession dominate the idea of place much more strongly than in Gk. usage.

3. Meanings of מָקוֹם in Comparison with the Greek τόπος.

a. Land, Locality. As in Gk. (→ 187, 16 ff.) מָקוֹם often means a land or locality, but with the distinctive feature that the sing. is always used, whereas the Gk. prefers plur. οἱ τόποι τῶν (→ 187, 22 ff.); the suffix is also most added unless a gen. or אֲשֶׁר expresses the relation in question, e.g., into the territory of the Canaanites, Ex. 3:8, the march of Israel into its land, Ju. 11:19; Naomi went out of the district in which she was, Rt. 1:7. LXX always transl. in the sing. But in LXX passages with no Hbr. original it follows the Gk. practice and prefers the plur., e.g., ἔμπειρος εἶ τῶν τόπων, Tob. 5:5, cf. 2 Macc. 9:23; 10:14; 12:18; 3 Macc. 2:26.

b. Town, Dwelling-Place. Since the sing. also denotes the land as the dwelling-place of a people it is often hard to say when the ref. is to a town. This is certainly so in Gn. 18:24 (par. עִיר), cf. 19:12-14; 26:7, also Dt. 21:19; cf. Ju. 19:13, 16; 1 S. 30:31; 1 K. 13:8, 16, 22, also in later LXX passages, often with a typical Hbr. αὐτοῦ, e.g., οἱ ἐν τῷ τόπῳ αὐτοῦ, 1 Εσδρ. 2:4; cf. Bel et Draco 39 Θ; 1 Macc. 10:13, also without 3 Macc. 4:3 (par. νομός and πόλις); Da. 11:43 LXX; Bel et Draco 23 LXX; 1 Macc. 10:40; 11:14 etc.; 2 Macc. 8:6; 10:17 etc. The plur. occurs only with כָּל־ and means "all towns," "all dwelling-places," Am. 4:6; Ezr. 1:4; Neh. 4:6, without πᾶς, 1 Εσδρ. 2:12. The sing. with כָּל־ denotes the totality of inhabited places, "everywhere," the consuming of the tithes by the priests, Nu. 18:31; dead bodies lying everywhere, Am. 8:3, the eyes of Yahweh, Prv. 15:3; cf. Mal. 1:11. [50] This use continues unchanged in the LXX, Wis. 19:22; cf. 1 Macc. 1:25 with the typical Hbr. pronoun: ἐπὶ Ἰσραὴλ ἐν παντὶ τόπῳ αὐτῶν. Independent of the Hbr. is κατὰ τόπον "in the relevant place," 2 Macc. 12:2; 3 Macc. 3:12; cf. 4:4; par. to κατὰ

---

[49] The similar אֶל־מָקוֹם אַחֵר in Nu. 23:27, cf. v. 13, means "elsewhere."

[50] Perhaps one should ref. here to Ps. 103:22: בְּכָל־מְקֹמוֹת מֶמְשַׁלְתּוֹ, for ἐν παντὶ τόπῳ τῆς δεσποτείας αὐτοῦ in ψ 102:22 presupposes the sing.

τὰς οἰκίας, 3 Macc. 4:18; cf. also 1 Macc. 12:4; 3 Macc. 7:12; for plur. κατὰ τόπους, cf. 1 Εσδρ. 2:4. [51]

c. Other Places. As in Gk. (→ 188, 36 ff.) all possible sites and places can be called מָקוֹם, e.g., the place where the ambush was set, Ju. 20:33; cf. 2 K. 6:8-10; 1 Macc. 11:69; the place where the Israelites were to camp, Dt. 1:33, a narrow place on the way, Nu. 22:26; cf. also Neh. 4:7 (2 Εσδρ. 14:7); Is. 22:23, 25; 2 K. 6:6; Ez. 17:16; 39:11; 2 Macc. 12:21. The context makes the ref. plain. מָקוֹם is also used in the expression "in such and such a place," 1 S. 21:3, [52] cf. 2 K. 6:8. Apart from instances to be treated later (→ lines 20 ff.) no special meaning developed. We do not find examples of "part of the body," "position," "grave-site" (→ 189, 32 ff.; 190, 3 ff.; 192, 28 ff.) in the Hbr. OT. [53]

4. מָקוֹם as the Promised Land.

מָקוֹם is not used technically for the promised land. In this respect the word is in competition with the much more common אֶרֶץ, with which it can also be used in parallelism, Jos. 1:2 f. Independently it may also denote the "place" which Yahweh has appointed for His people, Ex. 23:20; cf. Nu. 10:29; 2 S. 7:10; 1 S. 12:8. It is par. to נַחֲלָה (→ III, 769, 9 ff.) for the place to which each rightly belongs, Nu. 32:17 f., [54] no matter whether the ref. be to the whole people, the tribes, or individuals. The alternation of מָקוֹם and עַם in Nu. 24:11, 14 is to be viewed similarly. The man who dwells abroad is separated not only from his own people but also from his own place, 2 S. 15:19, cf. Prv. 27:8; Sir. 41:19. [55]

5. מָקוֹם as a Term for Holy Places. [56]

a. Original Canaanite Shrines. From the older parts of traditions preserved in Gn. and also Jos and Ju. (J and E) one may see that the wandering Israelite tribes found in the land holy places and cultic centres which the OT calls מָקוֹם. With the traditional aetiologies Israel took over these shrines as sanctuaries of Yahweh. In these texts we find in the OT a very ancient and perhaps original technical use of מָקוֹם, esp. for the gt. Canaanite shrines which then played a role in the history of Israel: Bethel, Gn. 28:11-19; 35:7, 13, 15; Shechem, Gn. 12:6; Gilgal, Jos. 5:9; Beer-sheba, Gn. 21:31. Gn. 12:6 ff. is a typical cultic story in which an adopted מָקוֹם is introduced thus. Abraham reaches the already existing holy place of Shechem with its oracular terebinth. It was obviously a Canaanite shrine. But now Yahweh appears to him here and promises him this land, and

---

[51] It is doubtful whether מָקוֹם itself can also mean "house." In Ex. 16:29 only LXX has the parallelism οἴκοι ὑμῶν — τόπος αὐτοῦ (HT תַּחְתָּיו — מְקוֹמוֹ); cf. also Nu. 32:17 f.

[52] LXX, of course, did not understand the Hbr. אֶל־מְקוֹם פְּלֹנִי אַלְמוֹנִי here and transl. ἐν τῷ τόπῳ τῷ λεγομένῳ Θεοῦ πίστις, Φελλανι Αλεμωνι, 1 Βασ. 21:3.

[53] The instances given, Lv. 13:19 for part of the body, 1 K. 20:24 for position, cf. Δα. 11:21; 11:38 LXX, and Sir. 49:10 for grave-site, are only special instances of the gen. meaning "place" with ref. to a man or thing.

[54] At Jos. 24:28 LXX has ἕκαστος εἰς τὸν τόπον αὐτοῦ for אִישׁ לְנַחֲלָתוֹ. In fact this Hbr. expression means the same as אִישׁ לִמְקוֹמוֹ in Ju. 7:7 → 194, 13 ff.

[55] ἀπὸ τόπου, οὗ παροικεῖς is the transl. of HT ממקום תגור.

[56] On what follows cf. H. W. Hertzberg, Art. "Hl. Stätten," RGG³, III, 156-160 (with bibl.); G. v. Rad, Theol. d. AT, I⁴ (1962), 32-43, 55-59 and passim; C. A. Keller, "Über einige at.liche Heiligtumslegenden," ZAW, 67 (1955), 141-168; 68 (1956), 85-97. → III, 233. 14 ff.; IV, 882, 1 ff.

he builds an altar to Yahweh there, v. 6 f. Thus the ancient holy place is associated with faith in Yahweh and the promise of the land. This shows that Israel took over the idea of מָקוֹם as a holy place only at the conquest, and had to change it decisively in so doing. [57] This is even clearer in the Bethel story. Bethel is introduced without details or explanations in Gn. 28:11 as הַמָּקוֹם: "And he came to the holy place and he took of the stones of the holy place." [58] The narrator thus assumes that this place was already a holy place and with the traditional aetiological story he also has the appropriate conclusion telling of the awesome sanctity of the place (מַה־נּוֹרָא הַמָּקוֹם הַזֶּה, Gn. 28:17), its naming (28:17. 19), and finally its consecration (28:18). The primary interest of the Israelite author is in the interpolated and disruptive passage Gn. 28:13-16 and here esp. in the saying יְהוָה בַּמָּקוֹם הַזֶּה (28:16), [59] which does not lead up at all to the name, and in the promise of the land (28:13 f.), which naturally has nothing whatever to do with the original aetiology. The pt. of the story is to give a theological basis, not now for the cultus at the place in question, but rather for the conquest of the land.

The appropriation of traditional aetiologies is not always so distinct, and in many cases even the existing cultic significance of such a place is no longer evident. But there can be no doubt that all the places called מָקוֹם in Gn., Beer-sheba in 21:31, Mahanaim in 32:2, Penuel in 32:31, Succoth in 33:17, were original cultic centres which Israel took over not only in fact but also theologically. [60] Sometimes the ref. to a special event in the history of the conquest replaces the older aetiology of such a shrine, cf. Gilgal in Jos. 4-5, [61] though the stereotyped conclusion of the original aetiology וַיִּקְרָא שֵׁם הַמָּקוֹם הַהוּא גִּלְגָּל (Jos. 5:9) occurs here even though no special cult is being established. The same expression is common in Ex., Nu., Ju. and 1 and 2 S. Often one may see here the ref. to an aetiology, cf. Massah and Meribah (originally a sacred well?) in Ex. 17:7, Kirjath-jearim in Ju. 18:12 and Perez-uzzah in 2 S. 6:8 (1 Ch. 13:11), which both served as stopping-places for the ark, 1 S. 6:21 ff.; 2 S. 6:8. The cultic background is obscure in Nu. 11:3, 34; 13:24; 21:3; Ju. 2:5; 15:17; 1 S. 23:28; cf. also 1 Ch. 14:11 (Baal-perazim) and 2 Ch. 20:26. Perhaps these are analogous constructs.

b. Zion and the Jerusalem Temple. [62] The Jerusalem temple occupies a special position as מָקוֹם inasmuch as the tradition ignores any link by cultic aetiology with the pre-Israelite holy place there must undoubtedly have been in Jerusalem. [63] Certainly Jerusalem before Dt. was one of many holy places in the land. But for Israel it is esp. the city of David (2 S. 6:12 etc.) and it takes on cultic significance only with the bringing of the ark there (2 S. 6:17). Whether it thereby became a holy place in the traditional sense is discussed in Nathan's prophecy in 2 S. 7:1 ff. The temple seems to have been understood originally as a place for the ark. The terminology in 1 K. 8:6 f. gives no evidence of a technical use of מָקוֹם: "the priests brought in the ark אֶל־מְקוֹמוֹ" and the cherubim covered with their wings מְקוֹם הָאָרוֹן." [64]

---

[57] On these matters cf. the OT theologies, also A. Alt, Art. "Israel," RGG³, III, 936-942; O. Eissfeldt "El and Yahweh," Journal of Semitic Stud., 1 (1956), 25-37.
[58] The transl. "of the stones which lay there" in some renderings (e.g., H. Menge) is an incorrect linguistic softening.
[59] Whether source criticism can clarify the relation of El and Yahweh is doubtful but this does not basically alter the obvious intention of the narrative.
[60] Cf. also Gn. 22 (cf. v. 14). The original name of the place has been lost and its significance and aetiology are obscure, cf. H. Gunkel, Gn., Handkomm. AT, I, 1³ (1910), ad loc. and G. v. Rad, Das erste Buch Mose, AT Deutsch, 3⁴ (1961), ad loc.
[61] M. Noth, Das Buch Jos., Handb. AT, I, 7² (1953), 25-27.
[62] For discussion (with bibl.) of Zion → VII, 292, 28 ff.
[63] Gn. 14 confirms this tendency in Israelite tradition.
[64] מָקוֹם is also used non-technically with the ark in 1 Ch. 15:1, 3.

Only with Dt. does there take place a fundamental change. In a rich formula which is constantly repeated the Jerusalem temple is called "the holy place which Yahweh your God shall choose ... to cause his name to dwell there," Dt. 12:5, 11 etc.; cf. 16:16; 17:8, 10; 18:6; 31:11. With this declaration of the Jerusalem temple as a holy place where Yahweh causes His name to dwell is directly linked the command to destroy all holy places in the land אֶת־כָּל־הַמְּקוֹמֹת, Dt. 12:2. [65] The name and function of prior Canaanite shrines are, of course, adopted herewith. [66] But the exodus tradition is also adopted that Yahweh "tabernacles" (שָׁכַן) among His people (2 S. 7:6) and gives it a place to dwell מָקוֹם לְעַמִּי (→ 195, 14 ff.), 2 S. 7:10. This terminology and concept established themselves later and they dominate the historical writing of Dt. and Ch., cf. esp. 1 K. 8:29 f. etc. (2 Ch. 6:20 f. etc.), [67] also Jos. 9:27; Neh. 1:9.

Other places in the land were no longer called מָקוֹם in the technical sense, [68] cf. the equation of the "hill of Zion" and the "holy place of the name of Yahweh Sabaoth" in Is. 18:7. Sometimes one also finds the combining of מָקוֹם with a word of the root קדשׁ, Jer. 17:12; Ezr. 9:8; Is. 60:13; cf. Ps. 24:3; [69] Qoh. 8:10.

c. This Place in the Prophets. Already in the Deuteronomistic 1 K. 8 we find הַמָּקוֹם הַזֶּה for the temple in vv. 29 ff. etc. (2 Ch. 6:40; 7:12 etc.). [70] It is noteworthy that the same expression is common in prophetic passages from Dt. on, esp. in the prophecies of disaster in Jer. At first the ref. seems to be mostly to Jerusalem, its inhabitants (2 K. 22:16-20), and the whole land of Judah (2 K. 18:25, cf. Zeph. 1:4; Jer. 7:20). But several passages in Jer. which have "this place" are less certain, and it is an open question whether the idea of the temple is not also present, cf. 14:13; but cf. 14:15; also 28(35):3 f. [71] The situation is obscure in passages more strongly influenced by Dt., esp. the temple address in Jer. 7. Acc. to the traditional reading this runs: "I will cause you to dwell in this place" (i.e., the land), [72] 7:3, 7, but the continuation is: "But go ye now unto my (holy) place which was in Shiloh (cf. 1 S. 1:24 etc.), where I caused my name to tabernacle at the first" (7:12), and then finally: "Therefore will I do unto this house (בַּיִת) over which my name is named ... and the place (מָקוֹם) which I gave to you and to your fathers, as I have done to Shiloh" (7:14). Obviously (הַזֶּה) מָקוֹם (הַ) is used as a double sense here. So, too, in other

---

[65] Cf. the juxtaposition of בְּכָל־מָקוֹם אֲשֶׁר תִּרְאֶה in Dt. 12:13 and בַּמָּקוֹם אֲשֶׁר־יִבְחַר יהוה in 12:14.

[66] Jerusalem as the holy place which Yahweh has chosen takes over all the functions of cultic sites in the land — each time this formula is repeated: the bringing of sacrifices, Dt. 12:14 and first-fruits, 12:26; 14:25; 26:1 f., the eating of sacrifices, esp. the Passover, 12:5-7; 14:23; 15:20; 16:2 etc., celebrating the main festivals, 16:16; 31:11, official decisions in judicial matters, 17:8,10.

[67] Since the prophetic situation of Dt. in the time of the wilderness wandering no longer applies here, the phrase "which Yahweh shall choose" is mostly dropped, but cf. 2 Ch. 7:12.

[68] LXX has τόποι for "high places" at 2 Ch. 34:6 (HT corrupt?), cf. 2 Εσδρ. 13:35.

[69] This is hard to date but cannot be before Dt. On בְּמָקוֹם קָדְשׁוֹ in Ps. 24:3 cf. the same expression in Ezr. 9:8; on כְּבוֹדֶךָ מָקוֹם מִשְׁכַּן in Ps. 26:8 cf. the passages in Dt. (→ 196, 31 ff.), also for Ps. 132:5, where מָקוֹם (יהוה) is also linked with the concept of time.

[70] That the phrase cannot just be taken adverbially in this context (1 K. 8:29 might suggest this: "the prayer which thy servant prays in this place, i.e., here") is shown esp. by 2 Ch. 6:40; 7:15, which speaks of "the prayer of this place."

[71] On the adv. use in Jer. → 194, 1 ff. This is found esp. in the autobiographical passages and in Baruch. The only instance of tied use in Jer. is in 17:12 with ref. to the temple.

[72] This rests on the traditional pointing of the HT, cf. LXX: κατοικιῶ ὑμᾶς. But one can also point so as to read: "I will tabernacle with you in this place (sc. the temple)," cf. ᾿Α (Syh): καὶ σκηνώσω σὺν ὑμῖν. Cf. on this whole question W. Rudolph, Jer., Hdbuch AT, I, 12² (1958), ad loc.

passages in Jer. [73] This intentional multiplicity of meaning is to be explained by the artificial Deuteronomic linking of מָקוֹם as shrine with the idea of מָקוֹם as the place where Yahweh causes His people to dwell. Whereas the prophetic protest with its threat of disaster is directed against the city, land and inhabitants, and מָקוֹם is meant in the sense of the ancient promise of the land, for the later Deuteronomic redactors the central problem is the destruction of the Jerusalem temple.

d. Post-Exilic Usage. The meaning established by Dt. is partially followed here. The Deuteronomic formula "the holy place where Yahweh causes his name to tabernacle" lives on only in works dependent on Dt. [74] In P and related works the cultic use of מָקוֹם is much more directly governed by the idea of the sanctity of a place or its precincts; ancient Canaanite concepts emerge again in this respect. In the priestly legislation the precincts of the tabernacle are מָקוֹם קָדֹשׁ, Lv. 6:9, 19, 20; 7:6; 10:13, 14 vl., 17; 14:13; 16:24; 24:9. מָקוֹם is also commonly used for individual cultic places, e.g., the place for slaying the whole offering, Lv. 4:24 etc.; 6:18 etc., the place for ashes and refuse, Lv. 1:16, clean and unclean places outside the camp, Lv. 6:4; 14:40 etc.; Nu. 19:9. Analogously specific parts of the temple are מָקוֹם, Ez. 41:11; 46:19 f., and the place where the temple stands as well as the temple itself, Ezr. 9:8 (2 Εσδρ. 9:8). The Aram. אֲתַר seems to be used similarly for the temple in Ezr. (2 Εσδρ.) 6:3, 5 and also for the place where it stands, Ezr. (2 Εσδρ.) 6:7, cf. 5:15. In all these instances LXX transl. τόπος. [75]

Only the LXX developed the term into a technical one for the holy place. In particular the translator of Ps. often goes beyond the original in using τόπος for the temple, e.g., for מָעוֹן in ψ 67:6 and 83:7, [76] for סֹךְ in ψ 75:3, and τόπος σκηνῆς for סָךְ in ψ 41:5, [77] cf. also ψ 131:7; 78:7. τόπος occurs for מָכוֹן at Is. 4:5; Sir. 36:12, with no Hbr. original Lv. 8:31; 10:18; Nu. 19:3. This technical use is quite clear in later histories written for edification, 1, 2 and 3 Macc. Here τόπος, which originally served as a transl. of Hbr. מָקוֹם in all its senses, receives a content equivalent to the Gk. τὸ τέμενος. But τέμενος is rare in the Gk. OT [78] and is never used for מָקוֹם. It is more common only in 1, 2 and 3 Macc., where it is used exclusively, however, for pagan shrines. [79] In 1, 2, 3 and 4 Macc. the Jewish temple is τὸ ἱερόν [80] or, including the precincts, ὁ τόπος. Both terms are clearly differentiated from τέμενος, cf. 2 Macc. 11:3 and 3 Macc. 1:9 f. with 1:13. [81]

In 1, 2, 3 and 4 Macc. the land is never called τόπος. "The holy place where God has planted his people" in 2 Macc. 1:29 is not the land but the temple, cf. 2 Macc. 5:19 f. Only

---

[73] Again in parts influenced by Dt.: Jer. 16:2-9; 19:3-6, 12; 32:37; 33:10, 12, and the Deuteronomic saying: "Innocent blood does not flow in this place," 22:3.

[74] The passages quoted from 1 and 2 Ch. (→ lines 13 ff.) are all copies of the corresponding verses in 1 and 2 S., 1 and 2 K., or analogous to them.

[75] τόπος also occurs for אֲתַר in Da. 2:35 Θ. Its use in 1 Εσδρ. 5:43, 49; 6:18, 26; 8:75 corresponds exactly to the passages from Ezr. (2 Εσδρ.) → lines 16 ff.

[76] LXX probably read מָעוֹן for מַעְיָן Ps. 84:7.

[77] ψ 26:5 transl. סֹךְ by σκηνή.

[78] Apart from 1, 2 and 3 Macc. only Hos. 8:14 for הֵיכָל; Ez. 6:4, 6 for חַמָּן (a difficult word probably denoting a special altar of incense, cf. W. Zimmerli, Ez., Bibl. Komm. AT, 13 [1956], 148 f.); also 4 Βασ. 21:6 vl.

[79] This applies also to 3 Macc. 1:13. In the dispute whether he should enter the inner sanctuary of the Jewish temple Ptolemy asks διὰ τίνα αἰτίαν εἰσερχόμενον αὐτὸν εἰς πᾶν τέμενος οὐθεὶς ἐκώλυσεν τῶν παρόντων.

[80] Elsewhere ἱερόν is not used at all in the Gk. OT, probably because of its pagan associations for the ancient translators, → III, 226, 5 ff.

[81] Only in 2 Macc. 1:14 and Bel et Draco 15-17 LXX is a heathen temple called τόπος, cf. also ἄσυλος τόπος, 2 Macc. 4:33 f. → 190, 1 f.

rarely is ὁ τόπος Jerusalem or Zion, 1 Macc. 6:57, 62, [82] but "the sacred precincts" are very commonly ἅγιος τόπος, 2 Macc. 2:18; 8:17; 3 Macc. 2:14, ἱερὸς τόπος, 4 Macc. 4:12, ὁ ἑαυτοῦ (sc. θεοῦ) τόπος, 2 Macc. 3:30; 10:7; 15:34 etc., but cf. also the common ὁ τόπος in the abs., 2 Macc. 3:2, 18, 38; 13:23 etc. The whole pt. is that God has recorded His power here, 2 Macc. 3:30, 38 f. etc., that He has dedicated this place, 2 Macc. 2:8, 18; 3 Macc. 2:16, and that He protects it from desecration, 2 Macc. 3:18; 3 Macc. 1:29; 4 Macc. 4:9. The sense of "holy place" still clings to the word even when the ref. is not the temple, e.g., for the place where the sacred fire is kept 2 Macc. 1:19, cf. 1:34 ff., also the place where Jeremiah hid the ark, 2 Macc. 2:8 f., cf. also 3 Macc. 6:30 f.; 7:20.

Historically, then, the land is no longer Israel's place even before the final expulsion from Palestine. The theological understanding of place is fully orientated to the temple as the holy place. As regards the resultant question of the righteous Jew concerning his place in the world, Wisdom's understanding of place (→ lines 16 ff.) attempts to give an answer.

6. Places in Creation.

Wisdom's understanding of place rests on presuppositions which are plainly distinct from the concept of a specific cultic centre as a holy place. The basis is the general usage which is found in Hbr. as well as Gk. and which in the Gk. sphere underlies the scientific (→ 191, 17 ff.) and cosmological (→ 192, 9 ff.) use, namely, that of "the right place for something or someone," e.g., for raising cattle in Nu. 32:1, camels in Gn. 24:31, camping in Gn. 24:25, dwelling in 1 S. 27:5; "seating" should also be mentioned in this connection, 1 S. 9:22; 20:25, 27. The place can be very gt., 1 S. 26:13, can become too narrow, 2 K. 6:1, cf. Is. 49:20, or cease to be there at all, Is. 5:8; cf. 28:8; Jer. 7:32; Neh. 2:14; 1 Macc. 9:45; 10:73. Not to have one's place is to cease to be. Hence it is continally said of the wicked that his place denies him when he perishes, Job 8:18; cf. 18:21; 20:9; Ps. 37:10. Friends are as unfaithful as streams which swell in season but when the heat comes they vanish from their place, Job 6:17; cf. with ref. to the Assyrians Na. 3:17.

The same terminology is used in mythological speech. Gog comes from his place in the farthest north, Ez. 38:15; disaster comes from the north too, Jer. 4:6 f. But this mythical, personifying way of speaking of historical powers is very rare. [83] No less rare is the mythical ref. to Yahweh's place. In analogy to the above passages (→ lines 28 ff.) Mi. 1:3 and Is. 26:21 say that Yahweh leaves His place in judgment, namely, heaven, and comes to earth. On the other hand Yahweh says in Hos. 5:15: "I will go and return to my place," i.e., heaven. [84] Elsewhere ref. to God's place has in view the temple. This is how "strength and gladness are in his place" in 1 Ch. 16:27 is to be taken in context. [85] The prayers which are made in the temple אֶל־הַמָּקוֹם הַזֶּה Yahweh will hear "in the place of his dwelling in heaven," 1 K. 8:30. [86]

---

[82] It is rare for places of no religious significance, cf. ἐν τόπῳ ἐπισήμῳ, 1 Macc. 11:37; also 1 Macc. 14:48; 2 Macc. 8:31; 14:22; 3 Macc. 5:44; 4 Macc. 5:1.

[83] Cf. the disputed Ps. 44:19.

[84] On the transl. cf. H. W. Wolff, Dodekaproph., I, Bibl. Komm. AT, 14, 1 (1961), 132, 134. It may be doubted whether מָקוֹם here means the lion's lair as part of the simile of 5:14 (Wolff, 147); cf. G. Fohrer, "Umkehr u. Erlösung beim Propheten Hosea," ThZ, 11 (1955), 165 f.

[85] The par. in Ps. 96:6 has בְּמִקְדָּשׁוֹ with ref. to the heavenly sanctuary.

[86] On the temple as מָקוֹם → 196, 29 ff. Ex. 24:10 f. is puzzling. LXX reads καὶ εἶδον τὸν τόπον, οὗ εἱστήκει ἐκεῖ ὁ θεὸς τοῦ Ἰσραήλ (v. 10) and καὶ ὤφθησαν ἐν τῷ τόπῳ τοῦ θεοῦ (v. 11). The first expression esp. is the typical rendering of a Hbr. original (→ 193, 14 ff.) but there is no equivalent in the present HT. One does not find τόπος here in the later transl. That the LXX is trying to avoid an anthropomorphism is doubtful in view of the Hebraic style (there is, of course, no ἐκεῖ in some MSS); cf. D. W. Gooding, The Account of the Tabernacle (1959), 20.

The problem arises when man's place begins to become sociologically and theologically doubtful and is no longer self-evident. For it is true of all men (not just the wicked) that they pass away and their place knows them no more, Ps. 103:16. The righteous, too, suffers this fate, Job 7:10. In the question of a fresh orientation, now with ref. to the cosmos, consideration is given to the right place of things in the world. Thus מָקוֹם and in the LXX τόπος (often with no Hbr. original) is used in many respects as in Gk. geography (→ 192, 1 ff.) and cosmology (→ 192, 9 ff.), though one cannot postulate direct dependence: "Mountains rise up and valleys sink in the place which God has ordained for them," Ps. 104:8; cf. Job 14:18; 18:4, "the sun returns in a day to its place," 1 Εσδρ. 4:34; cf. Qoh. 1:5, so too rivers, Qoh. 1:7. The early dawn, the light and the darkness have places appointed by God, Job 38:12, 19. Ref. may also be made to the place of all creation, Bar. 3:24.

Whereas this contemplation of God's creation gives new assurance to Job and the author of Ps. 103 f., it is for the Preacher only an indication of the pointlessness of all events in the world: "Everything returns to its place," Qoh. 3:20, cf. 6:6. In the Wisdom song in Job 28 (→ VII, 489, 34 ff.) knowledge of the places of precious stones is contrasted with the secret of the place of wisdom, 28:12, 20; only God knows its way and place, v. 23. Similarly abstract theological concepts are sometimes said to have their place like material things, [87] as when wrong is said to stand in the place of right and injustice in the place of justice, Qoh. 3:16, cf. Bar. 3:15. In close connection with this τόπος is used in the sense of "opportunity" in Sir. and Wis. But the ref. is not to opportunity in the secular sense as in Gk. lit., cf. the admonition not to give anyone an "occasion" to curse in Sir. 4:5. [88] τόπος denotes supremely the divinely given "possibility" of being. God gives the opportunity to repent, Wis. 12:10, the time and place to break free from wickedness, 12:20, an opportunity for mercy, Sir. 16:14. This transf. usage in Jewish Wisdom lit., which is sometimes based on a Hbr. original, is not to be explained merely by adoption of the corresponding transf. meaning in Gk. It presupposes the OT idea of place to the degree that it speaks of the divinely given place in which believing existence has its basis. In Wisdom this place is, of course, neither the land which God has given the people nor a holy place like the temple. Detached from any concrete concept, it is the making possible of salvation, repentance and mercy.

C. Later Jewish Usage.

In later Jewish lit. only one peculiarity need be noted, namely, the designation of God as place. This occurs in the Rabb. and Philo but not in Jos. [89] or the pseudepigr. lit.

1. Rabbinic Writings. Here (הַ)מָקוֹם is used like the true designations [90] God, Lord, Father in heaven: "One must satisfy men as one must satisfy הַמָּקוֹם," Sheq. 3, 2, [91] cf. also Ber., 5, 1; [92] Sota, 8, 1. [93] This usage begins in the first generation of the Tannaites with R. Jochanan b. Zakkai and R. Chanina b. Dosa, and it continues in the second with

---

[87] Cf. v. Rad, op. cit., 460 on Job 28:23. For the poem wisdom is something remarkably material which must even be located.

[88] HT here מָקוֹם.

[89] The use of τόπος in Jos. corresponds fully to that in other Gk. usage and has thus been dealt with in the survey of Gk. lit. → 187, 20 ff.; 188, 19 f. etc.

[90] Cf. on this E. Landau, Die dem Raum entnommenen Synonyma f. Gott in d. neuhbr. Lit. (1888), 30-45; A. Marmorstein, The Old Rabb. Doctrine of God, I (1927), 92 f., 109-113 etc. (with. bibl.).

[91] Prv. 3:4 is quoted: "Find favour and recognition in the eyes of God and man."

[92] In the older readings other MSS have לַאֲבִיהֶם שֶׁבַּשָּׁמַיִם instead.

[93] Other examples in Landau, op. cit., 31 f.; Marmorstein, op. cit., 92 f., 108 f.

R. Gamaliel II and R. Aqiba and the third with R. Meir and R. Shimon b. Yochai, but then recedes in the time of Rabbi, i.e., the last third of the 2nd cent. A.D. [94] In the Tosefta [95] the use of this term as a word for God is less common, but further examples are found throughout Rabb. lit. except in the Tg. The origin and significance of the designation are disputed. It is hard to say whether it arose after the destruction of the temple and in connection therewith or whether it already existed earlier. [96] Equally uncertain is whether philosophical or historico-religious factors influenced its development or simply the desire to avoid the more unequivocal designations by using substitutes [97] → III, 93, 13 ff.

2. Philo. In Som., I, 61-63 Philo takes τόπος in 3 ways: [98] a. as the place a body fills, b. as the divine *logos* which God Himself has filled with incorporeal forces, and c. as God Himself, since He includes all things in Himself. There is a connection with Rabb. usage inasmuch as God is called τόπος. But if one compares Philo's view of God as τόπος with the OT it is apparent that all the constitutive elements in a theological understanding of place, namely, the motives of the promised land and the holy place (→ 195, 11 ff.), are here abandoned in favour of a view of God as place absolutely in the cosmic sense. It is ἀσέβεια to ascribe to deity coming and going, Conf. Ling., 134; cf. Poster. C., 14; Leg. All., I, 44; Som., I, 64. [99] In statements connected with the idea of God as τόπος the influences of Hell. usage are plain to see, [100] as when it is said that God includes all things in Himself but is not Himself enclosed by anything, Fug., 75, cf. Conf. Ling., 136; Som., I, 63 and 185. God is the place of refuge for all things, Som., I, 63 Fug., 75. In His capacity as τόπος He has created room and place χώρα καὶ τόπος for all creatures, Conf. Ling., 136; cf. Fug., 77. But He also fills all things, Conf. Ling., 136; cf. Leg. All., III, 4.

An important question is how man understands himself in this world which as a whole has become a theological place in the special sense but in which there are no longer any places of God. For Philo the place of man is governed directly by the understanding of the cosmos, and hence we can read in very secular terminology: ἐγὼ μὲν οὖν οὔκ εἰμι τόπος, ἀλλ᾽ ἐν τόπῳ, καὶ ἕκαστον τῶν ὄντων ὁμοίως, Som., I, 64; cf. Leg. All., III, 51. In contrast to God every movement of earthly beings is a change of place, Conf. Ling., 135, cf. Sacr. AC, 68; Poster. C., 30. The Aristotelian doctrine of categories can also be applied to the definition of earthly existence, τόπος and χρόνος being substituted for πού and ποτέ (→ n. 36) and as irrevocable determinations of things differentiated esp. from the other categories, Decal., 30, also Poster. C., 111; cf. also Decal., 31; Som., I, 187.

Within the cosmos nature has assigned to all creatures their different places, the sea to fish etc., Det. Pot. Ins., 151. [101] But man is at home in all spheres, Op. Mund., 147. τόπος can also be used for cosmic spheres, Spec. Leg., I, 85; Vit. Mos., II, 101. [102] Yet it must be considered that man's being at home in the world is only apparent. Man does not receive his religious determination by submitting to the bondage of time and space and acknowledging his basic spatial distinction from God. The term τόπος occurs in a

---

[94] For instances of this use of the word cf. Marmorstein, *op. cit.*, 118.

[95] On the Lat. *locus* as a loan word to denote God in T. Sukka, 4, 28 *v.* K. H. Rengstorf, " לוקיס : locus," *Orientalische Stud. f. E. Littmann* (1935), 58-61.

[96] There is no certain instance of this designation prior to 70 A.D., cf. Bousset-Gressm., 316, but *v.* on Philo → lines 10 ff.

[97] Cf. Dalman WJ, I, 189 f. For attempts at explanation cf. Marmorstein, 92.

[98] The theologically unimportant part of Philo's usage has already been dealt with in relation to Gk. usage → 188, 30 ff.; 189, 18 ff.; 191, 8 ff. etc.

[99] Here and elsewhere Philo can have χώρα for τόπος, Som., I, 63.

[100] Cf. the passages from Corp. Herm. adduced → 192, 23 ff.

[101] τόπος and χώρα (χωρίον) are again interchangeable here, Det. Pot. Ins., 151 and 152; Rer. Div. Her., 241 etc.

[102] It is said of the Chaldeans that they made all things a harmony τόποις μὲν διεζευγμένων, Migr. Abr., 178; cf. 220.

further train of thought in Philo, namely, when it is said of the soul that it has left its heavenly place and come into the body as an alien land, Som., I, 181. Virtue and vice make manifest in their names and quasi-etymological derivations the antithesis of their spheres, Rer. Div. Her., 241. The wicked soul has no place to which it might ascend and is thus called ἄτοπος, Leg. All., III, 53. Though God is in no place (Poster. C., 14). it is said with ref. to the soul that God invisibly enters its sphere (χωρίον). One should thus make ready this place (τόπος) that it might be a dwelling worthy of God, Cher., 98.

The problem of the OT understanding of place is thus solved by spiritualising it; the philosophical language of Gk. cosmology had some influence here, as did also Gnostic tendencies. [103] When the OT text demands a positive understanding of the word τόπος, it is viewed as a cipher for the divine *logos* conceived of as spiritual space. By the *logos* the powers of God, who is otherwise inaccessible in place, are made available to the soul. As space God has completely filled the *logos* with incorporeal forces, Som., I, 62; cf. 127 (on Gn. 28:11). Similarly Gn. 22:3 f. (Som., I, 64-67), Ex. 24:10 (Som., I, 62) [104] and Gn. 18:33 (Som., I, 70) are referred to the *logos,* so that one has the impression that the equation of the *logos* with place is introduced only *ad hoc* to explain passages of this kind. Yet once Philo views the *logos* as place in another context. It is the place of the world of ideas which cannot be regarded as in a specific place ἐν τόπῳ τινί; it has no other place apart from the divine *logos*, Op. Mund., 17 and 20.

D. New Testament Usage. [105]

1. τόπος as a General Term for Place.

a. The influence of OT usage (→ 193, 14 ff.) or even directly of a Semitic original is plainly present in Jn. in the common combination of τόπος with ὅπου: ἐγγὺς τοῦ τόπου ὅπου ἔφαγον τὸν ἄρτον, Jn. 6:23; cf. 11:30; 19:20. [106] In translation an adverb of place and a relative pronoun are often enough: "there where," [107] e.g., εἰς τὸν τόπον, ὅπου ἦν 'Ιωάννης ... βαπτίζων, Jn. 10:40; ἐν τῷ τόπῳ ὅπου ἐσταυ-ρώθη, Jn. 19:41; [108] ἔμεινεν ἐν ᾧ ἦν τόπῳ, Jn. 11:6, cf. v. 30. This construction, which always indicates a Semitic foundation, is found elsewhere in the NT only in OT quotations [109] (Ac. 7:33 quoting Ex. 3:5; R. 9:26 quoting Hos. 2:1 [110]) and Rev. → 206, 15 ff.

Outside the sphere of direct Hebraic influence τόπος can serve to link up a story topographically. Here, too, an adverbial translation is often in place: "there" of the coming of the Levite in Lk. 10:32 or Jesus in Lk. 19:5; 22:40. The fact that such expressions occur mostly in Luke may be because he imitates Septuagint usage.

---

[103] On Jn. 14:2 f. → n. 152.

[104] Perhaps Conf. Ling., 96 (based on Ex. 24:10) belongs here: τότε γὰρ τὸν μὲν τόπον, ὃς δὴ λόγος ἐστί, θεάσονται acc. to the conjecture of H. Colson, Philo, IV, Loeb Class. Libr., 4 (1958), 60, n. 2 (against all the MSS and ed.).

[105] τόπος occurs 95 times, 74 in the Synpt., Jn. and Ac. (Jn. 17, Lk. and Ac. 37). It is rare in the Epistles, 9 times in Paul (4 in the adv. ἐν παντὶ τόπῳ [→ 203, 1 ff.] and 1 in OT quotation), 3 in Hbr., 1 in 2 Pt. It is more common in Rev. (8 times). It does not occur in Gl., Phil., Col., 2 Th., 2 Tm., Tt., Phlm., Jm., 1 Pt., 1, 2, 3. Jn. or Jd.

[106] ἐγγὺς ἦν ὁ τόπος τῆς πόλεως ὅπου ἐσταυρώθη in Jn. 19:20 means "the place of the crucifixion was near the city."

[107] But not Jn. 4:20, where τόπος may denote the temple → 204, 12 ff.

[108] Similarly ἐν τῷ τόπῳ in Jn. 5:13; 6:10 just means "there."

[109] But cf. εἰς τὸν αὐτὸν τόπον ὅπου καὶ πέρυσι, Herm. v., 2, 1, 1.

[110] ἐν τῷ τόπῳ οὗ in R. 9:26 does not mean "in the place that," "instead of" (Pr.-Bauer, *s.v.*) but "there where," cf. Mi. R.[12], *ad loc.*

One may compare the adverbial expressions ἐν παντὶ τόπῳ "everywhere" in 1 C. 1:2; 2 C. 2:14; 1 Th. 1:8, [111] the same with διὰ παντός, 2 Th. 3:16 (A* D* G 33 latt), [112] κατὰ τόπους, "here and there," Mk. 13:8 and par., πᾶς ὁ ἐπὶ τόπον πλέων, "from place to place," Rev. 18:17, [113] εἰς ἕτερον τόπον, "to another place," Ac. 12:17 [114] → 188, 36 ff.

b. To denote a specific place τόπος is used par. to πόλις, esp. in the Lucan writings; [115] τόπος is generally more common in Lk. than in Mt. and Mk. [116] In Ac. 16:3 ἐν τοῖς τόποις ἐκείνοις refers to the "towns" of Derbe, Lystra and Iconium (cf. Ac. 16:4: πόλεις); οἱ κατὰ τὴν Ἀσίαν τόποι in Ac. 27:2 denotes the "places," i.e., "harbours of the province of Asia." In both cases the plural may also be understood as "district." [117] Lk. 4:37 speaks more generally of "all the places" in the locality, cf. 10:1: Jesus sends His disciples out into every city and every "place." Possibly Ac. 12:17 also has in view another district. [118] When τόπος is more precisely defined by an adjective the stress is on this adjective, since τόπος alone can denote all possible places, cf. ἄνυδροι τόποι "waterless areas," Mt. 12:43; τόπος πεδινός "a field," Lk. 6:17; τόπος διθάλασσος "a mudbank in the sea," Ac. 27:41, [119] cf. also Ac. 27:29. [120] ἔρημος τόπος in the Synoptists (Mk. 1:35 and par.; 1:45; 6:31; 6:32 and par.) [121] is not always a desert but may be "waste place which men have abandoned," [122] though the expression can be identical with the noun ἡ ἔρημος. [123] Instead of an adjective a relative clause may define the place concerned more exactly (→ 193, 14 ff.), Mk. 16:6; cf. Mt. 28:6. [124]

c. τόπος is rare with the name of the place in question. But the Evangelists consistently refer to the τόπος Golgotha, the site of the crucifixion of Jesus, Mk. 15:22 and par.; Jn. 19:17. [125] Mk. 15:22 and Mt. 27:33 add that the Hebrew name means κρανίου τόπος in Greek, while Jn. 19:17 gives the Greek translation first and then the Hebrew original. [126] Luke takes a different path, introducing the place as the Septuagint introduces places in the wilderness wandering: ἐπὶ τὸν τόπον τὸν καλούμενον Κρανίον, Lk. 23:33 → 196, 24 ff.

---

[111] Cf. the title of Mart. Pol.

[112] Most MSS have ἐν παντὶ τρόπῳ.

[113] This is still a notable expression; for other possibilities cf. Loh. Apk., ad loc.

[114] → n. 49, also Pr.-Bauer, s.v. with other examples and bibl., but → n. 118.

[115] In Mt. only in οἱ ἄνδρες τοῦ τόπου ἐκείνου (Gennesaret), Mt. 14:35, which is reminiscent of the OT, cf. Gn. 26:7, also Gn. 19:12-14. As regards Mk. one may ref. only to 6:11 (or is the house in mind here? cf. v. 10).

[116] Lk. 4:37 puts τόπος in a sentence taken from Mk., so too Lk. 22:40.

[117] The plur. for "locality," which is common in secular Gk. usage (→ 187, 22 ff.) does not occur elsewhere in the NT, but cf. 1 Cl., 25, 1: Ἀνατολικοὶ τόποι.

[118] It is not clear where Peter goes since there is no concern for exact topography, cf. Haench. Ag.[13], ad loc.

[119] On this cf. Pr.-Bauer, s.v. διθάλασσος and Haench. Ag.[13], ad loc.

[120] Cf. the same usage in Herm. v., 1, 1, 3; 3, 1, 3; s., 6, 2, 6.

[121] For other instances of this expression cf. Pr.-Bauer, s.v. ἔρημος and → II, 657, 24 ff.; 658, 3 ff.

[122] Cf. Pr.-Bauer, s.v. ἔρημος.

[123] Thus Lk. 5:16 has ἐν ταῖς ἐρήμοις for the ἐπ᾽ ἐρήμοις τόποις of Mk. 1:45.

[124] The construction reminds us of the Semiticising speech of Jn. (→ 202, 22 ff.), but an adverb is not enough here, since the angel summons the women to inspect more closely the place of burial already known to them. The saying is omitted by Lk.; but cf. Ev. Pt. 13:56.

[125] On the meaning of the name and situation of the place v. J. Jeremias, Golgotha (1926), 1-7 and passim, also the comm.

[126] Jn. 19:13 follows the same procedure with ref. to Gabbatha.

Undoubtedly a very ancient tradition is preserved in this exact indication of place. An element which is important for the historical reality of the crucifixion has thus been kept consistently in the tradition. But it is open to serious question whether preservation of the memory of the place of the crucifixion was linked to the early rise of a cult at this place. The Lucan formulation cannot support this theory even though it leans so heavily on the usage of the OT. In Ac. 27:8 Luke is certainly not using the same expression with reference to a place which was cultically important: εἰς τόπον τινὰ καλούμενον Καλοὺς λιμένας. In both cases, then, he is simply imitating the style of the Septuagint. OT style is similarly imitated in Rev. 16:16: "the place called in the Hebrew tongue Armageddon."

2. Special Senses.

a. Temple.

The OT-Jewish use (→ 196, 29 ff.) of τόπος for the Jerusalem temple is continued in the NT in only a few instances. In the Synoptic Gospels it occurs only in Mt. 24:15: ἐν τόπῳ ἁγίῳ. In this way Mt. relates the mysterious allusion of Mk. (ἑστηκότα ὅπου οὐ δεῖ, Mk. 13:14) unequivocally to the temple; Da. 9:27 LXX and Θ undoubtedly made some contribution here. In Jn. 4:20 the Samaritan view that one should worship towards Gerizim is contrasted with the Jewish claim that Jerusalem is the only cultic centre: [127] ὁ τόπος [128] ὅπου προσκυνεῖν (→ VI, 764, 20 ff.) δεῖ. Here as in similar antithesis in Dt. (→ 197, 1 ff.) ὁ τόπος is the temple in the absolute, namely, the Jerusalem temple. Jn. 11:48 is also referring to the Jerusalem temple: καὶ ἐλεύσονται οἱ Ῥωμαῖοι καὶ ἀροῦσιν ἡμῶν καὶ τὸν τόπον καὶ τὸ ἔθνος. One can, of course, relate the saying to the city, [129] but the association of τόπος and ἔθνος is to be construed as "temple and people" as in later Jewish usage → 198, 31 ff.; [130] furthermore the meaning "city" is not found elsewhere in Jn. and is very uncommon in the NT generally → 203, 6 ff. In Ac. the reference of τόπος to the temple is in two passages very clear and theologically significant: Ac. 6:13 f. and 21:28. Here in the accusations against Stephen and Paul they are charged not only with arguing against the Law (Ac. 6:13; 21:28) and the people (21:28) but also with attacking the temple: Stephen speaks ῥήματα κατὰ τοῦ τόπου τοῦ ἁγίου [τούτου] [131] (Ac. 6:13) and has said of Jesus: καταλύσει τὸν τόπον τοῦτον (6:14); Paul teaches κατὰ ... τοῦ τόπου τούτου, has brought Greeks into the temple and desecrated τὸν ἅγιον τόπον τοῦτον (21:28). [132] ὁ τόπος οὗτος has been carefully selected and kept here in place of the customary τὸ ἱερόν [133] of Lk. and Ac. [134]

---

[127] Cf. Bau. J., ad loc.; Str.-B., I, 549-551.

[128] ὁ τόπος does not occur in ℵ.

[129] Cf. Pr.-Bauer, s.v. The comm. vacillate between the two senses.

[130] Cf. esp. ἀλλ᾽ οὐ διὰ τὸν τόπον τὸ ἔθνος, ἀλλὰ διὰ τὸ ἔθνος τὸν τόπον ὁ κύριος ἐξελέξατο, 2 Macc. 5:19. The situation is not the same in Pap., 2710, 6 (→ n. 15; Roberts-Skeat-Nock, 40 and 45 f.) since later Jewish usage cannot be presupposed there; cf. the people, law and temple in Ac. 21:28 → lines 27 ff.

[131] Though attested only in BC 69 pm it sy this may well be the original reading.

[132] τόπος also occurs twice for the temple in Stephen's speech at Ac. 7:7 (quoting Ex. 3:12 → n. 134) and Ac. 7:49 (quoting Is. 66:1 f.).

[133] Cf. Lk. 2:27, 37, 46; 4:9 etc.; Ac. 2:46; 3:1 etc.

[134] This is esp. clear in Ac. 6:14, where Lk. uses the Gospel phrase ἐγὼ καταλύσω τὸν ναὸν τοῦτον (Mk. 14:58), but alters the τὸν ναὸν τοῦτον of Mk. to τὸν τόπον τοῦτον. Quoting Ex. 3:12 in Ac. 7:7 Lk. also replaces ἐν τῷ ὄρει τούτῳ with ἐν τῷ τόπῳ τούτῳ.

These accusations against Stephen and Paul, which are not based on the tradition that Luke uses, are thus intentionally stylised by him. By means of ὁ τόπος οὗτος he ref. to the threats of disaster against the land, the city and the temple (→ 197, 16 ff.) and thus deliberately puts Stephen and Paul in the line of the OT prophets. Acc. to Lk. these apostles have the same role regarding the destruction of the second temple as Jeremiah did in relation to the destruction of the first temple. [135]

b. The Right Place For, Opportunity.

The use of τόπος for "the place which someone takes" or "which pertains to him" corresponds to current Greek usage → 190, 3 ff. Luke especially uses the word in this way, e.g., for placing by rank at a meal in 14:9, cf. 14:10, and for a place to stay in the inn, 2:7. The place of the layman in the meeting of the church might also be mentioned in this connection, 1 C. 14:16. [136] Whether this usage had already produced the technical sense of "position," "office," in the primitive Christian period is debated. Reference is mostly made to λαβεῖν τὸν τόπον [137] τῆς διακονίας ταύτης καὶ ἀποστολῆς in Ac. 1:25. But the circumlocutory way of speaking is of itself enough to show that a technical use of this kind cannot be presupposed here. [138] Rather τόπος in Ac. 1:25a bears the same meaning as in the statement which follows in 1:25b: "the right place for someone"; thus the empty place in the apostolic band goes to the one who is elected, [139] while Judas has gone to the place where he really belongs, namely, hell. [140] In both cases, then, τόπος is the place which is assigned by God and which man must fill either as a commission or as a punishment.

As in general Greek usage (→ 190, 18 ff.), so in the NT the transferred sense of "opportunity" is very closely related to that of "place for something": [141] to have no place and hence no "opportunity" for mission (R. 15:28), τόπον ἀπολογίας λαμβάνω, Ac. 25:16 → 190, 24. The contemporaneous influence of later Jewish usage (→ 201, 4 ff.) asserts itself when this opportunity is the divinely presented "possibility" of life and salvation. Here again theological matters are set forth as though they could be localised, → n. 87. What is meant is the basic theological

---

[135] Cf. also the fact that in his martyrdom Stephen suffers the fate of a prophet, Ac. 7:52.

[136] Cf. Pr.-Bauer, s.v. ἀναπληρόω and ἰδιώτης. The meaning "share of the laity" (in worship), which is advocated by G. H. Whitaker, "Ὁ ἀναπληρῶν τὸν τόπον τοῦ ἰδιώτου," JThSt, 22 (1921), 268, finds no par.

[137] ℵ ﬡ E pl read κλῆρον, influenced by the τὸν κλῆρον τῆς διακονίας of Ac. 1:17.

[138] E. Stauffer, "Jüd. Erbe im urchr. Kirchenrecht," ThLZ, 77 (1952), 203 has tried to show that τόπος is to be understood here in the light of the τόπος problems of the Qumran sect in connection with seating at table. He is followed by W. Nauck, "Probleme d. frühchr. Amtsverständnisses," ZNW, 48 (1957), 213 f. But cf. Haench. Ag.13, ad loc. and p. 1. Most of the Hbr. words adduced by Stauffer and Nauck have nothing whatever to do with the Gk. τόπος.

[139] In interpretation cf. Haench. Ag.13, ad loc.; G. Klein, Die zwölf Ap. (1961), 204-9; → 190, 5 ff.; → 199, 12 ff.

[140] ἴδιος τόπος is here a euphemism for hell, cf. H. Conzelmann, Die Ag., Hndbch. NT, 7 (1963), ad loc. → n. 153 f.

[141] Only rarely in the NT is τόπος used in a non-transf. sense to denote the right place for a thing, e.g., putting the sword back in its place (sheath), Mt. 26:52, the place where the nails were, Jn. 20:25 (the MSS vacillate between τύπος "mark" and τόπος, cf. Pr.-Bauer, s.v. τύπος; we should read τύπος in Jn. 20:25a and τόπος in 20:25b, Bau. J. and Bultmann J., ad loc.).

opening up of repentance, obedience etc.; thus it is said of Esau: μετανοίας τόπον
οὐχ εὗρεν, Hb. 12:17. What is expressed here is the Jewish and primitive Christian
view that man cannot control repentance at will. [142] A special divine act is needed
as in the sending of such prophetic figures as John the Baptist and Hermas. By this
act the τόπος μετανοίας becomes a reality. [143] Hb. 8:7 is to be understood similarly:
"For if that first covenant had been faultless, then should no place have been sought
for the second." What is sought is the divine act which establishes a new covenant.
R. 12:19 demands that the divine [144] wrath be allowed to work (δότε τόπον τῇ
ὀργῇ), [145] (→ II, 444, 9 ff.). [146] On the other hand, Eph. 4:27 warns against giving
place to the devil. [147]

But this transferred understanding of τόπος is also found in the NT in mythical
style, cosmic and heavenly being referred to as though they were places in a
geographical sense. [148] The aim of this usage is to depict theological realities which
are significant for the community. The link with mythical-cosmic speech is particularly
clear in Rev.: [149] All the mountains (→ V, 486, 21 ff.) and islands are to be moved out
of their places, 6:14b. [150] With direct theological implications it is said in 2:5 that
the candlestick of the disobedient congregation is to be removed from its place.
The cosmic background of this view of place is obvious, since behind the seven
candlesticks are seven stars (or planets?) (→ I, 504, 15 ff.) [151] which have their
own places in the cosmos. In the present context, of course, the reference is to the
eschatological possibility of the community. The possibility of existence which God
has given the community and the heavenly place of the candlestick are identical.
Similarly the mythical reference to place in Rev. 12 is a statement about the
theological place of the Church. The woman who symbolises the Church has in
the wilderness "the place which God has prepared for her" (12:6) so that she can
flee to her place in persecution (12:14). This reference to place is thus a promise

---

[142] Cf. Wis. 12:10; also Liv., 24, 26, 15 → n. 28. On the problem that God can seal off
repentance cf. Mi. Hb., ad loc.; → IV, 1005, 35 ff.

[143] Cf. also ἐν γενεᾷ καὶ γενεᾷ μετανοίας τόπον ἔδωκεν ὁ δεσπότης, 1 Cl., 7, 5.

[144] That the ref. is to God's wrath, not man's, is almost universally accepted by modern
transl., v. E. J. Goodspeed, Problems of NT Translation (1945), 152 f. But some patristic
exegetes seriously considered human wrath, cf. Smothers, 206-9.

[145] In interpretation cf. esp. K. Stendahl, "Hate, Non-Retaliation and Love," HThR, 55
(1962) 343-355.

[146] Against the attempt to understand this in the light of the modern Gk. δὸς τόπον τῆς
ὀργῆς "calm down" (D. B. Durham, "Acts 15:9; Romans 12:19," Class. Weekly, 36 [1942/
43], 29 f.) v. E. R. Smothers, "A Further Note on Romans 12:19," ibid., 37 (1943/44), 77-79
and Smothers, 206. A transl. like that of Pr.-Bauer, s.v.: "Give divine wrath a chance to
vent itself," is intrinsically correct, but it is still too weak and views God's wrath more as an
emotion than an act (like R. 1:18 ff.); this applies even more to Goodspeed's rendering (op.
cit., 154): "Leave room for God's anger."

[147] In illustration cf. Herm. m., 12, 5, 4, acc. to which the devil flees believers μὴ ἔχων
τόπον and comes to others ἔχων τόπον. Cf. "to execute the commanded actualising of
obedience" in 1 Cl., 63, 1, v. on this Pr.-Bauer, s.v. ἀναπληρόω.

[148] Cf. OT (→ 199, 28 ff.) and Jewish (→ 201, 24 ff.) usage, also τόπος in the cosmological usage of Hellenism → 192, 22 ff.

[149] The almost exclusive combination of τόπος with a possessive pronoun in Rev. is clear
evidence of the Jewish-OT background → 194, 6 ff.

[150] Oddly there is for this OT-sounding saying no par. in the OT or later Jewish lit.,
though apart from this the whole section Rev. 6:12-17 is made up of OT allusions, cf. Loh.
and Bss. Apk., ad loc.; but statements like Job 14:18 must have sponsored 6:14b.

[151] Cf. Bss. Apk., ad loc.

that God will sustain the Church's life. Conversely absence of place means destruction, the extinguishing of existence. When the dragon is expelled from heaven (Rev. 12:8) and when heaven and earth flee at God's appearing (20:11), the expression καὶ τόπος οὐχ εὑρέθη αὐτοῖς, which is taken from Da. 2:35 Θ, signifies their hopeless transitoriness, for only he who has his place can really endure. Outside Rev. there is only occasional reference to the heavenly place of the community or the individual, and now more in the interests of edification, Jn. 14:2; cf. 14:3. [152] But there is also a place of torment, Lk. 16:28. Thus it is said of Judas that he goes εἰς τὸν τόπον τὸν ἴδιον, [153] Ac. 1:25b. [154]

c. Place of Scripture.

This sense occurs only once in Lk. in an editorial saying at Lk. 4:17. [155] The various elements of common Hellenistic usage are thus seen at their clearest in Luke.

E. The Post-Apostolic Fathers.

On the whole the use in the post-apost. fathers is the same as in the NT. [156] One need stress only some moves towards the development of the sense "position," "office." Ac. 1:25 (→ 205, 12 ff.) cannot be regarded as the source of this development since some instances in the post-apost. fathers are certainly independent of it. The ἴδιος τόπος of the priest is mentioned along with the ἴδιαι λειτουργίαι of the high-priest and the ἴδιαι διακονίαι of the Levites in 1 Cl., 40, 5: "the earlier presbyters were extolled, for no one can push them out of their firmly established place," 44, 5. [157] Here as in Ac. 1:25 the place in the Church structure is related to the place in the hereafter. Less clear is Ign. Sm., 6, 1: "Even on heavenly powers judgment comes, hence a τόπος (office? heavenly rank?) should not puff up anyone." [158] ἐκδίκει σου τὸν τόπον ἐν πάσῃ ἐπιμελείᾳ in

---

[152] On the idea of the heavenly place of felicity cf. Bultmann J., ad loc. and for the interpretation of this mythical idea by Jn., loc. cit. In this context we cannot trace the origin and development of the idea, esp. as it has little to do with τόπος linguistically → IV, 580, 24 ff. One must undoubtedly speak of a Gnostic notion. We may simply ref. to the heavenly place of the soul in Philo Som., I, 181, cf. also the Coptic Ev. Veritatis (ed. M. Malinine, H. C. Puech and G. Quispel [1956]), 41, 4 - 42, 39 etc. and the Mandaean texts, and v. Bultmann J. on 14:1-4. Cf. Jonas Gnosis, I, 181-190 and 205-210.

[153] ἴδιος τόπος occurs only also in Herm. s., 9, 4, 7; 5, 4; 12, 4, but in another sense; yet cf. Ign. Mg., 5, 1 → n. 154.

[154] Cf. in the post-apost. fathers calling to the τόπος, 2 Cl., 1, 2, τόπος τῆς δόξης in 1 Cl., 5, 4; cf. Pol., 9, 2 and τόπος . . . μετὰ τῶν ἀγγέλων in Herm. s., 9, 27, 3. Barn., 19, 1 speaks of the ὁδός to the foreordained τόπος, cf. Jn. 14:2 ff.; → n. 152. The word is also used for "to have a place in the Church," Ign. Phld., 2, 2, and Ign. Mg., 5, 1 says everyone must go εἰς τὸν ἴδιον τόπον, namely, to life or death. In the tower allegory it is said of the stones used: ἔχουσιν τόπον εἰς τὸν πύργον τοῦτον, Herm. v., 3, 7, 5; cf. 3, 5, 5; 3, 9, 5.

[155] Cf. καὶ ἐν ἑτέρῳ τόπῳ λέγει to introduce another OT quotation, 1 Cl., 8, 4; 29, 3; 46, 3.

[156] Most passages in which τόπος occurs in the post-apost. fathers have already been used to elucidate NT usage, → n. 111, 117, 120, 143, 147, 153-155.

[157] Par. is: "You have forced out some ἐκ τῆς . . . λειτουργίας," 1 Cl., 44, 6.

[158] H. Schlier, Religionsgeschichtliche Untersuchungen zu d. Ign.-Br. (1929), 128 thinks the passages ref. to grades in Gnosticism, but cf. H. v. Campenhausen, Kirchliches Amt u. Geistliche Vollmacht² (1963), 112.

Ign. Pol., 1, 2 ref. more plainly to office, [159] cf. Herm. s., 7, 6; [160] Pol., 11, 1 *(locus)*. But these are isolated instances and in no sense bear witness to an established technical use. As in Ac. 1:25 we simply have an occasional variation on the expounded sense of "right place," "place for something." [161]

Köster

---

[159] The passage is not without difficulties. ἐκδικέω τινά means elsewhere "to get justice for someone," "to avenge him," ἐκδικέω τι "to take revenge for something," cf. Pr.-Bauer, *s.v.* For the necessary transl. here: "Exercise thine office uprightly," appeal is usually made to Orig. Comm. in Mt., 12, 14 (p. 98, 28 f.): οἱ τὸν τόπον τῆς ἐπισκοπῆς ἐκδικοῦντες, so Pr.-Bauer and Bau. Ign. Pol., *ad loc.*

[160] πάλιν ἀποκατασταθήσῃ εἰς τὸν τόπον σου (A εἰς τὸν οἶκόν σου, which is undoubtedly wrong, since this is to happen after his suffering and his house is to suffer with him, 7, 7) might ref. to restoration to his ecclesiastical office. But this is very uncertain.

[161] On the further development of this sense cf. Nauck, *op. cit.,* 213 f.

```
┌─────────────────┐
│                 │
│  † τράπεζα      │
│                 │
└─────────────────┘
```

Contents: A. Usage: 1. General Usage; 2. Dining-Table; 3. Moneychangers' Table; 4. Table for the Show-bread. B. Theological Table Sayings: 1. The Table as Mediator of Daily Bread; 2. The Table of Table Fellowship; 3. The Table of the Lord and the Table of Demons; 4. The Table in Congregational Worship.

A. Usage.

1. General Use.

τράπεζα ¹ (etym. from τετρα — πεζα "tetrapod") is found in Hom. Il., 11, 628; Od., 10, 354 etc.; it means "table" and is used in the LXX for שֻׁלְחָן, which originally means the "mat" or "leather" put on the earth for meals. ² From the sense of dining-table τράπεζα soon acquires the transf. sense of "meal," "foods," Hdt., I, 162, 1; Eur. Alc., 2; Soph. Oed. Tyr., 1464; Plat. Resp., III, 404d etc.; cf. esp. παρατίθημι τράπεζαν, Hom. Od., 5, 92; 8, 69; Tob. 2:2 S; Ac. 16:34 (→ 213, 9 ff.) Several OT passages come near to this sense, so 1 S. 20:27, 29, where לֶחֶם is par. to שֻׁלְחָן and LXX has τράπεζα, cf. also עָרַךְ שֻׁלְחָן Ps. 23:5; Prv. 9:2, LXX ἑτοιμάζω τράπεζαν. The transf. sense is common in the NT → 213, 1 ff.

2. Dining-Table. ³

The table developed in pre-historic times as a dining-table out of the cloth, leather, or wicker-work, or the metal or wooden plate, which was used to rest foods on, and which in the Near East is still used among the Bedouin, as often in simple circumstances, even to this day. ⁴

The form of the table, esp. its height, is determined in the main by the bodily posture adopted for eating. In earlier times, and often in the Near East to-day, we find crouching for meals with or without support on the ground, so that a tray on a low support is enough,

---

τ ρ ά π ε ζ α. Bibl.: On A.: J. Benzinger, *Hbr. Archäologie*³ (1927), 97 and 106; BR, 21 f., 522; Dalman Arbeit, VII, 218-224; also *Petra u. seine Felsheiligtümer* (1908); also *Neue Petraforschungen* (1912); K. Galling, Art. "Altar," RAC, I, 312 f., 333; S. Krauss, *Talmud. Archäol.,* I (1910), 58 f.; G. Kruse, Art. "mensa," Pauly-W., 15 (1932), 938-948; G. M. A. Richter, *Ancient Furniture* (1926), s.v. "Tables"; E. Ziebarth, Art. τράπεζα, Pauly-W., 6a (1937), 2194-2207; L. Ziehen, Art. "Altar," RAC, I, 312 f. On B.: J. Braun, *Der chr. Altar in seiner geschichtlichen Entwicklung* (1924), 48-65; F. J. Dölger, ΙΧΘΥΣ, II (1922), 12, n. 2 and 378, n. 5 f.; also "Der Kelch d. Dämonen," *Ant. Christ.,* IV (1934), 266-270; Harnack Miss., 612 f.; J. P. Kirsch, Art. "Altar," RAC, I, 334-6; Ltzm. K. on 1 C. 10:20; H. Mischkowski, *Der hl. Tisch im Götterkultus d. Griechen u. Römer*, Diss. Königsberg (1917); F. Wieland, "Mensa u. Confessio," *Veröffentlichungen d. Kirchengeschichtlichen Seminars d. Univ. München*, II, 11 (1906).
¹ The word is found in Mycenaean [Risch]. On the etym. cf. Boisacq, s.v.; Kruse, 937 f.
² Cf. Ges.-Buhl, s.v. Perhaps this explains the image in Ps. 69:22 or R. 11:9, cf. Zn. R., ad loc.
³ With the dining-table there was also the ἄβαξ "display table" and ἐλεός "kitchen-table."
⁴ Dalman Arbeit, VI, 45 f., 49, 73.

cf. Ez. 23:41. [5] Only in well-to-do circles did one sit in ancient times (in Israel already during the monarchy, 1 S. 20:5, 24), [6] on stools or benches at regular tables. The custom of reclining at table is occasionally found in Palestine in the pre-exilic period, Am. 3:12; 6:4; under Gk. and Roman influence it established itself in the Hell. age. At a Gk. banquet two guests would recline on a couch (κλίνη) at one table, at Roman feasts groups of three would recline on the three sides of a larger table, the open fourth side being used for serving. [7] In the imperial period one couch in the form of a half-circle (stibadium) was set up and used along with a sickle-shaped table. [8] In Palestine the dining-areas hewn out of sandstone in Petra give evidence of couches for two and three with a fourcornered middle area and also of stibadia with a round middle area. There is no table in these places. It is replaced by a 30 cm broad border on the couches or hollowed interior. [9] When the Rabb. make reclining at the Passover obligatory for every Israelite, Pes., 10, 1, [10] it may be assumed that the usual posture at ordinary meals was sitting or crouching. [11] At feasts acc. to Rabb. tradition [12] hors d'oeuvres were eaten on benches or seats in an antechamber while the guests were assembling and each said his own grace. The meal proper was taken at table in the dining-room, there was a common blessing, and table fellowship was thus constituted. The practice was to support oneself on the left arm and take the chopped up food with the right without knife, fork, or spoon, using instead bread and fingers, cf. Sir. 31:14; Mk. 14:20 and par.

This development is reflected in the terminology. The OT speaks always of sitting (ישב) at meals, though this does not exclude crouching: κάθημαι ἐπὶ τραπέζης (יְשַׁב אֶל־הַשֻּׁלְחָן), 1 K. 13:20, καθίζω ἐπὶ τραπέζης, Sir. 31:12, καθίζω δειπνεῖν ἐπὶ τραπέζης, Prv. 23:1, καθίζω φαγεῖν, Gn. 37:25; Ex. 32:6 etc. → III, 441, 14 ff. Only in the apocr. do we sometimes find words for reclining, ἀνάκειμαι, 1 Εσδρ. 4:11; Tob. 9:6 S, ἀνακλίνω, 3 Macc. 5:16, ἀναπίπτω, Jdt. 12:16; Tob. 2:1; 7:9 S, κατάκειμαι, [13] κατακλίνω, Jdt. 12:15, cf. συνανάκειμαι, 3 Macc. 5:39. [14] It is worth noting that Qumran, like the OT, speaks only of sitting at meals, 1 QS 6:4 f.; Damasc. 14:6 (17:4); [15] this applies to the Messianic banquet too, 1 QSa 2:11-22. [16]

In view of this practice it is surprising that in the NT, apart from an OT quotation (1 C. 10:7 = Ex. 32:6), the reference is always to reclining at table and never to sitting for meals. The terms found already in later parts of the LXX (→ lines 21 ff.; III, 441, 14 ff.) [17] are used in this connection. Apart from 1 C. 8:10 the

---

[5] Ibid., VI, 213 f.

[6] An upper chamber was furnished with a bed, table and stool for Elisha, 2 K. 4:10.

[7] Kruse, 940-942.

[8] Ibid., 942-944.

[9] Dalman Arbeit, VII, 223 f.; G. Rodenwaldt, Art. "Sigma," Pauly-W., 2a (1923), 2323 f.

[10] Cf. Str.-B., IV, 56 f.

[11] Dalman Arbeit, VII, 222; J. Jeremias, Die Abendmahlsworte Jesu³ (1960), 42, n. 8.

[12] Str.-B., IV, 615-620.

[13] Not in the LXX but elsewhere, cf. Jos. Vit., 222.

[14] In Aram. רבע is used for these words, in Rabb. Hbr. הסב, cf. Str.-B., IV, 56 f.

[15] שכב is used in the OT only for lying on couches to rest, cf. 1 QS 10:14.

[16] Excavations in Khirbet Qumran have not disclosed tables or seats in the dining-hall. But in the scriptorium fragments have been found which when put together give a small table 5 m long and 0.5 m high and parts of one or two smaller tables. These went with low benches along the wall. But this interpretation of the objects (which are made of bricks overlaid with mortar) by R. de Vaux, "Fouilles au Khirbet Qumrân," Rev. Bibl., 61 (1954), 212, is disputed by B. M. Metzger, "The Furniture in the Scriptorium at Qumran," Revue de Qumran, 1 (1958), 509-515, who thinks the objects are too low for benches and tables and were benches and foot-stools for the scribes; indeed, the universal practice of antiquity was not to write on tables but on the hands standing or the knees crouching.

[17] Dalman Arbeit, VII, 221; Jeremias, op. cit. (→ n. 11), 43, n. 1.

passages are all in accounts of the earthly ministry of Jesus. Since in Jesus' world the common practice in simple circumstances was sitting or crouching, i.e., except at feasts or banquets, one may assume that the words were used in a weak sense for "to sit down for a meal" and do not refer precisely to the bodily posture or the shape of the table.

Hence expressions meaning "to recline at table" do not always denote the reclining customary at special banquets (cf. Lk. 24:30) nor do they even presuppose a table, cf. ἀνακλίνω or κατακλίνω in Mk. 6:39 and par. At the Last Supper, then, it is not certain whether the chamber was furnished with couches, carpets, or mats (ἐστρωμένον, Mk. 14:15 and par.) [18] or whether a regular table was present. But the terms for reclining at table can include ref. to a table even though τράπεζα is not used. [19]

3. Moneychangers' Table.

The most familiar table of the artisan or trader is that of the moneychangers (from Plat. Ap., 17c). While other salesmen often displayed their wares on the ground, these put their coins on a table and thus came to be called τραπεζῖται, "table-men," i.e., moneychangers, bankers, [20] Lys. 'Αποσφάσματα, 1, 1; Demosth. Or., 36, 28; 49, 5; Mt. 25:27. On this basis τράπεζα comes to have the transf. sense of "bank," Lys., 9, 5; Demosth. Or., 33, 9 f. 24; 36, 6, also Jos. Ant., 12, 28, [21] cf. δίδωμι τὸ ἀργύριον ἐπὶ τράπεζαν, "to put (interestbearing) money in the bank," Lk. 19:23.

4. Table for the Show-Bread.

Of tables which served cultic purposes the NT mentions the OT [22] table for the show-bread: ἡ τράπεζα καὶ ἡ πρόθεσις τῶν ἄρτων, "the table and the showing of the bread," Hb. 9:2. [23]

There is nothing corresponding exactly to this phrase in the LXX or the HT. The closest in the LXX is ἡ τράπεζα τῆς προθέσεως in 'Εξ. 39:17 for אֶת־הַשֻּׁלְחָן . . . וְאֵת; לֶחֶם הַפָּנִים Ex. 39:36 and in 1 Ch. 28:16; 2 Ch. 29:18 for שֻׁלְחַן הַמַּעֲרֶכֶת, cf. 1 Macc. 1:22; Jos. Bell., 5, 217. We read of a table for the show-bread in the temple at Nob, 1 S. 21:7, in Solomon's temple, 1 K. 6:20; 7:48, [24] and the post-exilic temple, 1 Macc. 1:22; Jos. Bell., 7, 148. [25] It corresponds to the offering tables which were by the idols in pagan temples [26] and on which gifts to the deity not brought as burnt offerings were placed. [27] Hence it is called "God's table" like the altar (→ n. 42), 1 Cl., 43, 2.

The NT speaks of a cultic table in the non-biblical sphere only in 1 C. 10:21b → 213, 13 ff.

---

[18] Dalman Arbeit, VII, 223.
[19] Hence the following survey of passages with τράπεζα takes into account only one part of this usage.
[20] With κολλυβιστής Lys. Fr., 149 (Oratores Attici, ed. G. Baiter and H. Sauppe, II [1850], 193 f.); Mt. 21:12 and par.
[21] Cf. Ziebarth, 2194-2207.
[22] Elsewhere in the OT cultus tables are used to prepare the sacrifices in Ez. 40:39-43 (cf. G. Fohrer and K. Galling, Ez., Hndbch. AT, I, 13² [1955], ad loc.) and there are tables for unspecified purposes in 2 Ch. 4:8 (possibly for the lamps, 4:7 [Fohrer]).
[23] Cf. Rgg. Hb. and Mi. Hb.¹¹, ad loc.
[24] Acc. to Ez. 41:22 it measured 2 × 2 × 3 cubits.
[25] Cf. the depiction on the Titus arch, AOB, Ill. 509.
[26] Galling, 312 f.
[27] M. Noth, Das zweite Buch Mose, ATD, 5³ (1965), 167 f., 174. Cf. the Jewish designations in Str.-B., III, 718 f. Acc. to Philo the table for the show-bread, which he calls the holy table, Spec. Leg., I, 172; II, 161, is a model of the ideal table, Vit. Cont., 81; Congr., 168.

B. Theological Table Sayings.

1. The Table as Mediator of Daily Bread.

When the poor man in the parable in Lk. 16:21 hungers in vain for the crumbs which fall unnoticed as superabundance from the rich man's table, the rich man is blind to his neighbour. The same formula-type expression [28] occurs in an illustration in Mk. 7:28 and par.: The woman who does not belong to Israel seeks the help of Israel's God from Jesus out of the superfluity of His wealth and goodness. In R. 11:9 (= Ps. 69:22) [29] the table is a figure: The table by which Israel lives will become a snare that will cause it to fall in God's sight. Since the introduction to the quotation in R. 11:7 reminds us of 9:31, Orig. and Hilary were not mistaken to ref. the table here to the Law. [30]

2. The Table of Table Fellowship.

In four passages in Luke's works table is used in the theological context of table fellowship. In Lk. 22:21, the intimation of the betrayal, which in Mk. 14:18, 20 and par. is in two sections punctuated by the disciples' question, is compressed into a single saying, and the traitor is denoted by the expression: "The hand of him that betrayeth me is with me on the table," as compared with the rest of the tradition: "That dippeth with me in the (one) dish," Mk. 14:20 and par. The Lucan expression brings out more clearly than the parallel, which is in closer correspondence to conditions in Palestine, the fact that the traitor belongs to the circle to which Jesus had granted the closest fellowship, and especially regular table fellowship. [31] This whole circle, as the question of the disciples in Mk. 14:19 shows, is affected by the deed. Lk. 22:28-30 is also peculiar to Lk.: Sitting at the royal table is artificially connected with sitting on the thrones (Mt. 19:28): "That ye may eat and drink at my table in my kingdom."

The combination, which also occurs in Rev. 3:20 f., was perhaps found by the Evangelist in a special tradition, but terminologically its formulation is largely his own work, [32] esp. the emphatic ref. to the table. In the expression the common Synoptic idea that those who belong to Jesus will share with Him in the banquet of consummation (→ II, 34, 12 ff.), i.e., in eschatological salvation, [33] is given the more concrete form of sitting at the table of the Messiah King. The mode of expression reminds us of the constantly recurring OT sayings about coming to the king's table, cf. esp. 2 S. 9:7, where David confers the benefit: σὺ φάγῃ ἄρτον ἐπὶ τῆς τραπέζης μου. In the background is the current OT and Jewish idea of the meal of consummation → II, 35, 16 ff. [34]

[28] The idea occurs already in Ju. 1:7: βασιλεῖς... ἦσαν συλλέγοντες τὰ ὑποκάτω τῆς τραπέζης μου. The Rabb. lay down that scraps which fall from the table should be gathered at the end of the meal, Str.-B., IV, 526.
[29] On the form of the quotation Zn. R., ad loc.
[30] Cf. K. H. Schelkle, Pls., Lehrer d. Väter (1956), 386.
[31] On the meaning of this fellowship cf. L. Goppelt, Christentum u. Judt. im ersten u. zweiten Jhdt. (1954), 49-51; Jeremias, op. cit. (→ n. 11), 196-198. Peter's confession does not change this table fellowship into an intimation or anticipation of the final banquet (Jeremias, 197), for it is the confession of an embattled faith, not the expression of a firm insight. Expressions for table fellowship in τράπεζα do not occur in the NT or LXX, cf. ὁμοτράπεζος (→ n. 40) "table companion," Philo Spec. Leg., I, 120, συντράπεζος, "table companion," κοινὴ τράπεζα, Dg., 5, 7a, also וערוך השולחן היחד, 1 QSa 2:17 and also συνεσθίω (→ II, 693, 8 ff.), συμπίνω, Ac. 10:41 etc.
[32] Apart from Mt. 20:21 "his kingdom" occurs only in Lk. 1:33; 22:30; 23:42; "to eat and drink" is in Lk. (5:33; 7:33 f.; 10:7; 17:27) relatively more common than in the other Synoptists (only Mt. 11:18 f.).
[33] Mk. 14:25 par.; Mt. 8:11 par.; Lk. 14:24 par.; cf. Rev. 19:9.
[34] Cf. the meals with the Messiahs of Aaron and Israel, 1 QSa 2:17-21.

Twice in Ac. τράπεζα has the transf. sense of "meal" (→ 209, 10 ff.); the context is again that of table fellowship. The expression διακονεῖν (→ II, 84, 40 ff.) τραπέζαις (Ac. 6:2) has in view the common sacral meals of the primitive community in Jerusalem; the so-called community of goods gave to these a distinctive form not found elsewhere in primitive Christianity. The combination with τραπέζαις distinguishes this "serving" from the διακονία τοῦ λόγου (Ac. 6:4). διακονεῖν means here "to serve" and not specifically "to wait on" (→ II, 84, 40 ff.). Similarly τράπεζα does not meaning "dining-table" [35] or "table fellowship" [36] but "meal" (→ II, 84, 40 ff.), [37] so that the proper translation is: "to see to meals." [38] The other passage is Ac. 16:33 f., where the Philippian gaoler, when he and his house have been baptised, conducts the apostles into his own house and "sets a meal before them" παρέθηκεν τράπεζαν, → 209, 12 f. [39]

3. The Table of the Lord and the Table of Demons.

The saying about the τράπεζα κυρίου or δαιμονίων (1 C. 10:21b) refers to a table or meal which expresses cultic κοινωνία and not just table fellowship; this is clear from the argument for exclusiveness in vv. 14-20. With the cup of the Lord (1 C. 10:21a → VI, 156, 20 ff.) the table of the Lord is the table or meal which the Lord provides (1 C. 10:4) and which claims those who receive it for Him (1 C. 10:16). Similarly the table of demons is the table of the sacrificial meal, or the meal itself, which is dispensed by demons and which delivers up those who participate to them. [40] Paul is not arguing on the basis of Hellenistic ideas about communion with the gods in cultic meals, [41] but on the basis of the OT and Jewish sense that the sacrificial meal binds to the Lord of the altar (1 C. 10:18) and that

---

[35] Zn. Ag., ad loc.
[36] Pr. Ag., ad loc.
[37] One cannot follow the suggestion of Jackson-Lake, I, 4, 64 that the meaning is "money-changers' table," "bank," so that "general financial administration of the community" is in view.
[38] There is a close linguistic analogy in the community rule in Did., 11, 9 προφήτης ὁρίζων τράπεζαν: "a prophet who orders a table." If a prophet (supposedly) orders a meal for the poor and eats of it himself he is a false prophet.
[39] W. Nauck, Die Tradition u. d. Charakter d. 1 J. (1957), 174, cf. 153-165, suggests with others that this story of a meal of praise following baptism, Ac. 16:34, cf. 2:46, reflects what will soon be the baptismal eucharist.
[40] The gen. is both subj. and obj., cf. Bchm. 1 K. and Schl. K., ad loc. and the Jewish Chr. explanation in Ps.-Clem. Recg., II, 71: "He ... who has partaken of a sacrificial offering is not free of an unclean spirit. He has become a table companion of demons and has a part in the demon whose figure he has formed in his own spirit out of fear or love," and Ps.-Clem. Hom., 7, 3, 2 f.: "Over none of you do the demons have power if you have not previously contracted life fellowship with their chiefs; for it was legally established by God ... for the two chiefs that neither has power over a man unless he is first his table companion (ὁμοτράπεζος) and has resolved to do good or evil." Here the harmful effect of sharing the table of demons (7, 4, 2) is correctly shown to be divinely ordained (not just psychological), but it follows too closely a legal schema of retribution.
[41] Hence one should not see in his statements the Hell. idea of communion with the gods in the cultic meal. Such concepts vacillate between table fellowship (cf. Serapis as host and companion, Ael. Arist. Or., 8, 83 f. [Dindorf] or the invitation to δεῖπνον and εὐνή τοῦ Ἀνούβιδος, Jos. Ant., 18, 73) and patronage, cf. the invitation of Antonius εἰς κλείνην τοῦ κυρίου Σαράπιδος, i.e., to a meal which takes place in his honour and places under his patronage, P. Oxy., III, 523, 2 f. (2nd cent. A.D.). Further materials in Ltzm. K. on 1 C. 10:20 and Pr.-Bauer, s.v. τράπεζα. In context there is no thought of meals in the mysteries, → VI, 137, 14 ff.; 157, 15 ff.

behind the gods stand demons, → VI, 157, n. 88. The surrounding Hellenistic world probably influenced only his mode of expression. It calls the table where the sacrifice is made or from which it comes τράπεζα τοῦ θεοῦ. [42] Here, then, Paul does not use the common community term κυριακὸν δεῖπνον (1 C. 11:20 → II, 34, 4 ff.), but in analogy to the "cup of the Lord" he coins the impressive antithesis τράπεζα κυρίου — τράπεζα δαιμονίων. In so doing he follows the LXX, which calls the gods δαιμόνια (→ II, 10, 29 ff.) [43] and the altar of Yahweh τράπεζα κυρίου, Mal. 1:7, 12; Ez. 44:16. [44] But this linguistic dependence does not make the Lord's table an altar for Paul, nor does comparison with the cultic meal give the Lord's Supper a sacrificial character. [45] The common feature in the meals which sustains the argument is simply κοινωνία (→ III, 805, 8 ff.)) or participation. The self-proffering of the κύριος who is called upon in the εὐλογία and the power of the κύριοι named in dedication formulae summon the participants to conflicting dominions. For this reason one cannot alternate between the two meals. The Lord does not allow any gods but Himself, 1 C. 10:22.

4. The Table in Congregational Worship.

Early Christian worship was a feast embracing word and sacrament; alongside it were services of a missionary and catechetical character. Thus primitive worship took place in private houses as a gathering around tables in everyday use. Once the sacramental meal became detached from the general meal, a table which one approached was often used, [46] When in the 3rd century the elements were offered as a sacrifice (→ III, 189, 43 ff.) the table where the consecration took place was called an altar for the celebration. [47] But it was still an ordinary table specially prepared for the celebration. [48] Only from the later

---

[42] Ditt. Syll.[3], III, 1106, 99 (c. 300 B.C.); cf. 1022, 2 (4th cent. B.C.); 1038, 11 (c. 300 B.C.); 1042, 20 (2nd/3rd cent. A.D.).

[43] Is. 65:11 LXX: ἑτοιμάζοντες τῷ δαίμονι (לַגַּד, the god of luck) τράπεζαν, quoted in Just. Dial., 135, 4.

[44] Cf. also Test. Jud. 21; Test. L. 8; 1 QM 2:6 "table of glory" (for the tetragrammaton), also Str.-B., III, 419 f.

[45] As against H. Lietzmann, Messe u. Herrenmahl, Arbeiten z. Kirchengesch., 8 (1926), 180 f.

[46] As to the shape of the eucharistic table there are no direct pre-Constantinian witnesses. We have no archaeological data, and the artistic depictions are symbolical. A S. Callisto picture of the 3rd cent. A.D. shows 7 figures sitting in a half-circle behind an oval table-top symbolically characterised by loaves and fishes, cf. J. Wilpert, Die Malereien d. Katakomben Roms (1903), Plate, 41, 4; similarly the fractio panis in S. Priscilla in the 2nd cent., 15, 1. Only in two 2nd cent. pictures from S. Callisto can one make out the outlines of a table; it is a commonly attested round dresser with three legs at which those who serve it stand, cf. 38 and 41, 1. Dion. of Alex. uses for receiving the eucharist the expressions τῇ τραπέζῃ προσιέναι and τῇ τραπέζῃ παραστάντα, Eus. Hist. Eccl., VII, 9, 4. Conclusions from contemporary tables and later archaeological findings suggest that in the earliest period the eucharist was usually celebrated at round or sigma-shaped tables, cf. O. Nussbaum, "Zum Problem d. runden u. sigmaförmigen Altarplatten," Jbch. Ant. Christ., 4 (1961), 18-43. From Ign. Phld., 4 to Eus. Hist. Eccl., X, 4, 68 it is often stressed that there is only one altar for Christians, that of the eucharist. Hence even beyond the 4th cent. only one altar stood in churches.

[47] So for the first time expressly in Orig. Hom. in Jos., 2, 1 on 1:2; Cyprian ad Demetrianum, 12 (CSEL, 3, 1, 360); Ep., 43, 5 (3, 2, 594); 61, 2 (3, 2, 696); 63, 5 (3, 2, 704); 65, 1 (3, 2, 722); 72, 2 (3, 2, 776); 75, 17 (3, 2, 822); cf. The Second Book of Jeû, 46 (ed. C. Schmidt-W. Till, GCS, 45[3] [1959], 309). Acc. to Act. Thom. 49 a makeshift table could be made by spreading a cloth over a stool; tablecloths were first used only in the later imperial period, cf. Kruse, 942 and 944; T. Klauser, Art. "Altar," RAC, I, 349. Cf. on this Braun, 48-65; Harnack Miss., 612 f.; Kirsch, 334 f.; Wieland, 334 f.

[48] Wieland, 122 f.

3rd cent. on, and first in the East, was the eucharistic table honoured even *extra usum* as a holy place and left continuously in the one spot, Didasc., 15; Eus. Hist. Eccl., VII, 15, 1-5; X, 4, 44. [49] This table which had become a holy place could now be called either altar or table with appropriate preciser definitions. [50]

Goppelt

---

[49] Cf. Wieland, 126; F. J. Dölger, "Die Heiligkeit d. Altars u. ihre Begründung im chr. Altertum," *Ant. Christ.*, 2 (1930), 161-183; → n. 50.

[50] In the post-apost. fathers and 2nd cent. Apologists τράπεζα is never used in connection with the eucharist. Cl. Al. Paed., II, 1, 10, 6 mentions only the table of demons, not that of the Lord. But then τράπεζα with the appropriate definitions is often used for the eucharistic table. The 4th cent. Gk. fathers esp. call it "holy," Athanasius Ep. encyclica, 5 (MPG, 25 [1884], 229 A); Greg. Naz. Or., II apologetica, 8 (MPG, 35 [1886], 416 B); Or., 43, 56 (MPG, 36 [1886], 568 A). Its importance is stressed by laudatory attributes, e.g., βασιλικός, Chrys. Hom. in Hb., 17, 5 (MPG, 63 [1862], 133), ἀθάνατος, 13, 4 (107), θεῖος, Greg. Naz. Or., 43, 52 (MPG 36 [1886], 564 A), μυστικός, Carmina, II, 1, 1884 (MPG 37 [1862], 1161 A), πνευματικός and ἔνθεος, Or. V contra Julianum, 2 35 (MPG 35 [1886], 709 B). The Lat. fathers mostly use *altare*, but also *mensa*, e.g., Ps.-Cyprian Adv. aleatores, 11 (CSEL, 3, 3, 103). For further Gk. examples Dölger, *op. cit.*, 171-3 and A. Weckwerth, "Tisch u. Altar," *Zschr. f. Religions- u. Geistesgeschichte*, 15 (1963), 220 f.

τρεῖς, τρίς, τρίτος

A. Three in the Greek and Hellenistic Roman World.

Three plays no inconsiderable role in the divine world and esp. the cultus of antiquity. Divine triads [1] are common: Zeus, Poseidon, Hades, the rulers of earth, sea and the underworld; the judges of the dead; in Rome Jupiter, Juno, Minerva. [2] Orphic cosmogony often forms divine triads, Orpheus Fr., 12 (Diels, I, 11, 10-12); Orph. Fr., 54 (Kern, 130 f.). [3] Threefold execution of an act makes it definitive; threefold utterance of a word, expression, or sentence, gives it full validity and power. [4] The five invocations and petitions of an ancient prayer of the Roman Arval priests are repeated three times each, Carmina Latina Epigraphica, 1. [5] One must swear by Zeus three times, Aristoph. Ra., 305 f. [6] The dead are invoked three times, Ps.-Iambl. Theol. Arithm., 14; [7] Virgil Aen., VI, 506. To protect against accidents a specific saying (carmen) is said three times after taking one's place in a carriage, Plin. Hist. Nat., 28, 2, 4. A saying is recited three times to lull to sleep or to still the raging sea, Ovid Metam., 7, 146 f. Threefold performance of sacrificial actions underscores the request, Ps.-Iambl. Theol. Arithm. (→ n. 7), 15, p. 18, 5-7. [8] Other examples could be given, but one should not conclude that threefold

---

τρεῖς κτλ. Bibl.: J. B. Bauer, "Drei Tage," Biblica, 39 (1958), 354-358; E. v. Dobschütz, "Zwei- u. dreigliedrige Formeln," JBL, 50 (1931), 117-147; E. Lease, "The Number Three, Mysterious, Mystic, Magic," Class. Philol., 14 (1919), 56-73; R. Mayer, Die Verwendung d. Dreizahl als Stilmittel im AT, Diss. Freiburg (1944); R. Mehrlein, Art. "Drei," RAC, IV, 269-310 (Bibl. 309 f.); C. L. Mitton, "Threefoldness in the Teaching of Jesus," Exp. T., 75 (1964), 228-230; E. Norden, Agnostos Theos (1913), 348-354; G. Sauer, "Die Sprüche Agurs," BWANT, 84 (1963); O. Weinreich, "Trigemination als sakrale Stilform," Studi e materiali di storia delle religioni, 4 (1928), 198-206; Wnd. 2 K. on 12:8 f.; 13:13.

[1] The much quoted essay of H. Usener, "Dreiheit," Rhein. Mus., NF, 58 (1903) has a wealth of material, esp. from the Gk. and Rom. world, on divine triads, 1-48, three-headed mythical beings etc., 161-208; in threeness there is often development from two to three acc. to Usener, 321-342. The attempt at a mythological doctrine of numbers which concludes the essay (342-362) has come under mounting criticism. Lease's essay, which is also rich in materials, adduces divine triads, 57 f., cf. Mehrlein, 272-281, also W. Deonna, "Trois, superlatif absolu," L'Antiquité Classique, 23 (1954), 403-428. Many triads owe their existence as such to the ancient or modern tendency to systematise.

[2] On the Lesbian triad of Zeus, Hera and Dionysus disclosed by modern pap. discoveries v. Alcaios Fr., 129 (ed. E. Lobel and D. Page, Poetarum Lesbiorum Fr. [1955], 176), cf. C. Gallavotti, "La triade Lesbia in uno testo miceno," Rivista di filologia e di istruzione classica, NS, 34 (1956), 225-236 [Risch].

[3] Plat. Soph., 242c: τρία τὰ ὄντα, pts. without any further evidence (materially cf. Emped. Fr., 17 [Diels, I, 315-8]) to a pre-Socratic cosmology.

[4] For examples of cultic threes cf. esp. S. Eitrem, "Opferritus u. Voropfer d. Griechen u. Röm.," Skrifter utgitt av Videnskapsselskapet i Kristiania, II, 1 (1915), Index, s.v. "Drei"; Lease, 56-73; cf. Mehrlein, 282-8, for magic 288-291; also F. J. Dölger, Sol salutis[2] (1925), 93-103; Wnd. 2 K. on 12:8 f.

[5] Ed. F. Buecheler, I (1895).

[6] Cf. R. Hirzel, Der Eid (1902), 82 f.; for oaths by three deities, cf. 127; also Usener, op cit. (→ n. 1), 18-24.

[7] Ed. V. de Falco (1922), 16, 13 f.

[8] On three day fasts v. P. R. Arbesmann, "Das Fasten bei d. Griechen u. Römern," RVV, 21, 1 (1929), Index, s.v. "Fasttage."

performance or recitation was the cultic rule. In records of healing at the sanctuary of Aesculapius on the Tiber island we read of a process being carried out for three days (Ditt. Syll.³, III, 1173, 12 f., 15-17 2nd cent. A.D.) and in Ael. Arist. Or., 47, 71 (Keil) Aesculapius will not answer the first or second prayer; instructions are given to the sick person on the third. [9] Yet in the preserved records of 70 healings at Epidauros three is of no significance in the miracles, IG, IV², 1, 121, 122, 123 (4th cent. B.C.). With rules for pronouncing a saying three times (Preis. Zaub., I, 4, 208 f., 985 f.) we also find directions for recitation "once or three times" (1038) or seven times (958).

Aristot. Cael., I, 1, p. 268a, 10-15 traces back three in religious practices to the fact that men have received the ordinances (νόμους) of the no. three from nature. The Pythagoreans, acc. to him, say that three is the no. of the universe, that everything is limited by it, by beginning, middle and end. Such statements are common in lit. Three is perfect [10] because it embraces beginning, middle and end, Philo Quaest. in Gn., 3, 3 on 15:9, cf. 4, 8 on 18:6 f.; Plut. Quaest. Conv., IX, 3, 2 (II, 738 F); the Pythagoreans think that three among numbers and the isosceles triangle among figures is the basis of knowledge, Philo Quaest. in Gn., 4, 8. [The fact that groups of three occur in philosophical ethics and the theory of style, esp. in peripatetic authors, rests on the Gk. view of harmony and measure which regards the right as the mean between two extremes, cf. already Archiloch. Fr., 67a (Diehl³, III, 29)]. Three is characterised by fulness and solidity, Philo Quaest. in Gn., 4, 30 on 19:1; in Ex., 2, 100 on 27:1. Nature has produced three dimensions, Decal., 25, cf. Op. Mund., 102. Time is divided into three, Sacr. AC, 47 on Gn. 30:36, cf. Leg. All., III, 11 and II, 42. So is the soul, ibid., I, 70; III, 115. [11] There are three kinds of waters, Quaest. in Gn., 3, 3 [12] etc. Biblical ref. lead Philo to allegorical interpretations [13] of three, so Gn. 18:6 in Sacr. AC, 59 f. and Dt. 16:16 in Leg. All., III, 11. Many three passages are assembled in Ps.-Iambl. Theol. Arithm. (→ n. 7), 12-16, p. 14, 13 - 19, 20. It may also be mentioned that terms like τρισευδαίμων and τρισόλβιος convey a sense of perfection, 15, p. 18, 7-9, cf. τρίσμακαρ in Hom. Od., 6, 154 f. In Philo, e.g., there is a whole series of such constructs. [14]

B. Three in the Old Testament and the Septuagint.

Only in few of the passages in which it appears in the OT is three important as such. [15] When its use is not determined by the factual data in narratives etc. there may be formal reasons. Three persons are a group of their own, cf. the enumeration "the second, the third, and all that followed" in Gn. 32:19. When it is significant per se three is the number of completeness (→ lines 12 ff.). Thus the three sons of Noah are the ancestors of the whole race, Gn. 6:10. [16] Balaam blesses Israel three times, Nu. 24:10. The priestly blessing

---

[9] Cf. Wnd. 2 K. on 12:8 f.

[10] On numbers which are esp. perfect for Philo → 68, 8 ff. The ref. in K. Staehle, Die Zahlenmystik bei Philon v. Alex. (1931), 24-26 show that three itself is not so important as a starting-point for special discussions.

[11] For three in philosophical systematisation, esp. ethics, v. H. Merguet, Lexikon zu d. philosophischen Schriften Ciceros, III (1894), 696 f. on genera sententiae; → 225, 31 ff.

[12] Cf. Ps.-Iambl. → line 25 f. For deliberations on three both appeal to Hom. Il., 15, 189: τριχθὰ δὲ πάντα δέδασται, cf. Philo Quaest. in Gn., 4, 8; Ps.-Iambl. Theol. Arithm. (→ n. 7), 16, p. 19, 11 f.; the quotation is part of the fixed stock of literary material on three. Three is in fact very important in Hom., e.g., stylistically; for material cf. F. Göbel, Formen u. Formeln d. epischen Dreiheit in d. gr. Dichtung (1935), where other texts are also consulted.

[13] Acc. to Diog. L., IX, 46 Democr. wrote an ethical treatise Τριτογένεια.

[14] Cf. Leisegang, s.v.

[15] Cf. J. Hehn, Siebenzahl u. Sabbat bei den Babyloniern u. im AT (1907), 63-75. Hehn (75) rightly makes the critical observation that three is often used in the OT with no underlying relation.

[16] One often reads of three sons, to be taken as a round no., cf. 1 Ch. 23:8 f. with v. 10, v. 23 with v. 12, 19, 21 f. Job has a full no. of sons (7) and 3 daughters, 1:2; 42:13.

consists of three two-membered sayings of increasing fulness, Nu. 6:24-26. [17] The three-fold crescendo of Yahweh's promise in Hos. 2:21 f. is a complete confirmation of it. [18] The third performance of an action completes it, 1 K. 18:34, cf. 17:21. What is done three times successfully is not repeated but something else is done, 1 S. 19:19-22. In narrative, then, three can suggest that an event or group is complete. We find three Davidic heroes in 2 S. 23:16 f., 23, three friends of Job, Job 2:11; 32:1, 3, 5, three righteous men, Noah, Daniel and Job in Ez. 14:14, 16, 18, three friends of Daniel in Da. 3:23 f., three heavenly visitors to Abraham in Gn. 18:2, three flocks at the well in 29:2, three pages of Darius in 1 Εσδρ. 3:4, cf. the way in which the events of 1 K. 18:38 and 2 K. 1:10, 12 are given threefold form under the slogan "fire" in Sir. 48:3. Formulae are made impressive by threefold use of the same word in Jer. 7:4; 22:29; Ez. 21:32; [19] Is. 6:3. Systematisation is evident in the ref. to the three feasts when Israel must appear before Yahweh, Ex. 23:14, 17; 34:23 f.; Dt. 16:16; 2 Ch. 8:13. The three hours of prayer are presumed to be customary in Da. 6:11, 14, though it is not clear whether the point is the same in Ps. 55:17. [20] On the other hand there seems to be a liking for the use of three in the proverbial sayings of the Wisdom lit. which gather together in three that which is positively or negatively judged, that which is incomprehensible etc., Sir. 25:1 f. But three here may be developed into four, Sir. 26:5; Prv. 30:18, 21, 29, or it may be an expansion of two, Sir. 23:16; 26:28; 50:25; one finds the sequence two - three - four in Prv. 30:15. [21]

Three is a round number when found in the combination 2 - 3. This means a few times. God saves man's soul from the pit 2 or 3 times, Job 33:29, cf. 2 K. 9:32; Am. 4:8. Jehioakim reads 3 - 4 columns in Jer. 36:23; in parallelism one can find 2 - 3 and 4 - 5, Is. 17:6. [22] But what seems to be the formally similar "yesterday and on the third day" in the LXX is really different. It goes much further back and means "as before," Ex. 5:7, "for a long time," 1 Βασ. 14:21, negatively "never before," 4:7, πρὸ τῆς ἐχθὲς καὶ πρὸ τῆς τρίτης, "for some time," Ex. 21:29, ἀπ' ἐχθὲς καὶ τρίτης ἡμέρας, "before," Jos. 3:4, καθὰ ἐχθὲς καὶ τρίτην ἡμέραν "as before," "always," Jos. 4:18. In other time sayings three can mean a short or long period acc. to context. Israel wanders three days without water, Ex. 15:22. Someone is sought in vain for three days and all is done that can be done, 2 K. 2:17. A riddle cannot be solved in three days, Ju. 14:14. The plundering of booty lasts three days, 2 Ch. 20:25. There is a day and night fast for three days, Est. 4:16. The Jews beseech God for three days, 2 Macc. 13:12. In all these instances the three days seem a long time to those concerned. But then Hezekiah is to be well in three days, 2 K. 20:5. After two days Yahweh will give life to His people and on the third He will cause it to rise again, Hos. 6:2. In three days 80,000 perish, 2 Macc. 5:14. The time now is short. One should not overlook the fact that "on the third day" usually means here "the day after to-morrow," "the day after next," 1 K. 3:18; 1 Macc. 11:18. Three days can also be a postponement, a time for consultation, 1 K. 12:5, 12. Again three days can lead up to a decisive event on the fourth day, Jdt. 12:7, 10; cf. Ezr. 8:32 f. Three, which expresses already an extensive avenging of the sin of the fathers on succeeding generations (cf. Aesch. Sept. c. Theb., 743 f.: Guilt "remains" to the third member), is raised to four in Ex. 20:5; 34:7; Nu. 14:18; Dt. 5:9. Only in the third generation can Edomites and Egyptians enter the community of Yahweh, Dt. 23:9. The description of

[17] Bibl. in O. Eissfeldt, Einl. in d. AT³ (1964), 100, n. 1.
[18] B. Stade, "Die Dreizahl im AT," ZAW, 26 (1906), 124. For other instances v. Sauer, 79.
[19] Cf. J. Herrmann, "Zu Jer. 22:29; 7:4," ZAW, 62 (1950), 321 f.
[20] On the 3 hours of prayer in post-chr. Judaism cf. Str.-B., II, 696 f. The no. of prayer times presupposed in 1 QS 10:1-3; 1 QH 12:4-7 is uncertain.
[21] In such sayings one also finds 6/7 in Prv. 6:16, 9/10 in Sir. 25:7; v. W. Roth, "The Numerical Sequence x/x + 1 in the OT," VT, 12 (1962), 300-311. Cf. also Sauer, 87-91, on Prv. 30 ibid., 101-110.
[22] Not infrequently one also finds 1/2, cf. 10 instances including Sir. 38:17 in Roth, op. cit., 301.

the works of the Spirit in Is. 11:2 is three-membered, and so is that of the kingdoms of created things in Wis. 7:20. Threefold utterance of a saying emphasises its validity in a prophetic word like Is. 6:11; this then becomes a general stylistic device in poetry. [23]

C. Three in Jewish Literature.

Grouping in threes also has some importance in Judaism. That John Hyrcanus is honoured with the threefold office of king, high-priest and prophet (→ VI, 825, 19 ff.) is stressed by Jos. Ant., 13, 299; Bell., 1, 68; cf. for the future ruler, Test. L. 18:2. Three gifts were given Israel for the sake of three persons: the well of water for Miriam's sake, the pillar of a cloud for Aaron's and the manna *propter Moysen*, Ps.-Philo Antiquitates Bibl., [24] 20, 8. The ref. to the three nets of Belial (fornication, wealth and desecration of the sanctuary) in Damasc. 4:14-18 (6:10-11) are based on the three nouns in Is. 24:17, but with an obvious stress on three as the no. of completeness. In 1 QS 6:8 f. one finds the three ranks of priests, elders, people, in 2:19-21 priests, Levites, people; Damasc. 14:3 f. (17:1-3) adds proselytes. "The many" watch together "a third of all the nights of the year" in study of the Torah and praise of God, 1 QS 6:7 f. [25] On the three-year cycle of Torah readings → VII, 17, 5 ff. Three-membered sayings in lists of three important things etc. occur in, e.g., Ab., 1, 2, 5-7, 10, 15 f., 18; 2, 15-17 etc.; cf. Git., 3, 4: NN taught three things. God notes three things esp.: theft, idolatry, outrage, BM, 59a. Three as esp. guilty will not come back from purgatory, 58b. For triplets cf. Test. L. 18:3 f.; Jos. 2:5; Ps. Sol. 4:21; 8:5; 9:3, 5, 9; 15:3; for three-membered sayings the antitheses Test. Jos. 1:4, 5, 6.

D. Three in the New Testament.

1. a. It is often apparent at once that three is meant exactly. Thus it is used for the shipwrecks (→ IV, 891, 14 ff.) and the Roman beatings which Paul suffered, 2 C. 11:25, and for the three visits to Corinth, 2 C. 12:14; 13:1. Even though three takes on deeper significance in 2 C. 13:1, this does not alter its exactness. The three years in Gl. 1:18 are no less accurate than the fourteen in 2:1. The no. of tents in Mk. 9:5 and par. corresponds to the presence of Jesus, Moses and Elijah (→ VII, 379, 8 ff.), while the 4×3 gates in Rev. 21:13 are based on the 12 tribes of Israel and the four quarters of heaven, cf. Ez. 48:30-34 (→ II, 323, 15 ff.). Paul's saying about his rapture to the third heaven in 2 C. 12:2 is an adaptation to current ideas → V, 534, 25 ff. In Lk. 12:52 f. (→ IV, 1099, 17 ff.) the no. three arises out of the relationships; in the close quarters of a Palestinian house hostility exists between father and son and between son's wife and sister and mother. The par. Mt. 10:35, which is closer to Mi. 7:6, does not have the numbers. On the numbers in Jm. 5:17; Lk. 4:25 → II, 934, 27 ff.; IV, 640, n. 24. The no. 153 in Jn. 21:11 is usually explained as a triangular no. $(1 + 2 + 3 + 4 \ldots + 17 =$ 153) expressing totality, [26] though it is not clear why 153 is chosen. [27]

---

[23] On triplets v. S. Mowinckel, "Real and Apparent Tricola in Hebrew Psalm Poetry," *Avhandlinger utgitt av Det Norske Videnskaps-Akad. i Oslo,* II, 2 (1957); Ps. 93, 138 and 45 are examples, 13-15. On three as a literary device in the OT (the combination of three corresponding nouns etc.) there is a wealth of material in Mayer, 40-173 (non-biblical material for comparison, 215-278). Acc. to Mayer this device is most common in Dt., Ps. and the Prophets, 210.

[24] Ed. G. Kisch (1949).

[25] On the threefold division of the night v. Str.-B., I, 688-691.

[26] So, e.g., C. K. Barrett, *The Gospel acc. to St. John* (1955), *ad loc.*; J. A. Emerton, "The Hundred and Fifty-Three Fishes in Jn. 21:11," JThSt, NS, 9 (1958), 86-89 (with bibl.) connects it with the gematria of Hbr. letters.

[27] 17 is the sum of 10 and 7, the numbers of completeness or perfection, cf. Barrett, *op. cit., ad loc.* Critically cf. Bultmann J., *ad loc.* Cf. also H. Kruse, "Magni Pisces Centum Quinquaginta Tres (Jn. 21:11)," *Verbum Domini,* 38 (1960), 129-148.

b. Round numbers in three are more common in Ac., sometimes with preceding ὡς, 5:7, cf. Lk. 1:56. Only three occurs with numbers of months (7:20; 19:8; 20:3; 28:11 → IV, 640, 28 ff.) except at 18:11, though here again we have a round no. "Three days" occurs only in 9:9; 25:1; 28:7, 12, 17; the last four obviously denote short spaces of time. Other notes of time in Ac. confirm the fact that Lk. in his narratives intentionally binds events together by this means. For want of exact dates he has often to use round figures; this is patent in respect of the months.

2. The statements regarding the resurrection of Jesus in Mk. 8:31 and par.; 9:31 and par.; 10:34 and par.; Mt. 12:40; 27:63 f.; Lk. 24:7, 21; Jn. 2:19 f.; 1 C. 15:4; cf. Mk. 14:58 and par.; 15:29 and par. are fairly obviously related to Hos. 6:2 [28] → 218, 34 f.; II, 949, 12 ff.; VII, 29, n. 226. [29] But as in many other instances where the NT uses OT passages the "cause to rise again on the third day" is detached from its original context in Hos. 6:2. The idea of a short space of time, which possibly lies behind Hos. 6:2, no longer plays any part. In primitive Christianity the number three [30] derives from the Easter tradition [31] in which the day of the resurrection is the same as that of the discovery of the empty tomb or the first appearances of the Risen Lord.

3. In the NT, too, the ideas of few or many may be combined with three according to context → 218, 27 ff. [32] The use of three as a round number [33] can affect the way a statement is made. [34] Thus the fact that the owner has looked for fruit for three years on the fig-tree justifies an end to his patience; now he can no longer expect any harvest, Lk. 13:7 → VII, 755, 28 ff. When we find 2 - 3 the reference is obviously to few. Even to the smallest group of those who meet in invocation of Jesus He promises His presence, Mt. 18:20, cf. v. 19. Paul wants to limit as much as possible the number of prophets and of those who speak with

---

[28] No matter what the original image (cf. bibl. in G. Wagner, "Das religionsgeschichtliche Problem v. R. 6:1-11," AbhThANT, 39 [1962] 213, n. 153) the ref. in the saying about the people in Hos. 6:1 f. is not to physical resurrection in the lit. sense. On Hos. 6:2 v. F. Nötscher, Altorientalischer u. at.licher Auferstehungsglauben (1926), 138-146.

[29] Cf. further in this C. H. Dodd, Acc. to the Scriptures (1952), 77 f., 103; H. Grass, Ostergeschehen u. Osterberichte³ (1964), 136-8; B. Lindars, NT Apologetic (1961), 59-72 (cf. the review by C. F. D. Moule, ThLZ, 78 [1962], 681); U. Wilckens, Die Missionsreden d. Ag.² (1962), 78, n. 4 (with bibl.); J. Dupont, "Ressuscité 'le troisième jour,'" Biblica, 40 (1959), 742-761.

[30] There is no support for the idea that three is connected with the Jewish concept of the soul remaining near the body for three days after death, cf. on this E. Freistedt, Altchr. Totengedächtnistage u. ihre Beziehung zum Jenseitsglauben u. Totenkultus d. Antike (1928), 53-72. In primitive Christianity the resurrection of Jesus is not regarded as the return of a dead man to his former life but as an event analogous to the eschatological resurrection of the dead which takes place for all possibly a long time after the death of the individual. Cf. the bibl. → II, 948, n. 31, also Clemen, 96-108; J. Leipoldt, "Zu den Auferstehungsgeschichten," ThLZ, 93 (1948), 737-742.

[31] Cf. H. v. Campenhausen, "Der Ablauf d. Osterereignisse u. das leere Grab," Tradition u. Leben, Kräfte d. Kirchengeschichte (1960), 54 f.

[32] Cf. the three days in Lk. 2:46; Mk. 8:2 and par. → IV, 579, 17 ff.

[33] This also applies to ref. to "a third," Rev. 8:7-12; 9:15, 18; 12:4 → VI, 603, n. 67. A considerable number at least is in view. When R. Eliezer was excommunicated "the world was smitten: a third of olives, a third of wheat and a third of barley," BM, 59b. v. Str.-B., IV, 315.

[34] The three measures in Mt. 13:33 and par. remind us of Gn. 18:6 → II, 905, 17 ff.; Jeremias Gl.⁶, 146 f.; Dalman Arbeit, IV (1935), 120. There is certainly emphasis on the fact that quite a lot is in view.

tongues participating in divine worship, 1 C. 14:27, 29. In context the list in 1 C. 12:28 does not carry with it any ranking, cf. Gn. 32:20; → 217, 32 f.; *v.* Mt. 22:26. The "to-day, to-morrow, on the third day" of Lk. 13:32 reminds us formally of other groups ending with three; the last term here obviously means "the day after to-morrow" → 218, 36 ff. [35] Materially what is being said (→ 84, 3 ff.) is that God sets the term for Jesus' work, cf. Jn. 9:4; 11:9.

4. In NT sayings based on Dt. 19:15 "two or three" does not denote a small number but stands opposed to "only one" → IV, 490, 1 ff. The principle that one witness is insufficient judicially is formulated generally in Dt. 19:15 [36] and was applied thus in the Judaism of NT days. In Mt. 18:15-17 (→ II, 474, 4 ff.; III, 673, 17 ff.; IV, 490, 5 ff.) — there are three steps — the one who initiates the process is himself one of the two or three witnesses of the second saying. In 1 Tm. 5:19 f. the witness of more than one is a required presupposition for correction among the brethren [37] esp. in relation to the πρεσβύτερος. The allusion to Dt. 19:15 in 2 C. 13:1 (→ IV, 490, 16 ff.) obviously elucidates the earlier τρίτον. [38] The third performance of an action, as shown, makes it definitive → 216, 7 ff.; 218, 1 ff.; Paul is also speaking of an imminent definitive action in v. 2. He bases its definitive character on what was for him a familiar OT principle in which threeness is decisively important. He is obviously not putting any stress on μαρτύρων, [39] which shows how generally Dt. 19:15 can be taken. In 1 Jn. 5:7 f., as in 2 C. 13:1, τρεῖς takes precedence. The special reference here is to the agreement of three testimonies, v. 8b. [40] On the basis of the Torah rule Jn. 8:16-18 proves for Jewish readers the truth of the testimonies of the Father and Jesus by their agreement → IV, 498, 36 ff. Not Dt. 19:15, but 17:6 combined with Nu. 15:30 is expressly cited in Hb. 10:28. Nu. 15:30 imposes the death penalty for wilful transgression (→ IV, 490, 1 ff.) of God's will, cf. ἀθετήσας Hb. 10:28. [41] In Lk. 10:30-35 the conduct of the third traveller is distinguished from that of the other two, cf. τούτων τῶν τριῶν, v. 36.

---

[35] If with J. Blinzler, "Die literarische Eigenart d. sog. Reiseberichts im Lk.," *Festschr. A. Wikenhauser* (1953), 45 on Lk. 13:33 we omit σήμερον καὶ αὔριον καί, ἐχομένη in v. 33 means the fourth day, → VII, 273, 16 ff.

[36] The special ref. in Dt. 17:6 is to idolatry, in Nu. 35:30 to homicide. On the whole question cf. H. v. Vliet, *No Single Testimony. A Study of the Adoption of the Law of Dt. 19:15 par. into the NT*, Diss. Utrecht (1958).

[37] Schl. Past., 152; Dib. Past., ad loc. suggest the other "old men," J. Jeremias, *Die Br. an Tm. u. Tt., NT Deutsch*, 9⁸ (1963), ad loc.; H. v. Campenhausen, *Kirchliches Amt u. geistliche Vollmacht in d. ersten drei Jhdt.²* (1963), 160 etc. the assembly, cf. Dib. Past., ad loc. In the latter case v. 20 at least applies to the elderly.

[38] Cf. already Cramer Cat., V, 439, 9 f. ταῖς παρουσίαις ἀντὶ μαρτύρων ἐχρήσατο; also Ltzm. K., Bchm. 2 K., Wnd. 2 K., ad loc.

[39] Wnd. 2 K., ad loc. suggests threefold witness in the same words, but the material and textual context does not support this interpretation.

[40] On the history of exposition cf. W. Nauck, *Die Tradition u. d. Charakter d. 1 J.* (1957), 147-152; for his attempt, on the basis of a special usage of the Syrian church, to interpret πνεῦμα here as unction of the Spirit (153-182), cf., e.g., R. Schnackenburg, Review of Nauck, BZ, NF, 4 (1960), 297. On the comma Johanneum → V, 1003, n. 349; Schnckbg. 1 J.², 44-46 (with bibl.). A ref. to AZ, 64b: "Who is a resident alien (→ VI, 737, 6 ff.)? One who before three witnesses has pledged to worship no idols," might suggest that 1 Jn. 5:7 and Mt. 18:16 presuppose a legal proceeding in which there had to be three witnesses [Bertram].

[41] Cf. ἠθέτησαν νόμον μου, Ez. 22:26. Wilful rejection of the statute removes it, declares it invalid.

5. Threefold performance of an action or the threefold occurrence of an event shows that it is complete, finished, definitive, → 221, 15 f. "This was done thrice" in Ac. 10:16 (repeated word for word in 11:10) [42] declares God's will fully and incontrovertibly. "Thrice" obviously refers to what we are told in 10:13-15 or 11:7-9. The fact that the demand is issued three times, that Peter's objection follows three times, and that the objection is set aside three times, each time in the same words, shows what importance attaches to it all. The threefold prayer of Jesus in Gethsemane — the number is stressed in Mt. 26:44, cf. Mk. 14:41 (but not Lk. 22:42-46) — emphasises the urgency of concern, but above all Jesus with His threefold cry is quite certain of the will of the Father, → III, 49, 2 ff. A τρίς which is given emphasis by its very position characterises the intensity of Paul's desire in 2 C. 12:8; the negative reply in v. 9 is given in a statement by the Risen Lord → 59, 9 ff. One can hardly miss the fact that the incidents are in some sense parallel, though not intentionally so. The sending of a third servant in Lk. 20:12 underlines both the longsuffering of the Lord and also the obstinacy of the insubordination of the husbandmen, which reaches an unsurpassable climax in v. 14 f. Only in Lk. 23:22 is it recorded that Pilate asks a third time concerning the guilt of Jesus, and in so doing establishes definitively His innocence (οὐδὲν... αἴτιον, v. 4, 14), [43] cf. the express statement three times in almost exactly the same words in Jn. 18:38; 19:4, 6. The threefold denial of Jesus by Peter (Mk. 14:30 and par.; 14:72 and par.) shows how fully he departs from a relation of obedience and loyalty to Jesus in this situation → I, 470, 11 ff. That the emphatic τρίτον in Jn. 21:17 alludes to the threefold denial is quite possible but is not suggested by the text itself. [44] What is plainly accentuated in the context is Jesus' question as to Peter's love for Him; [45] this becomes a very penetrating question. Also emphasised by twofold repetition is Peter's answer and his commissioning by Jesus. Both these are fully valid. Jn. 21:14 stresses the fact that in the incident of vv. 4-13 Jesus revealed Himself a third time to the disciples as the Risen Lord. In this way vv. 4-13 are connected with 20:19-23, 24-29, and it is indicated that there is full certainty as to the fact of the resurrection, cf. ἤδη (v. 14).

6. τὰ τρία ταῦτα in 1 C. 13:13 is meant comprehensively. Faith, love and hope (cf. also → II, 532, 11 ff.; IV, 587, 36 ff.) are already associated in 1 Th. 1:3. They are related here to the ἔργον of the community which has its origin in faith (→ II, 649, 36 ff.). They relate to the work which grows out of love, to the patience which is based on hope in the Lord Jesus Christ. In Col. 1:4 f. faith, love and hope have a threefold temporal reference. On 1 Th. 5:8 → V, 310, 10 ff., on 1 C. 13:13 → I, 52, 2 ff., cf. also Hb. 10:22-24. The triad is firmly established in Paul. There is no evidence that he borrowed it. [46]

---

[42] The repeating of Ac. 10 in 11 is significant, cf. 10:44-47 and 11:15-17 and esp. 10:47 and 11:17. In 11:7-9 the conversation between the heavenly voice and Peter is repeated almost word for word because it is so important.

[43] As the author sees it this means that in some sense Pilate is innocent of the crucifixion of Jesus, cf. Ac. 3:13 etc.

[44] Zn. J., ad loc. thinks Jesus "thrusts the sting of remorse ever deeper into Peter's heart."

[45] The πλέον of v. 15 can hardly be explained in terms of Mk. 14:29 and par. There is nothing par. in either Lk. 22:33 or Jn. 13:37.

[46] On Porphyr. Marc., 24 → VII, 679, 16 ff. This is associated with 1 C. 13:13 by R. Reitzenstein, Historia Monachorum u. Historia Lausiaca (1916), 100-102, 242 f. Further bibl. — I, 51, n. 147; IV, 575, n. 2.

The triad God - Lord - Spirit (→ III, 107, 21 ff.) is also a fixed one in Paul, though the order varies. In the reverse order, as occasioned by the context, we find it in 1 C. 12:4-6 (→ VI, 434, 9 ff.), cf. Eph. 4:4-6. 2 C. 13:13 is clearly moulded by it (→ III, 807, 1 ff.); it is a promise like other simpler ones at the beginning and end of epistles (the two-membered promise of salvation becomes a three-membered one in 2 Jn. 3; 1 Tm. 1:2; 2 Tm. 1:2; cf. Jd. 2; → VI, 434, 13 ff.; → χάρις). [47] The formally opposite order: prayer by the Holy Spirit, the love of God, the mercy of our Lord Jesus Christ, occurs in Jd. 20 f. The three are closely connected in many other NT passages. A survey of the many NT statements in which God, Christ and Spirit are related without being explicitly set in juxtaposition [48] shows that these three are associated as the authors or agents of the work of salvation. As the numerous sayings in Paul show, the triad has its origin, not in theological reflection, but in the realities of the faith, proclamation, and liturgical life of the community. The fact that one can speak in the same sentence of God, Christ and the Spirit is rooted in the matter itself and it produces statements which are both far-reaching and comprehensive in content. Among these one may mention, e.g., 1 Pt. 1:2, which says that election (→ IV, 190, 20 ff.) is grounded in the work of God the Father, the Spirit and Jesus Christ, to whose obedience and saving death reference is made. [49] On Father, Son and Holy Spirit in Mt. 28:19 → V, 274, 28 ff.; 989, n. 279; VI, 401, 16 ff.; → υἱός. [50] On the triad God, the seven spirits and Jesus Christ in the promise of grace at the beginning of the letter in Rev. 1:4 f. → VI, 450, 7 ff. [51] On the probably ancient series God, Christ Jesus, angels in 1 Tm. 5:21 cf. Christ and the angels in Rev. 14:10 and "my Father" and "his angels" in Rev. 3:5, a passage related to 1 Tm. 5:21 not merely by the ἐνώπιον...; it is doubtful, however, whether this is a triad of equal entities. The same applies to Lk. 9:26. The serpent, the beast and the false prophet are an ungodly triad in Rev. 16:13 (cf. the πνεύματα τρία). There is a three-membered designation of God in Rev. 1:4 (→ III, 107, 17 ff.), 8; 4:8. [52]

7. With no special emphasis, three plays a certain role in parables and stories, [53] cf. the three gifts of Mt. 2:11, [54] the three types of people invited in Lk. 14:18-20, [55] the three servants mentioned as examples in Mt. 25:20-25; Lk. 19:16-21, [56] the three reasons why sowing was in vain in Mk. 4:4-7 and par. [57] A judgment is made more impressive

---

[47] 1 C. 16:23 f. makes it plain that these are promises; v. 24 cannot be a mere wish. On 2 C. 13:13 → V, 1011, n. 395.
[48] Collected in P. Gächter, "Zum Pneumabegriff d. hl. Pls.," Zschr. f. kathol. Theol., 53 (1929), 386-401; O. Moe, "Hat Pls. den trinitarischen Taufbefehl Mt. 28:19 u. ein trinitarisches Taufbekenntnis gekannt?" Festschr. R. Seeberg, I (1929), 181.
[49] This interpretation takes the governing nouns together as terms for the work of the triad. But → VI, 983, 30 ff.; in relation to the bibl. in n. 41 there → n. 40. On 1 Pt. 1:2 → V, 1011, n. 395. For a saying about Christ's obedience along with one about His death cf. Phil. 2:8; Hb. 5:8. Note the alternation of prep. in 1 Pt. 1:2. Sayings at the beginning of epistles are carefully formulated in fixed expressions.
[50] Cf. G. Delling, Die Zueignung des Heils in d. Taufe (1961), 94-6; G. Kretschmar, Stud. zu frühchr. Trinitätstheologie (1956), 5 f.
[51] The 7 spirits relate esp. to the throne angels, T. Holtz, "Die Christologie d. Apk. d. Joh.," TU, 85 (1962), 138-140.
[52] Cf. G. Delling, "Zum gottesdienstlichen Stil d. Joh.-Apk.," Nov. Test., 3 (1959), 124-7; there are Rabb. par. on the basis of Ex. 3:14. On the trisagion in Rev. 4:8 cf. Delling, 127 f. → n. 71.
[53] Bultmann Trad., 207 and 342 f.
[54] On the deduction that there were three magi v. W. Bauer, Das Leben Jesu (1909), 76 f. with bibl. [Bertram].
[55] Here the feast is a symbol of God's rule, cf. Mt. 22:2. On the two forms of the parable Jeremias Gl.⁶, 61-63, 175-196. There are 4 excuses in the Gospel of Thomas, Jeremias, 175 f.; Hennecke³, I, 210 f.
[56] Jeremias Gl.⁶, 55-60.
[57] Bibl. → VII, 546, n. 25.

when put in three forms, Mt. 5:22 → V, 420, 23 ff.; VI, 975, 6 ff. Jesus mentions three ways in which a host shows his solicitude, Lk. 7:44-46. The opinions of three groups on Jesus are recorded, Lk. 9:7 f. [58] Three temptations (→ VI, 34, 18 f.) show Jesus to be fully tried and tested, Mt. 4:1-11 and par. The threefold prediction of the passion underlines esp. the significance of the crucifixion, Mk. 8:31 and par.; 9:31 and par.; 10:33 f. and par.; cf. → II, 24, 10 ff. The conversion of Paul is recounted three times in Ac. to stress the fact that the Gentile mission was shown by God's special intervention to be divinely willed, 9:1-18; 22:6-16; 26:12-18. While certain groups of double parables [59] may well go back to Jesus, groups of three might have been assembled by the tradition, cf. Lk. 15:1-32. [60] In triple form Lk. describes the response of some who were ready for or called to discipleship (→ I, 213, 30 ff.), Lk. 9:57-62. Lk. also presents the teaching of the Baptist by means of three groups who all put the same question, 3:10-14. A principle is illustrated by three statements which in part agree word for word, Lk.6:32-34. Three warning examples are given in Jd. 5-7, three comparisons in 11, cf. Mt. 10:41 f. The task of the Paraclete is threefold, Jn. 16:8-11. Putting the one teaching in three short par. sayings can make it very impressive, e.g., with illustrations in Mt. 7:7 f.; Lk. 11:9 f. Futile self-concern is expressed in three questions in Mt. 6:31. The disciples' failure to understand the prediction of the passion is noted three times in Lk. 18:34 (peculiar to Lk.), cf. 9:45. Putting the same thought in three sayings is a stylistic device in 1 C. 1:26-28; the three οὐ . . . in v. 26 are conversely taken up again in v. 27 f. [61] In v. 30 the saying about the wisdom given in Jesus Christ is expounded in three closely related (τε καὶ . . . καὶ) nouns, cf. the three verbs in 1 C. 6:11, [62] the threefold we - you (you - we) in 1 C. 4:10, also 12b, 13a, the threefold . . . ὡς νήπιος, 13:11, the threefold οὐδένα . . . , 2 C. 7:2, the threefold τί ἐξήλθατε . . . , Mt. 11:7-9. Membership of the saved people is expressed three times and taken up in a threefold κἀγώ in 2 C. 11:22, cf. Gl. 3:28; 2 Tm. 1:7b, 11; Tt. 2:12b, 15a; R. 14:17; Rev. 1:9, the three pairs of nouns in R. 13:13, the three part. in Hb. 10:20, the three two-membered expressions with διά in 2 C. 6:7 f., also Phil. 3:2; 1 Cor. 15:52a, the three groups of Jews, Greeks and the community of God in 1 Cor. 10:32, or the three materially differentiated titles of Christ in Rev. 1:5a, the three-membered description of Christ's saving work in Rev. 1:5b, 6. 2 C. 6:4 f. is made up 3 × 3 expressions in ἐν. [63] On R. 11:36 [64] → V, 894, 17 ff., on Jn. 14:6 → V, 81, 5 ff. [65] Liturgical

---

[58] Cf. H. Sparks, "The Partiality of Luke for 'Three,'" JThSt, 37 (1936), 141-5. Acc. to J. Jeremias, "Jesus als Weltvollender," BFTh, 33, 4 (1930), 21, n. 1 using threes is a stylistic peculiarity of Jesus Himself; many instances are given. Not counting par., Mitton lists 64 examples from 4 sources (17 peculiar to Lk.). Acc. to him the findings support Jesus' own use of threes.

[59] Cf. Jeremias Gl.[6], 89-91.

[60] Ibid., 91 f. for other groups. On threes in Lk. R. Morgenthaler, "Die lk. Geschichtsschreibung als Zeugnis," I, AbhThANT, 14 (1948), 73-79.

[61] On v. 27, 28a cf. the three members in Jer. 9:22; 1 Βασ. 2:10 (not HT).

[62] Traditional acc. to G. Friedrich, "Christus, Einheit u. Norm d. Christen," Kerygma u. Dogma, 9 (1963), 235-258, esp. 246. For other ref. cf. Mayer, 279-282: The three nouns often occur in lofty style, so the song of praise Rev. 4:9. The par. δόξαν καὶ τιμὴν καὶ ἀφθαρσίαν in R. 2:7 or δόξα καὶ τιμὴ καὶ εἰρήνη in v. 10 perhaps suggest fixed usage. Cf. the 3 verbs of the confession of sin in 1 K. 8:47; 2 Ch. 6:37; Ps. 106:6, also Yoma, 3, 8 etc. and the 3 nouns Ex. 34:7.

[63] Cf. G. Friedrich, Amt u. Lebensführung (1963), 23, 34 f.

[64] In R. 11:33-35 v. 34a, 34b, 35 correspond in reverse order to the nouns πλοῦτος - σοφία - γνῶσις in v. 33, G. Bornkamm, "Der Lobpreis Gottes," Das Ende des Gesetzes[4] (1963), 72 f. The three-membered ἐξ - δι' - εἰς in v. 36 is related esp. to R. 9-11 by H. Schwantes, Schöpfung d. Endzeit (1963), 19.

[65] In some ways many of these passages (→ lines 19 ff.) often remind us of the tricolon of ancient rhetoric, of which Ps.-Long., 20, 1 says: When 2 or 3 figures form a group, they combine force, conviction and beauty. Cf. the examples from Sen. in E. Norden, Die antike Kunstprosa, I[3] (1915), 289 and Index, s.v. "Trikolon," also from the class. and Hell.-Rom. period E. Norden, "De Minucii Felicis aetate et genere dicendi," Wissenschaftliche Beilage zum Vorlesungsverzeichnis Greifswald (Easter 1897), 37-53. Cf. Jos. Bell., 4, 252b, 364b.

texts are sometimes in three lines, Eph. 5:14 (→ III, 990, 8ff.) or in three pairs of sayings acc. to the schema ab/ba/ab, [66] → VI, 416, 34 ff., 1 Tm. 3:16; both seem to be independent and not fragments of greater wholes. Finally ref. may be made to threefold indication of time in the doxology of Jd. 25.

E. Three in the Post-Apostolic Fathers.

To avoid abuse of hospitality the stay of travelling brethren is limited to 2/3 days in Did., 12, 2. If a prophet claims the community's hospitality for three days he is a parasitic false prophet, 11, 5 → VI, 860, 41 ff. When the herald proclaims three times that Polycarp has declared himself to be a Christian, the fact is definitively established, Mart. Pol., 12, 1. Trine immersion in Did., 7, 3 is based on baptism into the triune name, Mt. 28:19. The praying of the Lord's Prayer three times a day in Did., 8, 2 f. is connected with the Jewish practice → 218, 3 ff.; II, 801, 16 ff.; the altering of other Jewish customs is demanded in the context. Three eschatological signs pt. to the coming Christ, Did., 16, 6 f. → VII, 261, 8 ff. On Ign. Eph., 19, 1 → IV, 824, 23 ff. Love, faith, hope (→ 222, 31 ff.) are linked in this order, Pol., 3 2 f. Hope, righteousness and love are called δόγματα of the Lord in Barn., 1, 6. [67] In 10, 1 f. 9 it is stressed that Moses received three instructions, three prohibitions of meats, from God, which are to be expounded allegorically; Ps. 1:1 is related to these in 10, 10. In an allegorical application of Nu. 19 (with no specific ref.) to Christ's atoning work we read: 3 boys sprinkle the water of expiation as a witness for Abraham, Isaac and Jacob, who are great before God, 8, 4. The no. 318, IHT, in Gn. 14:14 is with 17:23 [68] expounded gematrically as the no. of Jesus the Crucifed (T cross), and circumcision is then related typologically to Him; Abraham received therein the instructions of three letters, 9, 7 f. The steps of penitence are apparently presented under the 3 guises of a symbolical woman, the Church, Herm. v., 3, 10, 2. 5. 9; 13, 1. [69] There are par. triads of closely related vices and complementary virtues in 1 Cl., 30, 8. [70] The triad Father, Son and Spirit in Did., 7, 1 (Mt. 28:19) occurs also as God, (Lord Jesus) Christ and (Holy) Spirit in 1 Cl., 46, 6 (with stress on εἷς or ἕν, cf. Eph. 4:4-6); 58, 2, God Father, Jesus Christ, Holy Spirit in Ign. Eph., 9, 1, (Jesus) Christ/Son, Father, Spirit in Ign. Mg., 13, 1 f. (→ VI, 451, n. 842). [71] The point that God is unchangeably characterised by His goodness is made in a statement referring to the three times οὗτος ἦν μὲν ἀεὶ τοιοῦτος καὶ ἔστι καὶ ἔσται, Dg., 8, 8. Cl. Al. shows acquaintance with the learned schemata of his day (→ n. 11) when he speaks of the threefold division of the soul in Strom., V, 80, 9, or the three kinds of goods among the peripatetics in II, 34, 1; IV, 166, 1 (cf. Aristot. Eth. Nic., I, 8, p. 1098b, 12-14), or the threefold nature of the Spiritual, Strom., I, 33, 1, or the three kinds of friendship, II, 101, 3. God has manifested Himself in three ways to the three peoples of Jews, Gentiles and Christians (cf. 1 C. 10:32 → 224, 28 f.), VI, 42, 1 f.

Delling

---

[66] a. with ref. to events on earth, b. in heaven; → ὕμνος.

[67] In the philosophical and popular tradition of antiquity there are canons with 2, 4 and 7 virtues, but not 3 [Dihle].

[68] Wnd. Barn., 355 f.

[69] Cf. Dib. Herm., 477.

[70] Cf. A. v. Harnack, "'Sanftmut, Huld u. Demut' in d. alten Kirche," *Festschr. J. Kaftan* (1920), 114-129.

[71] W. C. v. Unnik, "1 Clement 34 and the 'Sanctus,'" *Vigiliae Christianae*, 5 (1951), 204-208 shows that 1 Cl., 34, 6 does not pt. to liturgical use of the Sanctus in the world of 1 Cl. The same applies to Rev. 4:8 → n. 52.

┌─────────────────────┐
│ τρέχω, δρόμος,   │   → ἀγών, I, 134, 32 ff.
│ πρόδρομος   │
└─────────────────────┘

† τρέχω.

Contents: A. τρέχω in the Greek World: 1. In the Literal Sense; 2. In the Transferred Sense; 3. τρέχω in the Stadium. B. τρέχω in the Old Testament and Later Judaism: 1. The Septuagint; 2. Qumran; 3. Summary. C. τρέχω in the New Testament: 1. Paul; 2. Non-Pauline Writings. D. τρέχω in the Post-New Testament Writings.

A. τρέχω in the Greek World.

1. In the Literal Sense.

Though not common, and mostly [1] used only in the pres. and impf., τρέχω (Doric τράχω) [2] occurs from Hom. with synon. verbal forms derived from δραμ-. [3] Attic prose often has synon. θέω instead, so always in the expression θέω δρόμῳ, Thuc., III, 111, 2; Xenoph. An., I, 8, 18; cf. περὶ τοῦ παντὸς ... δρόμον θέοντες, Hdt., VIII, 74, 1. [4] Disregarding the special sphere of the race in the stadium (→ 227, 7 ff.) one cannot essentially differentiate the use of τρέχω (opp. βάδην, "step by step") [5] from that of comparable words in other languages. Literally τρέχω "to run" denotes the rapid forward movement of the feet, human, Hom. Od., 23, 207, animals, Il., 23, 392 f., e.g., "rushing on" in war, Xenoph. An., IV, 5, 18. With acc. obj. it usually corresponds to "to run through," e.g., Xenoph. Eq., 8, 1. [6]

2. In the Transferred Sense.

Here many inorganic objects may be the subj., ships in Theogn., 1, 856, a rapidly turning drill, Hom. Od., 9, 386. In the sense "to hasten on" the verb can be used of impersonal forces, e.g., ἠχώ, Callim. Hymn., 3, 245; ἔρις, Soph. Ai., 731, ὅρκος, Hes.

τρέχω . [1] Cf. Liddell-Scott, s.v.; Schwyzer, II, 258.
[2] An Indo-Eur. root dhregh- "to run" is assumed, but this is only partly supported by the forms in other languages, cf. Boisacq, Hofmann, s.v.; Pokorny, 273.
[3] With Sanskr. dramati "he runs" this belongs to a root drem-, related to the similar sounding drā- in Gk. ἀπέδραν "I escaped," Sanskr. drāti "he runs," cf. Frisk, s.v. δραμεῖν [Risch].
[4] θέω can sometimes be combined with ἐλαύνω, Aristoph. Eccl., 109; cf. the proverb Schol. in Eccl., 109 (ed. F. Dübner [1883], 316). On the text of this and its relation to the text of Aristoph. cf. I. van Leeuwen, Aristophanis Ecclesiazusae (1905), 20. This considers a nautical saying which like Aristoph. Eccl., 109 combines the verbs in a double negation: οὔτε θεῖν οὔτε ἐλαύνειν, "neither row nor sail." The fact that θέω was adapted to be used with other verbs in plays on words may be based on the intentionally ironical expression πλεῖ καὶ νεῖ καὶ θεῖ, Luc. Lexiphanes, 15 → n. 44.
[5] Cf. οὔτε βάδην ὑπήκουσεν, ἀλλ' ἀεὶ τρέχων, Xenoph. Cyrop., II, 2, 30. With ταχύ, Xenoph. An., IV, 6, 25, βάδην can mean "quick step," but there is still a difference from running in the sense of δρόμῳ θέω. Even on the track a ταχὺς βαδιστής is not a runner, Eur. Med., 1181 f.
[6] Cf. τρέχεις ἡμίονον "thou dost run like a hinny," Plut. Sept. Sap. Conv., 4 (II, 150b), v. D. Wyttenbach's note, ad loc., where other readings are rejected.

Op., 219, μῦθος, Eur. Ion, 529, cf. also Pind. Pyth., 8, 32 ff. [7] Used in a transf. sense of men τρέχω can mean gen. "to hasten," e.g., ὡς εἰς στεναγμοὺς καὶ γόους, Eur. Or., 959, with an emphasis on the necessary exertion, e.g., running for one's life: τρέχων περὶ τῆς ψυχῆς (→ 227, 21 f.; 229, 15), Hdt., IX, 37, 2. The part. with a finite verb is often used adverbially: ἀνὴρ ἄβουλος εἰς κενὸν μοχθεῖ τρέχων, [8] Menand. Mon., 51, cf. also Plato Comicus, 69, 2 (FAC, I, 510).

3. τρέχω in the Stadium.

Unlike τρέχειν in ordinary life this is distinctive in Gk. The fact that the Olympiads are almost always named after the victor in the race [9] shows perhaps more plainly than the surviving literary evidence what importance attached to this festal τρέχειν in the popular consciousness of antiquity. Expressions like Ὀλυμπία(σιν) δραμεῖν στάδιον, Plut. Apophth. Alexandri, 2 (II, 179d) or παρὰ ἓν πάλαισμα ἔδραμε νικᾶν Ὀλυμπιάδα, "he was victor at Olympia in all but one round," Hdt., IX, 33, 2 recall values far beyond the everyday. The στέφανος to be won at Olympia (→ VII, 619, 47 ff.) had only ideal worth; [10] a contestant of whom it could be said ἔδραμε νικᾶν Ὀλυμπιάδα had set aside material gain and devoted his powers to something higher. The verb τρέχω also shares in the popular religious motif originally connected with the Olympic games. [11] Like στάδιον (→ line 11), ἀγών (→ I, 134, 32 ff.) is also used as obj. with τρέχω, Eur. El., 883 f. [12] But this combination is usually not athletic in the strict sense but ref. to a situation in which the ability of a runner is needed but quickness of the feet does not decide and τρέχω does not have to be taken lit.: "to run a risk," Hdt., VIII, 102, 3, "to run for one's life," Dion. Hal. Ant. Rom., 7, 48, 3, [13] cf. Eur. Or., 878: ἀγῶνα θανάσιμον, also Alc., 489. Instead of ἀγών the danger itself may be named as the obj. of τρέχω: κινδύνων τὸν μέγιστον τρέχουσιν, Dion. Hal. Ant. Rom., 4, 47, 5. [14]

The high regard for winners in races which lies behind these expressions continued along with the valuing of all athletics [15] for many generations (→ line 8 ff.) and was typically Gk. But Gk., too, were the critical considerations urged from early days against athletics and races. From the standpt. of the πόλις Solon is supposed to have rated very low the value of the athlete in emergencies, with special ref. to the runner, Diod. S., 9, 2, 5,

---

[7] Cf. A. Drachmann, Scholia vetera in Pindari carmina, II (1910), 210; the figure of the runner in the arena perhaps had some influence here.

[8] If this were a ref. to running in vain (εἰς κενὸν τρέχω, → 231, 18 f.), the insight that it causes effort is pretty banal, nor does it affect only the unthinking. There is also no other instance of the combination of εἰς κενόν and τρέχω in non-bibl. Gk.

[9] Cf. J. Regner, Art. "Olympioniken," Pauly-W., 18, 1 (1939), 236; E. Meyer, *Pausanias' Beschreibung Griechenlands* (1954), 611 on Paus., V, 8, 5.

[10] "This glorifying ... in some sense made the victorious contestant the Gk. ideal of humanity," Regner, 233. Οὐ περὶ χρημάτων τὸν ἀγῶνα ποιοῦνται ἀλλὰ περὶ ἀρετῆς, Hdt., VIII, 26, 3.

[11] Regner, 235. The sites of games were called ἱερά, Plat. Leg., IX, 868a, cf. XI, 935b (→ III, 224, 24 ff.). Cf. rejection of the sanctity of sporting contests in Philo Agric., 113; Praem. Poen., 52, also Som., II, 168. But Philo calls sporting contests holy ἀγῶνες in Plant., 110; Flacc., 93; Omn. Prob. Lib., 112; Quaest. in Gn., 3, 20 on 16:2.

[12] It is also used with βῆμα (some 70 cm), Eur. El., 954, δίαυλος (double the length of the arena), Alexis Comicus, 235 (FAC, II, 486), δρόμος, Menand. Fr., 690 (Koerte, II, 218), λαμπάδες ("torch parade"), IG, II², 1028. Transf. τρέχω can denote a considerable span of life, Epicrates Comicus, 3, 14 (FAC, II, 350), cf. also Epigr. Graec., 231, 3 f.

[13] Cf. the same expression without acc. obj. → line 3 f.; also Ael. Arist. Or., 46, 261 (Dindorf).

[14] τρέχω in the transf. sense often ref., then, to length of life (→ n. 12) but mostly to human conduct in critical situations, not to that of life as a whole. Neither lit. not transf. is ὁδός used as an obj. of τρέχω outside the Bible.

[15] "An infinite number of times the diatribe sees a par. between the practice of virtue and athletics," Wendland Hell. Kult., 357, n. 1.

cf. Tyrtaeus Fr., 9 (Diehl³, I, 15 ff.). Xenophanes Fr., 2 (Diehl³, I, 65 f.) objected to overestimation of useless victories in sport as compared with intellectual achievement.[16] Plato warned against one-sided preference for bodily exercise at the expense of the ψυχή, Plat. Clit., 407e.[17] Acc. to Diog. L., VI, 70 f. Diogenes of Sinope contended for a healthy balance between ἄσκησις of soul and body, the one being incomplete without the other; but one should choose ἀντὶ τῶν ἀχρήστων πόνων τοὺς κατὰ φύσιν.[18]

This appeal to φύσις often associated with the name of Diogenes recurs often in the critical assessment of athletics by popular philosophy, namely, that of the Cynics.[19] Acc. to Dio. Chrys. Or., 9, 15 f. Diogenes says that to many animals there is given by nature an ability to run which man never achieves, so that it is useless for him to try to set records for running.[20] Acc. to Or., 9, 20-22 Diog. was able to persuade many visitors to the Isthmian games to treat the achievements of winners with disdain, to ridicule the athletes, or even to ignore them. But for all the scepticism the deeply rooted terminology of the race did not disappear. The spiritual contestant claimed it for his own activity[21] and applied it to the physical athlete only in a weakened or disparaging sense. The real Olympic victor is not the brilliant athlete who has run round the arena successfully but Diogenes: ἐπιτρέχων αὐτὸς ἐκήρυττε ἑαυτὸν νικᾶν τὰ Ὀλύμπια πάντας ἀνθρώπους καλοκἀγαθίᾳ, Ps.-Demetrius, 260. Similarly Dio. Chrys. Or., 8, 11 f. thinks those who wear the wreaths of victory and the contestants in the stadium lack σωφροσύνη[22] and the freedom of the authentic contestant, indeed, that they have never experienced true ἀγῶνες. Diogenes, however, is a true contestant who is a match for the πόνοι that disturb human life, cf. also Or., 9, 16-18, where the ability of the runner is relativised by a ref. to the superiority of many animals and disparaged by the assertion that speed is a symptom of anxiety. The better insight which is esp. needed is not attained by winning in sport. The example of the runner brings to light the inferiority of the one who excels physically as compared with the spiritual warrior and makes it possible to affirm this without self-contradiction. But the paradoxical distinction between a fully justifiable transf. use of the jargon of the arena and a much less justifiable literal use could not be consistently maintained. Thus Diogenes thinks the στέφανος (→ VII, 620, 24 ff.) is best adapted as an award for goats, for whom green food has at least some value, Or., 9, 13. He can also set the crown on a horse because it became Ἰσθμιονίκης in λακτίζειν. Or., 9, 22. On the other hand he crowned himself at the Isthmian games (9, 10 f.) because he wanted the value of victorious cynic philosophy recorded by a symbol from which the critic could not in fact detach himself.[23] The fact that philosophical criticism of athletics could not wholly rid itself of its vocabulary meant that the later reader of

---

[16] Acc. to Athen., 10, 5 (413c) the verses in Eur. Fr., 282 (TGF, 441) go back to him: κακῶν γὰρ ὄντων μυρίων καθ᾽ Ἑλλάδα οὐδὲν κάκιόν ἐστιν ἀθλητῶν γένους.

[17] Clit. is not authentic but comes from Plato's school [Dihle].

[18] Cf. Philo, who uses the language of the arena more richly (→ I, 135, 28 ff.) than any known author of his age for the wrestling of the ψυχή, cf. E. Norden, "In Varronis Saturas Menippeas observationes selectae," Jbch. f. Phil. Suppl., 18 (1892), 301.

[19] Cf. E. Weber, "De Dione Chrys. Cynicorum sectatore," Leipziger Stud. z. klass. Philologie, 10 (1887), 236-257; R. Heinze, "Anacharsis," Philol., NF, 4 (1891), 458-468; Norden, op. cit. (→ n. 18), 298-306; P. Wendland, Philo u. d. kynisch-stoische Diatribe (1895), 40-50; C. Hahn, De Dionis Chrys. orationibus, quae inscribuntur Diogenes, Diss. Göttingen (1896), 38-59; H. v. Arnim, Leben u. Werken d. Dio v. Prusa (1898), 264-6; J. Geffcken, Kynika u. Verwandtes (1909), 92, 104 etc.; W. Jaeger, Paideia, II (1944), 306-310; also "Tyrtaios über die wahre ἀρετή," Scripta minora, II (1960), 75-124.

[20] Cf. the similar judgment of Philo in Agric., 113-115.

[21] Abs. τρέχω is not used for exercise in virtue. For the changing of Heracles into the model of a spiritual warrior cf. O. Crusius, "Die Κυνὸς αὐτοφωνία d. Oinomaos," Rhein. Mus., NF, 44 (1889), 309-312 and R. Höistad, Cynic Hero and Cynic King (1948).

[22] Whatever the original reading this is how the end of Or., 8, 12 is to be understood.

[23] Cf. Philo → n. 11. Even the Jewish philosopher could not completely separate the vocabulary of the stadium from its origin, cf. Wendland, op. cit., 43, n. 3; J. Heinemann, Philos Werke, Schriften d. jüd.-hell. Lit. in deutscher Übers., 4 (1923), 135, n. 1.

athletic metaphors, these similitudines tritissimae Pauli Apostoli aetate, [24] is in a peculiar position; in the same author he can find the same sporting expressions with very different emphases, referring in the one case to necessary and valuable activity, in the other to that which is quite worthless.

B. τρέχω in the Old Testament and Later Judaism.

1. The Septuagint.

τρέχω occurs in Job 41:14 for דוץ "to leap," though רוץ was probably the original, [25] in Ez. 1:14 vl. for רצא-, in 2 Ch. 35:13 for רוץ hi, in all other passages for רוץ q. But רוץ is often transl. by compounds of τρέχω or other verbs, e.g., διώκω, → II, 229, 32 ff. Lit. the ref. is to the running of men (Gn. 18:7 etc.) or animals (Jer. 12:5 etc.). Is. 40:31 promises the endurance (→ III, 828, 24 ff.) needed to those who wait on Yahweh. רוץ is also used for "riding" in 2 K. 4:22. He who is not already a רץ "runner," "follower," by calling (1 S. 22:17 etc.) will have to run for various everyday or sacral reasons, e.g., to satisfy hospitality (Gn. 18:7), to bring good news (2 S. 18:19), in war (Ps. 18:30 HT; 2 S. 22:30), to save his life: τρέχει περὶ ψυχῆς (→ 227, 3 f., 21 f.), Prv. 7:23 LXX. It may also be just a matter of willing obedience, Gn. 24:17 (ἐπέδραμε); Nu. 17:12; 1 S. 3:5 → n. 5. In obedience to the divine order the sun lit. [26] runs its course, Ps. 19:5. [27] The cultus involves running in 1 S. 20:6; 2 Ch. 35:13. [28]

It is part of the special character of prophetic mission that Elijah, when the hand of God comes upon him, does something which otherwise only a trained רץ could do (→ line 12); he covers the considerable distance from Carmel to Jezreel ahead of the chariot of Ahab, 1 K. 18:46. It is possible that even later running was still important in the work of the prophet, for it is said of prophets without authorisation that God has not sent them and yet they have run, Jer. 23:21. Naturally this is not supernatural running as in Elijah's case, and it is perhaps to be explained by the fact that prophets of salvation should not lose any time with their good news, → line 14. But this hardly explains the use of "to run," which seems rather to have been part of following a prophetic mission. If one compares the concluding words of the two halves of Jer. 23:21 it seems that both, רוץ as well as הנבא, might have been regarded as marks of the prophet. Running is at any rate connected with the spreading of the prophetic message in Hab. 2:2. [29] But רוץ can have a transf. sense here and may denote reading: "to read with ease." Without mentioning prophetic mediation the Psalmist gives praise that Yahweh sends His Word to earth and it runs swiftly, Ps. 147:15 (ψ 147:4 → 226, 22 f.). In Job רוץ is twice used fig. [30] to describe the relation between God and man. Job has the impression that God is running like a warrior (→ VI, 509, 19 ff.) against him, Job 16:14. On the other hand the sinner runs as in battle against God, 15:26. It is not clear whether this is the negative counterpart of positive running in God's service as a general term for the work of the righteous. This use occurs in a phrase which is important as regards later development, namely, Ps. 119:32: "To run the way of God's commandments"; running here is an emphatic form of "walking," → VI, 570, 28 ff. The word is certainly not chosen merely for stylistic variety but corresponds to the readiness for zealous obedience expressed in

---

[24] Norden, op. cit. (→ n. 18), 300 f.

[25] Cf. F. X. Wutz, Die Transkriptionen in d. LXX bis Hier. (1933), 192-6, 377.

[26] So at least 1 Εσδρ. 4:34.

[27] There is no suggestion of a martial running of the נבור, cf. H. J. Kraus, Ps., I, Bibl. Komm. AT, 15, 1² (1961), ad loc.

[28] Hag. 1:9 mentions running off to one's own house in neglect of the cultic duty to rebuild the temple.

[29] Cf. F. Horst, Die zwölf kleinen Proph., Hndbch. AT, I, 14³ (1964), ad loc. LXX does not have τρέχω here, but διώκω without obj., which means the same.

[30] Cf. also the use of δρομεύς in a transf. sense for the transience of life, Job 9:25, cf. 7:6 vl.

v. 60 (→ 226, n. 5; 229, 16 f.) and fig. denotes the whole life and conduct of the righteous from the standpt. of the strenuous development of resources in connection with דֶּרֶךְ → V, 50, 14 ff. [31]

This combination of ὁδός and τρέχω is found in the retrospective ref. to the martyrdom of the 7 brothers in 4 Macc. 14:5: ἐπ' ἀθανασίας ὁδὸν τρέχοντες. Here Hell. terms are used out of regard for readers who think along these lines. The way is not that of obedience but the way of immortality. The idea suggested to the reader is that fearless hastening to death by torture is the final consequence of the brothers' consistent subordination of animal-alogical impulses and emotions to the *logos*, i.e., their whole manner of life. If the author is not speaking, as in 11:20; 13:15 etc., of an ἀγών, an ἀγὼν θανάσιμος (→ 227, 21 f.), or other sporting achievements, but of running on a way, he is formally adopting a biblical rather than a Greek (→ n. 14) use. Materially he means no other than the way of the commandments of Ps. 119:32. But since he is not directly dependent on this saying it may be assumed that in the days of 4 Macc. the idea of running on a way in sacred service was a more common one than the biblical data might suggest. [32]

2. Qumran.

Worth noting here is running in the exposition of Hab. 2:2 in 1 QpHab 7:3-5. [33] A special blessing is expressly emphasised here as the presupposition of running → 229, 22 ff. Whether running in this exposition be lit. a hastening to spread revealed truth or fig. the ready reading of the record, only the Teacher of Righteousness can fully accomplish and encourage the course of true proclamation or ready reading, i.e., with full understanding. To him God has disclosed the secrets contained in the prophetic Scriptures but not yet fully understood. Running, then, relates to the life work of this personage who gives directions for his disciples' life of faith. Of this circle of followers one might expect with a high degree of probability that in its theological deliberations high importance would attach to an image of authorised running in the service of divine revelation which corresponds closely to Ps. 119:32 (→ 229, 38 ff.) even though not directly dependent upon it. Finally, there comes from Qumran the saying 1 QH 5:21 f. in which the word probably ought to be supplied even if it is no longer contained in the text. [34] The amplified text reads: "And with the wretched of the offscouring (cf. 1 C. 4:13) my feet are (ready [to run]) with those who are cast down for righteousness' sake (who strive after righteousness?) to lift up together from the tumult all the poor in grace." Here as in Ps. 119:32 (→ 229, 38 ff.) and 1 QpHab 7:3-5 (→ lines 17 ff.) personal blessing is the presupposition of running: "Thou hast strengthened the counsel of truth in my heart and thence (follows) the covenant for those who seek it," 1 QH 5:9. In none of these passages does running have the power of attraction, but 1 QH 5:21 f. focuses on those who join the runner and are thus lifted up out of the confusion. It is this participation which gives real point to the running.

---

[31] Suspicions of the authenticity of אָרוּץ in Ps. 119:32 are without real foundation. It is impossible to say whether רוץ was used before in the same combination.

[32] A negative counterpart is ἔδραμον ἐν ψεύδει (for יִרְצוּ כָזָב) in ψ 61:5. He who in spite of the hostile intent of the heart brings words of blessing on the lips runs ἐν ψεύδει, i.e., he leads a false life.

[33] Cf. K. Elliger, "Stud. zum Hab.-Komm. vom Toten Meer," *Beiträge z. historischen Theol.*, 15 (1953), 154 f., 190 f.; O. Betz, "Offenbarung u. Schriftforschung in d. Qumransekte," *Wissenschaftliche Untersuchungen z. NT*, 6 (1960), 77, 85 f.; on the whole question A. Strobel, *Untersuchungen zum eschatologischen Verzögerungsproblem auf Grund d. späteren jüd.-urchr. Geschichte von Hab. 2:2 f.* (1961).

[34] Cf. A. Habermann, מגלות מדבר יהודה (1959), 120. But for a supplementary לָרוּץ only textual considerations are valid and not conclusions which might be drawn regarding the history of the term רוץ; cf. the very different suggestion of E. Lohse, *Die Texte aus Qumran* (1964), *ad loc.*

3. Survey.

One cannot assume that these are just accidental similarities even if one questions the amplification in 1 QH 5:22 or the authenticity of the traditional אָרוּץ in Ps. 119:32 → n. 31. Running means prompt obedience (→ 226, n. 5, 229, 15 f.) and often a special blessing is mentioned which makes this possible. In the Dead Sea Scrolls there is also apparent an eschatological expectation which demands swift obedience. Apart from 4 Macc. 14:5 the texts are not dependent on Hell. usage; there one sees how easy it was to combine the Hell. idea with others not dependent on it. But Philo and Jos. did not make use of this possibility. Philo does not employ τρέχω at all [35] and Jos. does so only in the everyday sense, cf. Bell., 6, 254, par. θέω.

C. τρέχω in the New Testament.

1. Paul.

The prayer ἵνα ὁ λόγος τοῦ κυρίου τρέχῃ in 2 Th. 3:1 reminds us of ψ 147:4 (→ 229, 31 ff.) and is to be interpreted in the light of this. But the five passages 1 C. 9:24-27; Gl. 2:2; 5:7; Phil. 2:16; R. 9:16, in which men are the subject, leave a first impression that the connection between literal τρέχειν and the transferred use varies considerably. [36]

Nevertheless Gl. 2:2 and Phil. 2:16 are very similar with their εἰς κενὸν τρέχω (Phil. 2:16 irrealis). Since the circumstances are different one may assume that the combination of εἰς κενόν with the verb τρέχω was a common use of the apostle's. Naturally the hypothetical employment does not mean that Paul considers the possibility that he might forfeit his own salvation and might thus have run εἰς κενόν. [37] He is rather contemplating the situation which would arise if on the Day of Judgment he were not accompanied by the host of believers whom it was his task to win and who are to be his καύχημα (→ III, 651, 28 ff.), Phil. 2:16. According to both passages his own running is the more significant, and the further from an εἰς κενόν, the more other men participate in it as the Galatian communities have done up to the time of their most recent trials (Gl. 1:6 ff.), ἐτρέχετε καλῶς, Gl. 5:7. We have here the same idea as that very probably found in Qumran (→ 230, 17 ff.), namely, that of a running on the basis of a higher commission and in company with others who are to be lifted out of the confusion.

In contrast the runner in the arena does not really need any supernatural commission. He runs with many others, yet not to lift them out of the ruck, but in competition for the prize (→ I, 638, 31 ff.) and with a view only to his own success. When Paul refers to the runner as an example (1 C. 9:24-27; Phil. 3:12-14 [38]) it may well be asked how far he adopts or corrects Hellenistic ideas (→ lines 32 ff.). In 1 C. 9:24-27 the athletic achievement of all who take part in the contest and the superiority of the victor over competitors who go away empty-handed are given due weight, and the metaphor corresponds to the matter in hand in respect of

---

[35] Compounds are found only rarely; Leisegang lists only ὑπερτρέχω in Mut. Nom., 215, but cf. διατρέχω in Ebr., 8; συντρέχω in Aet. Mund., 103; εὐθυδρομέω in Agric., 174; Leg. All., III, 323.

[36] "τρέχω is a common metaphor in Paul for his work (Gl. 2:2; Phil. 2:16; 2 Th. 3:1) or for effort (R. 9:16) or for manner of life (Gl. 5:7) in the spiritual sphere," Joh. W. 1 K. on 9:26.

[37] In this case one would have to take the sayings as though τρέχω were based on running in the stadium, → 233, 9 ff.

[38] Here διώκω without obj. replaces τρέχω.

preparation (→ II, 341, 43 ff.) and the expenditure of energy. But there is no reference to the fact that in the Christian race competitors have to be beaten. [39] If, then, Paul in 1 C. 9:24 mentions a part of the metaphor which does not correspond to the matter in hand, in Phil. 3:12 he keeps to the matter in hand even where the metaphor does not correspond to it. Irrespective of the metaphor he weaves the higher commissioning (→ 230, 32 ff.) into the section: ἐφ' ᾧ καὶ κατελήμφθην (→ IV, 10, 12 ff.) ὑπὸ Χριστοῦ Ἰησοῦ. This procedure [40] is quite understandable in terms of the presuppositions of Paul's common transferred use of τρέχω (→ 231, 18 ff.) and it shows why the runner in the arena could be considered as a model only with reservations.

The verb occurs quite unexpectedly [41] in R. 9:16: ἄρα οὖν οὐ τοῦ θέλοντος οὐδὲ τοῦ τρέχοντος, ἀλλὰ τοῦ ἐλεῶντος θεοῦ. This crisp statement emphasises in a third member the exclusively normative action of God after a two-membered rejection of human achievements. There are formal parallels as in Zech. 4:6 and Ass. Mos. 12:7. [42] The distinctive thing in R. 9:16, however, is that the two concepts of willing (→ III, 52, 17 ff.) and running do not stand in any immediately apparent [43] relation to one another. Probably [44] the image of the runner in the arena (→ 231, 35 ff.) is in the background here too. The reader of a religious-ethical text in antiquity would think of this first and it gave its impress to the word. [45] The negative point is that things do not depend on the man who puts forth all the power of his will in an ultimately autonomous attempt to win salvation. Hence they do not depend on the one who accomplishes such brilliant and yet superfluous achievements as the runner in the arena. [46]

2. Non-Pauline Writings.

Forgiving love in Lk. 15:20 impels the father to run towards the prodigal. Not so sure is why the unknown person mentioned in Mk. 15:36 and par. ran to the cross of Jesus to give Him vinegar to drink (→ V, 288, 24 ff.; VI, 159, 30 ff. and 160, n. 5.). Mk. 5:6 speaks of running under demon possession, [47] and also demonic in another way is the

---

[39] Though cf. Philo Agric., 120 f. → n. 18, 23.

[40] "The metaphor is constantly permeated by non-metaphorical expressions," W. Straub, Die Bildersprache d. Ap. Pls. (1937), 91.

[41] Wettstein, ad loc. thinks the way is prepared for it by the ref. to the hunter Esau, who would have to run, in R. 9:13. This is quite untenable, but it does correctly sense that a concrete understanding of τρέχω cannot be abandoned without some cogent reason.

[42] Cf. Mi. R.[12] on 9:16.

[43] Ibid., ad loc., acc. to which θέλω and τρέχω are Hell. verbs which do not originally belong together.

[44] One might be inclined to take τρέχω as a stop-gap which is not to be pressed and which is used because of an obvious liking for the two-membered negation, cf. Zech. 4:6; Ass. Mos. 12:7. The choice of τρέχω might be promoted by its replacing an original θέω. The combination θέλοντος - θέοντος would free the play on words from any pedantic question as to the meaning of the second part, which simply denotes doing or making an effort → n. 36. But the play θέλω - θέω has not been found thus far and it is hard to see why it should be spoiled by τρέχω. Another possibility is that Paul is reminding the Christian who runs either with (Gl. 2:2; 5:7; Phil. 2:16; 3:12 ff. → 231, 29 ff.) or without authorisation (cf. Jer. 23:21) that the decision is not finally in human hands, cf. Ac. 16:6 ff. But neither the sentence itself not the context suggests that Paul is thinking of the false prophets of ancient times or of himself and those like him. Thus all such considerations are at best unsure hypotheses.

[45] Mi. R.[12], ad loc.

[46] It is no surprise that the same author could view the same athletic achievement positively in a transf. sense and as useless in a lit. sense → 228, 34 ff.

[47] The reason for running is the same as for crying out → III, 900, 30 ff.

φωνή ... ἵππων ... τρεχόντων εἰς πόλεμον in Rev. 9:9 (→ VI, 514, 22 ff.; VIII, 229, 14). The running of the two disciples to the grave of Jesus in Jn. 20:4 is of symbolical significance, and so, too, is the difference in their speeds → VI, 102, 42 ff. It is probably connected with this that we read just before in 20:2 of Mary Magdalene running to these two disciples with news of the opening of the tomb, [48] cf. Mt. 28:8. τρέχω is used in a transf. sense (with the obj. ἀγών → 227, 18) only in Hb. 12:1 (→ I, 138, 20 ff.; IV, 491, 28 ff.).

D. τρέχω in the Post-New Testament Writings.

On the direct basis of Phil. 2:16 (→ 231, 18 f.) Pol., 9, 2, considering the ὑπομονή of deceased Christians, gives the assurance ὅτι οὗτοι πάντες οὐκ εἰς κενὸν ἔδραμον, ἀλλ' ἐν πίστει καὶ δικαιοσύνῃ, καὶ ὅτι τὸν ὀφειλόμενον αὐτοῖς τόπον εἰσὶ παρὰ τῷ κυρίῳ. For Paul himself running εἰς κενόν does not mean loss of the τόπος with the Lord (→ 231, 21 ff.) but loss of the καύχημα on His day. To be noted in the direction θέωμεν τὴν ὁδὸν τὴν εὐθεῖαν in 2 Cl., 7, 3 is the combining of the vocabulary of the arena with a running which embraces all life and conduct → 230, 1 ff., 23 ff. (θέω → n.44), to which ὁδός (→ n. 14) is added. [49] τρέχω is used in the lit. sense in Ev. Pt. 3:6; Mart. Pol., 7, 1. Ign. has neither the metaphor of the race nor τρέχω. Yet he has the compound συντρέχω 4 times (in the NT only 1 Pt. 4:4 in a transf. sense), so Ign. Pol., 6, 1, [50] where συντρέχετε might be taken as a special instance of the immediately preceding imp. συναθλεῖτε and hence derived from athletics. But the context is against this.

† δρόμος. [1]

1. Both in the lit. and the transf. sense the use corresponds for the most part to that of τρέχω (→ 226, 14 ff.). The noun means "course" and is used of horses, Hom. Il., 23, 375 etc. and men, 23, 758. A Persian messenger traverses more quickly than others τὸν προκείμενον (cf. Hb. 12:1) αὐτῷ δρόμον, Hdt., VIII, 98, 1. There is ref. to the journey of a day in Hdt., II, 5, 2 and the course of the clouds and heavenly bodies, Eur. Phoen., 163, [2] also a not always fortunate δρόμος in speaking, Ps.-Long Τέχνη ῥητορική, 569. [3] The noun often occurs in relation to contests, e.g., Soph. El., 741 f., cf. Pind. Isthm., 5, 60. In the transf. sense (→ 226, 21 ff.) it occurs in Hdt., VIII, 74, 1; cf. also the hexameter *vixi et quem dederat cursum Fortuna peregi*, Verg. Aen., IV, 653. [4] A track (for horses) is δρόμος already in Hom. Od., 4, 605, synon. γυμνάσιον, Ditt. Syll.³, I, 463, 14 (c. 246 B.C). Other meanings are "way" in Eupolis Fr., 32 (CAF, I, 258), "colonnade" in Plat. Theaet., 144c, "corridor" in Plat. Euthyd., 273 etc.

2. In the LXX δρόμος is used for מְרוֹץ Qoh. 9:11, מְרוּצָה 2 S. 18:27; Jer. 8:6; 23:10 and שְׁפָעָה Job 38:34 vl. The use hardly deviates from that elsewhere; ἐγένετο ὁ δρόμος αὐτῶν πονηρός in Jer. 23:10 is worth noting. It means much the same as Jer. 23:21 (→ 229, 22 ff.), i.e., running without authorisation.

---

[48] The secondary Lk. 24:12 may be mentioned in this connection too, → III, 39, 11 ff.
[49] "εὐθεῖα ὁδός of the race-track, but with a conscious echo of the 'straight path (of the Lord),' cf. Ac. 13:10; 2 Pt. 2:15," Kn. Cl., *ad loc.* An acc. with negative content referring to total behaviour occurs in the warning μήτε ἑτέρας δραμεῖν ἀταξίας ἢ ἀσελγείας, P. Lond., V, 1711, 33 f. (6th cent. A.D.).
[50] The choice of the compound rather than the simple form cannot be explained merely by Ign.'s liking for the prefix συν- (→ VII, 770, 11 ff.).
δρόμος. [1] On the formation cf. Schwyzer, I, 458.
[2] The examples mentioned by Pr.-Bauer, *s.v.* at the beginning hardly prove that the use of δρόμος in relation to the stars is a lit. one.
[3] Ed. A. Prickard, Libellus de sublimitate Dionysio Longino adscriptus² (1955).
[4] Cf. H. Conzelmann in Dib. Past. on 2 Tm. 4:7.

3. Philo speaks fig. of the δρόμος of nature, Plant., 9, the tongue, Det. Pot. Ins., 23, deliberation, Rer. Div. Her., 245, the eyes of the ψυχή, Plant., 22. Acc. to the judgment of the understanding the cosmos is a βραχὺς ὄρος τοῦ... ἀπαύστου δρόμου, Det. Pot. Ins., 89. He who turns to knowledge of the one may count as καλὸν δρόμον καὶ πάντων ἄριστον ἀγώνισμα νικῶν, Leg. All., III, 48. At the end of the life of Moses stands the εἰς οὐρανὸν δρόμος, Vit. Mos., II, 291.

4. In the three passages in which the simple δρόμος is used in the NT we have a terrestrially limited survey of the individual life whose termination may be expected shortly (Ac. 20:24 → 81, 16 ff.), is immediately at hand (2 Tm. 4:7 → 59, 19 ff.), or has already come (Ac. 13:25). The reference is not just to the biological course (→ 227, n. 12) but to a specific content. The δρόμος of John the Baptist (Ac. 13:25a) consists according to his own statement (13:25b) in unselfish heralding of the Messiah, that of Paul (Ac. 20:24b) in the fact that, as shown by the epexegetical καί, he has discharged the Master's commission without regard to his physical life, Ac. 20:24a. This is the task without whose successful execution Paul would have run εἰς κενόν (→ 231, 18 ff.). The use of δρόμος in Ac. is thus connected with that noted in respect of τρέχω in Paul's Epistles. To the point, then, is the concept of edifying speech in the classical and not the ironical sense.[5] In the three-membered statement τὸν καλὸν ἀγῶνα ἠγώνισμαι, τὸν δρόμον τετέλεκα, τὴν πίστιν τετήρηκα in 2 Tm. 4:7 δρόμος can be understood in the same sense as in the two verses in Ac., unless δρόμος and πίστις are felt to be closely related here (→ lines 10 ff.) and thus interrupt the unmistakable athletic jargon of 2 Tm. 4:7a and 4:8a. But if only πίστις interrupts this, δρόμος is adduced as what was from ancient times (→ 227, 8 ff.) the most impressive part of the ἀγών.[6]

5. If in 2 Tm. 4:7 the ref. to πίστις follows that to the δρόμος, the two are a unity in 1 Cl., 6, 2. Testimony is borne to the martyred Christian women: ἐπὶ τὸν τῆς πίστεως βέβαιον δρόμον κατήντησαν. To be able to stand before God in the δρόμος τῆς πίστεως is the concern of every Christian. But if weak women also can stand the course in such dreadful circumstances, even sceptical men can be assured of the certainty and constancy of the fixed course in their running. Author and readers think of this effect, of the strengthening of believers and arousing of others, when, abandoning the language of the arena, the text speaks of the βέβαιος δρόμος. Obviously they also have in view the imperishable crown of victory, though only the last part of the verse mentions this.[7] The ref. in 1 Cl., 20, 2 and Dg., 7, 2 is to the ordered course in the cosmos. In a personal address to Polycarp we find προσθεῖναι τῷ δρόμῳ σου, Ign. Pol., 1, 2. What is to be added to δρόμος may be seen esp. from σύνεσις (→ VII, 888, 4 ff.), κόπος in 1, 3 (→ III, 829, 17 ff.) and σπουδαῖος in 3, 2 (→ VII, 568, 6 ff.). He is to prove himself as ἀθλητής (→ I, 167, 35 ff.) in more than one field, 1, 3; 2, 3; 3, 1. In context the agonistic[8] demand προσθεῖναι τῷ δρόμῳ is not to be related to the sprint or race. The only thing to be gathered from προσθεῖναι is that Polycarp has still some distance to go. One should translate "supplement" or "augment" rather than "accelerate."[9]

---

[5] It may be noted that the use of δρόμος in Ac. is for Haench. Ag.14 on 13:15 enough — and rightly — to demonstrate a developing Chr. (Hell.) vocabulary of edification. His verdict is given a broader base by what he says about τρέχω. So far as δρόμος is concerned, the development occurs only in Luke; as a whole it took place earlier and not first in Hell.

[6] The echo of Verg. Aen., IV, 653 (233, 30 f.) is only formal, for any human life can be called cursus in that sense.

[7] If δρόμος here is the race-course (→ 233, 31 f.) and βέβαιος δρόμος is the point in the course where "the race is decided, victory is assured, the goal" (Kn. Cl., ad loc.), one should transl.: "They assuredly reached the goal in the contest of faith." This gives a par. to the last part of the saying. But there is no other instance of this use of βέβαιος δρόμος.

[8] J. Fischer, Die Apost. Väter (1956), 217, n. 4.

[9] Bau. Ign., ad loc.; Fischer, op. cit., ad loc.

† πρόδρομος.

1. This occurs as both noun and adj. and is found from Aesch. It means "running before," e.g., Aesch. Sept. c. Theb., 211. The ref. is often to those who hurry on with others following, Hdt., I, 60, 4, messengers, Eur. Iph. Aul., 424 and esp. troops, Hdt., IX, 14, cf. VII, 203, 1; Polyb., 12, 20, 7. It also occurs in relation to athletics, Poll. Onom., III, 148. [1] Winds are impersonal πρόδρομοι in Aristot. Meteor., II, 5, p. 361b, 24; Theophr. De ventis, 11, fruits in Hist. Plant., V, 1, 5, ships in Alciphr. Ep., I, 14, 1.

2. In the LXX πρόδρομος σύκου in Is. 28:4 means "early figs"; days reckoned as πρόδρομοι σταφυλῆς are mentioned in Nu. 13:20. Hornets are πρόδρομοι of God's avenging host in Wis. 12:8.

3. In the NT πρόδρομος occurs only once: ὅπου πρόδρομος ὑπὲρ ἡμῶν εἰσῆλθεν Ἰησοῦς (Hb. 6:20). The content of this clause certainly does not correspond materially to that of Jn. 14:2 f.; 17:24. But certainly, too, the formally surprising πρόδρομος, which thus far is not attested elsewhere in this context, was chosen with care. This forerunner is deliberately not called "our forerunner" but the forerunner "for us." [2]

In exposition one might ref. to the picture of the onrushing warrior (cf. ἀρχηγός Hb. 2:10), of the early fruit (cf. ἀπαρχή 1 C. 15:20), or the advance ship (cf. the nautical terms in Hb. 2:1; 6:1, 19; 13:9) → 226, 21 f. [3] But the last of these, acc. to which Jesus is compared to an advance ship, creates gt. difficulty, since just before there is ref. to the anchor and Jesus seems to be already the anchor. [4] Nor are the other suggestions satisfactory, so that an illuminating answer to the question of the derivation of πρόδρομος in Hb. is still to be sought. [5] Perhaps one should begin by pointing out that the last part of the parenthetical admonition in Hb. 5:11 - 6:20 corresponds to the last part of the interrupted presentation in 5:10: Jesus as High-priest after the order of Melchisedec (5:10 and 6:20). Preliminary to this in 5:8 f. is a survey of the whole work of Jesus both terrestrial and eschatological. It may be asked, then, whether the next to the last part of the admonition in 6:20a does not also correspond to next to the last part of the interrupted presentation. ὑπὲρ ἡμῶν seems to show that 6:20a is also meant as a survey of Christ's saving work. [6] It is quite conceivable that the word πρόδρομος corresponds to the content of 5:8 f. if the word ref. not just to the final end of the course but to the preceding course itself with all its tests and trials, so that the frequently observed concept of the commissioned and obedient running of the believer (→ 231, 4 f.; 233, 5 ff.) may be applied to Jesus Himself.

Jesus ran as believers now run, but by His running, which has reached its goal, that of those who obey Him πᾶσιν τοῖς ὑπακούουσιν αὐτῷ (Hb. 5:9) is alone made possible. Along these lines πρόδρομος is again part of the vocabulary of Christian edification (→ 234, n. 5). And more smoothly than on any other interpretation πρόδρομος fits into the priestly and sacral thinking [7] (→ III, 281, 17 ff.) which obtains at the end of the admonition.

Bauernfeind

πρόδρομος. [1] For details cf. C. Spicq, ""Αγκυρα et Πρόδρομος dans Hébr. 6:19-20," *Stud. Theol.*, III, 2 (1949), 185-7; also *L'Épitre aux Hb.*, II (1953), ad loc.
[2] Minusc. 489 adds ἡμῶν after πρόδρομος.
[3] The athletic race hardly calls for consideration.
[4] So E. Käsemann, *Das wandernde Gottesvolk*⁴ (1961), 147, n. 3, but cf. Mi. Hb., ad loc.
[5] Mi. Hb., ad loc.
[6] *Ibid.*, ad loc.
[7] *Ibid.*, ad loc.

τρυγών → VI, 63, 27 ff.

---

† τρώγω

---

1. The Usage.

a. τρώγω means lit. "to gnaw," "to bite," "(audibly) to chew," and it then takes on the weaker sense "to eat," first of herbivorous animals, Hom. Od., 6, 90, then men, Hdt., I, 71, 3, fig. Aristoph. Eq., 1077. In the later Hell. period, under Ionic influence, the word was often used popularly instead of ἐσθίω as the pres. of aor. ἔφαγον. [1]

b. The use in biblical Greek is in accord with this. τρώγω does not occur in the literature of Hellenistic Judaism, [2] but ἐσθίω fades out especially in later primitive Christian writings [3] and τρώγω comes to the fore, Jn. 6:54, 56 ff.; 13:18; Barn., 7, 8; 10, 2 f.; Herm. s., 5, 3, 7. The Synoptists usually have ἐσθίω, → II, 692, 28 ff. Mt. 24:38 has τρώγω for the profane eating which expresses abandonment to the world, [4] but ἐσθίω is used in 24:49. Lk. 17:27 puts ἐσθίω in the first sentence too; Luke probably found τρώγω rather vulgar. John, however, seems to follow a usage which generally replaces ἐσθίω with τρώγω. Whereas LXX Ps. 41:10 has ἐσθίω, Jn. 13:18, with no obvious dependence on the LXX and applying the place to Judas, again has τρώγω: ὁ τρώγων μου τὸν ἄρτον ἐπῆρεν ἐπ' ἐμὲ τὴν πτέρναν αὐτοῦ.

2. The Theological Meaning in Jn. 6.

The usage suggests that in Jn. 6:51c-58 the transition from ἔφαγον (6:52 f.) to τρώγω (6:54, 56 ff.) should be understood primarily as a grammatically based alternation between verbal forms. [5, 6] But the alteration of the verbal form can also throw light on the intention of the section. [7] From 6:51c "to eat" no longer has, as in 6:51b, the metaphorical sense of appropriating the self-proffering of Jesus in the word by faith, 6:35. It now means receiving His self-proffering in the eucharist by

---

τ ρ ώ γ ω . [1] Cf. in Latin *edo* and *manduco*, also in modern Gk. τρώγω and ἔφαγα, on this Bl.-Debr. § 101; J. Haussleiter, "'Εσθίω τρώγω," *Archiv f. lat. Lexicographie u. Grammatik*, 9 (1896), 300-302; Moult.-Mill., 644.

[2] This includes LXX, Ep. Ar., Philo and Jos. One may ref., however, to ἐκτρώγω in Mi. 7:4 LXX, κατατρώγω in Prv. 24:22e LXX; Ez. 23:34 'ΑΣΘ, ἀποτρώγω in Philo Vit. Cont., 40.

[3] It does not occur in the Johannine writings or post-apost. fathers; ἔδονται occurs in quotations at 1 Cl., 39, 9; 57, 6.

[4] Cf. already Demosth. Or., 19, 197; Plut. Quaest. Conv., I, 1 (II, 613b); VIII prooem. (II, 716e).

[5] B. Weiss, *Das Joh.-Ev., Kritisch-exeget. Komm. über d. NT*, 2⁹ (1902), *ad loc.*; Haussleiter, *op. cit.*, 301 f.; Cr.-Kö., *s.v.*; C. K. Barrett, *The Gospel acc. to St. John* (1955) on 6:54.

[6] We find the same alternation between the aor. which denotes the single act in the conditional clause and the iterative pres. part. in par. statements with πιστεύω too, cf. Jn. 6:54: ὁ τρώγων... ἔχει ζωὴν αἰώνιον and 6:47: ὁ πιστεύων ἔχει ζωὴν αἰώνιον, also 6:53: ἐὰν μὴ φάγητε and 8:24: ἐὰν... μὴ πιστεύσητε, cf. 11:25, 40.

[7] It is not that a new word is brought in to denote physical eating, as Zn. J. and Bau. J. on 6:54 suppose.

physical eating. [8] In 6:51, 53 the presentation of the gift unmistakably adopts eucharistic language [9] (→ I, 175, 34 ff.; 644, 14 ff.) and the eating is characterised as really corporeal by ἀληθῶς (-ής) (→ VI, 147, n. 20). If the intervening v. 54 breaks the many preceding references to ἔφαγον by using an expression with τρώγω which is repeated three times, this may underline at least the allusion to the eucharist.

This way of introducing the eucharist by the mode of expression is theologically significant. [10] In Jn. 6:51c-58 we do not have the fig. description of one of the Church's institutions but a direct continuation of the preceding revelatory address. [11] In its mode of expression the section is proclamation which summons to faith, but the formulation shows that this can be truly accepted only in the form of the eucharist. The self-proffering of Jesus by the word becomes the more concrete self-proffering by the eucharist and appropriation by believing hearing becomes correspondingly appropriation by believing eating. [12] The necessity of the eucharist to salvation, which in some sense is stated by Jn. 6:53 as is that of baptism by Jn. 3:5, is thus the necessity of the uncurtailed incarnation of the Word. The connecting line which we discover between Jn. 6:51c-58 and the address on the bread of life is thus an indisputable sign that they belong together. Elimination of this section would destroy the finest presentation of the relation between word and sacrament in the NT. [13]

Goppelt

---

[8] This is the climax of all c. 6, though ref. to the eucharist begins only with 6:51c, cf. O. Cullmann, "Urchristentum u. Gottesdienst," AbhThANT, 3⁴ (1962), 88-97; P. Niewalda, *Sakramentssymbolik im Joh. Ev.?* (1958), 14-22.

[9] In structure and content 6:51c corresponds to the bread saying in 1 C. 11:24b. The terms σάρξ and αἷμα, which occur together in Jn. 6:53, are the traditional designation of the eucharistic gift in Ign.

[10] Similarly Jn. 3:5 ref. to baptism.

[11] Stylistic arguments against the original connection of Jn. 6:51c-58 with the preceding address on the bread of life have been so convincingly refuted by E. Ruckstuhl, *Die literarische Einheit d. Joh.-Ev.* (1951), 220-271 that J. Jeremias, "Joh. 6:51c-58 — redaktionell?" ZNW, 44 (1952/53), 256 f. and E. Schweizer, "Das joh. Zeugnis vom Herrenmahl," *Neotestamentica* (1963), 371-3 have abandoned the thesis that the section is a secondary addition. This thesis, based on the disagreement of the section with the context and Johannine theology in gen., is supported by Bultmann J., ad loc. and G. Bornkamm, "Die eucharist. Rede im Joh. Ev.," ZNW, 47 (1956), 161-9. But the ref. to the death of Jesus which this section introduces into the c. links it to what precedes and what follows. That only His death completes His descent and makes Him a life-dispensing gift (Jn. 6:51c) is also emphasised in Jn. 3:13-16. The ref. to the death is taken up again in the ἀναβαίνω of 6:62, not just the καταβαίνω of 6:50 f. (as against Bornkamm, 165-9). H. Schürmann, "Jn. 6:51c — ein Schlüssel zur grossen joh. Brotrede," BZ, NF, 2 (1958), 244-262 develops this argument. P. Borgen, "The Unity of the Discourse in Jn. 6," ZNW, 50 (1959), 277 f. suggests a different and more dubious connection, namely, that 6:32-59 is a midrash on the quotation in 6:31, and that 6:49-58 is the naturally expected interpretation of φαγεῖν.

[12] If one misses the character of the section as proclamation and regards it as a disguised description of the eucharist it is misunderstood as the institution of a medicine of immortality (Bultmann J., ad loc.; Bornkamm, op. cit., 16) — an idea ruled out at once by Jn. 6:57 ὁ τρώγων με. The same misconception leads to Bornkamm's statement (162 f.): "There is no ref. here to faith." Jn. 6:54 is formulated as a par. of 6:47, not to replace faith by sacramental eating, but to bind the two together. 6:56b also presupposes a faith-relation, cf. Jn. 15:4. In discussion cf. T. C. Fritschel, *The Relationship between the Word and the Sacraments in John and in Ignatius,* Diss. Hamburg (1962), 38-90.

[13] We can put baptism and eucharist together under the later term sacrament because they are associated in Jn. 3:5; 6:53; 19:34; 1 Jn. 5:8 as already in 1 C. 10:1-4 — so long as we understand by the term what is common to them.

┌─────────────────────────────────┐
│ τυγχάνω, ἐντυγχάνω   │
│ ὑπερεντυγχάνω, ἔντευξις   │
└─────────────────────────────────┘

† τυγχάνω.

A. τυγχάνω in the Greek World.

1. From aor. ἔτυχον[1] there is formed with η-extension the perf. τετύχηκα and aor. ἐτύχησα (Hom.), also with infixed nasal[2] -γ- and -ανω the pres. τυ-γ-χ-άνω (in Hom. only twice). The fut. τεύξομαι comes from the full stem τευχ (= fut. mid. of τεύχω).[3]

2. In almost half the instances in Hom. τυγχάνω means "to hit" a target ref. to in the gen., e.g., breast in Hom. Il., 4, 106, cf. Il., 23, 857. At first the purely definitive aspect prevents development of the pres. and allows only that of the perf. to denote an accomplished state. When the act whose planned result is achieved is not denoted by τυγχάνω but by verbs like "smite," "throw," etc., the part. of τυγχάνω is often added, e.g., with βάλλω in Hom. Il., 12, 189 or οὐτάω in 5, 858. But with no apparent distinction of sense the part. of the other verb can also be put with τυγχάνω, e.g., βαλών in Hom. Il., 15, 581.[4] Elsewhere the obj. is not a target sighted by the marksman but in the military and sporting world the verb can mean more gen. "to do the right thing," "to succeed," e.g., Hom. Il., 23, 466. It can also mean "to obtain," e.g., of friendly conduct in Hom. Od., 15, 158, escort home, 6, 290. In other passages τυγχάνειν does not presuppose any planned or sought purpose, cf. being caught in deep sand (Il., 5, 587), nor does the subj. have to be a living creature but may be an object, e.g., the booty which accrues to someone: οὕνεκά μοι τύχε πολλά, Il., 11, 684. If there is no obj. it can easily be supplied, e.g., ἤμβροτες, οὐδ᾽ ἔτυχες, "thou hast shot wide and not hit," Il., 5, 287; in Hera's unwilling statement about mortals: τῶν ἄλλος μὲν ἀποφθίσθω, ἄλλος δὲ βιώτω, ὅς κε τύχῃ, Il., 8, 429 f. the generalising relative clause applies to both ἄλλος and the two verbal concepts are to be regarded as the logical subj. of τυχεῖν. When τυγχάνω is plainly intr., it often describes, esp. in Hom. Od., something that happens, a situation which arises, e.g., a ship just arriving, Od., 14, 334 (= 19, 291), or animals and men finding themselves somewhere, Il., 11, 116; Od., 12, 106. A geographical point can be described in this way too, e.g., the cliff situated round a harbour, Od., 10, 87 f.; cf. Il., 17, 748. In content a common factor in all these possible meanings is regard for what man cannot ordain and control. But usually, if not always, the idea of "chance"[5] would give a wrong impression, cf. the instances → lines 12 ff. Homeric poetry certainly does not want to portray the exploits of its heroes as mere strokes of fortune. But it presupposes that when a real hit is achieved it is always fortunate, that along

---

τυγχάνω. Bibl. G. Herzog-Hauser, Art. "Tyche," Pauly-W., 7a (1948), 1643-1689; H. Strohm, Tyche (1944), 83-88.

[1] This aor is originally related to the pres. τεύχω "to construct," "make," "bring about," Indo-Eur. dheugh ("to achieve a masterpiece"), cf. Germ. taugen (strictly perf.), cf. Hofmann, s.v.; Pokorny, 271; for another view, phonetically untenable, cf. Boisacq, s.v. [Risch]. Acc. to Strohm, 96 "the twofoldness of sense (reaching and happening) is expressed in the verbal stem."

[2] Cf. F. Kuiper, Die idg. Nasalpraesentia (1937), 157, n. 1, 167; Schwyzer, I, 701.

[3] On other forms cf. Pass. and Liddell-Scott, s.v.

[4] This shows that "at the heart is not the one who acts but the kind of action," Strohm, 86.

[5] The sense of the "accidental" as a conscious emptying of meaning or purpose is not native to the stem, Strohm, 86.

with the highly rated achievement another element is necessary. [6] No noun from the same stem is found in Hom. [7] Only later do we find Τύχη as a proper name, Hes. Theog., 360, then τύχη from Archiloch. Fr., 8 (Diehl[3], III, 6), Hom. Hymn. Cer., 420, Pind. Pyth., 8, 73. [8] The spread of this significant noun did not mean, however, that there was now implicit in the use of the verb a recognition of the concrete idea of τύχη or a confession of the personal Τύχη.

3. The post-Homeric use of the verb, esp. its spread as an auxiliary, rests on the development of the pres. stem, which made possible the expression of duratively understood processes and acts. The meaning underwent development inasmuch as in the intr. use the element of the accidental became much stronger than in Hom. (→ n. 5). Nestor escaped the death his brothers had to suffer because he ξεῖνος ἐὼν ἐτύχησε παρ' ἱπποδάμοισι Γερηνοῖς, was "by chance" a guest with the Gerenians, Hes. Fr., 15, 3. Later this sense predominates, e.g., "it so happened," Thuc., IV, 26, 6. The part. ὁ τυχών is used from the 4th cent. B.C. on for "a favourite": The kings and lords taken from a general choice were selected ὑπὸ τῶν τυχόντων, Xenoph. Mem., III, 9, 10. In the negative the part. then denotes the unusual: οὐ τὸν τυχόντα λόγον περαίνοντες "not to treat of a random thought," Plat. Leg., IV, 723e; the law-giver of the Jews is οὐκ ὁ τυχὼν ἀνήρ, Ps.-Long. Sublim., 9, 9. In the 3rd pers. sing. τυγχάνω after ὅταν, οὕτως and ὡς is often used formally for a situation not known in more detail, the subj. being mostly neut., "no matter how it may be," Thuc., V, 20, 2, "if it is so," Eur. El., 1169; τἀληθῆ ἄν εἴποι ἄκων, εἰ τύχοι, "a person might involuntarily tell the truth if that is how it turns out," Plat. Hi., II, 367a. This leads in Hell. times to εἰ τύχοι "for example": ζῷον ζῴου κρεῖττόν ἐστιν, ὡς ἵππος χελώνης, εἰ τύχοι, καὶ ταῦρος ὄνου Cleanthes acc. to Sext. Emp. Math., IX, 88. Similarly the part. neut. τυχόν [9] is used adverbially for "perhaps," Xenoph. An., VI, 20, or "occasionally," Ditt. Syll.[3], III, 1259, 8 (private letter, 4th cent. B.C.). [10] With the part. of a verb τυγχάνω may often (but cf. → 238, 14 f.) ref. to an unforeseeable concatenation of events; in this case the verb is best rendered adverbially, cf. δ... τυγχάνω μαθών, Soph. Trach., 370, ἔτυχον... στρατευόμενοι, Thuc., I, 104, 2, παρὼν ἐτύγχανον, Soph. Ai., 748. In this connection the part. ὤν means something might be so which was not to be expected, e.g., a sophist might become a merchant or a tradesman with wares, Plat. Prot., 313c. Other passages show that the idea of the truly unexpected can be less prominent and (in poetry and later prose) ὤν can be left out, as very occasionally in the otherwise strictly Attic prose of the class. age, e.g., Plat. Resp., II, 369b. τυγχάνω can thus be used as almost synon. with εἰμί. [11] This notably does not occur in mathematical statements, but in the Stoic philosophers τὰ ἐκτὸς ἐπικείμενα ("external reality") can be called τυγχάνον, Sext. Emp. Math., VIII, 11. Often in later use of τυγχάνω there is an inappropriate popularising, e.g., "contingent" for the loosely implied ref. to the broad sphere of the non-demonstrable. [12]

---

[6] "There is no stress... on the subj.; what matters is the way subj. and obj. meet, and here the richly attested sphere of 'hitting' in Hom. shows that the marksman knows the issue is not in his hands — as is in keeping with a basic Homeric concept," Strohm, 86.

[7] This was felt to be surprising quite early, Paus., IV, 30, 5, cf. Strohm, 85.

[8] Cf. Nilsson, I[2], 756; II[2], 200-210; H. Fränkel, Dichtung u. Philosophie d. frühen Griechentums[2] (1962), 557-9; O. Becker, "Pindars Olymp. Ode vom Glück," Die Antike, 16 (1940), 38-50.

[9] Cf. ἐξόν, Bl.-Debr. § 442; Schwyzer, II, 413.

[10] Cf. Deissmann LO, 121.

[11] Phryn. Ecl., 244 (Rutherford, 342) does not think the ἀρχαῖοι used the verb in this way. As far as class. Attic prose is concerned, the passages which have τυγχάνω and no ὤν are often debatable.

[12] On τυγχάνω as an auxiliary verb cf. Pass., s.v. In class. Attic prose ὤν occurs basically with τυγχάνω. In Hom., poetry, Ionic and esp. the koine it may be absent. The NT does not have τυγχάνω with ὤν. τυγχάνω is not isolated in this use: διατελέω, λανθάνω, φθάνω etc. are par. [Dihle].

B. τυγχάνω in the Septuagint.

1. The only Hbr. verb transl. more than once by τυγχάνω or the unique LXX compound κατατυγχάνω is מצא. The iron head which unnoticed becomes detached from the shaft of a swung axe hits the fellow-worker standing nearby, Dt. 19:5 (τυγχάνω), cf. Job 3:22 (κατατυγχάνω). [13] In Job LXX has the simple form in two other passages, neg. with grave as obj. in 17:1 and with shadow as obj. in 7:2. In Prv. 30:23 the ref. is to a despised woman who finally becomes a wife (ἐὰν τύχῃ ἀνδρός for תבעל). Where a known original lies behind LXX, τυγχάνω is very rare. [14] There was a feeling that the verb resisted equation with a Hbr. term.

2. Where there is no HT, e.g., 2 and 3 Macc., τυγχάνω is common, though not in theologically important passages. Predominant is the trans. use with gen. obj. in the sense "to obtain": ἀντιλήμψεως, 2 Macc. 15:7; 3 Macc. 2:33; βοηθείας 3 Macc. 5:35, γῆς (grave), 2 Macc. 13:7; εἰρήνης, 2 Macc. 4:6; 14:10; ἐλευθερίας, 3 Macc. 3:28 vl.; cf. also 1 Macc. 11:42; 2 Macc. 5:9; 14:6; 3 Macc. 7:10; Εσθ. 3:13e; 8:121; 1 Εσδρ. 8:53; Bel. 32. But we also find the intr. use. τυγχάνω is almost equivalent to εἰμί in Tob. 5:14; 6:1 S.; Wis. 15:19; 2 Macc. 5:8; 6:2. [15] Combination with the part. of another verb occurs in 2 Macc. 4:32; 9:1. εἰ ταῖς ἀληθείαις ταῦτα οὕτως ἔχοντα τυγχάνει in 2 Macc. 3:9 is an esp. clumsy question. Finally one might ref. to οὐ τῷ τυχόντι in 3 Macc. 3:7.

3. The noun τύχη denotes in Is. 65:11 a pagan deity whose worship is naturally to be rejected: ὑμεῖς δὲ... ἑτοιμάζοντες τῷ δαίμονι τράπεζαν καὶ πληροῦντες τῇ τύχῃ κέρασμα. The HT ref. to the gods of fortune גַּד and מְנִי, transl. δαίμων and τύχη; in some witnesses the order is reversed and τύχη is thus used for גַּד. [16] Apart from this τύχη occurs in the LXX only in Gn. 30:11. This is surprising in so comprehensive a Gk. work, but understandable from another angle. The noun is as good as avoided because in the noun, unlike the verb, an antithesis was felt to the very nature of OT piety. The exception is related to Is. 65:11 to the degree that there too in some witnesses (→ line 22 f.) τύχη stands for גַּד (גָּד); the only pt. is that in the name-giving cry of Leah after the birth of Gad בָּגָד or גָּד בָּא there is no trace of any protest against τύχη, Gn. 30:11. Acc. to the explanation of the name [17] the Hbr. suggested only spontaneous happiness with no thought of a connection with mythological fortune. The Gk. reader would see nothing about fortune in the name גָּד. The translator could either avoid the linguistically difficult connection (Σ ἦλθεν Γάδ) or choose another Gk. word at least to suggest it. Thus 'A selected εὐζωνία (εὐζωΐα). LXX, however, chose the freighted τύχη, but at least did so intentionally. The variants εὐτύχη, ἐντύχηκα, εὐτύχηκα, τετύχηκα, impetravi, beata facta sum, show that it was felt to be objectionable even after the rise of the LXX. [18]

---

[13] Elsewhere εὑρίσκω is preferred for מצא even when τυγχάνω is intrinsically possible, Gn. 4:14; Ex. 22:5; Nu. 15:32; 31:50; 1 S. 9:11 etc.

[14] In the statement וְאִישׁ מָשַׁךְ בַּקֶּשֶׁת לְתֻמּוֹ "a man had drawn his bow in his simplicity" in 1 K. 22:34; 2 Ch. 18:33, LXX not only avoids τυγχάνω but changes the sense with εὐστόχως.

[15] On the text. cf. P. Katz, "The Text of 2 Macc. Revised," ZNW, 51 (1960), 14.

[16] On the deities, about whom little is known cf. F. Cumont, Art. "Gad" in Pauly-W., 7 (1912), 433-435.

[17] Possibly the name derives from the stem גדד "to break in" and denotes sudden access of fortune, cf. M. Noth, Die isr. Personennamen (1928), 126 f.

[18] With the variants of Gn. 30:11 which remove τυγχάνω (→ lines 31 ff.) there is an opposite one at 2 Macc. 7:37. The last words of the youngest of the seven martyred brothers read in Cod A: καὶ σῶμα καὶ τύχην (instead of ψυχὴν) προδίδωμι περὶ τῶν πατρίων νόμων ἐπικαλούμενοι τὸν θεόν. There is no doubt but that ψυχήν is original. Unless we have a scribal error in A, one sees here a levelling down in which even in so serious a situation τύχη could be used before the prayer which then commences.

The offence might have been easily avoided by the use of a verb, but one can only conjecture why this course was not adopted. [19]

C. τυγχάνω in Hellenistic Judaism.

1. As regards the verb, there is nothing special compared with the LXX, cf. in Philo the trans. τυχεῖν in Leg. Gaj., 178: ὡς ἔτυχε, "as the matter stands," and εἰ τύχοι "for example," Ebr., 17; cf. Cher., 54; Leg. All., III, 86a, τυγχάνω with a part., Deus Imm., 171, ὁ τυχών, Op. Mund., 137. Cf. in Jos. "to get something," τιμῆς τε ἅμα καὶ ὠφελειῶν τυγχάνειν, Ant., 19, 129, ἐλευθερίας οὐ τυχόντες, Ap., 2, 128, then "to receive," e.g., τυχεῖν μερίδος "to receive a share of booty," Bell., 2, 598, "to reach the end," Bell., 2, 651; adv. cf. "already" in Bell., 1, 262, "then" in 1, 371, also 3, 77 and 290; ὁ τυχών occurs in Ant., 2, 120. Cf. in Ep. Ar. "to be present," 10, with a part., 30; οὐ τὴν τυχοῦσαν, 166.

2. The position changes, however, when the relation of the verb to the substantive τύχη is taken into account. Statements like that from 2 Macc. 7:37 Cod A → n. 18 were quite possible in Philo and Jos. Both used verb and noun together without restriction, Philo Virt., 122; Det. Pot. Ins., 109; Jos. Bell., 2, 207. Philo often comes close to the idea of a personal Τύχη, e.g., τίνι δ' οὐκ ἐφεδρεύεται ἡ τύχη διαπνέουσα καὶ συλλεγομένη ῥώμης; "for whom does not τύχη wait, drawing breath and gathering force?" Som., II, 146. [20] The way contemporaries used τύχη is repudiated by Philo, esp. Leg. Gaj., 1-6. Most men speak of it when they should be thinking instead of the divine logos, Deus Imm., 176. Yet to make himself intelligible to them, Philo often speaks as though he were one of them. [21] Jos., on the other hand, cannot keep his distance from the noun τύχη, for it was indispensable to him in depicting his transition from the Jews to the Romans, Bell., 3, 340-408. [22]

D. τυγχάνω in the New Testament.

1. The fact that man, even though very high demands are made on him, cannot "achieve" salvation on the basis of his own attainments, is unobtrusively brought out in the three passages in which τυγχάνω is used in this sense: ἵνα καὶ αὐτοὶ σωτηρίας τύχωσιν, 2 Tm. 2:10, ἵνα κρείττονος ἀναστάσεως τύχωσιν, Hb. 11:35, and οἱ δὲ καταξιωθέντες τοῦ αἰῶνος ἐκείνου τυχεῖν, Lk. 20:35. [23] A further passage about the λειτουργία (→ IV, 226, 22 ff.) of the heavenly High-priest is to the same effect: διαφορωτέρας τέτυχεν λειτουργίας, Hb. 8:6, cf. 5:4. By what power τυγχάνειν is possible is obvious in these verses. But when the object of τυγχάνω is earthly, as three times in Ac., we are given more precise information: ἐπικουρίας [24] οὖν τυχὼν τῆς ἀπὸ τοῦ θεοῦ, Ac. 26:22, πολλῆς εἰρήνης τυγχάνον-

---

[19] Cf. Thdrt. Quaestiones in Gn., 87 (MPG, 80 [1864], 196B); there Qu. 87 has the heading: διατί ἡ γραφὴ μέμνηται τύχης; Answer: Leah grew up in δυσσέβεια and was only a short time τὰ θεῖα πεπαιδευμένη; Jacob himself would not have spoken thus. If the ideas which governed the transl. were not along these lines, one has to take into account respect for a patriarch's wife, whose words would be reported as accurately as possible.

[20] M. Adler, Die Werke Philos v. Alex. in deutscher Übers., VI (1938), 250 transl. τύχη here by the goddess of fate. Cf. also A. Meyer, Vorsehungsglaube u. Schicksalsidee in ihrem Verhältnis bei Philo v. Alex., Diss. Tübingen (1939), 50-52.

[21] Cf. W. Völker, Fortschritt u. Vollendung bei Philo v. Alex., TU, 49, 1 (1938), 178, n. 5; E. Goodenough, The Politics of Philo Judaeus (1938), 12 and 76.

[22] On τύχη in Jos. cf. Flavius Josephus, De bello Judaico, ed. O. Michel and O. Bauernfeind, II, 2, Exc. 18.

[23] Materially one might compare these passages with Phil. 2:12 f.: ... κατεργάζεσθε· θεὸς γάρ ἐστιν ὁ ἐνεργῶν ...

[24] Cf. Haench. Ag.[14] ad loc.

τες διὰ σοῦ, Ac. 24:2, πρὸς τοὺς φίλους πορευθέντι ἐπιμελείας τυχεῖν, Ac. 27:3. Twice, again in Ac., unusual events are denoted by the intrans. part. in the negative: δυνάμεις τε οὐ τὰς τυχούσας ὁ θεὸς ἐποίει διὰ τῶν χειρῶν Παύλου, Ac. 19:11, οἵ τε βάρβαροι (→ I, 551, 27 ff.) παρεῖχον οὐ τὴν τυχοῦσαν φιλανθρωπίαν ἡμῖν, Ac. 28:2. The second of these verses refers to a → φιλανθρωπία which exceeds what one might normally expect of a stranger. The first, however, is not just saying that the sick became more healthy, or healthy in greater numbers, than usual; the reference is rather to the nature of the healings as then described in v. 12 → III, 213, 28 ff. [25] The Christian community has experienced various δυνάμεις but seldom along these lines. Paul uses εἰ τύχοι in the sense "for example" (→ 239, 22) in 1 C. 15:37 when giving a random instance. When εἰ τύχοι is used with reference to a great number in 1 C. 14:10: τοσαῦτα εἰ τύχοι γένη φωνῶν, the point is that an exact figure could be given only by chance: [26] "who knows how many." Paul once uses τυχόν (→ 239, 24 f.) for "perhaps" with reference to a journey which he has planned but is not yet sure about himself: πρὸς ὑμᾶς δὲ τυχὸν καταμενῶ, 1 C. 16:6. [27]

2. The verb could have theological significance only for readers whose thinking was basically Hellenistic. This explains its sparing use. Only the last 10 chapters of Ac. might be set alongside, e.g., the Books of Maccabees → 240, 10 ff. Far more important than the positive findings, and perhaps alone of any true importance, is the negative point that the simple path from the verb to the noun τύχη is not taken. Anyone who makes a comparison of the use in Philo (→ 241, 15 ff.) and Josephus (→ 241, 22 ff.) will see this vividly. In the NT message there is no room whatever for τύχη. In this respect there is continuity, not with the works of Philo and Josephus, but with the LXX → 240, 23 ff.

E. τυγχάνω in the Post-Apostolic Fathers.

God is the obj. of τυγχάνω in Ign. Eph., 10, 1; Sm., 9, 2, His grace (ἵλεώ σου τυγχάνωσιν) in 1 Cl., 61, 2, life in Dg., 9, 6, future and as compared with earthly "better" freedom for slaves in Ign. Pol., 4, 3, the blessings of the divine forbearance in 2 Cl., 15, 5. τυγχάνω is used for "reaching" port after weathering storms in Ign. Sm., 11, 3. τυγχάνω in the negative occurs in Herm. m., 10, 1, 5; s., 9, 26, 4 with ref. to vines that suffer neglect. Finally the figure of idols is the subj. in Dg., 2, 1. Twice τυγχάνω is used intrans. in the sense of εἰμί: ἐν σαρκὶ τυγχάνουσιν, Dg., 5, 8; τυγχάνων ἐπὶ γῆς, 10, 7; εἰ τύχοι means "perhaps," 2, 3.

† ἐντυγχάνω.

A. ἐντυγχάνω outside the New Testament.

1. This compound, found from Hdt. and Soph., means "to run up against something or someone," e.g., a bad situation, Soph. Ai., 433, stones and missiles flung by the enemy, Hdt., II, 70, 2, of the crocodile striking the back of the lure, Hdt., II, 70, 2, of lightning striking someone, Xenoph. Mem., IV, 3, 14, also lighting on a book, Plat. Symp., 177b or reading in it, Plut. De Romulo, 12, 10 (I, 24d). Often the ref. is to an encounter between

---

25 *Ibid., ad loc.* εἰ τύχοι is a formula, but not strictly the negative part.
26 Pr.-Bauer, *s.v.;* but cf. Bchm. 1 K., *ad loc.*
27 In Cod D syp Lk. 20:13; Ag. 12:15.

ἐ ν τ υ γ χ ά ν ω . Bibl.: R. Laqueur, Quaestiones epigraphicae, Diss. Strassburg (1904), 15-18.

men, Hdt., I, 134, 1. In this case the verb may simply ref. to the meeting or it may embrace more concrete aspects, companionship or conversation, Plat. Ap., 41b, or visiting for a special reason μηδ' ἐντυχὼν δύναιτ' ἂν ὧν ἐρᾷ τυχεῖν, "even if he makes a petition he cannot get what he wants," Soph. Fr., 85, 8 (TGF, 148); καὶ τοὺς ἐντυγχάνειν κατὰ σπουδὴν βουλομένους, Theophr. Char., 1, 3; cf. Ditt. Or., II, 664, 10 (1st cent. A.D.); 669, 46 (1st cent. A.D.). The point of the visit may be complaint, e.g., ἐνετύχομεν καθ' ὑμῶν "we have made petition against you," P. Giess., I, 36, 15 (2nd cent. B.C.), but often, later, it is advocacy ἐντυχόντων δ' αὐτῶν τῷ βασιλεῖ περὶ τούτων, Polyb., 4, 76, 9; cf. P. Amh., II, 142, 10 f. (4th cent. A.D.); P. Tebt., I, 183 (2nd cent. B.C.); → lines 34 ff. Religiously this may then be intercession, e.g., ἐντυχεῖν θεοῖς, Max. Tyr., 10, 1b, εἰδότες ὅτι... νυκτὸς καὶ ἡμέρας ἐντυγχάνει περὶ τούτων ὑπὲρ ὑμῶν, BGU, I, 246, 12 (2nd cent. A.D.). But fairly frequently ἐντυγχάνω intr. (→ 238, 27 ff.) can mean "to find oneself somewhere," Aristoph. Ach., 848; Eur. Alc., 1032; cf. Demosth. Or., 21, 88. In Thuc., IV, 132, 3 μὴ τοῖς ἐντυχοῦσιν means "the first actually present."

2. In the LXX ἐντυγχάνω is never controlled by a Hbr. equivalent, though one finds Aram. קרב pe'al in Da. 6:13. 1 Macc. always uses the verb with κατά and gen. in the sense "to complain," 8:32; 10:61, 63 f.; 11:25. 2 Macc. has it without prep. for "to complain." The positive "to solicit, petition" occurs in Da. 6:13; 3 Macc. 6:37 → lines 8 ff.; "to pray" in Wis. 8:21; 16:28. 2 Macc. ref. to ἐντυγχάνοντες, those who come into contact with the book as readers, 2:25; 6:12, or hearers, 15:39.

3. In Jewish Hell. writings ἐντυγχάνω is used in various senses for human relations, e.g., with gen. obj. κτείνειν τοὺς ἐντυγχάνοντας "to kill those who encounter one," Jos. Bell., 2, 305. But usually there is a specific obj.: "to meet (admit) envoys," Ep. Ar., 174, "to approach" someone with a request, Jos. Bell., 1, 278, 281, 298; Ant., 12, 18, "to turn" to God in prayer, Philo Vit. Mos., I, 173, "to raise" a complaint, Jos. Ant., 16, 170; Gr. En. 9:3, 10, "to have to do" with someone, Jos. Bell., 1, 256. In the case of a written work ἐντυγχάνω can mean starting reading, Philo Spec. Leg., IV, 161, reading itself. Jos. Ant., 1, 15; 12, 226, or encountering the contents, Jos. Bell., 1, 6.

B. ἐντυγχάνω (ὑπερεντυγχάνω) in the New Testament.

Here ἐντυγχάνω is twice used for "to approach someone with a complaint": ἐντυγχάνει τῷ θεῷ κατὰ τοῦ Ἰσραήλ (Elijah) "makes a complaint" to God concerning Israel, R. 11:2; Festus reports about Paul: περὶ οὗ ἅπαν τὸ πλῆθος τῶν Ἰουδαίων ἐνέτυχόν μοι, Ac. 15:24. In the sense "to intercede for" ἐντυγχάνω or ὑπερεντυγχάνω [1] ("to intercede for as a representative") occurs three times in the second half of R. 8. R. 8:26 f. says of the πνεῦμα (→ VI, 430, 23 ff.): ὑπερεντυγχάνει στεναγμοῖς ἀλαλήτοις (→ VII, 602, 7 ff.) and κατὰ θεὸν ἐντυγχάνει ὑπὲρ ἁγίων. In R. 8:34 Christ is the subject: ὃς καὶ ἐντυγχάνει ὑπὲρ ἡμῶν. Since Paul does not use the verb elsewhere and since τὸ ἐντυγχάνειν ὑπὲρ αὐτῶν (Hb. 7:25) is called the work of the High-priest who ever lives (→ 67, 20 ff.), these statements rest on an underlying theological idea which, applicable like παράκλητος (→ V, 812, 18 ff.) either to Christ or the Spirit, had already received a fixed form that is perhaps reflected in the ὅτι clause of R. 8:27b too. [2] In relation to the last things and the judgment (R. 8:34) as well as the present unattainability of the life of prayer (8:26 f.) the believer may know that he is not left in helpless isolation. There is an ἐντυγχάνειν for him which reaches up to the very top. [3]

---

[1] Not found before Paul.

[2] Cf. Mi. R.[12], ad loc.

[3] "Paul thus recognises a kind of movement between God Himself and His Spirit," Mi. R.[12], ad loc.

C. The Post-Apostolic Fathers.

In the post-apost. fathers the compound is of little theological significance. In 1 Cl., 56, 1; Herm. s., 2, 6; Pol., 4, 3 it ref. to intercession, and in Herm. m., 10, 3, 2, where ἐξομολογούμενος (→ V, 218, 41 ff.) follows at once, the meaning is very gen.: "not to ask" is the mark of the λυπηρός. "To approach" occurs positively in Mart. Pol., 17, 2, negatively in Herm. m., 10, 2, 5, "to read" in Dg., 12, 1.

† ἔντευξις.

1. The noun occurs from Plat. and corresponds gen. to ἐντυγχάνω. The ref. in Plat. Polit., 298d is to "encounters" of ships with pirates, gen. "dealings," Aristot. Rhet., I, 1, p. 1355a, 29, "conversation," Isoc. Or., 1, 20. "Address" is the sense in Dion. Hal. De Thucydide, 50. Theophr. Char., 5, 1; 20, 1 uses the word in the sense of "conduct," "deportment," Polyb., 1, 1, 4 for "being engaged" with a writing. In the sense "petition" ἔντευξις corresponds to ἐντυγχάνω "to petition" (→ 243, 2 ff.), P. Greci e Lat., 4, 338, 6 (3rd cent. B.C.); cf. Ditt. Or., I, 138, n. 10 (2nd cent. B.C.). A distinction can be made between mere petitioning and true asking: τὸ μὲν πρῶτον ἐντεύξεις ἐποιεῖτο ... μετὰ δὲ ταῦτα παρακουόμενος ἠξίου μετὰ δεήσεως, Polyb., 5, 35, 4 f. But in other cases there is no real distinction: δεδοικέναι δὲ μήποτε δηλώσας τὴν προκεχειρισμένην ἔντευξιν ἀποτύχῃ "the request which he had planned," Diod. S., 16, 55, 3 (1st cent. B.C.) Official petitions are commonly called ἔντευξις. Decision concerning the desires expressed was usually in practice a matter for officials but the address was to the king himself. One who thought the way to the exalted invisible power above visible rulers was no less open could also call a concern addressed to this power ἔντευξις, Plut. De Numa, 14, 8 (I, 70a).

2. In 2 Macc. 4:8 ἔντευξις means "conversation"; in Jos. Ant., 15, 79 the ἐντεύξεις are the claims of Cleopatra to Judaea.

3. In the NT the word occurs only twice in 1 Tm.: παρακαλῶ οὖν πρῶτον πάντων ποιεῖσθαι δεήσεις, προσευχάς, ἐντεύξεις, εὐχαριστίας ὑπὲρ πάντων ἀνθρώπων, 2:1, and πᾶν κτίσμα θεοῦ καλόν, καὶ οὐδὲν ἀπόβλητον μετὰ εὐχαριστίας λαμβανόμενον· ἁγιάζεται γὰρ διὰ λόγου θεοῦ καὶ ἐντεύξεως, 4:4 f. It is as well not to try to make too close a distinction between the synonymous terms.[1] But in 1 Tm. 2:1 thanksgiving for all men would not seem to make much sense unless "intercession" (→ II, 807, 32 ff.) preceded it; hence ἔντευξις is to be construed in this narrower sense. In 1 Tm. 4:5 the εὐχαριστία of v. 3 f. and comparison with 1 C. 10:30 suggest "prayer of thanksgiving." But perhaps we have here more than a stylistic device to avoid repeating εὐχαριστία. The reference could be to the "grace" which follows recitation of a text at meals, → IV, 118, 5 f.

4. Herm. uses the word for "prayer" like 1 Tm., but there may be slight shifts of sense in short sections. Thus in s., 2, 5 ἔντευξις occurs twice at the beginning with ἐξομολόγησις (→ V, 219, 29 ff.) and means "petitionary prayer," but in the καὶ δύναμιν μεγάλην ἔχει ἡ ἔντευξις which follows (cf. Jm. 5:16) the ref. is probably to "prayer" in a broader sense, as also in s., 2, 6 f. and m., 5, 1, 6; 11, 14; s., 5, 4, 3. In m., 10, 3, 3 the noun is closely related to ἐντυγχάνων in 3, 2 (→ lines 3 ff.); if it is said there that the ἔντευξις of the λυπηρός (→ IV, 322, 24 ff.) does not have the strength

---

ἔ ν τ ε υ ξ ι ς. Bibl.: Deissmann B., 117 f., 143 f.; R. Laqueur, Quaestiones epigraphicae, Diss. Strassburg (1904), 8-10; Mitteis-Wilcken, II, 1, 12-16.
[1] Cf. Dib. Past., ad loc.

to rise up to heaven, here and in the next sentences "petitionary prayer" is in view. But then the end of m., 10, 3, 3 reads: ἡ λύπη μεμιγμένη μετὰ τοῦ ἁγίου πνεύματος τὴν αὐτὴν ἔντευξιν οὐκ ἔχει, "has not the same δύναμις as the Holy Ghost without λύπη." Here, then, the earlier δύναμις is taken up into ἔντευξις and we are thus to transl. "power of prayer," cf. καὶ εἰληφὼς παρ' αὐτοῦ τοιαύτην ἔντευξιν, s., 5, 4, 4.

The usage in 1 and 2 Cl. differs from that in 1 Tm. and Herm. As the authors see it these works are to be regarded as ἔντευξις in their total contents: κατὰ τὴν ἔντευξιν, ἣν ἐποιησάμεθα περὶ εἰρήνης καὶ ὁμονοίας ἐν τῇδε τῇ ἐπιστολῇ, 1 Cl., 63, 2; ἀναγινώσκω ὑμῖν ἔντευξιν εἰς τὸ προσέχειν τοῖς γεγραμμένοις, 2 Cl., 19, 1. With the material explanation there is expressed here the fact that taking the contents to heart is a personal concern of the writers. In 2 Cl., 19, 1 this is adequately brought out by the rendering "address." [2] But in 1 Cl., 63, 2 the transl. "admonition" [3] (cf. Codex S: *supplicationem et exhortationem*) is too narrow; more to the point is: "The concern for peace and unity which we have stated in this letter." There is perhaps some kind of counterpart to the description of the two works as ἔντευξις in the request of Hb. 13:22: ἀνέχεσθε τοῦ λόγου τῆς παρακλήσεως, [4] and cf. more generally δεόμεθα ὑπὲρ Χριστοῦ in 2 C. 5:20.

Bauernfeind

[2] Cf. Hennecke, *ad loc.*
[3] Cf. Hennecke, Kn. Cl., *ad loc.*
[4] Cf. Mi. Hb.[12], *ad loc.*

τύπος, ἀντίτυπος,
τυπικός, ὑποτύπωσις
```

Contents: A. Usage: I. In Non-Biblical Greek: 1. τύπος; 2. ἀντίτυπος; 3. τυπικός; 4. ὑποτύπωσις. II. In Judaism: 1. Septuagint; 2. Philo. III. In the New Testament. B. Theological Significance in the New Testament: 1. The Scars in Jn. 20:25; 2. Example of the Obedience of Faith; 3. Teaching as Mould and Norm in R. 6:17; 4. τύπος as a Hermeneutical Term; 5. τύπος as the Heavenly Original according to Ex. 25:40.

## A. Usage.

### I. In Non-Biblical Use.

#### 1. τύπος.

Apart from two ref. of indeterminate age, an oracle in Hdt. (→ 248, 1 ff.) and an old Pythagorean rule in Plut. (→ 247, 5 ff.), τύπος occurs for the first time in Aesch. Sept. c. Theb., 488 etc. It derives etym. from τύπτω "to strike," but retains the sense of "blow" only in the ancient saying in Hdt., I, 67, 4 [1] → 248, 1 ff. Elsewhere the ref. is always to the impress made by the blow, what is formed, what leaves its impress, the form-giving form, hence form gen. as outline. This analysis is confirmed by the meaning of the derivates found for the first time in Democr. Fr., 135 (Diels, II, 114, 30; 115, 2 ff.): τυπόω [2] "to stamp a form," "to shape," "to form," τύπωσις, ἀπο-(ἐν-)τύπωσις "shaping," and τύπωμα "that which is shaped by an impress." From these basic senses

τ ύ π ο ς κ τ λ. Bibl.: On A.: A. v. Blumenthal, "τύπος u. παράδειγμα," Herm., 63 (1928), 391-414. On B. 2: A. Schulz, "Nachfolgen u. Nachahmen. Stud. über d. Verhältnis d. nt.lichen Jüngerschaft z. urchr. Vorbildethik," Stud. z. Alten u Neuen Test., 6 (1962), 308-331; W. P. de Boer, The Imitation of Paul, An Exeget. Study (1962), 17-24, 92-216. On B. 3: J. Kürzinger, "Τύπος Διδαχῆς u. d. Sinn v. R. 6:17 f.," Biblica, 39 (1958), 156-176; F. W. Beare, "On the Interpretation of R. 6:17 f.," NTSt, 5 (1958/59), 206-210. On B. 4: L. Goppelt, "Typos. Die typologische Bedeutung d. AT im Neuen," BFTh, II, 43 (1966), cf. 4-20; S. Amsler, "La typologie de l'AT chez S. Paul," RevThPh, 37 (1949), 113-128; R. Bultmann, "Ursprung u. Sinn d. Typologie als hermeneutischer Methode," ThLZ, 75 (1950), 205-212; J. Daniélou, Sacramentum futuri. Études sur les origines de la typologie bibl. (1950); C. H. Dodd, Acc. to the Scriptures (1952); R. V. G. Tasker, The OT in the New² (1954); E. E. Ellis, Paul's Use of the OT (1957), 126-139; K. J. Woollcombe, "The Bibl. Origins and Patristic Development of Typology," Essays on Typology (1957), 39-75; H. J. Schoeps, Paulus. Die Theol. d. Ap. im Lichte d. jüd. Religionsgeschichte (1959), 242-8; E. Starfelt, "Stud. i rabbinsk och nytestamentlig skrifttolkning," Studia theol. Lundensia, 17 (1959), 241-253, 284 f.; S. Amsler, L'AT dans l'église. Essai d'herméneutique chrét. (1960); K. Müller, Die Auslegung at.lichen Geschichtsstoffes bei Pls. Diss. Halle (1960); W. G. Kümmel, Art. "Schriftauslegung," RGG³, V, 1517-1520; C. Larcher, L'actualité chrét. de l'AT d'après le NT (1962), 489-513; H. Ulonska, Die Funktion d. at.lichen Zitate u. Anspielungen in d. paul. Briefen, Diss. Münster (1963); L. Goppelt, "Apokalyptik u. Typologie bei Pls.," ThLZ, 89 (1964), 321-344; K. Galley, Altes u. neues Heilsgeschehen bei Pls. (1965); A. Takamori, Typologische Auslegung d. AT? Eine wortgeschichtliche Untersuchung, Diss. Zürich (1966).

[1] [Line 13 f. by Dihle]. In the late Nonnus Dionys., 20, 351 τύπον βροντᾶιον "clap of thunder" should perhaps read κτύπον, also Soph. Phil., 29 στίβου γ' οὐδεὶς τύπος "no sound of a step," unless one should transl. "no trace of a step." The sense of "blow" attaches to τυπή, e.g., Hom. Il., 5, 887.

[2] This word occurs already in Gorg. Hel., 13.
```

τύπος develops an astonishing no. of further meanings which are often hard to define. In virtue of its expressiveness it has made its way as a loan word into almost all European languages. [3]

a. "What is stamped," "mark," Plut. Aem., 19 (I, 265d): τοὺς τύπους τῶν πληγῶν, Athen., 13, 49 (585c); Philo Vit. Mos., I, 119, "impress," e.g., of a pot in the ashes: χύτρας τύπον ἀρθείσης ἐν σποδῷ μὴ ἀπολείπειν, ἀλλὰ συγχεῖν, Plut. Quaest. Conv., VII, 1 (II, 727c), or which a seal leaves in wax, Eur. Hipp., 862 etc., "stamp," e.g., of a coin, Aesch. Suppl., 282 (metaph.); cf. Luc. Quomodo historia sit conscribenda, 10, of the sarcophagus for a mummy, Hdt., II, 86, 7, sunken or raised "relief": οἱ δὲ τοῖχοι τύπων ἐγγεγλυμμένων πλέοι, ibid., 148, 7; cf. 106, 2; 136, 1; 138, 3; Eur. Phoen., 1130; Paus., IX, 11, 3; ἐνταῦθά εἰσιν ἐπὶ τύπου γυναικῶν εἰκόνες. [4] A special use is for the "letter" engraved in stone: τὰ γεγραμμένα τύποις, Plat. Ep., 7, 343a; cf. Phaedr., 275a, plastic figure, Eur. Tro., 1074: χρυσέων ξοάνων τύποι, then "idol," Herodian, V, 5, 6; Jos. Ant., 1, 311: τοὺς τύπους τῶν θεῶν, cf. 322; 15, 329; Sib., 3, 14, more gen. "image," Anth. Graec., 6, 20, 6: σκιόεντα τύπον, "image in a mirror"; 7, 730; γραπτὸς ... τύπος "painted image"; Artemid. Onirocr., II, 45; children the image of their parents.

b. "Mould," "hollow form" which leaves an impress, Dio Chrys. Or., 60, 9: ἐκεῖνοι τύπον τινὰ παρέχοντες, ὁποῖον ἂν πηλὸν εἰς τοῦτον ἐμβάλωσιν, ὅμοιον τῷ τύπῳ τὸ εἶδος ἀποτελοῦσιν (of manufacturing figures of the gods); Luc. Alex., 21, "model," Aristot. Part. An., IV, 1, p. 676b, 9 f.: διὰ τὸ καθάπερ ἐν τύπῳ τὰ σχήματ᾽ αὐτῶν πλασθῆναι (→ 256, 25 ff.), and transf. ethical "example." But these senses are comparatively rare instead of the customary παράδειγμα, cf. also Plat. Resp., II, 377b: μάλιστα γὰρ δὴ τότε (in childhood) πλάττεται καὶ ἐνδύεται τύπος (the indicated example), also II, 379a; 383c; III, 396e; IV, 443c; Ditt. Or., I, 383, 212-219 (1st cent. B.C.).

c. If the stamp or impress is seen in and for itself as a form we get the meaning "outline," "figure," e.g., Emped. Fr. 62, 4 (Diels, I, 335): οὐλοφυεῖς ... τύποι χθονός "coarse earthly figures"; Aesch. Sept. c. Theb., 488; Ps.-Aristot. Physiognomica, 2, p. 806a, 32; Mirabilium auscultationes, 30, p. 832b, 15; Sib., 1, 380, transf. "outline" of what I think, Plat. Resp., VI, 491c; cf. III, 414a; Aristot. Eth. Nic., II, 2, p. 1104a, 1 etc.; also "basic features" in Plat. Resp., III, 403e; Crat., 432e; cf. Leg., IX, 876e: τὴν περιγραφήν τε καὶ τοὺς τύπους, sketch and chief forms of punishments as παραδείγματα for judges, also "kind," "type," Diod. S., 14, 41, 4: τῶν ὅπλων τὸν γένους ἑκάστου τύπον, "the kind of weapons corresponding to the nation"; Plat. Theaet., 171e; Resp., III, 397c; 402d; Iambl. Vit. Pyth., 23, 105, also "formulation" of a writing, e.g., Dion. Hal. Ep. ad Pompeium, 4: ὁ πραγματικὸς τύπος ("style," "form of expression"); Iambl. Vit. Pyth., 35, 259 (contents of a booklet); later for an imperial rescript, Justinianus Novellae, 113 praef. [5]

2. ἀντίτυπος.

Whereas the etym. derivation from τύπτω "to smite" is far less prominent in the meaning of τύπος than the idea of what is shaped, the reverse is true in respect of ἀντίτυπος. As adj. ἀντίτυπος and noun ἀντίτυπος (-ον) this occurs chiefly in senses

---

[3] In the Rabb. טוּפִיס, טְפוּס (טוּפְסָא) "form," "mould," "formula," in Lat. from Cic. Att., 1, 10, 3 and Plin. Hist. Nat., 35, 151, typus "figure," in French from the 14th century and German and the other languages from the 18th. Cf. the survey of the history of the loan word and its present use as an academic tt. (type; typology) in J. E. Heyde, "Typus. Ein Beitrag z. Bedeutungsgeschichte des Wortes Typus," Forschungen u. Fortschritte, 17 (1941), 220-223.
[4] Cf. typus "raised relief," Plin. Hist. Nat., 35, 151.
[5] Ed. R. Schoell and W. Kroll, Corpus iuris civilis, III⁴ (1912).

based on the thought of "to strike back" and only rarely for "antitypical." Aesch.
Choeph., 312 ff. supports the transl. of the oldest instance in the oracle in Hdt., I, 67, 4:
καὶ τύπος ἀντίτυπος, καὶ πῆμ' ἐπὶ πήματι κεῖται, as a retributive formula. The
interpretation in I, 68, 4 finds the τύπος in the anvil of a smith, the ἀντίτυπος in the
hammer, and the πῆμα in the iron on the anvil. 6 In detail one finds the senses a. "striking
back," the throwing back of a sound as an echo, Soph. Phil., 694, 1460, or of a light
as a reflection, Tryphiodorus Carmen, 519, 7 "sending back hard" of objects, Soph. Ant.,
134: ἀντιτύπᾳ δ' ἐπὶ γᾷ πέσεν, transf. "stiff-necked," "recalcitrant," Plat. Theaet.,
156a; Xenoph. Ag., 6, 2, "contrary," "inimical," Aesch. Sept. c. Theb., 521: τὸν Διὸς
ἀντίτυπον, "the adversary of Zeus"; Theogn., 1244; b. "antitypical," i.e., "corresponding," IG, 14, 1320, 4: ἀντίτυπον... τοῖς δακρύοις χάριτα, Nonnus Dionys., 8, 23;
Polyb., 6, 31, 8, then "reproduction," "copy," P. Oxy., XII, 1470, 6 (336 A.D.). In Neo-
Platonism, though not in Plato himself, ἀντίτυπος denotes the sensual world of appearance in contrast to the heavenly world of ideas, the αὐθεντικόν, Plot. Enn., II, 9, 6;
Procl. in Platonis Cratylum, 129; cf. 2 Cl., 14, 3: the flesh as ἀντίτυπος compared with
the spirit as αὐθεντικόν. In the NT the meaning of the term is redeveloped on the basis
of the specific use of τύπος → 253, 12 ff.

3. τυπικός.

The same applies to the rare adj. τυπικός a. "open to impressions," Plut. De virtute
morali, 4 (II, 442c), b. "corresponding to a type" (of fever), Gal. De typis, 4 (Kühn, 7,
471); Rufus acc. to Oribasius Collectiones Medicae, 8, 47, 11 (CMG, VI, 1,'1): τυπικῶς
νοσέω.

4. ὑποτύπωσις.

Acc. to the etym. derivation (→ 246, 16 ff.) ὑποτύπωσις occurs in the sense a. "model,"
Philodem. Philos. De Musica, 77; b. "sketch," Strabo, 2, 5, 18; Sext. Emp. Pyrrh. Hyp.
inscriptio.

II. In Judaism.

1. Septuagint. Here τύπος occurs only 4 times in the current senses "model" for the
construction of the sanctuary, Ex. 25:40 (תַּבְנִית), "idol," Am. 5:26 (צֶלֶם), "wording,"
"text," of a decree, 3 Macc. 3:30; Ep. Ar., 34 and (determinative) "example," 4 Macc.
6:19.

2. Philo. Philo often uses the word in the traditional way, esp. as a term in his
philosophy and hermeneutics → 258, 7 ff. 8

III. In the New Testament.

The NT occasionally uses τύπος in the traditional senses "mark" (Jn. 20:25),
"idol" (Ac. 7:43 = Am. 5:26), "text" (formulation and contents) of a letter (Ac.
23:25). In Paul, the Pastorals and 1 Pt. it is used 6 times for the determinative
"example" of the obedience of faith, also in R. 6:17 for Christian teaching as a
mould and norm. In the same circle of writings there occurs a new sense peculiar
to the NT. In 1 C. 10:6; R. 5:14 τύπος is a hermeneutical term for the OT "type."
A corresponding sense is borne by two words which are not found in the Septuagint

---

6 [Lines 1-3 by Dihle]. Thes. Steph. and Liddell-Scott, s.v. transl. τύπος here by "blow,"
but cf. v. Blumenthal, 409: "Where form lies on copy (conjectured -ῳ)."
7 Ed. G. Weinberger (1896).
8 For a survey cf. Müller, 81-84.

or Philo, namely, τυπικός in 1 C. 10:11 and ἀντίτυπος in 1 Pt. 3:21. Finally Ac. 7:44 and Hb. 8:5 develop out of Ex. 25:40 the sense of the heavenly "original" in distinction from the earthly ἀντίτυπος or "copy," Hb. 9:24.

B. Theological Significance in the New Testament.

1. The Scars in Jn. 20:25.

Jn. 20:25a: ἐὰν μὴ ἴδω ἐν ταῖς χερσὶν αὐτοῦ τὸν τύπον τῶν ἥλων "the (wound-) marks (traces, prints) of the nails" (in 20:25b we are to read τὸν τόπον τῶν ἥλων), [9] is the only verse in the NT which, in order to express the drastic nature of the request of the doubting disciple, explicitly mentions scars in connection with the appearances of the Risen Lord.

They are presupposed in Jn. 20:20 too: "He showed them his hands and his side," also in the par. tradition in Lk. 24:39: "Behold my hands and my feet." Acc. to one aspect of the tradition of the Easter appearances the Risen Lord is known, not by His appearance as such, but only by signs of His identity, esp. His way of speaking and acting. How far back this tradition of the scars (→ VII, 575, n. 24) as marks of identity goes we cannot say for certain. [10] One theory is that it is secondarily combined with the touching, which anti-docetically affirms corporeality, Lk. 24:39b. It is typical of Jn. that touching is demanded by doubt, is offered by the Lord, but is not done by the disciple. The decisive pt. is that the event establishes faith, not confirmatory knowledge. This distinguishes the NT statements from apocr. elaborations, Ign. Sm., 3, 2 (acc. to Hier. De viris illustribus, 16 [11] from Ev. Hebr.); Ep. Apostolorum, 11 f. (22 f.); [12] Ps.-Justin De resurrectione, 9 (Otto, III, 2, 242).

2. Example of the Obedience of Faith.

In Paul as in the Pastorals and 1 Pt., which are close to him in other ways too, τύπος occurs in the sense of a determinative "example."

In a similar sense we find not only ὑποτύπωσις (→ 250, 12 ff.) but in 1 Pt. 2:21 ὑπογραμμός, the "copy" a teacher gives the student, "example," "model" (→ I, 772, 10 ff.) and in Jn. 13:15; Jm. 5:10; cf. 2 Pt. 2:6; Hb. 4:11: ὑπόδειγμα, "example," "model" (→ II, 32, 34 ff.). (παρά-) ὑπόδειγμα often alternates with τύπος in LXX (Ex. 25:9, 40; 4 Macc. 6:19) and non-bibl. Gk. → 247, 22 ff. [13] The same applies to ὑπογραμμός → I, 773, 24 ff.

a. Paul says that he himself is an example to the community in Phil. 3:17 and 2 Th. 3:9. In 1 Th. 1:7 he praises the community for having become a model for others. In all three passages τύπος is related to the idea expressed by the verb μιμέομαι → IV, 667, 13 ff.; 670, 22 ff. τύπος is not the ideal which eros or a resolve of the will adopts as guide. As the term indicates and the context says, it is the model which makes an impress because it is moulded by God. 2 Th. 3:9 refers to the example of the apostle along with binding tradition (3:6) and authoritative direction (3:10 ff.). The example, then, represents what the word says and, like the word, it is effective only through faith. Both word and example bear witness to a reality, namely, divinely given life by faith, which summons and leads to faith and can be grasped only by faith. According to 1 Th. 1:7 the community, by receiving the word,

---

[9] A common slip, cf. Ign. Mg., 6, 1.
[10] The ref. to the στίγματα τοῦ Ἰησοῦ in Gl. 6:17 does not have the scars esp. in view, nor indeed the Risen Lord.
[11] Ed. E. C. Richardson, TU, 14, 1 (1896), 17.
[12] Ed. H. Duensing, Kl. T., 152 (1925).
[13] v. Blumenthal, 410.

has become an imitator of Paul and hence also of the Lord, and for its part it is now an example to others. The more a life is moulded by the word, the more it becomes τύπος, a model or mould. It is not a mould which forces nor is it an example which can be imitated. It can just be lived out again in freedom, namely, by faith. Along the same lines as in Paul, the exhortation in 1 Pt. 5:3 admonishes those who represent the word to become τύποι ... τοῦ ποιμνίου, "examples to the flock." The word cannot just be recited; it can be attested only as one's own word which shapes one's own conduct. The office-bearer is thus admonished: "Be thou an example of the believers, in word (i.e., preaching), in conversation," 1 Tm. 4:12; cf. Tt. 2:7: "In all things shewing thyself a pattern (in the doing) of good works" → 259, 18 ff.

b. The same idea is twice expressed in the NT by the derivate ὑποτύπωσις "model," which already in non-biblical Greek expresses especially this meaning of τύπος → 248, 24 f. According to 1 Tm. 1:16 Christ's dealings with Paul (→ IV, 385, 3 ff.) are a pattern which shapes the way of others to the faith, and according to 2 Tm. 1:13 the proclamation of Paul is a "model" of sound preaching.

3. Teaching as Mould and Norm in R. 6:17.

The idea of a moulded figure which thus serves as a mould has been found already in Paul, and it covers R. 6:17 as well. The disputed meaning of the statement [14] depends on the way παρεδόθητε and τύπος διδαχῆς are taken. External proximity to διδαχή suggests "to pass on" for παραδίδωμι, but the material context is speaking of the alternation between dependence on sin and dependence on righteousness. In v. 16 this is presented as the binding decision between two relations of obedience, in v. 18 as the appropriation of a slave. v. 17 connects the two. They were handed over by God to the new power (→ II, 170, 17 ff.; 499, 48 ff.) and also made obedient to it from the heart. For faith is in indissoluble antinomy both God's creation (R. 9:22 ff.; 2 C. 4:6) and also man's obedience (R. 10:14 ff.). They were made slaves of righteousness (6:18b), being delivered up by their calling (R. 8:28) or baptism (6:3) to a τύπος διδαχῆς, cf. Ac. 20:32. τύπος here is not just the outline, as though the reference were to a form of teaching, [15] whether that of Paul as distinct from other Christians [16] or the Christian form as distinct from the Jewish. [17, 18] τύπος is rather the impress which makes an impress, so that in context the teaching [19] can be described as the mould and norm [20] which shapes the whole personal conduct of the one who is delivered up to it and has become obedient thereto. [21]

---

14 Cf. the comm. of Theod. Mops. in Staab, 123; K. H. Schelkle, Pls., Lehrer d. Väter² (1959), 221 f.; the survey of more recent discussion in Kürzinger, 157-160.

15 Cf. Pr.-Bauer, s.v.; Mi. R.¹², ad loc.

16 B. Weiss, Der Br. an d. Römer, Kritisch-exeget. Komm. über d. NT, 4⁹ (1899), ad loc.

17 Ltzm. R., ad loc.

18 Kürzinger, 170 f. suggests another possibility: You accepted in baptism a service based on the type of teaching, namely, the baptismal confession, to which you were appropriated. But this hypothesis agrees neither with the philological presuppositions nor with Pauline theology.

19 διδαχῆς is to be taken as an appos. gen.

20 Cf. Zn. R., ad loc.: Doctrine "as the stamp which impresses on man a specific character moulded by it," cf. also Schl. R., A. Nygren, Der R.³ (1959), ad loc.

21 R. 6:17b is thus an important part of the text; it is an unjustifiable simplification to eliminate ὑπηκούσατε ... διδαχῆς as a gloss, as R. Bultmann proposes in his "Glossen im R.," ThLZ, 72 (1947), 202.

4. τύπος as a Hermeneutical Term.

In two passages Paul describes OT events as τύποι in order to show hermen-eutically that they point to the present eschatological salvation event.

a. The events which are said to have happened as τύποι in 1 C. 10:6 or τυπικῶς [22] in 10:11 are the things which befell Israel in the wilderness. Here manifestations of grace and judgments on sin form an indivisible material nexus. It is not the OT texts that are called τύποι, but the historical events, which are depicted in loose dependence on the OT. [23] The section 1 C. 10 did not arise out of scriptural exegesis. Rather the apostle's gaze moved from the situation of the community to the prior work of God in history, where he found light for the present. [24] In this way he hit on a series of events which God had caused to happen, and had recorded in Scripture, as τύποι for the end-time community, 1 C. 10:11. Both aspects are essential for τύποι, for both correspond to their content. A rule is not deduced from OT events for all God's further acts. [25] These events are under-stood as an indication of His corresponding dealings with the end-time community, the Church. The correspondence does not lie merely in external similarities between the events. It is to be seen primarily in the essential similarity in God's acts. Thus baptism is like the crossing of the Red Sea not merely in virtue of the basic passage through water, but beyond that as the basic deliverance where all who belong to God's people have their origin, 1 C. 10:1 f. The experiences of the community are also to be distinguished from those of Israel (→ VI, 146, 24 ff.; 437, 11 ff.), because the present events are eschatological, 10:11 → 254, 1 ff. Yet this distinction is not emphasised in 1 C. 10, since the intended exhortation is based on the similarity. This admonition deals with the two congregational rites which are already presented here unequivocally and exclusively as sacraments. These had been naturalistically misunderstood in Corinth along the lines of Hellenistic ideas of the divine → VI, 143, 1 ff.; 395, n. 381. [26] The point is to show that they should be interpreted as the saving acts of God who met Israel personally in salvation and judgment. Thus Paul opposes the God of the OT to any mythologising of the NT message by non-biblical Hellenistic ideas of God.

Analysis of the context raises the question how far the term τύπος expresses this significance of OT events. Exegetical discussion centres on whether τύπος here means "example," "model," which expresses a rule, [27] or technically "advance

---

[22] (A) 𝔄 DG al Ir^arm have the secondary but not inappropriate τύποι συνέβαινον for τυπικῶς συνέβαινεν.

[23] This is a basic distinction from allegorising, which takes the text metaphorically and usually moves away from it and from history, Goppelt Typos, 19; also Art. "Allegorie," RGG³, I, 239 f.; Woollcombe, 50-60; → I, 260, 14 ff.

[24] On the history of the tradition (Pentateuch, OT summaries, Jewish Midr., selection and adaptation by the Chr. community) cf. Str.-B., III, 405-416; Goppelt Typos, 173-6; Goppelt Apokalyptik, 329; W. Wiebe, Die Wüstenzeit als Typos d. messianischen Heilszeit, Diss. Göttingen (1939), passim; G. Martelet, "Sacrements, figures et exhortation en 1 C. 10:1-11," Recherches de Science Religieuse, 44 (1956), 325-359, 515-523; J. Jeremias, Die Kindertaufe in den ersten vier Jhdt. (1958), 38.

[25] As distinct from 1 Cl., where general historical analogies are sought.

[26] Cf. L. Goppelt, "Christentum u. Judt. im ersten u. zweiten Jhdt.," BFTh, II, 55 (1954), 128 f.; G. Bornkamm, "Herrenmahl u. Kirche bei Pls.," Stud. zu Antike u. Urchristentum² (1963), 138 and 143.

[27] So Joh. W. 1 K., ad loc.; cf. already Bengel, Schl. Erl., Schl. K., ad loc. Müller, 86-94 tries to take fuller account of the historicity of what is expressed by the term, but in the event he merely sublimates this explanation: τύπος denotes OT events in relation to ταῦτα as a

presentation" intimating eschatological events. [28] Our own analysis rules out the former and suggests that the word takes on here for the first time the technical sense in which it is often used in Christian literature subsequent to Paul → 253, 12 ff. Hence the best translations are "type" in 1 C. 10:6 and "typical" in 10:11, the words being used as hermeneutical terms and not in the usual sense.

b. This sense is demanded in R. 5:14: ᾿Αδάμ, ὅς ἐστιν τύπος τοῦ μέλλοντος. In the universal havoc he caused [29] Adam is for Paul a τύπος, an advance presentation, through which God intimates the future Adam, namely, Christ in His universal work of salvation → I, 141, 27 ff. [30] Against the background of R. 11:32 this may be gathered from the πάντας and οἱ πολλοί of R. 5:18 f. which expounds the antithetical correspondence (cf. ὡς — οὕτως, v. 18 f.) between Adam and Christ which also includes emulation (cf. οὐχ ὡς — οὕτως, v. 15 f.). [31] In content, then, τύπος, as in 1 C. 10, is the advance presentation which indicates higher correspondence. In this case the correspondence is antithetical. But this element is found already in the basic meaning. Thus τύπος can be the "hollow form" which makes an opposite impression on some other material, → 247, 18 ff. Paul [32] can adopt the term, which was familiar to him already in the sense of a moulding original (→ 249, 32 ff.), for a technical use consonant with this basic meaning. [33] To correlate

copy, i.e., a model, expressing a rule, and in relation to ἡμῶν as an example for concrete cases. "On the basis of their distinctive ability to represent at one and the same time this function of model and copy, they can be used to express the hermeneutical significance of the analogous interrelation of concrete historical complexes, i.e., their typological understanding," 93. But typological means that "OT events are raised to the level of a typical situation which can be actualised again and again historically," 91 f. The nearest approach is in the use of the term in Philo when he expresses hermeneutically the character of an OT saying as original and copy, → 258, 7 ff.

[28] Cf. Bchm. 1 K., Ltzm. K., ad loc.; Martelet, op. cit., 527.

[29] The statements about the destructive work of Adam point to the same traditional structure as those about the age of Moses. But they go much further beyond the bibl. account with the help of Jewish traditions and esp. in the light of the antithesis, Christ's saving work, Goppelt Apokalyptik, 229; cf. E. Brandenburger, Adam u. Christus (1962), 15-157, 240 f.; C. Colpe Die religionsgeschichtliche Schule (1961), 57-68; A. Vögtle, "Die Adam-Christus-Typologie u. der Menschensohn," Trierer Theol. Zschr., 60 (1953), 308-328; → I, 142, 26 ff.

[30] Schl. Erl., ad loc. transl.: "Who is a rule for him that is to come," but Schl. R., ad loc. expounds the point of the passage correctly: "Adam himself is the promise of Christ."

[31] "But the basic thrust of the τύπος is interrupted by the theme of emulation, which goes beyond any similarity. The two thought-forms of analogy and emulation are swallowed up in one another," Mi. R.[12], ad loc.

[32] There seem to be no preparatory stages for the technical use of τύπος in Paul, which is not attested before him. Philo has it in a hermeneutical sense, but in so fundamentally different a way that there is no connection between him and Paul → 258, 7 ff. The approach is a familiar one in the OT and Palestinian Judaism, but there is no word for it. The Rabb. סִימָן (סִמָנָא), which Str.-B., II, 140; III, 226 thinks is a par., means only "sign." The Hbr. אוֹת even in the sense of "symbol" or "sign" (LXX σημεῖον → VII, 216, 20 ff.) is only distantly akin, Is. 8:18; 66:19; Ez. 14:8 (cf. the vl. in the LXX); Sir. 44:16 (LXX ὑπόδειγμα). The closest is מוֹפֵת (LXX τέρας → 117, 9 ff.), which is often combined with אוֹת, in the sense of "augury": The prophet and the children given to him, as their divinely allotted names show, לְאֹתוֹת וּלְמוֹפְתִים, are set up by the Lord for Israel, Is. 8:18, cf. 20:3; אַנְשֵׁי מוֹפֵת in Zech. 3:8 are "men of augury," cf. also Ez. 12:6, 11; 24:24, 27.

[33] τύπος τοῦ μέλλοντος is stylistically a fixed expression (Mi. R.[12], ad loc.) which Paul often used, though not in 1 C. 15. Galley, 54-57 thinks Paul must have taken over τύπος since it is "only loosely suitable in the texts in which it occurs." This conclusion rests on a misunderstanding of both word and context. For the word acc. to Galley, 55 does not mean an indication but an image which as a shadow "is of less importance" than the reality.

these OT and NT events he employs neither the common εἰκών or ὁμοίωμα, both of which express only the relation of a copy, nor a word suggesting recurrence, like ἀποκατάστασις or παλιγγενεσία. The closest analogy is σκιὰ τῶν μελλόντων in Col. 2:17 (→ VII, 398, 13 ff.) This, too, suggests a linear, dynamic interconnection. But Paul could not use this expression, which applies to the statutes of Moses, either for Adam or for Israel's experiences in the wilderness → 258, 3 ff.

c. In primitive Christian literature the significance of OT phenomena for NT events is sometimes expressed by παραβολή, Hb. 9:9; 11:19; → n. 68; → 256, 16 f., and Paul himself can use the general ἀλληγορούμενα, Gl. 4:24; → I, 260, 10 ff. But these and similar terms (→ I, 141, 4 ff.; VII, 398, 31 ff.) are no more adequate than the OT words already mentioned to bring out the significance of the events which Paul calls τύποι. Hence it is not surprising that under Paul's influence τύπος became a hermeneutical term in the whole Church. It is already so familiar in 1 Pt. that this uses ἀντίτυπος in a corresponding sense and 3:21 says that baptism is an ἀντίτυπον to the deliverance of Noah. Noah was saved in the ark through the (penal) waters of the flood when these already reached his knees according to Gn. r., 32 on 7:7. One should thus translate 1 Pt. 3:21: "As a counterpart thereto baptism now saves you" (→ IV, 1116, 34 ff.), [34] → 258, 1 f.; 259, 34 ff.

d. In the post-apost. fathers τύπος occurs only in Barn. [35] (→ 256, 10 ff.) and Herm. [36] in a hermeneutical sense, but so naturally that it obviously must have become a current term throughout the Church. It is defined for the first time as such in Just. (→ n. 35) and lives on in Chr. lit. through the centuries like the mode of interpretation it denotes. [37] The Lat. fathers render it by *figura* (for the first time in Tert. Marc., 3, 16; 4, 40; 5, 7; De anima, 43) or the loan word *typus*. [38]

e. The hermeneutical term which Paul introduced was understood and accepted because it was a suitable expression for an approach already common in the community. Like the word that Paul coined for it, this has not been found anywhere in the non-bibl. sphere. [39]

---

[34] Linguistically it is natural to relate ὅ to ὕδωρ and to take ἀντίτυπον adj. and βάπτισμα as apposition, Wnd. Kath. Br., Wbg. Pt., Schl. 1 Pt., *ad loc.;* E. G. Selwyn, *The First Ep. of St. Peter*[4] (1952), 289 f. But δι' ὕδατος in 3:20 cannot be instrumental, Schl. 1 Pt., *ad loc.* It can only be meant locally like 1 C. 10:1 (Kn. Pt., *ad loc.*). Hence ὅ must have in view the previous act. διεσώθησαν δι' ὕδατος, just as βάπτισμα in 3:21 is meant as act. (ἀπόθεσις) and ἀντίτυπον must be a predicative noun, Kn. Pt., *ad loc.;* Goppelt Typos, 188 f.

[35] Barn., 7, 3; 8, 1 (12, 10?), esp. τύπος τοῦ 'Ιησοῦ, 7, 7. 10 f.; 12, 5 f., ὁ τύπος ὁ τοῦ σταυροῦ, 8, 1, τύπον σταυροῦ καὶ τοῦ μέλλοντος πάσχειν, 12, 2, τύπον . . . τοῦ λαοῦ, 13, 5. Cf. also Just. Apol., 60, 3: τύπος σταυροῦ, Dial., 40, 1; 140, 1: τύπος Χριστοῦ, Dial., 41, 1; 91, 2-4; 131, 4; 134, 3; basically 90, 2: ὅσα εἶπον καὶ ἐποίησαν οἱ προφῆται . . . παραβολαῖς καὶ τύποις ἀπεκάλυψαν, 114, 1: ἔσθ' ὅτε γὰρ τὸ ἅγιον πνεῦμα καὶ ἐναργῶς πράττεσθαί τι, ὃ τύπος τοῦ μέλλοντος γίνεσθαι ἦν, ἐποίει ἔσθ' ὅτε δὲ καὶ λόγους ἐφθέγγατο περὶ τῶν ἀποβαίνειν μελλόντων, cf. 42, 4. In the same way Melito of Sardis in his paschal homily, the most impressive testimony to the use of typology in the 2nd cent., distinguishes between τύπος and παραβολή, cf. J. Daniélou, "Figure et événement chez Méliton de Sardes," *Festschr. O. Cullmann* (1962), 284 f.

[36] Herm. calls his own visions τύποι of approaching events in the community, v., 4, 2, 5: τὸ θηρίον τοῦτο τύπος ἐστὶν θλίψεως τῆς μελλούσης τῆς μεγάλης, cf. 4, 1, 1; 3, 6 (hence perhaps also 3, 11, 4); s., 2, 2.

[37] Cf. L. Diestel, *Gesch. d. AT in d. chr. Kirche* (1869), *passim;* Goppelt Typos, 6-8; Daniélou, *passim;* Woollcombe, 69-75; P. Lundberg, "La typologie baptismale dans l'ancienne église," *Acta Seminarii Neotest. Upsaliensis,* 10 (1942); bibl. in Daniélou IX and G. Ebeling, Art. "Hermeneutik," RGG[3], III, 258-261 for individual verses; → n. 59.

[38] On *figura* or *typus* in the Lat. fathers cf. E. Auerbach, *Neue Dantestud.* (1944), 11-71.

[39] So also Ltzm. K. on 1 C. 10:11.

It crops up for the first time in prophetic eschatology, cf. the new exodus in Hos. 2:17; Jer. 16:14 f.; Dt. Is. 43:16-21; 48:20 f.; 51:9 ff.; 52:11 f., the new covenant in Jer. 31:31-34; Dt. Is. 54:9 f., the second kingdom of David in Am. 9:11 f.; Is. 11:1-10; Mi. 5:1; Jer. 30:9; Ez. 34:23 f.; 37:24, the new Zion in Is. 2:2 ff.; Dt. Is. 54:11-14, the new creation like Paradise in Is. 11:6 ff.; Dt. Is. 51:3. These depictions of the age of salvation as a renewal of earlier signs of salvation arose for various reasons. They were influenced by the idea, widespread around Israel (→ I, 389, 30 ff.; VI, 930, 18 ff., 45 ff.) [40] and often affecting the OT (→ I, 388, 3 ff.), that what was earlier returns or repeats itself periodically in the cosmic course of things, so that in particular the last age corresponds to the first. But the cyclic thinking which, based on observation of nature, stands behind this concept, was not really the decisive reason. [41] Nor was it the kind of historical thinking which allows for typical events. [42] The earlier manifestations of salvation are for the prophets a means of expression, [43] but not just this. The essential reason for this form of presentation is afforded by two considerations. First, the early manifestations are taken from the election traditions. Their renewal means, then, that the election fulfilled and displayed in them reaches its goal in spite of judgment. Again, the renewal does not just correspond to what has gone before; it transcends it. It overcomes not only judgment, but all that was inaccessible [44] because it is the fulfilment of election. If one describes as salvation history the continuity between the acts of God's election and the eschaton which arises simply out of God's electing, then it may be said that this shaping of prophecy has its controlling source in a thinking orientated to the consummation of salvation history. [45] In principle this gives to God's past action in salvation history a significance which Paul expresses when he calls it τύπος and evaluates it accordingly. This approach of OT prophecy is the origin of typology in the Pauline sense. [46]

As in the OT, so in the dependent Jewish writings the structure of this view of the election traditions is not uniform. In the main the thought of the consummation of salvation history, which lives by the present revelation of the word, becomes less prominent in these writings than the idea of recurrence and the need for depiction. The future eschaton is

---

[40] Cf. Bousset-Gressm., 502-6; G. van der Leeuw, "Urzeit u. Endzeit," *Eranos-Jhrbch.*, 17 (1949), 11-51; M. Eliade, *Der Mythos d. ewigen Wiederkehr* (1953); G. Schneider, *Neuschöpfung oder Wiederkehr? Eine Untersuchung zum Geschichtsbild d. Bibel* (1961).

[41] Following H. Gunkel, *Schöpfung u. Chaos in Urzeit u. Endzeit. Eine religionsgeschichtliche Untersuchung über Gn. 1 u. Apk. 12²* (1921), 366-9, H. Gressmann, *Der Messias* (1929), 149-283 tries to derive OT eschatology from the recurrence motif. W. Staerk, "Die Erlösererwartung in d. östlichen Religionen," *Soter*, II (1938) provides rich materials but stresses the "fundamental difference" between OT and ancient oriental eschatology, 178. For recent research cf. E. Rohland, *Die Bedeutung der Erwählungstraditionen Israels f. d. Eschatologie d. at.lichen Propheten*, Diss. Heidelberg (1956); S. Mowinckel, *He That Cometh* (1956), 149-154: Eichr. Theol. AT, I⁷, 336-341; A. Jepsen, Art. "Eschatologie im AT," RGG³, II, 655-662; G. v. Rad, *Theol. d. AT*, II⁴ (1962), 125-132; G. Fohrer, "Die Struktur der at.lichen Eschatologie," ThLZ, 85 (1960), 401-420.

[42] Fohrer, *op. cit.*, 418 mentions this reason among others.

[43] Rohland, *op. cit.*, 284-7: "Only to characterise the future as a new beginning is it depicted as a renewal of past acts of election, not because these are regarded as divinely established types of the future." Hence one should not speak of typology here, for this expresses recurrence in the sense of Barn., 6, 13 → n. 46.

[44] Cf. v. Rad, *op. cit.*, II, 285, cf. 377-387.

[45] This background may be seen only in Dt. Is., who in the prophetic word sees that God is the same in past and future and yet that what comes is also His new creation, Is. 43:13, 19; 44:7 f.; 45:21; cf. C. R. North, "The 'Former Things' and the 'New Things' in Deutero-Isaiah," *Festschr. f. T. H. Robinson* (1950), 111-126.

[46] Without going into the development of typology in the OT, Bultmann, 207 defines it phenomenologically as the "eschatologising of the motif of recurrence" and finds its principle in Barn., 6, 13: Ἰδού, ποιῶ τὰ ἔσχατα ὡς τὰ πρῶτα. But this def. and the implied derivation do justice neither to the typological approach of OT prophecy nor to Paul. They apply merely to the typology of Jewish apocalyptic and Rabbinism, which are overrun by the idea of recurrence → n. 48.

fantastically described as a return of Paradise (esp. in apocalypses) and the age of Moses (predominantly in the Rabb.) [47] In this form which is overrun by the idea of recurrence the typological estimation of the OT moved over from Judaism into NT Christianity too, Jn. 6:31; cf. Mk. 9:13 and par.; Mt. 11:14, cf. also Ac. 1:6; 3:22. [48] Yet always in Judaism, as in the OT, the typology relates to the future end-time, not the present, though this, too, is set in the light of Scripture. [49] Even in the Essene texts the present experiences of the community, though explained at times as an initiatory fulfilment of OT prophecies, [50] are never seen as typological correspondence to OT phenomena. [51] As the continuation of the holy remnant the sect sets itself under Scripture but it does not regard itself as inheriting a new election.

Something quite new is thus proclaimed when Jesus describes His person and work quite simply and yet most significantly as more than a renewal of OT events: "Behold, a greater than Jonah is here," i.e., one greater than the prophets is now calling to repentance, Mt. 12:41 f. and par.; "Behold, a greater than Solomon is here," i.e., a revelation of God's wisdom surpassing Solomon, Mt. 12:42 and par.; a greater than David is here, Mk. 2:25 f. and par.; a greater than the temple, Mt. 12:6; the Righteous One whose death is "the blood of the (new) covenant," Mk. 14:24 and par. These sayings correspond to the basic feature of all the work of Jesus. [52] This relates wholly to faith. His power is proved neither by Scripture nor miracles. These characteristically hidden sayings disclose the true meaning of His work to faith. Through this there is a self-proffering of God which corresponds to that of the OT and yet so surpasses it that the relation to God is now definitively made whole. This connection with OT events was a mark of the prophesied age of salvation. That age dawns in hidden form in the work of Jesus.

When along similar lines Paul expressly relates what has happened to the community through Christ to the OT, he expounds theologically an approach which Jesus Himself had initiated. In so doing he follows one of the first steps in the developing tradition of Chr. theology and takes many ref. to OT types from a long preparatory OT and Jewish evaluation of the election traditions of Israel along these lines. This way of relating OT phenomena to the present situation of the community is the central and distinctive NT way of understanding Scripture. [53] It is developed in various forms, sometimes as explicit comparison, sometimes as hidden allusion. For this reason, and even more because its definition is disputed, its scope in the NT is variously estimated by scholars. [54] Though

---

[47] Survey in Goppelt Typos, 34-47; Volz Esch., *passim*.

[48] To this kind of typology there applies what Bultmann, 210 says of typology in gen., that John (in 6:31), "toying with it, presses typological thinking *ad absurdum*."

[49] Goppelt Typos, 67 f.

[50] O. Betz, "Offenbarung u. Schriftforschung in d. Qumransekte," *Wissenschaftliche Untersuchungen zum NT*, 6 (1960), 75-82, 155-163; J. A. Fitzmyer, "The Use of Explicit OT Quotations in Qumran Literature and in the NT," NTSt, 7 (1960/61), 310-316.

[51] A. S. van der Woude, *Die messian. Vorstellungen der Gemeinde v. Qumran* (1957), 84, cf. 48 thinks the sect regarded its stay in the wilderness, i.e., Qumran, as an eschatological return of the age of Moses. But behind the similarities, which are very questionable for the Teacher of Righteousness, there is in my view no idea of the recurrence or renewal of past history but basically a biblicist identification of the present with the text of Scripture; the new covenant in Damasc. 6:19 (8:15); 8:21 (9:28); 20:12 (9:37) is at bottom only a readopted covenant, cf. Betz, *op. cit.*, 61-4.

[52] Acc. to these and other criteria these sayings in all probability go back to Jesus Himself. The way of understanding them was suggested to Jesus by current ideas of the eschatological prophet and just one, cf. E. Schweizer, *Erniedrigung u. Erhöhung bei Jesus u. seinen Nachfolgern*[2] (1962), 21-33, 53-62. But Jesus did not just take over these Jewish ideas. He related His own work at least as directly to the OT as the Teacher of Righteousness of Qumran. Cf. J. Schniewind, *Das Ev. nach Mk., NT Deutsch*, I[10] (1963) and *Das Ev. nach Mt., NT Deutsch*, 2[11] (1964), *ad loc.*; Goppelt Typos, 75 and 99-102.

[53] O. Schmitz, "Das AT im NT," *Wort u Geist. Festschr. K. Heim* (1934), 69; Goppelt Typos, 239; Ellis, 126, 147 f.; W. G. Kümmel, Art. "Schriftauslegung im Urchr.," RGG[3], V, 1519.

[54] Bultmann, 208-212; Goppelt Apokalyptik, 332-4.

it remains tied to current thought-forms in its mode of presentation, [55] rightly understood it is the decisive interpretation of Jesus, the Gospel and the Church. It shows us that these are eschatological events, and in what sense they are, [56] → 258, 42 ff.

In the post-apost. fathers, who often develop new ideas very one-sidedly, typology is either surprisingly unimportant or, when developed, it undergoes fundamental change. [57] This is a clear indication of the disappearance of the eschatological self-understanding of the apostles. In 1 Cl., which constantly ref. to the OT, there is one exposition which might be called typology acc. to the use of the term τύπος now emerging in Barn. The scarlet thread in Jos. 2:18 denotes Christ's blood, 1 Cl., 12, 7. This is an example of the basic change in the structure of typology. The typological interpretations which are developed and called τύποι in Barn. are similar, 7, 3. 6-11; 8, 1-7; 12, 2 f. 4-6; 13, 5 → n. 35. Here the similarity is not found in the essential features of God's action but in the outward form of OT events or their description. Here the types are not events, figures or institutions which point beyond themselves to something definitive, but concealed descriptions of what has now been manifested. Here typology is basically an allegorising of events and institutions. [58] As events can be called τύπος τοῦ 'Ιησοῦ, Barn., 7, 7. 10; 12, 5 f., so allegorically expounded sayings can be called παραβολὴ κυρίου, 6, 10 → n. 35 and 68. In Paul typology was a spiritual approach which was taught kerygmatically with a view to faith. Here it is a hermeneutical device which is offered with scribal argumentation as *gnosis*. In Barn. we find in extreme form the distortions of typology which have accompanied typological interpretation of the OT through the centuries right up to our own day (→ n. 37) and provoked objections to the method. [59] Acc. to its NT core, however, typology is theologically constitutive for an understanding of the Gospel.

5. τύπος as the Heavenly Original according to Ex. 25:40.

a. In Ex. 25:40 LXX, quoted in Ac. 7:44 and Hb. 8:5, the heavenly original of the tabernacle is called τύπος (for תבנית); elsewhere תבנית in this sense is transl. παράδειγμα by the LXX, Ex. 25:9 and 1 Ch. 28:11 f., 18 f., which ref. to models of the temple that David gave Solomon. Behind Ex. 25 stands the ancient oriental idea of a mythical analogical relation between the two worlds, the heavenly and the earthly, the macrocosm

---

[55] Goppelt Typos, 9 f.; J. Bonsirven, *Exégèse rabb. et exégèse paulinienne* (1939), esp. 324; J. W. Doeve, *Jewish Hermeneutics in the Synoptic Gospels and Acts* (1954), 91-118; K. Stendahl, *The School of St. Matthew* (1954), 183-202; W. D. Davies, *Paul and Rabb. Judaism*[2] (1955), 36-57; Ellis, 38-84; Müller, 64-179; Fitzmyer, op. cit.

[56] Goppelt Apokalyptik, 341 f.; on the term "eschatological" cf. F. Holmström, *Das eschat. Denken d. Gegenwart* (1936); R. Bultmann, *Gesch. u. Eschatologie*[2] (1964), 44-64; W. Kreck, *Die Zukunft des Gekommenen* (1961), 14-76; J. Moltmann, "Exegese u. Eschatologie d. Gesch.," *Ev. Theol.*, 22 (1962), 31-66; O. Cullmann, *Heil als Geschichte* (1965), 10-29.

[57] Goppelt Typos, 245-8; J. Klevinghaus, "Die theol. Stellung d. Apost. Väter zur at.-lichen Offenbarung," BFTh, 44, 1 (1948), 15-44.

[58] Thus H. de Lubac, "Typologie et allégorie," *Recherches de Science Relig.*, 34 (1947), 180-226, can rightly say that the distinction between typology and allegory is fluid in the fathers, though he overlooks the fact that they are basically different in thrust. Cf. Woollcombe, 72-5.

[59] On the use of the typological method in modern OT exposition cf. H. J. Kraus, *Gesch. d. historisch-krit. Erforschung d. AT von d. Reformation bis zur Gegenwart* (1956), 432-440; E. Fuchs, *Hermeneutik*[2] (1958), 192-204; *Probleme at.licher Hermeneutik. Aufsätze zum Verstehen d. AT*, ed. C. Westermann (1960); R. Rendtorff, "Hermeneutik als Frage nach d. Gesch.," ZThK, 57 (1960), 27-40; K. Frör, *Bibl. Hermeneutik. Zur Schriftauslegung in Predigt u. Unterricht* (1961), Index s.v. "Typologie"; E. G. Kraeling, *The OT since the Reformation* (1955); F. Foulkes, *The Acts of God. A Study of the Basis of Typology in the OT* (1955); A. Farrer, "Typology," Exp. T. 67 (1955/56), 228-231; R. A. Markus, "Presuppositions of the Typological Approach to Scripture," *The Church Quart. Review* 158 (1957), 442-451; *Essays on Typology*, ed. G. W. H. Lampe and K. J. Woollcombe (1957). Cf. also Amsler, 215-227; Goppelt Apokalyptik, 321-4, 337-343.

and the microcosm, so that lands, rivers, cities and esp. temples have their heavenly originals. [60] Faith in Yahweh adopts such ideas only infrequently. [61] In 1 Ch. 28:11 f., 18 f. the motif of Ex. 25 is transferred from the vertical plane to the horizontal plane in salvation history. David gives Solomon the model of the temple which God has given him. The mythical speculative background of the idea receives new prominence in Hell. Judaism. Whereas Palestinian apocalyptic and Rabbinism simply make the heavenly sanctuary a bit of heavenly geography and a depository for plans of the earthly sanctuary, [62] Hell. Judaism, Wis. 9:8 and esp. Philo see here a ref. to the difference in worth between the heavenly and earthly sanctuaries. Acc. to Phil. Leg. All., III, 102; Vit. Mos., II, 74 and 141 the relation between the models shown to Moses and the tabernacle is the same as that between the world of ideas in Plato's sense and the world of earthly phenomena.

b. The two NT passages Ac. 7:44 and Hb. 8:5 refer to Ex. 25 in evaluation, and there are other indications that they come from a Christianity influenced by Hellenistic Judaism. [63] Stephen's speech in Ac. takes two points from Ex. 25:40. First, the tabernacle was set up at God's command (Ac. 7:44, cf. v. 53), whereas Solomon's temple was an independent work of men (7:47-50). The temple, like Israel's entire conduct (7:51), contradicts God's way of proffering Himself, which is not tied to a place (7:2, 33 ff.). But the second point is the decisive one. There is a heavenly original, a τύπος, even above the tabernacle, which was the place of God's gracious self-proffering in the exemplary age of salvation (7:17). The speech is based on Jesus' saying about the temple, Ac. 6:14 = Mt. 26:61. Possibly there is even acquaintance with the idea that through Jesus there takes place the self-proffering of God which transcends the temple, Mt. 12:6. But it does not trace any line from the heavenly τύπος to Jesus. [64]

c. It is Hb. that directly connects Ex. 25:40 with Jesus' work of salvation. It does this within a broad typology characterised by concepts of its own independent of Paul. In Hb. 8:1 - 10:18 the primitive Christian confession of Jesus as Him who sits at the right hand of God (8:1; 10:12) is typologically interpreted in the light of the OT (→ III, 275, 1 ff.): [65] Christ achieves what the atoning action of the high-priest on the great Day of Atonement (Lv. 16) foreshadows. At the goal of His way He enters as the true High-priest with His own blood into the heavenly holy of holies before God, Hb. 9:11 f.; cf. R. 8:34. To characterise this heavenly high-priestly ministry of Christ as a real counterpart to the ministry of the OT, Hb. within this typology deduces from Ex. 25:40 that there is for the earthly sanctuary

---

[60] Eliade, op. cit., 16-24; K. L. Schmidt, "Jerusalem als Urbild u. Abbild," Eranos-Jbch., 18 (1950), 207-248.

[61] v. Rad, op. cit., II, 378.

[62] Str.-B., III, 700-704.

[63] On the historical context of Ac. 7 cf. M. Simon, St. Stephen and the Hellenists (1958), 78-116; C. Spicq, "L'Ép. aux Hébreux, Apollos, Jean-Baptiste, les Hellénistes et Qumran," Revue de Qumran, 1 (1958/59), 365-390.

[64] B. Reicke, "Glaube u. Leben d. Urgemeinde," AbhThANT, 32 (1957), 152-7 in a notable exegesis imports rather too much of Hb. 8:5 into Ac. 7. Wdt. Ag. on 7:43 f. also goes too far when he says the ref. to the heavenly typos disparages the temple as the copy of a copy. On the "tent of witness" in Ac. 7:44 and the "tent of Moloch" in 7:43 cf. Simon, op. cit., 55 f. In my view one should not stress every phrase in a quotation.

[65] Cf. Goppelt Typos, 196-205; J. van den Ploeg, "L'exégèse de l'AT dans l'ép. aux Hb.," Rev. Bibl., 45 (1947), 187-228; S. G. Sowers, The Hermeneutics of Philo and Hebrews. A Comparison of the Interpretation of the OT in Philo Judaeus and the Epistle to the Hebrews, Basel Stud. of Theol., 1 (1965), 105-126; S. Nomoto, Die Hohepriester-Typologie im Hb., Diss. Hamburg (1966).

(9:11), namely, the tabernacle (→ III, 278, 22 ff.; VII, 375, 26 ff.) as the ἀντίτυπον "counterpart" (9:24) and ὑπόδειγμα "copy" (8:5; 9:23; → II, 33, 14 ff.) a heavenly "original" τύπος (8:5 = Ex. 25:40). The former relates to the latter as the σκιά (8:5, cf. 10:1 → VII, 398, 31 ff.) to the ἀληθινόν (8:2; 9:24) or as the earthly (9:1), which human hands have made (9:11, 24) and which belongs to this creation (9:11), to the heavenly (8:5, 9:23), which is μείζων and τελειοτέρα (9:11).

This contrast reminds us of the cosmological speculations which Hell. Judaism, esp. Philo, links with Ex. 25:40. Acc. to Philo Leg. All., III, 102; Vit. Mos., II, 74 ff., 141; Som., I, 206, God both here and at creation (Op. Mund., 16. 19. 29. 36. 129) conceived first the ἀρχέτυπος, the archetype, the idea of the tabernacle, and then transferred it as a τύπος or παράδειγμα ("model") to the spirit of Moses; then acc. to this model Moses had a μίμημα, "copy," or σκιά, "shadow," made, namely, the earthly tabernacle which can be perceived by the senses. [66] The τύπος thus occupies acc. to this sense a middle position between the upper world and the lower, so that Philo can associate in with the ἀρχέτυπος in Som., I, 173 and with the μίμημα in Rer. Div. Her., 230 f.; Det. Pot. Ins., 83. Philo develops esp. the term ἀρχέτυπος which hardly occurs at all before him; it occurs in Philo some 76 times. [67]

In basic concept Hb. is obviously close to this speculation, but it is not dependent on it either in vocabulary or development. It follows Scripture in just calling the heavenly original τύπος and like the rest of the NT does not have ἀρχέτυπος. For the earthly copy again it does not have, like Wis. 9:8, μίμημα, but ἀντίτυπος, which is not found in Philo. Above all the vertical typology (→ lines 7 ff.), which is all-important in Philo, is in Hb. merely an aid to the presentation and characterisation of the horizontal. The earthly sanctuary goes with the first covenant (9:1) which acc. to promise will be replaced by one which is better and yet analogous, 8:7; 9:18. [68] The high-priestly ministry in the heavenly sanctuary is a metaphor from salvation history to interpret *intercessio* as the result of the eschatological work of salvation; it is not part of an apocal. or philosophical world-view. [69] Hence the concepts which express the relation of the earthly sanctuary to the heavenly denote OT types elsewhere in Hb. As the earthly tabernacle is ὑπόδειγμα καὶ σκιά, "copy and shadow," in 8:5, cf. 9:23, so, too, the Law, which is the cultic legislation in Hb., is σκιά, "a shadow," of eschatological expiation, 10:1, and the disobedience of Israel in the wilderness with all its consequences is ὑπόδειγμα, "an illustrative warning," for the community, not just an example, 4:11, cf. 2 Pt. 2:6. In this way the vertical theology makes the mode of typological intensification unmistakably plain both materially and linguistically. The comparative (κρείττων, 8:6; μείζων, 9:11), which Jesus developed (→ 255, 11 ff.), expresses an absolute and not just a relative intensifying, though correspondence, and hence continuity in salvation history, is not destroyed. Christ's work is presented as something eschatologically new which replaces God's OT institutions and yet achieves their intention. In essentials, then, the typology of Hb. agrees with that of Paul (→ 251, 13 ff.), though its development is original and the only relationship is through the gen. tradition of primitive Christianity.

In Hb., then, typology is a specifically biblical approach which overlaps and transcends

---

[66] Goppelt Typos, 59-62; Woollcombe, 62-4; U. Früchtel, *Die kosmologischen Vorstellungen bei Philo v. Alex.,* Diss. Hamburg (1962), 103-114.

[67] On the basis of this world-view Philo calls the figures in the fall story δείγματα τύπων, "typical examples," "which demand allegorical interpretation according to their hidden sense," Op. Mund., 157. Allegorising is for him a pressing on from the earthly copies to the heavenly originals.

[68] Hence, as a parenthetical note says, the first tent is itself παραβολή, "a similitude," pointing to the time of salvation as Isaac's restoration to Abraham does to the future resurrection, Hb. 9:8-10; 11:19 → V, 752, 6 ff.

[69] "To go into the (heavenly) sanctuary" is for Hb. (9:11 f.) the same as "going into heaven, there to come before God's presence for us," 9:24.

the mythical cosmic analogy thinking of antiquity, both the cyclic analogy between the world epochs and the vertical analogy between the upper world and the lower, by adopting them as forms of expression. This thinking always overruns typology when cosmic mythical reflection is stronger than the word of revelation in salvation history. Thus cyclic thinking invades Jewish apocal. and vertical thinking makes its way into Philo, and both very quickly permeate post-apost. Christianity. The upshot thus throws light on the structure of typological thought and its development. Its true root is the idea of consummation in salvation history. It expresses the certainty that the relation of God to Israel which is set under the word by God's work in history will in spite of every setback achieve its goal universally in new and yet corresponding demonstrations of the grace of God.

d. Horizontal as well as vertical thinking is already found in pregnant form in the post-apost. fathers. 1 Cl., regards the OT records as analogies from which one may read off the abiding cosmic order. In the background is a Stoic type of analogy thinking which is at once rational, historical and cosmic. Barn. expresses in an apocr. quotation the principle of once-for-all recurrence: "Lo, I make the last things as the first," 6, 13. But he does not relate this principle to scriptural exposition nor follow it, 256, 10 ff. The vertical analogy is found in a central place in Ignatius: The community is τύπος καὶ διδαχὴ ἀφθαρσίας, "type and doctrine of immortality," when it binds itself in unity with the threefold office, Mg., 6, 2 — for Paul the community apprehended by the word was τύπος, → 249, 33 ff. The threefold office takes this place in the community because it corresponds to the upper hierarchy of the total Church: προκαθημένου τοῦ ἐπισκόπου εἰς τόπον (Zahn conjectures τύπον) θεοῦ καὶ τῶν πρεσβυτέρων εἰς τόπον (conjecture τύπον) συνεδρίου τῶν ἀποστόλων, Mg., 6, 1 → n. 9. The analogy is indicated in Tr., 3, 1, though not here, by τύπος in the sense of "earthly copy": Ὁμοίως πάντες ἐντρεπέσθωσαν τοὺς διακόνους ὡς Ἰησοῦν Χριστόν, ὡς καὶ τὸν ἐπίσκοπον ὄντα τύπον τοῦ πατρός, τοὺς δὲ πρεσβυτέρους ὡς συνέδριον θεοῦ καὶ ὡς σύνδεσμον ἀποστόλων. χωρὶς τούτων ἐκκλησία οὐ καλεῖται. This vertical analogy [70] is not for Ign. an aid like the heavenly sanctuary or heavenly Jerusalem in Hb. 8 f. and 12:22 → 258, 22 ff.; it is the main point. It is closer to the analogy thinking of Philo and the Chr. Alexandrians than to Gnosticism in the strict sense. [71] The latter understands improper earthly phenomena, e.g., the crucifixion of Jesus in Act. Joh. 102, as symbols (συμβολικῶς) of the true events, e.g., redemption by *gnosis,* but for the rest it has a cyclic concept of the ἀποκατάστασις of all things, "the bringing back of the mixed to their proper place," Hipp. Ref., VII, 27, 4. 11. Hence one should not see any close analogy to Ign. in the corresponding Gnostic statement that the earthly Church, the pneumatics on earth, are ἀντίτυπον τῆς ἄνω ἐκκλησίας, Iren. Haer., I, 5, 6.

Goppelt

---

[70] But the admonition in Barn., 19, 7 par. Did., 4, 11 that the slave should be subject to his earthly master ὡς τύπῳ θεοῦ can hardly mean more than Col. 3:23 ff.
[71] Cf. Schmidt, *op. cit.* (→ n. 60), 244.

---

† τύπτω

Contents: A. Linguistic Relations and Usage: I. Linguistic Relations; II. Usage, especially in the Septuagint. B. Material Contexts of the Use in the New Testament: I. In the Preaching of Jesus; II. In the Passion Narrative; III. In Acts; IV. In Paul.

A. Linguistic Relations and Usage.

I. Linguistic Relations.

1. τύπτω is one of the many NT verbs meaning "to strike": δέρω (→ n. 39), κολαφίζω (→ III, 818, 17 ff.), κόπτω (→ III, 831, 6 ff.), μαστιγόω (→ IV, 515, 20 ff.), παίω, πατάσσω (→ V, 939, 29 ff.), πλήσσω, ῥαβδίζω (→ VI, 970, 25 ff.), ῥαπίζω. Its etym. root is τυπ-, (s)teup, cf. stupeo, "to stupefy by a blow," "to be rigid with astonishment."[1] As some of the above verbs (esp. κολαφίζω, μαστιγόω, ῥαβδίζω) denote specific kinds of blows, so did τύπτω originally: "to stamp on a mark," "to impress a figure etc." The result of this is τύπος (→ 246, 11 ff.), orig. the image on a coin etc. With the levelling down which began even before Hellenism τύπτω[2] was assimilated to other verbs with the gen. sense "to strike."[3] Like class. Attic, post-class. speech uses all the tenses and the later subsidiary form τυπτέω:[4] τυπτήσω (also τύψω, esp. in post-class. Gk.) ἔτυψα (from Hom. Il., 4, 531: τύψε, poetically and post-class. also ἔτυπον, koine ἐτύπτησα, perhaps a hyper-atticism), τετύπτηκα, τέτυμμαι (from Hom. Il., 13, 782, later also τετύπτημαι), ἐτύπην (from Hom. Il., 11, 191, post class. mostly ἐτύφθην). But in the Gk. of the LXX and NT τύπτω is used only in the pres. and impf.;[5] in the fut.[6] and aor. act. it is combined with πατάξω, ἐπάταξα (e.g., Lk. 22:49 f.,[7] sometimes

---

τ ύ π τ ω . Liddell-Scott, Moult.-Mill., s.v.; Phryn. Ecl., 152 (Rutherford); Pr.-Bauer, s.v.
[1] Cf. Boisacq, Hofmann, s.v. An original connection between τύπτω and κόπτω cannot be completely ruled out.
[2] τυπόω later came into use in the special sense "to stamp."
[3] How close τύπτω, πατάσσω and other verbs of striking are in the NT may be seen if one compares Lk. 6:29 and Mt. 5:39 for τύπτω and ῥαπίζω, Lk. 22:63 and v. 64 vl. (→ 264, 28 ff.) for τύπτω, δέρω and παίω, → V, 940, 11 ff. for παίω and πατάσσω. Cf. also, e.g., Lk. 12:47: δαρήσεται πολλάς, with Aristoph. Nu., 972: τυπτόμενος πολλάς (sc. πληγάς).
[4] Cf. Radermacher, 103.
[5] The way seems to be prepared for this development in Attic, cf. Lys., 13, 71: ὁ μὲν Θρασύβουλος τύπτει τὸν Φρύνιχον καὶ καταβάλλει πατάξας, ὁ δὲ Ἀπολλόδωρος οὐχ ἥψατο.
[6] We once find a periphrastic fut. of τύπτω in the NT: μέλλει τύπτειν, Ac. 23:3 → n. 63.
[7] Cf. also esp. 4 Βασ. 6:21 f.: "My father, shall I smite? (εἰ πατάξας πατάξω for הַאַכֶּה אַכֶּה). And he answered, Thou shalt not smite (οὐ πατάξεις): wouldest thou smite (τύπτεις) those whom thou hast taken captive..." ; 14:10 (Joash of Judah to Amaziah of Israel): τύπτων ἐπάταξας (הַכֵּה הִכִּיתָ) τὴν Ἰδουμαίαν, 1 Εσδρ. 4:8 (of the power of the king): εἶπε πατάξαι - τύπτουσιν.

also ἔπαισα, e.g., 2 Βασ. 6:7; Mk. 14:47) and in the aor. and fut. pass. with ἐπλήγην, Rev. 8:12 and πληγήσομαι, e.g., 2 Βασ. 11:15 (not in the NT). [8]

2. The most important word for "to strike" in the Hbr. OT is נכה. This occurs some 500 times, in the hi 480, and it is mostly transl. πατάσσω in LXX (344 times), and only 26 times by τύπτω. [9] In addition τύπτω occurs in LXX only once each for נגף at Ex. 7:27, כרת at 3 Βασ. 18:4, and חלק at Is. 41:7 "to hammer smooth."

3. In the Rabb. the reflexive use of τύπτομαι (κόπτομαι, πλήσσομαι) "to smite oneself" (in sorrow → 262, 10 ff.; 266, 7 ff.) corresponds to חבט hitp. in S. Dt., 308 on 32:5; Semachot, 8, [10] and to ספח pi and hitp [11] (→ III, 842, 2 ff.). כָּתַשׁ עַל הַלֵּב is the equivalent of τύπτω τὸ στῆθος (→ 262, 16 f.; 264, 13 ff.) in Midr. Qoh., 2 on 7:2 (→ 262, 18 ff.).

II. The Usage, especially in the Septuagint.

1. τύπτω can be used literally for striking in various ways, with the hand, fist, or foot, also a staff, stick, rod, whip and various weapons, e.g., spear, Hom. Il., 11, 191. sword, ibid., 4, 531. Various special meanings develop out of the basic gen. sense: a. "to smite mortally," "to deal a fatal blow," Hom. Il., 4, 531; 2 Βασ. 2:23, then gen. "to slay" [12] → V, 939, 31 ff., so Dt. 27:24 (cf. πατάξαι v. 25); Ju. 20:31, 39; [13] 4 Βασ. 6:22 (→ n. 7); 1 Ch. 11:16 (= 2 Βασ. 5:8); Ιεζ. 7:6 (9) → 268, 10 f.; 2 Macc. 3:39 → 268, 14 ff. etc.; cf. also Ac. 21:32 → 267, 8 ff.; b. "to smite an enemy (in the field)," 1 Βασ. 11:11: ἔτυπτον (Cod A ἔπληξεν) τοὺς υἱοὺς Ἀμμών, cf. 2 Βασ. 1:1; 4 Βασ. 14:10 (→n. 7); 3:24: τύπτοντες with ἐπάταξαν, 2 Ch. 28:23 (cf. v. 5); 1 Macc. 9:66; c. "to smite a land with destruction and extirpation," 1 Βασ. 27:9: καὶ ἔτυπτε τὴν γῆν καὶ οὐκ ἐζωογόνει (he did not leave alive) ἄνδρα καὶ γυναῖκα, cf. Rev. 11:6: ἐξουσίαν ἔχουσιν... πατάξαι τὴν γῆν ἐν πάσῃ πληγῇ.

2. With these more or less literal uses one finds various forms of transf. use, e.g., grief "stabbing" [14] the heart, Hom. Il., 19, 125: ὡς φάτο (Hera) τὸν (Zeus) δ' ἄχος ὀξὺ κατὰ φρένα τύψε βαθεῖαν, a man smitten in the heart by remorse and fear of God,

---

[8] Cf. Bl.-Debr. § 101, also Liddell-Scott, s.v. πλήσσω for examples of the mutual supplementing of verbs of smiting.

[9] Also 20 times by παίω, 17 by πλήσσω, 13 by κόπτω, 9 by μαστιγόω, 7 each by ἀναιρέω, ἀποκτείνω (→ n. 12), κατακόπτω, 6 by ἐκκόπτω, 5 by φονεύω, and another 30 times once or twice each by other verbs that have not much to do with striking [Bertram].

[10] Cf. G. Dalman, Jesus-Jeschua (1929), 174.

[11] The transl. render ספח by "to cross the hands" etc., v. Levy Wört, s.v.; Str.-B., I on Mt. 9:23; MQ 3:8 f. (transl. E. L. Rapp [1931]), or "to beat on the breast," so bMQ, 28b (transl. L. Goldschmidt, Der bab. Talmud, III [1899]); → III, 842, 3 ff. and n. 82. But cf. Gn. r., 22: ספח על פניו "to smite oneself on the face."

[12] Sometimes τύπτω in the sense "to strike" can be expressly distinguished from other verbs in the sense "to slay," so LXX: 1 Εσδρ. 4:8 from φονεύω v. 5, ἀποκτείνω v. 7, ἐκκόπτω v. 9; Ex. 2:11-14 from πατάσσω = ἀναιρέω, and Θ: Da. 5:19 from ἀναιρέω.

[13] In both cases Cod B has πατάσσω, but in Ju. its text is later and poorer than in other books of the LXX [Katz].

[14] τύπτω can also be the "stinging" of bees in Aristot. Hist. An., V, 21, p. 553b, 6, or wasps in Xenoph. Hist. Graec., IV, 2, 12, snakes in Anacreontea, 33, 10 (Diehl, IV [1913], 355); cf. παίω for the sting of scorpions, Rev. 9:5.

Is. 66:2 Θ (Cod 88): τυπτόμενον καρδίᾳ. [15] In another form of the same image in 1 Βασ. 1:8 it is the heart itself which is the stabbing or sorrow-causing agent: ἵνα τί τύπτει σε ἡ καρδία σου; In Hdt., III, 64, 1 τύπτω denotes the "pang" of conscience along with a thrust of sudden terror: When Cambyses heard the name of his brother Smerdis whom he had murdered, ἔτυψε ἡ ἀλήθεια τῶν τε λόγων καὶ τοῦ ἐνυπνίου. The only NT instance of this use is in 1 C. 8:12 for the wounding blow which one man deals to the συνείδησις of another, → 268, 23 ff.

3. τύπτω, mostly mid., for "to smite oneself" is used lit. in two ways: a. in training for the games, 4 Macc. 6:10: καθάπερ γενναῖος ἀθλητὴς τυπτόμενος (cf. 1 C. 9:27), and b. to express grief and remorse (→ III, 831, 6 ff.), e.g., beating the forehead (→ III, 845, n. 105), the breast (→ III, 835, 9 ff.; 842, 4 ff.), or both, [16] so Jos. Ant., 7, 252: David when he heard of the death of Absalom τυπτόμενος τὰ στέρνα καὶ τὴν κεφαλήν, Plut. Alex., 3 (I, 666a): The magi on the burning of the temple of Artemis in Ephesus διέθεον τὰ πρόσωπα τυπτόμενοι, Nonnus Dionys., 24, 184 f.: ἀμοιβαίῃσι ῥιπαῖς τυπτομένων παλάμῃσιν, "smiting themselves with the flat of the hand in mutual blows" (of the hands) (→ III, 832, n. 14). Lk. 18:13 (→ 264, 12 ff.) uses the act instead of the mid.: τύπτω τὸ στῆθος, or 23:48 (→ 266, 7 ff.) τὰ στήθη, both times for remorse. [17] On the reasons for smiting oneself → III, 831, 17 ff.; cf. also Vit. Ad., 8. The Jewish explanation of the custom [18] in Midr. Qoh., 2 on 7:2 [19] is a popular interpretation of this symbolic action: "Why does one smite on the heart (→ 261, 9 f.)? To say that all things (sc. sin and guilt and also all visitations) have their origin there."

4. From the lit. reflex use of τύπτω there again developed (→ 261, 25 ff.) a transf. use. τύπτομαι can mean (→ III, 831, 9 ff.; 834, 16 ff.; 845, n. 99) what beating the breast or brow seeks to express: lamentation and grief. It can denote "to lament," "to engage in mourning," Hdt., II, 40, 4; 61, 1b, also trans. as in the continuation of the last passage: [20] τὸν (ὃν) δὲ τύπτονται, οὔ μοι ὅσιόν ἐστι λέγειν, II, 61, 1c; cf. II, 42, 6; 132, 2. But this transf. use is almost exclusively restricted to the Ionic dialect; the Attic prefers κόπτομαι, e.g., Aristoph. Lys., 396: κόπτεσθ᾿ Ἄδωνιν, similarly the koine, e.g., 3 Βασ. 13:30 f. LXX; Jos. Ant., 6, 6, 377; hence there is no corresponding use of τύπτομαι in the LXX and NT. Only occasionally does one find this later, e.g., Luc. Syr. Dea, 6: μνήμην τοῦ πάθεος τύπτονται, "they mourn in memory of the death," sc. of Adonis. [21]

---

[15] Cf. ᾿A: πεπληγότα τὸ πνεῦμα (HT וּנְכֵה־רוּחַ).

[16] Acc. to A. Merx, Die vier kanonischen Ev. nach ihrem ältesten bekannten Texte, II, 2 (1905), 506, n. 1 smiting the breast is eastern, the forehead western (frontem percutere), cf. Lk. 23:48 Cod D → 266, 7 ff.

[17] Cf. in the same sense πατάσσω τὸ στῆθος Joseph and Asenath, 10, 1. 15, ed. P. Batiffol, "Le livre de la prière d'Aseneth," Stud. Patristica, 1 (1889), cf. Riessler, ad loc. It seems here the mid. τύπτομαι (κόπτομαι) τὸ στῆθος etc. is used for sorrow, the act. τύπτω (πατάσσω) τὸ στῆθος for remorse, so Jeremias Gl.[7], 142, n. 5. But one must be careful about distinctions of this kind, since κόπτομαι and κοπετός are used mostly for grief but also sometimes for remorse, cf. Jl. 2:12 LXX; Barn., 7, 5 → III, 851, n. 128. Cf. also Ev. Pt. 7:25 → n. 52. Fear and anxiety can also be reasons for the act as well as grief and remorse, e.g., Menand. Dyscolus (ed. H. Lloyd-Jones [1960], 674): ἔτυπτε τὸ στῆθος σφόδρα, because the girl's father had fallen in the well.

[18] From the surprisingly infrequent mention of τύπτειν the breast one cannot conclude that this was not a common practice (though it was not usual in prayer), cf. Jeremias Gl.[7], 142; the ref. given by Jeremias himself refutes this, for such a practice is presupposed in Midr. Qoh., 2 on 7:2. On the original magical significance of the action cf. G. Fohrer, Die symbolischen Handlungen d. Propheten (1953), 11.

[19] Cf. Str.-B., II, 247.

[20] The very next sentence Hdt., II, 61, 2 has κόπτομαι, also of mourning custom, but lit.: The Carians present καὶ τὰ μέτωπα κόπτονται μαχαίρῃσι → III, 831, 20 ff.

[21] Cf. H. D. Betz, Lukian v. Samosata u. d. NT (1961), 126-130.

B. Material Contexts of the Use in the New Testament.

τύπτω is used almost exclusively by the Synoptists, esp. Lk., and always in the lit. sense. It occurs elsewhere only once in Paul at 1 C. 8:12, here in a transf. sense.

I. In the Preaching of Jesus.

Luke in 6:29: τῷ τύπτοντί σε ἐπὶ τὴν σιαγόνα [22] πάρεχε καὶ τὴν ἄλλην, simplifies Mt. 5:39, which speaks of a blow (ὅστις σε ῥαπίζει) on the right cheek, not because this is more difficult to imagine (cf. Lk. 22:50 with Mt. 26:51), but because for him and his readers a blow with the back of the right hand (or with the left hand) was not particularly insulting. [23] It is enough for him to mention a box on the ears as such, [24] i.e., as an example of humiliation, and offering the other cheek for a second box on the ears as the epitome of refraining from self-assertion. In the parable of the slave who in his master's absence was entrusted with control over the whole household (Mt. 24:25-51 and par.) [25] and begins τύπτειν τοὺς συνδούλους αὐτοῦ (v. 49; Lk. 12:45 goes further and says he even beats the maidservants), the τύπτειν is a base abuse of power. Striking and carousing are an enviable prerogative of masters according to the opinion of slaves. [26, 27] The slave of the parable uses his chance temporarily to exchange the role of slave for that of master. To the offence of τύπτειν there corresponds by nature the punishment of διχοτομεῖν (Mt. 24:51 and par.), as offence and punishment often correspond, but with much enhanced severity, → II, 225, 17 ff. But perhaps διχοτομήσει is a mistranslation for "he will assign him blows"; [28] if so the punishment fits the offence exactly.

---

[22] Instead of ἐπὶ τὴν σιαγόνα (so also LXX 3 Βασ. 22:24 = 2 Ch. 18:23; cf. Hos. 11:4; Mi. 4:14; also Lam. 3:30: παίοντι ... σιαγόνα), literary speech prefers ἐπὶ κόρρης, so Plat. Gorg., 486c; 527a: τύπτω ἐπὶ κόρρης, Plut. Quaest. Conv., VII, 8, 4 (II, 713c): ῥαπίζω ἐπὶ κόρρης.

[23] Cf. the ref. in Str.-B., I, 342 (BQ, 8, 6 and T BQ, 9, 31) on striking with the inverted hand, i.e., the back of the hand. Hitting the right cheek with the back of the right hand might be the first part of a double box on the ears completed at once by slapping the left cheek. But the blow might have been with the left hand, which some peoples thought esp. humiliating, cf. 1 Εσδρ. 4:30: Apame, Darius' concubine, ἐρράπιζεν τὸν βασιλέα τῇ ἀριστερᾷ. Like Mt., Did., 1, 4 in its version of the saying ref. to the right cheek: ῥάπισμα εἰς τὴν δεξιὰν σιαγόνα.

[24] A slap in the face or box on the ears was often meant as an insult in antiquity, e.g., Hermippus Fr., 80 (CAF, I, 249): ἐγώ σου σήμερον τύπτων τὸ πρόσωπον αἱμορυγχίαν ("a bloody nose") ποιήσω, also 1 K. 22:24 when the false prophet Zedekiah boxes the ears of Micaiah b. Imlah before the kings of Israel and Judah; Job 16:10 (→ n. 40): they hit me disdainfully on the cheeks, also esp. Mi. 4:14; Is. 50:6 (→ 265, 12 ff.) and Mk. 14:65 and par.

[25] Lk. is original compared with Mt. when he ref. to only one servant and his different forms of behaviour, cf. W. Michaelis, Die Gleichnisse Jesu (1956), 76; Jeremias Gl.[7], 53.

[26] Being beaten was a big element in the slave's lot, cf. the ancient comedies, e.g., Aristoph. Pax, 743; Eubulus Fr., 60 (CAF, II, 185): The flautist who τύπτεται is probably to be thought of as a slave. Esp. in Roman comedy the verberari of slaves plays a gt. role; it is part of the slave's daily bread, Plaut. Asinaria, 628. In Plaut. Poenulus, 384; Curculio, 197 it even takes place on stage. Nor were things any better for female slaves, e.g., Menand. Dyscolus (→ n. 17), 195 f. In Plaut. Mercator., 396 the normal duties of a female slave are listed as weaving, grinding, cutting wood, cooking, spinning and being whipped [A. Thierfelder]. Hence the addition in Lk. 12:45 (→ line 13 f.) is true to life.

[27] Luc. Tim., 23 offers another example of a slave who, come to power, thinks he is acting like a master but in reality still behaves like a slave in that he τούς τε ἐλευθέρους ὑβρίζει καὶ τοὺς ὁμοδούλους μαστιγοῖ.

[28] So K. A. Offermann, Aramaic Origin of the NT (no date), 22 f., cf. Jeremias Gl.[7], 54, n. 6.

The point of the parable and esp. of the motif of striking depends in part on whether this is an original saying of Jesus [29] and hence an authentic parable or whether it is the work of the community with allegorical features. [30] In the former case the striking is a bit of embroidery in the picture of a servant who forgets the hour of responsibility. But even in this case it is probable, and in the latter case certain, that the parable does not have all Christians in view (cf. Lk. 12:41), but those who in the οἰκετεία (Mt. 24:45) or θεραπεία (Lk. 12:42) of Jesus are entrusted with a special ministry. [31] Since allegorical elements are not wholly alien to the parables, it is likely enough that in the picture of the striking and carousing slave Jesus wanted to warn those singled out by special responsibility against seeking to play the Lord in the time prior to the *parousia* [32] (cf. the echo in Paul at 2 C. 4:5, also 1 C. 4:21). The same is said positively, e.g., at Lk. 22:26.

The exemplary story of the Pharisee and the publican in Lk. 18:9-14 sets humble self-striking in juxtaposition to the humiliation of being struck, 6:29. The publican explains his τύπτειν τὸ στῆθος αὐτοῦ in the prayer: ὁ θεός, ἱλάσθητί μοι τῷ ἁμαρτωλῷ, v. 13. Jesus hereby shows that in spite of the conventional nature of this ancient practice (→ n. 18) beating the breast is here a spontaneous expression of a direct consciousness of sin [33] and desire for grace → I, 330, 27 ff., the only attitude which can stand before God, v. 14. It is thus just as radical a renunciation of self-assertion as the attitude in 6:29 → 263, 5 ff.

II. In the Passion Narrative.

In the passion narrative Jesus twice receives a powerful (→ 263, 13 ff.) and humiliating (→ 263, 5 ff.) beating, Lk. 22:63 f. and par.; Mk. 15:19 and par. and once there is a humble self-smiting in His honour (→ 266, 7 ff.), that of spectators at the foot of the cross, Lk. 23:48. As regards the former the striking of Jesus is in all accounts part of His mocking whether by the Jews (only the Synoptics) or the Roman soldiers (Mk., Mt., Jn.). In the first incident the verb τύπτω is used only as vl. in Lk. 22:64, in the second only in Mk. 15:19; Mt. 27:30.

The mocking of Jesus as prophet (Lk. 22:64 vl.) is a kind of blind man's buff. [34] He is blindfolded [35] and struck as a presupposition of the demand προφήτευσον

---

[29] Possible even acc. to Bultmann Trad., 125.

[30] So, e.g., W. Grundmann, *Das Ev. nach Lk., Theol. Handkomm. z. NT,* 3² (1961), 267.

[31] The very emphatic sing. in Mt. 24:45 par. may be explained by the frequency of the use of the slave in Jesus' parables, cf. J. Schniewind, *Das Ev. nach Mt., NT Deutsch,* 2¹¹ (1964) on 24:45. Whether the Antiochene Luke had the developing episcopate in view (Grundmann, *op. cit.,* 267 and n. 10) is doubtful, since he does not have it in Ac. (as distinct from the Past.).

[32] Cf. K. H. Rengstorf, *Das Ev. nach Lk., NT Deutsch,* 3¹⁰ (1965) on 12:41 ff. In interpretation cf. also A. Schlatter, "Die Kirche, wie Jesus sie sah," *Kirche im Aufbau,* 2 (1936), 9-11; C. H. Dodd, *Parables of the Kingdom* (1948), 158-160; Michaelis, *op. cit.,* 71-80; Jeremias Gl.⁷, 53-55; B. Reicke, *Diakonie, Zelos u. Festfreude* (1951), 236.

[33] Possibly in despair at the hopelessness of his position, cf. Jeremias Gl.⁷, 142; Grundmann, *op. cit., ad loc.*

[34] The guards who in Lk. pass the time thus until the meeting of the council in the morning might well have taken this game as a model. For the incident in the Sanhedrin with its dominant note of hate and scorn (in Mk. and Mt.) this is less likely. Lk. in his description might have had such a game in view, cf. its use in explaining κολλαβίζω in Poll. Onom., IX, 129; in this game one who has to cover his eyes with his hands receives a box on the ears, ὁ δὲ παίσας ἐπερωτᾷ ποτέρα τετύπτηκε, cf. W. C. van Unnik, "Jesu Verhöhnung vor d. Synedrium (Mk. 14:65 par.)," ZNW, 29 (1930), 310 f.; Hck. Lk., Grundmann, *op. cit., ad loc.*

[35] This is left out at Mk. 14:65 in the Western text (D a f sy⁸). The point of the striking is thus changed; they want "to teach Jesus to prophesy," i.e., drive out His prophesying

and the question (only Mt. and Lk.): τίς ἐστιν ὁ παίσας σε; As in the mocking by the Roman soldiers (→ 266, 3 ff.) rough handling is part of the game. This is why the Evangelists mention a second beating. [36]

In the text of almost all the older witnesses Lk. has only one striking, δέροντες, 22:63. But the 𝔎 text (followed by textus receptus) [37] reads in v. 64: καὶ περικαλύψαντες αὐτὸν ἔτυπτον αὐτοῦ τὸ πρόσωπον καὶ ἐπηρώτων αὐτὸν λέγοντες· προφήτευσον κτλ. Cod D reads similarly (with more assimilation to Mk. 14:65): καὶ περικαλύψαντες αὐτοῦ τὸ πρόσωπον ἔτυπτον αὐτὸν καὶ ἐπηρώτων λέγοντες· προφήτευσον κτλ., but leaves out δέροντες in v. 63. The original is perhaps retained in the mention of δέρειν and τύπτειν. [38] Lk. first says gen. in v. 63 that the guards mocked and mistreated [39] Jesus. He then depicts the mocking in which the mockers blind His eyes and smite Him. As in many other incidents in the passion story, so here the reference to OT scenes and figures was important for early Christianity, [40] in this case the figure of the Servant of the Lord in Is. 50:6 LXX: τὸν νῶτόν μου δέδωκα εἰς μάστιγας, τὰς δὲ σιαγόνας μου εἰς ῥαπίσματα, τὸ δὲ πρόσωπόν μου οὐκ ἀπέστρεψα ἀπὸ αἰσχύνης ἐμπτυσμάτων. Even to the wording the relation is plain. With the spitting [41] there is here a double striking. One is tempted to suppose that the incident was shaped as a fulfilment of the prototype. [42] In fact the correspondence of prophecy and fulfilment, of prototype and antitype, which is highly significant in salvation history, was so certain for the bearers of the primitive Chr. kerygma, that it must have seemed obligatory to them to follow OT originals in the phrasing and detailed presentation of the passion narrative → V, 700, 5 ff. At any rate it is here if anywhere, and not in the contemporary world around, that one is to seek any creative influences apart from the actual history. [43] The silent acceptance of mockery and smiting by Jesus, His radical renouncing of self-assertion, also corresponds to the prototype of the Servant, who does not defend himself but readily

---

(e.g., of the destruction of the temple) by blows; so Wellh. Mk., 125 f. The blindfolding is also left out by Mt., but the question τίς ἐστιν ὁ παίσας σε; (not in Mk.) explains the summons προφήτευσον.

[36] In Mk. (14:65), who ascribes this second striking to the servants, the sequence of κολαφίζω for mocking and λαμβάνω ῥαπίσμασιν for rough handling is plain, but it is confused in Mt. (26:67), who has two groups of Sanhedrists buffet Jesus (ἐκολάφισαν) and smite Him (ἐρράπισαν).

[37] So also the Itala, ed. A. Jülicher and K. Aland, III (1954), 254: et percutiebant eum (d ff² i l q, without eum a) or faciem eius (aur f), so, too, Vg.

[38] So also H. v. Soden, Die Schriften d. NT, I (1907), 1438, who gives as one reason that if 𝔎 had added, it would have followed the par. and chosen κολαφίζω or ῥαπίζω rather than τύπτω (only here), but cf. K. Aland, Synopsis quattuor Evangeliorum (1964), ad loc.

[39] δέρω can relate to the buffeting as Jn. 18:23, in the one case to the preceding ῥάπισμα δίδωμι, in the other the ensuing τύπτω (τὸ πρόσωπον 𝔎 text); καί then means "and indeed." If καλύπτω means covering the face (Cod D and Mk. 14:65) with a cloth, τύπτω means other blows, but it can mean that only the eyes are bound, so that the cheeks are left unprotected. But δέροντες can just mean "to maltreat" without ref. to this.

[40] One might think of other models: 1. the sufferers in the psalms of complaint, which offer many par. (e.g., Ps. 69:7); 2. Job (16:10 → n. 24); 3. Mi. 5:1: "They smite the ruler with a rod upon the cheeck."

[41] This, too, is left out by Lk., though he has it in the so-called third intimation of the passion (18:32 cf. Mk. 10:34). It is dropped with the mocking by the Roman soldiers. The main reason is that in Lk. Jesus is exposed only to the rough mockery and cruelty of the guards but in Mk. and Mt. to the hate and scorn of the Jewish leaders.

[42] Cf. M. Dibelius, Die Formgesch. d. Ev.⁴ (1961), 193 with n. 1; Loh. Mk. on 14:65.

[43] Apart from v. Unnik, op. cit. cf. G. Rudberg, "Die Verhöhnung Jesu vor dem Hohenpriester," ZNW, 24 (1925), 307-9.

offers himself for maltreatment and humiliation. [44] It also corresponds to Jesus' own saying in Lk. 6:29 → 263, 5 ff. [45]

The mocking by the Roman soldiers is a mocking of Jesus as king (Mk. 15:18 f. and par.). The soldiers strike Him with a stick on His thorn-crowned head [46] (Mk. ἔτυπτον αὐτοῦ τὴν κεφαλὴν καλάμῳ). It is probable that a traditional practice not only coloured the account in the Gospels but also inspired the soldiers themselves in their conduct. [47] A contrast to the Jewish police and Roman soldiers who buffet and strike Jesus is offered at Lk. 23:48 by οἱ ὄχλοι at the foot of the cross, τύπτοντες τὰ στήθη (καὶ τὰ μέτωπα Cod D → n. 16). Only Lk. enframes Jesus' march to death by such incidents of mourning → III, 846, 3 ff. The women who weep and bewail Jesus (v. 27) [48] make it plain that this is a proleptic mourning for the dead → III, 846, 3 ff. [49, 50] Similarly the τύπτειν τὰ στήθη of v. 48 can be understood as an expression of such mourning → III, 846, 5 ff.; 849, 4 ff. But since this dumb gesture of the people seems to be here a confirmatory Yes and Amen to the confession of the centurion (v. 47), [51] it is rather to be regarded like 18:13 (→ 264, 12 ff.) as a sign of self-contemplation and penitence, [52] → n. 17.

---

[44] There are non-bibl. par. for this, though for different reasons. Socrates thinks it right to let himself be beaten if country and laws demand, Plat. Crit., 51b: τύπτεσθαι and not τυπτόμενον ἀντιτύπτειν, 50e. But for all the outward similarity the inner distinction is all the greater in the attitude of the slave as compared with the athlete to τύπτεσθαι, Philo Leg. All., III, 201; Cher., 79-81.

[45] But cf. the Joh. par. to or version of the Synpt. mocking incident before the Sanhedrin, 18:22 f. and on this → 267, 14 ff.

[46] If the ἀκάνθινος στέφανος was an improvised copy of the diadem with which contemporary rulers were depicted on coins (cf. H. St. J. Hart, "The Crown of Thorns in Jn. 19:2-5," JThSt, NS, 3 [1952], 66-75 with ill.; Stauffer Theol., Ill. 15), if it was primarily meant as a caricature rather than torture, then one cannot presuppose a connection between it and the striking as one is gen. inclined to do. Yet if it was made of the prickly parts of date-palm, as Hart conjectures, it must have been painful in itself, and esp. so blows on the head covered by it.

[47] Cf. the bibl. in Bultmann Trad., 294, n. 1; Kl. Mk., Exc. on 15:15; also G. Bertram, *Die Leidensgeschichte Jesu u. der Christuskult* (1922), 72 f.; M. Nilsson, Art. "Saturnalia," Pauly-W., 2a (1923), 208 f., 210 f.

[48] Whether one can say that Lk. has used here the style of the lament for Tammuz (→ III, 835, 29 ff.) and that if the incident is historical Jesus Himself had fulfilment of the myth in view (so A. Jeremias, *Die Bdtg. des Mythos f. das ap. Glaubensbekenntnis* [1930], 22, 26) is very doubtful → IV, 795, 20 ff.

[49] For lamenting before death cf., e.g., Jos. Ant., 8, 273; 13, 399. In the case of Jesus the wailing of the men and women of Jerusalem is like that of near relatives for a condemned man on the way to execution, cf. the examples in Dalman, *op. cit.*, 174.

[50] Jesus' answer points to this too.

[51] This is how Ev. Pt. 8:28 understands the incident when it adds speech to the gesture: ὁ λαὸς ἅπας... κόπτεται τὰ στήθη λέγοντες ὅτι· εἰ τῷ θανάτῳ αὐτοῦ ταῦτα τὰ μέγιστα σημεῖα γέγονεν, ἴδετε ὁπόσον δίκαιός ἐστιν.

[52] The addition of the Old Latin Cod g¹: *dicentes: vae nobis quae facta sunt hodie propter peccata nostra; appropinquavit enim desolatio Hierusalem*, and the similar one of sy^sc, "and they said: Woe to us for what has happened, woe to us on account of our sins," both presuppose this interpretation. Obviously the lamenting is understood here as a present-eschatological fulfilment of Zech. 12:10 ff. (→ III, 849, 10 ff.), cf. Mt. 24:30; Rev. 1:7. The same applies to Lk. 23:27. It also means that the Jews took up Jesus' answer in v. 28 ff. and followed His direction. Ev. Pt. 7:25 has the same incident after the burial: τότε οἱ 'Ιουδαῖοι... γνόντες οἷον κακὸν ἑαυτοῖς ἐποίησαν, ἤρξαντο κόπτεσθαι καὶ λέγειν· οὐαὶ ταῖς ἁμαρτίαις ἡμῶν. ἤγγισεν ἡ κρίσις (cf. Jn. 12:31) καὶ τὸ τέλος 'Ιερουσαλήμ. A. Merx, *Die Ev. nach Mk. u. Lk. nach d. syr. im Sinaikloster gefundenen Palimpsesthandschrift* (1905), 506 regards this addition to Lk. 23:48 as original. This is not impossible but one cannot say that the text is "pointless" without it.

III. In Acts.

It is part of the picture of the apparently anti-Jewish presentation of Luke that in their contesting of the world-wide spread of the Gospel the Jews stop at nothing and continually resort to violence. The blows dealt in the process express the Jewish awareness how much is at stake. There is constant reference to τύπτειν in Acts. In 18:17 the Jews of Corinth [53] beat Sosthenes, the leader of their own synagogue, probably because he did not win his point with Gallio against Paul, cf. vv. 12 ff. In 21:27 f. the Jews of the *diaspora* in Jerusalem attack Paul and try to beat him to death, v. 31: ζητούντων τε αὐτὸν ἀποκτεῖναι. More so than in other NT passages τύπτω is here (v. 32) the uncontrolled and unrestricted battering of someone with a view to killing him (→ 261, 15 ff.), which is possible enough even though no sticks etc. are used. [54] Only the swift intervention of the commander of the Roman garrison prevents this outcome. On the other hand τύπτω in 23:2 is a blow on the mouth (→ VII, 700, n. 66) which the high-priest Ananias has administered to Paul. The incident is strikingly similar to that which Jn. (18:22 f.) has in place of the mocking of Jesus by the Jews → n. 45. [55] In the case of Jesus, however, a servant gives the blow on his own initiative, whereas the high-priest orders it in Paul's case. Nevertheless both blows are a punishment for unseemly speech, and like Jesus Paul defends himself: [56] "God shall smite (τύπτειν) thee, thou whited wall. On the one side thou sittest in judgment on me according to the law, on the other thou dost have me smitten (κελεύεις με τύπτεσθαι) contrary to the law." [57] Luke has Paul [58] pronounce here a common Jewish curse, [59, 60] with a play on the word τύπ-

---

[53] It is conceivable that πάντες denotes the pagan population of Corinth which seizes the opportunity for an anti-Jewish outburst. But the other interpretation is more likely, esp. if the ἀρχισυνάγωγος Sosthenes is the one who later appears as co-author of 1 C. The τύπτειν of his compatriots might have driven him to Paul, cf. G. Stählin, *Die Ag., NT Deutsch,* 5¹⁰ (1962), on 18:17.

[54] Zn. Ag. on 21:30 thinks some of the police under the temple captain had sticks; Haench. Ag.¹⁴ on v. 31 (n. 10) doubts this, since if it were so Paul could hardly have escaped without serious injury. Cf. Jos. Bell., 2, 176 f., where many Jews who were beaten (τυπτόμενοι) with sticks (ξύλα) died in consequence, also 2, 326, *v.* Schl. Mt. on 26:47 → V, 38, n. 11.

[55] One can hardly speak of an intentional par. (cf. Stählin, *op. cit.,* 13 f.) since Luke presents the scene quite differently in his Gospel.

[56] One can hardly deny a certain tension between the two incidents and Jesus' *logion* in Mt. 5:39; Lk. 6:29. But Jesus is not depicted as the silent suffering Servant in Jn. → 265, 23 ff. In His passion He is from first (13:3; 18:4 f.) to last the Lord of what happens, 19:30. Then in both cases, as distinct from Mk. 14:65 par.; 15:19 par., also Lk. 6:29 par., we have a flagrant breach of judicial procedure. Paul pts. expressly to this in Ac. 23:3b and Jesus in Jn. 18:23, cf. also Schl. J., *ad loc.*

[57] The questions in Plat. Hi., I, 292a-b sound similar: ἢ οὐκ ἔνδικος ὑμῖν ἡ πόλις ἐστίν, ἀλλ' ἐᾷ ἀδίκως τύπτειν ἀλλήλους τοὺς πολίτας; ... ἢ καὶ σύ με ἄκριτον ("without trial," "unheard") τυπτήσεις; Jesus also requests an orderly trial with His objection to unjust blows: μαρτύρησον περὶ τοῦ κακοῦ, Jn. 18:23.

[58] Cf. the similar curse on Paul's lips in Ac. 18:6: τὸ αἷμα ὑμῶν ἐπὶ τὴν κεφαλὴν ὑμῶν (also the Jews of themselves in Mt. 27:25), and in relation to himself 2 C. 1:23; R. 9:3 etc.; on this G. Stählin, "Zum Gebrauch von Beteuerungsformeln im NT," *Nov. Test.,* 5 (1962), 134-6; T. Klauser, Art. "Beteuerungsformeln," RAC, II, 222. There are no cursings of others in Paul's letters, but cf. Jd. 9.

[59] Cf. Shebu., 4, 13 (If anyone says:) God will smite thee, or: God smite thee similarly, this is the curse written in the Torah; cf. Dt. 28:21 ff.

[60] This is one of the things that shows the acquaintance of the Hellenist Luke with Judaica. Similar but not exactly the same curses were common in the Gk. world, e.g., κακόν σε κακῶς ἅπαντες ἀπολέσειαν οἱ θεοί (cf. Mt. 21:41), 4 times in Menand. Dyscolus, 138 f., 220 f., 600 f., 926 f., and cf. the self-curse in 311 ff.: (Pan and the nymphs) με ... ἀπόπληκτον ... ποιήσειαν, which is close to the biblical idea of God smiting.

τω. [61] The play on words suggests that the punishment should fit the crime, but also go far beyond it as in Lk. 12:45 f. and par. (→ 263, 14 ff.); for the τύπτειν of God wished in the curse is usually a mortal blow. [62] This is how Luke understood μέλλει τύπτειν. Indeed, it is less a curse than a declaration of judgment or prediction of cursing [63] whose fulfilment he himself lived to see, for in 66 the high-priest Ananias was murdered by the *sicarii* or Zealots, Jos. Bell., 2, 441.

God's smiting (→ V, 940, 1 ff.) might involve all kinds of blows of fate, cf. Dt. 28:22, 27 f., 35, e.g., plagues, Ex. 7:27: [64] ἰδοὺ ἐγὼ τύπτω πάντα τὰ ὅριά σου τοῖς βατράχοις (cf. Rev. 11:6), and esp. God's eschatological wrath and judgment, Ez. 7:9: Thou shalt learn that I, Yahweh, am he who smites [65] (LXX ὁ τύπτων). But usually the divine smiting is presented as a direct mortal blow, Gn. 8:21; Nu. 33:4; 2 S. 6:7; cf. 2 Βασ. 24:17: ἐν τῷ ἰδεῖν αὐτὸν (sc. David) τὸν ἄγγελον τύπτοντα ἐν τῷ λαῷ (the pestilence with which God snatches away the people through His angel, cf. Ac. 12:23); 2 Macc. 3:39: Heliodorus, smitten by God's angel (v. 26: ἐμαστίγουν αὐτὸν... πολλὰς ἐπιρριπτοῦντες αὐτῷ πληγάς), confesses: He smites and destroys (τύπτων ἀπολλύει) those who have come there (to God's holy city) with ill intent. The Hell. theology of Ep. Ar. modifies the idea of God's smiting in terms of clemency and instruction (cf. Prv. 3:12 = Hb. 12:6): οὐ κατὰ τὰς ἁμαρτίας οὐδὲ τὴν μεγαλωσύνην τῆς ἰσχύος τύπτοντος αὐτούς, ἀλλ' ἐπιεικείᾳ χρωμένου τοῦ θεοῦ. In opposition to this Paul and Luke stand on the soil of the OT and Palestinian Judaism.

IV. In Paul.

The only NT instance of a transferred use of τύπτω, and the only example in Paul's works, [66] is 1 C. 8:12: "But when ye sin so against the brethren, and wound their weak conscience (καὶ [67] τύπτοντες αὐτῶν τὴν συνείδησιν ἀσθενοῦσαν), ye sin against Christ." According to v. 10 the blow to the conscience of the weak brother is that the conduct of the strong leads him to act against his conscience. But τύπτω does not refer to the resultant pangs of conscience. It is actual damage in relation to his existence before God. This is shown by the other ways of expressing the same thing, v. 7: ἡ συνείδησις μολύνεται, v. 9 (cf. R. 14:13, 20): πρόσκομμα

---

[61] These and similar plays on words are common in Luke, cf. Lk. 23:48, also G. Holzhey in Stählin, *op. cit., s.v.* "Wortspiel."

[62] Cf. the exposition of Shebu., 4, 13 (→ n. 59) in bShebu., 36a with Ps. 52:5.

[63] If one takes τύπτειν σε μέλλει as fut. as Luke seems to (→ n. 6), cf. similar intimations of judgment in Gl. 5:10; 2 C. 11:15b; cf. 2 Tm. 4:14.

[64] For the connection with lit. striking cf. Ex. 7:17 and 7:27.

[65] Cf. among others G. Fohrer, *Ez., Hndbch. AT,* I, 13² (1955), *ad loc.* W. Eichrodt, *Der Prophet Hesekiel, AT Deutsch,* 22, 1 (1959), *ad loc.* wrongly thinks מַכֶּה (ה) = ὁ τύπτων is secondary.

[66] Only a clearly secondary addition to Tt. 1:11 in a Gk.-Lat.-Arab. minusc. of the 13th cent. (460) has τύπτω in the lit. sense. This contains a direction to the recipient, written in poor Gk., which is added for the sake of the link with ἐπιστομίζω (cf. Pr.-Bauer, *s.v.*): τὰ τέκνα οἱ τοὺς ἰδίους γονεῖς ὑβρίζοντες ἢ τύπτοντες (cf. Luc. Tim., 23 → n. 27) ἐπιστόμιζε καὶ ἔλεγχε καὶ νουθέτει ὡς πατὴρ τέκνα. With this cf. the command of the Book of the Covenant, which breathes the strict spirit of the OT, in Ex. 21:15 LXX: ὃς τύπτει πατέρα αὐτοῦ ἢ μητέρα αὐτοῦ θανάτῳ θανατούσθω. But one can hardly say that the addition to Tt. 1:11 achieves the high level of the NT.

[67] καί is meant explicatively here, cf. Bl.-Debr. § 442, 9. E. Käsemann, "Amt u. Gemeinde im NT," *Exeget. Versuche u. Besinnungen,* I³ (1964), 121 transl.: "When one breaks the conscience ..."

(→ VI, 753, 9 ff.), v. 13: σκανδαλίζει (→ VII, 355, 12 ff.), v. 11: ἀπόλλυται, cf. R. 14:15, 20, 23. τύπτω τὴν συνείδησιν is thus tantamount to "wounding the sense of faith, i.e., the fellowship of love which unites with God." It is offending in such a way that the brother's relation to God suffers serious harm.

Stählin

┌─────────────────────────┐
│ † τυφλός, † τυφλόω │
└─────────────────────────┘

Contents: A. τυφλός and τυφλόω in Greek Antiquity and Hellenism: I. The Meaning;
II. Blindness in the Literal Sense; III. τυφλός and τυφλόω in Comparisons and the Trans-
ferred Sense. B. τυφλός and τυφλόω in the Septuagint: I. Usage; II. τυφλός in the Literal
Sense; III. τυφλός in the Transferred Sense. C. τυφλός and τυφλόω and Their Equivalents
in Judaism apart from Philo: I. Usage; II. In the Literal Sense; III. The Transferred Sense of
Blind. D. Philo. E. τυφλός and τυφλόω in the New Testament: I. Usage; II. Blindness in
the Literal Sense; III. The Transferred Use of τυφλός and τυφλόω. E. τυφλός in the
Post-Apostolic Fathers.

A. τυφλός and τυφλόω in Greek Antiquity and Hellenism.

I. The Meaning.

1. The adj. τυφλός, [1] attested from Hom. Il., 6, 139 and Hymn. Ap., 172, is used lit.
for human blindness, also that of animals, e.g., Aristot. Hist. An., VI, 20, p. 574a, 27 etc.
As an attribute it occurs, e.g., with ὄψις, Eur. Cyc., 697, ὀφθαλμοί, Plat. Resp., VII,
518c, κόρη, Anth. Graec., 9, 123, and αἱ τῶν ὀμμάτων βολαί, Luc. Amores, 46.

Improperly τυφλός denotes objects without eyes, light, aperture, access: τυφλὸν
ἔντερον *(intestinum caecum)* "appendix," Gal. In Hippocr. epidemiarum librum sextum,
IV, 3 (CMG, 192, 6 f., 20), [2] τυφλαὶ ὁδοί, "cul-de-sacs," "blind alleys," Aristot. Hist.
An., IV, 8, p. 533b, 3, ῥύμη, P. Oxy., I, 99, 9 (55 A.D.), cf. P. Lond., III, 870, 8 (4th cent.
A.D.), etc. Not just "inability to see," but also "inability to be seen," is called τυφλός;
in this respect τυφλός means "invisible," "unclear," "hidden," "concealed," "dark," par.
κρύφιος, Plut. De Sollertia Animalium, 35 (II, 983d), par. ἀσαφής, Plut. Gen. Socr.,
18 (II, 587c), of cliffs, Anth. Graec., 7, 275, tracks, Plut. De Sollertia Animal., 10 (II,
966d).

──────────────

τυφλός κτλ. Bibl.: A. Esser, "Das Antlitz d. Blindheit in d. Antike," *Janus. Revue
internat. de l'histoire des sciences, de la médicine, de la pharmacie et de la technique*, Supplém.
Vol., 4[2] (1961); M. Friedmann, *Der Blinde in d. bibl. u. rabb. Schrifttum* (1873); J. Hempel,
"Heilung als Symbol u. Wirklichkeit im bibl. Schrifttum," *NGG Philosophisch-hist. Klasse*
1958/3 (1958); W. Herrmann, "Das Wunder in d. evangel. Botschaft. Zur Interpretation d.
Begriffe blind u. taub im AT u. NT," *Aufsätze z. Vorträge z. Theol. u. Religionswissenschaft*,
20 (1961); R. Herzog, "Die Wunderheilungen v. Epidauros," *Philologus Suppl.*, 22, 3 (1931);
E. Lesky, Art. "Blindheit," RAC, II (1954), 433-446; H. van der Loos, "The Miracles of
Jesus," *Nov. Test. Suppl.*, 8 (1965), 415-434; J. Preuss, "Bibl.-talmud. Medizin," *Beitr. z.
Geschichte der Heilkunde u. d. Kultur überh.* (1911), 313-324; O. Weinreich, "Antike Hei-
lungswunder, Untersuchungen zum Wunderglauben d. Griech. u. Römer," RVV, 8, 1 (1909).
[1] τυφλός is often associated with τύφω "to make smoke," "to smoke," though this -υ-
is long. It cannot be detached from Germanic words like Gothic *dumbs*, Old High German
tumb, Gothic *daufs*, Old High German *toup* etc., which also go back to an Indo-Eur. root
* *dhubh-, dhoubh-*, v. Boisacq, s.v., Hittite *duddumi-*. In Gk. other adj. in -λος are also used
for physical defects, e.g., χωλός "lame," v. P. Chantraine, *La formation des noms en grec
ancien* (1933), 238 [Risch].
[2] Cf. also Gal. De usu partium, 4, 18 (Kühn, 3, 333); Rufus Medicus in Oribasius Collectiones medic., 7, 26, 25 (CMG, 230, 23 f.); Aristot. Part. An., III, 14, p. 675b, 7. On the
"blind canal" (fallopian tube in the temporal bone) cf. M. Simon, *Sieben Bücher Anatomie
des Galen*, II (1906), Index, s.v.

2. The verb τυφλόω usually means act. "to make blind," "to rob of eyesight," e.g., τινά Hdt., IV, 2, 1; Eur. Rhes., 924, τινὰ βλέφαρον, Eur. Cyc., 673, ἑαυτόν Luc. Toxaris, 41, ὄψιν Eur. Phoen., 764, τὰς ὁράσεις, Plut. Quaest. Conv., V, 7 (II, 681d e), τὸν ἑτερόφθαλμον τυφλώσῃ καὶ τὸν δύ᾽ ἔχοντα, Aristot. Rhet., I, 7, p. 1365b, 18 f.; pass. "to go blind," "to lose one's sight," "to be blinded," Hdt., II, 111, 2, τυφλοῦμαι φέγγος ὀμμάτων, "to lose one's sight," Eur. Hec., 1035. Improperly τυφλόω act, means "to render ineffectual, blunt, unsuccessful, fruitless," pass. "to be ineffectual, unfruitful," τετύφλωται . . . μόχθος ἀνδρῶν, Pind. Isthm., 5, 56 f.

II. Blindness in the Literal Sense.

1. Normally in antiquity blindness means full loss of sight τυφλὸν τὸ μὴ ἔχον ὄψιν, Aristot. Metaph., VIII, 3, p. 1047a, 8 f.; Topica, VI, 6, p. 143b, 35, though the distinction between a little remaining sight and total blindness is fluid. [3] Par. to τυφλός is οὐχ ὁρῶν, Plat. Ep., 7, 335b etc., but opp. we find not only βλέπων, Aristoph. Pl., 665 f.; Fr., 259 (CAF, II, 121) but also ὀξὺ βλέπων, Plat. Leg., I, 631c, cf. Epict. Diss., II, 23, 11 etc., ὀξὺ ὁρῶν, Plat. Resp., VI, 484c, ὀξυδερκέστατος, Hdt., II, 68, 4. As in other languages τυφλός can be expanded hyperbolically to παντελῶς τυφλός, "stone-blind" Luc. De Domo, 18 or comparatively τυφλότερος, Strabo, 15, 686; Luc. Menippus, 21; Sib., 1, 370, cf. also μᾶλλον ἐποίησεν τυφλόν, Aristoph. Pl., 747. The blind, deaf and lame are often mentioned together, e.g., in Epidaurus-Wunder, 4 [4] → n. 23. In Plat. Crito, 53 we read of χωλοί and τυφλοί and then καὶ οἱ ἄλλοι ἀνάπηροι.

2. One cause of the widespread blindness in the southern Mediterranean countries was heredity ἐκ τυφλῶν τυφλοί, Aristot. Hist. An., VII, 5, p. 585b, 30, which might produce blindness at birth or later, Diod. S., 1, 59, 2; Plut. De Timoleone, 37 (I, 254), even old age, Dio C., 78, 14, 1; Hippocr. Epid., I, 12 (Littré, II, 678-682) etc. Plant or animal poisons, e.g., insects, snakes, are another cause, Ael. Nat. An., 4, 57; Apoll. Rhod., IV, 1523-5 (Seaton); Strabo, 15, 2, 7. Then we have wounds, e.g., in war, Epidaurus-Wunder, 32 → n. 4, accidents (11), exposure to bright light, e.g., lightning, Antiph. Fr., 195, 4 (FAC, II, 262), illness, Diog. L., IX, 3 f. etc. [5] Psychological causes are also sought, e.g., sorrow, tears in Anth. Graec., 7, 241 and 389. How far blindness can be due to sin is hardly discussed outside Judaism, → 283, 18 ff. It was realised, however, that apart from blindness due to fate, e.g., heredity, there was merited blindness, e.g., through overindulgence in alcohol, Mart., 6, 78, or other excesses, Aristot. Eth. Nic., III, 5, p. 1114a, 25-28, or affronting the gods etc. (for penal blinding cf. esp. → 272, 4 ff.). The rider Lenaios in Ael. Nat. An., 11, 31 reflects on the link between sin and blindness when his horse is blinded. [6]

3. Another common cause of blindness is the custom which was common in antiquity, the barbaric one of blinding (often τυφλόω), [7] practised or threatened by men as well as gods, whether in passion out of jealousy or revenge, or in war retribution, or for political

---

[3] Outside medicine, too, distinction is made between blindness and having one eye: τυφλὸς γὰρ οὐ λέγεται ὁ ἑτερόφθαλμος ἀλλ᾽ ὁ ἐν ἀμφοῖν μὴ ἔχων ὄψιν, Aristot. Metaph., IV, 22, p. 1023a, 4 f. (but cf. Epid.-Wunder, 69, Herzog, 34), also blindness and near-sightedness ἀμβλυωπία, Plut. Quaest. Conv., VIII, 9 (II, 732c). Acc. to Simpl. In Aristot. categorias 10, 101 (ed. C. Kalbfleisch [1907], 401, 7 f.) Chrysipp. also did not reckon the ὑποχυθέντες among the τυφλοί.
[4] Herzog.
[5] Corp. Hippocraticum esp. ref. to connections between bodily ailments, esp. eye inflammations, Hippocr. Προρρητικόν, II, 18-20 (Littré, IX, 44-48), impairment of vision, Gal. De usu partium, 10, 6 (Kühn, 3, 785-791) etc., and blindness, which is only rarely denoted by τύφλωσις Hippocr. Ἀφορισμοί, VI, 56 (Littré, IV, 576) or τυφλωθῆναι Hippocr. Κωακαὶ προγνώσιες, 218 (V, 632); conversely Hippocr. De Flatibus, 14 (CMG, 101, 2 f.) can use τυφλός in a transf. sense.
[6] Weinreich, 120 f.
[7] Ibid., 189-194; Esser, 36-74; Lesky, 436-8.

motives. Usually the men who follow this custom are barbarians or tyrants. The principle of *talio* is mentioned in Diod. S., 12, 4, 4; Diog. L., I, 57. The best example of self-blinding it that of Oedipus, who tries to atone for his incest with Iocaste in this way ἑαυτὸν τυφλώσαντα, Dio Chrys. Or., 11, 8; Soph. Oed. Tyr., 1268-79 etc. [8] There are also many examples of the punishment in myths, esp. by goddesses. Acc. to a common legend Helena is supposed to have punished Stesichorus with blindness for his railing poems Plat. Phaedr., 243a; Paus., III, 19, 11-13; Dio Chrys. Or., 2, 13; 11, 40; Tiresias suffered the same fate at the hands of Hera for insulting her, Ovid Metam., 3, 316-335; Luc. Dial. mortuorum, 28, 3 etc., or of Athena for seeing her in her bath, Callim. Hymn., 5, 82; Anth. Graec., 9, 606; Nonnus Dionys., 5, 337-342. [9] Men who attended the feast of the goddess Bona Dea also went blind, Cic. De domo suo, 105.

4. There are only a few not very precise literary ref. to the outward appearance of the blind. [10] The pt. to catch attention was their uncertain, groping gait, which was a favourite simile → 275, 19 ff. The blind stretch out their hands to find support, Plut. Alex. Fort. Virt., II, 4 (II, 336 f.). They feel their way along a wall by touch, Apoll. Rhod., II, 198 f. They use a stick to guide their feet, Callim. Hymn., 5, 127, cf. σκίπων... με ἀνήγαγεν, Anth. Graec., 9, 298: ἐπὶ σκήπτρῳ, Soph. Oed. Tyr., 455 f. They are glad of the help of a guide ἡγεμών, Eur. Phoen., 1616 or χειραγωγός, Plut. Comm. Not., 10 (II, 1063b); Artemid. Onirocr., I, 48 to protect them from accidents on the streets. Relatives esp. acted as such. The blind seer Tiresias says to his daughter ἡγοῦ πάροιθε, θύγατερ· ὡς τυφλῷ ποδὶ ὀφθαλμὸς εἶ σύ, Eur. Phoen., 834 f., and the blind Oedipus to Antigone κάθιζέ νύν με καὶ φύλασσε τὸν τυφλόν, Soph. Oed. Col., 21. But cf. also οἱ γὰρ βλέποντες τοῖς τυφλοῖς ἡγούμεθα, Aristoph. Pl., 15, τοῖς τυφλοῖσι γὰρ αὕτη κέλευθος ἐκ προηγητοῦ πέλει, Soph. Ant., 989 f., cf. τυφλὸν ὁδήγει, Ps.-Phocylides, 24 (Diehl³, II, 93) and Ovid Tristia, V, 6, 31. In antiquity Antigone is a symbol of more than ordinary care of and devotion to the blind, for in spite of all the threats of Creon and the pleading of her blind father to leave him she simply says τίς σε τυφλὸν ὄντα θεραπεύσει, πάτερ; Eur. Phoen., 1686.

Economic distress imposed another duty toward the blind. A few were well off, but the majority lived in dire poverty. Many blind men are beggars ἀλήμονες, Anth. Graec., 9, 13b, cf. ἀλητεύων, 9, 12. [11] To be sure, some are also singers and musicians, Hom. Od., 8, 62-64, poets, e.g., Homer, Suid., 251 (Adler, III, 526, 8 ff.), seers, e.g., Tiresias (→ n. 15) and philosophers, e.g., Democr. (→ 273, 8 ff.), even jurists, Cic. Tusc., V, 38, 112, statesmen, Valerius Maximus Dictorum factorumque memorabilia, VIII, 7, 4 f. [12] and kings, Hdt., II, 137, 1; Dio C., 51, 23, 4, [13] but such vocations were closed to the mass of less talented blind people. [14]

5. Although it was thought that the shutting out of sense impressions could lead to a more essential life, moral betterment was not *eo ipso* expected through blindness, and it

[8] On Democr.' blinding of himself → 273, 8 ff.
[9] For other instances cf. Esser, 150-170; Lesky, 437 f.
[10] Esser, 74-9.
[11] Cf. Diog. L., VI, 56; Ps.-Hdt. Vit. Hom., 13; Juv., I, 4, 115-8; Mart., 4, 30. Perhaps one may gather from the last ref. that the blind posted themselves at places of luxury where they could esp. count on sympathy or crowds, temples, markets etc. Blindness could be simulated to arouse sympathy, cf. Aristoph. Pl., 665 f. on the "blind" Neocleides, who is a better thief than those who have sight. But advantage could be taken of the blind, e.g., by palming off second-rate goods on them, Athen., 6, 7 and → n. 21.
[12] Ed. O. Holtze (1892).
[13] An advantage is that not only a stronger sense of touch but also a better memory compensates for failing sight: ἡ δὲ μνήμη... τυφλῶν ὄψις ἡμῖν ἐστιν, Plut. Def. Orac., 39 (II, 432b); Aristot. Eth. Eud., VIII, 14, p. 1248b, 1 ff.
[14] On the suffering of blind slaves breaking stones or mining brass and silver cf. Xenoph. Vect., 4 and Esser, 106 f.

was seen that it might even augment wickedness in a man, Plin. (the Younger) Ep., 4, 22; cf. also Plut. Suav. Viv. Epic., 12 (II, 1095a). There was a gen. conviction that blindness increased mental perception. Acc. to Aristot. De sensu et sensibilibus, 1, p. 437a, 15 f. the blind are more understanding than the deaf and dumb. Many think only the blind can be poets, Dio Chrys. Or., 36, 10; to be a seer esp. is linked to seeing with the inner eye and not seeing with the outer: Tiresias becomes a seer only when blinded, [15] cf. also Euenios, Hdt., IX, 93 f.; Phineus supposedly lost his sight so that he could be a seer, Apoll. Rhod., II, 178-184; Orph., 671-6 (Abel) etc. The philosopher Democritus even blinded himself so that the spirit should be distracted as little as possible, Cic. Fin., V, 29, 87. [16] But all this does not alter the fact that inability to see the world's beauty through loss of sight was for antiquity one of the worst blows of fate that could smite a man, Luc. Indoct., 2, and those threatened by "dreaded blindness" (Cic. Tusc., V, 38, 111) were plunged into despair. The eye was in antiquity the chief organ of sense → V, 319, 12 ff. Thus the blind were pitied, Epicharmus Fr., 34 (Diels, I, 203); Aristot. Eth. Nic., III, 7, p. 1114a, 25 ff. The κρείσσων γὰρ ἦσθα μηκέτ' ὢν ἢ ζῶν τυφλός (Soph. Oed. Tyr., 1368) of the chorus regarding Oedipus' self-blinding certainly corresponds to a widespread conviction, cf. Suet. Caes., II, 53, 3; Quintus Smyrnaeus Posthomerica, [17] 1, 76-82. Yet the philosophers still believe that the fate of blindness, for all its severity, should not overwhelm a man. Acc. to Plato only non-philosophers bewail loss of sight with vain lamentation, Tim., 47b. Sen. De Providentia, 5, 1 f. cannot regard blindness as a real evil, for, since it is sent by God, one can accept it, cf. also Cic. Fin., V, 28, 84. Finally the deaf and blind are not to be bewailed acc. to Diogenes of Sinope, but those who do not bear the pack (a play on ἀνάπηρος "maimed" and ἄνευ πήρας "without pack"), i.e., who do not lead the life of the sage who has no wants, Diog. L., VI, 33.

6. In gen. it was regarded as impossible to cure blindness. There were perhaps operations for cataracts as early as the 3rd cent. B.C. [18] and doctors sought with some success to prevent and treat incipient blindness, but only the supernatural powers of a god-like man or a god, not the skill of the physician, could restore sight to the blind. Acc. to Tac. Hist., IV, 81, e.g., the *remedium caecitatis* is one of the *multa miracula, quis caelestis favor et quaedam in Vespasianum inclinatio numinum ostenderetur.* [19] Even Apollonius of Tyana is not reported to have cured the blind. [20] The statement in Hippocr. Προρρητικόν, II, 19 (Littré, IX, 46): ἀδύνατοι ὠφελέεσθαι καὶ χρόνῳ καὶ τέχνῃ εἰς τὸ βλέπειν, is

---

[15] Acc. to Ovid Metam., 3, 316-8; Luc. Dialogi mortuorum, 28 etc. he received his talent as a seer from Zeus in consolation for being blinded by Hera; acc. to Callim. Hymn., 5, 121 f.; Nonnus Dionys., 5, 337-342 etc. Athena gave it to him in compensation for making him blind. But Oedipus' reproach against Tiresias: ὅστις ἐν τοῖς κέρδεσιν μόνον δέδορκε, τὴν τέχνην δ' ἔφυ τυφλός, shows that even a blind seer can be blind in his art, Soph. Oed. Tyr., 388 f.

[16] Cf. Cic. Tusc., V, 39, 113 f. with other examples of blind philosophers: Diodotus and Asclepiades. Cic. leaves open the factuality of Democr.' self-blinding.

[17] Ed. A. Zimmermann (1891).

[18] K. Kalbfleisch, "Ein griech. Zeugnis f. den Starstich aus dem 3. vorchr. Jhdt.," *Philol. Wochenschr.,* 44 (1924), 1037-9 ref. to the Stoic Chrysippus (→ n. 3); cf. P. Knapp, "Zur Frage d. Staroperation bei d. alten Griechen," *Klinische Monatsblätter f. Augenheilkunde,* 84 (1930), 277 f.; Esser, 32. Note what is said in Chrysipp.: τυφλότης μὲν γὰρ ἐξ ὄψεως γίνεται οὐκέτι μέντοι καὶ ἀνάπαλιν, cf. also Cels. Med., VII, 7, 6.

[19] A feature common in other miracles of healing, that the sick persons had been given up by doctors, does not occur in the case of the blind since it can be taken for granted here, Weinreich, 116; cf. 96, 195-7. Cf. also Paus., IV, 12, 10: ἀναβλέψαι παραλόγως δὴ μάλιστα ἀνθρώπων.

[20] J. Hempel, "Untersuchungen z. Überlieferung v. Apollonius v. Tyana," *Beiträge z. Religionswissenschaft,* 4 (1920), 45, n. 1. But cf. Philostr. Vit. Ap., III, 39: Another, blind in both eyes, was sent away seeing perfectly (of an Indian sage).

true not only of the injury mentioned there. [21] Curing blindness was conceivable only as a miracle or not at all. Sceptical voices sought to explain the curing of one born blind by Hadrian, not as a miracle, but rationalistically as an illusion, Aelius Spartianus De vita Hadriani, 25, 3 f. (Script. Hist. Aug., I, 26) [22] but they count for little against the many witnesses to the power of belief in miracle even in respect of blindness. The most familiar example is the frequently attested story of the healing of a blind man by Vespasian, Tac. Hist., IV, 81; Suet. Caes., VIII Vespasianus, 7, 2 f.; [23] Dio C., 66, 8. [24] But most such cures were done directly by miraculous acts of the gods. Often the punishment of making blind (→ 272, 4 ff.) was reversed (cf. ὁ τρώσας ἰάσεται, Suet. Caes., V, 43) when those made blind by divine penalty acknowledged their guilt, gave evidence of penitence, promised amendment, and visited the temple for prayer or sacrifice. [25] Athena restores sight to Ilus, Plut. Parallela Graeca et Romana, 17 (II, 309 f.), Apollo to Eurypylus, Paus., VII, 19, 7, cf. also Isis, Ovid Ep. ex Ponto, I, 1, 51-58. A certain Aischines who climbed a tree and looked into the abaton of Epidauros fell down and went blind as a punishment but besought the god for healing and his sight was restored, Epidaurus-W. 11 → n. 4. Sometimes sight is restored when a specific command of the deity is carried out, Paus., VII, 5, 7 f. and X, 38, 13, or other conditions are met. [26] But the miraculous healing power of the gods is not limited to reversing the penalty of blindness in penitent sinners. Isis can give sight to all who have lost it and who turn to her for healing, and she heals those whom physicians are powerless to aid, Diod. S., 1, 25, 5. Acc. to an epigram of Antipater of Thessalonica Artemis on the same day grants to a woman who is blind and childless both a child and also the "keenly sought rays of sweet light," Anth. Graec., 9, 46. Sight could also be had through other deities: Serapis Diog. L., V, 76; Athena Paus., III, 18, 2; Plut. De Lycurgo, 11 (I, 46a); Apophth. Lac., 7 (II, 227b), Bona Dea (cf. the inscr. re luminibus restitutis, CIL, VI, 68, 5 f.). Polymestor, made blind by Hecabe, prays to Helius εἴθε μοι ὀμμάτων αἱματόεν βλέφαρον ἀκέσαι' ἀκέσαιο τυφλόν, "Αλιε, φέγγος ἐπαλλάξας, Eur. Hec., 1067 f. But Aesculapius has special

---

[21] There were warnings against eye-doctors who negligently or with intent to deceive caused blindness. On the Nicarchus epigrams Anth. Graec., 9, 112. 115 (the doctor makes blind) and 9, 117. 126; Luc. Indoct., 29 cf. F. J. Brecht, "Motiv- u. Typengeschichte d. griech. Spottepigramms," Philologus Suppl., 22, 2 (1930), 48. On the comparison with Antiph. Fr., 259 (FAC, II, 294) → 277, 7 f. But negligence and hazarding of sight were condemned by strict medical ethics, cf. Esser, 33-5.

[22] Cf. the mocking of the deception of the priests of Aesculapius, Aristoph. Pl., 716-747. Similarly the blinding of Thamyris is not regarded as a miracle in Paus., IV, 33, 7, so Apollodorus Bibliotheca, I, 17 (ed. R. Wagner, Mythographi Graeci, I [1894]); Diod. S., 3, 67, 3; Dio Chrys. Or., 13, 21; Plut. De cohibenda ira, 5 (II, 455d), but as the result of an injury.

[23] Since it is both so close to the NT healings of the blind, and yet also so distant from them, the story may be given in context: "Vespasian, who against all expectation had mounted the throne as a wholly new prince, still lacked presence and divinely confirmed majesty. But this was granted to him. Two men of the people, one blind and the other lame, came before his tribunal and asked for healing. This had been promised them by Serapis in a dream. The god had promised that Vespasian would restore sight to the blind if he moistened his eyes with his spittle and the leg of the lame man if he would deign to touch it with his heel. Vespasian himself hardly believed this would happen. Hence he could not make up his mind to try. Finally, persuaded by his friends, he publicly attempted both and lo, not without success," M. Heinemann and R. Till, Sueton, Cäsarenleben⁴ (1951), 445.

[24] The MSS accounts differ: τὸν ὀφθαλμοῖς προσπτύσας (R Steph) or πηλὸν προσπτύσας (V C).

[25] Cf. Ovid Ep. ex Ponto, I, 1, 57 f.: saepe levant (sc. caelestes) poenas ereptaque lumina reddunt, cum bene peccati paenituisse vident.

[26] Cf. Hdt., II, 111: Stesichorus receives back his sight only after composing the palinodia → 272, 5 ff. When the blind Hermon of Thasos is cured at Epidauros and does not pay thanks ἴατρα the god makes him blind again: [ὁ θεός νιν] ἐποίησε τυφλὸν αὖθις, and only after coming back and sleeping again in the chamber of healing is he cured, Epidaurus-Wunder, 22 (Herzog), cf. also 55.

importance, Apart from Aristoph. Pl., 636 etc. and Ael. Arist. Or., 18 (Dindorf) [27] cf. esp. the votive tablets with ἰάματα on the walls of the eastern abaton at Epidauros → III, 197, 9 ff. The extant fr. of these ['Ἰά]ματα τοῦ 'Απόλλωνος καὶ τοῦ 'Ασκλαπιοῦ tell of many cures of the blind, [28] e.g., Epidaurus-Wunder, 65. Alketas of Halieis in a dream sees the god come to him and open his eyes with his fingers ἐδόκει οἱ ὁ θεὸς ποτελθὼν τοῖς δακτύλοις διάγειν τὰ ὄμματα, 18. Most instructive is the parody in Aristoph. Pl., 727-745, [29] where a cure is depicted with typical features. The suddenness of the miracle βλέπειν ἐποίησε τὸν Πλοῦτον ταχύ, Pl., 746 is stressed elsewhere in cures, cf. ἐξαπίνας, Epidaurus-Wunder, 65 → 288, 15. Apart from direct cures the god could also use or command medicine or magic as instruments. [30] Aesculapius, e.g., orders for a blind soldier a three-day cure with an ointment made of the blood of a white cock and honey, Ditt. Syll.[3], III, 1173, 15-18 (after 138 A.D.). Or by touching the miraculous altar the blind man himself receives the power to cure his blindness by the laying on of his own hands. [31]

III. τυφλός and τυφλόω in Comparisons and the Transferred Sense.

1. In view of the common nature and drastic effect of blindness in the life of antiquity it is no surprise that the blind man often figures in comparisons and proverbial expressions, though the no. is not as high as that of passages with the transf. sense. The *tertium comparationis* is usually the deficient vision or unsteady gait of the blind man. The fact that the ὀξὺ ὁρῶν and not the τυφλός is employed as watcher and keeper is used in Plat. Resp., VI, 484c as a comparison to show that philosophers ought to lead the state. A pointless dialectical method is like the uncertain gait of the blind ἡ γοῦν ἄνευ τούτων μέθοδος ἐοίκοι ἂν ὥσπερ τυφλοῦ πορείᾳ, Plat. Phaedr., 270d e, cf. also Plut. Galb., 1 (I, 1053); Alex. Fort. Virt., II, 4 (II, 336 f.) and Luc. Calumniae non temere credendum, 1, where ignorance is compared to a blind man walking in the dark. The cynic lifts up his voice and cries like Socrates: ἰὼ ἄνθρωποι, ποῖ φέρεσθε; τί ποιεῖτε, ὦ ταλαίπωροι· ὡς τυφλοὶ ἄνω καὶ κάτω κυλίεσθε· ἄλλην ὁδὸν ἀπέρχεσθε τὴν οὖσαν ἀπολελοιπότες, ἀλλαχοῦ ζητεῖτε τὸ εὔρουν καὶ τὸ εὐδαιμονικόν, ὅπου οὐκ ἔστιν, οὐδ' ἄλλου δεικνύοντος πιστεύετε, Epict. Diss., III, 22, 26. But other pts. of comparison are the pain and unalterability of blindness. Because ἄγνοια obscures things, darkens the truth and casts a shadow over every life, we are like those who wander in the dark μᾶλλον δὲ τυφλοῖς ὅμοια πεπόνθαμεν, Luc. Calumn. non temere cred., 1. To claim one can put ἐπιστήμη in a soul without it is acc. to Plat. Resp., VII, 518c just as much an illusion as οἷον τυφλοῖς ὀφθαλμοῖς ὄψιν ἐντιθέναι. Another common comparison is with the blind leading the blind: οὐδὲ ὁ ἄτεχνος τὸν ἄτεχνον (sc. διδάσκει) ὥσπερ οὐδὲ τυφλὸν ὁδηγεῖν δύναται τυφλός, Sext. Emp. Pyrrh. Hyp., III, 259; Math., I, 31. Acc. to Xenoph. Mem., I, 3, 4 Socrates regarded it as μωρία not to follow divine signs ἢ εἴ τις

---

[27] The ref. here is to a cure through the water of an Aesculapius fountain.

[28] Here again there is unbelief and mockery, against which Epidaurus-Wunder, 3 and 4 expressly warn. Thus the one-eyed Ambrosia of Athens laughs at cures and regards it as improbable and impossible that the lame and blind should be whole again, but in a dream in the ἱερόν the healing god comes to her and promises that if as ὑπόμναμα τᾶς ἀμαθίας she gives a silver pig as a votive offering she will be healed. He then slits her eye, drops in a φάρμακον, and the next day she is cured, Epidaurus-Wunder, 4.

[29] Weinreich, 95-100, 108 f.

[30] This applies esp. to cures in the imperial period where the god no longer appears and acts directly in a dream but orders ointments and magical rites to bring about the cure. The Aesculapius of this epoch is no longer the wizard and miraculous healer of the ancient *iamata* but a helper who advises and informs, Weinreich, 111. This does not imply doubt as to the possibility of divine aid. Rather men in this period expected each and everything from divine help, 113.

[31] Weinreich, 63 f., 115 f.; E. J. Edelstein and L. Edelstein, *Asclepius* (1945), I, 250 f.; II. 147. 153. 167. 169. 171.

αὐτὸν ἔπειθεν ὁδοῦ λαβεῖν ἡγεμόνα τυφλὸν καὶ μὴ εἰδότα τὴν ὁδὸν ἀντὶ βλέποντος καὶ εἰδότος. [32] But one who is physically blind may know the way intellectually, cf. Valerius Maximus Dictorum factorumque memorabilia (→ n. 12), VIII, 13, 5; Soph. Oed. Col., 1588 f.

Proverbial expressions which ref. to the fate and conduct of the blind are mostly paradoxical. Very common is καὶ τυφλῷ γε δῆλον: "even a blind man can see this," Plat. Resp., VIII, 550d, also V, 465d.; Menand. Fr., 98a (Koerte); Stob. Ecl., V, 1052, 12; Aristoph. Pl., 48 f. Also common is τυφλότερος τῶν σπαλάκων, Sib., 1, 370, also Cleomedes De motu circulari corporum caelestium, II, 1, 86; [33] cf. τυφλότερος ἀσπάλακος, Apostolius Centuria, 17, 35 (CPG, II, 695); Diogenianus Centuria, VIII, 25 (I, 309). τυφλῷ κάτοπτρον χαρίζῃ is also paradoxical, Plut. Proverbia, 27 (I, 346).

2. There are far more instances of metaphorical usage. τυφλός is used a few times for other parts of the body of the blind or for acts or objects, e.g., the hand, Eur. Phoen., 1699 etc., foot, Hec., 1050 etc., stick, Ion, 744, tapping, Plut. Suav. Viv. Epic., 12 (II, 1095a). Blindness is usually transf. to other spheres of sense or life, e.g., intellectual or moral blindness, and almost always with a negative accent. [34] It is noteworthy that though there is ref. to philosophical blindness antiquity does not speak of religious blindness except in Gnostic texts. The lit. and transf. meanings often merge: τυφλὸς τά τ᾽ ὦτα τόν τε νοῦν τά τ᾽ ὄμματ᾽ εἶ, Soph. Oed. Tyr., 371, or one can speak of the eye of the soul being blind, τυφλὸς γὰρ εἶ τῆς ψυχῆς τὸν ὀφθαλμόν, Luc. Vit. Auct., 18. Acc. to M. Ant., IV, 29 the man who falls asleep with his intellectual eye is blind τυφλὸς ὁ καταμύων τῷ νοερῷ ὄμματι. Spiritual blindness can be set in juxtaposition with physical sight. Thus Plato in Phaed., 99e fears he may be blind in ψυχή when he sees things with the bodily eyes.

a. τυφλός is most commonly used in the sphere of the capacity for knowledge and function of understanding. In a much quoted passage the νοῦς is the only sense not struck by blindness: νοῦς ὁρῆι καὶ νοῦς ἀκούει· τἆλλα κωφὰ καὶ τυφλά, Epicharmus Fr., 12 (Diels, I, 200), cf. Plut. De sollertia animalium, 3 (II, 961a); Alex. Fort. Virt., 3 (II, 336b); Max. Tyr., 11, 10 etc. All the sharper, then, is the complaint when it is called blind, cf. Soph. Oed. Tyr., 371 (→ line 18 f.) and also Procl. De providentia, 23, 12. [35] Blind and obtuse can be synon.; [36] esp. it is said of the masses: τυφλὸν δ᾽ ἔχει ἦτορ ὅμιλος ἀνδρῶν ὁ πλεῖστος, Pind. Nem., 7, 23 f., cf. Schol., [37] ad loc.: ἀνόητον. [38] The soul, too, is often called blind. Acc. to Democr. Fr., 72 (Diels, II, 159, 9 f.) the desires of the soul, when set strongly on something, blind it to all else αἱ ... ὀρέξεις τυφλοῦσιν εἰς τἆλλα τὴν ψυχήν. On the τυφλοῦσθαι of the ψυχή cf. also Plat. Phaed., 99e → lines 22 ff. Luc. Amores, 22 speaks of the τυφλὴ ἀναισθησία τῆς ψυχῆς. But more often than specific capacities and organs, man himself is called τυφλός to the degree that for some reason certain realities or spiritual phenomena do not come within his vision or his mental eye is blinded and he cannot see the nature of things any more. The classical example is that man's field of vision does not embrace destiny, and so in some sense every man is blind, i.e., as regards the future. It is said of what takes place in the

---

[32] Cf. Aśvaghoṣa, Buddhacaritam, 9, 64 (ed. R. Schmidt [1923]): "For how can one walk acc. to the faith of another like a blind man who is led in the darkness by another blind man?"

[33] Ed. H. Ziegler (1891), 158.

[34] An exception is the Indian saying: "He who ... is blind when it comes to looking on another woman ... triumphs as a great man in the world," O. v. Böhtlingk, Indische Sprüche. Sanskrit u. Deutsch, III² (1873), 5010.

[35] Ed. H. Boese (1960).

[36] τυφλόν τι κἀνόητον, Menand. Fr., 488 (Koerte), cf. Plut. Comm. Not., 10 (II, 1063a b). Plat. Phaed., 96c can use τυφλοῦμαι and ἀπομανθάνω as par.

[37] Ed. A. B. Drachmann (1927).

[38] Cf. οἱ πολλοὶ ἀποτετύφλωσθε, Epict. Diss., I, 16, 19.

future: τυφλόν ἐστι τοῦ μέλλοντος ἄνθρωπος, Plut. De Solone, 12, 10 (I, 84e), [39] cf. also τὸ δ᾽ ἐς αὔριον αἰεὶ τυφλὸν ἔρπει, Soph. Fr., 536 (TGF, 261), cf. also Stob. Ecl., V, 837, 14 - 838, 2. But usually not all men, only some groups are called blind, esp. in the moral and philosophical field. In the main the wealthy, lovers, the non-philosophical and non-experts are τυφλοί. Primarily it is wealth that robs men of intellectual and moral vision: τυφλοὺς τοὺς ἐμβλέποντας εἰς ἑαυτὸν δεικνύει, Menand. Fr., 77 (Koerte). [40] Wealth is like a poor optician πάντα βλέποντας παραλαβὼν τυφλοὺς ποιεῖ, Antiph. Fr., 259 (FAC, II, 294), cf. Stob. Ecl., V, 757, 5 f. The lover is also blind, [41] e.g., in relation to the beloved: τυφλοῦται περὶ τὸ φιλούμενον ὁ φιλῶν, Plat. Leg., V, 731e, [42] cf. Anth. Graec., 12, 106. Love of self blinds to oneself and esp. to one's faults, Gal. in Hippocr. epidemiarum librum sextum, IV, 14 (CMG, 217, 19 f.). [43]

In philosophy the earliest instance is Parmen. Fr., 6. 7 (Diels, I, 233, 5): κωφοὶ ὁμῶς τυφλοί τε are those for whom being and non-being are the same and not the same. Epict. Diss., II, 24, 19 calls philosophical ἄγνοια blindness: He who does not know who he is, why he has come into being, in what world he lives and with what companions, what is good and evil etc. κωφὸς καὶ τυφλὸς περιελεύσεται δοκῶν μέν τις εἶναι, ὢν δ᾽ οὐδείς. [44] The man who fears want and trembles lest he lack τὰ ἀναγκαῖα is also τυφλός, III, 26, 3. But it is said of the cynic: ὅπου δὲ προαίρεσις καὶ χρῆσις τῶν φαντασιῶν, ἐκεῖ ὄψει ὅσα ὄμματα ἔχει, ἵν᾽ εἴπῃς ὅτι "Αργος τυφλὸς ἦν πρὸς αὐτόν, III, 22, 103. τυφλός is esp. common among the sceptics. The wisdom of the sceptic Pyrrho boils down to knowing nothing, seeing nothing and hearing nothing, hence to being spiritually καὶ τυφλὸς ἅμα καὶ κωφός, Luc. Vit. Auct., 27. For the sceptic in Sext. Emp. Math., I, 302 the γραμματικός is blind to the διαλεκτικὰ θεωρήματα of Chrys., the μαθηματικά of Archimedes, and even more so the περὶ αὐτῶν γραφέντα ποιήματα. [45] Naturally one can also be blind to many other things in life, e.g., art, science and the beauty of the world, cf. Philodem. Philos. De Musica, 31 (p. 101); Plat. Resp., III, 411c d; Soph. Oed. Tyr., 389.

In Gnosticism [46] it is esp. unredeemed non-gnostics, dazzled by the world, who are blind [47] if and so long as they have not attained to saving *gnosis*. Like the favourite images of sleep and drunkenness, blindness is also used fig. for the state of ἀγνωσία in

---

[39] Cf. τῶν δὲ μελλόντων τετύφλωνται φραδαί, Pind. Olymp., 12, 9.

[40] Cf. Stob. Ecl., V, 757, 8 f. and Plat. Ep., 7, 335b, also ἆρ᾽ ὄλβος αὐτοῖς ὅτι τυφλὸς συνηρετεῖ (Stob. συνηρεφεῖ), τυφλὰς ἔχουσι τὰς φρένας καὶ τῆς τύχης; Eur. Fr., 776 (TGF Suppl. [1964], 606), cf. Stob. Ecl., V, 754, 9 f. Apart from riches, fear Liv., 44, 6, 17 and the libidines Cic. Tusc., I, 30, 72 can make blind.

[41] For the opp. view cf. Philostr. Ep., 52: τυφλοὶ οἱ μὴ ἐρῶντες.

[42] Quoted also Plut. De capienda ex inimicis utilitate, 7 (II, 90a). Acc. to Lucretius De rerum nat. (ed. J. Martin [1934]), IV, 1153 the *cupidine caeci* overlook all possible physical or spiritual blemishes.

[43] Cf. τυφλότης εἰς τὴν τῶν ἰδίων ἁμαρτημάτων γνῶσιν, Gal. de peccatorum dignotione, 5, 28 (CMG, 61, 11 f.).

[44] Epict. Diss., I, 18, 6 f. takes up again τὸν πεπλανημένον καὶ ἐξηπατημένον περὶ τῶν μεγίστων καὶ ἀποτετυφλωμένον... τὴν γνώμην τὴν διακριτικὴν τῶν ἀγαθῶν καὶ τῶν κακῶν with τὸν τυφλὸν καὶ τὸν κωφόν, cf. also Diss., II, 20, 37.

[45] Cf. also τετυφλωμένος καὶ κεκωφωμένος πρὸς τὰ τεχνικὰ θεωρήματα (sc. ὁ ἄτεχνος), Sept. Emp. Math., I, 34.

[46] Since the Gnostic texts of Nag Hamadi rest in part on ancient religious traditions and later Chr. Gnosticism shows the same basic view as pre-chr. Gnosticism, these texts are used here even though they are to be related in detail to the NT → 278, 21 f.

[47] Naturally the διάνοια (→ n. 52) or ψυχή of the non-gnostic as well as the man himself can be called blind or blinded, cf. ψυχὴ γάρ, μηδὲν ἐπιγνοῦσα τῶν ὄντων μηδὲ τὴν τούτων φύσιν μηδὲ τὸ ἀγαθόν, τυφλώττουσα δέ..., Corp. Herm., 10, 8. But the drop of light sent into the world is acc. to the will of Sophia chained by the chain of its incapacity for knowledge in order that this matter may be evident to the whole world in wretchedness because of its pride, blindness and ignorance, Sophia of Jesus Christ, 103, 17 - 104, 6, ed. W. C. Till, TU, 60 (1955), 247 f.

Gnosticism. But τυφλός and τυφλόω are not so commonly attested as σκότος, πλάνη, ὕπνος, μέθη etc., though they bear much the same sense. Thus in Ev. Veritatis [48] 29, 32 - 30, 15 ignorance is successively described as dream, sleep and blindness. In P. Oxy., I, 3 (= Gospel of Thomas, [49] 28) μεθύω and τυφλὸν εἶναι occur together in the same sense. If *gnosis* means salvation, τυφλός, denoting ignorance, embraces lostness and perdition. The Woe of Pist. Soph., 141 (GCS, 241, 25-32) is pronounced on the children of men who grope around like blind people in the dark. Up to the coming of light brought by the Revealer there is no difference between men, but "when (ὅταν) the light comes the one with sight sees the light and the blind man is the one who remains in darkness," Gospel of Philip, 56 (112, 5-9). [50] If everything here seems to be under predestination and both blindness and sight are foreordained, [51] other passages stress the fact that the Gnostic Redeemer has come to free the blind from their blindness: "But I have come to lead them out of their blindness that I may show to all the God who is over all," Sophia of Jesus Christ (→ n. 47), 125, 19 - 126, 5. Hence "blessed (μακάριος) is he who has opened the eyes of the blind," Ev. Veritatis (→ n. 48), 30, 14-16. Elsewhere full freeing from blindness is evidently expected only at death when the soul, freed from the body, leaves this world of darkness entirely. [52] "For (τότε) they will shed blind thought, trample (καταπατέω) the death of the powers (ἐξουσία) and rise up to boundless light...," The Nature of the Archons, 145, 5-8, [53] cf. Corp. Herm. Fr., 23, 41. The more important it is, then, that man who is already in this life on the upward way should not trust "blind leaders of the blind," Gospel of Thomas (→ n. 49), 34 in a sharper version based on Mt. 15:14. [54]

b. But what blinds man as well as man himself can be called τυφλός. Wealth esp. is blind, Plut. Apophth. Lac., 5 (II, 226 f.), [55] cf. Menand. Fr., 77 (Koerte). It is a τυφλὸς φίλος, ἀλλοπρόσαλλος ("inconstant," "capricious"), Anth. Graec., 15, 12. What makes blind can be personified in myth and τυφλός can be an attribute of the gods. Since the distribution of riches in this world seems to be arbitrary and unfathomable to men, the god of riches is himself thought to be blind. Thus from Hipponax. Fr., 29 (Diehl³, III, 89) [56] one finds the proverbial Πλοῦτος τυφλός. In the Schol. on Eur. Or., 256 [57] this is explained in relation to the prosperity of the unworthy, [58] but in Aristoph. Pl., 88-93 it is traced back to Zeus himself who smote Plutos with blindness in his youth to prevent him from distributing riches fairly, though cf. also 403 f. and 494 f. [59] The

[48] Ed. M. Malinine *et al.* (1956).

[49] Ed. A. Guillaumont *et al.* (1959).

[50] Ed. W. C. Till, *Patristische Texte u. Studien,* 2 (1963).

[51] Cf. Gospel of Philip (→ n. 50), 57 (112, 10-12): "Blessed (μακάριος) is he who exists before he came into being. For (γάρ) he exists who was and will be."

[52] R. McL. Wilson, *The Gospel of Philip* (1962), 116 obviously construes 56 (112, 5-9) thus. In the First Apoc. of James the Gnostic (James) learns from the Revealer (Jesus) that he will attain to Him who is (God) and be identical with Him when he rejects blind διάνοια and casts off the chain of the σάρξ which encircles him, cf. A. Böhlig and P. Labib, "Kpt.-gnost. Apok. aus Codex V von Nag Hammadi im Kpt. Museum zu Alt-Kairo," *Wissenschaftl. Zschr. der Martin-Luther-Univ. Halle-Wittenberg* (1963), Special Vol. 37.

[53] J. Leipoldt - H. M. Schenke, "Kpt.-gnost. Schr. aus d. Pap Cod v. Nag-Hamadi," *Theol. Forschung,* 20 (1960), 69-78.

[54] Cf. W. Schrage, "Das Verhältnis d. Thomas-Ev. zur synpt. Tradition u. zu den kpt. Evangelienübersetzungen. Zugleich ein Beitrag zur gnost. Synoptikerdeutung," ZNW, Beih. 29 (1964), 87 f.

[55] Cf. ἄπλουτον γὰρ οἴονται τὸν πλοῦτον καὶ τυφλὸν ἀληθῶς καὶ ἀδιέξοδον, Plut. Quaest. Conv., V, 5 (II, 679b).

[56] Cf. Amphis Fr., 23 (FAC, II, 322). In Luc. Tim., 20 Plutos is called οὐ τυφλὸς μόνον, ἀλλὰ καὶ χωλός.

[57] Ed. E. Schwartz (1887).

[58] Cf. τυφλὸς ὁ Πλοῦτος: ἐπὶ τῶν ἀναξίως εὐπραγούντων, Macarius Centuria, VIII, 60 (CPG, II, 223).

[59] Cf. also Luc. Tim., 27: He who does not see Plutos in his blindness is himself blind.

god of love is also τυφλός: τυφλὸς δ' οὐκ αὐτὸς ὁ Πλοῦτος, ἀλλὰ καὶ ὠφρόντιστος "Ερως, Theocr. Idyll., 10, 19 f., but we read less commonly of the blindness of Eros than of Plutos. [60] The same applies to the blind god of war Ares, Soph. Fr., 754 (TGF, 308): τυφλὸς ... οὐδ' ὁρῶν "Αρης συὸς προσώπῳ πάντα τυρβάζει κακά. [61] But there are many ref. to blind chance, fate or the god of fate: τυφλόν γε καὶ δύστηνόν ἐστιν ἡ Τύχη, Menand. Fr., 463 (Koerte), [62] cf. Diog. L., V, 82; Soph. Trach., 1104; Plut. Fort., 2 (II, 98a).

Gnostic texts also have the idea of the blind god or blind evil powers within a dualistic understanding of the world and redemption. Acc. to the Gospel of Philip (→ n. 50), 34 (107, 18 ff.) the πονηραὶ δυνάμεις are "blind throught the Holy Spirit," for they do not see their ministry to the saints. The blindness of the chief of the ἐξουσίαι consists in the pride and ignorance with which he regards himself as the only god, Nature of the Archons (→ n. 53), 134, 27. A voice out of incorruptibility teaches him better: "'Thou dost err (πλανᾶσθαι), Samael,' which means the god of the blind. His thoughts were blind," 135, 1 ff., cf. 142, 25 f. [63] Samael is interpreted as "blind god" as well as "god of the blind," Work without Title, 151, 15 ff. → n. 63. [64] Acc. to the same work Sophia Zoe mocks the decision of the ἐξουσίαι to make man in the words: "They are blind in ignorance," 161, 14 ff. It is plain that for all the mythological variation the blindness of the powers always consists here in darkness and ignorance as to their true role in the cosmologico-soteriological drama. Only in the Gnostic emanation theory ref. to in Iren. Haer., II, 17, 8 is the blindness of the emanation from *nous* defined as *ignorantia Patris*.

B. τυφλός and τυφλόω in the Septuagint.

I. Usage.

1. The adj. occurs some 20 times in the LXX for עִוֵּר and once for עַוֶּרֶת at Lv. 22:22, but mostly the word is used as a noun, often as a gen. attribute of ὀφθαλμοί, Is. 29:18; 35:5; 42:7; Job 29:15, more fully οἱ ἐν τῷ σκότει καὶ οἱ ἐν τῇ ὁμίχλῃ ὀφθαλμοὶ τυφλῶν in Is. 29:18. Par. is οὐχ ὑπαρχόντων ὀφθαλμῶν in Is. 59:10, and the opp. is βλέπων in Ex. 4:11. The OT uses τυφλός lit. in Ex. 4:11; Dt. 27:18, in fig. comparison Dt. 28:29; Is. 59:10 etc. and transf. Is. 42:18; 43:8 etc.

2. The verb occurs in the LXX only 3 times (for עִוֵּר), lit. only pass. τυφλοῦσθαι "to go blind," "to lose one's sight," Tob. 7:6 (only S, not BA), transf. act. "to dazzle" Wis. 2:21, [65] pass. ἐτυφλώθησαν οἱ δοῦλοι τοῦ θεοῦ, Is. 42:19. More common in the LXX is the compound ἐκτυφλόω which occurs 8 times and act. means lit. "to make blind" Ex. 21:26; 4 Βασ. 25:7; Jer. 52:11, while pass. ἐκτυφλοῦμαι is used for the extinction of sight Tob. 2:10; Zech. 11:17, [66] transf. Is. 56:10.

---

[60] Cf. A. S. F. Gow, *Theocritus*, II (1950), 198 f.

[61] A. C. Pearson, *The Fr. of Sophocles*, III (1917), 838; cf. Plut. Amat., 13 (II, 757b).

[62] Cf. Stob. Ecl., I, 91, 2 and 98, 10. Cf. ἡ πρόνοια τυφλόν τι κἀσύντακτόν ἐστιν, Nicostratus Fr. 19, 4 f. (CAF, II, 225). Then life can be called blind τυφλόν γε καὶ δύστηνον ἀνθρώπου βίος, Stob. Ecl., V, 827, 14. Cic. Lael., 15, 54: *non enim solum Fortuna caeca est, sed eos etiam plerumque efficit caecos, quos complexa est*.

[63] Cf. Act. Andr. et Matth. 24: καὶ ἀποκριθεὶς ᾿Ανδρέας εἶπεν τῷ διαβόλῳ· Πρὸς τί οὖν ἐπικέκλησαι ᾿Αμαήλ (Cod B II Ω read Σαμαήλ); οὐχ ὅτι τυφλὸς εἶ, μὴ βλέπων πάντας τοὺς ἁγίους; on Sammael for Satan in Judaism cf. Str.-B., Index, *s.v.*

[64] A. Böhlig and P. Labib, "Die kpt.-gnostische Schrift ohne Titel aus Codex II von Nag-Hammadi," *Deutsche Akad. d. Wissenschaften zu Berlin, Institut f. Orientforschung, Veröffentlichung* Nr. 58 (1962), 49.

[65] ἐτύφλωσεν (S) or ἀπετύφλωσεν (A B) γὰρ αὐτοὺς ἡ κακία αὐτῶν.

[66] The LXX uses other words as well as τυφλοῦμαι and ἐκτυφλοῦμαι for the same thing. These refer either to blindness or weak sight in old age: ἠμβλύνθησαν οἱ ὀφθαλμοὶ αὐτοῦ (sc. Isaac) τοῦ ὁρᾶν, Gn. 27:1, cf. ἠμβλυώπουν ... ἀπὸ γήρους αὐτοῦ, 3 Βασ.

II. τυφλός in the Literal Sense.

1. Apart from blindness ἀπὸ τοῦ γήρους the OT mentions other reasons cf. Tob. 2:10; Ex. 21:26. It also bears witness to the cruel practice of blinding; Samson's eyes were put out by the Philistines, Ju. 16:21, cf. also 1 Βασ. 11:2. Nebuchadnezzar had Zedekiah blinded, 4 Βασ. 25:7; Jer. 39:7; 52:11. The OT itself sets this under the *talio*, Ex. 21:24; Lv. 24:20; Dt. 19:21. [67] In Israel, too, blindness was a very severe handicap. [68] In Is. 35:5 f. the blind are the first in a list of companions in suffering often mentioned together: the blind, the deaf, [69] the lame, [70] and the dumb; in Ex. 4:11, however, they come last after the dumb, the deaf and the lame. [71] Sometimes the list of physical defects [72] is extended, Lv. 21:18; 22:22; cf. also Dt. 15:21.

2. The blind are specially protected in the laws of Israel. Blindness is among the μῶμοι (→ IV, 829, 18 ff.) which disqualify from sacrifice and from exercise of the priestly office, Lv. 21:18 ff. [73] But this cultic discrimination [74] does not imply rejection. God as Helper and Protector of the helpless demands humane treatment of the blind. One should not "curse the deaf or put a stumbling block before the blind" καὶ ἀπέναντι τυφλοῦ οὐ προσθήσεις σκάνδαλον, Lv. 19:14. Acc. to the ancient Dodecalogue of Shechem the man "who misleads a blind man on the road" is cursed ἐπικατάρατος ὁ πλανῶν τυφλὸν ἐν ὁδῷ, Dt. 27:18. In contrast Job in his final speech can confess with pride ὀφθαλμὸς ἤμην τυφλῶν, Job. 29:15. [75]

14:4; οἱ δὲ ὀφθαλμοὶ Ισραηλ ἐβαρυώπησαν ἀπὸ τοῦ γήρους καὶ οὐκ ἠδύνατο βλέπειν, Gn. 48:10; also 1 Βασ. 3:2 of Eli; οὐκ ἠμαυρώθησαν οἱ ὀφθαλμοὶ αὐτοῦ (sc. Moses), Dt. 34:7; οἱ ὀφθαλμοὶ αὐτοῦ (sc. Eli) ἐπανέστησαν καὶ οὐκ ἔβλεπεν, 1 Βασ. 4:15. It is uncertain what the main cause was (cataract etc.), Lesky, 434 f. with bibl. Several other expressions in prose and poetry are also used by the LXX for going blind: σκοτισθήτωσαν οἱ ὀφθαλμοὶ αὐτῶν τοῦ μὴ βλέπειν, ψ 68:24; ἐξέλιπον ἐν δάκρυσιν οἱ ὀφθαλμοί μου, Lam. 2:11, cf. ψ 68:4 and Dt. 28:65; καμμύσει τοὺς ὀφθαλμούς, Is. 29:10; οἱ ὀφθαλμοὶ αὐτῶν ῥυήσονται ἐκ τῶν ὀπῶν αὐτῶν, Zech. 14:12.

[67] Hempel, 248, n. 3.

[68] How hard their lot often was may be seen from the fact that the blind Samson in prison had to grind at the mill for the Philistines, Ju. 16:21.

[69] τυφλός occurs with κωφός at Lv. 19:14; Is. 29:18; 43:8.

[70] τυφλός occurs with χωλός at Lv. 21:18; 2 Βασ. 5:6, 8 (twice); Job 29:15.

[71] פסח in the HT (LXX) is analogous to many other passages which have עור and פסח together, Jer. 31:8; Dt. 15:21; 2 Βασ. 5:8, to be emended to פסח, Friedmann, 48, n. 1.

[72] On physical defects in Israel cf. L. Köhler, *Der hbr. Mensch* (1953), 39; Hempel, *passim*.

[73] Acc. to the rules about the condition of sacrifices the animal too is not to be blind, Lv. 22:22; there is a similar rule in the Law about the first-born of cattle, Dt. 15:21. Mal. 1:8 accuses unworthy priests of offering blind and defective beasts to God in sacrifice.

[74] It is debatable how far this applies to the obscure passage in 2 Βασ. 5:6-8 dealing with the capture of Jerusalem by David. It is plain that v. 6: οὐκ εἰσελεύσει ὧδε, ὅτι ἀντέστησαν οἱ τυφλοὶ καὶ οἱ χωλοί expresses the disdain of the Jebusites for the besiegers: Jerusalem is strong enough to be defended even by the blind and the lame. But the understanding of v. 8 is difficult. In v. 8a the ref. seems to be to David's hatred for the blind and the lame, though cf. K. Budde, *Die Bücher Samuel, Kurzer Hand-Komm. zum AT*, 8 (1902), *ad loc.*, who puts in a "not"; "David's soul does not hate the lame and the blind; they are not worthy opponents for him." "Truly David's heroes found lame and blind on the walls, all the Jebusites were as lame and blind to him." Perhaps v. 8a was added later: διὰ τοῦτο ἐροῦσιν· τυφλοὶ καὶ χωλοὶ οὐκ εἰσελεύσονται εἰς οἶκον κυρίου (κυρίου being thus an addition of the LXX). H. Windisch, "Kleine Beiträge z. evang. Überlieferung," ZNW, 18 (1917/18), 81 f. thinks that acc. to this proverb the blind and the lame were probably not allowed in the house because they brought bad luck. He cites G. Dalman, "Zion, die Burg Jerusalems," PJB, 11 (1915), 43 f. But it is not certain that the LXX first introduced exclusion from the temple. The HT might be forbidding access to the later temple (Budde, *ad loc.*), cf. Lv. 21:18.

[75] On leading the blind cf. also Ju. 16:26.

3. Since God as Creator fashions man acc. to His plan, blindness is not just a natural phenomenon or a matter of fate but God Himself is ultimately behind it τίς ἔδωκεν στόμα ἀνθρώπῳ καὶ τίς ἐποίησεν δύσκωφον καὶ κωφόν, βλέποντα (→ n. 17) καὶ τυφλόν; οὐκ ἐγὼ ὁ θεός; God asks Moses in Ex. 4:11. [76] Whereas there are no indications that blindness is regarded as a punishment for sin, in Dt. 28:28 f. blindness with madness and confusion is threatened as a penalty for those who do not listen to the Word of the Lord and keep His commandments. [77] As God sends blindness, so as the Almighty and All-merciful He can do what man cannot do (Ep. Jer., 36), namely, enable the blind to see again; He opens the eyes of the blind, κύριος σοφοῖ τυφλούς, ψ 145:8. [78]

III. τυφλός in the Transferred Sense.

1. Especially in the eschatological proclamation of the OT prophets blindness plays a gt. role in fig. expressions and comparisons and in the transf. sense, whether the theme be judgment or salvation. Zeph. 1:17 says of the gt. Day of the Lord, which is a day of trouble and distress, also of darkness, obscurity and night (v. 15), that men will wander around on this day like blind men, a fig. of speech for anxiety and confusion. In Is. 59:9 f. the sin of the people is branded and after a list of offences we read: ὑπομεινάντων αὐτῶν φῶς ἐγένετο αὐτοῖς σκότος, μείναντες αὐγὴν ἐν ἀωρίᾳ περιεπάτησαν. ψηλαφήσουσιν ὡς τυφλοὶ τοῖχον καὶ ὡς οὐχ ὑπαρχόντων ὀφθαλμῶν ψηλαφήσουσιν· καὶ πεσοῦνται ἐν μεσημβρίᾳ ὡς ἐν μεσονυκτίῳ, cf. Dt. 28:28 f.

2. In Dt. Is. most of the passages bear a transf. sense, usually with ref. to the exiles who are blind to God's words and deeds and cannot interpret aright what is going on around them. [79] The transf. sense is esp. incisive when the charge of spiritual blindness is paradoxically contrasted with the fact that they are not physically blind. Thus Is. 43:8 speaks of the blind people which yet has eyes; [80] "You blind, look and see," Is. 42:18. Blind watchers (par. dumb dogs) is an oxymoron in 56:10; man's being τυφλός [81] means "that they are all without knowledge" (LXX οὐκ ἔγνωσαν φρονῆσαι).

3. But it is above all in the prophetic message of salvation that the promise of the curing of blindness is a favourite theme of eschatological hope → 290, 5 ff. It is not always clear whether the meaning is lit. or transf. and often the two intertwine. Thus Is. 35:5: τότε ἀνοιχθήσονται ὀφθαλμοὶ τυφλῶν, does not merely ref. to fig. healing but also to the end of physical defects. [82] Is. 29:18, on the other hand, probably speaks only metaphorically: In that day the deaf will hear the words of Scripture and the eyes of the blind will see out of darkness and obscurity. In a special way the Servant of the Lord — himself blind in 42:19 [83] yet the light of the peoples in 42:6 — is ordained to open blind eyes, to lead the bound out of prison, and those who sit in darkness out of

---

[76] On Ps. 69:23 cf. A. Lods, "Les idées des Israélites sur la maladie, ses causes et ses remèdes," ZAW Beih., 41 (1925), 181 and 186.
[77] Cf. also Gn. 19:11; 4 Βασ. 6:18; Zech. 12:4.
[78] Cf. also the passive formulation in Is. 35:5 → 281, 29 ff.
[79] Herrmann, 12 f.
[80] Cf. also Is. 6:9 f. and on this Herrmann, 10 f. and F. Hesse, "Das Verstockungsproblem im AT," ZAW Beih., 74 (1955), 59-69; 83-91.
[81] So 'Α, Σ and Θ: LXX: ἐκτετύφλωνται.
[82] So B. Duhm, Das Buch Js., Handkomm. AT, 3, 1⁴ (1922), K. Marti, Das Buch Js., Kurzer Hand-Comm. z. AT, 10 (1900) and R. Kittel, Der Prophet Js., Kurzgefasstes exeget. Hndbch. z. AT, 5 (1898), ad loc.
[83] Acc. to Fohrer Is. 42:19 f. is an addition criticising Dt. Is. as the Servant of the Lord and subjecting his message to the Law. LXX has the plur. οἱ παῖδές μου. Acc. to Kittel, op. cit., ad loc. the servant is blind in order to make clear the antithesis to the normal, acc. to Duhm, op. cit., ad loc. "because he experiences divine revelations in word and deed and yet has not paid heed or understood, as further developed in vv. 23 ff."

the dungeon, 42:7. God Himself will be a guide to the blind on the way: ἄξω τυφλοὺς ἐν ὁδῷ, ᾗ οὐκ ἔγνωσαν, 42:16; [84] here again the lit. and fig. senses flow into one another. The decisive passage taken up in the NT is 61:1, where the messenger of joy says: εὐαγγελίσασθαι πτωχοῖς ἀπέσταλκέν με, ἰάσασθαι τοὺς συντετριμμένους τῇ καρδίᾳ, κηρύξαι αἰχμαλώτοις ἄφεσιν καὶ τυφλοῖς ἀνάβλεψιν. [85]

C. τυφλός and τυφλόω and Their Equivalents in Judaism apart from Philo.

I. Usage.

For τυφλός in the Talmud and Midr. one finds apart from Hbr. עוּר or Aram. עֲוִיר, עֲוִירָא esp. סוּמָא, whether for one who is born blind or for one who goes blind, in one eye or both. bMQ, 8a, e.g., speaks of someone blind in one eye סוּמָא בְּאַחַת מֵעֵינָיו, bTaan., 21a of someone blind in both eyes סוּמָא מִשְׁתֵּי עֵינָיו, bBek., 44a of both: עֵוֵר בֵּין סוּמָא בִּשְׁתֵּי עֵינָיו בֵּין סוּמָא בְּאַחַת מֵעֵינָיו "A blind man is both, blind in both eyes or blind in one eye."

II. In the Literal Sense.

1. Jewish statements about blindness are mostly within the framework of the OT and sometimes are *expressis verbis* interpretations of specific OT verses. OT sayings which ref. to the blind in the lit. sense are in part, however, taken metaphorically → 284, 31 ff. Judaism, too, thought there was no greater trouble and no greater or severer suffering than blind eyes, Midr. Ps. 146, 5 on 146:8. To bring out the full severity of the fate of the blind they are compared to the dead, bNed., 64b. [86] The blind man is euphemistically called סַגְיָא נְהוֹרָא "one who sees clearly" in Lv. r., 34, 14 on 25:29; jPea, 5, 5 (19a, 27); jKet., 11, 3 (34b, 66). [87] This is not making light of the lot of the blind but indicating that his spiritual light is all the brighter. [88] Above all he is supposed to have a sharper memory and enhanced intellectual powers; we often hear of famous blind scholars, e.g., R. Shesheth, R. Joseph etc. [89]

As in the OT (→ 280, 11 ff.), so in Judaism the blind are protected by law. Attempts were made in daily life to alleviate their lot by considerate treatment. Along with the fig. interpretation of Dt. 27:18 (→ 280, 16 ff.) the intention of the v. is retained even in the lit. sense. The blind know they will be protected from stones, holes, thorns and nettles, T BQ, 2, 12 (349); bMeg., 24b. [90] In other ways, too, the blind were looked after by others, → 283, 10 ff. We often hear of blind beggars, cf. bTaan., 21a; jKet., 11 (34b, 66). [91]

---

[84] Cf. also Jer. 31:8: "Behold, I will bring them from the north country, and gather them from the coasts of the earth, and with them the blind and the lame, the woman with child and her that travaileth with child ... " Here LXX Ιερ. 38:8 obviously read בְּמוֹעֵד פֶּסַח for בָּם עִוֵּר וּפִסֵּחַ. The HT shows that the blind in the lit. sense are not left behind by God on the return of His people.

[85] τυφλοῖς ἀνάβλεψιν for סְנוּרִים or עוּרִים is due to LXX misreading of אֲסוּרִים (cf. 'A, Σ and Θ: τοῖς δεδεμένοις). But τυφλοί makes sense for אֲסוּרִים since in the OT פקח is mostly used for the opening of the eyes, cf. Str.-B., II, 156 and J. Ziegler, *Untersuchungen zur LXX d. Buches Js.* (1934), 171 [Bertram].

[86] Str.-B., I, 524. Cf. bAZ, 5a; Gn. r., 71 on 30:1; Ex. r., 5 on 4:19; Tanch. תּוֹלְדוֹת, 7.

[87] Cf. also רוֹאֵי הַחַמָּה "seeing the sun," Ned., 3, 7, מִפְתְּחָא "one whose eyes are opened," jShab., 1, 3 (3a, 46); jSheq., 2, 6 (47a, 47), מְאוֹר עֵינַיִם "light of the eyes," bChag., 5b.

[88] A. Wünsche, *Neue Beiträge zur Erläuterung d. Ev. aus Talmud u. Midrasch* (1878), 126.

[89] For stories of the blind R. Shesheth bEr., 11b, Friedmann, 23-5, also 27 f., 56.

[90] Str.-B., I, 525.

[91] Cf. also Gn. r., 17 on 2:18 and Lv. r., 34 on 24:39. Acc. to jSheq., 5, 6 (49b, 32 f.) a blind man gave thanks in the fine words: Thou hast shown mercy to one who is seen but does not see; may the one who is not seen but does see be gracious to thee.

2. The blind were freed from some duties of the ceremonial law and had other privileges as well. [92] R. Jehuda liberated them from the penalties of scourging, excommunication and death, bBQ, 86b. Acc. to Chag., 1, 1 they did not have to appear before the Lord at feasts, cf. Men., 9, 8, while acc. to bBer., 30a they did not have to repeat the Eighteen Benedictions facing Jerusalem. Nor did they have to read the Haggada, though R. Joseph and R. Shesheth did, bPes., 116b. The Mishnah rules: The blind may recite and translate the shema-benedictions, Meg., 4, 6, but he may not read from the Torah, come before the ark or lift up his hands in priestly benediction; [93] cf. also 1 QSa 2:3-6. [94] He is not dispensed from keeping other statutes. Thus he must not go out with his stick on the Sabbath, T Yom Tob, 3, 17 (206), cf. bYom Tob, 25b. In some circumstances others must help the blind to fulfil the obligations of the Law. Thus acc. to Nidda, 2, 1 a blind girl must have someone to help her with the law of purification and to watch over her in the ritual bath. The blind are not to be witnesses or judges, bBB, 12b; 128a; T. Sanh., 5, 4 (423). Nor can they accuse their wives out of jealousy, bSota, 27a. Nor can they hand their wives bills of divorce, Git., 2, 5, cf. bGit., 23a. That they are finally subject to Jewish concepts of achievement and merit may be seen from a saying ascribed to the blind R. Joseph, bBQ, 87a, cf. bQid., 31a.

3. As sin and sickness are related (→ IV, 1092, 10 ff.), cf. bShab., 32b-33a, so acc. to the Jewish view blindness is a divine punishment (→ 281, 4 ff.; 284, 17 f.), cf. bTaan., 21a; Nu. r., 4, 20 on 4:16; bChag., 16a. Significant here is the familiar statement of the *ius talionis* that a man is punished where he sins. Samson sinned with his eyes and hence his eyes were put out, i.e., his blindness was a punishment for his lust, bSota, 9b; cf. Prv. 30:17, also bAZ, 65a. He who shams blindness will become blind, Pea, 8, 9; T. Pea, 4, 14 (24); he who cries out like a blind man: "Give to the blind," will one day have to do so in earnest, bKet., 68a; AbRNat, 3.

What about children born blind? The question of theodicy raised here is answered by a ref. either to the parents' sin or to God's prescience, though the sin of infants in the womb was also regarded as possible. [95] Acc. to R. Jochanan b. Dahabai (c. 180) children are blind because they (sc. the parents in sexual intercourse) look on that place. [96, 97] R. Josua b. Korcha, asking how God's righteousness can be reconciled with the fact that deaf and dumb and lame and blind people come into the world, answers by referring to God's wise foreknowledge which seeks to prevent a full development of evil impulses, Tanna debe Eliyyahu Zuta, [98] 23. [99]

4. Mythological and superstitious ideas also occur in explanation of blindness. Thus it may be traced back to demons, bShab., 108b; 109a. [100] Abimelech made Sarai blind by imprecation, bBQ, 93a. Isaac went blind when the tears of sorrowing angels fell into his eyes as he lay bound on the altar, Gn. r., 65 on 27:1. Abraham on the same occasion lifted up his eyes on high and saw the shechinah, and this resulted in blindness, *loc. cit.* and PREl, 32. But blindness may also be viewed as a divine blessing. When Esau takes daughters of Canaan to wife and Isaac is troubled by it, God says: "I blind his eyes so that he may not see and his worry may not increase, hence his eyes became blind," Tanch. תולדות, 8. A man who has an undutiful son or pupil will finally lose his sight, i.e., by

---

[92] For other examples Mak., 2, 3; T Mak., 2, 9 (440); bSota, 27a etc.

[93] Acc. to Str.-B., IV, 151 and Tanch. תולדות, 7.

[94] Acc. to 1 QM 7:4 the blind are also excused from the holy war.

[95] On this idea cf. Str.-B., II, 528 f.

[96] Acc. to Preuss, 314, 533 the *vulva* sexually understood.

[97] Cf. Str.-B., II, 529: "He who looks on the heel of a woman, his children will have physical defects," Kalla, 1, cf. Str.-B., I, 299.

[98] Ed. M. Friedmann (1902).

[99] Friedmann, 29 f.

[100] Examples in Friedmann, 12 and 52. On the demon Bath-Chorin who makes blind and deaf cf. Str.-B., IV, 517 and 525.

making him blind God will keep him at home so that he will not have to hear the jeering of people, Gn. r., 65 on 27:1. Naturally this kind of view does not rule out observation and discussion of the *causae proximae* of blindness, [101] e.g., the weakness of age, poison (→ lines 11 f.), injury, bBQ, 91a, blinding (→ 283, 20 ff.), [102] psychological causes, or the resultant weeping, bShab, 151b, Nu. r., 18, 22 on 16:35.

Normally Judaism does not expect any cure (→ 273, 25 ff.) for blindness [103] unless an angel prescribes the correct therapy as in the case of blind Tobit who, acc. to the direction of the angel Raphael, who at God's behest also heals R. Mathiya b. Cheresh (→ n. 102), is cured by his son with the gall of a fish, Tob. 11:7 ff. Miracles of healing are rare in Judaism (→ III, 129, 17 ff.), but there are instances of the blind being cured. The Midr. tells how by eating plants a blind man regained sight and one who had it went blind, Lv. r., 22 on 17:3; Nu. r., 18, 22 on 16:35; Midr. Qoh., 1 on 5:9, also by dipping in Miriam's well, Nu. r., 18 on 16:35. Ps.-Philo Antiquitates Biblicae, [104] 25, 12 tells of other cures: *Si quis de Amorreis caecus erat, ibat et ponebat oculos suos super eum* (sc. a very bright precious stone) *et recuperabat lumen.* Another cure is connected with penal blinding, bBM, 85b. [105] Acc. to Ep. Ar., 316 the tragedian Theodektes became blind when he wanted to put something from Scripture in a play. Suspecting his blindness was a punishment from God, he prayed to Him and later was cured. In this connection one finds a good deal of magic, superstition, and magical practice, e.g., bGit., 69a. [106]

In the Messianic age of salvation or renewal of the world Judaism expected the end of sickness and death and the healing of the blind: "Everything God has smitten in this world He will then restore. Thus the blind will be healed," Gn. r., 95 on 46:28. [107] This was based on prophetic promises for the last time and on God's proven deeds. [108] Acc. to M. Ex., 4, 9 on 20:18 [109] the end time corresponds to that of Moses, for there were no blind at the receiving of the Torah. Nor were there any blind, lame or deaf among the Israelites at the exodus. Because the Law was perfect, God did not will to give it to a defective people and hence He healed them, Pesikt., 106b. The blind have a certain priority in eschatological restoration: "When he comes to heal the world, he heals the blind first" (lit. here, as what follows shows, cf. also → line 33 f.), Midr. Ps., 146, 5 on 146:8.

III. The Transferred Sense of Blind.

1. When there is fig. or transf. ref. to blindness and its abolition in the eschaton, e.g., when Is. 35:5 is taken spiritually, the primary hope is that of the removing of blindness to the Torah, cf. Midr. Ps., 146, 5 on 146:8. The Messiah will be "the light of the

---

[101] Cf. Friedmann, 10-16; Preuss, 314 f.

[102] There are not many instances of this. Herod had the Pharisaic R. Baba b Buta blinded with spiky thorns, bBB, 4a. Acc. to bSanh., 27a there was blinding in a murder in the time of R. Abba b. Jakob. Various rabbis blinded themselves, R. Mathiya b. Cheresh to escape the temptations of the devil who had taken the form of a woman, Midr. Asereth ha-Dibberoth, 7 (A. Wünsche, *Aus Israels Lehrhallen,* IV [1909], 101 f.). This rests on the idea that the eye mediates sin, e.g., Midr. Cant., 2 on 4:1; Nu. r., 10 on 6, 2, cf. other examples in Str.-B., I, 302 on Mt. 5:29. But the blind are not immune from sin: "Is there not a blind man who can commit every abomination in the world?" S. Nu., 115 on 15:39.

[103] Preuss, 316.

[104] Ed. G. Kisch (1949).

[105] Cf. Str.-B., II, 267. It is uncertain whether the healing spittle of a son of Abuha mentioned in bBB, 126b has curative power in eye-diseases (so Rashi).

[106] Str.-B., I, 524 f.; Friedmann, 19.

[107] Cf. A. Wünsche, *Der Midr. Gn. r.* (1881), 469; cf. Tanh. ויגש, 8 and Midr. Qoh., 1, 4.

[108] Pesikt., 76a, 17 f. says with ref. to God: "I will open the eyes of the blind; he has done this of old, *v.* 2 K. 6:17," Str.-B., I, 594; cf. Lv. r., 27 on 22:27.

[109] Str.-B., I, 594 f.; Friedmann, 1 and 48.

peoples to open the eyes of the house of Israel which are as blind men to instruction . . . ,"
Tg. Is. 42:6 f. [110]

But blindness to the Law is not the only way or possibility of being spiritually blind,
as exposition of some OT passages shows. Whereas LXX and Tg. O. obviously take
Dt. 27:18 lit., Tg. J. I and II ref. it to an alien who is like a blind man, cf. also Tg. J. II on
Lv. 19:14. S. Lv., 11, 2 on 19:14 takes blind to mean unsuspecting and for BM, 5, 11 it
usually means ignorant. bPes., 22b et al. take Lv. 19:14 to ref. to leading astray and
incitement to sin. [111] The Rabb. often say that corruption makes blind on the basis of
Ex. 23:8 and Dt. 16:19, cf. Gn. r., 65 on 27:1; Tanch. תולדות, 8. M. Ex., 5, 20 on 23:8
takes blind to mean arbitrary exposition of the Torah rather than ignorance of it. In
Gn. r., 53 on 21:18 f. it seems that the unbeliever is called blind. But since the believer is
also the righteous man acc. to the Law, the sinner is blind, Ex. r., 30 on 22:1. In gen. the
transf. use is rare in Rabb. Judaism, as may be seen esp. in comparison with Philo → lines
35 ff. The lit. sense is easily predominant.

The Dead Sea Scrolls also offer few instances of the transf. use of blind. In a long
list of what is proper to the spirit of wrong (transgression, lying, folly etc.) one finds in
1 QS 4:11 "the tongue of blasphemy, blindness of eyes (וזרון עינים), deafness of ears,
stiffness of neck and hardness of heart." Acc. to Damasc., 16:2 f. (19:14 f.) the period
of Israel's blindness is fixed exactly. In Damasc. 1:9 (1:6) blindness is a figure for Israel's
search after God and inability to find Him without the Teacher of Righteousness. [112] In
Test. XII τυφλόω is often used transf. for the blinding of the νοῦς S. 2:7, the διάνοια
Jud. 11:1, the ψυχή 18:6, the διαβούλιον τῆς ψυχῆς 18:3. Even when there is ref. to
τυφλοῦν τοὺς ὀφθαλμούς the par. σκοτοῦν τὴν διάνοιαν shows that the metaphorical
sense is in view, D. 2:4. But the subj. of τυφλοῦν are not just vices like πορνεία and
φιλαργυρία Jud. 18:2, 3 or τὸ διαβούλιον τῆς νεότητος 11:1, but also τὸ πνεῦμα τοῦ
θυμοῦ D. 2:4 or indeed ὁ ἄρχων τῆς πλάνης καὶ τὸ πνεῦμα τοῦ ζήλου S. 2:7, cf.
J. 19:4. But the last of the seven spirits of error given man by Beliar πνεῦμα σπορᾶς
καὶ συνουσίας . . . τὸν νεώτερον ὁδηγεῖ ὥσπερ τυφλὸν ἐπὶ βόθρον, R. 2:8 f.

2. Jewish literature is not rich in proverbs or proverbial sayings in which the blind
figure. When someone hits on the right by chance it is said: "like a blind man at the
window," bBB, 12b; bNidda, 20b. Other examples are: "Where the blind are, a person
with one eye is said to see clearly," Gn. r., 30 on 6:9. "When a shepherd is angry with
his flock, he makes the bell-wether blind," bBQ, 52a. "A doctor at a distance is a blind
eye," bBQ, 85a.

D. Philo. [113]

1. Easily the majority of the instances of τυφλός in a transf. sense occur in Philo,
who uses the term almost exclusively for moral, philosophical and religious blindness.
Only seldom does he ref. to lit. blindness, Spec. Leg., IV, 198 (on the basis of Dt.
27:18). [114] More numerous are comparisons with the actions and destiny of the blind.

---

[110] Str.-B., I, 69. Cf. also Aggadath Bereshith (Warsaw, 1876), 69, 1 (47b) in Str.-B., I,
596: "In this world sins brought it about that the Israelites became deaf to the Torah and
blind so that they did not see the shechinah"; but in the Messianic age God will open the eyes
of the blind.

[111] Str.-B., III, 310-312, cf. also BM, 5, 11; bMQ, 17a and Str.-B., IV, 299.

[112] Cf. on this F. Nötscher, "Gotteswege u. Menschenwege in d. Bibel u. in Qumran,"
Bonner Bibl. Beiträge, 15 (1958), 81 f.; G. Jeremias, "Der Lehrer d. Gerechtigkeit," Stud. z.
Umwelt d. NT, 2 (1963), 160 f.

[113] Jos. only rarely has τυφλός or τυφλόω in a transf. sense: τυφλὸς ἦν τὸν νοῦν
᾿Απίων, Ap., 2, 142; τῇ διανοίᾳ τετυφλωμένον, Ant., 8, 30.

[114] Cf. also Virt., 5, where Philo reckons blindness πήρωσις et al. among the things
that are by common consent hard to bear δυσυπομόνητα.

A partial judge, e.g., must blunder along like a blind man with no stick or guide on which to rely, Spec. Leg., IV, 70, cf. also Virt., 172; Spec. Leg., III, 79. The ungodly are not unlike the blind, groping about at mid-day as in deep darkness, Rer. Div. Her., 250. The man who no longer has even the slightest particle of *nous* tumbles unexpectedly like a blind man and will continually slip and involuntarily fall, Deus Imm., 130. Sometimes one finds with blindness similar comparisons like deep sleep, Cher., 62, cf. also Virt., 172.

In the metaphorical use Philo mostly follows Plat. Leg., I, 631c and uses τυφλός to characterise πλοῦτος, the material treasures and goods of external wealth. [115] The crowd follows blind riches in the belief τὰ τοῦ λεγομένου τυφλοῦ πλούτου μόνα ἢ μάλιστα εὐδαιμονίας αἴτια, Spec. Leg., I, 25; but the true wealth which "sees," and which puts off the unreasoning, consists of perfect virtues and has its adornment and values in the soul, Fug., 19; Spec. Leg., II, 23. With πλοῦτος both ἀφροσύνη and also αἴσθησις and διάνοια are called blind: τυφλὸν καὶ ἄγονον καλῶν ἀφροσύνη, Som., II, 192, cf. Migr. Abr., 38, where the ἄφρονες are called τυφλοί. ἀμαθία is a τυφλὴ δέσποινα, Migr. Abr., 18. Absolutising of αἴσθησις is also condemned as blindness, indeed, αἴσθησις itself is τυφλή, Vit. Mos., II, 199. In Leg. All., III, 108 the one who leads the blind astray (Dt. 27:18) is wicked lust τυφλὸν γὰρ φύσει ἡ αἴσθησις ἅτε ἄλογος οὖσα, ἐπὶ τὸ λογικὸν ἐξομματοῦται "because it is bereft of the eye of thought." Hence blind αἴσθησις follows a blind leader, perception, 109. Strictly the blind should follow "seeing" thought, but νοῦς or ψυχή is deceived and follows blind leaders, 110. [116] Philo often speaks of τυφλὴ διάνοια or τυφλοὶ διάνοιαν: οἱ τυφλοὶ διάνοιαν are, e.g., those who are content with the lit. sense and do not take biblical texts allegorically, opp. μετελθεῖν ἐπὶ τὰς τροπικὰς ἀποδόσεις, Conf. Ling., 190 f., cf. Som., I, 164 opp. ὀξυδερκήσειν ... ὡς φυσιογνωμονεῖν καὶ μὴ μόνον τοῖς ῥητοῖς ἐφορμεῖν. Το neglect εὐσέβεια καὶ ὁσιότης is also to make the διάνοια blind, Spec. Leg., I, 54; Agric., 81. Finally Philo can call ordinary men blind because they choose evil rather than good, the ugly rather than the beautiful, the wrong rather than the right, the perishable rather than the imperishable, Rer. Div. Her., 76. Those who neither seek nor find but are content with the blind facts (τὰ τυφλά) of life create for themselves a τυφλὸν καὶ κωφὸν καὶ ἀνόητον καὶ πάντη πηρὸν βίον ἀβίωτον, Fug., 122 f.

2. Philo seldom uses τυφλόω. Only the νοῦς of the lover is discerning in relation to the beloved, πρὸς δὲ τὰ ἄλλα πάντα ἴδιά τε καὶ κοινὰ τυφλούμενον, Vit. Cont., 61. He who does not consider ὁ ἀπερίσκεπτος, blinded in the intelligence of the soul, διάνοιαν τυφλωθείς, with which alone he might understand being, has never even glimpsed this, but with his sense organs he perceives bodies in the world and regards these as the cause of all that comes to be, Ebr., 108, cf. also Leg. All., III, 231. Finally polytheistic idolaters are τυφλώττοντες περὶ τὸ θέας ἄξιον, Decal., 67.

E. τυφλός and τυφλόω in the New Testament.

I. Usage.

1. τυφλός occurs in the NT some 36 times in the lit. and 12 in the transf. sense; it also occurs in a parable. Only Mk. has it exclusively in the lit. sense, which is the more surprising in that he is familiar with the phenomenon of spiritual blindness. [117] Lk. has τυφλός twice in the parable in 6:39, also in the ambivalent quotation in 4:18

---

[115] Cf. Fug., 19; Som., I, 248 par. to deaf fame and unfeeling corpulence ἀναίσθητον εὐσαρκίαν, Sobr., 40; Rer. Div. Her., 48; Agric., 54; Praem. Poen., 54; Vit. Mos., I, 153; Jos., 258.
[116] Blind leaders of the blind (κεναὶ δόξαι) also occur in Virt., 7.
[117] Cf. Mk. 4:12; 8:18 and J. B. Tyson, "The Blindness of the Disciples in Mark," JBL, 80 (1961), 261-8; E. Schweizer, "Die theol. Leistung d. Mk.," EvTh, 24 (1964), esp. 344-8.

with ref. to the physically blind, cf. the one instance in Ac. at 13:11. But Mt., in addition to stories of healing the blind and general reports, also uses the word quite considerably in a transf. sense, esp. in the attack on the scribes and Pharisees. The lit. and transf. senses merge in familiar ambivalence in Jn. 9. Paul has the word only in the metaphor in R. 2:19. 2 Pt. 1:9 uses it fig., and Rev. 3:17 is also to be taken thus.

2. τυφλόω occurs three times in a transf. sense in the NT.

II. Blindness in the Literal Sense.

1. In most cases the NT uses τυφλός as a noun and in accordance with current practice elsewhere the ref. is to those blind in both eyes. Par. is μὴ βλέπων in Jn. 9:39, cf. μὴ βλέπων τὸν ἥλιον in Ac. 13:11. Removing of blindness is denoted by ἀναβλέπω in Mk. 10:51 f.; Mt. 11:5; Jn. 9:18 [118] etc., ἀνάβλεψις in Lk. 4:18, ἀνοίγω τοὺς ὀφθαλμούς or ἀνοίγομαι with subj. ὀφθαλμοί in Mt. 9:30; 20:33; Jn. 9:10 etc., βλέπω in Mt. 12:22; 15:31; Lk. 7:21; Jn. 9:25, ἐμβλέπω τηλαυγῶς ἅπαντα in Mk. 8:25.

2. The NT sheds little light on the social, legal and religious status of the blind. Interest does not focus on blindness as such, but on its cure. Most instances are thus found in accounts of healing → 288, 8 ff. On the other hand it is important and instructive, especially in comparison with the spiritualising and almost exclusively transferred use of Philo (→ 285, 35 ff.), that the blind are not the object of allegorising speculation but their plight is taken with full seriousness in its corporeality. The cry for help of the blind Bartimaeus ἐλέησόν με (Mk. 10:47) is quite traditional (cf. Ps. 6:2; 9:13 etc.) and yet it brings into fine and impressive focus the NT view of blindness → II, 485, n. 102. When Mk. 10:46 and Jn. 9:8 describe the blind as προσαίτης this is in keeping with the reality of the day (→ 272, 30 f.; 282, 30 f.), cf. ἐπαιτῶν in Lk. 18:35. As things were, begging was for many blind people the only means of livelihood, cf. also Lk. 14:13 f., 21.

The association of the blind with the deaf and lame [119] is traditional (→ 271, 18 f.; 280, 6 ff.) and may be due sometimes to summarising or OT quotation, yet it describes correctly the way in which these groups were linked by fate. Mt. 12:22 (which seems to be secondary as compared with Lk. 11:14) calls one and the same person τυφλὸς καὶ κωφός; blindness and deafness could occur together. About the only other point [120] is

---

[118] The common use of ἀναβλέπω does not enable us to say which of the blind had seen before and thus had sight restored, since ἀναβλέπω is used of the man born blind in Jn. 9:11, 15, 18.

[119] Cf. Mt. 11:5; 15:30; 21:14; Lk. 14:13; 14:21. Mt. 11:5 also has λεπροί and νεκροί, Mt. 15:30 κυλλοί, Lk. 14:13, 21 ἀνάπηροι and Jn. 5:3 ξηροί. Except at Mt. 15:30 and Lk. 14:21 the τυφλοί are always at the beginning or end for emphasis → 280, 6 ff.

[120] In view of the significance of the number two in the Gospels (Bultmann Trad., 343-6, esp. 345) one can hardly conclude from the δύο of Mt. 9:27 and 20:30 that the blind associated with one another in their sufferings. Whether the blind and lame had access to the temple (Mt. 21:14, not 2 Βασ. 5:8 → n. 74) cannot be decided in the absence of a Rabb. ruling along the lines of 2 Βασ. 5:8. Acc. to → III, 235, 29 ff. and J. Jeremias, Jerusalem z. Zeit Jesu³ (1962), 133 f. ἱερόν means the fore-court. With some plausibility a theological intention has been seen behind Mt. 21:14, cf. Loh. Mt., ad loc.; G. Strecker, "Der Weg d. Gerechtigkeit," FRL, 82 (1962), 19, n. 1; R. Hummel, "Die Auseinandersetzung zwischen Kirche u. Judt. im Mt.," Beiträge z. Evangel. Theol., 33 (1963), 94 f.

that the blind were led, Mk. 8:22; Lk. 18:40; Ac. 9:8; 13:11. [121] The only admonition about treating the blind properly is in Lk. 14:13: ὅταν δοχὴν ποιῇς, κάλει πτωχούς, ἀναπήρους, χωλούς, τυφλούς, cf. also 14:21. Nor is there any discussion of the reason for blindness except in Jn. 9:1 → 290, 28 ff. In Mt. 12:22 blindness and dumbness are traced back to possession by a demon as in Judaism → 283, 34 f. A solemn curse causes blindness in Ac. 13:11 (→ 272, 4 ff.), [122] but this is only temporary and it thus presupposes miraculous healing → 274, 8 ff.

3. At the heart of the NT statements about the τυφλός are the Gospel accounts of healing. [123] In style these differ little from similar accounts elsewhere (→ 274, 5 ff.) or from other NT miracle stories. [124] This is especially true of the accounts in Mk. 8 and Jn. 9, where there are some par. even in wording. [125]

Typical features of the NT stories are the cry ἐλέησον, [126] the separation of the blind Mk. 8:23, [127] the use of spittle (→ n. 23), [128] with washing in the pool of Siloam in Jn. 9, the laying on of hands Mk. 8:23, 25 [129] or touch Mt. 9:29; 20:34, [130] healing with a ref. to its suddenness [131] or difficulty Mk. 8:25, [132] and confirmation of the result. [133] Critical analysis suggests that some of these features might be secondary, e.g., touching the eyes in Mt. 9:29; 20:34, and the final δοξάζων τὸν θεόν· καὶ πᾶς ὁ λαὸς ἰδὼν ἔδωκεν αἶνον τῷ θεῷ in Lk. 18:43. [134] If one compares the accounts in Mk. 8 and Mk. 10 it seems that Mk. 10 stresses the dialogue between Jesus and the blind man and esp. the faith of the latter and Jesus' desire to help, v. 51 f. The accent falls, not on the miracle,

[121] Mt. 9:27: ἠκολούθησαν δύο τυφλοί (cf. also v. 28: προσῆλθον αὐτῷ οἱ τυφλοί) is not to be pressed; it is an abbreviation, cf. Mt. 20:29 f.; Mk. 10:46, but also Mk. 10:52; Mt. 20:34, and is meant to illustrate the πιστεύειν of v. 28. The same applies to Mk. Mk. 10:50 does not mean the τυφλός was not fully blind (V. Taylor, The Gospel acc. to St. Mark [1959], 449) but "the power of the coming miracle is already at work" in v. 50, Loh. Mk., ad loc.

[122] The mighty curse, the suddenness of the miracle παραχρῆμα, its confirmation καὶ περιάγων ἐζήτει χειραγωγούς and the effect on the pro-consul are stylistic traits. Haench. Ag.[14], 343, n. 5 rightly stresses the fact that Lk. wants to depict sudden blinding, not various stages, so that ἀχλύς is not a medical term. One must also concur in his criticism of Loisy, who thinks Bar-Jesus is meant to symbolise the blind Jewish people (346). But is Lk. illustrating the contrast to magic by superiority over it (347)?

[123] On the gen. features of healing in antiquity and the NT → III, 205, 5 ff., on healings of the blind → V, 347, 1 ff.; III, 211, 12 ff., cf. also Act. Andr. et Matth. 21; Phil. 128; Verc. 20.

[124] Cf. e.g., the striking similarity between Mk. 8:22-26 and 7:32-37 (Taylor, op. cit., 368 f.), though Taylor rightly rejects the idea of a mere variant or doublet.

[125] Cf. ἐπιχρίω (ἐπὶ) τοὺς ὀφθαλμούς which occurs only in Jn. 9:6 (p [66] אℵ D et al.), 11 and the Aesculapius inscr. → 275, 10 ff.

[126] Mk. 10:47; Mt. 9:27; 20:30; Lk. 18:38, redoubled after the threatenings of the crowd in Mk. 10:48; Mt. 20:31; Lk. 18:39, cf. also Mt. 15:22; 17:15; Lk. 17:13.

[127] Cf. Mk. 7:33, also Mk. 5:40 and Ac. 9:40.

[128] πτύσας εἰς τὰ ὄμματα αὐτοῦ, Mk. 8:23, ἔπτυσεν χαμαὶ καὶ ἐποίησεν πηλὸν ἐκ τοῦ πτύσματος καὶ ἐπέθηκεν αὐτοῦ τὸν πηλὸν ἐπὶ τοὺς ὀφθαλμούς, Jn. 9:6 (11, 15), cf. also Mk. 7:33; Weinreich, 97 f.; A. Jacoby, "Zur Heilung d. Blinden v. Bethsaida," ZNW. 10 (1909), 185-194; Hempel, 288; Str.-B., II, 15-17.

[129] Cf. also Mk. 6:5; 7:32; Lk. 4:40; 13:13; Weinreich, 14-37; Hempel, 286, n. 3 (with bibl.).

[130] Cf. Mk. 8:22 and also Mt. 8:3, 15; Mk. 1:41; 7:33; Lk. 5:13; 22:51. Weinreich, 1-75; Str.-B., II, 2 f.; Bultmann Trad., 237; H. Wagenvoort, Art. "Contactus," RAC, III, 404-421.

[131] Mk. 10:52; Mt. 20:34; Lk. 18:43; cf. also Mt. 8:3; Mk. 1:31; 2:12; Lk. 5:13; Jn. 5:9; Ac. 9:18, 34; Weinreich, 197 f.; → 275, 7 ff.

[132] Cf. Bultmann Trad., 237.

[133] εὐθὺς ἀνέβλεψεν καὶ ἠκολούθει αὐτῷ, Mk. 10:52, cf. Mt. 20:34; Lk. 18:43; ἐνέβλεπεν τηλαυγῶς ἅπαντα. καὶ ἀπέστειλεν αὐτὸν εἰς οἶκον αὐτοῦ, Mk. 8:25 f.; cf. also Mk. 1:31; 2:11 f.; 5:43 etc.; Bultmann Trad., 240.

[134] Cf. Lk. 9:43; 13:17; Weinreich, 116.

but rather on the trust of the blind man [135] and the healing power of Jesus' word. These are not confined to an inner sphere; they show their power against the blind reality and concrete physical affliction of blindness. [136] The significance of faith in healing the blind is then strongly emphasised by Mt. in 9:27-31. [137] Central here are the dialogue on faith and the healing formula: κατὰ τὴν πίστιν ὑμῶν γενηθήτω ὑμῖν, v. 29. [138] In the other healing Mt. locates the motive in Jesus' pity on the blind man, cf. the interpolated σπλαγχνισθείς in 20:34 [139] → IV, 1097, 20 ff. Like Mt., Lk. shortens Mk.'s narrative at many pts., but also makes it clearer (cf. ἀχθῆναι in 18:40 and ἐπυνθάνετο in 18:36) and closer to the style of such stories (→ n. 134), cf. the healing word and the praise of God.

Whereas there are hardly any parallels elsewhere for the stress on faith in healings of the blind, [140] there are several analogies to the account of Mk. 8:22-26 (→ n. 127-132), the best-known being the story of the cure by Vespasian → 274, 5 ff. [141] But one should not be led astray in this respect by the dramatic character of Mk.'s narrative. Mark himself relates the cure to 8:17 ff. and seeks by means of it to avoid false deductions from the preceding questions οὔπω νοεῖτε οὐδὲ συνίετε; (v. 17) οὐ βλέπετε; (v. 18) and οὔπω συνίετε; (v. 21). [142] This means that there is already a certain ambivalence in the use of τυφλός. [143] The blindness of the disciples,

---

[135] Cf. M. Dibelius, Die Formgesch. d. Ev.[4] (1961), 49; W. Jaeger, Die Heilung d. Blinden in der Kunst (1960), 8, 11. Taylor, op. cit., 447 finds the intention of the pericope in Mk. in its Messianic character as a preparation for the entry; E. Haenchen, Der Weg Jesu, Eine Erklärung d. Mk.-Ev. u. d. kanonischen Par. (1966), ad loc. compares the cry of the blind with that at the entry in 11:10, cf. also Loh. Mk., ad loc. and the survey in Kl. Mk. Possibly Mk. 10:46 ff. is correcting 10:35 ff. as 8:22 ff. does 8:17 ff. (→ 289, 14 ff.). One should compare the foolish request of the blinded sons of Zebedee for places of honour in the βασιλεία, which Jesus cannot grant, with the request of the blind beggar, which He fulfils. "The righteous stay blind, but the lowly see," J. Schniewind, Das Ev. nach Mk.[10] (1962), ad loc. The healed blind man follows Jesus to Jerusalem, cf. E. Schweizer, "Die theol. Leistung d. Mk.," Ev. Theol., 24 (1964), 351; U. Luz, "Das Geheimnismotiv u. die markinische Christologie," ZNW, 56 (1965), 15.
[136] On faith in the miracle stories → VI, 206, 18 ff., and esp. G. Ebeling, "Jesus u. Glaube," Wort u. Glaube[2] (1962), 236 f.; H. J. Held, "Mt. als Interpret d. Wundergeschichten," Überlieferung u. Auslegung im Mt., Wissenschaftliche Monographien z. AT u. NT, 1[4] (1965), 264-284.
[137] Alongside 12:22 ff. Mt., like Mk., has two healings of the blind, one (par. Mk. 10) on the way to Jerusalem (Mt. 20:29-34), the other (Mt. 9:27-31) with no par. in Mk., cf. Held, op. cit., 208 f.
[138] Held, op. cit., 168, 212 f., 222 f., 227 f.
[139] Ibid., 246. Held (210, n. 1) pts. out that by eliminating the intermediary role of the crowd Mt. lays stress on the immediate dealings between Jesus and the blind man.
[140] Apart from an Epidaurus inscr., on this cf. K. Latte, "Inscr. Graecae," Gnomon, 7 (1931), 113 f.
[141] Cf. also L. Szimonidesz, "Die Heilung des Blinden v. Bethesda u. Buddhas Gleichnis v. den Blindgeborenen u. dem Elefanten," Nieuw Theol. Tijdschr., 24 (1935), 233-259. Bultmann Trad. Suppl. (1958), 33 rightly dismisses as fantastic Szimonidesz' attempt to trace back the healing of the blind in Mk. 8 to a Buddhist parable. But cf. Loh. Mk., 159 f.: "The only distinctive thing about the story is that it has nothing distinctive compared with such non-christian accounts." Acc. to E. C. Hoskyns and F. N. Davey, The Riddle of the NT (1957), 117 f. Mt. and Lk. were aware of the closeness to these par. and to secular practice, and left out the story on this account. Taylor, op. cit., thinks "its bold realism" was the reason they left it out (369), also the fact that the second laying on of hands implies that the first was unsuccessful (372).
[142] Cf. Kl. Mk., ad loc.; Taylor, 97 f., 370; Grundmann Mk., 165; Luz, op. cit., 15. But Hck. Mk., ad loc. thinks Mk. 8:22 ff. is a prelude to what follows, cf. also A. Kuby, "Zur Konzeption d. Mk.-Ev.," ZNW, 49 (1958), 52 f.
[143] One is not to take the healing as a mere symbol. The blind man is not a symbol but the type of a blindness which may be either physical or spiritual.

expressed in their failure to understand, is answered by the healing of the blind. [144] διέβλεψεν καὶ ἀπεκατέστη, καὶ ἐνέβλεπεν τηλαυγῶς ἅπαντα, v. 25.

Jesus' healings of the blind are set in another light outside the accounts in the true sense. Here they signal with the other miracles the dawn of the eschatological age of salvation. Especially in Mt. 11:5 (→ II, 718, 1 ff.; VII, 246, 1 ff.) and Lk. 4:18; [145] 7:21 f. (→ III, 129, 43 ff.) the healings of the blind are a fulfilment of prophetic promise (→ 281, 27 ff.) and later Jewish expectation, cf. προσδοκάω Mt. 11:3; Lk. 7:19 f.

> Jesus' reply to the Baptist's question in Mt. 11:5 par. (Q) also has a polemical thrust in the debate between the Chr. community and followers of John, cf. the context. Mt. himself puts the healings under the rubric ἔργα Χριστοῦ of which he gives examples in c. 8-9. [146] Lk. puts ἐν ἐκείνῃ τῇ ὥρᾳ ... τυφλοῖς πολλοῖς ἐχαρίσατο βλέπειν (v. 21) between John's question and Jesus' answer, thereby making the messengers of John eye-witnesses of the miraculous signs. That the healing of the blind is esp. important for Lk. may be seen from the fact that with this he mentions only the healing of the sick and the demon-possessed, leaving out the χωλοί, λεπροί, κωφοί, νεκροί and πτωχοί mentioned in the quotation (v. 21).

The Johannine healing (Jn. 9), which is not behind the others in drama and realism, differs from its Synoptic counterparts especially in the fact that it is the cure of a man born blind (9:1, 2, 19 f., 32), it takes place on the Sabbath [147] (9:14, 16), and it has typical Johannine transparency, τυφλός being used by Jesus in a transf. sense in the ensuing discussion, vv. 39-41. The fact that this is the cure of a τυφλὸς ἐκ γενετῆς [148] illustrates the extraordinary and transcendent greatness of the miracle, cf. v. 32. But it is also points already to the symbolical horizon against which one has to understand the story: Man is by nature ἐκ γενετῆς blind to the light of revelation. [149] The same ambivalence characterises the dialogue between the disciples and Jesus about the reason for the blindness of the man born blind, v. 2 f. According to the disciples the man's blindness may be due to the sin of his parents. This is in accordance with the common OT and Jewish view that the parents' sin is

---

[144] Perhaps this explains the πάλιν κτλ. in v. 25. Dibelius, op. cit., 84 offers another explanation: The desire to instruct Christians endowed with healing power is the controlling interest in the depiction of a cure in stages. Haenchen, op. cit., ad loc. rightly rejects the idea of gradual healing and sees here the difficulty of a cure which emphasises the greatness of the miracle. Acc. to Bultmann Trad., 240, where we have par. for healing in stages, the depiction of successive progress is for effect (he leans on Strauss here). Van der Loos, 421 f. thinks this feature is obviously historical; it expresses the intention of Jesus "in part to manifest in His display of divine mercy to a man in need the omnipotence of His actions and His freedom in the method of treatment."

[145] If Lk. deliberately left out the healing of broken hearts and sought to present the Spirit as the prophetic Spirit rather than miraculous power (→ VI, 407, 20 ff., cf. M. Rese, At.liche Motive in d. Christologie d. Lk., Diss. Bonn [1965], 216, 228), τυφλοί is to be taken in a transf. sense.

[146] This and the mention of the lame and of lepers suggests that τυφλοί ref. to the physically blind, though the end of the story might indicate a metaphorical opening of eyes and ears, cf. Wellh. Mt. and Kl. Mt., ad loc.

[147] There is no special emphasis on this even though Jn. possibly saw in the process a clear ref. to breaking the Sabbath, cf. Bultmann J. on 9:6 and → VII, 28, 8 ff., esp. n. 222.

[148] On the phrase and materially cf. Paus., IV, 12, 10; cf. Acta Pilati, 6, 2: ἐγὼ τυφλὸς ἐγεννήθην.

[149] Cf. C. K. Barrett, The Gospel acc. to St. John (1956) on 9:1: "Mankind is not by nature receptive of the light (cf. 1:5, 10 f.). Man is spiritually blind from birth." Cf. Hipp. Ref., V, 9, 20.

visited on the children, [150] e.g., concretely in the form of blindness → 283, 18 ff., cf. v. 34. More difficult to explain is the view of the disciples that the man might have committed sin himself and been afflicted by blindness as a result. One can no more presuppose ideas of transmigration and reincarnation than the pre-existence of the soul and its pre-temporal fall. [151] Perhaps one may think in terms of isolated Rabb. statements to the effect that a child may sin in its mother's womb [152] or again the background may be the speculation that God's foreknowledge of future sin is the reason why He causes the man to come into the world blind → 283, 30 ff., [153] especially as Jesus' reply in v. 3b presupposes a differently orientated divine pre-science. [154] At any rate the question as to the why of the blindness, which is based on a dogma of retribution, is changed by the answer into a question as to its where-fore. This man is blind ἵνα φανερωθῇ τὰ ἔργα τοῦ θεοῦ ἐν αὐτῷ, v. 3b, cf. 5:36; 11:4 etc.

This shows that τυφλός is not meant equivocally only from vv. 39 ff. but already in the preceding verses. From the very outset the man born blind is a paradigm and symbol illustrating the truth of Jesus' saying that He is the light of the world, v. 5, cf. 1:9; 8:12, and that He has come in order that those who do not see may do so, 9:39. Yet even the impressive miracle of curing a man born blind evokes only embarrassment, strife, and rejection. Doubt is thrown on whether the cured man is really the same as the blind beggar, v. 8 f. It is contested whether the man who sees was ever blind, v. 18. Appeal is made to the Sabbath legislation, [155] v. 16. Ex-communication is pronounced, v. 34. Only the blind man himself confesses the One who has healed him. The Pharisees show, then, that Christ not only makes the blind to see (v. 39a) but also makes those who see blind (v. 39b, cf. 3:19).

III. The Transferred Use of τυφλός and τυφλόω.

1. If the whole story of the man born blind comes to a head in 9:35-41, it is clear that the τυφλοί of vv. 39-41 are those who cannot understand the σημεῖα of Jesus, who do not perceive His divine origin (v. 29), and who will not be called

---

[150] Ex. 20:5; 34:7; Nu. 14:18; Dt. 5:9; Jer. 31:29 f.; Ez. 18:20; Tob. 3:3 f.; cf. Str.-B., II, 529. Bau. J., ad loc draws attention to similar statements in Gk. tragedy, e.g., Aesch. Suppl., 434-6 etc.

[151] Bau. J., ad loc. rightly pts. out that neither in the usual Platonic-Hell. ref. nor in Slav. En. 23:4 f.; Wis. 8:19 f. nor among the Essenes (Jos. Bell., 2, 154-8; Philo Gig., 6-9; Som., I, 181) does one find the idea "that the soul in its pre-terrestrial state has stained itself with sin."

[152] Cf. the examples in Str.-B., II, 528 f., though with no specific ref. to blindness.

[153] K. Bornhäuser, "Meister, wer hat gesündigt, dieser oder seine Eltern, dass er blind geboren ist? Joh. 9:2," NKZ, 38 (1927), 433-7 suspects such ideas even though not acquainted with the ref. → 283, 30 ff. and he pts. to Rashi on Ex. 2:11 ff., where the slaying of the Egyptian by Moses is justified on the ground that Moses as a prophet foresaw that there would be none righteous among the progeny of this Egyptian if any such were born, cf. also bSota, 47a. Underlying both is the view that the unborn slain in the loins of sinful ancestors are not slain unjustly, since they would certainly have sinned if born and thus merited death, 437. The pt. missed by Bornhäuser that the slaying of the unborn may be traced back to God is supported by Midr. Tanna debe Eliyyahu (cf. on this Strack Einl., 220).

[154] Bultmann J. on 9:2 considers the possibility that the disciples' question poses an impossible alternative and is thus meant to show the absurdity of the dogma. Dibelius, op. cit. (→ n. 135), 89 thinks the form of the question suggests the ἐκ γενετῆς is added by Jn. and the man originally had become blind, cf. also Bau. J., ad loc. The points mentioned → 290, 22 ff. would explain the addition.

[155] Acc. to Rabb. statute the healing of a man born blind on the Sabbath was desecration of the Sabbath, cf. Str.-B., II, 533 f. → VII, 28, 20 ff.

out of the darkness of the world and their supposedly justified preconceptions into the light of the Revealer. In this respect the Jews and Pharisees play only a representative role. v. 40 f. makes it abundantly plain that their sin is not to see themselves as blind but to think they see and hence to censure the revelation with apparent perspicacity. [156]

Jn. 12:40 is adduced as a quotation from Isaiah. But τετύφλωκεν αὐτῶν τοὺς ὀφθαλμούς does not come from the LXX. [157] It is another rendering of וְעֵינָיו הָשַׁע. In distinction from Is. 6:10 and other quotations of the verse in the NT, God is in Jn. the author of the blindness, par. τὸ καὶ ἐπώρωσεν αὐτῶν τὴν καρδίαν. The blindness is that Jesus finds no faith in spite of His σημεῖα (v. 37); διὰ τοῦτο οὐκ ἠδύναντο πιστεύειν (v. 39) is based on the quotation.

Whereas in Jn. 12:40 God is the subject of τυφλοῦν, σκοτία is the subject in 1 Jn. 2:11. On the one side the blindness is caused by σκοτία acting as a force, while on the other it is the result of hatred of one's brother and walking in darkness, so that it is sin. Only through εἶναι and περιπατεῖν ἐν τῇ σκοτίᾳ does darkness get the power to make blind → VII, 444, 17 f. In content blindness is ignorance of the "whither." [158] The man who gropes about in darkness cannot know where the way leads, cf. Jn. 12:35.

2. The saying about blind leaders of the blind (Mt. 15:14 par.) who fall into the ditch with the blind they lead [159] comes from the Logia source, though originally as a detached saying. Its original form is better preserved in Luke (→ V, 100, n. 16) [160] but the original point escapes us. According to Lk. 6:39 blindness is suggested by the context (v. 37 f.) which forbids judging and criticising. Since man is blind to the μέτρον of his own sin and to the beam in his own eye, οὐ κατανοεῖς (v. 41) or οὐ βλέπων (v. 42), he should refrain from κρίνειν. [161] Mt. introduces the metaphor by ὁδηγοί εἰσιν τυφλοὶ τυφλῶν and relates it in a transf. sense to the Pharisaic interpretation of the Law. The blind leaders of the blind are blind to God's will [162] and to the Word of Jesus at which they take offence, cf. ἀκμὴν καὶ ὑμεῖς

---

[156] One should not restrict it, then, to "darkening of moral vision" and "self-satisfaction," J. H. Bernard, A Crit. and Exeget. Comm. on the Gospel acc. to St. John, II, ICC (1928), 340 f. Cf. Bultmann J., 256: "In the possession of their tradition, from which they draw their certainty, they are blind to the revelation which encounters them."

[157] LXX reads like Mt. 13:15 and Ac. 28:27: τοὺς ὀφθαλμοὺς αὐτῶν ἐκάμμυσαν, Is. 6:10.

[158] The question of the whence and whither is typically Gnostic, cf. Cl. Al. Exc. Theod., 78, 2 and Ev. Veritatis (→ n. 48), 22, 13 ff.

[159] There are many par. to blind leaders of the blind → 275, 34 ff.; 286, 19 ff., but none to πίπτειν εἰς βόθυνον. Jülicher Gl. J., II, 50 f. rightly supposes that OT passages like Is. 24:18; Ιερ. 31:44; Prv. 22:14; 26:27; Qoh. 10:8 lie behind this rather than going astray in the desert or falling in a river or against a wall. The nearest par. is Phil. Virt., 7, where those who strive after the riches τῶν κενῶν δοξῶν, τυφλῷ πρὸ βλέποντος σκηριπτόμενοι καὶ ἡγεμόνι τῆς ὁδοῦ χρώμενοι πεπηρωμένῳ πίπτειν ἐξ ἀνάγκης ὀφείλουσιν.

[160] Cf. Jülicher Gl. J., II, 52; Bultmann Trad., 82, 84, 97 etc.

[161] Cf. Bultmann Trad., 103: "How can you say you are a judge when you yourself are blind"; Jeremias Gl.[7], 37 f.; T. W. Manson, The Sayings of Jesus (1949), 57. Wellh. Lk., ad loc. emphasises more strongly the connection with v. 40: "A blind man is no guide (teacher) and a pupil no master — there is no authority apart from Jesus," cf. also B. Weiss, Die Ev. des Mk. u. Lk.[6] (1901), ad loc.

[162] Cf. G. Barth, "Das Gesetzesverständnis d. Evangelisten Mt.," Überlieferung u. Auslegung, Wissenschaftliche Monographien z. AT u. NT, 1[4] (1965), 82: "Their blindness shows itself in the traditions of the elders with which they equate God's real will."

ἀσύνετοί ἐστε; οὐ νοεῖτε κτλ. Mt. 15:16 f. According to the Pharisaic view the supposed blindness of those led by the blind leaders consists in their ignorance of the Law and tradition → 284, 32 ff. If Mt. does not directly regard this as unfounded, this in no way minimises his disputing of the qualities which the Pharisees claim for themselves as ὁδηγοί, cf. R. 2:19. Whether the others are in fact blind is irrelevant compared with the blindness of the Pharisees themselves, → V, 99, 20 ff.

This is continually argued against them in the great attack in Mt. 23 (v. 16, 17, 19, 24, 26). Twice they are accused of being ὁδηγοὶ τυφλοί (v. 16, 24) with no genitive attribute τυφλῶν. The blindness and folly of the Jewish authorities — the τυφλοί are also called μωροί in v. 17 (cf. the vl. in v. 19) — does not consist in their hypocrisy as this comes to light in the contrast between reality and appearance. It consists in their false exposition of the Law, cf. especially v. 17 and v. 19: τί γὰρ μεῖζον, which can neither perceive nor expound what is essential in the Law. But if the Pharisees and scribes are blind to God's will and the true intention of the Law, they are unmasked therewith as ὁδηγοὶ τυφλοί. Though they think they are ὁδηγοὶ τυφλῶν, in truth they are ὁδηγοὶ τυφλοί.

3. Paul is aware of a similar claim (R. 2:19), but his reference is to the Jews generally rather than just the scribes and Pharisees. The blindness of those who are not just τυφλοί but are also called οἱ ἐν σκότει, ἄφρονες and νήπιοι, consists, according to the Jewish view, in their not possessing the μόρφωσις τῆς γνώσεως καὶ τῆς ἀληθείας ἐν τῷ νόμῳ. Paul does not reproach the Jews for being blind but for living as those who do not see in spite of their undisputed ability to see. According to 2 C. 4:4 the God of this aeon has blinded the eyes of unbelievers, from whom the Gospel is concealed, that they do not see the light of the Gospel of the glory of Christ. In its dualism this reminds us strongly of Test. S. 2:7 (→ 285, 26), but Paul can dialectically attribute blinding and hardening [163] to God Himself (R. 9:18; 11:8, 10 → 281, 1 ff.) and the decision regarding unbelief, and consequently τυφλοῦσθαι, is made only with the preaching of the Gospel, → V, 557, 4 ff.; VII, 356, 37 ff.

4. Similarly 2 Pt. 1:9 does not describe deficient ἐπίγνωσις as such, but deficient fruitfulness of knowledge in virtue and the failure of virtuous striving for ἐπίγνωσις, as a τυφλὸν εἶναι, cf. v. 5 f.: ἐν δὲ τῇ ἀρετῇ τὴν γνῶσιν, ἐν δὲ τῇ γνώσει τὴν ἐγκράτειαν. [164] Rev. 3:17 says of the church of Laodicea that it regards itself as spiritually rich [165] and does not realise that in reality it is ταλαίπωρος καὶ ἐλεεινὸς καὶ πτωχὸς καὶ τυφλὸς καὶ γυμνός. Its blindness consists in self-deception regarding its complacency and self-satisfaction. As a cure it receives from Christ the counsel, κολλύριον (according to some MSS κολλούριον [166] [sc. ἀγοράσαι]) ἐγχρῖσαι τοὺς ὀφθαλμούς σου ἵνα βλέπῃς, v. 18. It is hardly worth asking what the eye-salve is. The only important point is that Christ (παρ' ἐμοῦ) can bring about the cure of blindness.

---

[163] Cf. the par. to ἐτύφλωσεν τὰ νοήματα αὐτῶν in 2 C. 3:14: ἐπωρώθη τὰ νοήματα αὐτῶν.
[164] μυωπάζω alongside τυφλός is difficult, since strictly it is a softening "to be nearsighted."
[165] πλούσιός εἰμι καὶ πεπλούτηκα is to be taken fig. with Bss. Apk., ad loc., and not related to material wealth, as against Zn. Apk., Had. Apk. and Loh. Apk., ad loc.
[166] With ref. to this ointment cf. the inscr. mentioned → 275, 10 ff. (Ditt. Syll.³, III, 1173, 15-18 [2nd cent. A.D.]).

F. τυφλός in the Post-Apostolic Fathers.

In the post-apost. fathers τυφλός occurs only twice at Barn., 14, 7. 9 in LXX quotations from Is. 42:6 f. and 61:1 f.

Schrage

+---
| † ὕβρις, † ὑβρίζω,
| † ἐνυβρίζω, † ὑβριστής
+---

A. The Usage in Greek.

ὕβρις is etym. obscure. The second syllable is originally connected with βριαρός "weighty," βρίθω "heavily laden." [1] Popular etym., as already in Hom., derives it from ὑπέρ along the lines of "beyond measure." [2] This is linguistically impossible but important historically. [3] With both noun and verb the range of meaning is very large. The noun means originally an act which invades the sphere of another to his hurt, a "trespass," a "transgression" of the true norm in violation of divine and human right. Arrogance of disposition is often implied, Hom. Od., 14, 262; 17, 431; cf. also Il., 1, 203. Thus ὕβρις stands contrasted with εὐνομία, δίκη (→ II, 178, 18 ff.) and σωφροσύνη (→ VII, 1097, 5 ff.) and calls for nemesis. [4] The ref. is to a wicked act, also insult, scorn, contempt, often accompanied by violence, rape, and mistreatment of all kinds. More rarely and later the noun also means something endured, e.g., Plut. Pericl., 12 (I, 158).

The verb ὑβρίζω, which is primarily trans. in formation, has the same range of meaning. From Hom. Od., 18, 381 it denotes intr. arrogant conduct and trans. "to harm,"

ὕβρις κτλ. Bibl.: G. Bertram, "Hochmut u. verwandte Begriffe im griech. u hbr. AT," *Welt d. Orients,* 3 (1964), 29-38; E. R. Dodds, *The Greeks and the Irrational,* II (1951), 28-63; W. Eberhardt, "Die Geschichtsdeutung d. Thukydides," *Gymnasium,* 61 (1954), 306-326; J. Fraenkel, *Hybris. Proefschr.* (1941); C. del Grande, *Hybris. Colpa e Castigo nell' Espressione poetica e letteraria degli scrittori della Grecia antica da Omero a Cleante* (1947); D. Grene, *Man in His Pride. A Study in the Political Philosophy of Thucydides and Plato* (1950); W. Jaeger, *Paideia. Die Formung d. griech. Menschen,* I-III (1934-47), *passim;* K. Latte, "Schuld u. Sünde in d. griech. Religion," ARW, 20 (1920/21), 254-298; H. Lewy, "Zur Vorstellung vom Neide d. Götter," ARW, 25 (1927), 194-7; Nilsson, I², 732-773; II², 559; S. Ranulf, "Gudernes Misundelse og Strafferettens Oprindelse i Athen," *Stud. over äldre Gräsk Mentalitet* (1930), 48-233: English ed. *The Jealousy of the Gods and Criminal Law at Athens,* I-II (1933/34), 32-160; H. G. Robertson, "Δίκη and Ὕβρις in Aeschylus' Suppliants," *Class. Rev.,* 50 (1936), 104-109; F. R. Walton, Art. "Hybris," RGG³, III, 497 (with bibl.); U. v. Wilamowitz-Moellendorff, *Der Glaube d. Hellenen,* II (1955), 114-123.

[1] The Indo-Eur. root would be *gʷer, gʷr(i)* (cf. also βρι, βαρύς, Lat. *gravis*) with prefix ὁ- from Indo-Eur. *ud-* "out from," *v.* Walde-Pok., I, 189, 685 f.; Boisacq, Hofmann, *s.v.* ὕβρις; Frisk, *s.v.* βρί and ὄβριμος. F. Kluge, *Etym. Wörterbuch d. deutschen Sprache⁶* (1905), 402 relates ὕβρις to *Übel,* but cf. Kluge¹⁷ (1957), *s.v.* This is derived from Old High German *uppi* from stem *ubja;* it is an "l" derivate of the root *ub* (cf. the prep. *über*). Evil is what is "beyond the norm," cf. J. and W. Grimm, *Deutsches Wörterbuch,* 11, 2 (1936), 6; cf. J. Murray, *A New English Dict.,* III, 2 (1891), *s.v.* "evil"; J. Franck and N. van Wijk, *Etym. Wb.* (1912), *s.v.* "euvel" = "overmoedig."

[2] In this sense Fraenkel, 6-9, 61 f., 67 coined the idea of conceptual etymology, cf. Thes. Steph., *s.v.* who ref. to *superbia* and F. Cornelius, *Idg. Religionsgeschichte* (1942), 283, 209, acc. to whom later synon. with ὑπερ- show how the Gks. themselves understood the word.

[3] Cornelius, *loc. cit.*

[4] Hubris (from the 5th cent. B.C.) includes man's pleonexia against deity, which is the real sin for the Gks., Jaeger, I , 228, cf. 246, 512; III, 221 f., 420, n. 131 and 133; also *Die Theol. d. frühen griech. Denker* (1953), 47. To the same area as ὕβρις belong esp. → ὑπερηφανία, ἀλαζονεία (→ I, 226, 28 ff.), αὐθάδεια (→ I, 508, 21 ff.) and πλεονεξία (→ VI, 266, 14 ff.). These words rather denote wickedness of disposition and the resultant sins of the tongue, so that they are not synon. with ὕβρις.

"damage," "injure," cf. Hom. Il., 11, 695, i.e., the injurious treatment of others even to rough handling. [5] From the class. age it is also common in the pass. [6]

ὑβριστής, derived from the verb, denotes a man who, sinfully overestimating his own powers and exaggerating his own claims, is insolent in word and deed in relation to gods and men. [7]

1. In Hom. ὕβρις is trespass beyond one's own sphere. ὕβρις and εὐνομία are anton. in human conduct, Od., 17, 487; cf. Plat. Soph., 216b. Often the arrogant, wild and unrighteous are contrasted with the hospitable who are minded to fear God, Od., 6, 120; 9, 175; 13, 201. The overweening come to a bad end (ἀτάσθαλοι), Od., 3, 207; 17, 588; 24, 282; Il., 11, 694 f.; 13, 633 f. Arrogance is an affair of supermen ὑπερηνορέοντες, [8] Od., 17, 581. The conduct of the free is esp. denoted by the group, Od., 1, 227; 24, 352 etc. [9] In Hes. [10] Theog., 307 ὑβριστής is connected with δεινός. In 514-6 it is characterised by the par. ideas of wickedness and overweening male force, cf. 996 and also Op., 134, 146, 191 f. [11] There is a warning against hubris, over which dike finally holds power, in 213 ff., cf. 238 f. Acc. to Hom. Hymn. Ap., 541 hubris is common among men. The dictum of Solon [12] Fr., 5, 9 f. (Diehl[3], I, 32): "Excess breeds wantonness," is adopted in Theogn., 153, and 751 says that lost and unrighteous man, sated with riches, falls into wantonness. But hubris means destruction, 43 f. Solon expects the gods to avenge every offence, though retribution may not always fall on the offender but often on his progeny. [13, 14] Hubris makes wealth unstable and it destroys arrogant giants, one reads in Bacchyl., 15, 57 ff. [15] Pind. Olymp., 13, 10 calls arrogance the mother of satiation. Εὐνομία, Δίκα and Εἰρήνα are contrasted with Ὕβρις here, 13, 6. 10 f. → 295, 10 f. [16]

2. Gk. tragedy deals with human hubris in the tragic sense. In Aesch. Pers., 808 it is set alongside godforgotten thoughts; the reward is divine τίσις, [17] cf. also 820 ff.; Ag., 217 ff., 374 ff., 750 ff. [18] There are the beginnings of a change when Aesch., though he regards the theft of fire as an act of defiant insolence, still sees in Prometheus a hero who made man independent of the gods. This raises the problem of hubris as an attempt on man's part to cross even the religious boundaries set for the individual in society and

---

[5] In modern Gk. the meaning is "to scold," cf. Moult.-Mill., s.v.

[6] Liddell-Scott, Moult.-Mill., Pape, Preisigke Wört., Thes. Steph., s.v.

[7] To break the rules of custom or law is in the first instance ἀδικία. It becomes ὕβρις when done out of overweening pride or arrogance. Thus the motive makes simple ἀδικία into an act of ὕβρις, cf. F. R. Earp, The Way of the Greeks (1929), 210 f. [Moule].

[8] Here and in other ref. the concept of hubris might be explained in terms of the prep. and synon., Fraenkel, 6-9.

[9] Cf. del Grande, 9-19, who thinks hubris is only possible between persons of the same social stratum.

[10] Cf. Jaeger, I, 102; Wilamowitz, II, 121; del Grande, 26-32.

[11] ὕβρις with ἀνήρ = ὑβριστής, cf. Hesiodi Carmina, ed. C. Goettling[3] (1878), ad loc.

[12] Cf. Fr., 3, 5 ff. (Diehl[3], I, 27 f.): The stupidity and greed of the citizens of Athens with their gt. hubris bring misfortune on the city, cf. 3, 31 (I, 29); on this Ranulf, 179 (Engl. 130 f.); acc. to del Grande, 48 for both Solon and Hes. all evil in society has its root in the false estimation of earthly goods.

[13] Solon takes offence at this and tries to avoid it in his legislation [Dihle].

[14] For Ranulf, 159 (122 f.), 181 (132 f.) the envy, caprice and cruelty of the gods are to the fore when they pursue human hubris with nemesis. This explains the orientation of the Gk. mind to moderation, self-limitation and harmony. Acc. to Fraenkel, 73 hubris is sociologically a transgressing of the limits of individuality.

[15] Fraenkel, 18.

[16] F. Dornseiff, "Peirithoos oder Apollon," Ath. Mitt., 66 (1941), 145 questions the supposed antithesis of hubris and aidos in Pindar.

[17] Jaeger, I, 329-331.

[18] Agamemnon is obsessed by fear of hubris, Jaeger, I, 324, cf. Nilsson, I[2], 751; Ranulf, 40, 128 f. (26, 96 f.).

to be himself. [19] Hubris is originally the ruthless or scornful right of might. But the view gains ground that the gods as bearers of nemesis oppose man's hubris with retribution, punishment and destruction. In the 5th cent., then, hubris becomes the class. expression of numinous fear, i.e., of the Greek sense of sin from the religious standpoint. [20] The gods do not love presumptuousness, Soph. Trach., 280. It breeds tyrants, Oed. Tyr., 873. It leads to senseless and futile excess and plunges the one who walks wickedly (ὑπερόπτης, 883) in word and work into sudden destruction. Finally it entails violation of reverence for the holy which Zeus must avenge if fear of the gods is not to perish altogether, 895-910. [21] An unsuccessful deed is shown to be hubris. For the sense of right and morality success is decisive. Failure, merited or unmerited, brings shame and loss. [22] The philosophical presuppositions change in Eur. The human norm replaces norms set by fate. [23] Hence hubris is no longer a religious concept though the mode of expression often seems to suggest it, cf. Heracl., 388; Or., 708. Hubris characterises human relations, negatively as scorn, contempt, or actively as hurt and violence, e.g., El., 68: "Thou has not scorned me in my misery." Acc. to Hipp., 474 it is hubris to want to be better than the demons, cf. Ba., 375.

3. In the Gk. historians hubris is an important factor in the course of events. In Hdt. the religious and metaphysical basis of the concept is plain. The hubris of the Persian plan of conquest (VII, 16 α 2) corresponds to the fundamental Persian attitude as Croesus sees it (I, 89, 2) but the deity leads Xerxes by a dream to the struggle for world-dominion (VII, 18; cf. also III, 80, 2; 81, 2 and the fable-like personifying of I, 189, 1; IV, 129, 2). [24] On this basis Thuc. develops a historico-philosophical theory of a purely immanent type. Sober prudence (I, 84, 2) is confronted by an attitude of untimely arrogance (II,

---

[19] The ethicising of the idea of hubris has many roots. Hurting one's fellow may be regarded as an offence against the gods, esp. where there is so social authority to punish the offence. Then the influential Delphic piety of the 6th cent. taught men to see in acts which violated law and hurt the the interests of others an overestimation on man's part and a violation of the intentions of the gods [Dihle]. Cf. also H. W. Stoll in Roscher, II 2767 f. Man's error, his wrong decision, is sin in the sense of Aristot. Poet., 13, p. 1453a, 15 f.; that he dare make such decisions is hubris in the sense of ancient drama, cf. P. van Braam, "Aristot.'s Use of ἁμαρτία," The Class. Quarterly, 6 (1912), 266-271. In practice hubris in the narrower sense is illegal violence and caprice as opposed to dike, which includes moderation and the principles of positive law, Aesch. Suppl., 418, 427, Robertson, 104-9. Finally cf. Dodds, 31: Between the encroachment which envious gods see in the too successful works of men and their punishment there is introduced the moralising assertion that success brings satiation which for its part breeds arrogance in word and act and even disposition. On this view every triumph is a fault (Aesch. Ag., 811-822; Hdt., I, 34) which calls down nemesis. Acc. to Eur. Iph. Aul., 1089-1097 the moral failing of the time is that escaping the envy of the gods is no longer the goal of human action. In Hom. Hymn. Ap., 541 one reads: ὕβρις θ', ἥ θέμις ἐστὶ καταθνητῶν ἀνθρώπων, cf. Dodds, 48: Zeus the heavenly father is originally the envious god who begrudges man what he most desires; but he becomes the terrible judge who strictly and pitilessly, though justly, punishes the chief sin of self-assertion as hubris.

[20] Cf. Braam, op. cit., 266-271; Cornelius, 137; Jaeger, I, 228; K. Kerényi, Die Religion d. Griech. u. Römer (1963), 109-122.

[21] On the motif of hubris in Soph. Oed. Col., 883; Ant., 480-6 cf. Ranulf, 49 f. (32 f.).

[22] There is thus a fixation on success, Latte, 256, 272.

[23] The ideal for Eur. is not keeping the mean but thinking higher than the human mean, cf. N. Söderblom, Kompendium d. Religionsgeschichte (1920), 389. But Eur. adopts traditional forms of expression, Wilamowitz, I, 15; cf. Jaeger, I, 419-449. In him too, then, hubris can be the fatal transgressing of the boundary between God and man [Dihle].

[24] For the connection between hubris and tyranny cf. Ranulf, 102 f. (67), 192-5 (139-142), who ref. to Hdt., also Aesch. Prom., 10, 34 f. (Zeus' tyranny); Ag., 938, 1409 f. (the people as a force to punish the hubris of princes); Soph. Ai., 1350; Oed. Tyr., 873. On Hdt., VII, 11-19 cf. Ranulf, 48 f. (31 f.); Fraenkel, 24-7; W. Aly, Volksmärchen, Sage u. Novelle bei Hdt. u. seinen Zeitgenossen (1921), 167-170, cf. 42 (ὑβριστὴς ποταμός, Aesch. Prom., 717 f. and on this → VI, 596, 4 ff. and n. 5) and 44.

65, 9). [25] Swift and unexpected affluence leads to hubris and punishment must follow, III, 39, 4 f.; 45, 4. [26] Acc. to Xenoph. [27] Hist. Graec., II, 2, 10 the decay of Sparta's power and the fall of Athens are divine judgments on human hubris. The anton. of ὕβρις is σωφροσύνη in Cyrop., VIII, 4, 14, cf. 1, 30; Ap., 19; Mem., III, 10, 5. Wealth can lead to arrogance, Cyrop., VIII, 6, 1. In An., III, 1, 21 the Persians represent hubris and acc. to III, 1, 13 a shameful overthrow (ὑβριζομένους ἀποθανεῖν) threatens the Gks.

4. In legal rhetoric one finds hubris technically from Aristoph. [28] In trials the main issue is the violence of the rich against the poor, Lys., 24, 15. 16. 18 etc. One finds violation of personal rights and forceful interference in the personal or domestic sphere, 1, 2. 4. 16, cf. also 2, 14; Aeschin. Tim., 87, 116, 188. In Demosth. Or., 21, 47; Aeschin. Tim., 15 the ὕβρεως γραφή contains the law of injuries and violations which exerted considerable influence and shaped the similar law in Alexandria, P. Tor., II, 3, 41-49 (3rd cent. B.C.); P. Fay., 12, 31 f. (c. 100 B.C.); ὕβρις with πληγαί, P. Hal., 1, 115; P. Hibeh, I, 32, 8 (3rd cent. B.C.). [29]

5. Socrates is not aware of arrogance and has no fear of seeming to be arrogant, Plat. Ap., 34c d, [30] thus helping to bring about his condemnation. Even acc. to friends he could be like a bold (ὑβριστής) satyr, Symp., 221e, cf. also 175e, 215b, 219c, 222a; Ps.-Plat. Alc., I, 114d. [31] Plato regards hubris as an essential cosmological and anthropological force. It is the negative side of eros. Eros μετὰ τῆς ὕβρεως is the basis of all destructive immoderation and disorder, Symp., 188a; Resp., III, 403a; Leg., VI, 783a; cf. Phaedr., 253d-e. The child is the most impudent being: ὑβριστότατον θηρίων, Leg., VII, 808d, cf. Euthyd., 273a. [32] The excesses and arrogancies of youth are esp. bad, Leg., X, 884 f. The hubris of youth is directed against the holy and also against parents and it is an attack on public life, Resp., VIII, 559d-560a, cf. Ps.-Plat. Def., 415e. Hubris has many names, forms and aspects, Phaedr., 238a, cf. Gorg., 525a; its consequences are injustice (Leg., III, 691c) and destruction (X, 906a). It is directed against subjects, the lowly and the defenceless, for whom the gods intervene in vengeance, Leg., VI, 761e, 777d; IX, 874c; XI, 927b-d. In the actuality of life there can easily be a vicious circle. Paideia brings victory but victory can result in licence, Leg., I, 641c, [33] cf. II, 661e, 662a. In Plat. hubris is not sin [34]in the bibl. sense but a power of fate which penetrates all areas of life and comes on man. In a very weak sense hubris can also be used of a mocker or a frivolous person, Prot., 355c.

6. With the mythical or philosophical usage of earlier times (which continued to exert an influence) and with the legal use, one also finds new applications in Aristot. In him, as earlier (→ 295, 13), ὕβρις can be sexual violation, Eth. Nic., V, 3, p. 1129b, 22; VII, 6, p. 1148b, 30; Pol., V, 10, p. 1311b, 19-25; Fr., 379, p. 1541a, 41. In a weak sense the verb can be a synon. of καταγελάω, χλευάζω, σκώπτω, Rhet., II, 2, p. 1379a, 29 ff., cf. Topica, VI, 6, p. 144a, 6 f. It also occurs pass. with ὀλιγωρία in Eth. Nic.,

---

25 Jaeger, I, 504.
26 Eberhardt, 317 f.; cf. Ranulf, 38 (24).
27 Jaeger, I, 497.
28 Fraenkel, 37 f., 42.
29 O. Gradenwitz, "Das Gericht der Chrematisten," APF, 3 (1906), 22-42, esp. 36; Moult.-Mill., s.v.; J. Partsch, "Die alexandrinischen Dikaiomata," APF, 6 (1920), 34-76, esp. 54-74; Preisigke Wört., s.v. (hubris in the sense of punishment); T. Thalheim, Art. ὕβρεως γραφή, Pauly-W., 9 (1916), 31.
30 Söderblom, op. cit., 389 f.
31 Jaeger, I, 211; the philosopher is περιττός, he submits to no norms, in the sense of Aristot. Metaph., 1, 2, p. 983a, 1; for he transgresses the envious limits drawn by the gods.
32 Cf. Plat. Leg., VII, 808d and on this → V, 601, 8 ff.
33 Jaeger, III, 300.
34 But cf. Latte, 292-8.

VII, 7, p. 1149a, 32, cf. Rhet., II, 23, p. 1398a, 25. As an expression of contempt ὕβρις means "maltreatment" with καταφρόνησις "scorn" and ἐπηρεασμός "ill-will," Rhet., II, 2, p. 1378b, 14 f. ὕβρις is also used act. for "arrogance" as a form of ἀδικία (→ I, 149, 33 ff.) with ἀσέβεια (→ VII, 185, 6 ff.) "offence against gods and men" and πλεονεξία (→ VI, 266, 14 ff.) "greed," De virtutibus et vitiis, 7, p. 1251a, 30 ff. Hubris in action is associated with pleasure, loc. cit., cf. Rhet., II, 2, p. 1387b, 23-30. The high-minded man is not to be confused with the arrogant, Eth. Nic., IV, 8, p. 1124a, 29 ff. To act arrogantly is very wrong, but hubris cannot be punished, for a presumptuous disposition is a gen. human complaint to which some (the rich and young) [35] are more prone and others less, Probl., 1, 16, p. 953a, 3-7. The wrong which results from hubris is to be distinguished from that which results from wickedness. ὑβρισταί go beyond the mean, Pol., IV, 11, p. 1295b, 9-11. Whereas war forces to righteous and considered action, the enjoyment of peaceful and quiet periods of prosperity produces transgressors. Peace and quiet are the goal of politics but they can be achieved only when wisdom, prudence and righteousness hold sway. Thus the question of hubris becomes in Aristot. a political problem, Pol., VII, 15, p. 1334a, 28 ff., cf. V, 2, p. 1302b, 5 f. and 11, p. 1314b, 24.

7. The later period brings no essential changes. In Polyb., 8, 12, 9 as already in Demosth. Or., 24, 143 ἀσελγής and ὑβρίζων are synon. Plut. Quaest. Conv., VIII, 6, 5 (II, 726d) characterises the ὑβριστής as by nature prone to (mocking) laughter, Quaest. Conv., I, 4, 3 (II, 622b). [36] Hence one finds ὕβρις καὶ φρύαγμα in Amat., 9 (II, 754c) and ὕβρις καὶ χλευασμός, Quaest. Conv., IX, 6, 1 (II, 741a). Sept. Sap. Conv., 3 (II, 148e) speaks of hubris in intercourse, 13 (II, 155 f.) of hubris against the law, cf. also Lib. Educ., 14 (II, 10c); there is pass. use in Lib. Educ., 12 (II, 8 f.); 15 (II, 11d); 17 (II, 13b). Hellas must endure violence, Pericl., 12 (I, 158). [37]

Thus hubris passed into common usage in many senses, some of them quite weak. It retains a certain emotional force as a poetic term. But in an age when more and more the problems of ethics and anthropology were being considered with the tools of rational thought this word which originally owed its content to myth could not become a tt. in philosophy. Hence hubris never became a key concept in Gk. thought. [38]

B. The Old Testament.

1. The main equivalent of LXX ὕβρις is גָּאוֹן with other derivates of גאה. The root גאה means in the first instance "to be or become high, lofty," then "to be proud, arrogant." The fig. which seems to lie behind this sense is that of the boiling or frothing of the sea, Ps. 46:3, [39] which is influenced by the myth of the uprising of the sea. Loftiness and pride גָּאוֹן are not intrinsically wrong. But to the degree they are linked with presumptuousness and defiant arrogance (→ n. 7) Yahweh comes to overthrow them, Am. 6:8; Jer. 13:9. [40] Lv. 26:19 and Ez. 7:24; 33:28 threaten Israel with the destruction of its glorious power if the people falls into disobedience, cf. foreign nations in Ez. 30:6, 18; 32:12 (Egypt); Zech. 10:11 (Assyria); Is. 13:19 (Babylon); Is. 23:9 (Tyre). Acc. to Ez. 16:49 f. pomp (גָּאוֹן), satiety and careless ease (→ line 13) lead to arrogance (גבה), cf. Ez. 7:20. [41] The destruction of the means of power on which they rely, of their גָּאוֹן (concretely), is the

---

[35] Nilsson, I², 736 f.; Fraenkel, 67.

[36] For laughter as a tt. for the affirmation of man as an autonomous being over against the Creator → III, 722, 24 ff.

[37] Cf. Nilsson, II², 559 for examples from the poetic fables of Babrius, 11, 43 (2nd cent. A.D.).

[38] Lines 26-30 are based on Dihle.

[39] Cf. the rising of the water and deepening of the river in Ez. 47:5.

[40] W. Rudolph, Jer., Hndbch. AT, I, 12² (1958), ad loc. emends acc. to v. 7: "so the great adornment is decayed . . . , " thus ruling out the transl. "pride."

[41] Cf. Dt. 32:15 and Solon's dictum that affluence breeds arrogance → 296, 15 f.

punishment of their sin, of the pride of the insolent and the arrogance of the tyrant, Is. 13:11. Here the Hbr. words are used psychologically or ethically. The OT is aware that pride is ineluctably followed by a fall, Prv. 16:18. This may be seen both in Israel (Hos. 5:5; 7:10; [42] Is. 9:8 f.; Jer. 13:17) and also in its enemies (Jer. 48:29 f.; Zech. 9:6; Zeph. 2:10). A proud and arrogant attitude is the true and fatal reason for their collapse. Sir. 10:8 almost seems to echo the principle of Thucydides that dominion passes from one nation to another by reason of violent arrogance. In Israel itself there is constant complaint about the encroachments of the wicked, Job 35:12, cf. 9. For the righteous the rule of wisdom is to hold aloof from the arrogant and not to take part in their exploiting of the poor, Prv. 16:19, cf. 8:13; 29:33; Sir. 10:6. The arrogant (גֵּאִים cf. Prv. 15:25; Ps. 94:2; 123:4; 140:5) seem to be a specific group in society and political life. [43] Claims to power, the suppression of the masses, i.e., the poor and a basic secularising of piety characterise them. Zeph. 3:11 promises their overthrow, cf. Ps. 36:12. In Sir. 10:12 ff. one finds a fundamental repudiation of this attitude. The beginning of pride is when a man engages in defiance [44] and turns away his heart from his Maker.

Derivates of the root גאה are mainly transl. in the LXX and Hexapla by ὕβρις and related terms or → ὑπερηφανία and related terms. Since these Gk. words correspond only to the negative side of גָּאוֹן etc. ὕβρις can be used only in passages in which it is appropriate to the meaning and context. Sometimes there are variations in understanding. Thus עַלִּיזֵי גַאֲוָתִי in Is. 13:3 ref. to heroes who "rejoice in my (sc. God's) majesty." But the LXX gives these heroes the task of executing God's wrath with joy and hubris, i.e., arrogance, [45] cf. Zeph. 3:11; cf. 2:15 (3:1), also Is. 23:7, 12; Na. 2:3. Jer. 13:17 HT has the difficult מִפְּנֵי גֵוָה (where we are perhaps helped by v. 15): [46] The prophet must weep because of the pride of the people of Jerusalem with which they provoke God. The LXX transl. lit.: ἀπὸ προσώπου ὕβρεως, but ὕβρις is taken as pass.: The people of Jerusalem must weep because of the violence they suffer.

In Sir. 10:12 f. גָּאוֹן means the same as זָדוֹן and both denote defiance and sin. In the Mas. גָּאוֹן and related terms can often be used positively for pomp (concretely) or pride (abstractly), but also negatively for arrogance or presumptuousness. No single action exhausts the Hbr. term and the meaning is open. But when the LXX uses ὕβρις it decides for a negative sense and brings the element of violence or actual encroachment into the text, e.g., Is. 28:1, 3; Am. 6:8; Zech. 9:6; 10:11; Jer. 13:9; Ez. 30:6; Lv. 26:19 etc.

2. The root זיד, like גאה, denotes first the bubbling up of water in the boiling of the sea or in cooking or simmering. In a transf. sense the verb (11 times Mas., once Sir.) is transl. "to be presumptuous," the noun זָדוֹן (11 times Mas., 10 Sir.) "presumptuousness," the adj. זֵד (16 times Mas., twice Sir.) "impudent" or "presumptuous." In the earlier canonical prophets it occurs only at 1 S. 17:28. It does not seem to occur in the prophetic tradition of the 8th cent. Is. 13:11 is primarily aimed at the proud rulers of Babylon and acc. to the traditional formulation attacks all arrogance anywhere in the world. Alien peoples are accused by the prophets of arrogance, opposition to Yahweh and rebellion against Him, Jer. 50:29-32 (Babylon); 49:16; Ob. 3 (Edom). Israel is similarly accused

---

[42] T. H. Robinson, *Die zwölf kleinen Propheten, Hndbch. AT,* I, 14³ (1964), *ad loc.* like H. W. Wolff, *Dodekapropheton, Bibl. Komm. AT,* 14, 1 (1961), *ad loc.,* transl. גָּאוֹן by "pride," H. Guthe in Kautzsch, *ad loc.* by "arrogance."

[43] H. Steiner, *Die Ge'im in d. Ps.* (1925), 22-30, comes to the conclusion, after a careful sifting of the background and ref., that the Sadducees are meant, cf. also Str.-B., II, 102, 105.

[44] יעז, which also belongs to the sphere of hubris (in Mas. only Is. 33:19 part. ni), and the more common עזז hi, e.g., Prv. 7:13; 21:29.

[45] The vl. παῦσαι for πληρῶσαι, if original (as thought by J. Ziegler, *Untersuchungen z. LXX des Buches Isaias* [1924], 64), creates a tension in the text which is not easily resolved.

[46] Cf. Rudolph, *op. cit., ad loc.*

in Ez. 7:10 (the king Zedekiah); Jer. 43:2 (those who seek refuge in Egypt). The same charge is found in historical accounts, e.g. the arrogance of the Egyptians against Yahweh and His people, Ex. 18:11; cf. Neh. 9:10, or of the Israelites striving against Yahweh, Dt. 1:43 (παραβιασάμενοι); Neh. 9:16, 29 (זִיד) hi alongside קָשָׁה עֹרֶף hi transl. τράχηλον σκληρύνω); Sir. 16:10 (σκληροκαρδία), and cf. the legislation of Ex. 21:14; Dt. 17:12, 13; 18:20, 22. In OT wisdom the word group takes on greater significance. In Prv. 13:10; cf. 11:2 it ref. to frivolous, contentious and dishonourable conduct. The basic sense of boiling up may still be detected in Prv. 21:24: עֹשֶׂה בְּעֶבְרַת זָדוֹן. In the Ps. זֵדִים seems to denote the same or a similar group or tendency as גֵּאִים → 300, 10 ff. They, too, are against the righteous, Ps. 86:14; 119:21, 51 etc. The reservoir of arrogance is sin, Sir. 10:13, 18, cf. 12:14, also 7:6; 9:12 (Mal. 3:15, 19); 11:9; 12:5; 13:1 ff.; 15:7. In Sir. 3:16 the parallelism of מֵזִיד and מַכְעִיס בּוֹרְאוֹ shows that arrogance is sin and is thus aimed against God. [47] The eschatological threat of Sir. 35:21 results from the same theocentric orientation. [48]

From the root זִיד only the noun is transl. 6 times by ὕβρις and related terms, though here there is considerable agreement between the Hbr. and Gk. words. But with ὑπερήφανος and related words (5 times) and ἀσεβής etc. (7) one finds ἁμαρτωλός at Sir. 12:14; 15:7, βλάσφημος at Sir. 3:16 etc., both more general and weaker, perhaps also to emphasises the religious character of the concept.

3. Since hubris is so broad and can denote disposition, attitude and conduct, sinful turning from or provocation of God, secularism, [49] as well as vainglorious arrogance, encroachments and tyranny against one's fellows, it is very hard to fix the limits of signification whether over against synon. or related Gk. words or with ref. to the equivalent Hbr. roots. In fact many Hbr. roots stand close in sense to hubris or are in context an expression of it. Thus one may ref. to רוּם, גָּבַהּ, גָּדַל "to be great, lofty, exalted," but also "to be boastful, proud, arrogant," e.g., Joel 2:20; Zeph. 2:10, where גָּדַל hi with חֵרֵף elucidates גָּאוֹן. In Zeph. 2:10 LXX ὕβρις is similarly elucidated: ὠνείδισαν καὶ ἐμεγαλύνθησαν ἐπὶ τὸν κύριον, cf. also Jer. 48(31):26; Is. 9:8; 10:12. For עֵינַיִם רָמוֹת Prv. 6:17 LXX has ὀφθαλμὸς ὑβριστοῦ, ΆΣ → ὑψηλός. Whether Is. 10:33 has arrogance in view with its simile of the high trees is questionable. But the LXX construed it thus, transl. רָמֵי הַקּוֹמָה by ὑψηλοὶ τῇ ὕβρει. Cod Β LXX also has ὕβρις for רוּם with גַּבְהוּת at Is. 2:17. Job 38:15 has → ὑπερήφανος for root רוּם; Prv. 21:4 Mas.: רוּם עֵינַיִם וּרְחַב לֵב LXX μεγαλόφρων ἐφ' ὕβρει θρασυκάρδιος. In Ps. 76:5 ΆΣ have ὑπερήφανοι τὴν καρδίαν for אַבִּירֵי לֵב. Cf. also the root גבה in Job 41:26; Is. 3:16, fig. too Ob. 4. It is linked with עֵינַיִם in Ps. 101:5 and occurs with רְחַב לֵב, cf. Prv. 21:4. The verbs גָּדַל, גָּבַהּ, רוּם are also linked with אַף or רוּחַ, thus pointing to the inner attitude for which LXX prefers ὑπερήφανος to ὕβρις, esp. as there is no current adj. from the stem ὕβρις, ὑβριστικός. נָשָׂא with נֶפֶשׁ at Prv. 19:18 Mas. is meant very differently, but LXX has for it εἰς δὲ ὕβριν μὴ ἐπαίρου τῇ ψυχῇ σου.

4. Other roots which might be connected with hubris are בָּעַט in Dt. 32:15; 1 S. 2:29 "to kick, despise," cf. 1 Βασ. 2:29: ἐπέβλεψας ... ἀναιδεῖ ὀφθαλμῷ. The root לִיץ [50] (in

---

[47] Fraenkel, 74; J. Hänel, Die Religion d. Heiligkeit (1931), 73: "An attack on God's majesty is human hubris."

[48] Disobedience to the Law or spoken will of God and arrogance in the sense of human autonomy are in a certain tension, since the latter entails practical atheism, cf. G. Bertram in G. Rosen, Juden u. Phönizier. Das antike Judt. also Missionsreligion u. d. Entstehung d. jüd. Diaspora (1929), 147, n. 100.

[49] Cf. A. Wendel, Säkularisierung in Israels Kultur (1934), 23: "Hence for the Israelites secularism or a secularising attitude are necessarily a leaving of the sphere of God's dominion, disobedience, rebellion and pride," cf. 116.

[50] H. N. Richardson, "Some Notes on ליץ and its Derivates," VT, 5 (1955), 163-179 opts for "talk freely or big, babbler" and applies this to Prv. 1:22; 19:28; 20:1 (p. 165 f., 172, 176).

all 32 times in Mas. and 4 in Sir.) found no uniform rendering in the LXX. The hubris group occurs among the many moral concepts found for it, Prv. 1:22; 19:28; Sir. 8:11. This involves sharpening compared with the sin of the tongue at issue in the Mas. "garrulity" or "ridicule." Similarly at Prv. 20:1 for הֹמֶה "noisy" one finds ὑβριστικός "violent" with ἀκόλαστος "unruly" for לִיץ. At Prv. 20:3 'A has the compound ἐξυβρίζω for גלע hitp "to break loose." קלל pi "to curse" in Lv. 20:9; 24:11-23 is transl. by variants with καθ- or ἐνυβρίζω. Other examples are 2 Βασ. 19:44; Ez. 22:7, cf. Lv. 20:9; Na. 1:14 E' (cf. Field, ad loc.); Prv. 6:33 Σ; 12:16 Θ; 1 Βασ. 17:10 (חרף). LXX also brings in ὕβρις at Prv. 19:10, 18 and thus alters the sense, esp. in the second v. The idea of hubris comes in because of a slip at Prv. 14:10, [51] cf. also 27:13 and Jer. 51(28):2. In the depiction of the wrong-doer in Job 15:20 ff. the translator replaced the image stiff-neckedness [52] by that of rebellion against God, cf. 22:12. ὕβρις seems to correspond both in sound and sense to the noun עֶבְרָה. [53] This comes from root עבר "to step over," hitp "to let oneself be caught away." עֶבְרָה might be understood as "presumption" at Is. 16:6; Jer. 48:30; Prv. 21:24; 22:8, cf. also Sir. 13:7; 16:8. But the translators hardly noted or regarded this. [54] On roots תעע 2 Ch. 36:16 (= 1 Εσδρ. 1:49), קלס Sir. 11:4, שׁחק Ju. 16:25, עלל Ju. 19:25 etc., ענה pi Ju. 20:5 → V, 631, 1 ff. On יְהִיר Prv. 21:24 → I, 508, 35 ff. On קשׁה also with עֹרֶף or צַוָּאר "neck" → V, 1028, 13 ff., cf. also Job 15:25-27 where ὕβρει corresponds to בְּצַוָּאר. On כְּסִיל → IV, 834, 16 ff. Other words like סלל hitp Ex. 9:17, עזז hi Prv. 7:13; 21:29, יעז part. ni Is. 33:19 (→ n. 44), [55] פחז Ju. 9:4; Zeph. 3:4 and עָתָק 1 S. 2:3; Ps. 31:18; 75:5; 94:4 might also be brought into the sphere of hubris in the sense of arrogance or insolence.

5. There are only a few instances from works only in Gk. or extant only in Gk. Wis. 2:19 ref. to worse than pride, i.e., to the mistreatment and torture of the righteous, who is to be condemned to a shameful death. [56] But in 4:19 the wicked will be delivered up to (spiritual?) torments among the dead (Is. 14:10 ff.) [57] for ever. In Est. 4:17d and 1-3 Macc. the group occurs in speeches and strongly rhetorical passages in varying senses from arrogance to violence. Hubris is used primarily to denote the attitude and conduct of the Gentiles. Esp. in opposition to them God is the One who hates hubris μίσυβρις (3 Macc. 6:9), obviously a new and unique expression.

C. Judaism.

1. Philo uses the group in various ways. He often speaks of "persecutions" of the Jews or "attacks" on them or the temple, Flacc., 58 f., 77, 79, 95, 117; Leg. Gaj., 191 and 302; Vit. Mos., I, 72. For the hubris of men in relation to one another cf. Spec. Leg., III,

---

51 LXX reads זד for זר. In 14:3, perhaps under LXX influence, גַּאֲוָה seems to have come into the Mas. for גֵּו, cf. B. Gemser, Sprüche Salomos, Hndbch. AT, I, 16² (1963), ad loc.
52 Cf. G. Hölscher, Das Buch Hi., Hndbch. AT, I, 17² (1952), ad loc.
53 P. de Lagarde, Anmerkungen z. griech. Übers. d. Prv. (1863), VIII thinks ὕβρις is a loan word from the Semitic (עֶבְרָה).
54 At Is. 16:6 LXX has ἐξαίρω with ὕβρις, ὑβριστής, ὑπερηφανία for other Hbr. words. In the other ref. it either uses another text or misunderstands the HT. עֶבְרָה is elsewhere "wrath" from עבר with orig. gajin for 'ajin → V, 392, 33 ff. cf. Ps. 7: בְּעַבְרוֹת, Hbr.: βεγαβρωθ (cf. Field, ad loc.), Θ: ἐν θυμῷ.
55 Also שדד "to offer violence," cf. G. Bertram, "Zur Prägung der bibl. Gottesvorstellung in d. gr. Übers. d. AT: Die Wiedergabe v. schadad u. schaddaj im Gr.," Die Welt d. Orients, 2 (1959), 502-513.
56 With Plat. Resp., II, 361e Wis. 2:12 ff. was used as a Messianic prophecy in the early Church, cf. E. Benz, Der gekreuzigte Gerechte bei Plato, im NT u. in d. Alten Kirche (1950), 41.
57 Volz Esch., 321-3.

173; Leg. All., III, 241; for that of men against women, III, 76, 78, 108 (Dt. 21:22 f.); Virt., 113; of women themselves, Spec. Leg., I, 281; III, 173 f. (Dt. 25:11), of "infringements" against parents, Spec. Leg., II, 245 and 254; Jos., 74, slaves, Spec. Leg., II, 83, debtors, Virt., 89, excesses at feasts, Vit. Cont., 42; Spec. Leg., III, 186; Flacc., 136. Hubris is one of many vices, Spec. Leg., I, 204; Conf. Ling., 117 (the building of the tower, Gn. 11:4). Boasters see presumption in admonitions to them, Spec. Leg., II, 18, cf. Leg. Gaj., 64 (πρὸς ὕβρεως). Hubris is often used for the "punishment," "dishonouring," imposed by a judge, with blows, Spec. Leg., III, 82, 168; Omn. Prob. Lib., 55. Other vices, including hubris, are condemned with murder, Decal., 170. Shame comes on the adulterer, Decal., 126, also on the perjurer, 86. The changing of hubris into a penal concept seems almost an inner contradiction, since there is no norm for hubris as a capricious act. Philo himself says hubris is in contradiction with law, Vit. Mos., II, 14. But it is in keeping with OT ideas as also with the pagan world that the criminal is without rights and is delivered up to the caprice of the executioner.

For Philo the Gentile world is permeated by hubris in many of its manifestations. This is true of the festivals with their violent excesses, Cher., 92, cf. also the mocking of Agrippa in Alexandria, Flacc., 32 and 40. The same applies to the games, Praem. Poen., 52; Agric., 113 and 116, to the dominant conceit in the cities with its scorn of men, Decal., 4, [58] to writers who squander their gifts on trash, Vit. Mos., I, 3. It is even true of the state which through its tax-gatherers grinds the people even after death with exactions and spoliations, Spec. Leg., II, 94 f. Philo hardly gets down to essentials. He adopts the ancient dictum of Solon that affluence breeds arrogance (→ 296, 15 f.), sometimes just alluding to it, Spec. Leg., III, 43; Poster. C., 99 and 145; Agric., 32; Abr., 228; Vit. Mos., II, 14 and 164; Virt., 163; Flacc., 91; Leg. All., II, 29; Op. Mund., 169: [59] Hubris is a common moral danger. Virtue is extolled in words, but in reality it is despised and mistreated, Mut. Nom., 196. Bodily desires threaten degeneration into sin (ἐξυβρίζω), Poster. C., 182. Understanding and senses lead so easily to arrogance, Leg. All., II, 70, cf. Det. Pot. Ins., 110. He who would follow God must avoid the society of licentious and wicked men, Praem. Poen., 100.

2. Joseph. finds hubris in OT history. [60] It is a recurrent motif from the story of Cain to the giants of Gn. 6. He esp. uses the noun ὕβρις. Less common is the verb with compounds, ἀφυβρίζω in Ant., 19, 357, περιυβρίζω in 18, 44. 260. 358, ἐξυβρίζω in 4, 189, ἐνυβρίζω in 1, 254, καθυβρίζω in 5, 148. Sometimes one also finds ὑβριστής "evil-doer," Bell., 3, 375; 5, 380 and ὑβριστικός, Ant., 2, 106, ἀνύβριστος "unmolested," Ant., 1, 208 f.; Bell., 17, 308; 7, 334; Vit., 80 and 259. Kinship with the hubris-concept of antiquity (→ 295, 7 ff.) and the proximity of synon. expressions are apparent in the description of the Sodomites, Ant., 1, 194; in their overweening presumption ὑπερφρονοῦντες in their own vast and wealthy sphere the Sodomites showed themselves to be evil-doers ὑβρισταί against men and irreverent ἀσεβεῖς vis-à-vis the divine; on account of this arrogance (they had to fall victim to punishment); Ant., 1, 100 and 113 (linked with tyranny in Nimrod); in 8, 253 and 277 the arrogance is against God, cf. 15, 135. For the rest the group expresses any kind of "defamation" (Ant., 16, 235), "ignominy" (17, 309; Bell., 4, 278), "shame," e.g., shameful peace (18, 47. 57. 60) or banishment (3, 266), "ravishing" (Bell., 6, 3), esp. of women (4, 560; 7, 377), also "encroachments" (Ant., 17, 316; 18, 1 and 6; 19, 160), "violence" (17, 297; Bell., 1, 269), "cruelty" (Ant.,

[58] E. R. Goodenough, *The Politics of Philo Judaeus, Practice and Theory* (1938), 30-40, esp. 38 f.

[59] Hubris was an important factor in the downfall of the Hell. world acc. to Philo (cf. Fraenkel, 1) and after him many Chr. apologists → 307, 5 ff. It is also to be viewed as a judgment on the pagan world when Philo regards arrogance due to ignorance as the essence of sin, cf. W. Völker, *Fortschritt u. Vollendung bei Philo v. Alex. Eine studie z. Gesch. d. Frömmigkeit* (1938), 64 f.

[60] K. H. Rengstorf placed at my disposal the lexical material he had already assembled on hubris (verb, noun and adj.) in Jos. Bell., Ap. and Ant., 1-7.

19, 129), "outbursts of rage" (19, 78), "mistreatment" (Ap., 1, 130), "making contemptible" (Bell., 7, 357; Vit., 408), "provocation" (Ant., 3, 311; 15, 129 etc.). The compounds too, as in Gk. gen., have no special sense, though the individual prep. give particular nuances and the sense can be strengthened or intensified. The concept of hubris often serves to characterise specific people, esp. the holders of political power, Ant., 18, 88. Hubris explains the fall of Israel and Judah, Ant., 10, 39, cf. 103. Hubris poisons human relations both on a large scale and a small. For this reason all self-assertion is ruled out by the Essenes, Bell., 2, 140. But all this hardly exhausts the great variety of Jos.' use of the group. [61]

3. The Dead Sea Scrolls, like the Wisdom lit., are against pride 1 QM 14:11: רמי קומה, cf. 1 QS 7:5: במרים, cf. Ps. 56:2. [62] Damasc. 2:19 (3:5): כרום ארזים גבהם וכהרים of bodily size is alluding to Gn. 6, cf. Sib., 1, 123. 312. רמי רוח in 1 QS 11:1 are arrogant men. In 1 QpHab 8:10 the ungodly priest is רם לבו, cf. 8:3: יהיר from Hab. 2:5, elsewhere only Prv. 21:24. In Damasc. 1:14 (1:10) איש הלצון ref. to the same ungodly priest as a "scoffer." [63] In 1 QS 4:9 גוה ורום לבב is listed in a catalogue of vices in which קנאת זדון also occurs in 4:10 with a par. in עברת זדון, Prv. 21:24. In Damasc. 1:15 (1:10) one finds גבהות עולם "their wicked (עול) pride." In 1 QH Fr. 3:15 we read חדל זדון: "presumption ceases." All these expressions, as the list of vices shows, are dealing with the sphere and operations of the spirit of corruption. Cf. also 1 Q 29:13, 3 (DJD, I, 132) רשע ושר גוה and also 1 QS 3:10 ff.; 4:9 ff. The root גאה with גאוה (גאון, גאות) occurs in the Scrolls only at 1 QH Fr. 55:2, but cf. 1 QS 4:9 גוה. [64]

4. Throughout Jewish eschatology one finds a kingdom of evil. Hubris is one of its marks. [65] The 12th petition of the Prayer of Eighteen Benedictions ref. to it: "Mayest thou root out the kingdom of arrogance (מלכות זדון), ... Yahweh who humbles the insolent (מכניע זדים)." [66] A political interpretation suggests itself, cf. Sib., 3, 352 (Rome). In the Rabb. tradition hubris occurs with זדון, which denotes wilful sin, גבה, גס, שחץ and derivates, Midr. Est., 4, 15; Dt. r., 4, 2 on 10:1 Raba (d. 352 A.D.) has said: "(The Torah) is not in heaven (Dt. 30:12), i.e., it is not found with him who proudly lifts up his mind," bErub, 55a. Pride is idolatry and denial of God, as is shown with the help of Prv. 16:5 with Dt. 7:26, the application of Is. 2:22, and on the basis of other passages, bSota, 4b, cf. also 5a. Ab., 4, 7 contains an important warning of Rabbi Ismael b Jose against the judicial office: "He who refrains from judging keeps himself from enmity, theft and vain swearing, but he who is bold in decision is a fool, an evil-doer, and of a haughty spirit." גס רוח or גס לב is not biblical, nor does it occur in the Qumran texts, which have רם לב etc. [67] Later Jewish and Jewish Hell. texts show that the hubris concept of the Gk. OT (→ 299, 31 ff.) was still alive and also influenced primitive Christianity

---

[61] In Jos. the importance of hubris in the historical depiction lies not only in the use of the term; it is the key to the author's understanding of history. Cf. W. Weber, *Josephus u. Vespasian. Untersuchungen z. dem Jüd. Krieg d. Jos.* (1921), 24 f., 66-79.

[62] H. Bardtke, *Die Handschriftenfunde am Toten Meer* (1953), 98; A. Weiser, *Die Ps., AT Deutsch,* 15⁵ (1955), *ad loc.*; A. M. Habermann, *Megilloth Midbar Yehuda* (1959), *ad loc.* does not read מְרֻם or מֵרֻם (LXX) but מָרִים from מרה "to be rebellious," but cf. K. G. Kuhn, *Konkordanz z. d. Qumrantexten* (1960), *s.v.* מר from מרר "to be bitter" (often in OT).

[63] A. S. van der Woude, *Die messian. Vorstellungen d. Gemeinde v. Qumran* (1957), 23 transl. "babbler" and ref. to Richardson, *op. cit.,* 177 f., 436.

[64] Cf. Habermann and Kuhn, *s.v.*

[65] Volz. Esch., 89.

[66] Str.-B., IV, 208-249, esp. 212 f., 216.

[67] Transl. P. Fiebig, *Pirqe' Aboth. Der Mischnatractat "Sprüche d. Väter"* (1906), 23, cf. also K. Marti and G. Beer, *Abot. Text, Übers. u. Erklärung* (1927), *ad loc.* For further Rabb. material *v.* Str.-B., II, 101-6; IV, 1072; Levy, I, *s.v.* גאה.

(→ 306, 25 ff.), though it did not undergo any further development, cf. Sib., 2, 259 (list of vices), 3, 455 and 529 (passion piety); S. Bar. 36:8; 48:40; 83:12 f.; Test. R. 3:5; B. 9:3 (a Chr. formulation); Test. Job [68] 15:6, 8; 41:4. Finally one might ref. to the apocalyptic statement in Sib., 4, 152-164 in which one finds together the two elements in hubris, the wicked act of destruction and impious joy at it.

D. The New Testament.

In the NT ὕβρις and related terms are only sparsely used. The noun occurs only 3 times, always in a pass. sense. The verb is used only trans. [69] There is only indirect ref. to the sin of hubris in ὑβριστής (twice).

1. The noun ὕβρις occurs in Ac. 27:10, 21 in words which Paul spoke to the sailors and his fellow-passengers before leaving Crete and then again at the height of the emergency. In both instances we find ὕβρις along with ζημία. The reference of both is to the "hardship," [70] "difficulty," "damage" and "loss" which are due to natural forces and which affect both the ship and its complement. [71] In the little list of sufferings in 2 C. 12:10 [72] the ὕβρεις are "difficulties" which according to Acts too Paul encountered on his journeys through the way, the weather, and the hostility of men → VII, 608, 2 ff. [73]

2. Paul uses the verb in 1 Th. 2:2 with reference to the sufferings (→ V, 924, 28 ff.) and ignominious handling (Ac. 16:12 ff.; Phil. 1:30) which he and Silas had to undergo at Philippi. The ὕβρεις inflicted on the missionaries, public whipping and imprisonment (Ac. 16:22-24), [74] are official acts of the authorities. ὑβρίζω has here the sense of "undergoing ignominious punishment." In Ac. 14:5 the content of ὑβρίζω ("to revile or maltreat") [75] is not defined. In Lk. 11:45 the rendering "to insult, slander" [76] does not quite do justice to the element of the proud or mockingly ironic in ὑβρίζω. The scribe is complaining that Jesus arrogantly attacks the leaders

---

[68] Ed. M. R. James, *Apocrypha Anecdota*, II, (1897).
[69] Bl.-Debr. § 148, 1; 152, 1; Helbing Kasussyntax, 23.
[70] On this sense *v.* Pr.-Bauer, *s.v.*
[71] If ἀσιτία in Ac. 27:21 ref. to sea-sickness, which can carry with it such mental manifestations as anxiety, dispiritedness and self-abandonment, the encouraging words of Paul — the hero does not suffer from sea-sickness — are well adapted to the situation. Sea-sickness is part of the hubris or hardship that had to be suffered. On the expression cf. Pind. Pyth., 1, 72 ναυσίστονος ὕβρις, "destruction bringing sorrow to ships." Hubris here has completely lost its ancient sense acc. to Fraenkel, 81 ref. to Ac. 27:21. On the literary question cf. Haench. Ag.[14], *ad loc.*, also E. Preuschen, *Die Ag., Hndbch. NT,* 4, 1 (1912), *ad loc.*
[72] A. Fridrichsen, "Zum Stil d. paul. Peristasenkatalogs 2 Cor. 11:23 ff.," *Symb. Osl.,* 7 (1928), 25-29.
[73] At 2 C. 12:10 ὕβρις is transl. in the Gothic Bible by *anamahts* "force," "mistreatment," and at Lk. 18:32 one finds *anamahtjan* "to mistreat," "do violence to." This verb is also used for ἀδικέω, ἀποστερέω, βιάζω, ἐπηρεάζω, συκοφαντέω, so that all these verbs might be synon. of ὑβρίζω. At 1 Tm. 1:13 ὑβριστής is transl. *ufbrikands* "despiser." Possibly the similarity of stem syllables in Gk. and Gothic (bri- and brik-) had some influence in this case. Here again the range of hubris seems to be still expanding. Cf. *Die Gotische Bibel*, II, ed. W. Streitberg (1960), *s.v.* and the various ref.
[74] Haench. Ag.[14], *ad loc.*
[75] But cf. Zn. Ag., *ad loc.*
[76] Jesus' address does in fact contain bitter irony, cf. B. Weiss, *Kritisch-exegetisches Handbuch über d. Ev. d. Mk. u. Lk., Kritisch-exeget. Komm. über d. NT,* I, 2[9] (1901), *ad loc.* R. Voeltzel, *Le rire du Seigneur. Enquêtes et remarques sur la signification théol. et prâtique de l'ironie biblique* (1955) was not available to me.

of His people with insulting mockery. The roughly handled messengers of Mt. 22:6 [77] are the prophets of the OT and perhaps also the apostles of the NT. They must suffer martyrdom; the term ὑβρίζω derives from the passion piety of Judaism → V, 907, 13 ff. In the third intimation of the passion the strengthening ὑβρισθήσεται (→ V, 634, 10 ff.) occurs along with ἐμπαιχθήσεται, Lk. 18:32: [78] Jesus is to suffer the fate of the righteous of the OT, the prophets and the martyrs.

3. ὑβριστής occurs only at R. 1:30 in a list of vices. [79] It is hardly a constituent part of such lists, but simply serves with many other terms to swell out the number of sins. ὑβριστάς is given strong emphasis by θεοστυγεῖς, which is to be taken as an adjectival attribute: [80] "despisers hated by God" as representatives of moral inferiority → 296, 3 ff. The expression θεοστυγεῖς ὑβριστάς presupposes rebellion against God, for the reference is to the disruption of human fellowship as a result of ungodliness. According to 1 Tm. 1:13 Paul described himself as a onetime blasphemer, persecutor and evil-doer. The three terms refer to the period when the apostle persecuted the community (1 C. 15:9; Gl. 1:13) or Christ Himself (Ac. 9:4, 5; 22:7, 8; 26:14, 15). The more specific use of ὑβριστής is not current in Paul. [81] The word characterises the persecution of the community as revolt against God.

4. Hb. 10:29 contains the only compound of the verb in the NT, namely, ἐνυβρίζω. Transgression of the Law of Moses brings death. How much more sharply will he be punished, then, who has sinned against Christ, trampled underfoot the Son of God, treated the blood of the covenant as profane, and done despite (ἐνυβρίσας) to the Spirit of grace. [82] The three statements are parallel and mean the same thing; similarly the three verbs καταπατήσας, κοινὸν ἡγησάμενος and ἐνυβρίσας correspond.

E. The Early Church.

The usage found in the NT only at Hb. 10:29 has a par. in 2 Cl., 14, 4: He who acts wickedly (ὑβρίσας) against the flesh (which was also the flesh of Christ) acts wickedly against the Church. [83] 1 Cl., 59, 3 (based on Is. 13:11) shows the influence of biblical developments on liturgical language in Christianity as well as in Judaism, where the

---

[77] W. Michaelis, Das hochzeitliche Kleid. Eine Einführung in d. Gleichnisse Jesu über die rechte Jüngerschaft (1939), 11-72; Jeremias Gl.⁷, 62 f. 65 f.

[78] G. Bertram, Die Leidensgeschichte Jesu u. der Christuskult (1922), 85, cf. also 72 f.; for the Gothic transl. → n. 73.

[79] S. Wibbing, "Die Tugend- u. Lasterkataloge im NT," ZNW Beih., 25 (1959), 88.

[80] So Zn. R., ad loc., 103. On rhetorical grounds Zahn links the neighbouring expressions in pairs.

[81] Materially overzealous service such as that of Paul in persecuting Christians is a sublime form of arrogance. Perhaps this is reflected in Phil. 3:6 when Paul calls himself a zealous persecutor of the community. He carried with him the same zeal and self-awareness into the Chr. apostolate. Cf. G. Bertram, "Paulus Christophorus. Ein anthropologisches Problem d. NT," Stromata. Festgabe d. Akademisch-Theol. Vereins (1930), 26-38, esp. 30-33 and → n. 73.

[82] Cf. Damasc. 5:11 f. (7:12): "And they profane their holy spirit and with a tongue full of railing speeches they open their mouths against the laws of God ...," cf. H. Bardtke, Die Handschriftenfunde am Toten Meer (1958), 263; cf. also Mi. Hb., ad loc.: Apostasy is rebellion (ὕβρις) and defamation of the Holy Ghost.

[83] The compound occurs in a similar connection in an addition to the Naassene sermon, R. Reitzenstein, "Griech. Lehren," Stud. zum antiken Synkretismus aus Iran u. Griechenland (1926), 166, 4: τὰς ἁγίας γραφὰς ... ἐνυβρίζουσι, cf. Hipp. Ref., V, 8, 1.

12th petition of the Prayer of Eighteen Benedictions invokes God, on the basis of Is. 13:11, as the One who humbles arrogant boasters. Often ὕβρις and related words are used in the sense of Christian endurance, Herm. m., 8, 10; Dg., 5, 15. In Herm. s., 6, 3, 4 the word occurs for the temporal punishment in which the righteous are exposed to indignities by unworthy men. The meaning of ὕβρις in Herm. s., 9, 11, 8 is obscure. Acc. to Just. Dial., 136, 3 the wicked rejection of Christ is directed against God Himself. At bottom pagans deride their own gods in their poetry, Apol., 4, 9. When they protect golden idols from theft this presupposes the scornful view these cannot protect themselves, Dg., 2, 7. To set up idols is to mock God, Just. Apol., 9, 3. Pagans mistreat the earth which they hold to be a goddess, Aristid. Apol., 4, 3. Tat. Or. Graec., 23, 1 adopts the philosophical criticism of the games when he states that hubris is crowned there instead of being punished. [84]

Sib., 6, 25 alludes to the mocking of Christ on the cross by means of the crown of thorns and the drink, cf. Test. B. 9:3; Act. Joh. 106 (p. 204, 8). He knows the evil they do to him. The charge of ὑβρίζειν against Jesus, to which there is only implied ref. in Lk. 11:45, is raised in Acta Pilati B 4:3 f. [85] on the ground of prediction of His resurrection. Here as in the NT examples of hubris etc. are neither numerous nor significant. Only the development of Chr. theology made the concept important. In the Chr. doctrine of tyrants in opposition to the state hubris as rebellion against God became from the 2nd cent. onwards a mark of the autonomous ruler hostile to God. Hipp., who died as a political prisoner in the Sardinian mines, worked out this teaching. [86] Aug. Enarratio, 2, 15 on Ps. 18 (MPL, 36 [1861], 163) calls *superbia* the basic sin which caused the fall and from which all schisms and individual sins derive. [87]

Bertram

---

[84] Cf. Philo's attitude to the pagan world → 303, 15 ff.

[85] C. v. Tischendorf, Evangelia apocr.² (1876), 295 f. On ὕβρις θεοῦ instead of κατάρα θεοῦ at Gl. 3:13 for קִלְלַת אֱלֹהִים Dt. 21:23 → III, 918, 18 ff. The pt. would not be that of Σ that he was hanged for despising God but that the hanging of Jesus on the cross is a mocking of God by the Jews. The OT formula would thus be given a new Chr. sense.

[86] J. Hashagen, "Über die Anfänge d. chr. Staats- u. Gesellschaftsanschauung," ZKG, NF, 12 (1930), 131-158, esp. 151.

[87] Aug. attacks esp. the *superbia* of the *docti huius saeculi*, cf. W. Kamlah, *Christentum u. Geschichtlichkeit. Untersuchungen zur Entstehung d. Christentums u. zu Augustins "Bürgerschaft Gottes"* (1951), 201-208.

† ὑγιής, † ὑγιαίνω

θεραπεία κτλ. → III, 128, 14 ff.
ἰάομαι κτλ. → III, 194, 1 ff.
ἰσχύω κτλ. → III, 397, 1 ff.
νόσος κτλ. → IV, 1091, 15 ff.

Contents: A. Profane Greek: 1. Etymology and Meaning; 2. Assessment of Health in the Greek-Hellenistic World. B. Septuagint. C. Hellenistic Judaism. D. New Testament. E. Post-Apostolic Fathers.

A. Profane Greek.

1. Etymology and Meaning.

The adj. ὑγιής occurs in a Hom. ref. (Il., 8, 524) which even antiquity knew to be inauthentic, and it is then found from the 5th cent. B.C. and taken in the direct sense of "healthy," [1] Hdt., III, 130, 3; 134, 1; Thuc., II, 49, 2; III, 34, 3 (σῶν καὶ ὑγιᾷ); Plat. Symp., 186b; ποιέω τινὰ ὑγιᾷ, Xenoph. Mem., IV, 2, 17; Plat. Charm., 156b. The derived verb ὑγιαίνω, from Theogn., 255; Hdt., I, 153, 1; Thuc., II, 58, 2 means "to be healthy," [2] e.g., as opp. to νοσέω and κάμνω, Plat. Gorg., 495e., 505a. A specific use is for mental health and the faculty of rational thought, Hdt., III, 33; Aristoph. Av., 1214; Eur. Ba., 948, opp. μαίνομαι, Plat. Lys., 205a; Theaet., 190c. Thus ὑγιής can have the gen. sense of "rational," "intelligent," "pertinent," e.g., in the one instance in Hom. Il., 8, 524: [3] ὑγιής μῦθος, "an intelligent or rational word," cf. also ὑγιής λόγος, Hdt., I, 8, 3; Dio Chrys. Or., 1, 49. Quite common is μηδὲν ὑγιὲς λέγειν, "to say nothing intelligent or even something false," Eur. Phoen., 201; Aristoph. Thes. 636; Pl., 274, hence "to lie" in Demosth. Or., 58, 36. Similar combinations are μηδὲν ὑγιὲς μηδ' ἐλεύθερον φρονῶ, Soph. Phil., 1006, cf. Eur. Andr., 448 or οὐδὲν ὑγιὲς διανοέομαι, Thuc., III, 75, 4; IV, 22, 2. Finally the group is used in relation to "true," e.g., οὐδὲν ὑγιὲς οὐδ' ἀληθὲς ἔχω, Plat. Phaed., 69b; cf. Plat. Phaedr., 242e; Resp., II, 372e; IX, 584a e; 589c; X, 603a b, also "firm," "constant," "reliable," Plat. Leg., I, 630b; Ep., 10, 358c; ὑγιῶς καὶ πιστῶς, P. Oxy., IX, 1187, 18 (254 A.D.), or "righteous," Plat. Resp., VI, 490c, or "whole," Plat. Gorg., 524e; 526d (of the soul); cf. ἰάσιμος, ἀνίατος "curable," "incurable," 525b-526b. ὑγιαίνω is often a greeting in letters, both at the beginning and at

---

ὑ γ ι ή ς κ τ λ .   Liddell-Scott, Pass., Pr.-Bauer, Preisigke Wört., Thes. Steph., s.v.; H. Diller, "Hippokratische Medizin u. attische Philosophie," Hermes, 80 (1952), 385-409; H. Ebbecke, "Gesundheit u. Krankheit vom Standpunkt d. Physiologie," Studium Generale, 6 (1953), 22-7; W. Ebstein, Die Medizin im NT u. im Talmud (1903); H. Flashar, "Die medizinischen Grundlagen d. Lehre v. d. Wirkung d. Dichtung in d. griech. Poetik," Hermes, 84 (1956), 12-48; H. Greeven, "Krankheit u. Heilung nach d. NT," Lebendige Wissenschaft, 8 (1948); W. Jaeger, Paideia. Die Formung d. griech. Menschen, II² (1954), 11-58; P. Kleinert, "Zur Idee d. Lebens im AT," ThStKr, 68 (1895), 693-732; L. Köhler, Der hbr. Mensch (1953), 33-47; W. Leibbrand, "Gesundheit u. Krankheit im abendländischen medizin. Denken," Studium Generale, 6 (1953), 32-9; H. Ruess, Gesundheit - Krankheit - Arzt bei Plato. Bedeutung u. Funktion, Diss. Tübingen (1957); J. Schumacher, Antike Medizin. Die natur-philosoph. Grundlagen d. Medizin in d. griech. Antike² (1963), 251-298 (with bibl.).
[1] Acc. to F. de Saussure, Recueil des publications scientifiques (1922), from *su "good" (Sanskr. su-) and root * gu̯iē (preserved in βίος and ζήω), hence "with good life," "living well" [Risch]. Cf. Boisacq, Hofmann, s.v.; Schwyzer, I, 298.
[2] On the formation of the verb cf. Debr. Griech. Wortb. § 222; Schwyzer, I, 733.
[3] At any rate it was already seen to be a later addition by the Homer philology of antiquity, cf. W. Leaf, The Iliad, I² (1960), 366. σῶς, which is not found in the NT, is Homeric, Liddell-Scott, s.v.

the end. [4] That the ref. is not just to bodily health may be seen from the parting on grave-stones in the sense "Farewell," CIG, II, 3706, 5; IG, 14, 2526, 6 f.

This broad range of meaning is rooted in the basic sense that the healthy is what is balanced according to the order of the whole. Already Alkmaion Fr., 4 (Diels, I, 215, 11 - 216, 4) thinks health is preserved by balance of forces (ἰσονομία τῶν δυνάμεων), namely, the moist, dry, cold, hot, bitter, sweet etc. Predominance of the one antithesis has a ruinous effect. Health rests on a balanced mixture of qualities: τὴν δὲ ὑγείαν τὴν σύμμετρον τῶν ποιῶν κρᾶσιν. [5] Obviously Alkmaion is harking back here to the ancient Pytha-gorean concept of harmony [6] which might well have its origin in the ethical and political sphere. [7] The group ὑγιής κτλ. is constantly used later in understanding the ordered relation between individual sections of society, Plat. Resp., II, 372 f.; III, 404-410; IV, 444d. [8] In Polyb., 28, 17, 12 the ὑγιαίνοντες are the "quiet," "reflective," as compared with the turbulent. This defining of the healthy as a mixture of different qualities and balance of extremes is adopted and applied in every age. [9]

2. Assessment of Health in the Greek-Hellenistic World.

While sickness and suffering as an experience of the uncertainty of human life are always felt to be a religious problem, health is mostly regarded as the normal, as what may be presupposed. In the earlier period, then, health figures only in Wisdom lit. with its rational character. Here it is specially valued from the very outset: ἀνδρὶ δ᾽ ὑγιαίνειν ἄριστόν ἐστιν, ὥς γ᾽ ἐμὶν δοκεῖ, Axiopistos Fr., 19 (Diels, I, 201, 17). Behind this stands a scholion which finely renders the average view: ὑγιαίνειν μὲν ἄριστον ἀνδρὶ θνατῶι, δεύτερον δὲ φυὰν καλὸν γενέσθαι, τὸ τρίτον δὲ πλουτεῖν ἀδόλως καὶ τὸ τέταρτον ἡβᾶν μετὰ τῶν φίλων, Scolia anon., 7 (Diehl, II, 183 f.). [10] There is a very high estimation of health in the ancient aristocratic ethic, Theogn., 255. [11] In Pind. Pyth., 3, 73 it is called ὑγίεια χρυσέα, while acc. to Critias Fr., 6 (Diels, II, 379, 13 f.) Ὑγίεια is the most joyous of the goddesses. [12] In philosophical teaching on values health is one of the ἀγαθά acc. to the Platonists and Peripatetics. It is the highest of the human goods which Plato distinguishes from divine goods and defines in Leg., I, 631c; V, 733e-734d.

---

[4] Ditt. Syll.³, III, 1259, 3 (4th cent. B.C.); P. Oxy., IV, 745, 10; BGU, I, 27, 3 f.; 38, 4 f.; II, 423, 3 (2nd. cent. A.D.); III, 846, 3 (2nd cent. A.D.); Ep. Ar., 41.

[5] On Alkmaion of Croton cf. E. Wellmann, Art. "Alkmaion," Pauly-W., 1 (1894), 1556; Schumacher, 66-81.

[6] Cf. the words of the anon. Pythagorean: τήν τε ἀρετὴν ἁρμονίαν εἶναι καὶ τὴν ὑγίειαν καὶ τὸ ἀγαθὸν ἅπαν καὶ τὸν θεόν. διὸ καὶ καθ᾽ ἁρμονίαν συνεστάναι τὰ ὅλα (Diels, I, 451, 11 f.) and: ὑγίειαν τὴν τοῦ εἴδους διαμονήν, νόσον τὴν τούτου φθοράν (I, 463, 26 f.). On Alkmaion and the Pythagorean school cf. Diog. L., VIII, 83; Aristot. Metaph., I, 5, p. 986a, 22; on this B. L. van der Waerden, "Die Harmonialehre d. Pythagoreer," Hermes, 78 (1943), 163-199.

[7] Ruess, 18; K. v. Fritz, Pythagorean Politics in Southern Italy (1940), V-IX and 94-104, but cf. W. Jaeger, Die Theol. d. frühen gr. Denker (1953), 268, n. 48, who finds the origin of the concept of mixture in early Gk. medicine and science. On the medicine of the Pythagoreans, Schumacher, 53-66.

[8] On the health of the state Jaeger, III, 47-49.

[9] Cf. Aristot. Metaph., I, 5, p. 986b, 23; 986a, 15; Diog. L., VIII, 26; for medicine Hippocr. Vict., 10 (Littré, VI, 482 f.); Vet. Med., 16 (CMG, I, 47 f.) and: ὅταν μετρίως ἔχῃ τὸ θερμὸν καὶ τὸ ψυχρὸν τῆς πρὸς ἄλληλα κράσεως, ὑγιαίνει ὁ ἄνθρωπος, Hippocr. Περὶ ἑβδομάδων, 24 (Littré, VIII, 647). On the Hippocratic view of health Schumacher, 198-202; E. Wellmann, Das Hygieinon d. Hippokr., Quellen u. Stud. z. Gesch. d. Naturwissenschaft u. d. Medizin, 4 (1933), 1, 1-5. For the concept to-day cf. Leibbrand, 32.

[10] Cf. Plat. Gorg., 451e; Aristot. Rhet., II, 21, p. 1394b, 13, but already Thales acc. to Diog. L., I, 37: τίς εὐδαίμων; ὁ τὸ μὲν σῶμα ὑγιής, τὴν δὲ ψυχὴν εὔπορος, τὴν δὲ φύσιν εὐπαίδευτος, Jaeger, II, 88.

[11] Cf. E. Schwartz, Ethik d. Griechen (1951), 59 f.

[12] On the goddess Hygieia cf. J. Tambornino, Art. "Hygieia," Pauly-W., 9 (1916), 93-7; O. Kern, Die griech. Religion, I (1935), 310; K. Kerényi, Der göttliche Arzt² (1956), 70, Ill. 30, 34; Nilsson, I², 440.

The art of healing thus holds an important place among the τέχναι, Gorg., 452a. Health is its τέλος, Aristot. Eth. Nic., I, 1, p. 1094a, 8. Since the healthy is the mean or the orderly, the way to health and its preservation is clear: All excess damages health, *ibid.*, II, 2, p. 1104a, 16 f. Rules of health are ordinances for the body, Plat. Gorg., 504c. One can tell the sick what manner of life will make him well, Plat. Resp., IV, 444d; Hippocr. Vict., I, 2 (Littré, VI, 468, 18), 32 (VI, 510, 13) etc. There is ref. to the sickness and health of the soul as well as the body. This usages increases in importance from Plato on, Plat. Tim., 86b. [13] σωφροσύνη is regarded as health of soul, Resp., III, 404e; IX, 571d; Phaedr., 231d. The soul is healthy and rational when the λογιστικὸν καὶ ἥμερον rules over the ἐπιθυμητικόν, IX 571c-572a. But basically bodily and spiritual health belong together, so that a man cannot have the one without the other, Charm., 156e-157c; Tim., 87d. This avoids overestimating purely physical processes, but on the other hand bodily healthy is given precedence of πλοῦτος, cf. the discussion of the hierarchy of values in Plat. Leg., V, 743d-744e; Euthyd., 279a b; 281.

In orthodox Stoicism the distinction between health of soul and health of body takes on profound significance. Since here only moral goods are ἀγαθά, bodily health is an ἀδιάφορον. But health of soul in analogy to that of body is defined as εὐκρασία, Stob. Ecl., II, 62, 15: εὐκρασία... τῶν ἐν τῇ ψυχῇ δογμάτων. Virtue follows health of soul, vice its sickness. In distinction from the Platonic and Aristotelian tradition, every πάθος is here a lack of reason and is thus viewed as sickness, II, 88, 8. [14] Posidonius opposed this view, since health of soul, the normal moral state, includes the inclination to failure and even vice, and hence does not correspond to bodily health as a proper functioning of the organs. [15] In the magic pap. ὑγίεια can be set alongside ζωή and σωτηρία and have the sense of "wholeness." [16] In Gnosticism there is little interest in health (→ II, 839, 21 ff.). Man is θνητὸς μὲν διὰ τὸ σῶμα, ἀθάνατος δὲ διὰ τὸν οὐσιώδη ἄνθρωπον, Corp. Herm., 1, 15, cf. Asclepius, I, 7b (Scott, I, 296, 28 ff.), 8 (300, 10 ff.).

B. The Septuagint.

1. ὑγιαίνω occurs in the LXX 41 times. There is no proper Hbr. original since natural life is not as such an object of theoretical consideration in the OT (→ II, 849, 6 ff., cf. also 843, 19 ff.). Health is part of life (חַיִּים), which is a divine gift (→ II, 844, 3 ff.). [17] In 9 instances ὑγιαίνω is the transl. of שָׁלוֹם (→ II, 402, 20 ff.) and denotes man's well-being, Gn. 29:6; 37:14; 43:27 f., cf. the hypocritical question of 2 Βασ. 20:9; also the thriving of cattle, Gn. 37:14. Βάδιζε ὑγιαίνων (for לֵךְ לְשָׁלוֹם) in Ex. 4:18 is a salutation: "Go in peace," cf. also Da. 10:19. All man's property may be included: σὺ ὑγιαίνων καὶ ὁ οἶκός σου καὶ πάντα τὰ σὰ ὑγιαίνοντα, 1 Βασ. 25:6. [18] ὑγιαίνω also means "to remain in good condition," Prv. 13:13 (for שלם). [19] cf. "to become healthy," Dt. 28:35 ᾿Α (רפא ni); Is. 38:9 Σ (חיה → n. 17). [20]

---

[13] Ruess, 3; Schumacher, 234 f.

[14] A. Bonhöffer, *Epict u. d. Stoa. Untersuchungen z. stoischen Philosophie* (1890), 262-284.

[15] Cf. K. Reinhardt, Art. "Poseidonios," Pauly-W., 22 (1953), 737-745; cf. here also the ref. from Gal. [Dihle].

[16] Preis. Zaub., 3, 576; T. Schermann, "Griech. Zauberpap. u. das Gemeinde- u. Dankgebet im 1 Cl.," TU, 34, 2b (1909), 41-4.

[17] Force and power work in it. Sickness is thus weakness חֳלִי, Dt. 7:15; 28:59, 61; Is. 38:9; Ps. 41:3, cf. חלה Gn. 48:1; 1 S. 19:14; 30:13; Is. 38:1. Similarly חיה can mean "to become healthy," Is. 38:9, 21; Jos. 5:8; cf. Ber., 5, 5 → II, 850, 19 ff.

[18] Cf. the Luc. form of 2 S. 11:7: εἰ ὑγιαίνει Ιωαβ καὶ εἰ ὑγιαίνει ὁ λαὸς καὶ εἰ ὑγιαίνει ὁ πόλεμος (!) καὶ εἶπεν ὑγιαίνει.

[19] LXX read יִשְׁלָם for יְשֻׁלָּם, cf. B. Gemser, *Sprüche Salomos*² (1963), ad loc.

[20] Ex. 1:19 Αλλ transl. the obscure חָיוֹת by ὑγιαίνουσιν.

2. ὑγιής occurs 10 times in the LXX. It is used for the "healthy" return of an army with some restriction of meaning as compared with the Hbr. בְּשָׁלוֹם "safe," "unharmed," Jos. 10:21. In Is. 38:21, cf. v. 9 we read that Hezekiah was restored to health after his prayer, ὑγιὴς ἔσῃ for חיה. [21] This shows there is no gulf between a purely natural life to which health also belongs and a life before God; the two belong indissolubly together, → II. 844, 33 ff.; 851, 15 ff. [22] In Sir. 30:14 ὑγιής is used for חי. Here health is definitely valued highly, cf. vv. 14-21 in praise of health. Hell. influences have been at work here, [23] as the dominant thought of the v. shows: "Health is better than riches" → 309, 19 ff. [24] To this corresponds the praise of the physician in 38:1-15. The statement that healing is from the Most High in v. 2 is taken to mean that God has created the physician, v. 1, 12. The physician works through means of healing given by God, v. 4 f. [25] Nor is the work of the apothecary forgotten, v. 7. Sin and sickness are still interconnected, but healing is not just on the basis of atoning sacrifice; it is also through the work of the physician, v. 12 f., 15. [26]

C. Hellenistic Judaism.

1. Joseph. [27] offers only few instances of a direct understanding of the word group, so Bell., 1, 647; 2, 31. He uses it primarily for rational thought and action → 308, 14 f. The ὑγιαίνοντες τῇ κρίσει are contrasted with the ἀνόητοι, Ap., 1, 222. διάνοια ὑγιὴς καὶ δικαία is promised to Solomon, Ant., 7, 381; he asks νοῦν ὑγιῆ καὶ φρόνησιν ἀγαθήν, 8, 23. Of a man it can be said: ἀκρατὴς ἦν ὑγιαίνοντος λογισμοῦ, Bell., 2, 31. Very generally: οὐδὲν or μηδὲν ὑγιές "nothing rational," Bell., 1, 7; Ant., 9, 118; 16, 340. Again: αἰτίαι οὐχ ὑγιεῖς, "irrational grounds," Ap., 1, 213; Bell., 5, 326: φρονέω ... οὐδὲν ὑγιές expresses an evaluation: "to have nothing rational or good in mind."

2. Philo of Alex. follows the Stoic understanding in his use of the group → 310, 15 ff. If the soul is healthy, sickness does little harm to the body, Virt., 3, 13 → 310, 16 f. [28] Health is present when desire is overcome, Det. Pot. Ins., 13. [29] The soul is healthy when "healthy thoughts" οἱ ὑγιαίνοντες λόγοι overpower passion and sickness, Abr., 223. Sickness as corruption of soul is the basis of all vice, Conf. Ling., 25. Agreement of all parts of the soul in iniquity is interpreted as the flood, Conf. Ling., 22 f. Here one sees the classical idea of the mutual relation of the parts of the soul. But the parts are qualified as healthy or corrupt. The healthy and true inclination of the soul can be pushed aside by the sick inclination, Agric., 164. The pillar of the healthy soul is the νοῦς. It must remain in man as the righteous man does in the race. If the νοῦς is healthy, man need have no doubt as to full redemption, Migr. Abr., 119, 124.

---

[21] Cf. the rendering of חיה pi by ὑγιεῖς ἀποδείξει in Hos. 6:2 E' (Field, ad loc.).

[22] OT wisdom would lead to this life by offering the way of life, Prv. 2:19; 5:6; 6:23; 10:17; 15:24. The teaching of wisdom is life and is healthy for the body, 4:22, cf. 14:30. In fact obedience to God's commands and well-being are not always in harmony, Job 21:7; Ps. 73:1-11, where v. 3 ref. to the health of the wicked.

[23] On Sir. cf. O. Eissfeldt, Einl. in d. AT³ (1964), 807.

[24] Cf. in Sir. 37:27-31 the call to a moderate way of life as the prerequisite for long life.

[25] Sir. 38:5 alludes to Ex. 15:23-25 in terms of an exposition offered in Tg. O. and also found in Philo Vit. Mos., I, 181-187 and Jos. Ant., 3, 6 f.

[26] Cf. also Lv. 13:15 f., where הַבָּשָׂר הַחַי "raw flesh" is oddly transl. τὸν χρῶτα τὸν ὑγιῆ and Is. 1:6 Σ which has ὑγιές for מְתֹם "something undamaged."

[27] K. H. Rengstorf kindly offered access to the Jos. concordance being prepared under his direction in the Institutum Judaicum Delitzschianum.

[28] Physical life is of little account gen. Thus there is little interest in health, though the body is the δεσμός of the soul, Leg. All., II, 57; III, 151; Det. Pot. Ins., 158; Ebr., 152; Rer. Div. Her., 68.

[29] Cf. H. Schmidt, Die Anthropologie Philons v. Alex. (1933), 45 f., 95 f.

D. New Testament.

1. As in the OT (→ 310, 28 ff.) health is not especially valued in the NT. How alien the group ὑγιής is to the Palestinian world may be seen from the proverb οὐ χρείαν ἔχουσιν οἱ ἰσχύοντες ἰατροῦ (→ III, 204, 31 ff.) ἀλλ' οἱ κακῶς ἔχοντες (Mk. 2:17 and par.). Only at Lk. 5:31 does one find ὑγιαίνοντες for ἰσχύοντες [30] → IV, 1095, 12 ff. Yet ὑγιής and ὑγιαίνω occur in the Jesus tradition. Jesus shows Himself to be the Victor over sin and suffering by His deeds. At His Word health is restored visibly (→ III, 211, 12 ff.), Mk. 5:34; Mt. 12:13; 15:31. In this regard Mt., Mk. and Jn. all use the adjective ὑγιής, cf. Mk. 5:34; Mt. 12:13; 15:31; Jn. 5(4):9, 14 f.; 7:23 (also Ac. 4:10). Lk. prefers the verb ὑγιαίνω, Lk. 5:31; 7:10; 15:27. Jn. especially claims that Jesus makes ὅλον (→ V, 175, 5 ff.) ἄνθρωπον "healthy" on the Sabbath, 7:23. [31] The work of the Revealer frees in this world for the new life which embraces man in his corporeality. The power to heal, to make whole, is also transmitted to the apostles according to Ac. 4:10 → V, 277, 21 ff.

2. 3 Jn. 2 has ὑγιαίνω in the salutation: περὶ πάντων εὔχομαί σε εὐοδοῦσθαι καὶ ὑγιαίνειν. This is borrowed from the epistolary formula of Hellenism (→ II, 162, 11 ff.; V, 114, 7 ff.) → 308, 26 ff.

3. The group takes on a new sense in the Pastorals. Christian proclamation and teaching (→ II, 777, 35 ff.) is called ὑγιαίνουσα διδασκαλία (1 Tm. 1:10; 2 Tm. 4:3; Tt. 1:9, 2:1), or ὑγιαίνοντες λόγοι (1 Tm. 6:3; 2 Tm. 1:13), or λόγος ὑγιής (Tt. 2:8). This terminology can be understood only against the Greek-Hellenistic background, → 308, 14 ff. To be avoided is the mistake of thinking that the reference is to the teaching which makes whole, whose goal is health of soul. [32] Sound doctrine is true and correct teaching in contrast to perverted doctrine, to μῦθοι (→ IV, 782, 11 ff.) καὶ γενεαλογίαι (→ I, 664, 4 ff.) ἀπέραντοι, 1 Tm. 1:4. This is the traditional teaching which is established and validated by the apostles and preserved by the office to which Timothy and Titus are called. But in the description of proclamation and teaching as ὑγιαίνουσα διδασκαλία there is a material definition which is important for understanding of the Pastorals. The concern of this teaching is not with a speculative soteriology slanted away from the world but with true, rational and proper life in the world, which as creation is characterised by order and reason. [33] Here, then, we have a non-speculative, pragmatic usage. Hence the admonition to ὑγιαίνειν τῇ πίστει (→ IV, 788, 30 ff.) is connected with the summons to a correct and orderly walk, Tt. 1:13; 2:2.

---

[30] Cf. Artemid. Onirocr., IV, 22 (p. 215, 17).

[31] Jn. 7:23 stands related to 5:1-18. There, too, one finds ὑγιῆ γίνομαι in 5(4):6, 9, 11, 14 f. It is also attested in healing inscr. from the Aesculapius sanctuary in Epidaurus, cf. R. Herzog, Die Wunderheilungen von Epidaurus (1931), No. 5, 11, 16, 23, 40 etc. K. H. Rengstorf, Die Anfänge d. Auseinandersetzung zwischen Christusglaube u. Asklepiosfrömmigkeit (1953), 16 thinks this indicates a polemic against the Aesculapius cult in Jn. But it is doubtful whether one can draw such conclusions from so general an expression.

[32] So W. Michaelis, Pastoralbr. u. Gefangenschaftsbr. (1930), 79 f.; cf. Dib. Past., 20. Michaelis, 84 tries to explain the designation of the Gospel as ὑγιαίνουσα διδασκαλία from the position of the Past. Teaching and proclamation are called sound because they avert the corrupting influences of the false teachers. Hence explanation in terms of philosophical usage is unnecessary. As the examples show, Gk.-Hell. usage is not specifically philosophical but represents the average undertanding. That fig. ideas may also be present is to be seen from 2 Tm. 2:17.

[33] Naturally we do not have here a philosophical rationalism, but the logical relating of faith and teaching to rational existence in the world.

E. Post-Apostolic Fathers.

The word group seldom occurs here. Prayer is made for the health of kings and rulers in 1 Cl., 61, 1. 1 Cl., 20, 10 in praise of the Creator ref. to the unstoppable springs created πρὸς ἀπόλαυσιν καὶ ὑγείαν. In Herm. s., 8, 1, 3 f.; 3, 1 the tree which represents the Law is called ὑγιές "sound." In s., 9, 8, 3. 5. 7, when the stones are tested by the Lord, the "strong" ones which can be used for building the Church are found ὑγιεῖς. s., 8, 6, 3 ref. to those who have not kept the seal (of baptism) ὑγιής, i.e., intact.

Luck

ὕδωρ

Contents: A. Water in the Ancient Oriental and Greek-Hellenistic World: I. Greek Usage; II. Meaning: 1. The Flood; 2. Water as Dispenser of Life; 3. Cleansing by Water. B. In the Old Testament-Jewish World: I. Usage; II. Meaning: 1. Literal Usage: a. Drinking Water and Irrigation; b. The Flood; c. Means of Cleansing; 2. Transferred Usage. C. In the New Testament: I. Water Literally and Metaphorically: 1. The Synoptic Tradition: a. Water as the Flood; b. Drinking Water; c. Cleansing Water; 2. In the Johannine Writings: a. Water as the Flood in Revelation; b. Drinking Water in Revelation and John's Gospel; c. Healing and Cleansing Water in John's Gospel; 3. 2 Pt. 3:5 f. II. Baptismal Water: 1. The Saying of the Baptist; 2. Water Baptism and Spirit Baptism in Primitive Christian Theology; 3. Interpretation of Baptism by Water Symbolism. D. The Baptismal Water in the Post-Apostolic Fathers and the Early Church: 1. Interpretation of Baptism by Water Symbolism; 2. Rules about the Water of Baptism; 3. Sanctifying of the Water of Baptism; 4. Holy Water.

ὕδωρ. On A. II: L. Deubner, *De incubatione*, Diss. Giessen (1899); A. Wünsche, *Die Sagen vom Lebensbaum u. Lebenswasser* (1905), 71-104, I. Goldziher, "Wasser als Dämonen abwehrendes Mittel," ARW, 13 (1910), 20-22; M. Ninck, *Die Bdtg. des Wassers in Kult u. Leben der Alten* (1921); H. Bonnet, "Die Symbolik der Reinigungen im ägypt. Kult," *Angelos*, I (1925), 103-121; A. King, *Holy Water. A Short Account of the Use of Water for Ceremonial and Purificatory Purposes in Pagan, Jewish and Christian Times* (1926); Ant. Christ., V (1936), 153-187; G. Spaltmann, *Das Wasser in d. religiösen Anschauung d. Völker*, Diss. Bonn (1939); M. Eliade, *Die Religionen u. d. Heilige* (1954), 217-246; F. Hartung, "Das Wasser im alten u. neuen Ägypten," *Naturwissenschaftliche Rundschau*, 10 (1957), 373-378; A. Hermann, "Der Nil u. d. Christen," *Jbch. Ant. Christ.*, 2 (1959), 30-69. On B. II: W. Brandt, "Die jüd. Baptismen oder das religiöse Waschen u. Baden im Judt. mit Einschluss des Judenchristentums," ZAW Beih., 18 (1910); also "Jüd. Reinheitslehre u. ihre Beschreibung in d. Ev.," ZAW Beih., 19 (1910), 5-55; T. J. Jones, "Quellen, Brunnen u. Zisternen im AT," *Morgenländische Texte u. Forschungen*, 1, 6 (1928); J. Thomas, *Le mouvement baptiste en Palestine et Syrie* (1935); O. Eissfeldt, "Gott u. das Meer in d. Bibel," *Stud. Orientalia J. Pedersen dicata* (1953), 76-84; P. Reymond, "L'eau, sa vie, et sa signification dans l'AT," VT Suppl., 6 (1958); O. Kaiser, "Die mythische Bedeutung d. Meeres in Ägypten, Ugarit u. Israel," ZAW Beih., 78² (1962). On C. I, 1: A. Büchler, "The Law of Purification in Mk. 7:1-23," Exp. T., 21 (1910), 34-40; G. Bertram, "Le chemin sur les eaux considéré comme motif de salut dans la piété chrét. primitive," Jubilé A. Loisy, I (1928), 137-166. On C. I, 2: T. Canaan, "Water and the 'Water of life' in Palestinian Superstition," *Journ. of the Palestine Orient. Society*, 9 (1929), 57-69; G. Widengren, *Mesopotamian Elements in Manichaeism* (1946), 185, s.v. "water"; F. M. Braun, "L'eau et l'Esprit," *Revue Thomiste*, 49 (1949), 5-30; C. H. Dodd, *The Interpretation of the Fourth Gospel* (1953), 297-300, 311-3; Bultmann J., 133-6; J. Daniélou, "Le symbolisme de l'eau vive," *Revue des Sciences Religieuses*, 32 (1958), 335-346; J. P. Audet, "La soif, l'eau et la parole," *Rev. Bibl.*, 66 (1959), 379-386; J. A. T. Robinson, "The Significance of the Foot-Washing," *Festschr. O. Cullmann* (1962), 144-7. On C. I, 3: J. Chaine, "Cosmogonie aquatique et conflagration finale d'après 2 Pt.," *Rev. Bibl.*, 46 (1937), 207-216. On C. II: For bibl. on baptism in gen. → I, 529 Bibl.; also G. R. Beasley-Murray, *Baptism in the NT* (1962); G. Kretschmar, "Die Gesch. d. Taufgottesdienstes in d. alten Kirche," *Leiturgia*, 5 (1964/5), 2-160; on the baptismal water: J. Steinbeck, "Kultische Waschungen u. Bäder im Heidentum u. ihr Verhältnis z. chr. Taufe," NKZ, 21 (1910), 778-799; J. Scheftelowitz, "Die Sündentilgung durch Wasser," ARW, 17 (1914), 353-412; A. Fridrichsen, "Johannes vattendop och det messianska eld dopet (Wasser-Feuertaufe)," *Uppsala Univ. Årsskrift* (1941); R. Wolf, *Aqua Religiosa. Die religiöse Verwendung v. Wasser im frühen Christentum u. in*

A. Water in the Ancient Oriental and Greek-Hellenistic World.

I. Greek Usage.

τὸ ὕδωρ "water" is found from Hom., e.g., Il., 16, 385; Od., 3, 300; 7, 277, plur. "waters" in Hom. only at Od., 13, 109, poetically in Soph. Fr., 271 (TGF, 189): ὕδασιν τοῖς ᾿Αχελῴου "in the waters of the Achelous"; Pind. Olymp., 14, 1: Καφίσια ὕδατα "the waters of the Cephisus"; Soph. Oed. Col., 1598 f.: ῥυτῶν ὑδάτων "flowing waters"; the plur. sense of flood is rarer, e.g., Eur. Hec., 451 f.: καλλίστων ὑδάτων πατέρα; Eur. Iph. Taur., 1192: πηγαῖσιν ὑδάτων, in the NT only Rev. 11:6; 16:5. There are many derivates and compounds, e.g., ἡ ὑδρία "water-jug" from Aristoph. Eccl., 678; Vesp., 926, in the NT Jn. 2:6 f.; 4:28; cf. Mk. 14:13 and par. ὑδροποτέω, "to drink water," from Hdt., I, 71, 3, in the NT 1 Tm. 5:23 ὑδρωπικός "dropsical" from Hippocr. ᾿Αφορισμοί, VI, 27 (Littré, IV, 570), in the NT Lk. 14:2.

II. Meaning.

From early times water occurs in three ways in human experience, as the flood which surrounds and menaces dry land, as the decisive dispenser of biological life and as the most important means of cleansing. In these qualities it takes on in religious thought a varied mythical and cultic significance and is also the object of rational consideration in natural philosophy and technology.

Thus in Egypt the Nile is not just given a place in myth and cultus but is also measured by gauges and irrigation is technically controlled. For the nature philosophy of Greece water is one of the elements → VI, 930, 14 ff. In religious thought it occurs in the ancient Orient, in Greece and also in Hellenism in three groups of ideas corresponding to the three qualities, and these may be illustrated by some examples.

1. The Flood.

Cosmogonies often have the world arise out of the primal flood. In the beginning acc. to the Babyl. epic Enûma-eliš, 1, 1-7, 160 (AOT, 109-121) were Apsu (the sweetwater ocean) and Mummu (and) Tiâmat (the saltwater sea of chaos and the dragon). Marduk slays Tiâmat and forms the universe from the two halves of her body.[1] In Egypt. stories of the beginning of the world the earth rises up from the flood as the primal hill.[2] For Hom. Il., 14, 200 f., 246[3] Oceanos is the origin of all things. The flood

---

seiner Umwelt, I, Diss. Leipzig (1956), cf. the review in ThLZ, 83 (1958), 730 f.; P. Wernberg-Møller, "Water, Wind and Fire (Lk. 3:16) and Orphic Initiation," NTSt, 3 (1956), 69-79; E. Rácz, Kultische Waschungen bei d. Ägypt. u. Juden u. ihr Verhältnis zur urchr. Taufe, mit bes. Berücksichtigung d. Qumran-Sekte, Diss. Vienna (1958); J. J. McGovern, "The Waters of Death," The Catholic Bibl. Quart., 21 (1959), 350-8. On D.: H. Pfannenschmid, Das Weihwasser im heidnischen u. chr. Kultus (1869); F. Dölger, ΙΧΘΥΣ, I (1928), 68-87; J. Zellinger, Bad u. Bäder in d. altchr. Kirche (1928); B. Neunheuser, "De benedictione aquae baptismalis," Ephemerides liturgicae, 44 (1930), 194-207, 258-281, 369-411, 455-492; F. Wiesehöfer, Das Weihwasser in d. Frühzeit des Christentums u. bei den klass. Völkern d. Altertums, Diss. Münster (1933); H. Scheidt, Die Taufwasser-Weihegebete im Sinne vergleichender Liturgieforschung (1935); T. Klauser, "Taufet in lebendigem Wasser! Zum religions- u. kulturgeschichtlichen Verständnis v. Did., 7, 1-3," Pisciculi f. F. Dölger (1939), 157-164; P. Lundberg, "La typologie baptismale dans l'Ancienne Église," Acta Seminarii Neotest. Upsaliensis, 10 (1942); E. Stommel, "Stud. z. Epiklese d. röm. Taufwasserweihe," Theophaneia, 5 (1950); also "Chr. Taufriten u. antike Badesitten," Jbch. Ant. Christ., 2 (1959), 5-14; A. Benoit, Le baptême chr. au second siècle (1953).

[1] Cf. A. Ungnad, Die Religion d. Babyl. u. Assyrer (1921), 25-47; H. Gunkel, Schöpfung u. Chaos in Urzeit u. Endzeit (1893), 16-29.

[2] Cf. the inscr. in A. de Buck, De egypt. voorstellingen betreffende den oerheuvel, Diss. Leiden (1922), 16 f.; Kaiser, 31 f., cf. 17 f.; A. Erman, Die Religion d. Ägypter (1934), 61-63.

[3] Cf. Nilsson, I², 34; H. Herter, Art. "Okeanos," Pauly-W., 17 (1937), 2349-2351.

of the Gilgameš epic, 11, 1-205 (AOT, 175-180) [4] reminds us of the primal flood but is not its return. This Mesopotamian story is developed in the Gk. myth of Deucalion and Pyrrha, but there seems to be no counterpart in Egypt. [5]

The cosmogony is in accordance with the view of the world. Acc. to Egypt. ideas the water of the Nile which is given to the land flows forth from "the living water in the earth," while to other lands is given "the living water in heaven" [6] which comes down as rain. [7] In Babylonia, too, there is distinction between the upper and the lower waters, Enûma-eliš, 4, 139 f. (AOT, 120). Among the Gks. the idea of an upper and lower ocean is less prominent, being replaced by that of the seas encircling the earth, Hom. Il., 18, 399; cf. Hdt., II, 23. [8] From this localising of water in the world arise theories as to the origin of earthly waters, concerning which Sen. De Quaestionibus naturalibus, III writes, then developing his own view: the aqua viva or nativa from the depths of the earth feeds springs, rivers and seas, while the aqua caelestis or collectiva streams to earth as rain only to seep away and disappear without a trace.

2. Water as Dispenser of Life.

A distinctive realm of ideas pertains to the water which men and animals drink and which causes plants to grow, esp. to springs and rivers. In the Gk. world springs and rivers are regarded as divine → VI, 596, 7 ff., [9] and there is a rich mythology connected with river-gods and nymphs, cf. Hom. Il., 21, 131 f.; 23, 147 f. etc. [10] The Egyptians in a song call the Nile "the Lord of the water which brings greenness" and they see in it the outflow of the primal flood from which everything derives, but not a gt. independent deity. [11] In the Isis cult the water of the Nile, which is holy and healing, plays an important role, Cl. Al. Strom., VI, 4, 37, 1; Apul. Met., XI, 10-11. [12]

The work of water in mediating natural life is sublimated in myths, cultic traditions and sagas. In Egypt water is given the dead to make possible his life in the hereafter, [13] and to provide him with cool water there, Book of the Dead, 17. [14] Acc. to the Babyl. myth Ištar was fetched back from the underworld by sprinkling with "living water," Ištar's Descent into Hell, 34-38 (AOT, 209). But it is denied to man, even to the wise Adapa: "They brought him the water of life, he did not drink it," Adapa-Myth, II, 62 f. (AOT, 145). [15] The Gk. world does not speak of a water of life which makes possible life in the hereafter or which brings back from the underworld. It ref. only to the drink of immortality which, except in legends, is reserved for the gods. In Hell. there arose the legend of Alexander's campaign for the water of life which confers immortality, [16] → III, 23, 16 ff. On the other hand the idea is widespread among the Gks. that drinking of the ἔνθεον ὕδωρ helps to bring about the ἐνθουσιασμός or ecstasy of prophecy. [17]

---

[4] Cf. also the flood stories in AOT, 198-201; Kaiser, 122-130.

[5] J. Riem, Die Sintflut in Sage u. Wissenschaft (1925), 10-14, 77 f.; cf. Book of the Dead, 175 (AOT, 6 f.).

[6] Cf. Erman, op. cit., 15 f.

[7] Cf. the Song to the Sun in A. Erman, Die Lit. d. Ägypter (1923), 360; Kaiser, 32.

[8] F. Gisinger, Art. "Okeanos," Pauly-W., 17 (1937), 2312 f.; H. Schäfer, Ägyptische u. heutige Kunst u. Weltgebäude d. alten Ägypter (1928), 85, 112.

[9] Spaltmann, 8-10, 23.

[10] Cf. Nilsson, I², 236-242, 450.

[11] Cf. Erman, op. cit. (→ n. 2), 16 f.; Ant. Christ., V, 153-6: Misconceptions of Gk. and Hell. authors regarding the Egypt. worship of the Nile.

[12] Cf. Ant. Christ., V, 156-160 and 153-175 gen.; J. Leipoldt, "Archäologisches zur Isis-religion," Angelos, I (1925), 127.

[13] Bonnet, 116 and gen. 114-117.

[14] Cf. G. Roeder, Urkunden z. Religion des alten Ägypten (1915), 237, cf. Index s.v. "Wasser"; also Ant. Christ., V, 169-171.

[15] Cf. F. M. T. de Liagre Böhl, "Die Mythe vom weisen Adapa," Die Welt d. Orients, 2 (1959), 416-431.

[16] Wünsche, 77-84; Ninck, 31-37.

[17] Ninck, 83-90.

3. Cleansing by Water.

The cleansing effect of water is everywhere sublimated to a religious celebration in the form of cultic washings. In Egypt idols, the king, priests and the dead had water sprinkled on them; the commonly depicted affusion corresponds formally to daily bathing. In the religious sphere it remains an act of purification which qualifies cultically. It is not a baptism for the remission of sins or for new birth. The sprinkling of the king is done by priests in divine masks accompanied by the saying: "I purify thee with life and salvation," and it is said of its effect: "Thou wilt be clean and shining through the water of life and salvation." [18] Here the cleansing effect seems to be related to the life-giving which can be mediated by washing as well as drinking, → I, 533, 1 ff. Among the Gks. it is a firm rule from earliest times that before prayer and sacrifice the hands should be cleansed by pouring water over them, Hes. Op., 724 f. Vessels of water were placed in the temples so that people might sprinkle themselves before entering the sanctuary, Just. Apol., 62, 1 → IV, 298, 42 ff. [19] For further details on rites of purification in the Gk.-Hell. world → IV, 296, 23 ff. If possible, living water or sea-water was used for this purification → IV, 297, 39 ff. [20] Sometimes the cleansing water was esp. sanctified by ceremonies, e.g., by being carried first round the altar, → 333, 23 ff. [21] In the mysteries sprinkling with water accomplishes a preliminary purification, Cl. Al. Strom., VII, 27, 6, but, so far as we can see, was practically never used in the true consecration. [22] The priest of Isis says before the cleansing sprinkling: *praefatus deum veniam,* Apul. Met., XI, 23; whether this ritual cleansing is supposed to wash away sins too is very doubtful. [23]

B. In the Old Testament-Jewish World.

I. Usage.

The LXX uses ὕδωρ both sing. and plur. for the Hbr. plurale tantum מַיִם. With the Hbr. word the verb is partly sing. and partly plur. The LXX ignores this vacillation and yet it can sometimes put plur. ὕδατα with a sing. verb, 2 Βασ. 5:20. The Hbr. usage has some distinctive features as compared with that of the LXX. Water is sometimes added to define more closely terms for bodies of water, since in the Near East it cannot be taken for granted that they will contain water, e.g., פַּלְגֵי מַיִם (LXX διέξοδοι ὑδάτων) brooks of water, Ps. 1:3; 119:136 (פֶּלֶג is the channel carved by flowing water) or עֵין הַמַּיִם "spring of water" Gn. 24:13 (LXX πηγὴ τοῦ ὕδατος); Ex. 15:27 (LXX πηγαὶ ὑδάτων). [24] With place-names water denotes a body of water close by, whether a spring, brook or small river, Jos. 11:5, 7: "by the water of Merom"; 16:1: "the water of Jericho"; Ju. 5:19: "by the waters of Megiddo." [25] מַיִם רַבִּים is often used for the sea, Is. 23:3; Ez. 27:26; Hab. 3:15; Ps. 29:3; 77:19; 107:23. [26]

This usage shows already that water is a gen. term for something which can appear in many forms: metereological phenomena like clouds, mist, haze, rain, snow, hail, dew, geographical like springs, brooks, streams, rivers, canals, ponds, lakes, seas, fountains and cisterns, biological as in drinking, domestic use and commercial use. Thus the ideas connected with water are not restricted to the concept itself but are also developed with the help of specific qualifications.

---

[18] Cf. the ill. and inscr. in Bonnet, 107 f.; Rácz, 4-56; Wolf, 1-12.
[19] Wolf, 27-9; Nilsson, I², 102.
[20] Paus., IX, 20, 4; Wolf, 160; Nilsson, I², 103.
[21] Wolf, 64.
[22] *Ibid.,* 153-177; J. Leipoldt, "Darstellungen v. Mysterientaufen," *Angelos,* I (1925), 46 f.
[23] Wolf, 166-168.
[24] Cf. Rev. 7:17; 8:10; 14:7; 16:4.
[25] Reymond, 104 f.
[26] Cf. H. G. May, "Some Cosmic Connotations of Mayim Rabbîm, 'Many Waters,'" JBL, 74 (1955), 9-21: The many waters are the onrushing chaotic elements.

II. Meaning.

The notions which the OT links with the term, on the basis of Israel's experience of salvation history, arise out of the water situation in Palestine and the ancient oriental view of the world. Since Israel lived in a country poor in water resources its statements about water are influenced by ideas concerning the provision of water.

1. Literal Use.

a. Drinking Water and Irrigation.

There is no assurance of water for either men or plants in Palestine. Water supply is always threatened. [27] Hence bread and water are given equal emphasis in the OT as vital necessities, Ex. 23:25; 1 S. 30:11 f.; 1 K. 18:4, 13; 22:27; 2 K. 6:22; Is. 3:1; 21:14; Ez. 4:11, 16 f.; Hos. 2:7; Job 22:7. Total fasting means doing without bread and water, Ex. 34:28; Dt. 9:9, 18; Ezr. 10:6; Jon. 3:7. The technique of providing water lies behind many OT stories: [28] "wells" (→ VI, 113, 11 ff.) are dug (בְּאֵר, τὸ φρέαρ), Gn. 26:18 f., 32; Is. 15:8; "cisterns" (בּוֹר, ὁ λάκκος), Gn. 37:20 etc., water is fetched from the well, Gn. 24:11, 20; 1 S. 9:11; 2 S. 23:15 f.; cf. Jer. 14:3, the "pitcher" which is carried on the shoulder (כַּד, ἡ ὑδρία), Gn. 24:14-18 etc., the "leather bottle" in which water is also carried (חֵמֶת, נֵבֶל, ὁ ἀσκός), Gn. 21:14 f.; Job 38:37, the "water-pot" (צַפַּחַת, ὁ φακός), 1 S. 26:11 f., the "conduit" (תְּעָלָה, ὁ ὑδραγωγός), 2 K. 18:17, the "trough" for cattle (שֹׁקֶת, τὸ ποτιστήριον), Gn. 30:38. The watering of tillable land [29] takes place in Palestine predominantly by precipitation, in winter by rain, in summer by dew and to a modest degree by water-courses. Artificial irrigation [30] on a limited scale was mostly reserved for gardens in antiquity, Dt. 11:10 f.

What falls to be said about the vital necessity of water is to be found in the basic OT witness concerning the provision of water for Israel in the desert wandering. The thirsty people, weak in faith, murmurs, Nu. 20:24; 27:14; Dt. 32:51; 33:8; Ps. 81:7; 106:32. Water is miraculously given, Ex. 17:2-7 (E and J²); Nu. 20:7-11 (P and J¹); cf. Ex. 15:22 ff.; Nu. 21:16 ff. This experience is the basis of the exhortation in Dt. 8:15; Ps. 78:15 f.; 105:41, worship in Ps. 114:8, and esp. the prophecy of the second exodus which is also portrayed as the return of Paradise, Is. 48:20 f.; cf. 41:17 f.; 43:20; 49:10; 35:6 f.; Jer. 31:9.

In the promise of the land the decisive thing is the assurance of watered tillable land on which the tribes which had lived as nomads on the steppes might settle, Nu. 24:7; Dt. 8:7; 11:11. The partial fulfilment makes the promise an eschatological expectation of the paradisial land, Is. 30:23 f.; Jl. 3:18 f. The prophecy of living streams flowing from Jerusalem and dispensing life views the Israel of the last time as an antitype of Paradise, Ez. 47:1 ff.; Zech. 14:8; cf. 13:1; Jl. 3:18; cf. Gn. 2:10 ff. Whereas the land of the age of salvation is to be watered by paradisial rivers, Yahweh is now confessed as the One who sends needed rain on the one side, 1 K. 18:41 ff.; Am. 4:7 f.; 5:8; 9:6, while on the other He can dry up even the rivers of Egypt and Mesopotamia, Is. 15:6; 19:5 f.; 50:2; Jer. 48:34; 50:38. Behind these confessions there does not stand any fixed notion of the way water is provided on the earth. The insight that water moves in a cycle of vaporising and drying up was restricted in antiquity to small circles of philosophical thinkers. [31]

As regards drinking water the central point is to be found in the promise of Is. 55:1: God Himself will give bread and water, i.e., what is strictly necessary for life → 325, 30 ff.

---

[27] Dalman Arbeit, I, 70-72; Reymond, 1-8.
[28] Dalman Arbeit, I, 524-536; Reymond, 125-159.
[29] Dalman Arbeit, II, 29-35, cf. I, 291-314.
[30] Dalman Arbeit, II, 219-241.
[31] Qoh. 1:7 thinks the cycle is mediated by the waters beneath the earth, cf. Plat. Phaed., 111c-113c; Ninck, 1-7.

This circle of ideas underlies what is said about water in the J creation story: The initially dead earth becomes a fruitful garden through the rise of the primal waters, Gn. 2:5 f. Acc. to a loosely attached note there proceed from the river that waters Paradise the four rivers which control the destiny of man in the Near East, Gn. 2:10-14. [32] The P story corresponds to a second group of ideas.

b. The Flood.

In accordance with a complex which often occurs elsewhere in the OT in strongly mythological form (Ps. 74:12 ff.; 89:9 ff.; Is. 51:9 → n. 38), the P story describes the earth as rising out of the sea of chaos. The Creator by setting up the firmament divides the waters, the sea of chaos, into the upper waters (→ 316, 4 ff.), the heavenly ocean of Job 36:27 f.; Ps. 29:3; 33:7; 148:4, whose blue shines through the firmament, and the lower waters, [33] Gn. 1:1, 6 ff.; cf. 7:11; 8:2; Ps. 104:2-9, also Ps. 89:10 f.; 93:3 f.; Job 38:4-11. Out of the lower waters there arises the earth which rests upon them and is encircled by them, Gn. 1:9; cf. Ps. 136:6; Prv. 8:27-29; 30:4; Is. 40:12 → 315, 25 ff.

At the flood (→ 315, 30 ff.) God's judgment acc. to P causes the waters above and below to come on the earth, Gn. 7:11, so that chaos returns. Acc. to J, however, it is simply that prolonged rain brings flooding, Gn. 7:12, 17b. Behind the original P story stand mythical traditions for which water is a chaotic force threatening the earth and its inhabitants. [34]

The relation of God to the flood became clear to Israel at the exodus from Egypt. He saved His people from their pursuers at the Red Sea by keeping back the flood from His people and then causing it to break over the pursuers, Ex. 15:21; 15:1-18; 14:21b, 27b (J); 14:16b, 22 (E). [35] This event is echoed again and again in the OT, Ps. 77:16, 19 f.; 78:13; 106:9-11; 136:13 ff.; Is. 51:10; 63:12; Neh. 9:11 etc. [36] There is a par. to this saving act in the story of the conquest in Jos. 4:23 (E?); Ps. 114:3, 5 when Israel passes through the Jordan, Jos. 3: (8,) 16; 4:18. [37] Another faint echo is when Elijah parts the Jordan in 2 K. 2:8. With God's historical intervention in the course of nature Israel declares against the surrounding nature religions the lordship of its God over creation. In these events water is the menacing flood. The Red Sea deliverance is sometimes depicted in the image of the conflict with the dragon which originally describes creation as an overcoming of the forces of chaos, Is. 51:9 f.; Ps. 74:13 f.; 106:9. [38]

The first two complexes relating to water live on in scholastic form in Rabb. Judaism, as may be seen merely from statements about the holy rock of the Jerusalem temple → VI, 96, 8 ff. This rock is the highest pt. of the earth which juts out like a dome from the lower waters. It stops up the primal flood so that this cannot wipe away the earth. But from it the water which rises up from the flood also flows in veins across the world. This water which makes possible the earth's fertility is released by the annual water ceremonies at the sacred rock during the Feast of Booths. In the age of salvation the

---

[32] "All the non-paradisial water which nourishes all cultures is as it were only a remnant or residue of the paradisial water . . . in the Orient water (is) the absolute basis of all cultural life," G. v. Rad, *Das erste Buch Mose, AT Deutsch,* 2⁶ (1961), *ad loc.* On the rivers cf. G. Hölscher, "Drei Erdkarten," SAH, 1944/48, 3 (1949), 35-44.

[33] Cf. also Gn. 49:25; Dt. 33:13; waters under the earth Prv. 3:20; Qoh. 1:7; Am. 7:4.

[34] For a historical discussion of the creation stories Kaiser, 117-130, for theological evaluation Eichr. Theol. AT, II⁵ (1964), 57-59, 105, 108 f.; v. Rad, *op. cit.,* Exc. on 2:4a; also *Theol. d. AT,* I⁴ (1962), 149-167, 371-4.

[35] In analysis of the tradition Kaiser, 130-134.

[36] G. v. Rad, *Theol. d. AT,* I⁴ (1962), 26 f., 189-192.

[37] Kaiser, 135-9.

[38] Cf. *ibid.,* 140-152 for a discussion. Acc. to Eichr. Theol. AT, II⁵ (1964), 72 these mythical images are increasingly poetic adornments; in particular the personification of the sea as the monster which Yahweh chases and binds by His rebuke, Job 38:10 f.; Ps. 104:7; 114:3 f. is independent of myth, though it could keep alive the myth of the chaos conflict.

river of Paradise will flow from this place. But far more than the first two groups the third group of OT ideas concerning water finds further development in Judaism.

c. Means of Cleansing.

(βαπτίζω → I, 529, 18 ff.; καθαρίζω → III, 414, 2 ff.; λούω → IV, 295, 11 ff.; νίπτω → IV, 946, 2 ff.).

Water is a means of cleansing the body, e.g., when offered to a guest so that he may wash his feet, Gn. 18:4; 19:2; 24:32; 43:24; 2 S. 11:8 → VI, 631, 23 ff., [39] or of washing clothes. [40] Yet the OT mentions partial or total washings of the human body or clothes almost exclusively as sacral purifications. With fire, blood and oil water is by far the most commonly used means of ritual cleansing, just as it was a means of sacral purification throughout the surrounding world of antiquity → IV, 296, 22 ff.; → 317, 1 ff.

Acc. to the laws of cleansing which are virtually all in P (esp. Lv. 11-15) ordinary water is normally used with no further qualification. For special purifications מַיִם חַיִּים (ὕδωρ ζῶν) "living, i.e., flowing water" is required (Lv. 14:5 f., 50 ff.) or a purifying water prepared from this (Nu. 19:17) מֵי נִדָּה (ὕδωρ ῥαντισμοῦ) Nu. 19:9, 13, 20 f., cf. Lv. 14:3-7, 49-52; also מֵי חַטָּאת (ὕδωρ ἁγνισμοῦ) Nu. 8:7. The water is used to cleanse men and objects by "sprinkling" נזה (περιρραίνω) Lv. 14:7, 51; Nu. 8:7; 19:18 f., 21 or זָרַק (περιρραντίζω) Nu. 19:13, 20, by partial washing, cf. רחץ (νίπτομαι τὰς χεῖρας καὶ τοὺς πόδας) Ex. 30:17-21; Lv. 15:11 (→ IV, 946, 15 ff.), by total washing, cf. רחץ (λούω → IV, 300, 26 ff.) Ex. 29:4; 40:12; Lv. 8:6; 14:8 f.; 15:5-8, 10 f. etc., or by dipping טבל (βάπτω or βαπτίζω, → I, 535, 12 ff.), cf. Lv. 11:32; 2 K. 5:14. With the bathing of the body the washing of clothes is often demanded too כבס (πλύνω) Lv. 14:8 f.; 15:5 ff., 10 f., 13; Nu. 8:7, 21. Finally it is frequently laid down that the entrails of sacrifices be washed with water, Ex. 29:17; Lv. 1:9, 13; 8:21; 9:14. These rites may be influenced by animistic ideas about powerful materials and magical actions but acc. to the OT statutes in their present form neither the water nor the act is ever efficacious as such. The rites take effect only as a fulfilment of the Law which separates Israel as the holy people of Yahweh and establishes even materially the distinction between holy and profane as gen. in antiquity. [41]

Since the cleansing rites are finally for the holy people, they can be viewed symbolically or eschatologically even in the OT itself. For the former, though with no express ref. to water, cf. Ps. 51:7: "Purge me with hyssop, and I shall be clean: wash me, and I shall be whiter than snow." For the latter it is no accident that we must turn to Ez., who is close to P. Acc. to Ez. 36:25 (→ 321, 26 ff.) God Himself will cleanse His people by an eschatological sprinkling of water, which is something that obviously no rites can do, cf. also Zech. 13:1 and the fig. description of eschatological remission as purification, Is. 4:4; Jer. 33:8; cf. Is. 1:15 f.; Jer. 4:14.

A distinctive act which is partly cultic and partly fig. is the washing of hands on blood guiltiness. Acc. to Dt. 21:6 the elders of a place, if they found in their district someone struck down by an unknown assailant, had to wash their hands in a stream over the blood of a slain heifer and swear their innocence in order to cleanse the place from blood guiltiness. [42]

In post-bibl. Judaism the Pharisees and Essenes, who sought to be the true Israel consecrated to God, develop the OT rites of cleansing in various ways into all-embracing

---

[39] Dalman Arbeit, VI, 136 f.

[40] *Ibid.*, V, 151-9.

[41] J. Döller, *Die Reinigungs- u. Speisegesetze d. AT* (1917); Eichr. Theol. AT, I[5] (1964), 78-82; v. Rad, *op. cit.* (→ n. 36), I, 285-293; Reymond, 228-234; → n. 46.

[42] As may be seen from the Mishnah rules, Sota, 9, 6 and the ref. in Jos. Ant., 4, 222 this cultic act lived on into NT times and occasioned a fig. use reflected in the expression "to wash one's hand in innocency," Ps. 26:6; 73:13.

systems → III, 418, 6 ff. Rabbinism takes the rinsing of the hands which the OT requires only for ministering priests, e.g., before partaking of the heave offering (cf. Ex. 30:19 f.), and makes it obligatory for all Israelites before meals, [43] → IV, 946, 18 ff. With the washings of the Pharisees proselyte baptism also arose; this was already gen. in NT times → I, 535, 21 f. [44] As regards the efficacy of these washings the Rabb. can teach: "By your life, the dead does not defile and water does not make clean, but it is an ordinance of the King of all kings" → III, 422, 14 ff. This radical but gen. accepted statement is also illustrated by the fact that Rabbinism divides water into six sorts or stages acc. to its suitability for ritual cleansing → III, 421, 19 ff.

While the Pharisees develop washings legalistically, for the Essenes these accomplish total cleansing along with inner purifying by the Spirit. Acc. to Jos. Bell., 2, 129 the Essenes took a bath daily before the mid-day meal (ἀπολούονται τὸ σῶμα ψυχροῖς ὕδασιν) as ἁγνεία "purification." Archaeol. discoveries in Qumran suggest that ritual washings were commonly practised there in basins of water. [45] The Qumran Scrolls contain only some basic rules of purification which apply both to daily washings and also to special baths, e.g., at reception. [46] Damasc. 10:10-13 (12:1 f.) contains technical rules similar to the Rabb. stages. Water for purification is not to be muddied nor should there be too little; it must be able to cover a man immersed in it. The cleansings seem to take the form of baths. Acc. to 1 QS 3:1-12; cf. 5:13 f.; Jos. Bell., 2, 138 a ritual cleansing of the body with water is useless if a man does not submit to the divine statutes as the community represents them, i.e., if he will not "cleanse himself by the holy spirit of the community in its truth." The "cleansing water" מי נדה 1 QS 3:4, 9; 4:21, or "water of washings" מי רחץ 3:5, or "water of cleanness" מי דוכי 3:9 is ordinary water, not water prepared acc. to the rite of Nu. 19. [47] Washings are necessary as well as conversion for cleanness, [48] i.e., total consecration. How they work is not said. They do not effect full and definitive cleanness, for they must be repeated regularly. The community looks ahead to a final cleansing. God will "sprinkle the spirit of truth like cleansing water" on the elect and thus remove the spirit of perversion from the body, 1 QS 4:21. [49] This prophecy takes up Ez. 36:25 but the water which in Ez. stands alongside the spirit is here a figure of cleansing by the Spirit.

2. Transferred Usage.

As elsewhere, so in the OT water is often used in metaphors and comparisons. [50]

a. The ability of water to quench thirst and nourish plant life is a metaphor: God is the source of living water, Jer. 2:13; cf. Ps. 36:9. The desire for Him or His Word is like

---

[43] Str.-B., I, 695-702; cf. Yadayim, ed. G. Lisowsky in *Die Mischna*, VI, 2 (1956).

[44] Cf. on this Str.-B., I, 102-113; J. Jeremias, *Die Kindertaufe in d. ersten vier Jhdt.* (1958), 28-34; N. A. Dahl, "The Origin of Baptism," *Festschr. S. Mowinckel* (1955), 36-52.

[45] R. de Vaux, "Fouilles de Khirbet Qumrân, Rapport préliminaire sur les 3e, 4e et 5e campagnes," *Rev. Bibl.*, NS, 63 (1956), 533-577; 1 QS 3:4 f. also mentions lakes and rivers, cf. Sib., 4, 162 ff.

[46] Acc. to O. Betz, "Die Proselytentaufe d. Qumransekte u. d. Taufe im NT," *Rev. de Qumran*, 1 (1958/59), 216-220 the ref. of 1 QS 3:4-9 is not to daily washings but to the rite of initiation, the bath for novices, cf. also W. Nauck, *Die Tradition u. der Charakter d. 1 J.* (1957), 167 f.

[47] As against J. Bowman, "Did the Qumran Sect burn the Red Heifer?" *Rev. de Qumran*, 1 (1958/59), 73-84.

[48] The emphasis on ritual cleanness may be seen from the terminology of 1 QS, cf. H. Braun, *Spätjüd.-häret. u. frühchr. Radikalismus*, I, *Beiträge z. histor. Theol.*, 24 (1957), 29, n. 5.

[49] R. Schnackenburg, "Die 'Anbetung in Geist u. Wahrheit' (J. 4:23) im Lichte von Qumrân-Texten," BZ, NF, 3 (1959), 88-94.

[50] Reymond, 107-116.

thirst for the water which is vitally necessary, Ps. 42:1; Am. 8:11 f. Those who belong to Him are like the flock drinking at the source of water, Ps. 23:2, or the tree by the brook, Ps. 1:3; Jer. 17:8. In the time of salvation Israel will be "like a watered garden, and like a spring of water, whose waters fail not," Is. 58:11. This imagery can also be applied to secular life, e.g., the relation to a woman in Prv. 5:15 f., 18; Cant. 4:15; Ez. 19:10, and in other ways Job 34:7; Ez. 17:5, 8; 31:4 f., 7, 14.

In the Dead Sea Scrolls 1 QH 8 uses the rather obscure image of planting by the water with ref. to the true community. This is like the "trees of life," 8:5 f., cf. Gen. 3:22; Ps. Sol. 14:3; Od. Sol. 11:18 f., which are hidden behind the lofty "trees by the water" 1 QH 8:6, 9, cf. Ez. 31:4 f., 14, the wicked, and which stretch out their roots to the מים חיים 1 QH 8:16, cf. 7. Perhaps here מים חיים is not living or flowing water as often in the OT but the water of life," [51] for it is close to מי קודש "holy water," 8:13, מקור חיים "source of life," 8:14, cf. Ps. 36:9, מעין רז "source of the mystery," 8:6, cf. "source of knowledge," 2:18; 1 QS 10:12; 11:3, and "drink of knowledge," 1 QH 4:11. Those who drink of the water of life are "eternal trees," 1 QH 8:12. They become Eden, 8:20, cf. 6:16 ff. But the trees by water will sink like lead in the flood, 8:18 f., cf. Ex. 15:10. The water of life is the revelation which is esoterically given in the community, cf. 1 QS 11:3-9.

Rabb. Judaism compares the word of the Torah or of scribes to water, Ab., 1, 11. [52] "To drink of the water of a scribe" is often used to describe the pupil relationship, 1, 4. [53] Damasc. calls false teaching "lying water" in 1:15 (1:10) 34 (9:28). Wisdom wants to give the ὕδωρ σοφίας to drink, Sir. 15:3.

b. As the flood, water is often in the OT a fig. of oppression, whether of the people in Is. 8:6 f.; cf. 28:2; Jer. 46:7 f.; 47:2; 51:55; Ez. 26:19, or individuals in 2 S. 22:17; Ps. 18:16; 32:6; 69:1, 14; 88:17; 124:4 f.; 144:7; Job 22:11; 27:20; Jon. 2:6. The all-covering breadth of water in a sea or river is compared to the knowledge of the Lord in Hab. 2:14; Is. 11:9 or to right in Am. 5:24, cf. 1 QH 10:14 f.; 11:1. There is frequent ref. to the roaring of water, Ps. 46:3; 65:7; Hab. 3:15, and in comparison Ps. 93:4; Is. 17:12 f.; Ez. 1:24; 43:2; cf. 1 QH 2:16, 27. [54] The heart failing for fear is compared to the running off of water, Jos. 7:5, cf. 1 QH 2:28; 8:32, 37, and death is like the spilling of water, 2 S. 14:14; Ps. 22:14, cf. also for other comparisons Dt. 12:16, 24; 15:23; Ps. 79:3; Lam. 2:19; Hos. 5:10. A final image is that of water bursting the dam (2 S. 5:20; 1 Ch. 14:11), flowing across the earth (Job 14:19) and flooding it (Is. 30:28, 30).

c. The cleansing function of water is also a common fig., but it is usually found with verbs of washing rather than the term water.

C. In the New Testament.

The distribution of the term in the NT is not just accidental. Apart from Eph. 5:26 it does not occur in Paul; this is in keeping with the non-graphic style of the apostle. It is most significant in the Johannine writings, whose vocabulary is influenced by the Baptist tradition.

I. Water Literally and Metaphorically.

1. The Synoptic Tradition.

In the Synoptic tradition ordinary water is set in the light of the eschatological event now present.

---

[51] So J. Maier, *Die Texte v. Toten Meer*, II (1960), 98.
[52] Cf. further Str.-B., II, 435.
[53] *Ibid.*, II, 436, 493, cf. also Sir. 24:30-33.
[54] Cf. ὡς φωνὴ ὑδάτων πολλῶν in Rev. 1:15; 14:2; 19:6.

a. Water as the Flood.

What Jesus does on Lake Gennesaret is a sign of His divine authority over water as the flood that threatens man. [55] The Gospel tradition calls the Galilean lake θάλασσα in Mk., Mt. and Jn. according to the OT-Jewish tradition. [56] Hence the stilling of the storm (Mk. 4:35 ff. and par.) takes on the character of a deliverance from peril at sea. [57] Lk. replaces [58] this word, which Greeks would find hard to understand, by λίμνη (5:1 f.; 8:22 f., 33) or some other formulation. At the stilling of the storm it is the raging of the water (τῷ κλύδωνι τοῦ ὕδατος) rather than the sea which is a threat, 8:24. The story has a twofold kerygmatic thrust. Jesus commands the storm and the sea as in the OT only God can do [59] and as He basically did in face of the flood at the Red Sea (→ 319, 20 ff.), Ps. 106:9. But He also summons His disciples to faith. To believe is to credit the God of Israel and to see His help present in Jesus. In the story of walking on the sea (Mk. 6:45 ff. and par.; Jn. 6:16 ff.) the coming of Jesus on the sea declares Him to be the One who like God Himself draws near to help His own, [60] while Peter's going to meet Him ἐπὶ τὰ ὕδατα "on the waters" declares what faith is (only Mt. 14:28 ff.; cf. Jn. 21:7): Faith walks over the flood of evil which engulfs unbelief → 319, 15 ff.; II, 461, 38 ff.

b. Drinking Water.

Drinking water also figures in a very simple, elementary, but for that reason all the more impressive form in the Synoptic tradition. A ποτήριον ψυχροῦ [61] "a cup of cold water" (in what is on the whole the more original form of the saying in Mt. 10:42; cf. Mk. 9:41 ποτήριον ὕδατος) is a little enough gift even in everyday Palestine, cf. μόνον. Yet the reward of a share in the kingdom is promised to it as mercy to the merciful, Mt. 5:7; 25:40, 45. But the man who lives only for himself, so that without being aware of it he denies even the tiniest help to those in need (Lk. 16:21), will thirst in vain for the slightest refreshment in the world to come (Lk. 16:24 ff.): "... that he may dip the tip of his finger in water, and cool my tongue." [62]

c. Cleansing Water.

Cleansing water occurs in three impressive scenes with its own symbolical and ritual significance. Whereas the woman who sinned much (Lk. 7:36-50) showed Jesus her attachment in every possible way, however singular, the Pharisee who invited Him held aloof. She sprinkled His feet with her tears and dried them with

---

[55] In Mt. 8:32; Mk. 9:22 and par. water is just the flood in which those who plunge drown with no specific theological point.
[56] Cf. Str.-B., I, 184 f.; Schl. Mt. on 4:18.
[57] Cf. Jon. 1:4 ff., 16.
[58] Cf. Jos. Bell., 3, 506. 515; 4, 456; 6, 349; Ant., 18, 28. 36.
[59] Cf. Ps. 65:7; 89:9; 107:28 f.
[60] Cf. Ps. 77:19; Job 9:8; Is. 43:16; cf. Sir. 24:5 (of wisdom); on this E. Lövestam, "Wunder u. Symbolhandlung," Kerygma u. Dogma, 8 (1962), 124-135.
[61] τὸ ψυχρόν "cold water," Hdt., II, 37, 3 etc., Hbr. דְּלִי שֶׁל צוֹנֵן T. Ber., 4, 16, but always ὕδωρ ψυχρόν in Jos., cf. Schl. Mt. on 10:42.
[62] The ref. to refreshment by water is to be found already in possible models for the parable, Jeremias Gl.⁷, 182.

her hair → VI, 630, 23 ff., but he did not even think of offering a foot-wash: ὕδωρ μοι ἐπὶ πόδας οὐκ ἔδωκας, Lk. 7:44. [63]

Mt. concludes the story of the trial of Jesus with an incident peculiar to his Gospel in which Pilate to protest his innocence λαβὼν ὕδωρ symbolically washes his hands, while the people accepts the guilt, Mt. 27:24 f. The scene is described in OT phrases, [64] and the hand-washing is to be seen against the background of OT-Jewish tradition. The Roman judge adopts this partly cultic and partly figurative custom (→ 320, 38 ff.) [65] to shift guilt before God from himself to the people.

The problems in ritual cleansing (sc. by water) are brought out by Jesus in a demonstration. He dispenses His disciples from the hand-washing before (and after) meals which had been enjoined in the Pharisaic Halachah (→ VI, 916, 1 ff.; III, 421, 31 ff.; IV, 946, 18 ff.), [66] Mk. 7:2 ff. and par. [67] → 321, 1 ff. He justifies this on the ground that the Halachah is invented by men to evade God's Torah, Mk. 7:6-13 and par. This verdict on the Pharisaic rites applies also to the washings of the Essenes. But Jesus' criticism of the Halachah would seem to have the abolition of the Torah itself as its goal. [68] Jesus sets aside the OT laws of purity, and with them the ancient concept of material cleanness and uncleanness, because He demands and effects the eschatological cleansing of the heart.

2. In the Johannine Writings.

Whereas in the Synoptic tradition various aspects of water in daily life are set in the light of the eschatological event enacted in the words and works of Jesus, water takes on a transferred eschatological significance in the Johannine corpus. In this regard the same ideas take on a more OT form in Revelation and a more Hellenistic form in the Gospel and 1 John.

a. Water as the Flood in Revelation.

In Rev. the OT ideas of water as the flood occurs in three figurative forms. The voice of the exalted Son of Man (1:15) and the proclamation of the eschatological victory of God (14:2; 19:6) are "as the sound of many waters." [69] The great whore

---

[63] This was not customary on invitations to banquets (Str.-B., IV, 615) but was possible in the case of someone like Jesus who came from the highways → 320, 6 ff. It is not meant that Simon himself ought to have washed His feet, which would be contrary to current practice → n. 93-95.

[64] W. Trilling, "Das wahre Israel. Stud. z. Theol. d. Mt.," Stud. z. Alten u. Neuen Test., 10³ (1964), 66-74.

[65] Cf. Orig. Comm. in Mt., II, 124 (GCS, 38, 259): Judaico usus est more . . . faciens non secundum aliquam consuetudinem Romanorum. But there are par. in the Graeco-Roman world, e.g., purifyings by washings after homicide, Hdt., I, 35, 1-4; Soph. Ai., 654 f.; Vergil Aen., II, 719 f. After sentencing to death the judge lifted up his hands to the sun and swore he was innocent of the blood of the condemned person, Const. Ap., II, 52, 1. The passage is assimilated to this practice in the Gospel of Nicodemus Act. Pilat., 9, 4 (Hennecke, I³, 340): "Then Pilate took water, washed his hands before the sun, and said, I am innocent of the blood of this just person."

[66] Brandt Reinheitslehre, 5-33; Büchler, 34-40.

[67] Mk. 7:3 is to be transl.: "They eat only when they have washed their hands with a handful (sc. water)."

[68] Cf. L. Goppelt, Christentum u. Jdt. im 1. und 2. Jhdt. (1954), 45 f.

[69] This common comparison (→ 322, 26 ff.) applies to God's voice in Ez. 43:2.

enthroned "on many waters" (17:1) is the world capital; [70] in v. 15 the waters [71] are then construed as the nations which the capital rules. In 12:15 the dragon tries to destroy the woman by spewing out "water like a river" behind her. The point of the image, behind which are mythical traditions, [72] is disclosed by basic OT concepts → II, 282, 14 ff.; VI, 604, 25 ff. The flood is an established metaphor for oppression, → 322, 22 ff. [73] The flight of the community is to the wilderness and its deliverance from the flood remind us of the basic redemption of Israel even though the details do not tally, → 319, 20 ff. What the metaphor is saying is that God's community as such is, like the Saviour of the world, saved from destruction by the adversary; he can only wage war with the rest of its progeny on earth, 12:17.

b. Drinking Water in Revelation and John's Gospel.

The intimation of judgment in Rev. speaks of drinking water cosmically: Earth refuses worship to Him who has made heaven, earth, the sea, and the fountains of waters, 14:7. Hence His judgment smites the rivers and fountains of waters (→ VI, 115, 9 ff.; 603, 23 ff.) so that the sweet water becomes wormwood (8:10 f.) [74] or blood (16:4 f, cf. 11:6; Ex. 7:17). While these judgments take away the water which is necessary for life, the drying up of the Euphrates (ἐξηράνθη τὸ ὕδωρ αὐτοῦ, 16:12) [75] with the sixth vial opens the way for the apocalyptic host from the East.

While the dwellers on earth (8:13; 11:10 etc.) are deprived of necessary water, those redeemed from the earth (14:3) are given the water of life to drink in the consummation. The water of life occurs four times in a variable figure freely modelled on OT prophecies. The Lamb, the Exalted One, will lead as Shepherd ἐπὶ ζωῆς πηγὰς ὑδάτων "to fountains of the water of life," 7:17 based on Is. 49:10; cf. Ps. 23:2 f. God Himself will give to the thirsty freely ἐκ τῆς πηγῆς τοῦ ὕδατος τῆς ζωῆς "of the fountain of the water of life," 21:6 based on Is. 55:1. The two other passages are linked with the idea of the new Jerusalem and the tree of life. A river of water of life (→ VI, 604, 29 ff.) will issue forth from the throne of God and of the Lamb, [76] 22:1. [77] Then we have the final promise of Rev. which in compressed form and with no particular emphasis uses again the image of the water of life freely given to the thirsty, 22:17, cf. 21:6. Whereas the OT prophecies in Is. 49:10 and Ez. 47:1-12 refer to real water, the passages in Rev. take water figuratively like Is. 55:1. The metaphor is explained by the appended ζωῆς, which does not occur in the OT verses. [78] The water of life might be a means to mediate life, the self-proffering of God and the Lamb in fellowship (21:22 f.), but not baptism or the

---

[70] Enthronement on many waters occurs in Jer. 51:13 with ref. to the geographical situation of Babylon and also in expression of its power and inaccessibility.

[71] Borrowing a common OT comparison, cf. Is. 8:6 f.; Jer. 47:2.

[72] Bss. Apk., 352-5.

[73] One should not ref. the waters allegorically (cf. Is. 8:7; Rev. 17:15) to the nations which are taken from earth and swallowed up in Hades because they have fallen victim to death, cf. Mt. 16:18.

[74] Cf. 4 Esr. 5:9.

[75] Cf. Is. 11:15; Zech. 10:11; 4 Esr. 13:43-47.

[76] No longer expected from the temple as in Ez. 47:1 ff., cf. Zech. 14:8; Jl. 3:18. Cf. also Rev. 21:22.

[77] By the river stands the tree of life (Rev. 22:2; cf. 22:14, 19; 2:7) rather than trees yielding fruits and healing (Ez. 47:12).

[78] Zech. 14:8 has מַיִם חַיִּים (ὕδωρ ζῶν) "living or flowing water" → 320, 13 f.

Spirit; [79] for all the passages which speak of the water of life refer to perfected believers, Basically, however, the water stands for life itself; [80] life is existence in fellowship with God.

Apart from Rev. the only work in the primitive Christian literature of the 1st century to speak of the water of life is John's Gospel. This connection is not accidental, though the difference in conceptual background should not be over-looked. Rev. uses OT promises as figures of the NT gift of salvation, but the Gospel begins with OT-Jewish monuments or institutions like Jacob's well in 4:5 f., 12 or the dispensing of water at Tabernacles to mediate the annual rainfall in 7:37a [81] and then develops Jesus' offer in antithesis to them with the help of ideas that are Gnostic and dualistic in form. Thus, as Jesus after the feeding of the multitude offers τὸν ἄρτον τὸν ἀληθινόν (6:32), so at Jacob's well He offers true water. He who drinks of the well will thirst again and again (4:13). The thirst for life expressed in thirst is not quenched → VI, 144, 30 ff. But Jesus leaves no more room for thirst, or, positively, He becomes in man a "well of water (→ VI, 116, 11 ff.) springing up to eternal life" [82] (4:14). The gift of Jesus quenches the desire for life because it gives birth to life in man. According to the OT view the perfected man no longer thirsts because he can always drink of the fountain; according to this dualistic way of speaking he no longer suffers thirst because he has the well of life within him. The new mode of expression corresponds to a fulfilment which surpasses the prophecy. In formally dualistic antithesis to the constitution of this creation Jesus' gift can be described as the true water because it effects a total renewal from within. His gift, living water, which becomes a well of water, is His Word (Jn. 8:37; 15:7), His Spirit (7:39 → VI, 442, 3 ff.; 14:17) and He Himself (6:56; 14:20; 15:4 f.) all in one → VI, 144, n. 81. In this sense the offer of living water (7:37 f.) is correctly interpreted by the Evangelist in 7:39. The obscure 7:38 (→ VI, 605, 28 ff.) does at least declare: "To drink is to believe." "He who believes in me (will experience) what Scripture says, Rivers of living water will flow from him," [83] → III, 788, 27 ff. The reference to Scripture has in view not a single OT text but the frequently promised eschatological dispensing of water → 318, 27 ff. He from whom the waters are to flow is the Promised One. [84] But it is quite possible the verse has the believer in view. Thus ὕδωρ ζῶν (4:10 f.; 7:38), in intentional anti-thesis to its traditional sense of "flowing water" (4:11), is construed as "the water which mediates life," "the water of life" (4:14; 7:38).

The historical setting [85] of the usage is plain. On the one side 1 QH (→ 322, 11 ff.) and even more so Rev. (→ 325, 19 ff.) develop what the OT says about water into the metaphor of the water of life. On the other the dualistic development of the idea is plain

---

[79] For a discussion cf. Had. Apk., ad loc.

[80] So also Had. Apk. on 22:1; Bss. Apk. on 7:17: ζωῆς is gen. qual.

[81] Already Zech. 14:16 f.; Taan., 1, 1 (Rabb. discussion c. 90 A.D.); RH, 1, 2; cf. J. Jeremias, "Golgotha," Angelos Beih., 1 (1926), 60-64.

[82] εἰς is to be taken with ἀλλομένου with ref. to the goal (as in 4:36; 12:25): "for eternal life" (Bau. J., ad loc.) or temporally: "for ever" (Bultmann J., 137, n. 3), but not spatially.

[83] κοιλία has here the special sense of "heart" or "inner being" found in the LXX → III, 788, 27 ff. For a discussion v. Bultmann J., 229, n. 2.

[84] Jesus is already compared to the sacred rock in 1 C. 10:4 → VI, 97, 13 ff.

[85] Discussions and materials in Bultmann J., 133-6 and Widengren, 185, s.v. "water of life."

(even more so than in Jn.) in Od. Sol. 30:1 (cf. 11:6 ff.), in Ign. R., 7, 2, [86] and much later in the Mandaean writings in which water of life is a fixed metaphor for the salvation which comes from above. [87] In distinction from the latter John's Gospel is materially rooted in OT thinking, but in a line of thought which leads from the Jewish Baptist movement to Gnosticism it develops the concept for the first time in the new way.

c. Healing and Cleansing Water in John's Gospel.

Two Johannine healings are linked to the common idea, based on medical experiences, that water has a curative effect. [88] The healing at the pool of Bethesda starts with the popular belief that the ruffling of the water from time to time (ὅταν ταραχθῇ τὸ ὕδωρ, Jn. 5:7, cf. the interpolation in 5:3 f.) would bring healing to the first to go down into it on such occasions. [89] Jesus' healing as a demonstration of eschatological grace sets aside these natural rules as it does also the Law — this is emphasised by the Evangelist — by taking place on the Sabbath (→ VII, 26, 30 ff.), 5:7 ff., 17, 20 f.

> In the other Sabbath healing Jesus puts clay made of spittle (→ VI, 118, 19 ff.) on the eyes of the blind man and tells him to wash it off in the pool of Siloam, 9:6 f. These measures do not help to accomplish the healing either magically or medically. [90] They are meant to show that Jesus' healing is an activity that transcends the Sabbath, 9:3 f., 14. [91] In this sense they are to be accepted with obedience as in the direction to Naaman in 2 K. 5:10 ff. (Jn. 9:7). As may be seen from the etym. note in 9:7 the Evangelist understands the process also to be metaphorical and symbolic. The man regains his sight through coming to Him whom God has sent. [92]

When Jesus miraculously provides the wine needed at the wedding at Cana in Jn. 2:1 ff. (→ V, 163, 21 ff.) He shows both by OT-Jewish and also by Hellenistic symbolism that He is the One who brings salvation. The reference to the origin of the wine perhaps carries with it, too, a kerygmatic declaration: The wine is attained from water which was set there "according to the purifying of the Jews" (2:6) for washing the hands and washing or sprinkling vessels → 320, 43 ff. Is this just an explanatory note or is it meant to express the fact that Jesus' gift of salvation replaces what was there before, in particular the Law (1:17)?

The foot-washing (→ III, 426, 25 ff.; IV, 305, 6 ff.; 947, 13 ff.; VI, 631, 4 ff.) sets forth in a sign what Jesus does for His own by His death. He shows them love εἰς τέλος to the uttermost, 13:1, cf. v. 34; 15:13. According to the order of this world the Rabbinic student was under obligation to serve his teacher and if necessary

---

[86] Cf. H. Schlier, "Religionsgeschichtliche Untersuchungen zu d. Ignatiusbriefen," ZNW Beih., 8 (1929), 146-8.

[87] Cf. Bau. J. on 4:14; K. Rudolph, Die Mandäer, II (1961), 61-6.

[88] H. Dechent, "Heilbäder u. Badeleben in Palästina," ZDPV, 7 (1884), 173-210; J. Preuss, "Waschungen u. Bäder nach Bibel u. Talmud," Wiener Medizinische Wochenschr., 54 (1904), 137-140, 185-8.

[89] Archaeolog. findings substantiate Jn. 5 and show that healings took place here in pre-Chr. times, cf. J. Jeremias, Die Wiederentdeckung v. Bethesda, J. 5:2 (1949), 24. The ruffling of the water is attested in pilgrim accounts but has not so far been explained technically, 12 f., 25 f.

[90] So B. Weiss, Das Joh.-Ev., Kritisch-exeget. Komm. über d. NT⁹ (1902), ad loc.

[91] Cf. Bau. J. on 9:6.

[92] There is no further symbolism in the passage as against Schl. Erl., ad loc.: "By covering it (the eye) He prepares light for it. The cover is not to remain; it drops away, but revelation takes place through the cover."

to wash his feet [93] as slaves had to do for their masters [94] and wives for their husbands. [95] By freely accomplishing this task (βάλλει ὕδωρ, [96] 13:5) Jesus declares that His work of salvation is service in the Synoptic sense (Mk. 10:43 ff. and par.), a demonstration of love. The symbolic action expresses two aspects of this demonstration. The loving service of Jesus cleanses His own before God (13:6-11) and it also pledges them to corresponding mutual service (13:12-20).

3. 2 Pt. 3:5 f.

The cosmogonic significance of water is touched on in the NT only in one passage, namely, 2 Pt. 3:5 f.: They do not realise that the heavens were of old and the earth was constituted out of water and by water in the power of God's Word. According to 3:7 (→ VI, 945, 16 ff.) the meaning is that heaven [97] and earth, the world, arose first out of and through water and perished in water (the flood).

OT-Jewish cosmogony simply speaks of the primal flood by which heaven is spanned and over which earth is built, Ps. 24:2; 136:6; Slav. En. 4, cf. in post-NT Christianity Herm. v., 1, 3, 4; also Theophil. Autol., I, 7; II, 10 and 13. Only in Ps.-Clem. Hom., 11, 24 is it taught "that water makes the universe but water has its origin from the movement of the Spirit and the Spirit proceeds from Him who is God over all." This cosmogony is developed in Ps.-Clem. to show that birth of water and the Spirit was intended by creation [98] and in 2 Pt. to carry through the parallel (already common in Judaism) [99] between the future destruction by fire and the flood. Both use non-bibl. Hell. ideas of emanation from elements. Unlike Thales: [100] ἐξ ὕδατος ... πάντα εἶναι καὶ εἰς ὕδωρ πάντα ἀπολύεσθαι, they do not have in view a physical process but rather that God's Word made heaven and earth from water as the original material and by water as the means, [101] just as it created man, e.g., from earth and by the Spirit, Gn. 2:7. [102]

II. Baptismal Water.

This is not the place to discuss the meaning of baptism but simply to investigate the ideas connected with the water of baptism.

---

[93] bBer., 7b with ref. to 2 K. 3:11: Elisha pouring water over the hands of Elijah; bKet., 96a: A student does for his teacher all the things a slave does for his master.

[94] M. Ex. on 21:2.

[95] bKet., 61a: When a woman brings four slaves with her in marriage she does not need to do housework, "yet she must pour him (her husband) a cup, make the bed, and wash his face, hands and feet." Basically these tasks are not viewed as slave labour but as proofs of love. When Chr. women wash the feet of the saints in 1 Tm. 5:10 this is certainly not wifely obligation or menial labour but a demonstration of the new service, cf. Lk. 7:38; 10:40.

[96] βάλλω ὕδωρ for filling with fluids is good Gk. (cf. Pr.-Bauer, s.v. βάλλω) and also finds a par. in Hbr., cf. Schl. Mt. on 9:17.

[97] συνεστῶσα (as we are to read) is attracted to γῆ but also goes with οὐρανοί (→ V, 514, n. 128; VII, 897, 27 ff.).

[98] H. J. Schoeps, Theol. u. Gesch. d. Judenchristentums (1949), 206 f.; G. Strecker, "Das Judenchristentum in den Pseudoclementinen," TU, 70 (1958), 196-209.

[99] Jos. Ant., 1, 70; T. Taan., 3, 1 (218); cf. Schl. Mt. on 3:11; → VI, 945, 16 ff.; 948, 1 ff.; R. Mayer, Die bibl. Vorstellung vom Weltenbrand. Eine Untersuchung über d. Beziehung zwischen Parsismus u. Judt. (1956), 114-125.

[100] H. Diels, Doxographi Graeci² (1929), 276b, 3-5.

[101] Though the idea occurs in Rabbinism it is not accepted; jChag., 2, 1 (77a, 15-24) says against the Amoraean Jehuda b. Passi: He who teaches the world in its original state was water offends against God.

[102] Cf. the statement ref. to the pot made by the potter, 1 QH 1:21: I am a clay vessel, kneaded with water, cf. 3:24; 12:25; 13:15; 1 QS 11:21 f.; J. C. Greenfield, "The Root 'GBL' in Mishnaic Hebrew and in the Hymnic Literature from Qumran," Revue de Qumran, 2 (1959/60), 155-162.

1. The Saying of the Baptist.

The saying of the Baptist in Mk. 1:8 and Mt. 3:11 and par. (→ I, 538, 13 ff.; V, 436, n. 380) is closely connected in its second form with Essene ideas. [103] The saying describes the imminent final event as the completion of that which has just begun. He who is to come will baptise with the Spirit (→ I, 537, 36 ff.; VI, 400, 7 ff.) and with fire [104] as John baptised with water. Baptism with water [105] is the initial eschatological cleansing which mediates the blotting out of sins and conversion. The coming One will complete this renewal by definitively creating the new and abolishing what is against God. This is how John himself already understood his baptism.

2. Water Baptism and Spirit Baptism in Primitive Christian Theology.

The combination of water baptism and Spirit baptism, which is prefigured in the OT and expressed in the saying of the Baptist, is taken up in various ways in primitive Christian theology. In Acts the saying of the Baptist is refashioned as the promise of the Spirit in the Easter appearances: John baptised with water but you will be baptised with the Holy Ghost, Ac. 1:5. This promise applies primarily to the receiving of the Spirit (→ VI, 413, 13 ff.) and not specifically to Christian baptism, Ac. 11:16. Furthermore the promise of the Spirit is formulated as the antithesis to John's water baptism in order to ward off a Jewish Baptist sect honouring John messianically (Ac. 19:1-7) and to clarify the relation between the washing and the endowment of the Spirit at Christian baptism in a specific missionary situation. If the uncircumcised receive the Spirit by believing hearing (Gl. 3:2), water cannot be denied to them (Ac. 10:47 f.; cf. 11:16 f.). According to this usage water is simply the baptismal element as in Ac. 8:36, 38 f.; it is not a figurative term for baptism itself. Certainly water is not meant as an efficacious element; the reference is to its use by men on the basis of the divine direction and the divine promise which is proclaimed, Ac. 2:38. According to this God will give the Spirit through this human action, not automatically, but in orientation to faith and the growth of the community, Ac. 8:16 f.; 11:17. [106]

The Johannine writings develop the same thought in a different way. According to John's Gospel the final point of the water baptism of John is that Jesus should be manifested thereby as the Bearer of the Spirit, since He receives the Spirit at it, Jn. 1:26 f., 31, 33. This is said to explain John's baptism and to answer the later disciples of John. 1 Jn., building on Jn. 1:29, 36, links baptism with death and declares that He has come through water and blood, i.e., through baptism at the Jordan and the cross, not through water alone, 1 Jn. 5:6. The latter was taught by the Docetic Gnosticism against which the epistle is written and which held that the heavenly Pneuma-Christ in baptism associated Himself with the man Jesus and parted from

---

[103] Acc. to 1 QS a present cleansing by the conversion which is made possible by the Spirit and by washings is to be followed by a total cleansing by the Spirit which is fig. described as sprinkling, while the impenitent will be destroyed by fire, 1 QS 4:13, 21; cf. 1 QSb 5:24 f.; Test. L. 18 → VI, 943, 31 ff.

[104] βαπτίζω does not mean "to immerse" but technically "to baptise," though it is meant fig. and does not ref. to Chr. baptism. Hence ἐν means "with" rather than "in" בְּ טבל.

[105] This must be understood in the light of the Baptist movement and its OT background as in 1 QS 4:21 → 320, 30 ff.; 321, 26 ff.

[106] Acc. to the Synoptic account of the baptism of Jesus He received the Spirit when He came up out of the water (Mk. 1:10 par.), hence in association with His baptism but not in it.

him at the passion, so that only the man died. [107] In accordance with His true coming Jesus is now fully attested by a threefold witness: the Spirit, the water, and the blood, 1 Jn. 5:7 f. Christ is attested by the historical events of His way when they are proclaimed and the Spirit speaks through this proclamation (Jn. 15:26; 16:7, 13) and specifically through its operation in baptism and the eucharist → IV, 498, 28 ff. The formula points to the latter, for according to John's Gospel what takes place now by water and the Spirit is Christian baptism (Jn. 3:5) and the flesh and blood which are efficacious through the Spirit are the eucharist, Jn. 6:53, 63. [108] This mode of expression suggests that the formulation in Jn. 19:34b is also referring to the two sacraments. [109] From the wound in the side which the fatal thrust of the spear opens near the heart there flow blood and water. [110] Perhaps [111] this note, which in context simply emphasises the onset of death, is also recalling the two sacraments and showing that they derive from the death of Jesus. In the passages which refer unambiguously to baptism (Jn. 3:5; 1 Jn. 5:6 ff.) ὕδωρ is always combined with πνεῦμα and hence it denotes, not baptism as a whole, nor water as the element, but the actual washing.

In the Pauline corpus Eph. 5:26 (→ IV, 304, 9 ff.) brings out the significance of washing in baptism: He (Christ) sanctifies it as He "cleanses it with the washing of water by the word." Christ Himself acts through baptism. He cleanses through the washing as He is at work through the Word. [112] The ῥῆμα is the baptismal formula, [113] the invocation of the name of Jesus over the washing in which the baptismal proclamation reaches its goal. Invocation of the name makes the washing baptism.

In a way which formally reminds us of Essene statements (→ 321, 10 ff.) Hb. 10:22 (→ VI, 983, 12 ff.) associates the washing and the spiritual cleansing in terms of operation: "Our hearts sprinkled from an evil conscience, and our bodies washed with pure water." The verse obviously has baptism in view and it characterises it as a total cleansing which replaces all previous purificatory rites. The body is washed with pure water, i.e., water dedicated to purifying, [114] and the heart is sanctified by sprinkling with the blood of Christ. [115]

Unlike this statement, which is developed in terms of existing rites, 1 Pt. 3:21 finds a sharp antithesis. Baptism is not a washing which cleanses from the filth of the flesh → II, 688, 11 ff.

---

[107] So the Gnostic Cerinthus in Ephesus in the early 2nd cent., Iren. Haer., I, 26, 1, and similarly the adversaries in 1 Jn.

[108] Cf. R. Schnackenburg, D. Joh.-Br., Herders Theol. Komm. NT, 13, 3³ (1963), 260-263. Acc. to Nauck, op. cit. (→ n. 46), 147-182 the passage ref. to a baptismal eucharist preceded acc. to Syr. liturgical tradition by endowment with the Spirit. But this ritualistic interpretation is in conflict with Johannine thinking.

[109] Cf. already patristic exegesis, Bau. J., ad loc.

[110] Orig. Cels., II, 36 makes this a physiological miracle by having blood and ὕδωρ καθαρόν flow forth. But the physiological side is open in the story. The attempted psychological explanations in Weiss, op. cit. (→ n. 90), ad loc. are wide of the mark.

[111] Acc. to Bau.; Bultmann J., ad loc. certain, not acc. to Zahn J., ad loc., uncertain acc. to Schl. J., ad loc. For other symbolical interpretations cf. Weiss, ad loc.

[112] ἐν ῥήματι here goes with both λουτρῷ and καθαρίσας.

[113] So Schlier Eph.³, ad loc.

[114] Cf. Ez. 36:25; Test. L. 8:5.

[115] Both through baptism; there is no distinction between ritual cleansing of the body by water and moral cleansing of the soul as in Philo Plant., 162: σώματα καὶ ψυχὰς καθηράμενοι, τὰ μὲν λουτροῖς, τὰ δὲ νόμων καὶ παιδείας ὀρθῆς ῥεύμασιν.

3. Interpretation of Baptism by Water Symbolism.

Already in the NT baptism is explained figuratively in terms of the various qualities of water, though no corresponding power is ascribed to the water. Like John's baptism, Christian baptism is often interpreted as a cleansing bath, Eph. 5:26; Hb. 10:22. Terms from the stem λούω are also used with no actual mention of water → IV, 303, 37 ff.; Ac. 22:16; 1 C. 6:11; Tt. 3:5; 2 Pt. 2:22. Twice the baptismal water is typologically expounded as the death-dealing and saving flood (→ 319, 15 ff.), 1 Pt. 3:20 f.: "Wherein (sc. in the ark) few... were saved by water, as an antitype of which [116] baptism doth also now save you." According to the Midrash [117] Noah went into the ark only when the water was already up to his knees; he thus went through the water of the flood into the ark. [118] Similarly 1 C. 10:1 f. compares baptism to the deliverance of Israel at the Red Sea. The people were baptised in the cloud (Ex. 13:21) and in the sea (Ex. 14:22) [119] → IV, 869, 36 ff. The tertium comparationis in both typologies is not passing through the water but deliverance through a flood which separates the saved from the lost. [120] This function of water makes it far clearer than the cleansing function that baptism is not to be repeated as cleansing usually is. In virtue of the crucifixion and resurrection it posits a completely new beginning which is comparable only to a dying with Christ in order to live with Him (R. 6) or a new birth (cf. 1 Pt. 1:3, 23; 2:2) and which brings into fellowship both with God and also with the people of the redeemed.

D. The Baptismal Water in the Post-Apostolic Fathers and the Early Church.

1. Interpretation of Baptism by Water Symbolism.

Interpretation of baptism by the functions of water is developed further in the post-NT writings. In the central vision of Hermas the Church appears as a tower which is established over water since previous generations (s., 9, 16, 4. 6) attained and will attain to salvation only through water, v., 3, 3, 5; s., 9, 16, 2; cf. v., 3, 2, 9; 7, 3. Though it has no effect on the interpretation there stands behind the vision the idea of a primal flood, the tower of the Church standing above the waters as earth was established above the flood at creation, v., 1, 3, 4. Barn., 11 interprets baptism allegorically in terms of OT statements about drinking water mediating life. Allegorically interpreted verses describe baptism as the reliable fountain of water (11, 5), as the water-course which brings fruitfulness (11, 6 f., 10), as the fountain of life which Israel rejects (11, 1 ff.). "We go into the water laden with sins and filth and rise up out of it bringing forth fruits in the heart, fear and hope in Jesus...," 11, 11. Esp. on the basis of the symbolical-allegorical mode of expression both Herm. and Barn. use for βαπτίζω and βάπτισμα (only v., 3, 7, 3; Barn., 11, 1) periphrases with water: "to go down into the water," Herm. m., 4, 3, 1, cf.

---

[116] ὅ relates to the preceding sentence; δι' ὕδατος is not instrumental but local. Cf. L. Goppelt, *Typos* (1939), 188 f.

[117] Cf. Midr. Hag. on Gn. 7:7.

[118] Just. Dial., 138, 2 allegorises: As Noah was saved, for he sailed on the water in the wood.

[119] As regards the source of this typology A. Merx, *Die vier kanon. Ev. nach ihrem ältesten bekannten Texte*, II, 1 (1905), 38 and Jeremias, *op. cit.* (→ n. 44), 38 recall the exegetical postulate of the school of Hillel on which proselyte baptism was grounded: Israel took a bath before being received into the covenant at Sinai. But at most this Rabb. speculation only helped to promote the Pauline typology.

[120] Cf. Goppelt, *op. cit.* (→ n. 116), 174, 188 f.; Lundberg, 112 f., 142-5.

s., 9, 16, 4; Barn., 11, 8, "to come up out of the water," Herm. s., 9, 16, 2, and both, Barn., 11, 11.

In the fathers baptism is then comprehensively explained with the help of the symbolical meaning of water derived from OT and non-biblical concepts. Esp. impressive are the statements in Tert. Bapt., 3-5. Water as the first element was the seat of the Holy Ghost and is more pleasing to Him than other elements ... It was the first to bring forth living creatures so that it is no accident that water can give life in baptism ... What previously healed only the body now heals the spirit too; what brought well-being in time now accomplishes salvation. The functions of water here explained simply as figures of the effect of baptism in the early Church, are now, on the basis of philosophical traditions which both Jews and Hell. associated with them, forces which were noted in baptism too. This will be apparent in the next two sections.

2. Rules about the Water of Baptism.

The form of baptism was never clearly specified or described in the NT. The Church no doubt followed Jewish models and esp. John the Baptist. In proselyte baptism men stood up to the hip in water and women up to their neck, and they either dipped the body into the water or poured water over it. [121] In John's baptism they probably stood in the same position and the Baptist immersed them or poured water over them. [122] According to every indication this was also the normal form of the earliest Chr. baptism. About the beginning of the 2nd cent. we find rules, if not about the mode of baptism, at least about the water to be used. Acc. to Did., 7, 1-3 baptism should be in running water ὕδωρ ζῶν, though it might be in standing water or water warmed in a tank. Even threefold pouring over the head will do. With this view the Syrian church behind the Did. follows OT-Jewish ideas acc. to which living water is preferable for purifications, → 320, 13 ff. This evaluation of the kinds of water [123] was already being crowded out toward the end of the 2nd cent. [124] when, as already customary in Just. Apol., I, 61, 3, baptism was usually administered in enclosed places rather than in the open. [125] It is perhaps with ref. to objections to this change that Tert. rejects even the relative grading of kinds of water represented by the Did.: "Hence it makes no difference whether one is baptised in the sea or in a pond, in a river or in a fountain, in a lake or in a tank," Bapt., 4. This statement is, of course, based on a typically post-apost. idea, namely, that of the sanctifying of the water → 329, 23 ff.

3. Sanctifying of the Water of Baptism.

From Ign. Eph., 18, 2 one finds in various forms the idea of a sanctifying of the water of baptism: "He was born and baptised to cleanse (καθαρίσῃ) water by his passion." This statement describes the institution of baptism in such a way that the common ancient idea [126] of a power mediated to the water is associated therewith. Water is cleansed or

---

[121] Benoit, 14, n. 57; Rácz, 90-93; Str.-B., I, 108, 110 f. The text does not explicitly state that the proselyte pours water over his body.

[122] The second possibility only acc. to Stommel Taufriten, 10. The typologies of 1 C. 10:1 f. and 1 Pt. 3:20 f. support it, but R. 6:4 presupposes immersion as practised from the 4th cent., Stommel Taufriten, 12 f.

[123] Hipp. Traditio apostolica, 21, 2 also demanded running water originally, with exceptions, but the transmission of the text is uncertain, cf. G. Dix, *The Treatise on the Apost. Tradition of St. Hippolytus of Rome,* I (1937), 33.

[124] Only the Jewish Chr. of Ps.-Clem. seem to speak exclusively of baptism "with the water of a fountain or river or the sea," Ps.-Clem. Recg., 4, 32. "Acc. to the manner of Moses you should lead him to a river or a fountain where is running water," Ps.-Clem. Contestatio, 1, 2 (GCS, 42, 3); cf. further Dölger ΙΧΘΥΣ, I, 84, n. 5.

[125] Cf. Klauser, 160.

[126] G. van der Leeuw, *Phänomenologie d. Religion*[2] (1956), 386-9.

sanctified [127] when set apart as a means of divine grace. The NT says this only of the eucharistic elements (→ VI, 157, 1 ff.), not of the water of baptism. But this founding of baptism is presupposed in the NT, for already in Mk. 1:9 ff. the baptism of Jesus is the basis and model of Chr. baptism. His entry into John's baptism makes this Chr. baptism after He has run His course. Jn. 19:34 and 1 Jn. 5:6-9 suggest this connection → 330, 3 ff.

Once the idea grew of an empowering of the water as well as an institution of the act, a corresponding epiclesis developed in the baptismal liturgy. Acc. to the NT the washing becomes baptism only with invocation of the name of Jesus over the act → 330, 17 ff. But from the 2nd cent. a preceding epiclesis over the water is gen.: *oportet* . . . *mundari et sanctificari aquam prius a sacerdote, ut possit baptismo... peccata... abluere.* [128] Various ideas cluster around this consecration. Acc. to Tert. Bapt., 4, cf. 8 the Spirit as a heavenly substance comes down on the water through the invocation of God and mediates to the water the power to sanctify. This very material explanation is an extreme view not shared by all. The epiclesis of Const. Ap., VII, 43 prays essentially only that the act of baptism which follows should have an effect corresponding to the promise.

4. Holy Water.

In the 4th cent. this sanctifying of the water of baptism merges with a hallowing of the water of lustration. From the 2nd cent. the custom had grown of washing the hands symbolically with water, as in Judaism and paganism (→ 317, 10 ff.; 321, 1 ff.), before prayer (cf. Tert. De Oratione, 13; Const., Ap., VIII, 32) or receiving or dispensing the eucharist (cf. Chrys. Hom., III in Eph. 1, MPG, 62 [1862], 28 f.). This lustration was done with unconsecrated water and was basically symbolic. In the 4th cent. there then developed the practice of consecrating water for use both in baptism and also in lustrations, and this gives us holy water. [129] Const. Ap., VIII, 29 has the formula of a dedicatory prayer which shows the multiple purpose: "Sanctify this water . . . and grant it effective power for the preservation of health, the curing of sickness, the driving out of demons, the warding off of all assaults through Christ our hope."

Goppelt

---

[127] Cl. Al. Ecl. Proph., 7, 1 (GCS, 17, 138): And the Saviour had Himself baptised . . . in order to sanctify all water for the regenerate, cf. also Tert. Adv. Judaeos, 8.

[128] Cyprian Ep., 70, 1 (CSEL, 3, 767), presupposed already in Iren. Fr., 35 (MPG, 7 [1882], 1247 f.); Tert. Bapt., 4; Orig. Fr., 36 on Jn. 3:5 (GCS, 10, 512) cf. Dölger, ΙΧΘΥΣ, 70-72. Hipp. Trad. apost., 21, 1 has a similar direction with no formula, cf. Dix, *op. cit.*, 33. For later development cf. G. Kretschmar, "Stud. z. früchr. Trinitätstheologie," *Beiträge z. hist. Theol.*, 21 (1956), 199-208; Stommel Studien, 7-34.

[129] V. Schultze, Art. "Weihwasser," RE, 21³ (1908), 56; S. Benz, Art. "Wasser," LexThK, X² (1965), 966.

┌─────────────────────┐
│ υἱός, υἱοθεσία   │   παῖς → V, 636, 24 ff.; πατήρ → V, 946, 10 ff.
└─────────────────────┘

Contents: A. υἱός in Greek: I. Classical Usage; II. Hellenism. B. Old Testament:
1. Linguistic Data; 2. בֵּן (בַּר) as a Term for Physical Descendants and Relatives; 3. בֵּן (בַּר)
as a Broader Term of Association; 4. בֵּן (בַּר) as a Term of Relationship; 5. בֵּן (בַּר) as a Term
for Relationship to God. C. Judaism: I. Hellenistic Judaism: 1. Septuagint; 2. Josephus;
3. Philo. II. Palestinian Judaism: 1. Duties of the Son; 2. Son as a Term of Relationship;
3. Israel and the Righteous as Sons of God; 4. The Messiah as Son of God. D. New Testament: I. υἱός without Reference to God: 1. Jesus as Son of Mary and Joseph; 2. Father and
Son as an Illustration of God's Care for Believers; 3. The Son as the Supreme Good; 4. υἱός

υ ἱ ό ς. Bibl.: Gen.: Cr.-Kö., s.v.; G. van der Leeuw, Phänomenologie d. Religion² (1956),
103 f., 124, 585 f., 738; S. Morenz, Art. "Sohn Gottes," RGG³, VI, 118 f.; Pr.-Bauer, s.v.;
Kühner-Blass-Gerth, I, 1, 506-8; Schwyzer, I, 573 f.; G. P. Wetter, "Der Sohn Gottes. Eine
Untersuchung über d. Charakter u. die Tendenz d. Joh.-Ev.," FRL, NF, 9 (1916). On A.:
L. Bieler, Θεῖος ἀνήρ, I (1935), 9-20, 134-140; II (1936), 41-74; P. Chantraine, Morphologie
historique du grec² (1961), 94-6; A. Debrunner, Review in Anzeiger f. idg. Sprach- u. Alter-
tumskunde, Beiblatt z. Idg. Forschung, 40 (1922), 13; Liddell-Scott, Pass., Thes. Steph., s.v.;
H. Usener, Das Weihnachtsfest² (1911), 71-8. On B.: P. A. H. de Boer, "De Zoon van God
in het OT," Leidse Voordrachten, 29 (1958); A. R. Johnson, The One and the Many in the
Israelite Conception of God (1942); J. Pedersen, Israel, Its Life and Culture, I-II³ (1954),
46-96; R. de Vaux, Les institutions de l'AT, I (1958), 71-87; P. Winter, "Der Begriff Söhne
Gottes im Moseslied, Dt. 32:1-43," ZAW, 67 (1955), 40-8. On C. and D.: B. W. Bacon,
"The 'Son' as Organ of Revelation," HThR, 9 (1916), 382-415; Bau. J. on 1:34; J. Bieneck,
Sohn Gottes als Christusbezeichnung d. Synpt. (1951); M. E. Boismard, "Constitué Fils de
Dieu (R. 1:4)," Rev. Bibl., 60 (1953), 5-17; G. Bornkamm, "Sohnschaft u. Leiden," Fest-
schr. J. Jeremias² (1964), 188-198; W. Bousset, Kyrios Christos² (1921), 45-49, 52-57, 151-
158, 248-259, 268-274; O. Cullmann, Die Christologie d. NT³ (1963), 276-313; Dalman WJ,
I, 219-237; J. Dupont, "Filius meus es tu," Recherches de Science Relig., 35 (1948), 522-543;
R. H. Fuller, The Foundations of NT Christology (1965); A. George, "Le Père et le Fils dans
les Év. synopt.," Lumière et Vie, 29 (1956), 27-40; also "Jésus Fils de Dieu dans l'Év. selon
S. Luc," Rev. Bibl., 72 (1965), 185-209; W. Grundmann, "Die Gotteskindschaft in d. Gesch.
Jesu u. ihre religionsgeschichtlichen Voraussetzungen," SDThFr, 1 (1938); also "Sohn Gottes.
Ein Diskussionsbeitrag," ZNW, 47 (1956), 113-133; F. Hahn, "Christologische Hoheitstitel,"
FRL, 83³ (1966), 280-346; E. Huntress, "'Son of God' in Jewish Writings Prior to the
Christian Era," JBL, 54 (1935), 117-123; B. M. F. van Iersel, "Der Sohn in d. synopt. Jesus-
worten," Suppl. Nov. Test., 3² (1964); Kl. Mk. on 1:11; J. Kögel, Der Sohn u. d. Söhne
(1904); W. Kramer, "Christus-Kyrios-Gottessohn," AbhThANT, 44 (1963); T. de Kruijf,
"Der Sohn d. lebendigen Gottes. Ein Beitrag z. Christologie d. Mt.," Analecta Biblica, 16
(1962); E. Lövestam, "Son and Saviour," Coni. Neot., 18 (1961); C. Maurer, "Knecht Gottes
u. Sohn Gottes im Passionsbericht d. Mk.," ZThK, 50 (1953), 1-53; O. Michel and O. Betz,
"Von Gott gezeugt," Festschr. J. Jeremias² (1964), 3-23; Moore, II, 119-140; J. Schreiber,
Art. "Sohn Gottes im NT," RGG³, VI, 119 f.; E. Schweizer, "The Concept of the Davidic
Son of God in Acts and its OT Background," Stud. in Luke-Acts (1966), 186-193; Str.-B., I,
476-8; III, 15-22; H. Virnekäs, Der Sinn d. Bezeichnung Jesu als Gottessohn im NT, Munich
(1959), On E.: A. Gilg, "Weg u. Bdtg. d. altkirchlichen Christologie," Theol. Bücherei, 4
(1955), 11-40; A. Grillmeier, Die theol. u. sprachliche Vorbereitung d. christologischen Formel
v. Chalcedon, I (1951), 5-202; Harnack Dg., I, 337-796; F. Loofs, Leitfaden z. Studium d.
Dogmengeschichte⁶ (1959), 59-97; R. Seeberg, Lehrbuch d. Dogmengesch., I³ (1922), 115-
248, 331-473.

in the Transferred Sense (Jn. 19:26); 5. Son of Abraham and Israel; 6. Son as a Term for Student; 7. υἱός as a Term of Relationship. II. Jesus as Son of God in the Tradition of the Community Prior to the Writing of the New Testament: 1. Jesus; 2. The Davidic Son of God: a. The Regency of the Exalted (R. 1:3 f.); b. Resurrection as Son of God (Ac. 13:33; 2:30 f.); c. The Baptism of Jesus (Mk. 1:11); d. The Separation of the Community from the World in the βασιλεία of the Son (Col. 1:13); e. The Transfiguration (Mk. 9:7); f. The Link with Ps. 110; 3. The Eschatological Role of the Son of God and the Absolute Use of ὁ υἱός: a. The Link with Son of Man Christology (1 Th. 1:10; Rev. 2:18); b. 1 C. 15:28; c. Mk. 13:22; d. Mt. 11:27; e. The Johannine Passages; 4. The Sending of the Pre-Existent Son of God; 5. The Miraculously Born and Miracle-Working Son of God: a. The Virgin Birth; b. The Miracle-Worker (Mk. 5:7); c. The Temptation of Jesus (Mt. 4:3, 6 and par.); 6. The Suffering Righteous as Son of God (Mt. 27:43). III. The Interpretation of the Divine Sonship of Jesus by the New Testament Writers: 1. Mark; 2. Matthew; 3. Luke and Acts; 4. Paul (Including Col. and Eph.): a. Apocalyptic Passages (1 Th. 1:10; 1 C. 15:28; Gl. 1:16); b. The Sending of the Son of God (Gl. 4:4 f.; R. 8:3 f.); c. The Suffering Son of God (R. 5:10; 8:32; Gl. 2:20); d. The Other References; 5. John: a. Eschatological Passages and the Absolute Use of ὁ υἱός; b. The Sending of the Son of God; c. The Son of God as the Content of the Confession; d. The Meaning of the Divine Sonship for John; 6. The Other Writings. IV. Men as Sons of God: 1. Works Apart from Paul; 2. Paul. E. υἱὸς θεοῦ in Primitive Christian Literature outside the New Testament: 1. Survey; 2. Meaning of υἱὸς θεοῦ in Early Church Christology.

A. υἱός in Greek.

I. Classical Usage.

1. The consistent paradigm of the O declension is first found in Attic only from the 4th cent. B.C. Examples of gen. υἱοῦ dat. υἱῷ acc. plur. -ούς occur on Attic inscr. from 300 B.C., e.g., IG, II/III², 2, No. 1534a, 47 (c. 275 B.C.); Demosth. Or., 23, 66; 44, 23; Menand. Dyscolus [1], 16; Fr., 334, 6 etc. The word is also written ὑός etc. In older epic, other dialects and esp. epic and derived poetry one finds a mixed paradigm: nom., acc., vocative υἱός υἱόν, υἱέ, gen., dat. υἱέος, υἱεῖ, plur. -εῖς, -έων, -έσι (-άσι), -εῖς, epic also gen., dat. sing. υἷος, υἷι etc. An older u-stem is to be seen in the forms of the mixed paradigm. [2] The presence of this u-stem strengthens the possibility of a combination of words for "son" from various related languages (Sanscrit, Gothic, Lithuanian etc.). [3]

2. From Homeric epic onward υἱός stands alongside παῖς for "son," in Hom. often for the sons of Zeus, e.g., Il., 5, 683; Od., 11, 568 → IV, 1025, 7 f. and other gods, e.g., Il., 13, 345; Hom. Hymn., 16, 2: υἱέες ἀθανάτων, Il., 16, 449; [4] plur. for the members of a people, e.g., υἷες Ἀχαιῶν, Il., 1, 162 etc.; Τρώων... υἱέας, Il., 23, 175, also Καπανήιος υἱός "son of Capaneus," Il.., 4, 367 etc. The almost complete avoidance of the word in the Attic tragedians shows that it was felt to be the least poetic, rather a terminological expression. υἱός is not restricted to the legitimate descendant, Il., 2, 727 etc. παῖς is more comprehensive (plur. "children") and when it does not mean "slave" it may carry, in distinction from υἱός, the nuance of the childlike: "the little son." In

---

[1] Ed. H. Lloyd-Jones (1960); with comm. by E. W. Handley (1965).
[2] Examples of υἱύς (also ὑύς and contracted to ὕς) in ancient Attic in IG, I², 571 and 663, also in Gortyn and Sparta. υἱός was dissimilated from υἱύς cf. Schwyzer, I, 573 f.
[3] The suffix -iu- in Gk. (* suius) seems to occur also in the Tocharian dialect B soy(ä) "son." The other Indo-Eur. languages have -nu-: sūnus (Sanscr., Baltic, Slavic), sunus (Germanic), cf. Pokorny, 913 f. Unexpected is Mycenaean dat. iiewei "to the son?", nom. iius uncertain, eventually also iios, v. A. Morpurgo, Mycenaeae Graecitatis Lex. (1963), 111 f., 118 [Risch].
[4] Basically cf. van der Leeuw, 585 f.

contrast υἱός is the anton. of θυγάτηρ: τοῦ καὶ δώδεκα παῖδες ... γεγάασιν, ἓξ μὲν θυγατέρες, ἓξ δ᾽ υἱέες, Od., 10, 5 f. and where it relates to inheritance and the sequence of generations, [5] e.g., Od., 20, 218 (cf. παῖς, 214); Hdt., I, 109, 4; III, 34, 5 (in Hdt.'s historical work παῖς occurs for "son" some 120 times, υἱός 6). υἱός is used abs. in Pind. Pyth., 8, 40 for the so-called epigoni, i.e., the sons of the seven against Thebes, and in Apoll. Rhod., I, 1351 f., where fitness as hostages is decided by ἀρίστους υἱέας ἐκ δήμοιο, i.e., "sons of full citizens." Hom. Il., 23, 175 is close to this. In Dion. Hal., 4, 4, 8 it embraces "sons" and "sons-in-law". [6]

3. Hom. and Hes. depict the Olympian circle of gods as a family dynasty. Zeus, the son of Kronos and Rhea, is πατὴρ ἀνδρῶν τε θεῶν τε, Hom. Il., 1, 544 etc. In the heroic age the gods had intercourse with mortals and children were conceived by mortal women. Thus in Gk. mythology Dionysus and Heracles were sons of Zeus by mortal mothers. They had the rank of gods under various conditions. Dionysus was a god from birth, though at times he had to strive for recognition. But Heracles led the toilsome life of a man and received apotheosis and reception into the Olympian circle only at death → 337, 22 ff. The apotheosis of heroes is not limited, however, to sons of the gods. [7]

4. A functional use of υἱός is indicated by mythological-genealogical constructions among which one might reckon the fact that the two physician-heroes of Ilias, Machaon and Podaleirios, are sons of Aesculapius, Il., 7, 731 (παῖδε); 11, 518. In Hes. Theog., 368 the rivers are sons of Oceanos. "Presumption" κόρος is a son of hubris acc. to an oracular saying in Hdt., VIII, 77, 1. Dionysus is υἱὸς Σταμνίου "son of the wine-pot," Aristoph. Ra., 22. Cnemon is Ὀδύνης ὑός "son of sorrow" in Menand. Dyscolus, 88, [8] cf. also Soph. Oed. Tyr., 1080. This genealogical model of abstract dependencies carries with it in principle the possibility of an extended use of the word.

II. Hellenism.

1. υἱός occurs as a translation in the style of oriental and especially Egyptian [9] rulers: "son of God," "son of Helios," "son of Zeus." Alexander the Gt. in his campaign was called "son of Ammon" (= Gk. "son of Zeus") by the Ammon oracle in the Libyan desert, Callisthenes Fr., 14a (FGrHist, IIb, 645). [10] The year 331 must count as an epochal one for the Gk. form of the ruler cult. From that date the Gk. form of the title was claimed esp. by the Ptolemies, cf. as the earliest witnesses Suppl. Epigr. Graec., 8, 504a, 6 (217 B.C.): υἱὸς τοῦ Ἡλίου, cf. Mitteis-Wilcken, I, 2, No. 109, 11, also Ditt. Or., I, 90, 3 (196 B.C.). In the Roman imperial period

---

[5] υἱωνός Hom. Il., 2, 666; IG, 5, 1, No. 1450 (1st cent. A.D.); P. Oxy., II, 261, 7 (1st cent. A.D.) and Attic ὑϊδοῦς "grandson," e.g., Plat. Leg., XI, 925a come from υἱός, not παῖς.

[6] υἱός drops out in mentioning the father's name Σωκράτης (ὁ) Σωφρονίσκου Ἀλωπεκῆθεν, "Socrates son of Sophroniscos of (Demos) Alopeke," Diog. L., II, 40; cf. also Schwyzer, II, 119 f.

[7] There are also many degrees and forms of deification. Immortality is not acceptance among the Olympian θεοί, F. Taeger, Charisma, I (1957, 60 with n. 40. Mythological accounts have many variations in detail and the religious bases are to be assessed differently in each case. For details and bibl. cf. H. J. Rose, A Handbook of Gk. Mythology (1958), pp. 134 ff., 182 ff.

[8] Cf. Handley, op. cit., 145.

[9] For a survey of the Egyptian background cf. Morenz, 118 f.; on the gen. basis van der Leeuw, 124; Taeger, op. cit., I, 191-208; II, 3-225. The material is readily accessible in L. Cerfaux-J. Tondriau, Le culte des souverains. Un concurrent du christianisme (1957), Index, III, s.v. "Fils de ..." (sc. Zeus etc.); for bibl. cf. also A. Dihle, Art. "Herrscherkult," RGG³, III, 280; W. v. Soden, Art. "Königtum," RGG³, III, 1714.

[10] Cf. H. Bengtson, Griech. Gesch.³ (1965), 334 f. and Taeger, op. cit., I, 191-6.

Divi filius was rendered θεοῦ υἱός, [11] e.g., for Augustus (BGU, II, 543, 3 [27 B.C.]; P. Tebt., II, 382, 21 [between 30 B.C. and 1 A.D.]; IG, 12, 3, No. 174, 2 [5 B.C.]).[12]

2. Comparatively late examples of a type of honorary title for leading citizens are found on inscr. The origin and nature of these inscr. is obscure. The ref. seems to be to a kind of honorary citizenship, perhaps in the form of adoption → 398, n. 7. They display a specific extension of the concept: υἱὸς τοῦ δήμου, Ditt. Or., II, 470, 10 with A 6 (c. 2 B.C.), cf. Ditt. Syll.³, II, 804, 10 (54 A.D.), etc., υἱὸς πόλεως, Ditt. Syll.³, II, 813, A 4; B 4 (1st cent. A.D.); IG, 5, 1, No. 37, 6 (2nd cent. A.D.), υἱὸς τῆς πόλεως φύσει δὲ Ἀπελλικῶντος, CIG, II, 3570,[13] υἱὸς Ἑλλάδος, Ditt. Syll.³, II, 854, 3 f. (1st cent. A.D.), υἱὸς τῆς πατρίδος, Inscr. Magn., 167, 5 (1st cent. A.D.), υἱὸς βουλῆς, IG, 5, 1, No. 595, 9; cf. 685, 4, υἱὸς γερουσίας, CIG, IV, 6843, 5 f.; υἱὸς φυλῆς, CIG, III, 4018, 10 etc.

3. υἱός (also voc. υἱέ) occurs (rarely) in pap. letters for people who are not relatives but are close (pupils), P. Strassb., I, 2, 1 (217 A.D.); P. Giess., III, 68, 2 (2nd cent. A.D.); P. Oxy., IX, 1219, 3 (3rd cent. A.D.).[14]

4. Among the Stoics, to whom the idea of divine sonship was suggested by doctrines of the unity of mankind [15] (Cleanthes' hymn to Zeus, Stob. Ecl., I, 25, 7, cf. Chrysippus Fr., 1022 [v. Arnim, II, 305]; Cic. De Legibus, I, 7, 23; Cic. Fin., III, 19, 64 etc.),[16] it is in Epict. Diss., I, 3, 2; 13, 3; III, 22, 81 etc. [17] that a filial relation comes into full focus. How far on the other hand the father-son relation was considered and reduced by him may be seen from passages like Diss., II, 16, 44: Heracles in his wanderings won many friends ἀλλ᾿ οὐδὲν φίλτερον τοῦ θεοῦ, "hence it was believed that he is the son of Zeus, and he was." Acc. to III, 24, 14-16 Heracles thought that God was the father of all the women and children abandoned by him, "for Heracles did not regard it as a mere phrase that Zeus, whom he held to be his own father, whom he named as such and directed his acts by him, is the father of men." [18]

---

[11] Deissmann LO, 294-6; cf. Deissmann B., 166 f. The Lat. differentiation between solemn *divus* and ordinary *divus* could not be expressed in Gk. in the transl. of *divus Iulius* or *Divi filius*. θεοῦ υἱός was the usual style. On the relation of *deus* to *divus* cf. Walde-Hofmann, 345. θεῖος, like *divinus*, meant "imperial," cf. Deissmann LO, 295 f.

[12] Cf. Preisigke Wört., *s.v.* υἱός. τοῦ Διὸς εἶναι υἱόν is even synon. with "to be ruler" in Dio Chrys. Or., 4, 21, cf. 27.

[13] Cf. K. Lanckoronski, *Städte Pamphyliens u. Pisidiens*, II (1892), No. 55. Further instances in W. Liebenam, *Städteverwaltung im röm. Kaiserreiche* (1900), 131 f.; cf. Deissmann B., 161-6, esp. 165 f. There are similar titles with θυγάτηρ etc.

[14] Further examples in Moult.-Mill. and Preisigke Wört., *s.v.* The voc. belongs to current post-class. usage, though it is rare even here; far more common is the class. ὦ παῖ, παιδίον, τέκνον. παῖς or παιδίον had become an appellative for "child" gen., cf. Epic. Fr., 177 (Usener): παιδία in line 25 as compared with υἱῶν in line 28.

[15] Grundmann Gotteskindschaft, 13-25.

[16] M. Pohlenz, *Die Stoa* (1948), 109.

[17] *Ibid.*, 339.

[18] C. Jakobitz and E. E. Seiler, *Handwörterbuch d. gr. Sprache* (1850) and Pape, *s.v.* are in error in citing ῥητόρων or ἰατρῶν υἱοί. There are no examples of this, though one finds some with παῖδες (→ V, 638, 5; cf. Liddell-Scott, *s.v.* παῖς). The first of the instances in Pr.-Bauer, *s.v.*, Ditt. Syll.³, III, 1169, 12 (c. 320 B.C.): υἱ[οὺς τοῦ θ]εοῦ (sc. Ἀσκληπίου) i.e., "physicians," cf. line 40, is an isolated one. Physicians constantly appeal to their god, Aesculapius, esp. the guild in Epidaurus. The second, Max. Tyr., 4, 2c is irrelevant here, since it ref. expressly to the sons of Aesculapius Machaon and Podaleirics → 336, 18 f.

5. υἱὸς τοῦ θεοῦ as the lofty title of Jesus and some Gnostics in the early Christian period is sometimes related by modern scholars to the Hellenistic idea of the θεῖος ἀνήρ. [19] But the roots of this notion do not reach back into the older Greek era. [20]

a. In Hom. θεῖος (→ III, 122, 17 ff.) is an epithet used for many heroes, e.g., Odysseus in Il., 2, 335 etc., Achilles in Il., 19, 297 etc., also with ἀοιδός Od., 4, 17 etc., βασιλεύς Od., 4, 621 etc., κῆρυξ Il., 4, 192 etc. This poetic use might reflect sacral ideas [21] but it is primarily a mark of epic style and forms no sure basis for investigation of concepts. In class. prose the following picture emerges: θεῖος, used of men, ref. either to their attitude to religious commands and thus means "pious," e.g., Plat. Resp., II, 383c: εἰ μέλλουσιν ἡμῖν οἱ φύλακες θεοσεβεῖς τε καὶ θεῖοι γίγνεσθαι, cf. Leg., II, 666d, cf. also the difficult Hes. Op., 727-732, which says a θεῖος ἀνήρ observes certain taboos, or else the irrational aspects of human action or capacity are emphasised, Plat. Men., 99d: τοὺς πολιτικούς . . . φαῖμεν ἂν θείους τε εἶναι καὶ ἐνθουσιάζειν, [22] cf. Xenoph. Oec., 21, 5: θεῖοι καὶ ἀγαθοὶ καὶ ἐπιστήμονες ἄρχοντες, also the toying with the predicate θεός or θεῖος for an eleatic philosopher in Plat. Soph., 216b-c: καί μοι δοκεῖ θεὸς μὲν ἀνὴρ οὐδαμῶς εἶναι, θεῖος μήν· πάντας γὰρ ἐγὼ τοὺς φιλοσόφους τοιούτους προσαγορεύω, cf. too the jesting-ironic sense in Plat. Phaedr., 242a: θεῖός γ'εἶ περὶ τοὺς λόγους. On the other hand men whose acts and gifts are above normal are called θεῖος; the Spartan who proved himself was styled θεῖος ἀνὴρ οὗτος by fellow-citizens, cf. Plat. Men., 99d and Aristot. Eth. Nic., VII, 1, p. 1145a, 27 f.; also ὡς ἀγαθοῖς καὶ θείοις τὴν φύσιν ἀμφοτέροις, Plut. De Lucullo, 46 (I, 523a). Aristot. Eth. Nic., VII, 1, p. 1145a, 18-24 defines a θεία ἀρετή as ἀρετῆς ὑπερβολή. But to such persons themselves a sacral character was never ascribed nor do they distinguish themselves by working miracles etc. [23] The features of θεῖος in later antiquity cannot be traced back smoothly to the earlier period. This does not mean that there were no people with charismatic traits.

b. The idea of divine charisma in mortals may be seen in Gk. poetry and biography, [24] cf. the seer Iamos in Pind. Olymp., 6, 29-63, Oedipus in Soph. Oed. Col., 1447-1666 etc., the poet Comatas in Theocr. Idyll., 7, 89 with the address θεῖε. But divine descent is ascribed to Iamos only in the form in which legends cluster around famous people → 339, 4 ff. Thus the ideas converge only haphazardly. The same applies to known historical figures to whom divinity is ascribed in some form, e.g., the Spartan general Lysander who was venerated as divine after the victory over Athens in 404 and to whom a cult was devoted in Samos (Duris of Samos in Plut. De Lysandro, 18 [I, 443b c]). Lysander must be viewed as a forerunner of the later divine kings → 336, 26 ff. [25] Emped. Fr., 112 (Diels, I, 354) says of himself he was regarded as a god: χαίρετ'· ἐγὼ δ' ὑμῖν θεὸς ἄμβροτος, οὐκέτι θνητὸς πωλεῦμαι μετὰ πᾶσι τετιμένος, ὥσπερ ἔοικα . . . But the ὑμῖν and

---

[19] Cf. Grundmann Gotteskindschaft, 25 f.; Bultmann Theol.⁴, 132 f.; Schreiber, 119 f. with bibl.

[20] Only a few examples may be given here. For materials cf. esp. Bieler, I, 9-20, 134-8; Usener, 71-4; Wetter, 4-20. The problem of the charismatic personality is dealt with by Taeger, I, passim in connection with the ruler cult.

[21] Even plainer in Hes. Theog., 81-103, cf. Bieler, II, 43-45.

[22] On θεῖος in Plato cf. J. van Camp and P. Canart, Le sens du mot ΘΕΙΟΣ chez Platon (1956); on the special role in the doctrine of enthusiasm cf. 414 f., also Taeger, op. cit., I, 143-5.

[23] The generous use of θεῖος ἀνήρ in Bieler, passim gives the wrong idea that there was a designation and fixed concept in this early period. Even with ἀνήρ or ἄνθρωπος, θεῖος is predicative; it is not a tt.

[24] Cf. on this Bieler, II, 45-7, 52-60, 82-95 and passim.

[25] Cf. Nilsson, II², 139-141.

ὥσπερ ἔοικα suggest some inner reserve. [26] As far as one can see Emped., let alone Lysander, was never called θεῖος, nor was his divine descent — our present concern — asserted. [27]

Legend busied itself with the birth of famous persons, esp. the philosophers Pythagoras, Plato etc. [28] The accounts contain what are obviously popular features, cf. Diog. L., VIII, 11: καί... οἱ μαθηταὶ δόξαν εἶχον περὶ αὐτοῦ ὡς εἴη Ἀπόλλων ἐξ Ὑπερβορέων ἀφιγμένος. [29] Neo-Platonic sources speak of Apollo as father, Porphyr. Vit. Pyth., 2, cf. Iambl. Vita Pyth., 2, 5-8. Diog. L., III, 2, appealing to Plato's sister's son Speusippus, says it was the talk of Athens that Plato's father Ariston tried by force to live with his wife in marriage until Apollo appeared to him; he then left his wife untouched until the delivery. There is a rather different version in Plut. Quaest. Conv., VIII prooemium (I, 717e). It is typical of these legends [30] that Plato is never styled υἱὸς τοῦ Ἀπόλλωνος; they never pressed on to υἱός predication. In Neo-Pythagorean and Neo-Platonic circles many such legends were created but there is still no υἱός predication, though the charismatic character of the θεῖος designation and the divine origin is emphasised strongly. [31] Plato is called θεῖος... καὶ Ἀπολλωνιακός in Anon. Vita Platonis, 2, [32] but not υἱὸς τοῦ Ἀπόλλωνος. Apollonius of Tyana is endowed with all the features of a charismatic personality in Philostr. Vit. Ap., IV, 31; V, 24 etc. He was also regarded as a god. Divine sonship is reported in I, 6, but in these words: οἱ μὲν δὴ ἐγχώριοί φασι παῖδα τοῦ Διὸς τὸν Ἀπολλώνιον γεγονέναι, ὁ δ' ἀνὴρ Ἀπολλωνίου ἑαυτὸν καλεῖ.

c. Finally one should mention here Simon Magus and other Gnostics of whom Celsus in Orig. Cels., VII, 8 speaks thus: ἐγὼ ὁ θεός εἰμι ἢ θεοῦ παῖς ἢ πνεῦμα θεῖον. We know their claims only from Chr. polemic. It is said of Simon not only that he called himself God's son (Mart. Pt. et Pl. 26) but also that he was worshipped as God (Act. Verc. 10). The υἱός formula is expressly mentioned with ref. to Dositheus in Orig Cels., VI, 11, cf. Cl. Al. Strom., III, 4, 30, 1 with ref. to Prodicos and his pupils who called themselves υἱοὺς μὲν φύσει τοῦ πρώτου θεοῦ.

d. As regards the question whether divine sonship is connected with the Hellenistic idea of the θεῖος ἀνήρ it is thus to be noted that θεῖος ἀνήρ is by no means a fixed expression at least in the pre-Christian era. θεῖος is mostly used predicatively → n. 23. Some are called θεῖοι without any ascription of a charismatic character → 338, 23 ff. Others have this character but never in the tradition are they called θεῖος → 339, 1 ff. The term is not, then, an essential element in these

---

[26] Cf. Kranz in the Suppl. to Diels, I, 500 f. on line 18.

[27] Bieler has assembled a good deal of material on divine descent etc. But it needs to be examined, since for our purpose it is not unimportant whether a man is called a god or a son of god or whether his descent is traced back to heroes or gods. Bieler, I, 134-8 lumps all these together.

[28] Further examples in Usener, 71-4; → n. 31.

[29] Cf. Diog. L., VIII, 41: ἐπίστευον (3rd pers. plur.) εἶναι τὸν Πυθαγόραν θεῖόν τινα.

[30] Orig. Cels., I, 37 evaluates them clearly, if polemically: "These are in fact legends, and the simple impulse to invent such things of a Plato was the belief that a man furnished with more wisdom and power than the average must have descended even physically from higher and divine seed," cf. Usener, 73.

[31] ὁ θεῖος Πλάτων, e.g., in Ps.-Plut. Consolatio ad Apollonium, 36 (II, 120d); cf. Cic. Nat. Deor., II, 12, 32: deus quidam philosophorum and Att., 4, 16, 3: deus ille noster Plato. The use in Cic. shows plainly that deus is not taken lit. but as an expression of reverence for the head of the school. θεῖος is richly attested in the Neo-Plat. philosophers who style themselves (cf. ὁ θεῖος Ἰάμβλιχος, Procl. In Tim., 341d) and others thus (Eunapius Vitae sophistarum, 6, 9, 3 [ed. J. Giangrande 1956]) etc. Gen. on the use of θεῖος for philosophers cf. Bieler, I, 17 f. and esp. n. 19.

[32] Ed. A. Westermann, Biographoi (1845), 389, 23 f.

notions. One cannot tell from the material even that such θεῖοι are usually sons
of gods. Apart from Greek stories of gods and heroes → 336, 10 ff., the express
claim that a mortal is a son of god occurs only in limited circles: 1. in connection
with doctors at a relatively early period (→ 336, 18 f. and n. 18), where the phrase
is functional and denotes membership of the profession by reference to the basic
deity Aesculapius; 2. in the ruler cult whose terminology suggests oriental (Egyptian) roots → 336, 26 ff.; 3. in the Gnostics combatted by Christian apologetic →
339, 22 ff.; 4. less explicitly in the biographies of philosophers in Neo-Pythagorean
and Neo-Platonic circles → 339, 4 ff. Even when legend invented a divine origin
for outstanding personages, this did not lead to υἱός predication → 339, 12 ff. The
more or less clear idea of divinity does not find linguistic expression, especially in
the form of stress on sonship. When, therefore, divine sonship is associated with
description as θεῖος this is quite accidental. The conceptual spheres of divine sonship and θεῖος may well be related, but the terminology does not support this
association.

W. v. Martitz

B. Old Testament.

1. Linguistic Data.

בֵּן (plur. בָּנִים) "son" is the most common term of relation in the OT (some 4850
instances). [33] In the st. c. apart from the usual בֶּן בֵּן in Gn. 49:22 is probably meant as
st. abs.) one finds the less common בְּנִי in Gn. 49:11, בְּנוֹ in Nu. 23:18; 24:3, 15 and בֶּן
in Dt. 25:2; Jon. 4:10; Prv. 30:1 and always before the name of the father of Joshua
נוּן. [34] The Aram. equivalent בַּר occurs in the Hbr. part of the OT [35] only at Prv. 31:2
in a text influenced by Aram., while Ps. 2:12 נַשְּׁקוּ־בַר "kiss the son" is corrupt. [36] There
are also 18 instances in the Aram. parts of the OT and a wealth of examples elsewhere. [37]
The form of the st. c. in the plur. בְּנֵי suggests a similar plur. formation to that for בֶּן.
בֵּן is probably not derived from the root בנה [38] nor from *banaj* (dropping the last syllable
and changing a to ä or e). [39] Like other terms of relationship [40] it seems to be a two-
radical, short-vowel word not derived from any root. The derivations suggested for בַּר

---

[33] In contrast בַּת "daughter" occurs only some 585 times.

[34] Cf. Ges.-K. § 96 notes; on the forms בני and בנו § 90 k-o.

[35] Cf. E. Kautzsch, *Die Aramaismen im AT* (1902), 24 f.; M. Wagner, "Die lexikal. u.
grammat. Aramaismen im at.lichen Hbr.," ZAW Beih., 96 (1966), 37.

[36] For the best solution cf. A. Bertholet, "Eine crux interpretum," ZAW, 28 (1908), 58 f.;
also "Nochmals zu Ps. 2:11 f.," *ibid.*, 93: וּנְשַׁקוּ בְּרַגְלָיו "kiss his feet."

[37] C. F. Jean - J. Hoftijzer, *Dict. des inscr. sémitiques de l'Ouest* (1965), *s.v.*

[38] So esp. F. Delitzsch, *Prolegomena eines neuen hbr.-aram. Wörterbuchs z. AT* (1886),
104; Köhler-Baumg., *s.v.* and derivates of בנה; but cf. T. Nöldeke's review of Delitzsch in
ZDMG, 40 (1886), 737. J. Barth, "Vergleichende Stud.," ZDMG, 41 (1887), 638-640 first
assumed derivation from a root בנה, but then in *Die Nominalbildung in d. semit. Sprachen*[2]
(1894), 6 he regarded the word as one of the biliteralia whose plur. rested on a fuller stem
בְּנִי or בנו.

[39] E. König, *Historisch-krit. Lehrgebäude d. hbr. Sprache,* II, 1 (1895), 101.

[40] Cf. the survey in G. Beer - R. Meyer, *Hbr. Grammatik,* I Göschen, 763/763a (1952),
94 f.

are also unsatisfying. [41] The relation between the two expressions, which are attested in various Semitic languages, [42] is to be explained by a sound-shift from bn to br (n to r). [43] The plur. with n even for br seems to show that bn was the original form, though no wholly convincing reason has been given for the shift. [44] An original i is to be assumed for the sing בֵּן (*bin*, cf. בֶּן־נוּן, בְּנָיָמִין). The vowel a in the plur. is perhaps to be understood in analogy to the dissimilation of Arab. i to a with i in the next syllable, [45] the Gk. transcriptions in Hexapla fr.: βανη for בְּנֵי ψ 17:46 and βαναυ for בָּנָיו ψ 88:31. [46]

2. בֵּן (בַּר) as a Term for Physical Descendants and Relatives.

a. Already in the use for descendants and relatives one sees the broad framework for possible expressions in which the basic sense leads on to information as to personal status. Naturally בֵּן first means the "son" begotten by the father and born of the mother, Gn. 4:17 etc., cf. בַּר Da. 5:22. Sons and daughters בָּנִים וּבָנוֹת are often mentioned together (Gn. 5:4) and in polygynous marriage the son of the slave-woman (Ju. 9:18) can be differentiated from the children of other wives. As the בְּנֵי הַנְּעוּרִים "sons of the young father" (Ps. 127:4) are esp. strong as the "first-fruits of his strength" (Gn. 49:3), the father's love is directed more to the בֶּן־זְקֻנִים "the son begotten in old age" (Gn. 37:3, cf. the expression in 21:2, 7). בֶּן־הַמֶּלֶךְ or בְּנֵי הַמֶּלֶךְ are usually princes as "sons of the king," Ju. 8:18; 2 S. 9:11; 13:4, with בַּר Ezr. 6:10 (cf. the "sons of Pharaoh" in 1 K. 11:20) and בֶּן־מֶלֶךְ (Ps. 72:1), in view of the parallelism with מֶלֶךְ is "the crown prince" who is enthroned, [47] while in 1 K. 22:26 f. the בֶּן־הַמֶּלֶךְ Joash mentioned after the שַׂר־הָעִיר Amon is a royal official with police duties, cf. also Jer. 36:26; 38:6; 2 Ch. 28:7. [48]

בֵּן and בַּר are also used for other degrees of relationship, "brother" in בְּנֵי אָבִיךָ Gn. 49:8 and בֶּן־אִמּוֹ Gn. 43:29, cf. Ju. 8:19; plur. Ps. 69:8, but בְּנֵי בִטְנִי Job 19:17, "grandson" in בְּנֵי בָנִים Gn. 45:10; Ex. 34:7 or just בָּנִים Gn. 32:1, "nephew" in בֶּן־אָחִיו Gn. 12:5, "cousin" in בֶּן־דֹּדִי Jer. 32:8, "daughter-in-law" in נְשֵׁי־בָנֶיךָ Gn. 6:18 or gen. "descendants" in מַלְכָּא וּבְנוֹהִי Ezr. 7:23. There is a similar use of בַּת, cf. Lv. 18:17.

---

[41] Cf. F. W. M. Philippi, "Das Zahlwort Zwei im Semitischen," ZDMG, 32 (1878), 37: "J. D. Michaelis and after him Gesenius relate it to the root ברא and construe it as 'the begotten,' but Bernstein and Levy derive it from ברר, the former construing it as *rudis*, *imperitus* or *purus*, *insons*, the latter as "shoot" proceeding from the stem, while finally Delitzsch thinks the Assyrian now teaches us that as בן goes back to בנה so does *bar* (Assyr. *nibra*) to ברא=ברה "to bring forth."

[42] Cf. C. Brockelmann, *Grundriss d. vergleichenden Grammatik d. semitischen Sprachen*, I (1907), 332; esp. Hbr. בן, Arab. *ibn*, Assyr. *bin* (usual only in *bin*, *binni*, "grandson"); Aram. בר, Mehri (South Arab.) *ber*.

[43] So already Philippi, *op. cit.*, 36-8.

[44] T. Nöldeke, *Neue Beiträge z. semit. Sprachwissenschaft* (1901), 135-140; Brockelmann, *op. cit.*, 332.

[45] Brockelmann, 253. But Nöldeke, *op. cit.* (→ n. 44), 135-140 thinks the shift from a to i is just as puzzling as that from bn to br.

[46] But cf. in the LXX 1 Ch. 7:35: Βανηελαμ for בֶּן־חֶלֶם and 2 Ch. 33:6: Γαι-βαναιεννομ for גֵּי בֶּן־הִנֹּם (B βανε, A βε, V βεν) as distinct from Γαιβενενομ in 2 Ch. 28:3 with a in the sing.

[47] The content of Ps. 72 suggests the enthronement of a new ruler (cf. H. J. Kraus, *Ps.*, Bibl. Komm. AT, 15² [1961], ad loc.) rather than that of a young ruler (H. Schmidt, *Die Ps.*, Hndbch. AT, I, 15 [1934], ad loc.). Throughout the Orient and also in Israel the judging mentioned in v. 1 is one of the tasks and rights of the king and there is no substance in derivation from the office of a "judge of Israel" (Kraus), the more so as the idea of such an office rests on very uncertain hypotheses.

[48] Cf. de Vaux, 183 f. with ref. to a Palestinian seal inscr. and Egypt. par.

Animals and plants also have בָּנִים בֵּן (בַּר) sing. and plur. is undoubtedly used for the direct offspring of animals, male or female, cf. Gn. 32:16; 49:11; Nu. 15:24; Dt. 22:6 f.; Zech. 9:9; Ps. 29:6; Job 4:11; 39:4; Ezr. 6:9. [49] The use of בֵּן for the "shoot" of a tree in Gn. 49:22 and perhaps for stars in Job 38:32 might also be mentioned. [50] In other cases, however, the ref. seems to be, not to young animals, but to individual male animals (→ 346, 3 ff.), [51] and in yet others there is a comprehensive use to denote membership of a species → 346, 27 ff. Finally sparks as offshoots of רֶשֶׁף "fire," "flame," i.e., as thrown off or produced by it, are also denoted, Job 5:7. [52]

b. In most instances בֵּן is a patronymic term to denote personal status. We are speaking of the ancient and widespread practice of appending appositionally to a man's name, whether in lists of people, in official introduction, or in repeated reference, the name of his father and in certain cases of other ancestors, thus showing that the one who bears the name is this man's son. [53] Deeply rooted genealogical thinking (cf. the lists of Jacob's twelve sons and similar genealogies especially in Genesis and 1 Chronicles) finds here a fixed, stereotyped expression. The individual is not isolated. He is seen in the organic context of his family and tribe. Here on the ground of blood-relationship in his basis, help and stay. Hence appeal to this takes precedence of the appeal to the cultic fellowship of faith, Gn. 50:17.

c. From the original feeling of the Israelites, their genealogical thinking, their concern for the continuation of the family and their desire for continual remembrance of ancestors, there follows a desire for many sons. These are a blessing and gift of God, Dt. 28:4-11; Is. 54:1; Zech. 8:5; Ps. 127:3-5; 128:3; childlessness is bad, Gn. 30:1 f.; 1 S. 1:11, or, like the early death of a child (2 S. 12:14 f.), it is a divine punishment, Gn. 20:18; Lv. 20:20; Dt. 28:18; 2 S. 6:23; Jer. 36:30; Hos. 4:9 f., unless it is a burden laid on a prophet for symbolic purpose, Jer. 16:2. Thus the command of Jer. to the exiles to marry and have children (Jer. 29:6) is an expression of the divine promise of life to those who seem to have fallen victim to extinction. Primarily the Israelite wants sons, for, while daughters leave the family in marriage, sons ensure its future, build new houses, and are the crown of the aged, Prv. 17:6; 23:24 f. Hence the blessing of the future wife, Gn. 24:60 [54] and the word of comfort to the mother who dies in childbirth: "Fear not, for thou hast (this time too) a son," Gn. 35:17; 1 S. 4:20. Only to a sinner does it happen that he has just daughters and no son, Nu. 27:1-3, or that almost all his sons die before him, 2 Ch. 21:17. The proportion of seven sons to three daughters is a good one for the

---

[49] יֶלֶד is also used for the young of animals, Is. 11:7; Job 38:41; 39:3.

[50] The sign of the lioness mentioned in Job 38:32 stands among the Arabs for cancer, which they do not have. Some stars of the virgin are called by them dogs baying after the lioness and בָּנֶיהָ ("company") might ref. to these. If so בֵּן here is used more generally.

[51] This sense is too one-sidedly stressed in Köhler-Baumg., s.v. בֵּן.

[52] The older transl. took רֶשֶׁף to be a bird (cf. G. Hölscher, Das Buch Hi., Hndbch. AT, I, 17² 1952, ad loc.), esp. in view of the ensuing עוּף and perhaps through a wrong ref. to בְּנֵי רֶשֶׁף to the god Resheph who is found in the Caratepe inscr. as rsp sprm and who stands in relation to specific birds, cf. on this F. Horst, Hi, Bibl. Komm. AT, 16 (1960), 81 f.; G. Fohrer, Das Buch Hi, Komm. AT, 16 (1963), ad loc.

[53] The use of just the patronymic formula without the name of the person can often be due to the practice of listing royal servants in hereditary positions simply by the name of the father from whom they have inherited the position. Cf. A. Alt, "Menschen ohne Namen," Kleine Schriften z. Gesch. d. Volkes Israel, III (1959), 198-213.

[54] Cf. the Ugaritic wedding blessing in V. Maag, "Syrien-Palästina" in Kulturgeschichte d. Alten Orient, ed. H. Schmökel, Kröners Taschenausgabe, 298 (1961), 490.

righteous and successful man, Job 1:2; 42:13, though we probably have here stereotyped, symbolical numbers. Often we read of gt. numbers of sons made possible by polygynous marriage, Ju. 8:30; 10:4; 12:9, 14; 1 S. 17:12; 2 S. 9:10; 2 K. 10:1; 2 Ch. 11:21; 13:21. In Ch. David gratefully regards his many sons as a gift from Yahweh, 1 Ch. 28:5. But it is a rare statement that someone else (1 S. 1:8; Rt. 4:15) or a place and name in Yahweh's temple (Is. 56:5) is better than sons. In the light of the connection of this position with rejection of the fertility cults of Canaan one can understand the abhorrence of child-sacrifices, Lv. 18:21; 20:1-5; Dt. 12:31; 18:10, but cf. Ez. 20:25 f.

d. In the patriarchal family the son is entirely under his father's authority, [55] with limitation of the power of life and death only in Dt. 21:18-21. The first-born son had some privileges, e.g., in seating (Gn. 43:33) and in receiving two-thirds of the inheritance (Dt. 21:17) as befitted the new head of the family. [56] He could forfeit these privileges through a grave offence (Gn. 35:22, 49:3 f.) or by his own renunciation (Gn. 25:29-34); the Law protected him against caprice, Dt. 21:15-17. There are not a few instances in which a younger or the youngest son was preferred over the rest, Isaac, Joseph, Benjamin, Ephraim, David, Solomon. But one may not deduce from these that the last-born had legal privileges. The father's liking is contrary to legal practice (Gn. 37:3; 44:20) or the preference rests on Yahweh's election (1 S. 16:12; 1 K. 2:15; Mal. 1:2 f.), cf. the way in which God rejected the offering of Cain the elder and accepted that of his younger brother Abel, Gn. 4:4 f.

Parental duty included care for the physical well-being of sons and esp. their up-bringing, which would include chastisement (Prv. 13:1, 24; 29:17) if a wise and good son was desired rather than a wicked and foolish one, Prv. 10:1; 17:25. After initial instruction by the mother (Prv. 1:8; 6:20) the duty of bringing up sons passed to the father. It included teaching to read and write, which is presupposed to be widespread in Dt. 6:9; 11:20; Ju. 8:14, vocational training, since the son would usually follow his father's calling, [57] and also moral and religious training, Ex. 10:2; 12:26 f.; 13:8; Dt. 4:9; 6:7, 20 f.; 32:7, 46.

As regards sons Wisdom teaching often ref. to their moral duties to parents, Prv. 1:8; 4:1; 6:20; 10:1; 15:5, 20; 17:21, 25; 23:24; 28:7; 29:3. The OT usually assumes that the good son is the normal one; he will naturally be submissive and obedient to his parents. Yet one should not miss the words of warning and admonition. Authoritative regulation was obviously necessary when the Decalogue laid on every son (even the adult) living in the family with his parents the duty of honouring them, → V, 963, 31 ff.

Sons are also responsible for their fathers, in civil law for debts (2 K. 4:1), in penal law for offences within the solidarity of blood-relationship, Jos. 7:24 f.; 2 S. 21:1-9; Est. 9:13 f.; Da. 6:25. The first protest against the latter responsibility, which was reciprocal, is in Dt. 24:16: "The fathers shall not be put to death for the children, neither shall the children be put to death for the fathers: every man shall be put to death for his own sin," cf. 2 K. 14:6. The idea of an analogous responsibility before God, who visits the father's sins on the sons, Ex. 20:5; 34:7; Nu. 14:18; [58] Jer. 32:18 (bewailed in Lam. 5:7

---

[55] On the *patria potestas* in the Jewish military colony of Elephantine cf. R. Yaron, *Introduction to the Law of the Aramaic Pap.* (1961), 41 f.

[56] Ex. 21:9 ref. to a right of daughters not found elsewhere, but cf. the story in Nu. 27:1-11 (and the supplementary qualification Nu. 36:1-13). The inclusion of Job's daughters in the inheritance is an exception (42:15). They have no claim to this; it is a gift. On Elephantine cf. Yaron, *op. cit.*, 65-78.

[57] Hence the priest who teaches is called "father," also Joseph when he gives counsel (Ju. 17:10; 18:19; Gn. 45:8). "Father" and "son" are used for teacher and student, 2 K. 2:12 and esp. in the Wisdom lit. → 345, 14 ff.

[58] The formula of Ex. 34:7; Nu. 14:18: "Yahweh visits the fathers' guilt on sons (and grandsons) to the third and fourth generation," occurs also in Ex. 20:5 but with the expansion לְשֹׂנְאָי, though it is not clear whether this ref. to the fathers or the sons: Is only the guilt of fathers who hate Yahweh visited on the sons or is the guilt visited only on descendants who

and bitterly derided by the exiles in Ez. 18:2), is opposed in Ez. 18:1-20, which advances a doctrine of personal responsibility even in religious matters. If the OT shows here an awareness of the problem of the generations, elsewhere it tells of serious tensions between father and son which can often lead with dramatic dynamism to a tragic conclusion. The story of the deceiving of the blind and aged Isaac by his son Jacob in Gn. 27 and then that of the moral depravity of Jacob's sons in Gn. 34; 35:22; 37; 38 (cf. 37:26: "What profit is it if we slay our brother and conceal his blood?") reflect the relations in semi-nomadic tribes. Then especially we have the tragedies of David's sons, Amnon and Absalom, which give us a glimpse of the abyss which could open up for the Israelites too.

e. Special sons inherit the promises of increase and possession of the land which were given to the patriarchs and which seemed constantly to be thrown in question by the lack of heirs or their destinies until they were finally carried out acc. to the divine will, providing both the religious basis for the claim of the expanding tribes to Palestine and also a starting-point for the development of the Hexateuch. [59] Of particular significance, too, are the children of Hosea and Isaiah, who have a place in the symbolical acts of their fathers, Hos. 1; Is. 7:3; 8:1-4 (but cf. Jer. 16:2). [60] So, too, does the Immanuel of the prophecy of Isaiah in 7:10-17, concerning whose person and role the views of exegetes differ widely. [61]

f. Equality with physical sons is conferred by adoption as a legal act by which someone of alien blood is recognised to be a child with full rights and duties. Already in early days adoption played a big part in Mesopotamia, [62] and it served to give childless couples descendants, to procure care in old age and gifts at death and to accomplish the freeing of slaves. [63] It is uncertain whether the OT anywhere mentions real adoption. [64] Perhaps there is an allusion in Est. 2:7, 15: "He took her (Esther) for his own daughter", and it is possible (though not certain) that Ps. 2:7: "Thou art my son; this day have I begotten thee" is an adoption formula → 351, 2 ff. The upbringing of Moses in Ex. 2:10 or Genubath in 1 K. 11:20 has nothing to do with adoption.

Instead the OT ref. to measures by which children were recognised as legitimate. A slave woman made pregnant by her master could give birth on the knees of her mistress, Gn. 30:3 (cf. 16:2), so that the child representatively born thus might count as coming from her womb. This is no doubt based on the older custom of the wife giving birth on her

---

hate Yahweh? Tg. O., ad loc. takes the latter view: כד משלמין בניא למחאי בתר אבהתהון, "in so far as the sons also sin after their fathers." Since there are examples of a similar use of ל (C. Brockelmann, Hbr. Syntax [1956] § 107i α) this is quite possible, and Ex. 20:5 thus interprets Ex. 34:7; Nu. 14:18 along the lines of Ez. 18:1-20.

[59] Cf. E. Sellin and G. Fohrer, Einl. in d. AT[10] (1965), 131-144.

[60] For details cf. G. Fohrer, "Die symbolischen Handlungen d. Propheten," AbhThANT, 25[2] (1967).

[61] Cf. the surveys in G. Fohrer, "Neuere Lit. z. at.lichen Prophetie," ThR, NF, 19 (1951), 295 f.; 20 (1952), 224 f.; also "Zehn Jahre Lit. z. at.lichen Prophetie (1951-60)," ThR, NF, 28 (1962), 69-72.

[62] Cf. H. Schmökel, "Mesopotamien," Kulturgeschichte d. Alten Orient (→ n. 54), 145 f. Legal difficulties because of the gt. no. of adoptions shed light on § 185 f., 191 of the Codex Hammurabi. On the proliferation of marketed adoptions to evade rules against sales of some properties cf. E. M. Cassin, L'adoption à Nuzi (1938).

[63] This is perhaps the pt. of the one adoption record from Elephantine, cf. Yaron, op. cit., 40 f.; Z. W. Falk, "Manumission by Sale," Journ. of Semitic Studies, 3 (1958), 127 f.

[64] S. Feigin, "Some Cases of Adoption in Israel," JBL, 50 (1931), 186-200 thinks ויולד in Ju. 11:1 is a provincialism "to adopt" and he alters the corrupt Ezr. 10:44 to make it ref. to adoption. But these proposals are not convincing. For an attempt to show that adoption was known in Israel cf. M. David, "Adoptie in het oude Israel," Mededeelingen d. Koninklijke Nederlandse Akademie van Wetenschappen, Afdeling Letterkunde, 18, 4 (1955).

husband's knees, whereby he acknowledged the child to be legitimate, Gn. 50:23 (cf. 48:12). From this practice, still known among the Bedouins, there arose a legitimacy rite known to the Greeks, Romans and Indo-Europeans gen., namely, that the father should take the new-born child on his knees, thereby recognising it. [65] In spite of many objections [66] Rt. 4:16 f. also seems to be a legitimacy rite. [67] When Naomi took to her bosom the child of the Levirate marriage of Boaz and Ruth she acknowledged it to be the legitimate child of her dead son. Job 3:12, however, ref. neither to adoption nor legitimation. [68]

3. בֵּן (בַּר) as a Broader Term of Association.

a. More broadly the plur. of בֵּן (בַּר) means "young men," "youths," Prv. 7:7; Cant. 2:3, and "children," Gn. 3:16; 21:7; 30:1; 31:17; Dt. 4:10; 29:21; Da. 6:25. [69] In this connection one might also mention בֶּן־בֵּיתִי in Gn. 15:3 and בְּנֵי בַיִת in Qoh. 2:7 "the slave(s) born in (my) house," cf. יְלִיד בַּיִת in Gn. 17:12.

בֵּן is also used in intimate address for younger companions, students or listeners (→ 357, 24 ff.) to whom the one speaking stands in the relation of a father (→ n. 57) or for whom the word is suitable because of membership of a specific group (→ 346, 18 ff.), 1 S. 3:6, 16; 24:17; 26:17, 21, 25; 2 S. 18:22; Prv. 2:1; 3:1, 21; 4:10, 20; 5:1; 6:1; 7:1. More rarely בֵּן expresses the fact that the one speaking regards the one addressed as subordinate, Jos. 7:19; 1 S. 4:16, or that the speaker is calling himself subordinate, 1 S. 25:8; 2 K. 16:7, "son" and "servant" being par. here, cf. also Mal. 1:6; 3:17.

b. With a fig. tendency the two persons whom Zachariah regards as worthy of Messianic leadership in the awaited end-time, Joshua and Zerubbabel, are called בְּנֵי־הַיִּצְהָר "sons of oil," "those anointed with oil." Things can also be related similarly, the arrow to the quiver (בְּנֵי אַשְׁפָּה Lam. 3:13) or the bow (בֶּן־קֶשֶׁת Job 41:20).

4. בֵּן (בַּר) as a Term of Relationship.

When the terms in a weaker sense express formal relationship, the reference can be to the member of a society, group, or fellowship.

---

[65] B. Stade, "'Auf Jemandes Knieen gebären' Gn. 30:3; 50:23; Job 3:12 u. אֲבָנָיִם Ex. 1:16," ZAW, 6 (1886), 143-156; A. G. Barrois, Manuel d'archéol. biblique, 2 (1953), 27 f.; Horst, op. cit. (→ n. 52), 49 f. Acc. to the Code of Hammurabi § 170 all that is needed for acknowledgement is that once in his life the father should call a slave's children "my children." Cf. also E. Schwyzer, "Der Götter Knie — Abrahams Schoss," Festschr. J. Wackernagel (1923), 292, cf. 283-293; H. Otten, Mythen vom Gotte Kumarbi, Neue Fr. (1950), 15.

[66] Acc. to W. Rudolph, Das Buch Rt., das Hohelied, die Thr., Komm. AT, 17, 1-3 (1962), 69-71, who rightly rejects the adoption thesis of L. Köhler, "Die Adoptionsform v. Rt. 4:16," ZAW, 29 (1909), 312-4, Naomi joyfully takes Ruth's son in her arms and so zealously vows to take care of him that neighbours goodnaturedly chaff her for acting as if he were her own. But his textual emendations are suspect and his objections to adoption do not apply to the legitimation needed in a Levirate marriage.

[67] Adoption may be ruled out since both parents are alive.

[68] Job 3:12: "Why did the knees prevent me? or the breasts that I should suck?" ref. to the mother's care and expresses the wish he might have found instant death instead. Cf. the Assurbanipal text in M. Streck, Assurbanipal u. d. letzten assyrischen Könige (1916), 348: "Thou wast weak, Assurbanipal, who sat on the knees of the goddess, the queen of Nineveh; of the four breasts put to thy mouth thou didst suck two, and hide thy face from the two others."

[69] But בֵּן זָכָר in Jer. 20:15 is "a male child" rather than "a son," "a boy."

a. As בֶּן־אָדָם Ez.2:1 etc.; Ps. 8:4 (plur. בְּנֵי הָ[אָדָם] Dt. 32:8; Qoh. 1:13 etc.), בֶּן־אֱנוֹשׁ Ps. 144:3 (Aram. Da. 2:38; 5:21; 7:13) or בְּנֵי אִישׁ Ps. 4:2; 49:2; 62:9; Lam. 3:33, man is a single member of a collective society (→ υἱὸς τοῦ ἀνθρώπου). The same is often true of בֵּן with names of animals. Thus בֶּן־בָּקָר in Gn. 18:7 means one of the herd, בֶּן־יוֹנָה in Lv. 12:6 (plur. בְּנֵי הַיּוֹנָה Lv. 1:14) "a single (male) dove," בְּנֵי הָרַמָּכִים in Est. 8:10 "single racing-mares." [70]

b. The expressions denote membership of a people, country, or place (acc. to the original [fictitious] gentilitial character of social and political groups in primitive societies). The plur. suggests "the individual men of." Thus there is ref. to בְּנֵי עַם "fellow-country-men" in Lv. 20:17; Nu. 22:5; Ez. 33:17; 37:18, בְּנֵי יִשְׂרָאֵל "Israelites" (not "sons" or "children" of Israel. The individual Israelite is אִישׁ מִבְּנֵי יִשְׂרָאֵל). בְּנֵי יְהוּדָה "Judaeans" in Jl. 3:6 (analogous to other tribes), בְּנֵי אַשּׁוּר "Assyrians" in Ez. 23:7, בְּנֵי בָבֶל "Babylonians" in Ez. 23:15, בְּנֵי אֱדוֹם "Edomites" in Ps. 137:7 etc., cf. the list of nations in Gn. 10, which also regards the race as a generative extension of Noah's family. The בְּנֵי הַמְּדִינָה in Ezr. 2:1 are "the men of the province (Judah)." Inhabitants of Jerusalem are sometimes called בְּנֵי יְרוּשָׁלַם Jl. 3:6 and בְּנֵי צִיּוֹן Is. 49:22; Ps. 149:2. [71] Dt. describes the rams as בְּנֵי בָשָׁן "bred in Bashan."

c. The terms also denote membership of a group or a vocational guild. Thus בְּנֵי נֵכָר "aliens" in Gn. 17:12; Is. 56:6, בְּנֵי הַגּוֹלָה "the exiles" in Ezr. 6:20; 8:35 (Aram. Da. 2:25 etc.; Ezr. 6:16), בֶּן־חוֹרִים "the liberated" Qoh. 10:17, בְּנֵי הַתּוֹשָׁבִים "resident aliens" in Lv. 25:45, בְּנֵי הָעָם "the common people" in 2 K. 23:6; Jer. 26:23 and בְּנֵי אֶבְיוֹן "the poor" in Ps. 72:4. The same applies to callings: בֶּן־הָרַקָּחִים denotes "a member of the guild or trade of the apothecaries" in Neh. 3:8, [72] בְּנֵי הַמְשֹׁרְרִים "the singers" in Neh. 12:28, among them subsidiary groups called by personal names, e.g., בְּנֵי קֹרַח Ps. 42 title etc., בְּנֵי הַכֹּהֲנִים "the priests" in Ezr. 2:61, בֶּן חֲכָמִים "a wise man" in Is. 19:11, and בְּנֵי הַנְּבִיאִים "the members of a prophetic group" or "the prophets" in 1 K. 20:35; 2 K. 2:3 etc., sing. בֶּן־נָבִיא Am. 7:14. [73] Sometimes בֵּן ref. to one of an animal species as the par. plur. shows: בְּנֵי צֹאן "small cattle" (par. "rams") in Ps. 114:4, בְּנֵי עֹרֵב "ravens" (par. "cattle") in Ps. 147:9, and בְּנֵי נָשֶׁר "eagles" (par. "ravens") in Prv. 30:17.

d. The terms denote sharing a nature or quality or fate, being taken captive and bound. Thus one finds בֶּן־חַיִל "the worthy," "reliable," 1 S. 18:17; 2 S. 2:7; 1 K. 1:52 etc., or the "martial," "courageous," Dt. 3:18; Ju. 18:2; 1 S. 14:52 etc., בְּנֵי שַׁחַץ "the proud (animals)," Job 28:8; 41:26, also בְּנֵי מֶרִי "the rebels" Nu. 17:10 (Ez.: בֵּית מְרִי), בְּנֵי בְלִיַּעַל "the useless," Dt. 13:14; Ju. 19:22, בְּנֵי שָׁאוֹן "the rowdy," Jer. 48:45, בֶּן־עַוְלָה "the wicked" Hos. 10:9; Ps. 89:22 etc., בְּנֵי נָבָל גַּם־בְּנֵי בְלִי־שֵׁם "the base and vile brood," Job 30:8, בְּנֵי עֹנִי "the afflicted," Prv. 31:5. Prv. 10:5 contrasts the בֵּן מַשְׂכִּיל and the בֵּן מֵבִישׁ, the "prudent"

---

[70] Cf. L. Köhler, רְמָכָה ZAW, 55 (1937), 173 f.

[71] Cf. W. F. Albright, "Abram the Hebrew," Bulletin of the American Schools of Oriental Research, 163 (1961), 47.

[72] But the sing. in Neh. 3:31 means the "son" of a goldsmith; similarly 3:8.

[73] This is not the place to take up the gen. question whether there were schools or disciples of the prophets, cf. J. G. Williams, "The Prophetic 'Father,'" JBL, 85 (1966), 344-8; the above expressions certainly cannot be given this sense. On the supposed disciples of Isaiah in Is. 8:16 cf. G. Fohrer, "The Origin, Composition and Tradition of Is. 1-39," Annual of Leeds Univ. Oriental Society, 3 (1961/62), 29-32. For discussion of the exegetical problem of Am. 7:14 cf. Fohrer's "Zehn Jahre Lit. z. at.lichen Prophetie (1951-1960)," ThR, NF, 28 (1962), 285-287.

and the "shameful." Falling under a specific fate is expressed by בֶּן־מָוֶת or בֶּן־תְּמוּתָה "to fall victim to death," 1 S. 20:31; 26:16; Ps. 102:21, בֶּן הַכּוֹת "to be subject to whipping," Dt. 25:2, בְּנֵי הַתַּעֲרֻבוֹת "hostages," 2 K. 14:14, בֶּן־גָּרְנִי "the threshed," Is. 21:10.

e. Finally the terms express belonging to a time or age: בֶּן־לַיְלָה "one night old" (grown overnight), Jon. 4:10, בֶּן־שְׁמֹנַת יָמִים "eight days old," Gn. 17:12, בֶּן שָׁנָה "one year old," Ex. 12:5 (cf. בֶּן־שְׁנָתוֹ Lv. 12:6; Ez. 46:13), בֶּן־שֵׁשׁ מֵאוֹת שָׁנָה "600 years old," Gn. 7:6 etc.

5. בֵּן (בַּר) as a Term for Relationship to God.

a. The OT often uses בֵּן and בַּר for beings which belong to the divine world or sphere but they are combined with other words for God, never with the name יהוה : [74] בְּנֵי (הָ)אֱלֹהִים Gn. 6:2, 4; Job 1:6; 2:1; 38:7, בַּר אֱלָהִין Da. 3:25, בְּנֵי אֵלִים Ps. 29:1; 89:6 and בְּנֵי עֶלְיוֹן Ps. 82:6. One of the first two expressions is also to be read in Dt. 32:8 → n. 77.

The fellowship of divine or heavenly beings can also be עֲדַת אֵל "God's assembly" in Ps. 82:1, קָהָל "congregation" and סוֹד "inner circle of the saints" who are "round about His (Yahweh's) throne," Ps. 89:5, 7. There is here a clear connection with ancient oriental ideas and phrases. In Gn. 6:1-4 we seem to have the revised fr. of an original mythical story [75] acc. to which the בְּנֵי (הָ)אֱלֹהִים had intercourse with women. It would appear that these were originally gods. But under the influence of his faith in Yahweh the narrator envisages them as angelic beings, [76] so that בֵּן expresses relationship to the sphere of Elohim. [77]

In Ps. 29:1; 89:6 the divine beings are בְּנֵי אֵלִים and in Ps. 89:5, 7 קְדֹשִׁים. [78] The underlying idea is again that of a pantheon under the supreme God whom the others worship and who rules terribly over them, esp. as קְדֹשִׁים goes back to Canaanite religion. [79] Ps. 29 also seems to rest on a Canaanite hymn into which Yahweh has been brought as the heavenly King on His throne [80] to whom the בְּנֵי אֵלִים and קְדֹשִׁים are subject. Since קְדֹשִׁים

---

[74] Cf. W. Herrmann, "Die Göttersöhne," Zschr. f. Religions- u. Geistesgesch., 12 (1960), 242-251; G. Cooke, "The Sons of (the) God(s)," ZAW, 76 (1964), 22-47.

[75] Mostly put in J, but O. Eissfeldt, Hexateuch-Synopse (1922), 9 *; Sellin-Fohrer, op. cit. (→ n. 59), 178 have the better suggestion of a third ancient source distinct from J and E.

[76] The older interpretations of pious men, sons of leading people or men seduced by demons may be set aside.

[77] In the reading [בני אל|] which is found in a fr. of Dt. 32:8 in 4 Q and which justifies doubt of the HT on the ground of the LXX the ref. is to Yahweh's court and in עֶלְיוֹן to Yahweh Himself, though the idea of a distribution of the peoples among divine beings may go back to a non-Israelite concept or formulation. Cf. P. W. Skehan, "A Fragment of the 'Song of Moses' (Dt. 32) from Qumran," Bulletin of the American Schools of Oriental Research, 136 (1954), 12-15; R. Meyer, "Die Bdtg. v. Dt. 32:8 f., 43 (4 Q) f. die Auslegung des Moseliedes," Festschr. W. Rudolph (1961), 197-209. Retaining the HT is hard to defend (so Moore, I⁵ [1946], 226 f.), however old the change to בני ישראל may be.

[78] Apart from the comm. cf. on Ps. 29 T. H. Gaster, "Ps. 29," JQR, 37 (1946/47), 55-65; F. M. Cross, "Notes on a Canaanite Psalm in the OT," Bulletin of the Amer. Schools of Oriental Research, 117 (1950), 19-21; on Ps. 89 cf. G. W. Ahlström, Psalm 89 (1959), 57-62.

[79] In Ugaritic one finds bn qds as a par. to "deity," "gods," Text, 137, 21. 38 (Gordon Manual, 167 f.); 2 Aqht, I, 4. 9. 14. 23 (181). Cf. also W. Schmidt, "Wo hat die Aussage: Jahwe 'Der Heilige' ihren Ursprung?" ZAW, 74 (1962), 62-66.

[80] So already H. L. Ginsberg, כתבי אוגרית (The Ugaritic Texts) (1936), 129 f.; cf. Kraus, op. cit. (→ n. 47), 235. In spite of the meteorological phenomena the hymn is undoubtedly to El, not Baal.

consistently in the OT means the heavenly beings around Yahweh and subject to Him, [81] this may also be taken to apply to the two Ps. The basic thought of the divine beings as gods is more plainly reflected in Ps. 29, and Ps. 89:5-8 shows how they have been reduced in power by Yahweh. [82] In both Ps., then, the pantheon of other gods has been degraded to the בְּנֵי אֱלֹהִים (אֵלִים) as Yahweh's court.

Canaanite ideas are even more plainly reflected in Ps. 82 [83] in which the divine beings are not only בְּנֵי עֶלְיוֹן in v. 6 but also עֲדַת אֵל and אֱלֹהִים in v. 1 [84] and their threatened end ("ye shall fall like one of the שָׂרִים," v. 7) may go back to the mythical fall of a member of the divine assembly. [85] But now Yahweh is supreme Judge in the heavenly council, not Elion. Yet the meaning of בְּנֵי עֶלְיוֹן is still vague for the poet. One might think of the supposed deities of other nations or — after their overthrow — the guiding and guarding angels set over the people, cf. Dt. 32:8 → n. 77; Da. 10:13, 20 f. One can hardly accept a mere ref. to human rulers or judges. [86]

Completely detached from the original connection with the divine world and mythology of Canaan are the depictions of the heavenly assembly in Job 1:6-12; 2:1-6. [87] The בְּנֵי הָאֱלֹהִים are heavenly or angelic beings wholly subject to Yahweh and gathered to report to Him and to receive orders. Among them is Satan (→ II, 73, 38 ff.), who is similarly subject and responsible to Yahweh. [88] On the other hand the parallelism of בְּנֵי אֱלֹהִים and stars in Job 38:7, which is part of the poem and not of the marginal story, again suggests the original link with a pantheon.

In Da. the ancient ideas are adopted and developed in a way corresponding to the comprehensive doctrine of angels in apocalyptic. Thus בַּר אֱלָהִין in 3:25 (only here sing.) is undoubtedly an angel, cf. the watchers and holy ones of 4:10, 14, 20 and the guardian angels of 10:13, 20 f. They are all to be equated with the thousands and tens of thousands who sat on thrones for the judgment, 7:9 f. The influence of ideas of divine beings, holy ones and a heavenly council is clear, while in the watchers one may perhaps see a reflection of the work of Satan in the prose narrative of Job. [89]

In the main the idea of a physical father-son relation between Yahweh and other divine beings or angels such as one finds elsewhere in the ancient Orient (cf. Is. 14:12) is obviously quite alien to the OT and is not even remotely suggested. Israel, especially under the influence of its Canaanite environment, did take over

---

[81] On this cf. M. Noth, "Die Heiligen des Höchsten," Gesammelte Stud. z. AT (1957), 274-290.

[82] The ref. to gods like Chemosh and Milcom in 1 K. 11:33 etc. shows that the idea of the existence of other gods for non-Israelite peoples was widely assumed prior to the exile.

[83] Cf. J. Morgenstern, "The Mythological Background of Psalm 82," HUCA, 14 (1939), 29-126; G. E. Wright, The OT against its Environment (1950), 30-41; M. Buber, Recht u. Unrecht, Deutung einiger Ps. (1952), 27-38; R. T. O'Callaghan, "A Note on the Canaanite Background of Ps. 82," Catholic Bibl. Quart., 15 (1953), 311-4; O. Eissfeldt, "El. u. Jahwe," Kleine Schr., III (1966), 390; Cooke, op. cit., (→ n. 74), 29-34.

[84] Cf. the analogous terms 'ly(nm), ilm and bn šrm for the gods Šhr and Šlm acc. to T. H. Gaster, "A Canaanite Ritual Drama," Journal of the American Oriental Society, 66 (1946), 71.

[85] Cf. the same idea in Is. 14:12 and the ref. to the arrogant king in Is. 14:12-15 and Ez. 28:11-19.

[86] Cf. the express treatment by Cooke, op. cit., 30-32.

[87] So also Herrmann, op. cit. (→ n. 74), 249.

[88] The fact that he is "in the midst" of the heavenly beings shows that he is one of them, cf. the use of the word in Gn. 23:10; 42:5; Nu. 17:21; 1 S. 10:10; Ez. 29:12. On Satan cf. G. Fohrer, "Überlieferung u. Wandlung d. Hioblegende," Festschr. F. Baumgärtel (1959), 46-48.

[89] The "leader of the host" in Da. 8:11, however, is Yahweh Himself rather than a subordinate as in Jos. 5:14.

the idea of a pantheon and a divine council according to which a series of divine beings, including at least in part the gods of other nations, exists under Yahweh the supreme God; at this stage the בְּנֵי הָאֱלֹהִים are the individual gods. But these are largely stripped of their powers and a theoretical as well as a practical monotheism develops. In connection with this the divine council becomes the court of Yahweh and its members are the heavenly beings, the angels, who serve Yahweh. Finally, then, בְּנֵי הָאֱלֹהִים denotes no more than membership of the divine world or sphere.

b. Three times in the OT the king is called God's son, 2 S. 7:14; Ps. 2:7; 89:26 f., and cf. the corrupt text of Ps. 110:3.[90] All these instances represent one aspect of the Jewish view of the Davidic monarchy[91] which influences the subsequent[92] Messianic promise (Is. 9:1-6, cf. v. 5). As the connection with the historical monarchy rules out a Messianic interpretation of these verses,[93] so the possible effect of ancient oriental ideas of sacral kingship is restricted in advance by the fact that the concept of a physical divine sonship of the king (birth from the deity) could find no place on the soil of the OT.[94]

The Nathan prophecy of 2 S. 7[95] is from an ancient source which tells of opposition to David's plan to build a temple (vv. 1-7, 17) and then adds in extended and reconstructed form the intimation that David's dynasty will be a lasting one, vv. 8-16, 18-29. Yahweh guarantees the perpetuity of the dynasty, cf. also 2 S. 23:5; Jer. 33:21; Ps. 89:3 f.; 132:12. He promises David's seed (זֶרַע 2 S. 7:12): "I will be his father, and he shall be my son" (v. 14, taken up again in 1 Ch. 17:13; 22:10; 28:6). Iniquities will be punished, but there will be no rejection, 2 S. 7:14b-15. If in the first instance the human relation of father and son is an example or model,[96]

---

[90] Cf. Kraus, op. cit. (→ n. 47), 752 f. Ps. 22:10; 27:10, however, can hardly ref. to the king adopted by God, as against A. Bentzen, "Messias, Moses redivivus, Menschensohn," AbhThANT, 17 (1948), 20.

[91] Perhaps Ps. 45:6 expresses the North Israel view if the אלהים is the king. But this is uncertain, since אלהים was perhaps put for יְהֶיֶה misread as יהוה and v. 6 is an abbreviation ("thy throne is [as] the [throne] of God"), or else אלהים goes with כסא ("thy divine [mighty] throne"). Cf. the discussion in C. R. North, "The Religious Aspects of Hebrew Kingship," ZAW, 50 (1932), 27-31; also M. Noth, "Gott, König, Volk im AT," Gesammelte Stud. z. AT (1957), 225; Kraus, op. cit., 331.

[92] On this cf. G. Fohrer, Das Buch Js., I, Zürcher Bibelkomm.[2] (1966) on 9:1-6.

[93] A. Vaccari, "De Messia 'Filio Dei' in VT," Verbum Domini, 15 (1935), 48-55, 77-86; J. de Fraine, "L'aspect religieux de la royauté israélite," Analecta Biblica, 3 (1954), 271-6.

[94] For the vast lit. on this problem cf. K. H. Bernhardt, "Das Problem der altorientalischen Königsideologie im AT," VT Suppl., 8 (1961); cf. also W. von Soden, op. cit. (→ n. 9), 1712-14. In the OT cf. Is. 14:12-15; Ez. 28. A certain approximation to the older Messianic interpretation is provided by the fact that champions of the theory of the sacral king in Israel embody the ideal Messianic figure in the actual king in Jerusalem as son of God and cultic representative of God.

[95] But cf. the partially divergent and very varied interpretations of L. Rost, "Die Überlieferung von der Thronnachfolge Davids," BWANT, III, 6 (1926), 47-74; S. Herrmann, "Die Königsnovelle in Ägypten u. in Israel," Wissenschaftliche Zschr. d. Univ. Leipzig, 3 (1953/54), 51-62; M. Noth, "David u. Israel in 2 S. 7," Mélanges bibl. A. Robert (1957), 122-130; G. W. Ahlström, "Der Prophet Nathan u. der Tempelbau," VT, 11 (1961), 113-127; E. Kutsch, "Die Dynastie v. Gottes Gnaden," ZThK, 58 (1961), 137-153; H. Gese, "Der Davidsbund u. die Zionserwählung," ZThK, 61 (1964), 10-26; on Nathan's prophecy cf. also G. v. Rad, Theol. d. AT, II (1960), 58.

[96] The Tg. stresses the fig. aspect by its rendering of the לְ in לְבֵן as "shall become as a son to me."

vv. 8-16 (with the extension vv. 18-29) belong to a wider context, as may be seen by comparison with the Egyptian royal story which served as the divine validation of the ruler at his coronation. [97] If Solomon, seeking to eliminate the constitutional defect of his accession without selection by or contract with the people, [98] derived his validation from Yahweh Himself within a royal story (1 K. 3:4-15), the period which followed regarded the divine legitimation of the Davidic dynasty as in every way desirable. 2 S. 7:8-16 served this end. Whereas 1 K. 3:4-15 related only to Solomon, the so-called Davidic covenant (2 S. 7:8-16) extended to the dynasty, and the royal covenant with the people, which David's successors usually did not make (2 K. 11:17 and 23:1-3 are exceptions), was transcended by that which God Himself had made. Although this is intrinsically a one-sided covenant obligating the superior, its reciprocity is indicated by the stress on the father-son relation. As a father or the chief wife could declare the son of a subsidiary wife or slave legitimate (→ 344, 28 ff.), so Yahweh declares legitimate the individual king apart from the dynastic basis by calling him His son and giving him a share in His fatherly rule. [99]

In Ps. 89 vv. 3 f. and 19-37 are poetic paraphrases of the divine legitimation of the Davidic dynasty in 2 S. 7. Appealing to this the complaint asks that affliction be removed and that the king acknowledged by Yahweh be saved from his enemies. In this connection vv. 26 and 27 say of David what applies also to his successors: "He shall cry unto me, Thou art my father, my God, and the rock of my salvation. Yes, I made him my firstborn, the highest of the kings of the earth." This corresponds in principle to 2 S. 7, the more so as any idea of a physical descent of the king from God is ruled out by the emphasis on his humanity in v. 19. But there is the distinction that the king of Judah is now exalted as the firstborn. This expression stresses a claim to unique privilege and is directed against the claims of other rulers. There can be no question of a divinisation of the king of Judah. Rather the Ps. uses the idea of his legitimation by Yahweh as a ground on which to seek Yahweh's help for the legitimate king.

The basic legal legitimation, which is to be distinguished from adoption (→ 344, 19 ff.), took concrete shape in the coronation ritual of Judah. [100] Only when Yahweh had acknowledged the new king as His son, established his full royal name (2 S. 7:9; 1 K. 1:47), granted him a first request (Ps. 2:8; 20:5; 21:2, 4) and invested him with his crown (2 K. 11:12; Ps. 21:3) and sceptre (Ps. 110:2) could he begin his rule. Ps. 2:7 is to be understood along these lines: "He said unto me, Thou art my son; this day have I begotten thee." It is doubtful whether the Ps. belongs to the actual enthronement, since the "he said" of v. 7 seems to be recalling an earlier declaration and hence can hardly be a divine oracle on the occasion. [101] If this is so, the Ps. is one for a time of trouble like Ps. 89 → lines 17 ff. The divine legitimation of the king is being set before him and his power over other nations established. All the

---

[97] Cf. Herrmann, op. cit. (→ n. 95), 59 f.

[98] Cf. G. Fohrer, "Der Vertrag zwischen König u. Volk in Israel," ZAW, 71 (1959), 1-22, but for a different view M. Noth, Könige, Bibl. Komm. AT, 9, 1 (1964), 40 f.

[99] On divine sonship as an expression of the original idea of the king's power as a person possessed of mana cf. Eichr. Theol. AT, I⁶, 296.

[100] On the coronation ritual cf. esp. G. v. Rad, "Das judäische Krönungsritual," ThLZ, 72 (1947), 211-216; K. H. Rengstorf, "Old and New Testament Traces of a Formula of the Judaean Royal Ritual," Nov. Test., 5 (1962), 229-244.

[101] There is no support for the idea of an annual enthronement at which the song was sung, Schmidt, op. cit. (→ n. 47), 5 f.

same, the declaration of Yahweh quoted here is a part of the coronation ritual, as the "this day" shows, and it is adduced as such. It is usually construed as an adoption formula, just as the father-son relation between Yahweh and the king is understood in terms of the law of adoption. But the concept in the basic passage 2 S. 7:14 (→ 350, 7 ff.) does not have its source in the adoption of an alien child but rather in the acknowledgment of the child of a concubine either by the father or the childless wife. In Ps. 2:7 the first part: "Thou art my son," might be taken as an adoption formula, [102] but the "this day have I begotten thee" fits in with this very awkwardly. It is thus better to assume that the acknowledgment of a child whom the slave has borne as a substitute for her mistress underlies the statement (→ 344, 28 ff.): "Thou art my son, this day I myself have begotten thee." This formula of acknowledgment is reapplied to the father and used in the coronation ritual. The Messianic promise of Is. 9:5: "Unto us a child is born, a son is given," speaks of birth rather than begetting and changes the acknowledgment into the people's shout of joy welcoming the ruler of the age of salvation "for us."

All this shows that the king of Judah was not God's son by nature and that he did not of himself enter the divine sphere by enthronement. He was acknowledged as son by a resolve of Yahweh, [103] and only thus could he have a share in the authority, possessions and inheritance of God. But if this is so, the question remains why the concept of son was used to express this. In explanation one should first point out that the Judaean coronation ritual, which includes legitimation of the king as son, is dependent in large part on that of Egypt in which Pharaoh's divine sonship is proclaimed. [104] The development of the Jerusalem ritual undoubtedly began quite early and may have been influenced already by the formulation in 2 S. 7:14. The Egyptian idea of physical sonship is changed into a legal one. This was made possible and facilitated by the fact that the description of the king as God's son has a further root in Israel's designation as God's son → lines 32 ff. As the election of Israel and God's assurances to it in the events of the exodus and Sinai constitute the form and basis of the idea of the election of David and his house and of the so-called Davidic covenant, so the concept of Israel's sonship is well adapted to serve as a model for the relation between Yahweh and the Davidic dynasty. [105]

c. Far more often than for the king the father-son relation is used to denote the relation of Yahweh to Israel or the Israelites. [106] Yahweh speaks of Israel as His firstborn son (Ex. 4:22; Jer. 31:9) whom He has called as His dear child (Jer. 31:20) out of Egypt (Hos. 11:1) and given a special place among the nations as the other sons (Jer. 3:19). Yahweh is similarly called the Father of Israel (Dt. 32:6, 18; Jer. 3:4; cf. Nu. 11:12). The totality of Israel consists of His sons and daughters (Dt. 14:1; 32:5, 19; Is. 43:6; 45:11; Hos. 2:1) which the wife Israel (Hos. 2:4) or Jerusalem (Ez. 16:20) has borne Him. In prophetic reprimand the additions "my" or "God's" may be left out or even replaced with adjectives which denote their guilt (Is. 1:2, 4; 30:1, 9; Jer. 3:14, 22; 4:22). The Israelites, too, speak of God as "our Father" (Is. 63:16; 64:7; Mal. 2:10). That there is no difference between

---

[102] Cf. the other positive or negative formulae behind 1 S. 18:21; Hos. 2:4; Tob. 7:12.
[103] Noth, op. cit. (→ n. 91), 222.
[104] v. Rad, op. cit. (→ n. 100), 211-216.
[105] Cf. G. Cooke, "The Israelite King as Son of God," ZAW, 73 (1961), 217 f.
[106] The occurences are not so rare as T. C. Vriezen, An Outline of OT Theology (1958), 144-147, imagines.

Israel as the son or the Israelites as the sons of Yahweh may be seen from the use of both expressions in Dt. 32:5-6, 18-19 and the parallelism between "my people" and "sons" in Is. 63:8; Jer. 4:22. Exceptions are Ps. 73:15 where the "generation of thy children" are the righteous and Mal. 1:6 where Yahweh's fatherhood relates to the priests. The father- or mother-son relation can also be used in comparisons: Yahweh pities, bears and comforts like a father or mother, Dt. 1:31; 8:5; Is. 66:13; Mal. 3:17; Ps. 103:13. Ps. 27:10 and 68:6 are to be taken similarly. In no case does the father-son relation express a connection between Yahweh and Israel which has arisen naturally and is by nature indissoluble. [107] Like the king, Israel and the Israelites are not the son or sons of Yahweh in a physical sense. Sometimes the terms can be used simply to describe the men belonging to a deity as worshippers of the deity, e.g., the Moabites as the "people of Chemosh" are called the "sons" and "daughters" of this god, Nu. 21:29, cf. Mal. 2:11; Jer. 2:26 f.

In particular the father-son relation serves to denote the two sides of the connection between Yahweh and Israel → V, 970, 30 ff. On the one side the distance between them and the subjection of Israel to Yahweh is stressed when the element of the father's dominion, possession and control and the corresponding element of the son's subordination are to the fore. This is most clearly brought out by the parallel expressions master and servant in Mal. 1:6. Dt. 8:5 uses the same idea when it points to Yahweh's fatherly dealings in His visitations; He is seeking to educate by punishing, cf. Prv. 3:12. Yahweh's legal claim to Israel which He has created, [108] His care for it, and the duties of Israel toward Him, are often mentioned in connection with the father-son relation, Ex. 4:22 f.; [109] Nu. 11:12; Dt. 14:1; 32:6, 18; Is. 1:2; 30:1, 9; 45:9-11; 64:7; Mal. 1:6; 2:10. On the other side the aim is to express the kindness and love of Yahweh, since this is presupposed as the responsible attitude of the father, Ps. 103:13. In this respect the idea of God as Father supplements His depiction as Husband, Shepherd and Redeemer. Along with these images it counterbalances the idea of Yahweh as Ruler and Judge and stresses the fact that He is bound to His people, which may thus appeal to His mercy, Is. 63:15 f. He has called it out of Egypt (Hos. 11:1) and given it preference over other peoples as His dear son and favourite child, Jer. 3:19; 31:20. The more bitter, then, is the disappointment that children so carefully brought up want no more of Him (Is. 1:2) and are corrupt, rebellious and untruthful, Is. 1:4; 30:1, 9; Jer. 4:22. But even so He still admonishes them to return to their loving Father (Jer. 3:14, 22) and promises them that He will receive them again as sons (Hos. 2:1).

The description of Israel as God's son is still influenced by the ancient eastern idea of the physical sonship of nations or men corresponding to notions of the physical divine sonship of lesser gods and many kings. Possibly the normal ancestors of Israel in pre-Mosaic times felt a kinship to the god of their tribes. Apart from the difficult divine names פַּחַד יִצְחָק and אֲבִיר יַעֲקֹב [110] there is perhaps an echo of this in the source of Ex. 4:22 f., which is influenced by the nomadic spirit. Here Yahweh calls the people "my"

---

[107] Cf. esp. Eichr. Theol. AT, I⁶, 31 f.

[108] On the connection of the father-son relation with the *imago dei* cf. Vriezen, *op. cit.* (→ n. 106), 120-122, 177.

[109] D. Daube, "Rechtsgedanken in d. Erzählungen des Pent.," *Festschr. O. Eissfeldt,* ZAW Beih., 77 (1958), 35-37, on the basis of the designation of Israel as Yahweh's son, considers the whole exodus story from the standpoint of the paternal right of redemption and reacquisition.

[110] Cf. W. F. Albright, *From the Stone Age to Christianity* (1949), 353.

first born son, while in later texts the personal suffix only denotes relationship. Similarly the original concept of physical sonship is perhaps reflected in the image of a marriage between Yahweh and Israel of which the Israelites are the issue, Hos. 2:4. Perhaps on account of these origins the idea of the father-son relation is comparatively late in Israel and is adopted only in altered form. For one thing, omission of the personal suffix "my" (most noticeable in Is. 1:2) rules out the possible notion of a physical descent of Israel or the Israelites from Yahweh. The belief now is that on the basis of His free decision and authority Yahweh acknowledges and legitimates Israel or the Israelites as belonging to Him. Furthermore Hosea gave a new interpretation to the traditional motif by pointing out that Israel the son proved itself ungrateful and sinned against the Father, 11:1 ff. Is. is even more critical, calling the sons even worse than the Father's cattle, 1:2 f. He often uses the term disparagingly as his more precise definitions show, 1:4, 30:1, 9. It is indeed a fixed expression for sinful and guilt-laden Israel.

d. That individuals could be seen in a father-son relation to Yahweh is revealed by personal names with "father" and "brother" as a theophorous element → V, 968, 20 ff. [111] There are, of course, no corresponding theophorous names with "son" in Israel. The OT mentions the Aram. Benhadad (son of Hadad) but does not see that Moses is the relic of a similarly constructed Egypt. name. Perhaps the idea of sonship is expressed in the names בְּדְיָה in Ezr. 10:35 and בְּדָן in 1 Ch. 7:17 by the term בַּד "twig," "shoot" from the plant world, the deity being thus represented as a tree (cf. Hos. 14:9) and the one who bears the name as its creation. [112]

C. Judaism.

I. Hellenistic Judaism.

1. Septuagint.

a. In the LXX υἱός is the usual transl. of בֵּן (בַּר). [113] One also finds quite often τέκνον (134 times) and παιδίον (19) with no regular grounds for selection of the broader term, though בֵּן can sometimes have the sense of "child" → 345, 10 f. There are in the LXX 19 other renderings of the simple בֵּן [114] and 21 equivalents of names in which the Hbr. word is dropped. This is common in the many statements about the age of men or animals (→ 347, 4 ff.), for which we find compounds like τριέτης, τριακονταέτης, ἑκατονταέτης or with greater numbers simple genitives like καὶ ἦν Νῶε ἐτῶν πεντακοσίων, Gn. 5:32.

Two passages suggest that there could be religious or theological reasons for using some other term than υἱός. In Ex. 4:23 Yahweh's order to Pharaoh שַׁלַּח אֶת־בְּנִי is transl. ἐξαπόστειλον τὸν λαόν μου. But this transl. rests on a more precise definition of content and on stylistic assimilation to the שַׁלַּח (אֶת־) עַמִּי which often follows, Ex. 5:1;

---

[111] M. Noth, "Die isr. Personennamen im Rahmen der gemeinsemitischen Namengebung," BWANT, III, 10 (1928), 66-75.

[112] Noth, op. cit., 149 f. (also בדיו). Ibid., 150-152 the name עֶגְלָיו is explained as st. c. so that the deity is represented as a bull and the bearer of the name as its young.

[113] Only in comparatively few cases is υἱός used for other Hbr. words, 14 times each for אִישׁ and בַּיִת, 4 for יֶלֶד or יָלִיד, once each for זֶרַע and מִשְׁפָּחָה and once each for 6 names of origin ending in i.

[114] ἀνήρ 1 S. 11:8; 17:53; Neh. 7:34; ἄνθρωπος 3 Βασ. 5:10, ἄξιος Dt. 25:2, ἀρνίον ψ 113:4, 6, ἄρσην Ex. 1:16, 22; 2:2, ἔκγονος Is. 49:15, εἶναι 2 Ch. 24:15, ἰός Lam. 3:13, κοιλία 1 Ch. 17:11, λαός Ex. 4:23, νοσσός (νεοσσός) Lv. 5:7 etc., οἶκος Jer. 23:7; Ez. 2:3, παῖς Prv. 20:7, πῶλος Gn. 49:11, σκύμνος Job 4:11, σπέρμα Dt. 25:5, συναγωγή Lv. 22:18.

7:26; 8:16; 9:1, 13; 10:3. In Hos. 11:1 נַעַר is transl. νήπιος and לְבָנַי τὰ τέκνα αὐτοῦ. In the Tg., too, the sing. is replaced by the plur. קְרִיתִי לְהוֹן בְּנִין, but most versions and the quotation in Mt. 2:15 follow the HT. [115] But in 11:1-7 there is frequent vacillation between the sing. v. 1, 4b, 5a, 6a and the plur. v. 2, 3, 4a, 5b, 6b, 7. The LXX does not eliminate this and the HT is severely disrupted by corruptions and glosses. Hence it is possible the original of the LXX had the plur. At any rate there seems to be no religious or theological reason for the LXX reading τὰ τέκνα αὐτοῦ. Hence no important conclusions can be drawn from the passages, esp. as elsewhere expressions which call Yahweh the Father of Israel of the Israelites and the latter His son or sons (→ 351, 32 ff.) are faithfully rendered and the various expressions for divine beings (→ 347, 9 ff.) are transl. by υἱοὶ τοῦ θεοῦ or ἄγγελοι Dt. 32:8; Job 1:6; 2:1; 38:7; Da. 3:25.

Fohrer

b. ὁ υἱὸς ὁ ἀγαπητός (→ 368, 5 ff.) occurs in Gn. 22:2, 12, 16 [116] (for יָחִיד) and then Ιερ. 38:20 (for יַקִּיר) uses it for Ephraim as the son whom Yahweh holds dear. πρωτότοκος might be taken corporatively in 2 Βασ. 19:44: πρωτότοκος ἐγὼ ἢ σύ, "I am older than thou." [117] "Sons of wisdom" occurs in Sir. 4:11, cf. 6:18 ff.; 39:13, "sons of the prophets" in Tob. 4:12, "of the righteous" in 13:10, 15, "of captivity" in 1 Esr. 7:11 ff., cf. Bar. 4:10, 14, "of Adam" in Sir. 40:1, "of Israel" in Tob. 13:3; Jdt. 5:23; Bar. 2:28; 1 Macc. 3:15; Ps. Sol. 18:3 etc., "of Jerusalem" in Ps. Sol. 2:3, 11; (8:21); cf. 2:6; 17:31; Bar. 4:10, 37, "of the covenant" Ps. Sol. 17:15, "of the people (of God)" Jdt. 12:8, cf. Ps. Sol. 17:31, "of aliens" (ἀλλογενῶν) 1 Macc. 3:45 (cf. ἀλλογενεῖς v. 36), "of the city" 4:2, "of presumption" 2:47.

c. The OT description of the Israelites as "sons of God" in Dt. 14:1 (→ 351, 37 ff.; 359, 31 f.) is adopted in Wis. 9:7; Ps. Sol. 17:27, cf. also Sib., 3, 702. God is even "he that begat us" in Sib., 3, 726. One finds υἱοὶ ἠγαπημένοι ὑπὸ σοῦ in Jdt. 9:4 and "sons of the Most High, the supreme living God" in Εσθ. 8:12q. Education and forgiveness play a great part in this divine sonship, Wis. 12:19-21, also God's mercy in Wis. 16:10, 21, 26, cf. 9:4, 7; 12:7, 19-21; 19:6. In sharp contrast to enemies are God's "children" in Wis. 18:4 (cf. παῖδες in 12:7); 3 Macc. 6:28, or the whole nation as God's son in Wis. 18:13; Sir. 36:16 vl. God treats these children as a father but rejects others, Wis. 11:10, cf. 3 Macc. 7:6. A new pt. is that the individual (→ 360, 10 ff.) says to God: "Thou art my father," Sir. 51:10 HT. [118] But not every Israelite (→ 355, 28 ff.) is a son in virtue of belonging to the people. The merciful is "as a son of the Most High," Sir. 4:10, and God warns the righteous as a υἱὸς ἀγαπήσεως and chastises him as a "firstborn," Ps. Sol. 13:9. [119] Acc. to Wis. 5:5 the righteous dwells after death among the "sons of God, i.e., the saints" → 347, 13 ff. But already on earth he calls God his Father (2:16)

---

[115] A. Baumstark, "Die Zitate d. Mt. aus dem Zwölfprophetenbuch," *Biblica*, 37 (1956), 296-313 conjectures that the quotation is taken from a missing original targum of essentially the same character as the ancient Palestinian Pent. targum; this is to be noted as against the Tg. reading above. Cf. also H. W. Wolff, *Dodekapropheton*, I, *Bibl. Komm. AT*, 14, 1² (1965); W. Rudolph, *Hosea, Komm. AT*, 13, 1 (1966) on 11:1.

[116] Acc. to Cod. Neofiti 1 on Gn. 22:1-14 Isaac offers himself willingly or binds himself on the altar; for his willingness cf. also Jos. Ant., 1, 232; Ps.-Philo Antiquit. Biblicae (ed. G. Kisch [1949]), 32, 2-4; cf. P. Winter, Review of G. Vermes, "Scripture and Tradition in Judaism" in *Durham Univ. Journal*, 55 (1963), 91; also H. J. Schoeps, *Pls.* (1959), 144-152. Cf. also Test. L. 18:6 and C. H. Turner, Ο ΥΙΟΣ ΜΟΥ Ο ΑΓΑΠΗΤΟΣ, JThSt, 27 (1926), 124 f.

[117] Cf. A. W. Argyle, "Πρωτότοκος πάσης κτίσεως (Col. 1:15)," Exp. T., 66 (1954/55), 61 f., 318 f.; but cf. H. G. Meecham, "Col. 1:15," *ibid.*, 124 f.

[118] Cf. the invocation of God as Father in Sir. 23:1, 4; Wis. 14:3 (→ V, 981, 5 ff.) but also Is. 1:2, cf. H. Wildberger, *Jesaia, Bibl. Komm. AT*, 10 (1965), *ad loc.*

[119] Cf. G. Bertram, "Der Begriff d. Erziehung in d. griech. Bibel," *Festschr. G. Krüger* (1932), 33-51.

and calls himself "God's son" (2:18, cf. 5:5), which is the same as God's servant (→ V, 678, 10 ff.) in 2:13 [120] → 378, 4 ff.; II, 267, 13 ff.

d. There is some hesitation about the title "son of God" (→ V, 978, 4 ff.) esp. in the Gk. sing. [121] The promised son of David is seen as God's son → 349, 17 ff.; 360, 16 ff. ψ 109:3 perhaps speaks of the divine birth of the Messiah: ἐκ γαστρὸς πρὸ ἑωσφόρου ἐξεγέννησά σε. [122] Dt. 32:43 LXX (as distinct from HT) calls the Israelites (cf. v. 5 f., 18-20) and the angels "God's sons." At v. 8b LXX reads ἄγγελοι θεοῦ for original "sons of God" → 347, 11 f. [123] Acc. to Ex. 4:22 Israel is the υἱὸς πρωτότοκος → VI, 873, 27 ff. On Hos. 11:1 → 353, 9 ff. At Jer. 3:19 Cod B offers the correct text: "I will set thee high among the nations." The other texts read like the HT: "I will establish thee as children," so that here institution into sonship and inheritance (→ 391, 21 f.) of the chosen land are connected, cf. ψ 2:7 f. On the other hand Is. 1:2 ref. to God's begetting (HT rearing) and exalting (→ n. 118) of sons, cf. also Sib., 3, 726.

2. Josephus.

"Son of God" is not found in Jos. → V, 979, 19 f. One should honour parents for they have their name in common with God the Father of all, of the whole human race, Ant., 2, 152; 4, 262. He is Father and Lord of the people of the Hebrews (5, 93) as of all (1, 20. 230; 2, 152). Even if God is called πατὴρ καὶ γένεσις τῶν ὅλων, this is interpreted by δημιουργὸς ἀνθρωπίνων καὶ θείων and is thus to be related to the Creator of men and angels, his rule over Israel being the climax of the statement. Jos. is obviously opposed to mythical ideas of sons begotten by God, for Ant., 7, 93 restates 2 S. 7:14 in such a way that the Davidic king cannot be confused with a son of this kind. [124] God is Creator, not Begetter. [125]

3. Philo.

Philo's usage is not uniform. It is accepted that God is Father of all and of everything → V, 956, 28 ff. Hence the cosmos can be called not merely the work of God and son of νοῦς (Migr. Abr., 193 f.) but also the younger "son of God" (Deus Imm., 31 f.). [126] Once inner spiritual laughter is called "son of God," Mut. Nom., 131. [127] More important are the ref. relating to man. Though Dt. 14:1 is quoted, not every man — Adam alone is singled out since he has God Himself as father and not a mortal (Virt., 204 → VII, 1053, 33 ff.) — nor every Israelite (→ 354, 30 ff.) is God's son, but only the doer of good, Spec. Leg., I, 318. Only good and outstanding men are called "God's sons" by Moses, while the wicked are "bodies" (Quaest. in Gn., 1, 92) or "sons of Adam" (Plant., 58 ff.). The sons of Israel are sons of him who sees God. If they cannot be called God's sons (Dt. 14:1) they should strive to become "sons of the firstborn logos" and hence "sons of one man," Conf. Ling., 145-148. [128] The wise man whom God chooses (ἐπιγράφω

---

[120] Taken to be a prophecy of Christ in Aug. Civ. D., 17, 20, cf. J. Reider, The Book of Wisdom (1957), 66 f.
[121] E. Burton, A Crit. and Exeg. Comm. on the Ep. to the Galatians, ICC (1921), 405.
[122] Not in the Hbr. text → 349, 10 f.; cf. George Père, 31.
[123] At Gn. 6:4 υἱοὶ τοῦ θεοῦ as HT; only Aʳ alters to ἄγγελοι → 347, 12.
[124] Cf. Jos. Bell., 7, 344: there is no κοινωνία between θεῖον and θνητόν even though the soul is invisible like God, 346; cf. also the expression οἱ θεοφιλεῖς ὄντες καὶ ὑπ' αὐτοῦ τοῦ θεοῦ γενόμενοι in Ant., 1, 106.
[125] Schl. Theol. d. Judt., 24 f.
[126] Cf. E. Schweizer, "Zum religionsgesch. Hintergrund d. Sendungsformel Gl. 4:4 f.; R. 8:3 f.; Jn. 3:16 f.; 1 Jn. 4:9," ZNW, 57 (1966), 204 f.; H. F. Weiss, "Untersuchungen zur Kosmologie d. hell. u. paläst. Judt.," TU, 97 (1966), 248-282.
[127] Or should ἐνδιάθετος go with υἱός?
[128] Cf. E. Bréhier, Les idées philosophiques de Philon d'Alex.² (1925), 170, 173, also 101; J. Pascher, Η ΒΑΣΙΛΙΚΗ ΟΔΟΣ (1931), 133.

"document publicly" cf. Som., II, 273) one may regard as an adoptive (εἰσποιητὸς υἱός) of God, Sobr., 56. This is the second birth without a mother which makes one a son of God, Vit. Mos., II, 209 f.; Quaest. in Ex., 2, 46; cf. Leg. All., III, 181 and 217; Rer. Div. Her., 62; Cher., 49; Congr., 7. The title "man of God" (→ I, 364, 30 ff.) is, however, more appropriate for the perfect and wise, Mut. Nom., 24-26 (cf. 125); Det. Pot. Ins., 162; cf. Sacr. AC, 9 f., and also for God's interpreter, the logos and prophet, Deus Imm., 138 f. The strict distinction between God and man upheld both in the OT and in Ep. Ar., 140 is more fluid in Philo, perhaps under the influence of the Hell. view of the sage → 339, 3 ff. [129] Thus the divinisation of Moses may be detected in Quaest. in Ex., 2, 29 notwithstanding the safeguard of emphasis on the distinction between God and man. [130] On the other hand miracles as God's acts are esp. typical of the Hell.-Jewish man of God on the basis of the OT model (Moses, Elijah), [131] but in the Hell. charismatic, apart from the didactic poem of Empedocles, this aspect is important only from the middle of the 2nd cent. A.D. It is thus possible that this idea found a place in the NT only by way of Hell. Judaism → 376, 14 ff. A more vital pt. is that Philo does not just personify the logos as an archangel and mediator, neither created nor uncreated (Rer. Div. Her., 205 f.; Conf. Ling., 146), and as an envoy or messenger of God (Rer. Div. Her., 205; Quaest. in Ex., 2, 13; Agric., 51 = Ex. 23:20; Cher., 35 = Nu. 22:31), but also sees in him God's image and organ (Det. Pot. Ins., 82 f.; Conf. Ling., 97 and 147), and indeed His firstborn son (Som., I, 215; Conf. Ling., 146). If he shares his sonship with the later cosmos (cf. Conf. Ling., 97) he is still the force which creates, sustain and orders the world (Agric., 51; Fug., 112) and the sinless mediator (108 f.; Som., I, 215). [132]

In general it may be seen that the hesitation to speak of the son of God (→ III, 92, 18 ff.) [133] was not by a long way so strong in Hellenistic Judaism as it was in Palestinian Judaism, → 360, 16 ff. But the title son of God was not used for the θεῖος ἀνήρ; [134] in fact, it is very rare in Hellenism too → 338, 1 ff. In Hellenistic Judaism great men are depicted after the model of Hellenistic charismatics on the

---

[129] D. Georgi, *Die Gegner des Pls. im 2 K.* (1964), 156-162.

[130] H. Windisch, *Pls. u. Christus* (1934), 103-108. When the angel addresses Seth as man of God in Vit. Ad., 41 this is quite normal, but in Slav. En. 7:4 the angels invoke the man of God as intercessor and in Test. Abr. 6 (p. 110, 12 f.) the angel himself is the man of God. Cf. also Test. Isaac, ed. W. E. Barnes, TSt, II, 2 (1892), Folio 13 verso (p. 143 f.): a spirit-endowed preacher.

[131] Georgi, *op. cit.,* 153-6.

[132] On the identity of logos and wisdom and the relation to the Plutarchian Hermes-Logos and the pre-Philonic doctrine of the powers of God cf. Schweizer, *op. cit.,* 200 f.; Weiss, *op. cit.,* 207 f.

[133] Hahn, 287.

[134] The Book of Joseph and Asnath (ed. P. Batiffol, *Stud. Patristica,* 1-2 [1889 f.]) is a special problem. 15:7 shows it was conceived in Gk. with the ref. to Zech. 2:15 LXX, cf. C. Burchard, *Untersuchungen zu Joseph u. Aseneth* (1965), 91-9. Acc. to 19:18 the saved community consists of sons and daughters of the living God over whom God will reign for ever. In 16:14 the sons of the Most High who eat manna are perhaps angels. In 6:2-6 however, in words that echo ψ 138:7, the dread of mortals at Joseph's appearing is described: "Where shall I, unhappy, flee? Where shall I hide from his face? How will Joseph, this son of God, regard me?" His character as such rests on indwelling light; no woman ever conceived this light. Similarly 13:13 contrasts the truth of his divine sonship with the false human opinion that he is a shepherd's son. Acc. to 25:5 he is a saviour for all Egypt. The statements are strongly reminiscent of a θεῖος ἀνήρ. But it is strongly affirmed that Jacob is his father, 22:4, cf. 7:5. In 23:10 his brothers simply say that their father is God's friend and their brother is as a son of God. In the background is probably the idea that Israel is God's son in whom God's Spirit dwells and who joins himself to the community of the proselytes, → I, 657, 4 ff. Cf. the Jewish prayer in Orig. Comm. in Joh., 2, 31, 190 on 1:6: "I am Israel, archangel of the power of the Lord and chief captain among the sons of God."

one side [135] and that of the biblical men of God through whom God works His miracles on the other. But the title son of God cannot be explained along these lines.

Schweizer

II. Palestinian Judaism.

1. Duties of the Son.

In the Jewish family sons received the covenant sign of circumcision the eighth day after birth and from early youth were instructed by their fathers in the Torah → V, 975, 20 ff. [136] When taught the Law the boy in his thirteenth year בַּר מִצְוָה (→ 358, 32 f.) becomes fully responsible for observance of the commandments from that time on → V, 647, 37 ff. Acc. to the Rabb. view the good impulse in him is now strong enough to resist successfully the evil impulse in him from birth. [137] Since the relation of son to parents is regulated by the Torah, the son must respect and honour them, esp. the father; [138] on this the Rabb. develop precise statutes → V, 974, 19 ff. cf. Qid., 31b, 32a. [139] If the son sees his father unwittingly breaking a commandment, he must not draw his attention to this directly, but even at this moment must still show due respect and say: "My father, is it written thus in the Torah?" But since even this might trouble his father the recommended form is: "My father, there is a verse written in the Torah which says ... ," Qid., 32a. [140] By the biblical quotation the son invites the father to see his own error. The obligation to honour one's father extends to death and even beyond, for when recalling his father a son should always be ready to say: "I will be an atonement for his (death-)couch," Qid., 31b. [141] This formula, which is to be used only during the first twelve months after death, obviously means that in the time his father is in the purifying fire of Gehenna the son is prepared to take from him some of the pangs he has to endure there. [142] Since the duties concerning the position of son to father embrace in the first instance instruction in the Torah and its careful learning, the relation of pupil to teacher can also be called that of a son (→ 345, 14 ff.) and can even be rated higher than that to one's natural father → V, 977, 18 ff. If a father renounces the honour due him, the renunciation is valid, but if a teacher does not claim the respect his pupil owes this is not possible, for the pupil has still to show the honour due, Qid., 32a. [143] Hence: "As pupils are called sons, the teacher is called father," SDt, 34 on 6:7. The one who instructs another in the Torah renders him the service a father must render his son and is thus as his father. [144] R. Resh Laqish (c. 250 A.D.) has said: "He who teaches the son of his neighbour the Torah, Scripture counts it as though he made him," bSanh., 99b. Whereas a father and mother have significance for and in this world, a teacher has significance in this world and the world to come, bSanh., 101a. For "his father has brought him into the world, but his teacher, who has taught him wisdom, brings him into the life of the future world," BM, 2, 11.

---

[135] Hahn, 293-5. The title is rare, cf. Georgi, *op. cit.*, 147, n. 4 Man of God is a more typical title, → 356, 4 ff. But cf. H. Braun, "Der Sinn d. nt.lichen Christologie," *Gesammelte Stud. z. NT u. seiner Umwelt* (1962), 255-9.
[136] On the duties of father to son cf. Moore, II, 127 f.
[137] Cf. Str.-B., IV, 468-470.
[138] Moore, II, 131-135.
[139] Str.-B., I, 708 f.
[140] *Ibid.*, 709.
[141] *Ibid.*, 708.
[142] Cf. E. Lohse, "Märtyrer u. Gottesknecht," FRL, 64² (1963), 99 f.
[143] Str.-B., I, 709.
[144] Cf. W. Grundmann, "Die νήπιοι in d. nt.lichen Paränese," NTSt, 5 (1958/59), 197 f.

As a son's duties are prescribed by the Torah, so all his way of life is fixed by it. In the Qumran and Rabb. lit. there are precise rules for each age. 1 QSa 1:6-19a says that in the end time the instruction of the young Israelite in the statutes of the covenant will take place from youth up. As בן עשרים שנה, "with 20 years," he will then join the roll. [145] The further stages are 25 years בן חמש ועשרים שנה 1 QSa 1:12 f., then 30 years בן שלושים שנה 1:13-18. The stages of human life are divided as follows in Ab., 5, 21; "With 5 years בן חמש שנים to Scripture, with 10 to the Mishnah, with 13 to (practice of) the commandment, with 15 to the Talmud, with 18 to the bridal chamber, with 20 to work, with 30 to maturity, with 40 to understanding, with 50 to counsel, with 60 to age, with 70 to old age, with 80 to hoary old age, with 90 to being bowed down, with 100 as dead and gone from the world." This list shows that in the years a son lives in his father's house his most important duty is study of the Scripture and its legal exposition. [146]

2 Son as a Term of Relationship.

As in the OT (→ 345, 25 ff.) so in the lit. of post-biblical Judaism בֵּן or בַּר is often used to denote the relationship which determines the nature of a man and the term which follows it often replaces an adj. The בְּנֵי מַעְרְבָא are for Babylonian Jews "the inhabitants of the west," i.e., Palestine (bNid., 51b) as distinct from the בְּנֵי מְדִינְחָא or בְּנֵי חַמְזְרָח, "the inhabitants of the east," i.e., Babylonia, [147] cf. also [148] בְּנֵי גוֹלָה "those who live in exile," AZ, 30b, בְּנֵי הָעִיר "the inhabitants of the city," Meg., 3, 1. Qid., 2, 3 distinguishes בֶּן־עִיר "inhabitant of a small town" from בֶּן כָּרָךְ "inhabitant of a city." Membership of a society is indicated as follows: בְּנֵי הַכְּנֶסֶת "members of a synagogal union," Bek., 5, 5, בְּנֵי חֲבוּרָה "members of a (Passover) society," T. Pes., 7, 15 (167), בְּנֵי הַחֻפָּה "sons of the wedding canopy" who are invited to the wedding, T. Ber., 2, 10 (4). The Israelites are בְּנֵי בְרִית "sons of the covenant (of circumcision)" and are distinguished as such from all Gentiles, BQ, 1, 2 f.; bBer., 16b. [149]

The following combinations express the fact that within the sphere in which he lives man is shaped by superior forces. All men are בְּנֵי הָעוֹלָם "sons of the world," but בַּר עָלְמָא דְאָתֵי or בֶּן־הָעוֹלָם הַבָּא "son of the world to come" is reserved for him who can be expected in the future world after the resurrection of the dead, bBer., 4a; bShab., 153a; bTaan., 22a. [150] The blessed are also בְּנֵי הָעֲלִיָה "sons of the balcony," bSukka, 45b, [151] but the damned בְּנֵי גֵיהִנּוֹם "sons of Gehinnom," bRH, 17a. Further examples which might be adduced are בַּר מִצְוָה "son of the commandment" under obligation to follow the commandments, bBM, 96a etc., בֶּן־הַרִיגָה "son of slaying," one who deserves death, bBer.,

---

[145] The age of 20 is more precisely described as follows: "And he shall not come near a woman to know her by intercourse until attaining twenty years, when he can know good and evil," 1 QSa 1:9-11. Cf. P. Borgen, "'At the Age of Twenty' in 1 QSa," Revue d. Qumran, 3 (1961/62), 267-277.

[146] Qoh. r., 1 on 1:2 does not ref. to the Law, however, but to the son's development into a man: "In the first year he is like a king's son resting in softness with all embracing and kissing him. In the second and third years he is like a swine because he puts his hands in the trough. In the tenth year he leaps like a kid. In the twentieth year he neighs like a horse, adorns himself and seeks a wife. If married he is like an ass (bearing a burden). If he begets children his face becomes as bold as a dog finding food and drink for them. When he finally grows old, he is like an ape." Cf. Borgen, op. cit., 269-275.

[147] Cf. the instances in Str.-B., I, 476.

[148] Ibid., I, 476-8 for material, cf. also the examples in Levy Wört., s.v.

[149] Str.-B., II, 627 f. for further examples.

[150] Ibid., I, 477, 830; IV, 837-9 for further examples, also Volz Esch., 341.

[151] Cf. Volz Esch., 341 and 418.

62b, בַּר מְהִילָא "son of circumcision," one who should be circumcised, bJeb., 71a. A man intensively occupied with the Torah is בֶּן־תּוֹרָה a "scribe," Tanch. בראשית, 2a. [152]

In the Dead Sea Scrolls sonship describes membership of the community of God's elect or of the race ruled by Belial. [153] On the one side are the בני אור "sons of light" 1 QS 1:9; 2:16; 3:13, 24 f.; 1 QM 1:3, 9, 11, 13, and on the other the בני חושך "sons of darkness" 1 QS 1:10; 1 QM 1:1, 7, 10, 16; 3:6, 9; 13:16; 14:17; 16:11. The former are also בני אמת "sons of truth" in 1 QS 4:5 f.; 11:16; 1 QM 17:8; 1 QH 6:29; 7:29 f.; 9:35; 10:27; 11:11; 16:18, or בני צדק "sons of righteousness" (→ n. 154) in 1 QS 3:20, 22, בני רצון "sons of the (divine) good-pleasure" 1 QH 4:32 f.; 11:9, or בני חסד "sons of grace" 1 QH 7:20. The latter are בני השחת "sons of the pit" Damasc. 6:15 (8:12); 13:14 (16:7), בני עול, or בני עולה "sons of iniquity" 1 QS 3:21; 1 QH 5:8 or בני אשמה "sons of guilt" 1 QH 5:7; 6:30; 7:11. A man's walk corresponds to the sphere in which he lives and by which he is shaped. The "sons of Belial" in 4 Q Florilegium 1:8; 1 QH 4:10 (?), cf. also Jub. 15:33 stand under the dominion of Belial, are led by the angel of darkness and wickedness, and walk in the ways of darkness, 1 QS 3:21. The "sons of his (God's) covenant" in 1 QM 17:8 are guided by the prince of light and walk in the ways of light, 1 QS 3:20. [154]

3. Israel and the Righteous as Sons of God. [155]

The OT statements about the divine sonship of the people of Israel (→ 351, 32 ff.) are taken up and developed by post-bibl. Judaism. Israel is called the people of the sons of God, the firstborn and only son of God, Sir. 36:11; 4 Esr. 6:58; Ps.-Philo Antiquit. Bibl. (→ n. 116), 32, 10. As God's sons Israelites are under God's protecting and guiding hand, Ass. Mos. 10:3. The promises of Ps. 2:7 and 2 S. 7:14 (→ 349, 9 ff.) are applied to the whole people in Jub. 1:24 f.: "They will do according to my commandments and I will be their father and they shall be my sons. And they shall all be called sons of the living God. And all angels and spirits will know and recognise them, that they are my sons and that I am their Father in constancy and righteousness and that I love them," cf. Jub. 2:20. [156] Test. Jud. 24:3 says of the future that God will pour out the spirit of grace, "and you shall be his sons in truth and walk in his commandments." [157]

The Rabb. lay impressive stress on the fact that Israel's divine sonship is grounded in the Law entrusted to it and will be seen in a walk according to the commandments of the Law. R. Aqiba derives from Dt. 14:1 the assertion: "Beloved are the Israelites; for they are called the sons of God. It was declared to them as a special love that they are called God's sons," Ab., 3, 14. Acc. to R. Jehuda b. Shalom (c. 370) God said to the

---

[152] Further examples in Str.-B., I, 477.
[153] Michel-Betz, 12-14.
[154] Cf. also "sons of the angels" in Eth. En. 69:4 f.; 71:1, cf. 10:7, 12, 15; 12:6; 14:6; "son of the serpent" in 69:12, "sons of man" in 12:1; 39:1; 64:2; 81:3; 93:11; Jub. 4:15-24 etc.; Ps.-Philo Antiquit. Bibl., 11, 1; Test. Jud. 24:1. While these expressions are to be taken lit., others simply denote relation, e.g., "sons of the earth" in Eth. En. 15:3; 86:6; 100:6; 102:3; 105:1, "sons of heaven" in 6:2; 13:8; 14:3; 101:1; cf. 39:1 f., "sons of Israel" in Ps.-Philo Antiquit. Bibl., 40, 8, "sons of righteousness" (→ line 8) in Eth. En. 93:2, "sons of the leader of the tribe" in Test. Zeb. 10:2, cf. L. 4:4, "son of the days" in Test. B. 1:6 [Schweizer].
[155] On the Rabb. cf. Moore, II, 203, 207; divine sonship was not lost through the fall [Schweizer].
[156] Cf. J. Jeremias, Abba (1966), 24, also Jub. 19:29, where, as in 2:20, God's election is the basis of Jacob's sonship, cf. also Test. Isaac 1:2, where Michael speaks to Isaac as the elect son, and Test. L. 4:2, where Levi's sonship rests on a resolve to be God's servant and minister. Acc. to Ps.-Philo Antiquit. Bibl., 33, 4 the Israelites are fig. "sons of Deborah" and acc. to Ass. Mos. 11:12 Moses is to nourish Israel "as a father his only son." On adoption cf. Ps.-Philo Antiquit. Bibl., 9, 16; 53, 3, also Test. Jos. 3:7 f.; Sib., 3, 254 [Schweizer].
[157] For further examples from the apcr. and pseudepigr. cf. Volz Esch., 99.

Israelites: "You have the wish to be singled out, that you are my sons? Busy yourselves with the Torah and observance of the commandments, so all will see that you are my sons," Dt. r., 7 on 29:1.[158] The same thought underlies the statement: "When the Israelites do God's will they are called sons; when they do not do God's will they are not called sons," jQid., 1, 8 (61c, 34 f.).[159] When God calls the Israelites His sons this expresses His election which was effected by the giving of the Law at Sinai and to which Israel should be obedient.[160] Midr. Ps., 2, 9 on 2:7 can thus ref. esp. to the fact that all parts of Scripture contain the same witness and speak of the divine sonship of the people, Ex. 4:22 in the Torah, Is. 52:13; 42:1 in the prophets, and Ps. 110:1; 2:7 in the hagiographa.[161]

The righteous in Israel are esp. God's sons → 354, 30 ff.[162] In Sir. 4:10 the admonition to treat orphans as a father and widows as one who stands in the place of a husband is linked to the promise: "Then God will call thee son and be gracious to thee and save thee from the pit."[163] God protects the righteous and will thus take vengeance on those who mistreat His sons and elect, Eth. En. 62:11.

4. The Messiah as Son of God.

The OT promises in which the royal anointed one is called God's son were not forgotten in post-biblical Judaism but were used with caution and not adduced without explanation. Both in the divine saying in Ps. 2:7 (→ 350, 35 ff.), which addresses the ruler as my son, and also in the promise of 2 S. 7:14 (→ 349, 17 ff.) to the house of David, "son of God" entails the acceptance of the ruler by God and his institution into the office of the anointed one which he is to discharge by divine authority.[164] Although sonship was not construed as physical descent in these OT sayings but rather as expressing the ruler's validation by God (→ 350, 30 ff.), Israel took good care lest the designation son of God might be falsely linked to the physical divine sonship which was so widely spoken of in the ancient Orient. It thus employed "son of God" only when quoting the Messianic promises and elsewhere avoided this term for the Messiah.[165]

---

158 Cf. Str.-B., I, 220.
159 *Loc. cit.*
160 Str.-B., I, 17-19.
161 *Ibid.*, III, 18 f. and Lövestam, 15-23.
162 Note that the "sons of God" of Gn. 6:2 are usually taken to be angels in Judaism, Ps.-Philo Antiquit. Bibl., 3, 1; cf. Eth. En. 106:5, and apart from the OT quotation there is no ref. to divine sonship in this connection, cf. Str.-B., III, 780-783. Angels are "sons of heaven" in Eth. En. 6:2 etc. (→ n. 154), also בני שמים in the Qumran texts: 1 QS 4:22; 11:8; 1 QH 3:22; 1 QH f 2:10. One also finds in the Rabb. another exposition acc. to which these sons are the great of the earth, Tg. O. on Gn. 6:2, 4; Tg. J. I on Gn. 6:2, 4; further examples in Str.-B., III, 783.
163 So acc. to the Hbr.; in Gk.: καὶ ἔσῃ ὡς υἱὸς ὑψίστου.
164 Hahn, 284 pts. out that in the OT tradition the title "son of God" is part of the Jerusalem style of the Davidic dynasty. Hence he rightly rejects other conjectured derivations, as against S. Mowinckel, *He that Cometh*[2] (1959), 368 f., who pts. to the son of man tradition, and G. Friedrich, "Beobachtungen z. messian. Hohenpriestererwartung in d. Synoptikern," ZThK, 53 (1956), 279 f., who weighs the possibility that the expected high-priest of the end-time might be called the son of God in Judaism. Grundmann Sohn Gottes, 113-133 suggests that "only in Essene priestly circles is there ref. to the sonship of the Messian. high-priest and this in a way related to the OT, i.e., in an adoptionist (→ 350, 30 ff.) sense," 117. On the priest as son of God on Syr. inscr. cf. J. R. Harris, "On the Name 'Son of God' in Northern Syria," ZNW, 15 (1914), 108-113 [Schweizer].
165 Dalman WJ, I, 223; W. G. Kümmel, "Gleichnis v. den bösen Weingärtnern," *Heilsgeschehen u. Gesch.* (1965), 215 f.; Jeremias Gl.[7], 71, n. 1; E. Schweizer, "Erniedrigung u. Erhöhung bei Jesus u. seinen Nachfolgern," AbhThANT, 28[2] (1962), 64, n. 265; van Iersel, 4, n. 7; also "Fils de David et Fils de Dieu," *Recherches Bibl.*, 6 (1962), 113-132.

Thus far there is no clear instance to support the view that in pre-Christian times Judaism used the title "son of God" for the Messiah. The Messiah is "my son" in Eth. En. 105:2, but this v. was added later, since it is not in Gr. En. [166] and has thus to be disregarded. The Lat. of 4 Esr. 7:28; 13:32, 37, 52; 14:9 uses *filius meus* for the Messiah, but the Gk. original is undoubtedly παῖς corresponding to Hbr. עַבְדִּי. [167] Thus all the apoc. ref. which might seem to testify to the Messianic title "Son of God" [168] fall to the ground. [169]

The Dead Sea Scrolls take up the OT sayings Ps. 2:7; 2 S. 7:14 and adduce them in connection with the Messianic expectation of the community. [170] Though the Messianic title "Son of God" is not expressly used here either, these sayings merit special notice. 1 QSa 2:11 f. gives rules for the "order (of seating) of worthy men who are (invited) to the gathering for the council of the community" אם יו[ל]י[ד [אל[ת]א אל[ת] המשיח אתם. [171] The lacunae cannot be filled with any certainty. If one reads יו[ל]יד [172] this does not have to be an allusion to Ps. 2:7, [173] but one might naturally suppose that the ref. is to God as the One who brings to pass the birth of the Messiah, cf. Is. 66:9. [174] One should then transl.: "When God causes the Messiah to be born among them." [175] In no case is one to see here a ref. to the physical divine sonship of the Messiah, nor should it be overlooked that the title "Son of God" is not in the MS and cannot be supplied. Yet the fr. of an eschatological Midrash found in Cave 4 shows that Ps. 2 was carefully read and expounded at Qumran. [176] Unfortunately the exposition of Ps. 2 breaks off after the introductory words following quotation of 2:1-2. But the Midrash on 2 S. 7:10-14 is contained in the preceding section. [177] The quotation is given up to 14a: "I will be his father, and he shall be my son." The exposition is then added: "This is the shoot of David who will come with the searcher of the law, who [. . .] in Zi[on at the en]d of

---

[166] Cf. C. Bonner, *The Last Chapters of Enoch in Greek* (1937), *ad loc.*

[167] Cf. the analysis of the tradition in → V, 681, n. 196, also Hahn, 285 and J. Bloch, "Some Christological Interpolations in the Ezra-Apocalypse," HThR, 51 (1958), 87-94, who thinks there might well be Chr. interpolations in 4 Esr.

[168] The Messianic Son of God passage Test. L. 18:6-8 cf. Jud. 24:1, 5 was probably influenced by the Chr. baptism story (→ 367, 23 ff.), cf. J. Gnilka, "Der Hymnus des Zacharias," BZ, NF, 6 (1962), 237, though cf., e.g., R. Meyer, *Der Prophet aus Galiläa* (1940), 67 f., cf. 149, n. 123 [Schweizer].

[169] Cf. E. Sjöberg, *Der verborgene Menschensohn in den Ev.* (1955), 47, n. 1; H. E. Tödt, *Der Menschensohn in d. synopt. Überlieferung²* (1963), 21, n. 5.

[170] Cf. esp. A. S. van der Woude, *Die messian. Vorstellungen der Gemeinde v. Qumran* (1957), 172-4 and *passim,* also K. G. Kuhn, "Die beiden Messiasse Aarons u. Israels," NTSt, 1 (1954/55), 168-179; K. Schubert, "Die Messiaslehre in d. Texten v. Chirbet Qumran," BZ, NF, 1 (1957), 177-197; M. Black, "Messianic Doctrine in the Qumran Scrolls," TU, 63 (1957), 441-459.

[171] For the text and proposals to fill the lacunae DJD, I, 110, but cf. M. Smith, "'God's Begetting the Messiah' in 1 QSa," NTSt, 5 (1958/9), 218-224; Y. Yadin, "A Crucial Passage in the Dead Sea Scrolls," JBL, 78 (1959), 238-241.

[172] One cannot accept the proposed יוליך in DJD, I, 117 ("when God ushers in") since ר can be read distinctly as the last letter.

[173] So R. Gordis, "The 'Begotten' Messiah in the Dead Sea Scrolls," VT, 7 (1957), 191-4; Michel-Betz, 11 f.

[174] Cf. M. Burrows, *More Light on the Dead Sea Scrolls* (1958), 300.

[175] If one wants to cling to "beget," one must take it along the lines of Ps. 2:7 as acceptance as a son → 360, 18 ff.

[176] Cf. J. M. Allegro, "Further Messianic Ref. in Qumran Lit.," JBL, 75 (1956), 176 f.; also "Fragments of a Qumran Scroll of Eschatological Midrašim," JBL, 77 (1958), 350-354.

[177] The OT text is quoted with some changes, Michel-Betz, 10. There is also a ref. to 2 S. 7:13, 16 in 4 Q Bt col. 4, 6-8. Cf. M. Baillet, "Un recueil liturgique de Qumran, Grotte 4: 'Les paroles des luminaires,'" Rev. Bibl., 68 (1961), 195-250. The decisive v. (2 S. 7:14) in the present context, however, is not quoted; Schweizer, 188.

the days, as it is written: And I will raise up the ruined booth of David (Am. 9:11). [178] This is the ruine[d] booth of David [wh]ich will stand to save Israel," 4 Q Florilegium 1:11-13. The OT saying acc. to which God will be the ruler's father and the ruler His son is adduced, but it is worth noting that no precise interpretation is given. Thus the title "Son of God" is not used in the Dead Sea Scrolls either except in OT quotations. [179] To be sure, the OT presuppositions for the use of the Messianic complex of 2 S. 7 are retained. [180] But Judaism in pre-Chr. times obviously avoided employing the title "Son of God" in order to ward off misunderstanding of the term in the non-Jewish world. [181]

This Jewish reservation naturally became all the stronger when Christians began to apply the title "Son of God" to Jesus of Nazareth. In Rabb. lit. there is only isolated ref. to Ps. 2:7 and the Messiah is never called the Son of God apart from the OT text. [182] The oldest instance of this is a Baraitha from bSukka, 52a which relates Ps. 2:7 to the Messiah ben David. [183] The other passages calling for consideration all come only from the age of the Amoraeans. Thus Midr. Ps., 2, 9 on 2:7 quotes sayings of R. Judan (c. 350) and R. Huna (c. 350) relating Ps. 2:7 to the Messianic king. [184] In the Tg. on Ps. 80:16 the וְעַל־בֶּן of the Hbr. is explained in terms of the Messianic king. [185] These few ref. to the Ps. stand in contrast with the many polemical sayings of the Rabb. which ref. to the uniqueness of God and plainly reject the idea He could have a son. [186] Since the Synagogue had to react sharply to the Chr. doctrine of the divine sonship of Jesus Christ, a Messianic interpretation of 2 S. 7:14 was no longer espoused [187] and a new sense was given to the words of Ps. 2 by reinterpretation. [188] The sayings about divine sonship are attenuated to mere comparisons so that Tg. Ps. 2 says: "Thou art dear to me as a son to his father, innocent as if I had this day created thee." [189] In this way Rabb. Judaism tried to eliminate the title "Son of God" from Messianic expectation, to expound fig. the OT passages in which the anointed one is called God's son, and thus to reduce considerably the importance of this designation. [190]

Lohse

---

[178] The quotation from Am. 9:11 is also found in Damasc. 7:16 (9:6).

[179] One may omit 1 QH 3:6-18 here, since the image of the pregnant woman who gives birth is not meant Messianically but expresses the sufferings of prayer. Cf. J. Maier, *Die Texte vom Toten Meer*, II (1960), 72 f.

[180] Hahn, 287 rightly states "that the motif of divine sonship in its developed form, in the sense of institution to office and the holding of dominion, belongs materially to the sphere of later Palestinian Judaism." But his conclusion goes beyond what the sources actually warrant: "Most probably even the titular use of 'Son of the Highly Praised' etc. was common already in the pre-Chr. tradition."

[181] The sources demand caution. Cf. Volz Esch., 174: "We must be cautious in claiming that the expression 'Son of God' for the Messiah was not used at all, or was not possible, in Jewish writings." Cf. also Bieneck, 25; Cullmann, 280 f.; Bultmann Theol., 52 f.; Löve-stam, 90.

[182] Str.-B., III, 19 f.

[183] *Ibid.*, 19; Lövestam, 19 f. M. Ex., 7 on 15:9 has "son of the king" in a comparison, but does not call the Messiah "Son of God," cf. Str.-B., III, 676 f. For the same comparison v. Yalqut Shim'oni, 2, 620 on Ps. 2:2, cf. Str.-B., III, 19.

[184] Cf. Str.-B., III, 19.

[185] *Loc. cit.*

[186] Str.-B., III, 20-22.

[187] *Ibid.*, 15 f., 677; Michel-Betz, 8; Lövestam, 89.

[188] On the basis of Ps. 89:27 the Messiah can be called "the firstborn," Ex. r. 19 on 13:2 (cf. Str.-B., III, 258), also in the explanation of Ps. 2 by Rashi possibly on the basis of older traditions (Str.-B., III, 673 f.); Tg. Ps. 89:27 reads: "I will also make him the firstborn among the kings of the house of Judah, the most high among the kings of the earth."

[189] Cf. Str.-B., III, 19 f.; Michel-Betz, 7.

[190] Lövestam, 20 f.

D. New Testament.

I. υἱός without Reference to God.

1. Jesus as Son of Mary and Joseph.

Jesus is presented as the son of the Virgin Mary (→ 376, 12 ff.; V, 834, 16 ff.) in Mt. 1:21-25; [191] Lk. 1:31; [192] 2:7 (→ VI, 876, 6 ff.). [193] The apparent contradiction to the genealogies (Mt. 1:16; Lk. 3:23) [194] is not felt so keenly because legal acknowledgment counts for more than biological descent. If in Mk. 6:3 [195] (but not the par.) the inhabitants of Nazareth call Him the son of Mary and list His brothers by name, this brings out the very natural character of the description; Joseph had obviously died early. [196] The par. (Mt. 13:55; Lk. 4:22; cf. Jn. 6:42) which call Jesus the son of Joseph characterise the blindness of men toward Him. [197] This is not because they fail to perceive the virgin birth but because they think they have said all there is to be said, whereas they have not even touched as yet on the true mystery of the origin of Jesus → VII, 138, 18 ff.

Whether Rev. 12:5 ref. to the birth in Bethlehem [198] or to the eschatological birth of the Christ of the *parousia* [199] is debatable. At any rate the Messiah is seen as the son of the Jewish or Chr. community. [200] A ref. to Mary seems to be ruled out by 12:17 and the heavenly character of the woman in 12:1 → II, 323, n. 18. [201]

---

[191] Joseph is more important here than in Lk. even though he is only the guardian, cf. G. Strecker, *Der Weg d. Gerechtigkeit* (1962), 53 f.; K. Stendahl, "Quis et unde? An Analysis of Mt. 1-2," *Festschr. J. Jeremias*² (1964), 95. Above all the title Immanuel is more important for Mt. (→ VII, 776, 10 ff.) than the birth (of which no account is given), *ibid.*, 103 → 380, 10 ff.

[192] The verse is almost a lit. quotation from Is. 7:14 LXX.

[193] The meaning of this v. depends on whether with it sysone reads γυναικί in v. 5 (so H. Vogels, "Zur Textgeschichte v. Lk. 1:34 ff.," ZNW, 43 [1950/51], 257-9) or ἐμνηστευμένῃ αὐτῷ (γυναικί).

[194] There is no art. only with Joseph, cf. N. Geldenhuys, *Comm. on the Gospel of Lk.* (1950), *ad loc.*, who puts ὤν ... 'Ιωσήφ in a parenthesis so as to make Eli the father of Mary.

[195] Kl. Mk., *ad loc.*; V. Taylor, *The Gospel acc. to St. Mark* (1952), *ad loc.* accept the vl. of p⁴⁵.

[196] E. P. Gould, *A Crit. and Exeget. Comm. on the Gospel acc. to St. Mark*, ICC (1896), *ad loc.*; B. H. Branscomb, *The Gospel of Mark* (1937), *ad loc.* E. B. Redlich, *St. Mark's Gospel* (1948), *ad loc.* sees here a lack of respect, cf. C. E. B. Cranfield, *The Gospel acc. to St. Mark* (1959), *ad loc.*

[197] In Jn. 1:45, however, "son of Joseph" is used innocuously like "of Nazareth," and only the latter causes offence.

[198] So most comm.

[199] Loh. Apk. Exc. on 12:18.

[200] Cf. Is. 66:6-9. Or son of wisdom, cf. Loh. Apk. on 12:13-18? Or of the Holy Spirit (equated with the community), cf. S. Pétrement, "Une suggestion de Simone Weil à propos d'Apoc. XII," NTSt, 11 (1964/65), 291-296? E. Lohse opts rightly for the Jewish community, *Die Offenbarung d. Joh.* (1966), *ad loc.*

[201] Cf. P. Prigent, *Apk. 12* (1959), 141-4; A. Feuillet, "Le Messie et sa mère d'après le chapître XII de l'Apoc.," *Rev. Bibl.*, 66 (1959), 55-86; J. Michl, "Die Deutung d. apok. Frau in der Gegenwart," BZ, NF, 3 (1959), 301-310; A. T. Kassing, "Das Weib, das den Mann gebar (Apk. 12:13)," *Benediktinische Monatsschr.*, 34 (1958), 427-433; O. Betz, "Das Volk seiner Kraft," NTSt, 5 (1958/59), 67-75; J. Kosnetter, "Die Sonnenfrau (Apk. 12:1-17) in d. neueren Exegese," *Festschr. T. Innitzer* (1952), 93-108; J. E. Bruns, "The Contrasted Women of Apoc. 12 and 17," *The Catholic Bibl. Quarterly*, 26 (1964), 459.

2. Father and Son as an Illustration of God's Care for Believers.

On Mt. 7:9 and par. → V, 992, 2 ff., on Lk. 15:11-32 → 365, 2 ff.; V, 983, 28 ff.; 994, 7 ff.,[202] on Hb. 12:5-8 → V, 621, 23 ff.; 1014, 5 ff. In the figurative saying Mt. 17:25 f. (→ II, 500, 35 ff.) believers are "sons of the king" (→ 341, 17 ff.)[203] and are free in contrast to subjects. The original story is trying to emphasise this,[204] not with reference to the Law but in respect of the temple and sacrificial cultus. Mt., however, seems to be stressing continuation in the synagogal fellowship which is possible in this freedom and which the Jewish mission always makes possible.[205]

3. The Son as the Supreme Good.

The horror of the eschatological tribulation is marked by the fact that fathers rise up against sons and sons against fathers, Lk. 12:53; → V, 983, 10 ff.[206] The seriousness of discipleship is proved by not loving even sons and daughters more than Jesus, Mt. 10:37 → IV, 690, 28 ff.; V, 982, 17 ff. On the other hand, the mercy of Jesus may be seen in His raising to life again of the widow's only son, Lk. 7:12.[207] The story is put in Lk. because of 7:22.[208] In Lk. 14:5 the υἱός who has fallen into a well[209] comes before the ox to strengthen the urgency of rescue even on the Sabbath, → V, 287, 16 ff.; VII, 24, 17 ff.[210]

4. υἱός in the Transferred Sense (Jn. 19:26).

In Jn. 19:26 the word of power from the cross makes the favourite disciple the son of Mary → IV, 643, 20 ff.[211]

---

[202] E. Fuchs, Zur Frage nach d. historischen Jesus (1960), 140 f., 153-5, 369-371 emphasises that the parable cannot be detached from what takes place in Jesus.

[203] It is open to question whether the physical sons of kings or members of their nations as distinct from subjugated nations are in view, cf. Kl. Mt., ad loc.

[204] Perhaps pre-Matthean oral tradition, cf. Strecker, op. cit., 200 f.

[205] R. Hummel, Die Auseinandersetzung zwischen Kirche u. Judt. im Mt. (1963), 103-106.

[206] Only in Lk. does the revolt of the younger generation against the older become reciprocal, cf. J. M. Creed, The Gospel acc. to St. Luke (1950), ad loc.

[207] In the par. raising of a girl by Apollonius of Tyana (cf. Kl. Lk., ad loc.) it is the bride/bridegroom relation that stresses the special severity of fate.

[208] A symbolical ref. to Mary and Jesus (cf. A. R. C. Leaney, A Comm. on the Gospel acc. to St. Luke [1958], ad loc.) is thus improbable; cf. rather 3 Βασ. 17:23, cf. v. Rad, op. cit. (→ n. 95), 379.

[209] The best witnesses read ὄνος, but this is the easier reading and might have crept in from 13:15, cf. A. Plummer, A Crit. and Exeg. Comm. on the Gospel acc. to St. Luke⁵ (1922), ad loc. The meaning is: "a child or even just an ox"; cf. also Kl. Lk., ad loc. The adduced par. BQ, 5, 6 absolves the owner of the well from responsibility in the case of the ox but not of the person, cf. Creed, op. cit. (→ n. 206), ad loc. M. Black, An Aramaic Approach to the Gospels and Acts² (1954), 126 suggests a play on words: son-ox-pit or ox-ass-pit.

[210] Mt. 12:11 f. gets the same effect by ref. to the only sheep of a poor man, with the conclusion: "of how much greater value is a man"; Lk. 13:15 explains that an ox or an ass has to drink even on the Sabbath.

[211] Did the story arise out of confusion with the Mary mentioned in Ac. 12:12, cf. Wellh. J., ad loc.? Does it represent the relation of Jewish and Gentile Christianity, Bultmann J., ad loc.? Is it a symbolic presentation of Mk. 10:30, C. K. Barrett, The Gospel acc. to St. John (1955), ad loc.? Or were John Mark and his mother Mary Magdalene the two at the foot of the cross, W. Hartke, Vier urchr. Parteien u. ihre Vereinigung zur apostol. Kirche, II (1961), 755-760 [Bertram]? Could the readers have been aware of all this? Might it not be that behind the story there simply stands the historical tradition that a disciple (John the son of Zebedee?) to whom the Fourth Gospel rightly or wrongly traces back its tradition took special care of Jesus' mother after His death?

5. Sons of Abraham and Israel.

Lk. 15:21, 24 (→ 364, 2 f.) show that one can be a son biologically without truly being a son. Only the father's word of forgiveness makes the son a true son and hence also a brother of the elder son, v. 32. [212] This is central in the question of descent from Abraham. In Lk. 19:9 this denotes membership of the people of Israel. [213] This alone is the basis of the gift of Jesus and salvation, not the zeal of Zacchaeus nor his readiness to restore ill-gotten gains → 104, 23 ff. But Gl. 3:7 (→ I, 9, 12 ff.; III, 784, 21 ff.; V, 1005, 5 ff.) and 4:22-30 (→ VI, 429, 4 ff.; VII, 131, 13 ff.; 285, 19 ff.) emphasise that only God's election determines who is a descendant of Abraham → VII, 545, 29 ff. Only Mt. 27:9 (quotation); Lk. 1:16 (→ III, 385, 7 ff.); 2 C. 3:7, 13 (→ III, 386, 33 ff.) refer to sons of Israel, denoting in each case pre-Christian Israel.

6. υἱός as a Term for Student (→ 345, 14 ff.). [214]

In Mt. 12:27 and par. Jesus calls the students of the Pharisees [215] who perform exorcisms "sons of the Pharisees." In Ac. 23:6 Paul describes himself as υἱὸς Φαρισαίων, [216] which hardly refers to his ancestors but rather to his teachers. The close relation of Mark to the apostle is expressed by υἱός in 1 Pt. 5:13 → V, 1005, 22 ff. [217]

7. υἱός as a Term of Relationship.

υἱός is also used in the NT along the lines of → 346, 30 ff.; 358, 11 f., mostly with a positive or negative evaluation: "sons of royal dominion" in Mt. 8:12; 13:38, [218] "of peace" in Lk. 10:6, "light" in Lk. 16:8; Jn. 12:36; 1 Th. 5:5 (→ φῶς), [219] "the resurrection" in Lk. 20:36 (→ 390, 8 ff.), "this aeon" in Lk. 16:8; 20:34, [220] "the wicked one" in Mt. 13:38, "the devil" in Ac. 13:10, [221] "Gehenna" in Mt. 23:15 → 358, 31 f., "disobedience" in Eph. 2:2; 5:6, "perdition" in Jn. 17:12; 2 Th. 2:3. The expressions "sons of the bride-chamber" in Mk. 2:19 [222] and "of thunder" in Mk. 3:17 are neutral.

---

[212] Cf. "this thy son" instead of "my brother" in v. 30 (32).

[213] The Church is not called Israel in Lk., cf. E. Schweizer, *Gemeinde u. Gemeindeordnung im NT²* (1962), § 5b.

[214] On the Jewish background cf. Grundmann, *op. cit.* (→ n. 144), 197-9.

[215] The relation to Mt. 12:24 establishes this sense, cf. Schl. Mt. on 12:27; M. J. Lagrange, *L'év. selon S. Luc.⁸* (1948); F. C. Grant, *The Gospel of Matthew* (1955); Leaney, *ad loc.* But Kl. Mt. and A. H. McNeile, *The Gospel acc. to St. Matthew* (1915), *ad loc.* see a more gen. ref. to the Israelites.

[216] The sing. is obviously a correction.

[217] Cf. Gl. 4:19; on this E. Güttgemanns, "Der leidende Apostel u. sein Herr," FRL, 90 (1966), 185-194; → ὠδίνω.

[218] In the past all Israelites, in the future only the disciples of Jesus, cf. Hummel, *op. cit.* (→ n. 205), 157. Kruijf, 161-5 is naturally right when he says that faith in the Son makes them sons of the βασιλεία, but the use of υἱοί is quite different from that of υἱὸς (θεοῦ).

[219] The addition "and the day" is original (B. Rigaux, *S. Paul, Les épîtres aux Thess.* [1956], *ad loc.*) and relates to the day of the *parousia*, v. 4 (→ II, 952, 16 ff.). Its reality confers vigilance. On Eph. 5:8 → φῶς.

[220] In the Rabb. only → 358, 27. Lk. 16:8 is esp. noteworthy here, for it has "sons of the light" alongside "sons of this aeon" → 359, 4 ff., cf. also Mt. 13:38 and Bultmann Trad., 190, n. 1.

[221] Is this meant as an antithesis to "son of Jesus," 13:6? Cf. Bau. Ag., C. S. C. Williams, *A Comm. on the Acts of the Apostles* (1957), *ad loc.*

[222] Rabb. par. in Schl. Mt. on 9:15; stylistically similar 1 Macc. 4:2.

II. Jesus as Son of God in the Tradition of the Community Prior
to the Writing of the New Testament.

1. Jesus.

Jesus Himself hardly ever used "Son of God." [223] Apart from instances in which
others applied the title to him, it occurs in the Synoptics only in the plur. → 389,
24 ff. This is not affected by an assertion which might go back to a special tradition,
namely, that of the mockers at the foot of the cross that Jesus styled Himself the
Son of God, Mt. 27:43 → 378, 1 ff. There remains only the contested point whether
Jesus used the absolute ὁ υἱός, Mk. 13:32; Mt. 11:27 and par. → 372, 6 ff.; 372, 22 ff.
As with all developed titles (→ υἱὸς τοῦ ἀνθρώπου) the originality of Jesus is
that while not adopting current categories in self-designation He actually expressed
and worked out more by His life and teaching than the titles themselves could ever
say. [224]

Apart from the version in Mt. 6:9 of what seems to be the original πάτερ of Lk. 11:2
"our Father" (→ V, 980, 17 ff.; 981, 9 ff.) is never used with ref. to God in the Gospels,
but always "my Father" and "your Father" → V, 987, 15 ff. Hence Jesus does not include
Himself among others in an "our Father." [225] He stands in a special if not precisely defined
relation to the Father, cf. ἀββά, for which there is no parallel → V, 984, 18 ff. [226] It is
most unlikely that this surprising linguistic innovation should be the work of the community → 391, 20 f. [227]

2. The Davidic Son of God.

a. The Regency of the Exalted (R. 1:3 f.).

The community from which R. 1:3 f. comes (→ V, 453, 15 ff.; VI, 416, 32 ff.;
VII, 126, 22 ff.) confesses Jesus as the son of David in the sense of 2 S. 7:12 ff. →
349, 17 ff.; 359, 22 ff.; 360, 16 ff. → υἱὸς Δαυίδ. [228] But this denotes only His work in
the earthly sphere. The eternal dominion promised to the son of David as Son of
God has been achieved, however, from Easter onwards. From His exaltation into
the realm of the Spirit He is the promised Son of God who in power (ψ 88:11, 18 and
already ψ 109:2 f.) exercises His royal dominion over the community as His people

---

[223] Cf. van Iersel, 3-26 and Hahn, 280 f. for an account of the investigation. As against
W. Lütgert, Gottes Sohn u. Gottes Geist (1905), 2 f. it is to be stressed that the theological
correctness of the designation does not depend on the usage of Jesus.

[224] Cf. already Dalman WJ, I, 230.

[225] van Iersel, 93-104, 113-116; W. Marchel, "Abba, Père. La prière du Christ et des
chrétiens," Analecta Bibl., 19 (1963), 154 f.

[226] Cf. Jeremias, op. cit. (→ n. 156), 56-67; also "Vatername Gottes" in RGG³, VI,
1234 f.; Marchel, op. cit., 103-176, who deduces from this "communauté de nature" with the
Father, 154, 169 f.

[227] Hahn, 320, though he thinks Jesus cries "Father" as any man may, so that restriction
to a special filial relation on the part of Jesus is secondary, 327 f. But cf. E. Hübner, "Credo
in Deum patrem," Ev. Theol., 23 (1963), 662, acc. to whom we become sons only after the
crucifixion, Mk. 14:36.

[228] So also Michel-Betz, 6; Fuller, 167. van Iersel, 73 recalls that the key words σπέρμα,
υἱός, ἀνάστασις also occur in 2 S. 7:12-14. On the Davidic character of "Son of God" in
R. 1:4 and the distinction from v. 3a (→ 384, 23 ff.) cf. K. W. Wegenast, "Das Verständnis d.
Tradition bei Pls. u. in d. Deuteropaulinen," Wissenschaftl. Monographien z. AT u. NT, 8
(1962), 70-75.

→ 381, 20 ff. In a distinctive way, then, the two titles which were identical in the OT (→ 349, 17 ff.), i.e., "son of David" and "Son of God," now succeed one another as two stages, [229] so that both continuity and also reinterpretation may be discerned. The royal rule of Jesus is now completely non-political and it is also given universal extension. Adoption Christology (→ 356, 1 f.; n. 156) is not quite the right term for it, since this implies antithesis to another concept and no such antithesis is present → 368, 12 ff. [230] Nevertheless it is true that the title "Son of God" primarily denotes a function of Jesus, for v. 4 simply states that at Easter Jesus took up His office as Messianic King over the community → 384, 23 ff.

b. Resurrection as Son of God (Ac. 13:33; 2:30 f.).

In Ac. 13:33 the divine sonship of Jesus begins at Easter. The "to-day" of institution as Son of God in Ps. 2:7 (→ 350, 35 ff.; I, 670, 20 ff.) is given this reference. [231] We thus have the same functional Christology as in R. 1:4. [232] The slogan ἀναστήσω helped to associate the Davidic prophecy and the resurrection of Jesus as suggested in R. 1:4 and to interpret Ps. 2:7 accordingly. [233] The focus of theological concern is the resurrection itself. This is not just the beginning of the regency of the Son of God which is important only for the community, though the exaltation motif (2:33, cf. 5:31) is still there. But as in Ps. 16:7-11 it is understood as the victory over death. If R. 1:3 stresses the link with salvation history, here again the central reference is not to a timeless dominion of the Exalted but to God's intervention in the unique act of the resurrection and its significance for the resurrection of believers.

c. The Baptism of Jesus (Mk. 1:11). [234]

In Mk. 1:11 the voice of God says: σὺ εἶ ὁ υἱός μου ὁ ἀγαπητός, [235] ἐν σοὶ εὐδόκησα → 354, 13 ff., 24 f.; II, 740, n. 7; IV, 739, 3 ff.; V, 530, 18 ff. The opening

---

[229] That R. 1:4 really denotes institution and not just the revelation of His divine sonship is shown by Boismard, 5, cf. ὁρίζω in Ac. 10:42; 17:31. Kruijf, 37 f. also stresses the functional character of the divine sonship in these statements.

[230] Cf. also van Iersel, 85 f.

[231] Cf. in support Schweizer, 186; Haench. Ag., ad loc.; Dupont, 530; Lövestam, 8-10, 37-48. But for another view cf. M. Rese, At.liche Motive in d. Christologie d. Lk., Diss. Bonn (1965), 114-123.

[232] Since Lk. no longer shares this Christology, he no longer uses the quotation, cf. U. Wilckens, Die Missionsreden d. Ag. (1961), 177 f. This suggests a pre-Lucan combination of texts in Ac. 13:33-35 (36), though Rese, op. cit., 132-136 questions this. It is perhaps typically Lucan that Paul, who is not fully accredited as a witness of the resurrection, should use proof from Scripture, cf. Rese, 131 f.

[233] Is. 55:3 belongs here and is thus quoted in v. 34, Schweizer, 187-9. Cf. the חַסְדֵי דָוִד and Ps. 16:10 which speaks of חֲסִידֶךָ = τὸν ὅσιόν σου and is a distinct resurrection text in v. 35; Lövestam, 53-55 and the review by T. Holz, ThLZ, 88 (1963), 203, also J. W. Doeve, Jewish Hermeneutics in the Synoptic Gospels and Acts (1953), 173; J. Dupont, "ΤΑ ΟΣΙΑ ΔΑΥΙΔ ΤΑ ΠΙΣΤΑ (Ag. 13:34 = Js. 55:3)," Rev. Bibl., 68 (1961), 91-114; Rese, op. cit., 126-128, cf. 123 f., 129-136. Ac. 13:36 ref. back to 2 S. 7:12. Remission of sins is proclaimed in v. 38 — already linked with the David tradition in Sir. 47:11, Schweizer, 190; cf. the key words εἰς αἰῶνα, διαθήκη, θρόνος in 2 S. 7:13, 16; 23:5; Ps. 89:3 f., 28 f., 36, 39, for remission of sins 2 S. 7:12 f. and Ps. 16:10 in Ac. 2:30 f. (remission v. 38); van Iersel, 78-83.

[234] Hahn, 340-6.

[235] G. D. Kilpatrick, "The Order of Some Noun and Adjective Phrases in the NT," Nov. Test., 5 (1962), 112 f. shows that this is to be taken as an adj., not a second title.

of heaven, the coming of the Spirit, and the sounding of the voice are eschatological events [236] so that we are to think of the king of the last time rather than an original παῖς [237] → V, 701, 9 ff.; [238] otherwise one would also expect that the title would have played a greater role in the NT. Mt. 4:3 (Q) also presupposes υἱός → n. 314. Mt. 12:18 might just as well be influenced by Mk. 1:11 as *vice versa*. [239] One is thus to view the statement along the lines of the expectation of the Davidic Son of God of Ps. 2:7, the more so as a Targum on Ps. 2:7 offers חביב = ἀγαπητός. [240] The usual explanation is a combination of quotations with Is. 42:1. As 4 Q Florilegium and the NT show, these were commonly followed. [241] But this is certainly no combination, since εὐδοκεῖν ἐν is not found in Is. 42:1 LXX, εὐδοκέω is an expression for the divine election (→ II, 740, 13 ff.) [242] and finds its best parallel in David's song in 2 Βασ. 22:20. What is said about adoption → 367, 5 ff. applies here too, but now institution into the office of the eschatological king is put already at baptism and the earthly work of Jesus is understood as the regency promised to the house of David and executed by God's commission. Thus far one cannot say for certain by what key image its content is determined → 377, 18 ff.; 378, 20 ff.; 380, 4 ff.; 381, 11 ff. [243]

---

[236] The opening of heaven in Is. 63:19 goes with the gift of the Spirit, v. 14: κατέβη πνεῦμα παρὰ κυρίου and v. 11: θεὶς ἐν αὐτοῖς (HT αὐτῷ) τὸ πνεῦμα τὸ ἅγιον. Cf. I. Buse, "The Markan Account of the Baptism of Jesus and Is. 63," JThSt, NS, (1956), 74 f.; cf. also Is. 63:11 LXX in Hb. 13:20 (ref. to the death and resurrection of Jesus). A. Feuillet, "Le baptême de Jésus d'après l'év. selon S. Marc (1, 9-11)," *The Cath. Bibl. Quart.*, 21 (1959), 468-490 sees behind Mk. 1:11 the exodus typology (473 f.) and hence the representation of the wilderness generation by the Messiah (476-490). On the opening of heaven without the gift of the Spirit cf. Ez. 1:1; S. Bar. 22:1; Jn. 1:51; Ac. 7:56; Test. L. 2:6 (the gift of the Spirit before). The closest par. are Test. L. 18:6 f.; Jud. 24:2; cf. Michel-Betz, 20 f.

[237] There are no instances of παῖς being replaced with υἱός, cf. A. Feuillet, "Le baptême de Jésus," *Rev. Bibl.*, 71 (1964), 325, but cf. Lk. 7:7 with Jn. 4:47.

[238] Revised J. Jeremias, *op. cit.* (→ n. 156), 192-6. Cf. also Bousset, 57; Dalman WJ, I, 227 f.; Maurer, 32; Grundmann Sohn Gottes, 125; Fuller, 193 f. Dupont, 526 sees the first influence of Ps. 2:7 on the Gospels at Lk. 3:22 Cod D. Rese, *op. cit.*, 132-5 considers whether Lk. was not the first to take up Ps. 2:7. But cf. P. Vielhauer, "Ein Weg z. nt.lichen Christologie?" *Aufsätze z. NT, Theol. Bücherei*, 31 (1965), 191; also "Erwägungen z. Christologie d. Mk.," *ibid.*, 205 f.

[239] ὁ ἀγαπητός esp. does not correspond to the HT, cf. G. Barth, "Das Gesetzesverständnis d. Evangelisten Mt.," *Überlieferung u. Auslegung im Mt.²*, *Wissenschaftliche Monographien z. AT u. NT*, 1 (1961), 118, who assumes the influence of the baptismal voice, so Strecker, *op. cit.* (→ n. 191), 68 f. (before Mt.), but not L. Cerfaux, "Les sources scripturaires de Mt. 11:25-30," *Ephemerides Theol. Lovanienses*, 31 (1955), 335 f., who conjectures reciprocal influence of Is. 42:1 and Ps. 2:7.

[240] Lövestam, 96; Cerfaux, *op. cit.* (→ n. 239), 335, but cf. Tg. Is. 42:1. Elsewhere only Gn. 22:2, 12, 16 (→ n. 365), to which Test. L. 18:6 probably alludes, cf. M. Black, "The Messiah in the Test. of Levi 18," Exp. T., 60 (1948/49), 321 f.; 61 (1949/50), 157 f., cf. 90 f. E. Best, *The Temptation and the Passion* (1965), 172 attempts explanation in terms of Isaac typology → n. 116.

[241] Midr. Ps., 2, 9 on 2:7 (→ 362, 14 f.) does combine Ps. 2:7 with Is. 42:1 but not with Ex. 4:22 (→ 355, 8 f.); Ps. 110:1 (→ 388, 8 ff.) and Da. 7:13 (→ 371, 10 ff.; Lövestam, 96 and 108), i.e., with all the passages the NT adduces for the Son of the God title, but not those directly influenced by Nathan's prophecy.

[242] G. Münderlein, "Die Erwählung durch das Pleroma," NTSt, 8 (1961/62), 266. E. Norden, *Die Geburt d. Kindes³* (1958), 132 f. gives Egypt. par.

[243] G. Kretschmar, "Ein Beitrag z. Frage nach dem Ursprung frühchr. Askese," ZThK, 61 (1964), 39, n. 30 (cf. 66 quoting Didasc., 9) shows that where Jesus' baptism is understood as adoption it opens the way to discipleship with the saying of Ps. 2:7 to the baptisand.

d. The Separation of the Community from the World in the βασιλεία of the Son (Col. 1:13).

Qumran terminology and strict separation between the community and the world [244] may be seen in Col. 1:12-14. [245] One may thus suppose that the phrase "son of his (God's) love" [246] comes from the same tradition, the more so as it reminds us of Mk. 1:11 → 367, 24 ff. [247] Here as in the passages influenced by the promise to David, i.e., R. 1:4 (→ 366, 22 ff.) and especially Rev. 1:5, [248] His royal dominion is that of the exalted Lord. It is characterised by the remission of sins which delivers from the power of darkness → n. 233; 248. By this the community is severed from the world, as at Qumran. But in the NT community there is a much greater hesitation to relate expectation of the Davidic Son of God to the community rather than the Messiah → 389, 23 ff.

e. The Transfiguration (Mk. 9:7) → IV, 868, 19 ff.; V, 701, 11 f.

Little further light can be shed on the origin of the story. [249] But the apocalyptic background is plain, [250] so that there again it would seem that the institution of Jesus as King of the end-time is the root of His designation as Son of God [251] → 378, 27 ff.; 389, 3 ff.

---

[244] The separation of the elect community from the sons of Belial and the wicked is the true theme in 4 Q Florilegium 1:7-17.

[245] Cf. κλῆρος τῶν ἁγίων, φῶς, ἐξουσία τοῦ σκότους, ἄφεσις τῶν ἁμαρτιῶν in Col. 1:12-14, cf. Ac. 26:18 and 1 QS 11:7 etc. (→ III, 762, 1 ff.; 763, 30 ff.; VII, 431, 22 ff.; 442, 1 ff., 21 ff.), also (→ VII, 125, n. 219) 2 Cor. 6:14 - 7:1, the only NT passage to share the term Belial with Qumran, also κύριος παντοκράτωρ with Rev. and 2 Βασ. 7:8, 25-27. Cf. E. Lohse, "Christusherrschaft u. Kirche im Kol.," NTSt, 11 (1964/65), 208 f.; K. G. Kuhn, "Die Schriftrollen vom Toten Meer," Ev. Theol., 11 (1951/52), 74 f.; J. Gnilka, "2 K. 6:14 - 7:1 im Lichte d. Qumranschriften u. d. Zwölf-Patriarchen-Test.," Festschr. J. Schmid (1963), 86-99; S. Wibbing, "Die Tugend- u. Lasterkataloge im NT," ZNW Beih., 25 (1959), 114; → n. 400.

[246] This corresponds to ἀγαπητός (→ 367, 24) and does not mean begotten of His love, cf. K. Romaniuk, L'amour du père et du fils dans la sotériologie de S. Paul (1961), 250.

[247] Or is the unusual expression linked historically with the εἰκών concept (→ II, 395, 29 ff.) cf. → n. 431; H. Wildberger, "Das Abbild Gottes, Gn. 1:26-30," ThZ, 21 (1965), 485 f.; E. Schweizer, "Die 'Mystik' d. Sterbens u. Auferstehens mit Christus bei Pls.," Ev. Theol., 26 (1966), 243, n. 19? If so it might have derived from the saying to which the hymn Col. 1:15-20 is linked by ὅς.

[248] In Rev. 1:5 (cf. Ps. 89:27) He is the Firstborn and the Ruler over all kings, then in a striking reinterpretation of the moon (Ps. 89:37b) the "faithful witness" and also the Redeemer from sins (Is. 40:2), while in Rev. 12:5; 19:15 He is Ruler over all peoples cf. also 2:27 (Ps. 2:9) → 389, 7 ff.; V, 940, 25 ff. VI, 494, 13 f.; 968, 7 ff.

[249] A Moses midrash (→ IV, 868, 18 ff.) has been suggested; it should be noted that Ex. 24:15 f. (LXX Ἰησοῦς) and 34:35 are closer in popular narration, cf. Ps.-Philo Antiquitates Bibl. (→ n. 116), 11, 15; 12, 1. Cf. 2 C. 3:18 and S. Schulz, "Die Decke d. Mose," ZNW, 49 (1958), 30, n. 149; H. Hegermann, Die Vorstellung v. Schöpfungsmittler im hell. Judt. u. Urchr. (1961), 113-5. W. Staerk ref. to the motif of conception of the Spirit in Die Erlösererwartung in den östlichen Religionen (1938), 323 f.

[250] Cf. S. Bar. 51:3 ff., cf. also Mt. 4:8; Rev. 21:10; Ez. 40:2 f.; 4 Esr. 13:35 f. (→ IV, 757, 1 ff.; V, 482, 14 ff.; II, 931, 6 ff.; IV, 856, 14 ff.) and esp. H. Riesenfeld, Jésus transfiguré (1947), 182-200, 223-5, 303-6.

[251] As against Hahn, 310-312, 334-340, who sees here the Son of God, cf. Vielhauer, op. cit. (→ n. 238), 207 f. This is true even if with Vielhauer and C. E. Carlston, "Transfiguration and Resurrection," JBL, 80 (1961), 233-240 one sees here an original resurrection story (in just criticism cf. C. H. Dodd, "The Appearances of the Risen Christ," Stud. in the Gospels [1955], 25; Hahn, 339, n. 1).

f. The Link with Ps. 110.

Mk. 12:35-37 (→ υἱὸς Δαυίδ) shows that the rule of the Son of David after His exaltation was understood with Ps. 110 as session at the right hand of God with the subjugation of His enemies. Where else could the promised throne be found? Even if the quotation was first used only in the Hell.-Jewish world, [252] it shows increasingly the more strongly apoc. idea that the subjugation of enemies is going on now but will be completed only at the *parousia*. Thus the tie between this and Son of Man christology (→ ὁ υἱὸς τοῦ ἀνθρώπου) might well be old, attesting to a not yet Hellenised exaltation christology, 384, 34 ff. [253] The same linking of the Davidic promise to Ps. 110:1 and to a subjugation of enemies which goes on up to the *parousia* [254] may be seen in the mosaic of quotations in Hb. 1:5-13, [255] while 5:5 f. [256] combines the ref. to the Son of David in Ps. 2:7 with Ps. 110:4 and thus introduces the high-priest motif which is so important for the author → 388, 15 ff. [257]

3. The Eschatological Role of the Son of God and the Absolute ὁ υἱός. [258]

a. The Link with Son of Man Christology (1 Th. 1:10; Rev. 2:18).

The eschatological role of the Son of God is plain in 1 Th. 1:10. Since the title is connected with the resurrection (→ 366, 26 ff.) and the concept of the atoning death (→ 383, 18 ff.) it might be that an exaltation christology which designated the One raised from the dead as God's Son was combined here with the idea of the saving function [259] of the Son of God who according to Paul was sent down from heaven to make expiation for sin → 383, 5 ff.; 386, 1 ff. A more likely theory, however, is that a saying originally about the Son of Man was reinterpreted by Paul on the basis of what were for him common associations with the title "Son of God," [260] which his churches could readily understand [261] → n. 265. The parallels support this.

---

[252] On Mk. 14:62 → 371, 1 ff.; 379, 7 ff. Since Jesus is מרא but not אדוני (S. Schulz, "Maranatha u. Kyrios Jesus," ZNW, 53 [1962], 134-143) Ps. 110:1 was hardly being related already to the *parousia* of Jesus in the Palest. community (Hahn, 287); this came only in the Hell.-Jewish community. But cf. E. Trocmé, *La formation de l'év. selon Marc* (1963), 95, n. 84; E. Lövestam, "Die Davidssohnfrage," *Svensk Exegetisk Årsbok*, 27 (1962), 81 f., who sees an authentic dominical saying here.
[253] Cf. G. Bertram, Art. "Erhöhung," RAC, VI (1964), 22-43; → n. 262.
[254] Cf. the express interpretation of Ps. 110:1 in Hb. 10:12 f.
[255] The collection of texts begins in v. 5 with Ps. 2:7 and 2 S. 7:14 (in the original) and passes on to the others with the catchword πρωτότοκος ψ 88:28; Ps. Sol. 18:4; it is enframed by Ps. 110:1 in v. 3 and v. 13. We also find the key words "throne" from 2 S. 7:13, 16 etc., "staff of his dominion" (cf. Ps. 2:9) and "anointing" from ψ 88:20 f. in v. 8 f. Ps. 46:6 f., which ref. to God, is quoted here with ref. to His Son, so that the Son is called θεός.
[256] Acc. to G. Schille, "Erwägungen z. Hohenpriesterlehre d. Hb.," ZNW, 46 (1955), 97 f., 104, 106 f. the first v. belonged to an early song and the second is the author's interpretation, but cf. G. Friedrich, "Das Lied d. Hohepriesters im Zshg. v. Hb. 4:14 - 5:10," ThZ, 18 (1962), 99.
[257] S. Aalen, "'Reign' and 'House' in the Kingdom of God in the Gospels," NTSt, 8 (1961/62), 238 f. thinks the Nathan prophecy has also influenced Jn. 14:1 ff.
[258] van Iersel, 175 (cf. the review by N. A. Dahl, JBL, 81 [1962], 294 f.) and Hahn, 281 have shown that this is separate from the expression Son of God.
[259] Cf. the materially closely akin formulation in R. 5:9.
[260] The Son of Man is never called the Son of God in Eth. En., Huntress, 118.
[261] G. Friedrich, "Ein Tauflied hell. Judenchristen," ThZ, 21 (1965), 502-516; cf. L. Legrand, "L'arrière-plan néotestamentaire de Lk. 1:35," *Rev. Bibl.*, 70 (1963), 172 f.

In the one v. in Rev. which speaks of the Son of God (Rev. 2:18 → 389, 7 ff.) this Son is described precisely as One like unto the Son of Man, 1:13-15. He is exalted here and is even regarded as identical with the Spirit who now speaks to the community through the prophet, 2:29 → VI, 449, 24 ff.; 450, 19 ff. But the function described by Ps. 2:8 f. which His disciples will one day fulfil in the eschaton but which He already discharges (2:26-28 → n. 248) will be stated in the same words in 19:15 (cf. 12:5) with reference to the Christ of the *parousia*. Here too, then, an apocalyptic Son of Man saying has been transferred to the exalted Son of God who already reigns over the community → n. 273; → 370, 7 ff.

A further observation shows how far the link goes. Ps. 110:1, which is related to the the exaltation of the Davidic Son of God (→ 370, 2 ff.), is already referred in Mk. 14:62 (→ 379, 6 ff.) to the Son of Man described in Da. 7:13 [262] and 1 C. 15:25-27 and Eph. 1:20-22 show independently that Ps. 8:6, which relates to the Son of Man, was also connected with Ps. 110:1. [263] The saying about the subduing of all foes could just as well ref. to the feet of the apocal. Son of Man as to those of the exalted Son of God [264] → 372, 7 ff.

b. 1 C. 15:28 (→ III, 329, 20 ff.).

ὁ υἱός occurs here in a highly apocalyptic context [265] with a pronounced subordinationist ring. The title "the Son" is appropriate, since it naturally suggests the counterpart "Father," while "Son of God" stresses supremacy over all "sons of men." The formula is thus designed to safeguard against a wild exaltation christology which forgets the still awaited consummation (→ n. 264) and which timelessly makes Him who is enthroned at God's right hand a second God. [266] In so doing, it also protects the older exaltation christology which, apocalyptically understood, leads on to the *parousia*. This happened before Paul, as Mk. 13:32 shows. [267] In this way the community avoids a unitarian concept of God on the one side and

---

[262] Mk. certainly ref. to the *parousia*. Possibly in a subordinate clause Da. 7:13 originally ref. to the exaltation of Jesus, cf. Schweizer, *op. cit.* (→ n. 165) § 3 f., but in any case an apocal. text was from the very first connected with Ps. 110:1. Did Ps. 80:17 (man of thy right hand = Son of Man) also have some influence (A. Bentzen, "Messias, Moses redivivus, Menschensohn," AbhThANT, 17 [1948], 40)?

[263] R. Schnackenburg, *Gottes Herrschaft u. Reich*³ (1963), 207.

[264] 1 C. 15:25 and Hb. 10:13 are future, Eph. 1:20 has a past ref.

[265] Though there is an undoubted relation to the milieu of Son of Man christology, one cannot explain the title directly as just a Greek reformulation of Son of Man (→ n. 268), cf. A. J. B. Higgins, "The OT and Some Aspects of NT Christology," *Canadian Journ. of Theology*, 6 (1960), 205-210, who thinks Son of Man and High-priest are (an early?) unity; Kruijf, 74-6, 93; Dupont, 524 f., also *Gnosis* (1949), 60 f. This view founders on the fact that while the NT ascribes to the Son of Man the *parousia* and judgment, it does not ascribe to Him rule up to the *parousia*.

[266] Cf. W. Grundmann, "Mt. 11:27 u. d. joh. 'Der Vater — der Sohn' Stellen," NTSt, 12 (1965/66), 48 f., though he thinks the abs. formula is the oldest christology which reaches back to the proximity of Jesus Himself, and is then developed secondarily into Son of Man and Son of God, 46.

[267] Naturally the chronology cannot be cleared up. No doubt Easter was from the very first interpreted as exaltation, but the dangers of exaltation christology might well have come to light in Hell-Jewish circles (which adopted Ps. 110:1 → 370, 4 ff.?). In answer there would be stress on apocal. sayings and Jesus as ὁ υἱός would be subordinate to the Father.

a doctrine of two Gods on the other. The theological concern of the later doctrine of the Trinity is thus protected. What can be pictured in this aeon only as a duality of God will be seen to be His unity in the consummation. Hence the Son does not possess a dignity alongside the Father and in competition with Him. He has his place within the one glory of God → 382, 24 ff.; n. 273.

c. Mk. 13:32 (→ I, 85, 20 ff.).

Since Lk. 12:8; Mk. 13:26 f.; Mt. 13:41; 25:31; Jn. 1:51 have the Son of Man and angels together, and Mk. 8:38 and par. have the triad Father, Son of Man, and angels, [268] Mk. 13:32 is also rooted in Son of Man christology [269] (→ ὁ υἱὸς τοῦ ἀνθρώπου). Again the apocalyptic question of the *parousia* is central [270] and there is stress on the Son's subordination to the Father. The reference here, of course, is to His earthly work. Jesus is God's delegate. In His whole life and teaching He brings about the encounter between God and the world. But He is not given a glimpse into the final decision regarding the time of consummation. In support of the derivation of the saying from Jesus [271] the title "Son" is not primary and the goal of the statement does not lie in it. [272] For origin in Palestinian Jewish Christianity it might be argued that this uses Son of Man christology, which already presupposes *parousia* with the angels, to restrict too specific expectation on the one side and too close an approximation of the exalted Lord to God on the other. [273] The fact that later Jesus' ignorance caused offence [274] is naturally no argument to the contrary. [275]

d. Mt. 11:27 (→ V, 992, 40 ff.; VII, 517, 14 ff.).

In Mt. 11:27 and par. we find ὁ υἱός with ὁ πατήρ. [276] That all things are given to the Son reminds us of Mt. 28:18b → II, 171, 1 ff.; 568, 34 ff.; V, 274, 28 ff.; VI,

---

[268] Cf. 1 Th. 3:13; 2 Th. 1:6 f.; 1 Tm. 5:21; Rev. 1:4 f. (→ VI, 450, 7 ff.); 3:5 with other titles. Once "Father" is used, Son of Man has to become Son of God, cf. Mk. 8:38 with Lk. 12:8 (or even Mt. 10:32 → ὁ υἱὸς τοῦ ἀνθρώπου?). Only in Mk. 1:13 do we find Jesus and angels without the title Son of Man.
[269] Fuller, 114. Perhaps originally a detached saying, van Iersel, 120-122.
[270] ἡμέρα and ὥρα are also apocal. terms, Mk. 14:25; Lk. 21:34 (Taylor, *op. cit.* [→ n. 195] on Mk. 13:32); Jn. 5:25-28; Rev. 18:10 (Loh. Mk. on 13:32). F. Dewar, "Chapter 13 and the Passion Narrative in St. Mark," *Theology,* 64 (1961), 99-107 sees the fulfilment in Mk. 14:35, 41 and compares the context 13:36 with 14:37 f. But this would be at most a secondary revision of the original apocal. saying.
[271] P. Schmiedel, Art. "Gospels," *Enc. Biblica,* 2 (1901), 1881; Loh. Mk., Grundm. Mk., *ad loc.;* V. Taylor, *The Names of Jesus* (1953), 57, also *The Person of Christ* (1958), 149; I. H. Marshall, "The Divine Sonship of Jesus," *Interpretation,* 21 (1967), 94 f.
[272] van Iersel, 123.
[273] Hahn, 327, n. 1; 328 f. Cf. E. Schweizer, "Der Menschensohn," *Neotestamentica* (1963), 80 f. The fact that in Mk. 8:38 as in Phil. 2:11 (→ 382, 26 ff.) the ref. to the δόξα τοῦ πατρός occurs in an apocal. context shows how strongly the latter concern is rooted in this stratum of the community.
[274] At Mt. 24:36 some Cod omit οὐδὲ ὁ υἱός. Higgins, *op. cit.* (→ n. 265), 204 f. thinks the saying without this is dominical. Bultmann Trad., 130 regards it as perhaps Jewish. Jeremias, *op. cit.* (→ n. 156), 40 ref. to the abs. Hell. ὁ υἱός.
[275] G. Harder, "Das eschatologische Geschichtsbild d. sog. kleinen Apokalypse Mk. 13," *Theol. Viat.,* 4 (1953), 95 f. thinks v. 30 is authentic, v. 32 an emendation.
[276] Bibl. → V, 992, n. 288, also Bultmann Trad., Suppl. (1962), 26 f. On the text cf. P. Winter, "Mt. 11:27 and Lk. 10:22 from the First to the Fifth Cent.," *Nov. Test.,* 1 (1956),

401, 16 ff. [277] It again points us to apocalyptic lines of thought [278] whose fulfilment the community finds in the present lordship of the Exalted. Mutual knowledge occurs in Hellenistic mysticism (→ I, 713, 18 ff.), [279] but in terms of ידע we are to think of election by the Father and acknowledgment by the Son, [280] as is typical of Qumran, [281] so that this saying, too, is rooted in the apocalyptic idea of the election and acknowledgment of the Son to whom the Father gives all power. [282] Conversely the Son knows the Father and works for His acknowledgment in the world. [283] As in the Johannine texts [284] (→ 385, 12 ff.) the stress here is not on subordination but on the function of representing God in the world. To be sure, the Son's power is that given Him by the Father, but the emphasis is on the unique position of the Son. Possibly the idea of the Logos as God's Son and Mediator of revelation had a part here as in Jn. → 356, 22.

112-127. Just. and others put the saying that no one knows the Father but the Son before the converse. J. Weiss, "Das Logion Mt. 11:25-30," Festschr. G. Heinrici (1914), 126 thinks this is original, since otherwise ὁ υἱός in the last clause would be superfluous. But if so it is hard to fit on the final member. Is then the shorter Lk. 10:22 Cod 1216, 1579a original? So essentially Winter, 148; Bultmann Trad., 171; R. Meyer, Der Prophet aus Galiläa (1940), 122 f. But it is badly attested and might be a scribal slip or free abbreviation. That Gk. feeling would later put God's unknowability before that of the Son is easy to understand, esp. as there are texts without the last clause.

[277] So also Bultmann Trad., 122; Dupont, op. cit. (→ n. 265), 59; Hahn, 323 f. Mt. 28:19 has ὁ πατήρ and ὁ υἱός in the baptismal formula (→ 380, 28 ff.), which perhaps goes back to the same tradition. The Synoptists do not elsewhere say that Jesus has this power, though they tell how He exercises it, Hahn, 324, cf. the remission of sins in Mk. 2:10. Since προσέρχομαι with verb is typical of Mt. (H. J. Held, "Mt. als Interpret d. Wundergeschichten," Überlieferung u. Auslegung, op. cit. [→ n. 239], 214-6). Mt. in 28:18-20 depicts an appearance of the One enthroned in heaven.

[278] Dupont, op. cit. (→ n. 265), 59 f. ἐξουσία and βασιλεία are also given to the Son of Man in Da. 7:13 f. We are not to think of the παράδοσις of mysteries, so E. Norden, Agnostos Theos⁴ (1956), 290-3; Cerfaux, op. cit. (→ n. 239), 333, also op. cit. (→ n. 239), 743, who also recalls Da. 2:21-29, which is suggested only by this context. But this means the title "Son" cannot be explained as equivalent to wisdom. At most only the linking of v. 27 with vv. 28-30 would help here, T. Arvedson, Das Mysterium Christi (1937), 230 f.

[279] Cf. K. Niederwimmer, "Erkennen u. Lieben," Kerygma u. Dogma, 11 (1965), 92-4.

[280] As against derivation from the Gnostic view of knowledge (→ I, 713, n. 83) by Arvedson, op. cit., 154 f. cf. Hahn, 323-6, 328, n. 5 also Kruijf, 66.

[281] Election, knowledge of God and revelation to others are related in 1 QS 4:22, cf. 1 QH 18:23 f., election and knowledge of God in 1 QS 11:15-18, cf. 11:3; 1 QH 10:27 f.; 14:12-15, 25; 1 QM 17:7 f., knowledge of God and revelation to others in 1 QS 9:17, election and revelation to others in 1 QSb 4:24-27, where the revealer for man, indeed, for the whole earth, is as an angel of the presence. For bibl. cf. C. Colpe, Die religionsgeschichtliche Schule (1961), 28, n. 1. Bacon, 385-394 even suggests a pre-Chr. saying ref. to Israel as God's elect son. A. M. Hunter, "Crux criticorum - Mt. 11:25-30," NTSt, 8 (1961/62), 245 with ref. to this idea and stress on the knowledge of God thinks Hosea is the ultimate root.

[282] Authentically dominical acc. to R. H. Fuller, The Mission and Achievement of Jesus (1954), 94 f.; D. A. Frövig, Das Sendungsbewusstsein Jesu u. d. Geist (1924), 231-3; Jeremias, op. cit. (→ n. 156), 47-50; van Iersel, 182; George Père, 29 f.; most assured dominical saying acc. to H. Schumacher, Die Selbstoffenbarung Jesu bei Mt. 11:27 (1912), 100, but cf. Hahn, 324; Dahl, op. cit. (→ n. 258), 295.

[283] Cf. Ex. r., 15, 8 on 12:1 f.: That God gives the world to Abraham means also that He can hide nothing from him, Grundmann, op. cit. (→ n. 266), 44; also E. Schweizer, "Die Kirche als Leib Christi in d. paul. Antilegomena," Neotestamentica (1963), 307-9. Acc. to Apc. Mos. 3 the Son knows God's secrets. On the apocal. revelation of mysteries cf. D. Lührmann, Das Offenbarungsverständnis bei Pls. u. in paul. Gemeinden (1965), 98-104, cf. 104-124.

[284] v. Iersel, 150 assembles the Joh. par., but ἀποκαλύπτω does not occur 160.

e. The Johannine Passages.

In Jn. 3:35 and 5:19-23(26) one may still detect the apocalyptic origin of the abs. ὁ υἱός. [285] If the Son is here viewed as the Father's delegate, the adoption and development of this usage in Jn. (→ 385, 5 ff.) and Hb. (→ n. 390) is readily understandable. In Him the Father Himself is seen, so that faith in Him means faith in the Father. The juxtaposition of ὁ υἱός and ὁ δοῦλος (Jn. 8:35 f. → II, 276, 10 ff.) points to a very different root. We have here the generic article of the image (→ 390, 13 f.), [286] but the reference to *the* Son, Jesus, and to eschatological abiding seems to be traditional. This may be seen from the unexpected mention of the permanent abiding of the Son as compared with the transitory position of the servant. In Hb. 3:5 f. (cf. 7:24) Moses is similarly ὡς θεράπων, Jesus ὡς υἱός, [287] and Gl. 4:7; R. 8:15-17 stress the lasting status of the son and heir (→ n. 400) in contrast to that of the servant [288] → 391, 11 ff.

4. The Sending of the Pre-Existent Son of God.

That a traditional line of thought or even a formula spoke of the sending of the Son of God even before Paul may be seen from the agreement of Gl. 4:4 f.; R. 8:3 f.; Jn. 3:(16), 17; 1 Jn. 4:9 in the expression: "God sent his son in order..." → III, 328, 7 ff.; 584, 37 ff. [289] God, not Father, is always the subject → 371, 18 ff. [290] The saving mission of the Son is always expressed in a ἵνα clause. Probably the reference should always be to "His" Son rather than "the" Son. [291] The verb for sending can

---

[285] S. Schulz *Untersuchungen z. Menschensohnchristologie im Joh.* (1957), 125-135 (as against J. Blank, *Krisis* [1964], 162 f.) claims an apocal. origin for both. 5:26 with its par. structure to v. 21 may also be noted here; in it too there is a secondary equation of ὁ υἱός with a very old υἱὸς ἀνθρώπου, 109-113. Cf. also S. Schulz, "Komposition u. Herkunft d. joh. Reden," BWANT, 81 (1960), 134-6. For kinship to Mt. 11:27 cf. Grundmann, *op. cit.* (→ n. 266), 44 f.

[286] Oddly enough there are hardly any par. (→ n. 416), only Apc. Shadrach (ed. M. R. James, TSt, II, 3 [1893] 6:5 has son and servant in antithesis, with a ref. also to the son's inheritance → n. 417. In the OT, however, son and servant stand in parallelism since sonship is understood primarily as obedience to the father → 345, 20. A. Böhlig, "Vom 'Knecht' zum 'Sohn'" *Wissenschaftl. Zschr. d. M. Luther-Univ. Halle-Wittenberg, Gesellschafts- u. sprachwissenschaftl. Reihe,*[6] (1957), 590 notes that the most obvious antithesis to the slave was the free man or the master. The son replaces these in the NT because in him both elements are contained, Mt. 17:25 f. (→ 390, 13 ff.). Acc. to Böhlig the terminology is perhaps to be understood in terms of court style.

[287] In the language of Hb. the contrast between the provisional and the definitive is described in 3:5 f., Kögel, 116 f. Moreover it is only here in the NT that we find ὁ υἱός without the accompanying Father, Grundmann, *op. cit.* (→ n. 266), 48, n. 3.

[288] Here related to the community, though its status as son and heir in Gl. 4:7 (sing. in spite of v. 6) is originally grounded in Jesus, 3:16, 29, where the concept of heir is introduced, 4:1, 4-7, cf. "joint-heir" in R. 8:17. An image like that of Mt. 17:25 f. (→ 390, 13 ff.) might be the source, so that secondarily a community which thinks apocalyptically would ground its freedom in that of the Son, but the development might well be the reverse, cf. K. Niederwimmer, *Der Begriff d. Freiheit im NT* (1966), 70-73.

[289] Kramer § 25a-c.

[290] ὁ πατήρ occurs from the first time in 1 Jn. 4:14 in a much weaker formulation, cf. Jn. 5:36; 6:57; 10:36; 20:21.

[291] Many witnesses read αὐτοῦ at Jn. 3:16, 17; 1 Jn. 4:9 also seems to have read Jn. 3:16 f. thus → n. 377.

be either (ἐξ)ἀποστέλλω, πέμπω, or δίδωμι. [292] What does Son of God mean in this schema? [293] Heavenly pre-existence is not intrinsically included [294] any more than in OT or NT references to the sending of the prophets or God's sending of Jesus, or in the claim that Zeus sent down philosophical preachers [295] or an emperor or king as redeemer. [296] Nor does mention of His Son have to include this, as shown by the full parallel of the sending of servants and the son (Mk. 12:1-9 → 378, 32 ff.) and the possibility of analogous explanation to → 367, 1 ff. But since the sending formula occurs only in Paul and John, who both presuppose an already developed christology in which the pre-existent Lord was depicted after the pattern of the logos or wisdom, [297] the formula probably had its roots in the same sphere.

Sending by God and the Son of God title [298] are combined only in the realm of the logos and wisdom speculations of Egyptian Judaism. [299] In fact the sending of the Son of God and the Spirit (Gl. 4:4-6) corresponds exactly to that of wisdom and the Spirit (Wis. 9:10, 17), [300] while the interrelating of Son and sons (Gl. 4:6) may also be found in Philo → 355, 34 ff. Here, then, is the root of a very different idea of the Son of God in which the heavenly closeness of the pre-existent Son to God is decisive and constitutes His significance as the One sent down from heaven to earth. [301] The community is thus given a form of speech by which it can distinguish

---

[292] That Jn. 3:16 does not mean giving up to suffering (Kramer § 26a) but sending (W. Popkes, Christus traditus [1967] § 13, 5d; 14, 2) is suggested by the par. 3:17 and esp. 14:16, which uses διδόναι with ref. to the Spirit par. πέμπειν in 14:26; 15:26; 16:7. Cf. Bau. J., ad loc.

[293] For what follows cf. Schweizer, op. cit. (→ n. 126), 199-208 with examples.

[294] Bousset, 153.

[295] Cf. Epict. Diss., III, 22, 56, 59, cf. also 1, 37 etc.

[296] σωτῆρα πέμψασα in the Priene inscr. Ditt. Or., II, 458, 35 (9 B.C.) is a conjecture with no support in the text, but cf. BMI, IV, 1, No. 894; Plut. Alex. Fort. Virt., 6 (II, 329c). In Sib., 3, 286 also the sending of the king from heaven means virtually his sending from the East, 3, 652, cf. too 5, 108 and 256; to the contrary only 5, 414 f.

[297] For Paul cf. E. Schweizer, "Zur Herkunft d. Präexistenzvorstellung bei Pls.," Neotestamentica (1963), 105-9; also "Aufnahme u. Korrektur jüd. Sophiatheologie im NT," ibid., 110-121. For John → IV, 133, 12 ff.; C. H. Dodd, The Interpretation of the Fourth Gospel (1953), 274-7. On the combination of Logos and Son of God cf. Jn. 1:1 ff. and also Hb. 1:2 (→ 388, 7 ff.); Rev. 19:13-15 (→ 371, 4 ff.).

[298] For the logos Philo Agric., 51; for sending Rer. Div. Her., 205; Cher., 35; Quaest. in Ex. 2:13, also Som., I, 103; for divine sonship → IV, 89, 15 ff., 34 ff.; W. Theiler in Philo v. Alex., ed. L. Cohn et al., VII (1964), 400 f.; for his high-priestly mediation → III, 272, 34 ff.

[299] Already before Philo Hell. Judaism explained God's work in the world with the help of the idea of divinely sent power, wisdom, or logos, cf. the more mythical notions of pagan Egypt. theology, cf. Schweizer, op. cit. (→ n. 126), 201 f., and under probable Egypt. influence the equation (combining sonship and sending) of Hermes, son of Zeus and Maia, whom the gods sent down from heaven, with the logos → IV, 87, 14 ff.; for similar Egypt. speculations, again very close to Philo's logos statements, cf. Plutarch, Schweizer, 200 f. That a Gnostic redeemer myth can hardly be presupposed (→ VI, 393, 18 ff.; VII, 1093, 7 ff.) is shown by the fact that the "Son" title in the formula of sending is not combined with exaltation or ascension, Kramer § 27d.

[300] Only here does Paul use ἐξαποστέλλω (Wis. 9:10), Schweizer, op. cit. (→ n. 297), 108.

[301] For the further history of the schema cf. Syr. Treasure Cave (ed. C. Bezold [1883]) 5:7, 13; Apc. Eliae 20:1 f.; Just. Ap., 63, 4 f. says the λόγος is God's Son because He knows God. Dial., 61, 1, 3 ff. describes the δύναμις λογική as υἱός, σοφία, ἄγγελος, θεός, κύριος, λόγος, ἀρχιστρατηγός. The Logos is also God's Son in Orig. Cels., II, 31; Cl. Al. Strom., VI, 39, 3. Iren. Epid., 9 has Son, Word, Spirit and Wisdom together, G. Kretschmar, Stud. z. frühchr. Trinitätstheologie (1956), 48 f. Simon Magus is said to have called himself

the sending of Jesus quite unequivocally from that of prophets and teachers and even angels. [302] Naturally the statement herewith made by the community went beyond the given thought-scheme from the very outset. In Hellenistic Judaism the Son is associated neither with the Father nor with men as He is in the Christian community. [303] Also lacking is the historical singularity and eschatological significance of the sending. But the NT conception of the Son of God pre-existent in heaven and sent down thence to earth might well go back to Hellenistic Judaism, even though this thinks more strongly in spatial categories than in temporal-eschatological categories → I, 401, 18 ff. In interpretation of Paul → 383, 5 ff., of John → 386, 1 ff.

5. The Miraculously Born and Miracle-Working Son of God.

a. The Virgin Birth (→ V, 829, 23 ff.; 835, 30 ff.; VI, 402, 2 ff.).

Only in Lk. 1:35 (→ II, 300, 20 ff.; VII, 400, 17 ff.) and not in Mt. 1 is the annunciation of the virgin birth linked to υἱὸς θεοῦ. As the one who has no human father Jesus is here called God's Son. The saying takes up the statement about the Son of God of the stem of David (Lk. 1:32 → 381, 20 ff.) and explains the title in terms of the creative power of the Holy Spirit and the δύναμις of God. If in the OT the election of the office-bearer by God is the basis of sonship, here the elective and creative act of God plays this role. But now the term Son of God is not the same as when the angels are called sons of God → 347, 9 ff.; 355, 6 f. It does not just denote a being which belongs to God's world and derives from the heavenly sphere → 375, 15 ff.

There seem to be no true historical par. [304, 305] At a pre-Lucan stage it may be that Jesus was called a Nazirite already chosen by God in His mother's womb acc. to Ju. 13:7. [306] If so the v. would go back to the same stratum of the tradition as 1:15 and only combination with the Son of the Most High of v. 32 would link it with Davidic expectation. [307] A pt. in favour of this is that already in Hell. Judaism the miracle-working and often miraculously born men of God of the OT were being presented in the garb of Hell.

δύναμις θεοῦ, Orig. Cels., V, 62; VI, 11. Cf. also Wetter, 8, 28 f., 40, 82-4. We find sending and Logos terminology together in Dg., 7, 2-4: God sends the Logos, not a servant or angel, the τεχνίτης and δημιουργὸς τῶν ὅλων, and indeed ὡς σῴζων. Finally Celsus shows the par. between the Chr. sending of the Son and the pagan sending of Hermes (-Logos), Orig. Cels., VI, 78.

[302] It is very striking that in contrast to the Gospels Paul never speaks of such sendings except in R. 10:15.

[303] M. J. Lagrange, "Les origines du dogme paulinien de la divinité du Christ," Rev. Bibl., 45 (1936), 33.

[304] E. Brunner-Traut, "Die Geburtsgeschichte d. Ev. im Lichte ägyptologischer Forschungen," Zschr. f. Religions- u. Geistesgesch., 12 (1960), 97-111; T. Boslooper, The Virgin Birth (1962), 135-186; for Gk. par. → 339, 7 ff.

[305] It is constantly assumed that θεῖοι ἄνδρες were called sons of God in the Hell. period, Bau. J. on 1:34; Braun, op. cit. (→ n. 135), 255-9; Sevenster, Art. "Christologie," RGG³, I, 1752; Schreiber, 119, but cf. → 340, 1 ff.

[306] D. Daube, "Evangelisten u. Rabb.," ZNW, 48 (1957), 119 f. even suggests an allusion to the story of Ruth: the fact that Boaz covered her is a spec. ref. to her chastity; → 377, 8 ff.

[307] H. J. Cadbury, The Beginnings of Christianity, I, 5, (1933), 357, n. 2; Rese, op. cit. (→ n. 231), 286-290. It is most improbable that Luke was the one to combine the traditional v. 35 with the concept of holiness (George Jésus, 190 f.).

charismatics. [308] If miracles on God's commission and in the service of proclamation are typical [309] of these, however, the title "Son of God" does not occur, though one does find the concept of derivation from God [310] → 339, 4 ff.; 340, 1 ff. Another possible root of the concept of the Son of God in the community is thus laid bare.

b. The Miracle-Worker (Mk. 5:7).

A similar development may be seen at Mk. 5:7 (→ V, 462, n. 7) in the cry of the demon-possessed: "Jesus, Son of the most high God."

The demonic cry in Mk. 1:24, which calls Jesus Ναζαρηνός and ὁ ἅγιος τοῦ θεοῦ, is undoubtedly rooted in the OT picture of the charismatics called σωτῆρες in Ju. 3:9, 15 (cf. 15:18), for in Ju. 13:7; 16:17 Ναζιραῖος [311] and ἅγιος θεοῦ are alternative translations of the same Hbr. term. [312] It is possible that even before Mk. the title was thought to be too weak and Jesus the miracle-worker was called Son of God after the analogy of a θεῖος ἀνήρ of divine origin → IV, 609, 23 ff. [313] Expectation of a Messiah who would drive out demons would be a step in this direction (→ Χριστός). It has been seriously argued, however, that Mk. himself was the one to make the substitution → 378, 25 ff. On Mt. 14:33 → 380, 8 ff.

c. The Temptation of Jesus.

Satan's question presupposes a tradition in which the Son of God manifests Himself primarily by His mighty acts. Since the title was hardly connected with the miracle-worker in pre-Chr. times, it was perhaps taken from Mk. 1:11 and par. [314] Materially, however, the pericope clearly takes issue with what was obviously a wide-spread misunderstanding of Jesus as a miracle-working man of God after the manner of Hellenistic Judaism. For here it is the devil who suggests a divine sonship that can be manifested and proved. [315]

---

[308] Georgi, op. cit. (→ n. 129), 145-167; cf. 258-265; cf. Fuller, 68-72; → 356, 4 ff.

[309] This seems to be important in charismatics only from the middle of the 2nd cent. A.D. (though → 356, 12 f.). Previously the sage, poet, or statesman ranked as such. Possibly oriental influence is at work here → 338, 28 ff.

[310] Cf. Just. Ap., 22, 2-6; Dial., 67, 2; Orig. Cels., I, 37 → n. 30. For the gt. differences → V, 835, 30 ff. and the express discussion in J. G. Machen, The Virgin Birth of Christ (1930), 324-379, cf. Kl. Mk. on 1:11.

[311] Mk. has Ναζαρηνός, an emendation of the traditional Ναζωραῖος (Mt., Lk., Ac., Jn.).

[312] The question: τί ἡμῖν καὶ σοί; might come from the same layer 3 Βασ. 17:18, cf. E. Schweizer, "Er wird Nazoräer heissen," Neotestamentica (1963), 52 f.

[313] So Hahn, 297-301. Cf. Jn. 6:69 b.syᶜ.

[314] So Dalman WJ, I, 226. It is thus hard to think the story could be handed down in Q without the account of the baptism. The Moses-Israel typology behind the Q version has been pointed out by J. Dupont, "L'arrière-fond biblique du récit des tentations de Jésus," NTSt, 3 (1956/57), 287-304. A contrast to Ex. 4:22 might have been sensed secondarily, Kruijf, 57.

[315] Q also stresses Jesus' miracles, but as the fulfilment of OT prophecy (Lk. 7:18-35) calling to repentance (Lk. 7:9; 10:13-15; 11:14-23, 29-32), cf. G. Bornkamm, "Enderwartung u. Kirche im Mt.," Überlieferung u. Auslegung, op. cit. (→ n. 239), 33 f., who shows that the miracles are no longer demonstrations of divine sonship but an expression of compassion, and that the understanding of divine sonship clearly moves away increasingly from the idea of the θεῖος ἀνήρ. Acc. to Apc. Esr. 4:27 antichrist, claiming to be God's Son, will work miracles.

6. The Suffering Righteous as Son of God (Mt. 27:43).

In Mt. 27:43 the chief priests mock Jesus in the words of the suffering righteous (Ps. 22:8) because He regarded Himself as the Son of God like the suffering righteous in Wis. 2:18. [316] In Wis. 2:13, 18 this designation is fully parallel to "servant of God" and is used of the righteous man (→ 354, 30 ff.) who, trusting in God as his Father, will be exalted among the sons of God after his passion and ignominious death. Since Son of God was combined only with this servant and not with the Messianic Servant of Is. 53, [317] this aspect of the tradition outside Mt. 27:43 (→ 379, 21 ff.) led only to the general thought that Son of God and suffering are not incompatible → 383, 18 ff., 26 ff.

III. The Interpretation of the Divine Sonship of Jesus by the New Testament Writers.

One can see Jesus simply as the son of Joseph (Jn. 6:42) or as God's son merely in the sense of a heavenly being (Mk. 5:7) and in so doing remain blind. By questions and misunderstandings the disciples of Jesus in following Him sought to learn by ever new interpretations in what sense He was son of Joseph and in what sense Son of God. They thus gave the concept Son (of God) ever new content to express the mystery that God is to be found present for man in Jesus.

1. Mark.

Mk. 1:11 adopts the title Son of God from the tradition → 367, 23 ff. The dialogue is merely between God and His Son. Prior to the first manifestation of Jesus Mark depicts here and also in the temptation story, in which only the Spirit, Satan and the angels appear with Jesus, the divine dimension in which the life and passion of Jesus will be enacted. It is heaven which here comes down to earth. This is even plainer in Mark's own 3:11. [318] What demons know as opposed to men goes beyond the tradition (1:24 → V, 117, 33 ff.). It is the fact that God's Son is present in the man Jesus. This is repeated in 5:7 → 377, 5 ff. In 9:7 (→ 369, 13 ff.; V, 101, 9 ff.) God Himself can impart the mystery of the divine sonship of Jesus to the three intimates. [319] This is possible only because after Peter's confession, in which Peter still does not quite reach the same level of knowledge as the demons, Jesus announced the suffering of the Son of Man, [320] 8:27-33 → ὁ υἱὸς τοῦ ἀνθρώπου. He thus tied all true insight to the condition of suffering discipleship, 8:34 - 9:1. Before the passion only the parable of 12:1-9 points to the son who again is sent to suffer

---

[316] Cf. also Damasc. 1:18-21 (1:13-16); 1 Cl., 16, 15 f. and H. Kosmala, *Hebräer-Essener-Christen* (1959), 291-3; Maurer, 25 f.; Hummel, *op. cit.* (→ n. 205), 115 f.

[317] Cf. Schweizer, *op. cit.* (→ n. 165) § 4c, 6a-d. Is. 53 did, of course, influence the more general picture of the suffering righteous, 32, n. 143; also M. Rese, "Überprüfung einiger Thesen v. J. Jeremias zum Thema d. Gottesknechts im Judt.," ZThK, 60 (1963), 28 (on Test. B. 3:8). On Is. 53 cf. also K. Euler, *Die Verkündigung vom leidenden Gottesknecht aus Jes. 53 in d. griech. Bibel* (1934), 85-91, 109-114, 122-148 [Bertram].

[318] The fact that ancient tradition is preserved in v. 7a, 9 f. can hardly be contested, cf. E. Haenchen, *Der Weg Jesu* (1966), *ad loc.*

[319] The σὺ εἶ of 1:11 becomes the οὗτός ἐστιν of proclamation.

[320] Compared with previous parabolic utterance (4:33) this is for Mk. the first open proclamation of Jesus (8:32a), cf. E. Schweizer, "Anmerkungen zur Theol. d. Mk.," *Neotestamentica* (1963), 100.

and to die. [321] Though it has been conjectured that the sending of the son was brought into the parable only because the community had already begun to speak in these terms (→ 374, 14 ff.), the reference is in no sense to pre-existence. On the contrary the sending is fully parallel to that of the servants, though surpassing it as the lord's supreme effort. Only in the midst of suffering can Jesus answer in the affirmative the high-priest's question whether He is the Son of God (14:61), [322] and this indeed in such a way that the reference to the apocalyptically understood exaltation and *parousia* of the Son of Man (→ ὁ υἱὸς τοῦ ἀνθρώπου) immediately gives precision to the answer, 14:62 → V, 210, 40 ff. Only in the moment when Jesus dies with a loud cry does the first man, a Gentile, confess that He was the Son of God, [323] 15:39. [324] One can thus understand why already in 1:1 (though the text is doubtful) [325] Mark sums it all up for his readers, who are in on the secret, by pointing them to the Son of God.

For Mark, then, the title Son of God expresses the mystery of Jesus as the One sent by God in a higher sense than any of the prophets. But in contrast to a christology which sees Jesus primarily as a miracle-worker Mark emphasises the point that one can truly see Him as the Son of God only if one understands that He shows Himself to be such in the passion, death and exaltation of the Son of Man. [326]

2. Matthew.

There is a fresh nuance in Matthew, since he takes over from the tradition the designation of the suffering Righteous as the Son of God, 27:43 → 378, 18 ff. Here the divine sonship of Jesus is concealed under the shame and cannot be demonstrated.

---

[321] Kümmel, *op. cit.* (→ n. 165), 214-7 thinks derivation from the community is more likely than from an original parable, but cf. Jeremias Gl.⁷, 74; van Iersel, 141-145.

[322] The ambivalent Christ title is thus interpreted in strongly Jewish terms → 381, 3 ff. A. J. B. Higgins, *Jesus and the Son of Man* (1964), 67 f. thinks this equation by the high-priest was historically quite possible.

[323] Bousset, 52 f., 55; P. A. van Stempvoort, "'Gods Zoon' of 'Een zoon Gods' in Mt. 27:54?" *Nederlandsch theol. tijdschr.*, 9 (1954/55), 79-89. As against C. Mann, "The Centurion at the Cross," Exp. T., 20 (1909), 564 one must say that what is meant is not "a son of God" but "the Son of God." The art. is not used with the predicate when it precedes the verb, E. C. Colwell, "A Definite Rule for the Use of the Article in the Greek NT," JBL, 52 (1933), 12-21; R. Bratcher, "A Note on υἱὸς θεοῦ (Mk. 15:39)," Exp. T., 68 (1956/57), 27 f.; cf. M. Zerwick, *Graecitas Biblica⁴* (1960), 171-5 and Mt. 4:3, 6; 14:33; 27:40, 43; Lk. 1:32, 35; Jn. 10:36. That neither the θεῖος ἀνήρ nor unity of God and man is meant is shown by Vielhauer, *op. cit.* (→ n. 238), 209.

[324] The development is palpable, but one is not to see behind this a schema of apotheosis, presentation and enthronement as though Jesus only became God's Son in the full sense with the crucifixion, Vielhauer, *op. cit.*, 212-4. For one thing it is doubtful whether Mk. takes the Son of God title so functionally that divine sonship only begins with institution to office. But the main pt. is that Jesus has already been proclaimed as Son of God by God and the demons.

[325] Cf. the survey in S. C. E. Legg, *Novum Test. Graece, Ev. secundum Marcum* (1935). For authenticity Bieneck, 35; Cullmann, 301, n. 3; it would be more likely if Mk. had understood the whole life of Jesus as ἀρχή of the Easter Gospel of the Son of God, cf. M. E. Glasswell, "The Use of Miracles in the Markan Gospel," *Miracles* (1965), 161 f.

[326] The Messianic secret thus amounts to this, that Mark gives stories of mighty acts but has Jesus forbid their proclamation before the passion because only in light of this could they be understood as signs of divine sonship which have nothing to do with magic. Cf. E. Schweizer, "Die theol. Leistung d. Mk.," *Ev. Theol.*, 24 (1964), 349, also *Das Ev. nach Mk.*, NT Deutsch, 1 (1967), 207 f.

It would appear from 27:40 that Matthew is intentionally correcting a wrong picture, for here the mockers at the foot of the cross adopt more or less literally the suggestion of the tempter: "If thou be the Son of God..." In 21:39, too, Matthew strengthens the reference to the crucifixion of the Son [327] → 378, 32 ff. Especially at the baptism of Jesus, where the voice of God is now a proclamation rather than an address (3:17 → II, 740, 15 f.), [328] the idea of the end-time king instituted as Son of God is corrected along the lines of the suffering Righteous in 3:15 → II, 198, 26 ff.[329] 14:33, where the miracle-worker is worshipped as the Son of God, is also to be regarded as taken from the tradition rather than formulated by Matthew himself. [330] Since the story of Peter's walking on the water is for the Evangelist a figure of discipleship, he finds in it the praise and confession of the Son of God to which all discipleship should lead. This is why he does not speak of the Son of God in connection with the virgin birth → n. 191. The quotation in 2:15, which is referred to the leading of God's Son out of Egypt to Nazareth and His growing up there under God's direction, is indeed more important for him. [331] It is taken from a tradition [332] which thinks of Jesus as fulfilling the destiny of Israel, so that the saying about Israel as God's son can be applied directly to Him. [333] That the title Son of God was already the customary one for Jesus may be seen in Mt. 26:63 (→ V, 465, 6 ff.; 989, n. 278) as compared with the rather different Marcan formulation, but especially in 16:16 (→ V, 211, 28 ff.), where the ambivalent title Christ, which Mark applies to Jesus only with considerable reserve, is interpreted by "Son of the living God," [334] so that the confession of Peter can be hailed as a divine revelation. Hence 17:5, in contrast to Mk., is no longer a first disclosure of the secret but a repetition of 3:17 which serves to strengthen the startled disciples (17:6 f.) and illustrates the promise to them. [335] Finally the title Son of God is adopted in 8:29 in contrast to Mk. 1:24, 34; 3:11. In 11:27 Matthew adopts a saying which already in Q sees in the Son the Revealer of all mysteries chosen and acknowledged by the Father → 372, 22 ff. A final stage is reached with the association of the names of the Father, the Son and the Holy Ghost in 28:19 → III, 108, 10 ff.; V, 274, 28 ff.; VI, 401, 16 ff.; 434, n. 678 (cf. 4 [5] Esr. 2:47). On Mt. 24:36 → 372, 6 ff.

3. Luke and Acts.

For Luke the title Son of God characterises Paul's preaching. Ac. 9:20. [336] For the rest it is not truly central. In Lk. 4:41 the invocation of Jesus as Son of God by the

---

[327] Kruijf, 140.

[328] οὗτος for σύ gives us a proclamation of what is true from 1:18 (cf. 2:15), cf. Strecker, op. cit. (→ n. 191), 125; Hummel, op. cit. (→ n. 205), 115.

[329] Schweizer, op. cit. (→ n. 165), § 2d-f shows that suffering is regarded as the content of the righteousness which is to be fulfilled.

[330] Much edited acc. to Barth, op. cit. (→ n. 239), 105 f.; Held, op. cit. (→ n. 277), 193-5. The tradition has interpreted the established title along the lines of "God-Man" → 356, 4 f. Mt. bases the Son of God predicate not only on the idea of the suffering Righteous but also on the miracles and expressly in 27:54 on the apocal. events. In 8:29 he leaves out the Ἰησοῦς of Mk. 5:7. For him, then, Jesus is not just the suffering Righteous but also the apocal. Son of God who achieves the miracle of new creation. Cf. G. Braumann, "Der sinkende Petrus," ThZ, 22 (1966), 404-7.

[331] Stendahl, op. cit. (→ n. 191), 101.

[332] Acc. to K. Stendahl, The School of St. Matthew (1954), 203-6 oral tradition; for Jewish par. cf. 194-202.

[333] Kruijf, 110-112.

[334] In Mk. not until 14:61 (→ n. 322); cf. Jn. 20:31.

[335] Mk. 9:10 is also left out, cf. Barth, op. cit. (→ n. 239), 99.

demons is picked up from Mk. 3:11 to give precision to the general statement of Mk. 1:34, but in Luke "Son of God" is expressly interpreted by the obviously more natural → Χριστός. [337] Lk. 22:70 formulated Jesus' affirmative answer to the question of His divine sonship with extraordinary care and with far greater caution than the acceptance of the closely related Christ title of Mk. 14:61; Mt. 26:63. By putting v. 69 first and leaving out Mk. 14:62c Luke also interprets the divine sonship along the lines of an elevation to the right hand of God (→ 379, 5 ff.) which is no longer apocalyptically limited and shaped by the *parousia*. The fact that in the centurion's confession in 23:47 (→ 379, 9ff.) Son of God is replaced with δίκαιος (→ II, 187, 27ff.) probably testifies to a desire to safeguard against exposition in terms of pagan sons of God. [338] The alteration in Lk. 3:22 Cod D can hardly be Luke's own. [339] As in Mk. 1:11 (→ 378, 20 ff.; 380, 4 ff.) the voice of God is thus addressed to Jesus. [340] Hence Lk. 9:35, like Mk. 9:7 (→ 378, 27 ff.), is a first revelation, not of course for the readers, but for the disciples. v. 31 and perhaps the reformulation of what the voice says [341] bring the naming as Son of God closer to the passion than in Mk. [342] Mk. 13:32 (→ 372, 6 ff.) is left out; Luke has no wish to refer to a restriction of knowledge of even the earthly Jesus. [343] Since Ac. 8:37 vl. (→ V, 211, 26 ff.) [344] does not seem to be by Luke himself and Lk. 4:3, 9; 8:28; 10:22; 20:13 stay close to the par. the only special Lucan material is in Lk. 1:32, 35.

Lk. 1:32 f. adopts the tradition of the Davidic Son of God (→ 366, 21 ff.) [345] which is also important in 1:69; 2:4; cf. Ac. 2:30 f.; 13:23, 33-36 etc. The formulation, however, may well go back in large measure to Luke himself. [346] The only part of 1:32 to go beyond the tradition is οὗτος ἔσται μέγας (which is analogous to 1:15) → VI, 837, 18 ff. [347] "Son of the Most High" is thus to be regarded as a formulation

---

[336] The quotations in Ac. 13:33-36, which are traditional (→ 367, 11 ff.), are put on Paul's lips. Cf. C. F. D. Moule, "The Christology of Acts," *Studies in Luke-Acts* (1966), 174.
[337] The very reverse of → 379, 5 ff.; 380, 17 ff. J. Blinzler, *Der Prozess Jesu*³ (1960), 106, n. 33 pts. to the equation in Lk. 4:41; Ac. 9:20, 22 and Dupont, 523, n. 2 to Mt. 27:54 and par.
[338] Or is Luke avoiding Son of God altogether? George Jésus, 193-5; Moule, *op. cit.* (→ n. 366), 165? Or is he giving an older version changed by Mk. for theological reasons → 377, 14 f.?
[339] Rese, *op. cit.* (→ n. 231), 300 f. supports a Lucan origin. But it is unlikely that 1:35 can be related to anything but the birth, so that the "today" of Ps. 2:7 would be difficult for Lk. A more probable explanation is that a copyist (before the Synoptics were assembled?) emended acc. to Ps. 2:7 → V, 701, n. 349; cf. H. W. Bartsch, *Wachet aber zu jeder Zeit* (1963), 51, who ref. to adoptionist tendencies in the Western text.
[340] The objectivity of the event is established by the reformulation in v. 21b, 22a. It is not said who baptised Jesus; 3:20 would not seem to support John.
[341] Rese, *op. cit.*, 303 f. asks whether the change to ἐκλελεγμένος links to ἐκλεκτός in 23:35, i.e., the passion (cf. H. Conzelmann, *Die Mitte d. Zeit*³ [1960], 51), while the final allusion to Dt. 18:15 suggests a second Moses, cf. J. Schniewind, "Zur Synoptiker-Exegese," ThR, NF, 2 (1930), 147.
[342] For stress on the passion cf. Lk. 24:26; Ac. 3:18 and Moule, *op. cit.* (→ n. 336), 167.
[343] The Son knows the day and hour, but it is not appropriate for men to know them, Ac. 1:6 f., cf. Conzelmann, *op. cit.*, 122, n. 2; 166, n. 2; George Jésus, 199 f.
[344] Perhaps there are traces of an ancient baptismal liturgy, Cullmann, 297.
[345] Schweizer, 191.
[346] κληθήσεται here (unlike 1:35) might denote election (→ III, 490, 19 ff.). βασιλεύω ἐπί is a Hebraism, Bl.-Debr. § 177. But υἱὸς ὑψίστου is against a Palestinian origin, cf. H. H. Oliver, "The Lucan Birth Stories and the Purpose of Luke-Acts," NTSt, 10 (1963/64), 222. "Υψιστος without θεός occurs in the NT only in Lk., Ac., cf. the throne of David, also ref. to the exaltation in Ac. 2:30, Jesus' royal dominion, Lk. 22:30; 23:42.
[347] Rese, *op. cit.*, 285 f.

of Luke which goes beyond "prophet of the Most High" (1:76 → VI, 840, 33 ff.)
→ VI, 402, 8 ff. The expectation of the rule of the Son of God in fulfilment of the
Davidic promises has been long since taken out of the political sphere and related
to the rule of the exalted Lord over His community → 367, 4 f. [348] The same applies
to 1:35, where the conceiving by the Spirit which Luke took from the tradition
(→ 376, 15 ff.) is the basis of the description as Son of God. [349] Hence v. 35 explains
v. 32. The strong reserve of Luke in relation to the title Son of God misunderstood
in terms of the divine sons of paganism shows that fundamentally he is not referring
to anything other than the election of God. But since naive utterances (→ 367, 5 ff.;
368, 12 f.) can give rise to an adoption-christology which expressly declares that Jesus
was no more than a man prior to His selection by God [350] there is the threat of a
parallel to the apotheosis of Greek heroes. If, then, the statements that the One
instituted by God as Son meets us in the work of Jesus are to be sustained, there
is need to investigate the basis of the divine sonship of Jesus in the election at His
birth or already in His pre-existence. Since Luke was not interested in the biological
question [351] he does not cross over the boundary to a metaphysical understanding. [352]
The only essential point is that the mystery of the birth of Jesus, which rests on
God's act rather than the procreative power of man, [353] is still maintained, → V,
834, 16 ff. [354]

4. Paul (Including Col. and Eph.).

a. Apocalyptic Passages (1 Th. 1:10; 1 C. 15:28; Gl. 1:16).

The fact that in Paul, too, the concept of the Son of God is taken from the Son
of Man sayings of the tradition may be seen from 1 Th. 1:10 (→ 370, 16 ff.; V, 522,
20 ff.). The fact that for Paul the idea contains both the dignity of the Son and
also His subordination to the Father is plain in 1 C. 15:28, which is not essential
in the context (→ 371, 17 ff.); the (Pauline?) interpretation of expectation of the
parousia [355] in Phil. 2:11b. (→ V, 214, 6 ff.) points in the same direction, the Father
being here too the One to whom final honour belongs. Both verses make it clear

---

[348] Since this is an original Chr. formula, even at an earlier stage of Lk. the fut. is already
contextually related to the time of the Exalted. It thus seems to me to be a mistake to see
here the Christ of the *parousia*, Hahn, 247 f. There is no par. for this in the NT, since even
1 Th. 1:10 (→ 370, 16 ff.) does not ref. to dominion after the *parousia*. The fut. in the message
of the angel prior to Jesus' birth are self-explanatory.

[349] The stress is on this. In view of the par. 2:23 there is no emphasis on Ἅγιον. It is
uncertain whether there is any allusion to Ps. 2:7, Rese, *op. cit.*, 287-9.

[350] Cf. H. J. Schoeps, *Theol. u. Gesch. d. Judenchristentums* (1949), 74-8 on the christology
of the Ebionites.

[351] Burton, *op. cit.* (→ n. 121), 413 emphasises that acc. to 3:38 Adam was not born of
human parents but was still a full man and not a demi-god; Hahn, 304-308.

[352] It is only here that C. G. Montefiore, *The Synoptic Gospels²* (1927), II, 162 locates
the break with Judaism, which is debating with Christianity rather than Jesus. Paul does
not think metaphysically either → 384, 12 ff. Cf. J. Jocz, "The Son of God," *Judaica*, 13
(1957), 130-132, acc. to whom Jesus' own understanding agrees with the later statements;
J. Weiss, *Das Urchristentum* (1917), 85-88.

[353] This is an essential statement in spite of the human images in which it is formulated.

[354] For further par. cf. Morenz, 118 and for 1 QSa 2:11 Michel-Betz, 15 f. On Jn. 1:13
→ 390, 13 ff.

[355] As R. 14:10-22 and also 1 C. 15:25 f. show, Paul undoubtedly understands Phil. 2:10,
11a as future. It is another matter whether the tradition was ref. to the past.

how much Pauline theology is orientated to God's power and honour as the goal of all history and how little a metaphysically conceived divine equality is the basis of what he says about the Son. Perhaps there is also an echo of apocalyptic Son of Man ideas in Gl. 1:16 → V, 359, 14 ff. [356]

b. The Sending of the Son of God (Gl. 4:4 f.; R. 8:3 f.).

Paul adopts a traditional thought pattern here (→ 374, 14 ff.), but completely reconstructs it. When timelessly valid wisdom statements, or similar statements describing a primal mythical event, were applied to Jesus, they were made into statements about a unique and definitive act. Paul brings this out into the open in Gl. 4:4 (→ III, 584, 37 ff.) when he speaks of the fulness of times. [357] The sending is also interpreted in terms of the predicate γενόμενος ἐκ γυναικός. This is used traditionally for all men, [358] but does not occur elsewhere in Paul. Perhaps even before Paul it had already been connected with the sending, though there are no examples in the other NT writings. This is supported by the fact that Paul adds the parallel γενόμενος ὑπὸ νόμον. He also takes it up again in the ἵνα clause which is variable in the formula (→ 374, 18 ff.): ἵνα τοὺς ὑπὸ νόμον ἐξαγοράσῃ. Both formulations obviously develop what is said in 3:13: Χριστὸς ἡμᾶς ἐξηγόρασεν ἐκ τῆς κατάρας τοῦ νόμου, γενόμενος ὑπὲρ ἡμῶν κατάρα. In other words, the formula which before Paul was explained in terms of the incarnation of the pre-existent Son is referred by him to the substitutionary death on the cross, 3:13b. [359] The statement about the incarnation is not enough for Paul. [360] It might be taken to imply no more than the coming of a heavenly teacher and revealer.

R. 8:3 f. is to be construed similarly → III, 18, 5 ff.; 951, 18 ff. Here again the formula is reinterpreted by the context. The preceding grammatically unrelated reference to the impotence of the Law shows by its very abruptness how important this thought is for Paul. If in the first instance ἐν ὁμοιώματι σαρκός (→ V, 195, 28 ff.), like γενόμενος ἐκ γυναικός in Gl. 4:4, simply denotes the incarnation as a whole, Paul puts the main accent on the judicial destruction of sin in the σάρξ of Jesus, [361] in the death of the cross according to the par. Gl. 4:4 → VII, 133, 25 ff. This is proved by the addition "as an offering for sin." [362] This means again that

---

[356] So U. Wilckens, "Der Urspr. d. Überlieferung d. Erscheinungen d. Auferstandenen," Dogma u. Denkstrukturen, Festschr. E. Schlink (1963), 83, who on the basis of R. 1:4 sees a par. to Ac. 7:56.

[357] Cf. Hb. 1:2; also Mk. 1:15; Eph. 1:10; Mk. 16:14 Cod W; Jn. 7:8 and → VI, 305, 18 ff. The προθεσμία of the Father in Gl. 4:2 is to be understood as → 166, 11 ff., but a more strongly legal expression is chosen in accordance with the image.

[358] Cf. 1 QH 13:14; 18:12 f., 16, 23; 4 Esr. 7:46, also Job 14:1; Mt. 11:11.

[359] Cf. the added θανάτου δὲ σταυροῦ in Phil. 2:8.

[360] This may also be seen in the fact that the sending is only a secondary motif in the context. It simply declares the coming of age of the heir, cf. Ltzm. Gl. on 4:5. But the seriousness of the statement forces a change in image. Man without the Son of God is not only a minor but a slave; the influence of the contrast between son and slave (→ 374, 6 ff.; 391, 21) may be seen here. Hence the theme is acceptance as son, not just coming of age, and only the fact of inheritance combines this again with the image of v. 1 f., cf. Schlier Gl. on 4:5.

[361] Cf. the exact par. → 391, 14 ff. In spite of vs. 7 ἐν τῇ σαρκί in R. 8:3 goes with the verb → VII, 133, 25 ff., cf. ἐν Χριστῷ in 8:2 (par. 6:23; 8:39 = διὰ Χριστοῦ 5:21; 7:25).

[362] This is usually regarded as a gloss with no support in the text. But if one notes that the formula occurs already in Lv. 9:2 f.; 12:6, 8; 14:22, 31; 15:15, 30; 16:3, 5 par. εἰς ὁλο-καύτωμα, 23:19 = εἰς θυσίαν σωτηρίου, 7:37 indeclinable, 5:6, 11 superfluous, it is probable that Paul adopts it to ensure liturgical or legal understanding.

the Law is vindicated without entailing man's eternal death → VI, 429, 30 ff.; 431, 1 ff. Paul, then, resolutely detaches the sending formula from the Hellenistic Jewish theology in which it has its roots. [363] If the connection with God's acts in the history of Israel had been abandoned there, the Son of God is here regarded once more as Abraham's heir (Gl. 3:13-16) and especially as the One who overcomes the curse of the Law.

c. The Suffering Son of God (R. 5:10; 8:32; Gl. 2:20).

Like the passages mentioned above R. 5:10; 8:32; Gl. 2:20 find the divine sonship of Jesus particularly in His suffering. "Son" describes the close bond of love between God and Jesus and thus emphasises the greatness of the sacrifice, [364] R. 5:8, but esp. 8:32, [365] → 364, 9 ff.; n. 116. There is also an echo of this bond of love in the title used in Col. 1:13 → 369, 1 ff. Though Paul certainly presupposes the pre-existence of the Son of God, he does not stress this traditional (→ 375, 7 ff.) topos. The Son of God title has for him the function of describing the greatness of the saving act of God who offered up the One closest to Him. The antithesis between adoptionist and metaphysical divine sonship (→ 367, 5 ff.) is inadequate for Paul because subordination (→ 384, 28 ff.) is no problem for him. The deepening of his understanding of the divine sonship as compared with the tradition lies rather in the fact that this is no longer grounded in the heavenly glory of the Exalted (→ 366, 27 f.) or general institution as King of the end-time (→ 368, 1 ff.) or apocalyptic expectations (→ 370, 15 ff.) but precisely in His suffering and rejection.

d. The Other References.

In R. 1:3 Paul makes υἱὸς αὐτοῦ the heading of the confession quoted, though it does not seem to fit too well with v. 4 → n. 228. As here, so also in R. 1:9; 2 C. 1:19; Gl. 1:16. [366] the Son of God is called the content [367] of the Gospel or of proclamation. The same is true in Eph. 4:13, except that here faith is understood primarily as knowledge of the Son of God, → I, 707, 4 ff. If the uniqueness of Jesus is safe-guarded in Palestinian fashion by the statement regarding the fulfilment of all God's promises in the end-time (cf. 1 C. 15:3-5) and Hellenistically by eternal being ἐν μορφῇ θεοῦ (Phil. 2:6), it is implied for Paul by the title of Son (→ 378, 32 ff.), so that in Gl. 1:16 this can connote all that was revealed to Paul at his call to be an apostle to the nations. On R. 8:29; Gl. 4:6 → 392, 4 ff. 1 C. 1:9 is of interest (→ III, 804, 24 ff.), for it is the only passage in the NT where "Son" of God occurs in rather attentuated fashion alongside Ἰησοῦς Χριστὸς ὁ κύριος ἡμῶν. This seems to indicate that originally the designation Son of God had nothing to do with

---

[363] Cf. K. Stalder, Das Werk des Geistes in d. Heiligung bei Pls. (1962), 134 f., n. 3, though the influence of Hell. Judaism was perhaps stronger than he allows for.

[364] On the distinction between offering by the Father and self-offering cf. Popkes, op. cit. (→ n. 292), § 16, 2b; 17:1c; on the question of the atoning death G. Fitzer, "Der Ort d. Versöhnung nach Pls.," ThZ, 22 (1966), 161-183.

[365] Ἴδιος in R. 8:32 to distinguish from the adoptive sons of 8:14 ff., for υἱὸς ἀγαπητός (which Paul does not use) in Mk. 1:11; 9:7; 12:6 (→ I, 48, 6 ff.); Mt. 12:18; Jn. 3:35; Col. 1:13; Eph. 1:6, cf. Romaniuk, op. cit. (→ n. 246), 219.

[366] That Paul saw the One exalted to heaven is stated in Ac. 9:3 ff. par. → n. 356.

[367] Cf. Mi. R., ad loc.

worship of the heavenly κύριος but had its roots in a very different christology strongly influenced by apocalyptic expectations, i.e., in the Easter experience of the community understood in these categories → 370, 4 ff.

5. John

a. Eschatological Passages and the Absolute Use of ὁ υἱός, → V, 999, 25 ff.

If the loving relation between Father and Son, which belongs theologically to a different sphere (→ 386, 6 f.; 387, 26 f.), [368] is also included in 3:35 f., the originally apocalyptic idea of the giving of power to the Son (→ 371, 17 ff.) and the authoritative character of the dominion of the Son are unmistakable. Under this rule neutrality is no longer possible, only faith or disobedience. The promise to believers is also influenced by → 374, 14 ff. The transfer of power [369] and the Father's love for the Son are also interrelated in 5:19-23, 26. There is an echo of an originally subordinationist tendency in v. 19 (→ 371, 16), but now in such a form that the accent is on the fact that the Father Himself truly encounters man in the Son. Thus the movement of the Father to the Son is no longer a single transfer of power; it is a lasting demonstration. [370] The definitive μείζονα ἔργα of the resurrection from the dead, which surpass all God's work in creation and preservation and which are here too ascribed to the Son, are related now to the awakening to faith which takes place already. [371] In distinction from Phil. 2:11b (→ 382, 26 f.) the same honour accrues to both Father and Son. [372] Similarly in Jn. 14:12 one may still detect the eschatological prospect of μείζονα (ἔργα) to the glorifying of the Father in the Son, but this is again related to the time of the Church. Finally the eschatological background is plain in 6:40. The reference is again to the enduring will of the Father rather than a single transfer of power. But this includes the gift of eternal life as resurrection on the last day through the Son. [373]

In the Johannine Epistles the use is more attenuated. The only thought to persist is that of the full representation of the Father by the Son. Without the Son one cannot have the Father and hence one cannot have eternal life, 1 Jn. 2:22-25; [374] 5:12; → II, 823, 39 ff. A fatal step is to abandon the doctrine of Christ, i.e., to lose the Son, 2 Jn. 9. Finally the absolute ὁ υἱός makes its way into the sending formula at 1 Jn. 4:14 → n. 290. [375]

---

[368] Cf. the motif of sending in 3:34, where proximity to the originally apoc. transfer of power gives it a strongly public character, cf. Blank, op. cit. (→ n. 285), 70-73.

[369] Δέδωκεν 5:22 and 3:35, ἔδωκεν 5:26.

[370] Naturally this is not mythically understood in Jn. as in Philo Conf. Ling., 63. It is never said that Jesus saw or heard in heaven what He teaches and does, Bultmann J. on 5:20, for Gk. and Hell. par. cf. 190, n. 2. It is not very likely that there is a common parable in the background, C. H. Dodd, "Une parabole cachée dans le quatrième Év.," RevHPhR, 42 (1962), 108-111; also P. Gaechter, "Zur Form v. Joh. 5:19-30," Festschr. J. Schmid (1963), 67.

[371] But cf. the traditional (→ n. 285) saying about the Son of Man in vv. 27-29. The fact that in the par. v. 25 "Son of God" replaces "the Son" suggests editorial revision. Higgins, op. cit. (→ n. 322), 165 regards v. 27 as tradition and v. 28 f. as Johannine redaction.

[372] But Jesus' words transcend pride and humility, Bultmann J., 186.

[373] In 17:1 "the Son" catches up "thy Son" and is thus par. to 11:4. In the textually uncertain 1:18 the μονογενὴς υἱός is expressly depicted as the Revealer of the Father → IV, 741, 2 ff.

[374] Cf. the eschatological layer 1 Jn. 2:28 f. → V, 653, 33 ff.

[375] But there is no sharp distinction between abs. and non-abs. use in John, cf. F. M. Braun, Jean le théologien, II (1964), 107.

b. The Sending of the Son of God.

John, too, is concerned to distinguish the sending of the Son from that of prophets and angels. He, too, presupposes pre-existence, → 374, 14 ff. But he again does not really find the uniqueness of Jesus here. Less strict in his terminology than Paul, he can even refer formally to the sending of the Baptist in the same way as to that of Jesus, → lines 33 ff. Like Paul, in Jn. 3:16 he interprets the sending formula as a reference to the greatness of God's act of love. The choice of the verb ἔδωκεν (→ n. 292) goes beyond anything in Paul in this respect. This shows the stress is on this point, not on a metaphysical statement as to the status of the pre-existent Lord → 384, 12 ff. But above all the sending formula points on to the crucifixion of Jesus (v. 14 f.), [376] so that we have the sending of the pre-existent One as in Gl. 4:4 f., but it is a sending to the cross. In v. 17 the giving of the Son is explained to be the salvation of the world and hence in Johannine fashion the gift of (eternal) life. This is repeated in 1 Jn. 4:9 (→ 374, 17) [377] and here again v. 10 defines the sending of the Son more precisely by referring to the expiatory character of His death. [378] Finally the claim of Jesus to be God's Son in Jn. 10:36-39 and 19:7, described in 10:36 as sending by the Father to do His works, leads to the death of Jesus. [379] His sonship is thus sharply distinguished from any sonship possible for believers, → 390, 26 ff. The significance of this sending of the Son is primarily explained in terms of the problem of God's remoteness and inaccessibility. It is thus understood as a demonstration of God's love which grants faith and therewith also deliverance from judgment and life in the true sense. John is thus closer to the concept of the Revealer, though he certainly does not regard Him as merely a prophet or teacher of wisdom who saves by pedagogic instruction or direction or the imparting of secrets. This is apparent in distinctive fashion in 1 Jn. 5:20 → IV, 967, 9 ff. Here salvation, in a way wholly parallel to Paul's ἐν Χριστῷ εἶναι (→ II, 541, 6 ff.), is described as being in God's Son. But this means being in authenticity (ἐν τῷ ἀληθινῷ, → I, 250, 25 ff.), not in evil (ἐν τῷ πονηρῷ). [380] At the point, then, where God invades the world in His Son, there is the world of the genuine and true in which alone is life worthy of the name.

c. The Son of God as the Content of the Confession.

The passages above quoted show already that the Son of God is for John the sum of the confession which divides from Jewish belief. Similarly in 1:34 it is sending by God (→ line 4 f.) which leads the Baptist to differentiate Jesus as the Son of God (→ V, 702, 1 ff.) from himself. The expression can also be equated with "King

---

[376] As Gl. 4:5 catches up the ἵνα clause in 3:13 f. (→ 383, 15 ff.), so does Jn. 3:16 v. 15.

[377] Dependence on Jn. 3:16 is evident no matter what view of authorship is espoused, cf. ἡ ἀγάπη τοῦ θεοῦ, εἰς τὸν κόσμον, τὸν υἱὸν αὐτοῦ (→ n. 291) τὸν μονογενῆ, ζήσωμεν.

[378] Cf. 1:7: "the blood of Jesus Christ, his Son" → I, 174, 18 ff.; III, 425, 24 ff.

[379] That these attacks presuppose the exclusive sense of God's fatherhood and Jesus' sonship is stressed by J. H. Greenlee, "'My Father,'" The Bible Translator, 6 (1955), 120 on Jn. 5:18.

[380] Cf. walking in the two spirits in 1 QS 3:18, perhaps with ref. to personal approach → VI, 559, 16 ff.

of Israel" (1:49) [381] or → Χριστός (→ 381, 2 f., cf. 11:27; [382] 20:31 [383]) without giving rise to any need to draw important conclusions from John's typical alternation of titles. Finally one finds in Jn. 3:18, cf. 1:12; 2:23 the formulation "faith in the name of the only-begotten Son of God." This emphasises even more firmly the fact that a specific confession is contained in the predicate and that deliberate utterance of the name in acceptance of God's unique acts in Jesus is decisive → V, 271, 38 ff. On the basis of 1:49; 20:31 one might ask whether the Son of God is for John especially close to the Hellenistic charismatic → 376, 27 ff. Now it is incontestable that Jesus is manifested by miracles, but titles of dignity in answer to His astonishing deeds are either very different (4:29; 6:14; 9:35) or are completely absent (2:11, 23; 4:39, 53; 11:45). On 5:25 → n. 371; on 6:69 → n. 313; on 8:35 f. → 374, 6 ff.; on 11:4; 17:1 → n. 373.

The Johannine Epistles present a similar picture. Jn. 20:31 is repeated in 1 Jn. 4:15; 5:5, though without the Christ title. Πιστεύω τῷ θεῷ is the same as πιστεύω εἰς τὸν υἱὸν τοῦ θεοῦ, 1 Jn. 5:10, cf. Jn. 9:35 vl. The sending formula is given in the abbreviated form that God has given eternal life, and this in His Son, 1 Jn. 5:11. There is also reference to the manifesting and coming of God's Son, 1 Jn. 3:8; 5:20. The content of God's witness is His Son, 1 Jn. 5:9. 1 Jn. 2:22 f. (cf. 2 Jn. 9) speaks of confessing the Son and the Father. "His (not: the) Son" occurs with the Father as the One with whom the believer has fellowship, 1 Jn. 1:3, cf. 7 → III, 807, 39 ff. "Name of the Son" occurs in 1 Jn. 3:23; 5:13.

d. The Meaning of the Divine Sonship for John.

When one considers what was already the formalised use of Son of God, especially in demarcation from false faith, one can hardly deny that the title has already become a cipher which presupposes a unity of essence between Father and Son without defining it more precisely. But when one examines the basic passages it is also evident that this unity of essence is grounded in the love between Father and Son and is thus an ever new unity of willing and giving on the part of the Father and of seeing, hearing, and responsive obeying on the part of the Son. [384] This unity is demonstrated in the acts of Jesus performed on the Father's commission, and it thus reminds us of the miracle-working Son of God. It is not an ephemeral unity which has to be attained and which might be broken off at any time, but is grounded in the depths of God's being and it thus reminds us of the Son of God who is sent out of His pre-existence. Thus Abraham and Isaiah already saw the Son of God, Jn. 8:56; 12:41. [385] Nevertheless, the heart of Johannine theology is not to be found

---

[381] "He who comes into the world" reminds us of the formulations → 374, 14 ff.

[382] But one does not have to agree with J. Howton, "'Son of God' in the Fourth Gospel," NTSt, 10 (1963/64), 227-234, in finding a typically OT root for the Son of God title whether in respect of historical development, which is very doubtful here, or of the Evangelist, who also uses expressions with a strong OT colouring in 1:41, 45, obviously in keeping with the situation of the first disciples. It is possible that John simply adopted a tradition more strongly influenced by Judaism.

[383] H. Riesenfeld, "Zu den joh. ἵνα-Sätzen," Studia Theol., 19 (1965), 216 f.

[384] Cf. Braun, op. cit. (→ n. 375), 108-112.

[385] Cf. Paral. Jerem. 9:13-20. Cf. also 1st Apc. James, ed. A. Böhlig and P. Labib, "Kpt.-gnostische Apokal., "Wissenschaftliche Zschr. d. M. Luther Univ. Halle, Sonderband (1963), 33, 16-24.

in these presuppositions but in the emphasis on the unity of love (→ V, 999, 25 ff.), which lives on in Jesus' dealings with His people. It must be conceded, however, that the understanding of divine sonship seems to be pushed much further here and that the use of the title as a cipher carries within it the risk of a purely metaphysical conception.

6. The Other Writings.

a. Hb. adopts the tradition of the Son of David who is exalted to eternal dominion, → 370, 9 ff. [386] This is plain in the introductory statement, [387] which contrasts the υἱός as κληρονόμος [388] with all that God said provisionally and by way of promise in the OT, and which gives a more precise description in terms of Ps. 110:1. Along the same lines the name Son [389] is taken to denote an infinitely higher, God-like (→ n. 255) dignity surpassing that of Moses (10:29), the OT priesthood (7:28 → 83, 7 ff.) and even angels (1:8). [390] If eschatological caution (→ 371, 21 ff.) is not forgotten with the adoption of Ps. 110:1b (→ n. 254), there is no limiting of the dignity of sonship. A characteristic of the author is his adoption of the high-priestly motif from Ps. 110:4 → 370, 11 ff. This is shown not so much by the express combining of Ps. 2:7 and 110:4 in Hb. 5:5 f. but rather by the by no means arbitrary fusion of the two in 7:28 and the quite natural juxtaposition of High-priest and Son of God in 4:14. The concepts of Son of 'God and High-priest (→ III, 278, 40 ff.), which are close already in Philo's view of the logos (→ 356, 15 ff.; III, 272, 34 ff.), are now conjoined → III, 276, 25 ff. [391] At the same time the Jewish notion of Melchisedec as an angel-like, heavenly mediator [392] exerts an influence, → IV, 568, 7 ff. It is true that the concept of the High-priest serves to unite what is said about the passion of the historical Jesus with His divine sonship, as had been done already in the tradition → 378, 1 ff.; 384, 7 ff. [393] Yet one should not overlook the fact that this seems paradoxical for the Son of God, 5:8 → V, 917, 5 ff. [394] Only in the exalted Lord who strides through the heavens are the Son of God and the High-priest one and the same (4:14), and the special position of the priest Melchisedec, who has neither father nor mother (→ III, 275, 1 ff.), serves specifically to describe the uniqueness of the Son of God, 7:3. Hence the title Son of God occurs in conceptual connection with His expiatory suffering only when

---

[386] On Davidic sonship in Hb. cf. E. Grässer, "Der historische Jesus im Hb.," ZNW, 56 (1965), 74-76.

[387] There are echoes of the introductory statement to R. in Hb. 1:1-4, Dupont, 536.

[388] Cf. also Ps. 2:8; Ps. Sol. 17:23; 1 Macc. 2:57.

[389] Cf. ὄνομα v. 4 and → 387, 3 ff., 21.

[390] Friedrich, op. cit. (→ n. 256), 105. Cf. → 374, 3 ff. Ὁ υἱός occurs abs. at 1:8 (equivalent to ὁ θεός); cf. 1:2; 5:8; 7:28.

[391] For the thesis of an early influence of the (Essene) Messiah-High-priest in the NT cf. Grundmann Sohn Gottes, 116; Friedrich, op. cit. (→ n. 164), 280-282. But cf. Hahn, 282-4, also J. Gnilka, "Die Erwartung d. messian. Hohepriesters in d. Schriften v. Qumran u. im NT," Revue de Qumran, 2 (1960), 425 f.

[392] A. S. van der Woude, "Melchisedek als himmlische Erlösergestalt in den neugefundenen eschatologischen Midr. aus Qumran Höhle 11," OT Studiën, 14 (1965), 370 f., cf. 354-373.

[393] G. Bornkamm, "Das Bekenntnis im Hb.," Stud. z. Antike u. Urchr.² (1963), 201 f.

[394] The word was perhaps inserted by the author into an existent hymn. It would thus express his own view of sonship, cf. Friedrich, op. cit. (→ n. 256), 108. On the paradox of suffering cf. Bornkamm, 195 f.

readers are warned against rejecting so great a Deliverer, 6:6; [395] 10:29. [396] On 2:10 f. → 391, 1 ff.; on 3:6 → 374, 11 ff.

b. In 2 Peter (1:17) one finds only the reference to Mk. 9:7 → 378, 27 ff. If the wording of the divine utterance corresponds rather to that at the baptism of Jesus (→ 367, 23 ff.), v. 17a shows that only dignity and majesty, and not in any sense divine election, are seen in the title Son of God. [397]

c. In Revelation "Son of God" occurs only in 2:18, presumably on the basis of Ps. 2:7 and as a material substitute for Son of Man → 371, 1 ff. The paucity of usage is the more surprising in view of the fact that πατήρ is fairly common and is used only with reference to Christ, who Himself is depicted throughout in terms of Ps. 2:7-9, cf. Rev. 2:26-28; 12:5; 19:15 → 363, 15 ff.; n. 408. [398] The title and concept Son of God are thus familiar to the author, but as in the case of other titles he adopts it only within the limits of what is possible for the Jew. [399] As the Lord of all earthiy rulers the Son of God is closer here to Jewish models, but precisely here too, as ὁ μάρτυς ὁ πιστός, He is the One who as Sufferer, shedding His blood, purchases His people for Himself, 1:5 → 369, 7.

IV. Men as Sons of God.

1. Works Apart from Paul.

Jewish tradition related the promised Son of David sometimes to the Messiah and sometimes to the community → 359, 21 ff.; 360, 18 ff. In the NT awareness of the uniqueness of the divine sonship of Jesus is determinative. Whether Jesus Himself expressed this, e.g., in the cry Abba, is less important than the fact that He and not the community has already risen again. There are thus powerful barriers against the democratising of divine sonship. Only in the Qumranic interpolation 2 C. 6:18 (→ n. 245) is the prophecy of Nathan extended to the present community, while Rev. 21:7 refers it to the overcomers living in glory after the *parousia*. [400] God is the Father of all (→ V, 990, 7 ff.) but this does not mean that all men are His sons. [401] There are hints of this only in Lk. 3:38; Ac. 17:28 (→ I, 684, 26 ff.; III,

---

[395] The question of Jewish (1 Th. 2:15) or Gentile (Mk. 10:33) guilt for the crucifixion is thus shown to be a false one, the community being told that the decisive guilt lies in their unbelief.

[396] Bornkamm, *op. cit.* (→ n. 393), 190-3 suggests the influence of a baptismal confession. As he sees it the root is Mk. 1:11, *ibid.*, 193 → 367, 23 ff. The link with the high-priest in Hb. 4:14 comes, of course, from Ps. 110:4, while that with the atoning death was already current.

[397] E. Käsemann, "Eine Apologie d. urchr. Eschatologie," *Exeget. Versuche u. Besinnungen,* I⁴ (1965), 150.

[398] Opposition to the emperor as God's son (cf. Rev. 19:13-15) might reflect later development, cf. Preisker ZG, 207.

[399] T. Holtz, "Die Christologie d. Apk.," TU, 85 (1962), 20 f., cf. 5-26.

[400] Ps. 2:8 f. is also referred to them → 371, 4 ff. Acc. to Rev., then, divine sonship cannot be ecstatically presupposed. On κληρονομέω and son → n. 417; III, 781, 30 ff.; Schweizer, 192, n. 11. The God/son relation of Rev. 21:7 (→ n. 408) shows the influence of Ez. 37:27 and 2 S. 7:14, cf. Rev. 21:3 and 2 C. 6:16 alongside 18.

[401] C. H. Dodd, *The Ep. of Paul to the Romans* (1932) on 8:16. W. Michaelis, Review of W. Grundmann, *Die Gotteskindschaft,* in *Deutsches Pfarrerblatt,* 44 (1940), 133 stresses that fatherhood does not demand divine sonship as a self-evident complement. Cf. also Cullmann, 282. On God as Father cf. also H. F. D. Sparks, "The Doctrine of the Divine Fatherhood in the Gospels," *Stud. in the Gospels* (1955), 241-262 and H. W. Montefiore, "God as the Father in the Synoptic Gospels," NTSt, 3 (1956/57), 31-46.

718, 31 ff.) (→ 354, 21 ff.), and both these passages have the creation in view, not a mythical or mystical begetting or the presence of a divine spark in man. Apart from → lines 19 ff. only Mt. 5:45 (→ V, 652, 38 ff.; 990, 21 ff.) speaks of a present sonship of the righteous man (→ 354, 32 f.) who takes the perfect love of the Father in heaven as his model. [402] Here, then, sonship is not given by nature. It is grounded in the fatherly love of God which first grants the possibility of obedience, and with it sonship. According to the parallel Lk. 6:35 sonship is actualised only eschatologically. [403] Mt. 5:9b par. v. 8b is to be taken similarly. [404] But here and perhaps also in Lk. 6:35 the correspondence between God's acts and those of the righteous man (as His son) probably has some effect, [405] while in Lk. 20:36 [406] eschatological divine sonship obviously derives from the description of the angels as God's sons (→ 355, 6 f.), so that the "sons of the resurrection" (→ 365, 23) are defined as beings in the heavenly sphere immune from death and corruption. The situation is different again, however, in Mt. 17:25 f., where we find the image of → 374, 7 f. (→ 364, 4 ff.). But the Matthean understanding of the disciples as sons of God also goes beyond the image. Freedom from the Law, which Jesus authoritatively claims for Himself, is conferred on the community too and makes it a company of free υἱοί. [407]

Rev. 2:26 f. shows already that eschatological life as a son of God (21:7) consists in an apocalyptic share in the lordship of Christ as God's Son. [408] John consciously bases the divine sonship of believers, as a present sonship, on that of Jesus. [409] He takes this from his tradition, for Jn. 1:12, [410] in a very close relation to the Johannine hymn to the Logos, and perhaps as part of it (→ VII, 139, n. 303), grounds divine sonship on the authority granted in the Logos. [411] If in the tradition, in close connection with the ideas of Hellenistic Judaism (→ 375, 14 f.), it was acceptance of the divine Logos at work in the world which conferred this authority, for John it is acceptance of the incarnate Lord in faith. [412] Yet for him Jesus is so uniquely God's Son from all eternity that he always without exception uses τέκνα [413] for believers

---

[402] On the demand for ethical perfection cf. Strecker, op. cit. (→ n. 191), 141.

[403] "Εσεσθε υἱοὶ ὑψίστου is par. to ἔσται ὁ μισθὸς ὑμῶν πολύς, while γίνεσθε in v. 36 again corresponds to the demand ἀγαπᾶτε in v. 35a.

[404] Kl. Mt., ad loc. and esp. H. Windisch, "Friedensbringer — Gottessöhne," ZNW, 24 (1925), 242 f.

[405] The divine sonship of the righteous in Wis. 2:18 is only manifest eschatologically (Wis. 5:5 → 354, 33 f.), equation with the angels again being included. It is possible, but not at all certain, that expectation of the Messiah as peacemaker made it easier to transfer the title son of God to peacemakers among the disciples, so Windisch, op. cit., 241, 248-251, who regards Solomon the peacemaker as the basis of the idea. If this is true the passages are close to → lines 18 ff.

[406] Not in Cod D etc.

[407] Jesus unites Himself fully with the disciples, cf. J. Schniewind, Das Ev. nach Mt., NT Deutsch, 2¹¹ (1964), ad loc. and → 389, 24 ff.

[408] Cf. 12:5; 19:15 (→ n. 248) and the idea of co-rule Mt. 19:28; Lk. 22:30; R. 5:17; 1 C. 6:2; 2 Tm. 2:12. In Rev. 21:7 (→ n. 400) the name Father is avoided, being reserved for Christ's relation to God (Lohse [→ n. 200]), ad loc.

[409] Cf. W. Grundmann, "Zur Rede Jesu vom Vater im Joh.," ZNW, 52 (1961), 214-230.

[410] Michel-Betz, 22 f.

[411] Against the view that there is ref. here to the virgin birth cf. P. Lamarche, "Le Prologue de Jean," Recherches de Science Religieuse, 52 (1964), 506-509; Cullmann, 304.

[412] The original ref. might be to the Logos in the world from creation; the Evangelist relates it to the earthly Jesus, cf. Schweizer Sophiatheologie (→ n. 297), 115 f.

[413] Burton, op. cit. (→ n. 121), 415 f. W. Sanday - A. C. Headlam, A Crit. and Exeget. Comm. on the Ep. to the Romans, ICC⁵ (1902) on 8:14-17 see in τέκνον the natural relation whereas υἱός includes recognised status and legal privileges. Mi. R. on 8:16 finds no distinction in usage. τέκνα θεοῦ occurs only in John and Paul.

(→ V, 653, 33 ff.), and they alone, never Jesus, are said to be born of God. [414] Finally Hb. 2:10 f. shows even more clearly from the theological standpoint that believers become sons of God only as the Son confesses them to be His brethren. [415] One sees a combination of Johannine and Pauline influence here.

2. Paul.

In Paul we find a considered theological grounding of the sonship of believers in that of Jesus, this time in connection with the saying about the sending of the Son to save those in bondage under the Law → 383, 6 ff. [416] The use of the quotation Hos. 2:1 in R. 9:26 shows already that the divine sonship awaited as the eschaton is fufilled for Paul in the community of Christ. For him, too, the apocalyptic aspect is no doubt primary. But the express handling of the theme in Gl. 4:4-7 and R. 8:3 f., 14-17 makes is plain that under the influence of Hellenistic Jewish εἰκών speculations the contrast between free son and servant on the one side and the inclusion of the community in the Son on the other played some part. The train of thought is parallel in the two passages. [417] Those ἐν Χριστῷ are one person with Christ. Believers are united to Him. They are thus heirs, Gl. 3:28 f.; R. 4:16 ff. God sends His Son (Gl. 4:4; R. 8:3 f.) in order that the curse and power of the Law may be broken (Gl. 4:5; R. 8:3 f.) and the community may live (Gl. 4:6; R. 8:4b-13 → VI, 433, 1 ff.) through His substitutionary death. Their sonship rests on this or is shaped by it, Gl. 4:5; R. 8:14, [418] In this sonship they cry Abba, Gl. 4:6; R. 8:15b → 366, 17 ff.; VI, 430, 23 ff. [419] Hence they are no longer slaves but free, Gl. 4:7a; R. 8:15a → 374, 6 ff. They are thus heirs too (Gl. 4:7b; R. 8:17), though this will be fulfilled,

---

[414] Dupont, 527 but → I, 671, 25 ff. On the other hand ἐκ τοῦ πατρός is used only with ref. to Jesus, Cullmann, 305. But cf. W. F. Lofthouse, "Fatherhood and Sonship in the Fourth Gospel," Exp. T., 43 (1931-2), 442 ff.

[415] Kögel, 118.

[416] Paul does not speak of the new birth because he emphasises that sonship dissolves an earlier and different relation to God, cf. Schl. R., 266.

[417] One finds the followed detailed presuppositions in Paul: Christians are children of Abraham → 365, 1 ff.; V, 1005, 4 ff.; the inheritance is reserved for Abraham and his seed, Gl. 3:18; Hb. 6:12, 17; 11:8, cf. Ac. 7:5; it consists in the promise, Gl. 3:18, 29; 4:28, 30; Ac. 7:5; Hb. 6:12 f., 17; 11:9; Jm. 2:5; but the inheritance is also promised to the Son or sons of God of David's stem → n. 400; Christ (Gl. 3:16, cf. Hb. 1:2, 4; Mk. 12:7) or His community (Gl. 3:7, 29; Ac. 20:32; Eph. 1:18; Hb. 1:14) takes Abraham's place; Abraham's children are God's children, Jn. 8:39, 41, cf. R. 9:8; sons are free (→ 374, 6 ff.) and are heirs, Rev. 21:7. In the NT the inheritance is very often future and eschatological, mostly with the βασιλεία as content, cf. E. Fuchs, Die Freiheit des Glaubens (1949), 106. In Philo cf. Migr. Abr., 94; Virt., 79; Congr., 23, also Rer. Div. Her., 101, 298; Vit. Mos., I, 155 and → n. 286.

[418] Schlier Gl. on 4:6 distinguishes between the possibility of sonship provided by Christ's coming and the reality given through the sacrament of baptism. But one should speak rather of the reality of sonship given by the death of Jesus and put into effect not in baptism but in the life of faith, i.e., prayer and hope, R. 8:14, cf. Schlier Gl. on 4:7. That R. 8 also confers the reality of sonship on those who have the Spirit, even though it will be manifested only at the eschaton, may be seen in vv. 19 ff., cf. on these A. Schlatter, Der Glaube im NT⁵ (1963), 397 f. Oe. Gl. on 4:7 ref. to divine sonship as the ontic ground for impartation of the Spirit, though the latter is the noetic ground for the former, cf. also S. Zedda, "L'adozione a figli di Dio e lo Spirito Sancto," Analecta Biblica, 1 (1952), 140-182.

[419] Whether the ref. is to liturgical or daily prayer (the Lord's Prayer?) (W. Bieder, "Gebetswirklichkeit bei Pls.," ThZ, 4 [1948], 28) or to a free cry of the spirit is debatable, cf. O. Kuss, Der R. (1959) on 8:15. T. M. Taylor, "'Abba Father' and Baptism," Scottish Journ. of Theology, 11 (1958), 62-71 suggests a baptismal formula in which the candidate confesses his obedience of faith and is accepted into God's family.

of course, only at the eschaton, R. 8:18 ff. → 355, 11; n. 288. Only then will they be manifested as sons (R. 8:19), though they are this even now. Up to then their proleptic being is a matter of faith, not sight. Plainly, then, Paul bases the sonship of the community on that of Jesus → 390, 18 ff. Hence what R. 8:15 (→ III, 902, 32 ff.) calls the "spirit of sonship" is the "Spirit of the Son" in Gl. 4:6. [420] The historical background (→ 355, 34 ff.) is still visible in R. 8:29. The fact that Christ, as Logos, is God's image underlies the possibility that believers will be fashioned in His likeness [421] and can thus return to the world of God → II, 396, 24 ff.; VII, 787, 34 ff. But once again this background has been completely reconstructed in terms of apocalyptic thinking. Believers already live as a new creation. This is the work of the Son of God who in His Spirit (Gl. 4:6) embraces a whole world and brings into being a new creation. Man is set in this at baptism and therewith becomes God's son. [422]

Schweizer

E. υἱὸς θεοῦ in Primitive Christian Literature outside the New Testament.

In primitive Chr. lit. outside the NT the term υἱὸς θεοῦ is used for Jesus Christ in widely varying proportions. This is true statistically. In Did. this christological title is very rare and it does not occur at all in 1 Cl. and 2 Cl. But in Ign. it plays a significant role. Barn. and Herm. show that the term gained ground in the first half of the 2nd cent. and became firmly rooted in Chr. usage. Just. and Iren. bear testimony that it had become one of the most important christological expressions and also that considerable theological problems were associated with it. The statistical findings reflect the theological development which opens with remarkable diversity and leads on to fixed formulae in the debate with Gnosticism. [423] As regards the earlier period there are signs of this theological development in the later NT writings. One need only ref. to the kinship between Hb. and 1 Cl., Ign. and John, or the Past. and Pol. It may be observed that the absence of υἱὸς θεοῦ for Christ in a work does not have to mean that the author of the work was unfamiliar with the divine sonship of Jesus as a theological statement.

1. Survey.

a. 1 Cl. never has υἱὸς θεοῦ but this is presupposed when 36, 4 f. says: "The Lord speaks as follows concerning His Son," and also when Ps. 2:7 f. and 110:1 are quoted. 7, 4 also shows familiarity with this Christ predicate: "Let us contemplate the blood of Christ and realise of what value it is to His Father." b. Did. [424] uses the triadic baptismal

---

[420] Cf. R. 8:15: setting in sonship → 399, 16 ff.; at Gl. 4:6 the gen. is missing in p[46] and Tert. Marc., 5, 6, but cf. R. 8:9; 2 C. 3:17b and W. Grundmann, "Der Geist der Sohnschaft," *Disciplina Domini*, 1 (1963), 180 f.

[421] J. Kürzinger, "Συμμόρφους τῆς εἰκόνος τοῦ υἱοῦ αὐτοῦ (R. 8:29)," BZ, NF, 2 (1958), 298 f. interprets: "To have a share in the form of His Son." Cf. also A. R. C. Leaney, "Conformed to the Image of His Son," NTSt, 10 (1963/64), 470-9. W. Thüsing, *Per Christum in Deum* (1965), 146 f., on the basis of the eikon concept, finds the focus of the understanding of the divine sonship of Jesus in the ontic divine likeness into which Christians are drawn, cf. 121-5 and → n. 247.

[422] Stressed in Grundmann, *op. cit.* (→ n. 420), 188-190, who traces back the chain of tradition to Jesus' own baptism.

[423] What is said about diversity at the beginning of the theological development offers a basically different aspect from that in, e.g., Grillmeier, 3 f. An important work in this connection is W. Bauer, *Rechtgläubigkeit u. Ketzerei im ältesten Christentum*[2] (1964).

[424] On the date of Did. cf. A. Adam, "Erwägungen z. Herkunft d. Did.," ZKG, 68 (1957), 1-47; J. P. Audet, "La Didachè, Instr. des Apôtres," *Études Bibl.* (1958), 187-210.

formula "in the name of the Father, and of the Son, and of the Holy Ghost" in 7, 1. 3. In the list of terrible events in the end-time in 16, 4 [425] we find the appearance of a world-leader ὡς υἱὸς θεοῦ → n. 315. c. At the beginning of the 2nd cent. Ign. in his letters uses υἱὸς θεοῦ several times; it is obviously a fixed and traditional expression. Eph., 4, 2 calls members of the community "members of His (God's) Son." In Eph., 20, 2 Christ is called υἱὸς ἀνθρώπου and υἱὸς θεοῦ, the former being simply "son of a man" rather than Son of Man in the Synoptic sense. Acc. to Mg., 8, 2 God has "revealed Himself through Jesus Christ His Son." In the foreword to R. Christ is called the μόνος υἱός of God. Sm., 1, 1 does not merely say He is θεός but calls Him also υἱὸς θεοῦ κατὰ θέλημα καὶ δύναμιν θεοῦ. There is also a series of statements which speak of the Father and thus presuppose Christ's divine sonship, e.g., Mg., 3, 1; 7, 1; Tr., 9, 2; Phld., 7, 2. For Ign. υἱὸς θεοῦ was plainly a current christological title. The same applies to Pol., cf. 12, 2, also Mart. Pol., 17, 3. d. Barn. shows that υἱὸς θεοῦ has a solid place in the christological vocabulary, though it does not play any special role in this letter. Christ has come to call sinners and "He then revealed that He is God's Son," 5, 9, cf. 5, 11 and 7, 9. Barn., 7, 2: "If now the Son of God who is the Lord and will judge the quick and the dead has suffered... let us believe that the Son of God could suffer for us," seems to suggest a credal formula. On the basis of a much edited and christianised OT quotation (Ex. 17:14, 16) in which υἱὸς τοῦ θεοῦ is added, 12, 10 says: "See again Jesus (the previous ref. was to Joshua), not son of a man but Son of God" τύπῳ δὲ ἐν σαρκὶ φανερωθείς. [426] Here, too, υἱὸς τοῦ θεοῦ stands contrasted with υἱὸς ἀνθρώπου, which is not a christological title but simply denotes human origin. e. In Herm. υἱὸς θεοῦ is common, esp. in s., 9, though in different connections and with different meanings. It does not occur in m., and only indirectly in v. at 2, 2, 8: "The Lord has sworn by His Son." The slave comparison is expounded in s., 5, 5, 2 ⟨ὁ δὲ υἱὸς τὸ πνεῦμα τὸ ἅγιόν ἐστιν⟩, [427] ὁ δὲ δοῦλος ὁ υἱὸς τοῦ θεοῦ ἐστιν. What follows then discusses why and in what sense the Son of God came as a slave and how this slave was then instituted as Son, 5, 3-6, 8. Understanding of the passage is complicated by what is said in the explanation of the allegory of the willow in s., 8, 3, 2. "This great tree... is the Law of God which is given to the whole world." [428] Here as elsewhere in Herm. it is clear that "Son of God" is a fixed traditional expression which the author finds it hard to define and which runs up against many inherited concepts. [429] Thus when s., 8, 11, 1 says that God wills that the calling which has taken place through His Son should be maintained, we simply have a traditional formula. How hazy it is in Herm. may be seen from its use in s., 9. At the beginning of the parable of the mountains the Holy Spirit is equated with the Church, and there is then added: ἐκεῖνο γὰρ τὸ πνεῦμα ὁ υἱὸς τοῦ θεοῦ ἐστιν, s., 9, 1, 1. It seems to be clear that the ref. is to God's Son before all worlds. [430] But in the interpretation of the allegory of the tower the rock and gate are called υἱὸς τοῦ θεοῦ in s., 9, 12, 1, the pre-existent and historical Son of God [431] being conjoined, whereas in s., 9, 12, 6 only the gate is the Son of God. All this shows that one should not press the statements of Herm. dogmatically. This is also evident in the following sections from s., 9 with its many more ref. to the Son of God. Here traditional formulae predominate, "the name of the Son of God" in s., 9, 13, 2. 3. 7; 14, 5 f.; 15, 2; 16, 3. 5. 7; 17, 4; 28, 2. 3, sometimes with "seal of the Son of God," i.e., Chr. baptism, s., 9, 16, 3, then in s., 9, 16, 5

---

[425] On Did., 16 cf. P. Vielhauer in Hennecke, II, 442-4.

[426] Cf. Wnd. Barn., ad loc.; P. Prigent, "L'Épître de Barn. I-XVI et ses sources," Études Bibl. (1961), 123 f.

[427] Whether ⟨ὁ δὲ υἱὸς τὸ πνεῦμα τὸ ἅγιόν ἐστιν⟩, which appears in some editions (e.g., Whittaker, 56) on the basis of a Latin witness, is original, is open to question in spite of Dib. Herm., ad loc.

[428] Cf. Dib. Herm., ad loc.

[429] Cf., e.g., s., 8, 3, 3: Michael.

[430] Dib. Herm., 602.

[431] Ibid., 575.

"the power of the Son of God" in which the apostles fell asleep — a traditional formula to depict graphically the descent of the apostles to Hades. When s., 9, 18, 4 speaks of the joy of the Son of God at the cleansing of the Church and s., 9, 24, 4 of the abiding of the progeny of true Christians with the Son of God, again too gt. dogmatic stress should not be laid on the sayings. The Son of God lives in the hereafter as one of God's entourage, but with no detailed consideration of His relation to the earthly Jesus. One may thus say that υἱὸς θεοῦ is for Herm. a traditional term for Christ which he integrates into his material without reflecting on the significance of the expression. The most important reason for this is that the sole concern of Herm. is to preach repentance. He has no theology, [432] and this is plain in his use of υἱὸς θεοῦ. f. How far the apocr. Gospels, which arose before the middle of the 2nd cent. or whose traditions stretch back to this period, applied the title υἱὸς θεοῦ to Christ, it is hard to say with exactitude. In particular it is most difficult to date the traditions behind these in large part fragmentary texts. Some fr. and many passages seem to indicate familiarity with this designation of Jesus. Thus acc. to Jerome Ev. Ebr. Fr., 2 [433] has "out of Egypt have I called my Son," Hos. 11:1, cf. Mt. 2:15. But sweeping conclusions can no more be drawn from this than from the equation in Epiph. Haer., 30, 13, 7 f. in which the version of the baptism pericope in Ev. Ebr. Fr., 3 [434] has the heavenly voice of Mk. 1:11 and Lk. 3:22 D. Both passages show that the Jewish Chr. Gospels followed the Synoptic tradition. But we learn nothing as to their own attitude to υἱὸς θεοῦ and its dogmatic significance. It is more difficult to interpret the fr. which one must attribute directly to Ev. Ebr. [435] Thus a Coptic fr. [436] speaks of the Father God who elected a power (═ Michael) and entrusted Christ to his care. In Fr., 4 acc. to Jerome, [437] which is a par. to the NT baptism story, the Spirit says to Jesus: "Thou art my firstborn Son." It is evident that this is a mythical-gnostic development of Hell. υἱὸς θεοῦ ideas which perhaps kept the concept intact but decisively changed the content. [438] g. The same applies to the Coptic Gospel of Thomas, though this does not have the term directly. Logion 37 speaks of the "Son of the Living One," Logion 44 of the Father and the Son, Logion 64 and 65 (parables) of the Son, and Logion 86 (cf. Mt. 8:20) of the Son of Man. But the Father here is ineffable primal light and the Son is the Revealer, not the Hell. υἱὸς θεοῦ. [439] Here as in Ev. Ebr. we see how Gnostic speculation used the title Son of God but associated it with other ideas and put it a context quite different from that of the NT and early Chr. writings. h. In the fr. of the Gospel of the Egyptians we do not find Son of God, but this tells us little in view of the ruinous state of this apocryphon. [440] On the other hand the title is used in the Gospel of Peter in a naive manner and under the influence of the canonical Gospels, cf. Ev. Petr. 3:6, 9; 11:45 f. This confirms the fact noted already in Herm. (→ 393, 22 ff.), namely, that υἱὸς θεοῦ established itself as a christological title in the first half of the 2nd cent., but in association with a wide variety of ideas. [441] i. With Justin and the other Apologists, then Iren., theological reflection begins. Son of God becomes a commonly found and much used title for Christ → 396, 31 ff.

---

[432] Ibid., 423.

[433] Cf. E. Klostermann, Apokrypha, II, Kl. T., 8³ (1933), 6; cf. Vielhauer, op. cit. (→ n. 425), I, 90 ff., who puts the fr. in the Ev. Naz.

[434] Klostermann, op. cit., 14; cf. Vielhauer, op. cit., I, 103.

[435] Cf. Vielhauer, I, 104-8.

[436] Cf. Klostermann, 5; Vielhauer, I, 107.

[437] Klostermann, 6; Vielhauer, I, 107.

[438] On the Gnostic character of Ev. Hebr. cf. Vielhauer, I, 105 f.

[439] Cf. E. Haenchen, "Die Botschaft d. Thomas-Ev.," Theol. Bibliothek Töpelmann, 6 (1961), 62-5.

[440] Cf. W. Schneemelcher in Hennecke, I, 109-117.

[441] On the adoption of the title in the Roman Creed cf. H. Lietzmann, "Symbolstudien," Kleine Schriften, III, (1962), 192-200.

2. Meaning of υἱὸς θεοῦ in Early Church Christology.

The paucity of sources warns us against schematisation and over-simplification. The varied statements cannot be reduced to over-hasty generalisations such as viewing the κύριος title as the common factor in all of them [442] or trying to find even at this early stage statements concerning the twofold being of the bearer of the title and His unity in Christ. [443] In relation to the NT one must be careful not to investigate non-NT witnesses solely from the standpt. of their relation to the NT.

If 1 Cl. (→ 392, 30 ff.) never uses υἱὸς θεοῦ but presupposes the title this is due to his concern to establish peace in Corinth. Christological exposition was unnecessary in this context. The υἱὸς θεοῦ predicate for Christ was avoided, since in view of its Hell. origin (→ 336, 26 ff.) many things clung to the expression which did not fit in too well with the world of thought of the author, who drew heavily on the legacy of Hell. Judaism. [444] This also explains the tendency towards a certain subordinationism. In 1 Cl., 36 Jesus is the Mediator of salvation through whom knowledge of God is imparted to man. He is begotten by God as Son — Ps. 2:7 f. is quoted — in order that God may be known through Him. Here the quotations from Ps. 2:7 f. and Ps. 110:1 (→ 392, 30 ff.) are characteristically interwoven into the admonition to obedience. The disobedient in Corinth are unambiguously equated with the foes of Ps. 110, 1 Cl., 36, 6. This does not rule out the fact that there are ideas of pre-existence in 1 Cl., cf. 16, 2: τὸ σκῆπτρον τῆς μεγαλωσύνης τοῦ θεοῦ, [445] the Lord Jesus Christ did not come arrogantly, but full of humility. This means that even before the incarnation Christ was the sceptre of the divine majesty; God exercised His power through Him. The stress is again on the resultant admonition to obedience rather than on pre-existence as such. [446] Nevertheless, the ideas of pre-existence and Christ's subordination to God seem to be the determinative factors in the christology of 1 Cl. [447]

Ign. uses υἱὸς θεοῦ far more often → 393, 3 ff. The thought of Christ's divine sonship has central significance for him. [448] Christ is called "God" as well as "Son of God." This description of Christ as θεός is not restricted by an added "our" or "my." Ign. is convinced of the true deity of the Lord. [449] He confesses the εἷς θεός who is Father and Creator. But Christ came forth from this one God. In Mg., 7, 2 He is called the One who proceeded from the one Father. The Logos concept is combined with the same προέρχομαι in Mg., 8, 2: "that there is one God, who revealed Himself through Jesus Christ His Son, who is His λόγος, who came forth from silence, who in all things pleased Him that sent Him." [450] Whether the προελθεῖν is to be construed as pre-temporal begetting in the later sense is a debatable pt. The expression occurs in Gnostic texts, where it means coming forth soteriologically. [451] Eph., 18, 2 - 19, 3, too, can be understood only when one is familiar with the Gnostic myth of the hidden Redeemer who comes down to earth and then ascends again. [452] This pagan-mythical notion is combined with the main elements in the Chr. tradition (the virgin birth and death of the Redeemer) and undoubtedly the

---

[442] So Gilg, 11-13.
[443] So Grillmeier, 31 etc.
[444] Thus Is. 53 is also quoted only with ref. to ταπεινοφροσύνη, i.e., Jesus as a model, 1 Cl., 16.
[445] Cf. Kn. Cl., ad loc.
[446] For pre-existence cf. also 1 Cl., 22, 1: Christ speaks through the Holy Spirit in the OT.
[447] Cf. also in 1 Cl., 42 the chain of tradition God-Christ-apostles-bishops. On the christology of 1 Cl. cf. also A. v. Harnack, Einführung in die alte Kirchengeschichte, Das Schreiben d. rom. Kirche an die korinthische aus d. Zeit Domitians (1929), 71-80.
[448] Cf. H. Schlier, "Religionsgeschichtliche Untersuchungen z. d. Ign.-Briefen," ZNW Beih., 8 (1929), on the relation to Jn. cf. 176 f.
[449] Cf. Jn.; on this Bau. Ign., 193 f.
[450] Cf. J. B. Lightfoot, The Apost. Fathers, II, 2 (1889), 126-8; Bau. Ign., ad loc.; Schlier, op. cit. (→ n. 448), 32-39.
[451] Cf. Schlier, op. cit. (→ n. 448), 35 f.
[452] Ibid., 5-32.

υἱὸς θεοῦ concept plays a special role in all this, since this originally pagan-Hell. term is well adapted to serve as a starting-pt. for speculative statements about the οἰκονομία of God manifested in the way of the Redeemer. One sees here the danger that christology might degenerate into mythological speculation. But Ign., with his sharp opposition to Docetism, emphasises that he sees in Christ not only divine essence but also flesh, Eph., 7, 2: εἷς ἰατρός ἐστιν, σαρκικός τε καὶ πνευματικός, γεννητὸς καὶ ἀγέννητος, ἐν σαρκὶ γενόμενος θεός, ἐν θανάτῳ ζωὴ ἀληθινή, καὶ ἐκ Μαρίας καὶ ἐκ θεοῦ, πρῶτον παθητὸς καὶ τότε ἀπαθής, Ἰησοῦς Χριστὸς ὁ κύριος ἡμῶν. [453] One might speak here of a pneuma-sarx christology, [454] though one should not lean too heavily on this schematic description. It should certainly be noted that if Ign. speaks so mythologically of the Son of God in Eph., 18, 2 ff. he regards him as a spiritual being of divine origin who became man and thus avoids either modal or dynamic monarchianism. In the background is the Son concept, and this shows itself to be a safeguard against such deviations. At any rate one can say that though different ideas jostle one another without being reconciled, the concept of the Son of God is central in Ign.

In Barn. υἱὸς θεοῦ is an established element in christology → 393, 13 ff. If interest focuses on the problem of the relation of the old and new covenants, [455] the author naturally cannot ignore christology completely. Christ is for Barn. God's pre-existent Son who took part in creation (5, 5) and assumed flesh for our sake. How else could men have abided His appearing, 5, 10? Barn. avoids Docetism by stressing what is strongly felt to be the paradox of His passion, 5, 1 - 6, 7. In spite of details regarding the passion of Jesus Barn. finds it hard really to explain the full humanity of the Son of God. The term υἱὸς θεοῦ is related esp. to the divine origin and nature of the Redeemer. Concern to combine this with the tradition of the man Jesus gives a hint as to the problem of all early church christology, and esp. the υἱὸς θεοῦ predicate.

In Herm. (→ 393, 22 ff.) there is no precise grasp of the christological relevance of the designation υἱὸς θεοῦ. [456] Nevertheless, acc. to the testimony of Herm. the statement that Christ is the υἱὸς θεοῦ is an inalienable constituent of the Chr. faith. The obscure co-existence of different expositions of the title (adoption in s., 5, link with angelology in s., 9) shows what problems it raised.

In Just. [457] the λόγος concept seems to be more important. But with it the υἱός concept is not just used, e.g., in passages which hark back to a regula fidei; [458] it also has theological relevance. Just. attempts something of gt. significance for the future development of christological teaching when he combines the Son and Logos concepts, or rather interprets the Son by the Logos. To understand aright the point of this interpretation of existing Chr. tradition one must start with the view of God. All those of whom the OT says that God revealed Himself to them did not see God the Lord but Him "who was God through the will of the Father, His Son," who became man, Dial., 3, 5; 127, 4. With the aid of the twofold sense of λόγος (reason and word) Just. can show how to conceive of the begetting of the Logos by God, Dial., 61, 2. This Logos, begotten as Son without anything being taken from or lost by the Father (cf. the example of fire in Dial., 128, 4), can be called ἕτερος θεός: θεὸς ἕτερός ἐστι τοῦ τὰ πάντα ποιήσαντος θεοῦ, ἀριθμῷ λέγω ἀλλὰ οὐ γνώμῃ, Dial., 56, 11. Just. wants to reconcile what Christians say about the υἱὸς θεοῦ Jesus Christ, who can simply be called θεός, with monotheism. The Logos

---

[453] For the text cf. Grillmeier, 30, n. 6, though the reading ἐν σαρκὶ γενόμενος θεός is to be regarded as original.

[454] *Ibid.*, 31.

[455] On Barn. cf. Bultmann Theol., 507-510, though he is too one-sided.

[456] Cf. Dib. Herm., 576.

[457] For bibl. cf. Altaner, 96-101; J. Quasten, *Patrologie*, I (1962), 196-219; *Bibliographia Patristica*, ed. W. Schneemelcher, 1 ff. (1959 ff.). C. Andresen, *Logos u. Nomos* (1955), 312-372, who gives prominence to Middle Platonism, is significant, but much too one-sided.

[458] Cf. A. Hahn, *Bibliothek d. Symbole*[3] (1897), 4 f.; Lietzmann, *op. cit* (→ n. 441), 220-3.

concept, in which Logos and Son are virtually synon., is a help here. The incarnation of the Logos through the Virgin Mary is presented as in the Synoptic tradition. There are, of course, many perils in this system. On the one side a subordinationist thrust is unmistakable, while on the other an inclination towards mythological pluralism is evident. [459] All the same, one should at least see that Just. struggled to grasp systematically what it means to speak of the υἱὸς θεοῦ and how this can be protected against a polytheistic interpretation. The philosophical concept of the λόγος, which is naturally rather different from the Johannine λόγος, [460] lay to hand for this purpose. But this raised the new problem of reconciling the Logos of the Apologists and the Logos of the Johannine Prologue. This is plain already in Tat. Or. Graec., 13.

Iren., too, identifies Son and Logos, but not in the same way as Just. He has a deep dislike for speculations which try to penetrate the ineffable mystery of the generation of the Son. Thus, while Iren. speaks of the Logos, he refuses to explain the birth of the Son by the analogy of the uttering of a human word, e.g., Haer., IV, 20. He thus comes closer to modalism.

The main stress in Iren. is on the problem of the true incarnation of the Son, e.g., Haer., III, 16, 3; 22, 1. Thus the Son of God becomes the Son of Man, of whom it must be said: Vere homo, vere Deus, IV, 6, 7. This is a christology of unity which has not altogether incorrectly been given the rather schematic title of logos-sarx-christology. [461] This theological understanding of the term Son of God makes sense in opposition to Gnostic speculation in which the historicity of God's revelation and saving work was lost. It is possible because from the very outset certain aspects of Gk. piety were associated with the concept of the υἱὸς θεοῦ.

Schneemelcher

† υἱοθεσία.

1. In the Greek World.

On the formation → I, 686, 20 ff., with n. 1. The word is attested only from the 2nd cent. B.C. [1] and means "adoption as a child"; there are, however, older verbal equivalents υἱὸν τίθεμαι and υἱὸν ποιέομαι in the sense "to adopt." [2]

---

[459] Cf. esp. Loofs, 97.

[460] It is unlikely that Just. used Jn. in spite of W. v. Loewenich, "Das Joh.-Verständnis im 2. Jhdt.," ZNW Beih., 13 (1932), 39-50.

[461] Grillmeier, 37 f.

υ ἱ ο θ ε σ ί α . Bibl. F. Brindesi, "La Famiglia Attica," Biblioteca di Cultura, 66 (1961), 31-85, cf. E. Berneker, Zschr. d. Savignystiftung f. Rechtsgesch., Romanistische Abteilung, 79 (1962), 519 f.; J. Dey, ΠΑΛΙΓΓΕΝΕΣΙΑ, NTAbh., 17, 5 (1937), 128-131; Deissmann NB, 66 f.; L. H. Marshall, The Challenge of NT Ethics (1946), 258 f.; T. Mayer-Mahly, Art. "Adoption" in Der kleine Pauly, 1 (1964), 71 with bibl.; U. E. Paoli, "Note giuridiche sul Δύσκολος di Menandro," Museum Helveticum, 18 (1961), 53-62; W. H. Russell, Teaching the Christian Virtues (1952), 233 f.; M. W. Schoenberg, "Υἱοθεσία. The Word and the Institution," Scripture, 15 (1963), 115-123; R. Taubenschlag, The Law of Greco-Roman Egypt² (1955), 133-6; L. Wenger-A. Oepke, Art. "Adoption" in RAC, I, 99-112; T. Whaling, "Adoption," Princeton Theol. Rev., 21 (1923), 223-235; H. J. Wolff, "Eherecht u. Familienverfassung in Athen," Forschungen z. röm. Recht, 13 (1961), 214 f.

[1] Earliest instances, inscr. Ditt. Syll.³, II, 581, 102 (200-197 B.C.); GDI, II, 2581, 218-222 (c. 180 B.C.), literary Nicolaus Damascenus Fr., 130 (FGrHist, IIa, 401, 19); Diod. S., 31, 26, 1 and 27, 5 etc.

[2] Cf. υἱὸς θετός Pind. Olymp., 9, 62, παῖδά τινα ποιέομαι, Hom. Il., 9, 494 f., and cf. the instances in Liddell-Scott, s.v. ποιέω, ποίησις, ποιητός, εἰσποιέω, τίθημι, θέσις, θετός.

a. Legal Presuppositions.

Obviously in ancient Greece adoption was not always strictly formal. In the civic law of Gortyn in Crete (probably codified in the 5th cent., but on a much older basis) adoption (ἄμφανσις, cf. Attic ἀναφαίνω "to proclaim") had to take place on the market-square before the assembled citizens and from the speaker's tribunal. The rules allowed adoption even when there were already male descendants. [3] In Athens ποίησις "adoption" seems to be a way of meeting the absence of such heirs. It is also permitted only for Attic citizens of legitimate descent. The adopted son is introduced to the family cultus, presented to the family, clan, phratria, and inscribed in the κοινὰ γραμματεῖα, Isaeus, VII, 1, which could not be done without the consent of the phraters (VII, 16), then at the people's assembly at the beginning of the Attic official year entered on the public roll (ληξιαρχικὸν γραμματεῖον), VII, 27 f. [4] The name of the adopted person did not change. [5] The continuity of the family and the family cultus was maintained by adoption, VII, 30, cf. II, 10. 36; IX, 7. Thus the legal process of adoption was often combined with making a will (διατίθεμαι), X, 9. [6] Not infrequently testamentary adoption included the duty of providing for the adopting parent. The adopted son entered at once into the rights of the parent and undertook out of the assigned income to keep the testator and his family to the end of their lives, Menand. Dyscolus (→ n. 4), 731 f., 739. Hence adoption was a way of providing for old age, Isaeus, II, 10. [7]

b. Religious Presuppositions.

In Greek there are no instances of adoption in the transf. sense. [8] Even when the ruler cult made its way into the Gk. world (→ 336, 26 ff.) the divinity of the ruler was viewed in terms of descent rather than adoption. For this reason the use of adoption terminology in a myth in Diod. S., 4, 39, 2 [9] is all the more noteworthy. After the deifying (ἀποθέωσις) of Heracles Zeus persuaded his spouse Hera to adopt him (υἱοποιήσασθαι); to this end Hera took him to her body and let him slip down to earth under her robes. She imitated the process of natural birth (μιμουμένη τὴν ἀληθινὴν γένεσιν). The pt. of this remarkable rite [10] was to confer legitimacy on the son of Zeus (→ 336, 13 ff.), this being regarded as necessary in addition to apotheosis. [11]

W. v. Martitz

---

[3] Cf. J. Kohler - E. Ziebarth, *Das Stadtrecht v. Gortyn* (1912), 71 f. and on common Gk. law 117-119.

[4] It could also be done informally, even by word of mouth, Menand. Dyscolus (ed. H. Lloyd-Jones [1960]), 729-739, cf. Paoli, 54. The adopted son had to declare assent, e.g., Menand. Dyscolus, 748, cf. Paoli, 57. In the law of Greco-Egypt. pap. men and women could adopt without being bound by special conditions (θέσις), Taubenschlag, 133-6. On the basically different relations in Roman family law cf. M. Kaser, *Das röm. Privatrecht, Hndbch. kl. AW,* 1 (1955), 57-60, 292-4; M. H. Prévost, *Les adoptions politiques à Rome sous la république et le principat* (1949), 18-29; L. Wickert, Art. "Princeps," Pauly-W., 22, 2 (1954), 2200-2222.

[5] In gen. only a paternal name was given with either φύσει or καθ᾽ υἱοθεσίαν etc.; the naming of both paternal names obviously became common in Greece under Roman influence, e.g., Ditt. Syll.[3], III, 1255 (2nd cent. B.C.) with par. in the comm., *ad loc.,* cf. the inscr. under → n. 1 and A. Wentzel, "Studien über die Adoption in Griechenland," *Herm.,* 65 (1930), 167-176.

[6] Cf. Paoli, 56.

[7] The title of honorary citizen (→ 337, 3 ff.) might go back to a special form of adoption, cf. V. Chapot, *La province romaine proconsulaire d'Asie* (1904), 165 f.

[8] Wenger-Oepke, 104 and 106.

[9] Cf. Lycophro Alexandra (ed. E. Scheer, I [1881]), 39 with schol., *ad loc.* (Scheer, II [1908], 31), cf. Dey, 128; Wenger-Oepke, 102.

[10] Diod. S., 4, 39, 2 notes that barbarians (which?) have this rite at adoption "to this day."

[11] On this need cf. Eratosthenes Catasterismi, ed. A. Olivieri (1897), Fr., 44; Dey, 130.

2. In Judaism.

The word does not occur at all in the LXX. [12] The thing itself is found in Philo for the relation of the wise to God, → 355, 36 f.; V, 957, 17 ff.

3. In the New Testament.

The term is used only for placing in sonship towards God and occurs only in Paul (including Eph.). The choice of the word shows already that the sonship is not regarded as a natural one but as a sonship conferred by God's act. But since υἱότης occurs only later one cannot be sure whether the term applies always to the act and not also to its result, R. 8:23; Gl. 4:5; → II, 275, 7 ff. Even so, the reference would still be to sonship resting on the act. This is true already of Israel's sonship in R. 9:4, [13] where God's covenants and promises seem to be associated with it and where the main point in what follows is that sonship be understood not as an assured sonship by natural descent or merit but as a sonship always dependent on God's free grace and to be received in faith. In Gl. 4:5 reception of sonship is identical with liberation from the Law → 391, 16 ff. Institution by God is again set forth as the only ground of sonship. [14] If R. 8:15 (→ III, 902, 32 ff.) presents the Spirit who governs the life of the community as the Spirit of sonship in distinction from the spirit of bondage, this is the same point. It is the all-transforming act of the Son that changes bondage into sonship. [15] Eph. 1:5 backs this with a reference to God's foreordination which rules out all the boasting of man with his natural or acquired qualities. An important point is that R. 8:23 can also describe υἱοθεσία as future, → V, 970, 1 ff.; VI, 422, 23 ff. This is not merely asserting that man can never possess this sonship, never have it in his hands, never be in a position where he no longer needs God. As opposed to an enthusiasm which thinks it has all things in sacramental transformation by baptism or even in the acceptance of the doctrine of justification, it is also making it plain that God follows a uniform course in His dealings with believers, so that sanctification acquires its meaning from the goal of the perfect and definitive consummation in which our body (→ VII, 1062, 1 ff.) will be redeemed from the conflicts of unbelief and error and death, so that faith becomes sight. [16]

Schweizer

---

[12] Adoption is also uncommon in the Rabb., Str.-B., III, 340. Cf. also P. Gaechter, *Das Mt.* (1963), 30 f. and bibl.; → 344, 23 ff.

[13] J. Jeremias, *Abba* (1966), 17. Jesus does not use the word. At most there is something of a par. in reacceptance into God's covenant in Lk. 15:22, cf. Wenger-Oepke, 107.

[14] Whaling, 223 f.

[15] A. Dieterich, *Eine Mithrasliturgie* (1903), 152 suggests the term is taken from the mystery cults, but cf. already A. v. Harnack, "Die Terminologie d. Wiedergeburt," TU, 42, 3 (1918), 103 f., who ref. only to OT roots. Cf. also K. Niederwimmer, *Der Begriff d. Freiheit im NT* (1966), 70-72.

[16] E. Gaugler, *Der Geist u. d. Gebet der noch schwachen Gemeinde* (enlarged occasional paper of the *Internationale Kirchliche Zschr.*, 51 [1961]), 26 f. W. Thüsing, *Per Christum in Deum* (1965), 119-125 stresses the difference from Gl. 4:5-7 and the connection with R. 8:29 → 392, 5 ff. For later development cf. F. Pfister, Art. "Kultus" in Pauly-W., 11 (1922), 2177 [Bertram].

---

† ὁ υἱὸς τοῦ ἀνθρώπου

Contents: A. The Linguistic Problem. B. The Historical Problem: I. The Impossibility
of an Israelite Genealogy of the Idea of the Son of Man: 1. General; 2. Old Testament
Concepts: a. Ezekiel; b. Psalm 80; c. The Personification of Israel; 3. Results. II. Non-
Israelite Background of Son of Man Messianology: 1. Untenable Hypotheses: a. Iran;
b. Babylonia; c. Egypt; d. Judaism; e. Gnosticism; 2. A Possible Hypothesis (Canaan);
3. Bearing on the Understanding of Son of Man. III. The Son of Man in Jewish Apocalyptic:
1. Daniel 7: a. The Vision; b. The Interpretation; 2. The Similitudes of Ethiopian Enoch:
a. Usage and Interpretation; b. The Exaltation of Enoch to the Son of Man; 3. The Sixth
Vision of 4 Esr.; 4. Data from the Synoptic Gospels; 5. Son of Man Expectation in the
Broader Compass of Jewish Messianology. C. The Son of Man in the New Testament:

ὁ υἱὸς τοῦ ἀνθρώπου. Bibl.: In gen. E. Brandenburger, "Adam u. Christus,"
Wissenschaftliche Monographien z. AT u. NT, 7 (1962); G. Iber, Überlieferungsgeschichtliche Untersuchungen z. Begriff d. Menschensohns im NT, Diss. Heidelberg (1953); H. Lietzmann, Der Menschensohn (1896); R. Otto, Reich Gottes u. Menschensohn³ (1954); J. Wellhausen, "Des Menschen Sohn," Skizzen u. Vorarbeiten, VI (1899), 187-215; also Einl. in d.
ersten drei Ev.² (1911), 123-130. On A.: M. Black, An Aramaic Approach to the Gospels and
Acts² (1953), 21 f., 236, 246 f.; J. Bowman, "The Background of the Term 'Son of man,'"
Exp. T., 59 (1947/48), 283-8; Dalman WJ, I, 191-219, 383-397; P. Fiebig, Der Menschensohn (1901); E. Sjöberg, " אדם בן נשׁא u. בר נשׁא im Hbr. u. Aram.," Acta Orientalia, 21 (1950/
51), 57-65, 91-107; G. Vermès, "The Use of Bar Nash/Bar Nasha in Jewish Aramaic," Contribution to M. Black, An Aram. Approach to the Gospels and Ac.³ (1967), Appendix E,
310-328. On B. and D.: J. Aistleitner, Die mythologischen u. kultischen Texte aus Ras Schamra
(1959); C. P. van Andel, De structuur van de Henoch-traditie in het NT, Diss. Utrecht (1955),
91-102; W. Baumgartner, "Ein Vierteljahrhundert Danielforschung," ThR, 11 (1939), 59-83,
125-144, 201-228; A. Bentzen, "Messias-Moses redivivus-Menschensohn," AbhThANT, 17
(1948); W. Bousset, Die Religion d. Judt.² (1906), Index, s.v. "Mensch," "Menschensohn,"
"Urmensch"; also "Hauptprobleme d. Gnosis," FRL, 10 (1907), 160-223; Bousset-Gressm.,
262-8, 350-5, 489-521; R. Bultmann, "Die Bdtg. d. neuerschlossenen mandäischen u. mani-
chäischen Quellen f. d. Verständnis d. Joh.-Ev.," ZNW, 24 (1925), 100-146; A. Christensen,
"Les types du premier homme et du premier roi dans l'histoire légendaire des Iraniens," I, II,
Archives d'Études Orientales, 14, 1 (1917), 2 (1934); C. Colpe, "Die religionsgeschichtliche
Schule," FRL, 78 (1961), Index, s.v. "Mensch," "Menschensohn," "Urmensch"; J. Coppens
and L. Dequeker, "Le fils de l'homme et les saints du Trés-Haut en Da. 7, dans les Apo-
cryphes et dans le NT," Analecta Lovaniensia Biblica et Orientalia, III, 23 (1961); G. R.
Driver, Canaanite Myths and Legends (1956); J. A. Emerton, "The Origin of the Son of
Man Imagery," JThSt, NS, 9 (1958), 225-242; A. v. d. Gall, Basileia tou Theou (1926), Index,
s.v. "Menschensohn"; C. H. Gordon, Ugaritic Literature (1949); J. Gray, "The Legacy of
Canaan," Supplements to Vetus Test., 5 (1957); H. Gressmann, "Der Ursprung d. isr.-jüd.
Eschatologie," FRL, 6 (1905); G. Hölscher, "Die Entstehung d. Buches Da.," ThStKr, 92
(1919), 113-138; H. L. Jansen, "Die Henochgestalt," Skrifter utgitt av det Norske Videnskaps-
Akad. i Oslo, 1939, 1 (1940); J. Jervell, "Imago Dei," FRL, 76 (1960), 37-70, 140-170, 257-
271; A. S. Kapelrud, Baal in the Ras Shamra Texts (1952); C. H. Kraeling, Anthropos and
Son of Man (1927); M. J. Lagrange, Le judaisme avant Jésus Christ³ (1931), Index, s.v.
"Fils de l'homme"; T. W. Manson, "The Son of Man in Da., Enoch and the Gospels,"
Bulletin of the John Rylands Libr., 32 (1949/50), 171-193 N. Messel, "Der Menschensohn
in d. Bilderreden d. Hen.," ZAW Beih., 35 (1922); B. Murmelstein, "Adam, Ein Beitrag

I. The Synoptic Gospels: 1. The Preaching of Jesus: a. Generic Use of "Man" Including the Speaker; b. Apocalyptic Titular Use of "Man"; c. Sayings of Jesus and Later Son of Man Sayings; d. The Son of Man as a Symbol of Jesus' Assurance of Consummation; 2. The Oral Tradition of the Primitive Community: a. First Stage; b. Second Stage; c. Third Stage; 3. The Literary Tradition of the Primitive Community: a. First Stage: Mark and the Special Lucan Source; b. Second Stage: Luke; c. Third Stage: Matthew; II. The Later Apocalyptic Tradition: 1. Ac. 7:56; 2. Rev. 1:13; 14:14; 3. Hb. 2:6; III. John's Gospel; IV. Reformulation as the Pneumatic, Heavenly, Macrocosmic Man: 1. Christ as the Second Adam: a. 1 Corinthians 15; b. Romans 5; 2. Christ as Eikon and Soma. D. The Son of Man in the Early Church: I. The Continuation of the Apocalyptic Tradition in Jewish Christianity; II. The Continuation of the Reformulation in Christian Gnosticism: 1. Sources; 2. General; III. The Son of Man Title in the Debate about Christ's Human Nature.

A. The Linguistic Problem.

1. The NT expression ὁ υἱὸς τοῦ ἀνθρώπου is an Aramaism in which there stands behind ἄνθρωπος a typically Semitic general or generalising concept of "man" that is then individualised by status constructus combination with an equivalent for υἱός. This combination is indeterminate in Hebrew too → 346, 1 ff.

---

z. Messiaslehre," WZKM, 35 (1928), 242-275; 36 (1929), 51-86; M. Noth, "Zur Komposition d. Buches Da.," ThStKr, 98/99 (1926), 143-163; also "Das Geschichtsverständnis d. at.lichen Apokalyptik," Gesammelte Stud. z. AT, Theol. Bücherei, 6 (1957), 248-273; also "Die Heiligen d. Höchsten," ibid., 274-290; H. Odeberg, "Föreställningarna om Metatron i äldre judisk mystik," Kyrkohistorisk Årsskrift, 27 (1927/28), 1-20; also The Fourth Gospel (1929); J. Pedersen, "Zur Erklärung d. eschatologischen Visionen Henochs," Islamica, 2 (1926/27), 416-429, L. Rost, "Zur Deutung d. Menschensohns in Da. 7," Festschr. E. Fascher (1959), 41-43; H. M. Schenke, Der Gott "Mensch" in d. Gnosis (1962), Index, s.v. "Menschensohn"; R. B. Y. Scott, "'Behold, He Cometh with Clouds,'" NTSt, 5 (1959), 127-132; E. Sjöberg, "Der Menschensohn im äth. Hen.," Skrifter utgivna av Kungl. Humanistiska Vetenskapssamfundet i Lund, 41 (1946); W. Staerk, "Soter. Die bibl. Erlösererwartung als religionsgeschichtliches Problem," I BFTh, II, 31 (1933), 37-9, 72-4, 151-3; also "Die Erlösererwartung in d. östlichen Religionen," Soter, II (1938), 421-476; Volz Esch., 262-8, 350-5, 489-521. On C.: M. Black, "Servant of the Lord and Son of Man," Scottish Journ. of Theol., 6 (1953), 1-11; J. Blinzler, Der Prozess Jesu³ (1960); G. Bornkamm, Jesus v. Nazareth⁵ (1960), Index, s.v. "Menschensohn"; Bultmann Trad., Index, s.v. "Menschensohn"; Bultmann J., Index, s.v. υἱὸς τοῦ ἀνθρώπου; H. Conzelmann, Die Mitte d. Zeit⁵ (1964); O. Cullmann, Die Christologie d. NT³ (1963), 138-198; M. Dibelius, Die Formgesch. d. Ev.⁴ (1961), Index, s.v. "Jesus u. Messiasgeheimnis"; F. Hahn, "Christologische Hoheitstitel," FRL, 83³ (1966), 13-66; L. van Hartingsveld, Die Eschatologie d. Joh.-Ev. (1962), 28-32, 63-9; A. J. B. Higgins, Jesus and the Son of Man (1964); J. Jeremias, Die Abendmahlsworte Jesu³ (1960); also Abba (1966), 15-67; also "Zur Geschichte d. Verhörs Jesu vor dem Hohen Rat," ibid., 139-144; also "Kennzeichen d. ipsissima vox Jesu," ibid., 145-152; also: "παῖς (θεοῦ) im NT," ibid., 191-216; also "Das Lösegeld f. Viele," ibid., 216-229; also "Die älteste Schicht d. Menschensohnlogien," ZNW, 58 (1967), 159-172; W. G. Kümmel, Verheissung u. Erfüllung³ (1956); W. Manson, Jesus the Messiah (1943), Index, s.v. "Jesus Christ"; W. Marxsen, Anfangsprobleme d. Christologie (1960), 20-34; also "Der Evangelist Mk.," FRL, 49² (1959); W. Michaelis, "Joh. 1:51, Gn. 28:12 u. das Menschensohnproblem," ThLZ, 85 (1960), 561-578; F. Rehkopf, "Die lukanische Sonderquelle," Wissenschaftliche Untersuchungen z. NT, 5 (1959), 97, No. 71; E. Schweizer, "Der Menschensohn," Neotest. (1963), 56-84; S. Schulz, Untersuchungen z. Menschensohnchristologie im Joh.-Ev. (1957); E. Sjöberg, "Der verborgene Menschensohn in d. Ev.," Skrifter utgivna av Kungl. Humanistiska Vetenskapssamfundet i Lund, 53 (1955); V. Taylor, The Names of Jesus (1953), 25-35; H. E. Tödt, Der Menschensohn in d. synpt. Überlieferung (1959); P. Vielhauer, "Gottesreich u. Menschensohn in d. Verkündigung Jesu," Aufsätze z. NT, Theol. Bücherei, 31 (1965), 55-91; also "Jesus u. d. Menschensohn," ibid., 92-140; A. Vögtle, "Der Spruch vom Jonazeichen," Festschr. A. Wikenhauser (1954), 230-277.

2. In the OT בֶּן־אָדָם — the determinate form בֶּן־הָאָדָם is not attested — occurs 93 times in Ez. as God's address to the prophet, and also another 14 times, always in a poetic or solemn context. [1] It is a lofty term for man, who in everyday speech is אִישׁ or אִשָּׁה or — rarely — אָדָם, which is mostly collective. Individual men are in most cases בְּנֵי הָאָדָם or בְּנֵי אָדָם.

3. In the Rabb. Hbr. of the Mishnah [2] בֶּן־אָדָם does not occur. "A man" is אָדָם אֶחָד in Ab., 6, 9, ordinary men בְּנֵי אָדָם, "someone" just אָדָם. [3] Mishnah Hbr. does not prove anything for Aram. [4] even if it be regarded as Hebraicised Aram. In 1 QS 11:20 ("What is בן־[ה]אדם among the marvellous works?") a second writer put the ה above the line and formed what is thus far the first determinate form in Hbr. It may be an Aramaism of the type בַּר נָשָׁא and if so points to Jewish Aram. [5]

4. In Aram. the earliest example is in the 3rd stele of Sfire, line 16 (before 740 B.C.): [6] "In the event בר אנש ('someone') dies, thou hast broken the treaty." In Aram., Nabataean, Palmyrenian and Hatrian inscr., [7] as in Aram. leather documents and pap. including those of Elephantine and Sakkara, אנש alone means both "man" collectively and also "a man," "somebody" in the sing. (for which we also find גבר and אִישׁ). [8] When Aram. became the language of Achaemenidian officialdom literary imperial Aram. [9] produced the first example of בר אנש in Da. 7:13. The determinate plur. בני אנשא occurs in Da. 2:38; 5:21. The determinate אנשא has a generalising sense in Da. 2:43; 4:13; 7:8 and a collective sense in 4:14, 22, 29, 30; 5:21; Ezr. 4:11, while the indeterminate אנש, as in pre-Persian and Persian inscr. and pap., means the individual man, Da. 5:5; 7:4; 6:8, 13, also in a pronominal sense in 3:10; 5:7; 6:13; Ezr. 6:11. Whether one may conclude from this that the sing. בר אנש was an esp. solemn expression [10] not used in everyday connections, or whether אנש and בר אנש were equivalent here in both ordinary and solemn style, [11] it is hardly possible to say; the latter is more likely. [12]

---

[1] Dalman WJ, I, 192; Sjöberg בן אדם, 57 f.

[2] Cf. C. Y. Kasovsky, *Thesaurus Mishnae,* I² (1956), 21-25, 383-5; on the instances in the Gemara → n. 15.

[3] Dalman WJ, I, 384.

[4] Cf. *ibid.,* 193.

[5] Vermès, 327.

[6] H. Donner and W. Röllig, *Kanaanäische u. aram. Inschr.,* I (1962), No. 224; cf. II (1964), 238, 265, 269, 271 f.

[7] Examples in C. F. Jean and J. Hoftijzer, *Dict. des inscr. sémitiques de l'ouest* (1965), 19, with an emphatic plur. only for Palmyrenian.

[8] Sjöberg בן אדם, 100 f. Cf. E. G. Kraeling, *The Brooklyn Museum Aram. Pap. New Documents of the Fifth Cent. before Christ from the Jewish Colony at Elephantine* (1953), 8, 5: אנש אחרן "somebody else"; 8, 8: . . . לא אנש "nobody."

[9] Non-literary examples from inscr. and pap. in Jean-Hoftijzer, *op. cit.,* lines 16-18 (only אינש/אנש both abs. and emphatic plur.).

[10] So Dalman WJ, I, 194, rather different later; → n. 23.

[11] Fiebig, 9 with ref. to כאנש in Da. 7:4.

[12] Fiebig, 57 f. concludes against Dalman: "If the Samaritans and already in pre-Chr. times bibl. Aram., also ancient parts of the Jerushalmi, and hence the Galileans, know not only אנש, respective אנשא, but also the formation with בר, one may assume that the Judaeans and Nabataeans or Palmyrenians in Jesus' time knew not only אנש or אנשא but also בר אנש or בר אנשא." Sjöberg בן אדם, 107 f. considers whether בר אנש in Da. should not be explained as due to popular influence, since it does not occur elsewhere in imperial Aram. whether in lit. or in the inscr. and pap. of the Persian period, which are in the

In the days of Jesus the expressions אנש, אנשא, בר (א)נש and בר (א)נשא were common in the Aramaic spoken in both Galilee [13] and Judea, [14] and all four could mean "man," "a man," "someone." [15] The two forms with בר could also have the generalising sense and the other two the collective sense of "man." [16] For "I" one does not find בר אנשא [17] but only ההוא גברא "that man." [18] But with specific pointing a speaker could include himself in ברנש [19] as well as בר נשא, [20] whose generic sense

---

same official style. But it is doubtful whether one can make so clear a distinction between literary and popular usage since there is no evidence of this in the pre-Persian period and the inscr. and pap. of the Persian period use the same language at that of the pre-Persian. The Sfire example (→ 402, 12 f.), unknown to either Sjöberg or Fiebig, shows that in Aram. both בר נאש and אנש were possible from the very first as indef. pronouns.

[13] Here one adduces the Aram. of j Talmud (ed. Venice [1523], reprinted Berlin [1925], cf. Krotoschin [1866] and Berlin [1920] and Midr. Gn. r. (ed. J. Theodor-C. Albeck [1912-1927 = Jerusalem 1965] and H. Odeberg, *The Aram. Portions of Bereshit Rabba*, I [1939]; on the generalising sense of the determinate form, II [1939] § 330; 334; 350, 1; 352, 1; 354, 1 and 3; 355), supported by the Samaritan (cf. Fiebig, 14-16 and Dalman WJ, I², 384 but cf. I¹, 193), cf. Tg. Pentateuchus Samaritanus (ed. H. Petermann-C. Vollers [1872-1891]), p. 16, 35 on Gn. 9:6 (ברנשה MS A and Ed); p. 427, 15 on Nu. 23:19 (בר אנש, line 37, MS A: בר אנשה).

[14] Cf. for this Gn.-Apocryphon of 1 Q (ed. N. Avigad and Y. Yadin [1956]) and (with Black Approach, 236) the oldest Tg. pal. (ed. P. Kahle, *Masoreten d. Westens*, II [1930]) in passages with no Hbr.; akin is the later Tg. J. II, now Codex Neofiti, I (Vermès, 315 f.); in the fr. known thus far (ed. M. Ginsburger [1899]) the findings are the same, cf. on Gn. 49:22, where the determinate form means "man" generically, Black Approach, 247.

[15] For Galilee cf. many examples of ברנש in j Talmud in the sense "a man," "man" (collectively) and "somebody" in Vermès, 316-9 and Fiebig, 35 f., also jBer., 2, 8 (5c, 49) and → n. 19; examples from j Talmud of בר נשא "a man," "man" may be found in Fiebig, 33-5 → n. 20. Examples from Gn. r.: בר נשא at 38, 13 on 11:28 (Theodor [→ n. 13], 363, 7), בר אינש → n. 19; at 79, 6 on 33:18 Theodor, 942, 2 has בר נש and Odeberg, *op. cit* (→ n. 13), 92, 8 בר נשא. Judaea: Gn.-Apocr. 21:13: לא...כל בר אנוש "no man," "nobody" (undoubtedly pre-Chr.). In Tg. pal. (→ n. 14) Gn. 4:14 (p. 7 → n. 19); Ex. 19:13 (p. 56) and Dt. 34:6 (p. 61) have the indeterminate form for "a man," "someone," while Gn. 9:5 f. (p. 31) has the determinate form for "man," but both interpretations are interchangeable, Bowman, 286; Sjöberg בן אדם, 98.

[16] So Fiebig, 59 f., though he does not distinguish between generalising and collective.

[17] But cf. P. Haupt, "The Son of Man = hic homo = ego," JBL, 40 (1921), 183 and Vermès, 320-327.

[18] E.g., Gn. r., 68, 12 on 28:12 (Theodor, *op. cit.*, 784, 6 - 785, 3): A man (חד בר נש) came to R. Jose b. Halafta and said to him: It has been revealed להההוא גברא (i.e., 'to me') in a dream..." There are 2 other instances in Vermès, 320 and more in F. Haupt, "Hidalgo and Filius Hominis," JBL, 40 (1921), 167-170.

[19] M. Black, "Unsolved NT Problems: The Son of Man in the Teaching of Jesus," Exp. T., 60 (1948/49), 34, cf. 11-14, 32-36 ref. to Gn. r., 7, 2 on 1:20 (Theodor, 51, 1; Odeberg, 8, 13), where Ja'aqob of Kephar Nebirayya (c. 350 A.D.) says of himself: "בר אינש who teaches a word of the Torah, shall he be whipped?" Some lines later (Theodor, 51, 6) we find מן מר for בר אינש in the same saying (Odeberg, 8, 21 reads here the vl. בר נש in Theodor, 51, 20). J. M. Robinson, *Kerygma u. historischer Jesus²* (1967), 187, n. 17 quotes this as a direct example of barnaš "I." Vermès, 321 f. also ref. to Nu. r., 19, 3 on 19:2 (par. Gn. r., 7, 2 on 1:20); jBer., 2, 8 (5c, 41); Tg. pal. (→ n. 14) on Gn. 4:14 (p. 7).

[20] E.g., jBer., 1, 5 (3b, 14-17) par. jShab., 1, 3 (3a, 64 - 3b, 3): "R. Shim'on ben Yohaiy (130-160 A.D.) said: "If I had stood on Sinai when the Torah was given to Israel I would have prayed the All-merciful to give בר נשא a twofold mouth, one for the study of the Torah and one for everyday use." Vermès, 323-6 also quotes jBer., 2, 8 (5b, 62-65); jKet., 12, 3 (35a, 9: בר נשא and בר נש); jSheb., 9, 1 (39d, 23-28).

was always apparent, or he could refer to himself in either and yet generalise at the same time.

5. As regards the NT this means that ὁ υἱὸς τοῦ ἀνθρώπου is a literal rendering [21] of the determinative בר (א)נשׁא [22] which is ambiguous in Greek.

As often in Aram. the determination covering all בר (א)נשׁא became meaningless in everyday use. Basically, then, the Aram. equivalent does not carry any different meaning from those mentioned → 402, 12 ff., only the special sense reflected in lofty style. [23] Nor can one in any given case choose with certainty between the four different senses (→ 403, 3 ff.), just as in everyday usage one of the other three terms might well be employed in place of בר אנשׁא.

Like the other three expressions בר אנשׁא cannot be used exclusively as a title. The special Messianic sense could occur primarily only in certain apocalyptic contexts and it could only approximate to a fixed title. In this regard, as in others, NT usage shows merely that there could be a certain emphasis on the determinate side. The determinate form undoubtedly became normative for "the man" in the Messianic sense, [24] but is was not reserved for this and the established determinate sense here

---

[21] ὁ υἱός can be understood only genealogically and not in individualising fashion in Gk. O. Moe, "Der Menschensohn u. der Urmensch," Stud. Theologica, 14 (1960), 119-129 begins with the Gk. sense, finds it confirmed in Lk. 3:38, where Jesus is finally the Son of Adam (and hence also the last or future Adam, 123), and thinks that in styling Himself thus Jesus had in view esp. Gn. 3:15 (124), since He "appeared as a born member of the present human race" (126) and accepted the responsibility of expiating the guilt of all mankind (127). Aramaic and historical research is here regarded as irrelevant and one should not follow it in trying "to explain the meaning of Jesus' self-description" by the idea of the primal man (129) as though Jesus wanted "to be man in the sense of primal man," 126.

[22] υἱὸς ἀνθρώπου is never used for the ordinary man in the Gospels as in Da. 7:13 LXX (Jn. 5:27 is Messianic), and οἱ υἱοὶ τῶν ἀνθρώπων for "men" occurs only at Mk. 3:28.

[23] Dalman WJ, I, 389: "bar enāš thus remains 'son of man' though we should sometimes put it differently." This is a not wholly satisfactory softening of the thesis of [1] (1898), 197: "'Son of man' is a correct transl. of ὁ υἱὸς τοῦ ἀνθρώπου but only to some degree does this transl. fit the Aram. בר אנשׁא," cf. 196: "If 'the son of man' were to be transl. back into Aram., we should have to say בּרֵהּ דֶּאֱנָשָׁא. The equivalent in Mishnah Hbr. would be בְּנוֹ שֶׁלְאָדָם."

[24] The indeterminate form is not yet a fixed title in Da. 7:13 (→ 421, 3 ff.) nor is it conditioned by the כ (Jn. 5:27; Rev. 1:13; 14:14 are dependent on Da.). The indeterminate בר נשׁ in Tg. Ps., 80, 18 (ed. E. Nestle, Psalterium Chaldaicum [1879]) is influenced by the indeterminate בֶּן־אָדָם in the bibl. text. The saying of R. Abbahu (c. 300 A.D.) against Christians in jTaan., 2, 1 (65b, 60), cf. Str.-B., I, 486, which does not ref. to Da. 7:13, has בֶּן־אָדָם because it is based on Nu. 23:19 and the determinate form was not in use elsewhere in Hbr. → 402, 1 ff. In the two Hell. Jewish examples sometimes adduced from Philo Praem. Poen., 95 (ἐξελεύσεται γὰρ ἄνθρωπος) and Sib., 5, 414 (ἦλθε γὰρ οὐρανίων νώτων ἀνὴρ μακαρίτης, 5, 256-259 is a Chr. interpolation) the influence of earthly national Messianism is so strong that these tell us nothing about Son of Man Messianology, i.e., with ref. to whether "man" is determinate or indeterminate. As regards the Philo ref. it is also doubtful whether it has anything to do with the son of man, since the basis is Nu. 24:7 LXX. In Hb. 2:6 the use of Ps. 8:4 prescribes the indeterminate form while 1 Tm. 2:5 and perhaps Phil. 2:7 (→ n. 472) may well reflect reformulation of Son of Man-Messianology, cf. the Chr. interpolation ὡς ἄνθρωπος in Test. S. 6:4 (R. H. Charles, A Crit. and Exeget. Comm. on the Book of Daniel [1929] on Da. 7:13). Of more weight than all these examples is the status emphaticus presupposed by ὁ υἱὸς τοῦ ἀνθρώπου in the Gospels and Ac. 7:56, while the art. in R. 5:15 and 1 C. 15:45 ff. proves nothing. On the usage of Eth. En. → 423, 12 ff. and that of Esr. → 428, 3 ff.

was not safeguarded against misconstruction in the everyday sense. In the Gospels a Messianic sense is connected only with the translation ὁ υἱὸς τοῦ ἀνθρώπου except at Jn. 5:27 (υἱὸς ἀνθρώπου).[25] This translation is not wrong, for it was deliberately differentiated from the common ἄνθρωπος, for which the original might also have been בר אנשא in many cases. But one has to concede that when בר אנשא, which originally meant only a man in the everyday sense, is rendered ὁ υἱὸς τοῦ ἀνθρώπου in Greek, then this is misunderstood or rather deliberately interpreted along Messianic lines. This is a possibility at Mk. 2:10 (→ 430, 33 ff.), Mk. 2:28 (→ 452, 6 ff. with n. 371), Mt. 8:20 and par. (→ n. 241), Mt. 11:19 and par. (→ n. 241), and Mt. 12:32 and par. (→ 452, 21 ff.; n. 406). But a Messianically intended בר אנשא could also be translated by (ὁ) ἄνθρωπος | (οἱ) ἄνθρωποι instead of ὁ υἱὸς τοῦ ἀνθρώπου. There is a possibility that this took place at Mt. 9:8: τὸν θεὸν τὸν δόντα ἐξουσίαν τοιαύτην τοῖς ἀνθρώποις cf. v. 6: ὅτι ἐξουσίαν ἔχει ὁ υἱὸς τοῦ ἀνθρώπου (→ 459, 17 ff.).[26] For conscious interpretation one might suggest 1 Tm. 2:5: ἄνθρωπος Χριστὸς ᾽Ιησοῦς (with v. 6 a rendering of Mk. 10:45); Hb. 2:6: ἄνθρωπος ... υἱὸς ἀνθρώπου (quoting Ps. 8:4); 1 C. 15:21b: δι᾽ ἀνθρώπου (cf. the quotation from Ps. 8:6 in v. 27 and ὁ υἱός in v. 28), 45-49: ὁ δεύτερος ἄνθρωπος ἐξ οὐρανοῦ (v. 47); R. 5:15: ἐν χάριτι τῇ τοῦ ἑνὸς ἀνθρώπου ᾽Ιησοῦ Χριστοῦ, and perhaps also Phil. 2:7: ὡς ἄνθρωπος.

The expression בר אנשא might originally be understood of man in the typical as well as the Messianic sense.[27] This is a possibility in the five sayings — lines 8 ff. But it will not do to explain all the sayings about the earthly work of the Son of Man along these lines,[28] since all the other sayings of the group permit of reference only to Jesus and not also to man as a type. The hypothesis that "the man" here is just a way of saying "I"[29] cannot be verified one way or the other.[30] The Messianic interpretation established by the translation ὁ υἱὸς τοῦ ἀνθρώπου was certainly normative for the faith of the primitive community. One need not ask what the Aram. equivalent would be in every instance, since the further history of ὁ υἱὸς τοῦ ἀνθρώπου lay only in the Gk. tradition once it had established itself as a Messianic title.

---

[25] The indeterminative use here might well go back to Da. 7:13, since Jn. 5:27 seems to lie historically between the apocalyptic Son of Man tradition and that of the primitive community (Iber, 117). Bultmann J., ad loc. suggests ἀνθρώπου was added on the basis of Da. 7:13. For other views cf. Schulz, 111-113.

[26] There is no instance in the Gospels, not even Mt. 4:4 or Jn. 8:40, where ὁ υἱὸς τοῦ ἀνθρώπου would fit better than an existing ἄνθρωπος.

[27] Cf. Dalman WJ, I, 196.

[28] So A. Meyer, Jesu Muttersprache (1896), 91-3; Wellhausen Sohn, 201; Wellhausen Einl., 123-5; Lietzmann, 51-3.

[29] Bultmann Theol.[3], 31; Schweizer, 70-72, 79-83 believes בר אנשא is used for "I" though with specific emphasis; he thus thinks the starting-pt. for the whole idea lies in sayings about the Son of Man at work on earth, but cf. Hahn, 23-26.

[30] Cf. the Rabb. findings → n. 18-20; already Dalman WJ, I, 204 f., 392 f.; Sjöberg Menschensohn Ev., 239, n. 3; Hahn, 24. There is nothing to show that ὁ υἱὸς τοῦ ἀνθρώπου can be a transl. of ההוא גברא (→ 403, 3), nor that Jesus used ההוא בר נשא in distinction therefrom, so F. Schulthess, "Zur Sprache d. Ev.," ZNW, 21 (1922), 248 f. and in spite of Dalman WJ, I, 205 J. Y. Campbell, "The Origin and Meaning of the Term 'Son of Man,'" JThSt, 48 (1947), 144-155.

B. The Historical Problem.

I. The Impossibility of an Israelite Genealogy of the Idea of the Son of Man. [31]

1. General.

The figure of the Son of Man undoubtedly attracted to itself the attributes of Yahweh, e.g., riding on the clouds in 4 Esr. 13:3, Da. 7:13, also Is. 19:1, that of the ruler whose glance causes quaking, 4 Esr. 13:3 cf. Ps. 104:32, that of melting all things by His voice, 4 Esr. 13:4 cf. Mi. 1:4, that of detaching the mountain, 4 Esr. 13:7 cf. Zech. 14:4, that of flaming smoke, 4 Esr. 13:10 cf. Is. 30:27 ff., violent storm and battle against the hosts of men → 428, 9 f. Such traits could be transferred to an eschatological Son of Man only if He was a heavenly being and not a mere earthly Messiah. They point directly to an origin of the concept outside the tradition of Israel.

There are clear indications that the author of Da. could not himself have created either the "man" symbol for God's eschatological rule or "man" as the representative of God's heavenly entourage or the true Israel → 422, 28 ff. a. As the representing of heathen kingdoms by beasts is borrowed (→ n. 164), the same might be postulated in relation to the "man." b. The "in the clouds of heaven," which in Da. 7:13 f. is made introductory to a scene by the order and a prep., has to be an attribute of the Son of Man or an adverbial ref. to His coming; if this is left unexplained in the interpretation, it is probably because the author could not explain it, having adopted the image. c: The heavenly being as which the man is depicted (→ 421, 14 ff.), being a representation of God's renewed dominion, might well have been a god before being demoted to angelic status in consequence of Jewish monotheism.

In 4 Esr., too, the differences between figure and interpretation (→ 428, 4 f.) suggest fragmentation and an alien tradition. As regards Eth. En. it seems evident that the Son of Man concept involves large-scale adoption of elements from outside Israel and Judaism which must derive in great part from the influence of a different total view and which in Judaism could not be combined with what was perhaps an already established Son of Man figure.

2. Old Testament Concepts.

An argument in favour of the presence of non-Israelite tradition is that one cannot construct a genealogy of the Son of Man concept in the OT alone.

a. Ezekiel. This applies first to derivation from the addressing of Ezekiel as בֶּן־אָדָם. This occurs 93 times in Ez., strengthened 23 times by אַתָּה. [32] If Jesus calls Himself ὁ υἱὸς τοῦ ἀνθρώπου (→ n. 28-30, 233), it has been claimed that this self-designation is to be understood in the light of Ez. since Jesus would not have such difficulty with this use as with Messianic predicates. As in Ez., it denotes true humanity which Jesus would understand in terms of the readiness for suffering of the Servant of the Lord of Dt. Is. [33] The element of suffering in Ez. consists in the solidarity of the prophet with his people on the path of suffering awaiting it. The term בֶּן־אָדָם could thus take on collective significance, for the people itself is addressed in the prophet who represents it. As against all this, however, the weakness and lowliness of the creature which the address emphasises in comparison with the majesty of the God of Israel does not have to mean that suffering

---

[31] Cf. Gressmann, 340-354; Kraeling, 130-151.

[32] This is no Aramaism (G. Fohrer, *Ez., Hndbch. AT,* 13² [1955], 17) but a Hbr. form denoting the individual of the species as distinct from the collective אָדָם (cf. Gn. 1:29).

[33] W. A. Curtis, *Jesus Christ the Teacher* (1943), 127-143; Cullmann, 163 also says that "Son of Man" on the lips of Jesus is at the same time an expression of humility.

is an essential element in the concept בֶּן־אָדָם. [34] Indeed one finds acceptance of the divine judgment already in Jer. 18:18 ff.; 20:7 ff. etc. (as co-suffering) and Is. 52:13 ff. etc. (as vicarious suffering). The relation of Ez. to his people is hardly one of representation or embodiment of the people. It is true that Jesus or the primitive community could have taken the address to the prophet in this sense. But even if this could be proved [35] they would not have been following the usual scribal interpretation whose understanding of man was rather after the traditions of P, [36] nor could the address as thus transmitted be the origin of the Synoptic Son of Man title in the majestic sense fashioned by suffering.

For the more precise relation of Ez. 1 f. to Da. 7 → n. 151.

b. Psalm 80. In Ps. 80:15, 17 the people of Israel is personified as a "man (אִישׁ) at God's right hand" and a "son of man" (בֶּן־אָדָם) whom God made strong for Himself. [37] Already, then, in pre-apocalyptic tradition it seems that the Son of Man was a collective entity. Yet this psalm cannot be regarded as the origin of the Messianic Son of Man. [38] For the conclusion of the allegory of vv. 8-15: וְעַל־בֵּן אִמַּצְתָּה לָּךְ, in which the son (v. 15b) personifies the vine Israel, does not fit the metrical structure and would thus be struck out by some as a doublet of v. 17b. [39] On this reading the people is asking for a king (v. 17) who sits at God's right hand (as in Ps. 110) and should guarantee Israel's salvation, though he cannot do this because in spite of his relation to God and his majesty (the man at God's right hand) he is weak and helpless before God like every man (בֶּן־אָדָם). [40] Originally, then, the son was regarded as an individual but the glossator made him collective by putting v. 17b (as 15b) at the end of the allegory of the vine and thus relating him unequivocally to Israel. [41] Historically this would be a comparable step to that from Da. 7:13 to Da. 7:27b → 422, 1 ff.

c. The Personification of Israel. Finally the personification of Israel, which apart from Ps. 80:17b is plain in many places and various strata of the OT, cannot be regarded as the root of the man-concept in apocalyptic. For one thing it is not constructive but simply fills out given concepts, as the relation of Da. 7:27 to 7:13 shows. For another the significance of Israel as the people of the end-time is not enough to explain the transcendence of the Son of Man nor His judicial work, which applies to Israel too.

3. Results.

It would seem, then, that one has to seek a non-Israelite background for the figure of the Son of Man. A basic principle from the very outset is that even if

---

[34] But cf. W. Eichrodt, "Zum Problem d. Menschensohns," *Ev. Theol.,* 19 (1959), 1-3.
[35] Lk. 19:10 (→ 453, 7 ff.; n. 415) might be related to Ez. 34:15 f., though this ref. to God's work, not the prophet's, Manson Son, 173.
[36] On the setting of Ez. in priestly usage, which likes to name אָדָם as a legal subject (Lv. 1:2; 13:2; Nu. 19:14), cf. W. Zimmerli, *Ez., Bibl. Komm. AT,* 13 (1954), 70 f.
[37] Black, *op. cit.* (→ n. 19), 11.
[38] Similarly the בֶּן־אָדָם of Ps. 8:4 is regarded as a king in whom the primal man of the ancient Orient still lives on. In this sense he was brought into connection with the Son of Man. Cf. A. Bentzen, "King-Ideology — 'Urmensch,' — 'Troonsbestijgingsfeest,'" *Stud. Theologica,* 3 (1950/51), 148-157. This modification of the primal man hypothesis is implicitly refuted → 410, 6 ff. On the Tg. on Ps. 8:4 (→ n. 24), which says non-messianically בַר נָשָׁא, cf. Bowman, 284.
[39] A. Bertholet in Kautzsch, 209; H. Gunkel, *Die Ps., Handkomm. AT,* II, 2⁴ (1926), *ad loc.*
[40] H. J. Kraus, *Ps., I, Bibl. Komm. AT,* 15, 1 (1960), *ad loc.*
[41] Ps. 80 did become important for Son of Man Messianology, though in a different sense; the Tg. interprets בֶּן־אָדָם by בַר נָשׁ both individually and Messianically, cf. Str.-B., I, 486; → n. 24; → 430, 18 ff.

such a background is found the Son of Man figure does not really derive from it nor can the significance of the figure either in Jewish apocalyptic or the NT be materially explained in the light of it. The point is simply to hunt out the conceptual materials, which are significant because the new Messianic understandings possible at various times could hardly have crystallised without them.

II. Non-Israelite Background of Son of Man Messianology.

1. Untenable Hypotheses.

a. Iran. The apocalyptic Son of Man can hardly be the Avesta Gaya-marətan or Middle Persian Gayōmart in a Judaised form, [42] for one cannot regard Son of Man and Gayōmart ("mortal life," meant as an appellative and not as a term for anonymity) as variations of one and the same prototypical primal man. [43] Such a figure with a proto-logical as well as an eschatological role can be proved between Zarathustra or the later Avesta on the one side and the 2nd cent. on the other neither directly nor with the help of deductions from the Zoroastrian or Zurvanitian Pahlavi lit. of the Sassanidian and early Islamic period. Even if he could, it would still be impossible to show why his original form Adam does not appear in the last time in Judaism and his eschatological form Saōšyant- [44] does not appear in the first age in Zoroastrianism or Zurvanism. The eschato-logical role [45] of Gayōmart is simply that acc. to the Ind. Bundahišn, 30, 7. 9 [46] he is the pioneer of the resurrection and not that dominion is given him over all peoples. If Saōšyant-were regarded as the returning Gayōmart, his activity as that of an earthly saviour would have to be distinguished from that of a Son of Man in heaven. [47] Again, the Indo-Iranian king of paradise, who is called Yama in the Rigveda and Yima in the Avesta, [48] is a protological figure. As ruler of the realm of the blessed dead Yašt (→ n. 44), 9, 8 ff.; 15, 15 f.; 19, 30-33; Vendidad, 2, [49] he is contemporary with every generation and does not come to all mankind as judge. [50] Appeal might be made to the Fravaši [51] as regards the Son of Man equated with Enoch (→ 428, 36 ff.) but not as regards the total imagery, e.g., in Da. [52] or 4 Esr. Nor is there any original unity of essence between Enoch and

---

[42] Cf. v. Gall, 409-419; W. Bousset, Die Religion d. Judt. (1903), 347 f.; Kraeling, 128-165.

[43] Cf. the attempt of Christensen, I, 33.

[44] v. Gall, 108 f. tries to overcome this difficulty by combining Gayōmart with the third Saōšyant. This goes beyond passages like Yasna, 26, 10 (ed. K. F. Geldner, Avesta, I [1886], 94); Yašt, 13, 145 (K. F. Geldner, Avesta, II [1889], 202), where the liturgical list from Gaya-(marətan-) to the victorious Saōšyant presupposes correspondence to beginning time and end time but not an identity of the two in either time, Colpe, 150.

[45] So v. Gall, 109, 126, 409, 437; Bousset-Gressm., 352.

[46] Ed. F. Justi, Der Bundehesh (1868).

[47] Thus assuming such a combination the Son of Man is just a variation of the earthly national Messiah of Israel, cf. H. Junker, Untersuchungen über literarische u. exeget. Pro-bleme d. Buches Da. (1932), 62 f. or Gressmann, 361-4, who suggests the Yama-Yima rather than the Gayōmart myth.

[48] Cf. Bousset-Gressm., 489 f. (only for the Messiah figure); Gressmann, 272-285, 362-4 (hence for the Son of Man too); Iber, 7 (direct genealogy). Acc. to H. Güntert, Der arische Weltkönig u. Heiland (1923), 374-6 Yima was the original of Gayōmart, whose name is an artificial construct of Persian theology.

[49] Ed. D. H. Jamasp, Vendidad (1907).

[50] Cf. Lagrange, 398.

[51] The Fravaši of the exemplarily righteous man Enoch is the Son of Man acc. to Otto, 319-321, who essentially follows Staerk Soter, II, though his additions (e.g., 471: "potential fulness of power," a vox media which fits the protective and sacrificial functions of the Fravaši and the judicial office of the Son of Man) are better adapted to show how unlikely the connection between Son of man and Fravaši is.

[52] Baumgartner, 220.

"his" Son of Man such as one may assume to exist between Iranian man sacrificing and seeking protection and his Fravaši. Furthermore the sources [53] do not ref. to the eschatological judicial office of the Fravaši.

b. Babylonia. Only on the basis of the unlikely thesis that the Son of Man was originally a second Adam can one associate the Babyl. Adapa [54] with the Son of Man. [55] Adapa himself has no eschatological, judicial or redemptive function. [56] Only linguistically is the designation zēr amelūti "seed (shoot) of humanity" [57] analogous to בר נשא; this has no bearing on the content. The primal sage found in Adapa may also be represented by Ea (Berosus Fr., 1, 4 f.; 3, 11 f. [FGrHist, III, C 369 f., 375 f.]: Oannes), [58] the Babyl. god of the sweetwater ocean and wisdom. A historically related Jewish antitype may be seen in the Son of Man of Eth. En. (the bringing of wisdom) and 4 Esr. (arising out of the sea). [59] Yet anything more is shattered by the fact that agreement of individual motifs does not prove the identity of the persons to whom they are attached. In Ea/Oannes the context of the motifs is a primal cultural act which cannot be a pattern for eschatological judgment.

c. Egypt. The hypothesis [60] that the Ancient of Days who gives the Son of Man world dominion in Da. 7 (→ 423, 6 f.) and the throne of glory in Eth. En. 62:5; 69:27-29 (→ 427, 25 ff.) is the same as the Egypt. world-ruler the sun-god, the aged Atum, and that the successor of Atum, a beautiful youth who is the sun-god Re (or Horus?), is the Son of Man, is close to the Canaanite theory → 415, 38 ff. But there is a difference in that on the Egypt. theory one has to postulate a unity of essence (however modified) between the Son of Man and the Ancient of Days, since the "pattern" sets before us different stages of the Egypt. sun-god, Atum in the evening and Re in the morning or at midday. Such a concept is remote from Da. 7. Furthermore the analogy applies only if Atum abdicates, but Re's abdication is attested as well. [61] The tertium comparationis, "beautiful youth," [62] is peripheral in relation to the Son of Man and on the Egypt. side applies only to Horus, whose entry into the alternation between Atum and Re is a special stage in the history of Egypt. religion. [63] In Egypt syncretistic equations of sun-gods

---

[53] Fully discussed and quoted in N. Söderblom, "Les Fravashis," RHR, 20 (1899), 228-260, 373-418.

[54] Ed. and transl. by J. B. Pritchard, Ancient Near Eastern Texts² (1955), 101, cf. E. A. Speiser, 101-3. Cf. P. Jensen, Art. "Adapa," Reallex. d. Assyriologie, 1 (1932), 33-5; F. M. T. Böhl, "Die Mythe v. weisen Adapa," Welt d. Orients, 2 (1959), 416-431; G. Roux, "Adapa, le vent et l'eau," Revue d'Assyriologie et d'Archéol. Orientale, 55 (1961), 13-33; D. O. Edzard, "Mesopotamien," Wörterb. d. Mythologie, ed. H. W. Haussig, I, 1 (1965), 39.

[55] Cf. A. Jeremias, Art. "Oannes-Ea," Roscher, III, 1, 586, n. 3 and H. Zimmern in H. Gunkel, Schöpfung u. Chaos in Urzeit u. Endzeit (1895), 148-151 and KAT, 520-3 (only Adam). A-da-ap may be linguistically related to Adam acc. to Speiser, op. cit., 101, n. * but in Gn. 2:5 - 5:5 Adam as proper name is much more intertwined with Adam as typical man than in the Adapa myth.

[56] Cf. A. Jeremias, Hndbch. d. altoriental. Geisteskultur² (1929), 98 and F. Jeremias in Bertholet-Leh., I, 599, but cf. Bousset-Gressm., 355, n. 3. When Sennacherib, who felt himself to be the renewer of the world, is lauded as Adapa's successor (cf. the letter to Assurbanipal in Pritchard, op. cit., 450), this denotes descent from a wise hero of primal days but not the transfer of a quality as redeemer.

[57] Only in a fr. from Assurbanipal's library, cf. Pritchard, op. cit., 102 D, line 12.

[58] Cf. the instances in Edzard, op. cit., 56 (s.v., Enki) and 117.

[59] So Jansen, 105-111.

[60] Cf. H. Gressmann, Der Messias (1929), 403-5.

[61] A. Erman, Die Religion d. Ägypter (1934), 37.

[62] Gressmann, op. cit., 403-5 ref. to the "charming countenance" of the Son of Man (only Eth. En. 46:1).

[63] A view of the sun as torch replaced that of the sun as man or disc — something which could always happen in Egypt, often for political or religio-political reasons, cf. H. Kees, Der Götterglaube im alten Ägypten (1941), 183, 230-233, 389-405, 423.

and transfers of predicates vacillate too much [64] to provide as a basis for the merging of the Ancient of Days into the Son of Man some hypothetical form in which the ancient cosmic god is clearly replaced by a young one. Since "like a man" in Da. 7 is merely descriptive, the idea of an underlying god with an animal's head (→ n. 150) can be ruled out.

d. Judaism. Rabb. speculations about Adam, whose outstanding qualities (as a collective entity for the race) at the beginning of the present aeon are thought to have contributed to an understanding of his eschatological antitype the Son of Man (and representative of Israel) as the initiator of the new aeon, [65] are originally purely protological. [66] Where speculations on man are also eschatological one may see the influence of other elements of which one is a heterogeneous view of the Son of Man or one of its developments, → n. 67; 430, 12 ff.; 470, 24 ff. The high estimation of Adam may be due to a special soteriological concern. But the fact that this leads to glorifying of the first man Adam, who nevertheless does not become the redeemer but whose majesty guarantees the glorifying of his successors, who without him stand in need of redemption, and the fact that no new figure is constructed to whom this concern is related, all this makes it highly improbable that the Son of Man is here the only exception. [67]

As regards Adam Qadmōnī or hā-Rišōn [68] the predicate "heavenly" is misleading. It denotes here the cosmic and universal character of the figure as determined by the heavenly dimension, while in the case of the Son of Man the ref. is to the place of His appearing. On the other hand, there is a close connection between the Adam-Kadmon idea on the one

---

[64] On equation of Re (in the morning rather than midday form) with Atum as Atum-Re-Harachte cf. W. Helck, "Ägypten," Wörterb. d. Mythologie, I, 1 (→ n. 54), 342 and 390: "Thus Re becomes not only the ruling cosmic god but also the primal creator-god. At the same time Atum becomes the form of the setting sun."

[65] The lit. which presents these hypotheses with many variations is the same as that for theories deriving the figure of the Son of Man from other spheres and need not be repeated here. The connection with other spheres rests on the theory that Adam speculation indicates the influence of the "oriental figure of the primal man" etc. in Judaism. We cannot accept this.

[66] They glorify Adam as protoplast, e.g., Sir. 49:16; Vid. Ad., 31-42; bSanh., 59b; 1 QS 4:23; Damasc. 3:20 (5:6) and many expositions of Gn. 1:26 in Jervell, 26-37, or else they view him as the prototype who fixed the destiny of coming generations, 4 Esr. 3:7, 21 f. etc.; S. Bar. 17:3 etc.; S. Lv. (ed. I. H. Weiss [1862]), 27a on 5:17 (→ V, 696, 1 ff., n. 310). Where the sources speak of the fall, either Adam's glory is restored, Vit. Ad., 41; Apc. Mos. 39, or there is no restoration and Adam's gigantic size (→ lines 8 ff.) is reduced, Str.-B., IV, 947; Schenke, 129, or Adam becomes mortal, Tanch. (ed. Stettin [1865]) בראשית, 8 (11b); S. Dt. (ed. M. Friedmann [1864]), 339 (141a) on 32:50; as regards influence on the mortality of the human race cf. Brandenburger, 45-64.

[67] Brandenburger, 69 with Jervell, 119 (→ I, 142, 25 ff.) pts. out that neither in the Rabb. nor in apocal. Judaism of the NT age is there any evidence that the second Adam had a soteriological function. Murmelstein, 258 f. thinks it was suppressed in anti-chr. polemic. But note the clearly Messianic man of Nu. 24:7 LXX: ἐξελεύσεται ἄνθρωπος ἐκ τοῦ σπέρματος αὐτοῦ (sc. Jacob/Israel) and 17: καὶ ἀναστήσεται ἄνθρωπος ἐξ Ἰσραήλ (both deviating from HT); also Test. Jud. 24:1; cf. N. 4:5: ἄχρις οὗ ἔλθῃ τὸ σπλάγχνον Κυρίου, ἄνθρωπος ποιῶν δικαιοσύνην καὶ ποιῶν ἔλεος . . . and Philo Praem. Poen., 95 (exposition of Nu. 24:7 LXX). Yet we do not find the attribute "second." The ref. must be to the earthly-national Messiah, cf. 2 S. 23:1-7 LXX, where ἄνθρωπος is either non-technical or it is influenced by Son of Man Messianology, so perhaps the vir in 4 Esr. (→ 428, 4), cf. G. H. Box, The Ezra-Apocal. (1912), ad loc. Just. Dial., 34, 2; 126, 1; 128, 1 f. is already christological and no more justifies the deducing of a first and second Adam typology than Sir. 24:28.

[68] These terms are reserved for the figure whose gigantic size reaches from one end of the world to the other, the macrocosm, so Tanch. תזריע, 10, 57 (Buber, 37); Gn. r., (ed. Venice, 1545), 8 (6a) on 1:26 etc.; Lv. r., 14 (114d) on 12:2; Pesikt. r. (ed. M. Friedmann, 1880), 23 (115a) etc.; bSanh., 38b.

side and the idea of the heavenly, i.e., macrocosmic man in Philo (→ lines 9 ff.) and Gnosticism (→ 412, 9 ff.) on the other. But this is insufficient basis for a redemptive activity of Adam-Kadmon which for its part might explain the function, if not the figure, of the Son of Man. Only in Gnosticism and not in Philo (→ lines 14 ff.) nor in Judaising magical prayer [69] is redemption brought by a hypostatically individuated figure. But this came about only by attaching a pagan prophet or the man Christ (→ 475, 37 ff.) to a cosmic pleroma related to Adam-Kadmon. Historical and eschatological elements were thus imported into the idea which did not originally belong to Adam-Kadmon. [70]

The nature of Philo's ἄνθρωπος οὐράνιος, which is akin to Adam-Kadmon, [71] forcibly prevents us from seeing here any counterpart to the apocal. Son of Man of the same historical genealogy. [72] The apocal. Son of Man far too plainly lacks, and has always lacked, a macrocosmic character (→ n. 71), a cosmological function as the best part of the world soul, [73] and an anthropological function as the best part of the human soul, [74] while the Philonic "man" far too plainly lacks individuality, participation in heavenly scenes, and an eschatological and as such specifically judicial function. It is thus impossible to claim even the remotest kinship between the two. This does not alter the fact that Paul (→ 471, 13 ff.), Eph./Col. (→ 472, 32 ff.) and some Gnostics (→ 474, 31 ff.), reinterpreting the heavenly quality [75] of the apocal. "man," could in fact understand Him as an ἄνθρωπος with the traits of Philo's "man." Nevertheless, the fact that certain concepts can merge syncretistically does not prove original relationship.

If the Son of Man is not an ἄνθρωπος οὐράνιος, is He perhaps σοφία in apocal. or mythological dress? [76] Jewish wisdom speculation (→ VII, 496, 16 ff.) belongs in part

---

[69] Preis. Zaub., 1, 195-222; 4, 1167-1227. Here the heavenly cosmic Adam, since he is invoked by the earthly Adam for salvation and draws the latter to himself, is a *salvator*, and since he cannot be completely differentiated conceptually or substantially from the petitioner, 4, 1177-1179, 1211-1213; 1, 209-211 he is also a *salvandus*, cf. E. Peterson, "La libération d'Adam de l' 'Ανάγκη," *Rev. Bibl.*, 55 (1948), 199-214 and Brandenburger, 77-81. This reminds us of philosophical σωτηρία but is closer to Gnosticism inasmuch as the cleft between the *salvator* and the *salvandus* who is enslaved to demons and fate is dualistic. Yet Adam does not come down to himself as in the developed Gnostic myth. Like the Naassene sermon, the prayer of the magic pap. is half-way to Gnosticism.

[70] Brandenburger, 246. 261.

[71] Cf. with the passages → n. 68 Philo Op. Mund., 25. 69. 134 f. 139; Spec. Leg., III, 83. 207; Rer. Div. Her., 230 f.; Leg. All., III, 96; also I, 31-108; II, 4; Plant., 18-20, 44; Conf. Ling., 41-3. 146.

[72] Cf. Bousset, *op. cit.* (→ n. 42), 248-255, 346-9; Bousset Religion, 307-9; Bousset Hauptprobleme, 194-7; Reitzenstein Ir. Erl., 104-111, 120 f.; Bultmann Bedeutung, 141; Bultmann J., 11 f., 12, n. 3; Cullmann, 141-4, 150-3.

[73] Cf. Conf. Ling., 24. 41; Det. Pot. Ins., 83; Som., II, 267; Omn. Prob. Lib., 111; Fug., 72; Rer. Div. Her., 57; Ebr., 140. For details cf. Jervell, 52-70; F. W. Eltester, "Eikon im NT," ZNW Beih., 23 (1958), 34-48.

[74] Cf. Det. Pot. Ins., 83; Agric., 9; Rer. Div. Her., 230-232; Poster. C., 58; Ebr., 140; Leg. All., III, 137; Cher., 130; Spec. Leg., I, 124; Vit. Mos., II (III), 135. Cf. Jervell, 60-64; Eltester, *op. cit.*, 54-58.

[75] Naturally presupposing equation with Jesus Christ; this adds some new features to ἄνθρωπος theology (→ 470, 23 ff.; 474, 24 ff.) which makes it hard to pick out the true origins.

[76] So J. Muilenburg, "The Son of Man in Da. and the Eth. Apoc. of Enoch," JBL, 79 (1960), 197-209, esp. 208 f., developing the insights of A. Feuillet, "Le fils de l'homme de Da. et la tradition bibl.," *rev. Bibl.*, 60 (1953), 170-202, 321-346 and Kraeling, 74-127, 154 f. The argument is that Son of Man statements, esp. in Da. and Eth. En., are very similar to what is said about hypostatised wisdom in wisdom speculation, but also Job 15:7 f.; Prv. 8:22-25, and Jewish interpretations of Gn. 1:28 f. (Jervell, 46-51); Ps. 8; Ps. 80 and Ez. 28 (cf. Bentzen, 39-47). Wisdom traditions contain cosmological, mythological, astronomical and protological-eschatological speculations, and speculations about the first man are connected with many of these. A linking of protological and eschatological speculation could lead to eschatological man from eschatological wisdom, the counterpart of the cosmological wisdom active at creation which in function symbolises the cosmos and converges on the glorified Adam.

at least (→ VII, 503, 4 ff.) to the same tradition as the idea of the Son of Man. But where there is a connection wisdom manifests the Son of Man (Eth. En. 48:7) or the Son of Man has wisdom (→ 425, 31 f.). This interrelationship of the two makes it most unlikely that the Son of Man is another version of wisdom, cf. also → 373, n. 278. Again, there are in detail considerable differences between the Son of Man concept and the wisdom myth of Eth. En. 42 (→ VII, 507, 20 ff.). Only when the Son of Man was interpreted as the heavenly and cosmic anthropos (→ 471, 26 ff.; 476, 7 ff.) could He be equated with σοφία. [77]

e. Gnosticism. When the primal man of Gnosticism is advanced as the original of the Son of Man the basis is often a specific theory of the relationship, influence, or identity between Gnosticism and other forces. In many cases this theory for its part rests on the construction of a genealogical connection between all available "man" figures. For this reason the relevant hypotheses are integral to theories already discussed, esp. the Iranian, [78] though this may not always be clear in detail. The originally imprecise connection between the Son of Man of the Gospels and the Gnostic anthropos teaching [79] might be defined more closely as the expression of an original kinship such as that between the Son of Man of apocal. and the idea of the heavenly or primal man in Gnostic and esp. Mandaean and Manichaean religion [80] or the agreement between Jesus' term for Himself and that of the redeemer in "popular Iranian belief" (de facto in Gnosticism and esp. among the Mandaeans). [81] Hypotheses which try to be more exact chronologically argue that Judaism took over an early form of the Gnostic anthropos, i.e., the victorious primal warrior who orginally goes back to Marduk and then interpreted this Messianically and as the one "like a man," [82] or that the Gnostic anthropos, around already in the 2nd cent. B.C., was adopted and altered in Jewish apocal. [83] Without passing first through apocal. and the Synoptic tradition, the Gnostic primal-man/redeemer doctrine had a direct influence on the Son of Man christology of John's Gospel. [84]

For all the variations in details the textual data support certain basic views which can be delineated clearly. "Man" with various predicates (perfect, first, eternal, immortal, male-female, pre-existent) is the supreme God (Father, living Father, Bythos, Father of truth, Nous, All), Apocr. Joh. [85] 22:9; 47:15; 48:3 f.; Gospel of Thom. [86] Logion 24 (86, 7 ff.), 106 (98, 18 ff.), work without title [87] 151, 19; 152, 2; 155, 26, the Ophite system,

---

[77] On the basis of the older identification of spiritualised ἄνθρωπος and σοφία as found, e.g., in Philo Rer. Div. Her., 126-8 etc.

[78] For the Gnostic anthropos as the Hell. or syncretised form of the Iranian Gayōmart cf. Kraeling, 85-127; Bousset-Gressm., 354 f.; Bousset Religion, 407; Bousset Hauptprobleme, 202-9; Reitzenstein Hell. Myst., 9-17, 181, 418; Ir. Erl., passim. Cf. Colpe, 9-56; Schenke, 16-33.

[79] Reitzenstein Poim., 81.

[80] Bousset, op. cit. (→ n. 42), 248-255, 346-9; Bousset Religion, 407; Bousset Hauptprobleme, 194-202, 215-223; Gressmann Ursprung, 364; Bousset-Gressm., 355.

[81] R. Reitzenstein, Das mandäische Buch d. Herrn d. Grösse (1919), 45 f.

[82] Kraeling, 142-5, 187.

[83] Reitzenstein Ir. Erl., 118-123; Bultmann J., 12; Cullmann, 141-154; S. Mowinckel, He That Cometh² (1959), 426 and 431.

[84] Bultmann J., 12 etc.

[85] Ed. W. Till, Die gnost. Schriften d. kpt. Pap. Berolinensis, 8502, TU, 60 (1955), cf. also Sophia Jesu Christi, ibid., 96, 12; on this Schenke, 6 f., 34-43. For Nag-Hammadi materials cf. M. Krause - P. Labib, "Die drei Versionen d. Apokryphon d. Joh. im kpt. Museum zu Alt-Kairo," Abhandlungen d. Deutschen Archäol. Instituts Kairo Kpt. Reihe, 1 (1962), Index, s.v. ⲣⲱⲙⲉ. On the "Son of Man" in this system → 475, 14 ff.

[86] Ed. A. Guillaumont - H. C. Puech - G. Quispel - W. Till - Y. Abd el Masih (1959), cf. E. Haenchen, Die Botschaft d. Thomas-Ev. (1961), 53 and 65.

[87] Ed. A. Böhlig - P. Labib, Deutsche Akad. d. Wissenschaften Berlin, Instit. f. Orientforschung, 58 (1962); cf. Schenke, 7 and 49-51.

Iren. Haer., I, 30, [88] Eugnostos the Blessed, Cod. Cairensis Gnosticus, III, [89] 76, 23 f.; 77, 10-14; 85, 10. 21 f.; 88, 6 f.; 89, 8 f., the Valentinians, Cl. Al. Strom., II, 36, 2-4; Epiph. Haer., 31, 5, 5; 36, 2, 2 f.; Iren. Haer., I, 12, 4, [90] and perhaps the Marcosites, Iren. Haer., I, 14, 3 (→ 475, 20 ff.), the Naassene Sermon, Hipp. Ref., V, 7, 3 - 9, 9, [91] the Sethian system, ibid., V, 19-22, [92] Zosimos Hypomnemata on the Stoicheion Omega, 5-10 [93] (here not clearly differentiated from the protoplast), the so-called Arab. Monoimos, Hipp. Ref., VIII, 12; X, 17, [94] the tractate on the three natures [95] and the Ptolemaeans and Colorbasaeans in Iren. Haer., I, 12, 3 → 475, 6 ff. Among many beings of the same rank in the highest pleroma one is (first, perfect, great, ineffable) "man" in Pist. Soph., 285, 16; 319, 19 f.; 329, 24, 26 f.; 330, 2, [96] in the Second Book of Jeû, 122, 16, [97] in Ancient Gnostic Work, 227, 2; 229, 15; 232, 6; 259, 6 etc., [98] and among the Mandaeans, e.g., Lidz. Ginza R., 118, 22-25. [99] A figure which is subordinate to the supreme God or His equivalent being in the pleroma, but which for that reason is all the more central in the pleroma and in mythological events, is called "man" in The Nature of the Archons, 139, 2; 144, 33, [100] in the Sophia Jesu Christi, 93, 15; 94, 9-11; 95, 5; 96, 12 etc., [101] among the Valentinians acc. to Epiph. Haer., 31, 5, 5, [102] in the Gospel of Phil., 108, 23 f.; 123, 19-22; 124, 1, [103] among the Sethians acc. to Hipp. Ref., V, 19, [104] in the Poimandres tractate, 12-15, [105] and in Manichaeism, e.g., Kephalaia, 51. [106] The influence of this figure, which is always an independent hypostatised Redeemer except in the Sophia Jesu Christi and Poimandres, may also be seen in the christology of Mart. Pt., 9 [107] and Act. Phil., 140. [108]

The following historical conclusions may be drawn from this. Intellectually considered the Gnostic "primal man" finds its origin in the microcosm-macrocosm idea according to which the structure of the cosmos is understood after the analogy

---

[88] On the "Son of Man" in this system → 475, 1 ff.

[89] Not yet ed., but cf. Sophia Jesu Christi (→ n. 85), 94, 9-11; 95, 5-9; 108, 2; 109, 5; 113, 14 f.; 115, 18, where Till in the app. pts. out the par. to Eugnostos. Cf. Schenke. 8 f. (older numbering of Cod I). On the "Son of Man" in this system → 475, 19.

[90] Schenke, 9. On the "Son of Man" in Heracleon → 475, 29 ff. and W. Foerster, "Von Valentin z. Herakleon. Untersuchungen über d. Quellen u. d. Entwicklung d. valentinianischen Gnosis," ZNW Beih., 7 (1928), Index, s.v. "Menschensohn."

[91] Schenke, 13 and 57-60; Colpe, 161 f.

[92] Schenke, 13.

[93] Ed. M. Bertholet - C. E. Ruelle, Collection des anciens alchimistes grecs, Texte Grec (1963), 230, 17 - 223, 2; cf. Schenke, 15 and 52-56.

[94] On the "Son of Man" in this system → 474, 31 ff.

[95] Not yet ed., cf. the photos in P. Labib, Coptic Gnostic Pap. in the Coptic Museum at Old Cairo, I (1956), 3 f., 7, 11-26, 27-36 (?), 37 f., 39 f. (?), 41-44, 45 f. (?), though these do not include the Cod. Cairensis Gnosticus, I, 122, 27 - 123, 19 which Schenke, 15 quotes from secondary sources. The vol. does not have the whole of the tractate on the three natures; there is more, but nothing on the heavenly man, in H. C. Puech and G. Quispel, "Le quatrième écrit gnostique du Cod Jung," Vigiliae Christianae, 9 (1955), 65-102.

[96] Cf. Schenke, 12.

[97] Ed. C. Schmidt, TU, 8, 1. 2 (1892); Schenke, 13.

[98] Ed. C. Schmidt, (→ n. 97); Schenke, 13.

[99] Schenke, 13 f.

[100] Ed. Labib, op. cit. (→ n. 95); Schenke, 7 f. and 59-63.

[101] On the "Son of Man" in this system → 475, 16 ff.

[102] Schenke, 9.

[103] Ed. W. Till, Patristische Texte u. Studien, 2 (1963); Schenke, 9-12. On the "Son of Man" in this system → 475, 32 ff.

[104] Schenke, 13.

[105] Nock-Fest, I, 1-28; cf. Schenke, 44-8; Colpe, 12 f.

[106] Ed. C. Schmidt - H. J. Polotsky - A. Böhlig (1940), 126 f.; Schenke, 108-119.

[107] Schenke, 98-100.

[108] Ibid., 100-103; cf. also Act. Joh., 100 (Schenke, 103-105).

of a man. [109] In the further development of this idea which leads on to Gnosticism this man is partly spiritualised into a universal pleroma (→ 413, 12 ff.) and partly focused on a central hypostasis within this pleroma (→ 413, 12 ff.). Occasionally even within one and the selfsame system he is presented both as the universal pleroma and also as the hypostasis at work within it, cf. the Valentinians. As a hypostasis he is the chief or best part in the macrocosm and microcosm, or, since these are so often spiritualised, he is the chief or best part of the world soul and the human soul, the heavenly man in the cosmos and the inner man in the outward earthly man. In this function other spiritual concepts can be used instead of that of man → 411, 19 ff. with n. 73 and n. 74 and → IV, 87, 25 ff.; 955, 23 ff.

> Gnosticism arises when the anthropos as the best part of the human soul is detached from itself as the best part of the world soul and a doctrine is developed which seeks to tie the two together again. The heart of this doctrine lies in the actual claim that an earthly prophet is the representative or incarnation of the best part of the world soul, as which he draws near to men, who have within them, detached from its origin, and sleeping, drunk, dead or unconscious, the best part of their soul. Such a claim might be raised by followers of the prophets, as in Chr. Gnosticism, or by a prophet himself, as in the case of Simon Magus. In principle it was thus quite possible in pre-Chr. times and did actually take place thus in Simon's case → VII, 90, 1 ff. But there is no known instance prior to the final redaction of Da. When such a claim is made not only is the upper man incarnated but the prophet is also mythologised or at least viewed docetically. His fusion with the pleroma was the first step towards a doctrine of the heavenly anthropos who is individuated and yet represents himself as the universal pleroma, descending and redeeming himself in the detached best parts of the human soul, which might also stand for a separated or darkened part of the cosmic dimension. Redemption can take place by invocation, revelation of identity, and reuniting. Where these things do not just happen in the present but are set in an eschaton, last judgment etc., one may see the influence of Jewish or Chr. eschatology. [110]

Basically the Gnostic anthropos has nothing whatever to do with the Son of Man of Jewish apocalyptic, nor is the latter to be understood in terms of the macrocosm-microcosm idea that lies behind the Gnostic anthropos doctrine. As regards the fact that in the case of the Gnostic anthropos the term "man" or identification with an earthly prophet can lead from hypostatisation to personification, the feature of personification is something it may perhaps have in common with the Jewish Son of Man. But this simply shows that the hypostatic thinking of the Orient lived on both in Judaism and also in syncretism. [111] The decisive differences are that the Son of Man acts only in the eschaton, not the present; that He judges; that where He redeems He acquits, but does not fuse with a part of Himself; that He stays in heaven and does not come down to men or to cosmic darkness, nor go back up again; that in no sense does He stand in natural union with the cosmos; and that He is just announced by prophetic, apocalyptic writers, not given living representation by prophets bringing gnosis.

---

[109] Bultmann J., 11.
[110] Shown in detail by R. Haardt, "Das universaleschatologische Vorstellungsgut in d. Gnosis," *Vom Messias zum Christus,* ed. K. Schubert (1964), 315-336.
[111] A special instance of this is anthropomorphism whose object in the case of the Son of Man was originally the divine world and in that of the anthropos the cosmos. With both it also made possible participation in heavenly scenes.

The hypothesis that the Son of Man statements of John's Gospel (→ 464, 30 ff.) display more fully than those of Jewish apocalyptic or the Synoptic Gospels the central features of the Gnostic anthropos myth is based on the following agreements: first, that the pre-existent Son of Man has come down from heaven; secondly, that He is exalted, the exaltation being strictly differentiated from the resurrection; thirdly, that His destiny is tied to that of believers, they too being exalted from a state of lowliness; and finally, that He is the Judge. [112] But the pre-existence statement gives real evidence of the Gnostic myth only if it applies to the totality of souls. There is nothing, however, not even the idea of katabasis, to show that this stands behind the Son of Man in the "inclusive" sense, especially behind Jn. 3:13. [113] The idea of man as a collective soul, which, if we ignore a series of hypostatic differentations in the redeeming world of light, involves parallelism or identity of redeemer and redeemed, [114] is not refuted, since the Evangelist is interested neither in cosmology, anthropology, nor the destiny of the soul; he was just not acquainted with it. It is most likely that for him or his source ὁ υἱὸς τοῦ ἀνθρώπου still meant "man" and this brought about an association with the heavenly man (→ 411, 9 ff.) current among his readers, though this was not a collective soul plunged into darkness nor a salvator salvandus. The katabasis concept is then a necessary result of connecting the historical account of Jesus' life on earth with the identification of the earthly Son of Man and the heavenly man, for which the way was smoothed by the ascension. For the post-resurrection and post-ascension community it was natural that there could be an anabasis only of One who had first come down → 466, 36 ff. Identification with a heavenly being, which made possible the katabasis concept, meant including in the total complex a pre-existence statement which was in no way compatible with a collective soul, though it did not owe its origin to faith in the ascended Son of Man but was present already in the wisdom or logos tradition (→ VII, 498, 3 ff.). The parallelism of anthropos and logos or sophia in this tradition (→ n. 77) might help to explain why the Gospel has a prologue about the Logos → 470, 1 ff.

If the Gnostic anthropos is exalted (→ line 3 f.), this is either the reuniting of the fallen part with the higher part (→ 414, 11 ff.) or the return of the higher part which had come down to the fallen part. But the ascended Jesus was not hypostatically sundered and He neither returns to His former place as higher part nor returns to Himself as lower part. When the Redeemer is also Judge in Gnosticism (→ line 6), one sees Jewish or Christian influence, and in some cases directly Johannine influence → n. 110. The judicial work of the Gnostic Redeemer is to be understood in the light of the substantial event that takes place in Gnosticism (→ 414, 26), and not vice versa.

2. A Possible Hypothesis (Canaan).

Since the deciphering of the Ras Shamra texts traces of Canaanite mythology have been seen in the three most important figures of Da. 7, (a) the fourth beast (→ 421, 10 f.), which occurs in the empire-schema of the Seleucid period and which cannot be

---

[112] Bultmann Bedeutung, 139.
[113] As against Bultmann J. on 3:13; Odeberg Gospel, 72-100; → 467, 3 ff.
[114] Bultmann Bedeutung, 140.

compared to any symbolical animal, (b) the Son of Man, and (c) the Ancient of Days. The fourth beast seems to be the chaos-dragon ltn [115] who was defeated by Anat or Baal, or the sea-monster Iam vanquished by Baal, [116] while the Son of Man has been identified as the storm-god Baal, who overcomes Ashtar, Iam, ltn or Mot and comes on the clouds, [117] and the Ancient of Days is equated with the gray-haired "father of years," [118] the king and creator El, who after the victory over the dragon institutes Baal as world-ruler or is driven out by him. [119] Perhaps the author combined with the vision of the four beasts a mythical fr. in which an ancient god abdicated in favour of a younger or nominated the younger as his successor; by so doing he made the one "like a man" the symbol of an empire. [120] Another possibility is that Da. 7 reflects ideas of the harvest-feast in which prior to the exile the victory over the chaos dragon and the enthronement of the victor as king were celebrated, and which played a decisive role in the rise of eschatology. [121]

The data are as follows. [122] The term 'ab šnm, which in the transl. "father of years" is claimed as a predicate of El, has been found four times intact in the Ugaritic texts. In III Baal, I, 8 [123] = I AB, I, 8 [124] = Gordon Manual, 49, I, 8 [125] Anat comes to El and bids him rejoice like Atrt and her sons at the death of Baal. [126] In II Aqhat, VI, 49 [127] =

---

[115] O. Eissfeldt, *Baal Zaphon, Zeus Kasios u. d. Durchzug d. Israeliten durchs Meer* (1932), 23-30.

[116] Gray, 71 and 208.

[117] Emerton, 232. Behind Baal as proper name, i.e., ba'al šamēm, there perhaps stands a proper name Hadad, cf. Kapelrud, 50-52, though cf. M. Pope, *El in the Ugaritic Texts* (1955), 47, 55-58, 95-100.

[118] Rost, 42, following H. Bauer, "Die Gottheiten v. Ras Schamra," ZAW, 51 (1933), 82; Pope, *op. cit.,* 32 f.; A. Bentzen, *Da., Hndbch. AT,* I, 19² (1952), 48 (on Da. 7:9), 61 with bibl.

[119] Kapelrud, 30-38, 86-98, though cf. O. Eissfeldt, *El im ugaritischen Pantheon* (1951), 53-70.

[120] Rost, 43; the continuation perhaps told how the young god was seated on the throne (to the right?) of the one who nominated him, or directly on the throne of the abdicating god.

[121] S. Mowinckel, *Psalmenstud.,* II (1921), 44-89, 254-263; A. Bentzen, *King and Messiah* (1955), 74-6. Emerton, 230-234 rejects Bentzen's interposing of the Davidic king. We need not discuss here Emerton's own way of connecting Da. 7 and the enthronement festival. Also rejected is J. Morgenstern, "The 'Son of Man' of Da. 7:13 f. A New Interpretation," JBL, 80 (1961), 65-77, acc. to which the Ancient of Days and the one "like a man" are based on the national god of Tyre in his two phases as Ba'al Šamem (an old god sinking into the underworld in the west) and Melkart (the son returning from the underworld to his people to rule, judge and bless it as a divine king). There is no basis in the text for this, and while Tyre's Melkart took on some of the character of Baal or Hadad he really corresponds to the Ugaritic Ashtar, who has nothing in common with the Son of Man at all, cf. V. Maag, "Syrien-Palästina," *Kulturgesch. d. Alten Orient,* ed. H. Schmökel (1961), 581-4. Furthermore the influence of the sun religion of Tyre on Israel in the days of King Hiram and its revival by Antiochus Epiphanes (with the equation of Ba'al Šamem's disappearance with the harvest feast and of Melkart's return in the spring equinox with the New Year Feast Dec. 18-25 — hence the close connection of Ancient and Days and Son of Man in Da. 7:13 f., composed under Antiochus) is all mere assumption. Morgenstern, 76 f., also "The King-God among the Western Semites and the Meaning of Epiphanes," VT, 10 (1960), 138-197 even goes so far as to regard the unity of Father and Son in Jn. 10:30 as a reminiscence of the theology of Tyre influencing the Galilean Jesus sect by way of Caesarea.

[122] Quoted from the ed. of Driver, the transl. of Aistleitner and the ed. of Gordon Manual. The ref. in all three are given.

[123] Driver, 108 f.

[124] Aistleitner, 18.

[125] Gordon, 44.

[126] In the imperfect I * Baal, VI, 2 (Driver, 106 f.) = I * AB, VI, 2 (Aistleitner, 17) = Gordon Manual 67, VI, 2 (not transl. Gordon, 42), where we have only šnm, we should supply the same for messengers of the underworld bringing El the news of Baal's death.

[127] Driver, 54 f.

II, D, VI, 49 [128] = Gordon Manual, II Aqhat VI, 49 [129] she comes to El to abuse the youth Aqhat who has refused the immortality she offered him. In II Baal, IV, 24 [130] = II AB, IV-V, 24 [131] = Gordon Manual, 51, IV, 24 [132] Atrt comes to El to get his assent to a palace for Baal. In VI Baal, III, 24 [133] = VI AB, III, 24 [134] = Gordon Manual, IX 'nt III, 24 [135] the artist god Ktr does the same to get from El orders to build the palace. [136] In all 4 passages we read: [137] tgly śd el wtbu qrš mlk 'ab šnm lp'n el thbr wtql tšthwy wtkbdnh. This may be transl.: "She penetrated the fields of El and came into the pavilion of the king, father of years; she did homage and fell at El's feet, she bowed down and did him honour," [138] or: "She climbed the mount of El and entered into the residence of the king the father, into the šnm, she bowed at the feet of El, she fell down and did him honour," [139] or: "She enters the abode of 'Il and comes into the domicile of the King, Father of Šnm. At the feet of 'Il she bows and falls, prostrates herself and honours him." [140] Until the word šnm is found in some other context [141] it might be not only the gen. plur. of šnt "year" but also the name of a residence or of a son of El. There are also other possibilities. [142] Furthermore "father of years" is not a convincing par. to "Ancient of Days."

Hardly more unequivocal is the other par. to Da. 7:9. šbt dqn "grayness of beard (or chin)" is said of El. [143] This is not a convincing par. to שְׂעַר רֵאשֵׁהּ כַּעֲמַר נְקֵא in Da. 7:9, esp. as beards are not peculiar to gods in the ancient Orient, [144] even when gray.

More important than this triviality regarding El are two characteristics of Aliyan Baal. [145] In the Baal cycle he is given 12 times the epithet rkb 'rpt "he who rides on

---

[128] Aistleitner, 73.

[129] Gordon, 91.

[130] Driver, 96 f.

[131] Aistleitner, 40.

[132] Gordon, 31.

[133] Driver, 74 f.

[134] Aistleitner, 34.

[135] Gordon, 25.

[136] It is not clear, however, that Baal is to get the palace. The damaged III * Baal, C, 5 (Driver, 76 f.) = III AB, C, 5 (Aistleitner, 47) = Gordon Manual, 129, 5 (Gordon, 11), where 'ab šnm is broken off after mlk, is to be filled in along the same lines; here Ktr is asked by El to build a palace for Im.

[137] Naturally with masc. verb forms in the 4th passage and that quoted → n. 136; the last word without n energicum wtkbdh. The passages are at times to be supplemented by one another.

[138] Similarly Driver → n. 123, 127, 130, 133.

[139] Aistleitner → n. 124, 128, 131, 134.

[140] Gordon → n. 125, 129, 132, 135.

[141] It occurs in the as yet syntactically unrewarding texts Gordon Manual, 1, 3. 6; 2, 26 and 107, 4, the first two being sacrificial hymns, the second a list of gods. Each time šnm comes after tkmn. Gordon, 111. 109 f. suggest a divine pair Tukamuna and Šnm. Aistleitner transl. "May this offering rise to the dwelling of the sons of El, to Tkmn and Šnm!" Perhaps this Šnm is a homonym of the other.

[142] Pope, op. cit., 33 suggests derivation as part. plur. masc. from a root šny related to Arab. sanā "to be noble." Eissfeldt, op. cit., 31, though he suggests šny, relates it to Hbr. שׁנה "to change," but Gray, 117, n. 1 objects that this is tny in Ugaritic.

[143] II Baal, V, 4 (Driver, 96 f.) = II AB, IV-V, 66 (Aistleitner, 41) = Gordon Manual, 51, V, 66 (Gordon, 32); V Baal, V, 2 (Driver, 88 f. = V AB, E 10 (Aistleitner, 30) = Gordon Manual VI 'nt, V, 10 (Gordon, 22); V Baal V, 24 f. (Driver, 90 f.) = V AB, E, 33 (Aistleitner, 30) = Gordon Manual, VI 'nt, V, 33 (Gordon, 22). In the last two the par. just before is simply šbth or šbt(k) "his" or "thy grayness," probably ref. to the hair or beard.

[144] As regards Ugaritic cf. the examples of dqn in G. D. Young, Concordance of Ugaritic, Analecta Orientalia, 36 (1956), No. 503.

[145] On the sobriquet Aliyan "the eminent," which suggests his dominant role in the pantheon as already presupposed in the Ras Shamra texts, cf. Kapelrud 47-50.

clouds." [146] Though not the son of El, but Dagan, his role as El's replacement is clearly brought out in the Anat Baal texts. [147]

It may be seen then that "father of years" and "grayness of beard" are dubious par. to the epithets of the Ancient of Days in Da. 7:9. Even if one accepts them, the latter cannot be traced back in unbroken tradition to the supreme god of Canaan, El, since the possibilities of a direct influence of Canaanite mythology on Jewish apocal. have not yet been demonstrated. It is more likely that in each case Yahweh faith has also to be taken into account, absorbing El-directed belief in a supreme God on the one side and constituting a final picture of God for apocal. on the other. Yahweh did not just at the start of the conquest take over the hypostases El Elyon, El Olam, El Bethel, El Šaddai and finally El God of Israel [148] and then when it was completed attract to Himself the predicates of Creator and King. He also united with Himself statements about Baal, and these prevent us from seeing directly in Baal the original only of the Son of Man. Yahweh too rides on the clouds (Is. 19:1, and materially Dt. 33:26; Ps. 68:33). It is He who has fought Leviathan (Is. 27:1; Ps. 74:14, materially Job 26:13) and Rahab (Is. 51:9; Ps. 89:10; Job 9:13; 26:12), in whom the chaos dragon of Canaan, in Ugaritic Iam (finally Iammu) or ltn, Lothan, still lives on. [149] Appearance as a man, which from the outset might apply to El as well as Baal, [150] is attributed to Yahweh in Ez. 1:26. [151] Possibly Baal was not

---

[146] II III, 10. 17 (Driver, 94 f.) = II AB, III, 11. 18 (Aistleitner, 38 f.) = Gordon Man., 51, III, 11. 18 (Gordon, 30); II V, 60 (Driver, 98 f.) = II AB, IV-V, 122 (Aistleitner, 42) = Gordon Man., 51, V, 122 (Gordon, 34); I * II, 7 (Driver, 104 f.) = I * AB, II, 7 (Aistleitner, 15) = Gordon Man., 67, II, 7 (Gordon, 39); III * A, 8. 29 (Driver, 80-83) = III AB, A, 8. 29 (Aistleitner, 51 f.) = Gordon Man., 68, 8. 29 (Gordon, 15 f.); IV, I, 7 (Driver, 116 f.) = IV AB, I, 7 (Aistleitner, 52) = Gordon Man., 76, I, 7 (Gordon, 49); IV III, 36 (Driver, 118 f.) = IV AB, III, 37 (Aistleitner, 54) = Gordon Man., 76 III, 37 (Gordon, 51); V II, 40 (Driver, 84 f.) = V AB, B, 40 (Aistleitner, 26) = Gordon Man. ʿnt, II, 40 (Gordon, 18); V III, 53 (sic) (Driver, 86 f.) = V AB, D, 35 (Aistleitner, 27) = Gordon Man. ʿnt, III, 35 (Gordon, 19); V IVa, 4. 6 (Driver, 86 f.) = V AB, D, 48. 50 (Aistleitner, 28) = Gordon Man. ʿnt, IV, 48. 50 (Gordon, 20); also I Aqhat I, 43 f. (Driver, 58 f.) = I D, 43 (Aistleitner, 77) = Gordon Man., I Aqhat, 43 f. (Gordon, 95).

[147] Kapelrud, passim. Cf. also C. Virolleaud, Légendes de Babylone et de Canaan (1949), 92-5. Behind it is probably the adoption into Ugaritic religion of an older Canaanite stratum, possibly also Hurrian and Hittite, focused on the god of storm and fertility, Gray, 116 f. J. Oberman, Ugaritic Mythology (1948), 84 elucidates Baal's relation to the ongoing authority of El.

[148] R. Dussaud, Les découvertes de Ras Shamra (Ugarit) et l'AT (1941), 168-174; O. Eissfeldt, "El u. Jahwe," Kleine Schriften, 3 (1966), 386-397.

[149] The gods Ashtar and Mot of vegetation myth, whose overthrow is only on the margin in the Ras Shamra texts (Kapelrud, 99-102), have left no trace in the OT.

[150] Ugaritic reliefs portray El with bearded face and horns jutting out under the high cap (C. F. A. Schaeffer, "Les fouilles de Ras Shamra-Ugarit," Syria, 18 [1937], 128, Plate 17), while Ugaritic statuettes and a relief depict Baal as a vigorously striding young man with a short apron and peaked cap from which horns jut forth, a shaft of lightning in his left hand and the thunder-club in his right, R. Dussaud, L'art Phénicien du seconde millénaire (1949), Fig. 29, 34, 35, 43. Horus and Re (→ 419, 17 ff.), on the other hand, have falcons' heads, cf. Helck, op. cit. (→ n. 64), 360, 389; G. Roeder, Die ägypt. Götterwelt (1959), Plate 11 (age of the Ptolemies).

[151] Acc. to Fohrer, op. cit. (→ n. 32), 182 there is a literary and theological connection between this passage and Da. 7. Ez. 1:28 ("This was the appearance of the likeness of the glory of Yahweh") does not ref. to the whole vision of the throne-chariot but only to the דְּמוּת כְּמַרְאֵה אָדָם of v. 26, since in the corresponding light-penomenon in 8:2-4 no chariot is seen but only דְּמוּת כְּמַרְאֵה אִישׁ. The kabod in human shape is like the Son of Man with clouds; Ez. (17:3 etc.) can also use beasts to symbolise enemies (Da. 7:1-18); the chariot motif of Ez. is echoed in the description of the throne with flames and fiery wheels in Da. 7:9. Furthermore, Da. 8:17 is the only v. outside Ez. (→ 406, 32 ff.) where a prophet is addressed as בֶּן־אָדָם, the whole scene recalling Ez. 2, W. Eichrodt, Der Prophet Hesekiel, AT Deutsch,

even known in Palestine in the Middle and Late Bronze Age. If one presupposes these OT traditions, then the Son of Man, even if it be postulated that Da. 7 suppresses a tradition which has it that He slew the fourth beast, does in fact play the part of Yahweh after the transfer of rule. Even the עִם עֲנָנֵי שְׁמַיָּא reminds us of the theophanies of Yahweh.

Yet in spite of such objections the Canaanite hypothesis does so far come closest to the actual facts. The mythographical similarity between the relation of the Ancient of Days and Son of Man on the one side and that of El and Baal on the other, which fits into the broader conclusion that older material lives on in the tradition of Israel and Judah (→ 347, 21 ff.), carries with it a nexus of motifs which is lacking in the parallels of motif on which the other hypotheses rely. This allows most easily a religio-historical connection.

The Ugaritic texts, however, do not represent exactly the mythology believed in Palestine. They do not contain a version of statements about El and Baal to which the ideas of Da. 7 and visionary discourses can be traced back historically. For in the OT Yahweh has the predicates of several Canaanite gods. For this reason we can no longer say whether there had already been in the Canaanite world a transfer of predicates of which thus far we have no evidence, so that apocal. is the revival and reconstruction of these traditions, or whether Yahweh with the undoubted union of predicates in Himself stands behind both the Ancient of Days and also the Son of Man, so that in the tradition which leads to apocal, we are to assume a hypothetical stage of new differentiation in the Ancient of Days and the Son of Man.[152] Yet either way, and on all the possible variations, the transfer of dominion from the Ancient of Days to the Son of Man would seem to go back to the wresting of power from an old god by a young one as this was handed down in Canaanite mythology, the rivalry between Baal and El in the Ras Shamra texts being thus far the closest par.

3. Bearing on the Understanding of Son of Man.

The historical findings warn us against putting too much stress on the human form of the figure at issue. This applies also to the crystallisation of the concept in the description "as a man" in Da., where angels are also presented in human form → 421, 14 ff. What we have here is not the adoption of the term "man" from myth but the depiction of an appearance. If the expression used, without the comparative word, in Enoch, 4 Esr., the world of Jesus and Jewish Christianity, is employed terminologically and given much stronger emphasis, one may assume, not that traditions of a cosmic heavenly macroanthropos, a protoplast put in the end-time, or an archetypal primal man were adopted (→ 408, 7 ff.), but rather that

---

22 (1965), ad loc. Naturally the visionary speech of Ez. played its part in the development of apocal. traditions. Yet what is said about Yahweh in human form (on the cloud as a form of theophany [→ IV, 905, 5 ff.] and symbol of the heavenly cf. also Ex. 16:10; 24:15-18; Lv. 9:24; Nu. 20:6; Ps. 104:3) represents a merging of divine attributes which are at times differentiated again in apocal.

152 Emerton's theory (240-242) cannot be proved, namely, that the Isr. enthronement feast adapted a Jebusite rite in which El Elyon was the chief deity with a higher rank than Yahweh, who after the conquest was equated with Baal in some circles. On this view Baal/Yahweh is the origin of the Son of Man. After David's capture of Jerusalem, in a way analogous to the usurpation of El's role by Baal, Yahweh was increasingly equated with El Elyon and thus became the chief God. El/Yahweh is thus the origin of the Ancient of Days. In some unknown fashion the tradition of two figures was retained up to the postexilic period and then reinterpreted in terms of Yahweh's pre-eminent position, the Son of Man being demoted to angelic rank but, like Michael and Metatron later, maintaining the predicates of might.

Jewish apocalyptic itself had been fruitful in developing the figure of the Son of Man. Always outside Da. 7:27b this was interpreted Messianically, and hence the fixed and determinate form could arise in the form of a title, as the Synoptic Gospels presuppose for the first time, → 404, 13 f. The differences in the functions of the Son of Man may be explained by the differences between the groups which expected Him and the times in which they did so. The fact that the story of the Son of Man concept may be read within that of Jewish apocalyptic itself does not rule out the possibility that it might be enriched by heterogeneous traditions which are not constitutive for a primal man concept, as in Enoch, or that it might form connections with frequently intermingled speculations about the macroanthropos, protoplast, or archetype, as in Hellenistic Judaism (→ n. 67; 430, 12 ff.), Christian speculations about Adam (→ 470, 24 ff.) and Gnosticism → 474, 26 ff.

III. The Son of Man in Jewish Apocalyptic.

1. Daniel 7.

a. The Vision.

Within Da. 7, and brought into the style of visionary depiction within the corresponding statements in v. 2, 4, 6, 7, 11, 21 by the introductory "I saw (in the night visions)" in v. 9 and v. 13, there is an independent little apocalypse consisting of v. 9, 10, 13, 14. [153] It describes how the Ancient of Days takes His place on the throne of tongues of fire with fiery wheels (v. 9), while thousands of thousands minister to Him and ten thousand times ten thousand stand before Him, and His court is set for judgment, for which the books are opened (v. 10). "And, behold, one like the Son of Man came in [154] the clouds of heaven, and came to the Ancient of Days, and they brought him near before him," v. 13. To Him was given eternal dominion, honour, and an indestructible kingdom, and all nations serve Him, v. 14. The עִם־עֲנָנֵי שְׁמַיָּא of v. 13 (→ IV, 905, 19 ff.) introduces the whole scene in v. 13 and v. 14 [155] and the אֲתֵה הֲוָא simply denotes a coming with the clouds denoting the superhuman majesty of the One like a man, [156] His supernatural origin, [157] divine likeness, [158] ascent from earth to heaven, [159] divine throne chariot, [160] or sphere, as opposed to watery chaos. [161] The expression thus tells us that the whole scene

---

[153] Beginning with v. 9 on metrical grounds acc. to Noth Komposition, 145. Acc. to Hölscher, 120 v. 11a is an addition from the Maccabean age; it belongs to a first series of additions acc. to Coppens-Dequeker, 24 f., 29. Noth Komposition, 145 thinks v. 11b is part of the original apocalypse vv. 2-7 and is related to the appended scene by v. 12. Rost, 42 thinks v. 14 is the conclusion, but Noth, 146 sees in it an editorial bracket. On the whole question cf. O. Plöger, Das Buch Da., KAT, 18 (1965).

[154] Transl. as in Scott, 128, who draws attention to the alternation of עַם and בְּ in Da., the rendering of עַם by μετά and ἐπί in Θ and LXX, and materially analogous passages like Ex. 19:9; 34:5; Nu. 11:25.

[155] Scott, 128-131.

[156] S. R. Driver, Daniel (1922), 88; Dalman WJ, I, 198.

[157] Volz Esch., 204.

[158] F. Hitzig, Das Buch Daniel (1850), 114.

[159] Manson Son, 174.

[160] Charles, op. cit. (→ n. 24), 186.

[161] J. A. Montgomery, The Book of Daniel (1927), 303.

takes place in the invisible heavenly world like that in Ez. 1. The visible clouds are a symbol indicating this. Another sign and pointer is the visionary כְּ, which is a mark of apocal. style from the days of Ez. [162] Along the lines of our historical findings (→ 419, 27 ff.) it is designed to describe what is seen without denoting it exactly. [163] It thus presents the appearance of the One who comes before the court without equating His attributes with those of an earthly man. If the clouds, which in the author's mind (עִם not עַל) represent the scenery, also become a vehicle for the One like a man, as in the case of Baal (→ n. 146), they do not conduct Him either up to heaven or down from it, but through it.

The One like a man comes after a lion with eagle's wings in v. 4, a bear in v. 5, a panther with four heads and four wings in v. 6, and a dreadful beast with ten big horns and ten little ones in v. 7 f. [164] If after these representatives of four empires [165] One like a man appears, [166] the context shows that it is not an ideal or archetypal man that is introduced, but that after the rule of the beast-powers [167] the eschaton is now represented by One like a man. That this One is a heavenly being, whether angel or God, is shown by the fact that in 10:16, 18 Da. is again dealing with a כְּמַרְאֵה אָדָם or כִּדְמוּת בְּנֵי אָדָם. [168] The context makes it plain that this is an angel → 348, 21 ff. In 7:18, 22, 25? (→ 422, 9 ff.), 27 the "saints of the most High" are not originally Israel, but heavenly beings. [169]

The four beasts represent empires which have exercised dominion. Eternal eschatological dominion is given, however, to the One like a man. Exercising power rather than representing a group is the *tertium comparationis* between the beasts and the One like a man. [170] Hence the One like a man is not the representative of a specific people or kingdom. He is a symbol of the eschatological dominion conferred on Him by God. [171] As such He suggests Messianic ideas without Himself being a Messiah. Only thus does there arise the question who will belong to a Messianic kingdom ruled by Him as this is implied by a symbol of dominion.

---

[162] Volz Esch., 11 f.

[163] Cf. Baumgartner, 216. The author, acc. to Rost, 41 f., did not add the particle but found it as in the case of the beasts.

[164] They represent the Babylonian Empire under Nebuchadnezzar (614 or 612 to 539 B.C.; in the vision of the colossus in 2:32, 37 f. the head of gold), the Median Empire, which did not arise after (6:1) but alongside the Babylonian (620-553 B.C., the breast and arms of silver in 2:32b, 39a), the Persian Empire with the 4 Achaemenidian kings known to the OT (Cyrus II, 559-529 B.C., Darius I, 521-486 B.C., Xerxes I, 485-465 B.C., Artaxerxes I, 465-424 B.C.; the belly and loins of brass in 2:32c, 39b), and the Macedonian Empire with 10 kings from Alexander the Gt. (336-323 B.C.) to probably Seleucus IV (187-175 B.C.) or his brother and the "little horn" Antiochus IV Epiphanes (175-164 B.C.) (the legs of iron and feet part of iron and part of clay in 2:33, 40-43).

[165] On the rise and earliest development of the four empire schema in the 6th cent. in the Iranian-Armenian-Assyrian sphere cf. Noth Geschichtsverständnis, 250-259.

[166] He corresponds to the stone of 2:34 f., 44 f. which crushes the iron and clay feet and thus topples the whole statue, ending world history with the Seleucid kingdom acc. to Noth Geschichtsverständnis, 262 f.

[167] On the beast symbols cf. Hos. 13:7 f. and Noth Geschichtsverständnis, 267-271.

[168] Cf. ὡς ὁμοίωσις υἱοῦ ἀνθρώπου Da. 10:16 Θ, ὡς ὁμοίωσις χειρὸς ἀνθρώπου Da. 10:16 LXX and ὡς ὅρασις ἀνθρώπου Da. 10:18 LXX and Θ.

[169] Cf. Procksch and Sellin, then Noth Heilige, 275-290. Cf., e.g., Ps. 89:5, 7; Job 5:1; 15:15; Prv. 9:10; 30:3; Sir. 42:17; Tob. 8:15; Damasc. 20:8 (9:33); 1 QS 11:7 f.; 1 QH 3:21. The only exception is Ps. 34:9 and on this cf. Coppens-Dequeker, 33-54.

[170] Origin offers no *tertium comparationis*, since the beasts come up out of the sea (v. 2 f.) while the One like a man was in heaven from the very first.

[171] It is not said whether a specific people will exercise this dominion. מַלְכוּתֵהּ/מַלְכוּ in v. 14a means a sphere of rule both spatially and temporally, but does not say who bears it.

b. The Interpretation.

In view of the par. עָם in 1 QH 3:21 f. the עַם קַדִּישֵׁי עֶלְיוֹנִין of v. 27b is to be transl. "host of the saints of the Most High" [172] with a ref. to heavenly creatures. When it is said here that מַלְכוּתָה and שָׁלְטָנָא is given to them, that this kingdom will last for ever, and that all powers will be subject to the host, both in wording and content this is so plain a par. to what is said about the One like a man in v. 14 that the latter becomes a representative of the saints of the Most High. This interpretation is briefly anticipated in v. 18 [173] and repeated in v. 22a. [174]

Problems arise with ref. to v. 25a. If יְבַלֵּא here means "he will destroy (wear down) (the saints of the Most High)" rather than "he will sorely vex them," [175] the par. "he will speak words against the Most High" seems to suggest that the saints are heavenly beings. But if one takes the stem baliya in all its senses, or reads the stem balā in the sense "to mistreat," "torment," then the ref. is not to the blasphemy of Antiochus Epiphanes but only to his oppression of the Jewish people. There seems to be a clear historical ref. in v. 25b c. If the "altering of times and law" denotes an attack on the divine order of the world and ordering of things, [176] the altering of the festal and cultic calendar takes concrete shape in measures against the cultic community in Jerusalem. If the saints are the subject of יִתְיַהֲבוּן in 25c, as in mostly supposed, then the Jewish people must be in view, for heavenly beings cannot be delivered into the hands of a conqueror. But even if זְמְנִין וְדָת are the subj. a ref. to the attack on the Jewish calendar is more likely than a ref. to the attack on the heavenly order of things which is implied thereby. In v. 21 the saints are very plainly the portion of God's people Israel which has remained righteous. [177] The "I beheld," which is not used elsewhere in the interpretation, points to a resumption of visionary style and introduces a new feature, the war of the last horn, which has now become a big one, Antioches IV Epiphanes, against the saints, the Jewish people. Whether v. 26b is referring to the victory of the Maccabees or the dawn of the heavenly kingdom it is no longer possible to say.

In the first stage of interpretation then (→ lines 1 ff.) the One like a man changes from a symbol of eschatological dominion to a representative of God's heavenly entourage that will rule the heavenly kingdom which in the end-time is to exercise

---

[172] קַדִּישֵׁי עֶלְיוֹנִין as a whole is a gen. epexegeticus of עַם, Noth Heilige, 284, cf. Coppens-Dequeker, 53. n. 186; the plur. ending in עֶלְיוֹנִין either goes with the whole st. c. combination and is thus a double plur. (but cf. Damasc. 20:8 [9:33]) or it is an assimilation to אֱלֹהִים, hence not "the saints among the lofty beings" etc., so O. Procksch, "Der Menschensohn als Gottessohn," Christentum u. Wissenschaft, 3 (1927), 429, cf. 425-443, 473-481.

[173] The v. is not materially related to the destruction of the beasts suggested in v. 17; this v. as an interpretation of the vision of the beasts has perhaps been sharply abbreviated in view of the (added?) interpretation of the vision of the Son of Man, Noth Komposition, passim.

[174] v. 22b is perhaps an unimportant addition which simply says קַדִּישִׁין, Noth Heilige, 287. v. 22a might be secondary alongside v. 21 (→ n. 176 f.) and v. 22b. Acc. to Coppens-Dequeker, 29 v. 22a perhaps belongs to a 1st series of additions and v. 22b to a 2nd.

[175] So Noth Heilige, 286, who derives from Arab. balā rather than the traditional baliya.

[176] So Noth Heilige, 286, who thus concludes that one cannot interpret it in terms of the Maccabean struggle as in v. 21. Acc. to Hölscher, 120 f. not only v. 21 and all v. 25 but also v. 20, 22 and 24 are additions from the Maccabean age. Acc. to Coppens-Dequeker, 27-33, v. 25a and v. 20, 22a, 24 belong to the first series of additions, while v. 25b and 21, 22b belong to the second.

[177] Cf. the ref. → n. 172, also Montgomery, op. cit. (→ n. 161), 95, 312; Charles, op. cit. (→ n. 24), 164-6, 192, and Bentzen, op. cit (→ n. 118), 57 f. for the view that v. 21 is an addition.

all power in place of earthly empires. This is a congenial interpretation in view of the reference to the dominion of the One like a man in the vision itself. In the second stage of interpretation (→ 422, 21 ff.) the saints of the Most High are that portion of the Jewish people which remained loyal to the ancient traditions of Israel in the days of the Maccabees. The One like a man thus becomes the representative of the true Israel which is to replace the empires. This interpretation, which introduces national hopes of consummation on earth, [178] is less congenial. In both cases the One like a man is a collective entity and He plainly takes on a saving eschatological function, though without being directly the Messiah or Redeemer. [179]

2. The Similitudes of Ethiopian Enoch. [180]

a. Usage and Interpretation.

In Eth. En. the Son of Man figures only in the similitudes of 37-71. The vv. in the vision Da. 7:9 f., 13 recur in reconstructed form in 46. Here, too, "man" is not a Messianic title; it simply describes the appearance of the heavenly being. [181] This is also indicated by the combining of expressions for the Son of Man with demonstrative pronouns which reproduce the Gk. def. art., [182] whereas the Messiah [183] and the Elect One, which the Son of Man can also be called, never have demonstrative pronouns. The main proof that this is not a title, however, is the alternation of expressions. There are three of these, and they are also composed exclusively of some of the 7 terms for man in Eth. En. [184] This is a strong argument for the view that while there are specific underlying terms in Gk. and Aram. (or Hbr.), there is no title.

The following are the combinations: [185] (a) only in the second similitude (45-47) walda

---

[178] Coppens-Dequeker, 54.

[179] Baumgartner, 214-7 discusses older exposition.

[180] The *terminus ad quem* of the form of Son of Man expectation in these is 70 A.D., since the destruction of Jerusalem would certainly be mentioned if it had already taken place. The *terminus post quem* is the Parthian attack of 40-38 B.C., to which there is ref. in 56:5. It is probably closer to the latter date than the former (→ V, 687, n. 245), though thus far the similitudes have not been found in the Dead Sea Scrolls. Sjöberg Menschensohn äth. Hen., 39 suggests the period between Herod and the first procurators. Chr. origin is espoused by J. C. v. Hofmann, "Über d. Entstehungszeit d. Buches Hen.," ZDMG, 6 (1852), 87-91; H. Weisse, *Die Evangelienfrage* (1856), 214-6; F. Philippi, *Das Buch Hen., sein Zeitalter u. sein Verhältnis zum Judasbrief* (1868); A. Hilgenfeld, *Die jüd. Apokalyptik in ihrer geschichtlichen Entwicklung* (1857), 148-184, in whose opinion the Messianic teaching has undergone Chr. revision.

[181] Wellhausen Sohn, 199 on v. 1: "When this has been said the first time exactly in the words of the passage in Da., there is no room for misunderstanding if it is shortened thereafter." It is often stated in the lit., however, that "man" has become a fixed title in En. as distinct from Da.

[182] Since the Eth. Gospel transl. renders ὁ υἱὸς τοῦ ἀνθρώπου without demonstrative pron., obviously because the context yielded the special sense in each case, one may assume that the demonstrative was chosen intentionally here.

[183] On the Messianology of c. 83-90, where the Messiah is a white bullock in an animal story, and where He leaves it to God to judge and to Elijah to fight against Israel's foes, cf. Pedersen, 416-429.

[184] Namely be'esī (< be'esīhū), sab'e, 'eguel (plur. 'egual, plur. of plur. 'egualāt) 'egual (plur. 'egualāt), heyāw (fem. heyāwt), daqīq (fem. daqāq) / daq, welūd / wald (plur. welūd), 'ed (plur. 'edāw). For the nuances, sometimes very fine, v. A. Dillmann, *Lex. linguae Aethiopicae* (1865), s.v., also *Chrestomathia Aethiopica edita et glossario explanata* (1865, new impress. 1950), s.v.; Manson Son, 177 f.

[185] Cf. also 'eguāla māwtā, 'eguāla 'emaheyāw (Gn. 1:27 transl. of ὁ ἄνθρωπος, Rom. 2:3 and 9:20 for ὦ ἄνθρωπε, Nu. 23:19 and Ps. 8:4 for υἱὸς ἀνθρώπου, Fiebig, 86) and daqīqa 'eguala 'emaheyāw. On the use of the concept elsewhere, also plur., → 359, n. 154.

sab'e (46:3, with zekū "that" in 46:2; 48:2 and zentū "this" in 46:4), this being closest to בַּר נְשָׁא, i.e., an individual out of a group of men in gen., plur. welūda sab'e "sons of men"; (b) only in the third similitude (58-69) and the appendix (70 f.) walda 'eguāla 'emaheyāw [186] (62:7; 69:27; with zekū 62:9, 14; 63:11; with 3rd pers. personal pronoun [for demonstrative] we'etū 69:26; 70:1; 71:17), בַּר אֱנָשׁ/בֶּן־אָדָם, i.e., an individual out of a collective, "man," [187] υἱὸς ἀνθρώπου; (c) walda be'esī (62:5; [188] with we'etū in 71:14 or 15 and twice [→ n. 188] in 69:29). [189] Among these the originality of walda sab'e is certain. The context in which it occurs gives plain evidence by other criteria that it is a source. [190] As regards the authenticity of walda 'eguāla 'emaheyāw and walda be'esī there is no agreement. [191] In view of the alternation of the last two and the agreement concerning them in the third similitude we may confidently see here a single Son of Man tradition. But this corresponds so well with walda sab'e statements in the second similitude, or overlaps them so greatly, that one may supplement them by each other even though they may come from different traditions.

In all three terms it is said of the Heavenly One in human form that He will drive from their camps and from the homes of believers the kings, mighty men, men of strength, sinners and world-seducers whose faces are covered with darkness and shame before Him and who plead with Him for mercy. He will eject them from their thrones, crush them, and extirpate them from the earth with His sword because they do not see whence their power

---

[186] In the Eth. Gospel transl. the usual rendering (without demonstrative) of ὁ υἱὸς τοῦ ἀνθρώπου, also in Eth. OT for בֶּן־אָדָם in Ps. 80:17 and Ez. 2:1, and בַּר אֱנָשׁ in Da. 7:13. Whether ὁ υἱὸς τοῦ ἀνθρώπου could also be the equivalent of the two other forms (so R. H. Charles, *The Book of En. Transl.*[2] [1912], *passim*, who expressly rejects υἱὸς ἀνθρώπου and deduces a pre-chr. Messianic designation from בַּר נְשָׁא) it is impossible to say.

[187] Acc. to Manson Son, 177 f. this sing. can also render כְּבַר אֱנָשׁ and בְּנֵי (or בֶּן־) כִּדְמוּת אָדָם / ὡς ὁμοίωσις υἱοῦ ἀνθρώπου. The plur. is welūda sab'e; a plur, welūda 'eguāla 'emaheyāw has not been found.

[188] In 62:5 and 69:29 (twice) some, mostly later MSS have walda be'esīt "son of woman" (acc. to Meyer, *op. cit.* [→ n. 28], 160 = son of Eve = son of the race of the mother of all living = man). This is not a Jewish Messianic title nor a Chr. emendation (cf. also L. Couard, "Der himmlische Messias," *Die religiösen u. sittlichen Anschauungen d. at.lichen Apkr. u. Pseudepigr.* [1907], 204-213, esp. 205) but an incorrect reading, cf. G. Beer in Kautzsch Apkr. u. Pseudepigr. on 62:5; Sjöberg Menschensohn äth. Hen., 9 and 42.

[189] Cf. Bowman, 287, who thinks walda sab'e is used for בַּר נְשָׁא and walda be'esī for בְּרֵהּ דִּגְבַר. In transl. the first and second combinations (→ 423, 22 ff.) are usually rendered "son of man" (cf. Beer, *op. cit.*, 188; A. Dillmann, *Das Buch Hen. übers. u. erklärt* [1853]; J. Flemming and L. Radermacher, *Das Buch Hen.*, GCS, 5 [1901], *ad loc.),* but cf. Lietzmann, 47. The third combination (→ 425, 4 f.) is sometimes differentiated as *Mannessohn* rather than *Menchensohn* (Beer, Flemming/Radermacher) or *Mannessohn/Sohn des Mannes* (Dillmann, Lietzmann except at 62:5), but this is misleading if no distinction is made between the first two. Charles, *op. cit.* (→ n. 186) simply has "Son of Man" for all three.

[190] Acc. to F. Stier, "Zur Komposition u. Literarkritik der Bilderreden d. äth. Hen.," *Festschr. E. Littmann* (1935), 70-88, esp. 76-83 the so-called "second vision-source," c. 46 and 48:2-7.

[191] Acc. to Messel, 7 f., 15-18 walda 'eguāla 'emaheyāw was put in for "the Chosen One" by an interpolator influenced by the Eth. NT. In contrast walda be'esī, or origin. more likely walda be'esīt, is from a third hand. Acc. to Stier, *op. cit,* 86 n. 1 these two terms, which belong to his source 38 and 39:2b; 45; 48:8-10; 50; 51; 58 and probably 61:6 ~ 63:12, also the doubtful 69:26-29, are secondary, since elsewhere "sitting on the throne of glory" (45:2; 51:3; 55:4; 61:8; 62:2, 3) is firmly linked only to the Elect One. For this view Messel and Stier develop arguments from Lietzmann, 47 f., but Sjöberg Menschensohn äth. Hen., 42 with n. 14 tries to show with Charles that the three terms are just different transl., it being natural that from c. 62 on either 'eguāla 'emaheyāw or generic be'esī should be used for sab'e (c. 46; 48) dependent on the st. c. walda.

was given to them, because they do not praise the Lord of spirits, but lift up their hands against Him and with unrighteous deeds oppress the earth and its inhabitants, 46:4-8; / 63:11; 69:27 f.; 62:9; / 62:5; 69:29.

In the terms walda sab'e "descendant of man" and walda 'eguāla 'emaheyāw "descendant of the race of those born of woman" it is said of Him that in hidden form He exists personally before the creation of the world, 48:3, 6; / 62:7, [192] that He will be manifested by God to the saints, the righteous, the elect, who hate the ways and works of the wicked world, 48:7; / 62:7; 69:26, that all of the dwellers on earth to whom He will be manifested will fall down before Him and bless, praise and worship Him, 48:5; [193] / 69:26. In the terms walda sab'e and walda be'esī "descendant of man" it is said of Him that He or His Word will be mighty before the Lord of spirits in eternity, 48:6; / 69:29. In the terms walda 'eguāla 'emaheyāw and walda be'esī it is said of Him that He will sit on the throne of glory and that judgment will be committed to Him, 69:27; / 62:5; 69:29. In the term walda sab'e alone it is said of Him that He looks like a man, 46:1, that His charm is like that of an angel, 46:1, that He is chosen by the Lord of spirits, 46:3; 48:6, that He is with the "Head of Days" at the time of the vision, 46:1, 2, [194] that He is named before Him, 48:2, that He reveals what is hidden, 46:3, that He has righteousness and uprightness, 46:3; 48:7, that He is the avenger and deliverer of the lives of the just, 48:7, that He is the staff of the righteous, the light of the nations, the hope of the afflicted, 48:4. In the term walda 'eguāla 'emaheyāw alone it is said of Him that after the condemnation of the wicked the Elect One will dwell or eat with Him and that (then? with Him?) they will ascend up from the earth, 62:14 f.

Since the Elect One of the second similitude is defined in exactly the same way as the walda sab'e and the latter is also said to be elect, since this predicate of election applies to the One like a man denoted by the other two expressions, [195] statements about the Elect One may also be adduced for the sake of completeness. [196] He is chosen by the Lord of spirits, 49:2, 4. He appears before Him, 49:2; 52:9. The Spirit and righteousness have been poured out upon Him, 62:2 f., righteousness will rule in His days, 39:6, He judges with penal destruction sinners, kings and mighty men, 48:9 f.; 52:2-9; 55:4; 62:2-13. Praise of the Lord of spirits and of the Elect One again merge into one another, 61:11-13. He sits on the throne of glory, 45:2 f.; 51:3; 55:4; 61:8; 62:2. New statements are that He will choose the righteous and the saints after the resurrection of the dead, 51:1 f. and that He will judge all the works of the saints in the heavens acc. to the standards of the Lord of spirits, and weigh their deeds with scales, 61:8 f.

Both final judgment (53:1 - 54:6) and also the state of deliverance (e.g., 50:1 as a refashioning) are painted in more detail in connection with the Elect One than with the three terms for the Son of Man. But this provides no necessary ground for differentiation between them. It is worth noting that in 39:6; 40:5; 45:3 f. statements are already made about the Elect One before any term for man appears (46:1). But the very breadth of the eschatology of the Elect One establishes the broadly Messianic significance of the man-concepts embedded in it. It must have been known to the Eth. translators and caused them to choose the combinations which distinguish this man from an ordinary man who

---

[192] Cf. Sjöberg Menschensohn äth. Hen., 83-115; Emerton, 235.

[193] One cannot be certain whether it is the One like a man or the Lord of spirits who is lauded here, cf. also 61:11-13.

[194] Re'esa mawā'el clearly echoes עַתִּיק יוֹמַיָּא in Da. 7:13.

[195] Unless these expressions later replaced the elect one and thus interpreted Him (correctly materially) as the Son of Man along the lines of the second similitude. If so this could only be a Jewish, not a Chr. interpolation. Messel, 3-32. J. Drummond, The Jewish Messiah (1877), 17-73; O. Pfleiderer, Das Urchristentum (1887), 312-4; W. Bousset, Jesu Predigt im Gegensatz z. Judt. (1892), 105-7 argue for the latter and cf. Lagrange, 242-4.

[196] Cf. Coppens' survey and discussion of Synoptic examples in Coppens-Dequeker, 78-83.

can be denoted by simple (→ n. 184) or combined (→ n. 185) expressions. [197] But even though the Messianic significance of the figure be assured, [198] "man" is not for this reason a title. [199] The man is not a personification of the Jewish people. [200] In spite of pre-existence He is not a mediator of creation like wisdom, in spite of His being with God He is not God's image, in spite of His name He is not the prototype of man. His functions define Him wholly and utterly as an eschatological figure. [201]

The fact that some statements about the One like a man in the similitudes depend on statements about the Ebed Yahweh in Dt. Is. (→ V, 687, 5 ff.) is beyond dispute. But the passion statements are not transferred. [202] One might seem to find them explicitly in Eth. En. 47:1, 4. But when we read there: "In those days the prayer of the righteous and the blood of the righteous one will rise up to the Lord of spirits" and "because ... the prayer of the righteous was heard and the blood of the righteous was avenged before the Lord of spirits," the gen. "of the just one" is not a predicate of the Son of Man but represents a collective sing. denoting the Jewish martyrs who suffered righteously.

b. The Exaltation of Enoch to the Son of Man.

Attached to the third similitude — and even from the literary standpt. it is probably an appendix — we find a depiction of the exaltation of Enoch "to that walda 'eguāla emaheyāw and to the Lord of spirits," 70:1. [203] If one may assume here that he is just elevated to them, what En. is saying about the exalted status is that an angel (Michael? or the Ancient of Days?) addresses him directly as walda be'esī (71:14) [204] who will practise righteousness; the righteous who walk on his way will no longer separate themselves from him. The appendix closes with the observation that length of days will be with this walda 'eguāla 'emaheyāw and that the just will walk in the name of the Lord of spirits from eternity to eternity. En., then, is neither the incarnation of the Son of

---

[197] The Messianological-eschatological context need be regarded as linguistically determinative only if the Aram. text was directly available for the Eth. as argued by E. Ullendorff, "An Aramaic 'Vorlage' of the Ethiopic Text of Enoch?" in Atti del Convegno Internazionale di studi etiopici, Accad. Nazionale dei Lincei. Problemi attuali di scienza e di cultura, 48 (1960), 259-267. The intermediary Gk. translators could have done this work for them already.

[198] The description of the Son of Man as the Anointed One in 48:10; 52:4 and passages which take up national hopes (cf. 50; 56; 46:4-8; / 63:11; 69:27 f. / 55:4; 62:2-13) confirm this thought without mixing national and apocal. eschatology as in 4 Esr. For details cf. Sjöberg Menschensohn äth. Hen., 140-6 and Jervell, 41, n. 73.

[199] The discussion in Sjöberg, op. cit., 40-60 suffers from his failure to distinguish between "Messianic" and "title."

[200] But cf. Messel, 84-8 who thinks the idea of a personal Messiah came into the tradition only through Chr. editing. If the close relation between the Righteous One and the righteous, the Elect One and the elect, is plain, one should not conclude from this or 49:3: "In him dwells the spirit of those who have fallen asleep in righteousness," that the Son of Man is, as taught by Murmelstein, 26; Otto, 153; Staerk Soter, II, 475, a — macrocosmic — personification of the eschatological community or a collective soul, cf. Sjöberg Menschensohn äth. Hen., 98-100

[201] M. Black, "The Eschatology of the Similitudes of Enoch," JThSt, NS, 3 (1952), 1-10.

[202] Sjöberg Menschensohn äth. Hen., 121-128, rev. J. Jeremias, ThLZ, 74 (1949), 406.

[203] G. Kuhn, "Beiträge z. Erklärung d. Buches Hen.," ZAW, 39 (1921), 240-275 finds in the exaltation of 71 a definitive though obscure and confused repetition of the provisional visionary translation of c. 14 f. This type of rapture is of central significance in Slav. En. (ed. A. Vaillant [1952]) and Hbr. En. The ref. here is not to the return of One previously incarnated, but to an exaltation, Sjöberg Menschensohn äth. Hen., 171-185 → III, 551, 39 ff.

[204] Charles, op. cit. (→ n. 186), ad loc. transl. 71:14, 16 in the 3rd person, not the 2nd, so that the Son of Man about whom En. has already received revelations is shown to him. The MSS do not permit this. Critical attempts to deal with the problem are made by H. Appel, "Die Komposition d. äth. Hen.," BFTh, 10, 3 (1906), 43-45 and Charles, op. cit., 142-144.

Man, [205] as though he had already come down to earth before as such, nor is there achieved a provisional mystical identity between the two figures, [206] nor are there two developments of the same primal man whose [207] unity is established again in the identification expressed here. The pt. is simply that En. is instituted into the office and function of the eschatological Son of Man, with perhaps a suggestion that the earthly man En. is transformed into the heavenly being, the Son of Man.

The probability seems to be that this enshrines the theology of a Jewish group [208] which had chosen as its hero the Enoch who in ancient times had been translated to heaven and initiated into all the divine secrets. Perhaps the head, founder, or teacher of the group had named himself after this Enoch. Son of Man eschatology did not arise under these followers of Enoch. It was presupposed, not initiated, by them. [209] They give it concrete form by assuming that their master, Enoch, was the future Son of Man and Judge of the world. This is analogous to the belief of primitive Christianity in the eschatological work of Jesus as the Son of Man. [210]

3. The Sixth Vision of 4 Esr.

The Son of Man concept is accompanied by another Messianology in 4 Esr., and the two eschatologies, which are represented by the Man and the Messiah, [211] go hand in

---

[205] Acc. to Odeberg Metatron, 1-20 the primal man incarnate in Adam lives on in Metatron at the earliest stage of the concept. Only later is Metatron equated with En., Hbr. En. 3-15. Odeberg concludes from this that En. is Metatron come down to earth and that his elevation symbolises the return of the divine brought down with him. Par. are seen to the Gnostic and esp. the Mandaean redeemer doctrine. There is a par. if the descent (one cannot say incarnation) of Enoch/Metatron is really to be presupposed, but Sjöberg Menschensohn äth. Hen., 172-185 contests this, and in any case the par. shows that the doctrine of a descending redeemer basically arises out of a macrocosm idea (exalted En. is as big as the whole world, Hbr. En. 9) only with the specific qualification of a prophet (→ 414, 19 ff.), and thus does not permit chronological deductions.

[206] The manner of identity is not considered, so that the objections of Staerk Soter, II, 68, n. 3 and S. Mowinckel, "Hen. og Menneskesønnen," Norsk Teol. Tidsskrift, 45 (1944), 57-69 are in some respects pointless.

[207] Cf. Jansen, passim, who from the outset finds Enoch in heavenly form behind the Son of Man and traces him back to Babyl. Ea/Oannes, whose main characteristic (he is the god of the ocean and wisdom) is the same as that of the earthly Enoch. On the historical question → 409, 8 ff.

[208] In essentials we follow van Andel, passim here, but we do not accept his thesis that the master of the sect mystically identifies himself with Enoch and like the Teacher of Righteousness of Qumran has left behind written halachah and divine mysteries, nor do we make any deductions regarding collective understanding of the Son of Man in the NT or His relation to the kingdom of God.

[209] Sjöberg Menschensohn äth. Hen., 154-9, 165, 167.

[210] Cf. C. K. Barrett, The NT Background (1956), 255.

[211] The Messiah is compared to a lion sicut leo, 11:37, cf. the interpretation in 12:31. Here the comparison gives Judah a symbol (Gn. 49:9) which is set against the eagle (4 Esr. 11:1-12, 31) for Rome. He is of the seed of David, 12:32 (cf. Mi. 5; Jer. 23:5-8; Ez. 34:23-31; Am. 9:8-15; Is. 9:11), so that He is not pre-existent like the Son of Man (13:26), though He is kept for the end of the days, 12:32. On filius meus, in 7:28 → 361, 4 ff. and n. 167. His fight against the wicked at the end of the days (11:37-46; 12:32 f.) is comparable to that of the Son of Man in 13:5, 30-38, 49, though without the fiery stream issuing from His mouth, 13:10, 27. The description of salvation is shorter (properly only 12:34: nam residuum populum meum liberabit cum misericordia, qui salvati sunt super fines meos, et iocundabit eos, quoadusque veniat finis dies iudicii) than we find with the Son of Man (cf. esp. 13:12, 23, 26, 40, 48), but He does not bring final judgment as the Son of Man does (cf. 12:34; 7:28: et iocundabit, qui relicti sunt annis CCCC. The Syr. figure of 30 yrs. here is based on the yrs. of Jesus' life). When the time of His dominion runs out, He will die, 7:29. Oddly no place of coming is stated apart from the fig. suscitatus de silva in 11:37, but Mt. Zion, which properly ref. only to the

hand with a third in which God ushers in the end directly. [212] The view of the end-time in which the Son of Man is central is to be seen with this qualification. It occurs only in the sixth vision, c. 13. The Son of Man is (only Syr. and Eth.) "(somewhat) as the form of a man," v. 2, [213] *ille* or *ipse homo*, v. 3, 5, 12, and *vir*, v. 25, 32, 51. [214] He is — but only in the interpretation — God's παῖς (→ V, 681, n. 196), v. 32, 37, 52, cf. the Messiah in 7:28. He was for a long time concealed pre-existently with God, v. 26. [215] He then comes *de corde maris*, v. 3, 51, and *cum nubibus caeli*, v. 3. [216] He arrives at the pt. in time when the nations wage war against one another, v. 31. He comes down on a hill (v. 6) which is explained to be Zion, v. 35. [217] From this hill He fights a countless host of ungodly men with a stream of fire issuing out of his mouth, vv. 5-11, 27 f. With this He destroys (v. 38) the nations (v. 33, 37, 49) as a punishment for their sins, v. 37. He thus protects the remnant of the people Israel (v. 49) [218] and gathers around Him a peaceful host (v. 12, 39, 47) which consists of the returning 10 tribes (vv. 40-47), or those who have good works and faith in the Most High (v. 23), or the remnant of the chosen people, v. 48. But this eschatological Israel cannot be a historical continuation of the earlier one. It must represent the new aeon. For as man fashions order among the *derelicti*, the Most High redeems His whole creation, v. 26. In the depiction of the conflict essential features of OT theophanies (the call to battle, discouragement, earthquake, darkness, the voice of Yahweh) are transferred to the Man (storm, earthquake, war, discouragement, fire from His mouth), just as the motif of the storm of peoples is part of a long Jewish tradition. [219]

Fighting the nations and ushering in the end, the Man does more and is more expressly the eschatological leader than in Da. 7. The comparative and fig. character which Da. sought to retain in his depiction is almost completely lost. The interfusion of national hopes now gives us (as with the Messiah) persons *qui cum eo sunt* (13:52). These cannot be angels [220] but only end-time heroes like Elijah, Enoch and Moses, esp. those of whom no death is reported. In a remarkable way the merging of the lofty figure of the Son of Man with the Messiah gives Him a predicate of lowliness through the transfer of the servant title. The constitutive idea of concealment in the heavenly world prior to His

---

Son of Man in 13:35, may be mentioned here. The version in c. 12 is more concretely related to world history than that of c. 7. The Messiah destroys Rome and world rule passes to Israel. The Messianic kingdom is not the same as God's rule, as in the OT. It is an intermediate kingdom at the end of the first aeon before the last judgment, cf. the par. material in Volz Esch., 226.

[212] 4:36; 5:4 f., 42; 6:6, 18-28; 7:43 f.; 8:55-61; 9:2. The OT idea of the day of Yahweh lives on here without being transferred to a Saviour (cf. Jer. 46:10; Is. 13 ff.; Jl. 2:1 f.; Zeph. 1:7 ff.), but judgment is not described so concretely. In 4 Esr. 7:29-44 (after the Messianic kingdom) it is balanced by national Messianic hope and in 6:7-28 (separation of the aeons) by apocal. hope.

[213] Wellhausen Sohn, 198 transl. *quasi similitudinem hominis*. The *ille homo* which follows ref. to this. The Lat. scribe jumps from the first *et vidi et ecce* to the second.

[214] In v. 32 *(filius meus, quem vidisti virum ascendentem)* the double acc. perhaps retains the element of comparison.

[215] *quem conservat Altissimus multis temporibus*. *Altissimus* is also used for God in 3:3; 4:2, 11, 34 (also *excelsus*). He is not knowable to dwellers on earth in 4:21, is the Creator in 3:4, the Consummator in 6:6. The Messiah and Son of Man are always subject to Him. When v. 32 says: *et tunc revelabitur filius meus*, this means that God will manifest Him, Sjöberg Menschensohn Ev., 47, n. 6.

[216] As distinct from Da. 7:13 (→ 420, 25 ff.) "in the clouds of heaven" ref. here only to the coming of the Man. The interpretation ignores it completely.

[217] This is probably based on national Messianic expectation.

[218] This is par. to the national hope of Israel that the eagle, Rome, will be destroyed by the Messiah described here as the lion (11:37; 12:31) and the seed of David (12:32), 11:39-46; 12:32 f. The remnant of Israel *residuus populus* is liberated thereby.

[219] Cf. Ez. 38 f.; Mi. 4:11; Zech. 14:2; Sib., 3, 663 ff.; Eth. En. 56; 90:16; Test. Jos. 1:9; S. Bar. 70:7-10 etc., and esp. Rabb. material about Gog and Magog, Str.-B., III, 831-840.

[220] So Gunkel in Kautzsch Apokr. u. Pseudepigr., *ad loc.*

manifestation [221] is not affected by this. The Son of Man is clearly differentiated as a person from His community.

The vision obviously represents a late stage [222] in the history of the Son of Man concept. It should not be heralded forthwith as the background of the Synoptic Son of Man tradition but does offer interesting par. to the observable enrichment of this tradition by other messianological traditions. In both cases certain features lose their distinctiveness in this process.

4. Data from the Synoptic Gospels.

Allusions to Da. 7:13 on the lips of Jesus might be secondary additions by the primitive community → 450, 6 ff.; 453, 20 ff.; 460, 9 ff. The Son of Man Messianology of Eth. En. is in detail reflected with notable paucity in the Synoptics (→ n. 260, 294, 342, 413) and it seems to belong so plainly to a special group (→ 427, 7 ff.) that it has little to tell us directly about the source of NT Son of Man Christology. [223] The Son of Man concept is advanced along with the idea of a political Messiah in 4 Esr. (→ 427, n. 211) and in this respect it is not comparable with Son of Man Christology. Furthermore it is relatively late, perhaps even later that the oldest Synoptic stratum. [224] In view of this we are driven to the conclusion that Jewish apocalyptic material does not provide an answer to the crucial question as to the incipient shape of the NT Son of Man concept in Judaism between 50 B.C. and 50 A.D. Even allowing, then, for the uncertainties which always beset the circular arguments of exegesis and history, one must conclude that the oldest stratum of the Synoptic tradition suggests a Jewish Son of Man tradition which provisionally constitutes a fourth source alongside those already mentioned.

We ref. to the texts assembled → 433, 8 ff. In this connection there is no need to try to say how far they are original to Jesus and how far they are to be assigned to the primitive community. The underlying Son of Man expectation is in principle to be attained by abstraction from the application to Jesus by Jesus Himself and (or) the community. The possibility of the development of a genuinely Jewish Chr. Son of Man Christology as an important phase in the history of Jewish Messianology has also to be taken into account. In detail these principial claims cannot lead to concrete statements so long as we can get no other information about the hypothetical bearers of this fourth Son of Man tradition.

5. Son of Man Expectation in the Broader Compass of Jewish Messianology.

In ancient Judaism Son of Man expectation stands in tension with a series of other eschatologies. [225] Among them are the this-worldly expectations of a political kingly

---

[221] Cf. Sjöberg Menschensohn Ev., 45-47.

[222] Sjöberg Menschensohn Ev., 48, n. 1 shows against Box, op. cit. (→ n. 67), 273 that the supernatural and national features in the picture of the Messiah (→ n. 211) merge as ideas for all the traditional character of c. 7, 12 and 13, but have not been pieced together editorially from different written sources.

[223] C. H. Dodd is critical in his "Die Grundlagen d. chr. Theol.," Ev. Theol., 12 (1952/53), 448. Acc. to him the similitudes are an isolated and marginal testimony and their pre-chr. origin is doubtful. Cf. Volz Esch., 188: Son of Man expectation is "not popular ... it is hardly known to the broad masses, but was presumably at home only in certain apocal. circles."

[224] B. Violet, "Die Apokalypsen d. Esr. u. d. Bar. in deutscher Gestalt," GCS, 32 (1924), p. XLIX f. sets the final redaction at c. 100 A.D.; the place is uncertain, perhaps Rome.

[225] For details cf. Bousset-Gressm., 222-268; Lagrange, 363-387; J. Bonsirven, Le Judaisme Palestinien au temps de Jésus-Christ, I (1934), 341-467; Schürer, II, 579-650; Moore, II, 323-376; Volz Esch., 173-229; R. Meyer, Art. "Eschatologie im Judt.," RGG³, II, 662-5; also "Messias im nachbibl. Judt.," RGG³, IV, 904-906 → 360, 15 ff.

Messiah (Davidic, cf. Ps. Sol. 17 f.; Sib., 3, or non-Davidic) [226] and a priestly Messiah, [227] the hope of an exalted Messiah and Intercessor like Enoch (→ II, 557, 12 ff.; IV, 856, n. 102), expectations of a return of ideal figures like Elijah (→ II, 931, 6 ff.) and Moses (→ IV, 856, 12 ff.) and expectation of salvation in which there is no central saviour. [228] If the Son of Man concept can sometimes be fused with one or other of these expectations, e.g., that of the Son of David in 4 Esr. 12:32; 13:3, 25 ff. or Enoch in Eth. En. 70 f. or Elijah in Mk. 9:12 f., it cannot be fitted into a single system within Jewish eschatology as a whole, nor does it occupy a pre-eminent position among the various expectations. As in the case of all the other eschatologies, one has to consider that it was only specific groups who expected a transcendent Saviour and as such the Son of Man. There is also the possibility of a more literary or even a purely literary reflection of this expectation.

Difficult to fit in is Sib., 5, 414-433. [229] This describes the work of a political kingly Messiah which again became very significant in the post-NT period. But when He is called ἀνὴρ μακαρίτης and is said to have come down from heaven οὐρανίων νώτων (5, 414, cf. 3, 286 οὐράνιος), this surely reflects Son of Man expectation. Unfortunately the passage does not allow us to make further deductions as to the expected figure which exerted an influence here, → n. 24.

On the other hand Judaism, [230] which apart from Da. 7:27 always interpreted the בר אנש of Da. 7:13 f. messianically, retained all the characteristics of the Son of Man, though His name was changed, usually to בר נפלי or Son of the clouds, [231] or else it was quoted in the original context and implicitly related to the Messiah. [232] Trypho in Just. Dial., 32, 1 recognised that a glorious and powerful Messiah will come acc. to Da. 7:13, though he denies that He was come in Christ crucified or that Christ will come again. He thus bears witness to a messianic interpretation of Da. 7:13 f. independent of the Chr. one (on this → n. 67).

C. The Son of Man in the New Testament.

I. The Synoptic Gospels.

1. The Preaching of Jesus.

a. According to the tradition Jesus probably referred to Himself three times as "man," perhaps in mashal form, when the desire for self-differentiation from God, another man, or animals gave occasion for this.

(a) In the story of the healing of the lame man in Mk. 2:1-12 Jesus says pointedly in v. 10: Not only God may forgive, but man too in Me, Jesus. [233] The word

---

[226] Cf. the Maccabees or the anti-Herod Galilean pretenders Hezekiah, Judas and Menachem; cf. esp. Jos. Ant., 18, 4-10, 23-25; Bell., 2, 433-458.

[227] Namely, a Messiah of Aaron or the Zadokites, cf. also the priest-prince of Test. L. 18.

[228] So Sir., Jub., Slav. En.; v. Bousset-Gressm., 222 and Volz Esch., 262-8, 350-5, 489-521.

[229] Cf. A. Kurfess (1951); linked by Bousset-Gressm., 224 with the 5th and 6th visions of 4 Esr.; S. Bar. 35-40; 53:10 f.; 69-74 and Rev. passim. Cf. also Sib., 5, 256-9 and on this → IV, 857, n. 110.

[230] Rabb. statements in Str.-B., I, 20, 67, 483-6, 843, 956-9; II, 287; III, 19, 147, 639; IV, 876 f., 1002; Bowman, 285 f. On Tg. Ps. 80 v. also → n. 41.

[231] Only R. Abbahu (c. 300 A.D.) in anti-chr. polemic, jTaan., 2, 1 (65b, 59 f.), Str.-B., I, 486, 959 → n. 24.

[232] E.g., Sanh., 98a; Jehoshua' b. Levi (c. 250 A.D.), Str.-B., I, 486, 843, 956.

[233] Since Jesus has Himself in view (this does not mean, of course, that [Son of] Man is a fixed self-designation, as Vielhauer Jesus, 122 f. seems to suppose when he argues for an opposing view), it was but a step for the community to make בר נשא a messianic title → 441, 34 ff. No antithesis to God is intended, and the community saw no rivalry between God and Jesus in respect of the power to forgive sins.

"man" is evoked by the need to reply to the objection of v. 7: Who can forgive sins but God alone? [234] which in turn, as in Lk. 7:45, is quite understandable in view of the saying in v. 5b: Son, thy sins are forgiven. [235] Jesus is not generalising in His use of the term "man." He is not setting up a general antithesis to God. He is simply meeting an objection which is controlled by the scribal view of God and does not take into account the messianic actualising of the remission of sins as this is effected by Jesus [236] → IV, 345, 4 ff.

(b) In Mt. 11:18 f. Jesus seems to be putting Himself on a level with the Baptist, though the primitive community regarded the subordination of the latter as important. [237] Again, Jesus is called "a glutton and winebibber" by opponents, which the later tradition would surely have found offensive. These two points leave no doubt as to the fact that v. 19 (→ VI, 140, 27 ff.) is an authentic dominical saying. [238] Is the title Son of Man original too? In Aramaic there are several reasons to expect בר נשא (→ 405, 8) as the equivalent. First, it is demanded by the ensuing ἄνθρωπος, where it is indispensable as a noun sustaining the participial equivalents of φάγος and οἰνοπότης. Again, it is the noun which links together John and Jesus as mes-

---

[234] The usage here is the same as in analogous cases in Galilean Aram. → n. 15-20. Mt. 4:4 shapes it when he has Jesus ref. to Himself in the ἄνθρωπος of Dt. 8:3. That there was not originally an "I" in Mk. 2:10 for which the community substituted a "man" in generalising self-designation seems to follow from the fact that the community did not usually call itself man but Israel, elect (chosen generation), saints (holy people), twelve tribes, Jerusalem, temple, priesthood, house, bride, body, flock, field, disciples, cf. E. Saunders, Art. "Gemeinde," *Bibl.-Historisches Handwörterbuch*, I (1962), 543; E. Schweizer, "Gemeinde u. Gemeindeordnung im NT," AbhThANT, 35² (1962), 28-79.

[235] For the material connection of v. 5b with the preaching of Jesus cf. W. Manson, *Jesus the Messiah* (1943), 41 f. and for the formal connection of the v. with what precedes and with the setting and substance of the story cf. Dibelius, 63-65, both in opposition to Bultmann Trad., 12-14, who thinks v. 5b rather than v. 6 marks the beginning of an interpolation that reflects community debates about its authority to forgive sins, which is neither based on the authority of Jesus, since this is projected back to Him by the community, nor conferred by God, since the authority is seen in opposition to God (v. 7). But this antithesis does not arise out of the question of the Pharisees: May not God alone forgive sins? since on Bultmann's theory the community itself put this question on their lips. Schweizer, 71 rightly pts. out that Jesus' table fellowship with sinners is in deed and in truth no other than remission of sins.

[236] Wellhausen Einleitung, 123, 129 f., cf. Wellhausen Sohn, 203 on Mk. 2:10: "In reply to the reproach that He is doing what it is not lawful for man to do Jesus makes the protestation that man has this power; though I am man, I have it (the accent, however, is not on the 'man' but on the 'may': man may forgive sins)." Wellhausen, then, begins expressly with Jesus' own self-awareness, which is not explicitly defined as messianic, cf. J. Wellhausen, *Einl. in d. ersten drei Ev.* (1905), 93 f.: Jesus claims authority to forgive sins "even though He is man, not because He is the Messiah." Many scholars, e.g., Bultmann Trad., 13; Tödt, 118 wrongly suggest that it is Wellhausen's view that what is originally maintained is the gen. power of man to forgive sins, as though Wellh. had said that Jesus claims authority to forgive sins because He is man.

[237] H. Braun, *Spätjüd.-häret. u. frühchr. Radikalismus*, II, *Beiträge z. hist. Theol.*, 24 (1957), 38, n. 1 makes the odd statement that "the reproach against Jesus in Mt. 11:19 stands in a later composition which formulates the relation between John and Jesus programmatically, but in itself it belongs to the very oldest stratum." The composition is later only in so far as it contains the messianic ὁ υἱὸς τοῦ ἀνθρώπου, not in so far as John and Jesus are set in programmatic relation, for to what community could one ascribe such a programme?

[238] Even the ἦλθεν does not need to look back to Jesus' earthly existence as a whole from the standpt. of the community (so Bultmann Trad., 164-8; → II, 668, 10 ff.), esp. as we have here the 3rd pers., not the 1st. Cf. Bultmann Trad., 168, n. 2. The orig. was אֲתָי, then with auxiliary verb. For Aram. senses which might back an original ἦλθον (1st pers.), cf. Jeremias Älteste Schicht, 166 f.

sengers of wisdom (→ VII, 515, 12 ff.); without it Mt. 11:19c and par. would be left hanging in the air: the ἔργα by which God is justified [239] are done by both men, and because they indicate the coming of the hour of decision, due note is to be taken of them. Thirdly, it should be observed that the antithesis to the ascetic John, who does not receive sinners, is best stated in the 3rd person, [240] and since the name Jesus is without parallel in a saying of Jesus about Himself (→ III, 287, 28 ff.) the only possibility is בר נשא: "John came neither eating nor drinking... Now there comes one [241] who eats and drinks..."

(c) The saying in Mt. 8:20 and par. is the same in both accounts. It has been expounded in different ways.

Some have interpreted it as biographical apophthegm based on Jewish wisdom. Originally man who is homeless on earth contrasts himself with the beasts. [242] This has been made into a saying of Jesus referring to His homelessness. But one should not detach the saying from its setting, which establishes the original relation of the logion to the situation of Jesus. [243] Furthermore, man is not in the least homeless acc. to secular Jewish wisdom. [244] The saying has also been viewed as a conscious expression of the humanity of Jesus in contrast to ὁ υἱὸς θεοῦ. [245] But the context makes a comparison only with animals. A third interpretation is that Jesus is referring to His life of need, i.e., to His concealment as the Son of Man, which in contrast and relationship is the prelude to His glory as such. [246] The primary ref. of the saying, however, is to discipleship and to the authority of the One who calls thereto; what those who are called must expect is not concealment but homelessness. [247] Finally, the saying has been viewed as an I-saying which brings out the character of discipleship, the title Son of Man being imported later. [248]

Since this is a dominical saying against whose authenticity no cogent arguments can be brought, the question can only be whether Jesus is here speaking of Himself non-messianically as a man. If so, this unusual mode of expression is occasioned

---

[239] Acc. to Jeremias Gl.[7], 162. Schl. Mt., ad loc. takes ἐδικαιώθη in the Palestinian sense "as justified, approved by God," not the Gk. sense: "was judged." Cf. also → II, 214, 28 ff. with n. 13, 14, also Kl. Mt., ad loc.

[240] But the 1st pers. is possible, and the title might have supplanted an "I," → 442, 10 ff.; 433, 2 f.; 446, 7 f. This is the view of Bornkamm, 207, though cf. Vielhauer Jesus, 125-127.

[241] On this possible transl. → 403, 3. Here, of course, בר נשא is not ordinary man (Bultmann Trad., 166 etc.), for Jesus and not just any man who eats and drinks is contrasted with the ascetic John. But man is not a title, cf. the due consideration and rejection of this view in Vielhauer Jesus, 127. Tödt, 108 f., who without linguistic discrimination thinks the title has its origin in the Palestinian community, views the whole from the standpt. of rejection by "this generation" in Mt. 11:16 and par.: "in the place, then, where Jesus' claim stands in sayings about the coming Son of Man, the designation Son of Man is introduced in statements about His present work."

[242] Schulthess, op. cit. (→ n. 30), 216-236, 241-258 (249: "Man, i.e., ordinary man like us, has not..."); Bultmann Trad., 27, 102; R. Bultmann, Jesus (1964), 142 f.

[243] Cf. Dibelius, 159 with emphasis on the interrelation of the almost formal Mt. 8:19-22.

[244] In spite of Vielhauer, 123-5, then, the contrast to the refuges of animals is historical rather than natural. Jesus is not homeless because He has no house and no friends to see to His support, but because, though not as the concealed Son of Man, He goes to Jerusalem to His death.

[245] Schl. Mt., ad loc.

[246] M. Dibelius, Jesus[4] (1966), 82; Sjöberg Menschensohn Ev., 238 f.; Schweizer Menschensohn, 79.

[247] Tödt, 113 f.

[248] Bornkamm, 207; cf. Tödt, 114.

by the statement which contrasts him with the beasts. Or is it that He Himself said: "I have no place to lay my head," and the community substituted the title? It is impossible to say for certain. But mutual support is lent to each other by the first possibility and the two analogies (Mk. 2:10 → 430, 32 ff. and Mt. 11:19 par. → 431, 8 ff.) in which there is a juxtaposition with God and another man. In other words, there is much to support the interpretation that even animals have dens but a man such as I, Jesus, has nowhere to lay his head.

b. Eight sayings of Jesus about the coming Son of Man yield a self-contained apocalyptic picture and seem to stand up to critical analysis.

(a) Mt. 24:27 and par. tells us how the appearing of the Son of Man was envisaged. Mt. in the second half (cf. 24:3, 37, 39) adds παρουσία (→ n. 255), [249] but in the first half he has the more concrete and perhaps on that account the older text. [250] The original would then be: "For as the lightning flashes from the rising of the sun and shines to the setting of the sun, so it will be with the Son of Man in his day." [251] The Son of Man will thus shine in heaven and will be perceived by all men, just as no one can miss lightning. This statement comes after a warning against following rumours and joining one of the numerous messianic pretenders [252] (Mt. 24:26), and it offers the consolation that there is no reason to fear the Messiah might go unrecognised. For it is not a matter of some Messiah establishing himself who has come out of earthly concealment, whether in the desert or in inner chambers, but rather of the epiphany of the Son of Man which will be visible to all and which does not permit of any deception. This thought, which plainly sets aside the idea of a political Messiah in favour of a heavenly bringer of salvation, constitutes a decisive argument for the authenticity of the saying. [253] If the terminology of the Day of Yahweh is echoed here, [254] this is no argument to the contrary, since what it amounts

---

[249] Cf. Kümmel, 32, n. 63.

[250] Tödt, 45.

[251] Lk. 17:24b: οὕτως ἔσται... does not mean that here the Son of Man is compared directly to lightning (in distinction from Mt.), but rather that (as in Mt.) the ref is to His visibility, which is like that of lightning, cf. οὕτως ἔσται... in v. 26b and Mk. 4:26. On ὥσπερ γάρ cf. the preface to the parable in Mt. 25:14, though there is no corresponding οὕτως (cf. Jeremias Gl.7, 100 f.) in view of the fact that a story is being briefly introduced, → 434, 5; n. 257. The tertium comparationis here is just the visibility (Zn. Mt., ad loc.; Str.-B., I, 954) of the coming of the Son of Man, not the fact that He comes from the East (so later on the basis of Mt. 24:27 the Syr. church, cf. E. Peterson, "Die geschichtliche Bdtg. d. jüd. Gebetsrichtung," Frühkirche, Judt. u. Gnosis [1959], 13), nor, as in 24:37 f., 43 f. the fact that He comes suddenly (so E. Grässer, "Das Problem der Parusieverzögerung in d. synpt. Ev. u. in d. Ag.," ZNW Beih., 22² [1960], 170; Bultmann Trad., 128; Conzelmann, 115, though cf. 69, n. 1), for the indications of place and the elements of surprise (ἰδού) in Mt. 24:26 are now avoided, and certainly not in favour of new ones.

[252] Not Son of Man pretenders as though Messiah and Son of Man were the same, as in the primitive Church, so Vielhauer Gottesreich, 75 f., as against whom Tödt, 306 f. argues that Mt. 24:26 is original compared to Lk. 17:23, Lk. being the first to blur the distinction between Son of Man and Messiah.

[253] So also Bultmann Trad., 163; Tödt, 206. The subj. of ἰδοὺ ἐν τῇ ἐρήμῳ... ἰδοὺ ἐν τοῖς ταμιείοις in Mt. 24:26 must be different from that in v. 27 (as against Vielhauer Jesus, 110), where γάρ does not indicate the subj. of v. 26 but underlies the warning imperatives. Since Mt. simply follows Mk. 13:21-23 in Mt. 24:23-25 one can only conjecture that the ref. is to the same figure, so that Mt. could continue without mentioning it again.

[254] Kl. Mt., ad loc.; Volz Esch., 188.

to is not the dogmatic combination of two heterogeneous hopes for the future but simply an adoption of the term "day," which hereby acquires again a multiple sense → II, 951, 38 ff.

(b) The element of suddenness comes to expression in Mt. 24:37 and par. [255] The point is that the Son of Man will surprise men as men going about their everyday tasks were surprised by the flood in the days of Noah. [256] Since the κατακλυσμός (Gn. 6-8) was the execution of a judgment on men, the comparison implies that the execution of judgment on all men begins with the epiphany of the Son of Man. One may conclude that the Son of Man Himself will execute the office of judge, not of advocate or prosecutor. According to Lk. 17:30 the present generation will be overtaken by the day of the Son of Man in exactly the same way as the people of Sodom were by the rain of fire and brimstone. [257] Like Noah (v. 26), Lot too (v. 28), who prepared for the disaster without knowing when it would strike, is an example of the way the present generation must prepare for the coming of the Son of Man. Thus the point of the final comparison as well, i.e., intimation of the unexpected coming of the Son of Man (v. 39), goes back in substance to Jesus Himself. [258]

Disregarding what some think is the secondary nature of Lk. 21:34-36, Lk. 21:36 might well confirm this: "Watch ye therefore, and pray always, [259] that ye may be in a position to escape all these things that shall come to pass, and to stand before the Son of man." [260] If one accepts the principle that inauthenticity has to be proved rather than authenticity,

---

[255] παρουσία is again secondary in Mt. → 459, 6 f. The plur. ἐν ταῖς ἡμέραις was perhaps shaped by Lk. in analogy to v. 22 (Tödt, 47) or else Lk., knowing the "days of Jesus" from the post-Easter standpt., introduced in both passages an extension of the working period of the Son of Man, the original ref. being to the day of sudden coming. Already in v. 22 the plur. may be based on the "days of the Messiah" (Str.-B., IV, 816-844). If so, it is older, though a certain fusion of Messiah and Son of Man eschatology may be descried. It may also, like the sing., denote a non-extended time (→ II, 950, 21 ff.), or it may be a short form of "the days when the Son of Man makes an end" analogous to "the days when Noah went into the ark."

[256] Mt. in v. 39 elucidates the carelessness which prevailed then by οὐκ ἔγνωσαν, and in so doing shifts the accent somewhat.

[257] This is a comparison or par., not a full parable. As in other comparisons (→ 433, 13; 434, 5) the Son of Man thus belongs originally to this complex of ideas. The special source (on this cf. Rehkopf, passim) made the connection, obviously to heap up the title (v. 24, 26, 30), though, as the par. in Mt. show, from an authentic if detached tradition which Mt. either used elsewhere or, in the case of Lk. 17:30, did not know. This is more probable than the conjecture of Bultmann Trad., 123; Kümmel, 31; Vielhauer Gottesreich, 74; Tödt, 45, that the comparison in vv. 28-30 is a secondary imitation of v. 26 f. with alteration of the figure. In an exact imitation the Son of Man saying would have to be at the beginning and not the end; on ἀποκαλύπτεται → III, 580, 32 ff. On the other hand, it is unlikely that Mt. left out the second comparison on purpose because it did not bring out so clearly as the first the unexpected onset of judgment, so Kl. Lk., ad loc.

[258] Jesus uses other double comparisons, cf. Lk. 12:49 f. (fire and water).

[259] The ἐν παντὶ καιρῷ goes with δεόμενοι, not ἀγρυπνεῖτε. ἐν παντὶ καιρῷ δεόμενοι means the same as πάντοτε προσεύχεσθαι in Lk. 18:1. One cannot, then, regard Lk. 21:36 as secondary compared to Mk. 13:33, as though imminent expectation had faded out in Lk. and men must watch at all times.

[260] σταθῆναι (etc.) ἔμπροσθεν usually denotes coming before a judge, Mt. 25:32; 27:11; 1 Th. 2:19; 3:13. Hence the further activity of the Son of Man as surety or prosecutor cannot be ruled out in Lk. 21:36; in Eth. En. too He is surety as well as judge (→ 424, 15 ff.), e.g., 69:29.

this saying will have to be attributed to Jesus. [261] The esoteric character which one would expect in analogy to other sayings (cf. Lk. 17:22; for v. 24, 26, 30; 18:8b → 457, 17 ff.) was possibly lost when the saying was attached to the Marcan material.

(c) The saying in Lk. 18:8, which undoubtedly comes from the pre-Lucan source, need not be separated from v. 6 f., in which Jesus presses home the parable of the unjust judge. [262] God will suddenly see that His elect, who cry to Him day and night, will get their rights, v. 8a. [263] But will the Son of Man, when He comes, find on the earth the faith which man must have to be of the elect (v. 8b)? The subject is not the coming of the Son of Man to earth but the faith which men have on earth. [264] According to Synoptic usage this can mean acceptance of the preaching of Jesus. Will the Son of Man, when He appears in heavenly judgment, be able to say that men on earth have responded to Jesus' summons to decision and confessed Him, obeyed His call for repentance, and persistently petitioned God as the widow did the unjust judge? [265] The point made here in a question is made again in Lk. 17:24, 26, 30, as an intimation and in Lk. 21:36 as a demand. If one cannot understand Lk. 18:8b more precisely, it must be regarded basically as part of Jesus' own preaching.

(d) In the confession before the supreme council in Lk. 22:69 and par. the Lucan version, which belongs to the special source of the passion narrative, is to be assessed independently of Mk. (→ 371, 10 ff.). [266] The expression from Da. 7:13, which recurs elsewhere (→ 450, 6 ff.) and the point of which is changed by the relating of μετὰ τῶν νεφελῶν τοῦ οὐρανοῦ only to ἐρχόμενον (→ 420, 26 ff.) has not yet been added here. [267] We simply have a judgment scene in heaven in which the Son of Man sits beside the supreme Judge. The allusion to Ps. 110:1, where the enemies of Him who sits at God's right hand are subdued under His feet, means that His activity is in closer agreement, not with that of the advocate or prosecutor, but rather with that of the judge himself. This fits in very well with what we find elsewhere → 433, 24 ff.; 434, 9; n. 260.

---

[261] As against Bultmann Trad., 126, who asks whether Lk. here was using a lost epistle of Paul, and Tödt, 89-92, who ascribes to Lk. a major role in formulating the passage.

[262] Cf. Jeremias Gl.7, 135, but not Vielhauer Gottesreich, 62.

[263] Jeremias Gl.7, 134.

[264] Hence the use of ἐπὶ τῆς γῆς corresponds to that in Mk. 2:10 and that of πίστις is the same as in Mt. 8:10 and not in Paul. The difficulty of finding an Aram. equivalent for πίστις is a gen. one in the Synoptic tradition and is no argument against Lk. 18:8b being original. One cannot say for certain what is meant by the πίστις which will qualify in the final judgment, so that the saying as a whole offers no sure basis for an understanding of Son of Man expectation.

[265] The deducing of God's hearing of prayer from the hearing of the petition by the implacable judge is not to be styled a conclusion a minore ad maius (Jeremias Gl.7, 136) but rather a peiore ad melius if we are to get the real pt. of the parable.

[266] But cf. E. Lohse, "Der Prozess Jesu Christi," Festschr. K. D. Schmidt (1961), 26 f. On ἀπὸ τοῦ νῦν δέ (also 1:48; 5:10; 12:52; 22:18; Ac. 18:6), cf. Lk. 16:16: ἀπὸ τότε. The Matthean ἀπ' ἄρτι is different (apart from 26:64 cf. 23:39 and 26:29, with no other instances in the Synoptists).

[267] Tödt, 94-97, who assumes dependence on Mk. 14:62, has to explain the alteration in Lk. speculatively as the elimination of the idea of the parousia in favour of a sessio ad dextram in God's kingdom which is effective already for the persecuted Church. In so doing he fails to note the antiquity of the saying.

The Lucan version is older than the Marcan, since Jesus here uses a veiled form of speech, not confessing Himself clearly to be the Messiah by ἐγώ εἰμι [268] and largely eliminating the element of apocal. vision by the use of a simple copula (ἔσται ... καθήμενος) rather than the visionary ὄψεσθε. [269] Only the elucidation of the periphrastic δύναμις (only Mk. 14:62 and par.) by τοῦ θεοῦ is perhaps secondary in Lk. [270] The argument for composition by the community, namely, that Mk. 14:62 is part of a planned series of self-sayings, does not apply to Lk. If one regards the quoting of Da. 7:13 as secondary one no longer has the idea of the exaltation of the Son of Man, which is unknown to Jewish apocal.; the saying is simply referring to His majesty. The authenticity of Lk. 22:69 can be contested only if the historicity of the whole judgment scene is called in question. [271] But this is to be investigated in relation to the individual elements, which may lead to different judgments in different cases. When the specific element Lk. 22:69 is considered in isolation, at most one can dispute only the place where it is put, [272] not the wording or point. The Son of Man appears at the judgment not merely as witness or advocate, but also, seated at God's right hand, as a participant in condemnation or pardon.

(e) Peculiar to Mt. in the saying 10:23 (→ 60, 9 ff.) in the charge to the disciples: "When they chase you from one city, flee to another, for amen, I say to you, You will not have finished the cities of Israel before the Son of Man comes." [273]

Only 10:5 f. in the same charge, and also peculiar to Mt., limits the mission of the disciples so plainly to Israel. For this reason the saying might be a key in the problem of the historical Jesus from the standpoint of consistent eschatology. [274] On this view it is an admonition to hurry, to proclaim the message to as many recipients of the promise as possible before the end. But one can also take the saying as a promise that the disciples will not have to endure persecution for long; [275] it is not that the disciples must make haste but that the last hour is hastening on. Along these lines there is expectation that the whole Palestinian church, which still pursues its mission in Israel and which is comforted by a Jewish Christian prophetic claim, will utterly perish. [276] But if the saying is

---

[268] Loh. Mk. on 14:62 thinks the variant σὺ εἶπας ὅτι ἐγώ εἰμι has some claim to authenticity since it would explain the variants in Mt. and Lk. B. H. Streeter, *The Four Gospels*[4] (1936), 322, pts. out, however, that σὺ εἶπας might come from Mk. 15:2, the answer in the council being thus assimilated to that given to Pilate. But the agreement between Mk. and Mt., whose πλὴν λέγω ὑμῖν does not make an unequivocal Yes out of the σὺ εἶπας, is still remarkable. The unambiguous ὑμεῖς λέγετε of Lk. 22:70 ref. to the title ὁ υἱὸς τοῦ θεοῦ.

[269] Also W. Bousset, *Kyrios Christos*, FRL, NF, 4[2] (1921), 17, n. 3 concludes on this ground that Lk. has the more ancient form of the Logion.

[270] There is no proof that δύναμις was used thus only in Galilee, so Loh. Mk., *ad loc.* as against the more gen. view of Dalman WJ, I, 165 and Str.-B., I, 1006.

[271] On this cf. H. Lietzmann, "Der Prozess Jesu," *Kleine Schriften*, II (1959), 251-263; M. Dibelius, "Das historische Problem d. Leidensgeschichte," *Botschaft u. Geschichte*, I (1953), 248-257; J. Blinzler, *Der Prozess Jesu*[3] (1960), 163-174; P. Winter, *On the Trial of Jesus* (1961), 27 f.; Jeremias Verhör, 139-144; Lohse, *op. cit.* (→ n. 266), 24-39.

[272] After Peter's denial in Lk., before in Mk., in both cases obviously for contrast.

[273] Cf. J. Jeremias, *Jesu Verheissung f. d. Völker*[2] (1959), 17 f. Perhaps the saying did not belong originally to the charge, since it is not in the par. to 10:22 (Mk. 13:13; Lk. 21:17 ff.; Mt. 24:9, 13) and bears no relation to v. 24, 25, cf. Vielhauer Gottesreich, 64 f.

[274] Cf. A. Schweitzer, *Gesch. der Leben-Jesu-Forschung*[6] (1951), 407 (*The Quest of the Historical Jesus* [1945], 358), who notes that non-fulfilment of Mt. 10:23 is the first delay in the *parousia* and thus provides the first fact in the story of Christianity which gives a lasting and otherwise inexplicable turn to Jesus' work.

[275] Tödt, 57.

[276] Cf. Schl. Mt., *ad loc.*; T. W. Manson, *The Sayings of Jesus* (1954), 182.

regarded as the work of the Jewish Chr. community, [277] why did not the community which fashioned it drop it again when the prophecy was not fulfilled (→ VI, 845, n. 402)? That in the short time between its formulation and its further transmission it won impregnable authority as a saying of the Lord is a more arbitrary hypothesis than that it really was a saying of the Lord. Furthermore, if it is not accepted as a saying of Jesus, it still finds a material parallel in the message that the divine rule is directly at hand, concerning whose non-fulfilment the community had to be convinced even after Easter. It is most unlikely that this reproduces a rival imminent expectation of such intensity as to give rise to such a saying. [278] Only as an authentic dominical saying can Mt. 10:23 have survived the tendency, which is particularly clear in Mt., to ascribe to Jesus a work among the Gentiles. [279] Only as such can it have failed to fall victim to the offence which would be taken at it as an unfulfilled prophecy. [280] Persecution of the disciples was to be expected even in the life-time of Jesus, just like Jesus' own suffering. [281]

The sayings fits in well with other testimonies to the expectation of the coming Son of Man. Whether the coming be regarded as to earth or in heaven is not clear, but the latter may be assumed in analogy to other sayings → 433, 10 ff.; 434, 7 f.; 435, 8; 435, 23.

The expression "sign (→ VII, 236, 18 ff.) of the Son of Man" which will appear in heaven is probably an older Synoptic tradition than Mk. 13:26 and par., which is plainly modelled on Da. 7:13. [282] It is hardly possible that there could be any other source for it than Jesus' own preaching. For Mt. the best place to put it was in the apocalyptic discourse parallel to the development in terms of Da. 7:13 f. (→ 450, 6 ff.) in Mk. 13:26. In all probability the sign of the Son of Man was neither a light-phenomenon nor the Son of Man Himself but the banner around which the eschatological people of God would rally. [283]

---

[277] So Bultmann Trad., 129 (chr. vaticinium of the missionary period); cf. Kl. Mt., ad loc. Acc. to Schweizer, 62 the saying arose at the earliest when the community began to ask whether missionaries should go beyond the borders of Israel. Acc. to Vielhauer Gottesreich, 65 the saying is an apocal. word of comfort for the time of eschatological persecution; an early Chr. prophet revealed it as the saying of the Exalted Lord.

[278] The revival of imminent expectation after Jesus' death, e.g., in Paul, is no contradiction but rather a confirmation of this thesis. For we do not have a rival hope, Son of Man expectation, but a continuation of kingdom of God expectation and hope of Christ's return (without the Son of Man title → n. 472). For further arguments → 438, 9 ff.

[279] Examples in Jeremias, op. cit. (→ n. 273), 29 f. Acc. to Sjöberg Menschensohn Ev., 134 the v. has claims to authenticity.

[280] J. Schniewind, Das Ev. nach Mt., NT Deutsch, 2¹¹ (1964), ad loc.

[281] Jewish eschatological expectation also has the two motifs of flight and promise of a speedy ending of affliction (Str.-B., I, 557 and 953), though a repetition of these motifs does not have to be merely literary and may be for historical reasons.

[282] The first of the two ref. to the Son of Man in Mt. 24:30 may well belong to Mt.'s special material rather than his exposition of Mk., for the combination with Zech. 12:12, 14 is obviously independent of the tradition expressed in Rev. 1:7 and the sign cannot yet be the cross as in Apc. Pt. 1 and Ep. apostolorum, ed. H. Duensing, Kl. T., 152 (1925), 16 (though cf. A. J. B. Higgins, "The Sign of the Son of Man," NTSt, 9 [1963], 382); a further pt. is that the whole expression is not, as one would expect with a secondary exposition, elucidated or reinterpreted (the "sign" of the parousia in Mt. 24:3 differs here from Mt. 24:30); it presents something hard to understand and veils what is said.

[283] For a light-phenomenon in view of Lk. 17:24 and Pesikt. r., 36 (161a-162a) cf. Str.-B., I, 161 and 954 ff. It is also possible not to take τοῦ υἱοῦ τοῦ ἀνθρώπου as an obj. gen.: "the sign which points to the Son of Man," but as an explicative gen. In this case the Son of Man Himself would be the sign of the end, though this is most unlikely acc. to Higgins, op. cit., 380-382. Most convincing is the argument of T. F. Glasson, "The Ensign of the Son of Man (Mt. 24:30)," JThSt, NS, 15 (1964), 299 f. who establishes both the sense of banner and also an elementary nexus of ideas → 429, 21 ff.

(f) In view of the fact that the title Son of Man, in contrast to others, occurs only on the lips of Jesus, one must assume that at least this basic core of sayings is authentic, at any rate as concerns the use of the title. [284] Only thus can one explain the increase in use of the title in dominical sayings. It is also unlikely that the community would have begun to formulate messianological sayings of Jesus before it formulated christological sayings about Him. Another argument for authenticity is that we find here a fourth tradition which is independent of Daniel, 4 Esr. and Enoch and which thus indicates the variability of Son of Man expectation in Judaism.

> This tradition could also have been developed exclusively in the churches. It is most probable, indeed, that there were charismatic circles which after the collapse of the last hopes for a political Messiah activated supranational apocal. expectations, awaited Jesus as the Son of Man, and thus became Jewish Christians rather than Jews. Nevertheless, three arguments, of which the second and third mutually support one another, tell strongly against the view that it is their Christology alone which is transmitted in the sayings of Jesus. First it contradicts all else that we know about primitive Chr. prophecy that anonymous leaders of these churches should prophesy directly as Jesus (rather than speaking in the name of Jesus or developing or remodelling actual sayings of Jesus, as later). Secondly, the age of enthusiasm in which this supposedly happened was extinguished far too quickly, and the independence of the Syr.-Palestinian communities controlled by it was far too weak compared with Jerusalem, to permit the success on this scale of the Son of Man oriented Christology which it alone espoused alongside other Christologies. Finally a theology of this sort, born of apocalyptic, is intrinsically most improbable, since elsewhere the first post-Easter enthusiasm was satisfied that the resurrection was the dawn of the new aeon, and from this point on, for all the lack of ecclesiastical organisation or sacral law, it is more a sign of the delayed *parousia* than of imminent expectation if in an eschatological *ius talionis* judgment is committed to the returning Son of Man. [285] Even the three non-messianic "man" sayings of Jesus (→ 430, 29 ff.) cannot offer any ground for putting a new Son of Man expectation on the lips of Jesus directly after Easter, since this would presuppose, in the face of both Jewish and Galilean Aram. usage, that a precise apocal. nuance was caught in the indefinite generalising בר (א)נשא. The only sound conclusion is that Jesus Himself was a prophet in this apocal. tradition and that He proclaimed Himself to be the Son of Man.

c. Parallel to these sayings there are in the preaching of Jesus four groups of statements which might well have become Son of Man sayings later.

> To the first group belong Lk. 22:27, where Jesus says of Himself: "I am among you as he that serveth" (→ 448, 23 ff.; cf. Mk. 10:45 and par.) and Lk. 22:48, where the original seems to be: "Judas, betrayest thou me with a kiss?" (→ 446, 29 ff.). In the

---

[284] But cf. H. B. Sharman, *Son of Man and Kingdom of God*[2] (1944), 83 etc.; Vielhauer Gottesreich, *passim;* Vielhauer Jesus, *passim;* H. Conzelmann, "Gegenwart u. Zukunft in d. synpt. Tradition," ZThK, 54 (1957), 281-3; also Art. "Jesus Christus" in RGG[3], III, 630 f.; H. M. Teeple, "The Origin of the Son of Man Christology," JBL, 84 (1965), 213-250; E. Käsemann, "Die Anfänge chr. Theol.," *Exeget. Versuche u. Besinnungen,* II[2] (1965), 99, who think Jesus did not speak of the Son of Man at all. Acc. to Lietzmann, 85, 93 the title was first used in Chr. apocalypses.

[285] As against E. Käsemann, "Sätze Hl. Rechts im NT," *Exeget. Vesuche u. Besinnungen,* II[2] (1965), 78-81; also "Zum Thema d. urchr. Apokalyptik," *ibid.,* 110 f.; also *op. cit.* (→ n. 284), 88-95, whose forceful arguments are stated above in his own terms. Bousset, *op. cit.* (→ n. 269), 5-19 also gives a convincing depiction of Jewish Chr. prophecy with its Son of Man Christology, but he does not think he can prove that Jesus did not use the title, 7-10 and 16, n. 3.

second group one may list Mk. 3:28 f., which belongs to eschatological proclamation without ref. to the person of Jesus and which originally runs: "All sins and all blasphemies can God forgive man. Only he who speaks a word against the Holy Ghost can never get forgiveness, but deserves condemnation for ever," → 442, 13 ff. If the unforgivability of rejecting forgiveness is threatened here, in Mt. 5:11 (ἕνεκεν ἐμοῦ → n. 308) those are called blessed who are despised and persecuted in the end-time (→ 443, 12 ff.), but cf. Lk. 6:22. A further group consists of sayings which state explicitly the significance of Jesus for His disciples, so perhaps Mt. 10:32 f.: He who confesses Him before men, He (or men) will confess in the last judgment; he who denies Him, He (or men) will deny → 442, 1 ff. Things are rather clearer in Lk. 22:28-30: For those who have stuck with Jesus during His trials He will appoint the kingdom of God as the Father has appointed it for Him, in order that all may share with Jesus in the eschatological banquet → 447, 26 ff. But cf. Lk. 12:8 and Mt. 19:28. Closely related in a fourth group are the enigmatic sayings of Jesus about His perfecting. A sign like that of the deliverance of Jonah is given to this generation in Mt. 12:39 and par. (cf. Mt. 12:40b and par. → 449, 5 ff.); Jesus will be perfected, Mk. 9:9 (→ 445, 11 ff), on the third day, Mk. 9:31 (→ 444, 20 ff.; cf. Lk. 13:32 → n. 310). Not to be separated from this perfecting is the suffering, Mk. 8:31 (cf. Mt. 16:21); 9:31; 10:33; 14:21a and par.; 14:41 (→ 445, 22 ff.), which Jesus must have related to Himself in the first person and which He must have regarded as in line with the typical fate of the prophet, Mt. 23:34-36 and par.; 23:37 and par.; Lk. 13:33 (→ n. 310), cf. Lk. 12:50 → 444, 13 ff.

Even if all these sayings became Son of Man sayings later, it is only in conjunction with them that Jesus' proclamation of the Son of Man achieves completeness. Without this, i.e., if the Son of Man sayings uttered by Him are isolated, Jesus would only be a preacher of repentance, a second Amos or a second Baptist. With the preaching of the Gospel it is the Lord's sayings about His perfecting which as an appendix to His Son of Man sayings transcend the preaching of repentance, and later, and by no means accidentally, attract to themselves the title Son of Man, which is thereby given a new range of meaning → 443, 17 ff. These sayings also pose a new question.

d. Did Jesus conceive of Himself as the apocalyptic Son of Man? This much-debated question hinges finally on the principle of identity and hence it is hardly possible to give an answer either way, [286] whether Yes [287] or No. [288] In the Palestinian mode of thought as yet uninfluenced by this principle one would expect neither explicit identifications (e.g., "I am the Son of Man," "I as Son of Man," "the Son of Man, I am he"), nor differentiations ("I and the Son of Man," "the Son of Man with me," "the Son of Man in my place"), nor implicit assumptions of this kind. This is the more true in that this mode of thinking still stands in the service of prophetic preaching → VI, 843, 26 ff.; 848, 3 ff. In such preaching the relating of two events or states to one another, e.g., the work of Jesus and the rule of God, is easily possible. Indeed it was prophetic preaching itself which set up the relation, and in turn the relation underlies this preaching in its prophetic tension and dynamic. Preaching as prophecy and its content, namely, a specific connection between

[286] Not even in the sense that Jesus intentionally leaves open the who of the Son of Man, the implicit thesis of Tödt.

[287] So, e.g., Cullmann, 157-165; E. Stauffer, "Messias oder Menschensohn?" *Nov. Test.*, 1 (1956), 81-102.

[288] Bultmann Theol.⁵, 29-34 etc.

present and future, shape one another reciprocally. This may still be said even of the relation between a present person and a future event. But a connection between person and person raises a problem in prophecy. If an identification is stated directly and explicitly, the dynamic element in the relation between the present and the future person is destroyed and the preaching loses its prophetic character. [289]

The prophecies of Jesus, in which He brings the eschatological future into the present, present the dawning end-time in three traditionally distinct and conceptually unintegrated schemes. We thus find sayings about His own perfecting with a not very clearly defined role in the eschaton, then proclamation of the kingdom of God, and finally the announcing of the Son of Man. These three views of the last time cannot be identified with one another, but they do not mutually exclude one another. We have here parallel symbols. Jesus' own role in the eschaton begins with the mere fact that He preaches the kingdom of God. [290] The kingdom of God and Son of Man ideas have a common origin, as Da. 7 shows, [291] and in the period which followed they did not drift so far apart [292] that their occurrence together in a new eschatological message (even if not in the same sayings) would be quite unthinkable. [293] If Jesus' own person in its eschatological role was associated with the figure of the Son of Man, then Jesus was neither a rabbi [294] nor a community member reflecting on the founder of his group, though a conceptual, messianic-dogmatic integration between Himself and the Son of Man raises the same difficulties as an integration between the day of the Son of Man and the rule of God.

Seven sayings about the coming Son of Man which stand up to criticism, those in the Lucan source (→ 457, 14 ff.) no less than the others, are in addresses to the disciples. One may deduce from this that prior to the confession of Lk. 22:69 Jesus announced the Son of Man only in esoteric speech. In this respect there is a parallel to what He says about His perfecting to various hearers and also to His proclamation of God's kingdom to the whole people of Israel. Just as the kingdom of God

---

[289] We find examples of this. The primitive community identified Jesus as the Son of Man, some disciples of Enoch did the same for him (→ 427, 11 ff.), Rabb. groups identified Elijah and Phinehas or in the future Elijah and Enoch or Elijah and Moses (→ II, 931, 16 ff.; 933, 9 ff.), while popular opinion identified Elijah and John the Baptist → n. 380.

[290] The poor are blessed already in the fact that blessedness is ascribed to them; they have a share in the kingdom as they have a share in the work of Jesus, cf. L. Goppelt, "Der verborgene Messias," Der historische Jesu u. der kerygmatische Christus³ (1963), 378. On the single sense of fut. and pres. statements cf. H. Conzelmann, Art. "Reich Gottes" in RGG³, V, 915 and O. Cullmann, Heil als Geschichte (1965), passim.

[291] The Son of Man is originally a symbol of God's kingly rule and the holder of the kingdom established therewith (→ 421, 21 ff.); He is then the representative of its bearers (→ 422, 6) and finally of Israel; on Da. 7:13 f. LXX → 373, n. 278.

[292] I. H. Marshall, "The Synoptic Son of Man Sayings in Recent Discussion," NTSt, 12 (1965/66), 336 ref. to the exercise of kingly rule by the Son of Man in Eth. En. 69:26-28. On the Son of Man / Jesus relation in analogy to the kingdom of God / work of Jesus relation cf. R. Schnackenburg, Gottes Herrschaft u. Reich³ (1963), 110-122.

[293] For this reason one should not rule out Son of Man intimation like the authors ref. to → n. 284, nor regard kingdom of God preaching as non-typical, like E. Bammel, "Erwägungen z. Eschatologie Jesu," Stud. Evangelica, III (1964), 3-32, for, as N. Perrin shows in his The Kingdom of God in the Teaching of Jesus (1963), 158-206, the apocal. as distinct from the Rabbinic basis of Jesus' preaching cannot be argued away.

[294] Even if in respect of the common address "rabbi," which simply means κύριε (J. Jeremias), one has in view (with U. Wilckens, "Offenbarung u. Gesch.," Kerygma u. Dogma Beiheft, 1 [1961], 50, n. 22) the fact that, e.g., Enoch (Eth. En. 15:1, cf. 12:3 f. and 91:1) as the recipient of apocal. revelation is materially called "rabbi."

and the Son of Man could not be in competition in this respect, so it is with Jesus and the Son of Man. The apocalyptic Son of Man is a symbol of Jesus' assurance of perfecting. With a shift from the assurance to the one who has it, the whole process may be interpreted as a dynamic and functional equating of Jesus and the coming Son of Man with the future perfecting of Jesus in view. On this view the primitive community then made of it a static personal identification accomplished already in the present Jesus, → lines 29 ff.

> In its bearing on the Messianic secret this would mean that Jesus was not already the Son of Man in hidden form, that He was not speaking ambiguous words in which "man" might be taken both messianically and also non-messianically, and that He was not applying the theology of a concealed Son of Man to Himself. If on the other hand the oldest Evangelist does develop a theology of the Son of Man secret, he did not invent this to explain the externally non-messianic character of the earthly work of Jesus but along with other aspects he was simply developing theoretically an implication in the dominical sayings about the coming Son of Man, namely, that for Jesus only His own work could enter the picture as the basis of the continuity between His own present function and the future function of the Son of Man. [295]

If Jesus speaks not only of the Son of Man but also of His own passion and perfecting, this is not necessarily a theological combination of Son of Man and Servant of the Lord messianology, for in His consciousness of suffering He continues the tradition of the martyr prophets (→ VI, 834, 29 ff.; 841, 22 ff.), of which the Servant of the Lord was one. His Messianic awareness grows at this point out of a unique (→ 455, 11 f.) extension of the atoning sufferings (→ n. 381) of individuals ἀντὶ πολλῶν which had been constantly enacted in Israel (→ VI, 540, 12 ff.; 542, 34 ff.) and not out of the continuity between the function of the future Son of Man and His own work standing under the sign of vicarious passion.

2. The Oral Tradition of the Primitive Community. [296]

a. First Stage.

(a) In the expectation of Christ's return which Easter faith made possible the eight future-apocalyptic Son of Man sayings mentioned → 433, 8 ff. could be applied directly to the returning Jesus without further development. On this basis the title Son of Man could easily be projected back into other sayings. This extension of the title was supported by the emphatic use of "man" for Jesus in the three sayings discussed → 430, 29 ff. This term could be given a Messianic sense confirmed by its translation into Greek as ὁ υἱὸς τοῦ ἀνθρώπου rather than ὁ ἄνθρωπος. Jesus, who heals the sick and forgives sins, who has no place for His head and follows a different commission from that of the Baptist, is no longer acting as a mere man but as the present Son of Man who is also destined to come again.

---

[295] Cf. A. Vögtle, Art. "Menschensohn im NT," LexThK[2], VII, 300 and Higgins, 202, though cf. Sjöberg Menschensohn Ev., 214-6.

[296] We are hypothetically including here all statements for which no literary origin can be found, esp. in the Evangelists. The three different stages are to be seen only in terms of the development of the tradition; they may overlap chronologically.

(b) Possibly Mt. 10:32 f. was reconstructed at this stage [297] if the original read: "Anyone who confesses me before men, him will men (one) [298] confess before ... [299] but whosoever denies me before men, he will also be denied before ... " In this case the subject of confessing or denying before God in the second clauses of the two halves of the saying is enigmatic, but along the lines of Mk. 9:40 and par. or Mt. 12:30 and par. or Mt. 11:6 obedience or disobedience to Jesus was decisive for the eschatological pardoning or condemning of His hearers. Conviction as to the role of Jesus as surety or prosecutor in the Last Judgment might have led to the substitution of the solemn title Son of Man (→ 447, 9 ff.) or to the first person in either the first half (Lk. 12:8) or the second (Mk. 8:38) or both. The first person might well have preceded the substitution of the title if indeed Jesus Himself did not actually speak in the first person Himself. [300]

(c) The saying about the blaspheming of the Holy Ghost (→ VI, 397, 9 ff.) derives either from the basic Mk. 3:28 f. [301] or from a tradition behind this and the independent form in Lk. 12:10. [302] This developed into a reference to speaking against

---

[297] Nowhere else does Mt. eliminate the Son of Man title, not even in his par. to Mk. 8:38 in 16:27; P. Vielhauer, "Gottesreich u. Menschensohn," *Festschr. G. Dehn* (1957), 68 thought he did, but there is a tacit correction in Vielhauer Gottesreich, 77; Mt. 16:21 only seems to be an exception, since the title is here put at the beginning of the whole section in 16:13 → 460, 21 f.; Mt. 5:11 is primary as compared with Lk. 6:22 → 443, 12 ff. On the other hand Mt. often adds it, 16:28; 24:39; 25:31; 26:2 — 19:28 is older than Mt. (→ 447, 19 ff.) — or he brings it in his special material, 10:23; 24:30, or introduces it in his own words, 13:37, 41. For this reason it is more likely that the title was not originally in 10:32 than that Mt. was inconsistent. This is one of the results of Jeremias Älteste Schicht, 168-170, which has given a new turn to Synoptic investigation.

[298] The pass., which can be traced back to אָתֵּדִי or מוֹדֵי, may be deduced from the par. ἀπαρνηθήσεται in the second half of Lk. 12:9, where it is not just a shorter variation on ὁ υἱὸς τοῦ ἀνθρώπου ἀρνήσεται, Vielhauer Gottesreich, 77 as against Kümmel, 38, n. 86.

[299] It is no longer possible to say what was the original term for the divine court. On the one side Lk. takes care to eliminate non-Gk. expressions, e.g., the twofold "before my Father in heaven" of Mt., but this does not have to mean that the original in the source was "before the Father in the heavens" (→ V, 985, 20 ff.); acc. to Dalman WJ, I, 173 the original here was "before heaven." But the Jewish πατήρ μου (σου, ἡμῶν, ὑμῶν) (ὁ) ἐν τοῖς οὐρανοῖς is a specific usage in Mt.; he puts it for θεός in 12:50 → V, 520, 17 ff.; 985, n. 252.

[300] Vielhauer Gottesreich 78 f. argues against authenticity on the ground that the whole saying has the singular feature that eschatological significance is ascribed to confessing or denying Jesus (obj. gen.), which does not fit in with Jesus' life, since a situation in which a decision for or against Him was demanded in human courts arose only with His passion and was pressing only in Peter's case. But since Jesus was consciously moving toward His passion (→ 444, 5 ff.) such a situation was to be expected for all His disciples, and the flight to Galilee was tantamount to a denial. Nor do we have to differentiate such a situation so sharply from gen. eschatological tribulation as Vielhauer does, Gottesreich, 78 f. and Jesus, 103 f. For further counter-arguments cf. Tödt, 308-312; these are valid even if one does not accept Tödt's view that Son of Man is original in the logion.

[301] For the priority of Mk. cf. Wellhausen, *op. cit.* (→ n. 236), 75; Wellhausen Einl., 67; more firmly Wellh. Mt. on 12:31; Bultmann Trad., 138; Dalman WJ, I, 209. Only ὅσα ἐὰν βλασφημήσωσιν (LXX rather than Semitic [so Loh. Mk., *ad loc.*] construction) is an explication of πάντα ... αἱ βλασφημίαι in community parlance.

[302] E.g.

כל חובין (or sing.) וכל גדופין (or sing)

(דִי אֲמִיר לְבַר נְשָׁא יִשְׁתְּבִיק or: יִשְׁתְּבִיק(ו) לְבַר נְשָׁא), in which לְ may be transl. as either "on the part of ..." or "against ..." Cf. Black Approach, 102 with n. 2; 273, n. 1. גְּדוּפָא is common for blasphemy, cf. Dalman Wört., Jastrow, Levy Wört., Levy Chald. Wört., *s.v.*; Str.-B., I, 1009-1019.

man, [303] unless this was already the point in what might well be the more original form in Lk. 12:10 (with the generic בר נשא). [304] Only what is spoken against man could later become what is spoken against the Son of Man → 452, 21 ff. The original saying about blaspheming the Spirit and the developed or related speaking against man imply that no actual sin which disrupts the relation of man and man and no blasphemy whereby man offends against God is beyond forgiveness. [305] But man can treat this offer lightly. He can blaspheme against the Spirit, i.e., the Spirit of prophecy, [306] that could be constantly expected even after the days of Malachi (→ VI, 812, 29 ff.) and had come again in the days of Jesus in such a way that conversion was tendered and remission granted with Him. In so doing man can reject the remission of sins.

(d) Finally the last beatitude in Mt. 5:11 and par.: "Blessed are ye, when men shall revile you, and persecute you, and shall say all manner of evil against you (falsely?)," [307] has been appropriately supplemented by a "for my sake" [308] → 448, 34 ff.

b. Second Stage.

The title Son of Man is now added to other sayings of Jesus.

(a) This applies especially to prophetic (Mk. 9:31; 8:31; 10:33; 9:9 → 441, 18 ff.) and situational (Mk. 14:41; 14:21a and par.; Lk. 22:48) intimations of the passion. The fact that Jesus (as speaker) combines vicarious suffering and the title Son of Man in the three versions of the prediction of the passion and in Mk. 9:9 suggests that the most probable historical conclusion is that which presupposes that Jesus in His dynamic projects for Messianic perfecting did sometimes speak of the coming Son of Man (→ 438, 1 ff.) and that He also had to reckon with His own

---

[303] E.g. כל מאמר דאמיר לבר נשא ישתביק. The suggestion in Wellhausen Sohn, 204 can stand only at this hypothetical stage. In spite of the absence of λόγον in Marcion Lk. 12:10 מאמר or a similar word must have been included in view of the par. in Black Approach, 277.

[304] So E. Percy, Die Botschaft Jesu (1953), 254; also Tödt, 282-8. On this view βλασφημέω is an alternative transl. for the more lit. λόγον λέγω εἰς (an Aramaism, Black Approach, 277) while ἁμάρτημα and βλασφημία are interpretative.

[305] Grundm. Mk., ad loc., a restriction clothed in the form of a conditional clause. Loh. Mk. ad loc. sees legal phraseology here.

[306] For Judaism the sin against the Spirit was the same as the sin against the Torah and it could not be forgiven, cf. Str.-B., I, 637 f.

[307] εἴπωσιν πᾶν πονηρόν is an alternative transl. of the striking Aramaism ἐκβάλωσιν τὸ ὄνομα ὑμῶν ὡς πονηρόν, Lk. 6:22, Black Approach, 97, 258, 274. The ref., then, is to the eschatological destiny of the accursed, cf. also Str.-B., II, 159.

[308] Among sayings of the same or similar content, pre-Easter or post-Easter, the ἕνεκεν expression does not occur in the version which by reason of its independent attestation in Lk. 17:33 and Jn. 12:25 must be regarded as the oldest. In the par. to Lk. 17:33 in Mt. 10:39 ἕνεκεν ἐμοῦ is thus added, so also Mk. 13:9 = Mt. 10:18; par. Lk. 21:12: ἕνεκεν τοῦ ὀνόματός μου, cf. Mk. 13:13: διὰ τὸ ὄνομά μου = Mt. 10:22; 24:9; Lk. 21:17. Mk., with his usual stress on preaching the Word (→ 456, 6 f. with n. 383), also adds καὶ τοῦ εὐαγγελίου in 8:35 and 10:29. The first time the ref. in Mt. 16:25; Lk. 9:34 do not agree, the second time Mt. has instead τοῦ ἐμοῦ ὀνόματος in 19:29 analogously to 10:22; 24:9 or εἵνεκεν τῆς βασιλείας τοῦ θεοῦ in Lk. 18:29. It would thus seem that ἕνεκα τοῦ υἱοῦ τοῦ ἀνθρώπου with καὶ τοῦ εὐαγγελίου and τῆς βασιλείας τοῦ θεοῦ belongs to the third stage of the tradition. The second stage, represented by ἕνεκεν ἐμοῦ, occurs in Mt. only in discourses to the disciples. Hence in 16:24 what is addressed to a wider circle in Mk. and Lk. is spoken only τοῖς μαθηταῖς.

violent death and hence also with suffering → V, 713, 16 ff. But as an ever fresh possibility this was not necessarily related to a specific titular role which had to be adopted. The upshot of all this is that the intimations of the passion would originally have an I as subject as they came from the lips of Jesus. [309]

This is supported by sayings acc. to which Jesus expected to meet the fate of the prophets in Jerusalem and then to be perfected after three days, [310] as it is also by sayings whose original imagery was not revised by the community, e.g., Mk. 2:19 f. (→ IV, 1103, 4 ff.; 1105, 11 ff.): "Shall the people at the wedding fast while the bridegroom is still with them? So long as they still have the bridegroom with them, they do not need to fast. But the days will come when the bridegroom shall be taken from them: then they may fast," or Mk. 10:38 (→ VI, 152, 6 ff.): "Can you drink the cup which I must drink, or submit to the baptism with which I must be baptised?" or Lk. 12:49 f. (→ I, 538, 28 ff.; VI, 944, 7 ff.; VII, 884, 4 ff.): "I have come to cast fire on the earth, and how I wish it were already kindled! I must undergo a baptism, and how tormented I am until it be finally accomplished!"

Under the sign of the newly accepted personal identity of Jesus and the Son of Man the community could now consistently unite the Messianic majesty of the Son of Man with Messianic lowliness and fuse them in the *kerygma* of Jesus, the suffering Son of Man.

The simplest version of the passion prediction in Mk. 9:31 (→ V, 713, 11 ff.) contains of the various elements of suffering only delivering up and death. It does not, like the first form, offer a ref. to the necessity of the passion acc. to Scripture nor does it explain who the builders of Ps. 118:22 are (the elders, chief priests and scribes); it simply refers to men. [311] Hence at this pt. it seems older than 8:31. The stress is on God's action, which is described as παραδίδοται. This is supported by the par. Lk. 9:44. Here we find only μέλλει παραδίδοσθαι εἰς χεῖρας ἀνθρώπων, which is perhaps an unabbreviated special tradition. The ἀποκτενοῦσιν αὐτόν (cf. 1 Th. 2:15) might have been added *ex eventu*, but it might also have been presupposed as the final outcome of the passion → 443, 23 f.
In the pericope Mk. 8:27-33 the true intimation of the passion in 8:31 ff. is linked to Peter's confession only by the reaction of Peter in v. 32b, 33, where he either rejects the fact of suffering or cannot understand its point. In this version of the prediction the δεῖ lays emphasis on the fulfilment of Scripture (cf. Mk. 9:12b; Lk. 17:25), namely, Ps. 118:22. In line with this the suffering is not said specifically to be rejection and death, the καί link being an argument against this. [312] The πολλὰ παθεῖν is indeed in tension with the passion narrative, where the suffering comes only after the rejection by the Sanhedrin. For its part the ἀποδοκιμασθῆναι, in its application of ψ 117:22, does not in itself have to denote concretely the rejection by the Sanhedrin. It could be older than παραδίδοται εἰς χεῖρας ἀνθρώπων in 9:31 and might well have been combined with ὑπὸ ἀνθρώπων. "To suffer much," which is not said elsewhere of Jesus, and "to be rejected of men" are

---

[309] Synoptic par. without the Son of Man title to the terms linked with it in the passion predictions, παθεῖν, ἀποδοκιμασθῆναι, ἀποκτανθῆναι, ἀναστῆναι (here the par. is not lit.) and παραδίδομαι may be found in Jeremias Älteste Schicht, 160 f. As in other places (→ 442, 13), the community could easily insert the title for בר נשא, so Mk. 9:31 (→ lines 20 ff). Even the Aram. play on words (→ n. 311) might have had its origin in the community.
[310] Mt. 23:37-39; Lk. 13:32 (cf. Jeremias παῖς, 211-214). In view of these sayings and esp. Lk. 13:33 one cannot view the visit to Jerusalem as the usual festal journey but only as a deliberate march to prophetic martyrdom.
[311] Perhaps a play on words → V, 715, 14 ff.
[312] Cf. for what follows L. Goppelt, "Zum Problem d. Menschensohns," *Festschr. f. K. Witte* (1963), 20-32, with examples, 22-27.

materially so plain and yet also so imprecise in detail that one can hardly see here a formulation *ex eventu* even if "to suffer" be adjudged a Greek summarising of one or many materially related Aram. terms. [313] On ἀποκτανθῆναι → 444, 27 f.

The passion prediction in Mk. 10:33 f. contains seven elements, delivering up, condemnation, handing over to the Gentiles, mocking, scourging and putting to death. These could have been added *ex eventu* but could hardly have been first formulated by Mark, since they do not entirely agree with his passion narrative. [314] They probably derive from Palestinian tradition, since only there would handing over to the Gentiles be a scandal. The heart of the passion prophecies in the second as well as the first version has been overshadowed here by the reflection of actual events. [315]

In the address on the descent from the mount of transfiguration in Mk. 9:9 (→ 454, 20 ff.) there is again reference to the Son of Man as in the three passion predictions, but now with a statement about ἀναστῆναι which, as the interpretative ἐκ νεκρῶν (cf. Ac. 17:3) would clearly seem to suggest, is fashioned by the community, [316] its function being to relate the event of the transfiguration to the glory of the resurrection. [317] Albeit suffering [318] and death are implied in ἀναστῆναι, the point in the discussion with the disciples is not resurrection faith as such, which was self-evident for later believers, but rather that the Son of Man specifically must rise again, [319] and that only then will the secret of His Messiahship be disclosed. The inability of the disciples to grasp this is a constant theme in Mk. [320] On Mk. 9:12 → 454, 24 ff.; II, 940, 4 ff.; 941, 11 ff.

If Mk. 14:41 at the end of the Gethsemane incident is part of a tradition which previously embraced vv. 32-35, 40, [321] we have in v. 42 an independent με which directly corresponds to the Son of Man who is to be delivered up and which must

---

313 Hahn, 51.

314 Loh. Mk., *ad loc.*

315 But note that Mt. 20:19 first puts σταυρόω for ἀποκτείνω and ἐγερθήσεται for ἀναστήσεται. ἀποκτείνω can also dencte stoning, after which the body had to be suspended on a cross. All three versions ref. at the end to the rising again: ἀναστῆναι or ἀναστήσεται μετὰ τρεῖς ἡμέρας. Both in literary form and also in the tradition ἀναστῆναι is older than ἐγερθῆναι and μετὰ τρεῖς ἡμέρας is older than the more precise τῇ τρίτῃ ἡμέρᾳ or τῇ ἡμέρᾳ τῇ τρίτῃ which are used except in Lk. 9:44. Behind this intimation of the resurrection after three days there may lie concealed a perfection saying as in Lk. 13:32; if so this would be an authentic saying, not the work of the community. ἀναστῆναι occurs in Mk. only the 4 times mentioned here, in Lk. and Jn. once each, in Ac. 4 times, in Mt. not at all for Jesus' resurrection. The usage goes back to the noun ἀνάστασις which does not distinguish between the gen. resurrection and that of Jesus. Elsewhere ἐγείρω is used, Loh. Mk. on 9:9 f.

316 Some think the whole incident of 9:9-13 and the alleged sayings of Jesus cannot possibly be historical, so Otto, 208; Loh. Mk., *ad loc.* and Dibelius, 228; on this view we simply have here "theology."

317 Tödt, 182; the v. with its ἵνα μηδενὶ ἃ εἶδον διηγήσωνται was the starting-pt. for W. Wrede, *Das Messiasgeheimnis in d. Ev.*² (1913), 40, who argued that the commands to keep silence were interwoven into the material only in the light of a conviction which the resurrection alone made possible, namely, that Jesus was the Messiah. Some suggest that the transfiguration and the ensuing discourse are really a resurrection story.

318 Black Servant, 9 f., following V. Taylor, *The Gospel acc. to St. Mark* (1952), *ad loc.*, thinks that Dt. 18:15 lies behind Mk. 9:7 and that the statement about suffering is possible only because the typology of the prophet Moses (cf. Ac. 3:22-26) was referred to Jesus along with features from the suffering servant. "The conjunction of a tradition that a coming Elijah and a coming Moses would suffer death is clearly not unconnected with, yet as clearly independent of, Mark. 9:1-13."

319 Kl. Mk., *ad loc.*

320 On the Messianic secret → 441, 8 ff.

321 So K. G. Kuhn, "Jesus in Gethsemane," *Ev. Theol.*, 12 (1952/53), 260-285.

go back to pre-Marcan tradition. [322] But quite apart from any hypothetical distinction of source and tradition it is quite evident that the situation itself gives rise to the announcement of the arrest with which Jesus knew He had to reckon at this time. In contrast (cf. Lk. 22:22 and Lk. 22:21) Mk. 14:41 develops a basic theological saying in which the moment of the arrest is stressed as the hour of the delivering up into the hands of sinners of the One whom God has appointed for the work of perfecting. [323] This is why He is intentionally given the majestic name of the Son of Man here → 447, 5 ff.

The delivering up of the Son of Man (Mk. 14:21) [324] comes within a betrayal saying which Mk. puts before the institution of the Lord's Supper (Mk. 14:17-21) and Luke after (Lk. 22:21-23). [325]

In this the με of Mk. 14:18; Lk. 22:21 or μετ' ἐμοῦ of Mk. 14:18, 20; Lk. 22:21, supported esp. by the older version Lk. 22:21, has so strong a claim to antiquity that the Son of Man title that follows would plainly appear to be secondary → 455, 30 ff. The following argument pts. in the same direction. Behind υἱός in Lk. and before it in Mk. the title is interrupted by μέν, stylistic allowance thus being made for the primarily adversative πλὴν οὐαί of Lk. 22:22b or οὐαὶ δέ of Mk. 14:21b, which is supported by an Aram. original (וִי בְּרַם or וְוִי). [326] One may assume, then, that the oldest attainable form: "For I must go," is not only Aram. but also a dominical saying, for formally it comes after the prediction of the betrayal and materially it clearly fits the situation in which the eucharistic words were spoken.

Now we have seen in other instances that a first person which was unemphatic due to the context or oblique case usually remained, whereas a preceding or ensuing emphatic first person was given added weight by the substituting of the Son of Man title (→ 445, 22 ff.; lines 12 ff.). So here the oblique με / μετ' ἐμοῦ of Mk. 14:18, 20, which fits the situation so well, might well have remained intact, whereas the following thetic I-saying, which reaches beyond the situation, attracted the title of dignity to itself, and thus became a saying about the Son of Man who is destined to die. [327]

The saying of Jesus to Judas (Lk. 22:48), which also belongs to the special source, is to be interpreted in connection with 22:21. In Lk. 22:21 the idea is that of betrayal

---

[322] It is not so certain as Kuhn, op. cit., 262 supposes that v. 42 is an editorial addition of Mk. to introduce the pericope of the arrest in vv. 43-52, for v. 43 would flow on quite smoothly from v. 41, noer does v. 42 fit very well at the end of Kuhn's narrative B vv. 33, 34, 36-38.

[323] Loh. Mk., ad loc.

[324] Cf. on this W. Popkes, "Christus traditus," AbhThANT, 49 (1967), 154-169.

[325] On the independence of the versions cf. Rehkopf, 8-30.

[326] The position of μέν in Lk. as distinct from Mk. is stylistically poor and it is not found elsewhere in the NT (Rehkopf, 14). One may thus deduce that this complement of πλήν / δέ (cf. M. E. Thrall, Gk. Particles in the NT [1962], 28) did not syntactically weave an existing title ὁ υἱὸς τοῦ ἀνθρώπου (perhaps based on בר נשא) more smoothly into the whole, but rather that μέν was felt to be necessary before Lk. when the title was introduced. If so, the title was first put in in Gk. In keeping with this is the fact that the Mk. account, secondary compared to Lk., takes a further step and in acc. with the tendency to multiply the use of the title puts it in a second time in v. 21b. Cf. H. Schürmann, Jesu Abschiedsrede Lk. 22:21-38 (1957), 6.

[327] As elsewhere (→ 444, 31 ff.), the primitive community might well have added the proof from Scripture κατὰ τὸ ὡρισμένον / καθὼς γέγραπται περὶ αὐτοῦ which we also find in other parts of the passion story. But the substance of the saying in the verbs πορεύομαι and ὑπάγω has a claim to antiquity, since these are different renderings of אֲזַל/הֲלַךְ as euphemisms for dying, Rehkopf, 16.

by a friend, while in Lk. 22:48 the handing over is by means of a sign of friendship. Lk. 22:21 presents Jesus' awareness that He will be handed over by one of those nearest to Him, while Lk. 22:48 portrays His grief at the way it is done. [328] Hence Lk. 22:48 does not supplement the story of the arrest; with the expression, not of reproach, blame, or warning, but of sorrow on Jesus' part, it is integral to it. But for this reason the υἱὸς τοῦ ἀνθρώπου, though pre-Lucan, has probably replaced a με as in Lk. 22:21.

(b) The title Son of Man is also integrated into Jesus' eschatological and I sayings. In the saying about the final destiny of those who confess or deny Jesus the Son of Man is put in for the anonymous authority which defends or accuses (→ 442, 1 ff.) or for Jesus Himself (→ 442, 11 f.), so that He confesses every confessor before the angels of God [329] as in Lk. 12:8 [330] and denies every denier [331] as in Mk. 8:38. [332] There thus arises a certain alternative to the firmly embedded tradition that the Son of Man Himself judges, [333] but it is not very strong, since defence or prosecution by the Son of Man means necessarily either pardon in the one case or condemnation in the other. Either way the Son of Man as the returning Jesus — no personal or material distinction is felt, [334] the Son of Man is in very truth Jesus — authenticates the fellowship of His earthly followers as a heavenly fellowship. In Mt. 19:28 and par., whether before or with Matthew, the title Son of Man replaces an I which still remains in the eschatological διατίθεμαι (→ II, 105, 27 ff.) in Lk. 22:29. In Mt., which refers to the rule of the Son of Man in the coming aeon rather than to His epiphany, the catechetical context of the attitude to possessions (Mk. 10:17 ff.) is supplemented by the promise to disciples who renounce possessions. They will sit on twelve thrones judging the twelve tribes of Israel as (καὶ αὐτοί) and when (ὅταν) the Son of Man shall sit on the throne of His glory.

Mt. thus imports the saying from without. But in Lk. too it occurs in table conversation (vv. 24-38) after the account of the Last Supper and the betrayal saying (→ 446, 9 ff.), which surely cannot be its original setting. [335] Lk. 22:28 puts the saying in a new situation, ἐν τοῖς πειρασμοῖς, but uses the original opening, [336] the Gk. δέ replacing an older

---

[328] Rehkopf, 51.

[329] Mt. 10:32 had no occasion to mention the "angels" (cf. Da. 7:10) and "saints of the Most High" (Eth. En. 61:10 → 422, 1 ff.), which were a firm part of the Son of Man tradition, for he did not have this tradition in mind. Acc. to Dalman WJ, I, 172 Jewish lit. did not use angels for God; it must have been added before or by Lk.

[330] The impersonal pass. ἀπαρνηθήσεται in the second half of Lk. 12:9 does not disturb the parallelism (Bultmann Trad., 117); perhaps the title was not firmly embedded in the logion.

[331] The "to be ashamed" in Mk. is community parlance, R. 1:16; 6:21; 2 Tm. 1:8, 12, 16; Hb. 2:11; 11:16. Hence the ἐπαισχυνθῇ in Mk. does not have to have a Pauline tinge, so Kl. Mk., ad loc. So far no Aram. word has been found (מאס ? כפר?) for which (ἐπ)αισχύνομαι and (ἀπ)αρνέομαι might be different transl. Perhaps in the Aram. tradition itself there was vacillation between כפר and חפר [J. Jeremias].

[332] On the logion in Mk. → 456, 1 ff.

[333] The judge is God, appearing before Him being expressed by ἔμπροσθεν or ἐνώπιον → V, 208, n. 27. But He cannot be the subj. of denial, as against Vielhauer Gottesreich, 77. ἀπαρνέομαι does not denote direct judicial rejection → I, 469, 25 ff.

[334] But cf. Bultmann Trad., 117; Otto, 122; Marxsen Christologie, 26 and many others.

[335] Jeremias Abendmahlsworte, 94 f.

[336] Bultmann Trad., 170 f.

ἀμήν (Mt.) and ἀκολουθέω (Mt.) being the original word for discipleship. [337] In Mt. the judicial work of the Son of Man is connected with παλιγγενεσία which here has a singular sense as the equivalent of God's rule (so originally Lk. 22:29) or the coming aeon (Mk. 10:30, omitted Mt. 19:29 → I, 688, 23 ff.). In Lk. 22:29 διατίθεμαι / διέθετο does not have to be a secondary assimilation to διαθήκη in v. 20 but as the word of the instituting of the new covenant might well have been used by Jesus Himself in analogy to the use of such images as building, the temple and the flock outside the eucharistic situation. [338] This is then the basis of v. 30a, as shown by the content and the use of the conj. ἔσθητε and πίνητε for the modal nuance implicitly contained in the older fut. καθήσεσθε. The point of the saying is thus: "Truly I say to you: You who have followed me, I appoint royal dominion for you as my Father has appointed royal dominion for me."

If this saying is at least comparable with authentic sayings of Jesus (→ n. 297-300), in what follows the existence of the twelve as a pre-Easter institution is subject to debate. [339] But this concerns only the version in Mt., since Lk. merely has ἐπὶ θρόνων [340] and the ref. to the twelve tribes does not have to mean that there is one throne for each. [341] In any case, in this notion there is no place for the concept of the Son of Man as judge, as in other passages → 434, 18 ff. It would thus seem that Mt. adds this along with παλιγγενεσία, esp. as ἐπὶ θρόνου δόξης αὐτοῦ is stylised acc. to apocal. notions in 25:31. [342] This is an argument for treating ἐν τῇ παλιγγενεσίᾳ... δόξης αὐτοῦ in Mt. as secondary, like ἵνα ἔσθητε... βασιλείᾳ μου in Lk.

In Mk. 10:45 the fact that the par. Lk. 22:27 does not have the saying suggests that v. 45b (→ 455, 5 ff.) might be a later elucidation of v. 45a. [343] Here the title Son of Man is to be explained after the pattern of sayings about the earthly ministry of the Son of Man (→ 438, 35 ff.), but now with a specific emphasis on serving → IV, 342, 12 ff. The ἐγώ in Lk. might well be original. The principle of discipleship is to be found in the example of Jesus, who did not just preach serving but by His own acts made it obligatory as a new manifestation of relations between men. The saying belongs unequivocally to Jesus' higher estimation of serving as compared with being served (Lk. 12:37; Mt. 25:42-44) and hence even formally it fits in perfectly with the basic sayings about serving in Mk. 10:41-44 par. Mk. might well have substituted the title Son of Man for the first person ἐγώ. On the λύτρον saying in Mk. 10:45b → 455, 18 ff.

In the final beatitude, already expanded by "for my sake" (→ 443, 12 ff.) in

---

[337] Aram. אזל בתר or אתא, דבק, נפק, though cf. Loh. Mt., ad loc.

[338] Jeremias Abendmahlsworte, 188. Perhaps an existing διατίθεμαι/διέθετο brought about integration into the present passage s.v. διαθήκη.

[339] Cf. Vielhauer Gottesreich, 68-71; G. Klein, "Die zwölf Ap.," FRL, 77 (1961), 36.

[340] The only instance in Lk. except for the quotations in 1:32, 52.

[341] One need not follow Tödt, 59 in setting the judging of the twelve tribes in tension with rejection of the request of the sons of Zebedee in Mk. 10:43-45, since they were asking for pre-eminence, not just for a place of rule or judgment. Cf. also Zn. Mt. on 19:28 and Kümmel, 41 (judging is not an alternative to co-rule).

[342] Tödt, 57 ref. here to Eth. En. 61:8; 62:2; 69:27; 45:3. Cf. also 108:12b etc.

[343] Cf. Kl. Mk., ad loc. Considered also by Jeremias Lösegeld, 227. The influence of Is. 53, which M. D. Hooker, Jesus and the Servant (1959), 74-7 and C. K. Barrett, "The Background of Mk. 10:45," NT Essays in Honour of T. W. Manson (1959), 1-18 question in relation to Mk. 10:45, is incontestable as regards the first half of the v.

Mt. 5:11, the title is added in Lk. 6:22, so that they are called blessed who are cast out [344] (originally "accursed" → n. 307) for the Son of Man's sake. [345]

c. Third Stage.

Several Son of Man sayings are now reconstructed.

(a) Most important is the explanation of the sign of Jonah in Lk. 11:30 [346] → III, 408, 15 ff.; VII, 233, 3 ff.

Originally this must have followed the request of the Pharisees for a sign and the rejection of this request by Jesus (Mk. 8:11 f. and Mt. 12:38 f. par. to δοθήσεται αὐτῇ), i.e., as a qualification of the rejection (Mt. 12:39 par.: εἰ μὴ τὸ σημεῖον ᾿Ιωνᾶ, Mt. adding τοῦ προφήτου), so that the whole would read: "How this generation seeks a sign! [347] Truly I say to you, no sign will be given this generation. [348] The sign of Jonah will definitely be given it." [349] In this enigmatic saying Jesus was threatening a divine attestation of His person which would press the unbelieving demand for validation to its logical extreme and thus show how perverted it was. [350] How the accrediting analogue to Jonah's redemption was to be worked out in this future was not stated. It thus demanded kerygmatic interpretation. Mt. 12:40 may be regarded as secondary compared with Lk. 11:30 → 459, 10 ff.

In relation to the sign of Jonah Lk. refers to the men of Nineveh and, although the Pharisees might dispute this exegetically, he argues that they had heard of Jonah's deliverance and accepted this as a sign. It is also assumed that the saying has in view the *parousia* of the Son of Man after His resurrection, though one might ask whether Jesus would have made this distinction. The reconstruction of the cryptic comparison of Jesus in mashal form thus becomes a full analogy. It is not that a miracle like that of Jonah will be given to this generation as a sign but rather that as Jonah was a sign to the Ninevites, so will the Son of Man be to this generation. The fact that neither the OT nor Rabbinic writings refer to the significance of the deliverance of Jonah for the Ninevites does not matter now. For it was not the job of the primitive community to pay attention to possible scribal objections. Its concern was to bear witness that the *parousia* of the risen Jesus will be the

---

[344] The ref. to expulsion from the synagogue, i.e., ἀφορίσωσιν and μισήσωσιν, seems plainly secondary. ὀνειδίζω can thus be taken in the legal sense "to curse," "to ban," cf. K. Bornhäuser, *Die Bergpredigt* (1923), 28 f.

[345] In Lk. 6:22 the Son of Man title is pre-Lucan, cf. Tödt, 114 f. who ref. to Mt. 11:19; 12:32 and 8:20 par. Lk. 6:23 is to be taken independently of the preceding title. Thus the ref. of Tödt, 114 f. to Mk. 8:38; Lk. 12:8 f. and Mt. 19:28 is misleading. The pt. is not that in virtue of fidelity to the confession of Jesus the Son of Man will guarantee the reward promised in v. 23.

[346] Cf. Vögtle, 230-277.

[347] For the exclamatory transl. of the τί of Mk. 8:12 cf. Black Approach, 89.

[348] Mk. 8:12b: εἰ δοθήσεται τῇ γενεᾷ ταύτῃ σημεῖον corresponding to (or אם) אין אתיהיב אתא להדין דרא is an asseveration in the form of an anacoluthon and is not conditioned by εἰ μὴ τὸ σημεῖον ᾿Ιωνᾶ (Lk. 11:29b).

[349] εἰ μὴ τὸ σημεῖον ᾿Ιωνᾶ in Mt. 12:39 par. is the remnant of an irregular asseveration (negative), לא (אתיהיב) אתא דיונה (or אם) אין. We have here a relative negation (cf. A. Kuschke, "Das Idiom d. 'relativen Negation' im NT," ZNW, 43 [1950/51], 263) in which a solemn or emphatic statement is clothed in the form of a negation or exception, so that the statement, since it presupposes another one or an exception is made to it, does not mean all that it seems to, cf. in the NT Mt. 15:24; Mk. 2:17; 9:37; Jn. 1:11 f.; 7:16; Mt. 25:29b and par.

[350] Vögtle, 246. On the meaning → III, 409, 21 ff. The objections of Tödt, 195 are thus shown to be without substance.

granting of the sign of Messianic accreditation which is promised to the unbelieving generation and which may be perceived directly. [351] But since Jesus the Son of Man will come in the *parousia* as judge, or at least as witness for the prosecution or defence, it is now too late to accept this as a validation of His preaching and hence to decide in favour of it. [352]

(b) Mk. 13:26 brings in a reference to Da. 7:13. The quotation occurs in the Synoptic Apocalypse in a passage (vv. 24-27) made up of traditional apocalyptic materials, [353] Is. 13:10; 34:4; Da. 7:13; Zech. 2:10; Dt. 30:4. Especially as regards the construction of a sequence of eschatological events [354] this does not seem to fit in too well with the message of Jesus (cf. the unknowability of the date of the end in Mk. 13:32-37; Mt. 24:42 f. and par.; 25:1-13; Lk. 17:26 f.). The direct reference to Da. 7:13 in Mk. 13:26, for which there is a parallel in the older tradition only at Mk. 14:62, diverges in the sense that in Jesus' preaching the Son of Man is presented in basic form with no biblical discussion. It would thus seem that vv. 24-27 do not go back to the oldest tradition [355] but have been added by the Jewish Christian community. [356] The idea behind them is that of interpreting Jesus' intimation of the end in terms of Son of Man prediction and of giving this the authority of a scriptural quotation. The idea of coming with the clouds is included (→ 435, 21) and the title Son of Man can be abbreviated to the absolute ὁ υἱός (v. 32) → 372, 9 ff.

(c) The introduction to the esoteric discourse on the Son of Man contains a new saying in Lk. 17:22. Here the title comes from the special source, since Lk. never uses it himself. [357] The "days" of the Son of Man (plural as in v. 26), which extend the event of the "day" (v. 24, 30), may be pre-Lucan or Lucan, → n. 255. Since ἐπιθυμεῖν with infinitive is a pre-Lucan form, Luke obviously found a reference to the sufferings of the disciples which awakened hope that the Son of Man would

---

351 Vögtle, 270.

352 Thus the community does not think this wicked generation will be led to repentance by the deliverance of the One whom God has sent nor is this the view of Jesus if the logion is authentic, as against Tödt, 195 f. The double saying which compares this generation with pagans (the queen of the south and the men of Nineveh in Mt. 12:41 f. and par., cf. Vögtle, 248-253) and which makes the preaching of repentance the *tertium comparationis* for the καὶ ἰδοὺ πλεῖον Ἰωνᾶ ὧδε (→ III, 409, 3 ff.) was perhaps linked already to the Son of Man saying in the source, originally in the Lucan order. On the omission of the sign of Jonah in Mk. 8:12 → n. 377.

353 Acc. to Bultmann Trad., 129 it is older than the Marcan revision. J. W. Bowman, *The Intention of Jesus* (1945), 55-58, who does not think Mk. 13 deals with the end of the world but regards it as a prophecy of the destruction of Jerusalem, is forced to excise vv. 24-27. The apocal. predictions in vv. 1-23 are, however, the same in content as vv. 24-27 and thus denote the end of the world, Kümmel, 88-97.

354 μετὰ τὴν θλῖψιν ἐκείνην, Mk. 13:24; καὶ τότε ὄψονται, v. 26; καὶ τότε ἀποστελεῖ, v. 27. This undermines the thesis of F. Busch, *Zum Verständnis d. synpt. Eschatologie; Mk. 13 neu untersucht* (1938), 98-106 that we do not have a chronological sequence but that the one last act replaces the apocal. drama, and that the Evangelist is just exhorting to patience rather than thinking of a time, Kümmel, 90.

355 Nor can one argue that only the Son of Man saying does, since it is the climax of the pericope.

356 Kümmel, 92-95 shows that the whole cannot be a purely Jewish apoc. but reflects the experiences of the Chr. community (v. 6, 9-11, 13, 21-23) and also contains authentic dominical sayings (v. 2, 28-37).

357 Rehkopf, 56.

end them. This suggests the work of the community, [358] although an authentic motif of Jesus is present, namely, that the day of the Son of Man will not be manifest in such a way that men may then adjust their conduct to it. Hence along the lines of the point in 17:21 (→ 149, 29 ff.) that the kingdom of God will come at a stroke, this fits in well with the (→ 433, 8 ff.) acknowledgedly authentic sayings about the unexpectedness of the appearance of the Son of Man, v. 24, 26. Noah (v. 26) and Lot (v. 28) are commended as examples of the way in which we should be ready for the catastrophe without knowing when it will strike.

(d) In the parable of the thief in Mt. 24:43 f. and par. (→ III, 755, 28 ff.) the coming of the Son of Man, for which the hearers are exhorted to be ready, is compared to the very different [359] breaking in of a burglar, for which a prudent homeowner should be prepared. [360]

The thief is a figure of speech for the last day in 1 Th. 5:2, 4; 2 Pt. 3:10, since this day will come on the unbelieving and impenitent like a thief, i.e., a stroke of fate. [361] Since the thief is not the Son of Man in 1 Th. it is possible that this equation was not original, esp. as Jesus did not usually predict the epiphany of the Son of Man in comparisons [362] but in apocalyptic-prophetic discourse. [363] The comparison is an understandable one in intimation of the approaching catastrophe to the crowds to whom Jesus was originally speaking. [364] Only when the primitive Church applied it to the situation of the delayed parousia could the accent shift to the coming One and the thief become a figure of speech for the Son of Man (cf. Rev. 3:3; 16:15). This finds expression in Mt. 24:44 and par. [365] The v. is not a

---

[358] But not in the sense: "You will desire to have lived then" (Schweizer, 61), since the ὄψεσθε repeats Jesus' hope for a future end of tribulation, cf. Jeremias Gl.⁷, 152. It does not rest on an authentic saying about the present Son of Man, but transfers the title to the present Jesus and then expects Jesus as the coming Son of Man.

[359] E. Fuchs, Hermeneutik³ (1963), 223.

[360] This differs from the parable of the door-keeper in Mk. 13:33-37 and par. (which precedes in Lk. and perhaps also in Mt. if Mt. 24:42 is a remnant of it). In this parable confident waiting for the master (Mk. 13:35; Lk. 12:37; Mt. 24:42), who has ordered the door-keeper to watch (Mk. 13:34b), is applied directly in Lk. 12:36a. The stress is now on waiting for an approaching event, not on the person of the one who comes. This stress must surely have been the basic one in Jesus' own preaching, cf. the parable of the steward which follows that of the thief in Mt. 24:45-51 and Lk. 12:42-46 and that of the ten virgins, which perhaps replaces the parable of the door-keeper in Mt. 25:1-13. The other parables of the parousia might also be mentioned → V, 866, 4 ff.

[361] Jeremias Gl.⁷, 47 thinks these passages are based on Jesus' parable, since the image of the thief does not occur in the eschatological vocabulary of Judaism.

[362] The theme of the parables is God's triumph in His βασιλεία and vigilance in view of the expected final tribulation.

[363] There is a difference here from Mt. 24:37-39 and par. (→ 434, 4 ff.; 459, 14 ff.) which Vielhauer Gottesreich, 73 f., n. 79 misses.

[364] The γινώσκετε, which must be seen as an imper., leads on to the application. The conditional clause in v. 3 suggests the uncertainty of the hour as distinct from apocal. depiction or calculation.

[365] Mt. found this so loose that he put in διὰ τοῦτο, cf. 12:31; 13:13. The real parable is not basically christological, as against Vielhauer Gottesreich, 73 f., n. 79. To presuppose the same relation of content and interpretation as Vielhauer does not count in favour of authenticity, cf. Bultmann Trad., 125; Tödt, 50, 307 f. Tödt, 82 contradicts himself when he finds three par. conclusions in Mt. 24:39, 42, 44 and ascribes the position of v. 44 to the Mt. redaction. One can claim this only for v. 39, 42 or for v. 43 and 44, and in favour of a concluding v. 44 one has to take into account the parable of the thief, which, as its position in Lk. shows, was originally connected with that of the flood. If the title kurios in v. 42 suggests a structuring of the Son of Man title (→ n. 404) and if the latter is actually of older rootage in the Synoptic tradition, which is not always so, cf. Tödt, 83, then this merely proves that Son of Man is older here, not original, as against Tödt, 50, 206.

free invention of the community. It might well have belonged to the immediately preceding comparison with the fate of the flood generation in Mt. or the appended ref. to the fate of the men of Sodom in Lk. It is perhaps a doublet of the Son of Man sayings in Mt. 24:37 and par. (→ 434, 4 ff.) or Lk. 17:30 — a doublet which was them remodelled to go with the parable of the thief. 366

(e) The Sabbath pericope in Mk. 2:23-28 seems to reflect community debates rather than the healing ministry → 430, 32 ff. It culminates in the logion in v. 27 (→ VI, 19, 28 ff.): "The sabbath was made for man and not man for the sabbath." 367 As to the authenticity of this saying there is a certain consensus. 368 But v. 28: "Hence בר נשא (→ 405, 9) is lord even of the sabbath," does not seem to be logical in going on to ascribe dominion over the Sabbath to man, 369 for we should have a genuine syllogism only if it were concluded, along the lines of the creation story, that man cannot be the slave of anything created, including the Sabbath. The authority of man to validate or cancel the Sabbath (→ VII, 22, 23 ff.) takes us a good deal further than a conclusion of this kind. The reason would seem to be that the community, conscious of its final liberation from the Jewish Law, was defending the plucking of ears of grain on the Sabbath, not by a reference to the χρεία of man (as in the pericope, v. 25), but by the supreme authority of the Son of Man. 370 In this respect it developed the position of Jesus vis-à-vis the Sabbath and defined it authoritatively with the aid of the Son of Man title. 371

(f) At one of these stages the man against whom one may speak and yet be forgiven (→ 443, 5 ff.) was interpreted Messianically, though only in the translation. The development of the saying in Lk. 12:10 (→ VI, 407, 13 ff.), according to which blasphemy against the Son of Man can be forgiven but not blasphemy against the Holy Spirit, was most likely in a post-Pentecost community which was conscious

---

366 This conclusion is supported by the fact that Ev. Thom. (→ n. 86), which has parables with the same freedom from allegorising interpretations as elsewhere only Lk.'s special material has (Jeremias Gl.⁷, 87), does not have in either version of this parable (Logion 21b [85, 6 ff.] and 103 [98, 4 ff.]) a comparison of the burglar with the Son of Man, Jeremias Gl.⁷ 46 and 94.
367 There is a similar relaxing of the Sabbath in Judaism, cf. M. Ex., 5 on 31:14: "The sabbath is given to you, not you to the sabbath." For the difference between this and Mk. 2:27 cf. E. Lohse, "Jesu Worte über den Sabbat," Festschr. J. Jeremias (1960), 85. On 1 Macc. 2:41 → VII, 8, 24 ff.
368 Lohse, op. cit., 85; Braun, op. cit. (→ n. 237), II, 70, n. 1; Loh. Mk., ad loc.
369 So Wellh. Mk.², ad loc.
370 Cf. Tödt, 122.
371 There are also linguistic arguments against v. 28 being an authentic saying of Jesus. In a gen. construction such as we have here the equivalent of κύριος would not be שַׁלִּיט (Wellhausen Sohn, 203), which is mostly abs. and usually goes with בְּ, but מר, רב, or derivates or בעל → III, 1084, 10 ff. Such expressions usually denote the owner or controller of something, which is a good deal less than what is meant by κύριος τοῦ σαββάτου. Or else, with gen., they apply in a transf. sense or directly to God and thus acquire a lofty sense comparable with that in Mk. 2:28, but this can hardly be intended by Jesus, since it is the disciples who are lords rather than Jesus. If this is correct v. 28 would be an addition of the community in which κύριος is used as an established term for Jesus. One might conjecture that this happened after and because the title came into the context of 2:1 - 3:7a (Jeremias Abendmahlsworte, 86, n. 1) at 2:10. On this view we should have neither a misunderstanding nor an interpretation of בר נשא, which → 405, 9 had to take into account when studying the term in isolation.

of possessing the Spirit and which, in the light of the faith in the risen and ascended Lord made possible thereby, viewed the earthly life of the Son of Man as a preparatory age of salvation. On this view rejection of Jesus would not be so serious a breach with God as rejection of the Spirit of the exalted Lord who was to be given after the resurrection of Jesus. [372]

(g) On Mt. 12:32 → n. 406; I, 104, 8 ff.; IV, 1114, n. 54.

(h) The end of the story of Zacchaeus in Lk. 19:10 is not the work of Luke [373] but is pre-Lucan, since Luke never uses ὁ υἱὸς τοῦ ἀνθρώπου on his own [374] and ἦλθεν seems to be combined with the Son of Man title already in pre-Lucan tradition, Mt. 11:19. Yet v. 10 might still be an addition to the story, describing the work of the Son of Man in sententious fashion. Lk. 19:10 (→ VI, 500, 27 ff.; VII, 991, 32 ff.): "For the Son of Man is come to seek and to save that which was lost," reminds us of Mk. 2:17b and par. and more remotely of Mt. 15:24. In a saying of Jesus like this the title was added before Luke or else the statement was completely reconstructed on the basis of some similar saying or Mk. 8:35. Possibly the saying belongs to the next and literary stage.

3. The Literary Tradition of the Primitive Community.

a. First Stage: Mark and the Special Lucan Source.

(a) Mark takes over from the tradition the confession before the Sanhedrin (Mk. 14:62 → II, 352, 29 ff.; III. 937, 9 ff.) and he adds to it the quotation from Da. 7:13 (→ 379, 5 ff.; 435, 20 ff.) which he had already adopted in the apocalyptic discourse (Mk. 13:26 → 450, 21 ff.). In both instances there is assimilation to apocalyptic tradition, especially Da. 7:13. In them ὄψονται and ὄψεσθε relate to the *parousia*, like ἴδωσιν (9:1). [375] More concretely and with fuller details [376] Mark has this proclaimed by Jesus both in the apocalyptic discourse and also in the confession before the supreme council. In the second instance the announcement is part of Jesus' full confession of His Messiahship. Here the fact that it is He who will come again as Son of Man directs our gaze primarily, not to the *parousia*, but to its proclamation and hence to the disclosure of His majesty to the whole world.

Originally the proclamation of majesty even to enemies might have been uttered first in the hearing before the Sanhedrin, but we also find it in the disputations with the scribes and Pharisees in 2:10 (→ 430, 32 f.; 441, 35) and 2:28 (→ n. 371). From the very first Jesus gives evidence of His authority to remit sins as the Son of Man

---

372 So also Tödt, 111, who thinks that the connection with the Beelzebul pericope is original. But this exposition does not presuppose that it is a free invention of the community. For a different view cf. W. Bousset, "Wellhausen's Evangelienkritik," ThR, 9 (1906), 9, who also concludes that Lk. has the saying in the original context. But → n. 388 and cf. also Schl. Mt. on 12:32.

373 So Bultmann Trad., 34; cf. → n. 35.

374 Rehkopf, 56.

375 Marxsen Mk., 54.

376 But these cannot be systematised as in E. Lohmeyer, "Gottesknecht u. Davidsohn," FRL, NF, 43² (1953), 125. On the combination of Christ, Son, Son of God and Son of Man in Mk. cf. P. Vielhauer, "Erwägungen z. Christologie d. Mk.," *Aufsätze z. NT, Theol. Bücherei,* 31 (1965), 199-214.

and also to subject the Sabbath commandments to Himself. Mark did not change the sayings in content. It is no longer possible to say how their position relates to what is often regarded as the planned beginning of the developing use of the Son of Man title in the first version of the passion prediction, 8:31 → 444, 29 ff. [377]

> In Mk. 3:28 f. the saying about blaspheming the Spirit (→ 442, 13 ff.) is not yet a Son of Man saying. Whether one may deduce from the plur. τοῖς υἱοῖς τῶν ἀνθρώπων (instead of the sing. of the tradition) that Mk. wanted to avoid a Messianic interpretation must be left undecided. In view of the construction of the sentence such an interpretation would have been unlikely. In the Gk. text τῷ υἱῷ τοῦ ἀνθρώπου must have established itself already as a solemn Messianic designation.

When the theology of the suffering Son of Man had developed between Jesus' expectation of suffering and the writing of Mk. (→ 444, 16 ff.), Mark consciously sought to establish it [378] from 8:31 onwards with the first version of the passion prediction after the Messianic confession at Caesarea Philippi. Since this was designed to prepare the way for his passion narrative, in the light of it he interpreted the "rejection" as condemnation by the chief priests and scribes and construed the perfecting saying in the light of resurrection faith by means of ἀναστῆναι, which is undoubtedly older than ἐγερθῆναι (→ n. 315), though it is still post-Easter (cf. Lk. 13:31 f.; Mk. 14:58).

The saying in 9:9, which depends on the passion prediction and is thus post-Easter (→ n. 316), is undoubtedly pre-Marcan. Dying, which implies suffering preceding resurrection, is here so transcended by the reference to the resurrection (→ 445, 16 ff.; IV, 248, 9 ff.) that Mark with his special interest in the suffering Son of Man (→ 456, 16 ff.) thought he should give it particular emphasis. This comes to expression in v. 12b, which so clearly interrupts the sequence that one must regard it as an interpolation. [379] Mark is giving a positive answer here to the question whether mortal suffering, which is said of the forerunner, [380] is also written concerning the Son of Man Himself. But he does this a little early, i.e., directly after the place where the Son of Man Jesus Himself confirms that there was a popular belief that Elijah must come first and restore all things, and before the reference to the passion of John. Perhaps Mark wanted to forestall the error that this passion would render that of the Messiah / Son of Man superfluous. In analogy to the passion predictions Mark puts his corroborative explanation in the form of a saying of Jesus.

---

[377] Acc. to Sjöberg Menschensohn Ev., 105 Mk. 2:10, 28 deviate from the Evangelist's plan, being accidental slips due to adoption of a tradition which was already firmly established. Mk. 8:12 is either a different saying from that about the sign of Jonah (→ 449, 5 ff.) or else Mk. left this out with the interpretation of the sign as the Son of Man because he laid special stress on Jesus' mighty deeds as full proof of His Messiahship and the threat of a miracle of accreditation was thus unnecessary, Vögtle, 273 f.

[378] But not the intimations of the passion as such, which begin already with the clear and easily understandable image of the bridegroom in Mk. 2:19 f., cf. Wrede, op. cit. (→ n. 317), 19 f., 83, 120, 124. On the possibility of the disclosure of the mystery of the divine rule in Mk. 9:7 within the framework of passion sayings about the Son of Man → 378, 27 ff.

[379] Loh. Mk., ad loc. Mk. himself must be the glossator, for the theory of a written addition before him or in the MSS after him runs into serious difficulties.

[380] By the equating of the slain Baptist of v. 13 with Elijah, whom popular belief expected as the forerunner, cf. Str.-B., IV, 784-789.

The second version of the passion prediction which follows in 9:31 gives no evidence of Mk.'s editing and the third in 10:33 f. was stylised by the tradition before him, not by Mk. himself, → 445, 4 ff. Mk.'s hand may be seen, of course, in the selection and arrangement of the three versions.

The substance of Mk. 10:45b: καὶ δοῦναι τὴν ψυχὴν αὐτοῦ λύτρον ἀντὶ πολλῶν, belongs to the oldest Palestinian tradition of dominical sayings and must go back to an authentic logion.

Along the lines of the eucharistic sayings Mk. 10:45b speaks of the sacrifice of righteous life in the end-time for the redemption of guilty life. That this takes place ἀντὶ πολλῶν, not just to set aside incurred guilt so that life may be resumed, but for the definitive reconciling of all in this aeon, which is now at its close, gives to the "for all" what is in comparison with the earlier sense (→ 441, 22 ff.) a new and extended Messianic signification. But the very fact that this new sense is implicit and is not made explicit by the adding of a Messianic title or the like supports the view that the saying is part of the original preaching of Jesus, who when He made His Messianic claim realised that He was destined to suffer vicariously → 443, 23 ff. Naturally, then, the saying came to Mk. from the very earliest tradition.

The saying becomes Mk's interpretation when combined with a Son of Man logion which he took from another tradition. The Son of Man logion dealt originally only with Jesus' person and service (→ 448, 25 ff.) and with the request of the sons of Zebedee it establishes for Mark the obligatory service of the disciples along with the previously conferred διακονῆσαι of the Son of Man. By adding the λύτρον saying Mark follows the tradition which combines Son of Man and suffering sayings (→ 444, 16 ff.). In so doing he brings out the depth of Jesus' serving and even *expressis verbis* he presses it to the climax to which it was already tacitly moving, namely, the giving of His life in the service of the redemption of all men. But by this addition he also takes from the λύτρον saying its eschatological edge [381] and makes it an incomparable paradigmatic basis for the self-humbling which is paraenetically demanded of the disciples here.

Of the two references to the Son of Man in the betrayal saying in Mk. 14:21 (→ 446, 9 ff.) the second possibly goes back to Mark, since it presupposes a distinction in sense which became clear only in the Greek tradition, namely, that between ὁ υἱὸς τοῦ ἀνθρώπου and ἄνθρωπος, which are perhaps deliberately contrasted here. It is an almost pedantic and certainly not indispensable amplification of the threat in Lk. 22:22: "But woe unto that man by whom he is betrayed!" in which the 3rd person is influenced by the secondary Son of Man title in v. 22a. It is no less secondary in the first half of the saying in Mark (→ 446, 12 ff.) and is repeated by Mark to give weight to the threat and also to stress the dignity of the Son of Man, whom one cannot betray and remain unpunished. In the Gethsemane scene, too, Mark adopted the title (14:41) → 445, 22 ff. That it occurs for the last time with a passion saying here is intentional. Now the passion itself will be depicted, and here the title is unnecessary. If Mark does not add it again, he is following the tradition in this respect no less than in his previous use of it.

---

[381] E. Lohse, "Märtyrer u. Gottesknecht," FRL, NF, 46² (1964), 121 f. It makes no difference whether the theologoumenon of expiatory suffering comes directly from Is. 53 or developed again independently from the Maccabean period, as Barrett, *op. cit.* (→ n. 343), 8-14 supposes. Neither possibility proves anything either for or against the actualising of the theologoumenon by Jesus.

In Mk. 8:38, which has only the second and negative half of a logion which the sayings tradition had in full (→ 442, 1 ff.), Mark found ἐπαισχύνομαι in the community tradition, [382] but did not put it in under the influence of Pauline usage (→ n. 331), for this is the only time he has the verb, whereas ἀρνέομαι and ἀπαρνέομαι are more common, e.g., at the beginning of this pericope in 8:34, and cf. 14:30, 31, 68, 70, 72. On the other hand καὶ τοὺς ἐμοὺς λόγους, [383] the changing of "before man" to "in this adulterous and sinful generation" (cf. Mt. 12:39) and the adding of a description of the coming of the Son of man in traditional apocalyptic terms, [384] for which the judicial forum is abandoned, may all be attributed to Mark. Mark weaves the whole logion into a passage about the disciples' way of suffering, 8:27 - 10:45. He possibly left out the first half to connect it with v. 36 f. For Mark the coming of the Son of Man was undoubtedly the return of the earthly Jesus to the earth — hence the addition τοῦ πατρὸς αὐτοῦ. [385] This interpretation is given to the whole series by the addition of 9:1, the coming of the kingdom of God ἐν δυνάμει. [386]

The main interest of Mark (for the Messianic secret, which is more a Son of Man secret → 441, 8 ff.) is undoubtedly to be found in sayings about the suffering Son of Man. This finds expression both in the treatment and also in the order. The sayings can hardly be grouped as pure present sayings on the one side and pure future on the other, for they deal with the perfecting of the earthly Jesus. Since the reference is to perfecting in suffering, there is here no alternative of lowliness or glory. At most one might cite the confession before the Sanhedrin in this respect. Without the aspect of perfecting we have only Mk. 2:10, 28 with a present reference and Mk. 8:38 and 13:26 with a future reference. According to what principles they were related to the passion sayings it is impossible to say.

(b) The special Lucan source adopts 17 sayings from the tradition. Of these at least 6 (6:22 → 448, 34 ff.; 7:34 → 431, 8 ff.; 9:58 → 432, 9 ff.; 19:10 → 453, 13 ff.; 22:22; 22:48) have the title Son of Man as a self-designation on the part of the present Jesus. The last two (22:22: betrayal announcement → 446, 9 ff. and 22:48: Judas' kiss → 446, 29 ff.) are to be understood here, in distinction from Mk. (→ 455, 30 ff.), in terms of the situation rather than in the context of perfecting through the passion, so that we do not have any passion statements. [387] All the sayings are

---

[382] On the Aram. variant in the tradition from which ἀρνέομαι might derive → n. 331.
[383] Cf. the corresponding expressions καὶ (ἕνεκεν) τοῦ εὐαγγελίου in 8:25 and 10:29. Confessing and denying presuppose a relationship to a person and not just to words, Tödt, 38. "Note that, in Mk. 8:38, λόγους is omitted by WK sa. If this is the original reading, then τοὺς ἐμούς = 'my own (People)'" [C. F. D. Moule].
[384] Vielhauer Gottesreich, 77, n. 97.
[385] The traditional apocal. Son of Man has no father. The idea of the divine sonship of Jesus is brought in here, cf. Kl. Mk., ad loc → 372, n. 268. Acc. to this view the ὅταν ἔλθῃ ... is secondary compared with Lk. 12:9, but only from a literary and not a material standpoint.
[386] Marxsen Mk., 140.
[387] There is a reminiscence of passion predictions in Lk. 24:7. Later development is suggested here by δεῖ, which is not common to the type (cf. Popkes, op. cit. → n. 324, 154 f.) and also by σταυρωθῆναι. Since the betrayal saying in Lk. 22:22 is not primarily an intimation of the passion and the title is not used in the secondary quotation at 17:25, which for all the power of the Son of Man is meant to recall His passion, the special source says nothing about the suffering Son of Man and it is thus questionable whether the saying of the angel

addressed to a mixed audience. In contrast the sayings about the coming Son of Man, with the exception of the confession before the Sanhedrin (22:69 → 435, 8 ff.), are all directed to the disciples. There are ten such sayings: 12:8; confessing and denying (→ 457, 12) and 12:10: blaspheming the Son of Man (→ 452, 21 ff.), [388] 12:40: He comes unexpectedly (→ 451, 9 ff.), 17:22, 24, 26, 30: days of the Son of Man etc. (→ 450, 20 ff.; 433, 10 ff.), 18:8: Will He find faith?, 21:36: Be watchful so that you may stand before Him, and 22:69. The interpretation of the sign of Jonah (→ 449, 5 ff.) is addressed to the ὄχλοι, and in the saying about the Ninevites (11:32) the καὶ ἰδοὺ πλεῖον Ἰωνᾶ ὧδε relates Jesus to Jonah in a way analogous to the Jonah-Son of Man relation, v. 30. Both support the view that the special source is thinking of the present Son of Man here, whereas the future Son of Man seems to be in mind in the interpretation preceding the queen of the south/Ninevites saying.

Of the eight sayings (→ 433, 8 ff.) whose authenticity as dominical logia seems to be beyond question, though belonging to a particular stratum is not a criterion, the special Lucan source alone contains six, Lk. 17:24, 26, 30; 18:8; 21:36 and 22:69. The fact that all of them apart from the last are addressed to the disciples seems to be historically significant (→ 440, 21 ff.) especially as the parallels to 17:24, 26 in Mt. 24:27, 37, though differing in composition, are also set in an address to the disciples. It is by no means obvious that the special source first put the sayings about the future Son of Man in esoteric preaching and those about the present Son of Man in exoteric preaching; no reason exists for such a distinction. Indeed, the theology of the special source would lead us to expect both groups of sayings to be distributed in both esoteric and exoteric preaching.

b. Second Stage: Luke.

In fitting the Marcan material into his source [389] Lk. first adopted Mk. 2:10 (→ 430, 32 ff.) and 28 (→ 452, 6 ff.) in 5:24 and 6:5 without change. From his own source he then added 6:22 and 7:34. [390] The Marcan material in 8:31, 38; 9:31 then offered a basis for Lk. 9:22, [391] 26, [392] 44, though Lk. perhaps also used a special tradition in 9:44.[393] Lk. omitted Mk. 9:9, 12 (→ 445, 11 ff.) with the whole pericope of the descent. [394] The record of the journey from the special source contains Son of Man sayings at 9:58;

---

in 24:7 should be cited in this connection, esp. as it echoes neither 17:25, 22:22 nor 9:44 → 444, 25 f. But one cannot prove that it was Luke who first formulated a Galilean prediction by Jesus of the delivering up, crucifixion and resurrection of the Son of Man, so Tödt, 141. From the standpoint of the tradition one cannot as yet place the saying, and the same applies to the isolated 17:25, from which the Son of Man title seems to be absent only by accident.

[388] The relation of 12:10 to 12:8 shows that in 12:10 the reference is to the future Son of Man in distinction from the original sense → 452, 21 ff.

[389] Jeremias Abendmahlsworte, 91 f.

[390] Here Lk. with ἐλήλυθεν for ἦλθεν (as distinct from Lk. 19:10) looks back to the work of John and Jesus and thus makes the saying of Jesus part of his own account, cf. A. Harnack, *Sprüche u. Reden Jesu* (1907), 17 f. τέκνων in v. 35 for ἔργων in Mt. 11:19 is a pre-Lucan transl. variant or a variant in the Aram. tradition.

[391] The ἀναστῆναι of Mk. 8:31 is changed here to ἐγερθῆναι. Thus what was perhaps a ref. to perfecting is interpreted as resurrection.

[392] On the coming of the Son of Man "in the glory ... of the angels" cf. Conzelmann Mitte, 161, n. 3.

[393] There is no ref. to death or to resurrection after three days. This tradition is not to be linked more closely, then, either to the special source or to Lk. 17:25 and 24:7.

[394] It is replaced by a summary in 9:37b leading to the cure of the epileptic boy.

11:30; [395] 12:8, 10; 17:22, [396] 24, [397] 26, [398] 30, [399] and 18:8. The Marcan material (10:33) then offers a model for the third passion prediction in Lk. 18:31, but 19:10 is again from the special source. Lk. omits Mk. 10:45, for he has the par. tradition from the special source without the Son of Man title in 22:27. On the other hand Mk. 13:26 (→ 450, 6 ff.) can be taken over virtually unaltered in Lk. 21:27. [400] 21:36 then comes from the special source. Lk. no longer uses the ref. from the passion story Mk. 14:21, 41, 62, since he already has the content of Mk. 14:21, 62 in his special source, which also contains 22:48; among other things the shorter account of the Gethsemane incident does not have the Son of Man saying of Mk. 14:41. Finally Lk. 24:7 has not yet been assigned to any source. One can only say that it is unlikely to be Lk.'s own work, since he never uses the Son of Man title independently. [401]

---

[395] The double saying (→ n. 352) is more original in the chronological sequence queen of the south/Ninevites than *vice versa*, esp. as the connecting catchword between v. 31 and v. 30 is more difficult thus (only τῆς γενεᾶς ταύτης) than it would be in the case of Jonah, Vögtle, 249 f. In Lk.'s version the Son of Man saying is connected with the double saying from the standpt. of the threat of judgment on this generation, whereas this idea is abandoned in Mt.'s version, Vögtle, 251. In Lk. 11:30 the Son of Man saying is connected with the sign of Jonah by ᾽Ιωνᾶς (→ 449, 22 ff.) and also by σημεῖον and τῇ γενεᾷ ταύτῃ, Vögtle, 249. This is a further indication that Mt. offers his own interpretation → n. 405. Lk. is closer here to the original Son of Man saying of the community.
[396] In Lk. 17:22 Luke did further work on a community saying (→ 450, 20 ff.) which he found in his special source. To make it more suitable as an introduction to the esoteric inter-pretation he put "day" in the plur., which delay in the *parousia* might explain. "The days of the Son of Man" are thus the earthly days of Jesus. Looking back to these the community hopes for their return with the *parousia*. It is admonished not to overdo expectation of the end. False Messiahs are already a threat, cf. v. 23. The Church, which is now prepared for a period on earth, must treat their proclamations of the end with restraint. The stylistically poor μίαν (τῶν ἡμερῶν) shows that Lk. is adapting expectation of the one "day" (→ n. 255), which is rightly left in v. 24 and v. 30, and it also proves that a saying about the coming Son of Man has not been made out of a saying which at its earliest stage referred to Jesus as the earthly Son of Man.
[397] The fusing of Messianology and the weakening of the imagery in 17:23 f. (as opposed to, e.g., 13:29) show that there is no longer any interest in a precise conception of the event.
[398] The beginning of the Son of Man saying in v. 26 is changed on account of the passion prediction in v. 25, which at some unknown stage was perhaps added by someone who for all the power of the Son of Man wanted to recall His passion, Vielhauer Gottesreich, 62, n. 28; Tödt, 98-100. With this ref. to the suffering Son of Man there perhaps arose a similar reason to that of v. 22 to speak of the days of the Son of Man, unless there is some other explanation of the plur. → n. 255. The impf. forms ἤσθιον, ἔπινον... etc. in v. 27 weaken the durative character of the periphrastic impf. ἦσαν... τρώγοντες καὶ πίνοντες, Mt. 24:38 (on the type cf. G. Björck, ῏Hν διδάσκων, *Die periphrastische Konstr. im Griech.* [1940]) [Risch]. But the original ref. was not to the suffering and toiling of men in Jesus' time, which He would end as the present Son of Man — if so, ἔσται would be, as is possible in principle, the sense-changing rendering of a pres. For the ἄχρι ἧς ἡμέρας εἰσῆλθεν Νῶε εἰς τὴν κιβωτόν and not "they did eat, they drank... until the day that Noe entered into the ark, and the flood came... ," is basic in v. 27, as Mt. 24:38 shows.
[399] In spite of extensive editorial work in Lk. 17, more than in the case of the sayings about the present בר נשא in Mt. 8:20 par.; Mt. 11:19 par.; Mk. 2:10, the Son of Man sayings in v. 24, 26, 30 cannot be detached from the preaching of Jesus nor regarded as secondary eschatologisings of logia in which originally Jesus spoke of Himself as the present Son of Man as in Mt. 11:19 etc. All Lk. does is to adopt Jesus' warning about the day of the Son of Man and use it in the service of exhortation.
[400] On ἐν νεφέλῃ for ἐν νεφέλαις cf. Conzelmann Mitte, 171, n. 1. Concrete apocal. details, the falling of stars in Mk. 13:25a, the gathering of the elect by angels in v. 27, are replaced by ref. to the distress of nations in Lk. 21:25b, 26a and ἀπολύτρωσις in v. 28.
[401] Rehkopf, 56.

Luke is faithful to his sources. One cannot find any specifically Lucan Son of Man Christology in his Gospel. [402]

c. Third Stage: Matthew.

From the sayings tradition common to the Lucan source Mt. takes over the saying about the lightning-like appearance of the Son of Man in Mt. 24:27 and the comparison of His coming with the sudden disaster of Noah's day in Mt. 24:37. In both instances he has the new term παρουσία → V, 865, n. 42. [403] He also takes over unaltered the end of the parable of the children at play in 11:19, the saying about the homelessness of the Son of Man in 8:20 (→ 432, 9 ff.; 441, 34 ff.) and the allegorical interpretation of the parable of the thief in 24:44 → 451, 21 ff. [404] In changed form he uses from the same sayings tradition the interpretation of the sign of Jonah (→ 449, 5 ff.), relating the swallowing up of Jonah to the rest of Jesus in the tomb, Mt. 12:40. [405] He uses similarly the saying about the blasphemy against the Spirit (→ 442, 13 ff.; 452, 21 ff.), which with peripheral variations he fuses with the Marcan version, Mt. 12:31 f. [406] By repeating the conclusion (up to παρουσία) of the authentic saying in Mt. 24:37 he achieves a new saying, Mt. 24:39.

From Mark Mt. takes Mk. 2:10 (→ 430, 32 ff.) and 28 in Mt. 9:6 and 12:8. In 9:6 he might well have been aware of the original meaning "man" (→ n. 236), which ref. to Jesus but is not Messianic if there is a generalising ref. in v. 8. But the generalising might be due to mistranslation of an Aram. expression with exactly the same meaning as

---

[402] Conzelmann Mitte, 159, n. 2, but cf. Tödt, 101-4, who sees the interrelation of sources differently.

[403] Mt. has in view Christ's return and he also reinterprets the OT idea of God's coming in theophany to save (Is. 40:10; 59:19 f.; Zech. 14:5) or to judge (Is. 13:9; Mal. 3:1 f.; Ps. 96:13).

[404] Furthermore the title Kurios in c. 24 f. becomes an equivalent of Son of Man, G. Bornkamm, "Enderwartung u. Kirche im Mt.," Überlieferung u. Auslegung im Mt.⁴ (1965), 38-41; Tödt, 82 f., 255, 262.

[405] In the process ἐγένετο Ἰωνᾶς τοῖς Νινευίταις σημεῖον is replaced by a quotation from Jon. 2:1b. Since the saving of Jonah from the fish is not mentioned here, neither is the resurrection of the Son of Man. The interpretation thus becomes a pure passion saying. Since the story of Jonah is no longer just a sign of reviving, but has won prophetic significance for the suffering of the Son of Man, the saying about the sign is elucidated by the addition of τοῦ προφήτου, in distinction from Mt. 16:4 (which is dependent on Mk. 8:12), where there is no need to lead up to a Son of Man saying. The queen of the south / men of Nineveh saying is rearranged so that the saying about the latter catches up the word Ἰωνᾶς — for the words τῇ γενεᾷ ταύτῃ and σημεῖον, which connected the Son of Man sayings backwards with the sign of Jonah saying and forwards with the double saying, are omitted in Mt.'s exegesis — and expands the Son of Man saying, which no longer speaks of the parousia to judgment, along the lines of the originally remote distinction between resurrection and parousia. The resurrection will be to judgment, and here the Ninevites will testify against this generation because it did not listen to the preaching of repentance by the Son of Man, which is greater than the preaching of Jonah.

[406] Wellhausen Sohn, 203; Bultmann Trad., 138. In 12:31b Mt. gives his own paraphrase of the sayings tradition and the Marcan tradition of the blasphemy against the Spirit, as the absence of τοῦ ἁγίου before βλασφημία shows, cf. Dalman WJ, I, 167. Acc. to Käsemann, op. cit. (→ n. 284), 100 Mt. 12:32 (→ 405, 10 f.) is in the style of an eschatological legal maxim. Mt. repeats and extends the blasphemy saying in 12:32b (hence 12:32 is not an explanatory doublet of v. 31, as Dalman WJ, I, 214 thinks) by adding τὸ οὐκ ἀφεθήσεται αὐτῷ, sc. the blasphemer against the Holy Ghost: "neither in this world, neither in the world to come." Between the paraphrases he has put in without material change the blaspheming of the Son of Man from the sayings source, 12:32a. The historical sequence of Lk. or his source (12:10: blasphemy against Jesus forgivable, blasphemy against the Spirit in the community not) is thus set aside.

in v. 6 → 405, 12 ff. Before 12:8 Mt. left out the original conclusion of the Sabbath debate (→ 452, 8 f.), since υἱὸς τοῦ ἀνθρώπου was now more important than ἄνθρωπος in gen. The second (→ 444, 20 ff.) and third (→ 445, 4 ff.) versions of the passion prediction are adopted by Mt. with only trifling stylistic changes in 17:22 f. and 20:18, as is also the conclusion of the betrayal saying (→ 454, 26 ff.) and the Gethsemane pericope (→ 455, 39 ff.) in 26:24, 45. [407] In his reformulation of the descent pericope the content of the two Son of Man sayings (→ 454, 20 ff.) remains, the second being relocated virtually unchanged, Mt. 17:9, 12. Mk. 10:45 (→ 455, 5 ff.) occurs without material change in Mt. 20:28 and the quotation Da. 7:13 in Mk. 13:26 (→ 450, 6 ff.) is given in a form closer to the LXX in Mt. 24:30b, cf. the quotations from Ps. 110:1 and Da. 7:13 in the confession before the council in Mt. 26:64 (→ 452, 21 ff.). [408] There is more alteration of the confession and denial saying when it is not taken from the sayings tradition (Mt. 10:32 f.) but from Mk. 8:38 (→ 456, 1 ff.) in Mt. 16:27. The coming, which Mk. added, is put first, prominence is thus given to the Son of Man title, and shame is replaced by a judicial act. In v. 28 the coming of the Son of Man is also added to the ref. to the kingdom of God which follows in Mk. Thus the judgment of the Son of Man and the beginning of God's rule, which are parallel symbols of the end-time in Jesus' preaching, are fused into a single event. In 19:28, where the pre-Matthean [409] judging Son of Man might have been combined with the βασιλεία on the basis of Lk. 22:29 f., the event is called παλιγγενεσία → 458, 1.

At Mt. 16:13 Mt. puts the Son of Man title from the passion proclamation at the beginning of Peter's confession at Caesarea Philippi and he adds it again in 26:2 in the introduction to the passion story. In both cases his aim is to set the passion theme that follows programmatically under a title of dignity. [410] He probably takes 10:23 unaltered from his special source: "Ye shall not have gone over the cities of Israel ...," [411] and the same applies to 24:30: the sign of the Son of Man. [412] In the introduction to the parable

---

[407] There is a different stress here only to the degree that Mt. leaves more space for Jesus' preaching. His Gospel thus loses the character of a passion story with prior traditions about the secret epiphany of the Son of Man, and in these prior and now extended traditions themselves the passion predictions and the λύτρον saying lose their sustaining function. Through the stronger emphasis on majesty in sayings about the future and present Son of Man, not just in exposition of Mk. but also in that of the sayings and special material, the passion sayings are also set in relief. It is obvious that Mt. does not want to disparage them, but to give them new dignity by paradoxically connecting them with majesty sayings. This is even plainer in passages which he alters.

[408] Here the more precise "hereafter shall ye see" resolves the paradox in which the One expected in glory was first to suffer. But Tödt, 76-8 overworks his correct insight here when he tries to prove a different use of the predicates "Christ" and "Son of God" before and after the break in Mt. 26:64.

[409] Or perhaps Mt. himself added the Son of Man title for the I in διατίθεμαι (Lk. 22:29) to show the identity of the βασιλεία τῶν οὐρανῶν with the dominion of the Son of Man and the connection between the exalted Lord of the Church and His lowliness and suffering as the Son of Man — there is allusion to this in ἀκολουθήσαντες.

[410] Iber, 51; Tödt, 79, n. 117; 139; N. A. Dahl, "Die Passionsgeschichte bei Mt.," NTSt, 2 (1955/56), 17-21; G. Bertram, "Die Leidensgeschichte Jesu u. d. Christuskult," FRL, 32 (1922), 8-13.

[411] In view of its fidelity to the source Mt.'s exposition of the saying in 10:23 comes to light only in the relation to the context. He is telling Chr. missionaries who in the course of their work are handed over to pagan authorities and Jewish synagogues (v. 17) and tried by them (v. 19) that the return of their Lord is imminent. This should strengthen them to endure to the end.

[412] Coming before v. 30b the saying about the sign of the Son of Man in 24:30a is designed to bring out Christ's judicial office, which was not clearly enough implied for the Chr. reader by the coming in glory. καὶ τότε κόψονται πᾶσαι αἱ φυλαί is put in to indicate the reaction of the peoples.

of the last judgment he puts the Son of Man for the king (25:31) [413] and he has two new Son of Man sayings in the interpretation of the parable of the wheat and the tares, 13:37, 41. [414]

Mt. takes Son of Man sayings from the logia material, Mark and his special source and uses them either in unaltered form [415] or with variations. He also fashions new sayings in relation to each of the three traditions. Mt. thus offers a synthesis of all the meanings which arose before him and through him. The Son of Man, always equated with Jesus, is the One who preaches on earth, the vicarious Sufferer, the One exalted as Lord of the Church, the One who comes again as Judge and Advocate in the last judgment, and the One who rules over the new aeon in His kingdom, the kingdom of God.

II. The Later Apocalyptic Tradition.

1. Ac. 7:56.

Stephen in his vision in Ac. 7:55 f. cries out: "Behold, I see the heavens opened, and the Son of Man standing (ἑστῶτα) on the right hand of God." Apart from the quotations in Hb. 2:6; Rev. 1:13; 14:14 this is the only or at least the earliest instance of the title Son of Man on other lips than those of Jesus. Since in v. 55

---

[413] Basically, as a demand for service to neighbours, even the very least, the parable of the last judgment goes back to Jesus, Jeremias Gl.⁷, 204-7; Vielhauer Gottesreich, 62 f. Mt. may well have stylised the opening by introducing the Son of Man title, the familiar attributes of glory from Eth. En., the throne of glory, the angels, cf. J. Schniewind, Das Ev. nach Mt., NT Deutsch, 2¹¹ (1964), ad loc.; Bultmann Trad., 130 f., 162; Jeremias Gl.⁷, 204; Tödt, 68-72; for originally the chief figure in the parable was the king, v. 34, 40, who stands for God as in Jewish parables, cf. Str.-B., I, 978 f. Mt. transferred the divine office of judge to the Son of Man, i.e., the earthly and returning Jesus (cf. the father of the king in v. 34), as in the exposition of Mk. 8:38; 9:1 in 16:27 f. (→ 460, 13 ff.) and as perhaps by the introduction of the Son of Man title into the Jewish Chr. tradition at Mt. 19:28 → 447, 9 ff.

[414] Sayings about the present and the future Son of Man occur in the interpretation of the parable of the wheat and the tares in Mt. 13:36-43. For Mt.'s authorship cf. Jeremias Gl.⁷, 79-83. In the meanings attached to the seven most important elements in the parable in vv. 37-39 the sower of v. 24 is the Son of Man, i.e., Jesus, v. 37. When we are then told that the angels will gather out of the kingdom of Jesus the Son of Man all things that offend and all the wicked (v. 41) so that the righteous shall shine forth as the sun in the kingdom of their Father (v. 43), it seems plain that the kingdom of the Son of Man, understood almost chiliastically, must be the Church, Kl. Mt., ad loc.; the only other ref. to it, here fut., is in Mt. 16:28, → 460, 15 ff. The kingdom of the Son of Man arose through combination of the future Son of Man with the kingdom of God. Under the rule of Jesus the Son of Man the Church moves on to judgment, which separates the good and the bad. This judgment, which is depicted apocalyptically in vv. 40-43 in what is rather more than an interpretation of the fate of the wheat and the tares (v. 30b), is effected by the same Son of Man, Jesus, through the angels, v. 41. He hereby merges His earthly βασιλεία into that of the Father, cf. Tödt, 64-8. The coming again of Jesus is here expected quickly. From the standpt. of the tradition the two sayings, whether individually or together, seem to be the last in the Synoptists.

[415] Lk. 19:10: "The Son of Man is come to seek and to save that which was lost," which is the end of the Zacchaeus story, is variously attested in a catechetical context in Mt. 18:11 and at the beginning of the Lucan journey in Lk. 9:56. In Mt. 18:11 D is for it and Θ against, in Lk. 9:56 vice versa. In Mt. 18:11 sy꜀ are for and syˢ against. Cod D and Lat for and the Sahid. and Boh. versions against, textus receptus for and the Ferrar group against. In Lk. 9:56 the Syr. split the same way as with Mt. 18:11, the Lat is for and D against, Fam 1 (Lake) is for and Egypt. against; for details cf. the survey in F. G. Kenyon-A. W. Adams, The Text of the Gk. Bible (1960), 162. The saying might well be secondary in both, and hence also the title, cf. ἀπεστάλην in Mt. 15:24 → n. 35.

as distinct from v. 56 οὐρανός is in the singular, [416] θεωρεῖν is replaced by ἰδεῖν, "opened" [417] is left out and there is reference to the δόξα θεοῦ as well as to Jesus, the Son of Man, standing on the right hand of God, importance thus being attached to God as well as to the Son of Man, one may assume that Luke found v. 56 in the tradition and introduced it in his own words in v. 55. This fits in with the fact that Luke does not seem to use the title Son of Man independently (→ 450, 21 ff.; n. 401) and perhaps it also shows that the concept was no longer a living one, or stood in need of explanation in the form in which it occurs here, for it is odd that the Son of Man stands rather than sits at God's right hand.

Does this simply mean that He was at God's right hand, for which one might use either καθῆσθαι or ἑστάναι? [418] This runs contrary to the usual practice of quoting the very significant Ps. 110 with its καθῆσθαι. Did Jesus rise to welcome the martyr? [419] Or to confess him as a witness in the judgment? [420] Such explanations are natural enough, but they are not attested elsewhere in the contemporary world and they are in any case taken from the context rather than the saying itself. Does the Son of Man stand to minister before God like the angels in Da. 7? [421] This contradicts all we know about His activity in the last judgment. Has He stood up to enter on His Messianic office, and is the *parousia*, then, immediately at hand? [422] In the light of Luke's modification of imminent expectation and its transfer into the age of the Church, [423] one would rather expect the Son of Man to remain seated if this were the implication.

Do we have here an adaptation of the idea that God rises up to come forth from His dwelling-place in wrath on behalf of His children (Ass. Mos. 10:3) or to confront His enemies (Is. 14:22; Ps. 3:7; 7:6 etc.) or to accomplish salvation (Ps. 12:5)? Since more stress is obviously laid here on the significance of the Son of Man than on that of God, this conjecture is probably closer to the mark. But one might still ask whether there was a real tradition which expressed this by the divine predicate of "standing." Perhaps the Samaritan tradition fits the bill.

Possibly ἑστῶτα is an indication that a Samaritan predicate of God, not the Mes-

---

416 The sing. is Lucan, not the plur. (only Lk. 10:20; on Ac. 10:11 → n. 417), cf. Haench. Ag.14 on 7:55 f.; → V, 530, n. 270.

417 But cf. θεωρεῖ τὸν οὐρανὸν ἀνεῳγμένον in Peter's dream in Ac. 10:11, which is from another source, acc. to J. Jeremias, "Untersuchungen zum Quellenproblem d. Ag.," *Abba* (1966), 249 f. an interpolation into the Antioch source which also contains the Stephen story. θεωρέω is thus pre-Lucan, "opened" is said of heaven only where a source has it. Cf. also Tödt, 274-6.

418 Cf. E. Preuschen, *Die Apostelgeschichte, Hndbch NT*, 4 (1912), ad loc.

419 Jackson-Lake, I, 4, 84; Bengel on Ac. 7:55: *quasi obvium Stephano;* cf. 4 Macc. 5:37. So also C. K. Barrett, "Stephen and the Son of Man," *Festschr. E. Haenchen* (1964), 32-4.

420 C. F. D. Moule, "From Defendant to Judge and Deliverer. An Enquiry into the Use and Limitations of the Theme of Vindication in the NT," *Bulletin of the Stud. Novi Test. Societas*, 32 (1963), 47; Cullmann, 161 and 188; cf. Higgins, 145.

421 Haench. Ag.14 on 7:55; Tödt, 274 is more precise: Ps. 110:1 might be combined with Da. 7:13 as in Mk. 14:62.

422 H. P. Owen, "Stephen's Vision in Ac. 7:55-56," NTSt, 1 (1954/55), 224-6 thinks that here (after Jesus' death = ἔξοδος in Lk. 9:31, εἰσελθεῖν into His δόξα in 24:26, ἀναβαίνειν into heaven in Ac. 1:2, 11, 22; 2:34 and καθῆσθαι at God's right hand in Lk. 20:42; 22:69; Ac. 2:34) we have the fifth stage on the way from Jesus' death to His coming again. After He has risen and entered on His office there follows as the sixth and last stage the ἔρχεσθαι of Lk. 9:26; 12:36-38 etc. This sequence is constructed without regard to the sources of Lk.'s work.

423 E. Grässer, "Die Ag. in d. Forschung d. Gegenwart," ThR, NF, 26 (1960), 164, and against the *parousia* motif cf. also Tödt, 276.

siah, [424] is here transferred to the Son of Man, just as Simon Magus [425] and his supposed teacher Dositheos [426] applied it to themselves. Yet even though there might be other Samaritan traditions in Ac. 7, [427] it is still not clear why a Samaritan predicate should here replace the traditional one. [428] For this is what would have had to happen, since we have no knowledge of a complete Samaritan variation on Son of Man Messianology that might have gained access here. If Samaritan origin is to be established, [429] the meaning of the divine standing will have to be ascertained with greater exactitude than the present examples allow. [430] Only with reservations, then, can one venture the opinion that acc. to the tradition in Ac. 7 the Son of Man takes God's place by ushering in the end in judgment and salvation. It is also possible, however, that the reference is simply to the current Samaritan meaning of קים as "the one who stands upright," "the living," as distinct from the dead who cannot stand any more. [431]

2. Rev. 1:13; 14:14.

In these two visions (→ V, 188, 17 ff.; VI, 946, 33 ff.) Christ is introduced by a description based on Da. 7:13, His apocalyptic character being denoted by the ὅμοιος of this verse. In the revival of apocalyptic evidenced by Rev. Christ has made good His position. The traditional view of the Son of Man is augmented by other heterogeneous materials [432] and consequently changed much more than in the

[424] It occurs as קים in the Samaritan liturgy, cf. M. Heidenheim, *Die samarit. Liturgie. Bibliotheca Samaritana*, II (1888), XXXVII and A. E. Cowley, *The Samaritan Liturgy*, I (1909), 54, 15 (Marqah, 4th cent.).

[425] Hipp. Ref., VI, 17, 1 in triadic form. On the Samaritan background of the Simon and Dositheos tradition cf. G. Widengren, "The Ascension of the Apostle and the Heavenly Book," *Uppsala Univ. Årsskrift*, 1950, 7 (1950), 49.

[426] Ps. Clem. Recg., II, 8 f., 11; but the accounts need to be studied afresh, cf. T. Caldwell, "Dositheos Samaritanus," *Kairos*, 4 (1962), 105-117.

[427] Samaritan motifs may be suspected in the factual tradition which diverges from the Jewish view of salvation history and which is typical of medieval Samaritan chronicles, cf. J. Jeremias, *Heiligengräber in Jesu Umwelt* (1958), 37 f.: Acc. to Ac. 7:16 Abraham bought the grave at Shechem from the sons of Emmor and not Jacob, Gn. 33:19; Jos. 24:32. It is a local tradition in Shechem that all the 12 sons of Jacob were buried there. Also worth noting is the stress on Dt. 18:15 on the lips of Moses (Ac. 7:37), for Dt. 18:15-19 was the *locus classicus* for the Messianic expectation of the Samaritans, cf. A. Merx, "Der Messias oder Ta'eb d. Samaritaner," ZAW Beih., 17 (1909), 43.

[428] One might think of adoption of a symbolising of the resurrection or an immanent polemic against Samaritan prophets in which, already in the tradition and then in Luke with the adoption and retention of ἑστῶτα in v. 55, the ἑστώς predicate is a subject of debate. It is not mentioned in relation to Simon in Ac. 8, but this may be accidental.

[429] But cf. Cullmann, 167-9, 186-193 and M. Simon, *St. Stephen and the Hellenists in the Primitive Church* (1958), 67-74.

[430] Still unexplained is the connection between the Samaritan "the standing one" and the divine predicate ἑστώς in Philo Som., I, 246: ὄντως ἑστώς. Philo's own interpretation gives no trace of a possible older sense. He finds it embedded in Ex. 17:6: ὅδε ἐγὼ ἕστηκα πρὸ τοῦ σὲ ἐκεῖ ἐπὶ τῆς πέτρας ἐν Χωρήβ, Som., II, 221, more loosely I, 241, and takes it to mean "immutable" or "constant," so also Som., I, 250; Poster. C., 30. The constant One should direct the inconstant, Mut. Nom., 91, and make it stand, e.g. Abraham (Mut. Nom., 87), who at first does not stand but falls down before Him who does, 54 and 57 etc. ἑστώς can also be used of the *logos* in Leg. All., III, 32. G. Kretschmar, "Zur religionsgeschichtlichen Einordnung d. Gnosis," *Ev. Theol.*, 13 (1953), 359, n. 1 (with further evidence) thinks the origin of the term is pre-Gnostic and eventually Samaritan.

[431] Memar Marqah (ed. J. Macdonald, ZAW Beih., 84 [1963]), I, 17, 5, 7 f. etc. Macdonald ref. in II, 48, n. 7 and 244, n. 130 to the fact that the Chr. Son of Man might be understood by the Samaritans as אישה "man" or אישה דאלה "man of God" (for Moses).

[432] Cf. Loh. Apk., ad loc.; J. Behm, *Die Offenbarung d. Joh.*, NT Deutsch, 11⁷ (1956), and E. Lohse, *Die Offenbarung d. Joh.*, NT Deutsch, 11⁹ (1966), ad loc.; Fiebig, 125 f.

primitive Synoptic tradition → 441, 27 ff. In the vision the coming One is seen as the Lord who is already present. In keeping with this integration of Messianological statements is the fact that Son of Man sayings are transferred to the Son of God → 371, 1 ff.

3. Hb. 2:6.

In c. 1 and c. 2, thinking in terms of the eschatological exaltation of Christ, the author refers a series of OT passages, especially from the Ps. (2:7; 104:4; 45:6 f.; 102:26-28; 110:1; 8:4-6; 22:22), to Christ. The image of apocalyptic enthronement, which could easily make its way into the preaching of exaltation, and indeed apocalyptic imagery as a whole, could be restrained only by emphasis on the ruling power of Christ. The author proves this from Ps. 8. Originally a hymn in praise of the lofty position God has given man in creation, the Ps. now refers to the eschatological majesty of Christ, beneath whose feet God has set all things. The Messianic use of Ps. 8 in apocalyptic [433] is not enough to explain its application to Christ. This would be effected more easily by the referring of υἱὸς ἀνθρώπου in v. 4 to the Son of Man. From this one may also infer that Christ is not an angel comparable to apocalyptic powers, as many Jewish Christian groups obviously maintained. [434] Like the majesty saying, ἠλάττωσας αὐτόν and δόξῃ καὶ τιμῇ ἐστεφάνωσας αὐτόν (v. 6) especially are to be understood in terms of the Christ of whom the community realised that He was the Son of Man and that He had suffered, Hb. 2:9 f. → 42, 11 ff.; → V, 852, n. 64. What was in the OT a saying about the majesty of creaturely man, a majesty limited by God's power as Creator, now becomes a saying about the majesty which is paradoxically ascribed to one who is lowly.

III. John's Gospel.

The twelve Son of Man sayings in Jn. [435] (→ n. 462) range from a faithful reproduction of the apocalyptic sense to a degree of reinterpretation which is almost reconstruction. Although Son of Man Christology is less prominent than other Christologies in Jn., its extensive relationship with them is also attested.

1. In the discourse of Jesus in 5:17-30, which follows a disputation with the Jews in 9b-16 and has as its theme the equality of the Father and the Son, vv. 27-29 constitute a unity. [436] The motifs of Da. 7:13 f. are taken up in v. 27: [437] "And (he)

[433] Not in the Rabb., cf. Rgg. Hb., ad loc.
[434] This is perhaps the element of truth in M. Werner, Die Entstehung d. chr. Dogmas² (1953), 302-321, while the NT saying is to be understood in the sense of W. Michaelis, Zur Engelchristologie im Urchristentum (1942), 121-8.
[435] Cf. R. Schnackenburg, "Der Menschensohn im Joh.-Ev.," NTSt, 11 (1964/65), 125-9, who also refutes the idea that the Son of Man concept had a stronger theological influence on the explicit logia in Jn. → 374, 1 ff. Cf. also E. M. Sidebottom, The Christ of the Fourth Gospel (1961), 84-88 and C. H. Dodd, The Interpretation of the Fourth Gospel (1953), 241-9.
[436] Their position in the discourse is disputed: vv. 19-23 speak of the Son in the 3rd pers., v. 24 in the 1st, v. 25 f. again of the Son (not the Son of Man) in the 3rd, v. 30 again in I style. But changes of person are typical of revelation discourses, so literary analysis is not absolutely necessary, cf. Mt. 11:27 and Dibelius, 284, n. 1 On the par. "Son of God" in v. 25 → 385, n. 371.
[437] There is agreement even to the indefinite ἀνθρώπου, cf. Schulz, 111, n. 2. One should not follow H. H. Wendt, Das Joh.-Ev. (1900), 121 f. and Bultmann J., ad loc. in excising this saying as an addition, since the υἱός without art. would not be Johannine, cf. 3:16, 17, 35, 36; 5:19-23, 26; 6:40 and van Hartingsveld, 28-30.

hath given him authority to execute judgment also, because he is the Son of man."
In isolation one might take this wholly in the future sense of Jewish apocalyptic.
But in the context of what precedes (v. 21 f.), [438] where the resurrection of the dead
to judgment is to be interpreted directly by making alive in a more spiritual sense,
the κρίσιν ποιέω [439] may be construed as the reaching of a judicial decision which
comes about with the present appearing of Jesus. [440] The introduction of the themes
of Da. 7:13 f. is not to be regarded, then, as a traditional apocalyptic reaction. [441]
The meaning of υἱὸς τοῦ ἀνθρώπου here is more in the direction of that of Son
in other places → 385, 4 ff.

The construction of c. 9 is parallel to that of c. 5, a miracle of healing being again
followed by controversy with the Jews and then by a discourse. In the conversation
with the man born blind whom the Pharisees have examined and rejected Jesus asks
him whether he believes in the Son of Man, v. 35. [442] Since the man has already confessed Jesus to be a prophet (v. 17) and one authorised by God (v. 33), it is obvious
that a new dignity is the goal of confession here [443] and that the man who has been
cured is not familiar with this, as his question καὶ τίς ἐστιν shows. Jesus' answer:
"Thou hast both seen him, and it is he that talketh with thee" (v. 37), shows that
the point of the question was: "Dost thou believe in me as the Son of man?" The
Evangelist thus values the title as a Messianic one and he sets it in the service of
his realised eschatology here. [444]

The two references in the bread discourse (6:27 → I, 644, 12 ff.) and the
eucharistic discourse (6:53) diverge even more plainly from their origin in Jewish
apocalyptic. The former discourse is about the bread of life which the Father will
give, which comes down from heaven (v. 32 f.), and which is identical with Jesus,
v. 35: ἐγώ εἰμι ὁ ἄρτος τῆς ζωῆς; in v. 27 the Son of Man / Revealer will Himself
give the bread. The saying in v. 53 is distinguished from its context both by the
solemnly formulated introduction and also by the genitive in ἐὰν μὴ φάγητε τὴν
σάρκα τοῦ υἱοῦ τοῦ ἀνθρώπου καὶ πίητε αὐτοῦ τὸ αἷμα. [445] The tradition of v. 53
represents already the stage [446] at which the Son of Man title replaced an "I" or

---

[438] van Hartingsveld, 30-32.

[439] This need not be regarded as a quotation.

[440] So also v. 24 εἰς κρίσιν ἔρχεσθαι, cf. Bau. J., ad loc. → II, 671, 20 ff.; III, 941, 22 ff.
Whether the κρίσις concept of Jn. occasions the sudden change from υἱός to υἱὸς ἀνθρώπου
one cannot say. At any rate this is not a secondary interpolation, since a primitive Chr. interpretation of Son of Man Messianology must itself have played some part in shaping the
Johannine concept.

[441] The question is open at v. 28 f., but we need not try to decide it here. Bultmann J.,
ad loc. pleads for assimilation to popular eschatology, Schulz, 113-5 and van Hartingsveld,
30-32 see a close connection with v. 27. Plain enough are the use of Da. 12:2 in Jn. 5:28 f.
and the difference in content from v. 24 f.: all who are in the graves will rise up to judgment
— for those who hear now, the hour of judgment has come already.

[442] On πιστεύω εἰς → VI, 222, 28 ff.

[443] Hence one should not take v. 35 as a statement rather than a question, as Schl. J., ad
loc. does.

[444] Reinterpretation of judgment as present has nothing whatever to do with Gnosticism
→ 415, 34 ff.

[445] 6:51c-58 are ascribed to an ecclesiastical redactor by Bultmann J., ad loc.; E. Schweizer,
"Ego-eimi," FRL, NF, 38² (1965), 151-3; J. Jeremias, "Joh. Literaturkritik," ThBl, 20 (1941),
43-6; the literary unity of the bread and eucharistic discourses is defended by E. Ruckstuhl,
Die literarische Einheit d. Joh.-Ev. (1951), 249, 264, 266 etc.; E. Schweizer, "Das joh. Zeugnis
v. Herrenmahl," Neotestamentica (1963), 371-396; J. Jeremias, "Joh. 6:51c-58 — redaktionell?"
ZNW, 44 (1952/53), 256 f.

[446] Acc. to Jeremias Abendmahlsworte, 101 f. Jn. 6:51c is an independent version of Jesus'
saying about the bread at the institution of the Lord's Supper.

"mine," → 443, 15 ff. Implicit already in the act of interpretative distribution is the Messianic dignity of Him whose body believers eat in the eucharistic bread and whose blood they drink in the eucharistic cup, and this is expressed by a title of dignity. The same applies in v. 27 (→ VII, 949, 8 ff.), where there is an obvious forward reference to the end of the discourse about the living bread. Already v. 27b presupposes the interpretation of the eucharistic bread as bread of life and the understanding of its Giver as the (suffering?) Son of Man.

But why and in what sense is the title Son of Man retained in the new interpretation? The arguments of the Jews which are dealt with in the discourses are docetic (v. 52) and in opposition to them it is maintained that there is real consuming of Jesus' flesh and blood in the Lord's Supper → III, 588, 12 ff.; VIII, 236, 18 ff. Thus the point of the Son of Man title is that the Redeemer has not assumed a sham body but has become true man. Similarly in v. 27c Jesus' endowment with the Spirit in baptism, [447] which is shown by the aorist to be a once-for-all and legally valid act, has taken on importance in the sense that τοῦτον here does not refer to a heavenly being but to a real man commissioned by God. In the final stage of interpretation the meaning of the Son of Man title is thus as radically altered as, e.g., in Ign. Eph., 7, 2; 20, 2. [448]

2. All the other Son of Man sayings are about the descent and the ascent, exaltation and glorification of the Son of Man. That this is as far from the original sense as the understanding in 5:27; 9:35; 6:27, 53 may be seen best from 3:13 ff. (→ II, 559, 30 ff.; V, 526, 9 ff.), where Son of Man occurs twice. This is in Jesus' answer to Nicodemus, 3:10-21. The Son of Man sayings in v. 13 and v. 14 are only loosely connected with one another and with what precedes and might well be taken as independent logia. Like 12:24b (→ 467, 20 ff.), v. 14b comes from developed (Palestinian) tradition, though one need not try to relate it to a specific Aramaic dialect. [449] Since according to 12:32 f. the Evangelist understands ὑψόω not only with reference to the ascension as in Ac. 2:33; 5:31; Phil. 2:9 but also with reference to the crucifixion, we have here a counterpart to the Synoptic passion predictions. It is now linked to the motif of the uplifted serpent (cf. Nu. 21:8), [450] and this must be pre-Johannine, Thus the content of the ancient passion prediction is concentrated on one aspect of the crucifixion, namely, the spatial lifting up on high. In this way the sense of זקף gradually becomes "to exalt" and the Greek rendering ὑψόω hastens this process. Since the reference is to the Son of Man, v. 14 presupposes already the exaltation of the earthly Jesus as Son of Man and looks back to it as a completed act of enthronement. The combining of Son of Man and exaltation is thus a declara-

---

[447] σφραγίζω (→ VII, 949, 8 ff.) belongs to the vocabulary of baptism, cf. Bau. J., ad loc. and Pr.-B., s.v.

[448] Cf. E. M. Sidebottom, "The Son of Man in the Fourth Gospel," Exp. T., 68 (1956/57), 231-5, 280-3. On the question of agreement with Ign. Eph., 7, 2; 20, 2 cf. H. Schlier, "Untersuchungen z. den Ignatiusbr.," ZNW Beih., 8 (1929), 149 f., 168 f.; H. W. Bartsch, "Gnostisches Gut u. Gemeindetradition bei Ign. v. Antiochien," BFTh, 2, 44 (1940), 67-9; C. Maurer, "Ignatius v. Antiochien u. d. Joh.-Ev.," AbhThANT, 18 (1949), 43 and 100.

[449] Iber, 150 f., quoting Schl. J. on 3:14, Schulthess and Torrey, tries to establish the ancient conjecture that the basis of ὑψωθῆναι is the ethpe'el of an Aram. זקף which can also mean "to be lifted up on the cross," "to be crucified."

[450] For the Chr. understanding of this motif elsewhere cf. Barn., 12, 5-7; Just. Apol., 60; Dial., 91, 4; 94, 1-5, 112, 1 f.

tion of Christian faith. The ground was at most prepared for this in apocalyptic [451] and it came to fruition in the belief in the ascension → IV, 8, 1 ff.

The introduction of this tradition into the Hell. world-view adopted in Jn. and the analogy to the long-established ascension concepts of antiquity (→ I, 519, 20 ff.; → n. 458), in relation to which Jesus' ascension must have seemed to be a special instance, necessarily meant a reinterpretation of exaltation as ascent into a transcendent world above. This sense, which reaches its full development in Gnosticism, may be detected already in v. 14, which from the standpoint of the tradition looks back to the exaltation → 466, 34 ff. One can then see almost directly in v. 13 how an ascension idea would necessarily arise out of it. This converges with existing notions of descent, the closest of which to the circle of Jn.'s Gospel is the myth of the descent of wisdom to men (Eth. En. 42).

Witness to the same firm connection between Son of Man and ὑψωθῆναι may also be found in 8:28 and 12:34. In 8:28 the Evangelist [452] has Jesus warn the Jews, and it is evident that "when ye have lifted up the Son of man" has here the secondary sense of "when ye have crucified." The threat that the judicial office of the Son of Man will come into effect only with His exaltation, and this by the Father's commission, is wholly within the traditional tension of the "already" and the "not yet" of the last judgment. The only new thing is that Jesus is already lifted up as the Son of Man and will not become the Son of Man only after His exaltation. In 12:34 the classical Son of Man expectation of Jewish apocalyptic finds recognition, for in spite of the title Χριστός in the question one is forced to say that the Jews share this here. The Evangelist has Jesus oppose to it the new picture of the Son of Man found already in 3:14 f. and 8:28. There are also echoes of 3:13 in 6:62, which is in a new section after the discourse on the bread of heaven (concluded in v. 59). According to the words of Jesus the offence His disciples took at the bread discourse will be exceeded by a new one, namely, at the ascension of the Son of Man into heaven, [453] which will leave the disciples in sorrow and confusion. [454] The relating of the Son of Man title to Jesus is so firm here that it is retained even in an exaltation saying. In a way rather different from that of 3:13 the descent or pre-existence statement [455] arises out of a linking of the Son of Man as a heavenly being, known

---

[451] In apocal. there is no instance of the Son of Man Himself being exalted; He appears and is manifested in heaven. Enoch is exalted to be Son of Man in Eth. En. 70 f. (→ 426, 15 ff.) but this shows precisely that he is not originally identical with the Son of Man (on the historical hypothesis that the primal man stands behind Enoch as well as the Son of Man → 427, 2 f.) and that the combining of the exaltation idea with the Son of Man theme is secondary. The same applies to the idea of a descent in Jewish mysticism and Gnosticism, → 474, 26 ff. On the material priority of ascent over descent in Jn., and not *vice versa* as in the Gnostic myth, cf. E. M. Sidebottom, "The Ascent and the Descent of the Son of Man in the Gospel of St. John," *Anglican Theol. Review*, 39 (1957), 115-122.

[452] Or his tradition; Bultmann J., *ad loc.* thinks 8:21-29 is an older independent section, G. Bornkamm, "Der Paraklet im J.," *Festschr. R. Bultmann* (1949), 34 f. notes a connection with the Paraclete sayings in the Parting Discourses.

[453] ὅπου ἦν τὸ πρότερον does not mean (so Bultmann J. on 6:62) lifting up on the cross.

[454] This does not mean, then, that after the sending of the Spirit the cross was no longer a scandal as suggested by Odeberg Fourth Gospel, 268 f., Schl. J., *ad loc.* and H. Strathmann, *Das Ev. nach Joh., NT Deutsch,* 4¹⁰ (1963), *ad loc.* in the light of v. 63.

[455] The ref. here is to pre-existence in relation to the life of Jesus, not the creation of the world.

as such from the apocalyptic tradition, to Jesus as the earthly Son of Man, known as such from the Synoptic tradition.

Only in 12:23 and 13:31 f. does the idea of glorification occur in the Son of Man tradition. When Jesus in His reply to Andrew and Philip says: "The hour is come, that the Son of man should be glorified" (12:23 → II, 249, 19 ff.), this echoes the Jewish tradition that God glorifies the Son of Man by solemnly enthroning Him in heaven. [456] But the idea that the hour of glorifying has come and its explanation in terms of the metaphor of the corn of wheat which dies (v. 24 → III, 811, 10 ff.) gives to the glorification the further significance of suffering. [457] If from the standpoint of the tradition the saying is thus on the same level as the Synoptic passion predictions, the ἐλήλυθεν relates it to Mk. 14:41. There is a similar but even more developed interpretation of the tradition in the double saying in 13:31 f. which introduces the Parting Discourses and which falls rhythmically into five members. A first point of interpretation is that the first three members offer the aorist ἐδοξάσθη. This makes sense only if the meaning of glorification as suffering, exaltation and enthronement finds its centre in the self-actualising epiphany of the Son of Man / Revealer that reaches its climax in relation to the parting, which will lead by suffering and death to exaltation and enthronement. [458] The future δοξάσει in the fourth and fifth members has this future reference. A second point of interpretation is that in the mutual relation of God and Son of Man (God glorifies Himself through Him and He glorifies God), in historical terms the relation of the εἰκών to God is adopted rather than that of the judging Son of Man to God. This fits in with the tendency, noted already at 5:27 (→ 465, 6 ff.), to assimilate the meaning of the Son of Man to the more general concept of Son in John's Gospel. [459]

Most of the nuances mentioned thus far may be caught in the first Son of Man saying in the Gospel at 1:51, which concludes the story of the call of Nathanael. The many traditions adopted and developed here entail a development in Son of Man Christology whose wealth of meaning is indicated programmatically at the very beginning of the Gospel, and this as the conclusion of a whole series of christologically relevant titles or designations. [460] The saying has been attached secondarily to the Nathanael story. [461] Possibly the underlying tradition was Jesus' saying before the supreme council in Mk. 14:62 and par. → 453, 19 ff. But with the omission of the "coming" the ὄψεσθε is made into an intimation of visionary seeing

---

[456] Schulz, 119 with ref. to Eth. En. 51:3; 45:3; 55:4; 61:8; 62:2, 5; 69:27, 29; 71:7.

[457] Cf. Cullmann, 191; → II, 253, 11 ff.

[458] But cf. Schulz, 122. On the polemic against other exaltation concepts implied in lifting up on the cross cf. G. Bertram, "Der religionsgeschichtliche Hintergrund des Begriffs d. 'Erhöhung' in d. LXX," ZAW, 86 (1956), 57-71; also Art. "Erhöhung," RAC, 6 (1966), 37 f.

[459] Hence one should not excise τοῦ ἀνθρώπου at 13:31, as sometimes suggested.

[460] Cf. H. Windisch, "Angelophanien um den Menschensohn auf Erden. Ein Komm. zu Joh. 1:51," ZNW, 30 (1931), 217 f.: Lamb of God in v. 29, 36, the One who baptises with the Holy Ghost in v. 33, Rabbi in v. 38, Messiah or Christ in v. 41, the One proclaimed in the Law and the Prophets in v. 45, Son of God in v. 49 and King of Israel in v. 49.

[461] The link is ὄψῃ-ὄψεσθε. The change from the sing. to the plur. is the bridge between the story and the logion. An editorial καὶ λέγει αὐτῷ was added even though Jesus was already speaking, so that we now have two competing introductions. Cf. also the double ἀμήν which serves to quote adopted tradition, W. Oehler, Zum Missionscharakter d. Joh.-Ev. (1941), 99, cf. Jn. 13:21 with Mk. 14:18; λέγω ὑμῖν also belongs to the original saying in 1:51. The differences are sharper than those between 3:11 and 3:12, so that Michaelis' (561-563) contesting of the original autonomy of 1:51 is not entirely convincing. Perhaps the Evangelist aimed to advance the train of thought in vv. 47-51 by appending traditions.

whose object is in time rather than a reference to the manifestation of eschatological events. [462] This anticipation of future revelation, which is not a de-eschatologising but a transposition into proleptic epiphany, corresponds in many ways to the baptism story in Mk. 1:10 f. It makes it possible for the apocalyptic tradition which Jesus referred to Himself (→ 441, 2 f.) to be expounded in terms of a different one. We do not refer to the baptism story, [463] nor to later Jewish myths about the stone of Bethel (→ V, 530, 3 ff.), [464] nor to Gnostic teaching about the relation of an earthly person to the heavenly prototype, [465] but to the simple story of Jacob at Bethel which underlies the last two interpretations mentioned. [466] Adducing Gn. 28:12, one cannot say for certain whether the angels serve the Son of Man living on earth or the Son of Man enthroned in opened heaven. [467] Since in Gn. 28:12 the ascent and descent of the angels relates to God rather than Jacob, who is just a spectator, the heavenly apocalyptic Son of Man might have been put in God's place here. But in John's Gospel what is true of Him is true of the earthly Son of Man too, and the verse can easily be taken to refer to the unbroken fellowship which there is between Jesus and the Father → I, 84, 11 ff.; 521, 12 ff. [468] Probably the logion intentionally has many meanings and bears testimony to the fellowship of both the heavenly and the earthly Son of Man with the Father, the ministry of angels to the Son of Man both in heaven and on earth, the judicial mandate of the Son of Man in the *eschaton*, and His present and future epiphany. [469]

---

[462] Cf. τὸν οὐρανὸν ἀνεῳγότα with τοὺς οὐρανοὺς διηνοιγμένους in Ac. 7:56. Jeremias Älteste Schicht, 163 shows that Jn. 1:51 is the only Son of Man saying in Jn. to go back to older tradition Mk. 14:62 and par., whereas all the others have another version in Jn. itself without the title, 3:13 in 20:17, cf. 6:38 and 6:42; 3:14 in 12:32; 5:27 in 5:22; 6:27 in 6:51; 6:53 in 6:54; 6:62 in 20:17; 8:28 in 12:32; 9:35 in 3:36; 12:23 in 11:4; 12:34 in 12:32 or 5:12, cf. 8:25; 13:31 in 11:4, a sign of community influence.

[463] So Michaelis, 571 f.: The unique event of baptism is promised as a lasting one, angels come from the Synoptic temptation story, ascending and descending is a way of denoting their ministering traffic between God and Jesus, and one need not seek further for its origin.

[464] J. Jeremias, "Die Berufung d. Nathanael," *Angelos*, 3 (1930), 2-5; L. Goppelt, "Typos," BFTh, II, 43 (1966 impr.), 224. The stone of Bethel, the sacred stone which God created before the world and from which He has extended it, the place of His presence on earth above which is also the door to heaven, does not figure in the story and in view of the Son of Man title it is unlikely that Jesus is to be regarded as a symbol of this kind for the dwelling of God and gate of heaven.

[465] Odeberg Fourth Gospel, 33-40: In Gn. r., 68, 18 the בו of Gn. 28:12 is related to Jacob, not the ladder; in the appended Is. 49:3 the "thou" is taken to signify "thine image engraved on high," so that the ascending and descending angels symbolise the link between the earthly Jacob and his heavenly image. The Son of Man who replaces him is thus to be understood inclusively, i.e., He includes believers who are adopted into unity with the Father through Jesus. But one should not ignore the apocal. background of the v. The Rabb. exegesis quoted is late and in the earlier LXX בו relates to the ladder. Furthermore the Evangelist, for whom the Son became flesh and did not leave an image in heaven, could not have held such a view. Windisch, *op. cit.* (→ n. 460), 221. Historical objections → 415, 1 ff.

[466] Schulz, 98-103.

[467] So G. Quispel, "Nathanael u. der Menschensohn," ZNW, 47 (1956), 281-3.

[468] So Bultmann J., *ad loc.*

[469] As in Jn. 4:12 there may also be a hint that Jesus is greater than Jacob; it would seem from Ps.-Philo Antiquitates Bibl., 21, 4 (ed. G. Kisch [1949], though this ref. only to a *vir* in respect of whom Jacob says: *non deficiet princeps ex Juda, neque dux de femoribus eius*) that some circles awaited Jacob as others did Elijah. But other associations such as Son of Man / vine Jn. 15, vine / Adam / Son of Man Ps. 80:15 f., vine / Israel / Jacob (Dodd, *op. cit.* [→ n. 435], 245 f.), Jacob / Logos / Son of Man (cf. Philo Conf. Ling., 146-8 on the Logos) are unlikely.

3. Possibly the use of the Son of Man concept is to be seen in analogy to that of the Logos concept in the Prologue, for whose insertion before the Gospel there are no inner reasons. If the Gospel is not too far removed from Aramaic usage, there is perhaps still a sense of the strict meaning of ὁ υἱὸς τοῦ ἀνθρώπου as "man," and we sometimes find this in a new connection → 466, 12 f. In virtue of the actualisation of His work, the heavenly "Man" approximates to the figure interchangeable with the *logos* in, e.g., the Philonic tradition → 411, 9 ff. What Jesus says about Himself as Son of Man showed the Evangelist that the Man had now come down or had been sent down and had become the Redeemer, and that in a different way as compared with earlier views the Logos, Nous, or Anthropos could dwell here below among men. If it could be said of the Anthropos that He came down, the corresponding statement about the Logos could not be: "He became ἄνθρωπος or σῶμα," for this would be tautology. Nor would it do to say: "The Logos came down," as in the case of Man, for this would leave open the most varied possibilities from inward psychological reality to an outward and even docetic figure. The only logical and unequivocal formulation was one which would have been quite impossible and non-sensical from a pre-chr. standpt., namely: "The Logos became flesh." In this central affirmation of the Prologue, which means the same as "the (Son of) Man came down," we find a bold consistency, which does not fight shy of paradox, in developing ideas which are now transcended under the impress of the Christ event; [470] for this reason one will seek in vain a religious par. to this affirmation. [471] Both the incarnation of the Logos and the earthly walk of the Son of Man express a new fact by which the redemption or rejection of man is decided.

IV. Reformulation as the Pneumatic, Heavenly, Macrocosmic Man.

1. Christ as the Second Adam → I, 141, 13 ff.

The hypotheses that in Paul's Adam/Christ typology Christ plays the role of an eschatological Adam, Primal Man, or other Redeemer figure raise just as serious difficulties as the view that a genuinely christological understanding of Adam comes to expression here. In the present context we can only assemble the arguments for the second possibility without coming out clearly for this view.

Linguistically it is possible that ἄνθρωπος in 1 C. 15:21, 47; R. 5:15 has the same sense as ὁ υἱὸς τοῦ ἀνθρώπου, as may be seen from the rendering of ὁ υἱὸς τοῦ ἀνθρώπου in Mk. 10:45 by ἄνθρωπος in 1 Tm. 2:5. [472]

---

[470] The difference as compared with earlier views is that the Logos is now met in the body and not just in spirit and that the heavenly Man no longer embraces the whole world with His physical counterparts, earthly men, and mediates *soteria* to them thereby, but that for each earthly man He becomes one man among others, takes their sin to Himself and shares their death. This is more and other than the historicising of a mythological event, cf. Dodd, 271-285.

[471] The ancient Iranian Ameša Spentas adduced by Bau. J., 9 are in many ways comparable to Philonic views of spirit in their middle position between God/heaven and man/earth. But their personification, which is not always unambivalent, is not incarnation. The Indian Avatāras are "descents" in which the gods do not walk in the flesh and which one is accustomed to call incarnations only under the influence of Chr. theology, cf. V. Moeller, "Die Mythologie d. vedischen Religion u. des Hinduismus," *Wörterb. d. Mythologie*, 3, Lfrg. 8 (1966), 44 f.

[472] In contrast ἄνθρωπος in Phil. 2:7 is doubtful. On the possibility that a developed Son of Man christology lies behind Phil. 2:6-11 cf. Cullmann, 178-186; A. Vögtle, "Der Menschensohn u. die paul. Christologie," *Studiorum Paulinorum Congressus Internat. Catholicus*, 1961 (1963), 212-4; J. Héring, "Die bibl. Grundlage d. chr. Humanismus;" AbhThANT, 7 (1946), 29-35. But the arguments in favour of this can be presented only within a broader discussion than the present art. allows, since the kind of starting-pt. offered by the Adam typology is

a. 1 C. 15:21, 27 f., 45-49.

The originally non-messianic Ps. 8 (v. 5 LXX: "What is ἄνθρωπος that thou art mindful of him? and the υἱὸς ἀνθρώπου that thou regardest him?... v. 7b: thou hast put all things under his feet") is used christologically for the first time in the Chr. tradition at 1 C. 15:27. The ὁ υἱὸς τοῦ ἀνθρώπου probably led to this. [473] The transition which it made possible to a term for the original sense of "man" converges with the qen. Pauline view that the Messiah is the Son of God become man. This man, who in 1 C. 15 initiates the resurrection of the dead (v. 23), is in v. 21 contrasted with the ἄνθρωπος by whom death comes. So long as we have no sure evidence of an existing schema of the first and second Adam it is simpler to assume that the antitype: ἐπειδὴ γὰρ δι' ἀνθρώπου θάνατος, καὶ δι' ἀνθρώπου ἀνάστασις νεκρῶν, [474] is developed for the first time in v. 21 rather than that it follows a given schema. [475]

Yet this typology is not developed homogeneously in vv. 45-49. Instead we find it combined with an older view. The point is the correspondence between two essentially different Adam-Anthropoi, a pneumatic-heavenly and a psychical-earthly, [476] the former being the macrocosmic, upper and first in the heavenly hierarchy (→ VI, 866, n. 3) and the latter the microcosmic, lower and second. Upper/first and lower/second are not actually found in these combinations. They are modern terms. First and second express an ontic, vertical sequence rather than a temporal and horizontal. [477]

With which of the two was Christ equated? Obviously with the pneumatic-heavenly. There are possibly three reasons for this: 1. The content of the whole of c. 15, in which Christ is the author of life, thus assuming the function of the πνεῦμα in pre-Chr. tradition; 2. Christ as the Exalted achieves the same quality as the heavenly Adam already had, cf. ὁ ἐπουράνιος in v. 48; 3. Christ as the apocal. Son of Man to whose coming again allusion is made in the futurist statements of c. 15 is also a heavenly figure, cf. ἐξ οὐρανοῦ in v. 47. The qualification "heavenly," which under 2. applies to the Kurios as the heavenly Ruler of present faith and under 3. applies to the Son of Man awaited from heaven, acquires herewith a metaphysical-cosmological significance [478] which could hardly be avoided in view of the basic ideas of the Corinthians. But this change is held within the limits set by the transforming of Son of Man christology into Adam/Anthropos soteriology.

The "first/second" hierarchy, however, does not remain within these limits, for it was robbed of all point by the future sense which the heavenly quality of the upper Adam

not available here. G. Friedrich, "Ein Tauflied hell. Judenchristen," ThZ, 21 (1965), 514 f. suggests with some cogency that 1 Th. 1:9 f. spoke originally of the Son of Man. When the song was taken over from the Jewish Chr. circles in which the sayings of the Logia source were collected, τὸν υἱὸν τοῦ ἀνθρώπου, which Gentile Christians would not understand, was replaced by τὸν υἱὸν αὐτοῦ → 370, 21 ff. On the possible influence of Son of Man images in Gl. 1:16 → 383, 3 f.

[473] Vögtle, op. cit., 206, 217. On the abs. ὁ υἱός in v. 28 → 371, n. 265.

[474] From the standpt. of the tradition it is thus on the same level as other Paul. typologies or, e.g., Eve/Mary, cf. W. Staerk, "Eva-Maria," ZNW, 33 (1934), 97-104 and Brandenburger, 241. Cf. also → I, 141, 14 ff. and Brandenburger, 239 f. on Mk. 1:12 f.

[475] Brandenburger, 72 concludes from ζωοποιηθήσονται in v. 22b that the Corinthians were already familiar with a correspondence including ζωή. If this is true, it can have arisen only out of a misunderstanding of the preaching of Christ.

[476] Brandenburger, 74 with n. 2. Acc. to 244 on 1 C. 15:22 the macrocosmic and not the Gnostic anthropos category is expressed in the interrelationship of εἷς ἄνθρωπος and πάντες ἄνθρωποι.

[477] Cf. Philo Op. Mund., 69-76, 136-140, though the man first created in Gn. 1 is κατὰ τὴν εἰκόνα γεγονώς etc. and the man of Gn. 2 is ὁ πρῶτος ἄνθρωπος. Here later creation denotes also a lower value which remains with the higher, cf. Leg. All., I, 31, 42, 53, 55.

[478] Cf. C. Colpe, "Zur Leib-Christi-Vorstellung im Eph.," Festschr. J. Jeremias, ZNW Beih., 26 (1960), 183.

acquired by identification with the returning Son of Man. This order could not be implicitly reinterpreted but had to be explicitly restructured, the ontic sequence becoming also a temporal one. Thus Paul, from the vantage point of the ἔσχατος Ἀδάμ of v. 45 or the δεύτερος ἄνθρωπος of v. 47, twice puts a πρῶτος before the ἄνθρωπος Adam of Gn. 2:7 who as ψυχὴ (not πνεῦμα) ζῶσα and ἐκ γῆς χοϊκός was truly the second in terms of the basic understanding. In so doing he expressly establishes a new sequence, polemically affirming that "nevertheless the psychic, not the pneumatic, is first, and only then does the pneumatic come." Christ, who as the Son of Man is the upper, pneumatic, heavenly, redeeming Adam/Anthropos, [479] still remains the last, the coming One → VI, 419, 16 ff.

b. R. 5:12-21 → 252, 6 ff.

In the full contrast between Adam and Christ in R. 5 Christ is (ὁ) εἷς ἄνθρωπος Ἰησοῦς Χριστός the first time in v. 15a, then (ὁ) εἷς in v. 17b, 18b, 19b, and Ἰησοῦς Χριστός in v. 21b. The term ἄνθρωπος is really superfluous here, since Jesus Christ is clearly enough denoted by His name, and the references to Adam, who is εἷς ἄνθρωπος only in v. 12 and 19a, and εἷς elsewhere in v. 15b, 16a b, 17a (twice) and 18a, does not absolutely demand it. [480] It is possible that there is an echo of the Gk. Son of Man title in v. 15c. This does not explain the contrasting of Christ and Adam, which would have been typologically possible even without the title, but it does at least make it easier. Again, it has no relevance to the Christology of the section, which rests on other presuppositions than apocal. Son of Man Messianology. [481] It simply shows that the term man can be reinterpreted in such a way that it takes on prototypical significance: Christ, the prototype of the new humanity, thus becomes the antitype of Adam. For this development from an apocal. to an eschatological-prototypical Man Christ fewer hypothetical steps are needed than for a development from the Gnostic Redeemer, who as the original macrocosm can have other designations as well as man (→ 414, 9 ff.), to εἷς ἄνθρωπος Ἰησοῦς Χριστός. [482] But there is no sign here that a view is presupposed such as that which may be deduced from 1 C. 15:45-49. [483] There is much to favour the view that from the standpt. of the tradition Adam-Christ typology belongs to the same stage as 1 C. 15 and is thus the creation of Paul, and that the term man — not the new thing behind it — is used with this only incidentally.

2. Christ as Eikon and Soma.

Finally the interpretation of the Son of Man Christ as the heavenly ἄνθρωπος might well have made it possible to equate Him with the equivalent of ἄνθρωπος, namely εἰκών (→ II, 395, 25 ff.), so that Christ now becomes the εἰκών τοῦ θεοῦ, 2 C. 4:4;

[479] Brandenburger, 156.
[480] For a different interpretation cf. Brandenburger, 69, n. 6. We follow in part A. Vögtle, "Die Adam-Christus-Typologie u. d. 'Menschensohn,'" Trierer Theol. Zschr., 60 (1951), 309-328 and M. Black, "The Pauline Doctrine of the Second Adam," Scottish Journ. of Theol., 7 (1954), 170-179.
[481] Brandenburger, 158-266.
[482] The "Gnostic ideas which are partly in the background" (Brandenburger, 227) or the "Adam-Anthropos ideas which figure expressly in 1 C. 15:21 f., 45 ff. and from which ... decisive light is shed on R. 5:12-21" (Brandenburger, 236), may be called here only "dualistic ideas concerning the origin of sin."
[483] Hence it is almost an argument from silence when Brandenburger, 70 says that "the basic idea to be presupposed is more fully fused with Pauline thinking in R. 5:12 ff. than in 1 C. 15."

Col. 1:15. [484] Hence Christ becomes pre-existent in exactly the same way as the λόγος (→ IV, 130, 11 ff.), though the stress is on the fact that He represents, i.e., reveals God as His image, just as God speaks in Him as λόγος.

This equation also has a cosmological aspect. In the hymn to Christ in Col. 1:15-20 Christ as εἰκών is the mediator of creation. Hence in Col. and even more so in Eph. He has a heavenly body of cosmic proportions. Here the equation carries with it the implications of the idea of the cosmic Anthropos, namely, that the universal Man fills the all and is also set above it as κεφαλή (→ III, 677, 18 ff.) or λόγος. The eschatological function of Christ as Redeemer of the cosmos as well possibly led to this deduction in His interpretation as man. [485]

D. The Son of Man in the Early Church.

I. The Continuation of the Apocalyptic Tradition in Jewish Christianity.

Acc. to the ὑπομνήματα of Hegesipp. [486] James, the Lord's brother, when asked by the scribes and Pharisees what the door of Jesus [487] is, answered with a version of the saying of Jesus before the supreme council in Mt. 26:64. The Son of Man title is used here in a repetition of the question. Conjugated verbs replace the part. of the quotations from the Ps. (→ 460, 10 f.): κάθηται without ὄψεσθε denotes the present dominion of the exalted Lord [488] and μέλλει ἔρχεσθαι His *parousia*. The element of eschatological judgment is thus retained [489] while the influence of a different soteriological sense on the use of the title may be seen in the fact that we have here the reply to a question about the way of salvation which Jesus has opened up. [490] Acc. to the legend (based on 1 C. 15:7) that James partook of the Last Supper and was the first witness of the resurrection [491] James vows that he will eat no more bread until he sees the Lord raised from the dead. In the words *Frater mi, comede panem tuum, quia resurrexit filius hominis a dormientibus* Christ releases him from the oath. The linking of the Son of Man title to the resurrection from the dead must be analogous here to Mk. 9:9 and par. (→ 445, 11 ff.; 454, 20 ff.). The Easter kerygma and Son of Man Christology are fused. The command of the Risen Lord to continue the table fellowship of earthly days is then added → I, 142, 4 ff.; → IV, 857, 8 ff.

The Palestinian Chr. Son of Man tradition still exerts an influence in the Ps.-Clem.

---

[484] F. Delitzsch, *Hebr. NT* (1883), uses צֶלֶם, which the LXX mostly transl. by εἰκών, at Col. 1:15. At Phil. 2:6, 7, however, he chooses the other word from Gn. 1:26, 27, transl. μορφὴ θεοῦ by דְּמוּת הָאֱלֹהִים and μορφὴ δούλου by דְּמוּת עֶבֶד. μορφή can thus denote both the divine glory and also the human lowliness of the Son of Man. At Is. 52:14 'A transl. מַרְאֵהוּ וְתֹאֲרוֹ by ὅρασις αὐτοῦ καὶ μορφὴ αὐτοῦ, but LXX has τὸ εἶδός σου καὶ ἡ δόξα σου. תֹּאַר means "beautiful, majestic appearance," and is used thus not only in Is. 52:14; 53:2 but also in the christologically important 1 S. 16:18 (David as type: ἀνὴρ ἀγαθὸς τῷ εἴδει) [G. Bertram].

[485] Cf. Colpe, *op. cit.*, 172-187.

[486] In Eus. Hist. Eccl., II, 23, 3-9.

[487] "Door of Jesus" is a metaphor for the way of salvation, cf. Ps. 118:20; Str.-B., I, 458 etc.; → III, 179, n. 80.

[488] Elucidated by the addition ἐν τῷ οὐρανῷ, which perhaps reflects a combination with the idea of the kingdom of God → 460, 15 ff.

[489] Cf. O. Cullmann, "Die neuentdeckten Qumran-Texte u. d. Judenchristentum d. Pseudoklementinen," *Vorträge u. Aufsätze 1925-1962* (1966), 241-259.

[490] Hence one can hardly say with E. Lohmeyer, *Galiläa u. Jerusalem* (1936), 68 f. that the older Son of Man concept lives on here in undiminished strength and purity, nor does either this passage or that in Eus. Hist. Eccl., III, 20, 4 (→ 485, n. 44) prove that it belongs originally to Galilee.

[491] Hier. De viris inlustribus, ed. W. Herding (1879), 2.

Hom. and Recg. and the Ker. Pt. [492] but it is remarkably transformed by the prophetology of these writings. The true Prophet of Judaism, who takes the form of the prophets sent to succeeding generations but who is always the same and finally comes to rest in or as Jesus (→ VI, 858, 2 ff.), [493] is called *filius hominis* in Recg., I, 60, 3; III, 61, 2 and υἱὸς ἀνθρώπου in Hom., 3, 22, 3, cf. also the indef. plur. υἱοὶ ἀνθρώπων in Hom., 2, 17, 2; 3, 26, 1. The def. sing. occurs only where Jesus (and He alone) is called the Son of Man. [494] In Recg., I, 60, 1-7 Jesus' claim to be the Messiah is contested on the basis of the Gospel tradition by a disciple of John and disputed by Simon the Canaanite with the help of His self-designation as *filius hominis*. Acc. to Mt. 11:11 John is *maior ... omnibus qui sunt filii mulierum; filius hominis* thus means "son of man." Defined thus, Jesus belongs to the more highly esteemed male prophecy of the Hom., while John is relegated to female prophecy. In the syzygy canon in Recg., III, 61, 2 the 7th syzygy consists of the *temptator* and the *filius hominis*. One may gather from this that the title of majesty is still used but only for the earthly Jesus, Christ (the 10th syzygy) being used with ref. to His eschatological function. In Hom., 3, 22, 1-3 the male/female scale is applied to Adam and his σύζυγος Eve. [495] As the first prophet of the truth, which is embodied in the male, while false prophecy, beginning with Eve, is female (3, 22 f. 27), Adam is sometimes defined by the same term and in the same sense as Jesus: ὡς υἱὸς ἀνθρώπου ἄρσην ὤν Adam proclaims what is essential for the coming aeon as the male aeon (ὡς ἄρσενι τῷ μέλλοντι αἰῶνι). The indef. plur. ref. to the whole series of sons of man, i.e., true prophets. Thus the Son of Man in Ker. Pt. is the prototype of humanity. [496] His first representation is the protoplast. [497] He has no macrocosmic dimension at all and hence should not be called the primal man. [498]

II. The Confirmation of the Reformulation (→ 470, 23 ff.) in Christian Gnosticism.

1. Sources.

In Gnostic and semi-Gnostic texts ὁ υἱὸς τοῦ ἀνθρώπου occurs sometimes along with other expressions denoting the macrocosmic primal man → 412, 18 ff. This gives us interesting insights into the Gnostic understanding of the Son of Man on the one side and the genesis of the Gnostic Redeemer doctrine on the other.

In the so-called Arab Monoimos the primal man is (ὁ) ἄνθρωπος, ὁ πρῶτος ἄνθρωπος or ὁ τέλειος ἄνθρωπος. [499] The second highest deity which emanated from the first and came into action at creation and in redemption is called ὁ υἱὸς τοῦ ἀνθρώπου, Hipp. Ref., VIII, 12; X, 17. Monoimos thus reached his doctrine of the Redeemer by adding Son of Man Christology to an Anthropos-Aeon speculation. [500]

---

[492] Cf. Iber, 17-25, though also H. J. Schoeps, *Urgemeinde, Judenchristentum, Gnosis,* (1956), 24; cf. G. Bornkamm, rev. H. J. Schoeps, *Theol. u. Gesch. d. Judenchristentums* (1949), also *Aus frühchr. Zeit* (1950), ZKG, 64 (1952/53), 196-204.

[493] Recg., II, 47, 2-4; Hom., 3, 20, 2.

[494] Iber, 19.

[495] Iber, 22, n. 49.

[496] Cf. Recg., I, 45, 2: *statuit ergo* (subj. God) *principem ... hominibus hominem, qui est Jesus Christus.* On the alternation of Son of Man and *homo* or *filius viri* cf. H. J. Schoeps, *Theol. u. Gesch. d. Judenchristentums* (1949), 81.

[497] Cf. Recg., I, 47, 3: *Si primus ... homo prophetavit, certum est quod et unctus sit.*

[498] This doctrine of the *successio prophetica* is adopted by Gnosticism and integrated into macrocosm-microcosm speculation. As in Rabb. Adam speculations the first prophet, Adam, stands as macrocosm in a relation to the microcosm which can be defined as conceptual identity. But in the Ker. Pt. there is no trace of this identifying of the ideal heavenly man (= macrocosm) with the protoplast, as Cullmann, 153 maintains.

[499] Examples in Schenke, 15.

[500] Colpe, 213.

Acc. to the Ophite system as presented in Iren. Haer., I, 30 the first man exists in the Bythos as primal light and is the father of all. The ἔννοια which proceeds from him is the second man, the Son of Man, Iren. Haer., I, 30, 1. [501] Since a feminine spiritual potency of the first man is not hypostatised here as a daughter but as his son, the latter concept must have been already to hand. Both "men" beget Christ with the feminine *pneuma*, and later Christ descends on Jesus and thus makes Him able to bring the gnosis which redeems, I, 30, 1-6. [502]

Iren. Haer., I, 12, 3 f. quotes with the Ptolemaeans and Colorbasaeans two strands which in typical fashion define the Anthropos as the creator of the twelve aeons, as the primal beginning and all-embracing power, i.e., as the macrocosm and also its spiritualisation. The redeemer who descends from him is the Son of the Anthropos, I, 12, 4. The Anthropos thus achieves an independent emanation which by established tradition was the Redeemer and which also, as the son, could bear the name of its father, Anthropos.

In the Copt. Apocryphon of Jn. (→ n. 85) both the chief father-god and his subordinate partner Barbelo bear the title "Man" with different attributes (perfect, first, eternal). [503] Their son, the Redeemer Christ, is called the "Son of Man." [504] This is also His name in the Sophia Jesu Christi, where His father is Man, but not the highest deity, only the second after the primal father, [505] and in the Nag-Hammadi work "Eugnostos the Blessed." [506]

The Gnostic Marcos also seeks to interpret the existing title in terms of his own presuppositions. [507] He seems to have used it as a basis for his docetic Christology. The Spirit, who descended on Jesus at His baptism to unite Himself with Him, designated Him the Son of Man. The significance seems to be still present here when it is said further: "Jesus is thus a name for the anthropos of the order of salvation, and it was given according to the likeness and form of the anthropos who was to come down on him and who assumed and held him; he (sc. the Redeemer) is himself the anthropos and the logos, the Pater and the Arrhetos, the Sige and the Aletheia, the Ecclesia and the Zoe," Iren. Haer., I, 15, 3.

Things are much the same in the Valentinian Heracleon Fr. No. 35, [508] where the designation of Christ as ὁ υἱὸς ἀνθρώπου (*sic*) makes him par. or subordinate to one of the many beings who are called man in the Valentinian system, cf. also Saying 102 of the Ev. Phil., where in Valentinian fashion the Son of Man is the Soter and partner of Achamoth and his father, the true man, the Christ and partner of the Holy Ghost. [509]

The Son of Man is rather different in the system of the Peratae in Hipp. Ref., V, 12, 7. [510] Express ref. is made here to the v. in Jn. (3:17) which states most pregnantly the role of the Redeemer in this group. But for the Son of God of the original, Son of Man is substituted. Obviously such great value was attached to the character of Christ as Anthropos that a higher legitimation was sought for it than Jn. offered in a restricted way → 466, 16 ff. On the other hand the Anthropos could qualify as Redeemer only by the identification of Christ with him. Hence this independently redeeming Anthropos was

---

[501] Cf. H. Leisegang, *Die Gnosis* (1924), 174-6 and Schenke, 7.

[502] Older analysis in Bousset Hauptprobleme, 162 and Lietzmann, 62-4 claims that the Anthropos and the second Anthropos or Son of the Anthropos belong to the pre-Chr. epoch of the Ophites, but examination of the confused system of the Ophites makes this thesis untenable, Iber, 4, n. 24.

[503] Examples in Schenke, 7, 34-43.

[504] Cod. Berolinensis Gnosticus, 47, 15 f. (ed. Till, *op. cit.* [→ n. 85]).

[505] *Ibid.*, 98, 11 f.; 101, 7; 102, 15 f.; 108, 2; 124, 2. 6; Schenke, 8.

[506] Cod. Cairensis Gnosticus, III (→ n. 89), 81, 13. 21; 85, 1 ff. (Schenke, 9).

[507] Iren. Haer., I, 14, 3; 15, 1; cf. 15, 3; Hipp. Ref., VI, 39-50, cf. VI, 51, 1-5 and Leisegang, *op. cit.* (→ n. 501), 339.

[508] Orig. Comm. in Joh., 13, 49 on 4:37.

[509] Schenke, 11; Iber, 5, n. 33 (ref. to Cl. Al. Exc. Theod., 58 f. and Orig. Cels., 8, 15).

[510] Cf. Leisegang, *op. cit.*, 144.

present in advance neither as redeeming nor non-redeeming. Only with the adoption of the redeeming Christ or Son of Man into the speculation did he come into being. Only thus did Anthropos become the established term. [511]

2. General.

In all these witnesses the υἱός in the title is understood genealogically. [512] This Gk. understanding naturally set it in the same relation to the heavenly universal man as that in which other emanations already stood. But it also made possible a direct identification with this first man, the upper Anthropos. This man attains thereby his position as the macrocosm behind all the hypostatic differentiations of the universe and the spiritual substance of all its hypostases. But he also takes on specific form as the progenitor of the Redeemer or of many redeemers. For this reason, and because the Redeemer is also identical with him, the upper Anthropos acquires directly a soteriological character which is typologically different from the pre-mythological σωτηρία constituted thereby as, e.g., in Philo → VII, 988, 1 ff.

It is thus the redeemer quality of the ὁ υἱὸς τοῦ ἀνθρώπου attested in the Chr. tradition, and specifically in Jn., which alters speculation about His Father, as the upper man was understood to be. Hence in some groups Son of Man Christology exerted an important influence on the development of the Anthropos as Redeemer. [513]

III. The Son of Man Title in the Debate about Christ's Human Nature.

The original meaning of the title Son of Man was also lost as orthodoxy gradually developed in the early Church [514] and controversies arose about the true human nature of Christ. Ign. Eph., 20, 2 already uses about Christ an expression possibly taken from a confessional formulation when it says that He is descended after the flesh from the house of David R. 1:3, τῷ υἱῷ ἀνθρώπου καὶ υἱῷ θεοῦ → 393, 5 ff. What Ign. is trying to express is the paradoxical unity of the "sarkic" and the "pneumatic" in Christ. Barn., 12, 10 however, refuses to accept the υἱὸς ἀνθρώπου descended from a main in antithesis to the υἱὸς τοῦ θεοῦ, → 393, 18 ff. Just. Dial. c. Tryph., 100, 3 [515] then says that Jesus called Himself Son of Man either because He descended from the line of David, Jacob, Isaac and Abraham by the Virgin or because He had Adam and the rest as ancestors, from whom Mary too descended.

The Son of Man title is esp. common in the work of Iren.; [516] if here, as in the other fathers, it has largely lost its NT character, nevertheless the Jewish Chr. tradition continues to find expression in this author → 473, 12 ff. The term is reserved exclusively for

---

[511] The ref. to the Son of Man in the Naassene Sermon (once each in the prologue and epilogue in Hipp. Ref., V, 6, 4 and V, 9, 2 f. and once in the sermon itself in V, 7, 33) are not relevant here. The term is used for the mode of being of the Anthropos as "stamped" or "inner" man (Iber, 15): this is a simple syncretistic addition by which the Chr. tradition is added to the others as a validating authority. The introduction of the Son of Man into the speculation did not have the same results as in other systems.

[512] Cf. Schenke, 154.

[513] The adoption and reinterpretation of other Christologies played a part here. The prophetic leaders of groups from which non-Chr. Gnosticism developed might well have been influenced by the same interpretations. What is said in C. Colpe, Art. "Gnosis," RGG³, II, 1652 is to be supplemented along these lines.

[514] Cf. the texts in H. Appel, *Selbstbezeichnung Jesu: Der Sohn d. Menschen. Eine bibl.-theol. Untersuchung* (1896), 1-3, also the survey of thinking from the Reformation to the 19th cent., 3-27.

[515] On the question of the suffering Messiah in the Dial. cf. Sjöberg Menschensohn Ev., 246-254; on the question of the hidden Messiah, *ibid.,* 80-82.

[516] There are 17 other terms, but a specific sense cannot be ascribed to any of these, cf. A. Houssiau, *La Christologie de Saint Irénée* (1955), 25-38.

Christ, [517] whereas other designations can be used more extensively. [518] Iren. uses *filius hominis* mainly for the entry into flesh demonstrated by the fact that Jesus was humanly born, of Mary, Haer., III, 16, 5; 19, 3; 22, 1; IV, 33, 2 and 11; V, 21, 1; Epid., 1, 3, 36. To His human being corresponds the divine. That the *filius dei* became *filius hominis* for our salvation (= becoming *filius dei*) is a central principle in the Christology of Iren., Haer., III, 10, 2; 16, 3 and 7; 17, 1; 18, 3 f.; 19, 1 f.; V, 21, 2 f. The Logos (*Verbum dei*) can also be said to have become the *filius hominis*, III, 18, 6; 19, 3; 20, 2; 22, 1; V, 17, 3; 21, 1 with stronger reliance on the Adam-Christ typology. If in one instance we find instead: *propter hoc enim Verbum Dei homo* (III, 19, 1), there is no difference between *filius hominis* and *homo*. [519] The alternation simply shows that Iren. knew the individuating sense of *filius* as well as the genealogical sense.

In Tert. Marc., IV, 10 (CSEL, 47, 444-9), cf. De carne Christi, 5 (70, 199-203), 15 (227-9) it is a logical conclusion that the man of whom Jesus is the Son can only be His mother: *Si ex deo patre est, utique non est ex homine. Si non ex homine, superest, ut ex homine sit matre.* Acc. to Orig. Comm. in Mt., 17, 20 on 22:1-14 Son of Man means that as God makes only men His servants, so that in a certain way man forthwith arises whom one may parabolically style thus (sc. servant), so also the Redeemer, who is first in service, finally becomes the Son of Man, even though He is truly the Son of God, God, and the image of God. Acc. to Eus. Hist. Eccl., I, 2, 26 Da. 7:13 as prophecy ref. to our Redeemer who in the beginning was with God as God and Logos and who was called Son of Man in virtue of His ultimate incarnation. Greg. Naz. Or., 36 repeats the alternatives of Just. → 476, 28 ff. Epiph. Haer., 57, 8, 7 f. quotes Da. 7:13 like Eusebius and believes that He, the Logos, was God, Spirit and power, but had to be perfected in the flesh among men. Acc. to Chrys. Hom. in Joh., 27, 1 on 3:13 (MPG, 59 [1862], 158) Jesus does not just call His σάρξ the Son of Man but His entire self in His lowlier οὐσία. He often describes His whole self both in terms of His deity and also in terms of His humanity. Hier. Breviarium in Ps. on 8:4 (MPL, 26 [1884], 888a) repeats *de facto* the Mariological explanation of Iren. Aug. Serm., 121, 5 on Jn. 1:10-14 (MPL, 38 [1841], 680) has the catallactic explanation of Iren.: For your sakes He who was the Son of God became the Son of Man in order that you who were sons of men might become the sons of God. Cyril of Alex. Ep. ad Nestorium, 4 (MPG, 77 [1864], 45b-c) says that σάρκα ἐμψυχωμένην ψυχῇ λογικῇ ἑνώσας ὁ λόγος ἑαυτῷ καθ᾽ ὑπόστασιν, ἀφράστως τε καὶ ἀπερινοήτως γέγονεν ἄνθρωπος, καὶ κεχρημάτικεν υἱὸς ἀνθρώπου, οὐ κατὰ θέλησιν μόνην, ἢ εὐδοκίαν, ἀλλ᾽ οὐδὲ ὡς ἐν προσλήψει προσώπου μόνου, while his younger contemporary Ammonius of Alex. Fr., 55 on Jn. 1:51 [520] emphasises that the ἐκ Μαρίας σαρκωθείς became man ἀληθείᾳ and not δοκήσει.

Colpe

---

[517] We are disregarding here the use in Gnostic systems mentioned in Iren. and in NT quotations which he adduces to show the correctness of his teaching and to fight the errors of the Gnostics. From Mt. Iren. quotes 8:20 (Haer., I, 8, 3); 11:19 (IV, 31, 2); 12:40 (V, 31, 1); 16:13 (III, 18, 4); 24:39 (IV, 36, 3); from Mk. 2:10 (V, 17, 2); 8:31 (III, 16, 5); 14:21 (II, 20, 5); from Lk. 17:28 f. (IV, 36, 3); 18:8 (IV, 33, 11); from Jn. 5:27-29 (V, 13, 1); from Ac. 7:56 (III, 12, 13); also Da. 7:13 (IV, 20, 11; IV, 33, 11).

[518] Thus in III, 19, 1; IV, 41, 2 man can be called the son of God when as the redeemed he does God's will.

[519] Neither from this nor from Adam-Christ typology can one deduce an influence of the myth of the primal man on the Christology of Iren. (so Staerk, I, 160, n. 1; II, 97 and Cullmann, 196).

[520] Ed. J. Reuss, *Joh.-Komm. aus der griech. Kirche*, TU, 89 (1966), 211.

---

† υἱὸς Δαυίδ

Contents: A. David and the Son of David in Judaism: 1. King David; 2. The Messiah of David's Lineage. B. Δαυίδ and υἱὸς Δαυίδ in the New Testament: I. King David: 1. David as God's Servant; 2. David as the Prophet of Christ; 3. David as a Type of Christ; II. Christ of David's Lineage: 1. The Davidic Sonship of Jesus in Christological Confession; 2. Christ as David's Son and Lord; 3. υἱὸς Δαυίδ in the Gospels; 4. The Davidic Sonship of Jesus in the Revelation of John. C. Δαυίδ and υἱὸς Δαυίδ in the Writings of the Post-Apostolic Age: 1. Δαυίδ; 2. υἱὸς Δαυίδ.

A. David and the Son of David in Judaism.

1. King David.

For Judaism David[1] is one of the righteous of Israel who have experienced God's grace in a special way and lived according to His will. Because he was obedient to God he was given the divine promise (2 S. 7:16) according to which he ἐκληρονόμησεν θρόνον βασιλείας εἰς αἰῶνας, 1 Macc. 2:57. In the song in praise of the fathers of Israel sung in Jesus Sir., David has a prominent position among the fathers. He distinguished himself already as a shepherd when he played with young lions as with baby-rams and with bears as with kids, Sir. 47:3; cf. 1 S. 17:34-36. As a warrior he won gt. renown through his victory over Goliath and the subjugation of the Philistines, Sir. 47:4-7. In none of his exploits did he neglect to give praise and glory to God; "with his whole heart he loved him who had created him and with his whole soul he rendered thanks to him," 47:8. Because he was faithful to God and at pains to see that God was honoured and extolled, the Lord forgave him his sins, lifted up his horn for ever, made with him a covenant of

---

υἱὸς Δαυίδ. Bibl.: On A.: Dalman WJ, I, 260-6; S. Mowinckel, *He that Cometh. The Messiah Concept in the OT and Later Judaism*² (1959), 280-345; E. Lohse, "Der König aus Davids Geschlecht. Bemerkungen z. messian. Erwartung der Synagoge," *Festschr. O. Michel* (1963), 337-345. On B.: W. Wrede, "Jesus als Davidssohn," *Vorträge u. Studien* (1907), 147-177; G. A. Danell, "Jesus David's Son," *Vid Åbodomens fot* (1949), 62-74; also "Did Paul Know the Tradition about the Virgin Birth?" *Stud. Theologica*, 4 (1950), 94-101; R. P. Gagg, "Jesus u. d. Davidssohnfrage," *ThZ*, 7 (1951), 18-30; E. Lohmeyer, "Gottesknecht u. Davidssohn," FRL, 61² (1953); O. Betz "Donnersöhne, Menschenfischer u. der davidische Messias," *Revue de Qumran*, 3 (1961/62), 41-70; B. van Iersel, "Fils de David et Fils de Dieu," *La Venue du Messie, Recherches Bibl.*, 6 (1962), 113-132; W. Michaelis, "Die Davidssohnschaft Jesu als historisches u. kerygmatisches Problem," *Der historische Jesus u. d. kerygmatische Christus*³ (1963), 317-330; O. Cullmann, *Die Christologie d. NT*⁴ (1966), 111-137; F. Hahn, "Christologische Hoheitstitel," FRL, 83² (1964), 242-279. On C.: J. Daniélou, Art. "David," RAC, III, 594-603.

[1] The name דוד is transl. in Gk. by Δαυίδ, Δαυείδ, or Δαβίδ (cf. Bl.-Debr. § 38 App., 39, 1), also Δαυίδης or Δαβίδης (so Jos.), cf. Pr.-Bauer, *s.v.*

monarchy and established his throne in Israel, 47:11. Thus David is lauded in Judaism both as the victorious ruler over Israel and also as the pious psalmist. [2]

Among David's martial exploits repeated ref. is made esp. to the victory over Goliath, which he gained with God's help, 1 Macc. 4:30; Sir. 47:4; 1 QM 11:1 f. In war he woula not take the water which some of his soldiers had brought from the enemy camp at the risk of their lives, but poured it out as a libation to God, 4 Macc. 3:3-16. This act of David was regarded by the author of 4 Macc. as an illustration of the fact that rational under-standing was in a position to vanquish the thrust of impulse and by the virtue of reason to meet with scorn all the dominant desires of impulse, 3:17 f. For Hell. Judaism David is thus an example of virtuous conduct. Although Jos. Ant., 6, 156 - 7, 394, in a long account of David's work which follows closely the biblical original, does not ignore the sin with Bathsheba (7, 130, 153, 391), David is still presented as ἄριστος ἀνήρ who evidenced πᾶσαν ἀρετήν (7, 390), brave and battle-tested in every situation, the model of a ruler, σώφρων ἐπιεικὴς χρηστός, πρὸς τοὺς ἐν συμφοραῖς ὑπάρχοντας δίκαιος φιλάν-θρωπος, ἃ μόνοις δικαιότατα βασιλεῦσιν εἶναι προσῆκε (7, 391). Because he was stained with blood in his various campaigns, he was not allowed to build a temple for God in Jerusalem. But he made all the preparations so that his son could carry out the project [3] and he praised God in psalms and songs of praise, 4 Macc. 18:15; Philo Conf. Ling., 149. [4]

In the strict legal circles of Palestinian Judaism David was presented soberly and without adornment. [5] Damasc. 5:2 (7:5) says that David did not keep the law of Dt. 17:17, which forbids a king to have several wives, but in excuse it claims that he had not read in the sealed book. "And the works of David rose up (to God) with the exception of the blood of Uriah, and God granted remission," 5:5 f. (7:7). The Qumran community honoured David as a poet and singer who in the Ps. gave praise to God in exemplary fashion. Acc. to 11 Q Psᵃ 27:2-11 (DJD, IV, 91 f.) he composed no less than 4050 songs in God's honour.

For Rabb. Judaism [6] David was a righteous man who set a good example in his study of the Torah. At midnight he was wakened by his harp to continue this study, bBer., 3b. Each Sabbath he sat the whole day searching the Torah, so that even the angel of death could have nothing against him so long as his mouth did not cease studying, bShab., 30b. With Moses David was a good guardian and leader of Israel and God forgave him the sin he committed, S. Dt., 26 on 3:23. [7] If he took the showbread from the priest for food on the Sabbath, his conduct can be excused on the ground that he was in mortal peril, → VII, 21, 28 ff. [8] David knew how to control the passion the evil impulse kindled, Lv. r., 23 on 18:3. The evil impulse could indeed have no power over him, bBB, 17a. The sin with Bathsheba, we are now told, is one he did not wish to commit, and in reality did not commit, bShab., 56a. Another view is that David did succumb to the temptation but Bathsheba had been divinely predestined for him from the six days of creation, bSanh.,

---

[2] Cf. apart from the literary ref. the depictions of David at Dura-Europos, which give prominence to the anointing of David as king, Cf. H. Riesenfeld, *Jésus transfiguré* (1947), 76; C. H. Kraeling, "The Synagogue," *The Excavations at Dura-Europos*, VIII, 1 (1956), 168: "For the members of the Jewish community at Dura-Europos to see before them at the very right of the central Torah Shrine of the House of Assembly a scene depicting the anointing of David, was inevitably a reminder of the divine promises concerning the Messianic king who was to come, the Lord's Anointed himself, a 'shoot out of the stock of Jesse' (Is. 11:1) and a son of David. In all probability the scene received its prominent position in order to perform precisely this function." Cf. also *ibid.*, 217-220; 225-227; Ill., 66 and 73-75.

[3] Cf. the account of Eupolemos in Eus. Praep. Ev., 9, 30, 3-8; cf. 1 Εσδρ. 1:3.

[4] Only here does Philo mention the name of David with ref. to his descendants, who were the υἱοὶ τοῦ τὸν θεὸν ὑμνήσαντος Δαβίδ.

[5] Cf. H. Kosmala, "Hebräer-Essener-Christen," *Studia Post-Biblica*, I (1959), 95.

[6] Weber, Index; Str.-B., Index *s.v.* "David"; W. Staerk "Die Erlösererwartung in d. öst-lichen Religionen," *Soter* II (1938), 56-58.

[7] Cf. Str.-B., IV, 177 f.

[8] *Ibid.*, I, 618 f.

107a. David unceasingly praised God, appeasing Him with songs of praise and thanksgiving, bBB, 14b. All the psalms were ascribed to him. If at the beginning of a psalm we read לְדָוִד מִזְמוֹר, this means that the shechinah descended on him and only then did he compose the song. But if we read מִזְמוֹר לְדָוִד, this means that he first composed the song and then the shechinah rested on him, bPes., 117a. In David's time it was revealed to all peoples that there is only one God, so that 150,000 proselytes came and joined Israel, Nu. r., 8 on 5:6. By his intercession David could bring heaven down to earth, bChag., 12b. Thus Rab (d. 247 A.D.) can say that the world was created only for David, bSanh., 98b. For in David's days the history of all mankind and not just of Israel reached its climax. [9]

2. The Messiah of David's Lineage.

The divine promise imparted to David by Nathan assigned eternal continuation to his house and monarchy, 2 S. 7:12-16 (→ 366, 23 ff.). Judaism linked with this promise the hope that God would one day after the pattern of David raise up the anointed ruler who would free his people and bring it glory and renown. The title Son of David occurs for the first time in Ps. Sol. (17:21), which belong to c. the middle of the 1st cent. B.C. This expression, which came into common use in Judaism, developed out of older ones like שֹׁרֶשׁ יִשַׁי "sprout of Jesse" (Is. 11:10) and צֶמַח (דָּוִד) "shoot (of David)" (Jer. 23:5; 33:15; Zech. 3:8; 6:12). It was with disillusionment and inner resistance that pious circles had watched the Hasmoneans annex to the dignity of the high-priest that of the king as well even though they were not of Davidic descent, Ps. Sol. 17:4-6. [10] When the Hasmonean dynasty was replaced and political independence was lost, the older hope revived that an eschatological ruler of the house of David would come, and it was widely held among the people.

In the broad depiction of Messianic rule in Ps. Sol. 17 the expectation of an anointed king who would be the Son of David found its clearest expression. [11] First there is a reminder of God's promise that David's kingdom would never end, v. 4. Then appeal is made to God that at the selected time He would raise up for Israel the king, the Son of David, to rule over it, v. 21. This king will throw off alien dominion, seize the holy city from the foe, purge it of the heathen, subdue the peoples, judge the tribes of Israel, and rule the land in purity and righteousness, so that nations will come from the ends of the earth to see his glory and to look on the glory of the Lord, vv. 21-46. He will rule as a righteous king who is taught by God Himself. In his days no wrong will be done, for all are holy and their king is the χριστὸς κυρίου,[12] the Lord's Anointed, v. 32.

Pharisaic in origin, [13] Ps. Sol. builds on 2 S. 7; the Qumran community expressly adopts this passage too, relating vv. 11-14 to the "shoot of David who will come with the investigator of the Law in ... Zi[on at the en]d of the days, as it is written: And I will raise up the fallen tabernacle of David (Am. 9:11). This is the tabernacle of David, which is falle[n, and it] will rise up to save Israel," 4 Q Florilegium 1:11-13. [14] The "(shoot)

---

[9] *Ibid.*, IV, 994.
[10] Cf. K. G. Kuhn, *Die älteste Textgestalt d. Ps. Sal.* (1937), 57 f.; also "Die beiden Messias Aarons u. Israels," NTSt, 1 (1954/55), 176 f.; Lohse, 337 f. Other groups obviously saw in the rule of the Hasmoneans a fulfilment of God's promises of salvation, cf. 1 Macc. 14:4-15.
[11] Cf. Bousset-Gressm., 228-230; Str.-B., IV, 800 f.; Volz Esch., 177 f.
[12] Read χριστὸς κυρίου, the reading χριστὸς κύριος being a Chr. emendation.
[13] Cf. esp. Ps. Sol. 17:42 f.: The Messiah will correct the people Israel, being not only the ruler but also, acc. to the Pharisaic view, the teacher of Israel.
[14] Cf. J. M. Allegro, "Fr. of a Qumran Scroll of Eschatological Midrašim," JBL, 77 (1958), 353. Am. 9:11 is also quoted in Damasc. 7:16 (9:6 f.) and the following equation is made: tabernacle of the king — books of the Law; king — community. That is, the divine promise is fulfilled in the community of the covenant in which the Law is set up again. Cf. O. Michel - O. Betz, "Von Gott gezeugt," *Festschr. J. Jeremias*[2] (1964), 9 f. The Rabb. also have a Messianic interpretation of Am. 9:11, bSanh., 96b, 97a, cf. also Str.-B., II, 728.

of David" is awaited "who will arise at the en[d of the days]," 4 Qp Isᵃ Fr. D 1 [15] and it is seen that this hope has its basis in Gn. 49:10 f., "for to him and his seed is given the covenant of royal dominion over his people for eternal generations," 4 Q Patriarchal Blessing 4, cf. 2. [16] The Messiah of Israel shall rule over His people as king and shall stand alongside the Messiah of Aaron. Acc. to the dominant ideas of the sect first rank is ascribed to the latter, for it is his task to guide the pure community of God, 1 QS 9:11; 1 QSa 2:11-22. [17]

Expectation of the Son of David who will liberate His people and expose the ungodliness of the Gentiles, judging their iniquities and bringing to light their evil deeds (4 Esr. 12:32), is so widespread in Judaism during the 1st and 2nd cent. A.D. that the title בֶּן דָּוִד is constantly used by the Rabb. as a Messianic designation, so R. Jose b Qisma (c. 110 A.D.) in bSanh., 98a, R. Jochanan b Torta (c. 130 A.D.) in jTa'an, 4, 8 (68d, 45), R. Jehuda b Il'ai and R. Nechemya (c. 150 A.D.) in bSanh., 97a and other scholars. [18] If it is not always expressly emphasised that the Messiah must be of Davidic lineage, it became the dominant conviction that only a descendant of David could exercise Messianic rule, [19] and that Bethlehem would thus have to be the birthplace of the Messiah, Tg. Pro. on Mi. 5:1. [20] Since the Messiah was to come as the second David, he could sometimes simply be called David. When Jerusalem will be built, David will come, bChag., 14a; bMeg., 17b. [21] Hence expectation of the age of salvation can be expressed in the saying: "The rule of the house of David comes," jBer., 3, 1 (6a, 58). If David's name is linked in this way with the eschatological hope, one may see that it is focused not so much on the person of the eschatological ruler but rather on the fact that the age of salvation comes with him and through him. For the faith and hope of Judaism the Messianic kingdom is incomparably more important than the Messianic king. [22]

In the prayers which the pious Jews prays every day the name of the Messiah of David's race is again mentioned, but with no further characterisation of His figure. [23] In the 14th Benediction of the Prayer of Eighteen Benedictions acc. to the Palestinian Rec. God is asked to have mercy "on the kingdom of the house of David, of the Messiah of thy righteousness." [24] The 15th Benediction of the Bab. Rec. runs: "May the shoot of David sprout forth quickly, and may his horn be lifted up by thy help. Blessed be Thou, Yahweh, who dost cause the horn of help to shoot forth." [25] Again in the Habhinenu Prayer, which sums up briefly the most important intercessory concerns, prayer is made for the shoot of David or the sprouting forth of a horn for David, thy servant. [26] In the

---

[15] Ed. J. M. Allegro, "Further Messianic Ref. in Qumran Literature," JBL, 75 (1956), 180.
[16] Allegro, op. cit. (→ n. 15), 174 f., cf. also the echo of Gn.49:10 in Test. Jud. 22:2.
[17] On expectation of the Davidic Messiah in the Dead Sea Scrolls cf. esp. A. S. van der Woude, "Die messianischen Vorstellungen d. Gemeinde v. Qumran," Studia Semitica Neerlandica, 3 (1957), 169-189; K. Schubert, "Die Messiaslehre in d. Texten v. Chirbet Qumran," BZ, NF, 1 (1957), 184-8; M. Black, "Messianic Doctrine in the Qumran Scrolls," TU, 63 (1957), 441-459.
[18] Dalman WJ, I, 260 f.; Str.-B., I, 525; Bousset-Gressm., 226; Volz Esch., 174 and the other ref. there.
[19] Cf. Str.-B., I, 11-13. Cf. also the relevant passages in Tg. Pro.; Dalman WJ, I, 261; Str.-B., II, 337.
[20] Other examples in Str.-B., I, 82 f.
[21] Other examples Str.-B., I, 65; II, 337; Volz Esch., 174. David here might be David returned from death, but is more likely the "second David" or the "Son of David," cf. Str.-B., II, 337.
[22] Cf. Volz Esch., 176; H. J. Schoeps, Pls. (1959), 89. Only thus can one explain why the Messiah does not figure in so many apoc. writings in post-bibl. Judaism. Important here is the statement in Mowinckel, 341: "The Messiah plays no part in the Jewish cult, except as a subject of prayer."
[23] Cf. Volz Esch., 174 f.
[24] Cf. W. Staerk, Altjüd. liturgische Gebete, Kl. T., 58² (1930), 13; Str.-B., IV, 213.
[25] Staerk, op. cit., 18; Str.-B., IV, 213.
[26] Text in Staerk, 20.

Musaph Prayers one of the gifts God is asked to give is the "sprouting forth of a horn for David, thy servant," and the "setting up of a light for the son of Jesse, thine anointed." [27] These texts show plainly that the widespread eschatological hope of the people was for a Messiah of the lineage of David.

The ideas of Judaism concerning the future age of salvation were by no means uniform. Many circles awaited a pre-existent Deliverer who would come down from heaven. Others expected an anointed priest. Some even thought that God Himself would intervene rather than a Messiah in the great eschatological convulsion. Nevertheless, it was the dominant view that from Judah "the shoot would come forth and the staff of dominion would sprout," Test. Jud. 24:4 f. [28] The Messiah-King would be an earthly man who would restore Israel's glory and renown after the pattern of David, subjugating the Gentiles and ruling with righteousness. Beyond this there was no more precise consideration of his person. Messianic expectation of the Son of David focused rather on the work he would do on God's commission. [29] When the Messiah comes there will be glory and renown and God will give His people a share in this through His instrument. [30] The Messiah of the lineage of David will be the executor of salvation, but not its basis, meaning and content.

B. Δαυίδ and υἱὸς Δαυίδ in the New Testament.

I. King David.

1. David as God's Servant.

In the NT David is called one of the outstanding righteous men of Israel and the παῖς θεοῦ, Lk. 1:69; Ac. 4:25. In Mt. 1:6 his father is 'Ιεσσαί, cf. Ac. 13:22, and it is added that David begat Solomon of the wife of Uriah. [31] Since David was born in Bethlehem this is called the πόλις Δαυίδ, Lk. 2:4, 11; cf. Jn. 7:42. In Mk. 2:25 f. and par. we read how David was once hungry and ate the showbread, which normally only the priests are allowed to eat → VII, 21, 28 ff. God raised up David to be Israel's king, Ac. 13:22. David εὗρεν χάριν ἐνώπιον τοῦ θεοῦ, but it was his son who built the temple for God, Ac. 7:46 f. As a witness of faith (Hb. 11:32) David sang God's praise in the Ps. and as a prophet he predicted future salvation, Mk. 12:36 f. and par.; R. 4:6; 11:9; Ac. 1:16; 2:25, 34; 4:25; 13:35. God Himself spoke through David, Hb. 4:7; the Holy Ghost spoke through his lips, Ac. 1:16; [32] 4:25; 13:35. David was inspired by the Holy Spirit, Mk. 12:36 and par. He is regarded as the author of the whole of Ps., passing on

---

[27] Text in Staerk, 23.
[28] Cf. the explicit depiction of expectation of a national Messiah and his work in Mowinckel, 280-345.
[29] Mowinckel, 337-345.
[30] After the destruction of Jerusalem (70 A.D.) and the breaking of the Bar Cochba revolt (135 A.D.) expectation of a political Messianic kingdom became less prominent, though the hope of a Messianic age was not abandoned, being preserved esp. in liturgical prayers. To prevent rebellion living members of David's house who might have played a leading part were eliminated, cf. Eus. Hist. Eccl., III, 12, 19 f., 32. Eus. also gives an account by Hegesipp. (III, 20) acc. to which two grand-nephews of Jesus were informed against as descendants of David and brought before Domitian, who let them go, however, because their hands were marked by toil and as labourers and common people they were not open to suspicion.
[31] Lk. 3:31 ref. to a son of David called Ναθάμ, cf. 2 S. 5:14; 1 Ch. 3:5; 14:4.
[32] Ac. 1:20 then quotes Ps. 69:25 and 109:8, cf. J. Dupont, "La destinée de Judas prophétisée par David (Ac. 1:16-20)," Catholic Bibl. Quarterly, 23 (1961), 41-51.

the inspired words of God and bearing his witness as a prophet in virtue of the divine spirit conferred upon him → 479, 2. 18 f. and 480, 2 ff.

2. David as a Prophet of Christ.

In the Ps. David made it plain that the divine promises did not refer to him but to Christ. The Messiah is his Lord rather than his Son, Mk. 12:36 and par., cf. Ps. 110:1 → 484, 17 ff. David did not ascend up to heaven, but he prophesied that the Messiah should sit on the throne at God's right hand, Ac. 2:34, cf. Ps. 110:1. If we read: οὐκ ἐγκαταλείψεις τὴν ψυχήν μου εἰς ᾅδην οὐδὲ δώσεις τὸν ὅσιόν σου ἰδεῖν διαφθοράν (Ac. 2:27, cf. ψ 15:10), David cannot have meant these words (v. 27) of himself but only of Christ, for everyone knows that David died and was buried, and his tomb may be seen in Jerusalem, Ac. 2:29. [33] It follows, then, that David spoke as προφήτης (Ac. 2:30), προϊδὼν ἐλάλησεν περὶ τῆς ἀναστάσεως τοῦ Χριστοῦ (2:31). Having served his generation, David fell asleep according to the will of God. He was gathered to his fathers and saw corruption. But the One whom God raised up did not see corruption (Ac. 13:36 f.), [34] so that the promise to David has found its fulfilment in Christ. The promises connected with David's name have now been redeemed: δώσω ὑμῖν τὰ ὅσια Δαυὶδ τὰ πιστά (Ac. 13:34, cf. Is. 55:3; → 367, n. 233), [35] ἀνοικοδομήσω τὴν σκηνὴν Δαυὶδ τὴν πεπτωκυῖαν (Ac. 15:16, cf. Am. 9:11 → VII, 374, 39 ff.; 378, n. 59). The divine saying according to which the tabernacle of David was to be restored has been fulfilled in the history of Jesus, so that according to the unanimous testimony of the prophets the Gentiles shall come to seek the Lord. [36]

3. David as a Type of Christ.

David does not merely predict coming salvation as a prophet. As God's servant and Israel's king he is also a type of the eschatological Ruler. The coming kingdom for which the expectation of the pious waits is the ἐρχομένη βασιλεία τοῦ πατρὸς

---

[33] Jos., too, ref. to David's tomb in Ant., 7, 392-4; 13, 249; 16, 179; Bell., 1, 61. Cf. J. Jeremias, *Heiligengräber in Jesu Umwelt* (1958), 57 and 129: "The prudent request for indulgence (ἄνδρες ἀδελφοί, ἐξὸν εἰπεῖν μετὰ παρρησίας πρὸς ὑμᾶς περὶ τοῦ πατριάρχου Δαυὶδ) with which Peter in Ac. 2:29 introduces his questioning of this relating (sc. that of Rabb. exegesis) of Ps. 16:8-11 to David shows he had reason to fear he might be charged with blasphemy if he declared David's corpse to be corruptible in order to prepare the ground for relating Ps. 16 to Christ. So deeply rooted already in NT times was the idea of the incorruptibility of the saints."
[34] Cf. G. Klein, "Die zwölf Ap.," FRL, 77 (1961), 157 f.; E. Schweizer, "The Concept of the Davidic Son of God in Acts and its OT Background," *Studies in Luke and Acts* (1966), 186-193.
[35] "The incontestable ὅσια of David' of the LXX text simply ref. to future salvation — in Dt. 29:19 the Hbr. חֶסֶד is transl. by τὰ ὅσια," F. Mussner, "Die Idee d. Apokatastasis in d. Ag.," *Praesentia Salutis* (1967), 227. Cf. also Haench. Ag., 14 *ad loc.*; J. Dupont, "τὰ ὅσια Δαυὶδ τὰ πιστά," *Rev. Bibl.*, 68 (1961), 91-114; M. Rese, *At.liche Motive in d. Christologie d. Lk.*, Diss. Bonn (1965), 123-9.
[36] The stress is thus on πάντα τὰ ἔθνη, Ac. 15:17. Am. 9:11 is quoted acc. to the LXX, so that its use would seem to derive from the author rather than James, the Lord's brother, though cf. the Messianic interpretation of Am. 9:11 in the Jewish tradition → n. 14 and Mussner, *op. cit.*, 299-301.

ἡμῶν Δαυίδ, Mk. 11:10.[37] Under David Israel's history reached its zenith, for God said of him: εὗρον Δαυὶδ τὸν τοῦ 'Ιεσσαί, ἄνδρα κατὰ τὴν καρδίαν μου, ὃς ποιήσει πάντα τὰ θελήματά μου, Ac. 13:22. The promise to raise up a final Deliverer of David's line God has now honoured by causing Jesus to come forth from the seed of David as σωτήρ for Israel, Ac. 13:23.

II. Christ of David's Lineage.

1. The Davidic Sonship of Jesus in Christological Confession.

In the confession shaped by the Jewish Christian community at R. 1:3 f. (→ 366, 22 ff.) the first line speaks of the fact that Jesus is of David's seed. This can hardly be a mere assertion of His lineage. It means that Jesus' time on earth is understood already as Messianic → VI, 417, 10 ff.; VII, 126, 22 ff.[38] As the Son of David He fulfilled the promises of Scripture and the hope of Israel. But the dignity which the Risen Lord received is contrasted with the Messianic expression ἐκ σπέρματος Δαυίδ[39] and it goes far beyond it → 367, 1 ff.; VI, 416, 32 ff. In 2 Tm. 2:8 we again find ἐκ σπέρματος Δαυίδ in a kerygmatic formula[40] and the reference here is to earthly life of Jesus.

2. Christ as David's Son and Lord.

The Christian community which confessed Jesus as the Christ in whom the Scriptures are fulfilled had to explain the relation between the Messianic υἱὸς Δαυίδ and the title of majesty κύριος. Discussion of the question finds literary reflection in the pericope Mk. 12:35-37 and par.[41] If one asks how it is possible that on the one side the Messiah should be said to be the υἱὸς Δαυίδ and on the other David himself calls Him κύριος (Ps. 110:1), this does not mean that the Davidic sonship of the Messiah is repudiated.[42] On the contrary, we have here an

---

[37] Cf. on this the Jewish "the rule of the house of David comes," jBer., 3, 1 (6a, 58) → 481, 19 f. On Mt. 21:9 → 486, 20 ff.

[38] Lohmeyer, 77: "Son of David — only the Master in His earthly life is called this, not the crucified and risen Lord."

[39] Cf. on this Bultmann Theol.[5], 52; M. E. Boismard, "Constitué Fils de Dieu (R. 1:4)," Rev. Bibl., 60 (1953), 5-17; E. Schweizer, "R. 1:3 f. u. d. Gegensatz v. Fleisch u. Geist vor u. bei Pls.," Neotestamentica (1963), 180-9.

[40] Cf. H. Windisch, "Zur Christologie d. Pastoralbr.," ZNW, 34 (1935), 214-6; Dib. Past., ad loc.

[41] Cf. Bultmann Trad., 145 f.; G. Bornkamm, Jesus v. Nazareth[7] (1965), 206; H. Conzelmann, Art. "Jesus Christus," RGG[3], III, 630.

[42] The story is often taken to mean that Jesus rejected the title Son of David and linked Himself instead with Son of Man expectation. Cf. the comm., ad loc. and van Iersel, 121-3. But there is no suggestion of conflict between Son of David and Son of Man. Cullmann, 132 f. thinks Jesus is resisting the view that the Messiah is of earthly descent. The Messiah whom David calls his Lord has to be greater than David and hence His decisive descent cannot be from David; He has to descend from someone higher. Acc. to G. Friedrich, "Beobachtungen z. messianischen Hohenpriestererwartung in d. Synoptikern," ZThK, 53 (1956), 286-9 what is rejected here is a false eschatology; institution as the Messianic High-priest is set in contrast to this: The High-priest is greater than the Son of David. J. Gnilka, "Die Erwartung d. messianischen Hohenpriesters v. Qumran u. d. NT," Revue de Qumran, 2 (1959/60), 416-8 deduces from Mk. 12:35-37 that Jesus regarded Himself as the Davidic Messiah but not along the lines of a political national Messiah.

obvious Haggada-question which points to a contradiction based on two passages of Scripture and still seeks to do justice to both. It is thus a matter of bringing the different statements into a correct relation to each other. [43] Behind Mk. 12:35-37 and par. stands the same Christology as that expressed in the confessional sayings R. 1:3 f. and 2 Tm. 2:8. The title υἱὸς Δαυίδ is referred to the earthly Christ while the Lord is the exalted One who according to Ps. 110:1 sits at the right hand of God (→ III, 1089, 33 ff.) and is thus greater than David, being called κύριος. Both christological titles are correct. Through the υἱὸς Δαυίδ a link is forged with the OT promises of a Messiah of the lineage of David, and the κύριος predication is based on Ps. 110:1. υἱὸς Δαυίδ denotes the Messiah in His work on earth, κύριος the risen and exalted Lord. [44]

3. υἱὸς Δαυίδ in the Gospels.

a. In Mk. the address υἱὲ Δαυίδ occurs only at 10:47 f. [45] The blind man whom Jesus is passing calls out to Him and ask for His compassion and aid. In calling Him the Son of David he expresses his hope for healing and deliverance from the Messiah. [46] The Evangelist adopts the title from the tradition that had come down to him without laying any special emphasis of his own on it.

b. Luke follows the Mk. pericope and nowhere else does he have υἱὸς Δαυίδ in his presentation of Jesus' work. Only in the infancy stories, which are strongly permeated by OT motifs, do we find frequent stress on the fact that Jesus is of the house and lineage of David. God can promise through the angel Gabriel that He will give Jesus τὸν θρόνον Δαυίδ τοῦ πατρὸς αὐτοῦ, Lk. 1:32 → 376, 13 ff. God has honoured this future promise by raising up Jesus of the family of David. [47] In the Benedictus God is extolled because ἤγειρεν κέρας σωτηρίας ἡμῖν ἐν οἴκῳ Δαυίδ παιδὸς αὐτοῦ, Lk. 1:69. Joseph is ἐξ οἴκου Δαυίδ, Lk. 1:27, cf. 2:4. Jesus is born in Bethlehem, Lk. 2:1-20. The Davidic sonship is thus plainly understood in the sense that Jesus was of Davidic descent. David is called his ancestor in the genealogy, Lk. 3:31.

c. The Davidic sonship of Jesus is emphasised even more strongly in Mt. than in the Lucan infancy stories. The Evangelist begins with the words: Βίβλος γενέσεως Ἰησοῦ Χριστοῦ υἱοῦ Δαυίδ υἱοῦ Ἀβραάμ (Mt. 1:1) and he uses the genealogy to prove that Jesus was the Son of David. In the list of names mentioned the

---

[43] Cf. D. Daube, The NT and Rabbinic Judaism (1956), 158-169, reviewed by J. Jeremias, ThLZ, 83 (1958), 349 f.; cf. also J. Jeremias, Jesu Verheissung für d. Völker² (1959), 45.

[44] Lohmeyer, 83 f. derives the title Son of David from the Galilean community and thinks "that the names Servant of the Lord and Son of Man and Son of David belong closely together and that the name Son of David was a later offshoot of the two older concepts on Palestinian soil." But this is an unproved conjecture.

[45] The title υἱὸς Δαυίδ does not occur at all in the sayings tradition.

[46] The title υἱὸς Δαυίδ is used in the Christology of the Jewish Chr. community. But it cannot be shown that the historical Jesus was already called this, though cf. Michaelis, 320 f.

[47] The Evangelists, like the primitive Chr. tradition, use the title Son of David in relation to the earthly life of Jesus rather than His future eschatological manifestation. OT style lies behind Lk. 1:32 f., though one cannot conclude from this, as Hahn, 247 f. does, that we have here a tradition which ref. originally to the eschatological work of Jesus. On Rev. 5:5 and 22:16, which transfer the Messianic title of Jewish expectation to the exalted Christ, → 487, 3 ff.

importance of king David is given emphasis by the concluding note that there are 14 generations from Abraham to David, 14 from David to the Babylonian captivity, and 14 more from this to Christ, Mt. 1:17. [48] In Mt. as in Lk. the Davidic sonship of Jesus is through the father, for at the end of the list the Evangelist mentions Joseph: τὸν ἄνδρα Μαρίας, ἐξ ἧς ἐγεννήθη ᾽Ιησοῦς ὁ λεγόμενος χριστός, Mt. 1:16. [49] In the story which follows Mt. tells how Joseph was a υἱὸς Δαυίδ, 1:20. He received Mary and Jesus by divine command and in this way Jesus was grafted into the race of David, 1:18-25. [50] For Mt. the Davidic sonship of Jesus is of special significance, for on this ground he can show the Synagogue that Jesus is the Messiah of Israel. For this reason Mt. does not just adopt from Mk. 10:47 f. the addressing of Jesus as υἱὸς Δαυίδ, Mt. 20:30 f. He also lays stress on the Jewish Christian confession of Jesus as the Son of God by introducing the title into many stories which tell of the saving work of Jesus. [51] In Mt. 9:27 the two blind men cry out: ἐλέησον ἡμᾶς, υἱὸς Δαυίδ. The woman of Canaan turns to Jesus with the request: ἐλέησόν με, κύριε υἱὸς Δαυίδ, 15:22. Having seen the mighty acts of Jesus the crowd asks in astonishment: μήτι οὗτός ἐστιν ὁ υἱὸς Δαυίδ; 12:23. This amazed question is to be regarded as an inkling of the truth in sharp contrast to the hostile attitude of the Pharisees, 12:24. [52] The Son of David in whom the hope of Israel comes to fulfilment is the Saviour who turns aside sorrow and heals sicknesses. When Jesus finally enters Jerusalem He is jubilantly greeted: ὡσαννὰ τῷ υἱῷ Δαυίδ, 21:9, 15. [53] Mt. no longer refers as Mk. does to the ἐρχομένη βασιλεία τοῦ πατρὸς ἡμῶν Δαυίδ, Mk. 11:10 → 483, 25 f.; I, 581, 7 ff.; II, 669, 35 ff. He associates the name David with confession of Jesus as the Messiah of God's people. In His earthly way Jesus has come to Israel as the Son of David in whom the promises of Scripture are fulfilled. But the community which confesses Him knows that He who has worked as the Son of David on earth is the Kurios and Son of God (Mt. 22:41-46) to whom all power is given both in heaven and on earth, 28:18.

d. In Jn. the Davidic sonship of the Messiah is mentioned only in the crucial question which refers to the contradiction that Jesus comes from Galilee and yet is supposed to be the Messiah, Jn. 7:41. Scripture says plainly, ὅτι ἐκ τοῦ σπέρματος Δαυίδ, καὶ ἀπὸ Βηθλέεμ τῆς κώμης ὅπου ἦν Δαυίδ, ἔρχεται ὁ χριστός, 7:42. The Fourth Evangelist does not seem to be presupposing either the birth of Jesus in

---

[48] The threefold 14 corresponds to the numerical value of דָּוִד, cf. J. Jeremias, *Jerusalem zur Zeit Jesu*³ (1963), 326; K. Stendahl, "Quis et unde?" *Festschr. J. Jeremias*² (1964), 101; Hahn, 242-6.

[49] Both Mt. and Lk. want to prove the Davidic descent of Jesus by His genealogy. But the names diverge so greatly that attempts to harmonise them have not been successful. It is more rewarding to note the theological accents which the Evangelists give the lists, Mt. 1:1 ᾽Ιησοῦ Χριστοῦ υἱοῦ Δαυίδ, Lk. 3:38: τοῦ ᾽Αδὰμ τοῦ θεοῦ.

[50] Cf. Schl. Mt., 7-9; Stendahl, *op. cit.* (→ n. 48), 102.

[51] Lohmeyer, 69-75; Michaelis, 318 f.; J. M. Gibbs, "Purpose and Pattern in Matthew's Use of the Title 'Son of David,'" NTSt, 10 (1963/64), 446-464; G. Strecker, "Der Weg d. Gerechtigkeit," FRL, 82² (1966), 118-120; R. Hummel, "Die Auseinandersetzung zwischen Kirche u. Judt. im Mt.," *Beiträge z. Evangelischen Theol.*, 33² (1966), 116-122.

[52] Cf. Hummel, *op. cit.* (→ n. 51), 118 f. In stressing the title Son of David the Evangelist is not so much pursuing a historical concern (Strecker, *op. cit.*, 118-120); he rather "emphasizes Jesus as the Son of David, in whom are fulfilled all legitimate Jewish Messianic hopes" (Gibbs, *op. cit.*, 463), and he is thus "contending for the Messiahship of Jesus predominantly under the royal title of Son of David," Hummel, 121.

[53] By adding τῷ υἱῷ Δαυίδ Mt. shows he is a Palestinian, J. Jeremias, "Die Muttersprache d. Evangelisten Mt.," *Abba* (1966), 258-260.

Bethlehem or His Davidic descent. The Christ whom he proclaims is not a Messiah whose legitimacy has to be proved by the criteria of Jewish Messianic expectation. [54]

4. The Davidic Sonship of Jesus in the Revelation of John.

Christ is twice called ἡ ῥίζα Δαυίδ in Rev. at 5:5 and 22:16. [55] He is the shoot which has sprung forth from the race of David (cf. Is. 11:1, 10), the Messianic Ruler who holds the key of David in His hands, 3:7. This picture is taken from Is. 22:22, but it is used in a new sense. What is meant is no longer the key to David's palace. It is the key to the door of the Messianic banqueting hall. As the eschatological scion of the house of David Christ holds in His hands the key with which He opens up the way to salvation. By the transfer of OT and Jewish titles to the crucified, risen and ascended Christ it is emphasised that the promises of God are fulfilled in Him.

C. Δαυίδ and υἱὸς Δαυίδ in the Writings of the Post-Apostolic Age.

1. Δαυίδ.

In most of the passages in which he is mentioned David is the singer of the Ps. and the prophet of Christ, Asc. Is. 4:21; 1 Cl., 18, 1; 52, 2; Barn., 10, 10; Just. Apol., 35, 6; 40, 5; 41, 1; 42, 3; 45, 1; Dial., 19, 4; 22, 7; 28, 6; 29, 2 etc. Only rarely is an event from his life referred to by way of example. Thus 1 Cl., 4, 13 ref. in warning to the fact that διὰ ζῆλος Δαυίδ φθόνον ἔσχεν... καὶ ὑπὸ Σαοὺλ βασιλέως Ἰσραὴλ ἐδιώχθη. In Just. Dial., 141, 4 it is deduced from his transgression of the Law in company with the wife of Uriah that the patriarchs were not allowed to take many wives as lovers and that polygamy was not, then, legitimate for David. [56] In Chr. preaching and teaching, however, the real importance of David is as a witness of Jesus Christ. Christians realise, with the Synagogue, that "all things will reach their end through the house of David" (Sib., 7, 31) and that the Messiah will comes as a shoot of the house of David (6, 16) and as the rod of David (8, 254). They appeal to the prophetic words in which David proclaimed Jesus Christ. He himself said prophetically in Ps. 110:1 that Jesus is not his Son but his Lord. From this one may see irrefutably πῶς Δαυίδ λέγει αὐτὸν κύριον, καὶ υἱὸν οὐ λέγει, Barn., 12, 10 f. Thanks are given in the eucharistic prayer: ὑπὲρ τῆς ἁγίας ἀμπέλου Δαυίδ τοῦ παιδός σου, ἧς ἐγνώρισας ἡμῖν διὰ Ἰησοῦ τοῦ παιδός σου, Did., 9, 2. This is said over the wine poured into the cup. The Messiah is the true vine whose wine is drunk at the celebration of the Lord's Supper. [57] The eucharist was introduced by the liturgical cry: ὡσαννὰ τῷ οἴκῳ [58] Δαυίδ, Did., 10, 6. This cry of jubilation refers to the coming of Christ who fulfilled the Davidic promises and will come again at the parousia. [59]

---

[54] Cf. Bultmann J., ad loc.; for another view cf. Michaelis, 327-330.

[55] Rev. 22:16 reads: ἡ ῥίζα καὶ τὸ γένος Δαυίδ.

[56] Cf. the exposition in Damasc. 5:2 (7:5) → 479, 21 ff.

[57] For details on ἄμπελος Δαυίδ cf. Kn. Did., ad loc.; M. Dibelius, "Die Mahlgebete in d. Didache," Botschaft u. Geschichte, II (1956), 119 f.: "The holy vine of David is thus the promised salvation. It must be presupposed that the expression is already an established symbol and that Hell. Judaism no longer has any specific passage in view."

[58] So acc. to the Coptic version. Acc. to other MSS: ὡσαννὰ τῷ θεῷ Δαυίδ cf. J. Jeremias, Die Abendmahlsworte Jesu⁴ (1967), 245, 250.

[59] In Ebionite circles the name of David was avoided or polemically depreciated. Criticism of the temple led to criticism of the kings who built it. Hence the Ebionites did not use the title Son of David for Jesus, cf. H. J. Schoeps, Theol. u. Geschichte d. Judenchristentums (1949), 242-7.

2. υἱὸς Δαυίδ.

Υἱὸς Δαυίδ is used by the early Church as a christological title, but it is regarded as a description of the Davidic descent of Jesus. [60] Ign. Eph., 20, 2 speaks of Jesus Christ, τῷ κατὰ σάρκα ἐκ γένους Δαυίδ, τῷ υἱῷ ἀνθρώπου καὶ υἱῷ θεοῦ, cf. R., 7, 3. Sm., 1, 1 calls Jesus Christ: ἀληθῶς ὄντα ἐκ γένους Δαυίδ κατὰ σάρκα, υἱὸν θεοῦ κατὰ θέλημα καὶ δύναμιν θεοῦ, γεγεννημένον ἀληθῶς ἐκ παρθένου. In Tr., 9, 1 we read: 'Ιησοῦ Χριστοῦ . . . τοῦ ἐκ γένους Δαυίδ, τοῦ ἐκ Μαρίας, and Eph., 18, 2 emphasises even more plainly that Jesus is of the house of David by His mother, the Virgin Mary: 'Ιησοῦς ὁ Χριστὸς ἐκυοφορήθη ὑπὸ Μαρίας κατ' οἰκονομίαν θεοῦ ἐκ σπέρματος μὲν Δαυίδ, πνεύματος δὲ ἁγίου. This idea is then maintained apologetically in Just. Dial., 45, 4 against the Jew Trypho: διὰ τῆς παρθένου ταύτης τῆς ἀπὸ τοῦ γένους τοῦ Δαυείδ γεννηθῆναι σαρκοποιηθεὶς ὑπέμεινεν, cf. 43, 1; 100, 3; 120, 2. From the 2nd cent. on it is the dominant view that Mary was of David's line and that Jesus was born as υἱὸς Δαυίδ through her. [61] Sometimes it is underlined that Joseph, too, was of the seed and race of David (Asc. Is. 11:2), [62] so that Jesus was of Davidic descent both on his mother's side and also on that of His foster-father, Joseph. [63]

Lohse

---

[60] There is an indirect indication of this in the tradition in Hegesipp. that two grandnephews of Jesus were brought before the emperor Domitian as descendants of David, Eus. Hist. Ecc., III, 20, 1 → n. 30.

[61] Cf. W. Bauer, *Das Leben Jesu im Zeitalter d. nt.lichen Apokr.* (1909), VI, 13-17, with further examples.

[62] Further examples in Bauer, *op. cit.* 4-6.

[63] On the use of the title υἱὸς Δαυίδ in the fathers cf. Daniélou, 597-603.

```
┌─────────────────────────┐
│ † ὕμνος,  † ὑμνέω,       │
│ † ψάλλω,  † ψαλμός       │
└─────────────────────────┘
```

ᾄδω   (→ I, 163, 40 ff.),   αἰνέω   (→ I, 177, 18 ff.),
δοξάζω (→ II, 253, 12 ff.),   μεγαλύνω (→ IV, 543, 8 ff.),
ἐξομολογέομαι (→ V, 213, 27 ff.).

Contents: A. The Greek Sphere: I. Usage; II. Greek Hymns to the Gods. B. The Old Testament and Judaism: I. The Word Groups in Translations of Jewish Literature; II. The Songs of the Old Testament and Judaism. C. The New Testament: I. The Word Groups in the New Testament; II. The Songs of Primitive Christianity. D. The Early Church: I. The Word Groups in the Apologists; II. The Songs of Early Christianity.

A. The Greek Sphere.

I. Usage.

1. ὕμνος (etym. uncertain) [1] is used by Hom. only in the combination ἀοιδῆς ὕμνος, perhaps "manner of song," Od., 8, 429. Pind. Olymp., 2, 1 addresses the songs which control the phorminx: [2] "What god, what hero, what man shall we extol?" In Aesch. ὕμνος often ref. to the song of the Furies (Ag., 1191), which has a constraining effect,

---

ὕ μ ν ο ς κ τ λ. A. Arens, *Die Ps. im Gottesdienst d. Alten Bundes* (1961); F. Behn, *Musikleben im Altertum u. frühen Mittelalter* (1954); R. Deichgräber, *Gotteshymnus u. Christushymnus in d. Urkirche* (1967); O. Eissfeldt, *Einl. in d. AT*³ (1963), 117-170, 599-613, 826-831, 887-891; H. Koller, "Das kitharodische Prooimion," *Philol.*, 100 (1956), 159-206; J. Kroll, *Die chr. Hymnodik bis zu Klemens v. Alex., Verzeichnis d. Vorlesungen an d. Akademie zu Braunsberg* (Summer Semester, 1921); H. J. Marrou, *Gesch. d. Erziehung im klass. Altertum* (1957), 198-208; E. Norden, *Agnostos Theos* (1923); É. des Places, "Hymnes grecs au seuil de l'ère chrétienne," *Biblica*, 38 (1957), 113-129; J. U. Powell, *Collectanea Alexandrina* (1925); J. Quasten, *Musik u. Gesang in d. Kulten d. heidnischen Antike u. chr. Frühzeit* (1930); J. M. Robinson, "Die Hodajot-Formel in Gebet u. Hymnus d. Frühchristentums," *Apophoreta, Festschr. E. Haenchen*, ZNW Beih., 30 (1964), 194-235; J. Schattenmann, *Stud. zum ntl.lichen Prosahymnus* (1965); E. Schweizer, "Erniedrigung u. Erhöhung bei Jesus u. seinen Nachfolgern," AbhThANT, 28 (1955); A. Sendrey - M. Norton, *David's Harp. The Story of Music in Biblical Times* (1964); W. S. Smith, *Musical Aspects of the NT*, Diss. Amsterdam (1962); O. Söhngen, "Theol. Grundlagen der Kirchenmusik," *Leiturgia*, IV (1961), 2-15; M. Wegner, *Das Musikleben d. Griechen* (1949); A. N. Wilder, *Early Christian Rhetoric* (1964), 97-125; R. Wünsch, Art. "Hymnos," Pauly-W., 9a (1914), 140-183.
[1] Cf. Boisacq, Hofmann, *s.v.* [Risch].
[2] The four-stringed instrument of antiquity, cf. H. Abert, Art. "Saiteninstrumente," Pauly-W., 1b (1920), 1761 f.; Wegner, 29 f., 222 f. (texts and ancient ill.), Plate 1; Behn, 80 f.; M. Wegner, *Griechenland Musikgesch. in Bildern*, II, 4 (1963), Index, *s.v.*

cf. ὕμνος δέσμιος in Eum., 306, cf. 332 f., 344 f.; ὕμνοις αἰτησόμεθα in Pers., 625, in both cases the song of the chorus. ὕμνος can also denote the text and melody, e.g., ὕμνον ποιέω, Hdt., IV, 35, 3 etc. The distinction of an author of divine songs is mentioned, e.g., by Ditt. Syll.[3], I, 449 (c. 243 B.C.). Cleochares wrote for the god ποθόδιόν (= προσόδιόν) τε καὶ παιᾶνα καὶ ὕμνον so that boys might sing them at the sacrifice of Theoxenia, ibid., I, 450, 3 f. (c. 227 B.C.). For to soothe or touch by songs (like Orpheus) cf. Eur. Alc., 359, to honour by hymns Hipp., 55 f., in Eur. and elsewhere mostly the religious song; ἱεροὶ ὕμνοι occurs in Aristoph. Av., 210, ὕμνοι with ᾠδαί in Av., 1743; the κίθαρις [3] is called the mother of hymns in Thes., 124. That invocation of the names of the gods is important in hymns is apparent from Hdt., IV, 35, 2 f., where the names of the authors are also transmitted. Plat. Leg., III, 700b d demands that the original distinction between εἴδη ... ᾠδῆς, ὕμνοι, i.e., εὐχαὶ πρὸς θεούς, and θρῆνοι (→ III, 149, 2 ff.) and παίωνες and διθύραμβοι [4] be maintained. Sung ὕμνοι θεῶν καὶ ἐγκώμια are associated with prayers, VII, 801e. In Plato's state anyone who introduces other ὕμνοι than those established can be prosecuted for ἀσέβεια (→ VII, 185, 8 ff.), 799b. The living should not be honoured by encomiums and hymns, 802a. Demosth. uses the word only in Or., 21, 51 for hymns after oracular prophecies. Epict. individualises the praise of God. In digging, ploughing and eating one should ᾄδειν τὸν ὕμνον τὸν εἰς τὸν θεόν· μέγας ὁ θεός who has granted us tools and given us hands, throat and belly. If others are blind to this, those who see should sing hymns to God on behalf of all; what else can I still do as a crippled old man, εἰ μὴ ὑμνεῖν τὸν θεόν; Epict. Diss., I, 16, 16-20, cf. III, 26 and 30.

2. ὑμνέω [5] means first "to sing a song" of praise, then with acc. of person or thing, e.g., "to praise the gods in choral song," Hom. Hymn. Ap., 158 f.; ποιηταὶ ὑμνήκασι περί ..., Thuc., I, 21, 1; Homer (cf. Hom. Hymn. Ap., 156-164 sang the dances of the women of Delos, Thuc., III, 104, 5. But then ὑμνέω means gen. "to extol," "to praise." Pericles says in a speech: ἃ ... τὴν πόλιν ὕμνησα Thuc., II, 42, 2, cf. "to praise" someone's ἀρετή, Xenoph. Hier., 11, 8, to be lauded as the saviour of peace, Jos. Bell., 1, 205, "to affirm solemnly," "to stress," Plat. Resp., II, 364a, "to (re)cite a law verbatim," Leg., IX, 871a. For common use in relation to the gods cf. Epict. (→ lines 20 ff.); one must praise God at the beginning of a feast, Xenophanes Fr., 1, 13 (Diels, I, 127). King and people "praised" God and sang all kinds of native songs when the ark was brought up into Jerusalem, Jos. Ant., 7, 80. Philo obviously uses the verb in the sense "to praise," e.g., God., 253; Vit. Mos., II, 239; Conf. Ling., 149, the no. 10, Congr., 89, righteousness, Rer. Div. Her. 161 etc., even when the ref. is to a song, Leg. All., II, 102.

3. ψάλλω perhaps meant orig. "to touch" (etym. [6] akin to ψηλαφάω), then "to pluck" the string, to cause it to spring, of the string of a bow, Eur. Ba., 784; Dio C., 49, 27, 4, "to play a stringed instrument," Aristoph. Eq., 522; Menand. Epit., 301, "to pluck" strings with the fingers (opp. κρούω τῷ πλήκτρῳ), Plat. Lys., 209b, with κιθαρίζω and καπηλεύω as not a manly activity, Hdt., I, 155, 4, cf. the antithesis: to bear weapons — ψάλλω, to play the flute, [7] to be a brothel-keeper and merchant etc., Plut. Apophth. Xerxes, 2 (II, 173c). When Alexander skilfully plays a stringed instrument at a feast his father reproaches him: "Are you not ashamed to play (ψάλλειν) so well?" Plut. Pericl., 1, 6 (I, 152 f.); of the ψάλλειν καὶ αὐλεῖν of γύναια at banquets, Plut.

---

[3] On the cither cf. H. Abert, Art. "Lyra," Pauly-W., 13a (1927), 2479-2485; Wegner, 32-7, 206-210 (ancient texts and ill.), Plate 7a, 8 f., 18 f., 29a, 31, 32a; Behn, 79, 81-3, Plate 46-8; Quasten, Index, s.v.; Wegner, op. cit. (→ n. 2), Index, s.v.

[4] These belong to Dionysus; Διθύραμβος is one of his names, Eur. Ba., 526. Cf. O. Crusius, Art. "Dithyrambos," Pauly-W., 5a (1905), 1203-1230.

[5] From Hes. Theog., 11 [Risch].

[6] Cf. Boisacq, Hofmann, s.v. [Risch].

[7] αὐλός is really an oboe acc. to Marrou, 198.

De Arato, 6, 3 (I, 1029e). In teaching: [8] διδάξει... κιθαρίζειν ἢ ψάλλειν, Ditt. Syll.[3], II, 578, 17 f. (2nd cent. B.C.). To practise one's τέχνη an ὄργανον is needed, one cannot play the flute without a flute nor ψάλλειν without a lyre, [9] Luc. De Parasito, 17. [10]

4. ψαλμός is "plucking" the string of a bow, Eur. Ion., 173; Herc. Fur., 1064, or "playing" a stringed instrument, Pind. Fr., 125, distinguished from κιθαρισμός in a list of victors (in a contest for young people), Ditt. Syll.[3], III, 959, 10. [11] Elisha was seized by the Spirit of God while engaged in ψαλμός, playing a stringed instrument, Jos. Ant., 9, 35, cf. also 7, 80; ᾠδή and ψαλμός are mentioned in the Bacchic procession, Plut. Alex., 67, 5 (I, 702c), αὐλοί, ψαλμοί, μέθαι among pirates, Pomp., 24, 5 (I, 631b); dances, tinklings, ψαλμοί and licentious nights are mentioned in the description of a Parthian Sybaris, Crass., 32, 5 (I, 564d), with φόρμιγξ (thus denoting the instrument?) De amicorum multitudine, 8 (II, 96e). [12]

II. Greek Hymns to the Gods.

The form and style of the Gk. liturgical hymn [13] may be seen in the tragedians [14] and Aristoph. [15] Not by chance it is put on the lips of the choruses here. The cultic songs [16] in the Gk. language which have survived from actual use were mostly put on

---

[8] But there is no mention of victors in the αὐλός, Marrou, 198. Aristot. Pol., VIII, 6, p. 1341a, 18-24 excludes it from instruction as οὐκ... ἠθικὸν ἀλλὰ μᾶλλον ὀργιαστικόν.

[9] On the lyre cf. Abert, op. cit. (→ n. 3), 2479-2485; also op. cit. (→ n. 2), 1761-1764; Wegner, 37-44, 215-220 (texts and ill.), Plate 2b, 16 f., 19, 21 f., 24 f.; Behn, 79, 83-90, Plate 49-52; Quasten, Index, s.v.; Wegner, op. cit. (→ n. 2), Index, s.v.

[10] Plut. Quaest. Conv., VII, 8, 4 (II, 713b) discusses the question of music at table; it can regulate the base soul by ἐπιψάλλειν and κατανλεῖν. Guests who have the muse within them one should not κατανλεῖν καὶ καταψάλλειν ἔξωθεν, VII, 8, 4 (II, 713e).

[11] On the difference between the two v. Plat. Lys., 209b → 490, 38 f.

[12] ψάλτης for a (professional) player of a stringed instrument seems to be rare, Plut. Pomp., 36, 4 (I, 638d). More common is ψάλτρια: Noble and cultured participants in a symposium do not need the foolish and childish pranks of women playing the flute and dancing, ψάλτριαι, Plat. Prot., 347d. The street-police keep a watch on women flautists, ψάλτριαι and κιθαρίστριαι, esp. to prevent overcharging, also garbage collectors, Aristot. Ἀθηναίων Πολιτεία, 50, 2 (ed. H. Oppermann [1961]); cf. Plut. De Cleomene, 12, 3 (I, 810a); Luc. Bis Accusatus, 16. ψαλτήριον is a stringed instrument; one should not listen to the flute and ψαλτήριον without words and song, that the spirit may be entertained and ennobled (v. already Plat. Leg., II, 669e, cf. Aristot. Pol., VIII, 6, p. 1341a, 24 f.); Plut. Quaest. Conv., VII, 8, 4 (II, 713c). For attacks on the emancipation of music from words cf. W. Jaeger, Paideia, II (1944), 298 f.; Söhngen, 87. On the ethical evaluation of music in antiquity v. A. J. Neubecker, Die Bewertung d. Musik bei Stoikern u. Epikureern (1956); earlier bibl. 100.

[13] On the genres cf. Wegner, 75-81. Originally in Gk. songs were specialised for the different cults and rites, as denoted by the ancient cultic cries (ἰὴ παιάν etc.). But this type of distinction obviously began to disappear in the 5th cent. The dithyrambos Bacchyl., 17, acc. to the concluding prayer, is addressed to Apollo rather than Dionysus, while the paean of → 492, 13 f. (strictly an Apollo song) is addressed to Dionysus. The encomium was origin. a song in praise of a man sung at a festal banquet or procession [Dihle].

[14] Cf. F. Adami, "De poetis scaenicis Graecis sacrorum imitatoribus," Jbch. f. klass. Philologie, Suppl. 26 (1901), 213-262; Wünsch, 162-4.

[15] The choral lyric develops out of the cultic song. Cultic songs are also the model for songs like the hymn of Alcaios Fr. B, 2a (ed. E. Lobel and D. Page, Poetarum Lesbiorum Fr. [1955], 125 f.) to the Dioscuri and highly personal songs like that to Aphrodite by Sappho Fr., 1 (Lobel and Page, 2 f.) [Risch].

[16] The Hom. Hymn. in hexameter are songs in praise of the respective deities and are not cultic, cf. Wünsch, 147-156, also Koller, 173-182. On the singing of hexameters ibid., 163-7 and the accompanying instrument, 159-163. The Zeus hymn of Cleanthes is a philosophical imitation of hymns to the gods, Stob. Ecl., I, 25-27. In another measure Aristot. in Fr., 5 (Diehl[3], I, 117-9) wrote a hymn to Ἀρετή. On this group cf. M. Meunier, Hymnes philosophiques d'Aristote, Cleanthe et Proclus (1935), v. also des Places, 116-123.

inscr. in the Hell. period. [17] Their types are well known to a cultured Jew of the Dispersion. Philo in Vit. Cont., 80 mentions hymns sung in festal processions, [18] at libations,
at the altar, and by a standing choir. Choirs sang them from an early period. Ditt. Syll.[3],
II, 695, 28 f. (after 129 B.C.) mentions girls' choirs for Artemis Leukophryene. In the
Hell. and esp. the imperial period we often read of boys' choirs; the poet of the hymn
teaches the sons of citizens to sing the song to the λύρα, II, 662, 12-14 (c. 165/164 B.C.
→ 490, 4 ff.). A choir of ephebes sings at the solemn opening of the temple of Dionysus
in Teos, CIG, II, 3062, 7-10 (age of Tiberius). There is ref. to a choir of 30 boys in CIG,
II, 2715a, 7 f. [19] ὑμνοδιδάσκαλοι are mentioned, III, 1115, 26 (1st cent. A.D.). [20] The
melodies for certain hymns have been preserved. [21] Many hymns are obviously shared
by the soloists and choir, or choir and other cultic participants. The refrains (→ 497, 3 f.)
or cultic cries which frequently end strophes bear testimony to this, so in the Dionysus
paean of a Philodamos of Skarpheia: [22] ἰὲ Παιάν, ἴθι σωτήρ / εὔφρων τάνδε πόλιν
φύλασσ᾽ / εὐαίωνι σὺν ὄλβῳ. We often find the isolated cry ἰὴ (ἰὲ) Παιάν after which
the genre called paeans took its name (παιάν is orig. an epiclesis for Apollo), [23] cf.
the Aesculapius hymn of Erythraea. [24] Hymns often have a related structure: invocation
of the god, praise of his birth, of his acts, and prayer for his coming.

There is sometimes a mixture of style in Gk. hymns to alien, e.g., Egypt. deities. In the
Isis hymn of Andros [25] the mode of self-revelation in I sayings, in which the deity itself
speaks, [26] is combined with Gk. elements in form (hexameter) and style. [27] In the Anubis
hymn of Kios (Bithynia), [28] of which only the opening — an address — has been preserved, the Gk. influence on the structure seems to be stronger. Finally ὕμνος becomes
a gen. term for praise of the gods, Ael. Arist. Or., 45, 4 (Keil), who distinguishes between
rhythmic prose address to the gods and the hymns of poets. [29] The stylistic elements used
by him are older, e.g., lists of predicates with οὗτος, [30] Or., 43, 29 f. (Keil), sometimes
with part., cf. 45, 29. 32 (Keil); [31] esp. with part. this is very significant in the encomium

---

[17] Nilsson, II[2], 60; Wünsch, 169 f.
[18] On the processional song cf. R. Muth, Art. "Prosodion," Pauly-W., 23 (1957), 856-863.
On the choral movement → n. 53.
[19] Cf. Dio C., 59, 29, 6: the sons of leading families are brought from Greece and Ionia
to sing the ὕμνος to Caligula. On school choirs in worship cf. M. P. Nilsson, Die hell. Schule
(1955), 70 f.; Marrou, 200-202.
[20] L. Ziehen, Art. "Hymnodoi," Pauly-W., Suppl., 7 (1940), 279-281. Cf. Ditt. Or., I,
56, 68-70 (cult for Berenice who died young, Ptolemy III).
[21] Examples in Powell, 142-8, 150-9.
[22] Powell, 165-9.
[23] Cf. T. Eisele, Art. "Paian," Roscher, III, 1246-1250; on the paean gen. cf. J. Wiesener,
Art. "Paian," Pauly-W., 18 (1942), 2340-2363.
[24] Powell, 136 f., also used in Ptolemais, Egypt. For a paean to Hygieia, associated with
Aesculapius, cf. at the end of the 4th cent. B.C. Ariphron Fr., 1, ed. D. Page, Poetae Melici
Graeci (1962), 422 f.
[25] The inscr. is put at the beginning of the 1st cent. A.D. v. W. Peek, Der Isishymnus v.
Andros und verwandte Texte (1930), 100. The verses of the goddess precede her statements.
The Isis hymn of Mesomedes (freedman of Hadrian, text in Peek, 145 and Powell, 198, v.
des Places, 125-8) describes in paeans (3rd person, then 2nd) the comprehensive work of the
goddess in nature and the widespread honour paid her.
[26] The so-called Isis hymn of Kyme or Io (Peek, op. cit. [→ n. 25], 122-4) is in ordinary
prose (not rhythmic); the text begins with the words of the goddess.
[27] An iambic Isis poem (inscr., 103 A.D.) in Peek, 129, which begins with I statements, in
the main puts only the prose I sayings in verse.
[28] The text is post-Augustan, cf. Peek, 138; text, 139.
[29] A prose address to a god is called θεολογία in the Iobakchoi inscr. Ditt. Syll.[3], III,
1109, 115 (before 178 A.D.). The ὑμνητής of a goddess is the author of Inscr., 1111; one
may guess from the text that his function was to praise the goddess.
[30] Isis hymn of Andros (→ n. 25), 34-39: ἅδε (with 1st person).
[31] Cf. Norden, 164 f.

to Augustus in Philo Leg. Gaj., 145-8. The final c. of Ps.-Aristot. Mund., 7, p. 401a, 12-27, cf. already 6, p. 397b, 13-24 etc., offers a prose hymn to Zeus. Some of the elements of rhythmic prose are used by Jos. or his source in praise of God, Ap., 2, 188-192. Menander (3rd cent. A.D.) deals theoretically with the different types of divine hymns in Περὶ ἐπιδεικτικῶν, Ι, 1-9. [32] The hymn in Corp. Herm., 13, 17-20 [33] reminds us of OT praise. In Corp. Herm. ὕμνος is close to εὐλογία, 13, 15, cf. the styling of the ὕμνος (1, 31) as εὐλογία (1, 30). In 1, 31 three lines begin with ἅγιος ὁ θεός, twice three with ἅγιος εἶ.

B. The Old Testament and Judaism.

I. The Word Groups in Translations of Jewish Literature.

1. In the LXX ὕμνος occurs 5 times for תְּהִלָּה "song of praise" at ψ 39:4; 64:2; 99:4; 118:171, cf. 2 Εσδρ. 22:46, 6 times for נְגִינָה in the title εἰς τὸ τέλος (→ 52, 37 ff.) ἐν ὕμνοις Ps. 6; ψ 53:1; 54 (in these 3 instances 'A has ἐν ψαλμοῖς, Σ διὰ ψαλτηρίων); 60; 66; 75, once for תְּפִלָּה ψ 71:20 (clearly ὕμνος is intentionally selected here, cf. the context), once for שִׁיר Is. 42:10 (also chosen in acc. with the context). The meaning of ὕμνος for the translators may also be seen in other places, e.g., 2 Ch. 7:6. [34] In the Hexapla תְּהִלָּה esp. is transl. ὕμνος, cf. for 'Α, Σ and Θ ψ 21:4, for Σ ψ 65:2, 8; 70:14; 144:1; Is. 43:21. [35]

2. As regards ὑμνέω most of the LXX instances are in Da. 3 (36 times), vv. 57-88 in the imp. with εἰς τοὺς αἰῶνας. In the main ὑμνέω is used for הלל [36] pi, cf. 2 Ch. 29:30 (twice); ψ 21:23; Ju. 16:24 B (A ᾔνεσαν); 2 Εσδρ. 22:24, then שִׁיר in ψ 64:14; Is. 42:10, ידה hi in Is. 12:4; 25:1, זמר pi in 1 Ch. 16:9; Is. 12:5, רנן q (of sophia; LXX pass.) Prv. 1:20; 8:3, רנן hi Sir. 39:35; the verb is also used plainly for magnifying esp. cultic. In 'A ὑμνέω occurs 8 times for הלל pi (more often than in LXX), 8 times in Σ, once in Θ; it is used once for ידה hi in 'A, twice in Σ, once in Θ; for רנן pi Σ has it at ψ 58:17; 89:14 etc. Where 'A, Σ Θ have ὑμνέω LXX usually has other verbs, esp. (ἐπ)αινέω, but also ἐξομολογέομαι, ἀγαλλιάομαι. There is, however, no difference in the understanding of ὑμνέω. [37]

3. ψάλλω occurs some 40 times in LXX for זמר pi, only Ps. apart from Ju. 5:3; 2 Βασ. 22:50; it is then used 10 times for נגן pi, only 1 and 4 Βασ., q only ψ 67:26, other forms of נגן ψ 68:13; Sir. 9:4. [38] The meaning is "to play a stringed instrument," 1 Βασ. 16:16 (κινύρα → n. 48), 17, 23; 19:9; 4 Βασ. 3:15. In these instances playing is not accompanied by song. When the original is זמר pi the influence of this verb possibly extends the meaning. But often the obvious sense is "to play," esp. when an instrument is mentioned ψ 32:2; 70:22 f.; 97:5 (cf. 4); 143:9; 146:7; Ps. 149:3, but also ψ 26:6; 56:8; 100:1 f.; 104:2; 107:2, where singing and playing go together, v. also ψ 17:50; 56:10

---

[32] Rhetores Graeci, III (ed. L. Spengel [1856]), 331-344.
[33] Cf. on this G. Zuntz, "On the Hymns in Corp. Herm., XIII," Herm., 83 (1955), 68-92.
[34] Cf. also Jdt. 16:13; 1 Macc. 4:33; 13:51; 2 Macc. 10:7, 38. ὕμνοι accompany sacrifices, 2 Macc. 1:30; one sings them when going into battle, 12:37. The Ps. Sol. 10, 14, 16 bear the title ὕμνος, while 2 f., 5, 13, 15, 17 f. have the title ψαλμός. But there is no discernible difference in style or content, cf. 3:1 f. → n. 71.
[35] Test. L. 3:8 says that in the third heaven ὕμνοι are constantly addressed to God, cf. G. 7:2.
[36] Cf. the sense "to extol," "to praise," 1 QS 10:17; 1 QM 14:12 (12:1; 19:13), often in 1 QH, esp. of God's name as always in 1 QM.
[37] Cf. also ὑμνέω "to praise" par. δοξάζω in Test. Jos. 8:5.
[38] ψάλλω does not occur in the LXX in works with no HT.

(cf. v. 9); 107:4 (cf. v. 3). Elsewhere the idea of praise by song as well as stringed instrument is suggested, [39] Ps. 9:11; ψ 29:5; 65:4. One may see this understanding in the LXX also when it has τῷ ὀνόματι for HT שֵׁם (acc.), Ps. 7:17; 9:2; ψ 60:9; 65:4; 67:5, cf. 65:2 (not 20:14), cf. (לְשֵׁם) ψ 17:50; 91:2; 134:3, also acc. אֱלֹהִים ψ 46:7, or personal pron. "thee" ψ 56:10; 107:4; 137:1, for which LXX has the dat. Hence one must take into account a shift of meaning in the LXX in other passages in which the idea of playing is not evident. In many places the thought of "to play" to Yahweh (in His honour) is a natural one, and this could be introduced into other passages, esp. when the Gk. equivalent contains esp. the idea of playing.

4. ψαλμός occurs over 50 times for מִזְמוֹר [40] (only Ps. titles), for נְגִינָה "taunting song," Lam. 3:14, "playing on a stringed instrument," Lam. 5:14 (uncertain meaning Ps. 4 title), for זִמְרָה Am. 5:23; ψ 97:5, "the playing of a stringed instrument" or the "stringed instrument" itself ψ 80:3. ψαλμός is also used for "playing on strings" (erroneously for עוּגָב "flute") at Job 21:12; 30:31, but cf. 1 Βασ. 16:18 (for נגן pi) and 2 Βασ. 23:1; ψ 94:2 (for זָמִיר) the "song accompanied by a stringed instrument," cf. ψ 146:1 (for זמר pi). This is clearly the meaning in the title too, also to Ps. 7 (for שִׁגָּיוֹן); ψ 45 (for שִׁיר, normally transl. ᾠδή, very common in Ps. titles) and in the title of the Psalter (for תְּהִלָּה) [41] in B (A ψαλτήριον, not in S). ψαλμός is used for the instrument נֵבֶל in ψ 70:22. [42]

II. The Songs of the Old Testament and Judaism.

1. Only a few remarks can be made on the songs of the OT, [43] with ref. for the most part to the LXX. As an example of an OT hymn [44] in the narrower sense one might adduce first ψ 135. It begins with a three-membered call for praise of God (ἐξομολο-γεῖσθε . . .), vv. 1-3. It then recounts God's acts in creation, vv. 4-9. He is next extolled

---

[39] Cf. זמר in the Qumran Scrolls: "to play" 1 QH 11:23, "to sing" 11:5; 1 QS 10:9; on the fig. use → n. 71.

[40] Not so far found in the Qumran literature [Rengstorf].

[41] Cf. "praise" in 1 QH 11:23; 1 QS 10:8; 1 QM 4:14, a specific "song" 14:2.

[42] In works with no HT ψαλμός occurs only at 3 Macc. 6:35: "song of praise," in connection with dances and festal banquets. ψαλτήριον is mostly used for names of instruments. כִּנּוֹר 5 times and נֵבֶל 8, ten-stringed in ψ 91:4. In Leisegang, s.v. the noun is the only word in the group ψαλ- in Philo: Jubal the father ψαλτηρίου καὶ κιθάρας, Poster. C., 111, from Gn. 4:21 quoted in Poster. C., 103, → VII, 77, 23 ff., cf. also Jos. Ant., 1, 64. Singers in the LXX are usually ψαλτῳδοί (ψαλμῳδοί only in the vl. at Sir. 47:9; 50:18; 1 Macc. 11:70), cf. ψαλτῳδέω (of temple singing) in 2 Ch. 5:13, ἱεροψάλται in 1 Εσδρ. 1:15 for the temple singers in Jerusalem → n. 48. Egypt. temple singers are to have someone in mind in ὕμνοι, Ditt. Or., II, 737, 16 f. (2nd cent. B.C.). If the word then denotes the singer gen. and not just the player (Dittenberger, ad loc.), this means that singing and playing are again related. Already in the non-Chr. sphere the word by its very structure differentiates between the temple singer or musician and the secular singer; the secular singer did not enjoy a good reputation → 490, 40 ff. The ψάλται and ψαλτῳδοί in 1 Εσδρ. 5:41 are secular singers (male and female). The term διάψαλμα, found over 75 times in ψ, is as difficult as the original סֶלָה; traditionally διάψαλμα is understood as a musical interlude. N. H. Snaith, "Selah," VT, 2 (1952), 43-56, esp. 54 recalls διαύλιον for "musical interlude" on the flute (Hesych., s.v.). He thinks that at סלה the choir sang "O give thanks unto the Lord for he is good, for his mercy endureth for ever" (→ n. 45), this being introduced at the beginning of the 4th cent. B.C., 55 f. Philologically cf. for סלה E. G. Hirsch, Art "Selah," Jew. Enc., 11 (1909), 161-3.

[43] On the Ps. gen. cf. H. Gunkel and J. Begrich, Einl. in d. Ps. (1933); Eissfeldt, 136-166: "Kultische Lieder"; Sendrey-Norton, 54-92, on the musical aspect, 64-81, on music in the OT Smith, 1-21 (with bibl.).

[44] For specific hymns in the OT v. Gunkel-Begrich, op. cit., 32-94; Eissfeldt, 141-6.

as the Liberator from Egypt and as Helper during the wilderness period and the conquest, vv. 10-22. He is praised gen. as Deliverer in v. 23 f. and the Giver of sustenance in v. 25. The call to worship is taken up again at the end in v. 26. We thus find all the decisive themes of the praise of God in the OT. The second half of each v. underlines the element of praise with its ὅτι εἰς τὸν αἰῶνα τὸ ἔλεος αὐτοῦ, which almost always breaks the sequence of clauses. This was obviously sung by a second choir or the cultic community, as also in the *diaspora*, cf. Philo → 497, 1 ff. The same "for his mercy endureth for ever" occurs also in ψ 117:1-4, where first the people (Israel), then the priests (the house of Aaron), then those who fear the Lord (all who fear the Lord, LXX) are summoned to offer praise. [45] The part. style of the HT is imitated in ψ 135 and even put for the Hbr. impf. in v. 18; v. 16b (the miracle of the rock which gives water) and v. 26b are added in the LXX. In Ps. 148 the thought of creation is central. The psalm as a whole is one long summons to all that God has created in heaven (vv. 1-6) and earth (vv. 7 ff.), esp. men (vv. 11-13), to praise God (αἰνεῖτε). The structure of Da. 3:52-90 (only LXX and Θ, probably orig. Hbr.) [46] is similar. The imp. εὐλογεῖτε is addressed to heaven and its powers etc. vv. 58-73, the earth and its parts and animals vv. 74-81, men v. 82 and esp. Israel, the righteous etc. vv. 83-87. In the second line of each v. ὑμνεῖτε καὶ ὑπερυψοῦτε αὐτὸν εἰς τοὺς αἰῶνας catches up the εὐλογεῖτε. The song in 1 Ch. 16:8-36 extols God's acts for His people vv. 9-22 and speaks of the praising of God by the nations vv. 23-29 and by (earthly) creation vv. 30-33. Here again the imp. plays a decisive role. ψ 145 also has a hymnic character. Here the part. style of the Hbr. in vv. 6-9a is retained by the LXX only in vv. 6-7b. In vv. 7c-9a end-forms are used and perhaps not directly for the sake of rhyme, though this is ending rhyme in vv. 7c-9a (inner rhyme in v. 8a b; in vv. 6-9 the order of words is exactly the same as the HT, as often in the LXX).

2. Apart from prayer the singing of psalms is associated with sacrifices in the temple acc. to 2 Macc. 1:30: οἱ δὲ ἱερεῖς ἐπέψαλλον τοὺς ὕμνους. The cultus is started again in the desecrated sanctuary of Jerusalem ἐν ᾠδαῖς καὶ κιθάραις καὶ κινύραις καὶ κυμβάλοις, 1 Macc. 4:54. For the tamid offering there were set psalms for each day, Ps. 92 for the Sabbath (so already the HT), 24 for Sunday, 48 for Monday, 82 Tuesday, 94 Wednesday, 81 Thursday, and 93 Friday (so LXX), Tamid, 7, 4.

3. Jos. also calls the songs of the OT ὕμνοι (εἰς τὸν θεόν), Ap., 1. 40. Ex. 15 is an ᾠδὴ εἰς τὸν θεόν, Ant., 2, 346 in hexameters; Dt. 32 is a ποίησις ἑξάμετρος, 4, 303. [47] To the story in Ex. 18:12 Jos. appends as a matter of course the ὕμνους τε ᾖδον, 3, 64. Those returning from the Feast of the Dedication do not feel the toils of the way for joy

---

[45] "For he is good, for his mercy endureth for ever" (Ps. 106:1; 107:1; 118:1; 136:1; only the second part 136:2-26) is in 2 Ch. 5:13; 7:3; Ezr. 3:11 a definite choral song (sung by the Levites apart from 2 Ch. 7:3), or a refrain (→ n. 42), or a specific part of the temple liturgy related to the thankoffering in Jer. 33:11. In 2 Ch. 20:21 f. "Praise the Lord, for his mercy endureth for ever" is sung by the singers of Yahweh at the commencement of battle; the miraculous help of Yahweh in v. 22 is obviously related thereto, cf. 1 QM 13:2, though there seems to be no exact par. here. Acc. to the context in which "for his mercy endureth for ever" occurs, it ref. to the fact that Yahweh is at hand to help His chosen people, cf. 1 Ch. 16:41; 2 Ch. 7:6. The solid place of כי טוב .... in the life of Judaism may be seen from 1 Macc. 4:24: after a victory in the Maccabean Wars the Jews praise God ὅτι καλόν (incorrectly ref. to ἔλεος), ὅτι εἰς τὸν αἰῶνα τὸ ἔλεος αὐτοῦ. On the whole subj. cf. K. Koch, "Denn seine Güte währet ewiglich," *Ev. Theol.*, 21 (1961), 531-544. Acc. to M. Weise, "Kultzeiten u. kultischer Bundesschluss in d. 'Ordensregel' vom Toten Meer," *Post-Bibl.*, 3 (1961), 72 f. the ref. in 2 Ch. 5:13 (also 20:21; 29:30) is to the Song of Asaph in 1 Ch. 16:8-36, possibly also in 1 QS 1:19.

[46] Cf. further Eissfeldt, 799.

[47] Cf. Eus. Praep. Ev., 11, 5, 7, also on Jos. Ant., 7, 305. ψαλμός is used in Jos. only for playing the zither → 491, 4 ff., Schl. Lk., 126 [Rengstorf].

ὕμνους εἰς τὸν θεὸν ᾄδοντες, 8, 124. The Levites, called ὑμνῳδοί, 7, 364, stand at sacrifice "in the circle with the musical instruments" and ᾖδον ὕμνους εἰς τὸν θεὸν καὶ ἔψαλλον, "as they were taught by David," 9, 269, cf. 7, 305: ᾠδὰς εἰς τὸν θεὸν καὶ ὕμνους, and also 364. David composed ᾠδὰς εἰς τὸν θεὸν καὶ ὕμνους in various metres, four and five feet, 7, 305; Jos. naturally wanted to stress that there was something corresponding to Gk. hymns in Judaism. Agrippa II appointed a group of Levites who performed lesser duties in the temple τοὺς ὕμνους ἐκμαθεῖν and naturally to sing; he was punished for these and other offences against the πάτριοι νόμοι. The cultic order is sacrosanct in respect of the singing of psalms in the temple, Jos. Ant., 20, 218. [48]

4. That the father in the *diaspora* taught his sons the Song of Moses in Dt. 32 (cf. also 2 Macc. 7:6) is mentioned in 4 Macc. 18:18; it is said just before that he sang psalms for them: τὸν ὑμνογράφον ἐμελῴδει ὑμῖν Δαυιδ, v. 15. Test. Job 14 [49] ref. to musical accompaniments, esp. on the ten-stringed κιθάρα → n. 48. Job plays it and the widows he supports sing songs to God after meals, ἔψαλλον (I) αὐταῖς καὶ αὐταὶ ὕμνουν.

5. Philo uses ὕμνος [50] regularly for the OT Psalms, clearly so in introducing quotations: ἐν ὕμνοις λέγεται, ᾄδεται (a quotation from the Ps. follows) etc., Fug., 59; Mut. Nom., 115; Som., I, 75; II, 242 and 245; Conf. Ling., 52; Migr. Abr., 157. [51] Philo often states expressly that ὕμνοι were sung; this brings out the significance of religious songs for the Jewish *diaspora*. The thankoffering enjoined in Lv. 7:12 includes hymns, praises, prayers, offerings and other thanksgiving, Spec. Leg., I, 224. Divine worship in the temple is described in terms of hymns, prayers and offerings, I, 193. The Passover is observed μετ᾽ εὐχῶν καὶ ὕμνων, II, 148 (→ 499, 12). The name Judas is a significant σύμβολον... τῶν... εἰς θεὸν ᾠδῶν τε καὶ ὕμνων (cf. Gn. 29:35; 49:8) Som., II, 33 f., cf. Plant., 135; the combination ὕμνοι and ᾠδαί occurs also in Spec. Leg., III, 125; Flacc., 122. Of all the good things we can "conceive" the best and most perfect is a hymn to the Father of all, Plant., 135. The one whom God endows with spiritual gifts must respond

---

[48] Stringed instruments which David introduced acc. to Jos. Ant., 7, 306 were the κινύρα, ten-stringed 1 QM 4:5, struck with a plectron (for כִּנּוֹר almost exclusively in the historical books in the LXX, κιθάρα in Ps. and Is., cf. 1 K. 14:7; Rev. 5:8; 14:2; 15:2), and νάβλα, twelve-toned, played with the fingers (LXX only in the historical books for נֵבֶל); the two occur together in 1 Βασ. 10:5; 2 Βασ. 6:5; 3 Βασ. 10:12; 1 Ch. 13:8; 15:16, 28; 16:5; 25:1, 6; 2 Ch. 5:12; 20:28; 29:25; 1 Macc. 13:51. The former is mentioned in 1 QS 10:9; 1 QH 5:30; 11:22, 23, the latter in 1 QS 10:9; 1 QM 4:5; 1 QH 11:23. Jos. Ant., 11, 128; 12, 142 ref. to the freedom of ἱεροψάλται from taxes. In the Hexapla ψαλτήριον (LXX κινύρα) occurs at 1 Βασ. 16:16 ᾽Α, 23 Θ, ψαλτήριον (LXX κιθάρα) ψ 42:4; Is. 16:11; 30:32 (also all three Σ, which has ψαλτήριον 8 times); cf. Sendrey-Norton, 113-131 (with Ill.).

[49] Ed. S. Brock, *Test. Iobi* (1968).

[50] Philo seems to use ᾆσμα only rarely for psalm (→ n. 51), cf. ψ 22 in Mut. Nom., 115, ψ 45 in Som., II, 246, cf. also for 1 Βασ. 2:1-10 in Deus Imm., 10; Mut. Nom., 143, for Nu. 23:19 (-24) in Migr. Abr., 113, Dt. 26:5-11 (not the LXX text) in Spec. Leg., II, 217, Ex. 15 in Leg. All., II, 102; Plant., 48; Ebr., 111; Conf. Ling., 35.

[51] Philo quotes the Ps. comparatively more than all other OT works apart from the Torah. A Ps. quotation is often used expressly as a proof from Scripture, i.e., to support Philo's statements, μαρτυρεῖ δέ μου τῷ λόγῳ τὸ παρὰ τῷ ὑμνογράφῳ εἰρημένον ἐν ᾄσματι τούτῳ (ψ 77:49), Gig., 17. In keeping is the fact that the inspiration of the Ps. is plain. Philo stresses their validity: ... προφήτης ... ᾧ καλὸν πιστεύειν, ὁ τὰς ὑμνῳδίας ἀναγράψας (ψ 22:1), Agric., 50, cf. εἶπέ τις προφητικὸς ἀνήρ (ψ 83:11), Rer. Div. Her., 290. Philo often ref. to an author of the Ps. but seems to mention David only in Conf. Ling., 149, cf. ὁ τοῦ Μωυσέως δὴ θιασώτης... ἐν ὑμνῳδίαις ἀνεφθέγξατο (ψ 36:4), Plant., 39, ὁ θεσπέσιος ἀνὴρ ἐν ὕμνοις λέγων (ψ 93:9), Plant., 29, τῶν Μωυσέως γνωρίμων τις ἐν ὕμνους εὐχόμενος (ψ 30:19), Conf. Ling., 39; cf. also (ψ 64:10) Som., II, 245; ὁ ὑμνῳδός (ψ 100:1), Deus Imm., 74. Philo also combines quotations from the Torah and the Ps.: Gn. 2:10 and ψ 36:4 in Som., II, 241 f.; Gn. 23:6 and ψ 64:10, *ibid.*, 244 f., cf. 246 and 248.

with the one thing he can give, λόγοις καὶ ᾠδαῖς καὶ ὕμνοις, Sobr., 58. The fact that Philo has definite ideas of the liturgical song may be seen from his remarks on Ex. 15. Two choirs may sometimes sing antiphonally, but also together; the leader is distinguished from the choir, Vit. Mos., I, 180; II, 256 f. (his discussion ranges beyond Ex. 15:20 f.), cf. Agric., 79-82 (Ex. 15:1, 21 is called an ἐπῳδός or "refrain" in 82). Ex. 15 is very important for Philo, Ebr., 111; Sobr., 13 etc. It is the ἱεροπρεπεστάτη ᾠδή, Som., II, 269. Philo calls Dt. 32 the μεγάλη ᾠδή, Det. Pot. Ins., 114, the ᾠδὴ μείζων, Poster. C., 121 (part of the Law) Plant., 59 etc. [52] He speaks very highly of Dt. 32: Moses gathered the home of mortals and house of immortals and caused the song of perfect harmony to sound forth in order that men might hear it and ἄγγελοι λειτουργοί etc.; the hierophant placed himself among the dancers in the aether etc., Virt., 73-75. For Philo, then, singing and dancing are not related merely among the Therapeutae, [53] Vit. Cont., 83-85. [54] Among these there is individual as well as choral singing; someone comes forward (ἀναστάς) and sings a hymn to God, whether a new one he himself has composed or an older one by earlier poets, then others follow κατὰ τάξεις "in due order." The rest join in the refrains of the songs sung by individuals, Vit. Cont., 80.

6. The fact that Judaism produced songs in the 2nd and 1st cent. B.C. was known even before the Qumran discoveries, though little attention was paid to it. [55] On the songs in the Dead Sea Scrolls, of which the collection in 1 QH represents only a part, [56] research has only just begun. [57] The songs of 1 QS 10 f. remind us of 1 QH. Songs have also been preserved in 1 QM 10:8 - 12:16 (cf. 12:7-16 with 19:1-8); 13:7 - 14:1 etc. Stringed instruments are often depicted on the coins of the Bar Cochba revolt. They perhaps express

---

[52] Dt. 32 is similarly called ἡ μεγάλη Μωσέως ᾠδή in Eus. Praep. Ev., 11, 5, 7. Philo uses ᾠδή for specific texts with ref. to Dt. 32 and Ex. 15, the latter in Som., II, 269; Vit. Mos., II, 257; Agric., 81.

[53] For the Gk. cultus cf. P. Thielscher, "Ein Blick auf d. Reigentänze d. griech. Tragödie," Das Altertum, 7 (1961), 3-19, v. inter al. Marius Victorinus: antiqui deorum laudes carminibus comprehensas circum aras eorum euntes canebant, quius primum ambitum, quem ingrediebantur a parte dextra, στροφήν vocabant; reversionem autem sinistrorsum factam completo priore orbe antistrophon appellabant. dein in conspectu deorum soliti consistere cantici reliqua persequebantur, appellantes id epodon, Marius Victorinus, Ars Grammatica, I, 16 (ed. H. Keil, Grammatici Latini, 6 [1874], 58). Thielscher 7-10. The depiction in Philo Vit. Cont., 84 uses the stock expressions from tragedy, στροφή, ἀντιστροφή, προσόδιον, στάσιμον, which denote first the movements and then the related songs. The interrelating of poetry, song and dancing is in some sense typically Greek, Söhngen, 86; Koller, 160 f. and esp. H. Koller, Musik u. Dichtung im alten Griechenland (1963), 112 etc.

[54] As regards εὐχαριστήριοι ὕμνοι in Vit. Cont., 87 cf. הורית in 1 QS 10:23. On the harmony of lower male and higher female voices in Philo Vit. Cont., 88 cf. Ps.-Aristot. Mund., 6, p. 399a, 15-17.

[55] H. L. Jansen, "Die spätjüd. Psalmendichtung, ihr Entstehungskreis u. ihr. 'Sitz im Leben,'" Skrifter utgitt av det Norske Videnskaps-Akad. i Oslo, Historisk-Filosofisk Klasse, 1937, 3 (1937), 55 etc. thinks most of the psalms from 200 B.C. are for instruction and are thus edificatory or didactic. S. Holm-Nielsen, "Den gammeltestamentlige salmetradition," Dansk Teol. Tidsskr. (1955), 135-148, 193-215 emphasises that there is a direct line from the canonical to the later Jewish psalms and that the latter were not just for private purposes but were also used to some degree in synagogue worship. On song and music in Judaism during the Hell. Roman period cf. Sendrey-Norton, 227-248.

[56] Cf. H. Bardtke, Die Handschriftenfunde am Toten Meer, II (1958), 132-4; M. Delcor, Les hymnes de Qumran (1962); J. A. Sanders, "The Psalms Scroll of Qumran Cave 11," DJD, IV (1965), 53-93. As regards the worship of the group it is natural to suppose they used the OT Psalter, Arens, 106 f. on 1 QS 1:28; 9:4 f.

[57] Cf. H. Bardtke, "Considérations sur les cantiques de Qumran," Rev. Bibl., 63 (1956), 220-3; also op. cit. (→ n. 56), 136-8; S. Holm-Nielsen, "Hodayot. Psalms from Qumran," Acta Theol. Danica, 2 (1961), who thinks many of the pieces were used in worship; G. Morawe, Aufbau u. Abgrenzung d. Loblieder v. Qumran (1961).

hope for a restoration of the temple cultus. [58] At all events the use of this symbol shows what importance Judaism ascribed to ψάλλειν in its religious life. [59] For the temple cf. also the description of the Feast of Tabernacles [60] in Sukk., 5, 4, in which we find stringed instruments and the singing of the Levites and also the singing and dancing of prominent men of piety in the court of women. [61]

C. The New Testament.

I. The Word Groups in the New Testament.

1. The word ὕμνος occurs only in Col. 3:16; Eph. 5:19. [62] The Word of Christ is alive in the community [63] in teaching and admonition (→ IV, 1021, 27 ff.) and [64] in the singing of songs for God, i.e., in these the community [65] praises God (τῷ θεῷ comes last for emphasis) from the heart [66] on account of the salvation which He has given by what He has done in Christ, Col. 3:16. In Eph. 5:19 praise is directed primarily to the κύριος, so that we have a hymn to Christ, [67] though the goal according to v. 20 is the same as in Col. 3:16, namely, that in Spirit-produced (→ VI, 291, 29 ff.) song [68] thanks are given to God for the event of salvation connected with the name of our Lord Jesus Christ. [69, 70] The expression ᾄδοντες καὶ ψάλλον-

---

[58] P. Romanoff, "Jewish Symbols on Coins," JQR, NS, 34 (1943/44), 161-177, 299-312, 425-440, esp. 429; specimens, 425.

[59] Comte du Mesnil du Buisson, Les peintures de la synagogue de Doura-Europos (1939), 51 thinks the "Orpheus" playing the kinnor on the west wall above the niche for the Torah is meant to be David. Like other depictions in the vicinity this has, he thinks, a liturgical ref., esp. to the use of Ps. in the synagogue.

[60] Romanoff links the symbol on coins to this, op. cit., 430.

[61] Str.-B., I, 682; II, 806 f. On the use of the canonical Psalter in synagogue worship cf. Arens, 160-202.

[62] For a good treatment of these passages cf. Söhngen, 3-14; cf. also Schlier Eph.[5] on 5:19.

[63] Loh. Kol. on 3:16 is mistaken in relating ἐν ὑμῖν to individuals. ἐν ὑμῖν "among you," in the community etc. is common in Paul. Of 18 instances in 1 C., 13 plainly have this sense: 1:10f.; 2:2; 3:3, 18; 5:1; 6:5; 11:18f., 30; 14:25; 15:12, and it is implied in 3:16; 6:19 on the basis of 14:25. In 6:2 the meaning is certainly not "within you," nor "for yourself" in 11:13. For Col. cf. 1:6.

[64] The admonition is not by songs (as against Smith, 175 f.; Eph. 5:19 has a different version; → VII, 523, 11 f.), Wilder, 110.

[65] ἐν τῇ χάριτι means "as controlled by the grace-event in Christ, cf. ἐν χάριτι Χριστοῦ Gl. 1:6; Söhngen, 10 suggests "on the basis of His grace." Against the transl. "with thanks" in Dib. Gefbr.[2], ad loc. cf. Dib. Gefbr.[3].

[66] Dib. Gefbr.[3], ad loc.; v. Eph. 5:19; ἐν corresponds to בְּ, cf. Ps. 9:2; ψ 85:12; 110:1; 137:1. Cf. also Smith, 172 f.: What is meant is "the engagement of the heart" (173), not a "silent song" (165 f.).

[67] That κύριος means Christ may be inferred at once in the Pauline corpus; v. 19b and the end of v. 20 are also formally balanced. Even if LXX influence is seen (ψ 26:6: ᾄσομαι καὶ ψαλῶ τῷ κυρίῳ) this does not alter matters.

[68] On the antithesis in Eph. 5:18 f. cf. Philo Vit. Cont., 89 with ref. to the singing of the Therapeutae at nocturnal meetings: "After they have intoxicated themselves until morning in this noble μέθη" → IV, 547, 7 ff.

[69] Cf. the quotation from an anon. work against Artemon (c. 200 A.D., perhaps Hipp.) in Eus. Hist. Eccl., V, 28, 5: How many ψαλμοί and ᾠδαί which were composed by believers from the very first praise (ὑμνοῦσιν) Christ as the Word of God; cf. H. Schneider, "Die bibl. Oden im chr. Altertum," Biblica, 30 (1949), 36.

[70] The thought of edifying is present as in 1 C. 14, patently so in Eph. 5:19: ἑαυτοῖς (on the reciprocal ἑαυτ- cf. Bl.-Debr. § 287). One may thus suspect that the ref. is to individual songs. For Col. 3:16c d cf. v. 16a (also b).

τες in v. 19b underscores v. 19a. The combination of verbs in this order is found in the OT, ψ 26:6; 56:8; 104:2; 107:2. The literal sense "by or with the playing of strings," still found in the LXX, is now employed figuratively. [71] There is nothing to suggest that ψαλμός and ὕμνος relate to texts of different genres → I, 164, 21 ff.; on the three-membered expression → 224, 28 ff. [72] In 1 C. 14:26 ψαλμός means a Christian song in general. [73] The individual himself has obviously composed this and sings it at worship [74] (→ 497, 12 ff.) in distinction from the other Spirit-produced parts of worship. This is a song τῷ νοῖ (→ IV, 959, 1 ff.), contrasted with glossolalia in v. 15.

2. The verb ὑμνέω does not have to refer (→ 490, 26 ff., 33 ff.) to a song which is sung. In Hb. 2:12 it is Christ who praises God → III, 513, 10 ff. Ac. 16:25 however (cf. Test. Jos. 8:5) might well have a song in view. The "singing recitation" of the second part of the Hallel (Ps. 114-118) [75] is the meaning of ὑμνέω in Mk. 14:26; Mt. 26:30 → 496, 21 f. The term is apt, for these psalms are full of praise and thanksgiving (on Ps. 118 → 495, 7 ff.; → IV, 274, n. 48).

3. R. 15:9 interprets the ψάλλω of ψ 17:50 by δοξάζω (→ n. 37), with a reference to worship. The praise of Gentile Christians for God's mercy to them in Christ is provided here with scriptural support. In Jm. 5:13 grateful [76] praise of Christ at home is denoted by ψάλλειν. On 1 C. 14:15 → line 8 f., on Eph. 5:19 → 498, 12 ff.

4. In Luke's writings ψαλμός also means the OT "psalm" (Ac. 13:33). [77] We also find the plural (Lk. 24:44) which already in Philo, with another word, denotes the Psalter → 496, 15 ff. Βίβλος ψαλμῶν (→ I, 616, 17 ff.) occurs too, Lk. 20:42; Ac. 1:20. The Psalms are thus regarded as an authoritative writing → n. 51; I, 747, 10 ff.; 758, 28 ff., cf. γέγραπται in Ac. 13:33, and cf. also Lk. 20:42; 24:44. [78]

---

[71] The music and esp. the playing on strings in 1 QS is probably fig. too (→ n.'39) in the sense of praise (on זמר "to praise" in the OT → 493, 29 ff.), v. P. Wernberg-Møller, The Manual of Discipline (1957), 144, n. 27. The same applies to Ps. Sol. 3:1: ὕμνον καινὸν ψάλατε τῷ θεῷ, v. 3:2; cf. ψαλμὸν καινὸν... καρπὸν χειλέων, 15:3. On the "new song" v. ᾆσμα καινόν ψ 32:3; 39:4; 95:1; 97:1; 149:1, ᾠδὴ καινή ψ 143:9, ὕμνος καινός Is. 42:10; Jdt. 16:13.

[72] Cf. Smith, 61-5. E.'Wellesz, A History of Byzantine Music and Hymnology (1949), 33 thinks the spiritual songs of Col. 3:16 are melodies sung to Alleluias and other cries of jubilation (after the Jewish manner).

[73] But cf. Schl. Jk., 85 with ref. to 1 C. 14:26: ψαλμός is "a word assimilated to the style of the Psalter," also with ref. to Col. 3:16 etc., cf. Holm-Nielsen, op. cit., 206. Gk.-speaking Judaism obviously does not make any gen. distinction between ὕμνος and ψαλμός or ᾠδή, cf. Ps. Sol. → n. 34; 495, 31 ff. Perhaps Jos. likes to make an addition to ᾠδή to show the song is religious → 495, 32; 496, 1 ff., also → 495, 31 f., 34 ff. But there is no sign that we have here different genres of religious song.

[74] The ref. to stringed instruments in heavenly worship at Rev. 5:8; 15:2 (→ I, 165, 16 ff. on 15:3) need not mean that such instruments might sometimes accompany the singing at primitive Chr. worship.

[75] Cf. J. Jeremias, Die Abendmahlsworte Jesu³ (1960), 49, n. 4; 246 f.; Str.-B., I, 845-9.

[76] A reason for thanks is also indicated in the εὐθυμεῖ (opp. κακοπαθεῖ → V, 937, 937, 18'ff.).

[77] The numbering of Ps. 2 as Ps. 1 in Orig. and others is perhaps due to Jewish influence, cf. Str.-B., II, 725.

[78] Transl. the Jewish term for the Psalter תהלים (cf. Eissfeldt) along with the Torah and the Prophets, → VI, 832, 36 ff.

ψαλμός occurs elsewhere in the NT at 1 C. 14:26 (→ 499, 5 ff.); Col. 3:16; Eph. 5:19 → 498, 8 ff.

II. The Songs of Primitive Christianity.

Attempts have been made to identify various primitive Christian hymns or hymnal fragments in the NT. But such identifications must remain hypothetical, particularly as there is in the NT no attempt — and this is a point worth noting in itself — to use the Greek style of metrical hymns → 502, 25 ff. The pieces in the NT which take the form of praise are in general so little controlled by any clearly discernible laws that for the most part judgment as to their character as hymns can claim only limited validity.

The style of Jewish song is plain in the Magnificat [79] and the Benedictus. [80] A fixed form of a different kind is apparent in Eph. 5:14 (which is shown to be traditional by its introduction as a quotation). This is probably a liturgical fragment [81] (a summons to the baptismal candidate?) but not the fragment of a song. Also fixed in form is 1 Tm. 3:16 with its six lines of praise. One hesitates to see here part of a larger whole, but the name of Christ must have preceded it. [82] The piece is plainly differentiated from the context by its style. Short sentences are used in formal balance and material contrast. Elsewhere we find longer sentences, sometimes with subsidiary clauses or participles. But sometimes the texts can contain short parts of sentences which are relatively autonomous. It is fairly generally recognised that Phil. 2:6-11 is a pre-Pauline song. [83] In any case the piece existed as a totality prior to the composition of Phil. As regards other passages one may

---

[79] From the lit. on Lk. 1:46-55: H. Gunkel, "Die Lieder in d. Kindheitsgeschichte Jesu bei Lk.," Festschr. A. v. Harnack (1921), 43-60; P. Winter, "Magnificat u. Benedictus — Maccabean Psalms," The Bulletin of the John Rylands Library, 37 (1953), 328-347.

[80] On Lk. 1:68-79 cf. Gunkel, op. cit. (→ n. 79); P. Vielhauer, "Das Benedictus d. Zacharias," ZThK, 49 (1952), 255-272; Winter, op. cit.; J. Gnilka, "Der Hymnus des Zacharias," BZ, NF, 6 (1962), 215-238; A. Vanhoye, "Structure du 'Benedictus,'" NTSt, 12 (1965/66), 382-9.

[81] Cf. F. J. Dölger, Sol salutis[2] (1925), 365-8; K. G. Kuhn, "Der Eph. im Lichte d. Qumrantexte," NTSt, 7 (1960/61), 341-5; Wilder, 116-8. Acc. to B. Noack, "Das Zitat in Eph. 5:14," Studia Theol., 5 (1952), 52-64 we have here an eschatological hymn. Cf. also G. Friedrich, "Ein Tauflied hell. Judenchristen 1 Th. 1:9 f.," ThZ, 21 (1965), 502-516.

[82] Cf. on 1 Tm. 3:16 Norden, 254-6; Dib. Past.[3], 49-51; Schweizer, 63-6.

[83] Cf. on this E. Lohmeyer, "Kyrios Jesus. Eine Untersuchung zu Phil. 2:5-11," SAH, 1927/28, 4 (1928); E. Käsemann, "Kritische Analyse v. Phil. 2:5-11," Exeget. Versuche u. Besinnungen, I[4] (1965), 91-5; O. Michel, "Zur Exegese v. Phil. 2:5-11," Festschr. K. Heim (1954), 79-95; Schweizer, 51-5 etc.; O. Cullmann, Die Christologie d. NT[4] (1966), 178-186 etc.; J. Jervell, "Imago Dei," FRL, 76 (1960), 203-8, 212 f., 227-231; → 18, 6 ff.; I, 473, 8 ff.; III, 353, 11 ff.; 661, 13 ff.; IV, 750, 16 ff.; V, 197, 3 ff.; VII, 956, 15 ff. Acc. to D. M. Stanley, "The Theme of the Servant of Yahweh in Primitive Christian Soteriology and Its Transposition by St. Paul," The Catholic Bibl. Quart., 16 (1954), 420-5, Phil. 2:6-11 is in origin Palestinian, then probably a part of the liturgy of Philippi, though whether in connection with the eucharist or baptism it is impossible to say, 424 f. Lohmeyer, 73 thinks an origin is Jerusalem is feasible, and Cullmann supports an orig. Aram., 179. But this is left open by L. Krinetzki, "Der Einfluss v. Js. 52:13 - 53:12 Par. auf Phil. 2:6-11," Theol. Quartalschr., 139 (1959), 157-193, 291-336; if Paul adopts a hymn he also modifies it, 160 f., 334 f. Acc. to J. M. Furness, "The Authorship of Phil. 2:6-11," Exp. T., 70 (1959), 240-3 there is nothing formally against Pauline authorship. N. Flanagan, "A Note on Phil. 3:20-21," The Catholic Bibl. Quart., 18 (1956), 8 f. ref. to the "very striking" par. between 2:6-11 and 3:20 f. Cf. also E. Fascher, Art. "Briefliteratur," RGG[3], I, 1413 f.; A. Feuillet, "L'hymne christologique de l'Épître aux Phil. (2:6-11)," Rev. Bibl., 72 (1965), 352-380, 481-507; J. Jeremias on Phil. 2:7: ἑαυτὸν ἐκένωσεν, Abba (1966), 308-313.

at least ask whether there can be any certainty how far the author of the writing in question is adopting formulations which he himself did not compose (as may often be the case), how far he introduces variations, and what he himself has perhaps added. [84] Certainly the idea that pre-Christian material was adopted must remain highly hypothetical. [85] The epistles commonly accepted as Pauline plainly contain parts which are distinctively stylised — though one cannot say that the supposed hymnal passages Eph. 5:14; 1 Tm. 3:16; Phil. 2:6-11; Col. 1:15-20 give evidence of any one style [86] — and yet in context these pieces cannot be described as hymns simply because of their lofty speech and integrated structure. [87] Often Col. 1:15-20 (13-20) is said to be a hymn which the author of Col. took over and augmented. [88] Other attempts to reconstruct hymns especially out of the NT Epistles have produced little agreement. [89] Elements of songs have perhaps been worked over in

---

[84] Cf. N. A. Dahl, "Adresse u. Proömium d. Eph.," ThZ, 7 (1951), 263: "Free models developed for the form of this type of praise."

[85] On Col. 1:15-20 → n. 88. E. Fuchs, *Freiheit d. Glaubens* (1949), 61 f. concocts a Gnostic lament out of R. 7:9, 7, 11, 10, 18 f., 24 (2 × 5 lines).

[86] E.g., 2 C. 1:3-7 "composed in solemn rhythm" (Wnd. 2 K., *ad loc.*, and cf. his detailed observations), "tailored specially to the existing relations" (Ltzm. K.[4], *ad loc.*, thus formulated *ad hoc*), cf. the introductory 1 C. 1:4-9, which, though structured, clearly anticipates the themes of the letter. Cf. also R. 8:33 f.; 8:35; 37-39; the 3 double-lines in 1 C. 15:42b-43 (each with a rhyme in the verb). Cf. also the 7 membered series in Phil. 3:5 f.: lines 1-5 contain 2 accents, while 5 and 7 have ending rhyme. One might also ref. to the list of tribulations in 2 C. 11:23-27, 29 f.

[87] This applies no less to a piece like 2 Tm. 2:11-13 → V, 216, 26 ff.

[88] Cf. Norden, 253, also 240-254; E. Käsemann, "Eine urchr. Taufliturgie," *Exeget. Versuche u. Besinnungen*, I[4] (1965), 34-51; W. Nauck, "Eph. 2:19-22 — ein Tauflied?" *Ev. Theol.*, 13 (1953), 366, cf. 362-371; Dib. Kol.[3], 10-21; Schweizer, 102 f., 110 f., 129 f.; H. Hegermann, "Die Vorstellung vom Schöpfungsmittler im hell. Judt. u. Urchr.," TU, 82 (1961); E. Bammel, "Versuch zu Kol. 1:15-20," ZNW, 52 (1961), 88-95; Jervell, *op. cit.*, 198-203, 210 f., 218-226. But J. Kroll, "Die Hymnendichtung d. frühen Christentums," *Die Antike*, 2 (1926), 261 favours Pauline authorship. Cf. too E. Percy, "Zu den Problemen d. Kol. u. Eph.," ZNW, 43 (1950/51), 183-7: Not orig. a Gnostic hymn (as against Käsemann) etc., though one cannot deny that 1:13 f. might "contain an echo of the liturgical life of the Pauline communities," 187. On this pt. cf. C. Maurer, "Die Begründung d. Herrschaft Christi über die Mächte nach Kol. 1:15-20," *Wort u. Dienst*, NF, 4 (1955), 84 f.; he also thinks Paul might well have composed the piece *ad hoc*, 84. Cf. too C. Masson, "L'hymne christologique de l'épître aux Col. 1:15-20," RevThPh, 148 (1948), 138-142; J. M. Robinson, "A Formal Analysis of Col. 1:15-20," JBL, 76 (1957), 270-287; S. Lyonnet, "L'hymne christologique de l'épître aux Col. et la fête Juive du Nouvel An," *Recherches de Science Religieuse*, 48 (1960), 93-100.

[89] Acc. to C. Maurer, "Der Hymnus v. Eph. 1 als Schlüssel zum ganzen Briefe," *Ev. Theol.*, NF, 6 (1951/52), 154, Eph. 1:3-14 was composed by the author *ad hoc*. Dahl, *op. cit.* (→ n. 84), 263 f. thinks the similarity between this and 1 Pt. 1:3-12 may be explained by the fact that "both borrow from the form of baptismal eulogies." One might note in this connection that it is becoming increasingly clear how gt. was the role of baptismal motifs in the NT generally. On 1 Pt. 1:3-12 Wnd. Kath. Br., *ad loc.* observes that almost throughout one may discern in this epistle a division into strophes and measured lines. Cf. the attempt of H. Preisker to pick out various elements of a primitive baptismal liturgy from 1 Pt., *ibid.*, 156-161. G. Schille, *Früchr. Hymnen* (1962), 65-73 finds a hymn of the Hell. community in Eph. 1:3-12. He also detects hymns behind Eph. 2:4-7, 10 (53-60); Col. 2:9-15 (31-37); R. 3:23-25 (60). E. Käsemann, "Zum Verständnis v. R. 3:24-26," *Exeget. Versuche u. Besinnungen*, I[4] (1965), 96-100 finds a Jewish-Chr. original in R. 3:24-26. Cf. Percy, *op. cit.* (→ n. 88), 180 f., n. 15. Cf. also J. Cambier, "La bénédiction d'Eph. 1:3-14," ZNW, 54 (1963), 58-104; S. Lyonnet, "La bénédiction d'Eph. 1:3-14 et son arrière-plan judaïque," *A la rencontre de Dieu, Mémorial A. Gelin* (1961), 341-352. Acc. to Jervell, *op. cit.* (→ n. 83), 208, 214-8 2 C. 4:4-6 was a baptismal hymn, and so perhaps was Hb. 5:7-10 acc. to G. Friedrich, "Das Lied vom Hohenpriester im Zshg. v. Hb. 4:14 - 5:10," ThZ, 18 (1962), 102-4, cf. 95-115.

1 Pt. 2:21-25. [90] The song-like portions of Rev. (cf. 11:17 f.; 15:3 f.) enable us to draw formal conclusions as to the style of hymns in the relevant Christian world. [91] But textually they can hardly have been taken from other sources, since they belong so fully to the various situations in the eschatological context. [92]

D. The Early Church.

I. The Word Groups in the Apologists.

Independently ὕμνος occurs here only in Just. Apol., 13, 2. It and ὑμνέω also occur a few times in OT quotations or under their influence, e.g., ὑμνέω in Dial., 106, 1 (ψ 21:23), cf. Dial., 106, 2. ὑμνέω is used in a quotation from Aesch. in Athenag., 21, 5. ψάλλω and ψαλμός are found only in Just. Dial., the one of David in 29, 2, Christians in 74, 3, in a quotation in 37, 1 (ψ 46:7 f.), the other always with ref. to a specific OT psalm apart from Dial., 22, 3, which quotes Am. 5:23 (plur. as against LXX). In the post-apost. fathers ὑμνέω κτλ. do not occur, while ψάλλω κτλ. are used only in the quotation at Barn., 6, 16.

II. The Songs of Early Christianity.

In the post-apost. fathers a common song of the whole community is obviously pre-supposed at Ign. R., 2, 2, cf. also Eph., 4, 1 f. Also in hymnal style are Eph., 7, 2 (cf. Ign. Pol., 3, 2) [93] and 19, 2 f. [94] Acc. to Socrates Hist. Eccl., VI, 8 [95] Ign. introduced antiphonal singing to Antioch and from there it spread to other churches. A Gnostic ὕμνος has come down to us in Act. Joh. 94 f. [96] In this the singer, Jesus, stands in the centre of a circle of disciples clasping hands, moving around Him, and responding to each line with Amen, cf. the dancing and singing girls of Herm. s., 9, 11, 5. At the sound of a stringed instrument Thomas strikes up the so-called wedding song in Act. Thom. 6 f. (in Hbr.; ὕμνησεν and ᾠδή occur in 8). The pearl song is called a ψαλμός in 108-113. The Naassene hymn (ψαλμός, ὑμνῳδέω, 10, 1) in Hipp. Ref., V, 10, 2 has been preserved in Gk. measures. [97] The first hymn of the Church in Gk. verses is in Cl. Al. Paed., III, 101, 3. It contains 65 short lines in anapaests. [98] The first Chr. song with notes is in

---

[90] Cf. R. Bultmann, "Bekenntnis- u. Liedfr. im 1 Pt.," *Coni. Neot.*, 11 (1947), 13 f.; E. Lohse, "Märtyrer u. Gottesknecht," FRL, 64 (1955), 184 f. E. G. Selwyn, *The First Ep. of St. Peter* (1958), 268-281 finds a primitive Chr. hymn in 1 Pt. 2:6-10 (text 281). On the basis of the similarities between 1 Pt. 2:4-10 and Eph. 2:19-22 Nauck, *op. cit.* (→ n. 88) constructs a song of three strophes out of the latter. Cf. R. P. Martin, "The Composition of 1 Peter in Recent Study," *Vox Evangelica*, 1 (1962), 29-42.

[91] Cf. G. Delling, "Zum gottesdienstlichen Stil d. Joh.-Apk.," *Nov. Test.*, 3 (1959), 107-137.

[92] On Plin. Ep., X, 96, 7 cf. the survey in J. Quasten, Art. "Carmen," RAC, II, 906, bibl., 910; *v.* esp. Dölger, *op. cit.* (→ n. 81), 103-118, 124 etc.

[93] Kroll, 20: "The hieratic style derived from the Semites; it loves asyndetic and colometric forms."

[94] Lohmeyer, *op. cit.* (→ n. 83), 64 f. attempts a division of Ign. Eph., 19, 2 f. into lines and strophes. On 1 Cl., 59-61 cf. Robinson, 213-8.

[95] Ed. E. Hussey (1853).

[96] ὑμνήσωμεν τὸν πατέρα 94, before the arrest of Jesus; this is obviously based on Mk. 14:26 and par.

[97] The song is in anapaests, each line closing with an iamb, cf. H. Usener, *Gr. Versbau* (1887), 90, n. 50; often with ending rhyme. On texts of the 2nd-4th cent. cf. A. Dihle, "Die Anfänge d. gr. akzentuierenden Verskunst," *Herm.*, 82 (1954), 182-199.

[98] Kroll, *op. cit.* (→ n. 88), 278. Kroll suggests it was sung to the cither but not at worship, 280. Cl. Al. Paed., II, 43 permits the accompanying of Chr. singing with stringed instruments (πρὸς κιθάραν ... ἢ λύραν ᾄδειν τε καὶ ψάλλειν) at feasts. Flutes were not allowed (41, 1) but trumpets and stringed instruments were accepted on the basis of the

P. Oxy., XV, 1786 (3rd cent. A.D.): "All glorious (creations) of God together ... should not keep silent and the light-bearing stars should not hold back ... All roaring rivers should praise our Father and Son and Holy Ghost, all powers should agree: Amen, Amen! Might (and) praise ... to the only Giver of all good things, Amen, Amen!" [99] Already in the 3rd cent. there is some opposition to the use of non-biblical hymns in Chr. worship. [100] The Council of Laodicea (4th cent.) forbade this. [101] But it could not be fully suppressed in the East. [102] The so-called biblical odes arose instead. [103] In keeping is the fact that Bible MSS in Gk. do not yet contain the collection of bibl. odes in the 4th cent., whereas all the Gk. MSS from the 5th cent. do. [104]

Delling

OT (41, 4). In contrast to Dionysiac choruses Cl. Al. Protr., 119, 1 f. speaks of the χορὸς σώφρων of Christians which is formed by the righteous who sing a hymn to the King of all while girls play on stringed instruments. A description is also given of angels and prophets and ref. is made to the θίασος which one joins. The depiction is influenced by formal par. to the Bacchic procession, cf. 120, 2, but the hymn and cither are Chr. Cf. A. Dohmes, "Der pneumatische Charakter d. Kultgesanges nach frühchr. Zeugnissen," *Gedächtnisschrift O. Casel* (1951), 35-53, on Cl. Al. cf. 42-5.

[99] Cf. Quasten, 101 f. We have here anapaests, at the end of the 3rd cent., cf. H. Abert, "Das älteste Denkmal d. chr. Kirchenmusik," *Die Antike*, 2 (1926), 286 cf. 282-290; cf. also Kroll, *op. cit.* (→ n. 88), 280. Cf. further E. Jammers, "Rhythmische u. formale Stud. zur Musik d. Antike u. d. MA," *Archiv f. Musikforschung*, 6 (1941), 159-162, 177; Wellesz, *op. cit.* (→ n. 72), 125-9, cf. on this E. Jammers, Review of *The New Oxford Hist. of Music*, II (1957) in DLZ, 79 (1958), 50 f.; further bibl. Smith, 54 f. The song can hardly be related to any specific biblical text, cf. ψ 92:3; Ps. 148:3b; (powers) ψ 102:21a. For acclamation cf. 3 Macc. 7:13, for Amen at the beginning and end of acclamation Rev. 7:12.

[100] Paul of Samosata, cf. Eus. Hist. Eccl., VII, 30, 10; v. Schneider, *op. cit.* (→ n. 69), 42.

[101] Canon 15. 69, cf. E. Werner, "The Conflict between Hellenism and Judaism in the Music of the Early Christian Church," HUCA, 20 (1947), 407-470, esp. 435.

[102] Werner, *op. cit.*, 457. On this whole matter Sendrey-Norton, 249-258.

[103] Schneider, *op. cit.* (→ n. 69), 42.

[104] A. Rahlfs, Septuaginta Societatis Litterarum Gottingensis, X (1931), 78; the odes are put after the Ps., 341-365.

| ὑπάγω | → πορεύομαι, VI, 566, 30 ff. |

1. Outside the Bible this verb, attested from Hom., means a. trans. strictly "to lead under," e.g., horses under the yoke, Hom. Il., 24, 279 etc., "to lead from under," e.g., out of range, 11, 163, "to lead someone somewhere," before a court, Hdt., IX, 93, 3, "to bring, seduce, lead astray to something," Eur. Andr., 428; Cyc., 507. In the mid. we find χώραν ὑπάγομαι "to subdue a country," [1] Jos. Ant., 7, 307, ὑπάγομαί τινα "to put oneself at someone's disposal," 5, 339, cf. 12, 398, in the perf. pass. part. "to devote oneself" to the service of Isis, 18, 70. It then means b. intr. (from Hdt.) "to withdraw," Hdt., IV, 120, 2; 122, 2. The imp. is common: "Go away," "be off," Aristoph., e.g., Vesp., 290, plur. "March," Ran., 174, in popular usage. [2] In Epictet. we often find it before another imp., in many cases with an ironical ring: "Go, persuade someone else," Epict. Diss., III, 23, 12, "Go rather ... " III, 22, 108 etc. In the pap. it often means "to go away," "to go on a journey," P. Oxy., X, 1291, 11 (30 A.D.), "to journey to," Preisigke Sammelbuch, 1, 998, 2 (16/17 A.D.), "to go to" someone, P. Tebt., II, 417, 4 (3rd cent. A.D.), "go and receive ... ," ibid., line 21 etc. [3]

2. In the LXX it occurs a. trans. only at Ex. 14:21 for הלך hi: Yahweh caused the sea to go back, and pass. 4 Macc. 4:13: "to be induced to" something, then b. intr. only Ιερ. 43(36):19 אֲ* and in the imp. sing. apart from Tob. 10:12 א in the wish ὕπαγε ὑγιαίνων 8:21 א; 12:5 א cf. 10:11 א. In the expression "to go forth in peace, safe and sound, comforted" (→ II, 406, 25 ff.) [4] the LXX does not use ὑπάγω but ἀπέρχομαι 1 Βασ. 20:13 etc., πορεύομαι 1 Βασ. 1:17 etc., sometimes βαδίζω 2 Βασ. 15:9. The wish ref. primarily to physical well-being, cf. esp. returning in peace in Ju. 11:31 etc., but then it includes confidence etc. as well.

3. The verb is used only intransitively in the NT.

a. The Pauline corpus, Hb. and Ac. do not use it at all, and in the Catholic Ep. it occurs only at Jm. 2:16 (→ 505, 21) and 1 Jn. 2:11. In the Synoptics is never occurs in all three at the same place, Mt. and Lk. alone never have it in common, and Mk. and Lk. only at Mk. 11:2 and par. In par. passages Lk. often has other words, cf. Mk. 1:44 and par.; 2:11 and par.; 14:13 and par.; 14:21 and par.; at Mk. 10:21 and par. Lk. omits the verb. But Lk. can use the word in his special material, 17:14b with πορεύομαι in v. 14a; 8:42 (Mk. ἀπέρχομαι); 10:3; 12:58 (in both these Mt. omits the phrase and Mk. the passage); here the author has borrowed from some other source. Ac. uses πορεύομαι,

---

ὑ π ά γ ω . J. Kalitsunakis, " Ὑπάγω," Byzantinische Zeitschr., 29 (1929/30), 228-232.
[1] ὑπάγομαι πόλιν, "to subjugate a city," occurs already in Thuc., VII, 46 [Risch].
[2] To use ὑπάγω in the sense of "to go away" is regarded as non-Attic, Thomae Magistri Ecloga Vocum Atticarum (ed. F. Ritschl [1832]), 368, 11-13.
[3] From ὑπάγω there has developed in modern Gk. the ordinary word for "to go," πάω (< ὑπάγω), aor. ἐπῆγα (< impf. ὑπῆγον), the new pres. πηγαίνω [Risch].
[4] For הלך "to go hence," "to die" we find in ψ 38:14: ἀπέρχομαι, cf. also ψ 77:39: the metaphor of the πνεῦμα πορευόμενον, Gn. 15:2: ἀπολύομαι ἄτεκνος, 25:32: πορεύομαι τελευτᾶν, 3 Βασ. 2:2: πορεύομαι ἐν ὁδῷ πάσης τῆς γῆς. In Test. L. 13:3, B. 2:4 ὑπάγω means gen. "to go," "to go away" [Bertram].

which is also very common in Lk. but which does not occur in the genuine Mk. (up to 16:8), though it is more common in Mt. than ὑπάγω, [5] cf. also Rev. [6] Mk. has ὑπάγω 8 times alone, Mt. 12 in his special material or in passages with no exact par. in Mk. or Lk. NT use of the verb confirms the fact that esp. in the intr. it is part of popular usage → 504, 9 ff. The NT does not have οἴχομαι, which is not altogether uncommon in the LXX (esp. in Jer.).

b. In the Synoptics the verb is used mostly in the imperative, in Mt. 17 times and Mk. 12 times (on Lk. → 504, 26 ff.). In 7 cases in Mt. (5:24; 8:4; 18:15; 19:21; 21:28; 27:65; 28:10) and 4 in Mk. (1:44; 6:38; 10:21; 16:7) another imperative follows with no connecting καί → 504, 10 ff. [7] Usually the prior imperative not only makes the expression more vivid but also prepares the ground for the specific direction and gives it added weight through tense expectation. Another group of imperatives is found primarily in healing stories → VI, 574, 13 ff. In the relevant sayings of Jesus what is asked for is granted. Indeed, the answer may be contained in the ὕπαγε, cf. Mk. 7:29. When ὕπαγε precedes the specific answer it lays stress on the fact that the cure depends on the Word of Jesus, Mk. 10:52. In healings at a distance an intensive trust in Jesus' Word is also required of the petitioner, Mk. 7:29; Mt. 8:13, cf. Jn. 4:50. In Mk. 5:34 the word of healing is accompanied by the OT saying: "Go in peace, full of confidence" (→ 504, 19 ff.; II, 411, 15 ff.), to which the authority proper to Jesus (→ III, 210, 8 ff.) gives a particular fulness (cf. Lk. 7:50, cf. on the other hand the empty use of the wish in Jm. 2:16). In the last temptation of Jesus according to Mt. 4:9 f. Jesus proves Himself to be the Victor (→ VII, 158, 23 f.) by ordering Satan to depart from Him, which Satan has to do, v. 11. On the other hand Peter in Mk. 8:33 and par. (→ VII, 158, 28 ff.) is only put in his proper place → V, 291, 15 ff. In Mk. 14:21 and par. the going up of the Son of Man to death is denoted by ὑπάγω (here Lk. has another form of the saying; on πορεύομαι → VI, 573, 41 ff.). The reference to the intimation of this in the OT supports this interpretation.

c. In Jn., which easily prefers ὑπάγω (32 times) to πορεύομαι, the word is used with a second imperative, and no connecting καί, only at 4:16 and 9:7. [8] In 17 instances the reference is especially to the going or going away of Jesus. πορεύομαι (→ VI, 575, 27 ff., with ὑπάγω in the same passage, 14:2-5; 16:5-7) and ἀπέρχομαι (16:7a b, cf. v. 5) are employed similarly. The mode of expression, which occurs especially in the Parting Discourses, is pioneered in 7:33; 8:14, 21 f. In 7:33-35 and 8:21 f. it first gives rise to misunderstandings after the common manner of Jn. The sense "to go on a journey" or "to go to one's death" seems to be implied. But for those in the know it is apparent already in 7:33 f. and 8:14 that what is meant is going to God. The Evangelist for his part states this in 13:3. Yet it is still concealed even from the disciples in 13:33, [9] 36 f.; 14:4 f. and 16:17, the

---

[5] Mt. often uses πορεύομαι in his special material and sometimes in contrast to par. in Lk. or Lk. and Mk.

[6] Discipleship of Jesus means going into the hidden, the unknown, Rev. 14:4. On ὑπάγειν into the unknown cf. Plat. Euthyphr., 14c [Bertram].

[7] Only Lk. 10:37 has πορεύου and another imperative, this time with καί in view of the emphatic σύ. Mt. 26:18 and Mk. 5:19, 34 are not to be cited in this connection. On other constructions → VI, 573, 35 ff. with n. 50.

[8] Not Jn. 9:11. We find the expression without and with καί in Rev. 10:8 and 16:1.

[9] Express ref. is made here to previous sayings of Jesus.

last instance of ὑπάγω in the special sense. The puzzle is solved for them only in
16:27-30 → V, 856, 22 ff. Obviously in his use of ὑπάγω as a term for the going
hence of Jesus the author is following his common practice [10] of employing words
with many meanings. If he also had "to die" in mind — perhaps in the light of
πορεύομαι [11] — he might be basing this on the kind of use found in Mk. 14:21 and
par. → 505, 25 ff. The fact that Jesus "goes to God" through death is also given
special emphasis elsewhere in Jn., v. 3:14 with 12:32; 12:32 f.; 13:27, 30-32; → II,
249, 19 ff. The deeper significance of the term may be seen in the interpretation
of the Evangelist (13:3) and the statements of Jesus Himself. In the first instance
ὑπάγω corresponds to the ἦλθον which denotes the Whence of Jesus, 8:14 [12] cf.
13:3; → II, 671, 29 ff.; I, 521, 8 ff.; 522, 19 ff. He who knows the Whence — and
this is he who also knows by whom Jesus is sent, 7:33; 16:5; → I, 404, 31 ff. — will
also know His Whither. The critical beginning of this going is the way of the cross,
13:1-4, [13] cf. 13:36. [14] With the exaltation which the going to the Father includes
Jesus is justified and shown to be the One who has fulfilled the divine commission,
16:10 → II, 202, 11 f. From another angle the future coming of Jesus (14:28a, cf.
16:17) also corresponds to the going of Jesus → VI, 575, 39 ff.

4. In early Chr. writings the verb plays no special role. Did., 1, 4 carries an allusion
to Mt. 5:41, Ign. Phld., 7, 1 to Jn. 3:8, 2 Cl., 4, 5 to Lk. 13:27 (though Lk. with ψ 6:9 has
ἀπόστητε, Just. Apol., 16, 11 ἀποχωρεῖτε). Elsewhere in the post-apost. fathers ὑπάγω
occurs only in Herm for "to remove oneself," "to go away," e.g., v., 4, 1, 2, "to attain,"
e.g., v., 3, 5, 1. The imp. is related to another imp. by καί, v., 3, 1, 7; 4, 2, 5; s., 8, 11, 1;
9, 10, 1; even here this usage does not seem to be purely pleonastic. The verb occurs in
the Apologists at Just. Dial., 76, 5 on the basis of Mt. 25:41 [15] (v. Ps.-Clem. Hom., 19, 2,
5; Mt. has πορεύεσθε) and Dial., 103, 6 on the basis of Mt. 4:10 Imperial text. The only
other use in the Apologists is in Tat., 31, 3: Others have "gone down" beneath time in
a chronological adaptation of Homer. Cl. Al. uses the term only trans. and fig.: The aim
of the Law is "to lead" us from unrighteousness to righteousness, Strom., III, 46, 1; pass.
"to be led" to faith, IV, 73, 5, "to be brought" to tears, Paed., II, 56, 3; mid. the devil
seeks "to make us pliable," Strom., IV, 85, 1; "to seduce" to wickedness (idolatry, Nu.
25:1 f.), II, 83, 3 (Philo Vit. Mos., I, 295 has ἄγω in the same connection).

Delling

---

[10] O. Cullmann, "Der joh. Gebrauch doppeldeutiger Ausdrücke als Schlüssel zum Verständnis d. vierten Ev.," ThZ, 4 (1948), 360-372.

[11] For the LXX → VI, 572, 1 ff.; 573, 41 ff.; cf. the misunderstanding in Jn. 8:21 f.

[12] Knowing the Whence and Whither of the Saviour is decisive for man's salvation.
That is, he needs to know Jesus as the One in whom God, revealing Himself, does His saving
work. But cf. the Gnostic interpretation in Bultmann J., ad loc.

[13] The foot-washing prefigures the ultimate (→ VIII, 56, 3 f.) service of Jesus on the
cross. v. 3a relates to the fulfilling of the saving act which God has charged Him to perform,
cf. 3:35.

[14] Cf. 12:26 in context, v. C. K. Barrett, The Gospel acc. to St. John (1955) on 13:36,
but cf. Bultmann J., ad loc. 14:28-31 also illustrates the above principle. Barrett on 14:4 also
has the crucifixion and resurrection in view in relation to this passage.

[15] If Just. Dial., 76, 5 is quoting Mt. 25:41 from memory, it is natural that he should bring
in the popular form so familiar to him from Mt. [Dihle].

ὑπακοή → I, 224, 17 ff.	ὑπακούω → I, 223, 28 ff.
ὑπαντάω → III, 625, 28 ff.	ὑπάντησις → III, 625, 28 ff.

ὑπέρ

Contents: A. ὑπέρ with Genitive: 1. Over, Beyond; 2. On Behalf of; 3. In the Place of; 4. With Reference to; 5. On Account of. B. ὑπέρ with Accusative. C. ὑπέρ as Adverb.

This prep. comes from the Indo-Eur. *uper*, Sanskr. *upari*, Gothic *ufar* and like all words orig. beginning with i it has a rough breathing. It has the gen. sense of "over," "across," "beyond," which with the gen. esp. developed a transf. meaning. The gen. is far more common than the acc.; the rare dat. occurs in dialects. In the Hell. [1] age ὑπέρ invades the spheres of περί and ἀντί, e.g., ἔλεγον ἀκηκοέναι ὑπὲρ ὑμῶν, Wilcken Ptol., I, 120, 14 f. (2nd cent. B.C.); ὑπὲρ τοῦ γάλακτος παρατιθεῖσαι μέλι "instead of milk," Ael. Var. Hist., 12, 45. In modern Gk. it has disappeared from living speech and has been replaced in some sense by ἐπάνω, ἀπάνωσ(ε), γιά.

A. ὑπέρ [2] with Genitive. [3]

1. Over, Beyond.

The local sense of "over," "beyond," is common in class. Gk., e.g., τοὺς δ' ὑπὲρ θαλάσσης πεζῇ ἑπομένους, Hdt., VII, 115, 2; τοξεύοντες ὑπὲρ τῶν πρόσθεν, Xenoph. Cyrop., VI, 3, 24, but in the Hell. age it is completely supplanted by the transf. use, which was widespread even earlier.

ὑ π έ ρ . Bibl. B. F. C. Atkinson, *The Theology of Prepositions* (1944), 13 f.; K. Berg, "Die Zeit d. Magna Moralia," *Wiener Stud.*, 52 (1934), 145 f.; E. H. Blakeney, "Ὑπέρ with Gen. in the NT," *Exp. T.*, 55 (1943/44), 306; Bl.-Debr. § 230 f., cf. 185, 3; G. Bonfante, "The Prepositions of Latin and Greek," *Word*, 6 (1950), 106-116; V. Brøndal, *Théorie des prépositions* (1950); J. Humbert, *Syntaxe grecque²* (1954), 298-344; J. Irigoin, "Note sur l'anastrophe des prépos. en grec," *Glotta*, 33 (1954), 90-100; Johannessohn Präpos., 216-219; Mayser, II, 2, 456-461; C. F. D. Moule, *An Idiom Book of NT Greek²* (1959), 63-5; P. F. Regard, *Contributions à l'étude des prépos. dans la langue du NT* (1919), 590-596; A. T. Robertson, *A Grammar of the Gk. NT³* (1919), 628-633, 667, 784; also "The Use of ὑπέρ in Business Documents in the Pap.," *Exp.*, VIII, 18 (1919), 321-7; Schwyzer, II, 518-522; D. Tabachovitz, *Die LXX u. d. NT* (1956), 55-86; Trench, 201-3.
[1] The surge in this period is due to Ionic influence [Dihle]. Examples in Mayser, II, 2, 450-454, 460 f.
[2] On the distribution in the NT cf. R. Morgenthaler, *Statistik d. nt.lichen Wortschatzes* (1958), 160, 183 f. On ὑπέρ in the Hell. period and the NT *v*. Mayser, II, 2, 456-461; Radermacher, 143-6.
[3] On whether this is orig. gen. or ablative cf. Robertson Grammar, 629 f.; Schwyzer, II, 520. Pokorny, I, 1105 thinks the gen. with ὑπέρ in the sense "in defence of" is a genuine gen. On ὑπέρ with gen. in the various NT writings *v*. G. Bonaccorsi, *Primi saggi di filologia neotest.*, I (1933), 529. For 6 instances of ὑπέρ with gen. in the NT there is 1 with acc.

In the NT "beyond" in a transf. sense is possibly the meaning in ὑπὲρ τῆς εὐδοκίας at Phil. 2:13 (→ II, 747, n. 33): "Who fashions a will and work in you beyond your own will," but → 514, 6 f.

2. On the basis of the idea of protection the closest meaning to the spatial use for "over" is "on behalf of," "in defence of," "for." [4]

a. In the NT the prep. occurs in various expressions, "to intervene for someone," "to stand by someone's side": [5] ὃς γὰρ οὐκ ἔστιν καθ᾽ ἡμῶν, ὑπὲρ ἡμῶν ἐστιν Mk. 9:40 and par.; cf. R. 8:31 (→ III, 117, 39 ff.), with λέγω Ac. 26:1, but cf. vl. With φρονέω, ὑπέρ in Phil. 1:7; 4:10 does not have the neutral sense "to think of someone" but the intensive sense "to be concerned about someone," [6] cf. μεριμνάω in 1 C. 12:25, ἀγρυπνέω Hb. 13:17, ἀγωνίζομαι Col. 4:12, συνυπουργέω 2 C. 1:11, πόνος Col. 4:13, διάκονος Col. 1:7: ἵνα μὴ εἷς ὑπὲρ τοῦ ἑνὸς φυσιοῦσθε κατὰ τοῦ ἑτέρου "to argue earnestly for one teacher at the expense of the other," 1 C. 4:6, cf. the combination with ζῆλος in 2 C. 7:7 and σπουδή in 2 C. 7:12; 8:16. Elliptically, with a word of commending or requesting that is to be supplied, one finds ὑπὲρ Τίτου at 2 C. 8:23.

b. After terms of sacrifice or dedication ὑπέρ has the literal or transferred sense [7] of "for."

(a) So with προσφορά, the sacrifice in the Jewish temple, Ac. 21:26, the ministry of the high-priest who is appointed "for" men in Hb. 5:1a (→ I, 313, 42 ff.; III, 277, 17 ff.) and who offers blood for himself as well as for the offences of the people, 9:7. In this connection one may note expressions which use ὑπέρ to denote the offering of life, or suffering and death, "in favour of" or "for someone." [8] In the background are Jewish concepts of the vicarious significance of the death of martyrs and the just. [9]

(b) Aquila and Priscilla are ready to give their lives for Paul, R. 16:4: τὸν τράχηλον ὑποτίθημι. Paul ref. to his own self-sacrifice: ἀνάθεμα... ὑπὲρ τῶν ἀδελφῶν μου, R. 9:3, and to his sufferings for the churches: δαπανήσω καὶ ἐκδαπανηθήσομαι ὑπὲρ τῶν ψυχῶν ὑμῶν, 2 C. 12:15, ὁ δέσμιος τοῦ Χριστοῦ Ἰησοῦ ὑπὲρ ὑμῶν, Eph. 3:1, χαίρω ἐν τοῖς παθήμασιν ὑπὲρ ὑμῶν, καὶ ἀνταναπληρῶ τὰ ὑστερήματα τῶν θλίψεων τοῦ Χριστοῦ ἐν τῇ σαρκί μου ὑπὲρ τοῦ σώματος, Col. 1:24 [10] → 511, 27 ff.

In christological sayings ὑπέρ is used to show the thrust of the work of salvation (→ III, 18, n. 77; V, 710, n. 435). The death and passion of Christ are for men and

---

[4] Cf. 4 Βασ. 19:34: ὑπερασπιῶ ὑπὲρ τῆς πόλεως, cf. also Hom. Il., 7, 449: τεῖχος ἐτειχίσσαντο νεῶν ὕπερ, and in Attic prose, e.g., καλῶς ὑπὲρ τῆς πόλεως ἀποθνῄσκειν, Isoc. Or., 4, 77, cf. 4, 75. Cf. also Plat. Phaed., 78b, Demosth. Or., 2, 4; on this Schwyzer, II, 521.
[5] Cf. Moult.-Mill., s.v.; F. M. Abel, Grammaire du grec biblique (1927), 223.
[6] Cf. R. P. Martin, The Epistle of Paul to the Philippians (1959), 62.
[7] Cf. on this Mayser, II, 2, 458.
[8] On this LXX use cf. Johannessohn Präpos., 216 f.
[9] E. Lohse, "Märtyrer u. Gottesknecht," FRL, 64[2] (1964), 64-110; J.Jeremias, "Das Lösegeld für Viele (Mk. 10:45)," Abba (1966), 217-224.
[10] On the background of the idea of the expiatory death of Jesus cf. J. Jeremias, "Παῖς (θεοῦ) im NT," Abba (1966), 199-216, also, e.g., Bultmann Theol., 48-50, 86-8, 293-300; L. Cerfaux, Le Christ dans la théologie de saint Paul (1951), 95-120; O. Cullmann, Die Christologie d. NT[4] (1966), 59-79; Lohse, op. cit., 113-146; E. Schweizer, "Erniedrigung u. Erhöhung," AbhThANT, 28[2] (1962), 72-5; F. Hahn, "Christologische Hoheitstitel," FRL, 83[3] (1966), 46-66. There is general agreement that the primitive Palestinian churches had already reflected on the theological meaning of the death of Jesus. How far this reflection went back to the historical Jesus is connected with the question of the self-awareness of Jesus, v. Cullmann, 59-68; Jeremias, 213-6 et al.

accrue to their favour. This employment of the preposition finds its NT starting-point in a formula of faith and confession which belongs to the oldest strata of Christian tradition. [10] A basic form of this occurs in Paul in the following phrases: Χριστὸς ὑπὲρ ἡμῶν ἀπέθανεν, R. 5:8, and: Ἰησοῦ Χριστοῦ τοῦ ἀποθανόντος ὑπὲρ ἡμῶν, 1 Th. 5:10, cf. the vl. περί, then including the resurrection: τῷ ὑπὲρ αὐτῶν ἀποθανόντι καὶ ἐγερθέντι, 2 C. 5:15. In argumentative variations one finds: (εἷς) ὑπὲρ πάντων ἀπέθανεν, 2 C. 5:14 f. twice; ὑπὲρ ἀσεβῶν ἀπέθανεν, R. 5:6; μόλις γὰρ ὑπὲρ δικαίου τις ἀποθανεῖται, R. 5:7 → IV, 1076, 9 ff.; [11] μὴ Παῦλος ἐσταυρώθη ὑπὲρ ὑμῶν; 1 C. 1:13. Outside the Pauline letters cf. 1 Pt. 3:18: περὶ ἁμαρτιῶν ἀπέθανεν, δίκαιος ὑπὲρ ἀδίκων. The findings are somewhat complicated by the fact that the kerygmatic formula exists in a parallel form which still has ὑπέρ and even relates it to ἁμαρτίαι but in another sense. An example is when Paul quotes directly the confessional formula: Χριστὸς ἀπέθανεν ὑπὲρ τῶν ἁμαρτιῶν ἡμῶν, 1 C. 15:3 → 511, 34 ff. [12] The formula ὑπὲρ ἡμῶν recurs in another connection in Pauline exhortation, namely, when the saving intent of the death of Jesus is adduced as a reason for concern for one's neighbour: μὴ τῷ βρώματί σου ἐκεῖνον ἀπόλλυε, ὑπὲρ οὗ Χριστὸς ἀπέθανεν, R. 14:15, cf. δι' ὅν in 1 C. 8:11.

Gl. 3:13 (→ I, 450, 1 ff.) and 2 C. 5:21 are passages in which Paul develops the atoning significance of the death and passion of Jesus with the help of typological trains of thought. [13] The former depicts the liberating effect of the act of salvation as analogous to the redemption of a slave (→ I, 126, 14 ff.): Χριστὸς ἡμᾶς ἐξηγόρασεν ἐκ τῆς κατάρας τοῦ νόμου, Gl. 3:13. The act which is equated with payment of the ransom consists in a sacrificial and vicarious acceptance of the ground of bondage: γενόμενος ὑπὲρ ἡμῶν κατάρα → I, 450, 1 ff. Jesus in His death vicariously took upon Himself (κατάρα is *abstractum pro concreto:* bearer of the curse) the mortal curse (Dt. 21:22 f. and 27:26) which the Law brings and itself represents. He did so ὑπὲρ ἡμῶν, i.e., it brought salvation to us, to those under the curse, both Jews and Gentiles according to the context and Gl. 4:3 ff., 8 ff. The train of thought leading to the words εὐλογία and ἐπαγγελία (v. 14) shows that the meaning of ὑπὲρ ἡμῶν here is "in our favour," though intrinsically the concept of substitution might suggest that it also means "in our place or stead," → 512, 23 ff. [14] This supports for its part the view that in this statement about the death of Jesus Paul took the expression ὑπὲρ ἡμῶν from kerygmatic formulae. The line of thought in 2 C.

---

[11] But cf. Plat. Symp., 179b: ὑπεραποθνήσκειν γε μόνοι ἐθέλουσιν οἱ ἐρῶντες . . . Ἄλκηστις . . . ὑπὲρ τοῦ αὐτῆς ἀνδρός.

[12] The formal distinction between ὑπὲρ ἡμῶν etc. and ὑπὲρ τῶν ἁμαρτιῶν ἡμῶν, and in the related senses of ὑπέρ, is not adequately considered in Lohse, *op. cit.*, 131-3; Hahn, *op. cit.*, 55-6; W. Kramer, "Christos, Kyrios, Gottessohn," AbhThANT, 44 (1963), 22 f.

[13] Cf. on this Schlier Gl., *ad loc.;* Robertson Use, 324-6; J. Hoad, "Some NT References to Is. 53," Exp. T., 68 (1956/57), 254 f. On the vocabulary of ransom v. Deissmann LO 275-281; Lohse, *op. cit.*, 156, though cf. W. Elert, "Redemptio ab hostibus," ThLZ, 72 (1947), 265-270.

[14] In Paul ἀντί is not used for sacrificial substitution. On the possibility of distinguishing between these related meanings v. Kühner-Blass-Gerth, II, 1, 468 f.; Trench, 201-3; Winer, 358, n. 3; Robertson Grammar, 630 f.; Deissmann LO, 132, n. 5; 281; Moule, 64; M. Zerwick, *Graecitas biblica²* (1949) § 64. One may note similarity and difference in the par. use of ὑπέρ and ἀντί in Iren. Haer., V, 1, 2; δόντος τὴν ψυχὴν ὑπὲρ τῶν ἡμετέρων ψυχῶν καὶ τὴν σάρκα τὴν ἑαυτοῦ ἀντὶ τῶν ἡμετέρων σαρκῶν, cf. the similar mode of expression with a threefold ὑπέρ in 1 Cl., 49, 6. In the sense "in the place of" ὑπέρ occurs already with ἄλλαγμα in Is. 43:3 f. LXX. Jos. Bell.,, 6, 57 tells of a soldier who is ready to offer his life "for" (ὑπέρ) Titus. On dying "for" (ὑπέρ, περί, δία, ἕνεκα) in the post-apost. fathers v. Pol., 9, 2; Barn., 5, 5; 7, 2, 14, 4; Ign. Sm., 2; 2 Cl., 1, 2. Cf. also Cl. Al. Quis Div. Salv., 23.

5:21 (cf. v. 15) is similar, and so, too, is the use of ὑπὲρ ἡμῶν. God has made the sinless One (τὸν μὴ γνόντα ἁμαρτίαν) the bearer of sin — again an *abstractum pro concreto:* ἁμαρτίαν ἐποίησεν. Here again ὑπὲρ ἡμῶν makes the transition from substitution to intention. The atoning (ἁμαρτίαν ἐποίησεν ὑπὲρ ἡμῶν) and reconciling (καταλλάγητε, v. 20; → 513, 15 ff.) death of Christ brings it about that the Christians of whom Paul speaks and the missionary world to which he goes are righteous in fellowship with Christ, i.e., they have a share in God's righteousness, cf. R. 10:3 f.

A typical group is formed by expressions of the same content in which ὑπὲρ ἡμῶν is combined with the verb (παρα)δίδωμι → II, 169, 20 ff.: [15] ὃς τοῦ ἰδίου υἱοῦ οὐκ ἐφείσατο ἀλλὰ ὑπὲρ ἡμῶν πάντων παρέδωκεν αὐτόν, R. 8:32; τοῦ υἱοῦ τοῦ θεοῦ τοῦ . . . παραδόντος ἑαυτὸν ὑπὲρ ἐμοῦ, Gl. 2:20; ὃς ἔδωκεν ἑαυτὸν ὑπὲρ ἡμῶν, Tt. 2:14, cf. Eph. 5:2, 25; in more developed form ὁ δοὺς ἑαυτὸν ἀντίλυτρον ὑπὲρ πάντων, 1 Tm. 2:6. Outside the Pauline corpus, too, one finds ὑπέρ combinations in forms which vary but which all go back to a common tradition: ὅπως χάριτι θεοῦ ὑπὲρ παντὸς γεύσηται θανάτου, Hb. 2:9; then with typological allusion to the rite of the Day of Atonement: ὅπου πρόδρομος ὑπὲρ ἡμῶν εἰσῆλθεν Ἰησοῦς, Hb. 6:20; with another obvious verb: Χριστὸς ἔπαθεν ὑπὲρ ὑμῶν, 1 Pt. 2:21. John says with reference to the saving death of Jesus: ἀποθνήσκω ὑπέρ, Jn. 11:50-52; 18:14; τίθημι τὴν ψυχὴν ὑπέρ, 10:11, 15; 13:37 f.; 15:13; [16] with a figure of speech taken from the cultic vocabulary of Judaism ὑπὲρ αὐτῶν ἁγιάζω ἐμαυτόν, 17:19 → I, 111, 35 ff. [17]

(c) What is the probable origin of ὑπὲρ ἡμῶν (ὑμῶν etc.) in statements about the death of Jesus? One might suggest a catechetical development of the kerygmatic formulation ὑπὲρ τῶν ἁμαρτιῶν ἡμῶν, 1 C. 15:3; → 509, 12 ff. Yet it seems to be nearer the mark to refer to a logion which has ὑπέρ expressions both in the Pauline tradition and also in two of the Synoptic parallels. We are speaking of the words of institution at the Last Supper (→ II, 133, 12 ff.; V, 716, n. 484), which seem to have been of significance in relation to the rise of the ὑπέρ statements treated above: τοῦτό μού ἐστιν τὸ σῶμα τὸ ὑπὲρ ὑμῶν (1 C. 11:24, cf. τὸ ὑπὲρ ὑμῶν διδόμενον Lk. 22:19); τοῦτό ἐστιν τὸ αἷμά μου τῆς διαθήκης τὸ ἐγχυννόμενον ὑπὲρ πολλῶν (Mk. 14:24, [18] cf. Lk. 22:20). The ὑπὲρ ὑμῶν in the cup saying in Mk. undoubtedly belongs to the oldest stratum of the Gospel tradition and an Aramaic original may be discerned behind the Greek. [19] The allusion to Is. 53 must have been there before the translation of the eucharistic sayings into Greek, for ὑπέρ does not occur in Is. 53:11 f. in the LXX, though πολλοί does. [20] Together

---

[15] On the so-called παραδιδόναι formulae cf. Jeremias, *op. cit.* (→ n. 10), 206; Schlier Gl. on 1:4; R. H. Fuller, *The Mission and Achievement of Jesus* (1954), 58 f.; Hahn, *op. cit.*, 62 f.; Kramer, *op. cit.*, 26 f.

[16] Cf. Jeremias, *op. cit.* (→ n. 10), 203 → 155, 29 ff.; G. Dautzenberg, "Sein Leben bewahren," *Stud. z. AT u. NT,* 14 (1966), 107-113. Cf. also E. A. Abbott, *Johannine Grammar* (1906), 276.

[17] Zahn, cf. *Apost. Vät., ad loc.,* puts ὑπέρ with ἁγνίζομαι at Ign. Eph., 8, 1; Tr., 13, 3 on the basis of the Syr., Arm., Copt. transl.

[18] The par. Mt. 26:28 has περὶ πολλῶν.

[19] J. Jeremias, *Die Abendmahlsworte Jesu*[3] (1960), 165 and 171; Hahn, *op. cit.*, 59-61.

[20] Jeremias, *op. cit.,* 171. Cf. the same concept in 1 Tm. 2:6; R. 8:32, and on the former C. Spicq, *Saint Paul, Les Ép. pastorales* (1947), 60 f. Cf. also Dg., 9, 2 λύτρον ὑπὲρ ἡμῶν. On πολλοί → VI, 543, 8 ff.

with the complex symbolism of the eucharistic action the sense "for all" interprets the death of Jesus as the saving act which is to the benefit of the people of God as orientated to humanity, and of humanity as directed to the people of God. [21] The ὑπὲρ ὑμῶν of the cup saying in Mk. probably represents the earliest stage of ὑπέρ phrases with a personal reference in statements about the death of Jesus. No matter how one may assess the direct influence of Is. 53:11 f. on the self-awareness of Jesus and primitive Christian christology, the beneficial quality (ὑπέρ) of the death of someone, even in the categories of Jewish martyr theology, can be understood only against the background of the sacrificial concepts of the OT. Exclusively an act of self-sacrifice, the negative fact of death can become a positive event which may produce fruitful results for others. [22]

(d) The development of the related ὑπέρ combinations in primitive Christianity can thus be sketched as follows. We find theological interpretation and par. extensions in the τὸ ὑπὲρ ὑμῶν of the bread saying in Paul at 1 C. 11:24 and also in Lk. 22:19, cf. also the cup saying in Lk. 22:20. One may also suppose that the christological ὑπὲρ ἡμῶν presented above is already in Paul a common catechetical application of the liturgical ὑπὲρ ὑμῶν. Yet the latter, too, occurs catechetically, e.g., in Eph. 5:2 vl. An interpretative ὑπὲρ ἡμῶν also made its way into the typological statement 1 C. 5:7. ὑπὲρ πάντων may be regarded as an exposition of ὑπὲρ πολλῶν in 2 C. 5:14 f.; 1 Tm. 2:6; the latter is a typical catechetical paraphrase of the logion Mk. 10:45 and par. ἡμῶν πάντων in R. 8:32 may be regarded as a mixed form. Theological reflection leads on from this to the Johannine ὑπὲρ τοῦ λαοῦ in Jn. 11:50; 18:14; ὑπὲρ τοῦ ἔθνους in 11:51 f., or ἡ σάρξ μου ἐστιν ὑπὲρ τῆς τοῦ κόσμου ζωῆς in 6:51. Another aspect of ὑπὲρ ὑμῶν (ἡμῶν) is brought out in the ὑπὲρ ἀσεβῶν of R. 5:6, cf. 8. The introduction of ὑπὲρ ἡμῶν (ὑμῶν, ἐμοῦ etc.) into christological (παρα)δίδωμι sayings is also part of the first Christian systematisation → 510, 9 ff.

The acceptance of suffering and death by Christians in discipleship of Jesus is also to the advantage of fellow-Christians: δαπανήσω καὶ ἐκδαπανηθήσομαι ὑπὲρ τῶν ψυχῶν ὑμῶν, 2 C. 12:15; ἀνάθεμα εἶναι ... ὑπὲρ τῶν ἀδελφῶν μου, R. 9:3, cf. 16:4; χαίρω ἐν τοῖς παθήμασιν ὑπὲρ ὑμῶν, καὶ ἀνταναπληρῶ τὰ ὑστερήματα τῶν θλίψεων τοῦ Χριστοῦ ἐν τῇ σαρκί μου ὑπὲρ τοῦ σώματος, Col. 1:24, [23] cf. Eph. 3:1, 13 (→ 508, 27 ff.). The parallelism of christology (ὑπὲρ ἡμῶν) and discipleship (ὑπὲρ τῶν ἀδελφῶν) is intentional in 1 Jn. 3:16.

In sayings about the death of Jesus an important role is also played by the expression ὑπὲρ τῶν ἁμαρτιῶν "for the expiation (or purging) of sins," cf. already the christo-

---

[21] We are pointed in the same direction by the materially related saying (which also alludes to Is. 53:11 f.) about the Son of Man who serves and gives His life in Mk. 10:45 par., in which ἀντὶ πολλῶν may be regarded as another rendering of ὑπὲρ πολλῶν → I, 373, 1 ff. Jeremias, op. cit., 171 and 174, also op. cit. (→ n. 9), 216-229; Cullmann, op. cit. (→ n. 10), 64; Lohse, op. cit. (→ n. 9), 117-122; Hahn, op. cit. (→ n. 10), 57-9. Dautzenberg, op. cit. (→ n. 16), 98-107; H. E. Tödt, Der Menschensohn in d. synpt. Überlieferung² (1963), 187-194. A link with Is. 53:11 is denied by C. K. Barrett, "The Background of Mark 10:45," Stud. in Memory of T. W. Manson (1959), 1-18; M. D. Hooker, Jesus and the Servant (1959), 74-9.

[22] On sacrifice → n. 10 and cf. H. H. Rowley, "The Forms and Meaning of Sacrifice," Worship in Ancient Israel (1967), 111-143; A. Kirchgässner, Erlösung u. Sünde im NT (1950), 69-71; M. Barth, "Was Christ's Death a Sacrifice?" Scottish Journ. of Theology, Occas. Papers, 9 (1961); L. Sabourin, Rédemption sacrificielle (1961), 302-327; G. Fitzer, "Der Ort d. Versöhnung nach Pls. Zu d. Frage d. Sühnopfers Jesu," ThZ, 22 (1966), 161-183; G. D. Kilpatrick, "L'eucharistie dans le NT," RevThPh, 97 (1964), 193-204.

[23] J. Kremer, Was an den Leiden Christi noch mangelt (1956), 196-201 cautiously decides for the meaning "for the sake of," cf. also L. Morris, The Apostolic Preaching of the Cross³ (1965), 62-4, 172 f.

logical teaching tradition quoted by Paul: Χριστὸς ἀπέθανεν ὑπὲρ τῶν ἁμαρτιῶν ἡμῶν, 1 C. 15:3, [24] then Paul's own version: τοῦ δόντος ἑαυτὸν ὑπὲρ τῶν ἁμαρτιῶν ἡμῶν, Gl. 1:4. [25] This phrase, which is by no means identical with the personal ὑπὲρ ἡμῶν etc., shows that the Aram. speaking community was already expounding the death of Jesus along the lines of Is. 53:5 Tg.: בַּעֲוָיָתָנָא "on account of our transgressions." [26] This is no less than a fundamental point of departure for the primitive Chr. interpretation of the death of Jesus as an atoning death. First there was awareness of the fact. Then reflection on its meaning began. Yet the transl. of Aram. ב by ὑπέρ still calls for explanation, since διά is a better equivalent in what seem to be the variant rendering of the same expression Is. 53:5 Tg. which Paul offers elsewhere: (παρεδόθη) διὰ τὰ παραπτώματα ἡμῶν, R. 4:25. One may conjecture that ὑπὲρ τῶν ἁμαρτιῶν ἡμῶν displays the influence of the formulations ὑπὲρ ἡμῶν (ὑμῶν, πάντων) which were already part and parcel of christological sayings.

(e) ὑπέρ alternates with περί in the concept περὶ ἁμαρτίας (-ιῶν) ("atoning sacrifice" → VI, 55, 6 ff.) which has its source in the sacrificial vocabulary of the LXX, cf. ἵνα προσφέρῃ δῶρά τε καὶ θυσίας ὑπὲρ ἁμαρτιῶν "for the purging of sins," Hb. 5:1b, in which ὑπὲρ ἁμαρτιῶν can go with the verb as well as δῶρά τε καὶ θυσίας, the former being more likely, cf. also Hb. 7:27; 10:12. Logically different senses of ὑπέρ are combined thematically in Hb. 9:7: ὃ προσφέρει ὑπὲρ ἑαυτοῦ (→ 508, 20) καὶ τῶν τοῦ λαοῦ ἀγνοημάτων. This explains the alternation of περί and ὑπέρ in similar expressions, e.g., περὶ ἁμαρτίας R. 8:3; Hb. 10:18 and in the MSS, e.g., 1 C. 1:13; Gl. 1:4. [27]

3. In the Place of.

It has been shown already that the sense "on behalf of" is sometimes very close to "in the place of," "instead of," "in the name of" → 509, 28 ff. [28] In all probability the word has the representative sense in Paul's saying about baptism for the dead (→ I, 542, 17 ff): ἐπεὶ τί ποιήσουσιν οἱ βαπτιζόμενοι ὑπὲρ τῶν νεκρῶν, 1 C. 15:29. None of the attempts to escape the theory of a vicarious baptism in primitive Christ-

---

[24] Exposition of 1 C. 15:3 ff. divides acc. to differing views on the basic questions of primitive Chr. tradition and the genesis of primitive Chr. theology. The tradition quoted by Paul is mostly regarded as Palestinian, so Jeremias, op. cit. (→ n. 10), 199 ff.; Lohse, op. cit. (→ n. 9), 113-6; Hahn, op. cit. (→ n. 10), 55-7, 197-213. Hell. Chr. tradition is supported by W. Heitmüller, "Zum Problem Paulus u. Jesus," ZNW, 13 (1912), 331, and more recently Kramer, op. cit. (→ n. 12), 29-34; H. Conzelmann, "Zur Analyse d. Bekenntnisformel 1 K. 15:3-5," Ev. Theol., 25 (1965), 1-11; P. Vielhauer, "Ein Weg z. nt.lichen Christologie?" Aufsätze z. NT (1965), 179-183.
[25] Schlier Gl., ad loc. Atkinson, 14 thinks ὑπέρ is causal here. On the background v. 3 Βασ. 16:18 f.: ἀπέθανεν ὑπὲρ τῶν ἁμαρτιῶν αὐτοῦ. Cf. also Pol., 1, 2.
[26] So esp. B. Klappert, "Zur Frage d. semitischen oder griech. Urtextes v. 1 K. 15:3-5," NTSt, 13 (1966/67), 168-173 with significant arguments from Tg. on Is. 53. Views are again divided as to the influence of Is. 53: positively cf. Joh. W. 1 K., Ltzm. K., ad loc.; Jeremias, op. cit. (→ n. 10), 199 f.; H. W. Wolff, Js. 53 im Urchr.[2] (1950), 97 f.; Lohse, op. cit. (→ n. 9), 114 f.; cf. L. Cerfaux, Recueil II (1954), 446-451; negatively Hahn, op. cit. (→ n. 10), 55-7, 201-3; Kramer, op. cit. (→ n. 12), 26 f.; Conzelmann, op. cit. (→ n. 24), 5 f.; Vielhauer, op. cit. (→ n. 24), 179-183.
[27] Mi. Hb.[12], 217 and n. 2; 281. Cf. Barn., 7, 3-6. Cf. also Moule, 64. On this Ez. 40:39; 43:21, 25; 44:29; 45:17, 22, 25; 46:20 LXX. The similarity to Gl. 1:4 suggests a firm catechetical link even outside Hb.
[28] This sense does not occur in Hom., but cf. Eur. Alc., 701; Thuc., I, 141, 7; Xenoph. An., VII, 4, 9; Plat. Gorg., 515c. Further class. examples in Trench, 201, Hell. in Mayser, II, 2, 460 f.; Moult.-Mill., Preisigke Wört., s.v. Cf. also L. Wenger, Die Stellvertretung im Rechte d. Pap. (1906), 203; Robertson Use, 321 f.; Abel, op. cit. (→ n. 5), 223 f.; Radermacher, 139.

ianity seems to be wholly successful. [29] If one thus presupposes that there may be baptism "for the dead," this implies that the dead, probably relatives, were unbaptised at death. We thus have a kind of substitution even if, as one may suppose, the candidate was baptised for himself as well as with respect to someone who had died unbaptised.

In Phlm. 13: ἵνα ὑπὲρ σοῦ μοι διακονῇ, Paul is speaking of the hypothetical ministry of Onesimus in place of the absent Philemon. [30] In 2 C. 5:14 f. there is a play on the two related senses of ὑπέρ. τῷ ὑπὲρ αὐτῶν ἀποθανόντι καὶ ἐγερθέντι in v. 15 is based on a kerygmatic formulation like that in 1 C. 15:3 (→ 511, 34 ff.) and the prep. thus has the primary sense of "on behalf or in favour of." But in the more forensic expression εἷς ὑπὲρ πάντων ἀπέθανεν in v. 14 the sense "in the place of" is predominant, as is shown by the development of the thought in the following clause: ἄρα οἱ πάντες ἀπέθανον. [31] The meaning is the same in καὶ ὑπὲρ πάντων ἀπέθανεν in v. 15a. The two vv. are thus a model of the shifting sense of the prep. and the way an author can exploit this. The representative sense "in the name of someone," which is close to the substitutionary meaning, occurs in 2 C. 5:20 (→ VI, 682, 13 ff.): ὑπὲρ Χριστοῦ οὖν πρεσβεύομεν ὡς τοῦ θεοῦ παρακαλοῦντος δι᾽ ἡμῶν· δεόμεθα ὑπὲρ Χριστοῦ, καταλλάγητε τῷ θεῷ [32] → 509, 33 ff. As a preacher of the Gospel the apostle is an authorised transmitter of the divine message and hence a representative of Christ. The urgent call of the apostle as he invites men to believe is thus a call which the exalted Christ Himself issues.

4. With Reference to.

In a weaker use ὑπέρ in the sense of "in defence or favour of" has a tendency to slip over into the meaning "with reference to." [33]

a. With various verbs and expressions ὑπέρ is used with the gen. of an abstract noun in a final sense: "with reference to," "as concerns" (→ VI, 53, 10 ff.), "for the sake of," "for." In the NT τὸ μυστήριον τοῦ εὐαγγελίου, ὑπὲρ οὗ πρεσβεύω ἐν ἁλύσει occurs at Eph. 6:19 f. "for the promotion of" the Gospel, "in the interests of" its propagation, the apostle is at work as an envoy of Christ and has to endure imprison-

---

[29] M. Raeder, "Vikariatstaufe in 1 K. 15:29?" ZNW, 45 (1955), 258-260 thinks the prep. is final here (ὑπέρ of purpose): baptism is "for the sake of the dead," i.e., to be reunited with dead Chr. relatives at the resurrection. For the probable meaning and for discussion v. Ltzm. K., ad loc.; E. B. Allo, Saint Paul, Première Ép. aux Cor.² (1956), ad loc.; Blakeney, 306; G. R. Beasley-Murray, Baptism in the NT (1962), 185-192; M. Rissi, "Die Taufe f. d. Toten," AbhThANT, 43 (1962); → I, 542, 17 ff. K. Staab, "1 K. 15:29 im Lichte d. Exegese d. griech. Kirche," Studiorum Paulinorum congressus internation. catholicus, 1961 (1963), 443-450 appeals to early comm. for the sense "for your bodies which otherwise remain dead," though it is hard to see how this fits in with the train of thought in 1 C. 15. Staab, 444 f. gives early ref. to vicarious baptism, which he regards as heretical. It should be noted that in 1 C. 15:29 Paul is ref. to a practice in Corinth, though he does not expressly repudiate it.
[30] Deissmann LO, 285, n. 2.
[31] Cf. Eur. Alc., 700 f.: κατθανεῖν... γυναῖχ᾽ ὑπὲρ σοῦ, and esp. Dt. 24:16 LXX: οὐκ ἀποθανοῦνται πατέρες ὑπὲρ τέκνων, καὶ υἱοὶ οὐκ ἀποθανοῦνται ὑπὲρ πατέρων, cf. also 4 Βασ. 14:6.
[32] ὑπέρ has another sense with πρεσβεύω in Eph. 6:20 (→ lines 27 ff.). On 2 C. 5:20 → VI, 682, 13 ff., cf. also Winer, 359. E. B. Allo, Saint Paul, Seconde Ép. aux Cor.² (1956), ad loc. and K. H. Rengstorf, Apostolat u. Predigtamt² (1955), 19, n. 52 find more emphasis in the second ὑπέρ than the first. The transl. by Pr.-Bauer, s.v. "as Christ's helper" or "by Christ" can hardly be correct.
[33] Cf. Kühner-Blass-Gerth, II, 1, 487. 548; Robertson Grammar, 629. 632; Moulton, 170 f.; Radermacher, 140. 143. 146; H. Widmann, Beiträge z. Syntax Epikurs (1935), 230 f. On the alternation of ὑπέρ and περί v. Johannessohn Präpos., 217 f.

ment in discharging this task. The difference in the train of thought and the meaning of the prep. should be noted in comparison with 2 C. 5:20 → VI, 682, 13 ff. Similarly it is said of the goal of the apostle's work: ὑπὲρ τοῦ ὀνόματος αὐτοῦ, i.e., "to further the preaching of the name of Christ," R. 1:5, cf. 3 Jn. 7, ὑπὲρ ἀληθείας θεοῦ "to demonstrate the truthfulness of God," R. 15:8, ὑπὲρ τῆς ὑμῶν παρακλήσεως καὶ σωτηρίας, "to your comfort and salvation," 2 C. 1:6a, cf. v. 6b; 12:19; 1 Th. 3:2. ὑπὲρ τῆς εὐδοκίας in Phil. 2:13 (→ II, 746, 26 ff.) probably means "to the fulfilment of (God's) counsel." [34] With εἰμί: ὑπὲρ τῆς δόξης τοῦ θεοῦ, "to manifest God's glory," Jn. 11:4.

b. With the gen. of person and verbs or verbal nouns of asking or praying the prep. means "for," cf. δέομαι Ac. 8:24, εὔχομαι Jm. 5:16 vl., προσεύχομαι Mt. 5:44; Col. 1:3 vl.; 1:9, [35] ἐντυγχάνω R. 8:27, 34; Hb. 7:25, ὑπερεντυγχάνω R. 8:26 vl., δέησις R. 10:1; 2 C. 1:11; 9:14; Eph. 6:19; [36] Phil. 1:4, προσευχή, R. 15:30, the two last-named with ἔντευξις and εὐχαριστία, 1 Tm. 2:1 f. The idea of asking is presupposed in the anacoluthon 2 C. 8:23: εἴτε ὑπὲρ Τίτου, κοινωνὸς ἐμός.

c. With pers. ὑπέρ means "about," "with reference to," [37] cf. οὗτός ἐστιν ὑπὲρ οὗ ἐγὼ εἶπον, Jn. 1:30, [38] but cf. the vl., Ἡσαίας δὲ κράζει ὑπὲρ τοῦ Ἰσραήλ, R. 9:27, with καυχάομαι, ἐγκαυχάομαι, καύχησις, καύχημα, cf. 2 C. 5:12; 7:4, 14; 8:24; 9:2 f.; 12:5a b; 2 Th. 1:4, with ἐλπίς 2 C. 1:7, εὐχαριστέω 2 C. 1:11b.

d. With an abstract concept ὑπέρ means "with reference to," "concerning," cf. ἐρωτῶμεν δὲ ὑμᾶς ... ὑπὲρ τῆς παρουσίας τοῦ κυρίου ἡμῶν, "in connection with the treatment of the parousia," 2 Th. 2:1, [39] ἀγνοεῖν ... ὑπὲρ ·τῆς θλίψεως ἡμῶν, 2 C. 1:8, but cf. the vl. [40]

5. On Account of.

Causally ὑπέρ is used to denote the cause or reason: [41] "on account of," "because of." In the NT it occurs with verbs and expressions of suffering, the reference being to Christians who endure hardships because of their faith.

Cf. πάσχω, Phil. 1:29 (→ V, 920, 14 ff.) — τὸ ὑπὲρ Χριστοῦ is an ellipse which anticipates the thought of suffering —, ὑπὲρ τῆς βασιλείας, 2 Th. 1:5, δεῖ αὐτὸν ὑπὲρ τοῦ ὀνόματός μου παθεῖν, Ac. 9:16, cf. 5:41 (→ V, 919, 18 ff.), ἀποθανεῖν ... ὑπὲρ τοῦ ὀνόματος τοῦ κυρίου Ἰησοῦ, Ac. 21:13, cf. Ign. R., 4, 1, ἐν ἀσθενείαις ... ἐν διωγμοῖς καὶ στενοχωρίαις, ὑπὲρ Χριστοῦ, 2 C. 12:10. With verbs and expressions of thanks and praise: εὐχαριστέω 1 C. 10:30; 2 C. 1:11; Eph. 5:20, δοξάζω R. 15:9. To

---

[34] Cf. Loh. Phil., ad loc.; Moule, 65, though Martin, op. cit. (→ n. 6), ad loc. thinks the ref. is to man's good will. Cf. also Ign. Eph., 16, 2: πίστιν θεοῦ ... ὑπὲρ ἧς Ἰησοῦς Χριστός ἐσταυρώθη "to the establishing and promoting of faith in God."
[35] Cf. also 2 Macc. 12:44: ὑπὲρ νεκρῶν εὔχεσθαι, a passage adduced in elucidation of 1 C. 15:29.
[36] Eph. 6:18 f.: δεήσει περὶ πάντων τῶν ἁγίων καὶ ὑπὲρ ἐμοῦ and cf. on this Schlier Eph., ad loc.; on the alternation of ὑπέρ and περί cf. too Mayser, II, 2, 452.
[37] On the relation of ὑπέρ and περί in this sense v. Schwyzer, II, 500 with n. 1; 503, 522; Mayser, II, 2, 339, 450-4, 456; Moult.-Mill., s.v.; F. Krebs, Die Präp. bei Polyb. (1882), 41 f.; Pr.-Bauer, s.v.
[38] Bl.-Debr. § 231, 1 also adduces 2 C. 8:23 in the same sense, so too Allo, op. cit. (→ n. 32), 228 → 508, 14 f.
[39] Cf. B. Rigaux, Saint Paul. Les Épîtres aux Thessal. (1956), ad loc.
[40] Cf. also 2 Macc. 12:43: ὑπὲρ ἀναστάσεως διαλογιζόμενος.
[41] On this Kühner-Blass-Gerth, II, 1, 486 f.; Schwyzer, II, 521; Abel, op. cit. (→ n. 5) 224.

denote the reason for prayer: ὑπὲρ τούτου τρὶς τὸν κύριον παρεκάλεσα, 2 C. 12:8: because of the angel of Satan. [42]

B. ὑπέρ with Accusative.

1. The original spatial meaning "beyond" (of direction) occurs only occasionally in the NT and apart from a variant [43] only in the transferred sense "exceeding," "above measure," "above," "more than."

κεφαλὴ ὑπὲρ πάντα "the head towering over all," Eph. 1:22, ὑπὲρ δύναμιν 2 C. 1:8; 8:3 vl. ὑπὲρ ὃ δύνασθε 1 C. 10:13, μὴ ὑπὲρ ἃ γέγραπται, "not beyond what is written" 1 C. 4:6, [44] μή ... ὑπὲρ ὃ βλέπει με 2 C. 12:6, ὑπὲρ ἃ λέγω ποιήσεις Phlm. 21. [45]

2. After comparatives it can have the same sense as ἤ and means "than" [46] after, e.g., an adjective or adverb in the comparative.

τομώτερος ὑπὲρ πᾶσαν μάχαιραν Hb. 4:12, φρονιμώτεροι ὑπὲρ τοὺς υἱοὺς τοῦ φωτός Lk. 16:8, μᾶλλον ὑπέρ Jn. 12:43 vl. [47] So, too, after verbs with a comparative sense: ἡσσώθητε ὑπὲρ τὰς λοιπὰς ἐκκλησίας, "you have been treated worse than the other churches," 2 C. 12:13. When the comparative sense is suggested by the context it means "more than": οὐκ ἔστιν μαθητὴς ὑπὲρ τὸν διδάσκαλον "a disciple is not more illustrious than his teacher," Lk. 6:40 and par., cf. also Mt. 10:24b, τὸ ὄνομα τὸ ὑπὲρ πᾶν ὄνομα "the name exalted above all other names," Phil. 2:9, cf. Ac. 26:13, οὐκέτι ὡς δοῦλον ἀλλὰ ὑπὲρ δοῦλον "no longer as a slave but as something better than a slave," Phlm. 16 (→ VII, 127, 22 ff.), τῷ δυναμένῳ ὑπὲρ πάντα ποιῆσαι "who can do more than all we may ask or think," Eph. 3:20, ὁ φιλῶν πατέρα ἢ μητέρα ὑπὲρ ἐμέ "more than me," Mt. 10:37a, cf. v. 37b (→ IV, 690, 28 ff.), προέκοπτον ἐν τῷ Ἰουδαϊσμῷ ὑπὲρ πολλοὺς συνηλικιώτας, "I made progress in Judaism beyond many of my contemporaries," Gl. 1:14 → VI, 714, 19 ff.

---

[42] Schwyzer, II, 521: "on account of."

[43] Hb. 9:5 D* E*: ὑπὲρ δ᾽ αὐτήν "above" the ark, cf. Bl.-Debr. § 230.

[44] Cf. R. 12:3: μὴ ὑπερφρονεῖν παρ᾽ ὃ δεῖ φρονεῖν and Moule, 92. P. Wallis, "Ein neuer Auslegungsversuch d. St. 1 K. 4:6," ThLZ, 75 (1950), 506-8: "That our example may not teach you 'too much' and that you have it in black and white"; cf. also K. L. Schmidt, "Nicht über das hinaus, was geschrieben steht," In memoriam E. Lohmeyer (1951), 101-9. On the attempt to treat this obscure expression as a gloss v. W. F. Howard "1 C. 4:6. Exegesis or Emendation?" Exp. T., 33 (1921/22), 479 f. and cf. also Moule, 64.

[45] ὑπέρ τι καὶ καθ᾽ ὑπερβολὴν ὑπερευφραίνομαι in Barn., 1, 2; → V, 734, 13 ff. and 2 C. 8:3 where ὑπέρ is a vl. of παρά. In the light of Eph. 1:22 Atkinson, 13 speaks of a ὑπέρ of authority.

[46] In class. and post-class. Gk. ὑπέρ (→ V, 734, 13 ff.) means, in distinction from the compar. gen. or ἤ, the measure which is beyond the fact expressed comparatively (even with no direct compar.), e.g., ὑπὲρ αἶσαν Hom. Il., 3, 59, οὐκ ἔστιν ὑπὲρ ἄνθρωπον Plat. Leg., VIII, 839d, ὑπὲρ ἑαυτὸν φρονῶν P. Tor., II, 8, 70 (119 B.C.). The replacing of a genuine constr. with the compar. gen. or ἤ by παρά or ὑπέρ is found only in Jewish and Chr. Gk. lit. and is to be explained as a Semitism (or in the NT a Septuagintism). The Hbr. use of מִן for a missing compar. is rendered by the similar παρά and ὑπέρ in Gk., e.g., οὐκ ἀγαθὸς ἐγώ σοι ὑπὲρ δέκα τέκνα; 1 Βασ. 1:8, cf. Hag. 2:9, οὐ κρείσσων ἐγώ εἰμι ὑπὲρ τοὺς πατέρας μου 3 Βασ. 19:4, cf. Hab. 1:8. This explanation is supported by the fact that the modern Gk. use of ἀπό (διά) for the compar. gen. or ἤ does not occur in Jewish or Chr. Gk. lit. [Dihle]. With the acc., ὑπέρ occurs only in the compar. sense in the LXX, Johannessohn Präpos., 219. It occurs after a superlative in Herm. m., 5, 1, 6. Cf. also D. Georgacas, "Grammatische u. etym. Miszellen zum Spät.- u. Neugriechischen," Glotta, 31 (1951), 227.

[47] p66 ℵ etc.; most MSS read ἤπερ.

C. ὑπέρ as Adverb. [48]

The adverbial use of prepositions is rare and occurs in the NT probably in only one instance of ὑπέρ at 2 C. 11:23: "in greater measure" ὑπὲρ ἐγώ (sc. διάκονος Χριστοῦ εἰμι). [49]

Riesenfeld

---

[48] Cf. Schwyzer, II, 422 and 518; Thes. Steph., IX, 160; Robertson Grammar, 629; Bl.-Debr. § 203, 230; Pr.-Bauer, *s.v.* Cf. Eur. Med., 627: ὑπὲρ ἄγαν. Westcott-Hort etc. at 2 C. 11:23 write ὕπερ. Wallis, *op. cit.* (→ n. 44), 507 f. sees an adv. use in 1 C. 4:6 as well.
[49] Cf. ἐγὼ μᾶλλον Phil. 3:4.

---

† ὑπεραυξάνω, † αὐξάνω

---

1. ὑπεραυξάνω is seldom found; in the intr. act. it means "to grow to the extreme limit," e.g., a fish which is already big, Plut. Fluv., 6, 2 (II, 1153c): in the mid. pass. it means "to attain very gt. power or authority," Andoc. Or., IV, 24," to achieve the highest position or status," Dio C., 79, 15, 2.

αὐξάνω or αὔξω[1] means act. trans. "to bring to growth," Philo Op. Mund., 113 "to increase" e.g., of fruits (par. τρέφω), Epict. Diss., III, 22, 5, "to promote," e.g., one's house (family), Philo Vit. Mos., I, 150, "to elevate someone, his position or authority" (opp. ἐλαττόω "to reduce"), Polyb., 21, 19. 11; (opp. ταπεινόω "to lessen the influence"),[2] 24, 10, 3; intr. (from. Aristot., e.g., Hist. An., VIII, 42, p. 629a, 21) "to grow," as a natural process, M. Ant., IX, 3, 2; φιλία... ηὔξησε Jos. Ant., 8, 58,[3] αὐξάνει τὰ κακά Aesopus Fabulae,[4] 216, 3, 15 (with τὸ κακὸν... αὔξεται, 216, 2, 21 f.), also "to rise" in repute, power etc., of Cicero, Dio C., 46, 4, 1, Augustus, 53, 20, 1, "to mount in authority, position," αὔξειν ἤρχετο, 53, 24, 1. In the mid. pass., too, it means "to grow," e.g., ὁ δὲ παῖς ηὔξετο Hdt., VI, 63, 2. "to grow" into a multitude of peoples, I, 58, "to increase," of the δύναμις of the Romans, Polyb., 2, 18, 9; often αὐξάνομαι alone means "to grow in might," e.g., Hdt., V, 77, 4; VI, 132; Demosth. Or., 2, 5. 7, of the ἔθνος, Polyb., 2, 40, 6, of states, Epict. Diss., II, 20, 26, of King Philip ηὐξήθη, Polyb., 25, 3, 9; Dionysus must be "magnified, exalted, glorified" δεῖ νιν... αὔξεσθαι Eur. Ba., 181-183, cf. the act Plat. Lys., 206a.

2. The compound does not occur in the LXX. The simple form is used 11 times for פרה q, apart from Gn. 26:22 always mid. pass. in the sense "to be or to become fruitful, numerous," often with πληθύνομαι → VI, 280, 13 ff. It is also found 8 times in the act. for hi, always meaning that God "makes fruitful, numerous," e.g., Gn. 41:52 (A ὕψωσεν),[5] also for פֹּרָת Gn. 49:22, of Joseph. The mid. pass. is used for גדל q, of boys etc. Gn. 21:8, 20; 25:27; Ju. 13:24 A, the act for pi: Yahweh "made" Joshua "great" in the eyes of Israel, Jos. 4:14, as a promise to David also 1 Ch. 17:10 (but v. BHK).[6] Then the mid. pass. is used for נשׂא ni, of power and authority, ηὐξήθη εἰς ὕψος ἡ βασιλεία αὐτοῦ 1 Ch. 14:2, cf. Nu. 24:7, for פרץ "to extend" (→ VI, 231, 10 ff.) Gn. 30:30; 2 Ch. 11:23, for רבה "to become numerous" 1 Ch. 23:17, for צלח (lit. "to succeed") Jer. 22:30; the act. for יצא hi "to cause to grow," Is. 61:11; the mid. pass. for חדשׁ hitp "to renew oneself," "to increase," of the new moon Sir. 43:8. With no HT the act trans. occurs in the free rendering ὁ δὲ κύριος ηὔξησεν τὸν Ιωβ at Job 42:10. The mid. pass. in the sense "to become great" of man or his position is found in Sir. 2:3, "to grow" of the embryo or the boy, 4 Macc. 13:20, 22. Ju. 5:11 B means: "May God magnify acts of righteousness in Israel" → line 19 f.

ὑ π ε ρ α υ ξ ά ν ω κ τ λ. [1] Both forms are attested from the 5th cent. B.C.; on their distribution v. Liddell-Scott, s.v. [Risch].

[2] Cf. Dio C., 45, 11, 4; the ταπείνωσις "diminution" of the power of the Egyptians is compared by Moses with the αὔξησις "exalting" of the Hebrews, Jos. Ant., 2, 238.

[3] On the related use of the mid. pass. and intr. act. in Jos. v. Schl. Mt. on 6:28.

[4] Corpus Fabularum Aesopicarum, I, 2, ed. A. Hausrath (1956/57).

[5] Ref. may at least be made here to the problems of the LXX transl. → lines 21 ff.

[6] At 1 Ch. 17:10 LXX arranged the HT consonants (נגד ל) differently and thus came up with גדל = αὐξάνω [Bertram].

3. In the NT the compound occurs only at 2 Th. 1:3 → lines 20 ff. Behind the use of the simple form there plainly stands the thought of growth in creation, especially in the plant kingdom. The expression derives from the figurative language of the Synoptic parables and not so much from the actual use of the verb in these [7] but rather from the general employment by Jesus of imagery connected with the annual round of sowing and harvest etc. Perhaps this also affects the already stereotyped language of Ac. The original thought is that of the scattered seed (ὁ λόγος) which grows, Mk. 4:3-9, 14-20 and par., cf. also Mt. 13:30. Ac. 6:7 offers the interpretation that the number of disciples increased, cf. 12:24; 19:20 → VI, 715, n. 77. The figure of speech is still evident in Col. 1:6 (→ III, 616, n. 1; on καρποφορού-μενον v. Mk. 4:20 and par.); the Gospel is here the seed which grows in the plant. Then v. 10 speaks of growing or increasing in the knowledge of God, which finds expression in the Christian life, [8] cf. 2 Pt. 3:18. 2 C. 9:10 is also based on processes in the plant world: [9] God causes the fruits of righteousness [10] to grow, i.e., He brings about readiness to give. [11] αὐξάνω in 1 C. 3:6 f. stresses most emphatically the fact that God does the really decisive thing for the life of the community in contrast to a false estimate of the work of Paul or Apollos in founding the community or promoting its growth. The figurative background is less evident when the reference is to that growth in the faith of the community which the apostle hopes for in 2 C. 10:15 or for which he gives thanks because it is so rich (ὑπεραυξάνει ἡ πίστις) in 2 Th. 1:3. In both instances the context shows that the faith which grows is an active one.

The simile is also that of the natural growth of man, [12] e.g., the baby in 1 Pt. 2:2: As the baby grows physically through milk, so the Christian steadily grows spiritually through the Word → I, 676, 26 f. [13] The body of Christ is also engaged in steady growth ordained by God (τοῦ θεοῦ) on the basis of Christ (ἐξ οὗ ... ἐπιχορηγού-μενον), Col. 2:19. In the first instance αὔξει here is intensive rather than extensive. The community derives its growing life from its Head. [14] To the growing of the community "from Him" there corresponds a growing "to Him" [15] which embraces its whole existence (τὰ πάντα), Eph. 4:15 f. → III, 680, 12 ff.; VII, 1074, 6 ff.

If the metaphor of physical growth in Eph. 4:16 finally merges into that of building (cf. already v. 12 → V, 145, 19 ff.), 2:21 speaks expressly of a growing building (→ IV, 887, 18 ff.; V, 156, 5 ff.) in which God dwells in, with and by His Spirit, v. 22.

---

[7] Cf. Mk. 4:8; Mt. 13:32; Lk. 13:19, but not the parables of God's kingdom in Mt. 6:28.

[8] The combination with καρποφορέω again shows that we have here an image from the plant kingdom.

[9] The context speaks of the sowing and ripening of grain.

[10] I.e., concrete action. Through God's gift and act the Corinthians are rich in possibility (→ VI, 281, 25 ff.) as well as willingness, v. 11. This is the presupposition of the ἁπλότης in v. 11.

[11] Cf. Wnd. 2 K., ad loc.

[12] This is meant lit. in Lk. 1:80; 2:40 → 517, 24 f.

[13] Growth in faith is not restricted to those just converted → I, 672, 26 f. As the newly born naturally want milk, so the Christian should want the Word. Milk is natural unadulterated food; hence the figure in 1 Pt. 2:2. There is no trace of sacramental or mystery notions.

[14] The man who does not cleave to the Head but slips into dependence on angelic powers (v. 18) does not share in this life of the σῶμα.

[15] The thought in Eph. 4:15 is not unconnected with v. 13 → VI, 302, 21 ff.

None [16] of these three metaphors nor an astral one [17] underlies Jn. 3:30. This is rather a deepening of the widespread Greek usage already attested → 517, 12 ff. [18] The point at issue is the increase of influence, authority, or power, elevation in position.

4. In the post-apost. fathers the compound is not used. But the simple form occurs in the quotation from Gn. 1:28 (→ VI, 280, 38 f.) in 1 Cl., 33, 6; Barn., 6, 12. Acc. to Herm. v., 1, 1, 6 God multiplied creatures for the sake of the Church, cf. 1, 3, 4; Gn. 1 lies behind this too, cf. also v., 3, 4, 1. Did., 16, 4: "When wickedness increases, there will be mutual hate," is related to Mt. 24:12 → VI, 282, 20 ff.

Delling

---

[16] Linguistically Ac. 7:17 reflects the LXX in a text dependent on Ex. 1:7.

[17] Bultmann J., *ad loc.* C. K. Barrett, *The Gospel acc. to St. John* (1955), *ad loc.* regards this interpretation as absurd. αὐξ(αν)ω and ἐλαττόομαι are undoubtedly used for the waxing and waning of light, esp. the sun, cf. Pr.-Bauer, *s.v.* But 3:30 does not seem to be connected in any way with the description of Jesus as φῶς in Jn. 8:12 etc.

[18] Intr. act. and mid. pass., cf. in LXX trans. act. The intr. use of the act. predominates in the NT, Mt. 6:28; Lk. 1:80; 2:40; 13:19; Ac. 6:7; 7:17; 12:24; 19:20; Eph. 2:21; 4:15; Col. 2:19; 2 Pt. 3:18, whereas in LXX the act. is used only trans. The mid. pass. occurs only at Mt. 13:32; Mk. 4:8; 2 C. 10:15; Col. 1:6, 10; 1 Pt. 2:2. On ἐλαττόομαι in Jn. 3:30 cf. Hb. 2:7, 9, and outside the Bible Liddell-Scott, *s.v.* → 517, 8 f. The act. of αὐξ(αν)ω and mid. pass. of a par. verb occur together in Ac. 7:17. A similar sense of the act. to that of Jn. 3:30 may be found in an apocryphon appended to Mt. 20:28 in D it etc.: ὑμεῖς δὲ ζητεῖτε ἐκ μικροῦ αὐξῆσαι καὶ (μὴ sy^c) ἐκ μείζονος ἔλαττον εἶναι, cf. *ad loc.* J. Jeremias, *Unbekannte Jesusworte*[3] (1963), 42.

ὑπερβαίνω → V, 743, 6 ff.

---

† ὑπερβάλλω,
† ὑπερβαλλόντως,
† ὑπερβολή

---

1. In Gk. ὑπερβάλλω originally means "to throw beyond," Hom. Il., 23, 843, "to excel someone in throwing," 637, then "to go beyond," Hes. Op., 489, gen. "to excel," "to stand out," e.g., ὑπερβάλλουσα εὐδαιμονία "supreme happiness," Artemid. Onirocr., IV, 72; [1] censoriously ὑπερβάλλω τὸ μέτριον "to transgress the proper measure (in enjoyment)," Democr. Fr., 223 (Diels, II, 192), cf. 235 (II, 192), also φεύγειν τὰ ὑπερβάλλοντα ἑκατέρωσε by keeping to the golden mean, Plat. Resp., X, 619a. Right conduct is the mean between the two extremes of ὑπερβάλλειν and ἐλλείπειν, thus bravery is the mean between foolhardiness and cowardice, Aristot. Eth. Nic., II, 7, p. 1107b, 1-4. ὑπερβαλλόντως means "in supreme measure," e.g., to be honoured, Demosth. Or., 26, 23, to admire, Xenoph. Ag., 1, 36. On the mid. → line 29 ff.

ὑπερβολή means censoriously "excess," opp. ἔλλειψις "deficiency"; the right is the mean between them, Democr. Fr., 102 (Diels, II, 163), ethically Aristot. Eth. Nic., II, 6 f.. cf., e.g., 7, p. 1107b, 9 f. 22 f.; approvingly οὐδεμίαν ὑπερβολὴν καταλείπων φιλοτιμίας showing "supreme" zeal, Ditt. Syll.[3], II, 545, 13 f. (c. 213 B.C.), cf. ἡ ὑπερβολὴ τῆς φιλίας "the supreme stage" of friendship, Aristot. Eth. Nic., IX, 4, p. 1166b, 1; fire is an extreme of warmth etc. (par. ἀκρότης), Ocellus Lucanus De universi natura, 27. [2] On the adverbial use cf. εἰς ὑπερβολὴν πανοῦργος, Eur. Hipp., 939 f., καθ' ὑπερβολὴν ἐν ἐνδείᾳ "extreme lack," Aristot. Pol., IV, 11, p. 1295b, 18, τὰς καθ' ὑπερβολήν... ἡδονάς, Eth. Nic., VII, 9, p. 1151a, 12 f.

2. In the literature of Judaism one finds ὑπερβάλλω in the LXX only in the following passages, where the basic sense of "going beyond" is the starting-point:[3] φόβος κυρίου ὑπὲρ πᾶν ὑπερέβαλεν "is above all things," Sir. 25:11; with double acc. "to outbid someone," 2 Macc. 4:24; ὑπερβάλλουσα ἀναγνεία "boundless infamy," 4:13, of torments 7:42, fear 3 Macc. 2:23; μεγάλως ὑπερβαλλόντως λελάληκας "exceedingly" great (boastful), Job 15:11; in the mid. μὴ ὑπερβάλλου, abs. as, e.g., Hdt., III, 76, 1 f., "do not delay" to be converted (for hitp עבר), Sir. 5:7, cf. Jos. Ant., 1, 25; 8, 362. The noun is used by the LXX only adverbially: καθ' ὑπερβολήν of immeasurable pains, 4 Macc. 3:18. In Philo we find the part.: "passing" even the limit of wickedness itself, Poster. C., 9, "unlimited" εὔνοια to relatives (with περιττή), Spec. Leg., III, 154, cf. Virt., 192; we cannot grasp (χωρέω) directly the superabundant blessings of God, Som., I, 143, cf. Mut. Nom., 64, cf. also comprehending (καταλαμβάνω) the all-surpassing power of God, Spec. Leg., I, 263, also ὑπερβάλλουσα δύναμις Mut. Nom., 250, [4] χαρὰ ὑπερβάλλουσα Leg. All., III, 217. Philo uses the noun gen. to denote a supreme measure, e.g., of ἀθεότης in Deus Imm., 21, ἀσέβεια in Decal., 91, loyalty Jos., 258, perfection Fug., 115. There is excess of εὐδαιμονία and μακαριότης where angels come, Abr., 115. God shows the overflowing of His riches and goodness παρίστησιν... τὴν ὑπερβολὴν

ὑπερβάλλω κτλ.
[1] Ed. R. Pack (1963), 294, 3.
[2] Ed. R. Harder (1926), 17, 15-19.
[3] Jos. too uses the mid. in this sense in Ap., 1, 133, with the act. Ant., 8, 279 [Rengstorf].
[4] Of the τιμή of Moses, Jos. Ant., 4, 14 [Rengstorf].

τοῦ τε πλούτου καὶ τῆς ἀγαθότητος ἑαυτοῦ, Leg. All., I, 34. Supreme testimonies of grace are shown to Abraham αἱ τῶν χαρίτων ὑπερβολαί, Abr., 39. But we find the censorious use too → 520, 8 ff. The royal way is the middle one between excess and deficiency, ὑπερβολή and ἔλλειψις, Spec. Leg., IV, 168. The plur. means "excesses" in Exsecr., 136.

3. In the NT the word group occurs only in the Pauline corpus. The part. of the verb is used in Eph. in statements relating to the saving event in Christ. When in Eph. 3:19 the apostle seeks on behalf of the recipients the gift of an understanding of the love of Christ for them enacted in His self-sacrifice, he also says that this surpasses all possibility of human comprehension. The statement "surpassing every measure that man can grasp" occurs also in Eph. 2:7, where it outbids another word of fulness, and then again in Eph. 1:19, where it tops μέγεθος → II, 314, 15 ff. On the combination with δύναμις in 2 C. 4:7 → lines 37 ff. Paul speaks of the boundless grace of God at work in the recipients — not to extol them but the χάρις — in 2 C. 9:14, cf. πλεονάσασα... περισσεύσῃ, 2 C. 4:15 → VI, 265, 21 ff., v. ὑπερε-πλεόνασεν, 1 Tm. 1:14. In the Pauline corpus ὑπερβάλλω also goes with πλοῦτος with reference to χάρις in Eph. 1:7, δόξα in R. 9:23; Col. 1:27; Eph. 3:16 etc. → VI, 328, 48 ff. It is thus used with many synonyms. Compared with the glory of the ministry of the old order of salvation that of the new is all-surpassing; basically it is indeed beyond comparison, 2 C. 3:10; a parallel term is περισσεύει in v. 9; in general → 520, 33 ff. Similarly ὑπερβαλλόντως follows περισσοτέρως (→ VI, 62, 33 ff.) in the list of sufferings in 2 C. 11:23. In comparison with those mentioned in v. 22 Paul shows himself to be "to an outstanding degree" (cf. the ὑπὲρ ἐγώ of v. 23 → 516, 2 ff.) a minister of Christ by the blows he has received.

The noun occurs only in R., Gl., 1 and esp. 2 C., mostly in the expression καθ' ὑπερβολήν, "exceedingly." When sin works death through the presence of the Law it shows itself to be sin "in the supreme sense," R. 7:13 → II, 359, 8 ff. In what is, if possible, the even stronger double phrase καθ' ὑπερβολὴν εἰς ὑπερβολήν, the reference is to the immeasurable, eternal and all-exceeding glory which is the work [5] of the affliction that is so small in comparison and that lasts so short a time, 2 C. 4:17. Yet in the very same letter Paul can use not only the more precise ὑπὲρ δύναμιν but also καθ' ὑπερβολήν (→ I, 557, n. 3), "surpassing all measure," of the burden of affliction laid on him in Asia. In an adjectival use 1 C. 12:31b calls the mode of Christian life described in 13:1-17 one which "far surpasses" ("a much superior way") the life controlled by charismata, 12:28-30. Finally Paul uses the expression to make a sharp statement about his own persecuting activity before he became a Christian (Gl. 1:13, cf. materially 1 C. 15:9; Phil. 3:6). In 2 C. 4:7 Paul uses the noun to show that it is God alone who works in him: [6] the "excess" of power — it is God's way to work lavishly — is God's alone, cf. 12:9. According to 12:7 (→ VII, 412, 17 ff.) Paul [7] holds back so that judgment on him should not go beyond what is normally seen in him or received from him, [8] and especially that it should not be based on the "abundance" of revelations vouchsafed to him. [9]

---

[5] This denotes what is for Paul a firm inner connection between affliction and participation in salvation.
[6] The continuation shows that the ref. is primarily to the apostle.
[7] sc. from accounts of revelations experienced, cf. the context.
[8] This is not very impressive acc. to the view of the recipients.
[9] One cannot say whether ὑπερβολή denotes the "fulness" or the "special" experience of revelations, v. Wnd. 2 K., 383.

4. In the post-apost. fathers only the part. of the verb occurs. It describes the gifts of God in 1 Cl., 19, 2; 23, 2 and His love in Dg., 9, 2 as "superabounding" and running over. The star which rose in Christ "exceeds" in brightness all other stars "in incomparable fashion," Ign. Eph., 19, 2. The noun relates to what is for pagans the exceedingly high measure of goodness achieved in love for enemies, 2 Cl., 13, 4. καθ' ὑπερβολήν ref. to the joy of the author at the rich gifts of the Spirit in the community, Barn., 1, 2.

Delling

ὑπερεκπερισσοῦ, ὑπερεκπερισσῶς → VI, 61, 21 ff.
ὑπερεκτείνω   → II, 465, 1 ff.
ὑπερεντυγχάνω   → 243, 30 ff.

---

† ὑπερέχω, † ὑπεροχή

1. In non-bibl. Gk. the verb means: a. "to hold over," e.g., the hand over someone, Zeus in Hom. Il., 4, 249, the hands, Apollo in 5, 433, of the gracious hand of God (par. ὑπερασπίζω), Philo Som., II, 265; b. mostly "to rise above" lit. e.g., Hom. Il., 3, 210, "to tower" over the earth (gen.), Philo Det. Pot. Ins., 107, τῷ ὕψει, Gr. En. 24:3. In this sense it is mainly transf., e.g., in possessions (opp. ἐλλείπω "to be wanting"), Aristot. Rhet., II, 10, p. 1388a, 4 f., "to surpass" those around in wisdom, Ps.-Xenoph. Cyn., 1, 11, as heaven is higher than earth, so the priesthood of God, i.e., that of Levi, "surpasses" the earthly monarchy, Test. Jud. 21:4, "to distinguish oneself" in war, Menand. Fr., 560 (Körte), mathematically "to amount to more," Philo Op. Mund., 109, cf. ὑπεροχή "surplus," loc. cit. In this sense the verb is often used in the part. with ref. to political or social position, e.g., that of towns (opp. ταπεινός), Isoc. Or., 4, 95, "prominent" men, Aristot. Pol., III, 13, p. 1284a, 33, all men honour τὰ ὑπερέχοντα ἰσχύι, Paus., VI, 3, 16, they slew those whom they saw as in any way excelling themselves, Dio C. Fr., 109, 10, abs. οἱ ὑπερέχοντες "those who stand out" by reason of possessions, power, regard, cf. already Aesch. Prom., 213, everyone flatters the ὑπερέχοντες, Polyb., 28, 4, 9, directions to one τῶν ὑπερεχόντων, Epict. Diss., I, 30, 1, the crowd copies τοὺς ὑπερέχοντας, III, 4, 3,[1] esp. "rulers" (→ 43, n. 24), par. δυνατοί, Plut. Maxime cum principibus viris philosopho esse disserendum, 1 (II, 776d), gen. the "highly placed" who carry the threat of ill, Artemid. Onirocr., II, 9 (p. 109, 25 f.),[2] esp. for the poor and slaves, II, 12 (p. 121, 21 f.), who are always burdensome, I, 77 (p. 85, 20 f.). Materially one might ref. here to the expression οἱ ἐν ὑπεροχῇ ὄντες "in a higher position," Polyb., 5, 41, 3, cf. ...δοκοῦντες, Epict. Ench., 33, 12, ἐν ὑπεροχῇ κείμενος, 2 Macc. 3:11, plur. ἐν ὑπεροχαῖς "in high positions," Diod. S., 4, 41, 1, also gen. οἱ ἐν ὑπεροχῇ ὄντες "the considerable inhabitants," P. Tebt., III, 734, 23 f. (141/139 B.C.); ὑπεροχή is used of the "power" of the gods (par. κράτος) in Ditt. Or., II, 456, 38 f. (27-11 B.C.), cf. I, 383, 74 f. (1st cent. B.C.), so also 2 Macc. 15:13; elsewhere the noun is par. to δυναστεία, Polyb., 6, 9, 4.

2. The LXX uses the verb, of which all instances are given, only in the sense "to surpass," intr. lit. for עדף "to exceed," of the hangings in Ex. 26:13 (par. πλεονάζον in v. 12), of money in Lv. 25:27, for ארך hi "to be long," 3 Βασ. 8:8; 2 Ch. 5:9 (cf. ὑπεροχή "height," Jer. 52:22), also transf. for יֵשׁ עוֹד "there is still more," Sir. 43:30. The verb is then used fig., Daniel "surpassed" (part.) all the wise men of Babylon, Da. 5:11, a day is distinguished (as a feast-day) from others, it stands out, Sir. 33:7, cf. materially R. 14:5. We then find the intr. use "to take precedence" in the sense "to be stronger" (Isoc., 4, 95) for אמץ "to be stronger" than any other people, Gn. 25:23, "to hold a higher position" than someone (gen.) for גָּדוֹל מִן Gn. 39:9 or גָּדַל מִן 41:40, abs. οἱ ὑπερέχοντες "rulers" in Wis. 6:5, cf. vv. 1-4. On the noun → line 23, 27 f.

3. In the NT the verb, which is fairly common in Phil., is used only in part. form and a transf. sense, → 515, 3 ff. In construing the relevant passages one should recall how widespread was the metaphor of standing out in non-biblical usage. Two of the uses discussed occur in the NT → lines 6 ff. and 10 ff., 32, 35 ff.

ὑπερέχω. [1] The verb occurs only as part. in Epict.
[2] Ed. R. A. Pack (1963).

a. The salvation given by God[3] completely "exceeds" what we can grasp or think[4] (→ IV, 959, 4 ff.), Phil. 4:7. With a reference in context to the religion of Judaism (→ II, 890, 27 ff.) the apostle says in Phil. 3:8 that the knowledge[5] of Christ Jesus (→ I, 710, 19 ff.) as his Lord[6] is absolutely supreme. Paul did not proclaim God's act in Christ καθ' ὑπεροχὴν λόγου ἢ σοφίας[7] (1 C. 2:1), i.e., after the manner of outstanding eloquence and wisdom,[8] in contrast to the teachers of wisdom in Corinth → VII, 519, 2 ff.; IV, 101, 23 ff.

b. Through ταπεινοφροσύνη (→ 21, 33 ff.) Christians come to the point of always regarding others as "excelling" themselves, Phil. 2:3b. This means that they do not try to make themselves out to be more than other members of the community, v. 3a. One should compare with this the materially similar sayings in Eph. 5:21; 1 Pt. 5:5 (→ 44, 28 ff.), and also R. 12:16b (→ 19, 34 ff.). The reference of the part. in 1 Pt. 2:13; R. 13:1 is political. In 1 Pt. 2:13 the king is superior to the governors of v. 14a and is thus the supreme ruler. In R. 13:1 the part. defines the authorities generally as those who bear rule → 43, 25 ff. In 1 Tm. 2:2 οἱ ἐν ὑπεροχῇ ὄντες corresponds to ὑπερέχοντες. The intercession of the Christian Church is for all who are in the position of rulers (→ 523, 24 ff.; VI, 529, 29 ff.). These are mentioned along with kings as in 1 Pt. 2:13. The possibility of a life without political unrest depends on them.[9]

4. In the post-apost. fathers the verb is used lit. in Herm. s., 9, 6, 1, transf. in the part. "outstanding" of fruits in s., 9, 28, 3 f. (cf. of adornment in Xenoph. Hier., II, 2). The meaning is "to take precedence" in Barn., 13, 2 quoting Gn. 25:23 (→ 523, 35 ff.), cf. also Herm. v., 3, 4, 2, part. "those in higher positions" in contrast to the hungry, Herm. v., 3, 9, 5, materially cf. Barn., 21, 3. The noun occurs only in the expression καθ' ὑπεροχήν to emphasise a verb, cf. 1 Cl., 57, 2, as vl. for καθ' ὑπερβολήν, Barn., 1, 2 → 522, 5 ff. This adv. καθ' ὑπεροχήν, which does not occur in the LXX or NT, is analogous to καθ' ὑπερβολήν → 520, 21 ff.; 521, 25 ff. In the Apologists the verb occurs only in Athenag. Suppl. in the sense "to excel" in wisdom, 23, 1, in wisdom and power (dat.), 6, 2, mathematically "to be over," 6, 1, ὑπεροχή "surplus" only 6, 1 → 523, 10.

Delling

---

[3] The expression "peace of God" occurs for the first time in Jewish texts in the Dead Sea Scrolls, 1 QM 3:5; 4:14 etc., acc. to C. H. Hunzinger, "Aus d. Arbeit an den unveröffentlichten Texten v. Qumran," ThLZ, 85 (1960), 151 f. Peace is an eschatological gift, G. Friedrich, *Der Br. an d. Philipper, NT Deutsch,* 8[10] (1965), ad loc.

[4] Note the tension, νοῦς — νοήματα.

[5] τῆς γνώσεως is a subj. gen. The expression corresponds to דעת יהוה → I, 698, 4 ff.; 706, 16 ff.; 707, 4 ff.; 707, 19 ff. Cf. also γνώσεως Phil. 3:8 τοῦ γνῶναι ... v. 10.

[6] Only here does Paul say "my Lord." The ground of lordship is in the "Christ Jesus."

[7] Subj. gen. Ltzm. K., ad loc. suggests "lofty" words and wisdom, cf. 2 Macc. 6:23 with ref. to age.

[8] Linguistically cf. Dio. C., 58, 5, 1: Seianus was so great τῇ... ὑπεροχῇ τοῦ φρονήματος through his "soaring" effort ... ὑπεροχή in the sense of "excess" is the opp. of ἔλλειψις, and between them μεσότης is the ἀρετή [Dihle]. Cf. Aristot. Eth. Nic., II, 9, p. 1109a, 20-22.

[9] Cf. "in ἡσυχία and peace and righteousness," Philo Exsecr., 157.

---

† ὑπερήφανος, † ὑπερηφανία

Contents: A. Profane Usage. B. Usage in the Greek Old Testament. C. Usage in Hellenistic Judaism. D. New Testament Usage; E. Early Church Usage.

A. Profane Usage.

ὑπερήφανος contains the prefix ὑπερ- (→ 507, 3 ff.) but in other respects is etym. obscure. [1] The meaning is "outstanding," "distinguished": courage Bacchyl., 17, 49 f., wisdom Plat. Phaed., 96a, cf. Gorg., 511d, work Symp., 217e, deeds or works Plut. Fab. Max., 26 (I 189b); Ages., 34 (I, 615d); Pericl., 13 (I, 159d), also in a good sense P. Oxy., III, 530, 28 (2nd cent. A.D.). But both adj. and the derived noun ὑπερηφανία are used in the main censoriously of pride, arrogance, boasting. ὑπερήφανος is between ὑβριστής and ἀλαζών, with which it is sometimes used together, Pind. Pyth., 2, 28; Aristot. Rhet., II, 16, p. 1390b, 33. Unlike the ὑβριστής, who acts violently in spite of divine and human law (→ 295, 7 ff.; 296, 3 ff.), and the ἀλαζών (→ I, 227, 12 ff.), the empty boaster who deceives himself and others by making the most of his advantages, abilities and achievements, the ὑπερήφανος is the one who with pride, arrogance and foolish presumption brags of his position, power and wealth and despises others. Both adj. and noun are used of men or supermen Hes. Theog., 149, their acts Solon Fr., 3, 36 (Diehl[3], I, 29), or their attitude to others Andoc., IV, 13; Plut. De Alcibiade, 4 (I, 193e), and also of gods and men Plat. Resp., III, 391c; cf. 399b (called νόσημα in the former passage as in Leg., III, 691a); Menex., 240d. Aesch. Prom., 404 f. ref. to the attitude of Zeus to the older gods. In Plat. Men., 90a the ὑπερήφανος πολίτης, who is puffed up and annoying, is contrasted with the honourable and respectable citizen. Acc. to Plat. Leg., III, 691a; Aristot. Rhet., II, 16, p. 1390b, 33; 17, p. 1391a, 33 f. luxury, ease and opulence are the soil in which ὑπερηφανία develops as well as ὕβρις → 297, 23 ff. In Demosth. Or., 13, 30 the ref. is to private houses which are not only more ornate (ὑπερήφανος) than those of most but are even more lavishly (σεμνός) furnished than public buildings. [2] In line with such traditions Hell. ethics is usually against ὑπερηφανία: εὐποροῦντα μὴ ὑπερήφανον εἶναι, [3] Stob. Ecl., III, 114, 3 f. Esp. under Stoic influence ὑπερήφανος came into the list of vices as we find it in Jewish Hell. and Chr. documents. [4]

ὑ π ε ρ ή φ α ν ο ς κ τ λ. Bibl.: Liddell-Scott, Pape and Pr.-Bauer, s.v.; S.Wibbing, *Die Tugend- u. Lasterkataloge im NT* (1959), 86-108.

[1] ὑπερήφανος, first found in Hes. Theog., 149, obviously derives from the Homeric part. ὑπερηφανέων Il., 11, 694, behind which there seems to be a ὑπερηφανής. The original sense is perhaps "visible above others" (-φανής from φαίνομαι with η as ὑπερηνορέων), but also possible is "having wealth (ἄφενος) beyond the rest" (ὑπερ-ηφανής for ὑπερ-ηφενής). But cf. Boisacq, s.v. and again Hofmann, s.v. The Attic ὑπερήφανος rather than the expected ὑπεράφανος (so Doric, cf. Pind. Pyth., 2, 28 and Bacchyl., 17, 49) suggests an origin in Ionic poetry [Risch].

[2] Cf. Hag. 1:4-9: God's honour is lightly esteemed.

[3] The saying is attributed to Cleobulus Fr., 20 (Diels, I, 63), the tyrant of Lindus (c. 600 B.C.), one of the seven sages.

[4] There is also a list of vices in the syncretistic Gnosticism of Corp. Herm., e.g., 13, 7, cf. Reitzenstein Poim., 231-3. On the gen. problem cf. A. Dieterich, *Nekyia* (1893), 163-194; Ltzm. R. on 1:31; Wibbing, 86-108 and *passim*.

B. Usage in the Greek Old Testament.

In the Gk. OT the adj. and noun are mostly used for גֵּאֶה, זֵד, לוּץ and cognates → 299, 31 ff. They occur predominantly in Ps. and the Wisdom lit. Sir. and the Hexapla transl. give them prominence ψ 85:14; Prv. 21:24; Mal. 3:15 (LXX read זֵדִים); Ez. 7:10; 30:6 etc. The parallelism or pleonastic usage of the HT means that ὑπερήφανος and ὑπερηφανία come to be used along with ὕβρις and other synon. [5] Sometimes the OT use is positive, e.g., the oath "by the pride of Jacob" in Am. 8:7 (but cf. 6:8 ὕβρις → 299, 36 ff.); Is. 28:1 'ΑΣΘ, 3 'ΑΣ (LXX ὕβρις); Εσθ. 4:17k (but cf. 4:17w). [6]

God is against pride Prv. 3:34 [7]; ψ 17:28 (עֵינַיִם רָמוֹת); Is. 2:12 (רָם); 13:11 (עָרִיץ); Da. 4:34 Θ (גֵּוָה). The Gk. transl. put it thus even when the word is not in the original HT, Hab. 3:13 Αλλ.; Job 38:15. [8] The legal term בְּיָד רָמָה in Nu. 15:30 ("intentionally") is rendered by ἐν χειρὶ ὑπερηφανίας after Dt. 17:12 (בְּזָדוֹן, LXX ἐν ὑπερηφανίᾳ). [9] Cf. also Gr. En. 5:8. At Zeph. 3:6 גּוֹיִם is misread as גֵּאִים → 300, 8 ff. At ψ 88:11 ὑπερήφανος is the transl. of Rahab, [10] at ψ 123:5 Ε' (Field, ad loc.) it occurs instead of the metaphor of swelling (זֵידוֹן hapax legomenon from זִיד) water. The righteous prays and trusts that God will destroy the proud ψ 93:2; Job 40:12; Jdt. 6:19. The ref. may be to the arrogance of one's own people Lv. 26:19 LXX; Hos. 5:5 'ΑΘ; 7:10 Θ [11] or to that of Israel's enemies, as in the oracles against foreign nations Is. 16:6; Ιερ. 31:29b LXX, 29a 'ΑΣΘ; Ob. 3; cf. Ιερ. 30:10. In Macc. all the Gentiles, foreign kings and generals, and sometimes typical figures of the past like Pharaoh, are characterised as "insolent" 1 Macc. 1:21, 24; 2 Macc. 9:4; 3 Macc. 1:27; 5:13; 4 Macc. 9:30, cf. also Sir. 48:18; Εσθ. 4:17d, the giants of Gn. 6 in Wis. 14:6, Sodom or Samaria in Ez. 16:49, 56; Sir. 16:8. In Ps. the enemies of the righteous are called arrogant ψ 16:10; 30:19, 24; 35:12; 58:13; 72:6 etc. → 300, 7 ff. Here, too, the LXX has sometimes introduced the term as in ψ 73:3, where LXX read a form of נשא hitp "to boast" for מַשֻּׁאוֹת "ruins" in the HT. In the Wisdom lit., esp. Sir., ὑπερήφανος and ὑπερηφανία take on the character of a negative ethical term denoting schematically the attitude which the righteous are to avoid, Ex. 18:21; Prv. 8:13; Sir. 10:7; 25:2. There is a warning against the results and consequences of this attitude in Prv. 13:10 'ΑΣΘ; Sir. 10:12; 21:4; 22:22; 23:8; 27:15, 28; 32:12; Tob. 4:13. Humility is an abomination to the proud Sir. 13:20; he has no reverent awe 32:18. Wisdom is far distant from arrogance 15:8 (Hbr. לֵץ "mocker"). The righteous keeps it out of his house ψ 100:7 (HT רְמִיָּה "deceit"; perhaps LXX presupposes root רום). ψ 118:21, 51, 69, 78 and 122 formulate in different ways the attitude of the righteous to the ὑπερήφανοι. [12]

---

[5] The verbs ὑπερηφανέω and ὑπερηφανεύομαι also occur a few times in the LXX and Hexapla transl., Neh. 9:10; 4 Macc. 5:21; Dt. 1:43 Αλλ. etc.

[6] At ψ 45:4 the transl. obviously related the suffix of the 3rd pers. sing. masc. in בַּאֲוָתוֹ to Yahweh, LXX ἐν τῇ κραταιότητι, Σ ἐν τῷ ἐνδοξασμῷ. Hence ἐν τῇ ὑπερηφανίᾳ αὐτοῦ in 'Α, Ε' S' (cf. Field, ad loc.) has also to be construed positively.

[7] HT לַלֵּצִים הוּא יָלִיץ "Hé mocks the mockers." In this form the saying could not be used by the Rabb. against presumption, cf. Str.-B., I, 202. Acc. to the HT God's action and man's obviously seem to be on the same level. Hence LXX transl. freely κύριος ὑπερηφάνοις ἀντιτάσσεται. The verb is to be taken abs.: God resists the proud. Cf. ψ 17:26 f.

[8] Vg bracchium excelsum, Luther as LXX, Arm. the haughty.

[9] Cf. Vg per superbiam, Luther "aus Frevel."

[10] Cf. ψ 86:4 Σ. רהב is read as רחב which often means "presumptuous" and in this sense is transl. ἄπληστος "insatiable" at ψ 100:5; Prv. 28:25 and θρασυκάρδιος at Prv. 21:4.

[11] B. Stade - A. Bertholet, Bibl. Theol. d. AT, II (1911), 95, 117, 123 etc., v. Index "Hochmut"; Bousset-Gressm., 134 f.; G. Bertram, "'Hochmut' u. verwandte Begriffe im griech. u. hbr. AT," Die Welt d. Orients, 3 (1964), 32-43.

[12] The attitude of the righteous is fashioned by faith in the eschatological reversal of all relations as in 1 S. 2:6, 7, cf. G. Bertram, "Der religionsgeschichtliche Hintergrund d. Begriffs d. 'Erhöhung' in d. LXX," ZAW, NF, 27 (1956), 60 f.

The Hbr. original here is always זֵדִים, which primarily denoted a party or trend that was scorned and rejected. [13]

C. Usage in Hellenistic Judaism.

Hell. Jewish writings adopted the OT development of the concept. In Ps. Sol. 2:2 etc.; [14] 4:24; 17:6 etc. the ref. is to inner and outer foes. In Test. R. 3:5 cf. G. 3:3; D. 5:6 "arrogance" is traced back to a spirit of error, to the spirit of hate or to Satan himself. [15] There is a warning against it in Test. Jud. 13:2 and in the list of vices in 18:3, cf. L. 17:11. In Sib. the "haughty" occur in the enumeration of sinners at the Last Judgment at 2, 268. "Arrogance" is also a predicate of the gt. historical peoples of the different centuries in 1, 392; 3, 183 and 732; 5, 90; 8, 168. Even where Chr. influence may be seen the terminology of Jewish Hellenism is decisive. Philo Virt., 171 claims on the basis of Nu. 15:30 that insolence is punished by God Himself. [16] Jos. in his historical presentation has the concept chiefly in the form of the verb ὑπερηφανέω, [17] pass. of Potiphar's wife in Ant., 2, 54, Dathan and his clan in 4, 38. Acc. to 6, 38 (cf. 1 Βασ. 8:6) God Himself is affected by the "insolence" of His people in wanting to choose a king. The ref. in Bell., 1, 384 is to the "insolent" handling of envoys and in 3, 1 to the "arrogance" displayed by the Roman emperor Nero. [18] In Ep. Ar., 170 the forbidding of the use of wild animals for sacrifices is symbolically interpreted as an avoiding of "arrogance." Acc. to 211 self-control guards against "arrogance," and in 262 recognition of the equality of men keeps the king from it. Ep. Ar., 263 follows the argument of Prv. 3:34, cf. also 269. In these passages the term does not serve to characterise the wicked but denotes a sin against which even those who mean well must be on guard.

D. New Testament Usage.

In the NT the noun ὑπερηφανία occurs only once and the adj. ὑπερήφανος five times. The usage is shaped by the OT and the Hellenistic Jewish tradition with its lists of vices. Thus Paul puts ὑπερήφανος in the list in R. 1:30 (→ 525, 28 f.) which portrays the corruption of idolatrous paganism. ὑπερήφανοι stands in fact and also conceptually (→ 525, 9 f.) between ὑβρισταί (→ 306, 9 ff.) and ἀλαζόνες. The group of divinely hated despisers of men, the arrogant and the boastful (or arrogant boasters) [19] is interrelated. According to the exposition of the early Church the arrogant are those who brag of what they have to the have-nots. [20] In the list of vices in 2 Tm. 3:2 ἀλαζόνες comes before ὑπερήφανοι. For

---

[13] Mostly referred to the Sadducees → 300, n. 43.
[14] Moore, I, 433; Volz Esch., 89, 223.
[15] Volz Esch., 310.
[16] Only the noun occurs in Philo and only here. It is used synon. with ἀλαζονεία which alone represents the OT concept in the par. Spec. Leg., I, 265. On the LXX reconstruction of the OT used by Philo → 526, 11 f.
[17] The verb ὑπερηφανέω "I am haughty," e.g., Polyb., 6, 10, 8, trans. "I treat someone haughtily," e.g., Diod. S., 23, 15, 4, occurs from the Hell. period and is not directly connected with the Homeric part. ὑπερηφανέων → n. 1 [Risch]. A subsidiary form in Jos. Ant., 4, 259 is ὑπερηφανεύω "to treat contemptuously" → n. 5.
[18] Ant., 1, 195 ref. to the arrogance of the Sodomites. This includes both contempt for others and ungodliness and is punished by God. Princes and adversaries are often charged with insolence; Jos. Ant., 11, 216; Bell., 2, 358; 6, 172 use the adj., Bell., 4, 575; 6, 169 the adv., Ant., 13, 35; 16, 4; 4, 289; 11, 194 the noun synon. with ὕβρις, and 16, 194; 20, 56; Bell., 1, 334; 5, 517 the verb. The adj. is once used positively for magnificent buildings, Ant., 10, 225. [I owe the ref. in part to Rengstorf.]
[19] Cf. Zn. R., ad loc.
[20] Gennadius in Staab, 360.

the author the two terms denote different forms of arrogance. [21] The moral chaos depicted in the list, which is disguised by a pious exterior, arises out of false teaching and characterises the last time. [22] The list of vices in Mk. 7:20-23, coming after 7:18 f., serves to elucidate further the saying of Jesus about purity (7:15) for the Hellenistic Christian community. [23] The substantive ὑπερηφανία in 7:22 comes between βλασφημία [24] "blasphemy" (of God) and ἀφροσύνη the ungodly attitude of fools → IV, 832, 1 ff. → φρόνησις. In the first instance ὑπερηφανία too is against God and stands in contrast to the humility which is proper in relation to God and which is full surrender to Him. It is the pride in one's own being and work which already in the OT tradition (→ 301, 19 ff.) denotes resistance to God and the haughty disdain with which others are treated. [25]

In Lk. 1:51 (→ VII, 421, 27 ff.), a verse from the Magnificat, we read that He scatters those who are proud in the imagination of their hearts. [26] διανοία goes with ὑπερήφανοι and cannot be construed with the verb as an instrumental dative: "He scatters what is proud in their imagination." [27] The Greek translation seems to presuppose that the ὑπερήφανοι are a group or party which has banded together → 300, 7 ff. To their scattering and the toppling of the mighty from their thrones there corresponds the exalting of the lowly. Materially the quotation from Prv. 3:34 (→ 526, 9 and n. 7) in 1 Pt. 5:5 and Jm. 4:6 [28] (→ 19, 3 ff. and 14 ff.) is to the same effect. According to the quotation ὑπερηφανία is wickedness in its final form. Its opposite is ταπεινοφροσύνη "humility" (→ 21, 32 ff.) and ταπείνωσις "lowliness" [29] (→ 10, 36 ff.; 20, 21 ff.). 1 Pt. 5:5 enjoins the humility which all owe each other. The proud are visited by God's wrath, Nu. 15:30 LXX. But He shows His grace to the humble, and in due time this means their elevation. The arrogant think they do not have to ask for forgiveness. [30] This exposition avoids a one-sidedly

---

[21] B. Weiss, *Krit. exeget. Handbuch über d. Briefe Pauli an Tm. u. Tt., Krit. exeget. Komm. über d. NT*, 11⁵ (1886), ad loc.

[22] Dib. Past.³, ad loc.

[23] Bultmann, Trad., 96 and 179.

[24] D puts both nouns in the plur. like the first six nouns in the list.

[25] Loh., Wbg. Mk., ad loc.

[26] The idea of the reversal of power and possessions was common in the piety of the Palestinian poor, W. Grundmann, *Das Ev. nach Lk., Theol. Handkomm. zum NT*, III (1961), ad loc.

[27] Kl. Lk., ad loc.

[28] Jm. 4:6 is missing from LP al. But the quotation cannot have come into the text from 1 Pt. 5:5; it dropped out through homoioteleuton in 4:6a. The text is in disorder, cf. the comm.

[29] In the Hell. world as in philosophy ταπεινός etc. are used disparagingly for an abject disposition. Philo uses the group both positively like the OT and also disparagingly like the world around him → 2, 6 ff.; 11, 38 ff.; 14, 43 ff. Philosophical ethics from Cleanthes Fr., 557 (v. Arnim, I, 127) adopted the Cynic-Stoic term ἀτυφία, developed by Antisthenes, as the opp. of τῦφος "arrogance," "megalomania." Already in Plat. Phaedr., 230a we find the formula: ζῷον θείας τινὸς καὶ ἀτύφου μοίρας μετέχον. Philo introduced the term into the Jewish-Hell. background of Christianity. In antithesis to τῦφος it had the negative sense of "without presumption," but then as in the Cynic-Stoic doctrine of virtue it came to denote the attitude of "humility" and "modesty" as that of the pious sage along OT lines, Philo Cher., 42; Spec. Leg., I, 309; II, 235; Praem. Poen., 59; Omn. Prob. Lib., 84; Vit. Cont., 38 f.; Virt., 16 f. and 178; Abr., 24 and 104 etc., often in an emphatic ethical religious context. In the Chr. tradition ἄτυφος occurs for the first time in Tat. Or. Graec., 29, 2 for the modesty of expression and the simplicity of the preacher of the biblical message. Later we find it in comm. to explain the NT ταπεινός κτλ., Orig. Hom. in Lk. 8 on 1:48 (GCS, 35); Didymus on Jm. 4:6 acc. to Cramer Cat., VIII, ad loc.

[30] Wbg. Pt., ad loc.

ethical interpretation. Man's attitude to God finds expression in his attitude to other men.

E. Early Church Usage.

There are similar expressions in early Chr. writings. Thus Christ is an example of humility in 1 Cl., 16, 2: "He did not come with boastful and arrogant pomp." In 1 Cl., 30, 1 "detestable insolence" is rejected and 30, 2 adds the quotation from Prv. 3:34, cf. also 59, 3. In 1 Cl., 35, 5 cf. 57, 2 there is an admonition to set aside "arrogance" and "boasting." "In love is nothing arrogant," 49, 5. Here arrogance is not just a quality of enemies of the community; it is a temptation for all Christians. [31] The same is true in Did., 2, 6; acc. to the list of vices in 5, 1 pride is one of the many sins that lead on to the way of death, cf. Barn., 20, 1. In the lists in Herm. m., 6, 2, 5; 8, 3 the shepherd as well as members of the community must be warned against the sins into which they might fall or have already fallen acc. to s., 8, 9, 1. There is also warning, admonition or confirmation in Ign. Eph., 5, 3 [32] (quoting Prv. 3:34) and Pol., 4, 3; Sm., 10, 2. Just. Dial., 85, 8 simply have a quotation from Is. 66:6 [33] with ὑπερήφανος in the sense of Prv. 3:34 or ψ 88:11. Heraclitus is called "arrogant" in Tat. Or. Graec., 3, 1. [34]

Bertram

---

[31] On the christological basis of humility cf. Kn. Cl. on 1 Cl., 16, 2, on the link with 1 C. 13:4 *ibid.* on 49, 5.

[32] Bau. Ign., *ad loc.* ref. to the play on words with ἀντιτάσσεται.

[33] LXX has ἀντικείμενοι for אֹיְבִים.

[34] Cf. Tat. Or. Graec., 29, 2 and on this → n. 29.

ὑπερνικάω   → IV, 945, 32 ff.   ὑπεροχή   → 523, 1 ff.
ὑπερπερισσεύω   → VI, 58, 16 ff.   ὑπερπερισσῶς   → VI 61, 21 ff.
ὑπερπλεονάζω   → VI, 263, 1 ff.   ὑπήκοος   → I, 224, 35 ff.

	διακονέω κτλ. → II, 81, 27 ff.
† ὑπηρέτης, † ὑπηρετέω	δοῦλος κτλ. → II, 261, 1 ff.
	θεραπεία κτλ. → III, 128, 14 ff.

Contents: A. Non-Biblical Usage and Its Roots: 1. Usage in Classical Greek and Hellen-ism; 2. The Linguistic Problem. B. Hellenistic Judaism: 1. The Septuagint, Apocrypha and Pseudepigrapha; 2. Philo; 3. Josephus; 4. Equivalents in Palestinian Judaism. C. The New Testament: 1. Usage Generally; 2. Difficult Passages: a. Ac. 13:5: John Mark as ὑπηρέτης of Barnabas and Paul; b. Jn. 18:36: ὑπηρέται of Jesus; c. 1 C. 4:1: Paul and Apollos as ὑπηρέται Χριστοῦ καὶ οἰκονόμοι μυστηρίων θεοῦ; d. Ac. 26:16: Paul as ὑπηρέτης καὶ μάρτυς of Jesus; e. Lk. 1:2: ὑπηρέται τοῦ λόγου. D. The Early Church.

A. Non-Biblical Usage and Its Roots.

1. Usage in Classical Greek and Hellenism.

In Gk. lit. ὑπηρέτης crops up for the first time in Aesch. Prom., 954 cf. 983 (→ lines 22 ff.) and at about the same time we also find the derived verb ὑπηρετέω as an established element in the literary speech of the tragedians (→ lines 25 ff) and Hdt. (→ 531, 20 ff.). Both terms and the related ὑπηρεσία have a precise sense from the very outset. This makes it likely that the controlling ὑπηρέτης, irrespective of its origin (→ 533, 9 ff.), had long since acquired its own developed individuality in usage. In this regard it is naturally important that the employment of the word through the centuries preserves the basic sense which is apparent at the very first in its literary use.

In the oldest ref. it is Hermes, the messenger of the gods, who is called ὑπηρέτης, i.e., θεῶν ὑπηρέτης (Aesch. Prom., 954), which in the context can only mean that he is executing the will of Zeus and thus has behind him the power and authority of Zeus as chief of the gods, cf. 983. The men of Delphi are ὑπηρέται of Apollo in the same sense since in his name they proclaim the will of him who declares himself in the oracle, Soph. Oed. Tyr., 712. Similarly Odysseus with ref. to Zeus as true ruler of the isle of Lemnos

---

ὑπηρέτης κτλ. Bibl. On A.: Liddell-Scott, Pass., Preisigke Fachwörter, s.v.; H. Geiss, Zur Bezeichnung d. dienenden Personals im Griech., Diss. Munich (1953); W. K. Hobart, The Medical Language of St. Luke (1882), 88 f., 224 f.; H. Kupiszewski - J. Modrzejewski, "ΥΠΗΡΕΤΑΙ. Etude sur les fonctions et le rôle des hyperètes dans l'administration civile et judiciaire de l'Egypte gréco-romaine," Journ. of Juristic Papyrology, 11-12 (1957/58), 141-166 (Bibl.); L. J. D. Richardson, ΥΠΗΡΕΤΗΣ, The Class. Quart., 37 (1943), 55-61; H. Schenkl, "Pythagoreersprüche in einer Wiener Hdschr.," Wiener Stud., 8 (1886), 262-281. On B.: W. W. Graf Baudissin, "Zur Entwicklung des Gebrauchs von 'ebed im religiösen Sinne," Festschr. K. Budde, ZAW Beih., 34 (1920), 1-9; J. B. Frey, L'ancien Judaïsme, spécialement à Rome d'après les Inscr. Juives, CIJ, I, p. XCIX; Schl. Theol. d. Judt., 98; E. Schürer, Die Gemeindeverfassung d. Juden in Rom in d. Kaiserzeit nach d. Inschr. dar-gestellt (1879), 28; Str.-B., IV, 147-9. On C.: Pr.-Bauer, s.v.; W. Hadorn, "Die Gefährten u. Mitarbeiter d. Pls.," Festschr. A. Schlatter (1922), 65-82; B. T. Holmes, "Luke's Descrip-tion of John Mark," JBL, 54 (1935), 63-72; K. Stendahl, "The School of St. Matthew," Acta Seminarii Neotest. Upsaliensis, 20 (1954), 32-5.

can say of himself regarding his affair with Philoctetes: ὑπηρετῶ δ' ἐγώ, i.e., he acts as Zeus wills and as covered by him, Soph. Phil., 990. Socrates regarded himself as under divine orders to support and guide his fellow-citizens, to care for their ψυχή, and he acknowledged the ὑπηρεσία entrusted to him by following the command without concern for his own person: ἐγὼ οἴομαι οὐδέν πω ὑμῖν μεῖζον ἀγαθὸν γενέσθαι ἐν τῇ πόλει ἢ τὴν ἐμὴν τῷ θεῷ ὑπηρεσίαν, Plat. Ap., 29d-30a, cf. Euthyphr., 13d e. This attitude gives to work for men and their affairs acc. to the will of the gods (ὑπηρεσία) a recognised advantage over purely cultic worship (θεραπεία → III, 128, 25 ff.), namely, that of trying to make religion and piety fruitful for both individuals and society. Euthyphr., 12e-16a. Following this pattern [1] Epictetus described the true Cynic, with his concern to help men paternally and fraternally for their own sakes, in terms of the category of divine ὑπηρέτης, and this with an express ref. to the fatherhood of Zeus: [2] οὕτως πάντων κήδεται... ὡς πατὴρ αὐτὸ ποιεῖ, ὡς ἀδελφὸς καὶ τοῦ κοινοῦ πατρὸς ὑπηρέτης τοῦ Διός, Epict. Diss., III, 22, 81 f. [3] We find the same thing when a saying of the Pythagoreans [4] has the direction: τὸν εὐεργετοῦντά σε εἰς ψυχὴν ὡς ὑπηρέτην θεοῦ μετὰ θεὸν τίμα. [5] In all these instances ὑπηρέτης κτλ. serve to characterise someone, whether man, god, or divine being, in terms of the fact that he stands and acts in the service of a higher will and is fully at the disposal of this will. [6]

This usage is not at all limited to the relation between men and gods or lesser gods and higher gods. In principle it may be applied to every sphere of human life. The military world offers good examples. Hdt., V, 111, 4; Thuc., III, 17, 3 call the carriers of shields or weapons ὑπηρέτης because they have always to be ready to obey the one they are assisting. [7] The meaning is the same when the immediate aides of a commander are called his ὑπηρέται, e.g., Plat. Euthyphr., 14a; Xenoph. Cyrop., VI, 2, 13. This usage continues into the class. military text-books, though now [8] ὑπηρέτης become a tt. for the officer whose job it is to supervise the provisioning of the troops, i.e., the quarter-master. In civil life the physician has his ὑπηρέτης [9] who not only assists him but also carries out minor medical tasks on the doctor's instructions and thus gradually becomes a physician himself rather than a famulus, Plat. Leg., IV, 720a. [10] A contractor has to have ὑπηρέται on whom he can rely, Plat. Euthyphr., 13e. [11] The same applies to judges, who leave it to their ὑπηρέται to carry out their sentences, e.g., executing those condemned to death, cf. Plat. Leg., IX, 873b; Phaed., 116b c. If ὑπηρέται seem to be executive organs here, they are this explicitly in the government and judiciary of Hell. Egypt, where the word is a tt. for officials of all levels and types on whom the functioning of the apparatus of state depends (→ n. 21), [12] esp. as the discharge of notary functions, including attestations,

---

[1] Cf. on this M. Pohlenz, Die Stoa, I² (1959), 328.
[2] Epict. likes to call his immanent God Zeus, not least because in this way the idea of the father of gods and men leads on smoothly to his basic concept of fatherly goodness with ref. to the world and society, cf. Pohlenz, op. cit., 338 f.
[3] On philanthropy in Epict. and its meaning for his ethics ibid., 336-8.
[4] Schenkl, 278, No. 105.
[5] Cf. also Sextus Sententiae, ed. A. Elter (1892), No. 319.
[6] Cf. the rule of Epict. Diss., III, 7, 36 for the philosopher as Zeus' ὑπηρέτης: ὡς ὁ Ζεὺς διέταξεν, τοῦτο ποίησον.
[7] Similarly the light troops supporting the heavily-armed hoplites as the core of the army are ὑπηρέται, cf. Aristoph. Av., 1185-7.
[8] Cf. Asclepiodotus Τέχνη τακτική, ed. W. A. Oldfather (1923), II, 9; VI, 3; Arrianus Tactica, ed. R. Hercher and A. Eberhard Arriani Scripta Minora² (1885), 10, 4; 14, 4.
[9] He may naturally have many ὑπηρέται forming the new generation.
[10] Cf. the whole passage Plat. Leg., IV, 720a-d and Hobart, 88 f. Medical aides already form a kind of special class.
[11] Cf. also Inscr. Magn., 239 (age of Hadrian?): ὑπηρέται οἰκοδόμων.
[12] Kupiszewski-Modrzejewski, esp. 141, 149, 165 f. A mark of the system is that the πράκτορες under the judges also have their ὑπηρέται, so Preisigke Sammelbuch, V, 7529, 15 f. (2nd/3rd cent. A.D.).

falls on these servants of the state as well. [13] If in the same age and sphere the assistant of the leader of a cultic union can also be called ὑπηρέτης, Preisigke Sammelbuch, V, 7835, 11 (between 69 and 57 B.C.?), [14] this shows that the word still retained its basic sense, denoting one who is charged to carry out the orders of another. Thus ὑπηρέτης can also be used to characterise a friend when he unselfishly helps his friend in something he wants, Plut. Adulat., 23 (II, 64c). [15]

Thus the use of ὑπηρέτης on Gk. and Hell. soil, though it seems to be varied, presents a uniform picture when the gen. sense is noted. The ref. is always to a service of any kind which in structure and goal is controlled by the will of him to whom it is rendered. This service is not just to a superior [16] with clear rights over the inferior; [17] it also implies acceptance of the subordination. [18] To this degree it is possible in principle for a ὑπηρέτης to dissolve the obligation in which he stands. On the other hand, while he is dependent and is usually paid for his services, [19] he may for his part enjoy considerable authority and power, [20] though this is tied to the function discharged by him. [21] In view of this it is best to translate ὑπηρέτης by "servant" and ὑπηρετέω by "to be at the disposal," "to render service."

The ὑπηρέτης is distinguished from the δοῦλος (→ II, 261, 20 ff.), always used for a slave, [22] by the fact that he is free and can in some cases claim a due reward

---

[13] Kupiszewski-Modrzejewski, 163-5.

[14] Cf. also Diod. S., 1, 73, 3: ὑπηρέται of the priests in Egypt, cf. also G. Thieme, *Die Inschr. v. Magnesia am Mäander u. d. NT* (1906), 33 and IG, 9, 1, 976 (4th/3rd cent. B.C.).

[15] The rule of Gorgias Fr., 21 (Diels, II, 305) handed down by Plut. (→ line 6), though with doubts as to its truth: ὁ μὲν γὰρ φίλος ... αὐτῷ μὲν ἀξιώσει τὰ δίκαια τὸν φίλον ὑπουργεῖν, ἐκείνῳ δ᾽ αὐτὸς ὑπηρετήσει πολλὰ καὶ τῶν μὴ δικαίων, goes beyond the natural obligation of friendship by binding a friend even when unlawful ends are sought, cf. W. Nestle, *Vom Mythos zum Logos*[2] (1942), 314.

[16] Cf. the early juxtaposition of ἄρχων and ὑπηρέτης: οὔτε ἄρχων οὔτε ὑπηρέτης ἦν αὐτῆς (sc. τῆς πόλεως), Plat. Resp., VIII, 522b, or ἄρχω and ὑπηρετέω, Aristoph. Vesp., 518 f., or ἀρχικός and ὑπηρετικός, Aristot. Pol., I, 13, p. 1260a, 23, but also Plut. Lib. Educ., 8 (II, 5e).

[17] Cf. Richardson, 55, acc. to whom the whole group denotes "unquestioning service in response to another's authoritative bidding." We see this in the usage of Plut. who has the term for all types of subordinates from domestic employees (De Cleomene, 13 [I, 810d]) to prefects (De Demetrio et Antonio, 1 [I, 956b]).

[18] Soph. El., 996 implies already that a call to ὑπηρεσία may be accepted or refused.

[19] In class. Athens the rowers of the warships and transports of the *polis,* who were recruited from the fourth and lowest class of citizens, the so-called thetes with little or no property, were paid for their services as ὑπηρέται. This was necessary on social grounds, since otherwise their families would have been left destitute. In contrast honorary service was expected from independent citizens, esp. the upper class, the ἄρχοντες, cf. on this A. Böckh, *Die Staatsverwaltung d. Athener*[3], I (1886), 345 and 642. Already in Homer θής is "one who serves for reward," as a free man (Geiss, 64), so that as applied to the thetes ὑπηρέτης perhaps rests on the pre-Gk. term for a paid worker, cf. W. Pax, "Sprachvergleichende Untersuchungen z. Etym. d. Wortes ἀμφίπολος," *Wörter u. Sachen,* 18 (1937), 77 → n. 20.

[20] This is clearest in Hell. Egypt with its organised administration through a hierarchical system of ὑπηρέται "officials" → 531, 32 ff. Members of the system were remunerated unless they were in the so-called order of liturgies (cf. F. Oertel, *Die Liturgie. Stud. z. ptolemäischen u. kaiserlichen Verwaltung Ägyptens* [1917], 36, 57, 412) which had to accept state offices on the basis of social position and their financial ability to do the job. In ancient Egypt there are examples of the remunerating of priestly ὑπηρέται by ἱερεῖς disposing of benefices. Diod. S., 1, 73, 3 → n. 14.

[21] This is esp. true of Hell. Egypt with the definite tendency of its government to embrace and control the whole population, Kupiszewski-Modrzejewski, 163-5.

[22] Cf. already Homer, who does not have δοῦλος but often uses the stem δουλ-, Geiss, 77, who ref. to Mycen. *do-e-ro.*

for his services. [23] But the ὑπηρέτης also differs from the διάκονος (→ II, 81, 38 ff.) and the θεράπων (→ III, 128, 17 ff.). In the case of the διάκονος the accent is on the objective advantage his service brings to the one to whom it is rendered, [24] while θεράπων characterises the servant as one who is dedicated with respect, willingness and zeal to his service on behalf of the other. [25] The special feature of ὑπηρέτης, however, is that he willingly learns his task and goal from another who is over him in an organic order but without prejudice to his personal dignity and worth.

2. The Linguistic Problem.

Traditionally ὑπηρέτης and its denominative ὑπηρετέω (→ 530, 15 f.) are taken to be compounds of ἐρέτης. This is found from Hom. Il., 1, 142 etc. in the sense of "rower," [26] and for its part it is viewed as the nomen agentis of a two-syllabled verb, Gk. ἐρέσσω, Attic ἐρέττω from ἐρετιω (Hom. Od., 9, 490) meaning "to row." [27] Hence the orig. sense of ὑπηρέτης is taken to be "under-rower." [28] But esp. on material grounds this etym. runs into difficulties, since there is no doubt that the idea of rowers on various levels which is implied in this definition, the lowest level being made up of ὑπηρέται, [29] does not agree with the historical facts. [30] No more satisfactory is the proposal that the ὑπηρέτης was originally the member of a rowing crew in the sense that as ἐρέτης he and his fellows were put under a superior, [31] this finally yielding the general sense of "one who receives orders." [32] For from the very earliest instances the usage offers no trace of any such ideas → 530, 22 ff. On the contrary, though it is true that the ὑπηρέτης has a superior when he acts as a rower, and has to follow his directions, it is not rowing as such which makes him a ὑπηρέτης, but only the fact that he rows according to directions. In other words, the usage shows that it is the relationship of service which is basic to the description of a rower as ὑπηρέτης and not some other factor → 532, 7 ff. [33] The e-re-ta found in the Cnossian tablets [34] Ce., 902, 11 (15th cent. B.C.?) and the Pylian

---

[23] Hence Plat. Polit., 289c rightly distinguishes ὑπηρέται from δοῦλοι. Acc. to him the basis of the distinction is the personal freedom of the citizen from whom service is required even though it is expected he will willingly comply, so that ἑτοιμότατα ὑπηρετεῖν is a mark of the ὑπηρέτης, 290a.

[24] διακονέω κτλ. imply "help," → II, 88, 25 ff. It does not matter whether the help is voluntary or not. Thus Hermes is both the διάκονος Aesch. Prom., 942 and also the ὑπηρέτης of Zeus → 530, 14 ff. and 22 ff. Plat. Resp., V, 467a combines διακονέω and ὑπηρετέω (in this order) with ref. to the duties of all in war: διακονεῖν καὶ ὑπηρετεῖν πάντα τὰ περὶ τὸν πόλεμον, Epict. Diss., II, 23, 11 makes a similar distinction. On διάκονος cf. also Geiss, 83-5.

[25] This is why θεραπεύω (→ III, 128, 16 ff.) could become a tt. for proper conduct in relation to parents, e.g., Plat. Resp., V, 467a and the cultus. On the older use of θεράπων cf. Geiss, 1-35.

[26] ἐρέτης in Hom. Od., 1, 280 is always in the plur., so already Mycen. e-re-ta → lines 25 ff.

[27] Cf. esp. Frisk, also Boisacq, Hofmann, s.v. ἐρέτης; Etym. M., s.v. ὑπηρέτης.

[28] Cf. Boisacq, s.v. ἐρέτης: "rameur en sous-ordre," "serviteur," Hofmann, s.v. ἐρέτης: "ὑπηρέτης m Diener (eigtl. Unterruderer)"; so also Joh. W., 1 K. on 4:1: "Ruderknecht."

[29] Cf. Richardson, 55.

[30] Cf. W. W. Tarn, Hellenistic Military and Naval Developments (1930), 126, 162-6; cf. on this also Richardson, 55 f.

[31] Richardson, 58-61. For him ὑπηρέτης is originally the "member of an organized team of oarsmen," 61.

[32] Ibid., 58.

[33] In this sense cf. also Geiss, 89 f.

[34] Ed. J. Chadwick and J. T. Killen³ (1964), 25.

tablets [35] An., 1, 1 etc. (c. 1200 B.C.) is certainly connected with sea-faring in later texts, [36] but in the older ones it seems to be the "title of a functionary" used for a kind of "local official." [37]

The complete independence of ὑπηρέτης in relation to ἐρέτης suggests that in spite of their phonetic similarity they are of different linguistic origin even if in the present state of research it is hard to come up with any convincing theory. [38] If ὑπηρέτης, like ἐρέτης, is in fact an original nautical term and is linguistically related to ἐρέτης, it is worth considering whether the development of ὑπηρέτης does not indicate that the word or stem preceding the verb ἐρέσσω did not suggest steering rather than rowing, including steering a ship as owner or helmsman. At any rate it is to be noted that Homer has a use of διερέσσω which would fit this very well, cf. ἑζόμενος δ' ἐπὶ τοῖσι διήρεσα χερσὶν ἐμῇσιν, Od., 12, 444; ἔπειτα δὲ χερσὶ διήρεσσα ἀμφοτέρῃσι νηχόμενος, 14, 351 f. May it not be, then, that assuming a boat manned by two men [39] ὑπηρέτης was originally the assistant of the owner or helmsman who took orders from him? If this is correct, ὑπηρέτης would be primarily a servant and would contain from the very first the element which always characterised the use of the term, namely, that the one called this is subordinate and is bound to obey, but as a free man, not a slave → 532, 17 ff.

B. Hellenistic Judaism.

1. The Septuagint, Apocrypha and Pseudepigrapha.

a. In view of the uniformity and yet also the breadth of the use of ὑπηρέτης in Hell. Gk. it is surprising that the group plays next to no role in the Gk. Bible. When it occurs, the use is similar to that in class. and Hell. Gk. The terms have to do with service which in manner and goal is controlled by a superior will but is rendered rather than imposed.

Only once in the LXX is ὑπηρέτης used for עֶבֶד, [40] Prv. 14:35: δεκτὸς βασιλεῖ ὑπηρέτης νοήμων, and this in such a way that one might speak of a Hellenising of the original in the sense that in Gk. it is of the nature and essence of the ὑπηρέτης to be in a position to carry out orders and tasks in the proper way → 531, 23 ff. [41] The ὑπηρέ-

---

[35] Ed. C. Gallavotti and A. Sacconi (1961), 23.

[36] Cf. A. Morpurgo, Mycenaeae Graecitatis Lex., Incunabula Graeca, 3 (1963), s.v. e-re-ta; M. Ventris - J.Chadwick, Documents in Mycenaean Gk. (1959), 183-194; L. R. Palmer, Mycenaeans and Minoans. Aegaean Prehistory in the Light of the Linear B Tablets² (1965), 145-150.

[37] L. R. Palmer, The Interpretation of Mycen. Gk. Texts (1963), 183 and 419, It is also very uncertain whether τοὶ ὑπηρέται τᾶν μακρᾶν ναῶν (Ditt. Syll.³, III, 1000, 31 [Doric Inscr. from Kos.; 1st cent. B.C.]) are "rowers" [Risch].

[38] We can only put a question. Can one think in terms of derivation from a stem ar (the α being lengthened to η), comparing verbs like ἀρέσκω, ἀρτίζω, ἄρχω which have the same extension to η, ε to η being very unusual (Boisacq, p. XII does not have it in his list)? If so, the ὑπηρέτης by linguistic origin might be the one who puts himself under another by reason of the other's higher rank (cf. ἄριστος, ἀρετή etc.), and this in such a way that he has no one under him. But the η in ὑπηρεσία does not support "ship's crew" since the process seems to be the same as with η in ὑπηρέτης (on ὑπηρεσία for "rowing crew" cf. Thuc., I, 143, 1; VI, 31, 3; VIII, 1, 2, also Polyb., 5, 109, 1) and there is much to suggest that this is secondary compared with "service." The first η in τριήρης is best left out of consideration.

[39] In this respect one might perhaps ref. to the clay model of a Byblos ship with two banks found in Byblos (3rd cent. B.C.), cf. Ill. in A. Jirku, Die Welt d. Bibel⁴ (1962), Plate 22a.

[40] Hbr. עֶבֶד is predominantly rendered by δουλ-words in the LXX; παῖς can also be used sometimes for עֶבֶד → II, 265, 24 ff.

[41] The basis of this strange rendering is perhaps to be sought in a stronger total understanding of עֶבֶד such as may be seen esp. in religious contexts in the later parts of the OT, Baudissin, 9.

ται τοῦ βασιλέως of Da. 3:46 Θ fit the same pattern to the degree that they are there to carry out royal injunctions. [42] ὑπηρεσία for עֲבֹדָה in Job 1:3 also belongs here if the word denotes Job's "servants" or "followers." [43] At Sir. 39:4 the Hbr. שָׁרַת pi lies behind the ἀνὰ μέσον μεγιστάνων ὑπηρετήσει which is said of the wise man; the idea of both voluntary and also honourable service is bound up with this word in the OT. [44]

Apart from these passages the group occurs in the LXX only in the apocr. Wis. of Sol. composed in Gk. [45] ὑπηρέτης is found only once here for the kings of the earth as servants, i.e., the executives in God's βασιλεία (6:4). But the verb is used 4 times at 16:21, 24 f.; 19:6 and the noun ὑπηρεσία twice at 13:11; 15:7. [46] In all these ref. ὑπηρετέω is plainly related to the movement of another's will: ἐπιταγή 19:6, θέλησις 16:25; ἐπιθυμία 16:21, the (will of the) Creator 16:24, [47] and the same is true in the case of ὑπηρεσία which always denotes service as such [48] and in this respect follows non-biblical usage → n. 38. [49]

b. The OT pseudepigrapha offer many examples of the group and show full continuity with non-biblical usage. This applies first to Ep. Ar. One sees here the vocabulary of government in Hell. Egypt (→ 531, 32 ff.) when there is ref. to χρηματισταὶ καὶ οἱ τούτων ὑπηρέται, i.e., district judges [50] and their "sub-officials" in Ep. Ar., 111 or when, adopting the military use of ὑπηρέτης, the author ref. to ὑπηρέται τῶν ταγμάτων "army paymasters" along with βασιλικοὶ τραπεζῖται the "royal bankers." [51, 52] It is part of the same pattern when ὑπηρετέω is used to describe the various tasks of temple priests assigned according to a single plan, 92. [53] In Test. XII Beliar (→ I, 607, 1 ff.) has at his disposal ὑπηρέται or "assistants" in the form of wicked angels which bring destruction, Test. B. 3:8, cf. 3:3. Test. Jos. 14:3 expressly connects personal freedom with ὑπηρετέω when the wife of the Egypt. official Potiphar says to her husband concerning the domestic slave Joseph: τί συνέχεις τὸν αἰχμάλωτον καὶ εὐγενῆ παῖδα ἐν δεσμοῖς ὃν ἔδει μᾶλλον ἄνετον εἶναι καὶ ὑπηρετεῖσθαι, [54] cf. Gn. 39:1 ff. The term, then, has lost nothing of its particularity among terms of service → 532, 17 ff.

2. Philo.

In gen. ὑπηρετέω and ὑπηρέτης (ὑπηρέτις) always have a personal ref. in Philo. As concerns the usage it makes no difference whether the controlling subject is God,

---

[42] So far no one has been able to explain satisfactorily how ὑπηρέτης came into the Gk. transl. at Is. 32:5.

[43] Neither here nor elsewhere in the LXX does the word ref. to service as an oarsman → 533, 9 ff., nor in Philo, → 536, 16 f.

[44] Cf. Ges.-Buhl, s.v. Nu. 4:23 Αλλ has ὑπηρετῆσαι ὑπηρεσίαν in place of the LXX λειτουργεῖν for MT לַעֲבֹד עֲבֹדָה v. Field, I, ad loc.

[45] Cf. J. Fichtner, "Die Stellung d. Sap. in d. Lit.- u. Geistesgeschichte ihrer Zeit," ZNW, 36 (1937), 115 f.

[46] Wis. 13:12 Cod A has ὑπηρεσία as vl. for ἑτοιμασία → n. 48. Possibly this is due to the influence of the preceding v. 11.

[47] Decisive here is the idea that the goal of everything is determined by the will of the Creator.

[48] Cf. ὑπηρεσία ζωῆς Wis. 13:11, ὑπηρεσία (→ n. 46) τροφῆς 13:12, πρὸς ὑπηρεσίαν ἡμῶν 15:7.

[49] The metaphor of the potter creating acc. to his own will is used in Wis. 13:11; 15:7 → n. 47.

[50] Cf. Liddell-Scott, s.v. χρηματιστής, H. G. Meecham, The Letter of Aristeas (1935), 74.

[51] Cf. on this F. Preisigke, Girowesen im griech. Ägypten (1910), 38.

[52] τάγμα denotes a large corps, perhaps a legion, cf. Preisigke Fachwörter, s.v.

[53] The ref. is to the Jerusalem temple.

[54] On the text v. R. H. Charles, The Gk. Versions of the Testaments of the Twelve Patriarchs (1908), ad loc.

a ruler, a person in high position, an ordinary man, or even a bodily organ which needs the support of another organ to perform its function. Thus it is said of the sense of smell that nature has cleverly made it ὑπηρέτιν γεύσεως a "handmaid of taste" or in some sense βασιλίδος προγευστρίδα ὑπήκοον "an obedient taster for the queen," Sacr. AC, 44. [55] It is in keeping with the introduction of the idea of obedience, cf. also Conf. Ling., 54; Plant., 55, that in many cases the manner of ὑπηρετεῖν is expressly grounded in precise directions, Migr. Abr., 14; ἐπιτάγμασιν ὑπηρετεῖν, Spec. Leg., III, 177, cf. ὡς ὑπηρετεῖν ἐξ ἀνάγκης ἅττ' ἂν προστάττῃ τὸ δεσπόζον, Conf. Ling., 91; νόμων προστάξεσιν ὑπηρετοῦντες, Omn. Prob. Lib., 7. [56] Thus one has always to think of compliance with lawful instructions when we read that an individual cannot build a city or even a house alone, but needs others as helpers: χρώμενον ὑπηρέταις ἑτέροις, Poster. C., 50, or when it is stated that God uses those who commit little sins that can be expiated rather than those who commit serious evil that cannot be expiated as helpers in punishing the latter: χρῆται γὰρ ὁ θεὸς τοῖς ὀλίγα καὶ ἰάσιμα διαμαρτάνουσι... ὑπηρέταις κολάσεως, Spec. Leg., III, 122, [57] or when angels are brought in as God's ὑπηρέται, Poster C., 92; Mut. Nom., 87; Deus Imm., 158; cf. Som., I, 143, though it is made clear that unlike human δεσπόται God does not need ὑπηρεσία, Det. Pot. Ins., 56, as indeed He does not need anything, Spec. Leg., I, 152 etc. When he calls priests and Levites ὑπηρέται in Sacr. AC, 132 f.; Spec. Leg., I, 152 (with λειτουργός here), Philo follows the specific Egypt-Hell. usage → 532, 1 ff. Yet when in Spec. Leg., I, 229 he calls the high-priest τοῦ ἔθνους ὑπηρέτης in his official function, he seems to be following a wholly Jewish idea, though one which is hardly expressed in a wholly clear or appropriate way → I, 416, 36 ff.

Philo has also the usual distinction between ὑπηρέτης and διάκονος (→ II, 88, 16 ff.) → 533, 1 ff. This may be seen in Gig., 12; Vit. Cont., 75 and esp. Jos., 241. Here Joseph styles himself a ὑπηρέτης καὶ διάκονος for his family, set up by God Himself. ὑπηρέτης ref. to his function as God's assistant while διάκονος ref. to the help he can be to his family in discharging this function. [58] As concerns θεράπων (→ 533, 4 ff.) the emphasis is more on the proper attitude of service than on the service itself, Sacr. AC, 133.

3. Josephus.

In the more restrained speech of Joseph., who unlike Philo makes little use of imagery, there is no reflection on the use of the group. Hence its employment in Jos. is always clear and self-contained, being governed by the idea of helping someone, the manner of help being dependent on this person, so that the motives do not affect the usage. The span of the use of ὑπηρέτης is very broad. Moses is God's "assistant" when he brings

---

[55] On this function cf. Plut. Bruta ratione uti, 7 (II, 990a), also Philo Ebr., 208 f., 215 f., where prominence is given to the οἰνοχόος "cupbearer" among other ὑπηρέται.

[56] Thus for Philo parents are θεοῦ ὑπηρέται πρὸς τέκνων σποράν, Decal., 119 so long as they obey the divine commandment of Gn. 1:28, cf. H. Schmidt, Die Anthropologie Philons v. Alex. (1934), 36 f. It is worth noting that in this connection parents stand in the same relation to God as a ὑπηρέτης to his ἄρχων → n. 16. Thus Philo can sometimes call a ὑπηρέτης of God His ὕπαρχος "viceroy" Decal., 178, who is His ὑποδιάκονος in carrying out the task assigned to him, cf. also Plant., 55; Rer. Div. Her., 171.

[57] Cf. [ὁ θεὸς...] κολάζει... ⟨δι'⟩ ὑπηρετούντων ἑτέρων... οὐκ ἄνευ μὲν ἐπικελεύσεως, Fug., 66 and esp. ὥστε τὰς μὲν τούτου χεῖρας (v. Ex. 21:13) ὀργάνων τρόπον (after the manner of instruments) παραλαμβάνεσθαι, τὸν δὲ διὰ τούτων ἀοράτως ἐνεργοῦντα ἕτερον εἶναι, τὸν ἀόρατον, Sacr. AC, 133. There is kinship here with the Palestinian halacha, cf. S. Dt., 229 on 22:8, cf. B. Ritter, Philo u. d. Halacha (1879), 29 f.

[58] In context ὑπηρέτης ref. more to the χάριτες of God in the applying of which Joseph is God's assistant, while διάκονος ref. more to God's δωρεαί which take concrete shape in the provision for Joseph's relatives through Joseph as God's ὑπηρέτης. The transl. in L. Cohn, Die Werke Philos v. Alex. in deutscher Übers., I (1909), 207 fails to bring this out. For Philo's mode of expression here cf. Deus Imm., 57; Gig., 12.

the chosen people out of Egypt, and he it is also who passes on God's commands, Ant., 3, 16, cf. 4, 317. [59] The Levite in the sanctuary is ὑπηρέτης τοῦ θεοῦ, Bell., 2, 321. Then we read of the royal "servant" in Ant., 15, 242; 19, 353, the "deputy" of Joseph in Egypt, Ant., 2, 110, [60] Ptolemaic (Ant., 12, 32) [61] and ·Roman "officials" (Bell., 2, 352). [62] Finally the word can mean "agent," e.g., in carrying out a plot (Bell., 1, 609), in unrestricted exploitation (2, 41), or in government (Ant., 12, 399; Bell., 2, 448), and "executioner's assistant" in Ant., 16, 232; Bell., 1, 655. Sometimes the use is military as in Ant., 15, 287: "member of the bodyguard," or 4, 317 alongside ὑποστράτηγος with ref. to Moses (→ line 1), as elsewhere in Hell. Gk. → 531, 20 ff. Transf. use is rare; Titus calls the sword ὑπηρέτης because in the hands of the enemy it can more easily snap the thread of life than any illness, Bell., 6, 49. Here as always the ὑπηρέτης is a co-agent, cf. συνεργέω in Bell., 4, 521-3. He has to carry out directions or express orders, cf. also Ant., 4, 37 and 214; Ap., 2, 230. This leads to the natural result that the one who gives the commission is responsible for what the ὑπηρέτης does. [63]

What applies to the noun applies also to the derived verb. [64] Thus Levites are expressly described as those who are to assist the priests in the ministry of the sanctuary: ὅπως ὑφηγουμένων τῶν ἱερέων ὑπηρετήσωσιν, Ant., 3, 258, while the ministry of the highpriest helps the people pledged to the cultus: δεῖ... ἡμῖν τοῦ ἱερατευσομένου καὶ ὑπηρετήσοντος ταῖς θυσίαις καὶ ταῖς ὑπὲρ ἡμῶν εὐχαῖς, Ant., 3, 189. Acc. to Ant., 1, 269 Jacob was at his mother's hand ὑπηρέτει τῇ μητρί when she prepared for Isaac the meal that would gain the birthright for the younger son. Here [65] as elsewhere ὑπηρετεῖν means the receiving of instructions, Ant., 6, 41; 8, 169; 10, 191; 12, 97 etc. or knowledge of the needs and wishes of others, and deliberate execution of them, 13, 225; 14, 60 and 99, cf. 12, 97 and 3, 107. [66] Hence the adj. ὑπηρετικός means "apt for service" in the sense of "helpful," 2, 158. In the case of Abraham when he offers up his son at God's command we find the expression ὑπηρετῆσαι τῷ θεῷ since he has undertaken to be ready to obey the will of God with his whole being, 1, 225.

It is in keeping with the basic sense of ὑπηρέτης that a δοῦλος (→ 532, 17 ff.) can also act as such (Bell., 2, 41), though normally the ὑπηρέτης is able to say yes or no. How far the functions of a royal state or government can be expressed by the term may be seen from Ant., 6, 40 f. This passage is also well adapted to show where Jos. draws the boundary between ὑπηρέτης on the one side and διάκονος (→ 533, 2 ff.) or θεραπεύω (→ 533, 4 ff.) [67] on the other, namely, in respect of the functional character of the activities described by the group and of those who exercise them.

4. Equivalents in Palestinian Judaism.

Establishing equivalents to ὑπηρέτης κτλ. in Palestinian Judaism at the beginning of the A.D. period is hampered by the fact that the OT does not offer any starting-pt. → 534, 18 ff. What is to many an obvious recourse to חזן as the Semitic equivalent raises many objections which are partly linguistic and partly material. The only other possibility

---

[59] Moses does what God demands of him (προστάσσω) and is thus His ἀγαθὸς ὑπηρέτης, Ant., 4, 49.

[60] Jos. probably has in view a high official under Joseph.

[61] We also read of βασιλικοὶ τραπεζῖται "royal treasurers" → 531, 24 ff.

[62] Petronius proves to be a negligent ὑπηρέτης of the emperor (opp. → n. 59) and may thus look for severe punishment.

[63] Cf. Jeroboam in Ant., 8, 221.

[64] Jos. also has the compound ἐξυπηρετέω which is a stronger form, Ant., 13, 67.

[65] Jacob is explicitly called πεπυσμένος.

[66] For needs as motives of ὑπηρετεῖν cf. Ant., 2, 158; 12, 152; 13, 67 and 225; 14, 99.

[67] Jos. always uses the verb and the related noun θεραπεία for cultic service. He does not have θεράπων as a religious term, v. Schl. Jos., 12 f.

is to ask whether the stem שמש is not adapted to fill the gap, as is desirable, though not essential, in relation to some NT passages.

Already Epiph. Haer., 30, 11 tried to find for Chr. office-bearers, whom he called διάκονος ἢ ὑπηρέτης, a Jewish model or parallel in the חַזָּן of Palestinian Judaism: 'Αζανιτῶν τῶν παρ' αὐτοῖς διακόνων ἑρμηνευομένων ἢ ὑπηρετῶν. The חַזָּנִים [68] had important functions in the Jerusalem temple, helping priests who were no longer officiating to disrobe (Tamid, 5, 3) or proclaiming to the working population the approach of the Sabbath by signals which would make possible observance of the commanded rest (T. Sukka, 4, 11 f.). It may be assumed that they belonged to the Levites. [69] In the older Rabb. period they seem to have been people of rank in the synagogue congregations, while in a later stratum the tradition connected them with subsidiary duties. [70] The equation of חַזָּנִים as lower temple servants [71] with the assistants called ὑπηρέται by Philo and Jos. is supported by this as also by their Levitical character → 536, 18 f. and 537, 2 f. But the question is whether these two factors are adequate for identification. Thus the stem behind חַזָּן suggests that the activity of the חַזָּנִים might have been originally supervisory or directing rather than supportive. Furthermore, if חַזָּן is the equivalent of ὑπηρέτης, there is no verb corresponding to ὑπηρετέω. Finally חַזָּן does not relate to any existing or accepted need as ὑπηρετέω obviously does, esp. in Jos. → 537, 23 f.

In the vocabulary of Rabb. Judaism the stem שמש occurs in the verb שִׁמֵּשׁ (always pi or hitp/nitp) and the noun שַׁמָּשׁ, which means "servant." The group occurs neither in the OT nor the Dead Sea Scrolls thus far published. The derivation is obscure. If it is really Egypt. in origin [72] this might explain some aspects of the usage. We have in view not merely the fact that in Tannaite traditions the verb usually relates to a person or thing [73] but also the fact that the goal is relief of a need. [74] Sometimes there are astonishingly close par. to the use of the word group in Philo and Jos. Cf. σκεύη πρὸς τὰς θυσίας ὑπηρετήσοντα in Jos. Ant., 3, 107 and שני כלים המשמשין מלאכה אחת in T BM, 10, 11 and the idea in Philo Spec. Leg., III, 177 that χεῖρες ... τοῖς ἡμετέροις ἐπιτάγμασιν ὑπηρετοῦσιν with the materially and formally related sentence of the Palestinian Amoraean Levi (c. 300 A.D.) to the effect that the hand is one of the members or organs of man which "serve" him משמשין acc. to his disposing רשות, Gn. r., 67, 3 on 27:33. The special feature of the group precisely in the earlier stage of its use is that it contains on the one side the idea of assistance in a specific situation and displays on the other an interest in the correct functioning of certain relations and obligations in a broader

---

[68] Cf. S. Krauss, Synagogale Altertümer (1922), 121-131; also Str.-B., IV, 147-9. For חַזָּן on inscr. cf. CIJ, II, 805 (391 A.D.), 855 (3rd/4th cent. A.D.).

[69] Krauss, op. cit. (→ n. 68), 122.

[70] Ibid., 124-6.

[71] So Schl. Theol. d. Judt., 98, cf. also Schl. Jos., 13 f.

[72] Acc. to M. Auerbach, Wörterbuch z. Mechilta d. R. Ismael (Buchstabe א) nebst Einleitung, Diss. Strassburg (Berlin, 1905), 50, n. 25, T. Nöldeke regarded the verb as an Egypt. loan word.

[73] So M. Ex. בא 1 on 12:1 (Horovitz-Rabin, 5, 20 f.):יהושע שמש משה ... אלישע שמש אליהו with ref. to men, ibid. בחדש יתרו 10 on 20:23 (239, 5 f.):דמות שמשי המשמשין לפני במרום with ref. (heavenly beings) to God (prohibition of images); T. Yoma, 4 (3), 20: שימש בכהונה גדולה of high-priests with ref. to the people, cf. T. Sukka, 4, 28; bYoma, 47a; T. Kelim BM, 6, 7 of vessels with ref. to the (cultic) purpose assigned to them.

[74] Cf. T. Kelim BQ, 6, 16; BM, 1, 7; 2, 5-7; 7, 9 f.; 10, 4 f.; BB, 7, 11. Very plain is T. Chag., 2, 9 (cf. T. Sota, 14, 9; Sanh., 7, 1) with its ref. to the fact that Shammai and Hillel, as their students grew in numbers, were no longer able to satisfy their needs in respect of teaching: לא שימשו כל צורכן. Cf. also bNed., 41a with the interpretation of וּבְחֹסֶר כֹּל in Dt. 28:48 by בלא שמש.

framework. Both materially and linguistically all this leads us from שמש to ὑπηρέτης κτλ. and suggests that this root and its denominatives should be considered when equivalents of the Greek word group are sought in Palestinian Judaism. [75]

C. The New Testament.

1. Usage Generally.

a. The word group is comparatively rare in the NT, unlike words in δουλ- and διακον-. Furthermore the common Gk. ὑπηρεσία does not occur at all, let alone other terms. The distribution puts Luke (Lk. and Ac.) and John (Gospel only) in first place with nine instances each, while Mt. and Mk. have only two each. There is only one example in Paul. The verb occurs only three times in Ac.

b. The noun ὑπηρέτης is always used in a general sense similar to that of classical and Hellenistic Greek (→ 530, 13 ff.) including Philo (→ 535, 8 ff.) and Josephus (→ 536, 30 ff.): "assistant to another as the instrument of his will," possibly in a system of integrated functions in which account is taken of specific needs. Connected with this is the fact that the specific function of a ὑπηρέτης is to be gleaned from the context in which he appears. This is true at any rate in most of the NT instances.

(a) In the version of the short parable of going to the judge in Mt. 5:25 f. [76] the ὑπηρέτης is the one to whom the judge commits the guilty party to put him in prison. The obvious reference here is to the "judicial servant" who is an instrument of the courts to execute sentences → 531, 30 ff. In the eschatological image he serves to illustrate the ineluctability of approaching judgment unless there is timely perception and conversion.

Lk. 12:58 uses πράκτωρ instead. This is not because Lk. uses the judicial procedure of Rome rather than that of (Rabb.) Judaism as the framework of the saying. [77] It is rather because he has a different figure in view, namely, the one who executes sentence on debtors who are unwilling or unable to pay → VI, 642, 18 ff. [78] Two different forms of contemporary judicial speech or practice are thus followed, [79] but in both cases παραδίδωμι denotes execution of the sentence → n. 78. Only from the context can one see that the parables are applied differently. Luke stresses the threatening situation in which the debtor finds himself, while Mt. focuses on his responsibility in relation to himself and his fate, a responsibility which he must accept in his own interests so long as there is still time.

(b) In the depiction of Jesus at worship in the synagogue at Nazareth (Lk. 4:16 ff.) the ὑπηρέτης is the one who takes from Him the scroll of Isaiah which

---

[75] One should pt. out, of course, that in jSanh., 19c, 38, cf. Str.-B., I, 290 the חַזָּן, סוֹפְרִים and שַׁמָּשׁ are mentioned together. With the scribes the חַזָּן and שַׁמָּשׁ are thus differentiated and this in such a way that the חַזָּן is in fact (→ 538, 14 ff.) a kind of overseer, while the lowest function among those mentioned accrues to the שַׁמָּשׁ, namely, that of executing.

[76] Cf. Jeremias Gl.⁷, 39; also Bultmann Trad., Index; Str.-B., I, 289 f.

[77] Jeremias Gl.⁷, 39, n. 3, cf. 22 with n. 2.

[78] Pr.-Bauer, s.v. πράκτωρ with ref. to Ditt. Or., II, 669, 15-18 and Wilcken Ptol., I, 118, 15-24 (136 B.C.), where the πράκτωρ is expressly differentiated from the τοῦ κριτηρίου ὑπηρέτης.

[79] Examples in Pr.-Bauer, s.v. ὑπηρέτης; for Jos. → 537, 5 ff.

He has just used (v. 20), [80] namely, the "assistant" of the president of the synagogue who has certain functions to perform, especially in worship, at the latter's direction. [81]

(c) Mostly ὑπηρέτης denotes the member of a group of servants who are under various authorities and are at their disposal to accomplish various goals. Authorities mentioned are the ἀρχιερεύς or ἀρχιερεῖς in Mt. 26:58; Mk. 14:54, 65, the chief priests and Pharisees in Jn. 7:32, 45 f.; 18:3; Ac. 5:22, 26; cf. Jn. 19:6, these groups being a comprehensive term for the Sanhedrin, and finally οἱ Ἰουδαῖοι in Jn. 18:12, 18, 22, again a comprehensive term for the groups represented in the Sanhedrin. In all these instances the reference is probably to the "officers" of the Sanhedrin.

The context of the passages seems to suggest that the "officers" or "servants" of the Sanhedrin are to be distinguished from the Levites serving as temple police, cf. Jn. 7:30, 44; 8:20; 10:39; Ac. 4:3. [82] Even when they perform police duties, it is correct to view this merely as part of their general task. The term allows this.

c. The verb ὑπηρετέω occurs only in Ac. at 13:36; 20:34; 24:23. It carries always the customary sense of "to help" according to the express will of another.

This is immediately apparent at Ac. 24:23. Paul as a prisoner in Caesarea is permitted by the procurator Felix to let his "own" help him. [83] This includes not merely seeing and supplying his needs but also meeting his wishes. Passages like Phil. 2:25; 4:18 (Epaphroditus as λειτουργὸς τῆς χρείας μου) are well suited to illustrate this. In Ac. 20:34 Paul, surveying his work in Asia Minor, says at Miletus: ταῖς χρείαις μου καὶ τοῖς οὖσιν μετ' ἐμοῦ ὑπηρέτησαν αἱ χεῖρες αὗται. In so doing he adopts a not uncommon metaphor of the day → 538, 27 ff. [84] It is not so easy to say what the reference of the part. is in 13:36: Δαυὶδ μὲν γὰρ ἰδίᾳ γενεᾷ ὑπηρετήσας τῇ τοῦ θεοῦ βουλῇ ἐκοιμήθη. [85] But the meaning of ὑπηρετέω makes it clear that it can be taken only with the τῇ τοῦ θεοῦ βουλῇ which follows. [86] David fell asleep when he had served the will of God. [87]

---

[80] Probably he had already given it to Him on the instructions of the ἀρχισυνάγωγος.

[81] A Jewish ὑπηρέτης Flavios Julianos is mentioned on a burial plaque in the catacomb of the Vigna Randanini in Rome CIJ, I, 172, but the inscr. gives no indication of the precise reference. Since the inscr. frequently suggest that those buried were synagogue officials one may surmise that a synagogue servant was meant, Frey 124, cf. XCIX following Schürer, 28 f.

[82] So J. Blinzler, Der Prozess Jesus³ (1960), 84-86: "Servants" of the Sanhedrin.

[83] It is not clear who the ἴδιοι are. We cannot decide whether they are fellow-believers (Pr.-Bauer, s.v. ἴδιος), relatives, or friends.

[84] The idea that Lk. is exaggerating because Paul by his work could not even provide for his own needs, let alone support his companions (Haench. Ag.¹⁴ ad loc. ref. to 2 C. 11:9), finds no support in the text in the use of ὑπηρετέω, for the verb never means "to provide for." Hence one also cannot conclude from the v. that it is the duty of congregational leaders not to live at the expense of the congregation, Haench. Ag.¹⁴, ad loc.

[85] For the various possibilities cf. Haench. Ag.¹⁴, ad loc.

[86] So correctly G. Stählin, Die Apostelgeschichte, NT Deutsch, 5¹¹ (1966), 179 though cf., e.g., Haench. Ag.¹⁴, ad loc.

[87] The real difficulty in v. 36, then, is ἰδίᾳ γενεᾷ, which is usually taken to mean "in his generation" or, dependent on ὑπηρετήσας (→ n. 86), "to his generation" (dat.). There is an antithesis behind the expression as indicated by Δαυὶδ μὲν ... in v. 36 on the one side and ὃν δὲ ... in v. 37 on the other. This is caused by applying David's statements about himself in the Psalter to Jesus along the lines of the Davidic Christ-prohecy, vv. 32 ff. One may thus suppose that this is also the reason for formulation in terms of ἰδίᾳ γενεᾷ, which is given emphasis by the γάρ. The point of the γεγέννηκά σε quoted from Ps. 2:7 in v. 33

2. Difficult Passages.

a. Ac. 13:5: John Mark as ὑπηρέτης of Barnabas and Paul.

According to the usage of the time ὑπηρέτης here can only mean that John Mark was at the disposal of Barnabas and Paul to meet their needs and carry out their wishes. They were the ones, then, who on the basis of their own work decided what he should do as their assistant. The specific nature of his work is not stated. One may gather from the designation, however, that for the author of Ac. it was functional, being determined by the apostolic task (Ac. 14:4, 14), with no need of details.

It rests on a misunderstanding of the use of ὑπηρέτης for bureaucrats in Hell. Egypt when Luke is taken to mean that John Mark carried a Gospel around with him. [88] Nor does the reading ὑπηρετοῦντα in D provide adequate grounds for thinking that Lk. ascribed only material service to Mark, [89] since the verb does not imply this.

b. Jn. 18:36: ὑπηρέται of Jesus.

Either the question what Jesus means by calling His disciples ὑπηρέται is wrongly put, since He is only saying that He would have ὑπηρέται to fight for Him if He were an earthly king, [90] or the emphasis is on the fact that Jesus is indeed a king and thus has ὑπηρέται who could fight for Him, but the Law of His kingdom does not permit this. In the latter case the reference must be to His disciples when before Pilate He speaks emphatically of οἱ ὑπηρέται οἱ ἐμοί. [91] This being so, they are royal ὑπηρέται such as we find in Josephus (→ 537, 2 f.), and they are given a designation which is not wholly inconsonant with their description as φίλοι in Jn. 15:15, since both designations, though differently, have to do with relationship, φίλος from the standpoint of the confidence of the prince and closeness to him, ὑπηρέτης more from the standpoint of working with him to accomplish his ends. [92]

Jesus' words sound like an appeal to the political authorities at the time of the composition of Jn. to be fair to Christianity and not to confuse it with a political movement. [93]

---

is divine generation, which David did not have. Hence David had to die and be gathered to his fathers, whereas Jesus, though He died too, was raised up again by God. This ἰδίᾳ γενεᾷ is designed to explain the fate of David (expressed by ἐκοιμήθη κτλ.) in distinction from that of Jesus. It is to be interpreted rather than translated "on the basis of his own (natural) generation." This use of γενεά is not unique, cf. Preisigke Wört., I, 285; it possibly underlies (→ I, 663, n. 7) the understanding of Is. 53:8 LXX in Ac. 8:33.

[88] Holmes, 69. A similar misunderstanding of current usage lies behind the view of C. S. C. Williams, *The Acts of the Apostles* (1957), ad loc. that John Mark is called ὑπηρέτης here because he provided the apostles with the OT material necessary for the proof from Scripture, acting as a translator in Greek speaking areas. F. F. Bruce, *The Acts of the Apostles*⁴ (1956), ad loc. suggests a secretary, while Jackson-Lake, IV, 143 are inclined to see in Mk. a bearer of the Gospel tradition.

[89] So Haench. Ag.¹⁴, ad loc.

[90] Cf. Bultmann J., ad loc.

[91] Bau. J., ad loc.

[92] Cf. Epict. Diss., III, 22, 95. J. H. Bernard, *A Crit. and Exeget. Comm. on the Gospel acc. to St. John,* ICC (1928), II, 610 f. makes the further suggestion that the ὑπηρέται were the heavenly legions of Mt. 26:52 f. → I, 139, n. 21. The context seems to be against this.

[93] Cf. Bau. J., ad loc.; G. H. C. Macgregor, *The Gospel of John* (1928), ad loc.; H. Strathmann, *Das Ev. nach J.,* NT Deutsch., 4¹⁰ (1963), ad loc. etc.

In no sense does it aim at the crown as charged, cf. v. 37. [94] The question remains, however, whether current use of ὑπηρέτης justifies our interpreting the ἀγωνίζεσθαι (→ I, 134, 29 f.) of the ὑπηρέται of Jesus as bloody conflict, → I, 139, n. 21. The word can certainly denote the use of weapons, but its use is not limited to this. It can also ref. to any exertion which involves the deploying of all our forces to attain success, victory, or deliverance. [95] This sense fits the situation of the disciples in the passion narrative of Jn. extremely well. On the one hand they dare not intercede for Jesus with Pilate in view of the charge against Him, v. 29. On the other hand they fit in with the divine counsel concerning Jesus by their passive attitude (v. 36b); though they do not realise it, this seeks His exaltation → ὑψόω.

c. 1 C. 4:1: Paul and Apollos as ὑπηρέται Χριστοῦ καὶ οἰκονόμοι μυστηρίων θεοῦ.

The point of the expression here is that Paul and Apollos do not work on their own but are executive organs of Christ. This means that all they preach, teach, order and do has its origin and basis in God's plan for the world as this is manifested in Christ. [96] Hence ὑπηρέτης here comes close to ἀπόστολος (→ I, 441, 12 ff.) [97] and the further description added by καί has the character of a more precise elucidation of the ὑπηρέται Χριστοῦ, making Paul and Apollos independent of the criticisms and evaluations of the Corinthian Christians and also protecting them against self-criticism on any grounds, vv. 3 ff. [98]

The first part of the description reminds us of the characterisation of the true Cynic as ὑπηρέτης τοῦ Διός in Epict. Diss., III, 22, 82 (→ 531, 10 ff.) or ὑπηρέτης, ὡς μετέχων τῆς ἀρχῆς τοῦ Διός in III, 22, 95, [99] though the figures of speech are not wholly co-extensive. [100] It was hardly by chance that Epict. used the simile of the οἰκονόμος for the Cynic. [101] When Paul tries to illustrate ὑπηρέτης Χριστοῦ with the help of οἰκονόμος, he is probably following Lk. 12:42 rather than Mk. 4:11 and par. as commonly held. There is moreover no tension between 1 C. 4:1 and 3:5, since Paul's self-designation there as διάκονος rests on the emphasis given to the gain accruing to the Corinthian church through Paul and Apollos: δι' ὧν ἐπιστεύσατε → 533, 2 f.; 536, 24 ff.; 537, 31 ff.

d. Ac. 26:16: Paul as ὑπηρέτης καὶ μάρτυς of Jesus.

In the singular combination of ὑπηρέτης and μάρτυς the καί is probably epexegetical (→ lines 11 ff. and n. 98), so that μάρτυς defines ὑπηρέτης more narrowly. Through the personal intervention of Jesus Saul the persecutor and

---

[94] So Zn. J., ad loc.

[95] Schl. J., ad loc. with ref. to Jos. Ant., 13, 193; 17, 81. Cf. also Preisigke Wört., I, s.v. ἀγωνίζομαι and V. C. Pfitzner, "Paul and the Agon Motif," Suppl. Nov. Test., 16 (1967). 110.

[96] Cf. Schl. K., 146 f.

[97] ἀπόστολος could not be used because Apollos was not an apostle and was not counted as such → I, 441, 13 reading ὑπηρέτης for δοῦλος.

[98] The καί is thus epexegetical.

[99] Cf. Heinr. 1 K., ad loc.; Joh. W. 1 K., ad loc.

[100] Cf. on this K. Deissner, "Das Sendungsbewusstsein d. Urchristenheit," ZSTh, 7 (1929/30), 772-790.

[101] Epict. Diss., III, 22, 3 offers no par., as against Ltzm. K., ad loc.

enemy (cf. v. 14 f.) has become the servant and assistant of Jesus, and this in such a way that he now acts on His behalf, making His cause his own → IV, 493, 27 ff. Once again there stands in the background a recollection of his appointment as an apostle: ἀποστέλλω σε, v. 17.[102]

For Lk. the ὑπηρέτην, which comes first, is obviously the constitutive term in the whole expression.[103] The emphasis, then, is not on what Paul receives as a possession or prerogative,[104] but on the task which the κύριος had laid upon him. It is quite logical that the task of the new apostle as a witness[105] should be defined in terms of an adoption and continuation of Jesus' own task, cf. v. 18 with Lk. 2:30 ff. The dominant position of ὑπηρέτης in the whole section is given further stress when Paul in what follows says about himself: οὐκ ἐγενόμην ἀπειθής, v. 19.

e. Lk. 1:2: ὑπηρέται τοῦ λόγου.

The term refers here to the sponsors of the Evangelist in the composition of his πρῶτος λόγος which contains the history of Jesus from the very beginning to His parting from them at the ascension, cf. Lk. 24:51. There can be little doubt but that they are the same as the preceding αὐτόπται with whom they are joined by a καί → IV, 115, 23 ff. The meaning of the difficult expression is to be sought in the fact that it establishes continuity between the preaching of Jesus and the history of Jesus → V, 348, 1 ff. Each has its basis in those who had a share in it. The choice of ὑπηρέτης makes good sense in this connection, since the word emphasises the fact that the αὐτόπται were not propagandists for their own views of what happened with Jesus but had unreservedly put their persons and work in the service of Jesus' cause.

τοῦ λόγου goes only with ὑπηρέται.[106] ὑπηρέται τοῦ λόγου presupposes that what was primarily the theme of autopsia has become the theme of preaching and the tradition.[107] The whole formula is probably Luke's own. This is supported by the fact that the use of λόγος is the same as that which characterises Acts → IV, 115, 16 ff.

D. The Early Church.

In their use of the noun the post-apost. fathers have nothing new compared with the NT. With ἄγγελος and ἄρχων it means "official" in the sense of "servant" Dg., 7, 2; cf. Barn., 16, 4, or with οἰκονόμος (→ 542, 11 ff.) and πάρεδρος it has the sense of "functionary" Ign. Pol., 6, 1. The diaconate is ἐκκλησίας θεοῦ ὑπηρέται in Ign. Tr., 2, 3; possibly this follows Jewish usage → 537, 35 ff. Ign. Phld., 11, 1 has the verb for the ministry of a deacon associated with him, and the meaning is much the same in Herm. m.,

[102] Correctly seen by Wdt. Ag. on 26:16.
[103] It is astonishing that the comm. mostly neglect the word, concentrating on μάρτυς.
[104] Haench. Ag.14, ad loc.: "Paul is ... depicted as a constant recipient of heavenly visions," but cf. Zn. Ag., ad loc.
[105] Here, too, Luke relates μάρτυς to the fact that Paul has seen the risen Jesus as κύριος, cf. 1:8 etc., v. E. Günther, ΜΑΡΤΥΣ (1941), 102-6, but → IV, 493, 27 ff. On the textual problem of Ac. 26:16 cf. M. Dibelius, "Der Text d. Ag.," Aufsätze zur Ag.4 (1961), 83.
[106] So Kl. Lk., ad loc. and many others. Ag. 26:16 (→ 542, 31 ff.) is calculated to support this.
[107] On the relation between an eye-witness report and an account in antiquity cf. E. Norden, Agnostos Theos (1913), 316-327.

8, 10; χήραις ὑπηρετεῖν, s., 9, 10, 2 and Barn., 1, 5 "to help," "to assist," the will of God being always in the background.

Later usage is along the same lines in Just. Apol., I, 14, 1; II, 2, 7, where ὑπηρέτης occurs along with "slave," but is a "free servant" receiving and carrying out orders as such.

Rengstorf

† ὕπνος,	† ἀφυπνόω,	
† ἐνύπνιον,	† ἐνυπνιάζομαι,	
† ἔξυπνος,	† ἐξυπνίζω	

ἐγείρω → II, 333, 1 ff.
καθεύδω → III, 431, 7 ff.
ὄναρ → V, 220, 7 ff.
ὅραμα → V, 371, 18 ff.

Contents: A. The Word Group among the Greeks: 1. Origin, Meaning and Use of the Stem ὑπν-; 2. Sleep as a Natural Process; 3. The Scientific View of Sleep; 4. Disparagement of Sleep; 5. Sleep and Death; 6. The God Hypnos. B. The Word Group in the Septuagint and Judaism. C. The Word Group in the New Testament. D. The Word Group in the Early Church and Gnosticism.

A. The Word Group among the Greeks.

1. Origin, Meaning and Use of the Stem ὑπν-.

ὕπνος from Indo-Eur. * supnos, derived forms * suepnos and * suopnos, Lat. sopor "deep sleep," somnus "sleep" (hence somnium "dream"), means "sleep." [1] The Gk. ὕπνος is not attested for "dream." [2] The expressions ἐν ὕπνῳ and καθ' ὕπνον are used for the experiencing of dreams (→ 546, 26 ff.) — esp. clearly in LXX for Hbr. חֲלוֹם (→ 550, 12 ff.) — but they simply mean "during sleep." [3] For "dream" we find ὄναρ (→ V, 220, 7 ff.) and ἐνύπνιον from ἐν ὕπνῳ (→ 546, 11 ff. and 26 ff.). The compound ἀγρυπνέω (→ II, 339, 1 ff.) originally meant "to sleep in the open" (ἀγρός + ὕπνος) i.e., wakefully, fitfully, and then came to mean "to watch" (→ 555, 6 ff.). [4] Denominative verbs are ὑπνόω, ὑπνώω, ὑπνώσσω (-ττω), all both intr. and trans., and ὑπνίζω trans. only. There are in all over 100 derivates and compounds in ὑπν-.

2. Sleep as a Natural Process.

Apart from ideas the Greeks connected with the phenomenon of sleep generally (→ III, 431, 12 ff.), the special significance of ὕπνος κτλ. will be presented here. ὕπνος is common already in Hom., mostly for natural sleep. The main epithets are adj. like γλυκύς

ὕπνος κτλ. Bibl.: H. Winneberg, Hypnos. Ein archäol. Versuch (1886); A. Jolles, Art. "Hypnos," Pauly-W., 9 (1916), 323-9; M. B. Ogle, "The Sleep of Death," Memoirs of the American Academy in Rome, 11 (1933), 81-117; O. Michel, "Zur Lehre vom Todesschlaf," ZNW, 35 (1936), 285-290; E. L. Ehrlich, "Der Traum im AT," ZAW Beih., 73 (1953), passim; J. G. S. S. Thomson, "Sleep: An Aspect of Jewish Anthropology," VT, 5 (1955), 421-433; P. Hoffmann, "Die Toten in Christus. Eine religionsgeschichtliche Untersuchung z. paul. Eschatologie," NTAbh, NF, 2 (1966), 186-206.

[1] Cf. Boisacq, Hofmann, s.v.; Walde-Hofmann, s.v. somnus, sopio, sopor. Cf. also W. Porzig, Die Namen f. Satzinhalte im Griech. u. im Idg. (1942), 345.

[2] Cf. the def. of a dream in Hesych., s.v. ὄναρ: καθ' ὕπνον φαντασία.

[3] Even the not uncommon plur., e.g., ἐν τοῖς ὕπνοις Plat. Resp., IX, 572b; ἐκ τῶν ὕπνων ... ἐγειρόμενος I, 330e does not mean dream; it simply expresses the fact that the state denoted by ὕπνος is always of limited duration.

[4] On ἀγρυπνέω cf. Hofmann, Frisk, s.v.; J. Wackernagel, "Vermischte Beiträge z. griech. Sprachkunde," Kleine Schriften, I (1953), 764 f.

(16 times), Od., 8, 445; Il., 23, 232, νήδυμος [5] = ἥδυμος "sweet," in Hom. only with ὕπνος (11 times), Od., 12, 311; Il., 10, 91, but also ἡδύς, e.g., in the recurrent double line: (Penelope) κλαῖεν ἔπειτ' 'Οδυσῆα, φίλον πόσιν, ὄφρα οἱ ὕπνον ἡδὺν ἐπὶ βλεφάροισι βάλε γλαυκῶπις 'Αθήνη, Od., 1, 363 f.; 16, 450 f.; 19, 603 f.; 21, 357 f. etc. The sleep which Hera cunningly intends for the father of the gods is "friendly" and "mild" ἀπήμων, λιαρός, Il., 14, 164. Sleep is ruler over all, πανδαμάτωρ, Od., 9, 372 f.; Il., 24, 5, lord of all gods and men, Il., 14, 233 → 549, 11 f. It is said of man that he "takes" the gift of sleep αἱρέω, Od., 16, 481, and the gods that they lay it on men βάλλω → line 3 f., or pour it over them ἐπιχεύω Od., 5, 492, καταχεύω 18, 188. The sleeper enjoys sleep τέρπομαι Il., 24, 3, and whether god or man is overpowered by it δεδμημένος Od., 15, 6, cf. Il., 14, 353. The derivative ἐνύπνιον occurs in Hom. only at Od., 14, 495 (= Il., 2, 56) as an adv.: θεῖός μοι ἐνύπνιον ἦλθεν ὄνειρος. This is a pointer to the rise of the later independent noun. Of other ὑπν- words Hom. has only ἄυπνος "sleepless" Od., 19, 591 and ὑπνώω "to sleep" (only part.) Od., 24, 4 (= Il., 24, 344).

After Hom. we still find many unreflecting ref. to sleep. It "overpowers" λαβεῖν the man who is tired with wine, Plat. Symp., 223b. Wine mediates ὕπνον τε λήθην "the sleep" which makes all the cares of life forgotten, Eur. Ba., 282. We also find the phrases "at the time of the first sleep" περὶ πρῶτον ὕπνον in Thuc., II, 2, 1, "shortly after going to sleep" μικρὸν δ' ὕπνου λαχών in Xenoph. An., III, 1, 11, cf. διὰ μέσων τῶν ὕπνων "in the middle of the night," Plut. Them., 28 (I, 126b). There are now more derived words than in Hom.: The heart "cannot sleep for fear" οὐχ ὑπνώσσει κέαρ Aesch. Sept. c. Theb., 287; a certain mixture of wine is in a special way ὑπνοφόρος, Plut. Quaest. Conv., III, 9 (II, 657d); means of cooling are ὑπνωτικὰ φάρμακα, III, 5 (II, 652c). Argus sleeps with alternately closed eyes ὀφθαλμοῖσιν ἀμοιβαδὸν ὑπνώεσκε, Quintus Smyrnaeus Posthomerica, 10, 191. [6]

With ὀνειρώττω one finds ἐν ὕπνῳ in Plat. Resp., V, 476c, cf. ἰδόντι ... ἐνύπνιον, Aristoph. Vesp., 25, ὄψιν τινὰ ἰδὼν ἐνυπνίου, Hdt., VIII, 54, as adv. (→ lines 11 ff.) ἐνύπνιον ἐστιώμεθα, Aristoph. Vesp., 1218. The dream is the locus of divine revelations, ἐπηγγείλατο δ' ἐμοὶ ὁ θεὸς κατὰ τὸν ὕπνον, Ditt. Syll.[3], II, 663, 26 (200 B.C.), cf. III, 985, 3 f. (1st cent. B.C.). A psychological explanation of dreams is offered in Hdt., VII, 16 β 2: ἐνύπνια ... ἐς ἀνθρώπους πεπλανημένα result from thoughts during the day, cf. Aristot. De insomniis, 3, p. 462a, 29 ff., cf. 8 f., who traces back dreams to τὸ φάντασμα τὸ ἀπὸ τῆς κινήσεως τῶν αἰσθημάτων though not rejecting their character as δαιμόνια, De divinatione per somnum, 2, p. 463b, 12 ff. Materially → V, 222, 4 ff. In Artemid. Onirocr. [7], I, 1 (p. 3, 9 ff.) a basic difference is seen between ὄναρ: τῷ μὲν εἶναι σημαντικῷ τῶν μελλόντων and ἐνύπνιον: τῷ δὲ τῶν ὄντων, and this recurs in similar form in Philo (→ 552, 24 ff.) → V, 221, 28 ff. [8]

3. The Scientific View of Sleep.

Various attempts were made to explain sleep. Among the Pre-Socratics [9] it was emphasised that it is not a ψυχικόν but a σωματικόν [10] and is thus to be explained along natural lines, whether as relaxing of bodily energy as in Anaxagoras acc. to Aetius De

---

[5] Acc. to Hofmann, s.v. orig. a slip for ἥδυμος, cf. Liddell-Scott, s.v. and for details M. Leumann, "Homerische Wörter," Schweizerische Beiträge z. Altertumswissenschaft, 3 (1950), 44 f. The etym. connection with Endymion, the eternally sleeping youth (→ 549, 20 ff.), and the rendering of νήδυμος by "enveloping," Jolles, 324, are thus untenable.

[6] Ed. A. Zimmermann (1891).

[7] Ed. R. A. Pack (1963).

[8] Cf. T. Hopfner, Art. "Traumdeutung," Pauly-W., 6a (1937), 2240-2244. Macrob. In somnium Scipionis, I, 3, 2 ff. has another def. of ἐνύπνιον, Hopfner, 2243 f.

[9] The relevant fr. have been preserved in the collection of philosophical sayings by Aetius, Plut. Plac. Phil., V, 23 and 25 (II, 909c-910b), cf. H. Diels, Doxographi Graeci (1874), 435-8.

[10] Acc. to Aristot. sleep has this in common with death: θάνατος ... μόνον σώματος οὐ ψυχῆς, Plut. Plac. Phil., 25 (II, 909 f.), cf. Aristot. De somno et vigilia, 1, p. 453b, 11 ff.

placitis reliquia (→ n. 9), V, 25, 2 (Diels, II, 30, 10 ff.) or as loss of warmth (→ 546, 23 f.), Empedocles acc. to Aetius, *op. cit.,* V, 24, 2 (I, 301, 17 ff.): τὸν μὲν ὕπνον καταψύξει τοῦ ἐν τῷ αἵματι θερμοῦ συμμέτρῳ γίνεσθαι, or by the withdrawal of blood into the blood-vessels φλέβας, Alcmaion acc. to Aetius, *op. cit.,* V, 24, 1 (I, 214, 18 ff.), cf. Diogenes of Apollonia acc. to Aetius, *op. cit.,* V, 24, 3 (II, 57, 30 ff.). In this regard sleep is regarded as a transitional stage to death → 548, 8 ff.; 551, 21 ff. In early medicine these theories were dispelled by concrete observation of the flow of blood into the inner part of the body during sleep. [11] Cf. esp. Hippocrates, e.g., Epid., VI, 5, 15 (Littré, V, 320): τὸ αἷμα ἐν ὕπνῳ εἴσω μᾶλλον φεύγει, *ibid.,* V, 4, 12 (V, 310); Περὶ φυσῶν, 14 (VI, 110). Often light or heavy sleep during sickness shows whether the state is not serious or fatal: ἐν ᾧ νοσήματι ὕπνος πόνον ποιέει, θανάσιμον... Hippocr. Aphorismi, II, 1 (IV, 470), cf. IV, 68 (IV, 526), Epid., VI, 7, 5 (V, 344). Exceeding the natural amounts of waking and sleeping, or sleeping by day, is bad (→ lines 24 ff.), and usually denotes illness: ὕπνος, ἀγρυπνίη, ἀμφότερα τοῦ μετρίου μᾶλλον γενόμενα, κακόν, Aphorismi, II, 3 (IV, 470), cf. Acut., 13 (II, 330 f.); Epid., I, 10 (II, 670); Progn., 10 (II, 134). In the work De somno et vigilia Aristot. starts with the thesis that the alternation of sleeping and waking is a basic phenomenon of animal life in gen., I, p. 453b, 11 ff. [12] Sleep is not a deactivation of the organs of sense, 2, p. 455b, 2 ff., but κατάληψις... τοῦ πρώτου αἰσθητηρίου, 3, p. 458a, 28 f. and as such ἡδονή, 2, p. 455b, 19 and ἀνάγκη to preserve life, 2, p. 455b, 26, cf. 3, p. 458a, 29 ff.; ἕνεκα τῆς σωτηρίας. In Zeno, too, one may read: τὸν δὲ ὕπνον γίνεσθαι ἐκλυομένου τοῦ αἰσθητικοῦ τόνου περὶ τὸ ἡγεμονικόν, Diog. L., VII, 158.

4. Disparagement of Sleep.

The disparagement of sleep in the philosophical tradition appears early. In Heracl. Fr., 73 (Diels, I, 167) sleep is used as a metaphor for the conduct of fools: οὐ δεῖ ὥσπερ καθεύδοντας ποιεῖν καὶ λέγειν. [13] If in Hom. the beneficial aspects of sleep are stressed (→ 545, 24 ff.), it can now be stated that in sleep the human νοῦς loses contact with its surroundings and even with its previous power of thought, Heracl. in Sext. Emp. Math., VII, 129 (Diels, I, 148, 10 ff.), or that the sleeper abandons the κοινὸς κόσμος and shuts himself up in his own world εἰς ἴδιον, Heracl. Fr., 89 (Diels, I, 171). For Prodicus Fr., 2 (Diels, II, 315, 8 ff.) sleep is a sign of inactivity and weakness; like drunkenness and gluttony it impairs thought, Diogenes of Apollonia in Theophr. De sensu, 44 (Diels, II, 56, 14 f.), cf. Democr. Fr., 212 (II, 188) on sleeping by day → lines 13 ff. Plat. demands that those who really want to live and think should cut down on sleep, for ὕπνος... πολὺς οὔτε τοῖς σώμασιν οὔτε ταῖς ψυχαῖς... ἁρμόττων ἐστίν, the sleeper is of no more use than the dead, Leg., VII, 808b-c; in sleep the θηριῶδές τε καὶ ἄγριον gains the upper hand over the λογιστικὸν καὶ ἥμερον, man becomes an arena of uncontrolled desires, Resp., IX, 571c, cf. VI, 503d; VII, 537b; IX, 572b. Stoicism speaks similarly of sleep. It robs man of half his life like a greedy creditor, Ariston in Plut. An aqua an ignis utilior, II, 12 (II, 958d). The philosopher's task is to watch on behalf of others ὑπερηγρύπνηκεν ὑπὲρ ἀνθρώπων, Epict. Diss., III, 22, 95. He must see to it ἵνα μηδ' ἐν ὕπνοις λάθῃ τις ἀνεξέταστος παρελθοῦσα φαντασία, III, 2, 5. Syncretistic religious lit. (→ 556, 9 ff.) can speak of ὕπνος ἄλογος

---

[11] In this light it could no longer be said that sleep is close to death → line 5 f. It is rather an indication whether dangerous illness is present or not → lines 10 ff.

[12] The theories of cooling of the body and flowing back of blood (→ lines 1 ff.) are discussed as the result rather than the cause of sleep in Aristot. De somno et vigilia, 3, p. 456a, 30 ff.

[13] Heracl. Fr., 75 (Diels, I, 168) can also call sleepers ἐργάτας... καὶ συνεργοὺς τῶν ἐν τῷ κόσμῳ γινομένων.

alongside μέθη and ἀγνωσία τοῦ θεοῦ, Corp. Herm., 1, 27. [14] Sleep belongs to the material world by which man is mastered κρατεῖται even though in himself he is ἄϋπνος ἀπὸ ἀϋπνου, "from a Father who needs no sleep," 1, 15, cf. 13, 4. This does not prevent the author of Poim. in 1, 1 from depicting the sleep τῶν σωματικῶν αἰσθήσεων, in which the διάνοια rises up to spiritual heights, as a preparation for receiving revelation → 550, 24 ff., cf. 1, 30. The view of Aristot. (→ 547, 16 ff.) is adopted in Stob. Ecl., I, 290, 23 ff. cf. Corp. Herm., 5, 6 f.

5. Sleep and Death.

If popular religion could only lament in face of death (→ III, 831, 5 ff.), philosophy stressed the nearness of death to sleep → 547, 5 f. Anaxag. in Stob. Ecl., IV, 1084, 4 f. (Diels, II, 14, 16): There are two διδασκαλίας ... θανάτου, τόν τε πρὸ τοῦ γενέσθαι χρόνον καὶ τὸν ὕπνον, and Heracl. Fr., 21 (Diels, I, 156, 2 f.): θάνατός ἐστιν ὁκόσα ἐγερθέντες ὁρέομεν, ὁκόσα δὲ εὕδοντες ὕπνος, cf. Aristot. Gen. An., V, 1, p. 778b, 29 f.: ὕπνος is the mean between τοῦ ζῆν καὶ τοῦ μὴ ζῆν, similarly Plat. Ap., 40c d. On the other hand pre-Hell. poetry only occasionally uses ὕπνος as a euphemism for death, [15] cf. Hom. Il., 11, 241: κοιμήσατο χάλκεον ὕπνον of the death of Iphidamas; Hes. Op., 116 of man's pleasant mode of death in the golden age: θνῆσκον δ' ὥς θ' ὕπνῳ δεδμημένοι.

Another picture is presented by the epigrams of the Hell. age, [16] cf. from the 2nd/ 1st cent. B.C.: τί πένθιμον ὕπνον ἰαύεις "why must thou sleep thy sorrowful slumber?" Epigr. Graec., 204, [17] from the 1st cent. A.D.: τὸν φθιμένων νήγρετον ὕπνον ἔχων "the sleep of the dead from which is no awaking," [18] cf. νήγρετον ὑπνώσας in Adaeus Anth. Graec., 7, 305, εὕδομες εὖ μάλα μακρὸν ἀτέρμονα νήγρετον ὕπνον, Moschus Bucolicus, 3, 104 (2nd cent. B.C.). [19] The sleep of death is sweet ἡδύς, Epigr. Graec., 312 (Smyrna, 1st/2nd cent. A.D.) [20] and brings forgetfulness ὕπνος ὁ λήθης, ibid., 223 (Miletus, 1st/2nd cent. A.D.). [21] With the statement that the sleep of death is end and dissolution [22] we find the idea that sleep is not just a euphemism for death but that there is an actual correspondence. On an epigram in Rome (1st/2nd cent. A.D.) the dead woman asks her spouse to say: Popilia sleeps οὐ θεμιτὸν γὰρ θνήσκειν τοὺς ἀγαθούς, ἀλλ' ὕπνον ἡδὺν ἔχειν, Epigr. Graec., 559. [23] The souls of the righteous live on: ὕπνος ἔχει

---

[14] Cf. E. Norden, Agnostos Theos (1913), 132 f.; Reitzenstein Poim., 241. On ἀγνωσία τοῦ θεοῦ and sobriety cf. 1 C. 15:34.

[15] For the history of this metaphysical identification in the class. and post-class. age cf. Ogle, 81-117; cf. Hoffmann, 186-190. κοιμάομαι is more widespread for the sleep of death, cf. Soph. El., 508 f. εὖτε γὰρ ὁ ποντισθεὶς Μυρτίλος ἐκοιμάθη. Cf. also κοιμητήριον "grave" and the Chr. def. in Chrys. De coemeterio et de cruce, 1 (MPG, 49 [1862], 393): διὰ τοῦτο καὶ αὐτὸς ὁ τόπος κοιμητήριον ὠνόμασται, ἵνα μάθῃς ὅτι οἱ τετελευτηκότες καὶ ἐνταῦθα κείμενοι οὐ τεθνήκασιν, ἀλλὰ κοιμῶνται καὶ καθεύδουσιν (cf. also Thes. Steph., V, s.v. κοιμητήριον) and κοίμησις "death," Sir. 46:19; 48:13; Audollent Def. Tab., 242, 30; cf. Radermacher, 108; Ogle, 88-114; → III, 14, n. 60.

[16] G. Kaibel, Epigr. Graec., 101 suspects syncretistic influences, esp. from the Phoenicians, cf. Ogle, 87, but P. Hoffmann, 188 f. takes a different view.

[17] Cf. E. Peek, Griech. Grabgedichte (1960), No. 438, 7; in the sleep of death the dead woman can refuse the drink of Lethe in Hades and thus remember her former happiness, lines 11 ff., cf. Peek, p. 320. This and the following inscr. are given so far as possible, acc. to Epigr. Graec. and Peek.

[18] Peek, No. 284, 2.

[19] U. v. Wilamowitz-Moellendorff, Bucolici Graeci (1905), 94.

[20] Peek, No. 391, 2, cf. 271, 8.

[21] Ibid., No. 334, 3.

[22] Ibid., No. 452, 1 ff. (Thracia, 2nd/3rd cent. A.D.), cf. 307, 4: ὕπνον ἔχουσα μακρόν (Thessaly, 2nd/3rd cent. A.D.).

[23] Ibid., No. 271, 7 f., cf. Callimachus (Anth. Graec., 7, 451).

σε... καὶ νέκυς οὐκ ἐγένου· εὔδεις δ' ὡς ἔτι ζῶν... ψυχαὶ γὰρ ζῶσιν τῶν ἄγαν εὐσεβέων, *ibid.*, 433 (2nd cent. A.D.). [24] The sleep of death brings redemption from the body and forgetting: ἀλγεινῶν λύσασα νόσων δέμας ἡδέι ὕπνῳ, λήθης δῶρα φέρουσ', for the ψυχή, the true I of the dead, leaves the body and mounts up to heaven, 312 (Smyrna, 1st/2nd cent. A.D.), [25] cf. the memorial inscr. of Antiochus I of Commagene (shortly before 31 B.C.), in which the soul goes on ahead to the throne of Zeus Oromasdos, while the body εἰς τὸν ἄπειρον αἰῶνα κοιμήσεται, Ditt. Or., I, 383, 40 ff. [26]

6. The God Hypnos.

The infrequent use of the metaphor of the sleep of death in the earlier period is perhaps connected with the mythological distinction between Ὕπνος and Θάνατος in popular religion. [27] Hom. already mentions a god Hypnos [28] (only Il., 14 and 16). He is the twin of Thanatos (→ III, 8, n. 2), has power over gods and men, Il., 14, 233 (→ 546, 6 f.), and can put even Zeus to sleep, Il., 14, 252. Acc. to Hes. Theog., 211 f., 758 f. he is the son of Nyx. In Soph. Phil., 827-9 the chorus of sailors invokes Hypnos and asks him to conjure away the sorrows of Philoctetes; [29] the respectful address runs: Ὕπνε... ὦναξ. To sleepers Hypnos imparts revelations, Luc. verae hist., II, 32. A cult of Hypnos in Troizen is attested only in Paus., II, 31, 3. An original belief in goblins and demons was perhaps changed by theological reflection into the idea of a god in the Gk. pantheon. [30] The iconography [31] of the god is varied and leaves many questions unsolved. There is often a link with Thanatos. Acc. to a version of the Endymion saga first found in Licymnius acc. to Athen., 13, 16 (564c), Hypnos loved the sleeper and allowed him to sleep with open eyes so as to be able to enjoy his countenance. This explains the saying Ἐνδυμίωνος ὕπνον καθεύδεις "thou sleepest with open eyes," acc. to Diogenianus Centuria, II, 48 (CPG, II, 25); Zenobius Centuria, III, 76 (CPG, I, 75). [32] For the rest

[24] Peek, No. 339.
[25] *Ibid.*, No. 391.
[26] Legend has it that the souls of many remarkable men could leave their bodies during life, e.g., Hermotimus of Clazomenai, who would fall into a sleep-like state when his soul left him to roam abroad and awaken when it returned, his body remaining unaffected, Apollonius Mirabilia, 3 (ed. O. Keller [1877], 44); cf. Plin. Hist. Nat., 7, 52, 174, or Aristeas, whose ψυχή flew out of his mouth in the form of a raven. Epimenides of Crete is supposed to have slept for 57 yrs. in a cave, Plin. Hist. Nat., 7, 52, 175, Diog. L., I, 109, being caught up to the gods in a dream during this period, Max. Tyr., 16, 1, cf. Suid., *s.v.* Ἐπιμενίδης: οὗ λόγος, ὡς ἐξίοι ἡ ψυχὴ ὁπόσον ἤθελε καιρόν, καὶ πάλιν εἰσῄει ἐν τῷ σώματι. Aristot.'s pupil Clearchus of Soli in his work Περὶ ὕπνου, which is mentioned in Jos. Ap., I, 176 and is close to occultism, tells of a magician who by a ψυχουλκὸς ῥάβδος takes the soul of a sleeper out of his body and causes it to rove abroad; Procl. in Rem. Publ., X, 614b c. (Kroll, II, 122), cf. H. Lewy, "Aristotle and the Jewish Sage acc. to Clearchus of Soli," HThR, 31 (1938), 205-235; F. Wehrli, *Die Schule d. Aristot. Klearchos* (1948), 47 f. On the problem cf. Nilsson, I², 618; Rohde, II, 91-99 with further examples. The basis of later Pythagorean and Orphic ideas is to be sought in these materials, Rohde, 99-102, cf. 413 f. On the gen. significance in religious psychology cf. W. Wundt, *Völkerpsychologie*, IV, 1² (1910), 254-261; G. van der Leeuw, *Phänomenologie d. Religion²* (1956), 326-337; for many instances from Judaism cf. E. L. Ehrlich, "Der Traum im Talmud," ZNW, 47 (1956), 134 f. with n. 4; → 553, 8 ff.
[27] Cf. O. Kern, *Die Religion d. Griechen*, I (1926), 262.
[28] Cf. B. Sauer, Art. "Hypnos," Roscher, I, 2, 2846-2851; Jolles, 323-9.
[29] On this cf. D. M. Jones, "The Sleep of Philoctetes," Class. Rev., 63 (1949), 83-5.
[30] Sauer, *op. cit.*, 2848.
[31] Cf. H. Schrader, *Hypnos, Winckelmann-Programm d. Archäol. Gesellschaft zu Berlin* (1926), 85; Jolles, 326-9; Winneberg, *passim;* bibl. Roscher, I, 2, 2848-2851.
[32] Cf. Sauer, *op. cit.*, 2848; E. Bethe, Art. "Endymion," Pauly-W., 5 (1905), 2557-2560; O. Gruppe, *Griech. Mythologie u. Religionsgeschichte*, Hndbch. kl. AW, V, 2 (1906), I, 280, n. 5; L. Lerat, "Trois petits bronces gallo-romains du Musée de Besançon," *Gallia*, 8

Hypnos is often a rival of Hermes ὑπνοδότης, who is viewed only as a bringer of sleep, not as sleep personified. [33]

B. The Word Group in the Septuagint and Judaism.

1. In the LXX ὕπνος occurs primarily (21 times) for Hbr. שֵׁנָה with the subsidiary forms שֵׁינָה Sir. 40:5; (42:9?), שְׁנָא, שְׁנָת [34] and once Aram. שְׁנָה. Conversely שֵׁנָה, שְׁנָת are always transl. by ὕπνος or the verb ὑπνόω except for Prv. 24:33 and perhaps 6:10, where LXX has νυστάζω. The related verb יָשֵׁן "to sleep" is transl. 13 times by ὑπνόω [35] (including Sir. 46:20), 4 by καθεύδω, 1 κοιμάομαι. Even more exclusive is the adj. יָשֵׁן, in Gk. ὕπνος twice and ὑπνόω 3 times. Finally ὑπνόω is used 17 times for יָשֵׁן, יָשַׁן or שֵׁנָה but only twice for לִין (Cod B Ju. 19:4 ηὐλίσθησαν for ὕπνωσαν) and once each for מוּת Sir. 46:20, נוּם and שָׁאַן. One may thus see that the root ὑπν- in Gk. corresponds almost exactly to the root יָשֵׁן. But it goes further. ἐν ὕπνῳ and καθ' ὕπνον occur 11 times for חֲלוֹם (including Sir. 40:6) and once for the verb חלם. For these Hbr. terms ἐνύπνιον and derivates are the equivalents in most cases, 57 out of 60. ὕπνος is also used 4 times for חָזוֹן or חֵזוּ and once for נוּמָה at Sir. 31:1; this is ὑπνώδης at Prv. 23:21. These shifting relations show that in Hbr. the "dream" is more sharply differentiated from "sleep" (יָשֵׁן[י]) and derivates) by terms of the root חלם than it is in LXX Gk. — this is because of the function of the dream as a means of revelation, → V, 230, 4 ff. In LXX Gk. the word almost always used for dream, along with ἐν ὕπνῳ and καθ' ὕπνον, [36] is ἐνύπνιον, which as a development from the stem expresses the connection with sleep.

With the gen. use of ὕπνος, cf. ὅταν δῷ τοῖς ἀγαπητοῖς αὐτοῦ ὕπνον [37] "he gives it his beloved in sleep" ψ 126:2, ἵνα τί ὑπνοῖς, κύριε ψ 43:24, ὕπνος is twice used in later texts as a euphemism for coitus: ἐκ γὰρ ἀνόμων ὕπνων τέκνα γεννώμενα, Wis. 4:6, cf. 7:2 We often read of revelatory sleep → III, 434, 38 ff.. Behind Jacob's vision in Gn. 28:10 ff. some see an ancient Canaanite incubation concept, [38] cf. Solomon's dream in the Gibeon temple: ὤφθη κύριος τῷ Σαλωμων ἐν ὕπνῳ τὴν νύκτα, 3 Βασ. 3:5. [39] If, esp. in the Wisdom lit., the dream is often regarded as a divine message, [40] cf. ἐν ὕπνῳ and καθ' ὕπνον in Gn. 20:3, 6; 31:10 f., 24; 40:9; 41:17, 22; Nu. 12:6; 24:4, 16 (→ 545, 13 ff.); [41]

(1950), 95-104; L. Curtius, "Redeat narratio," Mitteilungen d. Deutschen Archäol. Instituts Berlin, 4 (1951), 10-34. Cf. Balaam's revelatory sleep ἀποκεκαλυμμένοι οἱ ὀφθαλμοὶ αὐτοῦ Nu. 24:4, 16 → 550, 24 ff.

[33] Cf. G. Krüger, "Hermes u. Hypnos," Jbch. f. Classische Philologie, 9 (1863), 289-301; Jolles, 325; Nilsson, I², 509 f.

[34] Cf. Ges.-K. § 80g: subsidiary poetic form.

[35] ψ 120:4 א reads ἐξυπνόω. On the terminology in gen. cf. Thomson, 421-4.

[36] Never ὄναρ and ὄνειρος only at Wis. 18:17, 19; 2 Macc. 15:11; 4 Macc. 6:5.

[37] On the adv. use of שֵׁנָא cf. F. Bussby, "A note on שֵׁנָא in Ps. 127:2," JThSt, 35 (1934), 306 f., who sees a euphemism for sexual intercourse → lines 22 ff.

[38] With κοιμάω and καθεύδω one finds ἐνυπνιάσθη in v. 12 and ἐξηγέρθη Ιακωβ ἀπὸ τοῦ ὕπνου αὐτοῦ in v. 16.

[39] On incubation in the OT cf. Ehrlich, 13-55 where instances are discussed and a bibl. is given.

[40] Ehrlich, 123; G. v. Rad, Theol. d. AT, II⁴ (1965), 318 f., 323 f. In the Pentateuch E esp. ref. to revelations in dreams, cf. O. Procksch, Das nordhebräische Sagenbuch. Die Elohimquelle (1906), 195-7; H. Holzinger, Einl. in d. Hexateuch, I (1893), 207-9; Ehrlich, 134-6.

[41] The verb נפל, which is used in six of seven passages with תַּרְדֵּמָה "deep sleep" cf. Gn. 2:21; 1 S. 26:12 or "sleep of revelation" Gn. 15:12, is transl. ἐν ὕπνῳ with ref. to receiving revelation in Nu. 24:4, 16. One sees the pt. of תַּרְדֵּמָה in the description of Balaam's revelatory sleep, cf. the transl. θάμβος in 1 S. 26:12 (→ III, 5, 27 ff.), ἔκστασις Gn. 2:21; 15:12 (→ II, 450, 23 ff.; 459, 22 ff.), and on this G. Bertram, "Vom Wesen d. Septuaginta-Frömmigkeit," Die Welt d. Orients, II (1954-59), 275; Thomson, 422 f.

Da. 4:10; 7:2; 9:21 etc., it should not be overlooked that the dream can be sharply rejected as a means of revelation and equated with false prophecy Ἰερ. 23:25: ἃ προφητεύουσιν... ψευδῆ λέγοντες Ἠνυπνιασάμην ἐνύπνιον, cf. v. 32. Here dreams as θελήματα καρδίας v. 26 (→ 552, 24 ff.) are of little worth compared to the "word" דָּבָר of God, cf. Ἰερ. 34(27):9; 36(29):8; Dt. 13:2 ff..; 40:5 ff. etc. [42]

If the stem ὑπν- is linked to sloth in Prv. 6:4, 9 and sin in Ju. 16:14, 20 (→ III, 434, 22 ff.) and is a figure of the eschatological destruction of God's enemies in Is. 29:7 f., it also has metaphorical significance in the occasional OT ref. to the sleep of death, [43] cf. Ἰερ. 28(51):39: καὶ μεθύσω αὐτούς, ὅπως καρωθῶσιν καὶ ὑπνώσωσιν ὕπνον αἰώνιον καὶ οὐ μὴ ἐγερθῶσιν, cf. v. 57 ᾽ΑΘ or Job 14:12: ἄνθρωπος δὲ κοιμηθεὶς οὐ μὴ ἀναστῇ... καὶ οὐκ ἐξυπνισθήσονται ἐξ ὕπνου αὐτῶν. [44] Sleep also denotes the imperfect state of the soul (→ 547, 23 ff.). Thus king Antiochus, who tries to force the Jews to eat swine's flesh, asks the aged Eleazar: οὐκ ἐξυπνώσεις [45] ἀπὸ τῆς φλυάρου φιλοσοφίας ὑμῶν; 4 Macc. 5:11. When Sir. 22:9 teaches: συγκολλῶν ὄστρακον ὁ διδάσκων μωρόν, ἐξεγείρων καθεύδοντα ἐκ βαθέος ὕπνου, this is more than a mere comparison: The fool is in large measure a sleeper.

2. Later Jewish writings offer further nuances. The πνεῦμα τοῦ ὕπνου of Test. R. 3:1, 7 is puzzling and obscured by interpolations. It can be the spirit of creation and as such both the transport of nature and also the figure of death, or it may be the spirit of error πλάνης καὶ φαντασίας v. 7. Test. S. 4:9 says of envy: ἐν ταραχῇ διυπνίζει τὸν νοῦν. There is also ref. to the sleep of death: ἐκοιμήθη (v. ὕπνωσεν) ὕπνον αἰώνιον, Test. Iss. 9:9. The death of the patriarchs is repeatedly described in the words: ἐκοιμήθη ὕπνῳ καλῷ Test. Zeb. 10:6; Jos. 20:4; Β. 12:2 (c); cf. D. 7:1; A. 8:1. [46] ἐξυπνίζω thus comes to denote the apoc. raising of the dead in Test. Jud. 25:4 → 555, 10 ff. [47] Apoc. [48] develops the idea of the eschatological sleep of death, cf. Eth. En. 49:3; 91:10; 92:3; 100:5; S. Bar. 30:1; 36:11, cf. 11:4; 21:24. The dualistic anthropology which the encounter with Hellenism (→ 548, 26 ff.) presupposes [49] lies behind the ref. to the eschatological sleep of souls in 4 Esr. 7:91 (requiescunt), cf. v. 80, 88, even to the pt. of explicit depictions of the intermediate state. [50] If the state between death and the eschaton

---

[42] Cf. Ehrlich, 155-170; → V, 228, 40 ff.

[43] E.g., 1 K. 1:21; 2:10; Ez. 31:18; cf. Ogle, 89-93; Hoffmann, 190-5, who think this was a common euphemism in the ancient Orient, 190 (→ n. 16). Ogle, 89 rightly emphasises the distinction from the Hell. view.

[44] Cf. Da. 12:2; Job 3:13; ψ 12:4; 87:6; Sir. 46:20 (= מוּת). ψ 3:6 is first taken to ref. to the sleep of death in 1 Cl., 26, 2; Just. Apol., I, 38, 5; Dial, 97, 1.

[45] Surprisingly (ἐ)ξύπνιος means "clever" in modern Gk.

[46] R. H. Charles Test. XII thinks ὕπνῳ is always due to a misreading of שֵׁיבָה "age" (Iss. 7:9; B. 12:2 acc. to most witnesses) as שֵׁינָה "sleep" and he suggests γήρει. But the witness in 5 passages is not clear enough to support this. Cf. also G. Delling, "Jüdische Lehre u. Frömmigkeit in d. Paralipomena Jer.," BZAW, 100 (1967), 30 f.; cf. Sib., 1, 70 f. 301. 370 f.

[47] Cf. Michel, 287, n. 4.

[48] These ref. are important even though linguistically there is no connection with the stem ὑπν-. Only the text of Eth. En. 100:5 is known through discovery of the Gk., cf. C. Bonner, "The Last Chapters of En. in Gk.," Stud. and Documents, 8 (1937), 50: καὶ ἀπ᾽ ἐκείνου (sc. from the Day of Judgment on) ὑπνώσουσ[ι]ν ⟨οἱ⟩ εὐσεβεῖς ὕπνον ἡδύν, καὶ οὐκ ἔσται οὐκέτι ἐκφοβῶν αὐτούς.

[49] Cf. Thomson, 425 f. 428 f. 432 f. This Pythagorean-Orphic influence (→ n. 26) meant that the separation of the soul from the body in sleep could be asserted in the Jewish sphere too, cf. first Midr. Ps. on 11:7 (ed. S. Buber [1892], 102); Ep. Ar., 213-6; cf. Ehrlich, op. cit. (→ n. 26), 134 f. On the relation between many Talmud statements and Artemidorus' Book of Dreams (→ 546, 35 ff.) cf. 145 with bibl. → V, 234, 12 ff. The same views may be found in the Koran, cf. Sura 6, 60; 39, 43; S. Fraenkel, "Miscellen zum Koran," ZDMG, 56 (1902), 71 f.; Thomson, 425 f.

[50] Cf. Volz Esch., 256-272; PREl, 32 (p. 233); Ps.-Menand., 13 (ed. J. Land, Anecdota Syriaca, I, 1852): Living in the underworld involves sleep, cf. Riessler, 1048.

could thus be called sleep, it was natural to use sleep as a figure for the time of this aeon, [51] 4 Esr. 7:31 f., cf. PREI, 34 (p. 253 f.): "Sleep in the night is like this world and waking in the morning is like the world to come." Closely connected with this is the dualism of light and darkness for the men of this and the coming aeon, cf. Eth. En. 41:8; 108:11 ff. → VII, 431, 3 ff.; 433, 17 ff. [52] OT ideas of dreams as means of revelation are naturally found in even greater variety in post-bibl. Judaism → V, 231, 20 ff. [53]

3. In Philo ὕπνος [54] first means sleep as a natural process → 545, 21 ff. It is God's gift, Spec. Leg., I, 298. Familiar Hell. observations (→ 547, 23 ff.) are used when correspondence is seen between sleeping and waking and the resting or activity of the higher or lower forces of the soul, Leg. All., II, 30: ἥ τε τῶν αἰσθήσεων ἐγρήγορσις ὕπνος ἐστὶ (τοῦ) νοῦ ἥ τε τοῦ νοῦ ἐγρήγορσις ἀπραξία τῶν αἰσθήσεων, cf. Som., I, 80; Rer. Div. Her., 257; Leg. All., III, 183 (etym. ὕπνος — ὕφεσις "relaxation"). The word is often used to characterise those far from knowledge: ὁ δὲ βαθὺς καὶ διωλύγιος ὕπνος, ᾧ πᾶς κατέχεται φαῦλος, τὰς μὲν ἀληθεῖς καταλήψεις ἀφαιρεῖται, ψευδῶν δὲ εἰδώλων καὶ ἀβεβαίων φαντασμάτων ἀναπίμπλησι τὴν διάνοιαν..., Som., II, 162 (→ 551, 11 ff.), cf. οἷς πᾶς ὁ βίος ὕπνος καὶ ἐνύπνιόν ἐστι, Som., I, 121; ἀοκνότατον (with no hesitation) γὰρ ὁ ἐπιστήμης ἔρως, ἐχθρὸς μὲν ὕπνου, Ebr., 159, cf. Sobr., 5. In the paraphrase of Balaam's second oracle (Nu. 23:24) in Vit. Mos., I, 284: οὐ τρέψεται πρὸς ὕπνον, ἀλλ' ἐγρηγορὼς τὸν ἐπινίκιον ᾄσεται ὕπνον, sleep, which originally concludes the victorious day, is something which must be repelled as a last assault of the enemy so that the victory may be completed in the victory hymn. When Abraham comes to believe, he opens ὥσπερ ἐκ βαθέος ὕπνου the eyes of his soul and sees pure light, Abr., 70. Philo is a good Hellenist in thus depreciating sleep → 547, 23 ff. The OT legacy finds expression in his many ref. to visions (→ V, 231, 23 ff.). As in Artemid. (→ 546, 35 ff.) the ἐνύπνια are here disparaged compared to the ὄναρ, while in good Gk. both can be described as αἱ ἐν τοῖς ὕπνοις φαντασίαι (→ 546, 32 f.; → V, 231, 29 ff.), Som., I, 1; II, 20 and 137; Jos., 126 etc. ἐνύπνια belong to the sphere of the νοῦς which destroys truth, Leg. All., III, 229; cf. Migr. Abr., 19 etc. The distinction from ὀνείρατα may be seen plainly in what is said about the revelatory philosophical dreams of the Therapeutae in Vit. Cont., 26, cf. also τῶν θεοπέμπτων ὀνείρων in Som., I, 1 and also the title, which faithfully renders the intentions of Philo's two works on dreams which have survived → V, 231, 36 ff. ἐνύπνια can sometimes be a figure for the fact that life itself is like a dream: οὕτω καὶ τῶν παρ' ἡμῖν ἐγρηγορότων αἱ φαντασίαι τοῖς ἐνυπνίοις ἐοίκασιν, Jos., 126. [55] Philo never uses sleep for death → 548, 8 ff. But the nearness of the two may be seen in Leg. All., II, 27: Μωυσῆς φοβηθείς, μή ποτε ὁ νοῦς μὴ μόνον κοιμηθῇ, ἀλλὰ καὶ τελείως ἀποθάνῃ.

---

[51] In contrast to the sleep of this world are the angels who never sleep but praise God continually, Eth. En. 39:12 f.; 40:2; 61:12 and keep watch over His throne, 71:7 cf. Dob. Th., 186, n. 4. The monastic orders of the Acoemeti deriving from Messilinianism imitated this activity [Dihle].

[52] Cf. O. Böcher, Der joh. Dualismus im Zshg. d. nachbibl. Judt. (1965), 96-108; S. Aalen, Die Begriffe "Licht" u. "Finsternis" im AT, im Spätjudt. u. im Rabbinismus (1951), 158-236 and passim; E. Lövestam, "Spiritual Wakefulness in the NT," Lunds Univ. Årsskrift, NF, I, 55, 3 (1963), 8-24.

[53] On the Talmud cf. Ehrlich, op. cit., 133-145.

[54] With prep. we usually find the plur., esp. in relation to dreams, cf. ἐν βαθεῖ ὕπνῳ Philo Jos., 140 with ἐν τοῖς βαθέσιν ὕπνοις Migr. Abr., 190; καθ' ὕπνον Abr., 154 with κατὰ τοὺς ὕπνους Det. Pot. Ins., 172 (→ n. 3). Of verbs for sleeping Philo has ὑπνόω and καθεύδω only twice each; much more common is κοιμάομαι, which in similar contexts is used like ὕπνος.

[55] On the connection of this view with the ideas of Heraclitus cf. H. v. Arnim, "Quellenstud. zu Philo v. Alex.," Philologische Untersuchungen, 11 (1888), 94-6.

4. Joseph speaks ordinarily of sleep in Ant., 6, 37. 314. 363; 7, 48; ὕπνος βαθύς is a deathlike sleep, 5, 193 cf. 208. 4, 269 mentions the Jewish principle [56] that a poor man's cloak should not be pledged because it serves as a cover εἰς ὕπνον. Ref. is made in Ap., I, 176 to Aristot.'s work on sleep → 546, 32 ff. Philo's Hell. criticism of ἐνύπνια does not occur in Jos. → V, 232, 43 ff. The dream revelations of the OT are cheerfully accepted in Ant., 2, 10 f. 64. 80. 212; 5, 215; 7, 147, cf. ὄψεις ἐνυπνίων θεασάμενος of Pharaoh's dreams, 2, 75; ἐνύπνια of Isis, Ap., I, 294. 298. 312; the counsel of an ἐνύπνιον can be wrong, but the Jews do not cease from φυγεῖν εἰς ἐνύπνια, Ap., I, 207. The Orphic idea of the separation of the soul from the body in sleep (→ n. 26) is found in Bell., 7, 349 f.: Since souls do not have to sleep with the mortal body they can θεῷ ὁμιλοῦσαι κατὰ συγγένειαν predict the future; τί δὴ δεῖ δεδιέναι θάνατον τὴν ἐν ὕπνῳ γινομένην ἀνάπαυσιν ἀγαπῶντας; [57] sleep is thus a prototype of death.

C. The Word Group in the New Testament.

1. Words of the stem ὑπν- are used first for the natural process and state of sleep. Thus sleep is the locus and presupposition of a divine vision: ἐγερθεὶς δὲ Ἰωσὴφ ἀπὸ τοῦ ὕπνου ἐποίησεν ὡς προσέταξεν αὐτῷ ὁ ἄγγελος κυρίου, Mt. 1:24. ὕπνος here means sleep, not dream (→ 552, 24 ff.), for which Mt. has the stereotyped κατ' ὄναρ (→ V, 235, 3 ff. with n. 50), Mt. 1:20; 2:12, 13, 19, 22; 27:19. In Lk. 8:23 Jesus sleeps in the boat with the disciples: πλεόντων δὲ αὐτῶν ἀφύπνωσεν, before the storm breaks. This phrase rationalises somewhat the point of Mk. 4:38 and Mt. 8:24, where Jesus' sleeping (καθεύδω) during the storm is regarded as a sign of His dominance over the forces of chaos. [58] Later reflection took up this theme of the sleep of Jesus → 556, 5 f. There is an ordinary reference to the awakening of the Philippian jailor (ἔξυπνος δὲ γενόμενος Ac. 16:27), who was jolted out of sleep by the midnight earthquake and the accompanying phenomena.

2. It is in keeping with the reserved evaluation of dreams in the NT (→ V, 235, 16 ff.) that the group ἐνύπνιον "vision" and ἐνυπνιάζομαι "to have visions" occurs only twice. Jl. 2:28 is quoted in Ac. 2:17. [59] The parallelism of ἐνύπνια and ὁράσεις (→ V, 370, 19 ff.) shows that the dreams are revelations which Luke thinks are given with the new preaching given by the Spirit in prophecy and speaking with tongues. [60] In contrast is the soberness of Jd. 8, where the libertinistic and gnostic opponents who are under attack are denounced as οὗτοι ἐνυπνιαζόμενοι. In view

---

[56] Cf. Str.-B., I, 343 f.

[57] On the underlying dualistic anthropology cf. Bell., 3, 372-5 and esp. in 7, 340-358 the war speech of Eleazar, who calls on the Jews of Massada to sacrifice futile life, cf. 419 etc.

[58] In exposition cf. Loh. Mk., ad loc.; G. Bornkamm, "Die Sturmstillung im Mt.-Ev.," Überlieferung u. Auslegung im Mt.-Ev., Wissenschaftliche Monographien z. AT u. NT, I[4] (1965), 48-53; H. J. Held, "Mt. als Interpret der Wundergeschichten," ibid., 253 f.; H. Conzelmann, "Die Mitte d. Zeit," Beiträge z. hist. Theol., 17[5] (1964), 42 f.; W. Grundmann, Das Ev. nach Lk., Theol. Handkomment. z. NT, 3[2] (1964), ad loc. → III, 436, 8 ff.; VII, 199, 10 ff. The motif of the sleep of assurance during a storm also occurs in Jon. 1:5 f. Cf. D. W. Nowack, Die Kleinen Propheten, Handkomm. AT, III, 4 (1897), 178; cf. Ac. 27:14 ff.

[59] On the text E. Haenchen, "Schriftzitate u. Textüberlieferung in d. Ag.," Gott u. Mensch (1965), 166; ἐνυπνίοις does not occur in D; → V, 235, n. 51. In interpretation cf. U. Wilckens, "Die Missionsreden d. Ag.," Wissenschaftliche Monographien z. AT u. NT, 5[2] (1963), 32 f.

[60] Cf. the many visions depicted by Lk. at decisive pts., Ac. 9:10; 10:10; 11:5. Paul's dreams are recounted in Ac. 16:9; 18:9; 23:11; 27:23, though Paul himself does not associate revelations with dreams, cf. Gl. 2:2. The stem ὑπν- is for him too closely riveted to this aeon → 554, 20 ff.

of the brevity of the expression used in contrast to the description of the excesses of the adversaries, and in view of the predicative linking of the participle with the subject, we cannot agree with much modern exegesis [61] in seeing a reference to special ecstatic or visionary experiences. In accordance with a common pattern (→ 547, 23 ff.; 551, 11 ff.; 552, 12 ff.) what we have here is a metaphorical depiction of the state of the libertines as visionary and noctural blindness to the truth of faith → VI, 262, 36 ff. [62]

3. A similar idea lies behind the fact that the intimate disciples were drunk with sleep (ἦσαν βεβαρημένοι ὕπνῳ Lk. 9:32 peculiar to Lk.) on the Mount of Transfiguration → 556, 6 ff.; → III, 436, 4 ff. [63] Luke uses this concept on the one hand to explain the confusion of Peter (Mk. 9:6 par. Lk. 9:33) when the appearances vanished and on the other to make the transfiguration an anticipation of Gethsemane with the help of the deliberate distinction between the rapture of Jesus and the sphere of the stupefied disciples (cf. Lk. 22:39 ff.). This is then given emphasis by the passion prediction in 9:31. [64] The sleep motif sheds light on the episode of the sleep of the νεανίας [65] ὀνόματι Εὔτυχος, ... καταφερόμενος ὕπνῳ βαθεῖ ... κατενεχθεὶς ἀπὸ τοῦ ὕπνου, Ac. 20:9. [66] The story recounts an actual occurrence, [67] which explains the restraint of the author in face of the raising of the dead. [68] The idea of man's sinful stupor in relation to salvation might account for the reference to sleep along with the raising again → lines 4 ff. [69] The apocalyptic call to watch in R. 13:11 f.: ... ὅτι ὥρα ἤδη ὑμᾶς ἐξ ὕπνου ἐγερθῆναι ... ἡ νὺξ προέκοψεν, ἡ δὲ ἡμέρα ἤγγικεν, very plainly uses awaking from sleep as a metaphor for casting off bondage to the old aeon. [70] The antithesis of night and day, sleep and waking, darkness and light, drunkenness and sobriety which Paul adopts here finds a direct model in the eschatological imagery of the speculative and apocalyptic utterances of later Judaism (→ 551, 12 ff., 25 ff.; 552, 8 ff.) and is also common in Hellen-

---

[61] Cf. Kn. Pt., ad loc.; Wnd. Kath. Br., ad loc.

[62] So older exposition, cf. C. F. Keil, Commentar über d. Br. d. Pt. u. Jd. (1883) on Jd. 8; W. M. L. de Wette, Kurze Erklärung d. Br. d. Pt., Jd. u. Jk., Kurzgefasstes Exeget. Hndbch. z. NT, III, 1³ (1865) on Jd. 8; F. Spitta, Der zweite Br. d. Pt. u. d. Br. d. Jd. (1885) on Jd. 8.

[63] Cf. G Bertram, "Die Leidensgeschichte Jesu u der Christuskult," FRL, 32 (1922), 45; on the dream hypothesis J. Blinzler, "Die nt.lichen Berichte über die Verklärung Jesu," NTAbh, 17, 4 (1937), 106 f.

[64] Cf. Conzelmann, op. cit. (→ n. 58), 183 f. On Lk. 22:39 ff. cf. the analysis in T. Lescow, "Jesus in Gethsemane bei Lk. u. im Hb.," ZNW, 58 (1967), 215-239; on Lk. 22:45 cf. T. Boman, Die Jesusüberlieferung im Lichte d. neueren Volkskunde (1967), 208-211, who tries to differentiate various strata of the tradition by means of the ref. to the disciples' sleep.

[65] Cf. παῖς in v. 12; Haench. Ag.¹⁴, ad loc.

[66] The two statements are a kind of escalation suggested by the ἐπὶ πλεῖον of Paul's preaching, though the late reception of Ac. (cf. M. Dibelius, "Der Text d. Ag.," Aufsätze z. Ag.," FRL, 60⁴ [1961], 80 f.) gives colour to the theory of doublets (Pr. Ag. and Haench. Ag.¹⁴, ad loc.). If this is true the second statement has a better claim to be regarded as original in view of the non-class. ἀπό with the pass., as against Pr. Ag., ad loc., cf. the emendation in DH ψ 33 al.

[67] Cf. Dibelius, op. cit., 22 f.

[68] Cf. Haench. Ag.¹⁴ on the story. The differences from 1 K. 17:21 f.; 2 K. 4:34 ff.; Ac. 9:36 ff. are palpable for all the common features. Another pt. as compared with similar reports in the Gospels and Ac. is that death is due here to the youth's own negligence.

[69] The death is a real one, Haench. Ag.,¹⁴ ad loc.; H. Conzelmann, Die Ag., Hndbch. NT, 7 (1963), ad loc.

[70] Mi. R.¹³, ad loc.; Lövestam, op. cit. (→ n. 52), 25-45; H. Braun, Qumran und d. NT, I (1966), 185 f.

istic religion (→ 547, 43 ff.; 556, 9 ff.). For this reason R. 13:11 is not to be viewed merely as a reference to sleep as a figure of the time of uncertainty and watching, as, e.g., in Mt. 25:5 → III, 436, 41 ff. Here as in 1 Th. 5:4-8 the Christian brother must let himself be addressed in terms of his attachment to the world. The command to watch, with ἀγρυπνέω (→ 545, 16 ff.), occurs in other apocalyptic passages too, Mk. 13:33; Lk. 21:36; Eph. 6:18, and cf. also Hb. 13:17 → II, 338, 21 ff. In the list of Paul's sufferings ἐν ἀγρυπνίαις (2 C. 6:5; 11:27) occurs as a metaphor for the unwearying labours of the apostle; the deeply embedded disparagement of sleep may be detected here → 553, 31 ff.

4. The verses Jn. 11:11-13 undoubtedly play on the metaphor of the sleep of death. As already in Mk. 5:39 and par. (καθεύδω) what we have here is not just sleep as a euphemism for death → 548, 9 ff. The expression ἵνα ἐξυπνίσω αὐτόν (v. 11) presupposes an apocalyptic heritage → 551, 23 ff. [71] Just before the Evangelist has Jesus make the decisive statement (v. 4) that the illness of Lazarus will not lead to his death; the ambiguous κεκοίμηται in v. 11 (→ III, 14, n. 60) takes up this thought and in the typical style of the Gospel points us to the deeper background of actual death (v. 13 f.; on v. 17 and 39 → 134, 3 ff.) as a reality which is so only in appearance face to face with Jesus. [72] In v. 12 f. we have a superficial mis-understanding [73] on the part of the disciples. [74] In the interpolated v. 13 with its unique double construction περὶ τῆς κοιμήσεως τοῦ ὕπνου, "the rest which is sleep," [75] the idea of the sleep of death stands in stark contrast to the ordinary use of sleep. The theological statement which relativises the power of death by the reality of salvation moves on from the OT and apocalyptic basis beyond the asser-tions of Hellenistic religion, not using these to embellish the inevitable state of death (→ 548, 15 ff.) but proclaiming the basic powerlessness of death in the light of the resurrection → line 32 f.; V, 880, 38 ff.

D. The Word Group in the Early Church and Gnosticism.

The noun does not occur at all in the post-apost. fathers. The verb is found in 1 Cl., 26, 2 quoting Ps. 3: ἐκοιμήθην καὶ ὕπνωσα· ἐξηγέρθην, ὅτι σὺ μετ' ἐμοῦ εἶ with ref. to the sleep of death. Since καθεύδω does not occur in the post-apost. fathers, κοι-μάομαι and κοίμησις are the other words for "to sleep," both predominantly with ref. to death. The apoc. images of day and night, sleeping and waking, are found in connec-tion with the resurrection (→ lines 10 ff.) in 1 Cl., 24, 3, cf. 26, 2 while we have the common Hell. euphemism in 1 Cl., 44, 2; Ign. R., 4, 2; Herm. v., 3, 5, 1 (2 vl.); 11, 3; m., 4, 4, 1; s., 9, 15, 6; 16, 3. 5. 7. There is seldom ref. to natural sleep. [76] Compounds are

---

[71] Michel, 285-7.
[72] On the ambivalence of Johannine sayings cf. Bultmann J. on 3:3, n. 2.
[73] As against Bultmann J., 304, n. 6 this is a genuine Johannine misunderstanding, for the disciples did not know the eschatological background of the image, cf. O. Cullmann, "Der joh. Gebrauch doppeldeutiger Ausdrücke als Schlüssel zum Verständnis d. vierten Ev.," Vorträge u. Aufsätze, 1925-1962 (1966), 185, n. 13.
[74] Even if one cannot agree with Michel, 289 that the idea of the eschatological sleep of death was gen. known to primitive Christianity (cf. in criticism Hoffmann, 202 f.), in the light of v. 11 there is an obvious nearness to apoc. concepts → 551, 23 ff. M. Meinertz, "Theol. d. NT, II" in Die Hl. Schrift des NT übersetzt u. erklärt, Ergänzungsband, II (1950), 220-222, finds the Jewish idea of sleep in the intermediate state in the NT too, but → I, 148, 11 ff.
[75] Cf. Radermacher, 108, though he does not think the v. is an interpolation.
[76] So Herm. v., 2, 4, 1; s., 9, 11, 3. 6 (omittit vl.).

ἀφύπνωσα in connection with the sleep of revelation, Herm. v., 1, 1, 3, ἐπικαθυπνόω of the sleep of sin, Barn., 4, 13 ἀγρυπνία of watchful care, Barn., 21, 7. The use in the NT apocr. is for the most part a considered one. The disciples' sleep in Andrew's boat with Jesus miraculously steering (Act. Andr. et Matth. 8, p. 75, 10, cf. 16, p. 84, 7 f.) seems to be an example of trust in Jesus. Jesus' sleep in the boat (→ 553, 19 ff.) is seen as a test. In Act. Joh. 97 (p. 199, 8 f.) the theme of demonic drunkenness with sleep is used to explain the flight of the disciples at the arrest → 554, 8 ff. [77] Specific Chr. ref. to the sleep of death is found in the question of the heavenly voice to the risen Lord: ἐκήρυξας τοῖς κοιμωμένοις; Ev. Pt. 41. The Gnostic idea of sleep as ignorance and self-forgetfulness plays a role esp. in the pearl song [78] of Act. Thom. When the king's son in Egypt forgets his task and falls into a deep sleep εἰς ὕπνον κατηνέχθην βαθύν (Act. Thom. 109, p. 221, 11 f.) from which he is aroused only by a message from home: ἀνάστηθι καὶ ἀνάνηψον ἐξ ὕπνου (110, p. 221, 21 f., cf. 111, p. 222, 8; 223, 1), so that he can execute his task and return to his native court, [79] this image of the descent [80] into matter [81] and the sleep of oblivion means that a concept of religious syncretism (→ 547, 43 ff.) which has an established place in dualistic soteriology has been adopted into Chr. Gnosticism, cf. Act. Thom. 60 (p. 177, 9); 66 (p. 182, 17 - 183, 1), where the antithesis between the ὕπνος of men and the Lord ἄϋπνος ὤν (→ 548, 1 ff.) is underlined, similarly Act. Joh. 21 (p. 162, 20 f.). The image of sleep is used to express the hostile things of the κόσμος and of ignorance of God which one must leave like a dream in the night, Ev. Veritatis 29, 1 - 30, 11, [82] cf. Apocr. Johannis 58, 18 (p. 156); [83] Sophia Jes. Christi (→ n. 83) 120, 2 (p. 200); Pist. Soph. 111 (p. 183, 29 ff.); Lidz. Ginza R., 181, 31 ff.; L., 485, 10 ff. As drunkenness etc., sleep is a sign of man's bondage to the world. [84] He belongs to the darkness which light confronts → 552, 3 ff. [85] He is thus in the sphere of death, cf. Lidz. Joh., 168, 6 f.: "The mystery of death is sleep." Outside these dualistic concepts of the sleep of the soul the NT idea of death as sleep up to the resurrection of the dead may be seen in the description of graves as κοιμητήρια (→ n. 15) and in a theological view of death which Chrys. De coemeterio et de cruce, 1 (MPG, 49 [1862], 394) puts as follows: Since Christ died for the life of the world, we no longer call death θάνατος but ὕπνος καὶ κοίμησις. [86]

Balz

---

[77] Lines 2-7 are by Bertram.

[78] In criticism of the title cf. A. Adam, "Die Ps. des Thomas u. d. Perlenlied als Zeugnisse vorchr. Gnosis," ZNW Beih., 24 (1959), 48; A. F. J. Klijn, "The So-called Hymn of the Pearl," *Vigiliae Christianae*, 14 (1960), 154-164.

[79] On the influence of such ideas on the 13th cent. Patarenes cf. F. C. Conybeare, "The Idea of Sleep in the 'Hymn of the Soul,'" JThSt, 6 (1905), 609 f.

[80] For the exposition of the prince's journey as the way of the soul cf. Klijn, op. cit., 157-164. C. Colpe, "Die religionsgeschichtliche Schule," FRL, 78 (1961), 176 f. et al. suggest the Redeemer.

[81] Egypt is a symbol of the flesh, Conybeare, op. cit., 610; Adam, op. cit., 56 with n. 54.

[82] W. Till, "Das Ev. d. Wahrheit," ZNW, 50 (1959), 176 f.

[83] Ed. W. Till, "Die gnost. Schriften d. kpt. Pap. Berolinensis, 8502," TU, 60 (1955).

[84] Cf. H. Jonas, "Gnosis u. spätantiker Geist, I: Die mythologische Gnosis," FRL, 51³ (1964), 113-5.

[85] On the connection with Iranian dualism cf. Reitzenstein Ir. Erl., 5 f., 135, with Mandaean, 51-64; cf. K. Rudolph, "Die Mandäer, I: Das Mandäerproblem," FRL, 74 (1960), 149, n. 6.

[86] For many examples from the early Church cf. Ogle, 96-114.

ὑπογραμμός → I, 772, 9 ff.
ὑπόδειγμα   → II, 32, 33 ff.
ὑποδέω, ὑπόδημα → V, 310, 33 ff.

---

† ὑπόδικος

1. Profane Greek.

ὑπόδικος [1] (from Aesch. Eum., 260) denotes a person or thing which by reason of certain facts is so struck by penal δίκη (→ II, 178, 18 ff.) that he must be subjected to a trial, to judicial examination, prosecution and punishment: "guilty" in the sense of having offended against the law, "culpable," "judicially actionable," "accountable." The law says: ἐάν τις φάσκη ἀποβεβληκέναι, ὑπόδικον εἶναι, "if someone charges a man with throwing away his shield (sc. in the battle), that man must be brought to trial," Lys., 10, 9. Of things: οὐχ ὑπόδικα τὰ εἰκότα, "the (merely) probable is not open to accusation," Aristot. Rhet., I, 15, p. 1376a, 22, cf. Ps.-Aristot. Rhet. Al., 5, p. 1427a, 13. The thing a person can be tried for is in the gen.: τοῦ φόνου, "for murder," Demosth. Or., 54, 25; τῆς κακώσεως, "for neglect" (sc. of the duty of supporting parents), Isaeus, VIII, 32; ὑπόδικος θέλει γενέσθαι χρεῶν, [2] "he wants to be brought to trial for his debt," Aesch. Eum., 260; ὑπόδικος ἔστω τοῦ βλάβους, "he should be held accountable for the damage," P. Hal., 1, 241 (3rd cent. B.C.). The dat. is used for the court one comes before or more commonly the person to whom the right of complaint belongs: ἐὰν δέ τις ἀπειθῇ, τῷ τῆς περὶ ταῦτα ἀσεβείας εἰρημένῳ νόμῳ ὑπόδικος ὀρθῶς ἂν γίγνοιτο μετὰ δίκης, "if a person does not comply he may rightly and properly come under the law of ungodliness which regulates such matters," Plat. Leg., IX, 868e-869a; τῷ βλαφθέντι, Plat. Leg., VIII, 846b; τῷ παθόντι, Demosth. Or., 21, 10; τῷ ἀδικουμένῳ, P. Fay., 22, 9 (1st cent. B.C.).

2. Judaism

a. The word does not occur in the LXX. This is perhaps connected with the fact that the OT concept of law is not orientated to abstract δίκη but to the person of God and to human society. Hence we find ἔνοχος (→ II, 828, 16 ff.), which has the responsibility of the guilty in view, but not ὑπόδικος, which expresses rather the ineluctability of condemnation.

b. Philo has the term in connection with accountability: The owner of an animal which butts or gores people is to be held accountable ὥσπερ αἴτιος ὑπόδικος ἔστω, Spec. Leg., III, 145, and so too the shepherd who leads his flock on to unsuitable land, IV, 25, cf. 37. The ref. in II, 249 is to blood-guiltiness in desecration of the Sabbath: ὑπόδικος ἔστω τοῦ θανάτου; except in the case of premeditated murder the owner is not guilty if a slave he has struck does not die at once μηκέθ' ὁμοίως ὁ δεσπότης

ὑ π ό δ ι κ ο ς . Note: G. Schrenk collected and first sifted the material for this art.
[1] Cf. Pass., Moult.-Mill., Liddell-Scott, Pr.-Bauer⁵, s.v.
[2] One should read χρεῶν "for debt" (Scholion) and not χερῶν "for evil deeds" (Cod.).

ὑπόδικος ἔστω φόνου, III, 142, cf. also 121. In a normal judgment on those who are of noble houses but do not appropriate the virtue practised in them: ὑπόδικοι δ' ὑμεῖς οἱ ἐκ μεγάλων φύντες οἴκων "you are open to, worthy of punishment," Virt., 197. Of things: ἔτι δὲ ψεκτὰ τὰ ἐπαινετὰ καὶ ὑπόδικα τὰ τιμῆς ἄξια, "what is praiseworthy (to us) is reprehensible (to others), and what is honourable is deserving of punishment," Ebr., 194.

c. Josephus: ὑποδίκου [3] τοῦ τὴν δυναστείαν διοικοῦντος, "after the administrator of the kingdom had become subject to punishment," Vit., 74.

d. In view of the difference between Gk. and Jewish views of law it is hard to find an exact Rabb. par. to ὑπόδικος. The closest is חַיָּב "guilty," "responsible," whose stem came into the OT as an Aramaism, [4] e.g., Ez. 18:7; Da. 1:10, and which in the later Jewish period expresses the various kinds of legal accountability. It is thus used for the financial accountability of a debtor in BM, 12b, the obligation deriving from a commandment, e.g., to recite the shᵉma, Ber., 3, 1, the guilt incurred through transgressing a commandment, Shab., 1, 1, the liability to a penalty, e.g., חַיָּב מִיתָה jQid., 1, 1 (58d, 23). The Syr. transl. renders the ὑπόδικος of R. 3:19 (→ lines 19 ff.) by the etpaʿal of the corresponding verb. [5]

3. The New Testament.

In the NT the word occurs only at R. 3:19 → IV, 1074, 15 ff.; V, 443, 6 ff. "But we know that the law says what it says to those who are under the law," ἵνα πᾶν στόμα φραγῇ καὶ ὑπόδικος γένηται πᾶς ὁ κόσμος τῷ θεῷ. ὑπόδικος here denotes more than a general unspecified liability to punishment [6] but less than definitive condemnation. [7] It describes the state of an accused person who cannot reply at the trial initiated against him because he has exhausted all possibilities of refuting the charge against him and averting the condemnation and its consequences which ineluctably follow. [8] Since not merely the Gentiles but the Jews too, who look down on them, are forced by their own divinely given Law to accept this, the result is that every mouth will be stopped and the whole world falls under the judgment of God to condemnation, unless God Himself establishes a new right, which is what R. 3:21 ff. proclaims as a reality actually accomplished in Jesus Christ.

4. Apart from the NT ὑπόδικος does not occur in primitive Chr. writings, including the Apologists.

Maurer

---

[3] A. Pelletier, *Flavius Josèphe, Autobiographie* (1959), ad loc. conjectures ὑπὸ Μοδίου for ὑποδίκου, but this does not simplify the difficult text.

[4] Cf. M. Wagner, *Die lexikalischen u. grammatikalischen Aramaismen im at.lichen Hbr.* (1966), 52.

[5] F. Delitzsch, ספרי הברית החדשה [13] (1928) transl. מְחֻיָּב לִפְנֵי אֱלֹהִים.

[6] Zürich Bible "strafwürdig," cf the weak def. in Schl. R., ad loc.: "ὑπόδικος is the man who so acts that the law, δίκη, testifies against him and must defend what is right against him." There is more than a "must" here, for the attack on the guilty party has already been mounted by the law.

[7] Michel R., ad loc.: "ὑπόδικος ... corresponds to the κατάκριτος."

[8] Calvin Comm. in epist. Pauli ad Romanos, Corp. Ref., 77 (1892), ad loc. has the apt comment: *Illi enim os obstruitur, qui sic irretitus tenetur iudicio ne qua elabi possit.*

ὑποκρίνομαι, συνυποκρίνομαι,
ὑπόκρισις, ὑποκριτής, ἀνυπόκριτος

---

† ὑποκρίνομαι, † συνυποκρίνομαι, † ὑπόκρισις, † ὑποκριτής.

Contents: A. Classical and Hellenistic Greek: 1. Original Meaning; 2. Recitation, Acting; 3. Transferred Meaning. B. The Literature of Dispersion Judaism: 1. The Septuagint; 2. Philo and Josephus; 3. The Historical Problem. C. The New Testament: 1. The Synoptic Tradition; 2. Paul; 3. The Pastorals. D. The Post-Apostolic Fathers.

A. Classical and Hellenistic Greek.

1. Original Meaning.

a. The verb ὑποκρίνομαι [1] probably had the original sense "to explain," "to interpret," which is kept on into the Hell. period: [2] "interpreting" dreams, Hom. Od., 19, 535 and 555; Aristoph. Vesp., 53; Artemid Onirocr., IV, 22; [3] Philostr. Vit. Ap., II, 37 (p. 79, 6); "interpreting" oracular instructions, Hdt., I, 91, 6, cf. I, 2, 3; 78, 3; Plut. Caes., 43 (I, 728d); Strabo, 7, 3, 11 etc.; of the information of the θεοπρόπος, Hom. Il., 12, 228; cf. Od., 15, 170; Theocr. Idyll., 24, 67. Hence ὑποκρίνομαι can very rarely mean gen. "to take up the word," "to answer," e.g., Hom. Hymn. Ap., 171; Hom. Il., 7, 407; Od., 2, 111; ἀναβάλλομαί τοι ἐς τρίτην ἡμέρην ὑποκρινέεσθαι, "I postpone answering you for two days," Hdt., V, 49, 9; ἔφασαν θέλειν βουλεύσασθαι ἡμέρην μίαν καὶ ἔπειτα ὑποκρινέεσθαι, Hdt., I, 164, 2, cf. IX, 49, 1. This sense occurs only in Ionic, not Attic. [4]

b. The derived noun ὑπόκρισις [5] can thus mean — only in Ionic — "answer," Hdt., I, 90, 3; 116, 1; IX, 9, 1. But the nomen agentis ὑποκριτής, which almost always means "actor," probably derives from the orig. sense "to expound," "to interpret," rather than

---

ὑ π ο κ ρ ί ν ο μ α ι κ τ λ. Bibl.: Thes. Steph., Pape, Pass., Liddell-Scott, Pr.-Bauer, s.v. G. Bornkamm, Art. "Heuchelei," RGG³, III, 305 f.; P. Joüon, "ὑποκριτής dans l'évangile et hébreu hanaf," Recherches de science religieuse, 20 (1930), 312-7; L. Lemme, Art. "Heuchelei," RE³, 8, 21-4; A. Lesky, "Hypokrites," Festschr. U. E. Paoli (1964), 469-476; F. Pfister, Art. "Epiphanie," Pauly-W., Suppl., 4 (1924), 277-323.

[1] The aor. is mid. in class. Gk., mostly pass. in Hell.: συνυπεκρίθησαν Gl. 2:13, cf. Herm. s., 9, 19, 3, v. Bl.-Debr. § 78. The act ὑποκρίνω occurs only in Anecd. Graec., I, 449, 25 for judicial questioning. Only Suid., s.v. and Eustath. Thessal. Comm. in Il., 687, 20 mention a basic sense "to differentiate by degrees."
[2] Schwyzer, II, 525: "Homeric ὑπο-κρίνομαι (orig. 'to bring forth one's opinion from the depths of the heart, from concealment'), cf. Attic ἀπο-κρίνομαι."
[3] Ed. R. A. Pack (1963), 258.
[4] ὑποκρίνομαι in the sense "to answer" occurs only once in Thuc., VII, 44, 5, which may be regarded as an isolated Ionism, since elsewhere Thuc. always has ἀποκρίνομαι. Cf. the pre-Euclid. epigram of the Acropolis IG, I², 401 and Ps.-Aristot. Rhet. Al., 36, p. 1444b, 18 f.
[5] Only occasionally do we find ὑποκρισία "the art of acting," e.g., Anth. Graec., 16, 289.

"to answer": [6] The actor is orig. either an interpreter of the poet — cf. Plat. Resp., II, 373b: actors are ὑπηρέται of the poet like rhapsodists and choristers; similarly Charm., 162d — or he is "the speaker who through his interpretative words made intelligible the myth of which the songs of the chorus sang." [7] There is support for this derivation in Plat. Tim., 72b, where prophets are distinguished from mantics as the interpreters of their words and visions; this use of ὑποκριτής is not current elsewhere in Plat. and is thus shown to be pre-Platonic: τῆς δι' αἰνιγμῶν οὗτοι φήμης καὶ φαντάσεως ὑποκριταί. It is also attested in Pind. Fr., 140b, 15, with ref. to the role of the dolphin: δελφῖνος ὑπόκρισιν. In Attic, then, ὑποκρίνομαι means "to act." The actor's job is to present the drama or πρόσωπον assigned to him by artistic reciting accompanied by mime and gestures, τὰς τραγῳδίας ὑποκρίνεσθαι, [8] Aristot. Rhet., III, 1, p. 1403b, 23, the Antigone of Sophocles, Demosth. Or., 19, 246, Oedipus, Epict. Fr., 11 etc. The art of the actor ἡ ὑποκριτικὴ (τέχνη) is that from the moment he dons the mask his whole conduct on stage should be in keeping with his allotted role, Diog. L., VII, 160 (προσηκόντως); Luc. Piscator, 33. If he does a poor job the poet will chide him, Plat. Charm., 162d, transf. Teles (→ n. 13) Fr., 2 (p. 5). There are thus various gifts, τραγικοί Demosth. Or., 18, 313, and κωμικοὶ ὑποκριταί, 19, 193, and good and bad actors acc. to their abilities, 18, 313 and Aristot. Eth. Nic., VII, 6, p. 1184b, 8.

2. Recitation, Acting.

Essential in acting is declamation, i.e., the art ἐν τῇ φωνῇ, πῶς αὐτῇ δεῖ χρῆσθαι πρὸς ἕκαστον πάθος, and varying acc. to volume (μέγεθος), colour (ἁρμονία) and rhythm (ῥυθμός), Aristot. Rhet., III, 1, p. 1403b, 24-32. Hence elocution is also part of rhetoric. The early rhetoricians, the Sophists (Gorgias), considered the thing itself, but Aristot. was the first to present it as an established part of rhetoric. Under the title περὶ τῆς λέξεως he deals with it as the doctrine of linguistic expression in contrast to that of the material power of persuasion: οὐ γὰρ ἀπόχρη τὸ ἔχειν ἃ δεῖ λέγειν, ἀλλ' ἀνάγκη καὶ ταῦτα ὡς δεῖ εἰπεῖν, p. 1403b, 15-17. Though it δύναμιν μὲν ἔχει μεγίστην, it has not been investigated thus far because only later did it find an entry into the art of acting: ὑπεκρίνοντο γὰρ αὐτοὶ τὰς τραγῳδίας οἱ ποιηταὶ τὸ πρῶτον, 20-24, cf. Plut. De Solone, 29 (I, 95c). Later the art of speaking developed as an indispensable specialised skill both on the stage and in the market-place, not because it had anything essential to contribute to the matter itself but διὰ τὴν τοῦ ἀκροατοῦ μοχθηρίαν Aristot. Rhet., III, 1, p. 1404a, 7 f. As prizes are awarded to actors, so also to-day τοῖς κατὰ τὴν ὑπόκρισιν ῥήτορσιν, p. 1404a, 16-19. Oratory has the capacity for μίμησις in common with poetry: ὑπῆρξε δὲ καὶ ἡ φωνὴ πάντων μιμητικώτατον τῶν μορίων ἡμῖν, 21 f. But for this reason the rhetorical art of speech must be distinguished from that of the actor. The orator needs ὑποκριτική least when his speech has a descriptive style (λέξις γραφική) and most when it is free public speech on the market-place (λέξις ἀγωνιστική). Hence one must recognise and control the relevant style

---

[6] So acc. to a theory of later antiquity, cf. Poll. Onom., IV, 123; Hesych., s.v. ὑποκρίνοιτο Apollonii Sophistae Lex. Homericum, ed. I. Bekker (1883), s.v. ὑποκρίναιτο, Photius Lex., s.v. ὑποκρίνεσθαι, more recently Frisk, II, s.v. κρίνω, A. W. Pickard-Cambridge, The Dramatic Festivals of Athens (1953), 131 f.: the ὑποκριτής is the partner of the chorus who "answers" him. But cf. G. F. Else, "The Case of the Third Actor," Transactions and Proceedings of the American Philological Association, 76 (1945), 1-10: ὑποκρίτης was the name of the second or third actor who was added to the author as the actor that was originally alone with the chorus and who "answered" him. Against both theories Lesky, 475: "The use of the verb in no way favours the meaning 'answerer' for the nomen agentis derived from it."
[7] Lesky, 475. The actor in Attic drama might well have been the reciter of the ἱερὸς λόγος of the cultus [Dihle].
[8] Cf. also Aristot. De mirabilibus auscultationibus, 31, p. 832b, 19; Diod. S., 13, 97, 6; Plut. Demosth., 28 (I, 859b); Luc. De mercede conductis, 30; Nigrinus 24; Ps.-Demetr., 193.

in a given place if the speech is to accomplish what it is designed to do, III, 12, p. 1413b, 3 - 1414a, 7, cf. p. 1414a, 14-17: διὸ οὐχ οἱ αὐτοὶ ἐν πᾶσι τούτοις εὐδοκιμοῦσι ῥήτορες· ἀλλ᾽ ὅπου μάλιστα ὑποκρίσεως, ἐνταῦθα ἥκιστα ἀκρίβεια ἔνι· τοῦτο δέ, ὅπου φωνῆς, καὶ μάλιστα ὅπου μεγάλης. Plut. Vit. Dec. Orat., 8 (II, 845a b) tells us that when Demosthenes was at first a failure in the popular assembly he took lessons from an actor called Andronicus ὡς οἱ μὲν λόγοι καλῶς ἔχοιεν, λείποι δὲ αὐτῷ τὰ τῆς ὑποκρίσεως... ἐρομένου (sc. τοῦ Δημοσθένους) αὐτὸν τί πρῶτον ἐν ῥητορικῇ, εἶπεν, Ὑπόκρισις· καὶ τί δεύτερον, Ὑπόκρισις· καὶ τί τρίτον, Ὑπόκρισις. Thus instructed, Demosthenes went to the assembly and achieved a striking success with literally the same speech. Aristot.'s teaching on the art of speech was developed esp. by Theophrastus. [9] In this form it then passed into the tradition as an established part of rhetoric. ὑπόκρισις hears means the "delivery" of a speech, including mime and gesture, as distinct from εὕρεσις and λέξις, the material and linguistic conception.

3. Transferred Meaning.

ὑποκρίνομαι can also be used in a transferred sense, e.g., τὸ βασιλικὸν ὑποκρίνεσθαι, Aristot. Pol., V, 11, p. 1314a, 40, cf. Ep. Ar., 219. In particular a very common comparison is worth mentioning here, namely, that of human life with the stage and of conduct with the task of the actor. [10]

Most of the examples are from the later period, but the source is probably the Socratic school. [11] Plat. Phileb., 50b already compares life to a drama τῇ τοῦ βίου συμπάσῃ τραγῳδίᾳ καὶ κωμῳδίᾳ, cf. Leg., I, 644d e; VII, 803c. But the comparison with the actor became esp. important in the Stoic tradition. Aristo of Chios applied it to his doctrine of total adiaphoria as the τέλος of the life of the wise: εἶναι γὰρ ὅμοιον τῷ ἀγαθῷ ὑποκριτῇ τὸν σοφόν, ὃς ἄν τε Θερσίτου ἄν τε Ἀγαμέμνονος πρόσωπον ἀναλάβῃ, ἑκάτερον ὑποκρινεῖται προσηκόντως, Diog. L., VII, 2, 160. [12] There has also been handed down a similar saying of Bion: [13] Δεῖ ὥσπερ τὸν ἀγαθὸν ὑποκριτὴν ὅ τι ἂν ὁ ποιητὴς περιθῇ πρόσωπον τοῦτο ἀγωνίζεσθαι καλῶς, οὕτω καὶ τὸν ἀγαθὸν ἄνδρα ὅ τι ἂν περιθῇ ἡ τύχη. καὶ γὰρ αὕτη, φησὶν ὁ Βίων, ὥσπερ ποιήτρια, ὁτὲ μὲν πρωτολόγου, ὁτὲ δὲ δευτερολόγου περιτίθησι πρόσωπον, καὶ ὁτὲ μὲν βασιλέως, ὁτὲ δὲ ἀλήτου. μὴ οὖν βούλου δευτερολόγος ὢν τὸ πρωτολόγου πρόσωπον. εἰ δὲ μή, ἀνάρμοστόν τι ποιήσεις, Teles Fr., 2 (p. 5 f.). [14] As the actor Polos can play

---

[9] Cf. W. Kroll, Art. "Rhetorik," Pauly-W., Suppl., 7 (1940), 1075 f.

[10] Cf. esp. R. Helm, Lucian u. Menipp (1906), 44-53, bibl. 47, n. 1; also O. Gigon, Komm. z. 2. Buch v. Xenoph. Mem., Schweizerische Beiträge zur Altertumswissenschaft, 7 (1956), 98; M. Kokolakis, The Dramatic Simile of Life (1960); R. Aichroth, Schauspiel u. Schauspielervergleich bei Platon, Diss. Tübingen (1960). On the influence in the M. Ages up to the the 17th cent. cf. E. R. Curtius, Europäische Lit. u. lat. MA² (1954), 148-154.

[11] On this cf. Gigon, op. cit., 98, esp. the instances n. 59.

[12] The same comparison occurs in Epict. Diss., IV, 2, 10; cf. Cic. De Catone maiore, 18, 64; Paradoxa Stoicorum, 3, 26; Synesius De providentia, I, 13 (MPG, 66 [1864], 1241c); Max. Tyr., 7, 1a b.

[13] On Bion's dependence cf. O. Hense, Teletis reliquiae² (1909), CX f.

[14] Cf. Luc. Nec., 16; Dio Chrys. Or., 64, 27. The same comparison applied to the moment of death and elucidated with ref. to the dying Socrates is found in Teles (→ n. 13) Fr., 2 (p. 16); Epict. Diss., IV, 1, 165, cf. M. Ant., XII, 36: "As when the praetor releases an actor whom he had engaged. 'But I did not play the five acts, only three.' Correct, but in life the three are the whole play. For what is finished is decided by him who is responsible for both mixing and dissolving. Thou art not responsible for either. Go happily then, for he who dismisses thee is happy," cf. W. Theiler, Kaiser Marc. Aurel., Wege zu sich selbst, Bibliothek d. Alten Welt (1951), 293; cf. also III, 8; Cic. De Catone maiore, 19, 70; 29, 85 and Sen. Ep. morales, 77, 20: quomodo fabula, sic vita non quam diu, sed quam bene acta sit, refert; nihil ad rem pertinet, quo loco desinas.

equally well both Oedipus the powerful king in purple and Oedipus the poor beggar of Colonus, so the noble man can play any part assigned to him, Epict. Fr., 11, also Plut. Fr., 18, 15 (II, 834a). [15] Hence: μέμνησο, ὅτι ὑποκριτὴς εἶ δράματος, οἵου ἂν θέλῃ ὁ διδάσκαλος· ἂν βραχύ, βραχέος· ἂν μακρόν, μακροῦ· ἂν πτωχὸν ὑποκρίνασθαί σε θέλῃ, ἵνα καὶ τοῦτον εὐφυῶς ὑποκρίνῃ ἂν χωλόν, ἂν ἄρχοντα, ἂν ἰδιώτην. σὸν γὰρ τοῦτ᾽ ἔστι, τὸ δοθὲν ὑποκρίνασθαι πρόσωπον καλῶς· ἐκλέξασθαι δ᾽ αὐτὸ ἄλλου, Epict. Ench., 17. [16] We also find the simile in connection with pedagogic character formation: *Nobis autem personam imposuit ipsa natura magna cum excellentia praestantiaque animantium reliquarum*, namely, the role of *constantia, moderatio, temperantia* and *verecundia* to observe the *honestum* and *decorum* in behaviour towards others, Cic. Off., I, 28, 97, cf. 31, 114. Cf. already Xenoph. Mem., II, 2, 9: Socrates sets before a quick-tempered person the example of actors who remain inwardly unaffected ὅταν ἐν ταῖς τραγῳδίαις ἀλλήλοις τὰ ἔσχατα λέγωσιν, cf. the rhetor, who must be able to play perfectly the role of an angry person while remaining quite calm inwardly, Cic. Tusc., IV, 25, 55; Sen. De ira, II, 17, 1; Stob. Ecl., I, 550, 15 ff.

But the comparison can also be used negatively: the stage is a sham world and the actor a deceiver. Thus Luc. Icaromenipp., 29 compares false philosophers to actors whose mask and fine costume have been stripped off and the true self that remains is a γελοῖον ἀνθρώπιον ἑπτὰ δραχμῶν ἐς τὸν ἀγῶνα μεμισθωμένον. [17] Hippocr. De victu, 24, 8-11 (Littré, VI, 496) attacks even more sharply certain philosophers who seek to educate to an ἀδικέειν δικαίως: Ὑποκριταὶ καὶ ἐξαπάται, πρὸς εἰδότας λέγουσιν ἄλλα καὶ φρονέουσιν ἕτερα οἱ αὐτοὶ ἐξέρπουσι καὶ ἐσέρπουσι οὐχ οἱ αὐτοί· ἑνὶ δὲ ἀνθρώπῳ ἄλλα μὲν λέγειν, ἄλλα δὲ ποιέειν, καὶ τὸν αὐτὸν μὴ εἶναι τὸν αὐτόν, καὶ ποτὲ μὲν ἄλλην ἔχειν γνώμην, ὁτὲ δὲ ἄλλην. In so far as there is in ὑποκρίνομαι an element of unreality and deception, the verb can also take on the sense "to pretend," e.g., Demosth. Or., 31, 8: ὁρᾷς ὡς ὑποκρίνῃ μὲν δεδωκέναι τὴν προῖκα, φαίη δὲ κατ᾽ οὐδ᾽ ὁντινοῦν τρόπον δεδωκώς, the opp. of ὑποκρίνομαι being: τὰ γὰρ ἀληθῆ καὶ μὴ κακουργούμενα τῶν πραγμάτων ἁπλῶς. [18] Hence ὑπόκρισις takes on the sense of "pretext," "pretence," e.g., Appian. Rom. Hist., 7, 19, 83; 9, 61, 319; 12, 14, 48;

---

[15] Cf. the common theme of willing acceptance of a change of role ordained by fate, Luc. Navigium, 46: Impoverished rich men are like actors who come out hungry from the theatre where they have been illustrious kings. Cf. Luc. Nec., 16; Nigrinus, 20; Apologia, 5; Max. Tyr., 21, 1d; Horat. Sat., I, 1, 15-19; Ep., I, 17, 29; Sen. Ep. morales, 76, 31. The idea as such also occurs in Thuc., IV, 12, 3 [Luschnat].

[16] The same pathos may be seen in the dying words of the emperor Augustus in Suet. Caes., II, 99, 1; cf. Dio C., 56, 30; on this E. Hohl, *Augustus, Das Altertum*, 2 (1956), 241. Cf. the different emphasis in the Cyrenaican Aristippus and Diog. L., II, 8, 66; ἦν δὲ ἱκανὸς ἁρμόσασθαι καὶ τόπῳ καὶ χρόνῳ καὶ προσώπῳ καὶ πᾶσαν περίστασιν ἁρμοδίως ὑποκρίνασθαι, cf. on this Horat. Ep., I, 17, 29. Panaetius (Cic. Off., I, 30, 107) took from Aristippus the image of the two masks (*personae*), the general and the individual, which each man has to wear. Another use of the simile of the actor is in Plut. Praec. Ger. Reip., 21 (II, 816 f.): As the protagonist must adapt to the tritagonist (who usually played the tyrant acc. to Demosth. Or., 19, 247), so in the state the wealthy must be subject to the rulers even though these are poor.

[17] Cf. Luc. Apologia, 5; Piscator, 31; Gallus, 26; also M. Ant., III, 7, where in antithesis to a list of vices containing ὑποκρίνασθαι we read: ὁ γὰρ τὸν ἑαυτοῦ νοῦν καὶ δαίμονα... προελόμενος τραγῳδίαν οὐ ποιεῖ.

[18] Cf. also Demosth. Or., 18, 287; 19, 250 and Aristot. Eth. Eud., VII, 10, p. 1243b, 8: μηδ᾽ ὑποκρινόμενον μηδέτερον αὐτῶν ἐξαπατᾶν, Epict. Diss., II, 9, 19 f.: τί οὖν Στωικὸν λέγεις σεαυτόν, τί ἐξαπατᾷς τοὺς πολλούς, τί ὑποκρίνῃ Ἰουδαῖον ὢν Ἕλλην (so Schenkl); ... καὶ ὅταν τινὰ ἐπαμφοτερίζοντα ἴδωμεν, εἰώθαμεν λέγειν "οὐκ ἔστιν Ἰουδαῖος, ἀλλ᾽ ὑποκρίνεται" (opp. ἔστι τῷ ὄντι καὶ καλεῖται Ἰουδαῖος), Polyaen. Strat., VIII, 29: Nitetis, daughter of king Apries, becomes the spouse of Cyrus, letting herself be taken for many yrs. ὑποκριναμένη for a daughter of the Egypt. king Amasis; Diod. S., 19, 9, 2; Appian. Rom. Hist., 7, 16, 71; 14, 10, 34; Vett. Val., VII, 4 (p. 275, 19); also Luc. Pseudolog., 25: σοφιστὴν εἶναι.

Ps.-Luc. Amores, 3; M. Ant., I, 11; II, 5, 17; IX, 2; Plot. Enn., III, 2, 1, 46 f. [19] ὑπόκρισις in this sense is a vice: ὑβρίζει ἑαυτὴν ἡ τοῦ ἀνθρώπου ψυχή . . ., ὅταν ὑποκρίνηται καὶ ἐπιπλάστως καὶ ἀναλήθως τι ποιῇ ἢ λέγῃ, M. Ant., II, 16. [20] But although the deceptive element in ὑπόκρισις comes out in this usage, it is not true that ὑπόκρισις is intrinsically a deceiving. The element of representing, of μιμητικόν (→ 560, 33 ff.), is as such regarded positively.

In all classical usage ὑποκρίνομαι never became a term with a negative ethical ring and ὑποκριτής alone cannot denote the "hypocrite" but remains a *vox media*. The words always have additions which show whether the acting or pretending is in a given case to be viewed positively, negatively, or neutrally. Only in the Byzantine period does the word group acquire a direct negative sense under the influence of Christian usage. [21]

B. The Literature of Dispersion Judaism.

1. The Septuagint.

In distinction from classical usage the group occurs *in sensu malo* in the LXX.

Apollonius does not execute his bloody task in Jerusalem immediately but waits for the Sabbath τὸν εἰρηνικὸν ὑποκριθείς, 2 Macc. 5:25. Eleazar refuses ὑποκριθῆναι . . . ὡς ἐσθίοντα τὰ ὑπὸ τοῦ βασιλέως προστεταγμένα, 2 Macc. 6:21. He prefers death to such ὑποκρίνεσθαι, which does not befit his age, since otherwise many of the younger men would assume, Ἐλεάζαρον τὸν ἐνενηκονταετῆ μεταβεβηκέναι εἰς ἀλλοφυλισ-μὸν καὶ αὐτοὶ διὰ τὴν ἐμὴν ὑπόκρισιν . . . πλανηθῶσιν δι' ἐμέ, v. 24 f. No, he would rather choose death and give the younger generation an example of consistent keeping of the Law, v. 27 f. In the par. 4 Macc. 6:12 ff. he gives a similar answer to the advice of well-wishers that he cunningly dissemble (σὺ δὲ ὑποκρινόμενος τῶν ὑείων ἀπο-γεύεσθαι σώθητι, v. 15): μὴ οὕτως κακῶς φρονήσαιμεν οἱ Ἀβραὰμ παῖδες ὥστε μαλακοψυχήσαντας ἀπρεπὲς ἡμῖν δρᾶμα ὑποκρίνασθαι, v. 17. To play such a role in this situation would be to pervert a long life of adherence to the Law and to become an example of iniquity (ἀσεβείας τύπος) rather than of righteousness, v. 19f. In both cases the suggested stratagem of ὑποκρίνεσθαι involves a much worse ὑποκρίνεσθαι: a spectacle of apostasy from God and His Law, i.e., ὑπόκρισις as a sin, which does not befit a son of Abraham. In keeping is the use in other LXX passages in which the term occurs, [22] Sir. 1:28-30: Μὴ ἀπειθήσῃς φόβῳ κυρίου καὶ μὴ προσέλθῃς αὐτῷ ἐν καρδίᾳ δισσῇ. μὴ ὑποκριθῇς ἐν στόμασιν (vl. -τι) ἀνθρώπων καὶ ἐν τοῖς χείλεσίν σου πρόσεχε. Otherwise the Lord will one day bring everything to light, ὅτι οὐ προσῆλθες φόβῳ κυρίου καὶ ἡ καρδία σου πλήρης δόλου. The parallelism shows that ἀπειθεῖν φόβῳ κυρίου and ὑποκριθῆναι correspond, so fear of God and hypocrisy are opposites. It is deception (δόλος) not to turn to fear of God but to depart from it, a matter of the divided heart, cf. for καρδίᾳ δισσῇ Ps. 12:2; Sir. 5:14 f.; Jm. 1:8; 4:8. The relation of the righteous to God brooks no sin; righteous who sin are hypocrites. The use of ὑποκριτής in Job 36:13 is similar: "The impiously minded (HT חַנְפֵי לֵב LXX ὑπο-

---

[19] Cf. κατὰ ὑπόκρισιν "hypocritically," Polyb., 15, 17, 2; 35, 2, 13; ὑποκριτής "hypo-crite," Ep. Ar., 219; Achill. Tat., VIII, 8, 14; 17, 3.
[20] Cf. ὑποκρίνομαι in lists of vices, M. Ant., III, 7; VII, 69; ὑπόκρισις, I, 11; II, 5. 17; IX, 2; Epict. Diss., I, 25, 1.
[21] Lines 7-12 [Dihle]. On the use in late antiquity under Chr. influence cf. esp. the Aesop tradition, A. Hausrath, Corpus Fabul. Aesopicarum (1956-62): on ὑποκρίνομαι Aesop Syntipas, 50 (Hausrath, I, 2, 177); Aphthonius, 8 (I, 2, 136); Nicephorus Basilaces, 346 (I, 2, 186); Fabulae, 7, 1 (I, 1, 11); ὑπόκρισις Fabulae, 7, 3 (I, 1, 11); 81, 1 (I, 1, 107); 166, 1, 3 (I, 1, 192); Syntipas, 37 (I, 2, 171).
[22] Exception ὑποκρίνομαι "to answer" in Job 40:2 א*.

κριταὶ καρδίᾳ) heap up wrath." The context is governed by the contrast between sinners and righteous. God gives life and fortune to the obedient, death and perdition to the wicked. The latter are as such ὑποκριταί. In rendering חָנֵף by ὑποκριτής the transl. undoubtedly did not have in view a hypocrite who seems to be righteous without actually being so. Rather ὑπόκρισις obviously has for him the character of sin. This is so in Job 34:30: LXX transl. the difficult (corrupt?) HT מִמְּלֹךְ אָדָם חָנֵף מִמֹּקְשֵׁי עָם literally: βασιλεύων ἄνθρωπον ὑποκριτὴν ἀπὸ δυσκολίας λαοῦ. This shows plainly that here too ὑποκριτής is used for חָנֵף. The pt. is prevention of a wicked man from becoming king. For the Gk. transl. the wicked man is simply a hypocrite. [23] The ὑπόκρισις of the wicked consists in breaking the Law as such, Sir. 32:15: ὁ ζητῶν νόμον ἐμπλησθήσεται αὐτοῦ, καὶ ὁ ὑποκρινόμενος σκανδαλισθήσεται ἐν αὐτῷ, and 33:2: ἀνὴρ σοφὸς οὐ μισήσει νόμον, ὁ δὲ ὑποκρινόμενος ἐν αὐτῷ ὡς ἐν καταιγίδι πλοῖον. We often find the same rendering in the Hexapla transl., cf. Is. 9:16 ΑΣΘ; 32:6 ΑΣΘ; 33:14 ΑΣΘ; Jer. 23:15 Σ; ψ 34:16 Σ; Prv. 11:9 ΑΣΘ; Job 15:34 ΑΘ; 20:5 Α; 34:30 Θ; 36:13 Θ, cf. also ὑποκρίνομαι Prv. 16:28 Σ; ὑποκριτής Hos. 6:9 Σ, the ref. being to wickedness. There is thus a widespread usage acc. to which the Hbr. חָנֵף is transl. ὑποκριτής. In the OT, however, the adj. חָנֵף always denotes the wicked man who has alienated himself from God by his acts. [24] Nowhere do words of the stem חנף have the sense of dissembling or hypocrisy, and the LXX keeps faithfully to the meaning. [25]

It thus follows that when the transl. use ὑποκριτής for חָנֵף they take it in a directly pejorative sense. The ὑποκριτής is the ungodly man, the ungodly man is the ὑποκριτής. [26]

---

[23] Cf. Est. r., 1 on 1:1 with ref. to Ahasuerus.
[24] Cf. Köhler-Baumg., s.v. and F. Horst, Hiob, Bibl. Komm. AT, 16, 2 (1960) on 8:13: "Acc. to its root it denotes an act or attitude by which a state of sacral relation to the Godhead is intentionally set aside. Not least this can take place through sinning against God."
[25] LXX mostly transl. by ἀσεβής, πανάνομος, or ἄνομος, e.g., Is. 9:16: All are ἄνομοι, Is. 10:6: εἰς ἔθνος ἄνομον. חָנֵף is also synon. with חַטָּאִים Is. 33:14, רְשָׁעִים Job 20:5; 27:8, cf. Prv. 11:8 f., שֹׁכְחֵי אֵל Job 8:13. The opp. is צַדִּיק Prv. 11:8 f., cf. Is. 33:15, יְשָׁרִים Job 17:8, עָנִי Job 36:15, cf. 13. Hence the noun חָנֵף means "wicked act" in Is. 32:6, LXX ἄνομα. The verb חנף has a similar sense in Jer. 23:11: "Even the prophet and priest have become transgressors" ἐμολύνθησαν. Cf. also Is. 24:5: Jer. 3:1; Mi. 4:11; Ps. 106:38 and in the hi Jer. 3:2: וַתַּחֲנִיפִי אֶרֶץ "thou hast desecrated the land" also Nu. 35:33, cf. the noun חֲנֻפָּה Jer. 23:15: "Defilement μολυσμός has gone forth from the prophets over the whole land." In Da. 11:32 חנף hi has the sense "to seduce into falling away from God": "And those who offend against the covenant he shall lead into apostasy" ἐπάξουσιν Θ. Cf. the Accad. ḫanpu "wickedness" and Syr. ḫanpa "the ungodly," Köhler-Baumg., s.v. In Arab. ḥanif denotes the heathen, esp. the follower of the religion of Abraham, Joüon, 315 bibl.
[26] In Rabb. lit. too we find the same sense of חנף and derivates, cf. Levy Wört., Jastrow, s.v.: "Wherever חנף occurs in Scripture there is a ref. to heresy (idolatry)," Is. 33:14 being adduced in proof, Gn. r., 48, 6 on 18:1. Thus חֲנֵפָא means "the ungodly" and חֲנוּפָה or חֲנוּפְתָא "ungodliness." Yet the sense of "flattery" "dissembling," "hypocrisy" is prominent in Rabb. usage, cf. esp. the section "flattery" in bSota, 42b, and in this the saying ascribed to R. Eleazar: "A community in which flattery is to be found is repugnant like a menstruous woman," Job 15:34 being adduced (→ line 14). Further examples Str.-B., I, 388 f. Cf. also esp. Qoh. r., 4 on 4:1: "Rabbi Benjamin (bLevi, c. 325) ref. Qoh. 4:1 to those who pretend knowledge of the Torah חֲנִיפֵי תוֹרָה. All the world כל עמא thinks such a one is an expert in Scripture but he is not, not an expert in the Mishnah and he is not; he wraps himself in his cloak and has the phylacteries on his head — and lo, the tears of the oppressed ..., 'and there is none to comfort them'; then God says, It is incumbent on me to punish them, cf. 'Cursed be he who does the work of Yahweh deceitfully,' Jer. 48:10," Str.-B., I, 389. Acc. to Joüon, 315 this unique usage in the Semitic sphere might have developed from an orig. sense of the root ḥnf "to turn from," "to pervert," which underlies the usage in Arab.

2. Philo and Josephus.

a. In Philo and Joseph., too, ὑποκρίνομαι/ὑπόκρισις is almost always [27] used in a negative sense. Acc. to Philo Conf. Ling., 48 the unwise man is as ὑποκρινόμενος εὔνοιαν ... ἀληθείας ἐχθρός. ὑπόκρισις, "a worse evil than death," is "to conceal or dissemble the truth after the manner of theft," Jos., 68, cf. Fug., 156; Rer. Div. Her., 43. It is connected with ψευδῆ πλάσματα, Rer. Div. Her., 43, cf. Leg. Gaj., 22 and with δόλος, Spec. Leg., IV, 183 (exposition of Lv. 19:16: δόλῳ πορεύομαι), cf. Jos., 67: ἀδόλως καὶ καθαρῶς ἄνευ τῆς ἐχθρᾶς ὑποκρίσεως. It is in series with ἀπάτη, γοητεία, σοφίσματα, προσποιήσεις, Som., II, 40, and with θωπεία and κολακεία as δουλοπρεπέστατα Omn. Prob. Lib., 99, cf. Leg. Gaj., 162. To put on virtues one must expose (Deus Imm., 103) or put off (Migr. Abr., 211) ὑπόκρισις.

b. In Joseph. ὑποκρίνομαι is more a matter of refined political or strategical action. [28] A deceitful role is played (Bell., 1, 471) when, e.g., friendship is pretended, 1, 318 and 516, cf. 5, 18: φιλίαν πλασάμενος, in order to be able to work the better against the supposed friend. [29] But such ὑπόκρισις may be for a good end as in the case of Joseph and his brethren, Ant., 2, 160. [30] In any case ὑπόκρισις is a matter of false appearances, Ant., 16, 216 and the ὑποκριτής is a "hypocrite" like John of Gischala who ἕτοιμος μὲν ψεύσασθαι, δεινὸς δ' ἐπιθεῖναι πίστιν τοῖς ἐψευσμένοις, ἀρετὴν ἡγούμενος τὴν ἀπάτην καὶ ταύτῃ κατὰ τῶν φιλτάτων χρώμενος, ὑποκριτὴς φιλανθρωπίας καὶ δι' ἐλπίδα κέρδους φονικώτατος, Bell., 2, 586 f.

3. The Historical Problem.

In more or less the whole literature of Dispersion Judaism one thus finds a use of ὑποκρίνομαι/ὑπόκρισις which differs characteristically from that of classical and Hellenistic literature. With few exceptions the term is employed *in sensu malo*. The ὑποκριτής is bad as such and ὑπόκρισις is a form of wrongdoing. In this respect there is no question of presenting a righteous appearance so that the true face of evil is disguised. Hence the translation "hypocrisy" is hardly apt. What is meant is the "deception" which characterises evil as apostasy against God or opposition to Him. This conclusion demands an explanation, for there is nothing in the Greek tradition to suggest that the "evildoer" (חָנֵף) should be rendered by "actor" (ὑποκριτής), nor is there anything in the Hebrew expressions for "evildoer" to suggest his conduct be regarded as "acting." Nevertheless one can discern the general background which makes sense of this remarkable translation.

Test. B. 6:4 f. says that a good mind does not have two speeches, [31] one of blessing and one of cursing..., ὑποκρίσεως καὶ ἀληθείας, but only one speech; for πάντα δόλον ἢ ψεῦδος ἢ μάχην ἢ λοιδορίαν οὐκ οἶδε. Here, then, ὑπόκρισις means the same as

---

[27] ὑποκρίνομαι in the sense "to answer" occurs only in Jos. Bell., 1, 277 vl. ἡ ὑποκριτική for the art of acting occurs once in Philo at Leg. All., II, 75, cf. also Ep. Ar., 219 → 561, 16 f. In Philo Som., I, 205 ὑπόκρισις is a branch of rhetoric which the sage has to learn in the course of instruction.

[28] ὑποκρίνομαι/ὑπόκρισις as πανοῦργον, e.g., Bell., 1, 628; 4, 60; 5, 112, as τερατεία Bell., 1, 630. The way Abraham palms off Sarah as his sister before Pharaoh and Abimelech is a τέχνη, Ant., 1, 162, 207, 211.

[29] Cf. ὑποκρίνομαί τι, e.g., Bell., 2, 617; Ant., 7, 165 (sickness); Bell., 4, 60 (flight); 4, 347 (treachery); Ant., 13, 220 (μετριότητα). ὑποκρίνομαι often with the inf. "to act as if," e.g., Bell., 1, 516. 518. 520. 569; 4, 209; 5, 112; Ant., 12, 216; Vit., 36.

[30] Cf. Ant., 13, 220: ἀπεδύσατο (namely, as a mask) τὴν ὑπόκρισιν καὶ ὁ ἀληθὴς Τρύφων ἦν. Cf. the later Chr. addition to Test. A. 7:3: οὗτος σώσει τὸν Ἰσραὴλ καὶ πάντα τὰ ἔθνη [θεὸς εἰς ἄνδρα ὑποκρινόμενος].

[31] Cf. the "divided heart," Sir. 1:28 → 563, 37 ff.

δόλος and ψεῦδος, with ἀλήθεια as antonym. This antithesis of truth and deception is common in Test. XII, cf. G. 5:1; D. 6:8; 1:3; Iss. 7:4 f.; A. 5:3. The evil spirit practises deception, Test. D. 3:6, cf. 2:1, 4. The ref. is to wickedness as deceit, and what is deceitful stands opposed to the truth of God; deception is satanic and ungodly. The same antithesis of truth and deception occurs in Gr. En. 98:15 - 99:2, 9; 104:9, [32] where there is ref. to ἔργα ψευδῆ as opposed to keeping God's commandments. The same idea occurs also in the Qumran sect, cf. esp. the doctrine of the two spirits in 1 QS 3:13 - 4:26. Here the spirit of wickedness fights the spirit of truth and his acts are "iniquity and falsehood" רֶשַׁע וָשֶׁקֶר, "fraud and deceit" כַּחַשׁ וּרְמִיָּה, 4:9. Similarly in the ancient Iranian tradition we find the two spirits of lying (drug) and truth (aša) as the spirits of evil wickedness and obedient righteousness, cf. esp. Yasna, 30, 3-5. [33] The word drug [34] is very common in the Gathas to denote evil in conflict with the truth; [35] indeed, in Indo-Iranian religion lying is the gt. moral evil [35] and as such it typifies the nature of the evil spirit and its representatives. [36] For the deceitful element in lying is hatred and hostility against the good and the truth. This basic religious concept of original and essential dualism between falsehood and truth, uprightness and iniquity, had an influence not only on Judaism but also on the Mandaean and Manichaean tradition. [37] Through the mediation of Judaism its vocabulary may often been found in primitive Christianity too → ψεῦδος.

It is thus understandable that ὑπόκρισις should be numbered among the terms for evil as lying and deceit in the vocabulary of Dispersion Judaism. The bad man plays the role of a bad man. He disguises himself when he becomes an evildoer instead of the good man he ought to be according to God's Law, cf. Eth. En. 99:2. This dissembling is eo ipso wicked deception, opposition to the truth of God. It is still a puzzle, however, why it should be described as "acting". [38]

C. The New Testament.

1. The Synoptic Tradition.

In primitive Christianity as in the LXX the word group is always used in sensu malo. Jesus attacks his opponents [39] as ὑποκριταί because they can discern the signs which usually announce rain or the south wind, but cannot evaluate "this time"

---

[32] Ed. C. Bonner, The Last Chapters of Enoch in Gk., Stud. and Documents, 8 (1937).
[33] Ed. K. F. Geldner, Die heiligen Bücher d. Parsen, I-III (1886-95).
[34] "It corresponds perfectly to the Vedic term druh and thus denotes deception, falsehood," G. Widengren, Die Religionen Irans. Die Religionen d. Menschheit, 14 (1965), 77. Other instances in C. Bartholomae, Altiranisches Wörterb. (1904), 778 f.
[35] Widengren, op. cit. (→ n. 34), 63.
[36] Ibid., 78, bibl. n. 86.
[37] Cf. Lidz. Ginza R., p. 16, 24 f. 33 f.; for Manichaeanism cf. Kephalaia, I (ed. H. J. Polotsky, A. Böhlig [1940]), 51, 1-14; 80, 29-32; 81, 13-20; 179, 21-28.
[38] Cf. also Joüon, 316. One might ask whether the choice is based on the fact that the theatre and actors were regarded as a wicked pagan institution in pious Jewish circles, cf. Bousset-Gressm., 94. The early Church adopted the same view in its discipline, cf. Constitutiones eccles. Aegypt., 11, 4 (ed. F. X. Funk, Didascalia et Constitutiones Apostolorum, II [1905], 107); further examples in C. Andresen," Altchr. Kritik am Tanz — ein Ausschnitt aus dem Kampf d. alten Kirche gg. heidnische Sitte," ZKG, 72 (1961), 229, n. 34. Did Judaism regard the pagan actor as a supreme representative of wickedness?
[39] Not His disciples, as against W. G. Kümmel, Verheissung u. Erfüllung. Untersuchungen z. eschatol. Verkündigung Jesu³, AbhThANT, 6³ (1956), 15. When the disciples are addressed, as in the par. Mk. 13:28 f., ὑποκριταί is patently not used. It is reserved for adversaries. Its absence in the par. Mt. 16:2b-3 vl. robs the saying of its polemical edge and makes it a stylised maxim.

correctly, Lk. 12:54-56. They are ὑποκριταί, not because they dissemble hypocritically, but in view of the blatant contradiction between their sure δοκιμάζειν of signs of the weather and the tardy or absent δοκιμάζειν of the nearness of the kingdom of God as intimated in the preaching and acts of Jesus. [40] Similarly Jesus censures the contradiction on the part of His adversaries when they have no scruples about leading out cattle to be watered on the Sabbath but raise objections against the healing of a sick woman on the Sabbath (→ VII, 25, 14 ff.): they are ὑποκριταί, Lk. 13:15 f. [41] In the saying about the mote and the beam in Mt. 7:3-5 and par. the critical ὑποκριταί [42] refers to the wrong relation between the denounced failings of one's neighbour and one's own failings, which are ignored. He who judges thus does wrong, cf. R. 2:1 ff.; Jm. 4:11 f. In Mk. 7:6 the critical ὑποκριταί is aimed at the hypocrisy of opponents, as the appended quotation from Is. shows: "This people honoureth me with their lips, but their heart is far from me." They claim to be declaring God's will but in truth they are only trying to assert the παράδοσις τῶν ἀνθρώπων. Mt. sharpens the reproach by putting Mk. 7:8 before the Is. quotation, extending it (Mt. 15:3-6), and relating the ὑποκριταί to it. The charge of hypocrisy in this sense is generally characteristic of the theological polemic of the First Evangelist. [43] It was from this standpoint that he composed the great programmatic address against the representatives of the teaching tradition of Judaism, [44] introducing the seven Woes by the stereotyped formula: οὐαὶ ὑμῖν, γραμματεῖς καὶ Φαρισαῖοι ὑποκριταί, Mt. 23:13, 15 f., 23, 25, 27, 29. [45] The hypocrisy of the adversaries consists in the jarring contradiction between what they say and what they do, between the outward appearance and the inward lack of righteousness: οὕτως καὶ ὑμεῖς ἔξωθεν μὲν φαίνεσθε τοῖς ἀνθρώποις δίκαιοι, ἔσωθεν δέ ἐστε μεστοὶ ὑποκρίσεως καὶ ἀνομίας, v. 28. [46] Their hypocrisy is, therefore, sin; failure

[40] For this exposition cf. Kümmel, op. cit., 15 f. But Jeremias Gl.[7], 162 finds a menacing ref. to the nearness of the present age to the Last Judgment. The reproach is not directed "against the foolish speculation which tries to calculate when God's kingdom will come on the basis of cosmic signs," G. Bornkamm, Jesus v. Nazareth[7] (1967), 67 f. The figurative aspect has in view the ability of farmers (or sailors, Mt. 16:2b) to read the weather and should not be taken as a metaphor for apocal. calculations.

[41] G. Klein, "Die Prüfung d. Zeit (Lk. 12:54-56)," ZThK, 61 (1964), 380, n. 45; 387 thinks the ὑποκριταί in Lk. 12:56 and 13:15 is editorial. Since, however, it is not common in Lk. and seems to be taken from Q at 6:42, there seems to be good reason to regard it as pre-Lucan.

[42] It occurs in both versions and thus belongs to the original Logion.

[43] Cf. on this G. Strecker, "Der Weg d. Gerechtigkeit. Untersuchung z. Theol. d. Mt.," FRL, 82[2] (1966), 139-143.

[44] Cf. on this E. Haenchen, "Mt. 23," Gott u. Mensch (1965), 37, 49-54.

[45] Mt. took the stylising from Q, as may be seen from the 5 Woes in the Lucan par. at Lk. 11:52, 42, 39 f., 44, 47. This does not have ὑποκριταί at all, the ὑποκριταί of 11:39 (D b) and 44 (𝔎 Θ pl it) being secondary. But one should not on this account argue that the ὑποκριταί in Mt. is editorial, Strecker, op. cit. (→ n. 43), 139, n. 9; cf. Lk. 12:1, which at the end of the Woes in 11:37 ff. and in interpretation of the saying from Q in 12:2 f., adds the Marcan motif of warning against the "leaven of the Pharisees" (Mk. 8:15) and then gives the explanation: ἥτις ἐστὶν ὑπόκρισις τῶν Φαρισαίων. There seems to be no reason for this in the context and one can explain it only on the assumption that Lk. was familiar with the catchword ὑπόκρισις from the Woes tradition and brought it in here. This shows in turn that the word predates Mt.

[46] This sentence is editorial acc. to G. Barth, "Das Gesetzesverständnis d. Evangelisten Mt.," G. Bornkamm, G. Barth, H. J. Held, Überlieferung u. Auslegung im Mt., Wissenschaftl. Monographien z. AT u. NT. 1[4] (1965), 57, n. 2. On this basis the contradiction between the outer appearance and inner reality of conduct came to be regarded as the very essence of

to do God's will is concealed behind the pious appearance of outward conduct. The proportions of what is commanded are also distorted (→ I, 558, 6 ff.; III, 594, 3 ff.), the least significant commandment of pious custom being put to the forefront and τὰ βαρύτερα τοῦ νόμου being neglected, v. 23 → IV, 1064, 14 ff. The opposite of the ὑπόκρισις of the adversaries is simple and unassuming doing of God's will, the real righteousness with which the disciples ought to surpass by far the scribes and Pharisees, Mt. 5:20. Hence the disciples are not to be as the hypocrites. They must not give, pray, or fast so as to be seen by men. On the contrary, these things are to be done by them in the concealment in which only God can see them, Mt. 6:2-4, 5, 16. [47] The ὑπόκρισις of the adversaries consists in the fact that they are concerned about their status with men rather than their standing before God. They thus fail to achieve the righteousness which they pretend to have. Their hypocrisy will be their ruin in God's judgment: ἀπέχουσιν τὸν μισθὸν αὐτῶν, v. 2, 5, 16. The same will apply to Christians too if they act like the wicked servant in the parable, Mt. 24:45-51 and par. Sham Christians like this will be equated with Jewish hypocrites in the judgment: τὸ μέρος αὐτοῦ μετὰ τῶν ὑποκριτῶν θήσει (Mt. 24:51; Lk. 12:46: μετὰ τῶν ἀπίστων). In the story of the tax penny in Mt. 22:18 the ὑπόκρισις of the questioners sent by the Pharisees (Mk. 12:15) is seen through by Jesus and their cunning make-believe is branded as πονηρία. Jesus calls them ὑποκριταί in the same sense as He does those who commission them in Mt. 23. Luke characterises them as ἐγκαθέτους ὑποκρινομένους ἑαυτοὺς δικαίους εἶναι, 20:20. They are to pretend to be just, but Jesus unmasks their role as πανουργία, Lk. 20:23. [48] As Luke sees it, this role is a hubris which typifies the Pharisee, Lk. 16:15; 18:9.

2. Paul.

Paul uses the term only in Gl. 2:13. When the Jewish Christians whom James sent from Jerusalem arrived at Antioch, Cephas withdrew from table-fellowship with the Gentile Christians: καὶ συνυπεκρίθησαν [49] αὐτῷ οἱ λοιποὶ Ἰουδαῖοι, ὥστε καὶ Βαρναβᾶς συναπήχθη αὐτῶν τῇ ὑποκρίσει, 2:13. [50] Strife arose between Peter and Paul over this. Paul confronted Peter face to face because he was "convicted of wrong," 2:11. [51] It is in this light that we are to understand the use of

---

ὑπόκρισις in the speech of later antiquity as this was influenced by Christianity, cf. the Aesop tradition → n. 21. Yet it should not be overlooked that in Mt. ὑπόκρισις is not characterised gen. by the disparity of appearance and being, the outer and the inner, but by the fact that the ref. is to an essential feature of ἀνομία. It is precisely this reproach which later the Ps.-Clementines notably try to shift away from the Pharisees, cf. the examples in H. J. Schoeps, Theol. u. Gesch. d. Judenchristentums (1949), 145, n. 2.

[47] On the three-membered tradition in Mt. 6:2-4, 5 f., 16-18 cf. Bultmann Trad., 140 f.; E. Klostermann, "Zum Verständnis v. Mt. 6:2," ZNW, 47 (1956), 280 f.; J. Dupont, Les Béatitudes. Le problème littéraire — Les deux versions du Sermon sur la montagne et des Béatitudes² (1958), 159-163. ὑποκριταί belongs to the pre-Mt. tradition. Cf. Qoh. r., 4 on 4:1 (→ n. 26) and the other Rabb. examples assembled in Str.-B., I, 388 f.

[48] Lk. interprets Mk.'s ὑπόκρισις along the Gk.-Hell. lines. Cf. also Jos. → 565, 12 ff. On ὑποκρίνομαι with inf. cf. Bl.-Debr., 157, 2; 397, 2; 406, 1.

[49] On συνυποκρίνομαι cf. Polyb., 3, 92, 5 etc.; Plut. Mar., 14 (I, 413e); 17 (I, 415b); Ep. Ar., 267.

[50] τῇ ὑποκρίσει is to be taken as an instr. dat. "through their conduct, which Paul describes as ὑπόκρισις," Ltzm. Gl. ad loc., cf. Schlier Gl.¹², ad loc.

[51] κατεγνωσμένος (→ I, 715, 9 ff.) means "condemned" before God, not "in the sense that his own conduct had itself condemned him," Schlier Gl.¹², ad loc. Cf. Paul's verdict in Gl. 2:14a.

ὑποκρίνομαι/ὑπόκρισις here. Paul's charge (→ VII, 597, 29 ff.) is not that they deceived the envoys from Jerusalem by their sudden change of practice. Their ὑπόκρισις was not culpable tactical hypocrisy. [52] Nor was it that their present conduct was discordant with that they had done before. [53] Nor was it merely the inconsistency in the attitude of Peter, → VI, 110, 6 ff. [54] The real point was that by breaking off table fellowship between Jews and Gentiles in the one Church they οὐκ ὀρθοποδοῦσιν πρὸς τὴν ἀλήθειαν τοῦ εὐαγγελίου, Gl. 2:14. Thus Paul, in the short summary of his doctrine of justification that follows directly (Gl. 2:14-21), can stylise as a polemic against Peter what he has to say theologically to the Galatian churches in face of their falling away from the "truth" of the Gospel (1:6 f.). In both cases there is falling away from the truth of the Gospel of God with its essential implication of an equal fellowship between Jews and Gentiles. [55] Thus the use of ὑποκρίνομαι/ὑπόκρισις (Gl. 2:13) stands in close relation to the distinctive Jewish usage described above → 563, 13 ff.

3. The Pastorals.

The use of ὑποκριτής in the primitive Catholic polemic against heretics is to be explained by the meaning of "evildoer," "apostate." In the heretical teaching against which the Pastorals give warning the reference according to 1 Tm. 4:2 is to demonic teaching ἐν ὑποκρίσει ψευδολόγων. From the very outset and in every respect these λόγοι are "deceitful," for they contradict the words of the truth of God (cf. 4:3; 6:5; 2 Tm. 3:8; 4:4; Tt. 1:14) and this is ὑπόκρισις.

D. The Post-Apostolic Fathers.

As in the Past. the false teachers in Herm. are summarily described as ὑποκριταί, Herm. s., 8, 6, 5; 9, 18, 3; 9, 19, 2 f. Acc. to Did., 8, 1 the Jews are just ὑποκριταί [56] as Christians are in Rabb. texts. [57] ὑπόκρισις is apostasy from God and from orthodoxy. Repentance is open only to those who have not blasphemed their Lord nor betrayed the servants of God but ὑπεκρίθησαν through avarice and assimilated their teaching to the desires of sinful men, Herm. s., 9, 19, 3. [58] Cf. also Barn., 19, 2: "Thou shalt hate all that does not please God, μισήσεις πᾶσαν ὑπόκρισιν, do not forsake the commandments of the Lord," cf. Did., 4, 12. But the sense of "dissembling," "hypocrisy," is also found. [59]

---

[52] So, e.g., Schlier Gl.[12], ad loc.: "He sees primarily in Peter's separation the deceiving of the men from Jerusalem."

[53] So, e.g., Oe. Gl., ad loc.: "Hypocrisy because it was not out of conviction."

[54] So W. Schmithals, "Pls. u. Jk.," FRL, 85 (1963), 59.

[55] For Paul Peter's conduct, which influenced even Barnabas, was also a breach of the rulings of the Apostolic Council, cf. Gl. 2:14b with 2:6-9. The only motive he can think of is fear of the Jewish Christians from Jerusalem, 2:12, though cf. Schmithals, op. cit., 59 f. But the probable basis was the general authority of James which was recognised by Peter and even Barnabas as an Antiochene "apostle," which had arisen de facto prior to the Apostolic Council, and which had not been altered by the latter's resolutions; cf. O. Cullmann, Petrus, Jünger, Apostel, Märtyrer² (1960), 46, n. 4; U. Wilckens, "Der Ursprung d. Überlieferung der Erscheinungen des Auferstandenen. Zur traditionsgeschichtlichen Analyse v. 1 Kor. 15:1-11," Festschr. E. Schlink (1963), 64-72.

[56] Jewish Chr. usage has had an influence here, esp. as seen in Mt. → 567, 16 ff.

[57] Gn. r., 48, 6 on 18:1; cf. A. Schlatter, Die Kirche Jerusalems vom Jahre 70-130 (1898), 28.

[58] Cf. Dib. Herm. ad loc.

[59] Cf. the vl. of the Imperial text at Jm. 5:12, which forbids swearing with a moral exhortation rather than the threat of eschatological judgment: ἵνα μὴ εἰς ὑπόκρισιν πέσητε. This is also an exposition of the command that yes be yes and no no, since a mixture of yes and no would be ὑπόκρισις.

In Pol., 6, 3 the false brethren are those "who bear the name of the Lord ἐν ὑποκρίσει and thus lead unstable men astray." Acc. to Herm. v., 3, 6, 1 there are people who "have become believers but ἐν ὑποκρίσει, and no sin has dropped away from them," cf. "hypo-critical repentance" ἐν ὑποκρίσει μετανοέω, v., 8, 6, 2. 1 Cl., 15, 1 differentiates those who keep peace μετ᾽ εὐσεβείας from those who pretend to keep peace μεθ᾽ ὑποκρίσεως. Herm. m., 2, 5 makes distinction between recipients of alms in real need and recipients in pretended need. In Herm. s., 9, 27, 2 a heavenly reward is promised to those who "without guile ἄτερ ὑποκρίσεως receive the servants of God into their houses." Ign. Mg., 3, 2 orders obedience to the bishop κατὰ μηδεμίαν ὑπόκρισιν, since otherwise one will deceive not merely the "visible" bishop but also and above all the "invisible" bishop. In this sense, as a summary term for any kind of pretence or deception before God or man, ὑπόκρισις occurs in lists of vices, cf., e.g., 1 Pt. 2:1 with δόλος (→ 571, 5 ff., cf. 565, 34 ff.); Did., 2, 6; 5, 1; Barn., 20, 1; Herm. m., 8, 3.

† ἀνυπόκριτος.

1. This term occurs for the first time [1] in the LXX: Wis. 5:18 in a list of the weapons with which God defends the righteous against the wicked; as helmet He puts on κρίσιν ἀνυπόκριτον. Similarly Wis. 18:15 says of the hypostatised Word of God that as a fierce warrior it jumps down from heaven into the corruption of earth: ξίφος ὀξὺ τὴν ἀνυπόκριτον ἐπιταγήν σου φέρων. In both instances ἀνυπόκριτος, used of God's saving, eschatological work, denotes the unfeigned simplicity of that which is irrevocable and definitive. [2]

2. In the NT ἀνυπόκριτος is a fixed attribute of ἀγάπη in the hortatory tradi-tion of Hellenistic Christianity. In R. 12:9 Paul opens a series of general ethical admonitions with the demand that love be ἀνυπόκριτος. The statement stands alone and hence ἀνυπόκριτος is not elucidated. [3] One finds the same developed use in the description of apostolic life: ἐν ἀγάπῃ ἀνυποκρίτῳ, ἐν λόγῳ ἀληθείας, 2 C. 6:6 f. Perhaps the expression διὰ τῶν ὅπλων τῆς δικαιοσύνης τῶν δεξιῶν καὶ ἀριστερῶν, which is appended in v. 7, is meant as a summary of the various parallel expressions in v. 6. If so, then this, along with the reference to the "Holy Spirit" and the "power of God" in the series v. 6 f., would bring out the character of all these virtues as gifts which God has placed at the disposal of the apostles as divine weapons to keep them steadfast and active in the midst of all the pressures in the cosmos. On this view ἀνυπόκριτος, as in Wis. 5:18 (→ line 15 ff.), is saying that the unadulterated clarity, unfeigned simplicity, and unreserved totality of the definitive reality of God describe the character of the neighbourly love of Christians,

---

ἀνυπόκριτος. [1] All profane examples are post-NT. The meaning is "free from hypocrisy or pretence." Hesych., s.v. ἀνυπόκριτος interprets: ἄδολος, ἀπροσωπόληπτος, so also, e.g., Iambl. Vit. Pyth., 31, 188 "without (dissembling) acting," Ps.-Demetr., 194. The adv. ἀνυποκρίτως occurs in M. Ant., VIII, 5, 2 ἀνυπόκριτος or ἐνυπόκριτος is a tt. in punctuation, Schol. in Dion. Thr. Art. Gramm., 1, 4, ed. A. Hilgard, Grammatici Graeci I, 3 (1901), p. 24, 17 f.
[2] So correctly K. Siegfried in Kautzsch Apkr. u. Pseudepigr., I, ad loc. Cf. as correlates of ἀνυπόκριτος in the context of Wis. 5:18: ἀκαταμάχητον ὁσιότητα v. 19 and ἀπότομον ὀργήν v. 20.
[3] The statements which follow in R. 12:9b are in parataxis to v. 9a, so that even if they expound ἀγάπη they do not elucidate its special quality as ἀνυπόκριτος, so, e.g., Schl. R., ad loc.

so that its opposite, a love ἐν ὑποκρίσει, is not just feigned, assumed, deceitful love, [4] but all this as the outworking of a wicked non-correspondence to God's own attitude and work. This feigning of love is thus in conflict with the truth and clarity of God from which the acts and attitudes of Christians proceed. [5]

The same tradition stands behind 1 Pt. 1:22. In accepting the ὑπακοὴ τῆς ἀληθείας the baptised have dedicated their souls εἰς φιλαδελφίαν ἀνυπόκριτον. [6] They are thus summoned "to love one another inwardly from the heart." In the understanding of ἀνυπόκριτος the meaning of ὑπόκρισις as "deceit," "dissembling," is predominant, for the subsidiary clause explains the formula φιλαδελφίαν ἀνυπόκριτον. "Unfeigned love" is brotherly love ἐκ καρδίας which rules out πᾶσαν κακίαν καὶ πάντα δόλον καὶ ὑποκρίσεις καὶ φθόνους καὶ πάσας καταλαλιάς, 2:1. In 1 Pt. the theological argument governs the context of the demand for unfeigned love, as 1 Pt. 1:23 f. after v. 22 shows. In contrast, the structure of the corresponding statements in the Pastorals is ethically shaped. In keeping is the fact that πίστις here denotes orthodoxy or fidelity to the tradition, so that the attribute ἀνυπόκριτος can be combined with it. [7] According to 1 Tm. 1:5 love is the τέλος of the Christian message. It is ἐκ καθαρᾶς καρδίας καὶ συνειδήσεως ἀγαθῆς καὶ πίστεως ἀνυποκρίτου, i.e., love is the fruit of pure belief, [8] which is the subjective basis of Christianity, orthodoxy being the objective basis. *Fides qua creditur* shows its genuineness, its unfeigned character, its being ἀνυπόκριτος, in full acceptance of *fides quae creditur* as orthodoxy. Hence heresy is hypocrisy (1 Tm. 4:2 → 569, 17 ff.), as the context of 1 Tm. 1:5 shows. The office-bearer especially must be a model ἀνυποκρίτου πίστεως, and the author can praise Timothy for his unfeigned orthodoxy from childhood, 2 Tm. 1:5. ἀνυπόκριτος is used in a similar way in Jm. 3:17, where to the demonic and immoral "wisdom" of the false teachers the author opposes the heavenly-pure and morally blameless "wisdom" of orthodox Christians: ἡ δὲ ἄνωθεν σοφία ... ἀνυπόκριτος → VII, 524, 27 ff. Here, too, it is taken for granted that heresy is also immoral, "hypocrisy."

3. The same view may be found in the moralising exposition of a Gnostic dominical saying in 2 Cl., 12, 2 f. [9] The author can understand the saying that "two are one" only as a structural description of the virtue of truthfulness: ὅταν λαλῶμεν ἑαυτοῖς ἀλήθειαν καὶ ἐν δυσὶ σώμασιν ἀνυποκρίτως εἴη μία ψυχή.

Wilckens

---

[4] Schl. K., *ad loc.* takes ἀνυπόκριτος in this psychological sense: "That any imitation of love be rejected behind which the man who is chained by selfishness may conceal his lack of love." Cf. the more subtle exposition of Luther on the basis of his pastoral experience, Vorlesung über den R. 1515/16, WA, 56 (1938), 459 f.

[5] On this meaning of ὑπόκρισις in Paul → 568, 25 ff. On the theological nature of the exhortation in R. 12 cf. esp. E. Käsemann, "Gottesdienst im Alltag der Welt. Zu R. 12," *Exeget. Versuche u. Besinnungen*, II² (1965), 203 f.

[6] These two expressions indicate the two great spheres of the baptismal catechism, the faith tradition which is confessionally accepted as the truth, and the ethical traditions summed up in the commandment of love (here, as in 1 Jn., brotherly love).

[7] Cf. on this Bultmann Theol.³, 534; Dib. Past. on 1 Tm. 1:5.

[8] On πίστις and συνείδησις ἀγαθή or καθαρά together cf. also 1 Tm. 1:19; 3:9; 4:1 f.; Tt. 1:15.

[9] On the logion quoted in 2 Cl., 12, 2 cf. the Ev. Thom., ed. A. Guillaumont *et al.* (1959), Logion 22 (85, 20 ff.); in exposition cf. E. Haenchen, *Die Botschaft d. Thomas-Ev.* (1961), 52 f.

```
┌─────────────────┐
│ † ὑπόστασις      │
└─────────────────┘
```

Contents: A. Greek Usage: 1. Preliminary; 2. Medical and Scientific Usage; 3. ὑπό-
στασις as a Philosophical Term: a. Stoicism; b. Peripatus; 3. Middle Platonism; d. Neo-
Platonism; 4. General Usage; 5. Special Meanings: a. In Astrology; b. In the Papyri.
B. ὑπόστασις in Judaism: 1. Septuagint; 2. Apocrypha and Pseudepigrapha; 3. Philo and
Josephus. C. The New Testament: 1. Paul; 2. Hebrews. D. Further Early Christian Usage.

A. Greek Usage.

1. Preliminary.

The word ὑπόστασις is a verbal subst. of ὑφίστημι. Yet it has hardly any senses corresponding to the act. ὑφίστημι. It is almost always to be understood in the light of the
intr. and mid. ὑφίσταμαι. [1] But it reflects only one part of the varied meaning of ὑφίσταμαι. [2] Whereas the verb in the mid. and pass. can mean also "to conjecture," "to agree,"
"to undertake," "to offer" etc., the noun corresponds only to the following senses, which
can involve independent derivations of the noun from the verb: 1. "to stand under (as a
support)," 2. "to place oneself under (concealment)," 3. "to stand off from," "to deposit
oneself as sediment on the ground," and hence "to be," "to exist," 4. "to promise." From
these meanings we get the following meanings of the noun: 1. "support," 2. "ambush,"
3. "deposit," "sediment," trans. everything that settles, hence the philosophical sense
"existence," "reality," Lat. substantia, [3] 4. "lease," a technical meaning found already in
early Hell. pap. and arising independently from the verb in the 4th cent. B.C. → 579,
33 ff.
    Note should be taken of a special difficulty in assessing the use of ὑπόστασις. It is
inadvisable and even misleading to start out from a gen. or indeed a biblical use, [4] for
the earliest examples are not in the least gen., but belong almost exclusively to the
specialised vocabulary of science and medicine. In this sphere the word became a common

---

ὑ π ό σ τ α σ ι ς. Bibl.: Liddell-Scott, Moult.-Mill., Pr.-Bauer, s.v.; C. Arpe, "Substantia,"
Philol., 94 (1941), 65-78; H. Dörrie, "Ὑπόστασις. Wort- u. Bedeutungsgeschichte," NGG
philologisch-hist. Klasse, 1955, 3 (1955), 35-92; F. Erdin, Das Wort Hypostasis, Diss. Freiburg (1939); M. A. Mathis, The Pauline Πίστις — Ὑπόστασις acc. to Hb. 11:1, Diss.
Washington (1920); H. Ringgren, Art. "Hypostasen," RGG³, III, 504-6; A. Schlatter, Der
Glaube im NT⁵ (1963), 614-8; R. E. Witt, "Ὑπόστασις," Festschr. R. Harris (1933), 319-
343.
    [1] Cf. esp. the stress on this in Dörrie, 39; on the derivation cf. also Mathis, 124 f. and the
much too schematic derivation from senses of the verb in Erdin, 1 f.
    [2] Cf. Liddell-Scott, s.v.
    [3] Sen. Ep. morales, 58, 15 has substantia for ὑπόστασις in a Stoic quotation.
    [4] This produced the class. misunderstanding whereby Luther on Melanchthon's advice
transl. ὑπόστασις in Hb. 11:1 by "assurance" (→ 584, 27 ff.). It also hampers the otherwise
excellent enquiry of Dörrie, who begins with the non-philosophical use and in addition brings
in many bibl. ref., 37-46.
```
```

tt. from Hippocr. and Aristot. One should also note the technical use in the pap. from the 3rd cent. B.C. → 579, 33 ff. In contrast, we have almost no examples of the non-technical use of the noun in everyday speech of the class. period, though the verb is common enough in class. lit. [5] The only exceptions are Soph. Fr., 719 (Pearson) and Menand. Fr., 397 (Körte). [6] While ὑπόστασις has in the first of these a sense not found elsewhere, that of "ambush," [7, 8] in the second the meaning seems to correspond to scientific usage. [9] We are thus dealing with a word which was developed very early as a specialised scientific term. [10] The philosophical use which grew up later is dependent on this early specialisation. Even later the range of meaning hardly goes beyond the scientific and related philosophical sense. But this means that for ὑπόστασις in its later gen. usage we must avoid deriving all kinds of senses etymologically from the different meanings of the verb ὑφίστημι/ὑφίσταμαι.

2. Medical and Scientific Usage.

Only rarely, and inadequately attested, do we find here a meaning connected with the etymology: "support." In descriptions of dislocations of the hip it is said that in some cases the sick member can still serve as a support for the body; in Hippocr. Περὶ ἄρθρων ἐμβολῆς, 55 (Littré, IV, 240) the sense of "prop" for the main part of the hip is clear, [11] and we find the same meaning once in Aristot.: many-fingered four-footed beasts can use their front feet as hands ... οὐ μόνον ἕνεχ' ὑποστάσεως τοῦ βάρους, Aristot. Part. An., II, 16, p. 659a, 24. Ὑπόστασις is used here instead of ἔρεισμα, which we find elsewhere in this connection. [12] But this special use, restricted to only a few passages, [13] did not undergo any further development outside the field of anatomy. [14]

Much more significant and more widely influential, however, is the use of ὑπόστασις as a special term for "what settles." [15] Hippocr. uses it thus for the "sediment of urine," i.e., the cellular and crystalline elements in urine, e.g., in the sick οἷσιν ἐξ ἀρχῆς, ἢ

---

[5] E.g., Hom. Il., 4, 267; Pind. Olymp., 6, 1; 8, 26; Hdt., I, 196, 3 etc.; Plat. Phileb., 19a; Soph. Ai., 1091; Eur. El., 983; cf. Liddell-Scott, s.v. ὑφίστημι.

[6] Both examples in Socrates Hist. eccles., III, 7 (MPG, 67 [1859], 396a, ed. R. Hussey [1853], I, 400, 26 - 401, 7).

[7] But v. for the verb Hdt., VIII, 91; Eur. Andr., 1114.

[8] Already called an unusual meaning by the grammarian Irenaeus acc. to Socrates, III, 7: ... μὴ ταῦτα σημαίνειν, ἐφ' ὧν νῦν παραλαμβάνεται. Παρὰ μὲν γὰρ Σοφοκλεῖ ἐν Φοίνικι ἐνέδραν σημαίνειν τὴν ὑπόστασιν· παρὰ δὲ Μενάνδρῳ, τὰ καρυκεύματα..., cf. also Dörrie, 35 f.

[9] The ref. is to the "dregs of wine," cf. Dörrie, 47 f. The Menander passage in Socr. is explained by ὡς εἴ τις λέγοι τὴν ἐν τῷ πίθῳ τοῦ οἴνου τρύγα ("the deposit in the wine-jug") ὑπόστασιν.

[10] Hence the impression of the Atticist Irenaeus (→ n. 8) that the word does not belong in cultivated style: βάρβαρον ἀποκαλεῖ τὴν λέξιν.

[11] Cf. Hippocr. Κατ' ἰητρεῖον, 3 (Littré, III, 284) for a similar sense; at the operation the patient should support the doctor φυλάσσων ὑπόρρυσιν, ὑπόστασιν, ἔκτρεψιν. But the other words in this sentence are also obscure.

[12] Because of their gt. weight elephants use their fore-feet only as a support μόνον ἐρείσματός εἰσι χάριν, Part. An., II, 16, p. 659a, 27; cf. IV, 10, p. 689b, 19 etc.

[13] Those adduced seem to be the only passages where the word is used with ref. to the human or animal body, Dörrie, 38.

[14] Another example is Philo Mechanicus, 84, 9 (ed. H. Diels and E. Schramm, AAB, 1919, 12 [1920]), 32: ὑποστάσεις ἐπάλξεων "the lower parts" (substructure) of a rampart. The repeatedly adduced example of an act. "underpropping," i.e., ἡ τοῦ ξύλου ὑπόστασις Hippocr. Μοχλικόν, 25 (Littré, IV, 368) (so Erdin, 3) must be abandoned, since one should read ὑπότασις here (Kühlewein, II, 260), cf. Dörrie, 37, n. 1a; Liddell-Scott, s.v. ὑπόστασις B, II, 1.

[15] Cf. esp. Dörrie, 46-8, also examples for the corresponding use of the verb ὑφίσταμαι.

διὰ ταχέων ὑπόστασιν ἴσχει, "whose urine immediately or very quickly contains a sediment," Hippocr. Aphorismi, 4, 69 (Littré, IV, 526). [16] Galen, too, makes regular use of the word, e.g.: ... τὸ οὖρον, οὔθ' ὑπόστασιν ἴσχον οὔτε ἐναιώρημά [17] τι, Gal. De sanitate tuenda, IV, 4, 40 (CMG, V, 4, 2). [18] ὑπόστασις also denotes the parts of a mixture which settle at the bottom; γάλακτος ὑπόστασις in Hippocr. Περὶ ἀφόρων, 242 (Littré, VIII, 456) means "curds." [19] What is denoted by ὑπόστασις may thus be a fluid or semi-solid substance. [20] This is evident in the further use. Aristot. can sometimes use the term for solid deposits. Watery fluids are those like wine and urine [21] καὶ ὅλως ὅσα μηδεμίαν ἢ βραχεῖαν ἔχει ὑπόστασιν, Aristot. Meteor., IV, 5, p. 382b, 13 f. [22] But usually ὑπόστασις is anything that settles at the bottom no matter of what kind: ἡ τῆς ὑγρᾶς τροφῆς ὑπόστασις καὶ τὸ περίττωμα, urine as such and not just its solid sediment, ibid., II, 2, p. 355b, 7 f.; [23] cf. τὴν ὑπόστασιν τῶν ζῴων καὶ τὴν ξηρὰν καὶ τὴν ὑγράν, solid and fluid excrements, II, 3, p. 358b, 9 f. [24] But elsewhere in Aristot. the term is not restricted to anatomy, though most of the examples are in this field. Thus the slimy bottom of stagnant waters is ὑπόστασις: worms arise there ... ὅπου ἂν σύρρευσις γένηται ὕδατος γεώδη ἔχουσα ὑπόστασιν, Aristot. Hist. An., V, 19, p. 551b, 28 f., also stagnant waters as such formed from the collecting of rainwater rather than fed by springs: τῶν δὲ στασίμων τὰ μὲν συλλογιμαῖα καὶ ὑποστάσεις ... τὰ δὲ πηγαῖα, Aristot. Meteor., II, 1, p. 353b, 23 ff. [25] The gathering of clouds under the influence of cool winds can be called ὑπόστασις, the deposit of moist air: περὶ δὲ τὸν Νεῖλον μόνον τῶν ποταμῶν οὔτε νέφους ὑποστάσεις ὑπάρχουσιν, Diod. S., 1, 38, 7, also the deposit on the smelting of iron-ore, Polyb., 34, 9, 10 f., and finally the sediment in the process of fermentation ἡ τοῦ γεώδους ὑπόστασις, the wine which remains when the "air" has evaporated, [26] Theophr. De causis plantarum, VI, 7, 4. [27] There is no doubt but that we have here a widespread technical usage. Along these lines ὑπόστασις is what settles, what remains, the sediment, collection, deposit, or residue, in whatever form. A constituent part of the concept is that this is the part which can be seen, which manifests itself, which takes concrete shape. How far a non-technical use corresponded to the scientific use in the class. age is a matter of conjecture. The pap. examples of a special use which go back to the early Hell. period (→ 579, 33 ff.), and the common occurrence of the term in Diod. S. (→ 578, 11 ff.), which possibly derives from his sources, make it likely that ὑπόστασις was used in everyday speech in the 4th cent. B.C. But it was the scientific use which formed the starting-pt. for the further development of the term in philosophy.

---

[16] Cf. Hippocr. Coacae praenotiones, 146 (Littré, V, 614), cf. 389 (V, 670) etc.

[17] A tt. for non-isolated cellular elements which cause darkening.

[18] Cf. also Gal. De sanitate tuenda, IV, 4, 45 f. and IV, 6, 20; Comm. on Hippocr. De natura hominis; 158 (CMG, V, 9, 1) etc.

[19] The transl. "sediment of milk" (R. Kapferer, Die Werke d. Hippokr., 24 [1939], 134, cf. "dépôt du lait" in Littré's ed.) is misleading, since milk does not have any natural deposit.

[20] Hence καὶ ὑποστάσιας ἴσχῃ in Hippocr. Περὶ ἄρθρων ἐμβολῆς, 40 (Littré, IV, 176) is perhaps a gathering of pus.

[21] The technical medical sense may be seen here.

[22] The connection with the verb is plain: ἐνίοις (i.e., other fluids) μὲν γὰρ αἴτιον τοῦ μὴ ὑφίστασθαι, Aristot. Meteor., IV, 5, p. 382b, 15.

[23] Cf. II, 3, p. 358b, 9. The collection of urine in the kidneys is the ὑπόστασις of fluids circulating here, Aristot. Part. An., III, 9, p. 671b, 20.

[24] Cf. Meteor., II, 3, p. 358b, 12, also Part. An., II, 2, p. 647b, 28.

[25] It is doubtful whether ἡ δ' ὑπόστασις τοῦ κύματος (sc. ἐποίησεν) τὸν κατακλυσμόν in Meteor., II, 8, p. 368b, 12 should be adduced here. The ὑπόστασις of the wave formed by a contrary wind is usually understood as "resistance," Dörrie, 41, but "gathering" is perhaps better, and as a damming up this causes inundation.

[26] The ref. in Menand. (→ n. 9; 573, 4 ff.) is to be explained along these lines.

[27] For an express discussion of this passage cf. Dörrie, 47.

3. ὑπόστασις as a Philosophical Term.

a. Stoicism. In the sense it bore in scientific usage ὑπόστασις was first[28] brought into philosophy in Stoicism, [29] and it was plainly Pos. who gave the term its special philosophical nuance. There is no evidence that Chrysipp. used the noun in the technical sense. [30] He certainly uses the verb ὑφίσταμαι in his philosophical vocabulary both for the subsistence of unformed being prior to specific things and also for the becoming actual, the coming into existence, of primal matter. [31] It is no accident, however, that Pos., trained and important both as philosopher and scientist, was the first to give the noun its strict philosophical sense. In contrast to the double meaning of the verb in Chrysipp., Pos. obviously uses the verbal noun ὑπόστασις only in the second sense of the verb, namely, to come into existence, and he does so in a sense which derives directly from the scientific use: ὑπόστασις is being which has attained reality, which has come into existence. This usage is plain in the following quotation which probably describes the teaching of Pos.: [32] in the qualities which constitute the nature of an individual thing . . . δύο εἶναι τὰ δεκτικὰ μόρια, τὸ μέν τι κατὰ τὴν τῆς οὐσίας ὑπόστασιν, τὸ δέ τι κατὰ τὴν (sc. ὑπόστασιν) τοῦ ποιοῦ, Ar. Did. Fr., 27. Esp. important is the fact that here ὑπόστασις and οὐσία are clearly differentiated conceptually. [33] Whereas οὐσία is by nature eternal being (= primal matter) as such, its ὑπόστασις is real being which has entered into existence, being manifested in the reality of existence, as present in individual phenomena. These have the twofold ability to achieve actualisation ὑπόστασις of both being and attributes. To understand why ὑπόστασις could achieve philosophical significance in this way one has to realise that in Stoicism being was viewed materially as primal matter. [34] The rise of existence out of the ground of being is thus a physical process whose result can be described by the same word ὑπόστασις which served to denote corresponding phenomena in scientific jargon. But ὑπόστασις underwent a change which was decisive for its future development and which can be understood only on Stoic premises. Thus a distinction can be made only theoretically and not practically between primal matter and its actualisation. This problem found expression already in Pos. in connection with the use of ὑπόστασις. On the relation of primal matter to its actualisation Pos. says that primal matter ἡ τῶν ὅλων οὐσία καὶ ὕλη is as such without form or quality, but ἀεὶ δ᾽ ἔν τινι σχήματι καὶ ποιότητι εἶναι. διαφέρειν δὲ τὴν οὐσίαν τῆς ὕλης τὴν οὖσαν κατὰ τὴν ὑπόστασιν ἐπινοίᾳ μόνον, Ar. Did. Fr., 20. Distinction, then, is possible only conceptually. In fact primal matter always exists as actualised in form and quality. Thus ὑπόστασις comes to denote οὐσία in its actuality. But this also means that ὑπόστασις cannot mean the real, concrete phenomenon. For it is not at all self-evident to Stoicism that οὐσία issues in phenomena. Understanding the relation between these is precisely the problem in this monistic doctrine. The development of ὑπόστασις is linked to this problem. This is plain in the distinction between it and ἔμφασις. It is elucidated in a saying about heavenly phenomena which goes back to

---

[28] All earlier instances of a philosophical use are uncertain. Later doxographers often use the current ὑπόστασις to present older views. The relevant passages have been assembled by Witt, 320-323. There are no pre-Stoic examples at all.

[29] To have seen this and convincingly presented it is the merit of works like that of Witt, 323-9 and esp. Dörrie, 48-58. We can give only the most important points from these works here.

[30] Acc. to Dörrie, 52, n. 17 the word is from the doxographer in, e.g., the Chrysipp. quotation in Ar. Did. Fr., 25: τὸ κενόν . . . κατὰ γὰρ τὴν αὐτοῦ ὑπόστασιν ἄπειρόν ἐστιν, but cf. Witt, 323.

[31] For "subsistence" Ar. Did. Fr., 20. 37; Plut. Comm. Not., 50 (II, 1085e); for "actualisation" Plut. Comm. Not., 41 (II, 1081 f.). Cf. Dörrie, 49; other examples, 49-53 and Witt, 323 f.

[32] Dörrie, 51 and for what follows *loc. cit.*

[33] Only a theoretical and not a practical distinction can be made between ὑπόστασις and οὐσία → lines 27 ff.

[34] Cf. M. Pohlenz, *Die Stoa,* I² (1959), esp. 64-75.

Pos. [35] and is frequently adduced: τὰ μὲν καθ' ὑπόστασιν γίνεται, οἷον ὄμβρος, χάλαζα ("hail")· τὰ δὲ κατ' ἔμφασιν, ἰδίαν οὐκ ἔχοντα ὑπόστασιν ... as, e.g., the rainbow, Aetius acc. to Plut. Plac. Phil., III, 5, 1 (II, 894b), cf. τῶν ἐν ἀέρι φαντασμάτων τὰ μέν ἐστι κατ' ἔμφασιν as, e.g., rainbows etc...., καθ' ὑπόστασιν δὲ σέλα (lightnings), Ps.-Aristot. Mund., IV, p. 395a, 29 ff. [36] The distinction here is between non-substantial and substantial heavenly phenomena. Only the latter are καθ' ὑπόστασιν, and thus real, substantial actualisations of universal nature. [37] The fact that Pos. applied this distinction to more than heavenly bodies may be seen from another quotation: ταύτην (i.e., the side-surface of a body) δὲ Ποσειδώνιος ... καὶ κατ' ἐπίνοιαν καὶ καθ' ὑπόστασιν ἀπολείπει, Diog. L., VII, 135. This usage hardly underwent any further development in Stoicism itself. [38] But its implications are clear, cf. πῶς ἂν οὖν καταλαμβάνοιτο τὰ ἄδηλα, τῆς ἀποδείξεως ἀγνοουμένης; ζητεῖται δ' οὐκ εἰ φαίνεται τοιαῦτα, ἀλλ' εἰ καθ' ὑπόστασιν οὕτως ἔχει, Diog. L. IX, 11, 91. This shows very plainly that ὑπόστασις had come to denote the reality which is not immediately apparent but concealed behind mere appearance: a result of the use of the term by Pos. We shall have to return to this when dealing with the gen. use. But the term also occurs later in the popularisation of Stoic theology: Zeus is called the father of gods and men ... διὰ τὸ τὴν τοῦ κόσμου φύσιν αἰτίαν γεγονέναι τῆς τούτων ὑποστάσεως, ὡς οἱ πατέρες γεννῶσι τὰ τέκνα, Cornut. Theol. Graec., 9 (p. 9, 3). ὑπόστασις here is the actuality of those who descend from the divine father of all. [39]

b. Peripatus. Examples of the philosophical use of the word in the Peripatetics are first found in Alex. Aphr. Quaestiones, 3 (Bruns, II, 2, p. 8, 13). 17 (p. 30, 5) etc.; Comm. on Aristot. Topica, II, 4. [40] It is immediately evident that there is dependence here on the Stoic use. To assume a reality beyond individual things is impossible, of course, on Aristotelian presuppositions. There is a reality only in these things: The generic concepts exist ἐστὶν ὑφεστῶτα not in themselves ἀλλ' ἔστιν ἡ ὑπόστασις αὐτῶν ἐν τούτοις ὧν κατηγορεῖται, Alex. Aphr. Comm. in Aristot. Topica (→ n. 40), IV, 5 (p. 355, 13 f.). [41] But here as in Pos. ὑπόστασις is differentiated from what exists only theoretically: only κατὰ τὸ ὄνομα is being a unity, πολλὰ δὲ κατὰ τὴν ὑπόστασιν καὶ τὰ πράγματα, Themist. In Aristot. Physica paraphrasis, I, 2 (5, 2, p. 4, 27). This saying is thus to the effect that individual things have "essence" and "reality" in themselves, whereas Pos. ascribed ὑπόστασις to individual things only in so far as the being behind them actualised itself in them in contrast to being present only κατ' ἔμφασιν or ἐπινοίᾳ.

c. Middle Platonism. Unfortunately instances of the use of ὑπόστασις in this elusive period of the Academy are very sparse. [42] But the link in the development of the term from Pos. to Neo-Platonism is undoubtedly to be sought here. [43] The beginning of Neo-

---

[35] Dörrie, 55.

[36] On Stoic ideas in this pseudo-Aristot. work cf. W. Capelle, "Die Schrift v. d. Welt," Neue Jbch. f. d. klass. Altertum, Gesch. u. Deutsche Lit., 8 (1905), 529-568, esp. 547, n. 1; H. Strohm, "Theophr. u. Pos.," Herm., 81 (1953), 287; Pohlenz, op. cit. (→ n. 34), I, 361 f.; II² (1955), 177; Dörrie, 56.

[37] It is uncertain whether Pos. had a predecessor for this distinction in Boethus of Sidon (Peripatetic?), who is said to have viewed heavenly phenomena only πρὸς τὴν φαντασίαν, οὐ κατὰ τὴν ὑπόστασιν, Aetius acc. to Stob. Ecl., I, 223, 22 f. Dörrie, 56 emphasises that for Pos. phenomena which are not καθ' ὑπόστασιν can still have reality.

[38] On this antithesis cf. Dörrie, 57 f.

[39] Cf. on this Pr.-Bauer, s.v.; Mathis, 119.

[40] Ed. M. Wallies, Comm. in Aristot. Graeca, 2, 2 (1891), 161, 29; on this and what follows v. Dörrie, 58-61 and the material in Sext. Emp., loc. cit.

[41] Cf. on this passage Dörrie, 60.

[42] For this material ibid., 64-67; Witt, 327 f.

[43] The term has no role in later Stoicism. It does not occur at all in Epict. The use of the verb in Epict. Diss., I, 20, 17 and III, 7, 6 corresponds to older Stoicism and there is no trace

Platonic development may be found in the two instances of the noun ὑπόστασις in the Platonist Albinus (2nd cent. A.D.). For him the soul is οὐσία νοητὴ ἀμετάβλητος τὴν ὑπόστασιν, Alcinous Didascalicus, 25, 1. [44] Here as in Pos. (→ 575, 28 ff.) the ref. is to the actualisation of the ground of being. But now the actuality relates to the intelligible world, to which the soul belongs. [45] The second instance ref. to the basic ground αἴτιον "actualisation," 14, 3. [46] In Albinus the verb ὑφίσταμαι also occurs for the first time in connection with the development of hierarchical ontological thinking. [47]

d. Neo-Platonism. This phase in the history of ὑπόστασις, which is so important for the later development of the Christian doctrine of the Trinity, is of no significance as regards biblical usage, and can thus be very briefly sketched in this context. [48] Final separation from Stoic usage is achieved in the fact that ὑπόστασις can no longer be used with reference to matter. This is ἀληθινῶς μὴ ὄν, εἴδωλον καὶ φάντασμα ὄγκου (mass) καὶ ὑποστάσεως ἔφεσις (yearning for actualisation), Plot. Enn., III, 6, 7, 13. Actuality derives only from the one: ἐκ τῆς ἐν αὐτῷ (i.e., in the one) τελειότητος καὶ συνούσης ἐνεργείας ἡ γεννηθεῖσα ἐνέργεια ὑπόστασιν λαβοῦσα, V, 4, 2, 36. Thus ὑπόστασις as a term for the actuality derived from the one is finally synonymous with οὐσία: ὑπόστασιν δὲ εἶναι καὶ οὐσίαν ἐξ οὐσίας ἐλάττω μὲν τῆς ποιησαμένης, οὖσαν δὲ ὅμως, ἀπιστεῖν οὐ προσήκει, "That an actuality and an essence is always less than the essence which has produced it, yet is essentiality, is beyond question," III, 5, 3, 1. It is evident here that ὑπόστασις is a reality which is brought forth by another and higher essentiality, and yet it is also clear that one must still insist on ascribing ultimate being to the hypostasis thus brought forth. Hypostasis then, as the manifestation of the one which is dependent on true being and which is always at a lower stage, takes on the sense which it has retained up to the present day in the vocabulary of religion. [49] In the history of theology this development was an essential presupposition for the formulation of the early doctrine of the Trinity. [50]

4. General Usage.

Apart from the scientific and philosophical use, but certainly not entirely independent of it, the noun ὑπόστασις occurs for the first time in Polyb., [51] a generation or so before

---

of the influence of Pos. Dörrie, 65 f. adduces here the saying πᾶν τὸ ὄν ὑπόστασιν ἔχει of the Stoic rhetor Dio Chrys. Or., 26, 4 (Budé, II, 333, 15), which simply gives evidence of the continuation of the usage of Pos. On Dio Chrys., cf. Pohlenz, op. cit. (→ n. 34), 364-366.

[44] Platonis Dialogi, ed. C. F. Hermann, VI (1864), 177, 20. Alcinous is certainly identical with Albinus, cf. J. Freudenthal, Art. "Albinus," Pauly-W., 1 (1894), 1314 f.

[45] ὑπόστασις occurs in the same sense in Philo → 583, 18 ff.

[46] Hermann, op. cit. (→ n. 44), 169, 28.

[47] Dörrie, 67 quotes all the relevant passages.

[48] Cf. Dörrie, 68-74 and also F. Picaret, "Hypostases Plotiniennes et trinité chrétienne," Annuaire de l'école pratique des Hautes Études, Section des Sciences Religieuses (1917), 1-52; Dörrie, 73, n. 23; Erdin, 24-28.

[49] This terminology was already used in Neo-Platonism to interpret traditional mythology, cf. Plot. Enn., III, 5, 2, 36. On hypostases in the modern religious sense v. H. Ringgren, Word and Wisdom, Studies in Hypostatization, Diss. Uppsala 1947; Ringgren, 504-6 with bibl.

[50] On the further history of the term in the early Church cf. Dörrie, 75-83; Erdin, 46-86; E. Hammerschmidt, "Eine Definition v. Hypostasis u. Ousia während des 7. allg. Konzils: Nicäa II, 787," Ostkirchliche Stud., 5 (1956), 52-55.

[51] We may disregard here the occasional use in Soph. → 573, 4 ff.; cf. also the Menander Fr. → n. 9, 10.

Pos. with the first philosophical use → 575, 7 ff. The meaning in Polyb. is fundamentally the same: the reality behind appearances. But a consistent transl. is impossible (as in other cases), since very different things might be viewed as this reality. In οὐχ οὕτως τὴν δύναμιν ὡς τὴν ὑπόστασιν αὐτοῦ καὶ τόλμαν καταπεπληγμένων τῶν ὑπεναντίων, Polyb., 6, 55, 2 ὑπόστασις is par. to τόλμα, the "resolution" behind the visible deployment of force, cf. οἱ δὲ Ῥόδιοι θεωροῦντες τὴν τῶν Βυζαντίων ὑπόστασιν, the "resolution" of the Byzantines, 4, 50, 10. [52] But the chief reality behind phenomena is what we would call "plan," "purpose," "concern," not in the sense that this is present only theoretically or conceptually, but in such a way that it is actually present. Polyb., 4, 2, 1 considers it a καλλίστη ὑπόστασις to begin his historical presentation where the work of Aratus breaks off. Similarly Diod. S., 1, 3, 2 says that many historians did not complete the plan of their enterprise τὴν ὑπόστασιν τῆς ἐπιβολῆς and cf. on the value of a universal history: ἐξέσται γὰρ ἐκ ταύτης ἕκαστον πρὸς τὴν ἰδίαν ὑπόστασιν ("plan," "purpose," "enterprise") ἑτοίμως λαμβάνειν τὸ χρήσιμον, 1, 3, 7. [53]

ὑπόστασις has the same meaning in Diod. S. in a very different connection and on the basis of different source material. Often a political or military "plan" is called ὑπόστασις: Onomarchus prodded the Phocians into observing the "plan" of Philomelus τηρεῖν τὴν ὑπόστασιν τοῦ Φιλομήλου, Diod. S., 16, 32, 3, [54] cf. the Thebans "in accordance with their own plan" κατὰ τὴν ἰδίαν ὑπόστασιν combined all Boeotia into a single federation, 15, 70, 2; ἰδία ὑπόστασις here is "one's own plan," i.e., the reality behind one's actions and judgments, cf. also 1, 28, 7. [55] In other writers, too, the same applies. The Egyptians do not reckon the yr. by the sun nor months and days by the moon, ἀλλ' ἰδία τινὶ ὑποστάσει κεχρημένοι εἰσί, Geminus Elementa Astronomiae, 8, 16 (1st cent. B.C.). [56] The distinctive thing is not the "starting-point" [57] but the strictly held "basic conception" of a yr. of 365 days without any compensating addition and the resultant dislocation of the year and seasons. [58] In Cic. ὑπόστασις is the fundamental view and assessment of the situation, while πολιτεία is used for political events, Cic. Att., 2, 3, 3. [59]

In another context in which the word occurs twice in Diodor. we find the same meaning. In both instances there is ref. to the ὑπόστασις of an unfinished temple or tomb: [60] καθόλου δὲ τοιαύτην τῇ πολυτελείᾳ καὶ τηλικαύτην τῷ μεγέθει τὴν ὑπόστασιν τοῦ τάφου λέγεται ποιήσασθαι τοὺς βασιλεῖς, Diod. S., 1, 66, 6. This makes sense

---

[52] In both cases the ref. is not to the resistance as such but to the reality which feeds it, the power of resistance which is virtually present. This is esp. clear in the second case. As yet there has been no battle; ὑπόστασις is the resolution not to yield even though it leads to open conflict.

[53] Dörrie, 43 suggests the transl. "actualisation" for Diod. S., 1, 3, 2, but this will not do in Polyb., 4, 2, 1 or Diod. S., 1, 3, 7, and since the ref. in all three passages is to the ὑπόστασις of a historical work one may assume that the sense is always the same.

[54] Cf. Diod. S., 16, 33, 1. Cf. also the Ael. Fr. quoted in Suid., s.v. (Adler, IV, 676): In their revolt the Syrians carried the Phoenicians, their neighbours, into the same purpose of revolt εἰς τὴν αὐτὴν ὁρμήν τε καὶ ὑπόστασιν. The transl. "resistance" (Dörrie, 41) is untenable here as elsewhere → n. 52; on Dt. 1:12 and Jos. Ant., 18, 24 → 581, 2 ff.; 583, 33 ff.

[55] Here and in the preceding passage Dörrie, 38 f. transl. "disposition," but this gives too subj. a slant. The ref. is to the obj. reality outside the individual and finding its actuality in the obj. concept rather than the disposition.

[56] Ed. C. Manitius (1898); we find the same formula in 8, 25.

[57] So Dörrie, 38, n. 7.

[58] By selecting this word Geminus wants to express the fact that there is a profound reason for the dislocation, namely, to prevent the feasts always coming at the same times.

[59] Cf. Dörrie, 40.

[60] This has led some to transl. ὑπόστασις by "foundation" here, Dörrie, 38, cf. Liddell-Scott, s.v.: "foundation or sub-structure of a temple." This is an etym. short-cut which cannot be justified and makes no sense in the context. On Na. 2:8 LXX, also adduced for this meaning, → n. 102.

only if ὑπόστασις is taken to be the total plan of this royal tomb or pyramid. The second ref. in 13, 82, 2 is to the gt. temple begun in Sicily and what is meant is certainly not the foundation [61] but the "plan" of the whole temple as this may be seen from the completed parts compared with similar finished structures. This transl. is supported by the fact that what follows shows how this temple with its combination of side-walls and rows of pillars follows two different "types" of plans for temples. [62]

One may thus see that while it is impossible always to transl. ὑπόστασις by the same term, yet in a historian like Diod. S., even though he has it in different connections and takes it from different sources, the meaning is roughly the same in every case, namely, the total plan or basic conception in accordance with which concrete phenomena and acts are to be appraised.

This helps us to understand the not very common gen. use of the word in other authors of the Hell. period. [63] In a statement of sceptical philosophy in Sext. Emp. Math., X, 266 [64] ὑπόστασις as the reality responsible for the rise of phenomena is very closely related to the word γένεσις "origin" [65] and it stands in contrast to ἄρσις "cessation" as γένεσις is the opp. of φθορά, cf. Hermogenes De ideis, I, 10. [66] The basic reality" of time is its ὑπόστασις in Gal. De diaeta Hippocratis in morbis acutis, 3 (CMG, V, 9, 1, p. 372, 13) and it is worth noting that the least possible unit of time, the instant, is the reality which underlies all time. [67] The less informed the usage is philosophically, the more ὑπόστασις means simply "presence," "existence." But here, too, the philosophical background is plain to see, cf. ὑπόστασις in contrast to φαντασία, Artemid. Onirocr., 3, 14. [68] Cf. also the pun on philosophers who speak of ὑπόστασις: the art of the toady differs from rhetoric and philosophy in respect of the reality τὴν ὑπόστασιν, for the one makes possible a truly good life ὑφέστηκεν and the other does not, Luc. De parasito, 27.

5. Special Meanings.

a. In Astrology. Here ὑπόστασις means the "reality" of life present in the constellation at the hour of birth. Since this is a reality which is not yet actualised in appearance but which immutably lies behind phenomena, it seems not unlikely that the philosophical meaning has influenced astrological usage. [69] Cf. Ἀρχέτυπος λέγεται ὁ καλούμενος κλῆρος τύχης, τὰ δὲ τούτου τετράγωνα ὑπόστασις, Catal. Cod. Astr. Graec., VIII, 4, p. 227, 17 f.; cf. XII, p. 174, 2; also frequently in Vett. Val., e.g., the foreordained "reality" of the year, IX, 8, p. 347, 14. [70]

b. In the Papyri. From the 3rd cent. B.C. ὑπόστασις is a tt. in the pap. for a "lease" and also for the "aggregate of deeds of ownership." [71] As regards the former cf. [τῆς ἐν τῷ κγ (ἔτει) ἀπὸ τῶν ἀπολειπου]σῶν παρὰ τὰς ὑπ[οστάσεις, "with ref. to the

---

[61] The building was well advanced when the city was destroyed. Only the roof was missing; what follows ref. to pillars and side-walls.

[62] οὗτος ἑκατέρας τούτων μετέχει τῶν ὑποστάσεων, Diod. S., 13, 82, 3.

[63] Cf. also → 578, 11 ff., 16 ff. for other examples of the usage in Diod. S.

[64] Cf. on this Dörrie, 62 f.; Witt, 328.

[65] Cf. the popularised saying of Stoic philosophy in Cornut. Theol. Graec., 9 (p. 9, 3) → 576, 17 ff.

[66] Ed. H. Rabe (1913), 274, 9.

[67] Cf. the distinction, which goes back to Chrysipp., that ὑφεστηκέναι applies only to the present and ὑπάρχειν only to the past and future, Dörrie, 51 f.

[68] Ed. R. A. Pack (1963). Cf. the Stoic distinction between ὑπόστασις and ἔμφασις → 575, 38 ff.

[69] Cf. Dörrie, 38 and also his "Zu Hb. 11:1," ZNW, 46 (1955), 200. But Dörrie dwells too much on the sense of "initial situation," which is naturally contained in the sense given above.

[70] Other examples are Vett. Val., II, 40 (p. 124, 7); IV, 15 (p. 183, 29) etc.

[71] Cf. Preisigke Fachwörter, Preisigke Wört., Moult-Mill., s.v.

lands of those who have handed back their leases," [72] P. Tebt., I, 61b, 194 (118-117 B.C.). [73] The latter is plainest in the petition of Dionysa: Wives should add copies of their marriage contracts to their husbands' deeds of property ταῖς τῶν ἀνδρῶν ὑποστάσεσιν, P. Oxy., II, 237, 8, 26 (186 A.D.). [74] There is a difference between copies of a specific document like a marriage contract and ὑποστάσεις, the complete "documents" of a person's property which are to be kept in the archives to be valid. [75] It should be noted that ὑπόστασις is not the possession or land as such but the document which guarantees its actual possession. [76] Only in the course of time did the word come to have the transf. sense of "possession," so that much later ὑπόστασις and ὕπαρξις are synon., cf. P. Oxy., X, 1274, 14-16 (3rd cent. A.D.). The same applies in the pledge of liability: I will give no cause for encumbrance κινδύνῳ ἐμῷ καὶ τῆς ἐμῆς ὑποστάσεως, "and I guarantee this with my own person and all my possessions," P. Oxy., I, 138, 25 f., cf. 138, 30 f.; 139, 28 (all 610-612 A.D.). Other instances of this, like those adduced, are very late, [77] just as it is very late that the distinction between the ὑπόστασις "or deed" and the possession itself is no longer upheld, e.g., P. Oxy., III, 488, 17 (2nd-3rd cent. A.D.); P. Greci e Latini, 4, 286, 13 f. (3rd-4th cent. A.D.).

B. ὑπόστασις in Judaism.

1. Septuagint.

The noun occurs in LXX some 20 times [78] for 12 different Hbr. equivalents, though these are of little help as regards the meaning in the relevant passages. [79] The verb ὑφίστημι is used rather more often in LXX, mostly for Hbr. עמד in the sense "to endure," "to continue." [80] There is no apparent link between the use of the verb and that of the noun. In Dt. 11:6 ὑπόστασις is employed for Hbr. יְקוּם, [81] and such meanings as "substance" have been proposed. [82] The meaning of the HT is "ground" אֲשֶׁר בְּרַגְלֵיהֶם, but the LXX denotes "movable property": καὶ πᾶσαν αὐτῶν τὴν ὑπόστασιν τὴν μετ᾽ αὐτῶν. In Job 22:20, where יְקוּם seems to be the original, [83] ὑπόστασις denotes immovable property [84] as opposed to movable (κατάλειμμα), which is destroyed by fire. ὑπό-

---

[72] To speak of the arable land of villages (Dörrie, 45, n. 47) is not quite precise enough; what is meant is the land offered on lease, cf. P. Tebt., I, p. 218, ad loc.

[73] Similarly P. Tebt., I, 72, 111 (114-113 B.C.); II, 336, 7 (c. 190 A.D.); cf. P. Oxy., II, 370 (1st cent. A.D.). The oldest instance is P. Eleph., 15, 3 (3rd cent. B.C.).

[74] In the same technical sense P. Oxy., II, 237, 8, 34. 42 (186 A.D.).

[75] Cf. P. Oxy., II, p. 176.

[76] The alternative explanation that ὑπόστασις was first the possession and then the meaning document arose from this (Dörrie, 44 f.) is untenable. The oldest examples mean "document," not "possession."

[77] Cf. Preisigke Wört., s.v.

[78] 1 Βασ. 13:21, 23; 14:4 not attested in A. One might also mention three instances in the other transl. but not LXX: 1 Βασ. 14:1 ᾿Α; Jer. 20:5 Σ; 1 Βασ. 9:7 Αλλ (Job 22:30 Θ as LXX).

[79] Dörrie, 41, n. 23 rightly observes that ὑπόστασις must be understood wholly in terms of the Gk. in the LXX.

[80] E.g., ὑπέστησαν δὲ διακόσιοι ἄνδρες, 1 Βασ. 30:10; ἐὰν ἀνομίας παρατηρήσῃ, κύριε, κύριε, τίς ὑποστήσεται; ψ 129:3.

[81] Elsewhere in the OT only Gn. 7:4, 23, where it is transl. ἐξανάστασις or ἀνάστημα.

[82] Ges.-Buhl, s.v.

[83] HT reads קִימָנוּ "our adversary," but cf. BHK which proposes יְקוּמָם and G. Hölscher, Das Buch Hi., Hndbch. AT, I, 17² (1952), ad loc.; cf. G. Fohrer, Das Buch Hiob, Komm. AT, 16 (1963), ad loc.

[84] Dörrie, 44, n. 38, cf. 46 takes "substance" in Job 22:20 to mean "life," "property" or "estate."

στασις can be used in these passages since "property" is understood as the "basis of existence." In the first instance this is to be taken very concretely, cf. καὶ οὐχ ὑπελείποντο ὑπόστασιν ζωῆς [85] ἐν 'Ισραήλ, Jud. 6:4. [86] The ref. is to that whereby daily life is sustained. Related to this is the meaning "basis of power": καὶ τὴν ὑπόστασιν τῆς ἰσχύος σου ἐπὶ τὴν γῆν κατάξει, Ez. 26:11; [87] the word has a similar sense in 1 Βασ. 13:21, though this is not wholly clear in the LXX. In most of the instances mentioned thus far the use of ὑπόστασις is due to the perplexity of the translator, who hits on this Gk. term in an effort to explain etym. the meaning of an unusual Hbr. word.

In a whole series of other instances, however, the normal Gk. meaning of ὑπόστασις is plain. What is meant, usually in a transf. sense, is the "reality" behind phenomena, cf. ... ὅτι εἶπα ὅτι ἔστιν μοι ὑπόστασις τοῦ γενηθῆναί με ἀνδρὶ καὶ τέξομαι υἱούς, Rt. 1:12; the HT here is תִּקְוָה "hope." [88] But the Gk. word expresses rather the "reality which gives a firm guarantee." [89] We find this meaning esp. in the Ps. Man has no foundation of his own before God: μνήσθητι τίς μου ἡ ὑπόστασις· μὴ γὰρ ματαίως ἔκτισας πάντας τοὺς υἱοὺς τῶν ἀνθρώπων, ψ 88:48; also ἡ ὑπόστασίς μου ὡσεὶ οὐθὲν ἐνώπιόν σου· πλὴν τὰ σύμπαντα ματαιότης, ψ 38:6, [90] both times opp. ματαιότης, "vain delusion," cf. also ψ 68:3. [91] The foundation of life is with God, as ψ 38 (already quoted) states in the same word: καὶ ἡ ὑπόστασίς μου παρὰ σοῦ ἐστιν, v. 8. [92] If one catches here an echo of the astrological use (→ 579, 25 ff.), this is even plainer in οὐκ ἐκρύβη τὸ ὀστοῦν μου ἀπὸ σοῦ, ὃ ἐποίησας ἐν κρυφῇ, καὶ ἡ ὑπόστασίς μου ἐν τοῖς κατωτάτοις τῆς γῆς, ψ 138:15; [93] here ὑπόστασις is obviously the "life-plan" of man hidden with God. This leads to some other passages in which, as often in Gk. lit., the word means the "plan" (→ 578, 7 ff.) lying behind phenomena or visible action. καὶ εἰ ἔστησαν ἐν τῇ ὑποστάσει μου with ref. to the lying prophets in Jer. 23:22 is a materially apt rendering of וְאִם־עָמְדוּ בְּסוֹדִי. ὑπόστασις as an abstract term for

---

[85] ὑπόστασις ζωῆς is used for מִחְיָה.

[86] Cf. καὶ ὑπόστασιν οὐχ ἔχομεν, 1 Βασ. 9:7 Αλλ.

[87] HT מַצֵּבוֹת "the stone pillars"; cf. the transl. of מַצָּב the "camp" or "post" (?) of the Philistines by ὑπόστασις in 1 Βασ. 13:23; 14:4, cf. 14:1 'Α. The ref. can hardly be to the camp as a "hiding-place" (Dörrie, 40) but rather to the camp as the basis of their power. In the same context מַצָּב is also transliterated in LXX at 1 Βασ. 14:1, 6, 11, 15. In 2 Βασ. 23:14 the same Hbr. word is transl. ὑπόστημα, in Is. 22:19 οἰκονομία, in Jos. 4:3 no equivalent at all. It is evident that LXX did not quite know how to handle the term.

[88] תִּקְוָה is transl. ὑπόστασις at Ez. 19:5, → 582, 3 ff. Melanchthon's "assurance" at Hb. 11:1 has repeatedly been justified by ref. to this and to Rt. 1:12 and ψ 38:8 (ὑπόστασις for Hbr. תּוֹחֶלֶת "hope" → lines 17 ff.), cf. Dörrie, 39, esp. n. 11; also op. cit. (→ n. 69), 199, esp. n. 14; on Hb. 11:1 → 585, 32 ff.

[89] Cf. Dörrie, 39, n. 11: "Even if she could say she still had the basis and guarantee of having sons."

[90] In these two ref. ὑπόστασις is used for Hbr. חֶלֶד (Ps. 39:5; 89:47), which occurs elsewhere in the OT only at Ps. 17:14; 49:2 and Job 11:17 and is best transl. acc. to the Arab. as "that which has endurance, persistence," cf. Ges.-Buhl, s.v. If this is right, ὑπόστασις is very apt, agreeing both with the meaning of the Hbr. and also with ordinary Gk. usage. Less correct is the transl. of חֶלֶד by γῆ in ψ 16:14 or οἰκουμένη in ψ 48:2, cf. ζωή Job 11:17.

[91] ὑπόστασις in ψ 68:3, in supposed allusion to the basic Gk. meaning, seems to be a slavish rendering of מָעֳמָד.

[92] On the Hbr. equivalent → n. 88. The word ὑπόστασις undoubtedly has here the same sense as in ψ 38:6. The claim that v. 6 and v. 8 have the word in different senses rests on a confusion of the texts of ψ 38:6 and 68:3; Dörrie, 38.

[93] The HT רֻקַּמְתִּי "I am wonderfully made" Ps. 139:14, offers no support for ὑπόστασις unless one emends רֻקַּמְתִּי as the original HT, cf. F. Wutz, Die Transskriptionen v. d. LXX bis zu Hieronymus (1933), 199.

God's "counsel" corresponds to the more concrete Hbr. idea of His "council." [94] ἡ μὲν γὰρ ὑπόστασίς σου τὴν σὴν πρὸς τέκνα ἐνεφάνιζεν γλυκύτητα in Wis. 16:21 is to the same effect. The meaning "plan," "purpose," is very clear in Ez. 19:5: καὶ εἶδεν (sc. the lioness) ὅτι ἀπῶσται ἀπ' αὐτῆς καὶ [95] ἀπώλετο ἡ ὑπόστασις αὐτῆς, [96] καὶ ἔλαβεν ἄλλον..., " when she saw that it was torn from her and her plan was thwarted." [97] Dt. 1:12 is to be understood similarly: πῶς δυνήσομαι... φέρειν... τὴν ὑπόστασιν [98] ὑμῶν καὶ τὰς ἀντιλογίας ὑμῶν; par. to ἀντιλογίαι, ὑπόστασις means the "plans" of the Israelites against God. [99] Perhaps Ez. 43:11 should be listed here too. [100] Among the things which are to be noted concerning the future temple we read of ἔξοδοι (εἴσοδοι), προστάγματα, νόμιμα and ὑπόστασις. This might well ref. to the "plan" or "ground-plan" [101] of the temple.

One may thus see that the use of ὑπόστασις in the LXX presupposes a specific understanding of the term which corresponds exactly to Greek usage in the same period as previously sketched. Apart from the few passages in which the word is understood etymologically in a secondary sense, [102] ὑπόστασις is the "underlying reality behind something." As the "plan" or "purpose," or as "that which endures," enclosed in God, ὑπόστασις is used quite precisely for a variety of Hebrew equivalents.

---

[94] If this use of ὑπόστασις seems strange, it is only because attempts have been made to start from the etym. meaning "putting oneself under," Dörrie, 40, n. 20. In fact it agrees perfectly with the transf. Gk. sense of "plan." This is perhaps one of the most felicitous renderings of Hbr. סוֹד, for which LXX has no single word; it uses βουλή, συνέδριον, γνώμη, μυστήριον etc.

[95] καί is not in B 62. 147. 407 Eth. (cf. HT), but is to be read in spite of J. Ziegler, Ez., LXX Gottingensis, 16, 1 (1952). On misunderstandings due to its omission → n. 97.

[96] For HT תִּקְוָתָהּ "her hope."

[97] "Basis of existence," "meaning and purpose of life" (Dörrie, 39) will hardly do here, since 1. the two first statements are par. (both dependent on ὅτι and linked by καί) and thus relate to the foundering of the same plan, and 2. this understanding is against the context, for the basis of existence is not lost; the lioness has other young which she chooses for new purposes.

[98] For מַשָּׂאֲכֶם, which means "your burden" in Dt. 1:12. But note that מַשָּׂא can denote the prophetic saying through which God's hostile purpose is made known, cf. Is. 13:1; 14:28 etc.

[99] What is meant is naturally "opposition and a rebellious mind" (Dörrie, 41, cf. 46), but this is not the basic sense of ὑπόστασις. The real starting-pt. is "plan," as in the par. Ael. Fr., 59 (→ n. 54) adduced by Dörrie; on Jos. Ant., 18, 24 → 583, 38 ff.

[100] The Hbr. equivalent is not clear. In the Gk. text, after καὶ τὰς ἐξόδους αὐτοῦ (וּמוֹצָאָיו) one would expect καὶ τὰς εἰσόδους αὐτοῦ (וּמוֹבָאָיו) rather than καὶ τὴν ὑπόστασιν, and this is in fact added in 'Α Σ Θ. But in this case there is no equivalent for ὑπόστασις apart from וּתְכוּנָתוֹ at the beginning of Ez. 43:11 ("its establishment"), which is left untransl. in the LXX.

[101] ὑπόστασις occurs in this sense in Diod. S., 13, 82, 2 → 579, 1 ff. One may also ask whether the Hbr. equivalent of ὑπόστασις at Ez. 43:11 was not תָּבְנִית, at 43:10 some 20 MSS. read this for תְּכוּנִית, and it is not wildly improbable that in 43:11 LXX read וְתָבְנִיתוֹ for the וּתְכוּנָתוֹ of the present HT; תָּבְנִית "structure," "model" (v. Ges.-Buhl) is an exact equivalent of ὑπόστασις in this kind of context.

[102] Cf. esp. Dt. 11:6; Job 22:20; Ez. 26:11; 1 Βασ. 13:23; 14:4; v. ψ 68:3. One should ref. finally to καὶ ἡ ὑπόστασις ἀπεκαλύφθη in Na. 2:8, where ὑπόστασις is a slavish rendering of נצב ho "to be put." The Gk. of Jer. 10:17 is obscure: In transl. of a corrupt Hbr. text ὑπόστασις is used for the difficult hapax legomenon כִּנְעָה, cf. W. Rudolph, Jer., Hndbch. AT, I, 12³ (1968), ad loc.

2. Apocrypha and Pseudepigrapha.

In the apocr. and pseudepigr. ὑπόστασις is very rare. πᾶσα ἡ ὑπόστασις τῶν σπλάγχνων μου ἐχαυνοῦτο [103] in Test. Zeb. 2:4 is untranslatable until we know the Hbr. original. In ὀλεθρεῦσαι πᾶσαν ὑπόστασιν ἁμαρτωλῶν, Ps. Sol. 15:5 (cf. 17:24) ὑπόστασις has perhaps the sense of "basis," "power," as in Dt. 11:6; Job 22:20, or it might mean "plans," "designs." [104] The sense in ὅτι ἐν βρώμασίν ἐστι ἡ ὑπόστασις τῆς ἰσχύος, Test. R. 2:7, [105] is the usual one of "that which underlies." [106]

3. Philo and Josephus.

a. In Philo both the verb ὑφίσταμαι and the noun occur in theological and philosophical contexts. The verb denotes real existing as compared with mere appearance, so that in the full sense it can be used only of the soul and God, cf. ἐπεὶ καὶ ὁ θεὸς μόνος ἐν τῷ εἶναι ὑφέστηκεν, Det. Pot. Ins., 160. All else is only corporeal "existing" with no permanence; the this-worldly qualities of the soul are part of this: ὅσα τοῦ τῆς ψυχῆς ἀγγείου λέγεται... πλεονεκτήματα πρὶν ὑποστῆναι φθείρεται τῆς σωματικῆς οὐσίας ἀεὶ ῥεούσης, Poster. C. 163, cf. the contrasting of ὑποστῆναι and purely shadowy existence: οὐδὲν οὖν ἔστι τῶν ἀνθρωπίνων σπουδασμάτων ἔργον καὶ πρᾶγμα οὐδέν, ἀλλὰ σκιά τις ἢ αὔρα πρὶν ὑποστῆναι παρατρέχουσα, Deus. Imm., 177. This usage is like that of Middle Platonism → 576, 34 ff. The same is true of the one passage in which Philo uses the noun in his own formulation: ὁ δὲ νοητῆς ὑποστάσεως κόσμος ἄνευ ἡστινοσοῦν σχημάτων ὄψεως, μόνης δε διὰ τῆς ἀρχετύπου ἰδέας τῆς ἐν τῷ διαχαραχθέντι πρὸς τὸ θεαθὲν αὐτῷ εἶδος ἄνευ σκιᾶς μετακληθήσεται, Som., I, 188. [107] This instance is very important. It deals with the world of "intelligible reality" νοητῆς ὑποστάσεως which may be known only through the idea of the primal type to the degree that this is present in that which "was formed" in relation to the seen "original" εἶδος, ἐν τῷ διαχαραχθέντι. This intelligible world is without shadow ἄνευ σκιᾶς. In contrast is the cosmos which is known "by sensory perception" ἀπὸ τοῦ αἰσθητοῦ or by the "seeing of figures" σχημάτων ὄψις. It is apparent at once that terms are used here in philosophical garb which are central to the christology of Hb.: ὑπόστασις, χαρακτήρ, σκιά. [108] Apart from this instance there are two other examples of the term in Philo, but both occur in the exposition of a Stoic dogma, namely, in the polemic against the doctrine of ἐκπύρωσις: ἡ αὐγὴ (sc. of fire) ... καθ' ἑαυτὴν γὰρ ὑπόστασιν οὐκ ἔχει, rather it is made up of coal and flame, Aet. Mund., 88, cf. 92. [109] ὑπόστασις here means "real, substantial existence."

b. In Joseph. ὑπόστασις occurs only occasionally, [110] while the verb ὑφίστημι is used some 30 times. With ref. to the Jewish people we read in Ap., 1, 1: ὅτι καὶ παλαιότατόν ἐστι καὶ τὴν πρώτην ὑπόστασιν ἔσχεν ἰδίαν. What is meant is the "distinctive reality from which it derives its being." The opp. would be derivation of essence ὑπόστασις and origin παλαιότης from some other people. Ant., 18, 24: ἑωρα-

---

[103] Slip for ἐθολοῦτο? cf. Test. XII (Charles, ad loc.).

[104] → 580, 23 ff.; R. Kittel in Kautzsch Apkr. u. Pseudepigr. transl. "essence."

[105] A has only ὅτι τὸ βρῶμά ἐστι ἰσχύς. In Test. XII Charles rightly thinks ὑπόστασις and ἰσχύς might be doublets.

[106] It is not certain whether τοὺς μὴ ἔχοντας ὑπόστασιν ἀγαθῶν ἔργων might be the Gk. original of qui non habent substantiam bonorum operum in 4 Esr. Lat., Schlatter, 617. If so, ὑπόστασις is used for the "heavenly reality" corresponding to good works done on earth.

[107] In the ed. of L. Cohn and P. Wendland this passage is regarded as a Chr. interpolation, while Dörrie, 61, n. 1 thinks it is a Neo-Platonist interpolation. But it is in keeping with Philo's use of the relevant terms elsewhere and is in no sense Chr., but Middle Platonist.

[108] We shall return to this in relation to Hb. 1:3 → 585, 16 ff.

[109] Cf. esp. the passages from Stoic usage adduced → 575, 39 ff.

[110] Jos. Ap., 1, 1 and Ant., 18, 24; ὑπόστασις is textually uncertain in Ant., 14, 320.

κόσιν δὲ τοῖς πολλοῖς τὸ ἀμετάλλακτον αὐτῶν τῆς ἐπὶ τοιούτοις ὑποστάσεως, attests the sense of "resolution" found elsewhere too. [111] The ref. is not to the "endurance" of the martyrs [112] but to the "invisible reality" from which there springs both the visible endurance of the martyrs and also the political murder of relatives. [113]

C. The New Testament.

In the NT ὑπόστασις occurs 5 times [114] in various senses and contexts, twice in Paul and 3 times in Hb.

1. Paul.

The two instances in Paul are both in 2 C. [115] 2 C. 9:4 comes in the second of the two chapters on the collection. [116] Paul has commended the Christians of Achaia for their zeal in the matter compared to the Macedonians, 2 C. 9:2. He has also sent on helpers to prepare the way so that his boasting (→ III, 650, 23 ff.) will not prove empty in this respect (v. 3) and he and the Macedonians who accompany him will not find the Achaians unready: ἐάν... εὕρωσιν ὑμᾶς ἀπαρασκευάστους καταισχυνθῶμεν ἡμεῖς, ἵνα μὴ λέγωμεν ὑμεῖς, ἐν τῇ ὑποστάσει ταύτῃ, [117] 2 C. 9:4. It is natural to think that the expression takes up again the theme of boasting. [118] If so, the point is that Paul will be disgraced because of his previous boasting, that he will be unmasked as a liar. [119] But it is difficult to support this meaning of ὑπόστασις linguistically, [120] and it should also be noted that Paul is concerned about much more than whether his boasting had been right or wrong. He has expressed this concern already in v. 3. The following v. is not just a repetition of the same thought. Paul returns here to his real reason for sending on the brethren in advance. He wants to wind up the collection quickly and successfully. If he finds the Achaians unprepared, he will be confounded in his whole "plan," and not only he but the Achaians as well, since they have made this "project" of the collection their own.

---

[111] Cf. Polyb., 6, 55, 2; 4, 50, 10 → 577, 30 ff.

[112] The etym. derived sense of "constancy," "resistance" (Dörrie, 41, cf. Schlatter, 616) is untenable.

[113] Mathis, 118 f. is right here: "to cling to what is invisible, to which true reality is ascribed." The only pt. is that this is meant in its presence and results, namely, "resolution" rather than "clinging to it."

[114] The verb does not occur in the NT nor in primitive Chr. lit. apart from Dg., 7, 6 (cf. Mal. 3:2), a work which is part of the apologetic lit. of the late 2nd and 3rd cent. and not genuinely primitive.

[115] In neither of these does Luther transl. the word: for ἐν τῇ ὑποστάσει ταύτῃ he has "in such boasting."

[116] On the historical locus of 2 C. 9 cf. G. Bornkamm, "Die Vorgeschichte d. sog. 2 K.," SAH, 1961, 2 (1961), 31 f.; D. Georgi, "Die Gesch. d. Kollekte d. Pls. f. Jerusalem," Theol. Forschung, 38 (1965), 54-58.

[117] MSS 𝔐 pl sy add τῆς καυχήσεως. This is a secondary and, as will be seen, not very apt addition from 2 C. 11:17. Luther's transl. and K.J.V. are based on this, → n. 115.

[118] The sense of "confidence," "trust," "hope," which most comm. adopt both here and at 2 C. 11:17 on the basis of Luther's transl. at Hb. 11:1 (cf. Ltzm. K., ad loc.), is quite untenable.

[119] So Dörrie, 39: "In this situation, i.e., on the basis of overhasty praise."

[120] This is even clearer in the case of the transl. "matter." Mathis, 136 is misled here by the transf. sense of the word "matter," overlooking the fact that while the Gk. ὑπόστασις can mean "matter" it has no sense corresponding to the transf. use of the Eng. "matter" for "affair" etc.

Here, then, ὑπόστασις means "plan," "project," as often in general Greek usage (→ 588, 7 ff.) and the LXX (→ 582, 1 ff.). [121] ὑπόστασις has the same sense in the second instance in Paul. In 2 C. 11:17 Paul introduces his own list of boasts with the words ὃ λαλῶ, οὐ κατὰ κύριον λαλῶ, ἀλλ᾽ ὡς ἐν ἀφροσύνῃ, ἐν ταύτῃ τῇ ὑποστάσει τῆς καυχήσεως. In a foolish comparison of himself with the Corinthian apostles he is not speaking of that which is his true glory but accepting a "purpose" which is forced on him by his opponents. Hence he does not say "in what is my true glory" but ἐν ταύτῃ τῇ ὑποστάσει τῆς καυχήσεως, "in this purpose of boasting (which is forced upon me)." [122] It is plain that in this context ὑπόστασις is almost the very opposite of the reality.

2. Hebrews.

The passages in which ὑπόστασις is used in Hb. (1:3; 3:14; 11:1) are essentially much more difficult to assess. This is especially so in view of the fact that the word has usually been given different meanings and translations in the three, e.g., "essence" in 1:3, "steadfastness" in 3:14, and "standing" in 11:1. [123]

A more or less fixed and developed usage is plainest in 1:3: [124] ὃς ὢν ἀπαύγασμα τῆς δόξης καὶ χαρακτὴρ τῆς ὑποστάσεως αὐτοῦ. Here ὑπόστασις is parallel to δόξα. Both words are obviously describing God's essence → IV, 339, n. 5. It is thus inadvisable to render ὑπόστασις specifically by "essence." The translation should rather express the degree to which δόξα and ὑπόστασις denote two special qualities in God's nature that are both present in the Son as their ἀπαύγασμα (→ I, 508, 13 ff.) and → χαρακτήρ. The fact that these are developed theological terms and not just incidental metaphors is shown especially by the parallels in Philo (→ 583, 18 ff.), [125] above all for χαρακτὴρ τῆς ὑποστάσεως. In Hb. 1:3, as in Philo, ὑπόστασις denotes the actuality of the transcendent reality, i.e., God, while in distinction from this δόξα expresses His mighty "glory" → II, 247, 27 ff. As the "impress" (χαρακτήρ) of this "being" (ὑπόστασις) which alone is real in contrast to all earthly phenomena (σκιά in Philo [→ VII, 396, 39 ff.] and Hb. [→ VII, 398, 35 ff.]) [126] Christ is the wholly valid revelation of this transcendent reality of God. Here, then, ὑπόστασις as "invisible, transcendent reality" is a term in the vocabulary of dualism.

It is best to interpret the best-known of the NT ὑπόστασις passages primarily in this light, namely, the much quoted definition of faith in Hb. 11:1: [127] ἔστιν δὲ

---

[121] Schlatter, 617 agrees here but without adducing the corresponding Gk. usage.

[122] Schlatter, 617 is in full material agreement here. He rightly draws attention to the difficulties which arise when the transl. "confidence" is adopted.

[123] So Wnd. Hb., ad loc. Luther has "essence" in Hb. 1:3, "assurance" or "confidence" in the other two verses.

[124] Cf. esp. Wnd. Hb. Exc. on ἀπαύγασμα and χαρακτήρ, Mi. Hb.[12], ad loc.

[125] δόξα occurs occasionally in Philo as a theological term in the OT sense (→ II, 233, 36 ff.), but ἀπαύγασμα is used par. to εἰκών in the sense of "essential copy" of a prototype, Plant., 50 (→ I, 508, 8 ff.).

[126] Cf. Hb. 8:5, 10:1; for Philo cf. Som., I, 188 (→ 583, 18 ff.); → VII, 396, 18 ff.; 398, 30 ff.

[127] Cf. esp. Dörrie, 84-92; Mathis, 3-11, 141-151 and Dörrie, op. cit. (→ n. 69), 196-202; B. Heigle, Verf. u. Adresse d. Hb. (1905), 109-118; G. Hoennicke, "Die sittlichen Anschauungen d. Hb.," ZwTh, 45 (1902), 26-28; M. A. Mathis, "Does 'substantia' Mean 'Realization' or 'Foundation' in Hb. 11:1?" Biblica, 3 (1922), 79-89; M. Schumpp, "Der Glaubensbegriff d. Hb.," Divus Thomas, 11 (1934), 397-410; E. Grässer, "Der Glaube im Hb.," Marburger Theol. Stud., 2 (1965), 45-51, 99-102; → II, 476, 8 ff.; 522, 1 ff.; 531, 1 ff.; VI, 207, 15 ff.

πίστις ἐλπιζομένων ὑπόστασις,[128] πραγμάτων ἔλεγχος οὐ βλεπομένων. In translation of ὑπόστασις here and in Hb. 3:14 Melanchthon advised Luther to use the rendering "sure confidence."[129] Whereas all patristic and medieval exegesis presupposed that ὑπόστασις was to be translated *substantia* and understood in the sense of οὐσία,[130] Luther's translation introduced a wholly new element into the understanding of Hb. 11:1. Faith is now viewed as personal, subjective conviction. This interpretation has governed Protestant exposition of the passage almost completely,[131] and it has strongly influenced Roman Catholic exegesis.[132] It has also had a broader effect.[133] Yet there can be no question but that this classical Protestant understanding is untenable.[134] The starting-point of exposition must be that ὑπόστασις in Hb. 11:1 has to have not only a meaning like that in Greek usage elsewhere[135] but also a sense similar to that it bears in the other Hb. references.[136] It should also be noted that ὑπόστασις here is parallel to ἔλεγχος and that it occurs in a sentence full of central theological concepts. Now as regards ἔλεγχος it is evident that this does not mean subjective non-doubting[137] nor does it have anything at all to do with conviction; it bears the objective sense of "demonstration" → II, 476, 8 ff.[138] In the first instance, then, the ἔλεγχος of πράγματα οὐ βλεπόμενα is the proof of things one cannot see, i.e., the heavenly world which alone has reality, whereas in Hb. everything visible has only the character of the shadowy and frontal.[139] If one follows the meaning of ὑπόστασις in Hb. 1:3, then ὑπόστασις ἐλπιζομένων bears a similar sense: it is the reality of the goods hoped for, which

---

128 It is now gen. recognised that the comma must come after ὑπόστασις and not πραγμάτων, cf. the express discussion of this in Mathis, 10 f.

129 On Luther's long hesitation before finally choosing "confidence" cf. Dörrie, 89-91, who has also collected the corresponding ref.

130 On this cf. Dörrie, 85-89; Mathis, 12-83; on the M. Ages and esp. Thomas cf. Schumpp, *op. cit.* (→ n. 127), 403-410.

131 Even serious modern transl. follow this understanding, cf. H. Menge, "confident trust." So do the comm., *ad loc.,* cf. Mi. Hb.[12], *ad loc.* Wnd. Hb., *ad loc.* tries to get closer to the sense with his transl. "standing" ("confident reliance"), but the word still denotes a subjective state.

132 Cf. Schumpp, *op. cit.,* 401 f.

133 Tyndale under Luther's influence transl. "a sure confidence." The A.V. went back on this, returning to the traditional sense of "substance." But modern Engl. transl. have adopted Luther's view again, cf. A.R.S.V. (1946) "assurance." The N.E.B. (1961), while retaining the concept of *substantia,* offers the very subj. rendering "gives substance to our hopes," which amounts once again to "assurance." Cf. on the transl. of ὑπόστασις Dörrie, 85, n. 4; *op. cit.* (→ n. 69), 197, n. 5. The subj. understanding also dominates Engl. exposition, cf. T. H. Robinson, *The Ep. to the Hebrews,* MNTC, 7 (1953), *ad loc.:* "Now faith means we are confident."

134 Bengel, *ad loc.* rejected "confidence." But the impressive support of Schlatter, 617 f. for closer correspondence to the common use of ὑπόστασις fell on deaf ears. The time has come, however, when the linguistic labours of Mathis, Witt and Dörrie have made abandonment of the traditional Protestant exposition unavoidable.

135 This is well stressed by Dörrie, *op. cit.* (→ n. 69), 196-202, though his own interpretation is not satisfying.

136 Oddly enough even Dörrie, 85 and *op. cit.* (→ n. 69), 201 has not been able to free himself from the presupposition that has held the field since Luther, namely, that ὑπόστασις must have a different sense in B. 11:1 from that it bears in 1:3.

137 So Luther.

138 Cf. E. Käsemann, "Das wandernde Gottesvolk," FRL, NF, 37[2] (1957), 22; Mi. Hb.[12], 373.

139 Cf. Hb. 10:1 and esp. the distinction between the true sanctuary not made with hands and the prototypical earthly sanctuary in Hb. 8:1 ff.; 9:11 ff.

have by nature a transcendent quality. [140] Primarily, then, ἔλεγχος and ὑπόστασις do not describe faith [141] but define the character of the transcendent future things, and do so in the same sense as Philo (→ 583, 9 ff.) and other representatives of Middle Platonism (→ 576, 34 ff.) speak of the reality and actuality of God and the world of ideas. In a formulation of incomparable boldness Hb. 11:1 identifies πίστις with this transcendent reality: Faith is the reality of what is hoped for [142] in exactly the sense in which Jesus is called the χαρακτήρ of the reality of the transcendent God in 1:3. The one formulation is as paradoxical as the other [143] to the degree that the presence of the divine reality is found in the one case in the obedience of a suffering and dying man (cf. Hb. 5:7) and in the other in the faith of the community. But this is the point of Hb. Only the work of this Jesus and only participation in this work (= faith) are not subject to the corruptibility of the merely shadowy and prototypical.

In this light the meaning of the third and last ὑπόστασις reference in Hb. is evident without further ado. [144] We have become participants in Christ ἐάνπερ τὴν ἀρχὴν τῆς ὑποστάσεως μέχρι τέλους βεβαίαν κατάσχωμεν (Hb. 3:14). This statement is one of those central and fundamental admonitions in Hb. [145] which carry a summons to cleave to that which establishes faith. Hence ἡ ἀρχὴ τῆς ὑποστάσεως (Hb. 3:14) is to be compared with expressions like ἡ ὁμολογία τῆς ἐλπίδος (10:23) and ὁ ἀπόστολος ... τῆς ὁμολογίας (3:1). In such sayings there is no reference to the subjective attitude [146] of faith but always to its objective possession → V, 215, 35 ff. Thus ἀρχὴ τῆς ὑποστάσεως is a description of the reality on which the existence of the community rests, as Christ, the apostle of the confession, is the presence of the reality of God in which believers share. [147] The fact that there can be reference to a "beginning" (ἀρχή) of this paradoxically present reality of God is best elucidated by Hb. 3:2, which says of the σωτηρία that it had a wholly real and visible beginning with the proclamation of the Lord. [148] "To cling to the beginning of the reality (of God)" is thus the same as being confident to the very end of the reality of God which has in all actuality commenced in the life of the community, and this in the way in which this divine reality is present in faith (11:1). [149] It is plain, then, that in Hb. ὑπόστασις always denotes the "reality" of God which stands contrasted with the corruptible, shadowy, and

---

[140] This is very clear in the ensuing description of the things on which the hope of the examples of faith is set → VI, 207, 15 ff.

[141] Hence one should not ask how far faith is ὑπόστασις but what ὑπόστασις has to say about the nature of the things hoped for. Failure to see this means that Dörrie, 84 vacillates between the translations "reality" and "realisation."

[142] It is not, then, that faith lends "the full assurance of future actualisation to what we hope for" (Dörrie, op. cit. [→ n. 69], 202) but rather that the reality of what is hoped for is presupposed and faith is equated with it.

[143] Cf. R. Bultmann on Hb. 11:7, 27 → VI, 207, 15 ff.; cf. → IV, 951, 22 ff. on Hb. 1:3.

[144] Understanding of this v. is impossible if a difference from the usage elsewhere in Hb. is assumed, so Dörrie, op. cit. (→ n. 69), 201 f.

[145] On this cf. G. Bornkamm, "Das Bekenntnis im Hb.," Stud. zu Antike u. Urchristentum² (1963), 188-203; H. Köster, "Die Auslegung d. Abraham-Verheissung in Hb. 6," Festschr. G. v. Rad (1961), 97 f. → V, 884, 11 ff.

[146] Not, then, "the initial position," "the chosen attitude," Dörrie, op. cit. (→ n. 69), 201.

[147] Mathis, 139 f. expounds similarly.

[148] Cf. the correspondence between ἀρχή and ἐβεβαιώθη and that between ἀρχὴ τῆς ὑποστάσεως and μέχρι τέλους βεβαία in Hb. 3:14.

[149] Cf. the warning against ἀπιστία in Hb. 3:12, 19, which is the framework for the admonition to cleave to the ἀρχὴ τῆς ὑποστάσεως in 3:14.

merely prototypical character of the world but which is paradoxically present in Jesus and is the possession of the community as faith.

D. Further Early Christian Usage.

In the NT the technical use of ὑπόστασις was restricted to Hb., which in other respects, too, has a theological terminology influenced like Philo's by philosophical usage. It is in keeping with this that outside the NT the term does not recur at all until the vocabulary of philosophy begins to have a clear effect on Chr. literature. Even Just. does not use the word. It becomes common for the first time in his disciple Tatian, in whom it has a sense influenced by the usage of the Stoa (→ 575, 2 ff.) and Middle Platonism (→ 576, 34 ff.). [150]

For Tatian God is absolute ὑπόστασις, i.e., "absolute, underived reality," and as such the foundation of the whole world: ὁ γὰρ δεσπότης τῶν ὅλων αὐτὸς ὑπάρχων τοῦ παντὸς ἡ ὑπόστασις, Tat. Or. Graec., 5, 1. [151] In a fully Stoic sense ὑπόστασις is the "reality" of God as manifested in the cosmos, cf. καθὸ δὲ πᾶσα δύναμις ὁρατῶν τε καὶ ἀοράτων αὐτὸς ὑπόστασις [152] ἦν σὺν αὐτῷ τὰ πάντα," in so far as it is the total power and reality of things visible and invisible, the all was with him"; again: σὺν αὐτῷ [153] διὰ λογικῆς δυνάμεως αὐτὸς καὶ ὁ λόγος, ὃς ἦν ἐν αὐτῷ, ὑπέστησεν, 5, 1. The fact that Tat. also tries to distinguish this divine reality from actualised being brings to light the problems involved in adopting this philosophical term into theology. [154] In another context in Tat. ὑπόστασις is "the reality standing behind existence," so the ὑπόστασις τῆς σαρκικῆς ὕλης in which man exists unconsciously and in concealment before birth," 6, 2, or the "reality" which is visible only to God, ἡ ὁρατὴ αὐτῷ μόνον ὑπόστασις, in which man finds himself after death and from which God can raise him up, loc. cit., or the "reality" of demons, ἡ τῶν δαιμόνων ὑπόστασις, which arises out of matter and wickedness, 15, 3, [155] or the "reality" of the elements, which Tat. cannot worship, however, since they are real but not divine; he rejects the allegory acc. to which the gods are "realities" of nature permeating the elements φύσεως δὲ ὑποστάσεις καὶ στοιχείων διακοσμήσεις, 21, 3. There is another instance of the same philosophical use in Athenagoras: One part of the angels rebelled against God τῇ τῆς οὐσίας ὑποστάσει καὶ τῇ ἀρχῇ, Suppl., 24, 4. Diognetus, however, takes the common view that ὑπόστασις is the "reality" behind appearances. One should test with the understanding as well as the eyes, τίνος ὑποστάσεως ἢ τίνος εἴδους are the things called gods, Dg., 2, 1; it will then be seen that the underlying "reality" is only stone, metal, wood etc.

In Gnostic texts ὑπόστασις occurs already in the 2nd cent. A.D. and is undoubtedly borrowed from philosophy. [156] In the Valentinians acc. to Iren. Haer., I, 6, 2 [157] πνευματικὴ ὑπόστασις is the "hidden spiritual reality," the "true nature" of the pneumatic, which in the midst of worldly activity can suffer no more damage than does gold, that

---

[150] On ὑπόστασις in Tat. v. M. Elze, "Tat. u. seine Theol.," Forschungen zur Kirchen- u. Dogmengesch., 9 (1960), 65; Mathis, 13-15; Dörrie, 75; Witt, 332 f.

[151] Ed. E. Schwartz, Tatiani Oratio ad Graecos (1888), though this text is debatable; cf. here and in the other ref. Goodspeed's ed.

[152] Punctuation acc. to Elze, op. cit., 72. There is no real reason to cut out αὐτὸς ὑπόστασις here, Dörrie, 75, n. 5; Schwartz, op. cit.

[153] Division and αὐτῷ for αὐτῷ acc. to Elze, op. cit., 72.

[154] Elze, 65.

[155] Elze, 103.

[156] In the intr. and subscriptio of The Nature of Archons ὑπόστασις means "plan," "purpose" (→ 578, 7 ff.), v. the text in P. Labib, Coptic Gnostic Pap. in the Coptic Museum at Old Cairo, I (1956), 134, 20. 26-27; 145, 22, cf. H. M. Schenke, "Das Wesen d. Archonten," ThLZ, 83 (1958), 661-670.

[157] Cf. W. Völker, "Quellen z. Gesch. d. chr. Gnosis, Sammlung ausgewählter kirchen- u. dogmengeschichtlicher Quellenschr.," NF, 5 (1932), 115.

keeps its true nature τὴν ἰδίαν φύσιν even when cast in the mire. Similarly in the Apocr. Joh. the soul-hypostasis ΝϨΥΠΟϹΤΑϹΙϹ ΝΤΕ Τ⳩ΥΧΗ etc. out of which man is made is the "underlying reality" of the 7 essences of the soul of which the substances of the human body consist (bones, tendons, flesh etc.). [158] In another passage the ὑπόστασις [159] of the σάρξ is the "reality of earthly existence" which the redeemed use until they enter into eternal life, Apocr. Joh. Cod. II, 25, 34. [160] The first beginnings of an adoption of hierarchical thinking in the use of ὑπόστασις occur in the description of created man as the ὑπόστασις of the first perfect man as seen in a mirror, Cod. II, 15, 9-10. [161]

Tat. and the Gnostic texts bear witness to the introduction of the term ὑπόστασις into the Chr. vocabulary. But there is no straight line from this early Chr. use to the employment of the term in the catholic doctrine of the Trinity. One has rather to consider at every step the corresponding philosophical usage in the period concerned.

Köster

---

[158] M. Krause and P. Labib, "Die drei Versionen d. Apocr. d. Joh.," *Abh. d. deutschen archäol. Instituts Kairo, Kpt. Reihe,* I (1962), Cod. III, 23, 10; II, 15, 9-10; esp. clearly IV, 24, 17 f.

[159] In Cod. III, 33, 15 we find instead προσυπόστασις, which is not attested elsewhere, cf. Krause and Labib, *op. cit.* (→ n. 158).

[160] Krause and Labib, *op. cit.* (→ n. 158); cf. Cod. IV, 40, 9-10; not in W. C. Till, "Die gnostischen Schr. d. Kpt. Pap. Berolinensis," 8502, TU, 60 (1955), 65, 19.

[161] Cf. Cod. IV, 23, 27; but III, 22, 8 and Pap. Berolinensis, 8502, 46, 16 have πλάσμα instead.

ὑποστέλλω   → VII, 597, 13 ff.
ὑποστολή   → VII, 599, 1 ff.
ὑποταγή   → 46, 24 ff.
ὑποτάσσω   → 39, 22 ff.
ὑποτύπωσις → 246, 1 ff.

---

† ὑπωπιάζω

---

1. ὑπωπιάζω is the denominative verb of ὑπώπιον, which means the "part of the face under the eyes," also the eyes themselves or the whole face. [1] Aristot. Rhet., III, 11, p. 1413a, 19 ff. mentions as an example of metaphors that consist in hyperbole the ref. to a ὑπωπιασμένος which might be taken for a basket full of mulberries. The tertium comparationis is the pronounced red or blue colouring of the ὑπώπιον. Diog. L., VI, 89 tells how the Cynic Crates was "struck in the face" (ὑπωπιάσθη) by a certain Nicodromos and avenged himself by putting the name of the culprit on his disfigured face. Ὑπωπιάζω means, then, to strike someone on the face (under the eyes) in such a way that he gets a "black eye" and is disfigured as a result. The description of cities ravaged by war as πόλεις... δαιμονίως ὑπωπιασμέναι in Aristoph. Pax, 539 ff. stays fairly close to the literal meaning: the "face" of the cities has been disfigured by the blows suffered. In contrast, when Plut. Fac. Lun., 5 (II, 921 f.) says of certain people with ref. to their theories about the constitution of the moon ὑπωπιάζειν [2] αὐτοὺς τὴν σελήνην σπίλων καὶ μελασμῶν ἀναπιμπλάντας, this use has a real basis in the appearance of the facies lunae, but the sense is fig. "to defame," "castigate" (with words).

2. The LXX [3] has only the noun ὑπώπιον but in the sense "blow in the face," "contusion," Prv. 20:30: ὑπώπια καὶ συντρίμματα συναντᾷ κακοῖς. The Hbr. equivalent is חַבָּרָה. [4]

3. In the two instances in the NT [5] (Lk. 18:5 and 1 C. 9:27) [6] it is hard to decide between a literal and a transferred use. In Lk. 18:5 the unjust judge of the parable supports his decision finally to grant justice to the widow with the words ἵνα μὴ εἰς τέλος ἐρχομένη ὑπωπιάζῃ με. One cannot rule out altogether the possibility

---

ὑπωπιάζω. Bibl.: V. C. Pfitzner, "Paul and the Agon Motif. Traditional Athletic Imagery," *Suppl. Nov. Test.*, 16 (1967).

[1] Cf. Suid., s.v. ὑπώπια and ὑπωπιάζω (Adler, IV, 680 f.).

[2] A conjecture of Turnebus in the Ed. Basileensis (1542) of the Moralia for ὑποπιέζειν, and undoubtedly correct.

[3] These three lines are by Bertram.

[4] With an alteration of the Mas. pointing to חַבָּרוֹת פֶּצַע תַּמְרִיק בְּרָע the v. means that bloody stripes cleanse the will, B. Gemser, *Sprüche Salomos, Hndbch. AT*, I, 16² (1963), ad loc.

[5] The word does not occur in primitive Chr. lit. outside the NT.

[6] The vl. ὑποπιάζω and ὑποπιέζω "to suppress" (on 1 C. 9:27 cf. Bchm. 1 K., ad loc.) are secondary softenings. The image of the arena is added to that of the ring from v. 26 and what is meant is in fact brought out quite well.

that he is expressing apprehension lest one day the widow in her despair might hit him in the face → II, 426, n. 25.[7] If, however, one opts for the transferred sense the meaning depends on whether one construes εἰς τέλος temporally as "in the end," "finally" (→ II, 426, 18 ff.) or as a term of measure "totally," "completely" (→ II, 427, 18 ff.). This will yield either: "lest she finally expose me in a public scene,"[8] or: "lest she wear me out completely by her persistent coming."[9]

In 1 C. 9:26 f. Paul, after comparing the Christian life with the training of the athlete,[10] then goes on to speak of his own apostolic work in metaphors taken from the same sphere. As a runner he runs οὐκ ἀδήλως,[11] as a boxer he does not strike aimlessly in the air → VI, 916, 17 ff. But in the continuation ἀλλὰ ὑπωπιάζω[12] μου τὸ σῶμα καὶ δουλαγωγῶ he sets aside the details of the comparison in the interests of his particular point. He has in view the physical mistreatment he has received, the scars this has left on his body, the hardships to which his body is constantly exposed, and the results of these.[13] Nevertheless, no boxer pummels himself with blows nor does the defeated athlete become a slave of the victor. The expression is thus a figurative one. Paul forcefully subjects his resisting body to his apostolic ministry and makes it serve this → I, 137, 23 ff.[14] What is meant Paul tells us with radical consistency in R. 8:13 (→ VI, 643, 48 ff.): εἰ δὲ πνεύματι τὰς πράξεις τοῦ σώματος θανατοῦτε, ζήσεσθε. The power which vanquishes the body is thus the πνεῦμα. This and the passages cited (→ n. 13) make it plain that the reference is not so much to an ἐγκράτεια practised by the apostle as to chastisements which God lays upon him and their willing acceptance. According to 2 C. 12:7-10 the Lord can even use corporal chastisements (→ VII, 411, 19 ff.) which the angel of Satan (→ II, 17, 2 ff.) inflicts on the apostle — ἵνα με κολαφίζῃ (→ III, 819, 11 ff.) — to make him strong for his ministry. This rules out comparison with philosophical and religious ascetics of every kind (→ I, 494, 26 ff.; II, 340, 27 ff.).[15]

Weiss

---

[7] Pr.-Bauer, s.v.; Kl. Lk., ad loc. This interpretation underlies the introduction of the vl. ὑποπιάζω, cf. 1 C. 9:27 vl. → n. 6.

[8] Cf. Zn. Lk., ad loc.

[9] This is supported esp. by the presents ἐρχομένη ὑπωπιάζῃ. Cf. F. Field, *Notes on the Transl. of the NT* (1899), 71; Jeremias Gl.[7]; 153; Bl.-Debr. § 207, 3.

[10] Cf. L. Ziehen, Art. "Olympia," Pauly-W., 18, 1 (1942), 7 f.

[11] On the meaning v. Pr.-Bauer, s.v.

[12] On the vl. ὑποπιάζω and -ιέζω → n. 6.

[13] Cf., e.g., 1 C. 4:9 ff. (esp. v. 11: κολαφιζόμεθα); 15:10; 2 C. 4:8 ff.; 11:23 ff.

[14] The fact that Paul has abandoned the image in spite of his use of athletic terminology may be seen fully from the concluding final clause μή πως ἄλλοις κηρύξας αὐτὸς ἀδόκιμος γένωμαι. For if the κῆρυξ (→ III, 683, 1 ff.) also calls the names of the contestants (cf. J. Reisch, Art. "Agones," Pauly-W., 1 [1894], 850), he does not take part in the contest and cannot ἀδόκιμος γενέσθαι in comparison with them. There is even less reason to think in terms of a contest between κήρυκες (Reisch, 838 and 850); the ἄλλοις does not fit in with this.

[15] Cf. H. D. Wendland, *Die Briefe an d. Korinther, NT Deutsch*, 7[12] (1968), ad loc.

```
┌─────────────────────────────────────────────────┐
│  ὕστερος, ὕστερον, ὑστερέω,                        │
│  † ἀφυστερέω,  † ὑστέρημα,  ὑστέρησις              │
└─────────────────────────────────────────────────┘
```

Contents: A. Secular Greek. B. Septuagint. C. New Testament: 1. ὕστερος, ὕστερον; 2. ὑστερέω; 3. ἀφυστερέω; 4. ὑστέρημα, ὑστέρησις. D. Post-New Testament Writings. 1. Post-Apostolic Fathers and Early Patristic Literature; 2. Second Century Gnosticism.

A. Secular Greek.

1. ὕστερος, [1] found from Hom., has the basic sense "what is behind, after," in space "behind someone or something," but esp. time "the second" of two: Aristot. Pol., V, 10, p. 1312a, 4; "the next": τῷ ὑστέρῳ ἔτει "the next year," Xenoph. Hist. Graec., VII, 2, 10; ἡ ὑστέρα "the following day," Jos. Ant., 3, 236, cf. ὑστεραία 14, 73 and 464; Bell., 1, 342; "the later": ὑστέρῳ χρόνῳ "at a later time," Hdt., I, 130, 2, cf. Plat. Leg., IX, 865a; ἐξ ὑστέρου "later," Jos. Ant., 14, 100; "too late," ὕστερος ἐλθών, Hom. Il., 18, 320; κἂν ὕστερος ἔλθῃ, Aristoph. Vesp., 691; ὕστερος ἀφικνεῖται, Thuc., IV, 90, 1; with gen. of things: ὕστεροι δὲ ἀπικόμενοι τῆς συμβολῆς, Hdt., VI., 120; ὕστεροι δ' οὖν ἀφίκοντο τῆς ἐν Μαραθῶνι μάχης γενομένης μιᾷ ἡμέρᾳ, Plat. Leg., III, 698e; οἱ ὕστεροι as opp. of οἱ νῦν "those who come later," Jos. Ant., 18, 304, "descendants," "posterity," Eur. Tro., 13. Transf. ὕστερος can also express less worth: ψυχὴν μὲν προτέραν γεγονέναι σώματος ἡμῖν, σῶμα δὲ δεύτερόν τε καὶ ὕστερον, ψυχῆς ἀρχούσης, ἀρχόμενον κατὰ φύσιν, Plat. Leg., X, 896c; οὐσίᾳ καὶ γένει οὐδενὸς ὕστερος, Tim., 20a, cf. Isoc. Or., 16, 31; Soph. Ant., 746 (γυναικός); πάντα ὕστερα εἶναι... πρὸς τὸ... "everything stands in relation to something after," Thuc., VIII, 41, 1, cf. also μηδ' ἔμπροσθεν τῶν νόμων, ἀλλ' ὕστερος πολιτεύου, Aeschin. Or. in Ctesiphontem, 23, also ὕστερον αὐτὸν τοῦ νόμου καὶ τοῦ ἄρχοντος τιθέναι, Plut. Fab. Max., 24 (I, 188c). ὕστερος is also used in the logical sense, esp. in connection with dispositions, ἐν τῷ ὑστέρῳ λόγῳ, Antiphon. Or., 6, 14; Plat. Gorg., 503c; Jos. Ant., 7, 244. Aristot. has πρότερον and ὕστερον astrologically: ἔστι τὸ τῇ γενέσει ὕστερον τῇ φύσει πρότερον, Metaph., 1, 8, p. 989a, 15 f.; Phys., VIII, 7, p. 261a, 14 etc.

2. The adverbial use of ὕστερον, attested from Hom., e.g., Il., 1, 27; Od., 8, 202, is wholly par. to that of the adj., "secondly," "after," "later," "too late," "finally" in the spatial, temporal, or logical sense, e.g., περὶ τῶν ἐς ὕστερον "for the future," Jos. Ant., 1, 325.

3. The verb ὑστερέω, from ὕστερος, [2] first occurs from Hdt. and Eur., the primary sense being "to come after," "to come too late" (opp. φθάνω): κἂν μὲν φθάσωμεν,

---

ὕ σ τ ε ρ ο ς κτλ. Bibl. Liddell-Scott, Moult.-Mill., Pape, Pass., Pr.-Bauer, s.v.; Helbing Kasussyntax, 173-6; J. Kremer, "Was an den Leiden Christi noch mangelt. Eine interpretationsgeschichtliche u. exeget. Untersuchung zu Kol. 1:24b," Bonner Bibl. Beiträge, 12 (1956).
[1] Adj. ὕστερος with adv. ὕστερον is composed with suffix -τερο- as a contrasting concept from the stem υ(δ) as πρότερος is from πρ and is identical with Sanskr. uttara "the higher," "the one behind," formed from ud "upward." Cf. Schwyzer, I, 533; II, 517; Boisacq, Hofmann, s.v.
[2] Schwyzer, I, 726.

ἔστι σοι σωτηρία· ἢν δ' ὑστερήσῃς, οἰχόμεσθα, κατθανῇ, Eur. Phoen., 975 f.; ὑστέ-ρησαν (vl. ὑστέρισαν) ἡμέρῃ μιῇ τῆς συγκειμένης, "they came too late," i.e., "they missed the agreed date by a day," Hdt., VI, 89; κατόπιν ἑορτῆς ἥκομεν καὶ ὑστεροῦ-μεν, Plat. Gorg., 447a; διὸ δεῖ σπεύδειν καὶ μηδεμίαν ποιεῖσθαι διατριβήν, ἵνα μὴ πάθωμεν, ὅπερ οἱ πατέρες ἡμῶν· ἐκεῖνοι γὰρ ὑστερήσαντες (vl. ὑστερίσαντες) τῶν βαρβάρων..., Isoc. Or., 4, 164, opp. here σπεύδω with the goal of προτέρους ἐλθεῖν. Cf. Jos. Ant., 17, 303: Varus did not want to be too late to get his share. That with which one is too late is in the dat. τῇ διώξει, Thuc., I, 134, 2, τῇ βοηθείᾳ, Demosth. Or., 59, 3, and what is missed thereby is in the gen. τῆς μάχης ἡμέραις (vl. ἡμέρας) πέντε, Xenoph. An., I, 7, 12. Thus ὑστερέω often means failure in something: Μυτιλή-νης ὑστερήκει, "he came too late to save Mytilene," Thuc., III, 31, 2, cf. the πατρίς, Xenoph. Ag., 2, 1: ὑστερήσει γάρ μου τῆς παρουσίας "he will not catch me," Synesius Ep., 141;[3] ἄλλην δὲ χάριν οὐκ ἐπιζητῶ λαβεῖν παρὰ σοῦ ταύτης ὑστερήσας, Phalaris Ep. (→ n. 3), 20; so also pap., e.g., P. Oxy., I, 118, 30 ff. (3rd cent. A.D.): οὐδὲν γὰρ ὄφελος ὑστερησάντων τῶν χρειωδῶν τῇ παρουσίᾳ αὐτοῦ, "it is of no avail if one comes too late to things that demand one's presence." The acc. is found as well as the gen. in the pap., e.g., P. Hibeh, I, 65, 29 (c. 265 B.C.): ἵνα μη[θὲ]ν [εἰς ἐ]μὲ ὑστερήσῃ. The καιρός esp. is missed, Aristot. Sophistici Elenchi, 16, p. 175a, 26; Polyb., 2, 11, 3; Diod. S., 15, 27, 3; P. Greci e Latini, 4, 432, 5 (3rd cent. B.C.). Of persons and things ὑστερέω means "to be wanting," pers. Jos. Ant., 6, 235, things μηδὲν... ἢ τὴν βασιλείαν, 6, 194; with gen. ἀπωλείας καὶ θανάτου τυραννικοῦ, 15, 70; ὡς μήτε ὑστερεῖν τι ὑμῖν τοῦ ὑπαρχόντων δικαίων μήτε κτλ., BGU, IV, 1074 (275 A.D.); ὑστερούσης πολλάκις σποδοῦ, Diosc. Mat. Med., V, 75, 13. ὑστερέω abs. occurs in Wilcken Ptol., I, 20, 26 (163 B.C.): εἰς τὸ μηθὴν... ἡμᾶς ὑστερεῖν, cf. synon. ἐγλι-πεῖν, line 30. Derived from ὕστερος in the sense "standing behind something" is the meaning "to stand behind someone," "to be after someone," ἐμπειρίᾳ ὑστερῶσι τῶν ἄλλων, Plat. Resp., VII, 539e; μηδ' ἐν ἄλλῳ μηδενὶ μέρει ἀρετῆς ὑστεροῦντας, VI, 484d; πότερον ἔχει λόγον ὁ λόγος ἢ πάντως ὑστερεῖ, Ps.-Plat. Epin., 983d, also Jos. Bell., 1, 271: τῆς ἀρετῆς ὑστερίζει. Finally in Hell. one finds the sense "to lack something" equally in the pass. deponent and act.,[4] cf. μηδενὸς ὦν... ἀπέλαυον ὑστερῶσιν ἀγαθῶν, Jos. Ant., 1, 98; πλήθους, 5, 214, cf. also Demosth. Or., 19, 332: πολλῶν ὑστερῶν.

4. The nouns ὑστέρημα and ὑστέρησις are very rare in ancient lit. apart from the LXX and Chr. writings. For ὑστέρημα cf. Corp. Herm., 4, 10; αὕτη διαφορὰ τοῦ ὁμοίου πρὸς τὸ ἀνόμοιον, καὶ τῷ ἀνομοίῳ ὑστέρημα πρὸς τὸ ὅμοιον, 13, 1, where the initiate asks the mystagogue: σὺ δέ μου καὶ τὰ ὑστερήματα ἀναπλήρωσον οἷς ἔφης μοι παλιγγενεσίας ⟨γένεσιν⟩ παραδοῦναι προθέμενος ἐκ φωνῆς ἢ κρυβήν. We have here the underlying expression ἀναπληροῦν ὑστέρημα "to fill up what is lacking," which is also found in Chr. lit. → 598, 33 ff.; 600, 19 ff. Similarly Test. B. 11:5 (text uncertain): Αὐτὸς ἀναπληρώσει τὰ ὑστερήματα τῆς φυλῆς σου. Cf. also ἀναπληρώσειν τὸ λεῖπον, Jos. Ant., 5, 214. With "what is missing" ὑστέρημα can also mean "want" like ἥσσημα opp. προτέρημα, though there are only two late examples in secular Gk.: Achmes, Oneirocriticon,[5] 152 with par. λεῖψις and Eutecnius Παράφρασις εἰς τὰ τοῦ Ὀππιανοῦ κυνηγητικά, IV[6] with opp. πλεονέκτημα. ὑστέρησις always means "want," "need."

---

[3] Ed. R. Hercher, Epistolographi Graeci (1873).
[4] So Helbing Kasussyntax, 174. Cf. also Bl.-Debr. § 101 who ref. to ἀπορεῖν — ἀπορεῖσ-θαι. For ὑστερεῖσθαί τινος cf. Diod. S., 18, 71, 5: τῆς χρείας, Jos. Ant., 15, 200: μήτε οἴνου μήτε ὕδατος, P. Masp, I, 67002, 3, 14 (c. 522 A.D.).
[5] Profane text with Chr. redaction c. 900 A.D., ed. F. Drexl (1925), 111, 4.
[6] Ed. O. Thüselmann, AGG, NF, 4, 1 (1900), 37, 17.

B. Septuagint.

1. Whereas ὕστερος (4 times) and ὕστερον (15) are always used in a temporal sense "after," "later," the sense "to have a deficiency" predominates in the case of ὑστερέω [7] and ὑστέρημα. [8] In most instances [9] the Hbr. original here is חסר. [10] Ointment is not to be lacking on the head Qoh. 9:8, the mixing cup is not to be empty Cant. 7:3, riches do not allow lack of anything the soul desires Qoh. 6:2, wisdom promises its pupils to fill every lack of instruction or thirst of soul Sir. 51:24; the man who has God as shepherd lacks nothing ψ 22:1. Worth noting is ψ 38:5: "Tell me, Lord, my end and what is the number of my days, ἵνα γνῶ τί ὑστερῶ." The transl. has moralised here. The HT "how fleeting (חָדֵל) I am," becomes: "that I may know what I lack," i.e., that I am a sinner. [11] Synon. of ὑστερέω [12] are ἀπορέω Sir. 10:27 (vl. ὑστερῶν) and ἐνδέομαι Dt. 15:8 vl. Close to the sense of "having a lack" is that of "to come too late," "not to attain," as may be seen esp. in Sir. 11:11 f., where the two meanings are found together: ἔστιν κοπιῶν καὶ πονῶν καὶ σπεύδων, καὶ τόσῳ μᾶλλον ὑστερεῖται (מתאחר). ἔστιν νωθρὸς προσδεόμενος ἀντιλήμψεως, ὑστερῶν ἰσχύϊ (חסר כח) [13] καὶ πτωχείᾳ περισσεύει. The opp. in v. 11 is σπεύδων and in v. 12 περισσεύει. Cf. also: ἡμεῖς ἀκάθαρτοι ἐπὶ ψυχῇ ἀνθρώπου· μὴ οὖν ὑστερήσωμεν προσενέγκαι τὸ δῶρον κυρίῳ κατὰ καιρὸν αὐτοῦ ἐν μέσῳ υἱῶν Ισραηλ; (HT: לָמָה נִגָּרַע לְבִלְתִּי הַקְרִיב "why should we be cut off that we not ...") Nu. 9:7; ὃς ἐάν ... ὑστερήσῃ ποιῆσαι τὸ πάσχα (HT וְחָדַל לַעֲשׂוֹת הַפֶּסַח "not to do," "to abstain") Nu. 9:13; and esp. Hab. 2:3: ἐὰν ὑστερήσῃ אִם־יִתְמַהְמָהּ (sc. ὁ κύριος), ὑπόμεινον αὐτόν, ὅτι ἐρχόμενος ἥξει καὶ οὐ μὴ χρονίσῃ. Israel must abide with confidence the delay in God's sure coming. ὑστερέω ἀπό τινος in the sense "to remain far from, to avoid someone," occurs in Job 36:17: οὐχ ὑστερήσει δὲ ἀπὸ δικαίων κρίμα (no HT) and Sir. 7:34: μὴ ὑστέρει ἀπὸ κλαιόντων (HT אַל תְּאַחֵר מִבּוֹכִים). Very close here, unless it is to be construed thus, [14] is the causative use in the vl. of ψ 83:12, where we find ὑστερέω for στερέω.

---

[7] The act and mid. are used equally and promiscue.

[8] ὑστέρησις occurs only in the Hexapla transl., e.g., Job 30:3 Ἀ.

[9] The only exception is Sir. 13:4: Ἐὰν χρησιμεύσῃς, ἐργᾶται (sc. ὁ πλούσιος) ἐν σοί· καὶ ἐὰν ὑστερήσῃς, καταλείψει σε. The Hbr. original is כרע "to fall or sink down exhausted." In ἐὰν ὑστερήσῃς the translator finds an exact adversative match for ἐὰν χρησιμεύσῃς. He used the verb ὑστερέω in the sense "to be poor, needy" to gain an effect in the Gk. which the HT does not have.

[10] In 14 of 21 LXX and 6 Hexapla examples ὑστερέω is used for Hbr. חסר and in 9 of 10 examples of ὑστέρημα and ὑστέρησις in LXX and Hexapla we find Hbr. words of the root חסר. This root, found 63 times in Hbr., is transl. a total of 23 times by ὑστερέω and derivates.

[11] So Helbing Kasussyntax, 174. It is also possible the transl. simply wants to make the HT more concrete, in which case τί ὑστερῶ ref. to the span of time up to the end of the days: "how much is still wanting."

[12] Cf. also καθυστερέω 1 Ch. 26:27; Sir. 37:20; 16:13.

[13] So (for כֹּל) one should read with R. Smend, Die Weisheit d. Sir. erklärt (1906), ad loc.

[14] χάριν καὶ δόξαν δώσει· κύριος οὐ στερήσει (vl. ὑστερήσει) τὰ ἀγαθὰ τοὺς πορευομένους ἐν ἀκακίᾳ. If in the vl. one assumes identity of subj. with δώσει as in the reading στερήσει, which corresponds to HT (מנע "to withhold," "to refuse"), then we have the causative use of ὑστερέω found elsewhere only in later Chr. lit.; on τινά τινος v. the examples in Pass., s.v.; τινά τι occurs only in modern Gk., cf. A. Thumb, Hndbch. d. neugriech. Volkssprache² (1910), 33 in Helbing Kasussyntax, 175. Schleusner, s.v. quotes a vl. at Nu. 24:11: καὶ νῦν ὑστέρηκέ (for ἐστέρησέν) σε κύριος τῆς δόξης. This may be a scribal error. But the use of the compounds ἀφυστερέω (twice) and καθυστερέω (4 times) shows a plain drift towards the causative use, cf. 2 Εσδρ. 19:20: τὸ μαννα σοῦ οὐκ ἀφυστέρησας ἀπὸ στόματος αὐτῶν (HT מן as in ψ 83:12, elsewhere transl. [ἀπο]στερέω); cf. also Ex. 22:28; Sir. 16:13 in the reading of Cod B, cf. Helbing Kasussyntax, 175 f.

2. ὑστέρημα (6 times) always means "lack," either to denote the lack of something with gen. of what is lacking, not wherein there is lack, cf. Ju. 18:10; 19:19 f. and esp. Qoh. 1:15: διεστραμμένον οὐ δυνήσεται τοῦ ἐπικοσμηθῆναι, καὶ ὑστέρημα οὐ δυνήσεται τοῦ ἀριθμηθῆναι, i.e., when there is nothing present there is nothing to list, or in the sense of "need," "poverty," abs ψ 33:10: φοβήθητε τὸν κύριον, οἱ ἅγιοι αὐτοῦ, ὅτι οὐκ ἔστιν ὑστέρημα (אין מחסור) τοῖς φοβουμένοις αὐτόν, and also 2 Εσδρ. 6:9: καὶ ὃ ἂν ὑστέρημα (מה) ... ἔστω διδόμενον αὐτοῖς, the lack being always in the abs., not the comparative sense.

C. New Testament.

1. ὕστερος, ὕστερον.

a. The adjective occurs in Mt. 21:31: ὁ ὕστερος "the last-named," [15] cf. 1 Tm. 4:1. The reference here is to being led astray by false teachers who ἐν ὑστέροις καιροῖς will try to overthrow believers. The conceptual horizon is traditional apocalyptic eschatology (→ I, 513, 8 ff.). In this context the first Christian experiences of error, debate, and apostasy soon found a fixed locus, cf. Mk. 13:22 f. It is typical of the situation of early Catholicism, however, that the eschatological notions of tradition were obviously regarded as prophetic descriptions of the present experiences of the Church, which, as predicted by the holy apostles, had now reached full measure. Thus in a smooth transition the last times become later future times, i.e., "later" in terms of the sacred time of origin with Jesus and the apostles. Cf. similarly 2 Tm. 3:1: ἐν ἐσχάταις ἡμέραις with 4:3: ἔσται γὰρ καιρὸς ὅτε, and also 2 Pt. 3:3; Jud. 18 with 2 Pt. 2:1; J Jn. 2:18 with 4:1.

b. The adverb is always used in a temporal sense and is less common in the comparative sense of "later," "after" [16] than the superlative "finally." In the comparative it occurs at Mt. 21:30: ὕστερον μεταμεληθεὶς ἀπῆλθεν, and similarly at v. 32: ὑμεῖς δὲ ἰδόντες οὐδὲ μετεμελήθητε ὕστερον τοῦ πιστεῦσαι αὐτῷ, cf. also Hb. 12:11: All fatherly chastisement is at the actual time (πρὸς μὲν τὸ παρόν) painful, but later (ὕστερον δέ) it brings forth righteousness as its peaceable fruit for those exercised thereby. In antithesis to πρὸς τὸ παρόν, ὕστερον is probably eschatological: The present time before the end is the time for the exercise of faith, while the eschatological future will bring salvation as the fruit of this exercise. [17] In Jn. 13:36 Jesus answers the question of Peter ποῦ ὑπάγεις: "Whither I go, thou canst not follow me now; ἀκολουθήσεις δὲ ὕστερον." In this passage the meaning of ὕστερον is intentionally obscure. Only Peter's misconcep-

---

[15] On the textual question cf. on the one side Jülicher Gl. J., II, 374-381; Loh. Mt., 310-312; Jeremias Gl.⁷, 125, n. 2, who favour the text of Cod ℵ, and on the other J. Schmid, "Das textgeschichtliche Problem d. Parabel v. d. zwei Söhnen, Mt. 21:28-32," Festschr. M. Meinertz (1951), 68-84, who opts for the text of Cod B, but with a ref. to the third possibility (Cod D) championed by E. Hirsch, Frühgeschichte d. Ev., II (1941), 316 f. (Lachmann and Merx).

[16] So also Jos. Ant., 1, 217; 2, 315; 6, 68 and 170; 11, 140; Bell., 1, 3; Ap., 1, 11; Vit., 355 etc.

[17] The Wisdom theme of education through suffering is given an eschatological dimension here, cf. Mi. Hb.¹², ad loc. and esp. G. Bornkamm, "Sohnschaft u. Leiden," Festschr. J. Jeremias (1960), 188-198. For par. from early Catholic lit. cf. E. Grässer, "Der Glaube im Hb.," Marburger Theol. Stud., 2 (1965), 158-171. ὕστερον is taken in a non-eschat. sense by C. Spicq, L'Ép. aux Hébreux, II, Études bibliques (1953), ad loc. and J. Héring, L'Ép. aux Hébreux, Comm. du NT, 12 (1954), ad loc. (ὕστερον = "en fin de compte").

tion that it is a mere matter of continuing earthly discipleship, even though this be to death (13:37), is rejected in view of the denial which will actually follow (13:38). The possibility of earthly discipleship will be radically abrogated with the death of Jesus. ἀκολουθήσεις δὲ ὕστερον does not refer, then, to a later martyrdom of Peter. [18] What is meant is rather the same as in 12:26: "If any man serve me, let him follow me; and where I am, there shall also my servant be." Directly after 13:36-38 this thought is developed in 14:2 f. with reference to being with the exalted Lord.

In the superlative ὕστερον occurs esp. in Mt.: cf. Mt. 4:2 with Lk. 4:2; Mt. 21:37 with Mk. 12:6 and Lk. 20:13; Mt. 22:27 and Lk. 20:32 with Mk. 12:22 (ὕστερον instead of ἔσχατον); Mt. 26:60 with Mk. 14:57. Cf. also Mt. 25:11. The only other instance is Mk. 16:14.

2. ὑστερέω.

In the NT, as in LXX, the act. ὑστερέω and deponent ὑστερέομαι are used without distinction.

a. The basic sense "to come too late," "to be absent," occurs twice in Hb. in an eschatological connection. With a warning reference to the fate of the wilderness generation as dealt with in 3:7 ff., Hb. 4:1 reads: "Let us therefore take anxious care that none of you should venture to miss (not to attain to) the promise of entering into rest which has yet to be fulfilled." [19] To achieve the promise is the summons to Christians now as it was to the Israelites earlier. To Christians, as to the Israelites, the word of the promise is of no avail as such. What counts is the faith that relies on the word with reference to the fulfilment of what is promised, 4:2, cf. previously 3:12-14 and later 4:11-13 and especially 6:9-20; 10:35-39. There is thus a need to watch carefully, μή τις ὑστερῶν ἀπὸ τῆς χάριτος τοῦ θεοῦ (Hb. 12:15), [20] which would take place through failure in peaceful relations with all the brethren in the community and in sanctification (12:14), and which would be like the conduct of Esau, "who for one morsel of meat sold his birthright" (12:16).

Also in an eschatological context Paul, summing up the section R. 1:18 - 3:20 in a single statement, says in 3:23: All men fall short of participation in the glory of God. [21] But they are justified by God's grace which has been at work in the Christ

---

[18] Against this common assumption on the basis of Jn. 21:18 f., which is favoured by, e.g., Bau J., ad loc.; H. Strathmann, Das Ev. nach Joh., NT Deutsch, 4[10] (1963), ad loc.; W. Thüsing, "Die Erhöhung u. Verherrliching im Joh.-Ev.," NT Abh., 21, 1/2 (1960), 130 f., 275 f., R. Bultmann rightly protests in Bultmann J., 460 and n. 4; 461 and n. 4. C. K. Barrett, The Gospel acc. to St. John (1958), ad loc. takes middle ground.

[19] It is also possible to relate the inf. εἰσελθεῖν to ὑστερηκέναι; so Mi. Hb.[12], ad loc. and Héring, op. cit. (→ n. 17), ad loc.

[20] For ὑστερέω ἀπό cf. Qoh. 6:2 LXX; Jos. Ant., 6, 235; also Herm. m., 9, 4 f.: ἀπὸ πάντων τῶν αἰτημάτων σου ἀνυστέρητος ἔσῃ (i.e., acc. to the context: οὐδὲν οὐ μὴ λήψῃ τῶν αἰτημάτων σου). "ἀπό is possible because of the idea of separation and distance latent in the verb," Helbing Kasussyntax, 173.

[21] On this understanding of ὑστεροῦνται as "to miss," "not to attain to," δόξα θεοῦ is to be construed as the eschatological glory which acc. to the apoc. view the righteous will share and from which sinners are excluded, 4 Esr. 7:122-125; 9:31-37; S. Bar. 48:49 f.; 51:1-3; 54:15, cf. also Damasc. 3:17-20 (5:4 f.). This is the line taken by Ltzm. R., Mi. R., ad loc. and O. Kuss, Der Römerbr. übers. u. erklärt (1957), ad loc. But perhaps Paul is thinking of the loss of the glory of the first time with which Adam was invested, Apc. Mos. 20; Gn. r., 12, 5 on 2:4 (Wünsche, 52). If so, ὑστεροῦνται means "to lack." Zn. R., ad loc. is wide of the mark with his "to lack recognition on God's part."

event. Justification as the work of God's grace removes, then, the consequence of sin, the loss of participation in God's glory. With the justification of sinners God has also foreseen from all eternity their final glorification, cf. R. 8:29 f. and also 5:2; 8:17 f., 18; 9:23; 1 Th. 2:12.

b. With reference to things or circumstances rather than persons ὑστερέω means "to lack": ἕν σε ὑστερεῖ (→ 593, 19 ff.), says Jesus to the rich young ruler, Mk. 10:21. This man who has kept all the commandments of the Torah from his youth up (v. 20) lacks here and now, face to face with Jesus, this one thing: the renouncing of all his possessions and entry into discipleship of Jesus. Lk. 18:22 with its ἕν σοι λείπει reproduces the same sense as that of Mk. 10:21, but Mt. 19:20 has the ruler himself ask: τί ἔτι ὑστερῶ; The ἔτι involves a not inconsiderable shift of nuance, for instead of an absolute lack we now find the idea of an unfulfilled remainder to complete the correct observance of the commandments (→ 73, 29 ff.), cf. the reply of Jesus in Mt. 19:21: εἰ θέλεις τέλειος εἶναι, ὕπαγε κτλ. Jn. 2:3: ὑστερήσαντος οἴνου, probably means in context (2:10) "when the wine was finished" [22] and not, as one might at a first glance conclude from οἶνον οὐκ ἔχουσιν, "since wine was lacking."

c. In the NT, too, the most common sense is "to have a lack." The prodigal son begins to starve in the far country (ἤρξατο ὑστερεῖσθαι) when he has squandered his whole inheritance, Lk. 15:14. Jesus sends out His disciples without purse, satchel or shoes to proclaim the kingdom of God and when they come back He asks them: μή τινος ὑστερήσατε; Lk. 22:35. Paul gives thanks for the χάρις granted to the Corinthians in Christ Jesus (1 C. 1:4), which he then goes on to elucidate as follows: ὅτι ἐν παντὶ ἐπλουτίσθητε ἐν αὐτῷ (1:5) ..., ὥστε ὑμᾶς μὴ ὑστερεῖσθαι ἐν [23] μηδενὶ χαρίσματι, 1:7. The stress on the rich gifts which the congregation has received (1:5 f.), and which it dispenses in tense expectation of the close parousia of Christ (1:7), stands in unmistakable material contrast with the theological ambitions of the Corinthian pneumatics (cf. 1 C. 4:8). In relation to the weak in the community whose conscience is burdened by eating idol meats Paul agrees unequivocally: "Meat will not cause us to stand before God (in the imminent judgment): οὔτε ἐὰν μὴ φάγωμεν ὑστερούμεθα, οὔτε ἐὰν φάγωμεν περισσεύομεν," 1 C. 8:8. [24] But for this reason the strong who have γνῶσις (8:1, 4) should not harry the weak by their Christian freedom nor cause them offence, 8:9 ff. Paul himself knows how to be poor (ταπεινοῦσθαι) and how to have more than enough (περισσεύειν); "in each and everything I am content: to have enough and to be hungry, καὶ περισσεύειν καὶ ὑστερεῖσθαι," Phil. 4:12. [25] To Corinth he came

---

[22] Cf. Jos. Ant., 15, 200. This is also the pt. in the vl. of Cod ℵ* it syhmg: οἶνον οὐκ εἶχον, ὅτι συνετελέσθη ὁ οἶνος τοῦ γάμου, which Bultmann J., 80, n. 6 wrongly regards as the original reading. The non-Johannine abs. gen. might well belong to a pre-Johannine narrative, Barrett, op. cit. (→ n. 18), ad loc. is surely right here; he thinks the vl. is an ancient gloss. A. Smitmans, "Das Weinwunder v. Kana," Beiträge z. Gesch. d. bibl. Exegese, 6 (1966), 202, n. 3; 262 f. thinks the gloss is connected with an exposition hostile to marriage.

[23] For the rare ὑστερέω ἐν cf. Ditt. Or., I, 339, 22 (2nd cent. B.C.).

[24] περισσεύω is thus the opp. of ὑστερέω cf. 1 C. 12:24; Phil. 4:12. Cf. περισσεῦον — ὑστέρησις or ὑστέρημα Mk. 12:44 and par.

[25] Cf. the Stoic examples in v. Arnim, III, 567-581, 589-603, 705-715 and Epict Diss., III, 5, 7: ἐμοὶ μὲν γὰρ καταληφθῆναι γένοιτο μηδενὸς ἄλλου ἐπιμελουμένῳ ἢ τῆς προαιρέσεως τῆς ἐμῆς, ἵν' ἀπαθής, ἵν' ἀκώλυτος, ... ἵν' ἐλεύθερος. Similarly he says

in personal poverty, refusing to claim the apostolic right of being supported by the community: παρὼν πρὸς ὑμᾶς καὶ ὑστερηθεὶς οὐ κατενάρκησα οὐθενός, 2 C. 11:9. Hb. 11:37 describes the situation of the fathers in similar terms: ἐλιθάσθησαν, ἐπειράσθησαν, ἐπρίσθησαν, ... περιῆλθον ἐν μηλωταῖς, ἐν αἰγείοις δέρμασιν, ὑστερούμενοι, θλιβόμενοι, κακουχούμενοι... It was as such that as believers they became witnesses who were not to attain to the promise in their own lives but according to God's foreknowledge only along with Christians in the approaching eschatological consummation, 11:39 f.

d. Finally we also find the sense "to be after, behind someone." Twice in his debate with opponents in the Corinthian church Paul emphasises sharply that he was not behind the other apostles in anything, 2 C. 11:5; 12:11. But in relation to the common life of Christians in the community as the one body in Christ the rule applies that "God has integrated the body and the greater honour is given to him who counts for nothing (τῷ ὑστερουμένῳ [vl. -οῦντι]) so that there may be no rift in the body, but all the members may care for one another in the same way," 1 C. 12:24 f. In the context ὑστερεῖσθαι corresponds here to ἀσθενέστερα ὑπάρχειν in 12:22 and ἀτιμότερα εἶναι in 12:23, cf. τὰ ἀσχήμονα ἡμῶν, 12:23.

3. ἀφυστερέω.

The verb occurs in the NT only at Jm. 5:14 in the sense "to withhold." [26]

4. ὑστέρημα, ὑστέρησις.

In Mk. 12:44 cf. Lk. 21:4 Jesus lauds the poor widow who has put two mites in the offering box: πάντες γὰρ ἐκ τοῦ περισσεύοντος αὐτοῖς ἔβαλον, αὕτη δὲ ἐκ τῆς ὑστερήσεως (Lk. τοῦ ὑστερήματος) αὐτῆς πάντα ὅσα εἶχεν ἔβαλεν, ὅλον τὸν βίον αὐτῆς. Here, then, ὑστέρημα or ὑστέρησις as the opposite of περισσεῦον does not denote the lack of something, a remaining something needed for completion, but rather want in general, or poverty. This is Paul's usage too. In the collection which he organises in his churches for the saints in Jerusalem, there should be a balance between them: ἐν τῷ νῦν καιρῷ τὸ ὑμῶν περίσσευμα εἰς τὸ ἐκείνων ὑστέρημα, ἵνα καὶ τὸ ἐκείνων περίσσευμα γένηται εἰς τὸ ὑμῶν ὑστέρημα, 2 C. 8:14 → VI, 266, 5 ff. As the Gentile Christians should share the surplus of their earthly goods with the Jewish Christians in their time of physical poverty, so the latter should share their surplus of spiritual goods with the former, cf. R. 15:27 [27] → VI, 63, 21 ff. The collection, then, is not just designed to relieve the

---

to God: ἐνόσησα, ὅτε ἠθέλησας· καὶ οἱ ἄλλοι, ἀλλ' ἐγὼ ἑκών· πένης ἐγενόμην σοῦ θέλοντος, ἀλλὰ χαίρων, 9, cf. III, 10, 8: νῦν τοῦ πυρέττειν καιρός ἐστιν, τοῦτο καλῶς γινέσθω· τοῦ διψᾶν, δίψα καλῶς· ... οὐκ ἔστιν ἐπὶ σοί; τίς σε κωλύσει; cf. also IV, 4, 34. How fully Pauline and Stoic motifs merged at a later age may be seen from Aug. De vita beata, 4, 25 (CSEL, 63 [1922]) where a Stoic adage is quoted as a Chr. one: *nullus autem perfectus aliquo eget.* → VI, 21, 17 ff.

[26] VI. ἀπεστερημένος, cf. Helbing Kasussyntax, 175.

[27] Ltzm., Wnd. 2 K., J. Héring, *La seconde Ép. aux Corinth., Comm. du NT,* 8 (1958), *ad loc.* take the ἵνα clause to mean that as the Corinthians now extend financial help to the Jerusalem saints, so the latter will some day do to them. As against this cf. D. Georgi, "Die Gesch. d. Kollekte d. Pls. für Jerusalem," *Theol. Forschung,* 38 (1965), 65, who rightly interprets the saying in terms of the apoc. concept of the intermediate Messianic kingdom.

distress of the Jerusalem saints (προσαναπληροῦσα τὰ ὑστερήματα τῶν ἁγίων). It is also designed (→ III, 348, 21 ff.; IV, 283, 1 ff.) to lead the Jerusalem Christians to praise God for the obedience of faith of the Gentiles, who demonstrate herewith their fellowship with the Jews, 2 C. 9:12 f. [28] When Paul in Corinth would not take any gifts for his support from that congregation, the churches of Macedonia sent him gifts: τὸ γὰρ ὑστέρημά μου προσανεπλήρωσαν οἱ ἀδελφοὶ ἐλθόντες ἀπὸ Μακεδονίας, 2 C. 11:9. The point of ὑστέρημα may be seen clearly from the ὑστερηθείς of the preceding clause. What Paul did not take from the Corinthians, he received from the Macedonian brethren. [29] The expression (προσ-) ἀναπληρόω τὸ ὑστέρημά τινος — the genitive denotes the person who suffers the lack — seems to have been specially developed → 593, 35 ff.; 601, 18 ff. It is found in the same sense in 1 C. 16:17 and Phil. 2:30 too → VI, 306, 21 ff. In both cases the meaning is that someone in direct fellowship with Paul fills a lack for his community. This lack consists in the momentary spatial distance between the community itself and Paul. [30] Paul himself stresses the fact that he did not expect gifts from his churches, so that the utterance of his great joy at what is received is not meant καθ᾽ ὑστέρησιν (Phil. 4:11), i.e., it is not the joy of a poor person whose need has been met. Paul, as one who is basically in the position περισσεύειν καὶ ὑστερεῖσθαι (4:12 → n. 24), rejoices rather at the sharing of his church in his present distress (4:14), which, as often before, the present gift expresses, 4:15-18.

The meaning is not quite so plain in 1 Th. 3:10. After Timothy has come back with good news about the faith of the congregation, Paul has a longing to see the church himself (3:6) καὶ καταρτίσαι τὰ ὑστερήματα τῆς πίστεως ὑμῶν (3:9 f.). In accordance with the common NT use the genitive τῆς πίστεως ὑμῶν does not denote a deficiency of faith but a deficiency which exists for faith as such in the time before the end. [31] Needed by faith are the preaching, teaching and exhortation of the apostle and instruction and strengthening by God and the Kurios Himself, vv. 11-13, cf. R. 1:11. The community needs this to maintain its faith to the end. [32] The plural τὰ ὑστερήματα has the same sense as in 2 C. 9:12 and Col. 1:24.

Col. 1:24 is difficult and much contested → IV, 1097, 32 ff.; VII, 136, 5 ff.: [33] "Now I rejoice in my sufferings for you καὶ ἀνταναπληρῶ τὰ ὑστερήματα τῶν θλίψεων τοῦ Χριστοῦ ἐν τῇ σαρκί μου ὑπὲρ τοῦ σώματος αὐτοῦ, ὅ ἐστιν ἡ ἐκκλησία. Here again we find the fixed expression (ἀντ-) ἀναπληρόω τὸ ὑστέρημα. As Epaphroditus in Phil. 2:30 fills up the ὑστέρημα of the church in his own person as their envoy (→ lines 11 ff.), so Paul as an apostle of Christ represents the exalted Kurios to the Church. But the lack which he fills up herein consists in the θλίψεις τοῦ Χριστοῦ which the apostle takes upon himself in his sufferings (παθήματα) in this physical, earthly life. Christ Himself, whom he has to proclaim (v. 23, 25-27), is now in heaven (vv. 15-20) as the Head of His body, the Church (v. 18). As such He has overcome His sufferings. His place on earth, the place of

---

[28] In interpretation cf. Georgi, op. cit., 74 f.

[29] τὸ ὑμέτερον ὑστέρημα in 1 C. 16:17 is correctly transl. by Schl. K., ad loc. as "the lack which cannot be removed by you."

[30] On this cf. esp. Loh. Phil., ad loc.

[31] But cf. Dib. Th., ad loc.: "to help your faith where there is still something wanting," and similarly Dob. Th., ad loc. B. Rigaux, S. Paul, Les Ép. aux Thessal., Études bibliques (1956), ad loc. thinks that ὑστερήματα has here as in Herm., v., 3, 2, 2 the sense of παραπτώματα.

[32] Cf. Loh. Kol., 78; also Grundlagen paul. Theologie (1929), 121-6.

[33] Cf. Kremer and also M. Schmid, Die Leidensausage in Kol. 1:24, Diss. Vienna (1956).

His sufferings, is now taken by the apostle, who is honoured to be able to suffer for the Church as the body of Christ. [34]

D. Post-New Testament Writings.

1. Post-Apostolic Fathers and Early Patristic Literature.

a. For ὕστερον adv. always in a temporal sense cf. Papias acc. to Eus. Hist. Eccl., III, 39, 15 on Mark as the author of Mk.: οὔτε γὰρ ἤκουσεν τοῦ κυρίου οὔτε παρηκολούθησεν αὐτῷ, ὕστερον δέ, ὡς ἔφην, Πέτρῳ κτλ.

b. ὑστερέω means first "to lack something" (τινός), cf. the fine antithetical description of the Christian life in Dg., 5, 13: They are poor and make many rich (cf. 2 C. 6:10); πάντων ὑστεροῦνται, καὶ ἐν πᾶσι περισσεύουσιν, and also Ign. Eph., 5, 2: ἐὰν μή τις ᾖ ἐντὸς τοῦ θυσιαστηρίου, ὑστερεῖται τοῦ ἄρτου τοῦ θεοῦ. [35] Common too, however, is the sense "to be in want," "to be poor," "to starve," cf. Did., 11, 12 where the community is advised to send away wandering teachers or prophets who ask for gifts of money: ἐὰν δὲ περὶ ἄλλων ὑστερούντων εἴπῃ δοῦναι, μηδεὶς αὐτὸν κρινέτω. Herm. esp. issues the constant admonition to help the starving. [36] Barn., 10, 3 with pastoral directness refers to the rule that the sated usually forget the Lord while those who starve pray to the Lord, just as sows forget their master while feeding, but cry for hunger and are then quiet again when they have received food.

c. ὑστέρημα means "what is lacking" in 1 Cl., 38, 2: When the rich supports the poor, what is lacking is supplied δι' οὗ ἀναπληρωθῇ αὐτοῦ τὸ ὑστέρημα → 593, 35 ff.; 598, 33 ff. The word means "lack" in a religious sense in 2, 6: ἐπὶ τοῖς παραπτώμασι

---

[34] Dib. Gefbr., ad loc. (with bibl.) interprets the saying in terms of the so-called passion mysticism of Paul: "There is a certain number of sufferings which must be endured by His Church between Christ's resurrection and His coming again"; the apostle accepts these for the community → III, 143, 38 ff.; VI, 307, 11 ff. Loh. Kol., ad loc. emends this view by suggesting as a basis the apocal. idea of a fixed measure of suffering which must be filled up before the age of salvation can dawn. Christ accepted these sufferings, but not in full measure, and the apostle as a martyr has to complete the measure in his sufferings. Against this is the fact that ὑστέρημα never means a remainder which must be made up for completion (→ V, 933, n. 20) but a lack or deficiency in gen. The ref. is certainly not to an "insufficiency in Christ's accomplishment," as against H. Windisch, Paulus u. Christus (1934), 245. C. Masson, L'Ép. aux Philipp., Comm. du NT, 10 (1950), ad loc. finds the lack in the fact that Christ's work can be completed only with the finishing of the Gentile mission, cf. M. Bouttier, "Remarques sur la conscience Apostolique de S. Paul," OIKONOMIA. Festschr. O. Cullmann (1967), 102 f. But this is an intruded idea, for "what is lacking in Christ's sufferings" is filled up in the suffering of the apostle as such, not in missionary preaching. W. Michaelis (→ V, 933, 25 ff.) thinks sufferings are normal in view of the sayings of Jesus in Mt. 5:11; 10:17 f., while their lack is abnormal; hence apostolic sufferings make good the lack. G. le Grelle, "La plénitude de la parole dans la pauvreté de la chair d'après Col. 1:24," Nouvelle Revue Théol., 81 (1959), 232-250 thinks ὑστέρημα means lack in the sense of need, poverty (cf. 2 C. 8:14; 9:12 → 598, 20 ff.), so that τῶν θλίψεων τοῦ Χριστοῦ is to be taken as a descriptive gen.: In suffering the apostle shares the poverty and affliction of the lowly Son of God and he may rejoice in prospect of the end of sufferings which Christ has already reached as the exalted Lord. On this view ἀνταναπληρῶ means compensating rather than filling up.
[35] Cf. ἀνυστέρητός τινος in Ign. Sm. Prescript: Ἰγνάτιος... ἐκκλησίᾳ θεοῦ... πεπληρωμένη ἐν πίστει καὶ ἀγάπῃ, ἀνυστερήτῳ οὔσῃ παντὸς χαρίσματος, cf. 1 C. 1:7. Cf. also Herm. m., 9, 4 → n. 20.
[36] Acc. to Herm. m., 8, 10 the command to support the poor is in the group of second good acts which Christians must perform after faith, fear of God, love, concord etc., cf. s., 5, 3, 7; m, 2, 4. Judgment is threatened against those who neglect it, v., 3, 9, 6. It is a special duty of the bishop to care for the poor and widows, s., 9, 27, 2; v., 3, 9, 2. 4.

τῶν πλησίον ἐπενθεῖτε· τὰ ὑστερήματα αὐτῶν ἴδια ἐκρίνετε, cf. also Herm. v., 3, 2, 2: Purging of the sinner from his ὑστερήματα and ἁμαρτήματα in the Last Judgment. ὑστέρησις occurs in Herm. s., 6, 3, 4 in the gen. sense of "lack," "indigence" as a degree of eschatological punishment for sinners.

In early patristic works one might ref. to Cl. Al. Fr., 46, which excludes all ὑστερεῖν and hence all human desires from the ἄφθαρτος βασιλεία. [37] Typical and theologically interesting as a harmonising solution of the problems of primitive Chr. eschatology is the usage in Cl. Al. Ecl. Proph., 12, 1: τὰ τῆς γνώσεως τὰ μὲν ἤδη μετέχομεν, τὰ δὲ δι᾽ ὧν ἔχομεν βεβαίως ἐλπίζομεν· οὔτε γὰρ πᾶν κεκομίσμεθα οὔτε παντὸς ὑστεροῦμεν, ἀλλ᾽ οἷον "ἀρραβῶνα" τῶν αἰωνίων ἀγαθῶν καὶ τοῦ πατρῴου πλούτου προσειλήφαμεν. One should also note the christological statement which ref. to a ὑστερεῖν in relation to the Father as a ὑστεροχρονεῖν: οὐ δύναται δὲ τὸ αὐτὸ κατὰ τὸ αὐτὸ καὶ προχρονεῖν τῇ ὕλῃ, καθὸ αἴτιόν ἐστιν, ἅμα ὑστερεῖν καὶ ὑστεροχρονεῖν, καθὸ τῆς αἰτίας ἐστὶν ἔργον, Strom., VIII, 9, 29, 5.

2. Second Century Gnosticism.

In 2nd cent. Chr. Gnosticism the terms ὑστερέω and ὑστέρημα play an important role in the degree that as tt. in theology they denote the lesser worth of what is outside the original divine pleroma. Thus lower wisdom (→ VII, 512, 4 ff.; 513, 4 ff.) as the power which has fallen downwards is the ὑστερήσασα δύναμις inasmuch as it did not emanate from the original thirty but only from their fruits, [38] Iren. Haer., I, 11, 2. Again through apostasy there arose beyond the first dodecad τὸ μυστήριον τοῦ πάθους τοῦ ὑστερήματος from which visible things finally sprang, I, 18, 4. As ὑστέρημα and πάθος came from ἄγνοια, so reattained γνῶσις will set aside these results of ἄγνοια. But γνῶσις has nothing whatever to do with the soul, which is by nature ἐξ ὑστερήματος, I, 21, 4. Thus Gnostics, following Lk. 15:1-7, flee the place of the ninety and nine, i.e., ὑστέρημα, and strive back upward to the ἕν, Iren. Haer., I, 16, 2.

Wilckens

---

[37] Cl. Al. Fr., 46 (GCS, 17); the βασιλεία is παρουσία πάντων τῶν ἀγαθῶν.
[38] The demiurge is also called καρπὸς ὑστερήματος, Iren. Haer., II, 19, 9 cf. I, 19, 1; 17, 2; 16, 3; II, 1, 1; 3, 2; 9, 2; 28, 4. Cf. F. M. M. Sagnard, *La gnose Valentinienne et le témoignage de S. Iréné* (1947), 433 f. and 123 f., 561 the interpretation of the Fr. of Valentinus in Cl. Al. Strom., IV, 12, 89, 6 - 90, 1 which belongs to the ὑστέρημα complex.

ὕψος, ὑψόω, ὑπερυψόω, ὕψωμα, ὕψιστος

---

† ὕψος.

A. ὕψος in Non-Biblical Greek.

ὕψος, neuter of ὕψι, ὕψιστος, [1] occurs from Aesch., e.g., Ag., 1376 and Hdt., e.g.,
II, 175, 1 (with μέγεθος), and means in these ref. and frequently the dimension of height
compared to the other dimensions μῆκος, εὖρος, πλάτος, and βάθος (→ I, 517, 6 ff.),
which measures the same dimension downward. ὕψος can also be a high place, mountains,
highlands, heights, Xenoph. An., VI, 4, 3. Transf. it can be the "summit" of uncultivation,
Plat. Ep., 7, 351d or the "height" of dignity, Ps.-Aristot. Mund., 6, p. 398a, 12. [2] Later
it is used as the title "highness," P. Masp., I, 67002, 3, 21 (6th cent. A.D.) etc. [3] Aestheti-
cally the speech of the Muses is characterised as "sublime" by ὑψηλολογέομαι in Plat.
Resp., VIII, 545e. [4] The writer's work is called θεσπεσία "divine" and ὑψηλή in Euthyd.,
289e. In an ethico-aesthetic sense Aristot. uses μέγεθος for ὕψος, e.g., in the well-known
def. of tragedy, Poet., 6, p. 1449b, 25. In the Stoic tradition ὕψος is an ethical concept
from Zeno. The σπουδαῖος opp. φαῦλος is also ὑψηλός, for he has part in the ὕψος
or "sublimity" of the wise and noble man, Stob. Ecl., II, 99, 16 f. [5] Rhetoric combines the
ethical and aesthetic elements in the concept ὕψος. In Ps.-Long. Sublim. ὕψος is not only
the "climax" of speech which is reached through the dynamics of words [6] by an orator
who can transcend himself (1, 4); it also corresponds to a natural demand, to the metaphysical need of man, who is no base ταπεινόν nor ignoble being, 35, 2; 36, 1. [7] In contrast
to ὕψος is πάθος; it thus includes spiritual effects on man, 8, 4; cf. 39, 3. ὕψος and
πάθος are poetic aids, and the most violent natural phenomena such as thunder, lightning
and tempest must serve to bring out the divine and supernatural aspect of ὕψος, 34, 2 ff. [8]
All kinds of defects attach to ὕψος, 3-5; hence true ὕψος must be distinguished from false.
True ὕψος is μεγαλοψυχία in the sense of Aristot. Eth. Nic., II, 7, p. 1107b, 22 ff.; IV,
7, p. 1123a, 34 ff. Sublimity stands between arrogance and pusillanimity, Ps.-Long. Sublim.,
5, 8; 7, 9-11. [9]

ὕ ψ ο ς . Bibl.: R. Weber, Die Begriffe μέγεθος u. ὕψος in d. Schrift vom Erhabenen
(1935); H. S. Schultz, Der Aufbau d. Schrift περὶ ὕψους (1936); J. H. Kühn, "Υψος. Eine
Untersuchung z. Entwicklungsgeschichte des Aufschwunggedankens von Platon bis Poseidonios, Würzburger Stud. z. Altertumswissenschaft, 14 (1941); D. S. Marin, Bibliography
of the "Essay on the Sublime" (1967).
[1] Models are μῆκος / μήκιστος from Hom. Od., 5, 299 or βάθος from Aesch. Prom.,
1029 (βάθιστος, Hom. Il., 8, 14). On ὕψιστος → 614, 20 ff.; on the adj. ὑψηλός cf. Schwyzer,
I, 484, n. 3 [Risch].
[2] Liddell-Scott, Pape, Pr.-Bauer, s.v.
[3] Preisigke Wört., III, 201, s.v.
[4] Kühn, 86 finds the origin of later ὕψος theory in the Platonic idea of philosophical
rapture.
[5] Ibid., 73 and 90.
[6] I. Kant, Kritik d. Urteilskraft (1799), 79-112 distinguishes the dynamically lofty and the
mathematically lofty, following ancient trains of thought in this regard.
[7] Ps.-Long. Sublim., 9, 9 has among examples of the sublime in Homer's diction a quotation
from Gn. 1:3 as an example of lofty style in which the legislator of the Jews speaks of God.
Under Jewish influence Moses as the mediator of divine knowledge is put above Hom. here,
Kühn, 27. 31. 44; E. Norden, "Das Genesiszitat in der Schrift vom Erhabenen," AAB, 1954,
1 (1955), 5-23.
[8] Schultz, 38.
[9] Schultz, 23.

B. ὕψος in the Greek Old Testament.

In the LXX the use is manifold. Ref. to the measurement of height is common, Ex. 25:10, 23; 1 Βασ. 17:4 etc. (HT קוֹמָה, גֹּבַהּ), also to a high place, Ju. 5:18; 2 Βασ. 1:19 etc. (HT מָרוֹם). εἰς ὕψος denotes raising up in 1 Ch. 14:2 etc.; 2 Ch. 1:1 etc. מַעֲלָה. Transf. ὕψος means man's exaltation by God in Jdt. 13:20; Job 5:11 and human pride in Is. 2:11, 17 (vl. ὕβρις); 10:12 as a synon. of ὕβρις (→ 299, 32 ff.). Sometimes the ref. is more to an actual high position than to arrogance, Ez. 31:2, 7 (HT גֹּדֶל), cf. also 1 Macc. 1:40; 10:24. When ὕψος means heaven (frequently) the loftiness of God may be in view, or ὕψος may be a substitute for God. Thus in 4 Βασ. 19:22, in deviation from the HT, ὕψος is a clear par. of εἰς τὸν ἅγιον τοῦ 'Ισραήλ. The LXX has also made a change in ψ 72:8. HT has מִמָּרוֹם "down from above," perhaps in the sense of "out of pride." [10] But LXX has εἰς τὸ ὕψος "against heaven," against the Most High, i.e., God, with a ref. to wrong against Him, cf. 1 Ch. 15:16. [11] Prayer of Man. 9 has the same meaning: "I am not worthy to see and contemplate the loftiness of heaven," cf. ἀνάλαβε δὴ ὕψος (HT גָּאוֹן), Job 40:10. Cf. also the occasional transl. of מָרוֹם by ὕψιστος → 617, 20 ff. ψ 11:9 seems to have a different sense from the HT: "According to thy loftiness thou hast regard to the children of men." In ψ 74:6 LXX read צוּר for God (HT צַוָּאר) in 6b [12] and thus rendered לַמָּרוֹם "against the height" [13] by εἰς ὕψος "against the Most High," i.e., God. In 6a Σ has the LXX text but then follows the HT literally in 6b. Cultic בָּמוֹת are gen. τὰ ὑψηλά (with no art. and sing.) in the LXX. Sometimes, e.g., 2 K. 23:8; Is. 53:9; Ez. 43:7; Job 27:15 the high places are perhaps burial places. [14]

C. ὕψος in Judaism.

1. The idea of rapture [15] on high [16] underlies the later Enoch legend, Slav. En. 3; Eth. En. 14:8 f. (→ II, 556, 22 ff.). In S. Bar. and 4 Esr. "height" (sing. or plur.) is usually heaven and occurs in various connections. In S. Bar. 13:1 revelation comes from the φωνὴ ἐξ ὕψους. [17] Test. L. 2:8 ref. to the immeasurable height to which the third heaven extends.

---

[10] Cf. Ps. 73:6 and H. J. Kraus, *Psalmen, Bibl. Komm. AT*, 15, 1 (1960), 501.
[11] At Neh. 9:5 (2 'Εσδρ. 19:5) a variant reads ὄνομα δόξης σου καὶ ὕψους σου, cf. Is. 35:2.
[12] On the LXX transl. of צוּר as a term for God cf. G. Bertram, "Der Sprachschatz d. LXX u. der d. hbr. AT," ZAW, 57 (1939), 98-100.
[13] So F. Baethgen, *Die Psalmen, Handkomm. AT*, II, 2³ (1904), ad loc.
[14] W. F. Albright, "The High Place in Ancient Palestine," *Volume du Congrès Strasbourg, 1956*, Suppl. to VT, 4 (1957), 242-258 [Gooding]. Acc. to 2 K. 23:8 the cultic high places were defiled. Similarly in Ez. 43:7 the royal graves near the temple desecrated the high place of Yahweh acc. to the view of the prophet (HT cf. Vg, but not BHK and G. Fohrer, *Ez., Hndbch. AT*, I, 13 [1955], ad loc.); cf. also Is. 53:9 acc. to B. Duhm, *Das Buch Js., Handkomm. AT*, III, 1⁴ (1922), ad loc. and Job 27:15; here partly by HT, partly LXX and then the comm. במות for במה is derived from מות "death." ὑψηλός can also be a divine predicate sometimes in the sense of "lofty," cf. 2 Βασ. 22:48 Cod A (no HT); ψ 98:2; 112:4; 137:6; Lam. 3:41 (no HT); also ψ 17:48 (no HT). In the LXX ὑψηλός also seems to describe the place of revelation as "lofty" and hence "sublime," cf. Gn. 12:6; 22:2; Dt. 11:30.
[15] On this cf. G. Strecker, Art. "Entrückung" in RAC, 5 (1962), 461-476.
[16] In O. Sol. "height" or "heights" means heaven, cf. G. Diettrich, "Die O. Sal.," *Neue Stud. z. Gesch. d. Theol. u. d. Kirche*, 9 (1911), 119, n. 1. The righteous man lifts up his arms thither (21:1) for grace and exaltation by the Lord. There the truth will be confessed by the Gentiles (10:7) and the righteous man will get there in the spirit on his mystical heavenly journey (22:1, cf. 36:1, and on this W. Bousset, "Die Himmelsreise d. Seele," ARW, 4 [1901], 136-154); perfection obtains there (O. Sol. 26:7). The idea of translation on high comes from the story of Enoch in Gn. 5:24.
[17] This is found in Gk. in P. Oxy., III, 403, 13 f. (5th cent. A.D.), cf. Violet, 220.

In Jos. Ant., 8, 126 we find ὕψος καὶ μέγεθος εὐδαιμονίας ἄπειρον, "infinite height and greatness of bliss." [18]

2. In Philo's usage ὕψος takes on theological significance. [19] αἰθέριον ὕψος is metaphorical in Conf. Ling., 4. It is for Philo the highest stage in the knowledge of God. Ungodliness is man's attempt in his own strength to make the way to the knowledge of God easy and comfortable for himself, cf. Poster. C., 169; Vit. Mos., II, 285. [20] In Poster. C., 110 Philo expresses a particular view on style. This must be adapted to the subject-matter and should sometimes be sublime and sometimes simple. "Sublimity in expression" ὑψηγορία corresponds to what one would expect in Moses as the publisher of revelation, Det. Pot. Ins., 79; Rer. Div. Her., 4. In an ethico-religious sense Philo speaks of ὕψος ἀρετῆς. The way to virtue is also the way to God, Plant., 24. 145, cf. Ebr., 128; Som., I, 115. 150; Leg. All., III, 18 f. There is a Platonising and more dualistic understanding in Conf. Ling., 95. True ὕψος is opposed by false, which rests on human arbitrariness, Poster. C., 136. 169. Philo warns against this, Spec. Leg., I, 293; Som., I, 131; Vit. Mos., II, 96. [21] He opposes astrologers and esp. Posidonius, whom he regards as the champion of false ὕψος, Migr. Abr., 184, cf. also Mut. Nom., 67; Fug., 194.

D. ὕψος in the New Testament.

Rev. 21:16 portrays the cubic heavenly city → III, 344, 1 ff. [22] The length and breadth are given first. But the height, which is 12,000 furlongs, cannot be omitted, as attempted, perhaps intentionally, in one MS. [23] Eph. 3:18 (→ I, 518, 1 ff.) adds a fourth measurement (βάθος) to the other three. [24] Specifically Christian speculations obviously begin early on the basis of the distinctive terminology. [25]

---

[18] Cf. also Ant., 19, 296. The many other Jos. ref. are to the height and size of mountains, buildings and men. I owe the Jos. material to Rengstorf.

[19] Philo's style seems to be related to that of his older contemporary Ps.-Long. → n. 7; Kühn, 53-71.

[20] Kühn, 11.

[21] H. Leisegang, Der Heilige Geist, I (1919), 208.

[22] Bss. Apk., ad loc.; H. Odeberg, The View of the Universe in the Ep. to the Ephesians (1934), 13-20.

[23] There are related concepts of the eschatological Jerusalem in Sib., 5, 251 f. Here the height of the walls reaches to the clouds, but cf. Volz Esch., 372. Similar expectations are attested in the Rabb. tradition. But the measurements are more modest than in Rev. 21:16, cf. Volz Esch., 372 and Str.-B., III, 849 f. The idea of a square foundation and of a cube may have mathematical-astrological significance. The ref. is to heaven → VI, 532, 12 ff.; VII, 337, 27 ff.

[24] Cf. Plat. Resp., VII, 528d. Plato describes astronomy as φορὰ βάθους, the science of moved bodies, cf. Reitzenstein Ir. Erl., 235, n. 1; Poim., 25, n. 1 and on this Clemen, 344. 410, also Dib. Gefbr. on Eph. 3:10; Dib. Herm. on v., 3, 2, 5. The arrangement of the four dimensions could pt. to Gnostic-type speculations (→ 134, 32 ff.) which might have influenced the NT views without either author or readers being aware of it. In context the formula is designed only to express the all-embracing power of the love of Christ. A. Orbe, "Los primeros herejes ante la persecucion," Estud. Valentinianos, V (1956), 218-236 traces the influence of the Eph. passage in early and heretical exposition and also its intellectual and religious setting, esp. the theme of cosmic crucifixion, cf. the review by G. Bertram, ThLZ, 91 (1966), 907-910. At Eph. 3:18 Vg has sublimitas et profundum, cf. 1 C. 2:10: profunda Dei. But for βάθος at R. 11:33 Vg has altitudo (Dei) and for βαθέα τοῦ σατανᾶ (vl. βαθέα τοῦ θεοῦ ἀλλὰ τοῦ σατανᾶ) at Rev. 2:24 altitudines Satanae.

[25] Thus the cross with its 4 arms is interpreted as follows. It pts. up to the deity and down to the humanity of Jesus. The length and breadth describe the spread of the Gospel north and south and east and west into the whole world. Or a ref. may be seen to humiliation and exaltation, the descent to Hades and the ascension, cf. Severian of Gabala (d. after 409), ad loc. acc. to Staab, 311.

In Eph. 4:8 f. (→ I, 610, 28 ff.) there is confession of the exaltation of Christ (→ 611, 10 ff.) in the words of Ps. 68:18. [26] The Psalmist has in view Yahweh's triumphant ascent of the hill of God after victory over the enemies of Israel, who are led as prisoners in the procession. [27] Similarly Eph. 4:8 f. refers to Christ's ascension. The battle and victory which would furnish prisoners for the triumph, for the entry into heaven (ὕψος), perhaps take place on the upward way, i.e., in the sphere of the hostile planets. Ascent and descent contain the same motif. The Christ who has come down to earth is from above, and He returns to His heavenly home in the ascent on high → III, 510, 7 ff. [28] The forms of expression are very similar to those of the Gnostic Redeemer myth. They offer the Christian community a comprehensive view of both the earthly and also the heavenly history and figure of Christ. In Lk. 1:78; 24:49 ὕψος has a primarily spatial ref. "the height of heaven." This is God's seat, and everything that comes from it comes from God Himself. Thus "height" becomes almost a term for God → 603, 8 ff. ἀνατολή (→ I, 352, 37 ff.) ἐξ ὕψους [29] is an astronomical-astrological concept. [30] Lk. 24:49 seems to confirm the usual view of 1:78, for ἐξ ὕψους δύναμιν simply means δύναμις ὑψίστου (Lk. 1:35 → II, 300, 20 ff.; VI, 402, 14 ff.) or δύναμιν ἐπελθόντος τοῦ ἁγίου πνεύματος, Ac. 1:8. [31] In Jm. 1:9 [32] ὕψος is to be taken in the sense of exaltation in rank. In contrast to the rich man, who is threatened with destruction if he does not humble himself as a member of the body and boast of this abasement, the lowly man may boast of his "exaltation" ὕψος by God. [33]

---

[26] Just. Dial., 39, 4. 5; 87, 6 ref. to Christ's "going up into" heaven (ἀνέλευσις) on the basis of this v.

[27] Kraus, op. cit. (→ n. 10), ad loc. Older Rabb. tradition ref. Ps. 68:18 to Moses, cf. Str.-B., III, 596-598.

[28] J. Kroll, "Gott u. Hölle," Stud. d. Bibliothek Warburg, 20 (1932), 11 etc. F. J. Dölger, Ant. Christ., II (1930), 316 f. (in spite of M. Meinertz) thinks the ref. of Eph. 4:8 f. is to the descent into Hades.

[29] Cf. Is. 4:2. In the HT צֶמַח is par. to פְּרִי, so that the original means the "shoot which Yahweh causes to grow," cf. O. Kaiser, Der Prophet Js. Kap. 1-12, AT Deutsch, 17 (1960), ad loc., who pts. out that the "shoot of Yahweh" was not taken Messianically until Tg. Pro., ad loc. Is. 4:2 LXX has the picture of God's shining forth: ἐπιλάμψει ὁ θεός, Σ ἔσται ἀνατολὴ κύριος "the Lord" (᾿ΑΘ ἔσται ἀνατολή) for צֶמַח. At Jer. 33:15 (no LXX) Θ has for the announced shoot of David צֶמַח צְדָקָה: ἀνατολὴν δικαίαν, Σ ἀνατολήν, δικαιοσύνην ποιήσει, cf. Jer. 23:5 ᾿Α: βλάστημα τοῦ δικαίου, Σ βλάστημα δίκαιον. The Lucan formulation is close to the form in Test. Jud. 24:4 ὁ βλαστὸς θεοῦ ὑψίστου Cf. on this A. Jacoby, "᾿Ανατολὴ ἐξ ὕψους," ZNW, 20 (1921), 205-214. F. Delitzsch, ספרי הברית החדשה (1880), transl. Luke's phrase by גֹּהַּ מִמְּרוֹם, but there is no OT basis for this.

[30] Cf. P. Vielhauer, "Das Benedictus d. Zacharias (Lk. 1:68-79)," Aufsätze z. NT (1965), 37-41. Rev. 8:13 etc. ref. to revelations in heaven.

[31] Cf. πνεῦμα ἀφ᾿ ὑψηλοῦ Is. 32:15. In ἰσχὺν τοῦ βραχίονός σου at Is. 51:9 LXX is not ref. to the arm of God as HT but to the arm of the Messiah, 1 QIsᵃ at 51:5 also seems to presuppose a Messianic interpretation (acc. to BHK). HT has "my salvation" and "my arm" and ref. both to Yahweh, but the Q text reads "my salvation" and "his arm," so that salvation = saviour (the Messiah) and the arm is the Messiah's. The same applies at Is. 62:11, where HT ref. impersonally to Jerusalem's salvation while LXX proclaims the coming of the Saviour. Cf. J. V. Chamberlain, "The Functions of God as Messianic Titles in the Complete Qumran Isaiah Scroll," VT, 5 (1955), 366-372; G. Bertram, "Praeparatio Evangelica in d. LXX," VT, 7 (1957), 241-244.

[32] Cf. Dib. Jk.¹¹, 58 and ad loc.

[33] G. Bertram, Art. "Erhöhung," RAC, 6 (1966), 26 f.

E. ὕψος in Early Christianity.

The usage of the post-apost. fathers remains within the sphere of that of the Bible, 1 Cl., 36, 2; 49, 4; 59, 3; Ign. Eph., 9, 1. In Barn., 20, 1 one finds ὕψος δυνάμεως in the sense of "arrogance." Did., 5, 1 has ὕψος between θρασύτης and ἀλαζονεία in a negative sense for "pride," "insolence." In Dg., 7, 2 τὰ ἐν ὕψεσιν occurs in a list which embraces all creation. In the Apologists ὕψος occurs only in OT quotations.

† ὑψόω, ὑπερυψόω.

A. ὑψόω in Non-Biblical Greek.

In non-bibl. Gk. ὑψόω is late and rare. We find it in Hippocr. Praecepta, 7 [1] (Littré, IX, 258) and it means "to lift up," "to raise on high," "to exalt" both lit. and transf. Thus Plut. Cons. ad Apoll., 5 (II, 103 f.) warns against hubris and ref. to the inconstancy of fate: ῥᾳδίως τὰ ὑψηλὰ γίγνεται ταπεινὰ καὶ τὰ χθαμαλὰ πάλιν ὑψοῦται. In Hell. the idea of elevation by gods and heroes and in mystical experience is a vital one. [2] Thus Corp. Herm., 11, 20 reads παντὸς δὲ ὕψους ὑψηλότερος γενοῦ. One finds the same usage in Plat. Leg., X, 905a: ὑψηλὸς γενόμενος. [3] But the verb does not occur in Plat. or Aristot. Corp. Herm., 4, 5 has ἑαυτοὺς ὑψώσαντες. In the magic pap. one reads: ὡς τὸν Ὄσιριν ὕψωσας, οὕτως ὕψωσον σεαυτήν, Preis. Zaub., I, 4, 2989 f. (4th cent. A.D.). [4] There is astronomical or astrological use e.g., in the 2nd cent. in the philosopher Theo. Smyrnaeus, 135, 2 [5] and in Vett. Val., III, 4 (p. 140, 7). [6]

B. ὑψόω in the Greek Old Testament.

There is rich material in the LXX. ὑψόω and compounds (esp. ἀν- and ὑπερ-) occur for about 20 Hbr. verbs some 260 times. [7] The most common originals are נשא, רום and גבה. When גדל is transl. ὑψόω it is hard to get the original sense, cf. Is. 1:2. There are many instances of religious usage, cf. exaltation of God or His throne in ψ 96;9; Jer. 17:12. God manifests Himself in His loftiness by intervening in the course of events, Is. 2:11, 17; 5:16; 12:4, 6; 30:18; 33:10 (with δοξασθήσομαι); 40:25 cf. Mi. 5:8; ψ 45:11; 63:8. The righteous constantly ask God for this revelation of His loftiness, ψ 7:7; 9:33; 17:47; 20:14; 56:6, 12; 88:14; 93:2; 107:6; Nu. 14:17. In these passages we find pass. forms in a mid. sense. [8] The righteous exalt God in the cultic hymn or liturgy, i.e., they praise Him, so that ὑψόω is almost synon. with ὑμνόω and δοξάζω, Ex. 15:2; 2 Εσδρ. 19:5; ψ 29:2; 33:4; 98:5, 9; 106:32; 117:28; 144:1; Δα. 3:52-88. As God's name alone is exalted ψ 148:13, so He alone can elevate and exalt men, Gn. 24:35; 26:13; 41:52 vl.; Jos. 3:7; 1 Βασ. 10:23; 3 Βασ. 16:2 etc. The Psalter, too, offers many examples, e.g., in the I-style ψ 3:4; 9:14; 17:49, cf. also 1 Βασ. 2:1; 1 Ch. 17:17 (HT makes no sense); [9] 25:5. ὑψόω

ὑ ψ ό ω . [1] ὑψόω derives from ὕψος as the opp. ταπεινόω from ταπεινός, v. Debr. Griech. Wortb. § 205. Hippocr. Praecepta, 7 seems to be only Hell. ὑψόω also occurs in Polyb., 5, 26, 12 [Risch].

[2] G. Bertram, Art. "Erhöhung," RAC, 6, 22-43; also "Der religionsgesch. Hintergrund des Begriffs d. 'Erhöhung' in d. LXX," ZAW, 68 (1956), 57-71.

[3] J. Kroll, "Gott u. Hölle. Der Mythus vom Descensuskampfe," Stud. z. Bibliothek Warburg, 20 (1932), 327, n. 2 assumes Plato's influence on Plut.

[4] The magic text on the raising of magic plants in astrological imagery denotes fetching up from the underworld.

[5] Ed. F. Hiller (1878).

[6] Liddell-Scott and cf. also Moult.-Mill., s.v.

[7] αἴρω and compounds (→ I, 185, 19 ff.; 186, 20 ff.) are used much more (some 530 times) by the transl. The word includes negative aspects → I, 185, 35 ff.; 186, 29 ff.

[8] Cf. Bl.-Debr. § 307, 314.

[9] Cf. K. Galling, Die Bücher Ch., Esr. Neh., AT Deutsch, 12 (1954), ad loc.; W. Rudolph, Hndbch. AT, I, 21 (1955), ad loc.

can almost mean "to deliver," "to redeem" in ψ 149:4 and perhaps helped to establish a rising belief in resurrection ψ 9:14 (→ II, 852, 22 ff.). [10] "Exaltation" is imparted esp. to the people of Israel Is. 4:2; 63:9; ψ 36:34; 88:17; 148:14, cf. 2 Βασ. 5:12. The ref. is to the elect of God, the king, the anointed, in ψ 88:20; 109:7 vl.; 1 Βασ. 2:10; the righteous ψ 111:9, cf. Prv. 14:34; 18:10; ψ 144:7 vl.; Job 36:7. [11] Exaltation contains an element of joy, ὑψόω is the transl. of צָלַל at ψ 107:8, ἀνυψόω of גִּיל polel at Sir. 40:26, cf. also ψ 144:7, where ἀγαλλιάσονται is a vl. of ὑψωθήσονται (HT יְרַנְּנוּ). Exaltation means drawing close to God; the righteous man who is meek and humble may hope for this and claim it ψ 149:4; 74:8. 11; 112:7; Ez. 17:24; Δα. 12:1; 1 Βασ. 2:7. This is esp. true of the Servant of the Lord as proclaimed in Is. 52:13. Here ὑψωθήσεται occurs with δοξασθήσεται for the overcoming of all earthly abasement and it is thus strengthened and underlined. [12] Exaltation is also glorification. The way is thus prepared for the christological statements of the NT → 610, 12 ff. Abasement is also finally given a fixed position as the presupposition of the exaltation of the righteous. To turn abasement into exaltation and lowliness into loftiness is the affair of God alone and it will be a sign of the time of salvation. Similar inversion by man is a sign of disorder and ruin, Εσθ. 1:1k; Ez. 21:31. [13] Part of the abasement and suffering of the righteous is that God can lift up their adversaries, Lam. 2:17; ψ 88:43. But arbitrary arrogance is ungodliness (→ 295, 1 ff.) Hos. 13:6; Mi. 6:12 (not the HT); [14] Is. 3:16; 10:15; 19:13; [15] 4 Βασ. 19:22 (Sennacherib); Jdt. 9:7 (the Assyrians); Ἰερ. 31:29; Ez. 28:2, 5. 17; 29:15; 31:10; Δα. 4:22; 8:25; 11:12, 36 f.; cf. also ψ 12:3; 36:20, 35; 139:9; 2 Ch. 26:16; 32:25. There is a warning against this type of pride in Dt. 8:14; 17:20; ψ 65:7; 74:5; Prv. 18:12.

C. ὑψόω in Judaism.

In Hell. Judaism LXX influence may be seen in Ep. Ar., 263; Jos. Bell., 2, 219; 3. 171; 5, 523; 7, 306 and 313; the use is secular. [16] Ps. Sol. 1:5 bewails the exaltation, i.e., the arrogance of sinners. Acc. to Sib., 3, 585 Israel is raised up to be a prophet. Test. R. 6:5 refers to secular exaltation, cf. Test. Jud. 21:8. In Test. N. 5:3 exaltation has an astral character. Test. Jos. 1:7 takes up the antithesis of abasement and exaltation; ὑψόω and δοξάζω occur together in 10:3, cf. 18:1. On Enoch's exaltation → 603, 23 f. In the Dead Sea Scrolls רום, which is a common HT original of ὑψόω, acquires a certain significance when "raising up" from death in 1 QH 6:34; 11:12 means awakening or resurrection. [17] In context 1 QH 15:16 f. also has an eschatological character. But the ref. in 1 QH 6:8

---

[10] G. Bertram, "The Problem of Death in Popular Judaeo-Hell. Piety," Crozer Quart., 10 (1933), 257-287.

[11] The combining of exaltation and God's righteousness in the last two ref. (cf. also ψ 88:14-17) might be taken in a Pauline sense by a Chr. reader.

[12] K. F. Euler, "Die Verkündigung vom leidenden Gottesknecht aus Js. 53 in d. griech. Bibel," BWANT, 66 (1934), 96-99, 143 f. HT Is. 52 f. has three synon. for exaltation, גָּבַהּ, נָשָׂא, רוּם. The Hexapla transl. are content with the theologically indifferent renderings ἐπαρθήσεται and μετεωρισθήσεται. But LXX introduces christologically significant terms and is thus a praeparatio evangelica. On Is. 53:8 LXX → II, 853, 30 ff.; acc. to Euler, 128 f. it ref. to the ascension of Is.

[13] Acc. to Ez. 21:31 HT the king is humbled in punishment, turban and crown (the marks of majesty) being stripped from him. The LXX ref., however, is to the evil he has done by abasing the lofty and elevating the lowly.

[14] Mi. 6:12c is a gloss based on Ps. 120:2 f. acc. to BHK, ad loc. and T. H. Robinson, Die zwölf kleinen Propheten, Hndbch. AT, I, 14² (1954), ad loc.

[15] At Is. 19:13 LXX reads נָשָׂא ni "to be proud" for HT נָשָׁא ni "to be deceived."

[16] I owe the Jos. material to Rengstorf. There are no Philo ref. acc. to Leisegang.

[17] S. Holm-Nielsen, "Hodayot, Psalms from Qumran," Acta Theol. Danica, 2 (1960), 121, n. 172; F. Nötscher, "Zur theol. Terminologie d. Qumrantexte," Bonner Bibl. Beiträge, 11 (1956), 151, cf. Index s.v. "Auferstehung." But the passage is open to debate.

is to the awakening of a remnant as the pure community. Acc. to 1 QM 17:7 Michael's rule will be exalted over heavenly beings and so will that of Israel over mankind. [18] bErub., 13b deals with abasing and exalting in the human sphere. The ref. is to the ranking of the various Rabb. schools. [19]

D. ὑψόω in the New Testament.

1. The OT motif of the exalting of the lowly and humbling of the lofty (→ 607, 13 ff.) [20] occurs in a new formulation at Mt. 23:12; Lk. 14:11; 18:14 as part of the Jesus tradition. The deviations of the texts in comparison with one another are slight; Lk. 16:15b is harsher. Along the lines of the OT revelation of God all exaltation on man's part is repudiated → 607, 18 ff. Exaltation is the act of God alone. [21] The passive form of the sayings avoids mentioning God's name in the usual OT way. The active occurs in Lk. 1:52; Ac. 13:17; Jm. 4:10; 1 Pt. 5:6. [22] According to 2 C. 11:7 the exaltation of the community consists in the fact that the Corinthians are made worthy to receive the Gospel and therewith the glory of Christ (for nothing) → 17, n. 45. The thought of social stratification is alien to the NT. Exaltation is blessing. This is especially plain in the saying of Jesus at Capernaum in Mt. 11:23; [23] Lk. 10:15. The eschatological element is clearer in 1 Pt. 5:6. But ὑψόω always has an eschatological reference for the Christian hearer and reader; [24] this is made explicit in Phil. 2:5 ff.

2. Within the framework of a pre-Pauline confession of Christ Phil. 2:9 [25] presents a statement about Christ's exaltation ὑπερύψωσεν. Obedience to the death of the cross is viewed in terms of the antithesis "humiliation" (→ 18, 10 ff.) as this is presented in the LXX (→ 6, 1 ff.). Raising up from death is also institution as

---

[18] A. S. van der Woude, *Die messianischen Vorstellungen d. Gemeinde von Qumran* (1957), 143 f.; J. Carmignac, *La règle de la guerre des fils de lumière contre les fils de ténèbres* (1958), 239 f.

[19] Str.-B., I, 921 with further materials.

[20] W. Baumgartner, *Israelitische u. orientalische Weisheit* (1933), 24 maintains that genuinely Chr. elements are surprisingly not very prominent in primitive Chr. exhortation, e.g., in Jm.

[21] As in En. (→ 603, 23 ff.) the exaltation of the righteous might be thought of in terms of rapture or ascension, H. Grass, *Ostergeschehen u. Osterberichte*[2] (1964), 229 f. also "Zur Begründung des Osterglaubens," ThLZ, 89 (1964), 407 f.; E. Schweizer, "Erniedrigung u. Erhöhung bei Jesus u. seinen Nachfolgern," AbhThANT, 28[2] (1962), 27 f.

[22] On the relationship of these two passages v. Dib. Jk.[11], 269 f. 272.

[23] Cf. Kl. Mt., *ad loc.*

[24] It is debated whether the Messiah concept or that of exaltation is the more basic in the Synoptic tradition. Acc. to Mk. 12:36: 14:62 cf. also 8:38 the exaltation of the earthly Jesus might be expected without any connection with His death and passion. Enthronement and exaltation were identical as the content of imminent expectation and apart from the resurrection the Easter event meant institution to heavenly glory, cf. the discussion in F. Hahn, "Christologische Hoheitstitel. Ihre Geschichte im frühen Christentum," FRL, 83[3] (1966), Index, *s.v.* "Erhöhung" and Index of Ref. Hahn, 251 thinks the expectation of eschatological enthronement was weakened by the theme of exaltation tied to the resurrection. Cf. also G. Bornkamm, "Der Auferstandene u. der Irdische, Mt. 28:16-20," in G. Bornkamm - G. Barth - H. J. Held, *Überlieferung u. Auslegung im Mt., Wissenschaftliche Monographien z. AT u. NT*, 1[4] (1965), 289-310; E. Grässer, "Das Problem d. Parusieverzögerung in den synpt. Ev. u. in d. Ag.," ZNW Beih., 22[2] (1960), 172-7; P. Vielhauer, "Ein Weg z. nt.lichen Christologie?" *Aufsätze z. NT* (1965), 141-198; J. M. Robinson, *Kerygma u. historischer Jesus*[2] (1967), 228-230; A. W. Argyle, *The Christ of the NT* (1952), 145-173.

[25] Robinson, *op. cit.*, 166 f. and Index on Phil. 2:5-11; E. Käsemann, "Krit. Analyse v. Phil. 2:5-11," *Exeget. Versuche u. Besinnungen*, I[4] (1965), 51-95.

the Lord before whom every knee shall bow in worship. [26] The use of the compound here is independent of the liking of Hellenistic Greek for composites; it is a genuine strengthening. By the conferring of the title Jesus receives the highest position, that of cosmocrator. [27] The fact that God Himself gives Him this position indicates the natural restriction of His dominion, 1 C. 15:27. The point of the humiliation and exaltation is not, as exegesis has commonly assumed, an ethical understanding of the conduct of Jesus along the lines of attainment and reward. It is rather an eschatological, soteriological explanation in the sense of the anthropos myth. [28]

Faith in the exalted Lord is expressed by Paul in other ways as well. He preaches the Crucified as the Lord of glory (1 C. 2:2, 8) [29] who has revealed Himself to him as the Exalted One in conversion and calling, in visions and auditions. The apostle himself stands, then, in the same tension between abasement and exaltation, between his human weakness and the power at work in him, i.e., the grace of the Lord, 2 C. 12:8-10.

3. As concerns the antithesis between exaltation and the earthly sufferings and temptations, the statements in Hb. about ὑψηλός (1:3; 7:26) correspond to the confession of Phil. 2:5-11. Christ has sat down at the right hand of the majesty on high. [30] This ἐν ὑψηλοῖς is the place of God's throne, [31] higher than heaven, and thus separated from sinners and from the sufferings and trials through which Christ had to pass, 7:26. [32] Since there are no ref. to the burial, resurrection and resurrection appearances in Hb., the concept of the denouement here is that of the exaltation of Jesus from the cross to heaven, i.e., to God's throne. [33]

4. In Ac. (2:33; 5:31) exaltation stands immediately alongside the common formula of the resurrection or awakening of Jesus (→ II, 39, 5 ff.; V, 356, 5 ff.; 524, 17 ff.). In 2:33 it denotes institution at the right hand of God [34] and the inauguration of rule. It is also the presupposition of the outpouring of the Spirit and the expressions of the Spirit in the Pentecost community seen and heard by those addressed. Along with the eye-witness, Scripture proof for the exaltation is adduced from Ps. 110:1, which sheds light on the rising up of Jesus (not David, 2:34a) into heaven. 5:31 lays stress on the soteriological aspect. Exaltation to be Prince and Deliverer as the Author of salvation takes place in order to grant

[26] Cf. ψ 95:10 with the additamentum christianum: e ligno in Just. Dial., 73, 1 etc.: The Lord enters into His glory directly from the cross.

[27] Hahn, op. cit., 120 f.; G. Bornkamm, "Zum Verständnis d. Christushymnus Phil. 2:6-11," Stud. zu Antike u. Urchr.[2] (1963), 177-187; cf. Robinson, op. cit., 167: The Easter event, i.e., the institution of Jesus as cosmocrator, is the basis of Christian preaching.

[28] Käsemann, op. cit. (→ n. 25), 94 f.

[29] E. Käsemann, "1 K. 2:6-16," Exeget. Versuche u. Besinnungen, I[4] (1965), 271-3.

[30] The allusion to Ps. 110 in Hb. also pts. to the OT basis of Christ's exaltation, cf. Hahn, op. cit., 126-132.

[31] Cf. Rgg. Hb., 13, who ref. to Eth. En. 51:3 etc. Exaltation to the throne of God implies sharing in God's cosmic rule.

[32] On the high-priestly ascension of Christ cf. Wnd. Hb. Exc. on 8:2 → V, 527, 34 ff.

[33] E. Käsemann, "Das wandernde Gottesvolk. Eine Untersuchung z. Hb.," FRL, 55[2] (1957), 150: "The existence of the dying Jesus is already shot through by the glory of the exalted Lord, since His dying signifies already His exaltation"... "Golgotha is no longer regarded as a profoundly earthly fact but as the beginning of the ascension of Jesus."

[34] τῇ δεξιᾷ is a dat. loci; the formulation is influenced by Ps. 110:1, cf. Haench. Ag.[14], ad loc. H. Braun, "Zur Terminologie der Acta von d.Auferstehung Jesu," Gesammelte Stud. z. NT u. seiner Umwelt[2] (1967), 173-7 stresses God's initiative at the exaltation by the dat. "at the right hand of God" and the resultant subordinationist trend in the Christology of Ac., which is in keeping with the pass. character of the resurrection of Jesus. G. Schille, "Die Himmelfahrt," ZNW, 57 (1966), 183-199, thinks the idea of ascension from the cross or on the day of the resurrection is original.

repentance and the remission of sins to Israel. There is no antithesis between humiliation and exaltation as in Phil. 2:5-11. The resurrection and ascension, which the author could equate with the exaltation, are seen as a necessary consequence. [35]

5. In Jn. [36] ὑψόω has intentionally a double sense in all the passages in which it occurs, 3:14; 8:28; 12:32, 34. [37] It means both exaltation on the cross and also exaltation to heaven. [38] ὑψόω denotes the event of salvation. As looking at the brazen serpent saves life in Nu. 21:8 f., so the man who believes in the exalted Son of Man has eternal life in Jn. 3:14 f. The tertium comparationis between the serpent and the Son of Man is lifting up. ὑψόομαι is used for the changing of Jesus' sphere of being in the same way as ἀναβαίνω (→ I, 519, 1 ff., cf. Jn. 3:13; 6:62), πορεύομαι (→ VI, 575, 27 ff., cf. Jn. 7:35, and ὑπάγω (→ 505, 29 ff., cf. Jn. 7:33; 8:14, 21 f.). [39] At one and the same time it both intimates and also obscures what is to come. The expressions all denote parting from the earthly sphere and return to the heavenly home, i.e., death; [40] death is the presupposition of exaltation and transfiguration. [41] But ὑψόω refers also to the mode of death. 8:28 and 12:32 with their ἐκ τῆς γῆς do not rule this out. Since in 8:28 it is the adversaries of Jesus who are to exalt Him, the most natural sense is indeed "to bring to the gallows." In reality, however, they exalt Him as the Ruler and Judge who will Himself pronounce sentence on them. [42] In Jn. 12:32 f. (→ VI, 722, 4 ff.) the Evangelist himself relates exaltation in the first instance to the crucifixion. Hence 12:32 makes discipleship of the cross constitutive for the disciples. [43] Jn. 12:34, an objection on the part of the crowd which might

---

[35] Bultmann Theol.[3], 48. 84; G. Bertram, "Die Himmelfahrt Jesu vom Kreuz aus u. der Glaube an seine Auferstehung," Festschr. A. Deissmann (1927), 187-217; U. Holzmeister, "Der Tag der Himmelfahrt d. Herrn," Zschr. f. Kathol. Theol., 55 (1931), 44-82; T. Steinmann, "Systematisches aus d. historischen Theol.," ZThK., NF, 8 (1928), 304 f., with ref. to the thesis of ascension from the cross, pts. to the need for a strong supporting structure of current soteriological and christological constructs. For M. Goguel, La foi à la résurrection de Jésus dans le Christianisme primitif. Étude d'histoire et de psychologie religieuses (1933), 105-117 the certainty of Christ's exaltation to heavenly life and Messianic glory is the starting-pt. J. Héring, Le royaume de Dieu et sa venue. Étude sur l'espérance de Jésus et de l'apôtre Paul (1937), 147-183 relates the exaltation and glorification, not just to the resurrection, but already to the baptism and transfiguration; P. Menoud, "Remarques sur les textes de l'ascension dans Luc-Actes," Festschr. R. Bultmann, ZNW Beih., 21[2] (1957), 148-156; K. H. Rengstorf, Die Auferstehung Jesu. Form, Art u. Sinn d. urchr. Osterbotschaft[5] (1967), 71 f., 146-154 attacks a confusion common from the time of Schleiermacher, namely, that of the resurrection and the reception into glory, of Easter and the ascension, on the basis of the concept of exaltation.
[36] W. Thüsing, "Die Erhöhung u. Verherrlichung Jesu im Joh.-Ev.," NTAbh, 21, 1. 2 (1960), 3-37; on this R. Bultmann, "Zur Interpretation d. Joh.-Ev.," ThLZ, 87 (1962), 1-5.
[37] O. Cullmann, "Der joh. Gebrauch doppeldeutiger Ausdrücke als Schlüssel zum Verständnis d. vierten Ev.," Vorträge u. Aufsätze 1925-1962 (1966), 176-186.
[38] Behind lie Syr.-Aram. or Hbr. words which have a double sense (cf. Germ. "aufheben"). Thus זקף is both the impaling of a wrong-doer (Ezr. 6:11) and the consoling lifting up of one who is bowed down. Cf. G. Kittel, " אִזְדְּקֵף = ὑψωθῆναι = gekreuzigt werden. Zur angeblichen antiochenischen Herkunft d. 4. Evangelisten," ZNW, 35 (1936), 282-5. זקף is the old Aram. word for "to lift up," "to hang up," and it occurs in the gen. sense in 1 QS 7:11 in an obscure connection. Cf. also רום or Syr. aphel from this 'arīm "to take away" (cf. F. Schulthess, "Zur Sprache d. Ev.," ZNW, 21 [1922], 220) and נשא (used by F. Delitzsch, ספרי הברית החדשה [1880]).
[39] Bultmann J., 109, n. 1.
[40] Bultmann J., 110, n. 2.
[41] Is. 52:13, and on this Euler, op. cit. (→ n. 12), 98.
[42] Bultmann J., ad loc.
[43] Ibid., ad loc.

originally have been the continuation of 8:28, sets ὑψοῦσθαι, the Redeemer's return to His heavenly home along the lines of the Gnostic myth, in antithesis to expectation of His eternal Messianic kingdom on earth. Jesus does not deal with the objection. His transfiguration (12:23; → II, 249, 19 ff.) and exaltation are His perfecting (19:30). Exaltation in Jn. is crucifixion in the sense of the OT type of the serpent and it is also receiving up into heaven from the cross. The assumption that the reference here is to the pneuma of Jesus which was parted from His body in death [44] makes it possible to combine the idea of exaltation with that of the resurrection and ascension.

6. Whether the NT reference be to awakening, resurrection, reception, ascent, rapture (diastasis, Lk. 24:51), enthronement (Mt. 26:64; Ps. 110:1), or royal dominion (Lk. 22:29 f.; 1 C. 15:25), all these can be summed up in the one word "exaltation." [45] They all denote the vanquishing of the lowliness of the earthly Jesus. The tension between abasement and exaltation, which is found already in the life, suffering and death of the righteous of the OT (→ 607, 7 ff.), is resolved hereby. [46] At the same time, on the basis of the king-ideology and messianology of the OT, which are understood christologically and soteriologically, and also under the influence of Enoch typology and the concept of the Son of Man in Daniel, a starting-point is provided for the apocalyptic structuring of eschatological expectation.

---

[44] J. Jeremias, "Zwischen Karfreitag u. Ostern. Descensus u. Ascensus in der Karfreitagstheologie d. NT," ZNW, 42 (1949), 198-201.

[45] G. Bertram, "Die Leidensgesch. Jesu u. der Christuskult," FRL, 22 (1922), 58 f. 96; O. Cullmann, "Die ersten chr. Glaubensbekenntnisse," Theol. Stud., 15² (1949), 52, cf. the review by R. Bultmann, ThLZ, 74 (1949), 42: The pt. of the confession is to confess Christ as the One who from His exaltation is the Ruler of every present; E. Lichtenstein, "Die älteste chr. Glaubensformel," ZKG, 62 (1950), 36-43, cf. H. E. Tödt, Der Menschensohn in d. synpt. Überlieferung² (1962), 168-170; cf. E. Schweizer, "Der Menschensohn," Neotestamentica (1963), 76: The exaltation of Jesus was the heart of proclamation; the Easter event was understood "first as exaltation, i.e., divine vindication (1 Tm. 3:16) ... and not strictly as resurrection in the sense of the overcoming of death." Similarly W. Hartke, "Vier urchr. Parteien u. ihre Vereinigung zur Apostol. Kirche," I, Deutsche Akad. d. Wissenschaften zu Berlin. Schr. d. Sektion f. Altertumswissenschaft, 24 (1961), 365; cf. also G. Barth, "Das Gesetzesverständnis des Evangelisten Mt.," Bornkamm - Barth - Held, op. cit. 125-8 and on this J. Rohde, Die redaktionsgeschichtliche Methode (1966), 56 f. Further Hahn, op. cit. (→ n. 24), 215, 217, 126-132; H. Braun, Gesammelte Stud. z. NT u. seiner Umwelt² (1967), 243-282; O. Cullmann, Die Christologie d. NT⁴ (1966), 211-213.

[46] W. Thüsing, "Erhöhungsvorstellung u. Parusieerwartung in d. ältesten nachösterlichen Christologie," BZ, NF, 11 (1967), 95-108, 205-222; 12 (1968), 54-80, 223-240 has already even in detail distinguished the various opinions on the relation between expectation of the parousia and the concept of exaltation. The latter is implied in the sayings about Jesus' authority in the Logia source and the miracles and epiphanies of the Synoptic tradition. In the post-Easter stratum the sayings of Jesus are presented as sayings of the Risen and Exalted One who is identical with the earthly Jesus. His authority is a means of displaying His dominion as the exalted Lord. Similarly Jesus is the Revealer in the Joh. discourses. The idea of exaltation is explicit in the preaching of God's rule. The various christological sketches for present, past and future form an essential unity. The concept of exaltation is faith in the christologically determined presence of the completion of salvation, 213. The unequivocal orientation to the eschata (in Rev.) in no way prejudices the concept of exaltation, the conviction as to the present power of Jesus and its present operation, 232. Thüsing, 104 f. ref. to C. H. Dodd, The Apostolic Preaching and Its Developments (1936), 70-73: realised eschatology, J. A. T. Robinson, Jesus and His Coming (1957), 100 f.: inaugurated eschatology, and R. Bultmann, "Ist die Apokalyptik die Mutter d. chr. Theol.?" Exegetica (1967), 477: present eschatology.

Between exaltation and resurrection there is no antithesis. [47] (Potential) exaltation is implied already by the acknowledgment of Jesus as Messiah, Christ, and Lord by His disciples. Logically priority seems to belong to the concept of exaltation. [48] For an understanding of the life of Jesus this thought is a necessary contrast to His humiliation. Exaltation is on the one side the presupposition of His coming again and it thus has eschatological significance. [49] But it does not imply translation into the invisibility (Jn. 14:19; 16:16 → V, 362, 8 ff.) and inaccessibility (Jn. 7:34) of another world. It is not so much a change of place as institution to power and glory, enthronement. This is on the other side the basis of the subjection of all creatures on earth, in heaven and under the earth to the dominion of the exalted Lord and hence of the Christ cult in a cosmic sense → III, 353, 11 ff.; 274, 29 ff. [50] In keeping with this is the formation of the Christian community with its claimed universal ecclesiology. The hymn of confession in Phil. 2:6 ff. possibly had its origin in the baptismal liturgy of this community. [51]

From the standpoint of the tradition the Johannine and Synoptic miracle stories and the Synoptic epiphanies, esp. the transfiguration on a high mountain (→ 603, n. 14), seem to be anticipations of future glory and exaltation. [52] The empty tomb which puzzled and scared the disciples and other adherents (Mk. 16:8) is also explained by the thought of exaltation. Acc. to Mk. 14:62 (cf. Lk. 22:69) Jesus takes His place on God's throne; He becomes the Lord, Ruler and Judge through God and alongside God → 372, 16 f. and n. 273. [53] He has thus entered into glory and shares the glory of the Father. With time the provisional nature of this position is less and less regarded. Belief in exaltation in the first instance implies (or is at least connected with) eschatological expectation. But it becomes more and more prominent, while imminent expectation and apocalyptic eschatology part company → n. 46. It remains the basic concept of all Christology, esp. as the reawakening and resurrection formed an effective corrective to docetic evaporation, → n. 24. Not only in the Gnostic world [54] and monophysite circles but also in the main body of the Church the idea of the cosmic Christ could appeal to the concept of exaltation. [55]

---

[47] The two concepts are already terminologically related in the OT. Ps. 9:13 speaks of the plight of the petitioner whom Yahweh lifts up out of the sphere ("gates") of death. For Pharisaic exegesis this was a testimony to belief in the resurrection, cf. the Qumran texts adduced → 607, 29 ff. The LXX reader could also relate humiliation and exaltation to the death and resurrection, esp. when they have a christological connection. Ac. 17:31 takes Ps. 9:8 christologically as a ref. to the Exalted Lord as the future Judge, a man whom God has raised up from the dead. With the current NT formulation the ἀναστήσας αὐτὸν ἐκ νεκρῶν might be regarded as a free transl. of Ps. 9:13: מְרוֹמְמִי מִשַּׁעֲרֵי מָוֶת, cf. LXX ὁ ὑψῶν με ἐκ τῶν πυλῶν τοῦ θανάτου.

[48] W. Herrmann, Der Verkehr d. Christen mit Gott im Anschluss an Luther dargestellt⁷ (1921), 233, quoted in Grass, op. cit. (→ n. 21), 408 f.

[49] Thüsing, op. cit. (→ n. 46), 104-108.

[50] Hahn, op. cit. (→ n. 24), 145-9, 231-241; G. Friedrich, "Beobachtungen z. messianischen Hohepriestererwartung in d. Synpt.," ZThK, 53 (1956), 265-311; A. Ehrhardt, "Ein antikes Herrscherideal. Phil. 2:5-11," Ev. Theol., 8 (1948/49), 101-110; also "Nochmals: Ein antikes Herrscherideal," ibid., 569-572; on this Käsemann, op. cit. (→ n. 25), 64 f. 87 f.

[51] Käsemann, op. cit. (→ n. 25), 95 and G. Friedrich, "Das Lied vom Hohepriester im Zshg. v. Hb. 4:14 - 5:10," ThZ, 18 (1962), 101.

[52] Bertram, op. cit. (→ n. 35), 189 f. (ref. to Apc. Pt. 3:6 etc.); H. P. Müller, "Die Verklärung Jesu. Eine motivgeschichtliche Studie," ZNW, 51 (1960), 56-64; on this Hahn, op. cit. (→ n. 24), 339.

[53] Hahn, op. cit., 327-333.

[54] Ibid., 348, 350; Holzmeister, op. cit. (→ n. 35), 46 ref. to Act. Joh. 102 and Iren. Haer., V, 31, 1; E. Güttgemanns, "Der leidende Ap. u. sein Herr," FRL, 90 (1966), 69 quotes Act. Joh. 98, the epiphany of the Risen Lord to John and the vision of the cross of light on Good Friday at the 6th hour (the hour of death acc. to Mk. 15:33-37).

[55] G. Bertram, "Ev. Joh. 14:9 u. das gnostische Christusbild," Akten d. 7. Internationalen Kongresses f. Chr. Archäologie Trier, 1965.

E. ὑψόω in Early Christianity.

In the post-apost. fathers the verb occurs a few times in the sense "to be arrogant," Did., 3, 9; Barn., 19, 3, cf. 6; Herm. m., 11, 12; s., 9, 22, 3. In the Apologists it is found only in Just. Apol., 50, 3; Dial., 13, 2; 32, 6 etc. and only in OT citations Is. 52:13; ψ 109:7 etc. In Act. Thom. 37 elevation above the earth, above the earlier state, is a presupposition of the vision of Christ. Test. B. 9:3 κύριος... ἐπὶ ξύλου ὑψωθήσεται is usually taken to be a Chr. interpolation. [56] Test. Jos. 1:7 is also suspect in this regard. [57] In the Chr. Syr. inscr. from Mothana and Bosra [58] the word is used in the same sense as δοξάζω, as in Jn.'s Gospel. [59] The eschatological leveling of hills and valleys ὑψώσει δὲ φάραγγας is proclaimed in Sib., 8, 234; ὑψόομαι has the sense of "arrogance" in 8, 419.

† ὕψωμα.

1. ὕψωμα in the Non-Biblical Sense.

ὕψωμα is late and rare. [1] It means "eminence," "high place," e.g., ὑψώματα βουνῶν Sib., 8, 234, τῆς πόλεως, Preisigke Sammelbuch, II, 5114, 8 (7th cent. A.D.). [2] As an astronomical or astrological word it means "culmination," ἀστέρας ὑψώματα καὶ ταπεινώματα λαμβάνοντας, Plut. Sept. Sap. Conv., 3 (II, 149a); Sext. Emp. Math., V, 33 and 35; Vett. Val., II, 25 (p. 92, 29); τῷ ἰδίῳ ὑψώματι ὃ καλοῦσι Ὥρου γένναν (winter solstice), Preis. Zaub., II, 13, 388 f. (4th cent. A.D.).

2. ὕψωμα in the Septuagint and Hellenistic Judaism.

LXX has ὕψωμα negatively only at Job 24:24 for רום in the sense of "arrogance" and positively at Jdt. 10:8; 13:4; 15:9 for "lifting up" par. to καύχημα and γαυρίαμα. The Hexapla translators often render במות "high places" and sometimes other words by ὕψωμα, 1 Βασ. 9:12; ψ 17:34; Ez. 6:6 ʼΑ; ψ 73:3 Σ; Is. 33:16 ΣΘ; Ex. 28:39 Θ etc. In the last v. the ref. is to the turban of the high-priest as a mark of dignity. In Qoh.10:6 ʼΑ the ref. is to high position. Philo Praem. Poen., 2 underlines the sublimity of the Ten Commandments; they are fashioned in the height of heaven ὕψωμα τοῦ ἀέρος. All the texts point to the Hell. and Jewish Hell. background of early Christianity and they show how broad is the range of meaning of ὕψωμα.

---

[56] M. Philonenko, "Les interpolations chr. des Testaments des Douze Patriarches et les Manuscrits de Qumran," I, RevHPhR, 38 (1958), 309-343 tries to prove that these are sectarian Jewish interpolations, not Chr., cf. esp. 314, 331.

[57] Acc. to Ign. Eph., 19, 2 the exalted Christ reveals Himself as cosmocrator through the universe (represented by the stars) by the rising of a new all-eclipsing star, cf. Ps. 110:3. The world secret of the conception, birth and death of the Lord is manifested by His exaltation, Ign. Eph., 19, 1.

[58] Ed. R. Dussaud - F. Macler, *Voyage au Safa et dans le Djebel-ed-Druz* (1901), 167, No. 35; ed. W. K. Prentice, *Publication of the Princeton-Univ. Archaeol. Expedition to Syria in 1904/05,* III: "Greek and Latin Inscr. in Syria," by E. Littmann and W. K. Prentice (1907-14), No. 574.

[59] The same use occurs also in the pagan sphere, cf. E. Peterson, "ΕΙΣ ΘΕΟΣ Epigraphische, formgeschichtliche u. religionsgeschichtliche Untersuchungen," FRL, 41 (1926), 176.

ὕψωμα. [1] Thes. Steph., Liddell-Scott, Moult.-Mill., Preisigke Wört., *s.v.*
[2] Cf. U. Wilcken, "Pap.-Urkunden," APF, 1 (1901), 165.

3. ὕψωμα in the New Testament.

In the NT the word is used only at R. 8:39 and 2 C. 10:5. In R. 8:38 [3] we have a list of occurrences, powers and places which might separate from God and hinder the work of His love. ὕψωμα is an astrological (→ 613, 16 ff.) term. [4] But it simply denotes the place on high which belongs to creation. It is the sphere in which astrally conceived powers [5] (1 C. 15:24; Col. 1:16; Eph. 1:21) hold sway. On His ascent Christ has victoriously pierced this sphere as the wall of partition [6] (Eph. 2:14) between heaven and earth or God and man (Col. 2:15) and has gone on to take His place on high ὑπεράνω, ἐν ὑψίστοις at God's right hand (Eph. 1:20). ὕψωμα is thus among the created things which are subjected to Christ, Eph. 1:22; 1 C. 15:25, 27; Hb. 2:8. The love of God revealed in Christ penetrates creation and thus penetrates the ὕψωμα at all times too. [7] In 2 C. 10:5 ὕψωμα means a "fortress with high towers." [8] Not real ramparts [9] behind which opponents barricade themselves but the overweening attitude of man's spirit (→ IV, 287, 13 ff.) is what resists true knowledge of God. Paul uses the common imagery of the *militia Christi* [10] but the campaign on which he embarks is a spiritual one.

4. ὕψωμα in Early Christianity.

There is an echo of Paul's usage at R. 8:39 in Act. Joh. 23. Here οὐρανῶν ὕψωμα is listed among the ungodly powers.

† ὕψιστος.

A. ὕψιστος in Non-Biblical Greek.

The superlative ὕψιστος is found from Pind. and Aesch. and with the rare comp.

---

[3] W. L. Knox, *St. Paul and the Church of the Gentiles* (1960), 106 tries to explain R. 8:38 f. along the lines of astrology. Neither the present nor future conjunctions of the stars in their significance for the present or future, nor the culmination or declension of the planets, whether hostile or friendly in their strength or weakness, can separate from the love of God [Moule].

[4] Reitzenstein Poim., 80, n. 3 gives an example of the sense "height."

[5] W. Gundel, Art. "Astrologie," RAC, 1 (1950), 825-7.

[6] Cf. Ign. Tr. rec. longa, 9, 4 (ed. F. X. Funk and F. Diekamp, Patres Apostolici, II³ [1913]) and on this H. Schlier, "Religionsgeschichtliche Untersuchungen zu d. Ignatiusbr.," ZNW Beih., 8 (1929), 21. Schlier has other par. to Eph. 2:14 from the Mandaean tradition and the Acta Thaddaei in Eus. Hist. Eccl., I, 13, 20. J. Kroll, "Gott u. Hölle. Der Mythos vom Descensuskampfe," *Stud. d. Bibliothek Warburg,* 10 (1932), 103, n. 1 claims that the Ign. interpolation is dependent on Eph. 2:14.

[7] We find the rule of stellar forces over man's destiny in Judaism too. But the Rabb. assume that Israel itself is not subject to this. Astrological superstition seems to be stronger in Hell. Judaism, cf. H. Gressmann, "Die Aufgaben d. Wissenschaft d. nachexilischen Judt.," ZAW 43 (1925), 19-23, who speaks of a Jewish astral religion; Str.-B., II, 402-5 and IV, Index *s.v.* "Astrologen," "Astrologie"; Ltzm. Gl. on 4:3; Dib. Gefbr. on Col. 2:8, 15.

[8] Chrys. Hom. in 2 C. 21:2 (MPG, 61 [1862], 543) explains the word by πύργωμα. The verb ὑψόω is also often used for the raising of fortifications, 1 Macc. 14:37; Jos. Bell., 1, 146; 3, 171, cf. Ltzm. 2 K. and Wnd. 2 K., *ad loc.*

[9] Bchm. 2 K. and Wnd. 2 K., *ad loc.*

[10] A. v. Harnack, *Militia Christi. Die chr. Religion u. der Soldatenstand in den ersten drei Jhdt.* (1905), 15 and 93.

ὕψιστος. Bibl.: W. Drexler, Art. "Hypsistos," Roscher, I, 2 (1886-1890), 2856-2858; F. Cumont, Art. "Ύψιστος" in Pauly-W., 9 (1914), 444-450; W. W. Baudissin, *Kyrios als Gottesname im Judt. u. seine St. in d. Religionsgeschichte,* I-IV (1929); IV, 82, Index *s.v.* עֶלְיוֹן; 89 *s.v.* Ζεὺς ὕψιστος.

ὑψίων Pind. Fr., 213 is formed from adv. ὕψι, [1] there being no adj. posit., though one finds the neuter ὕψος from Aesch. Ag., 1376. ὕψιστος is at first purely poetic; much later we find a religious use. It means "highest," "loftiest." [2] The neut. of the adj. denotes the "highest place" and is used, e.g., for the peaks of the Caucasus which are close to the stars, Aesch. Prom., 720. Transf. we find it with the wreath Pind. Pyth., 1, 100, with winning Isthm., 1, 51, fear Aesch. Suppl., 479, evils Pers., 331 and 807. It is a predicate of Zeus [3] in Pind. Nem., 1, 60; 11, 2; Aesch. Eum., 28; Soph. Phil., 1289. Zeus is the god on the highest mountain who is also god and lord of heaven. [4] He is also the supreme guarantee of justice and can thus be regarded as the most high in a moral sense. We read of a temple to Ζεὺς ὕψιστος at Thebes in Paus., IX, 8, 5, cf. also II, 2, 8; V, 15, 5. There are also non-literary ref. to Ζεὺς ὕψιστος. Inscr., 10, 1 f. [5] (29 B.C.). A society named after him existed c. 60 A.D. [6] From Bizya in Thrace, [7] which is to be regarded as the real home of the ὕψιστος cult, [8] and also from Miletus we have Theos-Hypsistos inscr., Ditt. Or., I, 378 (1st cent. A.D.); II, 755 and 756. [9] Mithra is the most high in an Antaradus inscr. [10] Jewish influence, which cannot be ruled out, e.g., in Palmyra and seems to be present in older inscr. from c. 200 B.C. (→ 618, 22 ff.), may be regarded as a manifestation of religious syncretism.

B. עליון in Semitic Usage.

The OT tradition probably depends on a Syr.-Canaanite designation אל עליון or עליון. The title itself does not occur in the Ras Shamra texts, but in these the Creator God, who is both Father of mankind and King, has in fact the position of the supreme God. [11] Philo Byblius (64-141 A.D.) acc. to Eus. Praep. Ev., 1, 10. 14 f. appeals to a Phoenician historian Sanchunyaton c. 1300 B.C. [12] In him he found a term for God which he trans-

---

[1] Boisacq, Hofmann, s.v.; Schwyzer, I, 631, 10. The comp. ὑψίτερος is also formed directly from ὕψι, Theocr. Idyll., 8, 46 [Risch].

[2] Zeus is already ὕπατος if not ὕψιστος in Hom. Il., 5, 756; 8, 22. 31; Od., 1, 45. 81; 24, 473 etc. [Dihle]. In class. Gk. ὕψιστος is only a superlative [Risch]. For Hell. and bibl. usage cf. Bl.-Debr. § 60, 2 and Radermacher, 67 f.: "In popular speech the comp. can very gen. take over the functions of the superlative." "Almost all the superlatives found in popular lit. are elatives, i.e., they are used to express the highest possible degree of perfection." The elative contains an abs. statement, not a relation or comparison.

[3] Cf. A. B. Cook, Zeus. A Study in Ancient Religion, I, 2 (1925), 876-889.

[4] Cf. Bertholet-Leh., II, 336 f.; F. Heiler, Erscheinungsformen u. Wesen d. Religionen, Die Religionen d. Menschheit, 1 (1961), 457.

[5] Ed. O. Rubensohn, "Neue Inschr. aus Ägypten," APF, 5 (1913), 163.

[6] Attested in P. Lond., 2710 in C. Roberts, T. C. Skeat, A. D. Nock, "The Guild of Zeus Hypsistos," HThR, 29 (1936), 40 f., cf. 39-88; J. A. Montgomery, "The Highest, Heaven, Aeon, Time etc. in Semitic Religion," HThR, 31 (1938), 143-150.

[7] Montgomery, op. cit., 143.

[8] The chief gods of cities in the Near East were often given the title of Zeus Hypsistos in the Hell. age, C. H. Dodd, The Bible and the Greeks (1935), 12. One also finds Zeus Olympios and Zeus Megistos, cf. O. Eissfeldt, Tempel u. Kulte syr. Städte in hell.-röm. Zeit (1941), 31 f., 48-50, 83, 90-92.

[9] Cf. also the votive inscr. to Zeus Hypsistos from Palmyra in M. Lidzbarski, Ephemeris f. semitische Epigraphik, II (1908), 295 f., Gebeil, ibid., 324 and Abedat in the Byblus district: Votive inscr. on an altar to Zeus Hypsistos, ed. E. Renan, Mission de Phénicie (1864), 234, cf. Drexler, 2856-2858.

[10] Ed. Renan, op. cit., 103 f. Cf. E. Schürer, "Die Juden im bosporanischen Reiche u. die Genossenschaften d. σεβόμενοι θεὸν ὕψιστον ebendaselbst," SAB, 1897 (1897), 213 f. Cf. F. Cumont, Textes et monuments relatifs aux mystères de Mithra, I (1896), 92; Cumont, 444-450. Here doubt is cast on Renan's reading; Mithra is not the previously mentioned ὕψιστος. Jewish influence may be ruled out here, Baudissin, III, 83.

[11] O. Eissfeldt, Ras Schamra u. Sanchunjaton (1939), 12-30; J. Aistleitner, Die mythologischen u. kultischen Texte aus Ras Schamra übersetzt² (1964), 15-20 etc.

[12] Eissfeldt, op. cit., 67-70.

literates as ἐλιοῦν and renders by ὕψιστος. If this is correct the name of the Most High is attested for the 2nd millennium B.C. [13] It certainly occurs on Stele 1 of Sfîre 754 B.C. [14] A pre-Israelite cult of the Most High which was taken over by Israel may perhaps be hinted at or presupposed for Jerusalem in texts like Gn. 14:19-22; 1 S. 2:10; Ps. 46:4. [15] A supreme God who was the cultic God of the Jebusites in Jerusalem and who was fused with Yahweh after the capture of the city might also lie behind the angel in 2 S. 24:17. [16] To a limited degree some of the concepts of the pre-Israelite, Canaanite El religion represented by El Elyon in Jerusalem were assumed into the faith in Yahweh. Nevertheless, one cannot speak of a cultic tradition of the Most High in Jerusalem, for only in the post-exilic period, and esp. in the Ps. of the sons of Korah (46:4; 47:2; 87:5b), is the ancient traditional term that was connected with the place, and remained dormant, employed again with any frequency. In relation to the ideology of Jerusalem it becomes an expression of the echatological hopes and expectations of the community focused on Zion as the throne of God. Ps. 82:6; 47:2; 97:9, which might be regarded as Jerusalem accession psalms, ref. to the עליון. Ps. 18:7-15 = 2 S. 22:8-16 contains the account of what might be an original Canaanite theophany of this עליון. The divine designation עליון occurs 31 times in the OT, only in poetry outside Gn. 14 and always without art. What is meant is the High One, the One who dwells on high (on mountains, in heaven), the Lofty One. It is a title of majesty for Yahweh of an archaic hymnal type [17] and like Shaddai it occurs as a proper name. אלה שמיא, אלהי שמים seems to have the same content. In 1 Εσδρ. 2:2; 6:30; 8:19, 21; Δα. 2:18 f. this is transl. by ὁ ὕψιστος or ὁ θεὸς ὁ ὕψιστος etc., [18] cf. also Δα. 4:23. In the OT עליון always ref. to the one God of Israel. In the Ps. it usually stands alone as a noun, but elsewhere it is mostly an adj. [19] The presence of the idea of the Most High or the Most High God in the surrounding world, which is

---

[13] H. Bauer, "Die Gottheiten v. Ras Schamra," ZAW, 51 (1933), 96 f.; Eissfeldt, op. cit., 114-6. The Eliun of Philo Byblius might be the Aliyan of Ras Schamra. Cf. also in the Hittite and Hurrian language the mythical tradition of the father of the gods Kumarbi who overthrows Anu the god of heaven [Risch]. H. G. Güterbock, "Hittite Mythology," Mythologies of the Ancient World, ed. S. N. Kramer (1961), 155-172; G. Steiner, Der Sukzessionsmythus in Hesiods Theogonie u. ihren orient. Par., Diss. Hamburg (1958).

[14] H. Donner - W. Röllig, Kanaanäische u. aram. Inschr., I (1962), 222, n. 11; cf. Montgomery, op. cit., 143 f. and J. Hempel, Report on P. S. Ronzevalle, "Fragments d'inscr. aram. des environs d'Alep," ZAW, 50 (1932), 182: Elyon is shown by these to be an independent ancient Syr. god, cf. also H. Bauer, "Ein aram. Staatsvertrag aus d. 8. Jhdt. v. Chr. Die Inschr. d. Stele v. Sudschin," Archiv f. Orientforschung, 8 (1932), 1-10, also E. Kutsch, Art. "Melchisedek," RGG³, IV, 843 f.

[15] Cf. H. J. Kraus, Ps., Bibl. Komm. AT, 15, 1 (1960), 197-205. R. Rendtorff, "El, Ba'al u. Jahwe, Erwägungen z. Verhältnis v. kanaan. u. isr. Religion," ZAW, 78 (1966), 277-291, warns against the theory that Yahweh was pushed into El's role as supreme god of the pantheon. He finds more differences in El worship in the patriarchal period. Adoption of the cultic tradition of Jerusalem by Israel was essentially much later. On the whole one must allow that the fusion of features of the Canaanite gods (El, Baal), with the Yahweh religion of Israel took place in many stages whose details need to be investigated further.

[16] Cf. G. Wanke, "Die Zionstheologie d. Korachiten in ihrem traditionsgeschichtlichen Zshg," ZAW Beih., 97 (1966), 46-54, 103-117, who contests present findings with particular ref. to H. Schmid, "Jahwe u. die Kulttraditionen v. Jerusalem," ZAW, 67 (1955), 168-197, cf. esp. 175. 185, who acc. to Wanke, 109 prepared the ground for the theory of a Jerusalem cultic tradition.

[17] Kraus, op. cit. on Ps. 7:17.

[18] For the equation of Hypsistos and Baal Shamen cf. Eissfeldt, op. cit., 90-92; F. Heiler, D. Religionen d. Menschheit in Vergangenheit u. Gegenwart (1959), 503-506, 513, 1062: Zeus Megistos as Baal Shamen. In Preis. Zaub., I, 4, 1060. 1068 (4th cent. A.D.) we find the equation of Βαλσάμης and ὕψιστος. It rests on an intentional by-passing of syncretistic misunderstandings that in Da. (LXX) אלא שמיא is transl. by ὁ κύριος ὁ ὕψιστος, cf. R. Hanhart, "Fragen um die Entstehung d. LXX," VT, 12 (1962), 159 f.

[19] Baudissin, II, 257. 305; III, 223.

given emphasis by the use of divine terms and theophorous personal names of the root עלה in other Semitic dialects, [20] combines with the OT statements themselves to suggest a pre-Israelite deity in the Canaanite or Syro-Phoenician sphere which took over the features of the Syr. Baal Shamen and could thus become a great universal deity instead of a local god → n. 15, 18. [21]

עליון occurs 6 times in the Dead Sea Scrolls. 1 QS. 4:22 ref. to knowledge of the Most High. The term is par. to אל in 1 QS 10:12; 11:15. In 1 QH 4:31; 6:33 we find אל עליון, [22] and in Damasc. 20:8 (9:33) the members of the sect (or the angels?) are "saints of the Most High." The title thus lives on in the community but with no special emphasis. עליון is rare in the Rabb. tradition. We find it in the first petition of the Prayer of Eighteen Benedictions. [23]

C. ὕψιστος in the Septuagint.

Apart from a few passages in which it is used topographically ὕψιστος is always a term for God in the LXX. In all the HT verses which have עליון as a divine title the translation is ὕψιστος. The Hexapla transl. follow suit. Only 'A apparently brings in ὕψιστος for the Messianic king at ψ 88:28. [24] LXX also uses ὕψιστος for other Hbr. words, [25] e.g., at Job 31:28 for ממעל from the same root עלה, and often for רום and מָרוֹם, which contain the concept of loftiness, cf. Is. 57:15. In מָרוֹם the basic local sense of "in the height" may still be seen, cf. the transl. of Job 16:19; 25:2; [26] 31:2; [27] ψ 70:19; 148:1. But מָרוֹם is a term for God, Ps. 92:8; [28] Mi. 6:6; [29] Is. 57:15; ψ 55:3 'A. The primary pt.

---

[20] *Ibid.,* III, 82, n. 1; 116; H. Gressmann, "Die Aufgaben d. Wissenschaft d. nachbiblischen Judt.," ZAW, 43 (1925), 18 f.

[21] O. Eissfeldt, "Jahwes Verhältnis zu 'Eljon u. Schaddaj nach Ps. 91," *Die Welt d. Orients,* II (1954-1959), 343-8. Against the thesis that 'Eljon is the chief deity in Dt. 32:8 and that Yahweh is subordinate cf. W. F. Albright, "Some Remarks on the Song of Moses in Dt. 32," VT, 9 (1959), 343 f. He adduces the text of the Qumran Fr. with benê 'Elôhîm, by which the LXX reading is confirmed. The Qumran Fr. is ed. by P. W. Skehan, "A Fr. of the 'Song of Moses' (Dt. 32) from Qumran," *Bulletin of the American Schools of Oriental Research,* 136 (1954), 12, and cf. Skehan's "Qumran and the Present State of OT Studies," JBL, 78 (1959), 21. Cf. also R. Meyer, "Die Bedeutung v. Dt. 32:8 f., 43 (4 Q) für die Auslegung d. Mosesliedes," *Festschr. W. Rudolph* (1961), 197-209. The concept of Yahweh as Elyon in the sense of the Great King (LXX ὕψιστος) points to the Persian period; Wanke, *op. cit.* (→ n. 16), 94-7 sees in Dt. 32:8 f.; Ps. 82:1, 6 early stages in the equating of Yahweh and Elyon, this being completed in Is. 14:14. The supremacy of Yahweh over all gods and kings also seems to be present in Ps. 48:2 f., which relates to Sennacherib and the events of 701. The psalmists were no more aware of these stages and distinctions in the terms for God than the transl.

[22] S. Holm-Nielsen, "Hodayot. Ps. from Qumran," *Acta Theol. Danica,* 2 (1960), 85, n. 75; 121, n. 171.

[23] Str.-B., II, 99.

[24] Kraus, *op. cit.* (→ n. 15), 623: "To the incomparability of Yahweh corresponds the singular top position of His representative on earth." 'A assumed this, for his transl. is not just mechanical here.

[25] Gressmann, *op. cit.* (→ n. 20), 18 f.

[26] H. Windisch, "Friedensbringer — Gottessöhne. Eine religionsgeschichtl. Interpretation d. 7. Seligpreisung," ZNW, 24 (1925), 245.

[27] HT: שׁדי ממרומים, LXX: ἱκανὸς ἐξ ὑψίστων, cf. G. Bertram, "Zur Prägung d. bibl. Gottesvorstellung in d. griech. Übers. d. AT. Die Wiedergabe v. schadad u. schaddaj im Griech.," *Die Welt d. Orients,* II (1954-1959), 502-513; also "ΙΚΑΝΟΣ in d. griech. Übers. d. AT," ZAW, 70 (1958), 24 f.

[28] It is not necessary to suppose that LXX read מְרֹמָם (Kraus, *op. cit., ad loc.*).

[29] Only here אלהי מרום, corresponding to אלהי השמים, cf. Sanchunyaton's deity Σαμημ-ροῦμος = שמי מרום in Montgomery, *op. cit.* (→ n. 16), 145 f., who finds support here for Hypsistos in Sanchunyaton → 615, 22 ff. with n. 13.

is that God is in heaven, on high, not that He is Lord over heaven, though reinterpretation along cosmic lines is not far distant. [30] In 1 Εσδρ. 6:30; 8:19, 21; Δα. 2:18f. LXX transl. אלה שמיא by ὕψιστος or κύριος ὁ ὕψιστος (→ 616, 20 ff.). ὕψιστος is esp. common in Sir., [31] 44 times, with HT in 23 of these. In the latter the original 10 or 11 times is עליון (אל), [32] but the word is also used for Yahweh at 12:2; 43:2; 48:5, and other Hbr. terms in 13 or 14 other instances. After κύριος, then, ὕψιστος is the most common divine name in Sir. It is used only for the God of Israel and always as a proper name. In phrases like θεὸς ὕψιστος and κύριος (ὁ) ὕψιστος it is a noun in apposition: the one God who as such is high above all else.

D. ὕψιστος in Judaism.

In 4 Esr. [33] altissimus is the main name for God. It is the Lat. for ὕψιστος, which is used for עליון, this in turn having replaced Yahweh. Altissimus is also used in the Vg of the OT and NT along with the elative and perhaps more apt excelsus, Gn. 14:19; 2 Βασ. 22:14; ψ 46:3 etc. ὕψιστος and equivalents occur, too, in the apocr. and pseudepigr. [34] at Tob. 1:4, 13; Jdt. 13:18; 2 Macc. 3:31; 3 Macc. 6:2; Jub. 7:36; Gr. En. 10:1; Sib., 3, 519. 580; O. Sol.11:2;[35] 35:1, more frequently Test. XII: S. 2:5; 6:7; L. 3:10; 4:1 f.; 5:1, 7 etc. In Jos. the cultic-liturgical term ὕψιστος is less prominent, though cf. Ant., 16, 163. In Philo as well there are only a few examples. In Leg. All., III, 83 [36] Philo guards against polytheistic misunderstanding with a ref. to Gn. 14. The idea of the Most High lifts theological thinking above matter. Loftiness of thought should correspond to Him, the Most High. One detects a certain apologetic interest when Flacc., 46 calls the Jerusalem temple the temple of the Most High God, cf. Leg. Gaj., 137. 278. 317. The gt. spread and popular use of the divine name Most High in Hell. Judaism may be seen from synagogue inscr. with the dedication τῷ ὑψίστῳ θεῷ, e.g., from Athribis in Egypt, Ditt. Or., I, 96, 5 (c. 200 B.C.), [37] or from towns in Asia Minor like Laodicea, Miletus, Stratonice etc. Esp. impressive is the invocation of the ὁ θεὸς ὁ ὕψιστος in the so-called vengeance prayers of Rheneia, Ditt. Syll.³, III, 1181 (c. 100 B.C.). [38] The votive inscr. quoted → 615, 10 ff. (from Fayum) might well be Jewish or under Jewish influence. [39] There might also be Jewish influence in the Palmyrenian votive inscr. "to the Most High God." [40]

The widespread concept of the ὕψιστος in the Hellenistic age has two roots: the Greek term for Zeus (→ 615, 6 ff.) and the Semitic עליון (אל) (→ 616, 2 ff.). In the OT and orthodox Judaism עליון and the equivalent ὕψιστος are an exclusive designation and indeed a proper name of the one God who is on high → lines 6 ff. But in the age of Hellenism the title becomes the instrument of a self-depiction of Judaism adapted to the ends of apologetic and propaganda, [41] even if it does not

---

[30] Baudissin I, 307 etc., cf. also the summary III, 677.

[31] Ibid., III, 223, cf. I, 425.

[32] Ibid., I, 408-428.

[33] Ibid., II, 150.

[34] Ref. in Str.-B., II, 99.

[35] A. Adam, "Die urspr. Sprache d. Salomo-Oden," ZNW, 52 (1961), 141-156 discusses the secondary Gk. text of Ode 11, ed. M. Testuz, Pap. Bodmer, 10-12 (1959), 49-69.

[36] J. H. Kühn, ΎΨΟΣ. Eine Untersuchung z. Entwicklungsgeschichte d. Aufschwungsgedankens v. Plat. bis Pos. (1938), 54, 65; Dodd, op. cit. (→ n. 8), 12.

[37] Dodd, op. cit. (→ n. 8), 13, cf. 11-13 with further material; cf. also Schürer, II, 500; III, 174, n. 70.

[38] Cf. on this Deissmann LO, 351-362.

[39] Rubensohn, op. cit. (→ n. 5), 163.

[40] Some 120 have been found, cf., e.g., Ditt. Or., II, 634 (162/3 A.D.) and also J. Starcky, "Autour d'une dédicace palmyrénienne à Šadrafa et à Du'anat," Syria, 26 (1949), 60.

[41] The tendency to exalt and venerate a Most High God was one of the ways Gk. piety approximated to monotheism. Judaism could meet this half-way, cf. Dodd, op. cit., 12. There

sink to the level of being an expression of the syncretism which made inroads into Judaism.

There are examples of this among the texts already quoted, cf. the votive inscr. from Athribis (→ 618, 24). The clearest instance is the use of the Hypsistos title in syncretistic Judaism in the Crimea in guilds of σεβόμενοι θεὸν ὕψιστον in the cities of Pantikapaeum, Gorgippia, Tanais, which belongs in part to post-Chr. Judaism. [42] Their influence may be detected also in Chr. sects in the ancient Church, the Coelicolae and the Messalians. [43]

E. ὕψιστος in the New Testament.

1. In the NT the formula ἐν τοῖς ὑψίστοις occurs twice in the story of the entry: ὡσαννὰ ἐν τοῖς ὑψίστοις (Mt. 21:9; Mk. 11:10) and δόξα ἐν ὑψίστοις (Lk. 19:38). It also occurs in the Christmas story: δόξα ἐν ὑψίστοις (Lk. 2:14). In the entry story we really have an invocation of God, the name of God being replaced by a designation of place in Jewish fashion. [44] In Lk. 2:14 as in 19:38 God in the highest is meant. But in its antithetical form the present text tends to emphasise the parallelism of the two parts of the sentence. [45] Thus ἐν ὑψίστοις becomes an attributive designation of place for δόξα [46] and corresponds herewith to ἐπὶ γῆς as a location for εἰρήνη: Glory on high for God and on earth salvation for mankind → II, 747, 23 ff. [47]

2. ὕψιστος occurs nine times in the NT as a term for God (→ 617, 12 ff.). Seven instances are in the Lucan tradition including Acts. In the infancy stories the expected child of Mary is called the Son (→ 381, 20 ff.) of the Highest, by whose creative power He is begotten, Lk. 1:32, 35. [48] In similar vein Zacharias calls the forerunner the prophet of the Most High in Lk. 1:76. In Mk. 5:7; Lk. 8:28 the demon-possessed person or the demon (→ III, 708, n. 50) addresses Jesus as the Son of God the Most High. Similarly the girl with a spirit of soothsaying (Ac.

---

thus arose in paganism Judaising cultic guilds worshipping the god Sabbatistes or the ὕψιστος, cf. M. Hengel, "Die Synagogeninschr. v. Stobi," ZNW, 57 (1966), 169 and G. Delling, "Die Altarinschr. eines Gottesfürchtigen in Pergamon," Nov. Test., 7 (1964), 74, n. 3.

[42] Schürer, op. cit. (→ n. 10), 200-225.

[43] G. Krüger, Art. "Himmelsanbeter," RE³, 8, 84; N. Bonwetsch, Art. "Messalianer," RE³, 12. 661-4; G. Rosen and G. Bertram, Juden u. Phönizier, Das antike Judt. als Missionsreligion u. d. Entstehung d. jüd. Diaspora (1929), 53 f. 145, n. 83. The father of Greg. Naz. belonged to the Hypsistarians acc. to Greg. Naz. Or., 18, 5 (MPG, 35 [1857 f.] 989 f.); cf. Ant. Christ., V, 59.

[44] This is confirmed by the form of the cry in Acta Pilati A, 1, 4 (ed. C. Tischendorf, Evangelica Apocr.² [1876], 219), which first gives the Hbr. wording transliterated into Gk.: ὡσαννὰ μεμβρομῆ βαρουχαμμᾶ ἀδοναί, then the transl.: σῶσον δὴ ὁ ἐν τοῖς ὑψίστοις. εὐλογημένος ὁ ἐρχόμενος ἐν ὀνόματι κυρίου. OT usage corresponds to this and we also read in Ps. Sol.: ἔνδοξος ἐν ὑψίστοις κατοικῶν.

[45] The Clementine Liturgy seems to follow Lk. 2:14; 19:38: ὕψιστε ἐν ὑψηλοῖς κατοικῶν, Const. Ap., VIII, 11, 2. The juxtaposition of God and man seems to be stressed in Lk. 2:14 when the ἐν with ἀνθρώποις is left out in important readings like it vg^cl Ir^lat.

[46] Luther's "on high" is ambiguous. Vg has in altissimis at Lk. 2:14 (so also Mt. 21:9) and in excelsis at Mk. 11:10; Lk. 19:38; avoidance of the misleading superlative corresponds better to the OT expression, cf. Zn. Lk., ad loc.

[47] Salvation here is meant eschatologically. The Hbr. basis may be seen in 1 QH 4:33; 11:9; Fr., 34, col. 2, 5 (DJD, I, 154), cf. C. H. Hunzinger, "Neues Licht auf Lk. 2:14 ἄνθρωποι εὐδοκίας," ZNW, 44 (1952/53), 85-90 and "Ein weiterer Beleg zu Lk. 2:14 ἄνθρωποι εὐδοκίας," ZNW, 49 (1958), 129 f.; R. Deichgräber, "Lk. 2:14: ΑΝΘΡΩΠΟΙ ΕΥΔΟΚΙΑΣ," ZNW, 51 (1960), 132; Holm-Nielsen, op. cit. (→ n. 22), 78 and 184.

[48] The "power of the Most High" is the Spirit of God, 1 QH 7:6 f., cf. Test. L. 16:3.

16:17) greets Paul and his companions as servants of God the Most High. [49] In Lk. 6:35: υἱοὶ ὑψίστου, we have a construction found already in the OT (→ 617, 18 ff.) whereby the divine name "the Most High" replaces an indication of place intended to avoid the name of God, namely, "on high." [50] In Ac. 7:48 the divine name "the Most High" deliberately stresses in context the transcendence of God. The author in his depiction [51] uses the OT name of God in Hellenistic form as a designation which gives emphasis to this aspect. In Hb. 7:1 the OT phrase "priest of the most high God" with reference to Melchisedec is taken from Gn. 14:18, but it has no material significance as regards the divine name. [52]

Both quantitatively and qualitatively ὕψιστος as a divine name is on the margin of the NT tradition. Notwithstanding Lk. 6:35 Jesus seems not to have used it. ὕψιστος does not correspond to the NT revelation of God no matter whether it be understood as a solemn liturgico-hymnal expression of sublimity, a religious philosophico-theological term to denote transcendence, or a traditional proper name for God.

F. ὕψιστος in Early Christianity.

Apart from liturgical use this term for God, which is essentially controlled by the OT (→ 616, 16 ff.), found little place in the religious consciousness of early Christianity. ὕψιστος occurs in 1 Cl. only in OT quotations or reminiscences at 29, 2; 45, 7 etc. There is a sonorous formulation in Ign. R. prescript: ἐν μεγαλειότητι πατρὸς ὑψίστου. Things are much the same in the Apologists where, apart from a NT formula in Aristid., 15, 1, OT quotations and NT ὕψιστος allusions are found only in Just. Apol., 33, 5; Dial., 19, 4; 22, 9 etc. There is no independent use of the divine name ὕψιστος at all. Worth noting, however, is the ascribing of the title ὕψιστος to the exalted Lord, to Christ, in the Gnosticising apocr. Acts, e.g., Martyrium Andreae prius 14: [53] ὦ σταυρέ, μηχάνημα σωτηρίας τοῦ ὑψίστου. In Act. Thom. 39; [54] 45; 49; 78; 150 Thomas is hailed as an apostle of the Most High. Jesus is addressed: Ἰησοῦ ὕψιστε, 48, and He is styled ὕψιστος παρὰ τοῦ μεγίστου, 143. The antithetical sentences δόξα τῇ ὑψίστῳ σου (vl. τῇ ὑψώσει σου) βασιλείᾳ (delendum βασιλείᾳ?) ἥτις δι' ἡμᾶς ἐταπεινώθη (80) have a liturgical character. Here deductions from NT faith are drawn regarding the exalted Lord. The ὑψωθείς has become the ὕψιστος and the confession of Phil. 2:9 is thus put into practice by transferring the OT name for God to Christ. He is the Kyrios and Hypsistos of the Chr. community.

Bertram

---

[49] At Lk. 8:28 τοῦ θεοῦ is not in D 892 al. Is the meaning here and in Ac. 16:17 "son of God the lofty one" or "of the Most High"? Haench. Ag.[14], *ad loc.* pts. out that the incident in Mk. 5:1 ff. par. takes place in Gentile territory. Mk. 5:7 has the same text as Lk. 8:28, but τοῦ ὑψίστου is not in Mt. Since Mt. 8:28-34 seems to be secondary with its abbreviating and embroidery — two demon-possessed, on doubling or the number two cf. Bultmann Trad., 345 — he perhaps shortened the address. Originally the story had for Jesus the full title "son of God the lofty One," or syncretistically, in keeping with the content of this almost comic story, "son of the Most High."

[50] In the par. 5:45 Mt. has τοῦ πατρὸς ὑμῶν τοῦ ἐν οὐρανοῖς, cf. 6:9 in the Lord's Prayer, though Lk. here is content with a simple πάτερ (11:2). If this is original, ὁ ἐν οὐρανοῖς in Mt. 5:45 and esp. ὕψιστος as a term for God are secondary in dominical sayings. Zn. Lk., 293, n. 64 pts. out that in the OT ὕψιστος is used on the lips of Gentiles or where the ref. is to Gentiles.

[51] Cf. Haench. Ag.[10], *ad loc.* but also Haench. Ag.[14], *ad loc.* on this.

[52] The style "high-priest of the Most High God," is attested for the Hasmonean period in bRH, 18b. but there do not seem to be any contemporary examples, cf. Str.-B., II, 100.

[53] Ed. R. A. Lipsius - M. Bonnet, *Acta Apostolorum Apocr.*, II, 1 (1898), 55, 4.

[54] *Ibid.*, II, 2 (1903), 156, 13.